D1592030

THE ENCYCLOPEDIA OF EPIC FILMS

THE ENCYCLOPEDIA OF EPIC FILMS

Constantine Santas
James M. Wilson
Maria Colavito
Djoymi Baker

ROWMAN & LITTLEFIELD
Lanham • Boulder • New York • Toronto • Plymouth, UK

3/11/15
WW
$125.00

Published by Rowman & Littlefield
4501 Forbes Boulevard, Suite 200, Lanham, Maryland 20706
www.rowman.com

10 Thornbury Road, Plymouth PL6 7PP, United Kingdom

Copyright © 2014 by Rowman & Littlefield

All rights reserved. No part of this book may be reproduced in any form or by any electronic or mechanical means, including information storage and retrieval systems, without written permission from the publisher, except by a reviewer who may quote passages in a review.

British Library Cataloguing in Publication Information Available

Library of Congress Cataloging-in-Publication Data

Santas, Constantine.

The encyclopedia of epic films / Constantine Santas, James M. Wilson, Maria Colavito, Djoymi Baker.

pages cm

Includes bibliographical references and index.

ISBN 978-0-8108-8247-8 (cloth : alk. paper) — ISBN 978-0-8108-8248-5 (ebook) 1. Epic films—Encyclopedias. I. Wilson, James M., 1959– II. Colavito, Maria Maddalena. III. Baker, Djoymi, 1972– IV. Title.

PN1995.9.E79S25 2014

791.43'65803—dc23 2013033410

™ The paper used in this publication meets the minimum requirements of American National Standard for Information Sciences—Permanence of Paper for Printed Library Materials, ANSI/NISO Z39.48-1992.

Printed in the United States of America

CONTENTS

ACKNOWLEDGMENTS

I WOULD LIKE TO THANK Stephen Ryan, senior acquisitions editor at Rowman & Littlefield, for his vision in conceiving this epic project, and then giving my coauthors and myself the opportunity to bring it to fruition. I'd like to thank my brother, Dr. Gerasimos Santas, of University of California, Irvine, for his unrelenting support and continuing philosophical discussions of Platonic and Aristotelian ideas on the ancient epic; scholar/librarian Joseph M. Dmohowski, of Whittier College, for sending materials and copies of his own works and for his two-year correspondence on subjects related to epic film; L. Robert Morris of Toronto, Canada, author of *Lawrence of Arabia*, for his assistance, long telephone calls, and discussions on the epic film; Greek scholars Dr. Spyros Vrettos and his wife, Dr. Vivi Kopsida-Vrettou, for their ideas on the epic and continued support of my project; and finally Dr. Peter Lardner, son of Ring Lardner Jr., for loaning me his sister's, Kate Lardner's, book, *Shut Up, He Explained: The Memoir of a Blacklisted Kid*, which gives a vivid picture of the era of blacklisted authors, Michael Wilson, Carl Foreman, and other screenwriters of epic scripts during the House Un-American Activities Committee investigations. I would also like to express my thanks to my colleagues and coauthors in this project for their hard and inspiring work, and to my family, Mary, Xen, Ari, and Christiana, for their heartfelt support. And a note of thanks to Danielle Costello, of Valdosta State University, for helping me put the manuscript together and for Harikleia Sirmans for compiling the index.

The following are my colleagues' notes on the subject:

Dr. Djoymi Baker would like to acknowledge the support of her family, Paul, Ava, and Finn, throughout the lengthy writing process, as well as the assistance of the library staff at the University of Melbourne.

Dr. James M. Wilson would like to thank Peggy Dyess and Diane Nyquist, of Flagler College, for their research assistance; Steve Skipp and Chris Chaya for their audio visual magic; and Alan Woolfolk, vice president of Academic Affairs, for sabbatical time. A special thanks to Dr. Leonard R. Bruguier for his inspiration (*Mitakuye Oyasin*) and Tamara Wilson for her support and love.

Dr. Colavito would like to thank Dr. Constantine Santas and his wife, Mary, for their support and guidance throughout the journey; Dr. Antonio de Nicolas, her husband and mentor, for always providing encouragement; Dr. Rex Emerick, colleague and friend, who helped her with project management and general good counsel; and lastly her maternal grandparents, who taught her the art of ancient technologies and how *every picture tells a story*, even the moving ones.

Constantine Santas

INTRODUCTION

DEFINITIONS AND AIMS

BEFORE IT BECAME a term in film, *epic* was known from the literary tradition, going back millennia. The word *epic* itself derives from the Greek "epos," meaning "word," "tale," "story," a "prophecy," "oracle," and, in literary terms, "a poem written in heroic verse,"[1] that is, poetry composed in hexameter dactylic lines, or "heroic measure,"[2] as are the poems of Homer. Western and world literatures are filled with epics: Babylonian, Greek, Roman, Hindu, Anglo-Saxon, African, and other literary masterpieces can be cited,[3] but language has retained and used the term *epic* to describe a real-life event, an achievement that entails great effort, a struggle to attain something important, or to describe an action that brings about admirable results. Any venture of large proportions—a war, a trek, an exploration—could be, and has been, categorized as an epic. A social struggle, a trial, a lengthy football game going into overtime, an election campaign of unusual length—these endeavors associated with size, length, complexity, and heroic action could be classified as epics. In the fictional sense, the word goes back to numerous literary works in the West[4] and throughout the world—tales of fights against monsters, of hard-fought victories, lengthy adventures, and heroic achievements of many kinds.

When film came into existence in the late nineteenth and early twentieth centuries, it adopted the term *epic* for films that were lengthy, spectacular, live with action, and often filmed in exotic locales, with large casts and budgets big enough to often intimidate producers and directors, but the effort and extravagance needed to mount an epic film paid off handsomely at the box office, for the genre became a favorite with audiences almost immediately. It survived the tribulations of World War I, World War II, and the Great Depression, and it has retained its basic characteristics of size and glamor for more than 100 years. Length was, and is, one of these traits, as franchises have replaced the once monolithic three to four hours duration of past eras. Popular stars as leads have studded epic yarns, and epics have given rise to new stars: Clark Gable was a sure bet for *Gone with the Wind* (1939), but Peter O'Toole rose to stardom with *Lawrence of Arabia* (1962), and Harrison Ford found his fortunes with the *Indiana Jones* franchise, which lent him his big-screen image in the late twentieth century. From Greta Garbo and Elizabeth Taylor, to Meryl Streep, Sigourney Weaver, and Natalie Portman, women, too, have held their status or rose to fame as leads in epics. Even youth—Daniel Radcliffe in the Harry Potter series (2002) and Elijah Wood in the *Lord of the Rings* trilogy (2001)—have joined the company of superheroes, helping to attract, and pin to their seats, the younger generations of theatergoers. Spectacular action, lengthy adventure sequences filled with suspense and danger, and monstrous villains and daredevil heroes have captured the imagination of audiences, and although the form has evolved during its many decades of existence, these elements have been retained, refined, and modernized to suit the tastes of each new generation.

The enormous appetite of audiences for adventure spectacle has had its effects, some immediate and palpable: epics have often broken box-office records and garnered more Oscars and other awards than any other genre in film. Some examples include D. W. Griffith's *The Birth of a Nation* (1915), which netted $18 million, an enormous amount for the times, and *Gone with the Wind*, David O. Selznick's epic of the Civil War, which made more than $77 million[5] in its initial opening, a record that was not broken for decades, in addition to its thirteen Oscar nominations and eight Oscar wins. *Ben-Hur* (1959) netted eleven Oscars, a record that was not broken until *Titanic* (1997), and *The Lord of the Rings: The Return of the King* (2003) also garnered eleven wins. The *Lord of the Rings* trilogy's (2001–2003) box-office returns are estimated to have neared $3 billion, and some of today's superhero blockbusters have opening weekends that pull in $50 million to $100 million. Today's big franchises, for instance, *Star Wars* and Harry Potter, count their worldwide grosses in billions, and the trend does not seem to show signs of taking a plunge any time soon.

Despite all that, the epic film has not achieved the one thing it has probably yearned for: critical recognition and respect as a genre. Most serious critics[6] regard it as an empty spectacle intended for mass entertainment, lacking substance or social significance, as, for instance, other genres have achieved: drama, social issues films, film noir, and especially what most critics cherish, "art" movies, which come out eclectically in prestigious DVD and Blu-ray editions, with critical commentaries by film scholars, for example, "The Criterion Collection," which rarely, if ever, has included an epic film. Whether such bias is deliberate is not the point here.

The aim of *The Encyclopedia of Epic Films* is to offer a selection of films categorized as epics; note and recognize them amid the plethora of mass production, for the genre is immensely prolix; and describe them in the most fundamental way, in alphabetical order, regardless of chronology, merit, popularity, and Oscar (or other awards) wins. Whether or not this collection will enhance the position of the epic as "high art" is, again, not our aim. As identified, described, and analyzed—admittedly in a relatively rather modest size—it is hoped that each entry will be judged as an individual epic or as part of a significant genre that will aspire for greater recognition, study, and significance as part of live film, which has honorably survived its relatively short time of existence.

LITERARY AND HISTORICAL BACKGROUNDS

The epic is an ancient form of literature, written or orally delivered as early as 3000 B.C.[7] *The Epic of Gilgamesh*, composed in Akkadian by Sumerian poets around 2000 and translated into Semitic tongues in the seventh century B.C., is the story of Gilgamesh, who, after the death of his friend Enkidu, embarks on a search for a wise man who has survived the flood to gain the secret of immortality. *Enuma Elish*, the Babylonian epic of creation, composed between 1500 and 1200 B.C., establishes the dominance of various deities and proclaims the god Marduk ruler of the heavens and earth. Homer's *The Iliad* and *The Odyssey*, oral compositions recited through the Greek world of antiquity since the eighth century B.C. and written down in the age of Peisistratus in the sixth century, project indelible heroic archetypes of cunning and bravery that have since exerted great influence on Western literary thought. Homer's imitators, the poets of the so-called Ionic school, or "cyclical" poets, undertook to complete the cycle of *The Iliad* and *The Odyssey*, devising an introduction up to the beginning of *The Iliad* and finishing the story of the war by adding the death of Achilles, the arrival of his son, the sacking of Troy, and the return of the heroes to their homelands.[8] Of these poets, Laches of Mytilene wrote *The Little Iliad*, which details the destruction of the city in four books, and which is criticized by Aristotle in *The Poetics* for its lack of structure.[9] These poems were usually inferior in literary merit, and only fragments of them survive. Other poets, more practically minded and following the models left by Hesiod in his *Works and Days*, written in the eighth century B.C., recommend honorable pursuits, expounding on the fruits of honest labor and urging explorations into the world of art and industry. Hesiod also wrote the *Theogony*, which became the source of myths about the genesis of the gods and provides a larger view of the progression from the divine to the human order. Hesiod's poems, which were generally influential in later antiquity, are preoccupied with didactic subjects and were intended for teaching (*didaskein*), a tradition followed by the Alexandrians, Callimachus (around 250 B.C.), Phranius, and Apollonius of Rhodes, famous for his *Argonautica*.

On the whole, the Hellenistic period, culturally fragmented and imitative, adhered to the tradition of Hesiod, producing some worthwhile didactic epics on subjects as varied as astronomy (Aratus of Sicyon), medicine, and geography, and even as trivial as angling and hunting.[10] The didactic epic was also a favorite subject of Roman poets and can be found in Lucretius's *On the Universe*, Virgil's *Georgics*, and Ovid's *The Art of Love*.[11] As seen by these examples, the epic form continued to expand and proliferate, becoming larger in scope and subject matter during the classic and later antiquity but producing no more literary epics equivalent to Homer's. The Roman authors, although often imitating Greek styles and themes, were by and large preoccupied with patriotic topics and narratives of their own history. Livius Andronicus translated *The Odyssey*; Naevius detailed the Punic Wars; Ennius wrote in hexameter in imitation of the Homeric meter; Cicero wrote an epic on Marius; Varro reproduced the *Argonautica* tale following the Greek model; and Virgil, who lived in the Augustan Age, composed *The Aeneid*, reputedly at the request of Emperor Augustus, to glorify the founding of the Roman Empire.

Virgil's epic spawned numerous imitators during the Middle Ages, and Virgil became the leading figure and spiritual guide of Dante in his wandering through the *Inferno* and *Purgatorio* in *The Divine Comedy*, where the subject matter becomes human salvation. The Middle Ages generally ignored both Aristotle's guidelines of the epic and Homer's epics, which were written in Greek and were not available in translations until the fourteenth century.[12] Medieval epics with Christian themes became prevalent during the "dark" ages, epics differing both in form and content from the Greek and Roman prototypes of the classical periods. Some of these, *Beowulf*, *Chanson de Roland*, and *Sir Gawain and the Green Knight*, to name a few, were epics whose spirit of heroism was permeated by chivalric and Christian virtues, for instance, combating sin and a medieval knight's quest for salvation.

Even Geoffrey Chaucer's *Canterbury Tales* and Giovanni Boccaccio's *The Decameron*, while not strictly epics in the traditional form (they are called "frame epics," requiring a narrator for each tale[13]), expressed ideas conforming to the beliefs of Christian morality that the medieval society espoused. Both of these authors possessed satirical bends and were preoccupied with castigating such social evils as greed, deception, and church corruption. Dante's *The Divine Comedy* was the culmination of these epics and projected ideas and paradigms not only for the condemnation of sin, but also pointing to the road of reaching heaven. The form of these narratives was changing, for Dante's story was told in the first person, but the epic format still expressed itself in verse, in this case the terza rima, a verse form that reputedly stood for the poem's allegorical meaning (the Trinity). In the English language, verse formats (prosody) evolved from the medieval narratives and became the ten syllable iambic pentameter, which remained in force until the end of nineteenth century.

Numerous poets in the twentieth century, T. S. Eliot, W. H. Auden, Robert Greeley,[14] among others, who showed no taste for long-verse epics, wrote poems that revisited the epic hero in his contemporary transformations, a seer or visionary meandering through the chaos of modern life, as with Eliot's Tiresias in *The Waste Land.* Some long-verse epic narratives on the grand scale were attempted in the twentieth century, showing a resurgence of the epic form in the lengthy poem by Nikos Kazantzakis, *The Odyssey: A Modern Sequel* (1936), clearly an extension of the Homeric tale, and in *Omeros* (1990), by Derek Walcott, a story set in the Caribbean, with many parallels to the Homeric poems, and in others.[15]

Although maintained in such sporadic works, the epic form relinquished its domain to the novel, which acquired epic dimensions in the eighteenth century in the works of Daniel Defoe, Jonathan Swift, Samuel Richardson, and Henry Fielding, whose narratives established the wandering hero, explorer and discoverer of lands. The novel acquired new dimensions in the nineteenth century in the massive works of Honoré de Balzac (*Pére Goriot*), Charles Dickens (*A Tale of Two Cities*), Fyodor Dostoyevsky (*The Brothers Karamazov*), and Leo Tolstoy (*War and Peace*), whose exploration of psychological and social conflicts invested the medium with fresh outlooks and social relevance. In the twentieth century, the novel flourished in the pioneering works of James Joyce (*Ulysses*), Marcel Proust (*Remembrance of Things Past*), D. H. Lawrence (*Sons and Lovers*), Thomas Mann (*The Magic Mountain*), Nikos Kazantzakis (*The Last Temptation of Christ*), William Faulkner (*Absalom! Absalom!*), George Orwell (*Nineteen Eighty Four*), Vladimir Nabokov (*Lolita*), and Umberto Eco (*The Name of the Rose*), among others; their works introduced such techniques as the narrator's voice as the primary means of narration (stream of consciousness), the establishment of the multiple point of view, and the break from the syntagmatic, or chronological, order of narrative.

The novel was, in part, a transformation of the epic form, although its prose format deprived it of the grandiosity of the Homeric hexameter or the elegant beat of the iambic pentameter of English poetry. But in many ways, the novel functioned like the ancient epic: it carried on the narrative tradition with its multiple plots and descriptions of grand spectacular scenes (*War and Peace*), and, while in written rather than oral form, it addressed large audiences, often elaborating on themes with significant social or national issues. Its most significant characteristic was the development of a viable prose narrative style that made the epic novel available to the masses. The novel expanded its geographical boundaries and social horizons and achieved unmatched popularity during the time of its greatest triumphs—the late nineteenth and early twentieth centuries. Using its scope and power, the novel dominated audiences as "emphatically" as the ancient epic form had, and, for a while, it became the dominant form of literary expression. That is, this was the case until film came along, to borrow from it as one borrows from a parent, antagonize it at times,[16] and compete for attention. Film, derivative and autonomous at the same time, has assimilated the main characteristics of the epic form, and, at least from an aesthetic point of view, it bears a striking resemblance to both the novel and the ancient epic.[17]

THE EPIC GENRE IN AMERICAN MOVIES

When film arrived in the early twentieth century, epics, of historical necessity, derived their subjects from the literary forms available to them, as much from antiquity as from the plethora of epic novels that had flourished in the previous (19th) century. These existing literary works, from Alexander Dumas Sr., Honoré de Balzac, Charles Dickens, Jules Verne, Leo Tolstoy, and Emile Zola, to mention the most prominent, became a means of reflecting social changes that had become the feeding ground for modern cultural myths: the numerous scientific discoveries of the previous century; prophecies of moon landings, as in the novels of Verne; momentous social events, for example, the Civil War, the massive immigration to the New World, and the movement of pioneers to the American West; folklore and the supernatural, as in the legends Frankenstein and Dracula; or (and) literary works of previous centuries that had described large conflicts, wars of liberation for instance. Even a brief list of early epics is a testament to that: *A Trip to the Moon* (Georges Méliès, 1902), *A Great Train Robbery* (Edwin Porter, 1903), *Ben-Hur* (Motion Pictures Patens Company, Fred Niblo, William Wyler, 1907, 1926, 1959), *The Count of Monte Cristo* (Biograph, 1909), *Cabiria, Quo Vadis* (Piero Fosco, 1914), *The Birth of a Nation* (D. W. Griffith, 1915), *Intolerance* (Griffith, 1916), *The Fall of Babylon* (Griffith, 1919), *Nosferatu* (F. W. Murnau, 1922), Napoleon (Abel Gance, 1927), *Gone with the Wind* (Victor Fleming, 1939), *Jesse James* (Henry King, 1939), and many more are a testament to the myth-making power of the epic film. Later in the century, the epic film achieved its greatest popularity during the 1950s and the 1960s, spurred by the rivalry of television and the arrival of the wide screen.

Although epic film production waned in the following decades, it by no means disappeared, and epic films continued into the 1970s with the gangster epics *The Godfather* (Francis Ford Coppola, 1972), *The Godfather Part II* (Coppola, 1974), *The Godfather Part III* (Coppola, 1990), *Apocalypse Now* (Copolla, 1979); the 1980s with *Gandhi* (Richard Attenborough, 1982) and *A Passage to India* (David Lean, 1984); and even into the 1990s and beyond, although some critics have prematurely announced the epic's demise.[18] Yet, a look at the epics produced in the last two decades (1993–2013) alone will convince skeptics that the epic form has made a thunderous comeback, with *Schindler's List* (Steven Spielberg, 1993), *The Age of Innocence* (Martin Scorsese, 1993), *Amistad* (Coppola, 1997), *Titanic* (James Cameron, 1997), *The Patriot* (Roland Emmerich, 2000), *Gladiator* (Ridley Scott, 2000), *Pearl Harbor* (Michael Bay, 2001), *Black Hawk Down* (Scott, 2001), *Gangs of New York* (Scorsese, 2002), *Master and Commander* (Peter Weir, 2003), *The Last Samurai* (Edward Zwick, 2003), *Cold*

Mountain (Anthony Minghella, 2003), *The Lord of the Rings: The Return of the King* (Peter Jackson, 2003), *Troy* (Wolfgang Petersen, 2004), *The Aviator* (Scorsese, 2005), and *Lincoln* (Spielberg, 2012), to mention only the most prominent. The resurgence of the epic film is partly owed to advances in technology—digital photography, for instance—that materialized in the tendency to popularize the sci-fi thriller and fantasy epic, going back to the days of the *Star Trek* series, *Aliens*, and *Close Encounters of the Third Kind*, and continuing into modern times with the *Star Wars* episodes I through VI, the *Iron Man* films, Harry Potter and the sequels, and the *Lord of the Rings* trilogy. The dozens of superhero epics that flood the screens each summer further attests to the longevity of the epic, albeit now a child of computer-generated imagery (CGI) technology.

The enduring popularity of the epic film can be partly explained by the continuing appeal of its larger-than-life personae, and partially by its stress on action and spectacle, but mainly because of its embracing of popular trends and ideals that define or represent an era. Today, for instance, when terrorist threats have replaced the fear of the Cold War (feeding materials for the James Bond series), the battle of good against evil has become the trademark for modern epics, including fantasy epics. In the mere span of 100 years, epic film has re-created, reshaped, and expanded the heroic images and archetypes of the past, connecting them to the present: from Gilgamesh to Hercules, Icarus to Luke Skywalker, Orestes to Hamlet, Odysseus to James Bond and Harry Potter, Moses to Superman, and Buddha to Gandhi, epic film has revisited and retooled these heroic images as no other narrative medium has, perpetually using them for its own ends while forging new ones.

From the outset, epic film has feasted on the collective myths of East and West, dipping into the inexhaustible resources of stories from the Bible; Greek, Egyptian, Babylonian, Roman, and medieval cultures; and, today, Oriental and Eastern myths (*Crouching Tiger, Hidden Dragon* is a recent example). Developing technologies have allowed[19] the epic film to bring into our consciousness heroes who can fly (*Superman*) or reach the moon and stars (*Apollo 13*, *Star Wars*). According to Otto Rank, such heroes—including Moses, Hercules, Oedipus, Siegfried, and Jesus[20]—lived lives that exhibited the basic components of the heroic saga: a high or divinely marked birth preceded by barrenness or prohibition; a prophecy warning of the perils of such a birth (Oedipus); a loss or wandering of the infant in a far-off land (Moses, Jesus); a recovery or suckling of an infant by an animal (Romulus, Remus); a discovery of distinguished parents (Oedipus); a revenge, if appropriate, to his mission (Hamlet); and the achievement of rank or honors, or both.[21] The hero, often conceived as both a tribal and religious leader (Jesus, Moses), may be exiled or die in the end (Oedipus, Hamlet), but his action has cleansed his land of a pestilence (Oedipus) or brought about the end of a corrupt system (Hamlet). We are told that Myths "are, by nature, collective and communal; they bind a tribe or a nation together in that people's common psychological and spiritual activities."[22]

And film is one of the most visible expressions of the renewal and perpetuation of myths and thus can be seen as the embodiment of humanity's most cherished dreams and desires. In one form or another, whether in film or another medium (in Mozart's and Wagner's operas, or in Mahler's symphonies, for instance), the epic form has related to communal myths more than any other form, and it will continue to thrive and prosper as long as audiences find a deeper need for it. It is safe to maintain that, at least for the time being, the epic film has captured (even in its most popular forms) and given expression to the need for the mythic hero more than any of the other cinematic forms.

According to anthropologists and myth critics, an archetype is a universal symbol, a phenomenon common to all cultures, even those isolated from one another by geographical ties.[23] In a Jungian sense, archetypes find expression in "tribal lore, mythology, fairy tales, religious systems, and primitive art."[24] They reside in the collective unconscious, which is a "part of the psyche [that] was the first to evolve and now provides the necessary links with humanity's ancestral past."[25] As an archetypal character, the hero undergoes trials and adventures in cyclical patterns that involve submersion, mystical death, and regeneration. All western mythical heroes were subjected to these cycles and thus undertook a quest, progressing from initiation to maturity, and finally making a victorious return to the tribe.

While conceding that epic heroes are representative of their tribe's hopes, aspirations, or fears, one must also admit that a certain strand of the epic is capable of embodying heroes that leave their imprint on the collective psyche in a manner that elevates them to the status of universal mythic heroes. It is their "drawing" power as archetypes that make them such attractive screen personas, capable of inspiring crowds of viewers, who are then reminded, in their collective consciousness, of desires that remain unfulfilled and can be satisfied by their projected visual counterparts on the screen. Such are warriors of extraordinary merit; so are so-called prophets—even in the most secular of societies—who can be seen as mythological heroes; and so are saviors of humanity, who, even the in the most technological of societies, can be seen as mythical heroes. Such are lovers who arouse sexual passions in both sexes, and men or women of nature who bring man back in touch with lost paradises. In film, such heroes are often depicted in all three (and many more) categories: warriors responsible for ridding humanity of Hitler: General MacArthur, General Eisenhower, General Patton; these figures have been depicted in epic films. Gandhi and Martin Luther King Jr. have both been subjects of films—although their actual personas may have surpassed film's imagery of them—while the mythical heroes of the technological age can easily be found in James Bond, Luke Skywalker, and Superman, as well as Batman, Spider-Man, Iron Man, and many others in the digital age.

SELECTING EPIC FILMS

With hundreds of possible entries, we had to be extremely selective to accommodate the need of fairly representing the genre in this rather large work. The genre is not pure. It has its parameters; length; multiple plot strands; spectacle; and a hero, man or woman, who represents tribal, national, or general human interests—as is the case with science fiction epics that describe aliens attacking or threatening the planet. Most of these characteristics are inherited from antiquity, as we have seen.

But film soon acquired its own traits. It was a visual medium requiring large casts; sets often built at great expense (especially for epics); and, as time progressed, stars, and often megastars, to represent such heroes as modern or ancient kings, adventurers, explorers, and space heroes, not to mention famous female leaders of antiquity or modernity, including Cleopatra, Marie Antoinette, Queen Elizabeth I, and Karen Blixen. Heroes of the West, for example, Jesse James and Wyatt Earp, came into play, and Hollywood stars Paul Newman, Kirk Douglas, John Wayne, James Stewart, Peter Fonda, and many others have had a share in bringing them to life and keeping legends alive. Big stars and studios with elaborate sets the likes of Paramount, MGM, and Warner Bros., not to mention the wide expanses of the West, were easily available in Hollywood, which took full advantage of its facilities and reputation of making big movies, and, thence, the epic film became a Hollywood phenomenon. There, it was possible to employ thousands of directors, writers, cinematographers, and technicians of every kind, while big-name, popular stars, under contract to various studios, were readily available to play the often larger-than-life heroes or heroines the epics required.

Almost entirely by popular demand, Clark Gable was cast as Rhett Butler in *Gone with the Wind* (1939), the big Civil War epic/romance that set the stage for the stream of great epics to come, especially after the close of World War II. Other great (and often not so great) leads in Hollywood epics have included Ramon Novarro in *Ben-Hur* (1927), Robert Taylor in *Quo Vadis* (1951), Charlton Heston in *The Ten Commandments* (1956), William Holden in *The Bridge on the River Kwai* (1957), Heston in *Ben-Hur* (1959), Kirk Douglas in *Spartacus* (1960), Heston in *El Cid* (1962), Elizabeth Taylor in *Cleopatra* (1963), Richard Burton and Peter O'Toole in *Becket* (1964), Marlon Brando in *The Godfather* (1972), Meryl Streep in *Out of Africa* (1985), Mel Gibson in *Braveheart* (1995), and Daniel Day-Lewis in *Lincoln* (2012), to mention some of the most memorable roles. This does not include stars in secondary roles, for instance, Rod Steiger, Anthony Quinn, Claude Rains, Sir Ralph Richardson, Charles Laughton, and Peter Ustinov, and such vamps as Hedy Lamarr (*Samson and Delilah*, 1949), Anne Baxter (*The Ten Commandments*), and Sophia Loren in *El Cid* and *The Fall of the Roman Empire* (1964).

Since the spectacular Hollywood epics were made in approximately four decades—the 1930s, 1940s, 1950s, and 1960s—with a brief hiatus during World War II (1939–1945), our main selections come from this period. The big Hollywood epic, which lasted until the mid-1960s, may now look like a dinosaur, an extinct species, as it fell by the wayside, along with demise of the Hays Code and the big Hollywood moguls who ran out of cash after several disasters at the box office, namely the remake of *The Mutiny of the Bounty* (Lewis Milestone, 1962), *Cleopatra* (Joseph L. Mankiewicz, 1963), *The Greatest Story Ever Told* (George Stevens, 1965), and several others; however, this historical decline of the big, spectacular epic, which some critics called the "epic of excess,"[26] does not mean that the epic is dead or forgotten.

The Birth of a Nation, *Gone with the Wind*, *The Ten Commandments*, *Ben-Hur*, *Spartacus*, and *Lawrence of Arabia*, to stay strictly with Hollywood, are, thanks to restoration and digital technology, as alive as they ever were, perhaps even more so because of the fact that they cannot be reproduced. And if they are attempted again, they will never be the same. The cast of thousands and the magnificent sets are gone, now replaced by CGI technology that can do, or pretend to do, the same thing, for the massive crowds of extras in those dinosaurs have been replaced by digitals dots. Consider that in the modern epic *Troy*, two models of Greek ships—the famous 1,000 ships of Homeric legend—were used, digitally multiplied to fill the seas. When *Cleopatra* was filmed in 1963, the ships were real ships; in fact, it was said that *Cleopatra* now commands the largest fleet in the world.

Although the magnificent epics of that bygone era are a thing of the past, that does not mean the extinction of the genre. When the grandiose epic declined, the great studios failed or turned to conglomerates that financed and distributed films in general. The public tastes turned to shorter and more socially relevant topics, with such popular hits as *The Graduate* (Mike Nichols, 1967), *Easy Rider* (Dennis Hopper, 1969), *Midnight Cowboy* (John Schlesinger, 1969), and *Carnal Knowledge* (Nichols, 1971). Action blockbusters like *Jaws* (Spielberg, 1975) gave audiences more thrills than the rather heavy-handed epic in its decline of the 1960s, and such franchises as *Superman*, *Rocky*, *Star Wars*, *Indiana Jones*, *Alien*, and many others that continue to this day gradually took over and redefined the epic form as related to changing tastes and newer means of doing business. After *Gandhi* and *A Passage to India*, both of which were filmed in exotic locales in India, epics became gangster yarns (the three *Godfathers*). War movies (*Saving Private Ryan*, Spielberg, 1998), revivals (*Titanic*), and digital and computer-generated adventure spectacles and franchises dominated the screens in the first decade of the twenty-first century.

We have included some of the most preeminent epics in our selection (*Avatar*, Cameron, 2009), while franchises and superhero epics have been placed in appendix A, given in shorter entries. Foreign-language epics appear in appendix B. The choices in the latter category are necessarily eclectic, as foreign-language films in general are considered art films, shown with subtitles in art-house theaters, and rarely distributed as mainstream movies. While the western is primarily an American enterprise, exploring history and myth of legend, it is a genre that has been explored for its own sake, as have film noir, comedy, musical, and other American genres and subgenres. Only the most prominent examples are included, for instance, *The Searchers* (John Ford, 1956), *How the West Was Won* (Ford, 1962), *Once Upon a Time in the West* (Sergio Leone, 1968), and a few others. We have also excluded the James Bond franchise, since the Bond movies are adventure thrillers, and a much-discussed genre of their own, with one exception, *The Spy Who Loved Me* (Lewis Gilbert, 1977), which is incorporated to illustrate the archetypal Bond villain. The war epic is included, but only sparingly, because as are the blockbuster franchises, it is a genre of its own.

Still, this is a sizable selection, written by four authors, and, as might be expected, there are several points of view—not discouraged by any means. We hope that this resource illustrates the characteristics of the great epic and its major or minor relatives and that it will encourage further study. The format is simple: included in each entry are crew and cast credits, AA nominations and wins, DVD and Blu-ray versions available, and the duration of each film. While notes are optional, each essay in the main list contains references (bibliography), which, in some cases, are quite extensive. No effort has been made to classify the epics according to merit or mark an entry by stars (****) or other measurements (A, B, etc.), for these are usually commercial variables, not necessarily or by agreement reflecting an epic film's standing. CS

Notes

1. Henry George Liddell and Robert Scott, *Greek-English Lexicon* (London: Oxford University Press, 1964), 309.
2. Seventeen-syllable dactylic lines, a dactyl being a three-syllable foot, of which the first is accented.
3. This list includes *The Little Iliad*, by Laches of Mytilene; Hesiod's *Works and Days*; *Argonautica*, by Apollonius of Rhodes; Virgil's *The Aeneid*; *The Bhagavad Ghita*; *Beowulf*; *Chanson de Roland*; and many other medieval epics. For further details, see Constantine Santas, *The Epic in Film: From Myth to Blockbuster* (Lanham, MD: Rowman & Littlefield, 2008), 6–8.
4. See Constantine Santas, "The Literary Origins of the Epic: Myth and Tradition," *The Epic in Film: From Myth to Blockbuster* (Lanham, MD: Rowman & Littlefield, 2008), 6–9.
5. Susan Sackett, *Box Office Hits: Hollywood's Most Successful Movies* (New York: Billboard Books, 1990), 14.
6. I am referring, in particular, to Andrew Sarris's total omission of any discussion of the epic film genre in his book *"You Ain't Heard Nothing Yet": The American Talking Film History and Memory, 1927–1949* (New York: Oxford University Press, 1998), 31–129.

7. Derek Elley, *The Epic Film: Myth and History* (Boston: Routledge and Kegan Paul, 1990), 9. See also *The Oxford Companion to English Literature* (q.v.).

8. Oscar Seyffert, *Dictionary of Classical Antiquities*, revised and edited by Henry Nettleship and J. E. Sandys (Cleveland and New York: Meridian Books, 1964), 219.

9. Aristotle, *Poetics*, Book XIII. See Charles Kaplan and William Davis Anderson, *Criticism: Major Statements*, 4th ed. (New York: St. Martin's Press, 2000), 28–29.

10. Seyffert, *Dictionary of Classical Antiquities*, 220.

11. For a detailed analysis of the subject of the didactic epic, see Monica Gale, "Didactic Epic," in *A Companion to Latin Literature*, edited by Stephen Harrison (Maltin, MA: Blackwell, 2005), 101–15. Also in Peter Toohey, *Epic Lessons: An Introduction to the Ancient Didactic Epic* (London: Routledge, 1996).

12. Katherine Callen King, ed., *Homer* (New York and London: Garland, 1994), 2.

13. A frame epic, or frame story, establishes a working framework of a group of people assembled for some social function, each undertaking to tell a story with a common theme. *Ship of Fools* (1965) is a film that corresponds to that format.

14. John Alexander Allen, "The Hero," in *Hero's Way: Contemporary Poems in the Mythic Tradition*, edited by John Alexander Allen (Englewood Cliffs, NJ: Prentice Hall, 1971), 127.

15. King, *Homer*, 12. King also cites the poems of Constantine Cavafy, Rainier Maria Rilke, and George Seferis as belonging to the epic genre (see "Introduction," xx–xxv). The epic in verse continues in our days, although sporadically, in such postmodern works as Antonio T. de Nicolas, *Moksha Smith: Agni's Warrior-Sage; An Epic of the Immortal Fire*, new ed. (New York, London, and Shanghai: Writers Club Press, 2001–2003).

16. See Joy Gould Boyum, *Double Exposure: Fiction into Film* (New York: New American Library, 1985), 23.

17. For more on the historical background of the epic literary form, see the "Selected Bibliography."

18. See Richard Corliss, "Maybe Nobody Told Martin Scorsese the American Film Epic Was a Dead Form," *Time Magazine*, December 23, 2002, p. 66, on Martin Scorsese's *Gangs of New York*.

19. Generally referring to CGI, along with 3D, streaming channels, and DVD and Blu-ray editions, mostly of restored or "Director's Cuts" editions of older movies.

20. Wilfred L. Guerin, Earle Labor, Lee Morgan, Jeanne C. Reesman, and John R. Willingham, *A Handbook of Critical Approaches to Literature*, 2nd ed. (New York: Harper & Row, 1979), 162–64.

21. Otto Rank, *The Myth of the Birth of the Hero* (New York: Vintage Books, 1959), 65.

22. Guerin, Labor, Morgan, Reesman, and Willingham, *A Handbook of Critical Approaches to Literature*, 156.

23. Philip Wheelwright, *Metaphor and Reality* (Bloomington: Indiana University Press, 1962). Quoted in Guerin, Labor, Morgan, Reesman, and Willingham, *A Handbook of Critical Approaches to Literature*, 156–57.

24. James F. Iaccino, *Jungian Reflections within the Cinema: A Psychological Analysis of Sci-Fi and Fantasy Archetypes* (Westport, CT: Praeger, 1998), 1.

25. Iaccino, *Jungian Reflections within the Cinema*, 1–2.

26. See Vivian Sobchack, "'Surge and Splendor': A Phenomenology of the Hollywood Historical Epic," in *Film Genre Reader II*, edited by Barry Keith Grant (Austin: University of Texas Press, 1995), 280–303.

A

THE ADVENTURES OF ROBIN HOOD (1938)

DIRECTORS: Michael Curtiz, William Keighley
WRITERS: Norman Reilly Raine, Seton I. Miller
PRODUCER: Hal B. Wallis (uncredited) (Warner Bros., First National)
DIRECTORS OF PHOTOGRAPHY: Tony Gaudio, Sol Polito
EDITOR: Ralph Dawson
ART DIRECTION: Carl Jules Weyl
COSTUMES: Milo Anderson
MUSIC: Erich Wolfgang Korngold
CAST: Robin Hood: Errol Flynn. Maid Marian: Olivia de Havilland. Sir Guy of Gisbourne: Basil Rathbone. Prince John: Claude Rains. Will Scarlett: Patric Knowles. Friar Tuck: Eugene Pallette. Little John: Alan Hale. High Sheriff of Nottingham: Melville Cooper. King Richard the Lion-Heart: Ian Hunter. Bess: Una O'Connor. Much: Herbert Mundin. Bishop of the Black Canons: Montagu Love. Sir Essex: Leonard Willey. Sir Ralf: Robert Noble. Sir Mortimer: Kenneth Hunter. Sir Geoffrey: Robert Warwick. Sir Baldwin: Colin Kenny. Sir Ivor: Lester Matthews. Dickon Malbete: Harry Cording. Captain of Archers: Howard Hill. Proprietor of Kent Road Tavern: Ivan F. Simpson as Ivan Simpson
AA: Best Art Direction (Carl Jules Weyl), Best Film Editing (Ralph Dawson), Best Music, Original Score (Erich Wolfgang Korngold)
AAN: Best Picture (Warner Bros. and First National)
DVD: Turner Entertainment and Warner Home Video, 2003
BLU-RAY: Warner Home Video, 2008
DURATION: 102 minutes

This beloved 1938 version of the Robin Hood myth remains a perennial favorite and the touchstone for all other film versions. It is also one of the best showcases of early (and expensive) Technicolor, or as one poster proclaimed, "A Technicolor Triumph," given full rein of lush colors that had previously been held at bay by Technicolor's Natalie Kalmus, who oversaw the technology's use on set and had been concerned not to overwhelm an audience more accustomed to black and white. She was convinced otherwise for this project,[1] and the result is breathtaking, particularly in the intensity and combination of colors in Milo Anderson's costumes.

While the characters are storybook heroes and villains, this is precisely the point: a fairy-tale Robin Hood, in which the impeccable cast takes evident delight. In England, in 1191, the deceptively charming and effete Prince John (Claude Rains) takes no small pleasure in learning that his brother, King Richard the Lion-Heart (Ian Hunter), has been captured upon his return from the Crusades. With the assistance of Sir

Guy of Gisbourne (a wonderfully brooding Basil Rathbone), John uses Richard's misfortune as a pretext for raising more taxes to free him, all the while intending to keep the ransom for himself. Their banquet is interrupted by Sir Robin of Loxley (Errol Flynn), a Saxon lord brave enough to protest the ill treatment of his people by the Norman aristocracy and John's scandalous plans to assume the throne.

Robin is declared an outlaw and takes to Sherwood Forest with those loyal to Richard and those who have suffered under Prince John, among them Much the Miller's son, Will Scarlett (Patric Knowles), Friar Tuck (Eugene Pallette), and Little John (Alan Hale). Hale also played the role of Little John in the 1922 *Robin Hood* (Allan Dwan), starring Douglas Fairbanks Sr., and again in the 1950 *Rogues of Sherwood Forest* (Gordon Douglas). Robin's outlaws attack a Norman party carrying the ransom taxes (in scenes directly mirroring those from the 1922 version) and force Sir Guy and the bumbling and cowardly Sheriff of Nottingham (Melville Cooper) to wear rags. The king's ward, Maid Marian (Olivia de Havilland), is disdainful of Robin, until his entourage proclaims that they will not keep the stolen money but rather use it to free Richard. When Robin shows her how they tend to the needy, Norman or Saxon, she begins to see him in a new light, their attraction and growing affection for one another told through the love theme by Erich Wolfgang Korngold.

Robin releases the infuriated Norman nobles, who decide to hold an archery contest to lure Robin with the promise of a golden arrow to be presented by Marian herself. Robin cannot resist, and the tournament is a showpiece of the film, with Robin splitting his competitor's arrow to win, but also ensuring his capture. Robin is to be publically hanged, but Marian bravely goes to his men and suggests a rescue plan. The freed Robin climbs her balcony to thank her, and the pair profess their love for one another.

Meanwhile, at a local Saxon inn, the Bishop of the Black Canons (Montagu Love) overhears a man call his traveling companion "sire," and the wily Bishop hurries to tell Prince John that King Richard has secretly returned to England. A former knight is sent to assassinate him, and Marian is arrested when Sir Guy discovers her trying to send word to Robin. But Marian's nurse Bess is able to warn her sweetheart Much (Herbert Mundin), who intercepts the assassin. For his part, Richard has heard tales of Robin's loyalty, and a disguised Richard conspires to have himself captured by the merry outlaws of Sherwood Forest. Richard reveals his true identity to Robin's entourage, and, as Prince John is planning to have himself crowned king the next day, he will need their help. The outlaws persuade the Bishop of the Black Canons by point of blade to let them pose as religious men and gain access to the castle. John's coronation plans are interrupted, and after an exciting sword fight with Robin, Sir Guy is slain and Marian rescued. King Richard, restored to his rightful place on the throne, orders the jubilant Robin to wed the willing Marian, and the film ends with their departure.

Robin's heroic exploits were given a grand treatment beyond an ordinary swashbuckling adventure film, with the budget for the film reaching an exorbitant $2 million (in 1938 dollars). Warner Bros. had been known for its gangster films, headed by James Cagney and Edward G. Robinson, as well as musicals, but the enforcement of the Motion Picture Production Code in 1934, essentially a code of conduct that prohibited screen immorality, put an end to the gangster genre in this era. Warner and its stable of actors had to reinvent themselves, switching from law breakers to law enforcers (in such films as William Keighley's *G-Men* of 1935) and producing prestige pictures and historical and literary adaptations. For *The Adventures of Robin Hood*, the studio distributed educational tie-in material to emphasize the highbrow aspirations of the film. Flynn was brought in on the strength of his performance in *Captain Blood* (1935, in which he costars with Olivia de Havilland), whose director, Michael Curtiz, was also brought in to the project when Warner Bros. felt that the early scenes directed by Keighley lacked the necessary verve (although a *Variety* review of the film cites illness as the official reason given at the time[2]). Replacement director Curtiz went on to have a memorable career that included the films *Casablanca* (1942) and *Mildred Pierce* (1945), but Flynn did not like working with him (to put it mildly), for he felt the director was reckless with the safety of his actors.[3]

The Adventures of Robin Hood was Warner's most expensive undertaking, but the risk paid off. It was a phenomenal critical and commercial triumph. The *New York Times* raved, "here, romantics, is a tale of high adventure, wherein blood is spilled and arrows fly, villains scowl and heroes smile, swords are flashed and traitors die—a tale of action, pageantry, brave words, and comic byplay." As for Prince John and his cohorts, "how the children's matinees will hiss them! We couldn't. We enjoyed them all too much."[4] *Variety* called the film "cinematic pageantry at its best."[5] In 1948, the film was given a successful "Warner Bros. EPIC RE-RELEASE" (as the trailer proclaimed). The film won three Academy Awards but lost Best Picture to Frank Capra's *You Can't Take It with You* (1938), for Columbia Pictures.

The figure of Robin Hood himself cannot be found in the reign of either Richard or John, but he is mentioned briefly in the Middle Ages, while the surviving ballads have much that suggests a late medieval, fourteenth-century England. The tradition of Robin as champion of the people is even later in the seventeenth century. It is this later tradition that *The Adventures of Robin Hood* mostly follows, by virtue of its historical advisor and Elizabethan specialist F. M. Padelford. As for the conflict between the Normans and Saxons depicted in the film, the Norman Conquest of England was in 1066, and John Aberth notes that by 1191, the two peoples were, in fact, completely "assimilated."[6]

In any case, each era reinvents its mythic heroes to resonate with its own time. Ina Rae Hark argues that the film "encompasses the double concerns of the Americans in the late 1930s, a transitional period between the crisis of the Depression and the coming war in Europe."[7] Thus, Prince John represents oppressive and racist tyranny exercised in the specific economic form of crushing taxes, and Robin's solution is the redistribution of wealth.

In doing so, Robin is, of course, prepared to break the law. Flynn's Robin is a "liminal" in-between figure who pays no heed to proper boundaries—between noble and commoner, Norman and Saxon (he shelters both if they are in need), civilization and wilderness. Robin may have the most power in Sherwood Forest, but it is partly his slippery ability to move with uncanny freedom between spaces, and evade or escape capture, that so infuriates the Normans. Robin's (much commented on) tights enable him to move freely, show off Flynn's physique, and emphasize his natural skill—he has no need for armor (an early costume design with an aristocratic Robin in chain mail was abandoned[8]).

Flynn and de Havilland made eight films together and are rumored to have been romantically involved during the making of *The Adventures of Robin Hood*, although in 2009, at the age of ninety-two, de Havilland finally broke her silence and said that although the pair fell in love, they never took their relationship further.[9] Regardless, the on-screen chemistry between the pair is evident. Flynn's reckless real-life exploits and star persona[10] perfectly underscore Robin's own humor and daring. Indeed, the film might have had quite a different feel if Warner Bros.' first choice, James Cagney, had not fallen out with the studio. DB

Notes

1. Peter Jones, "Glorious Technicolor," *The Adventures of Robin Hood*, directed by Michael Curtiz and William Keighley (Turner Entertainment and Warner Home Video, 2003), DVD.

2. "The Adventures of Robin Hood," *Variety*, 1938, www.variety.com/review/VE1117796684/ (27 May 2012). The production history of the film is detailed in various excellent accompanying documentary supplements to the two-disc special DVD restored edition of the film, headed by historian Rudy Behlmer, particularly Jeff Kurtti, "Welcome to Sherwood: The Story of The Adventures of Robin Hood," *The Adventures of Robin Hood*, directed by Michael Curtiz and William Keighley (Turner Entertainment and Warner Home Video, 2003), DVD. On educational publicity, see John Aberth, *A Knight at the Movies: Medieval History on Film* (New York and London: Routledge, 2003), 167.

3. Errol Flynn, *My Wicked, Wicked Ways* (London: Aurum, 1960, 2005), 202, 297.

4. Frank S. Nugent, "The Adventures of Robin Hood," *New York Times*, 13 May 1938, http://movies.nytimes.com/movie/review?res=EE05E7DF173FB72CA0494CC5B67994886896 (27 May 2012).

5. "The Adventures of Robin Hood," *Variety*.

6. Aberth, *A Knight at the Movies*, 150–55, 163, 168. Stephen Knight, *Robin Hood: A Complete Study of the English Outlaw* (Oxford, UK, and Cambridge, MA: Blackwell, 1994), 24, 262–88.

7. Ina Rae Hark, "The Visual Politics of *The Adventures of Robin Hood*," *Journal of Popular Film* 5, no. 1 (1976): 4.

8. John Aberth, *A Knight at the Movies*, 168.

9. Emily Andrews, "Errol Flynn? He Never Had His Wicked Way with Me, Says *Gone with the Wind* Star Olivia de Havilland," *Daily Mail*, 17 June 2009, www.dailymail.co.uk/tvshowbiz/article-1193489/Errol-Flynn-He-wicked-way-says-Gone-With-The-Wind-star-Olivia-Havilland.html (27 May 2012).

10. See Flynn, *My Wicked, Wicked Ways*.

Bibliography

Aberth, John. *A Knight at the Movies: Medieval History on Film*. New York and London: Routledge, 2003.

"The Adventures of Robin Hood." *Variety*, 1938, http://www.variety.com/review/VE1117796684/ (27 May 2012).

Andrews, Emily. "Errol Flynn? He Never Had His Wicked Way with Me, Says *Gone with the Wind Star* Olivia de Havilland." *Daily Mail*, 17 June 2009, www.dailymail.co.uk/tvshowbiz/article-1193489/Errol-Flynn-He-wicked-way-says-Gone-With-The-Wind-star-Olivia-Havilland.html (27 May 2012).

Flynn, Errol. *My Wicked, Wicked Ways*. London: Aurum, 1960, 2005.

Hark, Ina Rae. "The Visual Politics of *The Adventures of Robin Hood*." *Journal of Popular Film* 5, no. 1 (1976): 3–17.

Knight, Stephen. *Robin Hood: A Complete Study of the English Outlaw*. Oxford, UK, and Cambridge, MA: Blackwell, 1994.

Nugent, Frank S. "The Adventures of Robin Hood." *New York Times*, 13 May 1938, http://movies.nytimes.com/movie/review?res=EE05E7DF173FB72CA0494CC5B67994886896 (27 May 2012).

AGORA (2009)

DIRECTOR: Alejandro Amenábar
WRITERS: Alejandro Amenábar, Mateo Gil
PRODUCERS: Fernando Bovaira, Álvaro Augustín (Mod Producciones, Himenóptero, Telecinco Cinema)
EXECUTIVE PRODUCERS: Simón de Santiago, Jaime Ortiz de Artiñano
CINEMATOGRAPHER: Xavi Giménez
EDITOR: Nacho Ruiz Capillas
ART DIRECTION: Frank Walsh, Jason Knox-Johnston, Matt Gray, Stuart Kearns, Dominique Arcadio
COSTUMES: Gabriella Pescucci
MUSIC: Dario Marianelli
CAST: Hypatia: Rachel Weisz. Davus: Max Minghella. Orestes: Oscar Isaac. Ammonius: Ashraf Barhom. Theon: Michael Lonsdale. Synesius: Rupert Evans. Aspasius: Homayoun Ershadi. Cyril: Sammy Samir. Olympius: Richard Durden. Isidorus: Omar Mostafa. Theophilus: Manuel Cauchi. Medorus: Oshri Cohen. Hesiquius: Charles Thake. Prefect Evragius: Harry Borg.

Peter: Yousef Sweid. Hierax-Parabolano: Clint Dyer
AA: None
AAN: None
DVD: Paramount Pictures and Transmission, 2010. With running commentary by director Alejandro Amenábar.
Blu-ray: Region B/2, Dolmen Home Video, Fox, Tobis, 2010
Duration: 122 minutes

Agora is an "ancient world" epic set in the Egyptian city of Alexandria in the fourth century A.D., loosely based on historical events. Focusing on the life of the talented and charismatic female astronomer and teacher Hypatia (in a complex portrayal by Rachel Weisz), the film charts her life, along with the shift from the dying days of the Pagan Roman Empire to the emergence of a new Christian rule.

Hypatia teaches at the famous Library of Alexandria, the repository of all knowledge in the Western world. She is courted by her student Orestes (Oscar Isaac), but she rejects him by presenting him with her menstrual blood in front of the class, a scene based on a true event.[1] Hypatia's slave, Davus (Max Minghella), is also besotted by her, and after his conversion to Christianity—a faith that was legal in this era but still disparaged by the Pagan ruling elite—his first prayer is to beg his new God not to allow any other man have her.

When the Christians use the public meeting space called the Agora to disparage the Pagan gods, Hypatia is unable to dissuade her peers from violent revenge, but the attack turns against them, and the Pagans are pursued back to the library by an unexpected hoard of Christians. With the Pagans locked in the library and surrounded by the siege of Christians, the two groups await the intervention of the emperor himself.

The Pagans are eventually pardoned for beginning the fight, but the price is the library itself. Hypatia and her fellow scholars scramble to save what few documents they can. Although initially drawn to help Hypatia, Davus is repelled by her dismissive attitude to the slaves and instead joins his fellow Christians in destroying the library. He returns to rape her but changes his mind and is officially "freed" by a shaken Hypatia.

In the second half of the film, the city is now majority Christian. Davus is a Christian monk, and a converted Orestes has become prefect. A series of strikes and counterstrikes between the Christians and the Jews within the city ensue, and Orestes struggles to maintain control. The nonreligious Hypatia is now a trusted friend and advisor to Orestes, but in the conservative Christian climate, this alignment is frowned upon. The hard-line bishop of Alexandria, Cyril (Sammy Samir), sermonizes about the proper demure place of women in an obvious reference to Hypatia, and he demands that Orestes kneel to him and the Bible. Orestes walks out, causing a power crisis. Hypatia is captured by the monks despite Davus's thwarted attempts to warn her of her impending assassination. Outnumbered by the other monks, Davus suffocates Hypatia himself, with her consent, to save her from the suffering and indignity of death from the mob by stoning. Hypatia's actual demise was more grisly than presented in the film—there was no Davus, and the Christians skinned her alive.[2]

No religious group emerges from *Agora* with the moral high ground. The well-known past cruelties of the Roman Empire toward Christians are simply replaced by an equally oppressive, violent, and intolerant Christian rule. Even the nonreligious Hypatia, who proclaims tolerance, displays ingrained prejudices against slaves. As the Christians carry out a mass slaughter and expulsion of the city's Jewish population, a powerless Orestes exclaims that he was "naïve . . . to think we had finally changed." In his DVD commentary, director Alejandro Amenábar comments that Orestes' lament is one that could apply to the "human race throughout history," and Amenábar intended to create a particular evocation of the Holocaust.

Hypatia strives to unravel the mysteries of the cosmos while this religious and political turmoil surrounds her. In Hypatia's day, the preferred cosmological theory was that of Ptolemy, with Earth at the center of the cosmos and the five known planets, or "wanderers," revolving around it in circular orbits. To fit in with the observed looping movement of the planets, each was also said to undertake a second, smaller circular motion. Despite being widely accepted, Ptolemy's model was criticized for its perceived inelegance. Aristarchus of Samos (d. 230 B.C.E.) was the earliest astronomer known to have suggested that the Earth was one of the planets and that all the planets orbited the Sun.[3] Although this idea had not been taken seriously by subsequent scholars, Hypatia reconsiders this heliocentric concept and comes up with what was then a radical notion that the planets—including Earth—make elliptical orbits around the sun. This cosmological discovery would not come to light again until the scientific revolution of the seventeenth century. As none of Hypatia's own work survives, this part of the film is a historical embellishment, but as a narrative device, it functions as a symbol of the knowledge lost at the Library of Alexandria and the folly of human intolerance. Hypatia rejects both religion and men in favor of astronomy, her driving passion. Her insistence on the right to question ultimately brings about her downfall.

Amenábar intersperses the action with shots of the Earth taken from space, an unusual move for this genre, paralleling Hypatia's struggles to understand the cosmos. This vantage point suggests that the events in Alexandria are petty and small, yet emblematic of our human foibles.

Amenábar had previous international success with the atmospheric ghost story *The Others* (2001), and he received an Oscar for Best Foreign Language Film for *The Sea Inside* (2004). Regrettably, *Agora* did not attract as wide an audience as it deserved and did not have extensive theater distribution in the United States. Hypatia is an intellectual heroine, and the romantic interests that are often given greater focus in female-lead epics are dispensed with early on (even if they continue to motivate Orestes and Davus). These thwarted romantic possibilities perhaps contradict audience expectations, particularly as this is a character and era not well known to the general public. It is probably also telling that Amenábar was criticized for using a story about early Christianity to explore links with contemporary Islamic fundamentalism and the oppression of women.[4]

Variety gave the film a mixed review, suggesting that a "certain heaviness of style and lack of an emotional pulse could pose problems for mass audience acceptance, at least in the United States," but the *New York Times* found it "chilling," noting that the "skeptical and the secular also need stories of martyrdom and rousing acts of cinematic preaching."[5] *Agora* won a number of Spanish Goya Awards in 2010, including Best Cinematography (*Mejor Fotografía*) for Xavi Giménez and Best Original Screenplay (*Mejor Guión Original*) for Alejandro Amenábar and Mateo Gil. DB

Notes

1. Maria Dzielska, *Hypatia of Alexandria*, translated by F. Lyra (Cambridge, MA: Harvard University Press, 1995), 50. On the historical Hypatia, see also Michael Deakin, *Hypatia of Alexandria: Mathematician and Martyr* (Amherst, NY: Prometheus Books, 2007).

2. Alejandro Amenábar, "Commentary," *Agora*, directed by Alejandro Amenábar (Paramount Pictures and Transmission, 2010), DVD.

3. T. S. Kuhn, *The Copernican Revolution: Planetary Astronomy in the Development of Western Thought* (Cambridge, MA: Harvard University Press, 1957, 1985), 42.

4. Amenábar, "Commentary."

5. Todd McCarthy, "*Agora* (Spain)," *Variety*, 18 May 2009, www.variety.com/review/VE1117940282/ (7 January 2012); A. O. Scott, "*Agora* (2009): Love amid the Togas and the Intolerant," *New York Times*, 27 May 2010, http://movies.nytimes.com/2010/05/28/movies/28agora.html?scp=1&sq=agora&st=cse (7 January 2012).

Bibliography

Deakin, Michael. *Hypatia of Alexandria: Mathematician and Martyr*. Amherst, NY: Prometheus Books, 2007.

Dzielska, Maria. *Hypatia of Alexandria*. Translated by F. Lyra. Cambridge, MA: Harvard University Press, 1995.

Kuhn, T. S. *The Copernican Revolution: Planetary Astronomy in the Development of Western Thought*. Cambridge, MA: Harvard University Press, 1957, 1985.

McCarthy, Todd. "*Agora* (Spain)." *Variety*, 18 May 2009, www.variety.com/review/VE1117940282/ (7 January 2012).

Scott, A. O. "*Agora* (2009): Love amid the Togas and the Intolerant." *New York Times*, 27 May 2010, http://movies.nytimes.com/2010/05/28/movies/28agora.html?scp=1&sq=agora&st=cse (7 January 2012).

ALEXANDER THE GREAT (1956)

DIRECTOR: Robert Rossen
WRITER: Robert Rossen
PRODUCER: Robert Rossen (United Artists, MGM Studios)
CINEMATOGRAPHER: Robert Krasker
EDITOR: Ralph Kemplen
ART DIRECTION: André Andrejew
COSTUMES: David Ffolkes
MUSIC: Mario Nascimbene
CAST: Alexander: Richard Burton. Philip of Macedonia: Fredric March. Barsine: Claire Bloom. Aristotle: Barry Jones. Darius: Harry Andrews. Attalus: Stanley Baker. Parmenio: Niall MacGinnis. General Memnon: Peter Cushing. Demosthenes: Michael Hordern. Eurydice: Marisa De Leza. Cleitus: Gustavo Rojo. Philotas: Ruben Rojo. Pausanias: Peter Wyngarde. Nectenabus: Helmut Dantine. Aeschenes: William Squire. Antipater: Friedrich Ledebur. Ptolemy: Virgilio Texeira. Roxane: Teresa Del Rio. Arsites: Julio Peña. Spithridates: Jose Nieto. Nearchus: Carlos Baena. Perdiccas: Larry Taylor. Harpalus: Jose Marco. Hephaestion: Ricardo Valle. Stateira: Carmen Carulla. Aristander: Jesus Luque. Drunken Woman: Ramsey Ames. Amytis: Ellen Rossen. Ochus: Carlos Acevedo. Olympias: Danielle Darrieux
AA: None
AAN: None
DVD: MGM, 2004
BLU-RAY: Currently unavailable
DURATION: 130 minutes

Alexander the Great is a historical CinemaScope epic based on the life of the young Macedonian (played by Richard Burton) who conquered Greece and Asia, before his untimely death at the age of thirty-three. Burton had "sword-and-sandal" success with Henry Koster's 1953 epic *The Robe*, but, at thirty, looks too old to convincingly play a teenaged Alexander. He is also hampered by truly atrocious and distracting blond hair, sitting oddly against a dark and persistent five o'clock shadow. But there were even more pressing difficulties for the production, which was filmed mostly in Spain. It had exceeded its initial $2 million budget, and, much to the chagrin of writer, producer, and director Robert Rossen (best known for *All the King's Men*, 1949; *The Hustler*, 1961; and *Lilith*, 1964), the original three-hour running time was drastically cut at the insistence of the studio.[1] The result is understandably disjointed.

The first half of the film is the most compelling, depicting Alexander's teenage years as he struggles with an overbearing mother (Danielle Darrieux as Olympias) who declares him a god, and his paranoid father, Philip "The Barbarian" of Macedonia (Fredric March). Alexander becomes a pawn in his parents' bickering and upon being made regent tries to assert some sense of independence by laying waste to a rebelling city. He clearly loathes his father, who behaves with drunken dishonor after victory and discards Alexander's mother to marry a much younger woman.

Alexander saves his father's life in battle only to later stand back as his mother manipulates his friend Pausanias (Peter Wyngarde) into assassinating Philip. Olympias then kills Philip's new wife and her infant son, much to Alexander's distress. These caustic family relationships lay the foundations for Alexander's psychology as leader, and yet little time is left for his own rule in the second half of the film, where it loses structure and focus.

The youthful Alexander gains the admiration of the disparate Greek city states by speaking of "unity and strength," but once he comes to power, he meets resistance in the form of the Athenian general Memnon (Peter Cushing), who questions whether such a goal can simply be enforced by a dictator. When Alexander invades Persia, the exiled Memnon tries to help the Persian emperor, Darius (Harry Andrews), in the hope of securing freedom for Athens. Darius unwisely rejects his advice and then abandons Memnon on the battlefield to be slain by Alexander (the real Memnon survived only to die from illness some time later).[2] Alexander subsequently claims Memnon's widow Barsine (Claire Bloom) as his lover. Although her attraction to Alexander is evident, Barsine is disturbed to see another woman flung into the dirt by one of Alexander's men, presumably after being raped. Alexander is hardly reassuring, saying, "You will be treated according to your rank." Barsine retorts, "My rank is hers. I will share both her glory and her shame." As Barsine, Bloom has little to work with, but this brief scene is one of the film's best, for its time a rare and cutting commentary on the price women pay for the "glorious" wars of their men.

Alexander proves himself to be a talented strategist, continually defeating the Persians despite being outnumbered. After fleeing another losing encounter, Emperor Darius is murdered by his own men for refusing to abdicate in favor of Alexander, but Alexander is moved by Darius's final message that Alexander should marry his daughter Roxane (Teresa Del Rio) so that "our worlds may become one."

The celebrations of victory are short-lived. Alexander unsettles his men by proclaiming himself a god and stating his intention to conquer the world. In trying to outdo his father's legacy, Alexander nonetheless begins to resemble him in his drinking and paranoia. Alexander's old friend Cleitus (Gustavo Rojo) drunkenly declares that "it is by the blood of Macedonians [. . .] that you have grown so great!" Alexander spears him in the back but is immediately and desperately remorseful, announcing that it is time to return home.

Alexander finally marries Roxane in a group ceremony to bring about peace and unity, but he collapses at the celebration. He prays for his apotheosis and in his dying breath says that his empire should go to "the strongest."

Roxane and Barsine are by his side as he dies, and yet the real Alexander's main love interests were men. But this is 1955, and, instead, Alexander is presented as a young man struggling with an Oedipal complex, resenting his father and wrestling with an overly close maternal relationship. His wife Roxane is barely on-screen, but she was evidently more interesting than we are lead to believe here, as Plutarch tells us she killed her rivals after Alexander's death (*Life of Alexander*, 77.4).

The historical Alexander was a contradictory figure.[3] After all, this is the invader that the pre-Islamic Persians understandably referred to as "Alexander the Accursed."[4] As much as Alexander himself wanted to be Achilles (Plutarch tells us that Homer's *The Iliad* was his "most precious" possession, *Life of Alexander*, 26.1), it is a model of heroism that remains problematic for contemporary audiences. Alexander's lover Barsine declares that her Persian homeland is corrupt and needs Greek intervention, but who would a Cold War audience side with, given that the Athenian Memnon sees himself as fighting for freedom from Alexander's enforced "unity"?

Writer/director Rossen had been blacklisted in 1951 due to his former membership in the Communist Party and his refusal to name party members for the House Un-American Activities Committee. In 1953, he requested to reappear and confirmed a list of members' names provided to him by the committee. It was during this difficult time that Rossen began preparing *Alexander the Great*. Rossen intended to show the corruptive influence of power, as Alexander's professed aim of unity instead becomes a destructive force.[5] And yet Burton's Alexander never seems convincingly idealistic in the first place, his late change of heart in favor of peace perhaps too neat, such that *Alexander the Great* remains a deeply ambiguous film.

While *Variety* noted that no expense seemed to have been spared in either its spectacle or its "talented international cast," it nonetheless criticized Rossen for being unable to hold the viewer's interest, "resulting in some long, dull stretches."[6] By contrast, the *New York Times* praised the film's complex characters and concluded that it was "an overlong but thoughtful and spectacular entertainment."[7] It was not a financial success. DB

Notes

1. Alan Casty, *The Films of Robert Rossen* (New York: Museum of Modern Art, 1969), 34.
2. Michael Wood, *In the Footsteps of Alexander the Great* (Berkeley and Los Angeles: University of California Press, 1997), 51.
3. For the ancient sources on Alexander, see Dawn L. Gilley and Ian Worthington, "Alexander the Great, Macedonia, and Asia," in *A Companion to Ancient Macedonia*, edited by Joseph Roisman and Ian Worthington (Oxford, UK: Wiley-Blackwell, 2010), 186–207.
4. Shahrokh Razmjou, "Religion and Burial Customs," in *Forgotten Empire: The World of Ancient Persia*, edited by John Curtis and Nigel Tallis (London: British Museum Press, 2005), 154.
5. Casty, *The Films of Robert Rossen*, 5, 9, 28–33.
6. "Alexander the Great," *Variety*, 1956, www.variety.com/review/VE1117796725/ (10 March 2012).
7. A. H. Weiler, "Screen: A Saga of Ancient Titans; 'Alexander the Great' Is Sweeping Pageant," *New York Times*, 29 March 1956, http://movies.nytimes.com/movie/review?res=9e0defd71430e23bbc4151dfb566838d649ede&scp=1&sq=alexander%20great%20Richard%20Burton&st=cse (10 March 2012).

Bibliography

"Alexander the Great." *Variety*, 1956, www.variety.com/review/VE1117796725/ (10 March 2012).

Casty, Alan. *The Films of Robert Rossen*. New York: Museum of Modern Art, 1969.

Gilley, Dawn L., and Ian Worthington. "Alexander the Great, Macedonia, and Asia." In *A Companion to Ancient Macedonia*, edited by Joseph Roisman and Ian Worthington, 186–207. Oxford, UK: Wiley-Blackwell, 2010.

Razmjou, Shahrokh. "Religion and Burial Customs." In *Forgotten Empire: The World of Ancient Persia*, edited by John Curtis and Nigel Tallis, 150–80. London: British Museum Press, 2005.

Weiler, A. H. "Screen: A Saga of Ancient Titans; 'Alexander the Great' Is Sweeping Pageant." *New York Times*, 29 March 1956, http://movies.nytimes.com/movie/review?res=9e0defd71430e23bbc4151dfb566838d649ede&scp=1&sq=alexander%20great%20Richard%20Burton&st=cse (10 March 2012).

Wood, Michael. *In the Footsteps of Alexander the Great*. Berkeley and Los Angeles: University of California Press, 1997.

ALEXANDER: DIRECTOR'S CUT (2004)

DIRECTOR: Oliver Stone
WRITERS: Oliver Stone, Christopher Kyle, Laeta Kalogridis. Based on the biography *Alexander the Great*, by Robin Lane Fox.
PRODUCERS: Moritz Borman, Thomas Schuly, Jon Kilik, Iain Smith (Warner Bros., Intermedia Films, Pacifica Film)
CINEMATOGRAPHER: Rodrigo Prieto
EDITORS: Thomas J. Nordberg, Yann Herve, Alex Marquez
ART DIRECTION: Jonathan McKinstry (supervising), Kevin Phipps (senior)
COSTUMES: Jenny Beavan
MUSIC: Vangelis
DISTRIBUTOR: Constantin Film, Warner Bro.
CAST: Alexander the Great: Colin Farrell. Queen Olympias: Angelina Jolie. King Philip II: Val Kilmer. Ptolemy Soter I: Anthony Hopkins. Hephaestion: Jared Leto. Roxana: Rosario Dawson. Cassander: Jonathan Rhys Meyers. Craterus: Rory McCann. Cleitus: Gary Stretch. Antigonus: Ian Beattie. Perdiccas: Neil Jackson. Young Alexander: Connor Paolo. Aristotle: Christopher Plummer. Parmenion: John Kavanagh. Bagoas: Fransisco Bosch. Attalus: Nick Dunning. Nearchus: Denis Conway. Darius III: Raz Degan. Euridice: Marie Meyer. Young Ptolemy: Eliot Cowan. Pausanias of Orestis: Toby Kebbell. Porus: Bin Bunluerit. Stateira: Annelise Hesme.
AA: None
AAN: None
DVD: Warner Bros.: *Alexander*, 2004; *Alexander: Director's Cut*, 2005; *Alexander Revisited: The Final Cut*, 2007
BLU-RAY: Currently unavailable
DURATION: *Alexander*, 175 minutes; *Alexander: Director's Cut*, 167 minutes; *Alexander Revisited: The Final Cut*, 214 minutes

Alexander: Director's Cut is the second of three versions of the same film about Alexander III of Macedon (356–323 B.C.E.), best known as Alexander the Great. Directed by Oliver Stone and nearly universally derided critically despite a purported fifteen years in development, it is a didactic epic about Alexander inspired by a philosophical treatise found on a charred papyrus roll near Macedonia dating to the era of King Philip II.[1] Within this frame, Stone forges in Alexander's persona a classical epic theme of the hero who must pay the penalty for the crimes of his ancestors—with a neo-Orphic twist.

The historical Alexander was born to King Philip of Macedonia (although fabled to be the son of the god Zeus) and Olympias, princess of Epirus. This famed conqueror, who never lost a battle, died at the age of thirty-three without naming a successor to his vast Macedonian Empire. Stone's story begins years later, after the wars of succession had ended, leaving Alexander's former schoolmate and military companion, Ptolemy, as ruler of Egypt.

The action of *Alexander* is structured as a didactic frame narrative[2] in which a now aged Ptolemy (Anthony Hopkins) narrates his written historical memoir of Alexander to a cleverly named scribe, Cadmos.[3] Ptolemy begins his story with a reflective tone of reverence, saying, "He was a god, Cadmos, or as close as anything I've ever seen," but he also introduces the philosophical topic of his discourse, the dual nature of all humans, as he subtly slips sand through his fingers: "All men reach and fall . . . reach and fall." Ptolemy wears a now-broken ring, which is the same ring that Alexander (Colin Farrell) releases at the moment of his death in a scene that appears twice in the film, at the beginning and toward the end. In that death scene, we see a pale Alexander lying beneath the canopy of a Persian fan, and at the moment of his death, the *faravahar* of the Zoroastrian god of light, Ahura Mazda, depicted on that fan, merges into the winged eagle (a symbol of the divine Zeus and purported true father of Alexander), as in a symbolic apotheosis of the hero reminiscent of Ganymede's[4] mythic abduction by the king of the gods. These elements tease that we are about to see a classical heroic epic: a ring, the sand, the name of the insignificant scribe, the eagle. And *they do serve as tokens in this film*, but not in the sense that they do in the epic prophesy of a *heroic* narrative. Here, they are symbolic props for a more modern story—a literary one, a historical one. For this epic, although *about* a hero, is not a heroic epic.

Stone intentionally juxtaposes the Apollonian literate world of Egypt with the Dionysian dithyrambic actions of Alexander throughout the film by cutting between the action (Alexander) and narration (Ptolemy) scenes of the two characters. The action scenes include Alexander's youth (emphasizing his strong bonds with his mother, Olympias, and his lifelong companion, Hephaestion); the taming of his horse, Buchephalas; two elaborate military scenes (at Gugamela and India); and numerous exotic festival scenes shot at various locations during the journey to the east. The narrative interprets what we have seen. This does not help the heroic plot, but again, this is not a heroic narrative. Stone's intertextual theme here, based on the Orphic text of Derveni, is this: there is a human battle within us between the savage forces entombed within us (the Orphic dust of the Titans), which needs to be expunged, and the glory of Dionysian *enthusiasmos* (the god within), which also needs to be released. The conflicting tension serves as Alexander's quest: finding the mean between his mother's way and his father's way—both born of noble divine mythic origins, and both of which need to be fulfilled through his own actions.

The trouble is they conflict with one another. His mother's way preaches a path of love but purports to make a man weak; his father's way dictates that only through steel and suffering and overcoming fear is one's glory achieved. Even though these conflicting worldviews are dramatically depicted in mythopoetic sequences early in the film—his mother's initiatory training of young Alexander about human nature through the use of her snakes, and his father's cavernous journey through the walls of myth in the underground caves at Pella—this subject does not work for the screen because the conflict cannot be resolved through a unity of action, but only through philosophical contemplation, and this requires a literary or initiatory medium, not film, for its delivery. Stone's solution is to resort to flashback and parallel scene constructions out of chronological order to emphasize the correlations in Alexander's mind in an attempt to unravel the development of Ptolemy's narrative for the screen. The method fails, although the intent is noble.

Once examined within its mythopoetic context, *Alexander* wakes from its literary Tartarus and can be revived for evaluation. The choice of the myth of the ancestors of the human race as springing from the ash of the Titans is perfect for the denouement of the plot.[5] The action highlighting the heroic pathos occurs appropriately at the beginning and the end.[6] The symbols are precise; for example, the ring, symbolizing the handing over of the responsibility of civilization from one generation to the next, is completed.[7] The action and parallels move clearly. Unfortunately, those viewing the film come expecting to see a historical biopic; instead, they witness dramatic scenes from an ancient philosophical mystery rite of the *pharmakos*,[8] and, as unwelcome voyeurs (like King Philip, who prophetically lost an eye when spying upon his wife Olympias consorting with a snake in initiation), they become somewhat horrified and certainly confused.

Nevertheless, Stone's *Alexander* does reveal its true mission, albeit with a twentieth-century bent, through its didactic, if not heroic, message, adding more proverbial fuel to the critical fire. The Alexander of Oliver Stone, in the end, leaves the earth as a Promethean Titan, thereby resolving the family conflict, but is this resolution the one of biography, myth, or history? And what does this resolution leave for us as his final legacy?

For Stone, Alexander's mission was all about action: "'In the doing, always in the doing' will ring for me as Alexander's theme, his *crie de coeur.* And if he leaves us in the end with more questions than answers, his are grand questions well worth asking."[9]

And what of Alexander's character? Stone suggests that he was not an imperialist, but a sort of

> proto-man, an enlightened monarch naturally in search of one land, one world—the unity . . . of the womb. If Alexander had had a longer life, his empire might have yielded . . . the global world centers we have today but with *one world government*, centered on enlightened monarchy, or barring that, some form of governing body.[10]

Perhaps at the end of it all, however, it is the reflections by old Ptolemy in the film that capture the essential truths about Alexander's authentic legacy, despite the Apollonian restraint under which they were spoken or the literary *acroteria*[11] through which they survived: "The truth is never simple and yet it is. The truth is we did kill him. By silence we consented . . . because we couldn't go on. But by Ares, what did we have to look forward to but to be discarded in the end like Cleitus? After all this time, to give away our wealth to Asian sycophants we despised? Mixing the races? Harmony? Oh, he talked of these things. I never believed in his dream. None of us did. That's the truth of his life. The dreamers exhaust us. They must die before they kill us with their blasted dreams." And so with films. MC

Notes

1. The *Derveni Papyrus.*

2. The purpose of didactic epics, as the name indicates, is to teach. While they can vary in subject matter, from medicine, to geography, to dog rearing, they include standard features, including an introduction outlining a thesis about the Ages or Races of Humans in some mythic or philosophical preamble and a triangular structure: a teaching narrator, a named "student" to whom the epic is being "taught," and an unnamed audience of "hearers/readers."

3. Cadmos is the name of the founder of the House of Thebes (which also includes the god Dionysos). He is also said to be the inventor of the Greek (Phoenician) alphabet, according to Greek myth. The name (not necessarily the same person) is also related to a founder of the Samothracian Mysteries, where, according to Plutarch, Alexander's parents met during an initiation ceremony and where Alexander was conceived.

4. Ganymede was a beautiful young male youth who was abducted by Zeus on Mt. Ida. Taking the form of an eagle, Zeus snatched the boy and made him the immortal cupbearer to the gods. Zeus gave immortal horses to Ganymede's father, Tros (founder of Troy), in exchange for the boy. Ganymede is related to Alexander on his mother's side. (Tros was the mortal twin brother; Dardanus was the immortal twin brother by Zeus in that family line. Alexander is from the immortal line and thus related to Zeus here, as well.)

5. Alexander is descended from two lineages of Titans, both of whom are associated with the founding of the Samothracian Mysteries, although from different lines of succession. On his father's side, he is descended from Heracles through Zeus, son of the Titan Cronos (or directly through Zeus, son of Cronos). From his mother's side, he is descended from Achilles, through Dardanus, through Electra, daughter of the Titan Atlas.

6. The scene of Alexander's death and apotheosis symbolizes the philosophical passion of Prometheus through his torment and conciliation with the god Zeus. In retribution for deception, Zeus punishes Prometheus (himself a son of the Titan Iapetus) by having his (Zeus's) eagle torment him for thousands of years (by having him chained to a rocky mountain cliff while his liver is pecked out and regrown) until their conflict

is reconciled by the intercession of Heracles via Atlas, thus reuniting both branches of the Titanic family line.

7. *Pseudo-Hyginus, Astromomica 2.15:* "Prometheus (Zeus) bound with an iron chain to a mountain in Scythia named Caucasus . . . [but later] freed him from his chains. But he didn't go so far as to free him from all binding, since he had sworn to that, but for commemoration bade him bind his finger with the two things, namely, with stone and with iron. Following this practice men have rings fashioned of stone and iron, that they may seem to be appeasing Prometheus."

8. One who suffers unjust trials.

9. Oliver Stone, "Afterward," 11 January 2006, www.oscarworld.net/ostone/Alexander_Afterward_Jan_11.pdf (15 February 2012).

10. Stone, "Afterward." According to Josiah Ober of the Department of Classics at Princeton University, "Historian Arnold Toynbee once put forward a counterfactual speculation that has gained certain fame. What would have happened if, instead of dying at thirty-two, Alexander the Great had made it to old age? Toynbee saw Alexander conquering China and dispatching naval expeditions that would circumnavigate Africa. Aramaic or Greek would become our lingua franca and Buddhism our universal religion. An extra quarter-century of life would have given Alexander the chance to achieve his dream of One World, becoming, in the process, a kind of benevolent advance man for a United Nations, ancient style."

11. *Acroteria* are architectural ornamentations placed at the apex of ancient Greek temples.

Bibliography

Fox, Robin Lane. *The Making of Alexander.* Oxford, UK, and London: Rowman & Littlefield, 2004.

Gale, Monica. "Didatic Epic." In *A Companion to Latin Literature*, edited by Stephen Harrison, 101–15. Maltin, MA: Blackwell, 2005.

Hathorn, Richmond L. *Greek Mythology.* Beirut, Lebanon: American University of Beruit, 1977.

Ober, Josiah. "Conquest Denied: The Premature Death of Alexander the Great." In *What If? The World's Foremost Military Historians Imagine What Might Have Been*, edited by Robert Cowley, 37–55. New York: Penguin Putnam, 2000.

Santas, Constantine. *The Epic in Film: From Myth to Blockbuster.* Lanham, MD: Rowman & Littlefield, 2008.

Stone, Oliver. "Afterward." 11 January 2006, www.oscarworld.net/ostone/Alexander_Afterward_Jan_11.pdf (15 February 2012).

West, M. L. *The Orphic Poems.* Oxford, UK: Oxford University Press, 1983.

ALIEN (1979)

DIRECTOR: Ridley Scott
WRITERS: Dan O'Bannon, Ronald Shusett
PRODUCERS: David Giler, Walter Hill, Gordon Carroll (Brandywine Productions, 20th Century Fox)
CINEMATOGRAPHER: Derek Vanlin
EDITORS: Terry Rawlings, Peter Weatherlay
MUSIC: Terry Goldsmith
CASTING: Mary Selway
CAST: Captain Dallas: Tom Skerritt. Executive Officer Kane: John Hurt. Navigator Lambert: Veronica Cartwright. Warrant Officer Ripley: Sigourney Weaver. Science Officer Ash: Ian Holm. Engineer Brett: Harry Dean Stanton. Engineer Parker: Yaphet Kotto. Alien: Balaj Baedjo
AA: None
AAN: None
DVD: 20th Century Fox, 2003. Two-disc edition digitally restored and recut by Ridley Scott.
BLU-RAY: Currently unavailable
DURATION: 116 minutes (director's cut)

Alien should belong to the category of horror movie, rather than science fiction, or be regarded as a combination of both, a voyage of epic scope. It is Ridley Scott's big-screen success, after the *Duellists* (1977), which is a story of a feud between two French officers during the Napoleonic Wars, but which was only a modest box-office success. *Alien* became a hit and catapulted Scott into the ranks of first-rate moviemakers; it was followed by *Aliens* (1986), directed by James Cameron, and after that by a series of lesser movies that perpetuated the title but not the quality of the first two. Scott made one more science-fiction film, *Blade Runner* (1982), and of late (2012), he launched a big-budget project of real epic proportions, *Prometheus*, which has been viewed by many as a "prequel" to *Alien*. There is possibly a connection, for in *Prometheus*, a mega-spaceship is launched to detect the origins of archeological finds on Earth and the existence of another planet, but the motive for this exploration seems to be metaphysical, rather than a space exploration or commercial galactic transaction. *Alien* features a spaceship, *Nostromo*, returning to Earth after a successful voyage into space, hauling a load of 20 million tons of valuable ore in a huge secondary vehicle/refinery attached to the main spacecraft. *Nostromo* is occupied by seven crew members, each of whom has a specific function in running or supervising the mission, which is to land the ship and its cargo safely on Earth.

But things do not go exactly as planned. As *Nostromo* is nearing its destination, a signal is received from an unknown origin that awakens the crew from their stasis, which they exit in an unspecified period of time.[1] After a discussion, with which not all agree, they go along with Science Officer Ash's (Ian Holm) recommendation, and three of them—Navigator Lambert (Veronica Cartwright, who played young Cathy in Hitchcock's *The Birds* in 1963), Captain Dallas (Tom Skerritt), and Executive Officer Kane (John Hurt)—are dispatched to explore the origin of the signal. Following a rough landing on a strange planetoid, where they walk in their space suits, they explore the rough terrain and are eventually attracted by a horseshoelike structure that must have crashed on the surface. Strangely enough, this structure resembles the spaceship that Elizabeth Shaw, the sole survivor of *Prometheus*, rode in to continue her exploration. (This is a linkage that reinforces the idea that the latter was meant as a prequel to *Alien*.)

As the three enter the cavernous structure, they are stunned by the menacing, eerie atmosphere of the place, which, again, resembles that of the cave where the members of that ship wander in *Prometheus*. They find a gigantic alien being that seems to have been turned inside out. It emits some kind of radio transmission, which Ripley (Sigourney Weaver) interprets as a warning, but the three continue their exploration, and, when Kane finds some strange egglike beings, one of them springs out and engulfs his face. He is carried back to the ship against the wishes of Ripley, who points out that this is a violation of quarantine. The creature on his face resembles a large crab (nicknamed the "facehugger"), with humanlike claws, and when one of those is cut, an acid drips from it and burns the ship's floor. The facehugger is soon found dead, Kane seems out of danger, and the crew prepares to go into stasis and resume their trip. But, while they are having dinner, Kane goes into what looks like an epileptic fit, and soon a snakelike creature with a sharp "Scyllalike" head (the "chestbuster") springs from his bowels and disappears into the crevices of the ship.

One by one, the crew members are eliminated, as the creature grows to its full size: Brett (Harry Dean Stanton) is attacked and killed while looking for a cat on the ship, and Dallas is attacked and killed while searching for the monster. The rest of the crew, with Ripley now in charge, decide to abandon *Nostromo* and escape into the ship's shuttle, but they cannot do so, as it will not hold more than three people. As she checks the computer, Ripley discovers—she must have suspected something all along—that Ash is an android programmed to return the *Nostromo* to its owner, carrying the Alien with it. Ash attacks her and tries to choke her to death, but Parker (Yaphet Kotto) and Lambert intervene and decapitate Ash, whose head, still capable of speech, predicts that they will all perish. Soon Lambert and Parker are also killed, and Ripley manages to get into the shuttle, with the cat, but she discovers that the Alien is there, hiding. After a struggle, she puts on her space suit and separates from *Nostromo*, which explodes into space. The creature is in the shuttle, but Ripley manages to eject it, and when it tries to crawl back in through one of the exits, she blasts it into space. Ripley then communicates with the Earth base, relays what has occurred, and places herself and the cat in a stasis cell to await six weeks, hoping to be picked up when they come close to the horizon border. The movie ends there.

The viewer remains captive to the events in the interior of the ship (save the short exploration outside). It is a claustrophobic environment, and the viewer lives the terror moment by moment. Only the seven crew members are shown during the film, along with the Alien in its various regenerations and the curious cat, which is the only other creature that escapes destruction, sensing the presence of the Alien better than humans and hiding in places that the Alien cannot locate. Until the first attack on Kane, the crew members are seen as carefree souls, not particularly surprised or haunted by any fear about the failure of their mission. Two of them smoke cigarettes, as the protocol of spaceship life does not prohibit such a practice in the 1970s (an anachronistic action for today's viewer, but a device for showing the terror they are undergoing—Lambert in particular). We are not told who has employed them or anything about their previous adventures in space.

The plot is tight and economical, without any of the metaphysical, anthropological, or pseudoscientific and theological gadgetry that plagues the plot of *Prometheus*; however, there are obvious parallels. In both cases, the crews are attacked by alien creatures, not sympathetic to the human race, whatever that might be. *Alien*'s economy, however, and its avoidance of gratuitous philosophizing, helps create a tension that is lacking in the subsequent movie, decades later. In addition, *Alien* has a better heroine. While Elizabeth Shaw in *Prometheus* does not lack courage or dedication, Warrant Officer Ripley displays cunning and the guts of a seasoned fighter against odds. When alone vis-à-vis the tenacious monster, she exercises her only option, to be as heartless and cold-minded with it as Bowman is when disconnecting HAL in Stanley Kubrick's *2001: A Space Odyssey*. She is a survivor, and the audience roots for her. The other female character, Navigator Lambert, is nervous throughout the adventure and smokes compulsively, but she fights the monster bravely before succumbing.

There are obvious Hitchcockian elements in the story. As in Hitchcock's *The Birds*, man is attacked by a creature of nature other than a human. The attack comes unexpectedly and without reason. Both attacks seem apocalyptic, although in *Alien* there is design, for Science Officer Ash is an android, reminding us of David in *Prometheus* and HAL in *2001*. Ash is planning the elimination of the crew so he can triumphantly return to his "makers"/employers with an alien on board. What the idea is behind his behavior remains a mystery. In that sense, *Alien* does not explain the phenomena, interactions between man and nature, and the mystery remains unresolved. Also, as in *Prometheus*, the surviving member is a woman—launching into an unknown destination. There is a connection, for in both movies crews are fighting the unknown and seem ill-equipped to do so. The suspense is created by the unexplained mysteries in the universe, but in *Alien*, it is the fear of the unknown, as the plot is simple and unencumbered by metaphysical or even scientific question. The unknown evil and the potential of the unknown danger are the elements of this plot. CS

Note

1. This setup seems similar to the one used in Stanley Kubrick's *2001: A Space Odyssey* (1968), the purpose of this being to save life materials, nutrition, and oxygen for the long voyage.

Bibliography

Goodwin, Archie. *Alien: The Illustrated Story*. Illustrated by Walt Simonson. New York and London: Titan Books, 2012.

Scanlon, Paul. *The Book of Alien*. Illustrated by Michael Gross. New York and London: Titan Books, 2012.

ALL QUIET ON THE WESTERN FRONT (1930)

The greatest war book that has yet been written.

—Redacteur Stohr, Germany

DIRECTOR: Lewis Milestone

WRITERS: George Abbot, Maxwell Anderson, Del Andrews, C. Gardner Sullivan, Lewis Milestone. Based on the novel by Erich Maria Remarque of the same name.

PRODUCER: Carl Laemmle Jr. (Universal Pictures)

CINEMATOGRAPHER: Arthur Edeson

EDITOR: Edgar Adams

MUSIC: David Brockman

CAST: Paul Bäumer: Lew Ayres. Westhus: Richard Alexander. Franz Kammerich: Ben Alexander. Albert Kropp: William Bakewell. Herr Meyer: Edmund Breese. Lieutenant Bertinck: G. Pat Collins. Peter: Owen Davis Jr. Müller: Russell Gleason. Detering: Harold Goodwin. Leer: Scott Kolk. Professor Kantorek: Arnold Lucy. Mrs. Bäumer: Beryl Mercer. Behn: Walter E. Rogers. Tjaden: Slim Summerville. Himmelstoss: John Wray. Stanislaus Kaczynski: Louis Wolheim. Classroom Student: Arthur Gardner

AA: Best Director (Lewis Milestone), Best Picture (Universal Pictures)

AAN: Best Screenplay (George Abbot, Maxwell Anderson, Del Andrews), Best Cinematography (Arthur Edeson)

DVD: Universal Cinema Classics, 2007

BLU-RAY: Currently unavailable

DURATION: 138 minutes

Antiwar movies touching the epic scale are few and far between, but when they arrive, they remain in the ranks, and often in popular appeal, for a long time. Aside from *All Quiet on the Western Front*, a classic that has endured, one can mention Stanley Kubrick's *Paths of Glory* and David Lean's *The Bridge on the River Kwai* (both released in the same year, 1957), and later, *Saving Private Ryan* (1998), by Steven Spielberg, who acknowledged his debt to Lewis Milestone's (and Erich Maria Remarque's) masterpiece.[1] For good measure, one can add Jean Renoir's *Grand Illusion* (1937), Francis Ford Coppola's *Apocalypse Now* (1979), and Oliver Stone's *Platoon* (1984), the last two both polemic diatribes on the Vietnam War. This rather sporadic and eclectic short list excludes dozens of others, but for sheer scope and dramatic intensity, these will do for the moment. *All Quiet on the Western Front* was the first sound film to win Academy Awards for Best Director and Best Picture. It was ranked fifty-fourth in the American Film Institute's (AFI) best 100 movies until 2007, is still ranked seventh in the AFI's ten best epics category, and has won a permanent place in the Library of Congress National Film Registry.

The success of *All Quiet on the Western Front* as an antiwar movie is mostly due to the fact that it discards the usual trappings of war movies—generals giving orders to their staffs and planning attacks, and the consciously cultivated nationalistic attitude that separates "us," the good guys, from the "bad guys" we fight against and generally the good guys/bad guys mentality. War in most war movies is fought for a righteous cause; that is what separates this movie from its relations in the genre. This movie is told from a German point of view, negating the idea that Germany fought on the wrong side in World War I and World War II.[2] The German soldiers were thus placed in a "no man's land," and war is the same thing, no matter who fights it and what it is fought for. Much like Hemingway, Remarque himself had fought in war, and, in some ways, the two resemble one another, for both write about what war was actually like, the difference being that Hemingway veers into romance. His great antiwar novel, *A Farewell to Arms* (never really made into a satisfactory movie), ends with the death of his beloved Catherine Barkley, an English nurse whom he had met while he was wounded. Remarque's novel is pure war. Fictional elements are minimized, and the intent is to describe war as it is, not as it has been glamorized by poets, playwrights, novelists, and filmmakers, who, for the most part, have seen war as an adventure where the good guys—that is, our side—almost always win.

Remarque, and subsequently Milestone, add a subtle touch to all this by placing the concept of war into the mentality of the idealist. A teacher urges his teenage students to enlist when war breaks out, and his entire class answers his enthusiastic call. On the board we see the opening words of *The Odyssey*,[3] about a man of many devices, a warrior who had returned from Troy after he had scored a great victory; he later quotes the Romans, saying, "*Dulce et decorum est pro patria mori*" ("It is sweet and proper to die for one's country").

The war is thus defined from a double point of view. It is given from the older generation—teachers, parents, and older folks who do not fight but gladly send their sons to fight for the fatherland, and the younger generation, who fight the actual war. The speech of Professor Kantorek represents the older point of view, and the film is an attempt to expose war's shallowness and falsity. With gleaming eyes, Kantorek bursts out in dithyrambic odes describing the glories of dying for the fatherland, and the naïve students of his class, enthusiastic youths who believe him, except one, who cowers before the prospect of fighting, enlist—all twenty of them.

The teacher represents the old German idealism expressed in Romantic terms by the poets Goethe and Schiller, and in the grandiose Nordic myths that gave roots for the grandiose Wagnerian compositions, or the heroic myths sung by Homer and the Romans. Remarque explodes these myths in his book, and Milestone's film follows suit when it shows what the reality of war means. The myths of youth dying for glory are also placed against the reality of modern warfare. The 300 of Leonidas fought with spears, arrows, and swords, not that this was an easy way of dying, but modern war is a relentless barrage of shells exploding, even during the hours of rest; there is no respite from the horrors of modern warfare, which, in essence, started with World War I. Tanks and artillery and aerial bombardment were everyday means of battle; bunkers and trenches replaced the open battlefields of the eighteenth century and even the ranks of the Napoleonic battles; and the fighting became a constant nightmare, lasting twenty-four hours.

Once the group of twenty young men enters this modern inferno, they immediately become aware of its horrors and shed all notions of a war fought for any reason other than killing or being killed. Fights are a series of struggles against extinction, starving because of poor supplies, or mutilation. Friends see friends getting killed, being maimed, or going insane. Idealism is entirely wiped out in the first hours of battle. Brutality touches everything, from poor rations that are improperly distributed, to hunger and filth, to misery and ill health, to seeing friends die or become wounded. Above all, there is terror.

Hence, reality is juxtaposed to idealism. The key figure is one of the teacher's students, Paul Bäumer (Lew Ayres), who shared his teacher's idealism when he enlisted but has become the first to realize how empty those words were. Like a Hemingway character, he becomes the pivotal voice, that of the author (Remarque), for it is through him that the author, and subsequently the filmmaker, speaks. Shocked, Bäumer soon adapts to the new situation, but without losing his goodness or his humanity. He helps others when he can, but he is clear-eyed and understands that what he is engaged in is a fraudulent action. Not rebellious-minded, he performs his duty as best as he can, but his accumulated experiences open his eyes to the enormity of the crime, that war is nothing but a collective massacre without purpose or logic. When he stabs an opponent, a middle-aged Frenchman who lies wounded next to him in a hole, he tries to revive him and keep him alive, begging to be forgiven by him. The Frenchman dies, and Bäumer searches his pockets and finds his military card and a picture of his wife and a little girl. He vows to send his family letters, telling them how bravely their loved one died.

War is thus reduced to its essence: a massive slaughter of humans fighting and killing total strangers. When during a bunker conversation of veterans there is a brief exchange of why wars occur, one answer is that one nation offends the other, and then the offended one declares war. One of the soldiers laughs and asks how that can be. How can a German mountain offend a French plain? Another offers the explanation that the Kaiser had not had wars, and every Kaiser needs one to make a name for himself. A third suggests that those who initiate war—generals, prime ministers, and other leaders—should fight it out themselves, with gloves in the mud, if necessary, not have others fight it for them.

In this film, we do not see generals giving orders, and no strategic planning is shown. No rationale is given for either side, and we only see the events from the point of view of the men who are fighting. This entirely strips the war of its idealism, its raison d'être, or any kind of glamour. When Bäumer returns home on leave after he has been wounded, he goes to a pub where war is being discussed by a group of men who are all bickering about the mode of attack and the speed with which German forces should march into a parish. In his school, his old teacher recognizes Bäumer and urges him to speak to a group of youngsters—boys of no more than sixteen—of the glory of fighting for one's country. Bäumer simply speaks the truth, telling the young people that fighting is about killing or being killed, nothing else. One of the youths shouts that he is a coward. Disillusioned, Bäumer cuts his leave short and returns to the front, where at least there is no room for lying, for there people really know what war is.

Thus, *All Quiet on the Western Front* defines war: a struggle between two—or more—parties who are intent on inflicting bodily damage on one another. War is nothing but killing those whom you are ordered to kill. You have no choice, and any reason not to fight is considered treason and punished harshly. War is a fight for extinction. The message is not imaginary. More people were killed in World War I than all the wars of the last 200 or 300 years combined; millions were killed in just one battle—Verdun. But that is not the only point made in the film. The most important point is what war is in concept, carefully built up by centuries of idealistic sayings—"pro patria" and so forth—used universally and almost exclusively by those who are not doing the fighting, a concept that this film juxtaposes with the reality of war. The film says nothing about defending one's country in case of invasion or attack. It says nothing about wars that threaten one's existence. Those have been left for other movies to address, with little effort made to defend such an attitude, for anyone is capable of understanding defense.

All Quiet on the Western Front takes the subject to a higher level. It can be said that most wars have been fought on false pretenses—pretenses largely invented by those who use mottos lightly, to satisfy their own self-importance. Here it is not a general but a teacher who sends young people to battle. Generals usually have no choice, but a teacher can be deluded by the "glories of the past." Heroes have died heroically, defending their own. True enough. But it is also a myth that all men who have fought are heroes, or leaders. Most are common folk, wrenched from their families or common employments, given arms, trained to kill, and then kill or get killed.

No matter how one judges this film, whether as a condemnation of war, or just of an absurd war, or whether it holds that war in general is absurd, viewers cannot deny its effectiveness, for its relentless realism leaves the modern reader, who, some eighty years later, has become accustomed to much more violence on the screen, breathless with wonder and horror. Remarque's story and Milestone's worthy screen imitation of it tell it exactly like it is—and no one has ever told that story better. CS

Notes

1. See Mike Mayo, *VideoHound's War Movies: Classic Conflict on Film* (Detroit, MI: Visible Ink Press, 1999), 131.
2. It is interesting to note that Hitler never allowed this movie to be shown in Germany during World War II and that the movie's antiwar message also diminished its box-office value in the United Sates.
3. Ἄνδρα μοι ἔννεπε Μοῦσα πολύτροπον. ("Tell me, Muse, of the man of many stratagems.")

Bibliography

Mayo, Mike. *VideoHound's War Movies: Classic Conflict on Film.* Detroit, MI: Visible Ink Press, 1999.

Norman, Barry. *The 100 Best Films of the Century.* New York: Carol Publishing Group, 1990.

Remarque, Erich Maria. *All Quiet on the Western Front.* Cutchogue, NY: Little, Brown and Company, 1929.

———. *All Quiet on the Western Front.* Translated from German by A. W. Wheen. London: Folio Society, 1966.

AMADEUS (1984)

Director: Milos Forman
Writer: Peter Shaffer
Producer: Saul Zaentz (Saul Zaentz Company)
Cinematographer: Miroslav Ondricek
Editors: Michael Chandler, Nena Daneric, T. M. Christopher (2002 director's cut)
Art and Set Direction: Patrizia von Brandenstein, Karen Kerney
Costumes: Theodore Piskek
Music: Sir Neville Mariner
Sound Mixers: Mark Berger, Tom Scott, Todd Bockenheide
Makeup Artists: Paul LeBlank, Dick Smith
Cast: Antonio Salieri: F. Murray Abraham. Wolfgang Amadeus Mozart: Tom Hulce. Costanze: Elizabeth Berridge. Joseph II: Jeffrey Jones. Emanuel Schikanender/Papageno: Simon Callow. Leopold Mozart: Roy Dotrice. Katerina Cavalieri: Christine Ebersole. Count Orsini-Rosenberg: Charles Kay. Parody Commendatore: Kenny Baker. Papagena: Lisbeth Bartlett. Frau Weber: Barbara Byrne. Young Salieri: Marin Cavina. Count Van Strack: Roderick Cook. Kapellmeister Bonno: Patrick Hines. Archbishop Colleredo: Nicholas Kepros. Baron Van Swieten: Jonathan Moore. Father Volger: Richard Frank
AA: Best Picture (Saul Zaentz), Best Director (Milos Forman), Best Actor (F. Murray Abraham), Best Adapted Screenplay (Peter Shaffer), Best Art Direction (Patrizia von Brandenstein, Karen Kerney), Best Costume Design (Theodore Piskek), Best Sound (Mark Berger, Tom Scott, Todd Bockenheide), Best Makeup (Paul LeBlank, Dick Smith)
AAN: Best Actor (Tom Hulce), Best Cinematography (Miroslav Ondricek), Best Editing (Michael Chandler, Nena Daneric, T. M. Christopher)
DVD: Warner Home Video, 2002. Two-disc director's cut.
Blu-ray: Warner Home Video, 2009
Duration: 163 minutes (202 for director's cut)

Amadeus could be classified as a musical, but it is not, or as a biopic, but that is not exactly the case either. It could be described as a "biographical fantasy," as Charles Kiselyak aptly calls it,[1] or all of the above. The reason for its inclusion here, in an encyclopedia of epic films, is that it is unescapably of epic scope. Aside from its sheer length of 163 minutes (expanded to 202 minutes in the director's cut), *Amadeus* features an epic sweep of an era, in the late eighteenth century. It generally defines Vienna, Austria, as the capital of world culture, particularly classical music, brought to its zenith, a feat that was possible mostly because it had the royal patronage of Joseph II (1741–1790), in many ways a child of the Enlightenment. Despite his growing political fears (his sister Marie Antoinette had seen warning signs of the impending popular uprising in France), Joseph was known for his sponsorship of the arts and culture, and he was even called the "musical emperor." Under him, important composers flourished, Gluck, Haydn, Mozart, and Salieri, to mention a few of the most prominent. Mozart's operas changed the landscape of the opera genre, since his compositions, especially *The Abduction from the Seraglio* (*Die Endführung aus dem Serail*), in 1781, brought about a change from baroque elements of composers like Handel and acquired the rococo, or classical form, which Mozart explored and perfected with his subsequent major operas, *The Marriage of Figaro*, *Cosi Fan Tutti*, *Don Giovanni*, and *The Magic Flute*. These compositions laid the foundation for a musical form that was destined to influence the greatest operatic works for the next 100 years. Music became a dominant factor in human culture, shaping and readdressing its reason for existence.

Peter Shaffer, who wrote the stage play on which the movie is based, has his principal character, Salieri, proclaim the following about the renaissance of music:

> You, when you come, will be told that we musicians of the eighteenth century were no better than servants: willing servants of the well-to-do. This is quite true. It is also quite false. Yes, we were servants. But we were *learned* servants. We arrived, each of us, *fully trained*, and we built together—like the masons who built the great cathedrals—a gigantic Palace of Sound, its foundations grounded deep in the Disciplines of Beauty. Lines of strict counterpoint were set to the strengths of the spirit; lines of strict harmony stretched to the touch of the senses. And we said to our so-called betters, '*Enter*—and we will celebrate your lives.'[2]

But aside from its cultural influence, *Amadeus* is basically a story of the collision of two major musicians who vied for dominance in the musical world of eighteenth-century Vienna. Shaffer shaped the plot of the movie from his own stage play, *Amadeus* (1980), which had broken records in both Europe and the United States, and it was only a matter of time before it was turned into a major film. Saul Zaentz, an independent producer from Berkeley, sought the services of Milos Forman, with whom he had collaborated in the award-winning *One Flew Over the Cuckoo's Nest*, in 1975. Forman, a leader in the Czech New Wave, had fled Czechoslovakia after the Soviet invasion of that country in 1968, and it wasn't until the making of *Amadeus* in the early 1980s that he went back to its capital, Prague, where the major interior and exterior scenes were filmed. Prague offered a unique environment since many of the buildings, among them the wooden opera house known as Tyl Theatre, where Mozart had performed, were still intact. It was an ideal place to make a film of this scope and one that required such meticulous attention to period settings.[3]

The film begins at the end, with a series of flashbacks, as the elderly Salieri (F. Murray Abraham), now in a psychiatric ward for having attempted suicide, is feeling guilty for having murdered Mozart (Tom Hulce). The year is 1823, thirty-two years after Mozart's death in 1791. Salieri, now in his seventies, looks haggard, wrinkled, his hair thin and disheveled, a bandage that looks like a towel tied around his neck. A priest, Father Volger (Richard Frank), a much younger man, is seen coming into the ward to ask the ailing Salieri to confess his sin. As it is, the confession provides the springboard for the plot. (In the stage play, Salieri speaks directly to the audience.) It also shows Salieri to be a multidimensional character, as he is seen changing from one guise to another as the film progresses. He is now an old man in decay who no longer needs to hide anything; on the contrary, his confession, detailed and passionate, seems to cleanse him, as he tells of his deep-seated resentment of having been abandoned by God, who "implanted the desire" to be a great musician in him but "made him mute."

As he now recalls his court days, when he was the emperor's favorite, he is seen in his wig and official costume, strutting about, the all-powerful and conniving royal servant to Joseph (Jeffrey Jones), who often calls him "*cattivo*"—bad boy—for his evasive answers. He has risen to the enviable rank of court composer and is teaching many pupils, with a generous allowance, allowing him to live a life of luxury. He is also Joseph's most intimate advisor, accommodating and flattering the vain monarch, bragging to the priest, "Actually the man had no ear at all! But what did it matter? He adored my music!" Salieri maintained a close relationship with other courtiers of Italian extraction, among them the overbearing Count Orsini-Rosenberg (Charles Kay), opera director, dominant in choosing what was to be staged and blocking what he didn't like, while at his side stood the bumbling and aging Kapellmeister Bonno (Patrick Hines), now reduced to a mere lackey to the emperor.

Salieri is also seen at his home, without his wig, either composing a tune to please the emperor or in acts of sacrilege, as when he defiantly tosses the crucifix into the fire, vowing to block God's choice and destroy Mozart. F. Murray Abraham handles these guises with slick mastery, projecting an insecure, troubled man torn by his envy and admiration for Mozart, for he is the only person who truly understood Mozart's genius. Thence his envy intensifies, as he sees "that obscene little creature" threatening to steal his glory. His moments of pathos come to light as he, now an old and forgotten man and free to tell all, confesses to the priest.

The second, and main, line of action begins with the entrance of Mozart into the picture. We are shown Salieri snooping around in Archbishop Colleredo's (Nicholas Kepros) chambers, walking into a room where delicacies for the party are being brought in. As he is picking a chocolate cherry, he hears screaming and soon sees Costanze (Elizabeth Berridge) being chased by Mozart and overhears their intimate talk, during which Mozart teaches his fiancée how to spell scatological expressions backward. Shocked, Salieri follows Mozart into the music chamber, where the archbishop is exhibiting Mozart's talents in Vienna. He hears his music, then looking at his written composition by the piano, marvels at how such an "obscene, vulgar creature" could write such music, "the voice of God."

From that point onward, Salieri knows that Mozart is a serious challenge to his reputation and standing with the emperor, and he vows to do anything to prevent any complications. Subsequently, there are scenes where Mozart confronts the emperor and his courtiers, and he wins his first battle when he persuades Joseph to allow for a German opera, *The Abduction from the Seraglio*, to be written and performed in German, despite the vehement protests of the Italian faction. "But, Majesty, German is too brute a force," mutters a dejected Bonno, but in this case, Mozart wins the day, and his opera triumphs with audiences—only to be criticized by Orsini-Rosenberg for containing "too many notes." "Cut a few," says the emperor, who was bored by the length of the play. "Which few did you have in mind, your Majesty?" responds a stunned Mozart.

Another crisis develops when Salieri pays a naïve servant girl to offer herself as a servant to Mozart and be an informer about Mozart's composing. Later, as Mozart is giving a concert before the emperor, Salieri sneaks into his apartment and discovers that he is composing *The Marriage of Figaro*, based on a play by Pierre-Augustin Caron de Beaumarchais that had been forbidden by the emperor for fomenting revolutionary ideas, and thence banned in France. Mozart passionately pleads with the emperor, who finally consents to allow the play to go on, but Orsini-Rosenberg manages to tear off several pages of the composition, claiming that including "a ballet" in a play is against his majesty's wishes. But the scheme fails, as the emperor visits the theater during rehearsals and demands that the ballet music be restored. Still, the opera fails to attract larger audiences, and it lasts only nine performances. It later had a triumphant revival in Prague, and it continues to be one of the most frequently performed Mozart operas.

Meanwhile, much else has happened in Mozart's life. Against his father's wishes, he marries Costanze, and when Leopold (Roy Dotrice) arrives in Vienna, he finds the couple living in poverty and Costanze pregnant. The film quickly cuts into later events of the 1780s, the latter part of which shows Salieri's relentless attempts to block any Mozart success, as the action frequently shifts into his older persona as the shocked priest hears him relating his tale of vindictiveness. When Leopold dies, Mozart composes *Don Giovanni*, which is performed only five times outside of Vienna. Salieri attends all five performances, while explaining to the priest that Mozart, haunted by guilt for his father's death, re-creates the old man's vengeance in the statue of the Commendatore, a scepter "beyond the grave," punishing his philandering son by dragging him into hell.

As Mozart's health deteriorates, he is preparing a new German opera, *The Magic Flute*, to be performed in the countryside by Emanuel Schikanender's (Simon Callow) troupe, for which Mozart is promised "half the gate." A man in a mask visits Mozart in his apartment, as the representative of someone who wishes to commission a requiem for a large sum of money. Eager for funds, Mozart accepts. Pressed by both sides, and while Costanze leaves for Baden to take baths, Mozart faints during the performance of *The Magic Flute* and is carried to his apartment by Salieri, always present at a Mozart performance, and there he "helps" Mozart complete his compositions of the requiem, aiming to steal the work and, after Mozart's death, perform it as his own during Mozart's funeral. Costanze arrives in time and demands that Salieri leave the house, but Mozart dies before he can answer her. Neither Costanze nor Salieri attend Mozart's funeral, a paltry affair, where the corpse of the composer is brought in a cart, in a sack, and tossed into a common grave.

Amadeus was not without its critics, some of whom complained that it is based on shaky historical grounds, as there is no definitive proof that Salieri actually poisoned Mozart or that the events portrayed in the film are accurate. Crucial points of

Shaffer's stage play were altered, as noted here, and the fact that Mozart was a Freemason is omitted in the film. Some viewers also complain that the director's cut in the 2002 DVD edition (and subsequently in Blu-ray) contains a significantly altered version of the briskly paced original theatrical release of 1984, while the added thirty minutes would probably be unacceptable in theaters today. Some of the previously deleted scenes indeed add information, but not dramatic intensity. Still, *Amadeus* remains a monument of epic moviemaking, for, in addition to its length, it delineates a clash of musical titans, and it is unparalleled in its authentic reproduction of an important period of musical history, while its dialogue maintains an aura of modernity palatable to modern audiences. It sparked a renewed interest in classical music, and it honorably holds its position as a richly textured reproduction of Mozart's musical genius. CS

Notes

1. See Charles Kiselyak, "The Mozart Firmament," on *Amadeus Pioneer Special Edition*, directed by Milos Foreman (Pioneer, 1995), audio CD.
2. Peter Shaffer, *Amadeus* (London: Samuel French, 1981), 9.
3. The brilliant, award-winning designs and sets were supervised by Patrizia von Brandenstein, who collaborated with Forman in Prague, reproducing authentic models from Mozart's day. See Kiselyak's essay on the *Amadeus Pioneer Special Edition* CD, with analog channel commentary by Forman and Shaffer, photographs, and two music CDs.

Bibliography

Amadeus Pioneer Special Edition, directed by Milos Foreman (Pioneer, 1995), audio CD.

Anderson, Emily. *The Letters of Mozart and His Family*, 3rd ed. 3 vols. New York: Palgrave Macmillan, 1989.

Einstein, Alfred. *Mozart: His Character, His Work*. London: Oxford University Press, 1945.

Shaffer, Peter. *Amadeus*. London: Samuel French, 1981.

Solomon, Maynard. *Mozart: A Life*. New York: Harper Collins, 1995.

AMERICA, AMERICA (1963)

DIRECTOR: Elia Kazan
WRITER: Elia Kazan
PRODUCER: Elia Kazan (Warner Bros.)
ASSOCIATE PRODUCER: Charles H. Maguire
CINEMATOGRAPHER: Haskell Wexler
EDITOR: Dede Allen
ART DIRECTION: Gene Callahan, Vassilis Photopoulos
COSTUMES: Anna Hill Johnstone
MUSIC: Manos Hadjidakis
CAST: Stavros Topouzoglou: Stathis Giallelis. Vartan Damadian: Frank Wolff. Isaac Topouzoglou: Harry Davis. Vasso Topouzoglou: Elena Karam. Odysseus Topouzoglou: Salem Ludwig. Abdul Osman: Lou Antonio. Stavros's Grandmother: Estelle Hemsley. Hohanness Gardashian: Gregory Rozakis. Thomna Sinnikoglou: Linda Marsch. Gabaret/Anarchist: John Marley. Vartuki/Prostitute: Joanna Frank. Aleko Sinnikoglou: Paul Mann. Aratoon Kebabian: Robert H. Harris. Sophia Kebabian: Katherine Balfour. Mehmet: George Foundas (uncredited). Turkish Official: Dimos Starenios (uncredited)
AA: Best Art Direction, Black-and-White (Gene Callahan, Vassilis Photopoulos)
AAN: Best Director (Elia Kazan), Best Picture (Warner Bros.), Best Writing–Screenplay (Elia Kazan)
DVD: Warner Home Video, 2011. With running commentary by film historian Foster Hirsch.
DURATION: 174 minutes

Kazan's *America, America*, filmed in the Alfa Studios, in Athens, Greece, with footage shot in Istanbul and Mexico, is the only epic-length movie Kazan directed in his long and distinguished career. The film describes the harrowing adventures of its young protagonist, Stavros, as he tries to reach the United States, the land of promise, from the depths of his native Anatolia.

The story brings to life an almost identical journey of one of Kazan's uncles, Frank, who came to the United States as an immigrant from Turkey in the late nineteenth century, started at the bottom, became prosperous, and consequently brought the rest of his family to the country, including young Elia himself. Although based on the life of a close relative, the transformational story bears affinities to Kazan's own life, and the film is, to a degree, considered autobiographical.

By the time *America, America* was made (1963), Kazan had already achieved the status of legend as one of the major U.S. directors with such masterpieces as *A Tree Grows in Brooklyn* (1945), *A Streetcar Named Desire* (1951), *On the Waterfront* (1954), and *A Face in the Crowd* (1957), among others; however, along with his notable status, he also carried with him the stigma of being an informer, since he had testified before the House Un-American Activities Committee (HUAC) in 1952 and revealed names of fellow members of the Communist Party, of which he had been a member from 1934 to 1936. The guilt Kazan felt for the rest of his life—and the disgrace attached to it—became a theme in some of his movies, in which a hero suffers a conflict of interest resulting from his abandoning principle for expedience.[1] As we shall see, this also becomes a theme in *America, America*.

Kazan, who had studied the "naturalistic" acting method in the Group Theatre, modeled after Konstantin Stanislavski's Art Theatre in Moscow, under Lee Strasberg in the 1930s, later became one of the cofounders of the Actor's Studio in New York, where a number of a younger generation of actors, including Marlon Brando, Montgomery Clift, and James Dean, among others, were trained in what came to be known as method acting. According to this method, an actor's inner feelings must parallel those of a hero on the screen, a technique that sharply contrasts the stereotypical image that the Hollywood studios of the 1930s and 1940s had scrupulously adopted. For the most part, Hollywood stars were typecast, their image carefully honed to play adventure or romantic leads. A string of great stars, Clark Cable, Cary Grant, Errol Flynn, James Stewart, and Gregory Peck, for a few examples, were under contract to the major studios, whose interest was to preserve their stars' wholesome image, while certain chameleonic actors, Alec Guinness, for instance, would sink their own personalities into the character they played. A method actor is exactly the opposite, as his roles are suited to express his or her own inner turmoil on the screen, some doing so with great distinction, winning Oscars in the process.

Kazan had that idea in mind when he cast the twenty-two-year-old Greek actor Stathis Giallelis, whom he brought in from Athens, to be groomed to play the role of Stavros Topouzoglou in *America, America*, learning English in the process. This movie is considered by some, Foster Hirsch in his DVD commentary, for one, to be Giallelis's quintessential work, an epic that sums up his own life's adventure, but also those of all who chose the path of immigration to this country. While this epic's ethnic diversity may be the gist of the story line, the personal element embodied in its hero is its central theme. A young Greek, born in the depths of Anatolia, where Armenian and Greek minorities lived oppressed by the Ottoman Empire, decides to escape to freedom and a better life in the United States.

Kazan's young hero accomplishes that feat, but not before he is subjected to humiliation, beatings, robbery, deception, theft, and numerous other degradations. The theme is built on that character's dogged determination to succeed despite all adversity. Initially a naïve boy—"just a kid," as the commentator puts it—Stavros changes when he recognizes that sheepish submission, or even honest hard work, will not suffice to achieve his goal. Experience teaches him that to succeed, he must be an opportunist, at times casting scruples aside. Although tortured by his growing guilt, his body language shows that he is not entirely divested of his essential humanity. Kazan balances these antithetical impulses in his hero who struggles to survive, but who also resists temptation when opportunity for a carefree life is offered him.

Young Stavros is first seen digging snow with a fellow Armenian, Vartan, loading the chunks on their truck to sell to their village's customers, a menial and demeaning job. Stavros' family lives in a village of Anatolia, hundreds of miles from Constantinople (Istanbul), where Stavros' uncle, Odysseus, has a rug business and can assist the young man in getting a pass for the United Sates. It is his father who implants in Stavros the idea of going to the United States. Isaac (Harry Davis), a patriarchal figure with a family of several sons and daughters, is seen buckling the knee before the local Turkish official, but he soon tells his son that he has "inner honor" and urges him to seek his fortunes elsewhere. Stavros sets out on foot to visit his old grandmother, a hermit witch who lives in a cave, to ask her for money for his trip, but the fierce old woman, who looks like a withered deity (Estelle Hemsley, who played her, was an African American actress), hands him a dagger instead, pointing out that the only way to escape shame is to fight. On his way there, Stavros had met a bedraggled young Armenian, Hohanness (Gregory Rozakis), going to Constantinople on foot, with dreams of going to the United States. Seeing him coughing and wearing worn shoes, Stavros gives him his own footwear, a gesture that pays dividends later.

Meanwhile, his family collects their valuables, and Stavros starts out leading a donkey with his possessions on the beast's back. His first setback comes when a wily Turk, Osman (Lou Antonio), befriends him but later accuses him of thievery, and Stavros' possessions are confiscated. He hides some coins in his mouth while being beaten and robbed, and Osman, who follows him, asks for the remaining coins and prepares to kill him, pouring contempt on the "civilized Greek," who will suffer forever "like a sheep" under the mighty Turk. But while Osman turns his back to pray to Allah, Stavros jumps on him and, after a brief fight, kills him with the dagger his grandmother had given him. He throws it away in disgust, but moments later, he collects it, placing it inside his belt. This is his first initiation to violence and the beginning of his transformation from a subject uncomplainingly suffering abuse into a man who seeks his freedom—by any means, fair or foul.

When in Constantinople, Stavros finds his relative, Odysseus Topouzoglou (Salem Ludwig), who offers him a job in his modest rug-selling business. He also tips him off about a rich merchant who has four "plain" daughters ("one plainer than the other") and is looking for bridegrooms. Stavros is at first revolted by his relative's suggestion, not wanting to become a "gigolo," marrying for money. He leaves Odysseus and joins Gabaret (John Marley) and his anarchist group, working as a "hamal," a demeaning term reserved for those who carry heavy loads on their backs, like beasts of burden. While Gabaret is preparing to use dynamite and rob a bank, a Turkish detachment arrives and razes them down with bullets, killing most. The Turks carry the dead bodies in a cart to drop them from a cliff, but Stavros, miraculously still alive, drops off the cart and drags himself to his relative's door.

In an abrupt cut, we next see him dressed as a dandy, sporting a mustache and attending a church where the rich carpet seller and his daughters are also present. Through his cousin's introduction, he ingratiates himself with Aleko Sinnikoglou (Paul Mann), who invites him to his home, where one of his daughters, the soulful but uncomely Thomna (Linda Marsch), falls in love with him. Sensing that Stavros hides a secret, Thomna passionately implores him to stay and be happy with her, his future assured. Stavros, evidently in love with her, struggles to resist security and domestic happiness. In fact, his obsession with reaching the United States grows, but he is now conflicted, for, in reality, he dislikes his ruthless pursuit of his goal at the expense of another's happiness. Despite his feelings, he gets his tickets and embarks on a ship that carries hundreds of others, who, like him, have chosen to go to the new land of opportunity.

Meanwhile, Stavros has met another woman, Sophia Kebabian (Katherine Balfour), the middle-aged wife of a wealthy American, Aratoon Kebabian (Robert H. Harris), who is sailing back to the United States on the same luxury liner that carries hundreds of immigrants. Hohanness is also on board, traveling with a group of eight youths bonded to Agnastis (uncredited actor), under the obligation to work for him for two years without wages. When Kebabian suspects his wife's liaison with Stavros, he vows to take steps to prevent him from reaching American soil. While Stavros is ready to swim ashore, Hohanness, tubercular and sure that the authorities will turn him back, and remembering his friend's earlier kindness, jumps from the ship at night during a party, leaving his papers on his shoes before he jumps. Agnastis, knowingly and needing the extra man, tells the authorities that Stavros is Hohanness, hiding the fact that the latter had jumped to his death. The port official at Ellis Island believes the lie and allows Stavros to enter, but not before changing his fake name of Hohanness to Joe Arness, saying to him, "now you are baptized again without the benefit of the clergy." We next see Stavros, all smiles, wearing the straw hat Sophia had sent to him, along with her servant, Bertha (not credited), as a parting gift, along with $50, which Stavros dutifully sends to his parents. We see him overjoyed, shining shoes and tossing a coin in the air. His goal is accomplished—he has reached the United States.

Aside from its length, the movie has several characteristics of the epic. Photographed in stark black and white and rich in detail as the landscape changes from a snowcapped eastern Anatolia, to the barren countryside with huts made of clay, to a perilous road trip through the length of Turkey, to the busy city of Constantinople, the journey offers the viewer a panorama of characters, the devious and the downtrodden, the rich and the poor. Aleko, the prosperous carpet-seller, represents the bourgeois class, thriving under the Turks. Aleko is as egotistical with his male-dominated family as with his parasitic brothers, who loosen their belts after a big meal. Kazan deftly avoids direct political statements, not blaming the Turks for being brutal slave drivers, but he closely documents the conditions Armenians and Greeks lived in for centuries. Kazan's interest centers on the miseries of those living under abject slavery and their struggles to escape. His hero's deep-seated desire is to get away to the Promised Land. The movie is, in fact, more about the United States than the land of slavery that Stavros evidently despises, although the United States is shown only briefly at the end of the movie, when Stavros appears with other escapees from Bulgaria and Rumania. But even more than that, the story is about Stavros' epic journey, his realization that subjection and peaceful means will not help him achieve his goal. He experiences the whole gamut of human emotions—living as a helpless boy with a stern father, having a recalcitrant but inspired grandmother who shows him the way, and becoming a mature man, a modern wily Odysseus of many tricks, ready to fight by any means, emotionally sensitive but determined, and eventually triumphant. His is an epic journey indeed. CS

Note

1. For a detailed description of Kazan's conflicts in testifying before the HUAC and his ensuing testimony, see Elia Kazan, *A Life* (New York: Da Capo, 1988), 448–49, 459–64.

Bibliography

Ciment, Michel. *An American Odyssey*. London, Bloomsbury Publishing, 1988.

Kazan, Elia. *A Life*. New York: Da Capo, 1988.

Schickel, Richard. *Elia Kazan: A Biography*. New York: HarperCollins, 2005.

THE ANDROMEDA STRAIN (1971)

Director: Robert Wise
Writer: Nelson Gidding. Based on a novel by Michael Crichton.
Producer: Robert Wise (Universal Pictures)
Cinematographer: Richard H. Kline
Editor: Stuart Gilmore, John W. Holmes
Art Direction: Boris Leven, William H. Tuntke, Ruby R. Levitt
Costumes: Helen Colvig
Music: Gil Mellé
Special Effects: Douglas Trumbull
Cast: Dr. Jeremy Stone: Arthur Hill. Dr. Charles Dutton: David Wayne. Dr. Mark Hall: James Olson. Dr. Ruth Leavitt: Kate Reid. Karen Anson: Paula Kelly. Jackson: George Mitchell. Major Manchek: Ramon Bieri. General Sparks: Peter Hobbs. Dr. Robertson: Kermit Murdock. Grimes: Richard O'Brien. Senator from Vermont: Eric Christmas. Lt. Shawn (Piedmont Team): Mark Jenkins. Sgt. Crane (Piedmont Team): Peter Helm. Wildfire Computer Sgt. Burk: Joe DiReda. Lt. Comroe: Carl Reindel. Toby (Technician): Ken Swofford. Clara Dutton: Frances Reid. Air Force Major: Richard Bull. MP Capt. Morton: John Carter
AA: None
AAN: Best Art Direction–Set Decoration (Boris Leven, William H. Tuntke, Ruby R. Levitt), Best Film Editing (Stuart Gilmore, John W. Holmes)
GG: None
GGN: Best Original Score (Gil Mellé)
DVD: Universal Pictures, 2003
Blu-ray: Currently unavailable
Duration: 125 minutes

The Andromeda Strain purports to be a previously classified account of a near disaster in which an extraterrestrial organism came to Earth on a fallen satellite, killing most of the residents of the small New Mexico town of Piedmont, as well as the soldiers sent to retrieve the satellite. The film charts the efforts of expert scientists who are drafted in from their regular jobs under the lead of Dr. Jeremy Stone (Arthur Hill) to investigate the organism at a state-of-the-art underground facility known as Wildfire and prevent a worldwide catastrophe. In fact, the film is fictional, based on the 1969 best-selling novel by Michael Crichton, the first to be published in his own name, as he previously used pseudonyms to prevent any disruption to his medical studies. *The Andromeda Strain* is Crichton's only film appearance, where appropriately enough he is a medic in the background when Dr. Mark Hall (James Olson) is reluctantly pulled out of the operating theater to join "Project Scoop."

Rounding out the main team is the recalcitrant Dr. Ruth Leavitt (an excellent performance by Kate Reid, whose character was a man in the original book) and Dr. Charles Dutton (David Wayne), with assistance from Wildfire employee Karen Anson (Paula Kelly). Stone and Hall are taken to

Piedmont in protective suits and find dead bodies throughout the town. Just as they are about to leave with the retrieved satellite, the pair discovers two survivors: a six-month-old infant and an old man, Jackson (George Mitchell), who are taken back to the Wildfire research laboratory and placed in quarantine.

The scientists undergo a series of unusual decontamination procedures as they descend lower and lower into the facility. The team then undertakes animal experiments and confirms that the infection is airborne. (Some of these scenes are difficult to watch, a discomfort not allayed when director Robert Wise recalls that they got the monkey to collapse by starving it of oxygen and then reviving it, a method approved by the animal welfare observers at the time.[1]) Once the source of the organism is found on the satellite, Leavitt undertakes tests to find whether anything inhibits its growth, but she misses a vital result when the flashing red display seems to immobilize her.

The team argues with government officials to get an atomic bomb dropped on the town of Piedmont, only to urgently rescind when they realize that the organism, now given the code name Andromeda, could, in fact, use the nuclear energy to grow out of control. When Dutton's lab becomes contaminated with Andromeda, alarms sound and the flashing red warning lights prompt a fit in Leavitt, but Hall realizes it is epilepsy and not Andromeda and encourages Anson to help her. With time running out for Dutton, Hall theorizes that their patients have survived because the baby's excessive crying is causing his blood to become too alkaline, while the elderly Jackson has made his blood too acidic by self-treating an ulcer with cheap alcohol. Leavitt's lab results confirm the hunch, but when they notice that Dutton's lab rat is alive, they realize that Andromeda has mutated into a noninfectious form.

But the danger is far from over. Andromeda begins to break down the lab gaskets and spread, prompting the self-destruct sequence to initiate. The self-destruct is nuclear, so it will, in reality, give Andromeda new energy to grow and mutate further. Hall has the key to disable it, but when he is cut off by the lockdown, he is forced into a central core to reach the upper levels, while being shot at by lasers designed to stop escaped lab animals. Staggering from the effects of the lasers, Hall disables the self-destruct just in time. Aboveground, the now nonhazardous Andromeda drifts out to sea, where it is neutralized by rain and the alkaline sea water.

In reviewing the film, *Variety* wrote that "*The Andromeda Strain* is a high-budget 'science-fact' melodrama, marked by superb production, an excellent score, an intriguing story premise, and an exciting conclusion," but it found the film too "literal and talky."[2] The *New York Times* criticized the film's lack of pace and action, suggesting that, "Crichton put his novel together as if from a collection of note cards—a story outline beefed up with a lot of semiscientific data."[3] Crichton, in fact, deliberately rejected the formal elements of a regular novel by modeling the book on scientific journals, intended to be all the more chilling for its detachment.[4] Beyond his success as a novelist, Crichton is best known for *Jurassic Park* (Steven Spielberg, 1993, based on Crichton's 1990 novel of the same name) and for creating *E.R.* (1994–2009) for television, but he also occasionally directed (*Westworld*, 1973).

In keeping with science-fiction paradigms, the military is foolishly dismissive of science, the government is not to be trusted, and a creeping sense of paranoia is emphasized by Gil Mellé's electronic score and the claustrophobia of the lab. Even for the genre, it is unusual for the scientific process itself to be amplified to form the narrative so centrally. The search for scientific truth is rendered in heroic terms, yet the source of danger is brought to Earth by technology, and the film ends by questioning whether we would be so lucky to avert disaster a second time.[5] As Justin E. A. Busch argues, the multi-image split screen and the isolation measures of the lab in *The Andromeda Strain* emphasize the breakdown in communication, knowledge, and even humanity.[6] That the underlying anxiety of the film goes beyond the space age in and of itself becomes clear when the scientists discover that the Wildfire facility was truthfully designed to research and potentially harness biological weapons, and Dutton, for one, can understand why so many young people are disillusioned enough to want to simply drop out.

Although primarily a science-fiction film, *The Andromeda Strain* borrows tools from the more traditional epic to give its subject a sense of historical importance and heroic consequence—a previously secret history of humanity's most perilous moment. Wise (best known for *The Sound of Music*, 1965, and *The Day the Earth Stood Still*, 1951) and his cinematographer, Richard H. Kline, make particularly stunning use of CinemaScope, with Wise deciding to use an additional "split-field diopter," a half-lens that enables greater depth of field than otherwise possible with CinemaScope. The curved, color-coded Wildfire facility interiors (one set repainted for the five levels) and stainless-steel central core are perhaps too beautiful to be a real lab, but they are nonetheless striking tangible spaces, at once contemporary and futuristic. Many of the technologies displayed within the film itself are now commonplace, but at the time they were a significant special-effects challenge to Douglas Trumball (who worked on the 1968 Stanley Kubrick film *2001: A Space Odyssey* and subsequently Ridley Scott's 1982 *Blade Runner*).

David Wayne (who plays Dutton) won two Tony Awards for his stage work and managed to snare Marilyn Monroe in Jean Negulesco's 1953 *How to Marry a Millionaire*, but he was primarily a TV actor, and none of the leads were especially well known. This was a deliberate strategy by Wise to make the characters more credible as scientists, in keeping with the conceit of a real event.[7] By contrast, when *The Andromeda Strain* was remade in 2008 as a TV mini-series, Benjamin Bratt took the lead, but the program was not compared favorably to the original film, which is now held in high esteem. DB.

Notes

1. Laurent Bouzereau, "*The Andromeda Strain*: Making the Film," 2001, *The Andromeda Strain*, directed by Robert Wise (Universal Pictures, 2003), DVD.
2. "The Andromeda Strain," *Variety*, 1971, www.variety.com/review/VE1117796769/ (12 May 2012).
3. Roger Greenspun, "Screen: Wise's *Andromeda Strain*," *New York Times*, 22 March 1971, http://movies.nytimes.com/movie/review?res=9804E1DA1530E73BBC4A51DFB566838A669EDE (12 May 2012).
4. Laurent Bouzereau, "A Portrait of Michael Crichton," 2001, *The Andromeda Strain*, directed by Robert Wise (Universal Pictures, 2003), DVD.
5. For the Apollo missions, NASA did indeed take quarantine measures to guard against contamination, but they would not have been sufficient if there had indeed been a problem. Sergio Pistoi, "The Andromeda Strain," in *The Science of Michael Crichton*, edited by Kevin Robert Grazier (Dallas, TX: BenBella Books, 2008), 11–12.
6. Justin E. A. Busch, *Self and Society in the Films of Robert Wise* (New York: McFarland, 2010), 114.
7. Bouzereau, "*The Andromeda Strain*: Making the Film."

Bibliography

"The Andromeda Strain." *Variety*, 1971, www.variety.com/review/VE1117796769/ (12 May 2012).

Busch, Justin E. A. *Self and Society in the Films of Robert Wise*. New York: McFarland, 2010.

Greenspun, Roger. "Screen: Wise's *Andromeda Strain*." *New York Times*, 22 March 1971, http://movies.nytimes.com/movie/review?res=9804E1DA1530E73BBC4A51DFB566838A669EDE (12 May 2012).

Pistoi, Sergio. "The Andromeda Strain." In *The Science of Michael Crichton*, edited by Kevin Robert Grazier, 1–17. Dallas, TX: BenBella Books, 2008.

ANNA KARENINA (2012)

DIRECTOR: Joe Wright
WRITER: Tom Stoppard. Adapted from Leo Tolstoy's novel of the same name.
PRODUCERS: Tim Bevan, Paul Webster, Eric Felner (Universal Pictures, Focus Features)
CINEMATOGRAPHER: Seamus McGarvey
EDITOR: Melanie Anne Oliver
PRODUCTION DESIGN: Sarah Greenwood, Katie Spencer
ART DIRECTION: Thomas Brown
COSTUMES: Jacqueline Duran
MUSIC: Dario Marianelli
CHOREOGRAPHER: Sidi Larby Cherkaoui
CAST: Anna Karenina: Keira Knightley. Count Alexei Vronsky: Aaron Taylor-Johnson. Prince Alexei Karenin: Jude Law. Count Stepan ("Stiva") Oblonsky: Matthew Macfadyen. Konstantin Levin: Domhnall Gleeson. Daria (Dolly) Oblonsky: Kelly McDonald. Kitty: Alicia Vikander. Countess Vronskaya: Olivia Williams. Countess Lydia: Emily Watson.
AA: Best Costume Design (Jacqueline Duran)
AAN: Best Cinematography (Seamus McGarvey), Best Original Score (Dario Marianelli), Best Production Design (Sarah Greenwood, Katie Spencer)
DVD: Focus Features, 2012. Feature commentary by director Joe Wright.
BLU-RAY: Focus Features, 2012
DURATION: 129 minutes

Joe Wright's *Anna Karenina* is one of the many adaptations of Leo Tolstoy's celebrated novel to reach the screen, and it is certainly one of the most original. Previous versions include the Greta Garbo masterwork of 1936, while the novel was also turned into a movie 1946, with Vivien Leigh. And Keira Knightley had to compete with those greats, not to mention numerous TV miniseries versions, as well as the seven Russian takes on the work, as Joe Wright notes in his commentary in the DVD "Bonus Features."[1] Wright had previously worked with Knightley on *Pride and Prejudice* (2005) and *Atonement* (2007), and his choice of his favorite actress seemed to him and his producers the best choice to play one of literature's most alluring, complex, and tragic heroines. The rest of the cast, especially his choice of Jude Law for Anna's husband, Alexei Karenin, and Matthew Macfadyen, who had played Knightley's lover Darcy in *Pride and Prejudice*, to play her brother, Count Stepan ("Stiva") Oblonsky, also seemed fortuitous. Wright also collaborated with Tom Stoppard, one of England's top screenwriters, known for his *Shakespeare in Love* and many other screenplays. Stoppard produced a first-rate script, condensing Tolstoy's massive work into a plot and allowing for decent characterizations.

But Wright's most important innovation was the staging of the film in an actual theater, having a gigantic set built to accommodate the various scenes of the drama, with compartments that included a dancing hall, a cabaret, and an opera house, not to mention the most intimate quarters where the drama of Anna and her infidelities and the effects of her actions on her husband and numerous friends and relatives played out. The quick transitions, nimble camera work, and adept choreography by Sidi Larby Cherkaoui give the impression of an operatic work or a ballet, which was Wright's aim. Although the movement seems to retard the pace of the narrative, it actually produces the opposite effect of constantly changing emotional states, from the exuberant dances to embarrassing flirtations between Anna and Vronsky (Aaron Taylor-Johnson), to gossipy moments, to the tense emotion of the lovers' encounters, to the tragic moments at the end.

The plot mainly runs along the same lines as Tolstoy's work, which actually has two plots, one revolving around the other: Anna's story takes precedence, but the romance between Konstantin Levin (Domhnall Gleeson) and Kitty (Alicia Vikander) also remains a core element in the novel. Levin is Oblonsky's friend and a wealthy agriculturalist, with a large estate on which freed former serfs work. He comes to Moscow to court Oblonsky's young (eighteen years of age) sister in law, Kitty, who turns him down, hoping to be offered a proposal of marriage from one of Russia's "golden boys," the cavalry officer Count Vronsky. Disheartened, Levin returns to his farm after a brief visit to his sick brother in Moscow, and he remains there until later in the plot, when he again thinks he can regain the attention of Kitty.

Levin is Tolstoy's alter ego, in many ways the real hero of the story: although an aristocrat with wealth, he is closer to the land and the people who live there. There is the joy of life in him, which Tolstoy describes with unforgettable force in the scene of scything the ripe wheat given briefly in the movie. Of course, in the movie, Levin's role is diminished, as Anna's takes center stage, and he is seen as a rather surly, disappointed suitor who comes to life late in the movie, when Kitty, the woman he has pursued, finally accepts him. In the movie, Levin and Anna meet only once. This device allows the story's plot to have two endings, one unhappy (Anna's separation and death) and a happy one (Levin's having found happiness in marriage and a new life of love and work).

As some critics have pointed out, the story line, at times, seems overwhelmed by its style: Dancing, choreography, quick scenic transitions within the set, and dazzling camera work take over the stage, while the actual story of Anna's alienation from her husband and her attraction to Vronsky develops between the lines, as it were. For a Tolstoy drama, the first part of the movie seems a lighthearted mélange of elegant belles of the Russian society of the times and costumed young aristocrats showing their flair for mindless merriment, something the likes of Federico Fellini put on the screen in the mid-twentieth century—the Russian *La Dolce Vita.* In some respects, music men with trumpets blaring, accordion players, and others with clarinets screeching while workers rush to work is almost a mimicking of a scene from *Eight and a Half.*

But the drama quickens in the second part of the story, as the exuberant dancing is replaced by the sober subtleties of the drama. Anna "crosses the Rubicon," in Wright's words,[2] when she asks Vronsky to stay in St. Petersburg instead of going to a new location with the army. They soon make love, and Anna becomes pregnant. Social gossip flares up during a horse race, which causes a serious clash between Anna and her enraged husband, who threatens to divorce her. Karenin refuses to forgive her, but when Anna is near death after her birth of her child, he goes to her and forgives her. Vronsky is there, too, and he seems a broken man. He and Karenin meet to console one another, but things deteriorate again, as Anna is socially stigmatized, and Vronsky turns his attention to the young and rich princess Sorokina, at the bequest of his mother. Anna now approaches the stage of paranoid breakdown, as she has lost her lover (or thinks she has), husband, son, and young daughter, and she has also become a social pariah. In desperation, desperate and in flight of reality, she jumps into the tracks of a passing train and kills herself, crying, "Oh God, forgive me!"

Meanwhile, Levin has married Kitty, and they soon have a child of their own. The movie ends in a field, where Karenin is sitting on a chair, while two children, Serozha, his and Anna's son, and Annya, Anna's little girl, play among the blooming yellow flowers.

Critics have taken Wright to task on several accounts. One is the style with which he chose to narrate the story: a large stage, a pat puppet theater,[3] where movement freezes, and where frenzied dancers whirl around a large dancing floor, while dramatic episodes are pushed to the side. One critic criticized the ballet scenes, adding that Ophüls and Powell-Pressburger, who made choreographed dramas in the 1960s, wisely chose stars who could perform on both the dramatic and artistic levels, but, as Wright explains in his feature-length commentary, he employed fifty professional dancers for the key musical numbers, and that Alicia Vikander was a Swedish ballet dancer who had chosen an acting career. Taylor-Johnson was also an adept dancer; thence that criticism seems unfair, at least as far as these two are concerned.

But the same critic, Karen Backstein of *Cineaste Magazine*, finds the Keira Knightley performance to be the "big black hole" in the movie, "sucking in energy and illuminating nothing."[4] Tolstoy's Anna, Backstein asserts, had both grace and beauty, and "while Knightley does have the latter, she sorely lacks the former."[5] Other critics disagree. Oliver Lyttleton found Anna's performance to be a progression, moving "from strength to strength,"[6] while Knightley collaborators in the film[7] praise her intense concentration and thorough knowledge of Tolstoy's work. Some insist that Knightley was the overwhelming choice for this role. Knightley herself says in her commentary (see "Bonus Features," "Keira as Anna") that the heroine is a combination of classic and modern heroine. Admittedly, Knightley's body language and voice are almost totally modern, but that can be seen as a strength here, while, in her first collaboration with Wright, *Pride and Prejudice*, her mannerisms were at times out of place. The reason might be that Jane Austen's work was rendered in the original English, and change of tone will affect interpretation, while Tolstoy's work comes to us in translation, and Stoppard's script has something decidedly modern to it.

Anna, as Emma Bovary in Flaubert's work, suits the modern mold of a woman who is led astray by passion, and since antiquity, women like Phaedra (both in Euripides and Racine) are played over and over again; Phaedra in Jules Dassin's work *Phaedra* (1961) and Rosy (in David Lean's *Ryan's Daughter*) come back to life as tragic heroines in one fashion or another. In his commentary, Wright observes that Anna, while flagrantly deceiving her husband, is not a heroine that is hated by the audience, and that Tolstoy himself developed feelings of affection for her while writing the novel.[8] Knightley achieves that delicate balance of playing a sinner whom an audience cannot hate. Far from being a big black hole, Knightley actually lifts the movie from a well-staged soap opera to a dramatic work of classic, even epic dimensions. CS

Notes

1. "Bonus Features," *Anna Karenina*, directed by Joe Wright (Focus Features, 2012), DVD.
2. See "Director's Commentary," on both the DVD and Blue-ray, and "Bonus Features." The Rubicon is a river near Rome, and an army crossing is meant to be a declaration of war against Rome.
3. "Director's Commentary," *Anna Karenina*.
4. Karen Backstein, "*Anna Karenina*," *Cineaste Magazine*, XXXVIII, no. 2 (Spring 2013): 55.
5. Backstein, "*Anna Karenina*."
6. Oliver Lyttleton, "Review: *Anna Karenina* Is a Bold Reimagining of a Classic That's (Mostly) Thrilling and Inventive," *Playlist*, 31 May 2012, Blogs .indiewire.com (5 September 2012).
7. Weber, Wright, Vikander.
8. "Director's Commentary," *Anna Karenina*.

Bibliography

Backstein, Karen. "*Anna Karenina*." *Cineaste Magazine*, XXXVIII, no. 2 (Spring 2013): 55.

Lyttleton, Oliver. "Review: *Anna Karenina* Is a Bold Reimagining of a Classic That's (Mostly) Thrilling and Inventive." *Playlist*, 31 May 2012, Blogs .indiewire.com (5 September 2012).

Tolstoy, Leo. *Anna Karenina*. Translated by Richard Peaver and Larissa Volokohnsky. New York: Penguin, 2002.

ANTHONY ADVERSE **(1936)**

Director: Mervyn LeRoy
Assistant Director: William H. Cannon
Writer: Sheridan Gibney. Based on Hervey Allen's novel.
Producers: Hal B. Wallis, Jack L. Warner (Warner Bros.)
Cinematographer: Tony Gaudio
Editor: Ralph Dawson
Art Direction: Anton Grot
Music: Erich Wolfgang Korngold, Leo F. Forbstein
Cast: Anthony Adverse: Fredric March. Angela Guisseppi: Olivia de Havilland. Don Luis: Claude Rains. Vincent Nolte: Donald Woods. Maria Bonnyfeather: Anita Louise. John Bonnyfeather: Edmund Gwenn. Faith Paleologus: Gale Sondergaard. Denis Moore: Louis Hayward. Father Xavier: Henry O'Neill. Mother Superior Maria José: Eily Malyon. Tony Guisseppi: Luis Alberni. Elisha Jorham: Joseph Crehan. Mrs. Jorham: Clara Blandick. Carlo Cibo: Akim Tamiroff. Brother François: Pedro de Cordoba. Neleta: Steffi Duna. Napoleon Bonaparte: Rollo Lloyd
AA: Best Supporting Actress (Gale Sondergaard), Best Cinematography (Tony Gaudio), Best Musical Score (Leo F. Forbstein), Best Editing (Ralph Dawson)
AAN: Best Art Direction (Anton Grot), Best Assistant Director (William H. Cannon), Best Picture (Warner Bros.)
DVD: Currently unavailable
Blu-ray: Currently unavailable
Duration: 141 minutes

Based on Hervey Allen's 1933 1,200-page novel, the lavish Warner Bros. production includes two staged operas and scenes covering three continents, mountains, jungles, and the ocean. Mervyn LeRoy's $2 million adaptation of the sprawling novel purported to be about how people cannot conquer fate, but ironically, the film proves that choices people make define their characters and their futures. It is 1775, and the film opens with a horse-drawn carriage racing to Château de Besance, nearly bowling over road workers. Inside the carriage, Marquis Don Luis (Claude Rains), an abusive, power-hungry man who is much older than his new wife, Maria (Anita Louise), chastises her for her flirtatious behavior. Maria is pretty and submissive but not in love with him. He is also upset that he has not been able to consummate the marriage because of gout, suggesting sexual inadequacy. He is going to a bath for the cure. A lone rider follows them to the gate of the mansion. It is Denis Moore (Louis Hayward), Maria's true love.

Alone in her room, Maria prays to the Virgin Mary to let her forget Denis, but she forgets her prayer when she receives a note from Denis asking her to meet him. After the summer is over, she tells him, "I'm yours now, all yours," suggesting she is pregnant. They plan her escape from Luis, but that same night, now that his foot has healed, Luis plans to finally consummate their marriage. She hides in her room and waits by the window for Denis. Luis finds her and prevents her from leaving, swearing the world will never know she embarrassed him. Denis arrives the next morning, but Luis, Maria, and their servants have left. He catches up to them at an inn in Issoire, France. Luis, one of the best swordsmen in Europe, sneaks up behind Denis, sword drawn, and forces him to duel, killing him. They leave immediately, and after living on the road, they arrive at a chalet in the Alps in the dead of winter. Maria dies giving birth to a boy, who Luis leaves at the Convent of the Holy Child in the seaport of Leghorn (Livorno, Italy) with Maria's Madonna statue. Luis visits Maria's father, John Bonnyfeather (Edmund Gwenn), who lives in Leghorn. He is greeted at the door by Maria's former servant, Faith Paleologus (Gale Sondergaard), who is now the housekeeper. She is ambitious and attracted to Luis's money and power. Luis tells Bonnyfeather he buried Maria and her child in the mountains.

At the convent, the boy is baptized Anthony on January 17, 1773, St. Anthony's Day. He is allowed to stay in the girl's school, although he may not have contact with them. At ten years of age, he is so isolated that he practices saying his name to hear it said aloud. The nuns and Father Xavier (Henry O'Neill) are his only human contacts. Because he tests his boundaries, Mother Superior Maria José (Eily Malyon) decides to apprentice him to a merchant in Leghorn and chooses John Bonnyfeather at the Casa de Bonnyfeather. On the way to Bonnyfeather's, Anthony is stripped of his robe by street urchins. He is forced to enter his new world naked. Inside, Bonnyfeather immediately recognizes Anthony's resemblance to his daughter and her Madonna statue among Anthony's belongings. Realizing that Luis lied, he decides that Anthony will remain a foundling. Because he is "a child of sorrow, a child of adversity," Bonnyfeather gives him the last name of Adverse.

Anthony grows into a handsome young man, with responsibilities at the Bonnyfeather business and a love for Bonnyfeather's servant's daughter, Angela Guisseppi (Olivia de Havilland). Tony Guisseppi (Luis Alberni), her father, has spent all his money on lottery tickets, while Anthony has purchased one, with hopes of using the winnings to marry Angela. The night the lottery ticket is to be chosen, Bonnyfeather invites sea captain Elisha Jorham (Joseph Crehan) and his wife (Clara Blandick) to dinner. Tony wins the lottery and is brought to the Bonnyfeather gate by a crowd, having won 40,000 scudi. He buys one carriage for each member of the family to return to the home of his ancestors. Anthony tries to prevent Angela from going, but she insists, joining the parade of twelve carriages as they leave town. He is prevented from following her by some local men, including one who becomes his best friend, Vincent Nolte (Donald Woods).

Two years later, in 1796, Napoleon Bonaparte's (Rollo Lloyd) troops are in Northern Italy. Bonnyfeather closes his business and revises his will to include his employees, but the remainder of his estate is to go to Anthony, if he is still living when Bonnyfeather dies. If he is not living, the remainder will be divided between Faith and the Convent of the Holy Child. Nolte and Adverse decide to attend an opera put on by a company from Milan. When Adverse sees that Angela is one of the soloists, he meets her at the inn where she is staying. Adverse wants to get married, but she does not believe that Bonnyfeather would give his consent, so they marry secretly. After the wedding, Bonnyfeather tells Adverse of his plans to send him to Havana to collect a debt owed to him by the firm of Don Carlos Gallego and Son. He needs to leave immediately to avoid a coming French blockade at Gibraltar. Adverse agrees if he can take Angela with him. Adverse is to meet Angela at the convent at noon, but he misses her and does not see the note she leaves that says Napoleon has ordered their troupe to Rome instead of Venice.

Adverse is welcomed to Havana by Carlo Cibo (Akim Tamiroff), Bonnyfeather's representative in Cuba. Cibo says there is nothing left of the Gallego company except for a slaving outpost in Africa. He tells Adverse that he needs appropriate clothes and takes him to his tailor. While riding in a carriage through Havana, Adverse sees a slave being whipped. A passing monk, Brother François (Pedro de Cordoba), tries to prevent the whipping, but the owner whips both men. Adverse brings François into the carriage, and Cibo hides him on his estate because it is illegal to interfere with an owner and his slave.

When Adverse goes to Africa to recover the Gallego funds, François accompanies him.

The story picks up on the day that Gallego and Son, because of Adverse's oversight, settles the Bonnyfeather debt; therefore, Adverse will be free to go back to Europe. Adverse buys slaves from Arab traders and ships them to the United States. Neleta (Steffi Duna), his housekeeper and lover, is concerned that he plans to leave, but he says that for the first time in his life his name means something and that he has been paying a debt to himself of wealth and power. Bonnyfeather has not written him, and Adverse believes that he no longer cares about him. François, who rescues slaves too frail to be sold, reminds Adverse that the time has come for him to leave, but the last ship before monsoon season leaves without him.

Adverse begins self-loathing and becomes feverish. He walks through the jungle rain, and, finding the cross outside François's hut, he kneels in the mud before it. François finds him, and Adverse calls him "Father Xavier." Adverse is moved to his own bed. While under the fever, he repeats lessons learned from Father Xavier. As he recovers, Adverse expects François to visit him, but Neleta secretly prevents it. Claiming she is master now, Neleta threatens to take François's rescued slaves away on a slave ship and sends men to hurt him. After he recovers, Adverse rides into Francois's shack and finds him dying in the mud by the cross. With considerable effort, François makes him promise he will leave for Europe. Adverse promises and François dies. He returns to Leghorn a "lonely, embittered man."

Back in Italy and wearing a new outfit that reflects his new life, Adverse finds the Casa de Bonnyfeather closed, Bonnyfeather dead for more than a year, and Vincent Nolte in Paris and Napoleon's banker. Faith is due to get the inheritance and is surprised when he arrives. Adverse believes he is related to Bonnyfeather, and Luis, who is also there, realizes it is true. After Adverse leaves, Faith uses a portrait of Maria to blackmail Luis into marrying her.

Adverse leaves for Paris, but in the mountains, on a snow-covered mountain pass, Luis's carriage lies in wait to push Adverse's coach into a canyon; however, because Adverse's driver sees the hidden coach, he avoids the fall. Luis and Faith watch from the mountainside while their servant, coach, and horses go over the edge. They arrive at Nogent L'Artaud, outside Paris, before Adverse does, and Luis reports Adverse as an English spy. Napoleon's soldiers arrest Adverse upon his arrival. Nolte convinces the soldiers to release him. Nolte is with Napoleon because he advanced funds to him. Napoleon is unable to repay the debt until he receives a gold shipment from Mexico, but it cannot be shipped to France because of an exorbitant tax. Adverse and Nolte follow Napoleon to Paris, where Mademoiselle Georges, an opera singer and Napoleon's lover, works as their intermediary. Adverse still hopes to find his wife, because they "pledged ourselves to the future of the name given to me."

Mademoiselle Georges dances with Napoleon at a large masked ball, but when the other dancers unmask at midnight, she sees Adverse, becomes upset, refuses to unmask, and quickly leaves the dance. Adverse is informed Angela has a cottage outside Paris. He visits her, and she introduces him to his son, "Anthony." A watching soldier reports to Napoleon, who decides to send Adverse to the United States to collect the gold, which will be smuggled into New Orleans and then shipped to France. Later, Angela says he must go to the United States, but that she cannot go with him. She will be singing in an opera, which Adverse will attend that evening.

At the Paris Opera, the premiere of *The Duchess of Ferrara* with Mademoiselle Georges as the Duchess, has Napoleon, Josephine, Luis, Faith, Nolte, and Adverse in attendance. Adverse does not find Angela's name in the program, but hears her singing lead while in silhouette. Once she is onstage, he realizes she is Mademoiselle Georges and leaves early. In a moment to herself, Angela sheds a tear and says good-bye to him. His son and his mother's Madonna wait for him in his room. There is a note from Angela leaving him their son, who wants to go with him. Explaining their shared last name, Adverse explains, "It's a new name, son. Three people made it. Father Xavier gave it a mind, Brother François a soul, and your mother a heart." JMW

Bibliography

Stevens, George. *Conversations with the Great Moviemakers of Hollywood's Golden Age at the the American Film Institute.* Westminster, MD: Knopf, 2006.

Wakeman, John. *World Film Directors: Volume 1, 1890–1945.* New York: H. W. Wilson, 1987.

ANTONY AND CLEOPATRA (1972)

Director: Charlton Heston
Writers: Charlton Heston (screenplay), William Shakespeare (play)
Producer: Charlton Heston, Peter Snell (Folio Films, Izaro Film)
Cinematographer: Rafael Pacheco
Editor: Eric Boyd-Perkins
Art Direction: Jose Alarcont, Jose Alguero
Costumes: Wendy Dickson
Music: John Scott, Augusto Algero
Cast: Marc Antony: Charlton Heston. Cleopatra: Hildegard Neil. Enobarbus: Eric Porter. Octavius Caesar: John Castle. Marcus Aemilius Lepidus: Fernando Rey. Alexas: Juan Luis Galiardo. Octavia: Carmen Sevilla. Pompey: Freddie Jones. Schoolmaster: Enrique Alba. Menas: Peter Arne. Varrius: Luis Barboo. Menecrates: Fernando Bilbao. Scarus: Warren Clarke. Soothsayer: Roger Delgado. Proculeius: Julian Glover. Canidius: Sancho Gracia. Eros: Garrick Hagon. Thidias: John Hallam. Charmian: Jane Lapotaire. The Messenger: Joe Melia. Iras: Monica Peterson. Mardian: Emiliano Redondo. Ventidius: Aldo Sambrell. Soldier: Felipe Solano. Agrippa: Douglas Wilmer
AA: None
AAN: None
DVD: Warner Bros., 2011
Blu-ray: Currently unavailable
Duration: 148 minutes

Charlton Heston adapted William Shakespeare's play *Antony and Cleopatra* for the screen, taking the director's chair for the first time when Orson Welles and Laurence Oliver were unavailable. Heston had his first big break in a Broadway stage production of *Antony and Cleopatra* in 1947, in which he played the role of Caesar's lieutenant, Proculeius (alongside Katharine Cornell as Cleopatra, whom Heston rather sweetly refers to as "Miss Cornell" throughout his autobiography),[1] but he always saw in *Antony and Cleopatra* a particular cinematic affinity. Heston notes, "*Antony and Cleopatra* not only happens in Rome and Sicily and Athens and Egypt and on the seas that separate them, it is about the differences and the distances between those countries. . . . The play, in fact, cries out for a camera."[2]

The story takes place during the political alliance between Marc Antony (Heston), Marcus Aemilius Lepidus (Fernando Rey), and Octavius Caesar (an appropriately chilly John Castle). When Antony receives word that Pompey (Freddie Jones) is raising an army against the triumvirate, he leaves the arms of his lover, Cleopatra (Hildegard Neil, after Anne Bancroft turned the part down), and returns to Rome. The three leaders meet at a gladiatorial training school, the political machinations in the owner's box cross-cut with the bloody encounter below (while the concept has merit, the execution in the editing is somewhat jarring). Relations between the three leaders are tense; however, the alliance is strengthened when it is decided that the newly widowed Antony will marry Caesar's sister, Octavia (Carmen Sevilla). But Marc Antony's friend Enobarbus (Eric Porter) doubts that the new arrangement will prevent Antony from returning to his Egyptian queen in one of the most famous speeches from the play.

Cleopatra, meanwhile, is not pleased to hear of her lover's marriage, and her ladies in waiting do their best to calm her. The poor messenger is brought back in to describe her rival, his efforts to appease the queen effectively comical. The triumvirate confronts Pompey, but they are able to come to a satisfactory power-sharing arrangement without bloodshed. As the group drinks and celebrates, Pompey dismisses a suggestion that he take the opportunity to rid himself of his rivals, but later it is Pompey himself who is slain at the behest of Caesar.

Antony and Octavia depart for Athens, but it is not long before he abandons her for Egypt. The relations between Antony and Caesar having soured, Caesar sends his forces to Egypt, and, ignoring advice, Antony meets them at sea. Cleopatra joins the fleet against strong objections, which seem justified when she flees the battle. Antony follows her, abandoning the fleet. He is instantly regretful, and although he has an angry confrontation with his lover (Heston does well in a rage), they reconcile. Antony interrupts Cleopatra apparently considering betraying him to a messenger of Caesar. When he forgives even this, Enobarbus decides to leave his master, defecting to Caesar's camp, where he is met with evident disdain. Unable to bear his shame, Enobarbus flings himself off a cliff.

When Antony meets Caesar in battle on land, the Egyptian troops betray him, standing aside to let Caesar's forces through, and Antony is only just able to flee his capture. Cleopatra confines herself and her ladies in her monument, sending word to Antony that she is dead. In despair, Antony falls on his sword but survives long enough to be reunited with Cleopatra before he dies.

As Caesar's soldiers arrive, Cleopatra looks down from her apparently safe vantage point from the monument. The soldiers suddenly form a stairway with their shields, and Caesar's officer Proculeius (Julian Glover) is able to disarm the startled Cleopatra (an innovative staging solution to the scene devised by Joe Canutt,[3] even if the set exterior is somewhat underwhelming). Proculeius admits that Caesar will display her triumphantly in Rome, and upon receiving no convincing reassurance from Caesar himself, the queen takes her life with the aid of a poisonous snake.

The physical and geographical challenges that present themselves in staging the play are, by contrast, the heart of the cinematic epic and its emphasis on expansive space, spectacle, and excess, although the budgetary restrictions are in evidence in Heston's *Antony and Cleopatra.* Despite Heston practically being the embodiment of the historical epic thanks to his lead roles in Cecil B. DeMille's 1956 *The Ten Commandments* and William Wyler's 1959 *Ben-Hur*, a Shakespearean film epic was seen as a more doubtful box-office prospect. The disastrous production blowout on Joseph L. Mankiewicz's 1963 film *Cleopatra*, starring Elizabeth Taylor, had made the studio executives wary of the epic genre (Heston recalls that producer "Dick Zanuck jumped back from the [*Antony and Cleopatra*] script like a scalded cat"[4]), but the money was eventually found and the film shot in Spain. Joe Canutt, the son of Yakima (Yak) Canutt, who had been second director on

Ben Hur, was brought on board to direct the action sequences. Indeed, some of Yak's work makes it into *Antony and Cleopatra*, by virtue of galley scene outtakes from *Ben Hur* that were then used for the Battle of Actium,[5] but to (unfortunately) uneven effect.

Much to Heston's disappointment, *Antony and Cleopatra* had a generally poor reception. Although *Variety* called it "impressively mounted and well played,"[6] Heston summed up the situation as a "critical disaster,"[7] and the film was only given a limited theatrical release.[8] DB

Notes

1. Charlton Heston, *In the Arena: The Autobiography* (London: HarperCollins, 1995), 76–84, 448.
2. Heston, *In the Arena*, 430–31.
3. Heston, *In the Arena*, 451.
4. Heston, *In the Arena*, 435.
5. Heston, *In the Arena*, 449.
6. "Review: *Antony and Cleopatra*," *Variety*, 1972, http://variety.com/1971/film/reviews/antony-and-cleopatra-1200422846/ (14 June 2013).
7. Heston's difficult experience making the film and its poor reception is detailed in his journal, Charlton Heston, *The Actor's Life: Journals, 1956–1976*, edited by Hollis Alpert (London: Allen Lane, 1976, 1978), 332–69, 372–74, 380, 382, 388, 392, 414, 417.
8. The DVD version of *Antony and Cleopatra* was released in 2011, but it runs 10 minutes shorter than the original release, cutting a scene where Antony takes his leave from Cleopatra.

Bibliography

Heston, Charlton. *The Actor's Life: Journals, 1956–1976*. Edited by Hollis Alpert. London: Allen Lane, 1976, 1978.

———. *In the Arena: The Autobiography*. London: HarperCollins, 1995.

"Review: *Antony and Cleopatra*." *Variety*, 1972, http://variety.com/1971/film/reviews/antony-and-cleopatra-1200422846/ (14 June 2013).

APOCALYPSE NOW (1979); *APOCALYPSE NOW REDUX* (2001)

Director: Francis Ford Coppola
Writers: John Milius, Francis Ford Coppola, Michael Herr. Inspired by *Heart of Darkness*, by Joseph Conrad.
Producer: Francis Ford Coppola (United Artists)
Cinematographer: Vittorio Storaro
Art Direction: Dean Tavoularis, Angelo P. Graham, George R. Nelson
Editors: Richard Marks, Walter Murch, Gerald B. Greenberg, Lisa Fruchtman
Music: Carmine Coppola, Francis Ford Coppola
Sound Mixers: Walter Murch, Mark Berger, Richard Beggs, Nathan Boxer
Cast: Colonel Walter E. Kurtz: Marlon Brando. Captain Benjamin L. Willard: Martin Sheen. Lieutenant Colonel William Kilgore: Robert Duvall. Jay "Chef" Hicks: Frederic Forrest. George "Chief" Phillips: Albert Hall. Lance Johnson: Sam Bottoms. Tyrone "Mr. Clean" Miller: Laurence Fishburne. Captain Colby: Scott Glenn. Freelance Photographer: Dennis Hopper. Playmate of the Year: Cynthia Wood. Miss August: Linda Beatty Carpenter. Miss May: Colleen Camp. *Playboy* Agent: Bill Graham
Cast (additional in *Redux*): Hubert de Marais: Christian Marquand. Roxanne Sarrault: Aurore Clément. Francis de Marais: Roman Coppola. Gilles de Marais: Gian-Carlo Coppola. Christian de Marais: David Oliver. Phillipe de Marais: Michel Pitton. Gaston de Marais: Franck Villard
AA: Best Cinematography (Vittorio Storaro), Best Sound (Walter Murch, Mark Berger, Richard Beggs, Nathan Boxer)
AAN: Best Picture (United Artists), Best Supporting Actor (Robert Duvall), Best Art Direction (Dean Tavoularis, Angelo P. Graham, George R. Nelson), Best Director (Francis Ford Coppola), Best Film Editing (Richard Marks, Walter Murch, Gerald B. Greenberg, Lisa Fruchtman), Best Writing–Screenplay Based on Material from another Medium (John Milius, Francis Ford Coppola, Michael Herr)
DVD: Lionsgate, 2006
Blu-ray: Lionsgate, 2010. Two-disc special edition. Includes *Apocalypse Now Redux*.
Duration: 153 minutes; *Redux*, 202 minutes

Apocalypse Now and *Apocalypse Now Redux* are the original and extended-cut versions of director Francis Ford Coppola's archetypal war epic set in Vietnam during the American conflict there. Thematically inspired by the novella *Heart of Darkness*, by Joseph Conrad, the films have been acclaimed for their authentic depiction of the ambivalent and rationalizing *zeitgeist* of the Vietnam experience from both proponents and opponents of the war itself, while fervently eliciting visceral catharsis at both individual and cultural levels. The plot chronicles the mission of Captain Benjamin Willard of the U.S. Army Special Operations during one of his tours of duty, in which he is charged with "terminat[ing] with extreme prejudice" the command of the decorated but insurgent Colonel Walter E. Kurtz of Special Forces. Accompanied by a crew of four, Willard's journey is simultaneously a top-secret mission executed in a PBR boat snaking up the fictional Nung River to Cambodia and a serpentine quest to uncover the rationale behind its and his absurd purpose.

Significantly, these two editions of the film were produced more than two decades apart, and this unique production history delivers structurally different works, each of which reveals different aspects of the epic form, in some ways making them two very unique pieces. Taken together, however, this corpus of work reproduces a mimetic experience similar to the pathos and logos one would hope to achieve after the cathartic experiences of a cultural war, with *Apocalypse Now* portraying the immanent visceral response and somewhat ambivalent resolution, and *Apocalypse Now Redux* providing historical distance, back story, and a didactic dimension that concludes with general resolve. Most importantly, it succeeds in achieving this effect through the classic epic elements of unity of action, heroic temperament, and reversals, thereby elevating this work from merely a historical epic about an American war to an American classic about an archetypal war.

Apocalypse Now **(1979)**

> If something seems right to you, but your mind's diseased, don't think that's wisdom.
>
> —Euripides, *The Bacchae*

The literary inspiration for *Apocalypse Now* has intriguing and significant origins, and, in many ways, it involves writer John Milius. Milius, fresh out of college and rejected by the American draft, took up a teacher's challenge claiming that no one had done justice to Joseph Conrad's 1902 novella *Heart of Darkness* in film. So, in 1969, Mr. Milius penned the original screenplay that was to become this film, calling it *The Psychedelic Soldier*. No doubt with sardonic intent, he later renamed his work *Apocalypse Now* in response to a popular antiwar button that proclaimed "Nirvana Now" (the word *nirvana* referring to the Buddhist state of Enlightenment).[1] But the true blossoming of this napalm and nirvana masterpiece occurred with the addition of a few other crucial elements. These included Francis Ford Coppola's decision to cowrite, produce, and ultimately direct the film, after George Lucas stepped out of the project to pursue another film (*Star Wars*); Coppola's insistence on shooting on location (in this case primarily in the Philippines, and with much publicized difficulty); and his selection of the production crew that engineered the exquisite verisimilitude of the somatosensory experiences produced through the cinematography and sound production.

As promised, Milius does justice to Conrad's work. The similarities between the plot elements of *Heart of Darkness* and *Apocalypse Now* are obvious in both character development and broad overall action: a captain and his team of men leave civilization and sail up a dangerous river on a mission into foreign territory in search of a person, encountering adventures along the way and discovering upon arrival that the reputed host of their destination is suffering from a derangement of the senses. From here, the story deviates, primarily due to a disagreement between Milius and Coppola about how the story *should* end. The Milius version had a final battle;[2] Coppola admits to tacking on a Grailesque fugue at the film's conclusion[3] in an attempt to soften the Milius bloodbath. Ironically, however, it is not in its *similarities* but in its *deviations* from Conrad that this work truly demonstrates the archetypal and almost formulaic epic elements that cause it to be regarded as a classic of the epic form, while simultaneously deepening the original chaotic sense of anomie already present throughout the development, production, and later reception of this piece.

The epic elements in *Apocalypse Now*—length, spectacle, catharsis, and *anagnorisis*—are all present in the work; however, the distinctive interplay between the heroic temperament and the unity of action in this film is what evokes the hallmark and characteristic markings of the true archetypal origins of this epic plot: the ancient mythos of Apollo/Dionysos *pharmakos*,[4] as episodically introduced in Homer, the tragedians, and the Epic Cycles through the characters Achilles, Odysseus, Thersides, Philoctetes, and Atreidae.

Apocalypse Now begins anachronistically with a sound track heralding *The End* as opening credits run. The helicopters and ceiling fans in the opening scene dizzy the senses as they fuse with one another. Captain Willard's (Martin Sheen) inverted face is juxtaposed to a face of a statue of a pagan god (often characterized as Buddha). Willard is a fighter in a war zone, but the scene opens with him in a hotel. He is not fighting during a war. He is awaiting a mission, and thus at the opening, in the absence of the chaos of a war outside, he re-creates the war inside by a self-induced derangement of the senses, smashing his "icon" (image) in a mirror while mimicking Eastern martial arts kata gestures before ultimately succumbing to a Dionysian stupor.

We learn he has no ties to home. When he does get a mission, it is to "terminate with extreme prejudice" the command of a U.S. colonel in a mission that does not exist. Willard begins as a Hollow Man. During the plot, which is basically Willard being escorted up the Nung River while he digests the dossier of Kurtz's (Marlon Brando) biography before assassinating him, we observe through voice overlay his internal dialogue and reasoning in trying to comprehend why this man should be terminated. As Willard gets closer to the target of his mission, his reasoning becomes such that he almost embodies Kurtz to the point of becoming him, as a crucial scene reveals. (This is the Sampan scene, where Willard becomes so obsessed with fulfilling his mission that he savagely kills an innocent civilian woman in cold blood just because her "ailment" is getting in the way of his "work.") At this turning point, Willard is feared by the crew, and the film's journey becomes a *nekuia*, a ritual journey to the underworld in which the viewers are unwitting participants.

Spectacle includes both overt demonstrations of martial prowess and disturbing moments that are the subjects of internal delusions, those that evoke the horror of the emotional tone of Euripides in *The Bacchae*, as in the scenes at Kurtz's camp, populated with severed heads and deafening auditory droning of dithyrambic voices. But there are other moments of anamnesis, where we witness, in the midst of appalling action, the aural voice-over of a cool and rationalizing Willard, mimicking the similitude of a philosopher in the character of Socrates himself. Yet, other times, as in a total void of all sensibilities, we are rationally assaulted with the famed Kurtz, purportedly insane and visually set amid unspeakable atrocities, appearing in shadow, placidly pontificating or reciting (prophetically) passages from T. S. Eliot's "The Hollow Men." The only element commonly left droning throughout each of these impressionistic sequences is the anxiety-driven intertextual message: Kill him; "he contradicts their lies."[5] But as in some distant prophecy uttered by an oracular deity long since silenced, it becomes more and more difficult to discern to whom this message applies the longer the film drones on.

> What people thought would happen never did.
> What they did not expect, the gods made happen.
> That's what this story has revealed.
>
> —Euripides, *The Bacchae*

Apocalypse Now Redux (2001)

> Come friend, you too must die, Why moan about it so?
> There will come a dawn or sunset or high noon
> When a man will take my life in battle too—
> Flinging a spear perhaps
> Or whipping a deadly arrow off his bow.
>
> —Homer, *The Iliad*

Apocalypse Now Redux is the 2001 extended-cut version of the classic 1979 war epic *Apocalypse Now*, by director Francis Ford Coppola. It includes an additional forty-nine minutes of action and significant sequence editing to the original film. The twenty-two-year hiatus between the production of this film and its predecessor produces a clearer understanding of Coppola's mature vision of his project. And in the end, what was born as a script by John Milius, whose title, *Apocalypse Now*, was spawned as a sardonic response to the "Nirvana Now" antiwar protest buttons during the Vietnam conflict, may well have been reborn in its karmic *Redux* form as an archetypal epos designed to teach and warn about the dangers of taking any sides in the complex paradox that emerges when one confuses the illusion of human agency with the precision of Nature's capriciousness.

Although taking inspiration from Joseph Conrad's *Heart of Darkness*, *Apocalypse Now Redux* moves beyond Conrad's literary borders and Milius's *Psychedelic Soldier* (perhaps due to the deviation from Conrad in teleology from commerce to war and Coppola's general penchant for auteurship). Seeped as it is in symbolism and allegory, its cultural ancestors also include (aesthetically) *The Bacchae* of Euripides and *Siddhartha* by Hermann Hesse, and (didactically) *The Birth of Tragedy* by Friedrich Nietzsche; but most importantly, its *epic* foundations are firmly rooted in the complementary archetypal patterns of the "epic hero" marked in *The Iliad* and *The Odyssey* of Homer, in the mythos cycles of the heroes of the House of Atreus (Agamemnon and Menelaus) and in Achilles and Odysseus, and overtly in the Grail cycle of the Fisher King.

Archetypal epic elements regarding the unity of action in this film are intentional[6] and successfully articulated through the didactic use of a primordial cosmology where humanity is blindly impelled to action between the universal imperatives of eros and eris (love and strife) and trapped within the natural morphology of an elemental world of a Nature ruled by blind fate. This is made evident in a powerful scene from new footage where Willard is confronted by Roxanne (Aurore Clément), who reveals the following truth to him: "There are two of you, can't you see? One that kills and one that loves." Here form is impelled by action, not thought, and the space of the film is determined by the parameters of the elements, as Coppola describes, saying, "The film is made of four basic units or elements: FIRE (night bombings), WATER (the beach and the river), AIR (the wind of helicopter + monsoon), and EARTH (mud, holes, bomb craters, green foliage)."[7] The heroic space of action, then, is small, for in this universe, there are only two choices: coming together or breaking apart. The other possibilities are the purview of poets or philosophers, thus the need for narrative voice-over in this film.

Here, unlike in traditional films, character does not refer to personalities per se, but rather *those unities of action* that move the plot. This is a ritual mythos; each persona is representative of an aspect of the primary action moving to conclusion (which, in this case, is Captain Willard in eris with Kurtz). Examined in this manner, then, the boat is the soma (corpse body) of Willard, and his mission is the annihilation of his own *character* (a preconceived and now false collection of attributes from a previous life) as he sails up the river (here the primordial river is in the underworld, be it Acheron, Styx, Lethe, or Samsara) to meet and dissolve his demiurge. (Coppola states in his notes that The River itself is another character in this film.[8]) This is an *archetypal underworld* visit, and the other characters in the boat are aspects of Willard himself that he must discard as he moves closer to the end of his journey to meet his self-made demiurge: Kurtz.

Tokens reminiscent of other classical motifs are scattered about in the film, and, at times, they add comic relief along the way. For example, we first meet Captain Benjamin Willard's literal deus ex machina, Lieutenant Colonel William Kilgore (Robert Duvall) (who flies down from the 1st Squadron 9th Air Cavalry helicopter, Death from Above) when he comes to deliver "death cards" to victims he's just massacred. It is he who guides Willard to the entrance to the mouth of the Nung River and from whom Willard "steals" the surfboard ("Golden Bough") that is to play so prominently in later scenes. In the tragic and transforming Sampan scene there is a "puppy" (Cerberus) that is also taken without comment by the men, and it stays with the boat until the end of the journey. Mr. Clean's (Laurence Fishburne) ceremonial burial is reminiscent of Elpenor's death in *The Odyssey*; Chief's (Albert Hall) eris with Willard throughout the film, as well as his ritual death, recall the animosity between Odysseus and Philoctetes and demonstrates in modern film that classical study of the methods for breaking down the heroic will in eris: through force, persuasion, or deceit.[9] These and other scenes from *Redux* lend a combination of a journey *toward* and a journey *from* feeling to this film, although not necessarily concluding with a *nostos* (homecoming).

In one scene from newly added footage, Willard is specifically asked if he will return home after the war. His answer is "no." By the time they reach the destination where the denouement of the film will take place, only two passengers are left on the boat with Willard: Chef (Frederic Forrest), a tuned-out on dope chef from Louisiana who extols the virtues of sensuality and physical pleasures, but at the expense of hyper vigilance and fear, and Lance (Sam Bottoms), a professional surfer from California whose journey begins with him as a clean-cut kid and transforms him into a psychedelic, fatigue-painted participant in Kurtz's troop of ritual warriors.

There seems to be little evidence of eris between Kurtz and Willard, and we learn of Kurtz only from clippings from a dossier of literary sources, as narrated by Willard along the journey. We hear of his *bios and kleos* (*life and glory*), although Willard seems more impressed with Kurtz's *kleos*, but clearly disturbed by his *bios*, for it is after reading a letter from Kurtz to his son that the Sampan incident occurs and causes the death of an innocent woman by the impatient and, at last, *intentional* hand of Willard. "Everybody gets what they want. For me, what I wanted was a mission, and for my sin, they gave me one," remarks Willard at the beginning of the film.

What was Willard's sin? In the end, the Chief is dead by a savage hand after a stray blow by a poisoned arrow pierces his back, right through the heart. Clean is shot randomly while listening to the admonitions of his mother on a cassette tape to return home safely; Chef's head is savagely served to Willard as he sits helpless and caged in Kurtz's kingdom. And surfer Lance dances, haplessly immersed among the dithyrambic throng of revelers awaiting the movement of the next tide of that ineffable *River*. And "Mistah Kurtz—he dead."[10] "But in the final shot of the film, it's the immense, silent statue of the Buddha that dominates the image, surviving the last glimpses of a helicopter, napalm, the PBR, and Willard's face."[11] And there's the river. "The river laughed. Yes, so it was, everything came back, which had not been suffered and solved to its end, the same pain was suffered over and over again."[12] MC

Notes

1. Peter Cowie, *The Apocalypse Now Book* (Cambridge, MA: Da Capo, 2001).
2. Cowie, *The Apocalypse Now Book*, 43.
3. Cowie, *The Apocalypse Now Book*, 86.
4. See Gregory Nagy, *The Best of the Achaeans* (Baltimore, MD: Johns Hopkins University Press, 1986), 253, for a description of this ritual of the scapegoat associated with Apollo.
5. Cowie, *The Apocalypse Now Book*, 25, quoting Francis Ford Coppola, referring to the character of Kurtz.
6. Cowie, *The Apocalypse Now Book*, 35: "It is the intention of the filmmaker to create a broad, spectacular film of epic action-adventure scale that however is rich in theme and philosophic inquiry into the mythology of war; and the human condition."—(sic) F. F. Coppola.
7. Cowie, *The Apocalypse Now Book*, 34.
8. Cowie, *The Apocalypse Now Book*, 38.
9. Bernard Knox, *The Heroic Temper* (Berkeley: University of California Press, 1983), 119.
10. T. S. Eliot, "The Hollow Men," in *The Complete Poems and Play, 1909–1950* (New York: Harcourt, Brace and World, 1971), 56–59.
11. Cowie, *The Apocalypse Now Book*, 161.
12. Hermann Hesse, *Siddhartha*, translated by Gunther Olesch, Anke Dreher, Amy Coulter, Stefan Langer, and Seymon Chaichenets. Project Gutenberg EBook, June 2011.

Bibliography

Collins, Derek. *Immortal Armor: The Concept of Alkē in Archaic Greek Poetry*. Lanham, MD: Rowman & Littlefield, 1998.

Cowie, Peter. *The Apocalypse Now Book*. Cambridge, MA: Da Capo, 2001.

Eliot, T. S. "The Hollow Men." In *The Complete Poems and Play, 1909–1950*. New York: Harcourt, Brace and World, 1971.

Euripides. "The Bacchants of Euripides." In *The Bacchants of Euripides and other Essays*, edited by A. W. Verrall and translated by A. W. Verrall, 26–64. Cambridge, UK: Cambridge University Press, 1910.

Harrison, Jane Ellen. *Epilegomena and Themis*. New York: University Books, 1962.

Hathorn, Richmond L. *Greek Mythology*. Beruit, Lebanon: American University of Beruit, 1977.

Hesse, Hermann. *Siddhartha*. Translated by Gunther Olesch, Anke Dreher, Amy Coulter, Stefan Langer, and Seymon Chaichenets. Project Gutenberg EBook, June 2011.

Homer. *The Iliad*. GoodReads, http://www.goodreads.com/quotes/search?utf8=%E2%9C%93&q=Come+friend%2C+you+too+must+die%2C+Why+moan+about+it+so&commit=Search (29 September 2012).

Knox, Bernard. *The Heroic Temper*. Berkeley: University of California Press, 1983.

Nagy, Gregory. *The Best of the Achaeans*. Baltimore, MD: Johns Hopkins University Press, 1986.

———. "The Epic Hero." In *A Companion to Ancient Epic*, edited by John Foley, 71–89. Oxford, UK: Wiley-Blackwell, 2009.

APOCALYPTO (2006)

Director: Mel Gibson
Writers: Mel Gibson, Farhad Safinia
Producers: Mel Gibson, Bruce Davey (Icon Productions)
Cinematographer: Dean Semler
Editor: John Wright

Art Direction: Theresa Wachter, Roberto Bonelli, Naaman Marshall
Costumes: Mayes C. Rubeo
Music: James Horner
Sound Editors: Sean McCormack, Kami Asgar
Sound Mixers: Kevin O'Connell, Greg P. Russell, Fernando Cámara
Makeup Artists: Aldo Signoretti, Vittorio Sodano
Cast: The Village—Jaguar Paw: Rudy Youngblood. Seven: Dalia Hernández. Blunted: Jonathan Brewer. Flint Sky: Morris Birdyellowhead. Turtles Run: Carlos Emilio Báez. Curl Nose: Amilcar Ramírez. Smoke Frog: Israel Contreras. Cocoa Leaf: Israel Ríos. Mother-in-Law: María Isabel Díaz as Isabel Diaz. Old Story Teller: Espiridion Acosta Cache. Young Woman: Mayra Serbulo. Sky Flower: Iazua Larios. Village Girl: Lorena Heranandez. Wife: Itandehui Gutierrez. Eldest Daughter: Sayuri Gutierrez. Fish Hunter: Hiram Soto. First Temple Sacrifice: José Suárez. The Holcane Warriors—Zero Wolf: Raoul Trujillo. Middle Eye: Gerardo Taracena. Snake Ink: Rodolfo Palacios. Hanging Moss: Ariel Galvan. Drunkards Four: Bernardo Ruiz. Cut Rock: Ricardo Diaz Mendoza. Ten Peccary: Richard Can. Monkey Jaw: Carlos Ramos. Buzzard Hook: Ammel Rodrigo Mendoza. Speaking Wind: Marco Antonio Argueta. Vicious Holcane: Javier Escobar. The City—High Priest: Fernando Hernandez. Oracle Girl #1: Maria Isidra Hoil. Oracle Girl #2: Aquetzali García. Laughing Man: Abel Woolrich. Chilam: Antonio Monroi as Antonio Monroy. Man on Temple Top: Nicolás Jasso. Slave Auctioneer: Ronaldo Eknal. Woman Auctioneer: Miriam Tun. King: Rafael Velez. Queen: Diana Botello. Head Chac: Joaquin Rendon
AA: None
AAN: Best Makeup (Aldo Signoretti, Vittorio Sodano), Best Sound Editing (Sean McCormack, Kami Asgar), Best Sound Mixing (Kevin O'Connell, Greg P. Russell, Fernando Cámara)
DVD: Buena Vista Home Entertainment/ Touchstone, 2007
Blu-ray: Touchstone, 2007
Duration: 138 minutes

After the success of *Braveheart* (1995) and the controversy of *The Passion of the Christ* (2004), Mel Gibson returned to the epic to depict the final days of the Mayan civilization before Spanish arrival in the sixteenth century, with characters speaking the Yucatec Maya language. *Apocalypto* begins by introducing us to Mayan jungle-dwellers hunting a tapir, as Jaguar Paw (Rudy Youngblood) makes fun of Blunted (Jonathan Brewer) by making him eat the balls of the animal as a supposed cure for his infertility. The jesting is cut short when a tribe arrives on their land, their leader, Fish Hunter (Hiram Soto), asking simply for safe passage after their village was sacked. Jaguar Paw wants to know more of their story, but his father and leader, Flint Sky (Morris Birdyellowhead), restrains him, saying that fear is infectious and should not be brought back to their village. The same marauder Holcane warriors later attack their own village, and Jaguar Paw only just manages to lower his young son and pregnant wife, Seven (Dalia Hernández), into a dry well before being taken prisoner. The surviving adults are taken away, their distraught children following helplessly until the adults cross a river and the children must remain behind to fend for themselves. On the difficult journey, they are taunted by the Holcane Snake Ink (Rodolfo Palacios), who clashes with leader Zero Wolf (Raoul Trujillo). As the prisoners are taken through a village decimated by disease, an infected young girl makes a disturbing, if enigmatic, prophecy of the Holcane warriors' immanent death.

As they near the Mayan city, it is clear that the surrounding crops have failed, and many people are going hungry. The prisoners are taken through the chaotic city center, filled with many different classes of painted peoples, toward a pyramid. The women are taken to the slave market, while the men are painted blue and taken into the heart of the pyramid, where they see disturbing paintings of blue men being decapitated. At the height of the pyramid, Jaguar Paw watches his men have their hearts cut out and heads cut off before the Mayan king, but as he is dragged onto the altar, an eclipse is taken to be a sign of the sun god's appeasement, and he is momentarily spared.

Zero Wolf sends the men into a cruel game, whereby they must run toward freedom in their jungle home but are speared or clubbed down before they can escape. Jaguar Paw, however, is able to outsmart the Holcane, who pursue him through the dead cornfields and into the jungle. Although injured, Jaguar Paw's intimate affinity with the jungle and knowledge of its terrain enables him to continually outwit his pursuers. He is even able to harness the power of his namesake. Indeed, Jaguar Paw is no longer simply a desperate, if clever, man. As Andrea Stone, scholar of the Mayans, argues, "Slathered in black mud, eyes aglow, Jaguar Paw rises from the jungle floor transformed into his animal alter-ego," an indomitable hero "of mythic proportions."[1] It is this transformed Jaguar Paw who is able to prevail. As he rescues his wife, son, and newborn baby, the family looks out upon the Spanish fleet and decides to make a new life without engaging with the visitors.

The ending is bitterly ironic, because the new beginning Jaguar Paw seeks will be thwarted by colonization, and his heroic efforts have, in this sense, been in vain. By contrast, Traci Ardren, a scholar of the Mayans, takes the opposite view, arguing that the message conveyed by the "arrival of clearly Christian missionaries (these guys are too clean to be conquistadors)" is this: "The end is near and the savior has come."[2] That Gibson is a conservative Catholic is well known, and it was only a few months prior to the film's release that he became a pariah for making offensive anti-Semitic remarks when arrested for drunk driving. These two factors influenced the reception of the film as a conservative justification for Christian colonization, a perspective perhaps encouraged by the film's opening quote from Will Durant: "A great civilization is not conquered from without until it has destroyed itself from within."[3] Durant was not writing on the Mayans, but rather on the fall of the Roman Empire and the coming of Christianity. Durant continues, stating, "The essential causes of Rome's decline lay in her people, her morals, her class struggle, her failing trade, her bureaucratic despotism, her stifling taxes, her consuming wars."[4] By extension, then, Gibson makes the same argument of the Mayan civilization.

What Gibson depicts in the film is aspects drawn from Mayan culture (as well as outside cultures) between 200 B.C.E. and the early sixteenth century A.D., compressed into the same filmic time space. The considerable Mayan achievements in mathematics and astronomy are not depicted (an eclipse would not have been a surprise event), while the villagers do not represent communities during this considerable time span.[5] Vivian Sobchack has argued that the Hollywood historical epic is not about history per se, but rather a particular type of filmic experience, characterized by visual excess and a feeling of "general historical eventfulness" rather than specific, historically accurate events.[6] In other words, what we get in *Apocalypto* should come as no real surprise, nor should be its affective ability.

Reviews were notably conflicted, being both enthralled and disturbed. In light of Gibson's anti-Semitic outburst, the *Guardian*'s Peter Bradshaw balked at the masses of naked corpses, victims of Mayan sacrifice, writing, "Did he realize what images and ideas he was invoking? . . . It could be that this is the nearest he will ever come to some form of cinematically constituted apology."[7] Despite the controversy, *Apocalypto* performed respectably at the international box office. DB

Notes

1. Andrea Stone, "Orcs in Loincloths: A Mayanist Looks at *Apocalypto*," *Archaeology: A Publication of the Archaeological Institute of America*, 3 January 2007, http://archive.archaeology.org/online/reviews/apocalypto2.html (4 July 2013).
2. Traci Ardren, "Is *Apocalypto* Pornography?" *Archaeology: A Publication of the Archaeological Institute of America*, 5 December 2006, http://archive.archaeology.org/online/reviews/apocalypto.html (4 July 2013).
3. Will Durant, *Caesar and Christ: A History of Roman Civilization and of Christianity from Their Beginnings to A.D. 325* (New York: Simon & Schuster, 1944), 665.
4. Durant, *Caesar and Christ*, 665.
5. Andrea Stone, "Orcs in Loincloths." See also David Freidel, "Betraying the Maya: Who Does the Violence in *Apocalypto* Really Hurt?," *Archaeology: A Publication of the Archaeological Institute of America*, 60, no. 2, March/April 2007, http://archive.archaeology.org/0703/abstracts/maya.html (4 July 2013).
6. Vivian Sobchack, "'Surge and Splendor': A Phenomenology of the Hollywood Historical Epic," in *Film Genre Reader II*, edited by Barry Keith Grant (Austin: University of Texas Press, 1995), 285, 286.
7. Peter Bradshaw, "Apocalypto," *Guardian*, 5 January 2007, www.guardian.co.uk/film/2007/jan/05/actionandadventure.drama (6 July 2013).

Bibliography

Ardren, Traci. "Is Apocalypto Pornography?" *Archaeology: A Publication of the Archaeological Institute of America*, 5 December 2006, http://archive.archaeology.org/online/reviews/apocalypto.html (4 July 2013).

Bradshaw, Peter. "Apocalypto." *Guardian*, 5 January 2007, www.guardian.co.uk/film/2007/jan/05/actionandadventure.drama (6 July 2013).

Durant, Will. *Caesar and Christ: A History of Roman Civilization and of Christianity from Their Beginnings to A.D. 325*. New York: Simon & Schuster, 1944.

Freidel, David. "Betraying the Maya: Who Does the Violence in *Apocalypto* Really Hurt?" *Archaeology: A Publication of the Archaeological Institute of America*, 60, no. 2, March/April 2007, http://archive.archaeology.org/0703/abstracts/maya.html (4 July 2013).

Sobchack, Vivian. "'Surge and Splendor': A Phenomenology of the Hollywood Historical Epic." In *Film Genre Reader II*, edited by Barry Keith Grant, 280–307. Austin: University of Texas Press, 1995.

Stone, Andrea. "Orcs in Loincloths: A Mayanist Looks at *Apocalypto*." *Archaeology: A Publication of the Archaeological Institute of America*, 3 January 2007, http://archive.archaeology.org/online/reviews/apocalypto2.html (4 July 2013).

APOLLO 13 (1995)

DIRECTOR: Ron Howard
WRITERS: William Broyles Jr., Al Reinert. Based on the book *Lost Moon*, by Jim Lovell and Jeffrey Kluger.
PRODUCER: Brian Grazer (Imagine Entertainment, Universal)
CINEMATOGRAPHER: Dean Cundey
EDITORS: Mike Hill, Daniel P. Hanley
SOUND EDITORS: Rick Dior, Steve Pederson, Scott Millan, David MacMillan
ART DIRECTION: David J. Bomba, Bruce Alan Miller
SET DECORATION: Michael Corenblith, Merideth Boswell
COSTUMES: Rita Ryack
MUSIC: James Horner
SPECIAL EFFECTS: Robert Legato, Michael Kanfer, Leslie Ekker, Matt Sweeney
CAST: Jim Lovell: Tom Hanks. Fred Haise: Bill Paxton. Jack Swigert: Kevin Bacon. Ken Mattingly: Gary Sinise. Gene Kranz: Ed Harris. Marilyn Lovell: Kathleen Quinlan. Barbara Lovell: Mary Kate Schellhardt. Susan Lovell: Emily Ann Lloyd. Jeffrey Lovell: Miko Hughes. Jay Lovell: Max Elliott Slade. Blanch Lovell: Jean Speegle Howard. Mary Haise: Tracy Reiner. Pete Conrad: David Andrews. Jane Conrad: Michelle Little. Deke Slayton: Chris Ellis. NASA

Director: Joe Spano. Henry Hurt: Xander Berkeley. Glynn Lunney: Marc McClure. John Young: Ben Marley. Neil Armstrong: Mark Wheeler. Buzz Aldrin: Larry Williams. EECOM White, Sy Liebergot: Clint Howard. Walter Cronkite: himself (archive footage)

AA: Best Film Editing (Mike Hill, Daniel P. Hanley), Best Sound (Rick Dior, Steve Pederson, Scott Millan, David MacMillan)

AAN: Best Actor in a Supporting Role (Ed Harris), Best Actress in a Supporting Role (Kathleen Quinlan), Best Art Direction–Set Decoration (Michael Corenblith, Merideth Boswell), Best Effects–Visual Effects (Robert Legato, Michael Kanfer, Leslie Ekker, Matt Sweeney), Best Music–Original Dramatic Score (James Horner), Best Picture (Brian Grazer), Best Writing–Screenplay Based on Material Previously Produced or Published (William Broyles Jr., Al Reinert)

DIRECTORS GUILD OF AMERICA AWARD: Ron Howard

DVD: Universal Pictures, 2002

BLU-RAY: Universal Pictures, 2010

DURATION: 140 minutes

"Houston, we have a problem." That this phrase, uttered by astronaut Jim Lovell in the film *Apollo 13*, has burned itself into the Western consciousness, and not the real phrase, "Houston, we've had a problem,"[1] is indicative of the power of film to shape the popular imagination and its understanding of history. *Braveheart* (Mel Gibson, 1995) may have won the Oscar for Best Film over *Apollo 13*, but it is the latter that is, by far, the most accurate of the pair, being closely based on Lovell's own memoir. Aside from its most famous misquote, many lines of the film's dialogue come directly from the memoir, and also from the official mission transcripts. At first glance, the Apollo 11 mission, which saw Neil Armstrong become the first human to stand on another world, might seem the more natural story to bring to the big screen, but as Tom Hanks notes, the fate of the crew of Apollo 13 taps into an ancient story type that continues to find resonance with audiences: the heroic quest to return home against great odds.[2] Indeed, Apollo 13's command module was named Odyssey in honor of both Arthur C. Clarke's science-fiction work *2001: A Space Odyssey* (filmed by Stanley Kubrick in 1968), which depicts the wonders and perils of space exploration, and Homer's epic *The Odyssey*[3] (c. 750 B.C.E.), which recounts the Greek myth of Odysseus's heroic but perilous journey home from the Trojan War.

The film begins with the tragic loss of the Apollo 1 crew, who died in 1967 during a training routine when fire broke out in the command module, with design flaws preventing their escape. Moving forward to 1969, astronaut Jim Lovell (Tom Hanks, striking a balance between hero and awed everyman) is hosting a party to witness the moon landing (this, the real Lovell tells us, did not, in fact, take place, but it is a convenient way to introduce the main characters).[4] At the party is the Apollo 11 backup team, namely Lovell himself, along with Fred Haise (Bill Paxton) and Ken Mattingly (Gary Sinise), scheduled to make their own moon landing on Apollo 14.

But Lovell and his crew are brought into the Apollo 13 mission when Alan Shepard, head of the original crew, has problems with an ear infection. Despite Lovell's excitement, his wife Marilyn (Kathleen Quinlan) is anxious about the number 13 and is plagued by nightmares. Although the crew make light of suggestions of bad luck surrounding the number 13, a blow is, in fact, looming. A mere two days before the launch, Mattingly is taken off the team when he is exposed to the measles, being the only team member never to have had them previously. Swinging bachelor Jack Swigert (Kevin Bacon) gets the position in his stead, but there is evident tension between Haise and Swigert during their last-minute training. The real Lovell reveals that this subplot regarding concerns for Swigert's abilities was an invention of the film to build the drama of a rookie astronaut gaining the respect of his crewmembers. In reality, they all got along well and were not concerned about him.[5] Indeed, Swigert was a specialist on malfunctions of the command and lunar modules.[6]

On the day of the launch, 11 April 1970, the astronauts suit up while the team at mission control, headed by Gene Kranz (Ed Harris), go through their own paces. Marilyn decides at the last minute to attend, offering support to Haise's very pregnant wife Mary (Tracy Reiner) (the real Marilyn is just in front of them as an extra). Although engine five cuts out early, the crew gets the go-ahead, and Lovell announces, "Looks like we've just had our glitch for this mission."

The Lovell family arrives at mission control to watch the crew's television broadcast (although the eldest child, Barbara [Mary Kate Schellhardt], puts up typical teenaged resistance), only to be informed that none of the networks are actually showing the footage, deciding that the public has lost interest in the moon. Sharing their disappointment is Jim's mother Blanch (played by Ron Howard's mother, Jean Speegle Howard), who is confused when the television in her nursing home is not showing her son as expected.

Following the "broadcast," the crew is asked to perform some routine procedures, and Swigert stirs the oxygen tanks, as instructed. But unknown to either the crew or mission control, there is a problem with the wiring on one of the tanks, which causes a massive explosion. In the chaotic aftermath of the blast, Lovell notices that they are venting oxygen into space.

At mission control, Kranz tries to restore order among his increasingly panicked team. The White Team Electrical, Environmental, and Consumables Manager, Sy Liebergot (EECOM for short, played by Ron Howard's brother Clint),[7] tells Kranz that the Odyssey Command Module is dying. When their efforts to stop the leaking oxygen fail, and with only fifteen minutes of oxygen left in the command module, the crew is forced to make a hasty move into the lunar module. The crew cannot judge their position in space due to all the debris, and they must make sure the guidance information is taken to the lunar module, albeit via pencil and paper.

On Earth, a distressed Marilyn watches the television report of the crisis while trying to get information from NASA and doing her best to remain composed in front of her children. Mission control tries to work out how to get the crew safely home with limited oxygen and fuel, given that the lunar module was only designed to support two men for two days on the moon. When it is realized that the crew is also going to run out of battery power unless they start shutting things down, Mattingly is brought into the simulator to work out how to salvage enough power for reentry (the real Lovell recalls that there were several people working on the problem).

Meanwhile, the carbon dioxide levels in the lunar module start to climb dangerously high, but the men are unable to simply bring across another filter from the command module because they are different shapes. Mission control is able to work out how to put a square peg into a round hole, using spare bits and pieces the crew has at hand. As the temperature drops and Haise falls ill with a urinary infection, tempers flare between Haise and Swigert until Lovell intervenes. A difficult course correction using only the Earth in their window for guidance helps bring them together. Mattingly finally comes up with a reentry plan, diverting some of the lunar module's batteries to supplement the command module.

The reentry into Earth's atmosphere is tense, for no one can tell whether the explosion has damaged the command module's heat shield, and the worst is feared when the crew remain out of contact for longer than the usual three-minute communication blackout. Among the elation at mission control and the Lovell household when the crew finally makes contact, Kranz sits down silently, absorbing the enormity of the events. As Janet Maslin writes for the *New York Times*, "Better even than Mr. Howard's sure hand with this fascinating material is his film's unexpected restraint. *Apollo 13* understands the difference between movie bravado and real courage."[8] This restraint is also evident in James Horner's Oscar-nominated orchestral score, which is interspersed with music of the era.

The real Jim Lovell notes that the actors for *Apollo 13* ended up spending more time in zero-g aboard NASA's KC-135 airplane than real astronauts.[9] And although it is the human story that is most compelling in *Apollo 13*, the film is notable for its special effects, particularly the launch sequence, which copies some scenes from the original footage using models and computer effects, but also added scenes from vantage points that would, in fact, be impossible to create in real life. These computer effects, and the machines used to create them, stand in stark contrast to the equipment the Apollo 13 team was working with: Lovell brags that at the Vehicle Assembly Building at Cape Kennedy, they have a "computer that can fit into a single room." Upon reviewing the film, Roger Ebert wrote, "America's space program was achieved with equipment that would look like tin cans today. . . . Today . . . it would be safer and cheaper—but we have lost the will . . . we lost something crucial to our vision."[10] Indeed, the film ends as the crew is boarding the USS *Iwo Jima* (where the filmic Lovell is greeted by the real Lovell), and looking back on the lives of his colleagues since that day, Lovell wonders when we will be going back to the moon.

The film won director Ron Howard the Directors Guild of America Award, but, controversially, he was not nominated for Best Director at the Oscars (he would go on to garner this award for *A Beautiful Mind* of 2001 and was nominated for 2008's *Frost/Nixon*). DB

Notes

1. Jim Lovell and Jeffrey Kluger, *Apollo 13* (Boston and New York: Houghton Mifflin, 1994, 2000), 95. Originally published as *Lost Moon*.
2. "Lost Moon: The Triumph of Apollo 13," *Apollo 13*, directed by Ron Howard (Universal Pictures, 2002), DVD.
3. Hamish Lindsay, *Tracking Apollo to the Moon* (London: Springer, 2001), 265.
4. Jim Lovell, "Commentary," *Apollo 13*, directed by Ron Howard (Universal Pictures, 2002), DVD.
5. And although later the film implies that if Swigert is unable to dock the Service Module with the Lunar Module, the whole mission would fail, in reality, Lovell comments that either he or Haise would have been perfectly able to take over and complete the docking. Lovell, "Commentary."
6. Lindsay, *Tracking Apollo to the Moon*, 265.
7. See Sy Liebergot, with Dabid M. Harland, *Apollo EECOM: Journey of a Lifetime* (Burlington, Ontario, Canada: Collector's Guide Publishing, 2003).
8. Janet Maslin, "*Apollo 13*, a Movie for the Fourth of July," *New York Times*, 30 June 1995, www.nytimes.com/1995/06/30/movies/film-review-apollo-13-a-movie-for-the-fourth-of-july.html (28 April 2013).
9. Lovell, "Commentary."
10. Roger Ebert, "*Apollo 13*," *Chicago Sun-Times*, 30 June 1995, www.rogerebert.com/reviews/apollo-13-1995 (28 April 1995).

Bibliography

Ebert, Roger. "*Apollo 13*." *Chicago Sun-Times*, 30 June 1995, www.rogerebert.com/reviews/apollo-13-1995 (28 April 1995).

Liebergot, Sy, with Dabid M. Harland. *Apollo EECOM: Journey of a Lifetime*. Burlington, Ontario, Canada: Collector's Guide Publishing, 2003.

Lindsay, Hamish. *Tracking Apollo to the Moon*. London: Springer, 2001.

Lovell, Jim, and Jeffrey Kluger. *Apollo 13*. Boston and New York: Houghton Mifflin, 1994, 2000.

Maslin, Janet. "*Apollo 13*, a Movie for the Fourth of July." *New York Times*, 30 June 1995, www.nytimes.com/1995/06/30/movies/film-review-apollo-13-a-movie-for-the-fourth-of-july.html (28 April 2013).

ARARAT (2002)

DIRECTOR: Atom Egoyan
WRITER: Atom Egoyan
PRODUCERS: Atom Egoyan, Robert Lantos (Alliance Atlantis Communications, Serendipity Point Films)
CINEMATOGRAPHER: Paul Sarossy
COSTUMES: Beth Pasternak
MUSIC: Mychael Danna
CAST: Ani (Mother): Arsinèe Khanjian. Raffi: David Alpay. Celia: Marie-Josèe Croze. David: Christopher Plummer. Edward Saroyan: Charles Aznavour. Rouben (Screenwriter): Eric Bogosian. Actor Playing Clarence Usher: Bruce Greenwood. Ali, Actor Playing Jevdet Bey: Elias Koteas. Arshile Gorky: Simon Abkarian. Young Gorky: Garen Boyajian. Philip: Brent Carver
AA: None
AAN: None
CANADIAN GENIE AWARDS: Best Film of the Year (Atom Egoyan, Robert Lantos), Best Actress (Arsinèe Khanjian), Best Supporting Actor (Elias Koteas), Best Costume Design (Beth Pasternak), Best Original Score (Mychael Danna)
WRITERS GUILD OF CANADA PRIZE: Atom Egoyan
DVD: Alliance, Canada, 2011. Two-disc set.
BLU-RAY: Currently unavailable
DURATION: 115 minutes

Born in Egypt of Armenian descent, Canadian auteur Atom Egoyan operates independently of Hollywood studios, employing a relatively small number of actors, as in a theatrical troupe, somewhat in the manner of Ingmar Bergman. A musician and a writer of all his scripts, most derivatives of novels, Egoyan works within a limited range of subjects, geographically as well as thematically, achieving a level of subtlety uncommon in mainstream movies. Most of his movies are localized stories dealing with complex family problems and community themes that transcend cultural and historical boundaries, rarely expanding to other geographical latitudes. His style has perhaps alienated mainstream audiences, for he chooses to tell his tales elliptically, in nonchronological sequence, and his fractured story lines are sometimes difficult to follow. He works at once in the past, present, and future, and time fragmentation may inhibit the immediate impact of some of the scenes, causing one to reconstruct them—or resort to a second viewing. Thus, theme is built at the expense of linear chronology, as the pieces fall together as a memory exercise, when one needs to reconstruct the whole. Egoyan, who won several awards at Cannes, in 1994 for *Exotica*, in 1997 for *The Sweet Hereafter*, and for *Felicia's Journey* in 1999, rarely delves into the epic form, but *Ararat* is an epic—albeit be an "intimate" one—due to its historicity and subject matter.

Of the handful of genocide epic films that exist, most have to do with the extermination of the Jews in the concentration camps by Hitler during World War II—the event that came to be known as the Holocaust. Little is known, or accepted as fact, about the genocide of Armenian populations by the Turks in 1915,[1] as World War I was about to start. That is the dilemma that the makers of *Ararat* faced when they decided to film the events of this obscure event, which has remained "underground," as far as public consciousness of it is concerned, for more than eighty-five years, although it is well substantiated and has been commented on by scholars.[2] The movie is, however, heralded not as history, but an artistic representation of the attitudes of various parties involved, as they strive to sort out the past through various means—books, photographs, paintings, video footage, a film that is being made on the subject—to arrive at some comprehensive view of how such events might have evolved and what credibility is due to them. Various points of view collide, and relationships are built, cohering at the end, if one is patient enough to relate and juxtapose their strands.

That is the reason Atom Egoyan, who coauthored and directed this epic, decided to produce it elliptically, that is, foregoing the usual narrative technique of most epics—the chronological flow of events that lead to a conflict that is resolved with a victory over the forces of evil.[3] Rather, Egoyan chose to approach his subject with as much indirection as possible, practically "hiding" his true objective—one assumes to present as much of the naked truth as possible—and couching it in layers of structural palimpsests and codified objects that need to be peeled off and interpreted, one by one, or viewed simultaneously, enhancing the meanings of one another and provoking the viewer to reach a conclusion or sound understanding of these events.

Thus, the movie can be analyzed by setting up these levels against one another—or one with the other, or all of them simultaneously. In separating these levels and sorting out the various codifications, one can look at them in several ways: (a) This is "method" film, one that attempts to avoid clichés and stereotypical descriptions common to usual epic formulas—the straight chronological description, for instance; (b) This is a film whose ultimate goal is to bring to the viewer's conscience a momentous, but forgotten, event, the genocide of a large portion of a national entity, bringing closure to those who survived that event; (c) This is a story of complicated relationships between generations, different ethnic groups, or family members, and even strangers; and (d) This is a film whose interpretation depends on "reading" the transcriptions of objects, the transformations of codes, for example, a button on a painting, a pomegranate, a book, a digitally reconstructed mountain—objects that become connective symbols in a series of transformations that evolve into meaning for the reader. Finally (e), history (the film tells us) is reconstructed not by a single narrative, or "objective truth," but by the interaction of perceptions, memories, art representations of conflicts between individuals and groups that need to be reconciled, and, perhaps most important, an open mind that needs to see prima facie actualities from more than one point of view. Film is not a vehicle of history; however, it can be a significant means of awakening interest in an event that to some may seem ambiguous, untrue, unpleasant to remember if true, or illusory. Through codification and interrelation, film can reconstruct memories, describe attitudes and fears, or provide those connections that make up the fabric of truth. Ultimately, film is iconic, and it cannot reproduce history. It can awaken consciousness.

Let's elaborate further on the aforementioned points. In his DVD "Commentary," Egoyan describes both his method and the historical basis for the film and explains that he chose to bring the story to the screen by ways of indirection, dwelling on "symbols," which are essential to decode and relate the images, and by superimposing levels and sections of incidents, seen or remembered, one upon the other, so the viewer can see these from a number of reflexive angles; these groupings interrelate, but not in chronological order, although the stories in the film evolve chronologically.

There is an artist's painting of a mother and her son, and a button that hangs from it; the artist struggles to give expression to his feelings, which are the subject of the picture—which is their object. The artist, with whom the picture begins, is Arshile Gorky, well known in 1930s, painting a picture of his mother and himself as a boy; the picture shows him covering a missing button from his overcoat with a bunch of flowers his mother had put in his hand. A button hangs from a string over the photograph, and we assume that is the button that his mother had later sewn on the overcoat. According to Egoyan, the button is a fetish, for it keeps his memory of his mother alive. The photograph itself, another important node, has become the basis for the sketch, toward which the camera pans in the opening shots, which, in turn, is the model for the painting the artist is painting (in 1934). We later learn that the painting is hanging in a Toronto museum and is used by Ani (Arsinèe Khanjian), a university professor who has written a book on the Armenian genocide, as a basis for her public lectures on the subject.

The story, however, has already moved to the present (which is hard to determine at first). As a customs officer, David (Christopher Plummer) stops a passenger who is carrying a pomegranate in his bag, telling him he can't bring such an object into the country. The elderly fellow cuts the pomegranate with his knife and eats it, thus demonstrating that he has bypassed the law. The old fellow's name is Edward Saroyan (Charles Aznavour), and he is about to enter the country to make a movie about the Armenian extermination. His mother had died in Van, Armenia, where the genocide had taken place. The film is going to be about this incident, and as the story progresses, we learn that the script, written by Rouben (Eric Bogosian), will contain materials about Gorky (Simon Abkarian) taken from Ani's book. Here a triangle is introduced, consisting of Ani, her son Raffi (David Alpay), and Raffi's stepsister Celia (Marie-Josèe Croze), the daughter (from another mother) of Ani's second husband. Ani's son Raffi is a carrying on an affair with Celia, a fact highly resented by Ani. Raffi's father, obviously of Armenian extraction, has attempted to assassinate a Turkish official, is now dead, and has been labeled a "terrorist." Celia accuses Ani of having pushed her father off a cliff, but the latter contends it was a suicide. Celia's anger is expressed when she asks hostile questions, interrupting Ani during her lectures.

Meanwhile, we follow another strand of the story, which is happening at this precise moment—the present-present—as the same customs officer stops Raffi, who is returning from Armenia, and inquires about the contents of several canisters, which Raffi claims are films he took while he had visited Ararat (the Van area is not there—but this is poetic license) for the purposes of the making of the aforementioned film. He refuses to open them, saying that light would ruin the negatives. This incident, which runs throughout the story, "frames" Egoyan's film, providing the "solution" (denouement) of the whole.

But the story contains another level of relationships—and this part can be called the story of David, whose son Philip (Brent Carver) has a lover, Ali (Elias Koteas), a Canadian actor who is half Turk, and who is playing a part of in the movie Saroyan is making. Ali is overjoyed to get the part, but his heart breaks when he has to play Jevdet Bey, a sadistic Turkish official who orders the torture of boys and is possibly responsible for Gorky's mother's death. Ali cannot bear the guilt of being of Turkish descent or accept the Armenian genocide as a fact. Saroyan knows his problems, but he has a good actor in his hands and does not want to lose him. He sends him a bottle of champagne with Raffi.

The movie is made and is being exhibited on its premiere night at a Toronto theater, when Ani receives a phone call from her son, begging for her help. David has opened the canisters and finds that they contain cocaine, although Raffi has continued, up to the last moment, to claim that they were film. He had been taking the footage he wanted with his camcorder, and he had gone to Ararat on his own, not for the sake of Saroyan's picture. A guard there had helped him and, in exchange, asked him to bring the canisters into the country. David lets him go, and Raffi rejoins his mother.

Every object produces this reflexive act: Next, a book comes into our consciousness; it has been written by a talented female author of Armenian extraction and has now become the source of a film script, which, in turn, is the movie that is being made—a movie about the Armenian genocide, directed by Edward, who is the son of one of the surviving women (to be seen at the end of the movie as a child). The woman author, Ani, is the surviving widow of a man who died attempting an act of terrorism; her son, Raffi, is carrying on an affair with the daughter of her second husband, who committed suicide, a fact disputed by his daughter, Celia. Raffi is consumed by his passion to discover the actual location of Mount Ararat, which borders what was considered the Armenian land of Van, now Turkey; a moment later we see him confronted by a customs agent, David, who has suspicions that the youngster is smuggling drugs in the film canisters he has brought from his trip abroad. The interrogation continues—through intercutting for the duration of the film—an actual twenty-four hours. Now David, who is about to retire—this being his last interview—has a son, Philip, who also has a son, and as the four sit at the table, the young child asks a friend of Philip's, Ali, whether he believes in God. Ali, an actor of Turkish extraction, seeks a job in Edward's movie, and a moment later we see him jump for joy when he hears he got the part—at the same time we learn that he and Philip are lovers. The movie (which is, of course, a movie within a movie), in its plethora of overlapping plots, establishes an axis, and that is David's interrogation of Raffi, and this scene, interrupted to show the other plot segments, constitutes beginning-middle-end (so to speak), if one keeps track of the development of theme and time. David, knowing that Raffi did not think that he was lying, lets him go.

That establishes the main premise of the film—that reality, including what happened in past historical periods, is always subject to the interpretation of those who received it through tradition, personal choice, or individual bias. A Turk living in Canada and playing the person who committed these atrocities—or was an executioner—is unable to accept a historical truth that somehow implicates him, and wants to let things alone, let the past be past; he, too, lives in a new country, and why not look to the future and forget the past? When Ali raises these questions with Saroyan, asking him if he chose him to play the part because he was Turkish, the latter refuses to answer or argue the point with him, for a director, as he admits, wants an actor who can play the part; he does not want to argue whether the part the actor plays is true history. Raffi, on the other hand, whose father was killed when trying to assassinate a Turkish official and is presently called a terrorist, will not let Ali off the hook so easily, as he compares the part Ali plays—Jevdet Bey—to Hitler, and that is the breaking point between the two. There can be no reconciliation. Ali is humiliated, more in denial of the genocide as ever, and perpetually hostile, and he leaves Raffi and the champagne the latter offered him with a final look of hatred.

Three levels of reality are established here. One is the historical fact of the genocide; the other is the film about it, a film based on true witnesses and history; and then the film (which we watch), which is relating what happens when a film attempts to mix reality with filmmaking. A film, no matter how well documented, remains a fictional event; one can accept its "truths," another can dispute them or totally deny them. No matter how one equates truth with film narrative, there can be no actual belief, or belief must remain "suspended." It cannot be otherwise, for a film is a highly artificial and illusory construct, no matter how biased its premises are. David lets Raffi go, for he sees that this young man absolutely believed that the canisters could not contain drugs; the canisters were given to him by a trusted friend. The trust itself had a factual basis, and yet that basis was smashed as soon as the canisters were opened and cocaine was found in them. Was Raffi guilty of lying? No, because he believed he was telling the truth. One always transfers reality to his own subjective plane. Ali could not accept that his compatriots had committed the atrocities described in the film. In a way, the film Egoyan was making lets him go, too, for Ali absolutely (or almost) could not believe what he heard, but history, as illustrated by David, is harsh and impartial. David is Egoyan. He is the customs officer who understood innocence—for Raffi was innocent of a falsehood—but who also did not believe that the innocence of a person is enough to conceal a horrible historical fact—which offends even the descendants of the perpetrators. The film also says you cannot bury truth. The past must be dug up and preserved, no matter how horrid, for without such knowledge, we are not as human as we ought to be. Forgive, perhaps; forget, no. A film can do its part, not in the same terms as history, but its contribution is, nonetheless, not less valuable. CS

Notes

1. According to Merrill D. Peterson in his *"Starving Armenians": America and the Armenian Genocide, 1915–1930* (Charlottesville: University of Virginia Press, 2004), 201, the Armenian genocide by the Turks took place during an extended period of time, starting in the nineteenth century and continuing beyond the end of World War I. See the review by James Libby, professor emeritus, Embry-Riddle Aeronautical University, in the *Register of the Kentucky Historical Society* 102, nos. 3/4 (Summer/Autumn 2004): 357.

2. Peterson, *"Starving Armenians,"* 201.

3. Egoyan provides this view in his "Commentary" in the 2003 DVD Miramax Edition of *Ararat.* (Miramax and Disney provide the usual disclaimer on DVD commentaries, stating that what is said there is for the purposes of entertainment only and does not reflect the views of Miramax or Disney.)

Bibliography

Libby, James. *"Ararat." Register of the Kentucky Historical Society* 102, nos. 3/4 (Summer/Autumn 2004): 357.

Peterson, Merrill D. *"Starving Armenians": America and the Armenian Genocide, 1915–1930.* Charlottesville: University of Virginia Press, 2004.

THE ASSASSINATION OF JESSE JAMES BY THE COWARD ROBERT FORD (2007)

DIRECTOR: Andrew Dominik

WRITER: Andrew Dominik. Based on the novel by Ron Hansen.

PRODUCERS: Ridley Scott, Jules Daly, Brad Pitt, Dede Gardner, David Valdes (Warner Bros., Jesse Films, Scott Free Productions)

CINEMATOGRAPHER: Roger Deakins

EDITORS: Curtiss Clayton, Dylan Tichenor

MUSIC: Nick Cave, Warren Ellis

CAST: Jesse James: Brad Pitt. Robert Ford: Casey Affleck. Zee James: Mary-Louise Parker. Frank James: Sam Shepard. Mary James: Brooklynn Proulx. Tim James: Dustin Bollinger. Wood Hite: Jeremy Renner. Sarah Hite: Kailin See. Ed Miller: Garret Dillahunt. Dick Liddil: Paul Schneider. Ted Levine. Dorothy Evans: Zooey Deschanel. Charley Ford: Sam Rockwell. Albert Ford: Jesse Frechette. Wilbur Ford: Pat Healy. Martha Bolton: Alison Elliott. Henry Craig: Michael Parks. Narrator: Hugh Ross

AA: None

AAN: Best Supporting Actor (Casey Affleck), Best Cinematography (Roger Deakins)

DURATION: 159 minutes

The Assassination of Jesse James by the Coward Robert Ford's main theme is "celebrity." Reading the symbolism created by the framing, lighting, and image manipulation, the film is more specifically about acting and celebrity. To give the film its historical look, director Andrew Dominik and cinematographer Roger Deakins studied images from different media, including "images from past films, still photographer's work, paintings, even architectural magazines," not to re-create them, but to create a "melancholy feel of the piece, the emotions were within this kind of imagery."[1] Deakins says, "Because the film was this kind of poetic reimagining of [this Western tale], we made certain images that looked like they came from an old picture book, as if they came from an old box camera."[2]

One critic describes the results as "some of the most evocative work of [Deakins's] career and defining forever what we might call the Victorianising of the West."[3] Much of the imagery during the narration evokes sepia-toned, grain, blurred vignettes of the early days of photography. To achieve the desired imagery, Deakins shot some sections with lenses that had their front elements removed. Deakins did this to achieve a "distorted color fringing and vignetting [that] I felt reflected the kind of feel of photographs from the time."[4] These images are used in the goal of revealing character.

Dominik follows the novel's model by using an omniscient narrator. When the film opens, the narrator (Hugh Ross) reveals that, at only thirty-four years of age, Jesse James (Brad Pitt) has unhealed bullet wounds, granulated eyelids, constant paranoia, and two children who do not know his real name. His neighbors believe him to be rich and leisured and to have a common touch. He and Frank James (Sam Shepard) wait for darkness to fall in Blue Cut, Missouri, where they recruit "local gangs and country rubes" to assist in robbing a train. Jesse tells stories about Lincoln, "a tyrant," and his wife Mary Todd, who went into hysterics during a full moon. When Robert Ford (Casey Affleck), a young man eager for celebrity, sits down to listen to the stories, the others get up for chow. Ford wanders into the woods overlooking the railroad to see Frank. He tries to ingratiate himself. "I honestly believe I'm destined for great things, Mr. James." Frank tires of him and pulls a gun on him to make him leave. Frank is the boss and the brains of the outfit, but after twenty-five bank and stage robberies, he has lost his drive to continue. He quotes Shakespeare's "Sonnet 62," saying, "for this sin there is no remedy, it is so grounded inward in my heart." Robert asks Jesse to be a member of the gang, and Jesse says he can join.

The gang, hooded and waiting for the train, snuffs lanterns and waits in the darkness. Light from the train engine slats through the woods like a Zoetrope—a metaphor for filmmaking. Jesse stands on railroad sleepers piled on the tracks. The light from the train dramatically lights his silhouette. The train stops, and Jesse convinces the men inside the mail car to open the safe. When it is opened, they do not find the $100,000 they expected. Afterward, Charley Ford (Sam Rockwell) asks Frank to "gauge their courage" to make them regular sidekicks. Frank says that they should "shed that idea," and that they've given night riding up for good. Robert talks to Jesse and reads him a description of Jesse from a newspaper clipping. He has also read *The Train Robber, or, a Story of the Jesse James Boys*, by R. W. Stevens. James tells him, "They're all lies you know."

Back at his home, Jesse smokes behind his house. Frank leaves without saying anything. Jesse pulls snakes out of a can and says snake skins fried in garlic are good eating. He names them after his enemies. Jesse tells Robert to let Charley and Wood Hite (Jeremy Renner) "get their gatherings together." Robert reports this to them and lords it over Wood. Charley tells Robert that he will be doing menial work. Robert has to help move Jesse (posing as Thomas

Howard) into another house at night. Robert sees himself as helper to the family. He goes with Jesse to the saloon in Topeka. Robert listens to conversations, offering nothing, learning the way, not the meaning, as if he were "writing a biography or preparing an impersonation." James eventually asks him, "Do you want to be like me or be me?" Robert is sent away.

Robert goes to his sister's farm forty miles away. His sister, Martha Bolton (Alison Elliott), rents rooms to Robert, Charley, and other members of the James Gang. Dick Liddil (Paul Schneider), a womanizer, attempts to seduce Martha, and when she spurns him, he moves on to her daughter. Upstairs, Robert puts his mask from the Blue Cut robbery in a box of James artifacts under his bed, as if they are pieces of the "true cross."

As Robert bathes outdoors, Dick walks up and wants to know why Jesse asked Robert to stay longer. Robert says he's "not at liberty to say," pretending he did something more important than move furniture. Dick warns him, saying, "If you connive behind his back he'll come after you with a cleaver," and he asks if Jesse said that he (Dick) and a man named Jim Cummins were in cahoots. Dick puts a gun up to Ford's cheek and tells him not to tell Jesse. Robert returns to the house and finds Charley and Wood making fun of his hood. He says, "Cross me again and I'll put a bullet through your head."

The rest of the gang goes to Kentucky to Wood's father's (Major George Hite) place. Knowing that he would cause trouble, Wood warns Dick to stay away from his beautiful new wife, Sarah (Kailin See). The first night, Wood has to call Dick inside from his seduction of Martha on the porch. Ignoring Wood's prohibition, Dick has sex with her in the outhouse.

Jesse moves his family from Kansas City after four of the Blue Cut robbers are arrested. Jesse rides to Ed Miller's (Garret Dillahunt) house. Ed says that Jim told him that Jesse was planning on killing the guys that got caught. Ed also reveals that they considered capturing Jesse for the $600 reward but insists he does not need the money. Jesse suggests going into town, where he will buy him dinner. Ed agrees. Shown in flashback later, Jesse kills Ed while they ride through the darkness.

Jesse takes Dick to find Jim. They find Jim's nephew, Albert Ford (Jesse Frechette), who is also a young cousin of Robert and Charley. Jesse beats Albert to obtain information about Jim's location. Unsuccessful, Jesse leans against his horse and cries, revealing the pressure on him. Dick returns alone to Martha's house. When Wood realizes he is there, he tries to ambush Dick with one of Robert's guns, but Robert shoots Wood in the head. Robert and Wilbur Ford (Pat Healy) take Wood's body out to a creek bed and cover it with snow. Jesse shows up soon thereafter. Afraid he knows about the death of his cousin, Dick hides in a closet. Jesse, always suspicious, notices Robert's nervousness. Robert begins a comparison of his life and Jesse's; both are sons of preachers and the youngest of a number of brothers. Jesse says he wants to take one of the Fords with him. Because of Robert's odd behavior, he decides to take Charley. While riding away, Jesse asks Charley if he has seen Wood lately. Charley says, "No, not at all." When they are on the trail, Jesse and Charley cross a frozen creek. Jesse asks if he ever considered suicide. Jesse shoots down through the ice.

Robert visits the Kansas City police commissioner, Henry Craig (Michael Parks), and asks where he can find Dick Liddil. The governor honors Craig at a party where Robert acts like "he's the belle of the ball." Robert makes a deal with the governor to deliver Jesse in ten days. Craig tells Robert to return to Elias's grocery store in Richmond and await instructions from Sheriff James Timberlake. Jesse and Charley come to the store, and Jesse decides bring Robert along, but Charley warns Robert that Jesse is suspicious of him. Robert tells him he has ten days to arrest Jesse.

Jesse takes the Ford brothers to his house, where his wife is not pleased to see Robert and his daughter are afraid of him. Jesse discusses his plan to rob the Wells Bank in Platte City. Jesse uses Robert to act out how he will approach the bank's cashier, drawing a knife and putting it against Robert's throat. That night, Jesse and Robert sleep in the children's room. Robert imagines using a gun on Jesse, but Jesse is also awake, and holding a gun in his hand. Jesse gives Bob a nickel-plated pistol to apologize for his behavior. While the family and Charley are at church, Robert surveys the house, trying on Jesse's persona.

Jesse's depression and paranoia eventually cause him to seek death at Robert's hand. Jesse brings a paper back from his visit to town, but he has yet to read it. Robert sees a headline that reads, "The arrest and confession of Dick Liddil." Robert hides the paper. When Jesse reads the article, he takes off his holster, puts it on a couch, and says there's dust on a picture. He stands, posing, in front of the picture on the wall, waiting for Robert to see his cue. Robert takes his position behind him, fulfilling his role, and shoots him. Jesse's wife comes in, Robert sits down, and Charley leaves. Robert telegraphs the governor. The photo of Jesse in his coffin becomes as popular as photos of the Sphinx and the Taj Mahal.

A year later, on a New York stage, Charley and Robert reenact Jesse's death. Charley plays Jesse, and Robert plays himself. By October 1883, Robert is more famous than the president, eventually "killing" Jesse 800 times on stage. Charley becomes more like Jesse; he becomes paranoid, afraid that Robert might put a live round in the pistol. One night someone in the audience calls Robert a coward but will not admit it when Robert orders the house lights to rise. When the lights dim again, the man repeats himself. Robert jumps into the audience. Charley never mails letters to Jesse's widow begging for forgiveness, and he eventually shoots himself. Robert visits a bar and hears a musician (Nick Cave) sing about "Robert Ford, that dirty little coward." Robert shoots the floor and corrects the entertainer on how many children Jesse had but not the cowardice charge.

Robert opens a bar in Creede, Colorado. He tells his waitress that he has no real memory of the shooting and aftermath, but that he expected applause. He regrets killing Jesse. His notoriety is attractive to Edward O'Kelley who had a "generalized wish for revenge against Robert Ford." O'Kelley received a life sentence for second-degree murder for killing Robert, but he only served eight years after being pardoned by the governor. There were no eulogies, famous photographs, or staged reenactments for Robert Ford. JMW

Notes

1. Dustin Luke Nelson, "A Modest Lens: An Interview with Roger Deakins," *InDigest*, www.indigestmag.com/deakins1.htm (8 September 2013).
2. Scott Macaulay, "Roger Deakins: Sticking to the Script," *Focus Features*, 7 January 2012, http://focusfeatures.com/article/roger_deakins__sticking_to_the_script (8 September 2013).
3. Nick James, "War, Lust, Spies, and Quaint Conceits," *Sight and Sound* 17, no. 11 (November 2007): 38–42.
4. Roger Deakins, "Lens Selection and Leading the Viewer's Eye," *Roger Deakins Forum*, www.rogerdeakins.com/forum2/viewtopic.php?f=2&t=19&start=0+ (8 September 2013).

Bibliography

Deakins, Roger. "Lens Selection and Leading the Viewer's Eye." *Roger Deakins Forum*, www.rogerdeakins.com/forum2/viewtopic.php?f=2&t=19&start=0+ (8 September 2013).

Hansen, Ron. *The Assassination of Jesse James by the Coward Robert Ford*. New York: Knopf, 1983.

James, Nick. "War, Lust, Spies, and Quaint Conceits." *Sight and Sound* 17, no. 11 (November 2007): 38–42.
Macaulay, Scott. "Roger Deakins: Sticking to the Script." *Focus Features*, 7 January 2012, http://focusfeatures.com/article/roger_deakins__sticking_to_the_script (8 September 2013).
Nelson, Dustin Luke. "A Modest Lens: An Interview with Roger Deakins." *InDigest*, www.indigestmag.com/deakins1.htm (8 September 2013).

ATONEMENT (2007)

DIRECTOR: Joe Wright
WRITER: Christopher Hampton. Based on the novel by Ian McEwan.
PRODUCERS: Tim Bevan, Eric Fellner, Paul Webster (Universal, Studiocanal, Relativity Media, Working Title)
CINEMATOGRAPHER: Seamus McGarvey
EDITOR: Paul Tothill
ART DIRECTION: Ian Bailie, Niall Moroney, Nick Gottschalk, Sarah Greenwood
SET DECORATION: Katie Spencer
COSTUMES: Jacqueline Durran
MUSIC: Dario Marianelli
CAST: Robbie Turner: James McAvoy. Cecilia Tallis: Keira Knightley. Briony Tallis, Age 18: Romola Garai. Briony Tallis, Age 13: Saoirse Ronan. Older Briony: Vanessa Redgrave. Grace Turner: Brenda Blethyn. Lola Quincey: Juno Temple. Paul Marshall: Benedict Cumberbatch. Leon Tallis: Patrick Kennedy. Emily Tallis: Harriet Walter. Police Inspector: Peter Wight. Tommy Nettle: Daniel Mays. Frank Mace: Nonso Anozie. Sister Drummond: Gina McKee. Luc Cornet: Jérémie Rénier. Fiona Maguire: Michelle Duncan. Pierrot Quincey: Felix von Simson. Jackson Quincey: Charlie von Simson. Danny Hardman: Alfie Allen. Frenchman #1: Michel Vuillermoz. Frenchman #2: Lionel Abelanski. Interviewer: Anthony Minghella
AA: Best Music Written for Motion Pictures–Original Score (Dario Marianelli)
AAN: Best Art Direction (Sarah Greenwood, Katie Spencer), Best Cinematography (Seamus McGarvey), Best Costume Design (Jacqueline Durran), Best Picture (Tim Bevan, Eric Fellner, Paul Webster), Best Performance by an Actress in a Supporting Role (Saoirse Ronan), Best Writing–Adapted Screenplay (Christopher Hampton)
BAFTA AWARDS: Best Film (Tim Bevan, Eric Fellner, Paul Webster), Best Production Design (Sarah Greenwood, Katie Spencer)
GG: Best Motion Picture–Drama, Best Original Score–Motion Picture (Dario Marianelli)
DVD: Universal Pictures, 2007
BLU-RAY: Universal, 2007
DURATION: DVD, 118 minutes; Blu-ray, 123 minutes

Perfectly cast and beautifully shot, *Atonement* tells the tale of lovers separated and lives destroyed when a naïve thirteen-year-old girl misunderstands her glimpses into the sexual world of adults. Based on the best-selling novel of the same name by Ian McEwan (whose previous novel, *Amsterdam*, won the 1998 Booker Prize), the film necessarily omits some events, yet captures its sense of both loss and lyricism. *Atonement* won an Oscar for Dario Marianelli's score but lost Best Picture to *No Country for Old Men* (Scott Rudin, Ethan Coen, Joel Coen, 2007).

At first, *Atonement* appears to be merely a stylish British historical-class drama, but the film plays with those expectations. In 1935, the upper class Tallis family is enjoying the privileges of a leisurely summer on their country estate, among them the beautiful but somewhat aloof Cecilia (Keira Knightley), down from Cambridge, where she has been studying alongside the housekeeper's son, Robbie (James McAvoy). Her brother Leon (Patrick Kennedy) observes in "Cee" a telling animosity toward Robbie, but the youngest member of the Tallis family, Briony (played by several different actresses as she ages), is keen to have Robbie attend the family dinner and see a performance of her first play.

Briony reconsiders her opinion of Robbie when she sees him seemingly ordering Cecilia to strip and jump into a fountain. We later see the event from the adults' perspective and realize that it is Cecilia who takes the initiative to retrieve a broken vase from the water. The film frequently revisits past events in this manner to unravel the young Briony's misconceptions, but by film's end, we find that it is the elderly Briony who is herself reconstructing her memories and filling in the gaps with the benefit of adult hindsight.

Also at the Tallis household in the summer of 1935 is the teenaged Lola (Juno Temple) and her younger twin brothers Pierrot (Felix von Simson) and Jackson (Charlie von Simson)—relatives staying under sufferance after their mother ran off with her lover. The twins undermine Briony's play, and Leon's friend, Paul Marshall (Benedict Cumberbatch), flirts inappropriately with Lola.

Meanwhile, Robbie makes several attempts at writing a letter of apology to Cecilia for his behavior at the fountain, one of which is sexually explicit—the "c-word" is emblazoned on the big screen. He accidentally gives this version to Briony to deliver to Cecilia. The curious Briony is shocked when she reads its contents, later confiding to Lola that she believes Robbie to be dangerous. This opinion is confirmed when she discovers Robbie seemingly attacking Cecilia in the library. The pair is, in fact, making love (in one of the most erotic and best-edited love scenes to have been put to film), having declared their feelings for one another.

When the twins run away, the dinner party searches the gardens, and Briony interrupts a man raping Lola, assuming the attacker to be Robbie. Later, when Robbie returns with the twins, he is taken into custody to the disbelief of both Cecilia and his mother.

Robbie is sent to prison, but, with the advent of war, is given the choice to enlist. We next find him in Northern France, wounded, stranded, and trying to retreat with two other soldiers, Mace (Nonso Anozie) and Nettle (Daniel Mays). Their arrival on the beach at Dunkirk, with its incongruous set of images—horses being shot, men singing hymns, fairground rides—is one long five-minute take, which soon became known as "The Shot."[1] Filmed with a Steadicam used on a golf buggy, on foot, and on a rickshaw, and featuring 1,000 extras (with assistant directors in uniform to move them into shot several times over), the effect is as stunning as it is sobering.[2] When he sees the masses of soldiers on the beach, Mace swears and exclaims, "It's like something out of the Bible." This is the only sequence in the film given the truly expansive treatment we associate with the filmic epic, at the same time underscoring the themes of tragedy and fate that are played out by the characters throughout the film but—we sense—could just as easily have been told through any one of the other soldiers we see weeping, fighting, or playing on the beach.

Robbie becomes delirious, dreaming of his mother and being reunited with Cecilia, who is now a nurse in London and has cut off ties with her family. The pair writes to one another and long for a life together after the war. Briony is also a nurse, plagued with guilt now that she realizes that it was Paul, who has since married Lola, who was, in fact, the rapist. We also learn that Robbie was her first—and seemingly only—crush, adding a jealous motivation to her earlier misdeeds. Briony visits Cecilia and Robbie and promises the understandably incensed couple that she will do what she can to make things right.

But this encounter is a fantasy of the dying seventy-seven-year-old Briony (Vanessa Redgrave), who, in a television interview for her new and last book, *Atonement*, reveals that she found it hard to end the story with the truth of Robbie's death at Dunkirk and Cecilia's death in a London underground station bomb shelter. Briony never got to confront the pair, and aside from a brief meeting in a London café before Robbie is sent off to war, the couple is never reunited. It is only in Briony's invented ending that Robbie and Cecilia get to frolic on the beach near Dover at the end of the war.

Joe Wright previously directed Keira Knightley in *Pride & Prejudice* (2005), while her romantic lead in *Atonement*, James McAvoy, was best known at this time for his role as Idi Amin's physician in the acclaimed *The Last King of Scotland* (Kevin Macdonald, 2006). For its part, *Atonement* received quite contrasting reviews, from those moved by Wright's "mastery of nuance and epic"[3] to the "bored and annoyed."[4] Ian McEwan suggests that the film version of his novel is particularly good at creating a "sense of an expanse of time,"[5] which we might expect of a historical epic, but it is the way that *Atonement* brings these devices to bear upon a story about storytelling, the power and danger of inventing stories, and the play of memory that makes the film particularly compelling. DB

Notes

1. S. T. Van Airsdale, "The Oscars: Nominated *Atonement* Cinematographer—Who, Me?" *Vanity Fair*, 23 January 2008, www.vanityfair.com/online/daily/2008/01/the-oscars-nomi (12 January 2013).
2. Joe Wright, "Commentary," *Atonement*, directed by Joe Wright (Universal Pictures, 2007), DVD.
3. Roger Ebert, "*Atonement*," *Chicago Sun-Times*, 7 December 2007, http://rogerebert.suntimes.com/apps/pbcs.dll/article?AID=/20071206/REVIEWS/712060301 (12 January 2013).
4. S. T. Van Airsdale, "The Oscars: *Atonement*, Jane Fonda, and the Impossible Dream," *Vanity Fair*, 15 February 2008, www.vanityfair.com/online/daily/2008/02/the-oscars-aton (12 January 2013).
5. "The Making of *Atonement*," *Atonement*, directed by Joe Wright (Universal Pictures, 2007), DVD.

Bibliography

Ebert, Roger. "*Atonement*." *Chicago Sun-Times*, 7 December 2007, http://rogerebert.suntimes.com/apps/pbcs.dll/article?AID=/20071206/REVIEWS/712060301 (12 January 2013).

Van Airsdale, S. T. "The Oscars: *Atonement*, Jane Fonda, and the Impossible Dream." *Vanity Fair*, 15 February 2008, www.vanityfair.com/online/daily/2008/02/the-oscars-aton (12 January 2013).

———. "The Oscars: Nominated *Atonement* Cinematographer—Who, Me?" *Vanity Fair*, 23 January 2008, www.vanityfair.com/online/daily/2008/01/the-oscars-nomi (12 January 2013).

AVATAR (2009)

Director: James Cameron
Writer: James Cameron
Producers: James Cameron, Jon Landau (20th Century Fox, Dune Entertainment, Ingenious Film Partners)
Cinematographer: Mauro Fiore
Editors: Stephen E. Rivkin, John Refoua, James Cameron
Production Design: Rick Carter, Robert Stromberg, Kim Sinclair
Costumes: Mayes C. Rubeo, Deborah L. Scott
Music: James Horner
Sound Editors: Christopher Boyes, Gwendolyn Yates Whittle
Sound Mixers: Christopher Boyes, Gary Summers, Andy Nelson, Tony Johnson
Special Effects: Joe Letteri, Stephen Rosenbaum, Richard Baneham, Andrew R. Jones
Cast: Jake Sully: Sam Worthington. Neytiri: Zoë Saldana. Grace: Sigourney Weaver. Colonel Miles Quaritch: Stephen Lang. Trudy Chacon: Michelle Rodriguez. Parker Selfridge: Giovanni Ribisi. Norm Spellman: Joel David Moore. Moat: CCH Pounder. Eytukan: Wes Studi. Tsu'tey: Laz Alonso. Dr. Max Patel: Dileep Rao. Corporal Lyle Wainfleet: Matt Gerald. Private Fike: Sean Anthony Moran. Cryo Vault Med Tech: Jason Whyte. Venture Star Crew Chief: Scott Lawrence. Lock Up Trooper: Kelly Kilgour. Shuttle Pilot:

James Pitt. Shuttle Copilot: Sean Patrick Murphy. Shuttle Crew Chief: Peter Dillon. Tractor Operator: Kevin Dorman. Dragon Gunship Pilot: Kelson Henderson. Dragon Gunship Gunner: David Van Horn. Dragon Gunship Navigator: Jacob Tomuri

AA: Best Art Direction (Rick Carter, Robert Stromberg, Kim Sinclair), Best Cinematography (Mauro Fiore), Best Visual Effects (Joe Letteri, Stephen Rosenbaum, Richard Baneham, Andrew R. Jones)

AAN: Best Directing (James Cameron), Best Film Editing (Stephen E. Rivkin, John Refoua, James Cameron), Best Music Written for Motion Pictures–Original Score (James Horner), Best Sound Editing (Christopher Boyes, Gwendolyn Yates Whittle), Best Sound Mixing (Christopher Boyes, Gary Summers, Andy Nelson, Tony Johnson), Best Picture (James Cameron, Jon Landau)

GG: Best Director–Motion Picture (James Cameron), Best Motion Picture–Drama

GGN: Best Original Score–Motion Picture (James Horner), Best Original Song–Motion Picture (James Horner, Simon Franglen, Kuk Harrell for "I See You"), Best Motion Picture–Drama

DVD: 20th Century Fox, 2010

BLU-RAY: 20th Century Fox, 2009

DURATION: 162 minutes

James Cameron's almost obscenely expensive science-fiction epic (estimates of the final cost vary widely, but *BusinessWeek* cites $380 million[1]) is the "highest-grossing film of all time, having taken $2.782 billion worldwide."[2] *Avatar* marks a milestone in feature-film computer animation, motion-capture technology, and immersive 3D, such that "we feel like we've actually been there, not watched it on a screen."[3] A veteran of both science fiction (the *Terminator* films, 1984 and 1991; *Aliens*, 1986; *The Abyss*, 1989) and the epic (*Titanic*, 1997, which was groundbreaking in its day but whose effects already look stale), what Cameron presents in *Avatar* is really a futuristic, revisionist western: *Dances with Wolves* (Kevin Costner, 1990) in space. If the plot offers nothing new (it was widely criticized for its simplistic rendering), visually its entirely computer-generated imagery astounds.

The extended version of *Avatar* begins in a grimy city on Earth in the year 2154, where paraplegic former marine Jake (Sam Worthington) drinks too much, picks fights, and dreams of flying. Informed of the death of his scientist twin brother, Jake is offered a job on Pandora, a moon of the planet Polyphemus,[4] where humans are mining for the precious (and clumsily named) unobtanium. The moon boasts an atmosphere toxic to humans and an array of deadly wildlife, but there is a more pressing impediment to the mining—an indigenous humanoid population called the Na'vi who seem curiously impervious to bribery. Jake joins a team of scientists who periodically inhabit "avatars," genetically engineered bodies that meld human and Na'vi DNA and can be remotely controlled from emitter beds. The group's leader, Grace (Sigourney Weaver), is none too pleased to be given a soldier, but Jake can make use of his twin's expensive avatar and prevent it from simply going to waste.

Jake is delighted to have the ability to walk and run via his huge blue, alien avatar, and, despite Grace's frosty reception, he manages to get along with fellow team members Norm (Joel David Moore) and Max (Dileep Rao). The expedition is not really a scientific one, however. Grace's team is tolerated only so that they may be used to persuade the Na'vi to relocate to facilitate the commercial mining operation, headed by Parker Selfridge (Giovanni Ribisi) and protected by Colonel Miles Quaritch (Stephen Lang).

On his first foray into the wilderness of Pandora, escorted by pilot Trudy Chacon (Michelle Rodriguez), Jake is pursued by a fierce dinosaur-like creature, and he narrowly escapes. As night descends, the team is forced to abandon him to the many nighttime dangers of the jungle. Just when it seems that Jake will die at the hands of an animal pack, he is rescued by a Na'vi woman, Neytiri (Zoë Saldana), who only resists killing him herself because a seed from their sacred tree lands on her arrow, a sign from their deity, Eywa. Despite this sign, Neytiri is understandably hostile toward Jake, until a multitude of the special seeds envelop him. The awed Neytiri takes him to her father, the tribe's leader, Eytukan (Wes Studi), and her mother Moat (CCH Pounder), their spiritual leader. Having learned English from Grace's team, the tribe is able to communicate with Jake, and as a warrior society themselves, they are intrigued by him. By virtue of the sacred tree's approval, Neytiri is ordered to teach Jake their ways, even though they are doubtful of his ability to truly understand. Grace is appreciative, if a little jealous, of the breakthrough. Her previously good relations with the tribe evaporated when Na'vi were killed at her school for daring to rebel against the human "sky people."

The need for Jake's intervention is pressing, for the tribe lives on a rich unobtanium deposit, and Quaritch enlists Jake to gather information vital to removing the Na'vi from their home. Upon learning Jake's true purpose, Grace moves her operation to a remote outpost but does not directly admonish Jake, for she needs him to foster a way back in with the tribe.

Jake learns the ways of the Na'vi, eventually undertaking the perilous final stage of selecting a flying pterodactyl-like creature known as banshees. Mocked by his rival, Tsu'tey (Laz Alonso), who is betrothed to Neytiri, Jake nonetheless succeeds in mastering a banshee. Although Jake continues to provide valuable intel to Quaritch, he refuses an offer to return home and receive surgery to restore his legs. Jake wants to undertake the final initiation into the tribe, hoping to use his new status to persuade them to leave their home peacefully. Neytiri takes Jake to a sacred site where they can connect to their ancestors, and the pair mate, but in the morning, the newly bonded pair awaken to find the humans bulldozing the site. An incensed Jake attacks the vehicle and is spotted by Quaritch, who realizes that Jake can no longer be relied upon.

With the possibility of a peaceful relocation seemingly gone, Selfridge orders the destruction of the gigantic tree that is home to the Na'vi. Among Quaritch's team, only Trudy withdraws, exclaiming, "I didn't sign up for this shit." The Na'vi home is a burning wasteland, the shattered survivors retreating to the sanctuary of the sacred tree of souls. Among the dead is Eytukan, and Neytiri angrily rejects Jake for what she sees as his betrayal.

Although the human form of Jake and the scientific team are placed under arrest, Trudy helps them escape, taking the emitting machines even farther into the jungle in preparation for the anticipated hostilities. Jake's offer to help the Na'vi is rejected, but when he bonds with the most fearsome flying creature known as Toruk, the tribe is awed at his feat, and even Neytiri and Tsu'tey accept him back into the fold. The Na'vi attempt to permanently transfer Grace's consciousness into her avatar in view of her extensive wounds suffered during the escape from base, but the attempt comes too late. The grief-stricken Jake proclaims his intention to fly with Toruk and unite the tribes against the human sky people.

Meanwhile, Selfridge and Quaritch plan to destroy the tree of souls before they are overrun by the incoming Na'vi, also hoping to quash the people's will to resist once their sacred site is destroyed. The Na'vi bows and arrows are ostensibly no match for the technological flying craft and weaponry of the humans, but their knowledge of the difficult terrain affords them some advantage. They nonetheless struggle until Eywa responds to Jake's prayers, sending the fearsome creatures of the jungle against the infantry. Faced with defeat, the enraged Quaritch climbs into an exoskeleton fighting suit, and Neytiri engages him in battle only to be pinned under an animal. Jake arrives just in time to prevent her death, but Quaritch realizes that he does not have to engage with Jake's avatar, seeking instead to destroy his human form. Neytiri pulls herself clear and kills Quaritch with her bow and arrow, but Quaritch has damaged the mobile lab, and Jake's human body lies in the throes of death, saved by Neytiri just in time. The Na'vi expel all but a select few humans, among them, of course, Jake, but Jake elects to be transferred to his avatar, relinquishing his human body forever.

Grace's research reveals a literal, scientific basis for the Na'vi's reverence of Eywa, namely a connection of plant roots that function as a detectable planetary neural network. When Jake connects with the tree of souls, he confesses to Eywa that humans have already killed their own Earth Mother (a fact better served by the theatrical cut where we are left to imagine the hellhole that home has become). This ecological message is intertwined with *Avatar*'s postcolonial identification with a displaced and exploited culture. That a marine of seemingly average intelligence (but presumably with the untapped potential of his twin) is able to heed Eywa's call to heroic duty suggests that there is hope for the traditional perpetrators of such exploitation—in other words, our own Western culture. And yet as Jonathan Romney points out, it is "of course . . . a white man—in digital blue face, as it were—who is the real hero of the Na'vi victory."[5]

Randy Malamud notes that the Na'vi's own culture is not without the patterns of domination that the film ostensibly rejects.[6] Much is made of the harmonious, symbiotic connection between the Na'vi and the animal life of Pandora. And yet the Na'vi join with their equine or flying mounts not as a result of some meeting of minds, but rather through an imposition of Na'vi will. Neytiri tells Jake that when he chooses a banshee, he will know it chooses him back because it will try to kill him. It is difficult, then, to imagine how a banshee might communicate that they do *not* accept a Na'vi. As Malamud points out, there is a disturbing "no means yes" rape ideology underlying this ritual connection with the natural world, all which suggests that the film is more conservative than it sets out to be. At least two sequels are planned. DB

Notes

1. Ronald Grover, "IMAX, the Box-Office Supercharger," *BusinessWeek*, 7 January 2010, www.businessweek.com/magazine/content/10_03/b4163030932030.htm?chan=rss_topStories_ssi_5 (7 June 2013).
2. Ben Child, "James Cameron to Use Underwater Motion Capture for *Avatar* Sequels," *Guardian*, 8 April 2013, www.guardian.co.uk/film/2013/apr/08/james-cameron-avatar-sequels (7 June 2013).
3. Kenneth Turan, "*Avatar* Restores a Sense of Wonder to the Moviegoing Experience," *Los Angeles Times*, 17 December 2009, http://herocomplex.latimes.com/uncategorized/avatar-restores-a-sense-of-wonder-to-the-moviegoing-experience/ (7 June 2013).
4. The name Pandora comes from Greek myth, being the woman who opens a jar given by the gods and so releases all ills into the world, but hope remains within (Hesiod, "Works and Days," 82–83), while Polyphemus was the Cyclops who refused to show the hero Odysseus proper hospitality (Homer's *The Odyssey*, Book IX)—the latter a somewhat ironic choice given the film's narrative of colonial exploitation.
5. Jonathan Romney, "*Avatar*," *Independent*, 20 December 2009, www.independent.co.uk/

arts-entertainment/films/reviews/avatar-james-cameron-163-mins-pg-1845569.html (7 June 2013).

6. Randy Malamud, "Animals on Film: The Ethics of the Human Gaze," Georgia State University, 2010, www.english.gsu.edu/pdf/Spring.pdf (7 June 2013).

Bibliography

Child, Ben. "James Cameron to Use Underwater Motion Capture for *Avatar* Sequels." *Guardian*, 8 April 2013, www.guardian.co.uk/film/2013/apr/08/james-cameron-avatar-sequels (7 June 2013).

Grover, Ronald. "IMAX, the Box-Office Supercharger." *BusinessWeek*, 7 January 2010, www.businessweek.com/magazine/content/10_03/b4163030932030.htm?chan=rss_topStories_ssi_5 (7 June 2013).

Malamud, Randy. "Animals on Film: The Ethics of the Human Gaze." Georgia State University, 2010, www.english.gsu.edu/pdf/Spring.pdf (7 June 2013).

Romney, Jonathan. "*Avatar*." *Independent*, 20 December 2009, www.independent.co.uk/arts-entertainment/films/reviews/avatar-james-cameron-163-mins-pg-1845569.html (7 June 2013).

Turan, Kenneth. "*Avatar* Restores a Sense of Wonder to the Moviegoing Experience." *Los Angeles Times*, 17 December 2009, http://herocomplex.latimes.com/uncategorized/avatar-restores-a-sense-of-wonder-to-the-moviegoing-experience/ (7 June 2013).

THE AVIATOR (2004)

Director: Martin Scorsese

Writer: John Logan. Based on *Howard Hughes: The Secret Life*, by Charles Higham.

Producers: Graham King, Michael Mann, Sandy Climan, Charles Evans Jr. (Forward Pass, Appian Way)

Cinematographer: Robert Richardson

Editor: Thelma Schoonmaker

Art Direction: Dante Ferretti, Francesca Lo Schiavo

Costumes: Sandy Powell

Cinematographer: Howard Shore

Cast: Howard Hughes: Leonardo DiCaprio. Katharine Hepburn: Cate Blanchett. Ava Gardner: Kate Beckinsale. Spencer Tracy: Kevin O'Rourke. Noah Dietrich: John C. Riley. Juan Trippe: Alec Baldwin. Senator Owen Brewster: Alan Alda. Professor Fitz: Ian Holm. Jack Fryew: Danny Huston. Jean Harlow: Gwen Stefani. Errol Flynn: Jude Law. Johnny Meyer: Adam Scott. Glen Odekirk: Matt Ross. Faith Domergue: Kelly Garner. Katharine Houghton: Frances Conroy. Robert E. Gross: Brent Spiner. Louis B. Mayer: Stanley DeSantis. Joseph Breen: Edward Herrmann. Roland Sweet: Willem Dafoe

AA: Best Supporting Actress (Cate Blanchett), Best Cinematography (Robert Richardson), Best Art Direction (Dante Ferretti, Francesca Lo Schiavo), Best Costume Design (Sandy Powell), Best Film Editing (Thelma Schoonmaker)

AAN: Best Picture (Graham King, Michael Mann, Sandy Climan, Charles Evans Jr.), Best Director (Martin Scorsese), Best Actor (Leonardo DiCaprio), Best Supporting Actor (Alan Alda), Best Writing–Original Screenplay (John Logan), Best Sound Mixing (Tom Fleischman, Petur Hliddal)

BAFTA Awards: Best Film (Graham King, Michael Mann, Sandy Climan, Charles Evans Jr.), Best Makeup and Hair (Morag Ross, Kathryn Blondell, Sian Grigg), Best Supporting Actress (Cate Blanchett), Best Production Design (Dante Ferretti)

DVD: Miramax, 2005. Two-disc edition.

Blu-ray: Warner Home Video, 2007

Duration: 169 minutes

By 2005, Martin Scorsese had been waiting for his Best Director Academy Award for what seems almost half a century. He had made a meaningful and well-mounted epic the previous year—*Gangs of New York* (also nominated for Best Director)—and had directed some colossi that have left their mark on American movies, including *Taxi Driver* (1976), *Raging Bull* (1980), *The Last Temptation of Christ* (1988), *Goodfellas* (1990), and *Cape Fear* (1991). The list is significant. His heroes are social pariahs, psychopaths and killers, outcasts, underground men—and mostly men—whose lives are complicated, "mythical" in a negative sense, not the heroes who win in the context of the American work ethic, as does Hillary Swank's character in *Million Dollar Baby* (Clint Eastwood, 2004, which won for Best Director and Best Picture the same year).

The object of most Scorsese movies has been the creation of American myths, and *The Aviator* is no exception. Myth is closely associated with an archetypal hero, a leader of his tribe who is attempting to mold public opinion, carry out an ambitious project, or bring a worthwhile goal to the level of social consciousness. In making movies, Scorsese has shown preferences for representative types—fictional or from real life—who strive to achieve goals that seem unattainable to the common run of humanity, but who are also plagued by self-destructive tendencies that often prevent them from reaching such goals. Inner turmoil, physical disabilities, distorted pictures of the environment they live in—these and other failings often lead a person to antisocial behavior, frustration, isolation, and violent action. In the Scorsese canon, examples abound: Travis Bickle, Jake Motta, Jesus Christ, Frank Pierce—such characters do not display the charismatic qualities of a typical archetypal hero the public is used to: Superman, Batman, a Western gunman, or an epic Moses, nearly flawless characters whose function becomes to save humanity from the bad guys.

Rather, Scorsese's heroes fit the mold of the antihero, for their faults overwhelm whatever good intentions their actions imply. Yet, they, too, want to do some good or reach some goal, no matter how distorted that goal may become in their minds. A Travis Bickle, for instance, smoldering with suppressed rage, sets out to "clean up" New York City, which he perceives as corrupt, to win an immaculate virgin and also rescue a child prostitute from her pimp. In the end, he comes unhinged and resorts to violence. Jake Motta has the drive to become a world-class boxer, but his insane jealously of his brother and explosive temper destroy his marriage. Scorsese's Christ doubts his divinity and battles the temptations of the flesh, but he finally defeats the devil and the promise of domestic happiness and achieves salvation through crucifixion. Frank Pierce, a New York paramedic and driver of an ambulance, has vowed to save as many lives as he can when called to a rescue. In delineating such heroes, Scorsese works against the mainstream stereotypes usually offered by Hollywood, preferring to show the rough edges of a character who often comes through as an unpleasant type, too repulsive or rough-hewn to win an audience's unequivocal sympathy. On the other hand, Scorsese's characters are carefully drawn and given in concrete detail through the use of visual or verbal minutiae.

The art of Scorsese thus requires character development, rather than dependence on plot complications, the preferred mode of the average Hollywood flick. His movies become studies in character rather than escapist adventures, and whatever plot comes into play is usually episodic. A biopic format, therefore, places unusual pressures on a director who, as Scorsese does, pursues integrity of characterization while trying to lure an audience with an entertaining tale, as every movie must do. Scorsese manages admirably in this respect, for entertainment, which is largely dependent on crafting and scripting, has always been present. His movies have not lacked popularity and have won Oscars, although not one for Scorsese himself, despite numerous nominations (an exception is *The Departed*, 2006, which finally won him an Oscar for Best Direction—well deserved, it seems). We are reminded that Alfred Hitchcock never won an Oscar for Best Director either, and Hitchcock commanded immense popularity, being called the "Master of Suspense." Scorsese eschews suspense—and thence plot—dwelling on character, tone, art direction, thematic development, and, very decidedly, violence. His is an exploration of the American psyche, delving deeply into the causes of personal failure.

That is why *The Aviator* is something of an anomaly, for the depiction of Howard Hughes, both an icon and a rogue in the popular mind, depends on the notion that America's values were shaped in turmoil, both personal and tribal. That is his theme in his previous epic, *Gangs of New York*, which shows the clashes between the Natives—American-born "super-patriots"—and the newcomers, the immigrants from Ireland whose arrival helped mold the heterogeneous mixture that formed New York as a city and the United States in general. In the mid-nineteenth century, America was still in the process of being born. In the mid-twentieth century, America was "flying," in both a literal and metaphorical sense, toward becoming the world's sole superpower. In *The Aviator*, Scorsese chose the one figure that embodies these elements. Howard Hughes influenced his times and helped shape the future of aviation in this country, and the movie strives to present him as one of the builders of the new empire, despite all his personal eccentricities and failures.

Every movie is a result of form and format. Here the form (or genre) is the epic, while the format is biography told in chronological sequence. Of necessity, this is a lengthy movie (nearly three hours), while the emphasis on character dictates a chronological sequence. Other forms are available to biography, a flashback technique, for instance, which became the structural device of *Citizen Kane*, a film with which *The Aviator* bears certain resemblance. Both films present flawed characters, but *The Aviator* strives to present its hero in a positive light. Hughes (played by Leonardo DiCaprio) is a pioneer, a visionary, destroyed by illness and socially castigated for his excesses. The film wisely sections off a portion of his life—his rise and triumphs—and does not take it upon itself to describe his later years, during his decline. It begins in the late 1920s, when Hughes arrived in Hollywood, and ends in the mid-1940s, covering a period of approximately twenty years and presenting the man in his rise and maturity. Hughes died in 1976, after years of isolation and instability, and he was long forgotten as a major player in American life by that time. Scorsese aimed at presenting him at his best, during his most creative moments, but he documents some of his failures, eccentricities, and the beginning of his disintegration—in the midst of his final triumph, the airlifting of the largest plane in the world. He is seeing him as an American "Icarus," defined, like the Greek flawed hero, by his desire to fly, but "scorching" his wings by flying too close to the sun.

Thus, as biographies go, the film achieves some coherence, at least thematically. The first scene shows Hughes as a boy, being washed by his mother, and this image serves as a metaphor of Hughes's later obsession with cleanliness, showing a symptom of the neurosis that made his life a misery. There is a jump from early childhood to seeing a man negotiating the making of planes and directing a movie of vast scope—*Hell's Angels*. It is 1927 when the young Hughes is introduced, and the action proceeds from that point onward, unfolding sequentially. Scorsese chose to use no flashbacks, not wanting to interrupt the flow of his narrative, but the exact chronology is not always given, nor is there a sense of historical recognition of the period, outside of costuming, sets, and the general ambience of the era given mostly during the few moments at the Coconut Club, a famous entertainment spot in Hollywood during the 1930s.

After Hughes completes *Hell's Angels* at the phenomenal cost of $4 million (and subsequently *Scarface*, in 1932), he has established himself as a major filmmaker, but his interests take a decisive turn, for he now embarks on his meteoric career as an aviator. He becomes more famous for his transatlantic flights, including his triumphant flight around the world in four days, than for his movies, performing daring pilot stunts, some of which result in serious accidents. He wins in love as well, wooing Katharine Hepburn, then a rising star, and they remain lovers for several years. After a turbulent breakup with her, he makes several movies, including the controversial *The Outlaw*, the "sex western" with Jane Russell. Hughes has a run with the Motion Picture Association of America in a memorable confrontation, during which he uses "mathematics" to measure the exposed cleavages of various female stars of the time. After that he devotes most of his time to aviation; becomes the owner of Trans World Airlines (TWA), attempting to establish transatlantic air transportation; and continues to experiment with plane design, building the giant "The Hercules" as an experimental carrier on a huge scale, always striving for increased speeds to accommodate intercontinental travel, which Hughes had envisioned as possible and the way of the future. His health, mental and physical, deteriorates significantly, and he barely survives one crash. He collides with a prominent senator, Owen Brewster (Alan Alda), and appears before a senate committee, where his practices are questioned, while attempting to establish TWA as a carrier to rival PAN AM. The movie ends with his triumphant flight of The Hercules, the largest plane ever built, which he himself flies in the Los Angeles harbor.

Obviously, a plot of this sort seems episodic with no lever to propel it forward, and no suspense created, as, again, for instance, in *Citizen Kane* we have the mysterious word "Rosebud" that becomes the springboard for investigation, which gives the film its structure. Lack of plot design, with no suspense to speak of, the film must have compensating values to create its appeal and, therefore, win an audience. Scorsese seems to try to achieve this through the building of character in episodic sequences that become increasingly intense—as he did with Jake Motta's biography in *Raging Bull*. This technique is not unfamiliar to him, and one could cite examples of films in which the director has toiled to avoid the tried formula of well-plotted epics—*Lawrence of Arabia, Titanic, Schindler's List*—all of which rely on plot complication, or an "arc," as David Lean used to call it. Thus, Scorsese's character Hughes, well given by DiCaprio (also one of his leads in *Gangs of New York*), has to carry the weight of a linear narrative, and it is the strength of this performance—plus a few other passable-to-excellent performances—that will carry the day.

Scorsese always chooses heroes with flaws, those whose aims sometimes come in direct conflict with members the tribe—whether they be politicians, other tycoons, or, in the gangster world, other gangsters. His archetypes may possess stamina, vision, and extraordinary intelligence, but they are also plagued by all kinds of excesses—a mania to dominate, a willful disregard of the opinion of others, or a haunting by fears and destructive sexual obsessions. Hughes had most, or all, of these pluses and minuses. When he came from Texas as a young man, already wealthy from a sizable inheritance in oil, he embarked on a project that bordered on insanity—to make the most expensive movie ever, but true and real to life as possible, for he wanted to show to the public what a real plane dogfight really looked like; so he established cameras on all the planes flying, and the final realism of those scenes attests to the correctness of his vision. He did not spare his money and was almost always at the brink of bankruptcy, but when he undertook a project, he spared no means, no money or effort, putting his life at risk, for he would fly the planes himself, recklessly risking his life in the process.

Hughes's vision was that air travel had a future; therefore, he needed to lead the way in building bigger and faster planes—planes that would circumnavigate the globe. He set the example himself by flying around the earth in four days, an unprecedented feat, demolishing the still-standing record of Charles Lindbergh, who had flown across the Atlantic a few years earlier.

DiCaprio's portrait of Hughes is built on the contrasting character traits of Hughes—his strong drive, intelligence, and charisma are counteracted by his numerous ailments, most of them mental. He did not lack self-assurance; in fact, he had an excess of it, but that brought him into collision with rival air tycoons, while his amorous pursuits riddled his life with scandal, disappointment, and intense suffering. He verges on insanity, and he has moments of mental imbalance, rage, seclusion, or total loss of self-control and presence. He recovers during the senate hearing to deliver a stunning rebuttal to a corrupt senator and displays nerves of steel when he finally manages to take off flying The Hercules (well-named). His ego is immense, for he considers himself a person above an average politician—even a senator—or a movie star: "You are a movie star," he shouts at Cate Blanchett, playing Katharine Hepburn, "nothing else!" Although the movie offers a limited showing of his amorous adventures, enough time is given to his affairs with Hepburn and later with Ava Gardner (Kate Beckinsale), and his infidelities to them and whomever he dated. He dismisses Gardner's justified accusations that he will go with any underage girl (he did), saying he loves only her.

Despite all that, DiCaprio's Hughes comes through as a noncorrupt character, bent on his ideals, fighting his numerous character weaknesses, and going insane with the idea of a future dynasty in aviation that would promote the good of humankind. As such, *The Aviator* is a movie with a backbone, for, although episodic, and at times slow, it focuses on an archetype—a man of his times, going along with his times, but attempting to show the way. It has always been thus, and Howard Hughes is presented in this film as a great American, a hero, not an underground man, but finally forced to share the latter's destiny, at least as far as his personal happiness was concerned. CS

Bibliography

Floyd, Jim. *The Avro Canada C102 Jetliner*. Erin, Ontario, Canada: Boston Mills Press, 1986.

Higham, Charles. *Howard Hughes: The Secret Life*. New York: St. Martin's Griffin, 2004.

Maguglin, Robert O. *Howard Hughes, His Achievements and Legacy: The Authorized Pictorial Biography*. Long Beach, CA: Wrather Port Properties, 1984.

Wegg, John. *General Dynamic Aircraft and Their Predecessors*. London: Putnam, 1990.

B

BARABBAS (1961)

DIRECTOR: Richard Fleischer
WRITER: Christopher Fry. Based on the novel by Pär Lagerkvist
PRODUCER: Dino De Laurentiis (Columbia Pictures)
CINEMATOGRAPHER: Aldo Tonti
EDITOR: Raymond Poulton
MUSIC: Mario Nascimbene
CAST: Barabbas: Anthony Quinn. Rachel: Silvana Mangano. Pontius Pilate: Arthur Kennedy. Sara: Katy Jurado. Peter: Harry Andrews. Sahak: Vittorio Gassman. Rufio: Norman Wooland. Julia: Valentina Cortese. Torvald: Jack Palance. Lucius: Ernest Borgnine
AA: None
AAN: None
DVD: Sony Pictures Home Entertainment, 2002
BLU-RAY: Currently unavailable
DURATION: 137 minutes

Barabbas is an epic based on the 1950 historical novel of the same name by Nobel Prize–winning Swedish author Pär Lagerkvist and starring Anthony Quinn in the title role. Set in Jerusalem and Rome during the decades following the death of Jesus, it chronicles the fictionalized bios of Barabbas, the criminal condemned to death whose life was spared (and in whose place Jesus died) due to the technicality of a ritual celebration. The action of the film moves according to the internal meanderings of Barabbas' conscience, as he struggles with the burden of having been the one chosen to live, or as he sees it, as the one "sentenced to life" after Jesus had taken away his own death. In the end, this unfinished man completes his alchemical spiritual journey and achieves light.

Barabbas opens in medias res (following the story line from the New Testament passion narrative), with Pontius Pilate (Arthur Kennedy) bantering with the crowd in Jerusalem, asking them whom they would prefer to be released from jail in observance of the sacred custom, Jesus, "whom some call a king," or the "rebel assassin" Barabbas. Without a decision made, Pilate returns inside, at which time we see Barabbas locked inside his dark cell with the only light filtering inside coming from a small window. While the Romans scourge and mock Jesus, placing upon him a crown of thorns and a royal robe, another soldier walks toward Barabbas' cell. Then, as Jesus is brought out before the crowd in his kingly garb, and the crowd begins to cheer wildly, the guard notifies Barabbas that he is to be set free. As Barabbas emerges from the dark cell and into the light, his eyes become transfixed on the sun. He views Jesus, and seeing the cross, also recognizes his (Jesus') impending death. Shielding his face from the light and

Jesus, Barabbas exclaims, "Light plays tricks on you." Meanwhile, we see Pilate symbolically washing his hands of the offense of shedding innocent blood.

Once freed, Barabbas returns home to seek his lover Rachel (Silvana Mangano). When he is greeted enthusiastically, but inquisitively by his friends, he tells them he was released to celebrate a holiday and that he was very lucky. They crown him "King Barabbas," and he, too, dons the clothing of a mock king (in a parallel manner to the way in which we recently saw Jesus being attired). But despite his excitement, he longs for Rachel, although he is told that Rachel is changed and now thinks of nothing but the prophet from Nazareth. Barabbas turns and glances out the window; there he sees Jesus walking with the cross, and also his Rachel, mourning by the window for that prophet whom he now recognizes.

When Rachel sees him and he approaches her, she runs to her bedroom, and he follows her trying to be with her, but she refuses and he forces himself on her exclaiming, "I will not be made a fool of." She replies, "He came from God." But Barabbas counters, "God could look after his own and you can look after me." At that very moment, the lights go out in the sky. (In the New Testament, we recognize this as the moment of the eclipse at the death of Jesus, and it is.)

Barabbas, believing he has gone blind, is told by Rachel a different interpretation of the events: "Even light has left us now that we've killed him." Barabbas stumbles in the darkness out to the hill of the Crucifixion, where frightened mourners are observing the events. He witnesses the eclipse and the light slowly reemerging; he sees Jesus being taken down from the cross and also being buried inside the tomb and the tomb sealed shut. He finds Rachel there and tells her that the prophet is dead. She says come back in three days, which he does, and finds the tomb empty. Rachel is also there and tells him that now he should know that it is true that he is risen. He tells her that all he knows is that the tomb is now empty, and that his friends must have taken the body to go on with the story. Why? Because, why would they crucify anyone just because he said "love one another"?

On a mission to find the truth, Barabbas seeks the disciples to find out where they hid Jesus. He finds them hiding together and asks them why they are afraid. Because they stole the body? While there he sees Peter making a net and asks him why. Peter answers that Jesus told them that their fish will be men, because their job will be to draw men into the light, and just as fish struggle and gasp and die when they are taken out of the water, so will humans when they are taken out of the Spiritual Light, destined for mortality and not Immortal Life.

The scene cuts and we next find an inebriated Barabbas, woman in tow, exclaiming how he is now going to be "brought back to life."[1] He laments, "It's not my fault that I am alive." He taunts a blind man into looking at him and then becomes horrified when he realizes that the man cannot see him. He then comes upon a small group of people listening to a woman speaking about the coming of a future kingdom. It is Rachel, and she is illegally preaching the Good News to a group of followers. When Barabbas starts heckling her and causing a disturbance, it calls attention to her, the authorities arrest her, and she is publicly stoned to death, which Barabbas witnesses. Later, in a fit of anger and grief, he viciously kills a man and is captured.

Brought once again before Pontius Pilate, Barabbas is sentenced to death, but once again, due to an odd law that must be followed that states that men released during sacred rituals may never be killed,

Barabbas is instead sentenced to life imprisonment, and his first stop is the sulphur mines of Sicily. Barabbas responds by reflecting, "He's taken my death . . . that light wasn't light; that wasn't dark. I've got my light, and *you* can't have it."[2] During his twenty-year sojourn down through the bowels of the mines, he learns from one of the fellow prisoners how to stay alive by covering his eyes, and he also is burdened by the company of Sahak (Vittorio Gassman), another younger prisoner who becomes his prison partner. Sahak is a Christian who is at once mortified and intrigued when he learns the identity of Barabbas. He frequently questions Barabbas about his recollections of the day of the Lord's death and Resurrection, which serves as a constant reminder to Barabbas of the reason for his infernal internment.

An unexpected tragedy (a fire in the mines) once again proves lucky for Barabbas, who is one of only two survivors, the other being his partner. As Barabbas is pulled from the rubble into the light, he once again has the vision of the light that he saw on the day he was released from prison at Jesus' trial.

They are still condemned prisoners, however, so unable to be freed, they are sent off to work a farm where we find them basking in the bright sunshine and salting the fields with a plow.[3] One day, Sahak again begins to question Barabbas about the days of Jesus, and when Barabbas begins to get angry because he notices that Sahak proudly wears his prisoner's medal with an engraved cross on it, Sahak questions him, asking, "What other man's death could have troubled you so long?" And Barabbas, who wears the sign of Tiberius on his chest, has Sahak engrave a cross on the medal, too.

Another turn of events changes their fate once again, and they are whisked to Rome at the whim of the prefect's wife, to be trained to become gladiators. This section of the film contains the majority of the traditional sword and sandal spectacle scenes, including gladiator fights, chariot races, and massive crowds of spectators. Barabbas, an old man, is caught amid a small underground group of loyal Christians who protect one another within the gladiator ranks thanks to the Christian trainer Lucius (Ernest Borgnine). When the group is discovered, Barabbas denies his faith. He tells them, "I have no god; I tried to believe." Others are executed, including his friend. Some are taught a lesson by having to fight, unarmed except for a lance, against Torvald (Jack Palance), the greatest gladiator, who is armed on a chariot.

As predicted, this culminating scene pits the old, wise Barabbas against the young, vengeful Torvald. In a stunning and exciting scene, Barabbas kills the young gladiator and is set free. His first act is to recover the body of Sahak and deliver it to the catacombs for Christian burial. He tells the trainer, who is there with the others reciting mass, that it is something he has to do. The trainer is not so kind to him in return. "You believe because it suits you," says the trainer. "Jesus was killed because of me. Why me? Why did he choose me? Where are you? I'm lost. Show me the way. Which way should I go?" laments Barabbas, as he searches through the labyrinthine passages of the catacombs for the trainer, who dissolves into the darkness.

At last, Barabbas emerges from the crypt. He realizes that the city is burning and is told that the Christians set it on fire, so he begins setting everything aflame, believing that the end of the world must be near, as was told to him by Sahak and Rachel. In a frenzied state of mental intoxication, he is picked up by the authorities and thrown into jail, where he meets Peter (Harry Andrews), along with other Christians who have also been imprisoned. There he hears the truth; it is the emperor, not the Christians, who set Rome ablaze. The end of the world, alas, is not here. Barabbas asks, "Why can't God make himself plain?" Peter tells him that being the farthest, "you, Barabbas were the nearest," and that "by the conflict, you will know Him." And finally, "The kingdom is within."

The last scene is a crucifixion of all the Christians. Barabbas is on the cross. He remembers that it was the sixth hour when there was darkness and then says, "I give myself up into your keeping. It is Barabbas." Then he dies, and the film ends.

Barabbas continues to entertain audiences even today, despite its seemingly preachy outer appearance. Although frequently placed among the throng of either biblical or sword and sandal sagas of its era, this film technically fits less the religious epic category in form, and more the forerunner of the modern antiepic subgenre[4] due to its modern theme of this protagonist's internal turmoil as he attempts to seek a twisted spiritual guidance through a combination of casuistry and superstition amid an ambivalent and rudderless world bereft of a moral compass. As the archetypal antihero whose fall has caused his fortune and whose fortune has caused his fall, in *Barabbas* we witness the walking embodiment of the psychological effects of the mark of Cain in cinematic humankind, and also his transmutation. MC

Notes

1. The spiritual transformation of Barabbas follows the symbolic stages of spiritual alchemy in this film, utilizing the alchemical substances of mercury, sulphur, and salt to mark the significant scenes of transformation, followed by an anabasis or katabasis to mark the soul's movement. The intoxication of Barabbas represents the first stage of his spiritual transformation, represented by the alcohol (wine) as the symbol of Mercury/Dionysos, the vital energy. This element in spiritual alchemy serves as catalyst, or *psycopomp*, allowing the initiate to instigate the will to traverse the anabasis and katabasis stages necessary for transformation to occur. See Manly P. Hall, *The Secret Teachings of All Ages* (New York: Philosophical Research Society, 2003), 502–10.
2. In spiritual alchemy, sulphur represents the second stage in the spiritual transformation of Barabbas. He is in the underworld; this represents a katabasis in the epic journey. Sulphur is the stage designed to purify the life spirit, usually by fire. Hall, *The Secret Teachings of All Ages*, 502–10.
3. Salt is the third element in spiritual alchemy. It represents the physical body in the foundational state. The initiate is now ready for spiritual work. Hall, *The Secret Teachings of All Ages*, 502–10.
4. Constantine Santas, *The Epic in Film: From Myth to Blockbuster* (Lanham, MD: Rowman & Littlefield, 2008).

Bibliography

Hall, Manley P. *The Secret Teachings of All Ages*. New York: Philosophical Research Society, 2003.

Santas, Constantine. *The Epic in Film: From Myth to Blockbuster*. Lanham, MD: Rowman & Littlefield, 2008).

BARRY LYNDON (1975)

DIRECTOR: Stanley Kubrick
WRITER: Stanley Kubrick. Adapted from the novel *Memoirs of Barry Lyndon, Esq.* (1844), by William Makepeace Thackeray.
PRODUCER: Stanley Kubrick (Peregrine, Hawk Films, Warner Bros.)
CINEMATOGRAPHER: John Alcott
EDITOR: Tony Lawson
ART DIRECTION: Ken Adam, Roy Walker, Vernon Dixon
COSTUMES: Milena Cononero, Ulla-Britt Söderlund
MUSIC: Leonard Rosenman
CAST: Redmond Barry: Ryan O'Neal. Capt. Potzdorf: Hardy Kruger. Lady Lyndon: Marisa Berenson. Chevalier Bali Du Bari: Patrick Magee. Nora Brady: Gay Hamilton. Capt. Grogan: Godfrey Quigley. Belle (Barry's Mother): Marie Kean. Lord Ludd: Steven Berkoff. Reverend Samuel Runt: Murray Melvin. Sir Charles Lyndon: Frank Middlemass. Boy Lord Bullington: Dominic Savage. Lord Bullington: Leon Vitali. Capt. John Quin: Leonard Rossiter. Lord

Wendover: André Morell. Bryan Lyndon: David Morley. Narrator: Michael Hordern. The Girl (Lieschen): Diana Körner. Capt. Feeny: Arthur O. Sullivan. Seamus Feeny: Billy Boyle. Lord Hallam: Anthony Sharp
AA: Best Art Direction–Set Direction (Ken Adam, Roy Walker, Vernon Dixon), Best Music–Original Song Score and/or Adaptation (Leonard Rosenman), Best Cinematography (John Alcott), Best Costume Design (Milena Cononero, Ulla-Britt Söderlund)
AAN: Best Director (Stanley Kubrick), Best Picture (Stanley Kubrick), Best Literary Adaptation (Stanley Kubrick)
DVD: Warner Home Video, 2001
Blu-ray: Warner Home Video, 2010
Duration: 185 minutes

Barry Lyndon could be called a protracted art movie rather than an epic, but one could counter that Stanley Kubrick had already established his epic credentials with *Paths of Glory* (1957), *Spartacus* (1960), *2001: A Space Odyssey* (1968), and *A Clockwork Orange* (1971). While *Paths of Glory* and *Spartacus* adhere to the classic Hollywood mode, the three that followed carved a new path that enlarged both Kubrick's legacy and the epic format itself. Kubrick's epic opus is marked by an overt or implied polemic tone and antiestablishment bias that place those works outside the typical epic venture, where a hero triumphs against evil forces. *Barry Lyndon* progresses as a series of striking frames, a succession of pictorial compositions of a painter offering tableaus for the viewer to absorb before the camera obliges by moving on to the next frame. The camera zooms in and off a frame, allowing the viewer just enough "time" to absorb the full effect of that composition. Still, the epic mode is preserved, since, aside from length, the story deals with an archetypal figure that travels through his destined path, achieves his height of success through guile or brawn, and falls because of character flaws that also mark him as a tragic hero.

Kubrick drew selectively from William Makepeace Thackeray's novel, using only a portion of Barry Lyndon's life, that dealing with his rise and fall. Although the story unfolds during a period of years, even decades, we know nothing of Barry's childhood, or his old age—which can only be surmised. Redmond Barry (Ryan O'Neal), an Irish youth orphaned after his father's death in a duel, flees his homeland after a sex scandal. He was made to believe that he has shot to death a rival for the hand of his cousin, the flirtatious Nora Brady (Gay Hamilton). After being robbed by a clever highway robber, he is recruited into King George's army, which then, around 1750, was fighting the Seven Years' War in Europe, where England was allied with Prussia against France and several other nations. When Barry deserts, he falls into the hands of a sadistic Prussian officer, Captain Potzdorf (Hardy Kruger), who forces him into service in the Prussian Army. During a battle, Barry saves Potzdorf's life. He is decorated and given a post in the Prussian police force and asked to spy on a newcomer in Berlin, Chevalier de Balibari (Patrick Magee), a sharpshooter who is also an Irishman. Barry and de Balibari soon become vagabond gamblers, fleecing vain European aristocrats and traveling throughout Europe, living a luxurious but shiftless existence. Barry eventually attracts the attention of Lady Lyndon (Marisa Berenson), a fabulously wealthy and beautiful aristocrat who is married to Lord Lyndon, an ambassador of King George's in Europe, and an invalid. The latter soon dies in a fit of rage when he discovers Barry's duplicities, and a year later Barry and Lady Lyndon marry. He assumes her name and is henceforth called Barry Lyndon. A son, Brian, is born to them.

After reaching the peak of his career in wealth and status, Barry suffers various setbacks resulting mainly from his dissolute way of life, his callous behavior toward his wife, and especially from his disputes with Lady Lyndon's older son, Lord Bullington (played by Dominic Savage and Leon Vitali), who sees through him and becomes his mortal enemy. Barry's mother, who has moved in with her son at the Lyndon estate, advises Barry that his status, and thence that of his young son Brian, will not be secured until he acquires a peerage, thence becoming Lord Lyndon. In pursuit of a title, Barry spends colossal sums of money bribing officials, thus squandering the large fortune inherited by his wife. The turning point in his reversal of fortune comes during a concert, when, provoked by his stepson, Lord Bullington, now a young man, Barry breaks out into a rage and attacks him in front of his aristocrat friends, who know of his pariah origin and never forgive an upstart. Isolated and spurned by the society into which he has forced himself, Barry now takes to drinking, while Lady Lyndon attempts to kill herself. This brings back her son, who challenges Barry to a duel. In a panic, Bullington misfires, but Barry, having gained the advantage, fires into the ground. In a cowardly act, Bullington shoots Barry, whose leg soon has to be amputated. Dejected, poor, and a cripple, Barry is offered the annual sum of five hundred guineas on the condition that he never return to England. We hear through the narrator's voice that he has become a gambler in Europe, but his former luck does not hold this time.

The film excels in cinematic techniques, masterly integrated into an organic whole. Sets and costumes were based on works by that period's paintings, especially William Hogarth, whose tableaus are imitated. Lighting of interiors seems natural, as many scenes were filmed by candlelight to appear as real and authentic as possible. The deliberately slow pace acquires a certain rhythm, frequently enhanced by the tempo of the music of Bach, Vivaldi, Handel, Mozart, and especially Schubert, whose *String Trio in B Flat Major* (D. 581) punctuates the scene of Barry's seduction of Lady Lyndon. The second movement of the trio starts at the moment Lady Lyndon, the Reverend Runt (Murray Melvin), her invalid husband in his wheelchair, and her young son approach, as the camera zooms in on the little group. They catch the eye of Barry, who, sitting in a balcony, the eye-patched Chevalier across from him, decides that sharpshooting is no longer a satisfactory way of life—he needs to aim higher, to marry into wealth. As the melancholy cello notes of the trio fill the air, the narrator's resonant voice, retaining its tone of omniscience, externalizes Barry's thoughts.

Next, the camera cuts to a card table, where a group of people sit by candlelight. A cello sets the tone of the scene as Lady Lyndon exchanges glances with Barry, sitting across the table from her. Then, escaping the watchful eye of Reverend Runt, she walks into the balcony, at a measure pace, following the rhythm of the cello notes, as Barry is now seen walking toward her, the piano notes regulating his step. As he kisses her, the violin takes over. Cut to a scene in a boat, where Barry and Lady Lyndon sit side by side, now the music obligingly following the action, as the narrator tells that he has gained regular access to her company. On most occasions, music is usually a generalized sound, but in this scene, the music leads the action, choreographed, as it were, like a ballet movement. Point of view is enhanced by the detached speaker who, in the rich voice of Michael Hordern, maintains the narrative line as it follows the fortunes of Barry, offering sardonic comments on warfare, the social milieu, history, and fate. Hordern's voice resonates with irony and sarcasm, but also with compassion for the human condition. Counterpointed by the music, it has the effect of a Greek chorus.

This spectacle, which Kubrick so methodically pieced together, represents a historical period—the eighteenth century—depicting the manners, fashions, speech, and environments with the aura of authenticity. The devastation of war, for instance, is apparent in one of the "minor" episodes of that war—as the narrator acerbically calls it—when an entire detachment of English soldiers marches to drumbeat against another detachment of the French Army, who shoot them down to the beat of the drum. In the war scenes of *Barry Lyndon*, neither the victors nor the defeated are closely identified (with the notable exceptions of Potzdorf and Grogan, played by Godfrey Quigley), nor does it matter who wins. War is shown as a cruel, inhuman, unexplained, and totally absurd activity. The epic spectacle makes this possible, and any abbreviation of the form would have resulted in a lesser effect.

Often, as far as his vision is concerned, Kubrick refuses to be pinpointed. It is, however, possible that the epic form enables him to carry out a larger picture of a thematic meaning in a film. In *Barry Lyndon*, the epic form allows sufficient space for the individual story to be told, but also for a filmmaker to develop ideas on more complex levels. Thus, the epic becomes the means of encompassing a larger vision of humanity's frailties, its triumphs and losses, generosities and acts of cruelty. More often than not, Kubrick's epics allow the filmmaker to undertake film stories (several adaptations of literary works) with pessimistic messages—or at least messages that show the negative sides of humanity. *Barry Lyndon* is a trip to the past, as much as *A Clockwork Orange* and *2001: A Space Odyssey* are trips into the future. These projections are visions of societies that have either become too mechanized and automated, or where anarchic forces are loosed upon the world.

Barry Lyndon offers us a glimpse into the past, which we almost always tend to idealize; however, this film's action, which takes place more than two centuries ago, shows a decadent, corrupt, and savage society (despite its superficial refinements). Europe is dominated by murderous mercenary armies that kill and pillage. Alliances of convenience (England and Prussia) do not even make geographical sense. Not even a philosopher could explain the causes of the Seven Years' War, the narrator intones. And the dominant class is riddled with spies, deceit, corruption, and fraud. Inherently, and potentially a decent man, Barry is a product of his environment and time, and, to survive, he commits various fraudulent actions, eventually and through tragedy gradually becoming aware of who and what he is. Barry is caught in the whirling injustices and fraudulent schemes of his times. Naïve at first, he grows more cagey as he gains experience and achieves success, but finally, decrepit and wounded, he marches out of the sphere he had entered, a broken man in body and spirit, but at least worthy of attention for his one noble act, not shooting his enemy when he could, which was also his downfall.

Criticized as wooden in the lead role, Ryan O'Neal still commands admirable poise, for here he only defines a man who is passive by nature, receiving more blows than he gives (although he excels in a boxing match with a larger man), showing himself capable of intrigue, and gaining the woman he loves. But his passive nature is not quite up to confrontation with real viciousness, which comes in the face of the young, Hamlet-like Bullington. Barry, adept at deceiving decadent aristocrats, cannot face malice, vindictiveness, and real hatred. He is not entirely equipped to confront human malevolence, hesitating to gun down an unworthy opponent. He pays dearly for his one noble act. There can be nothing more ironic, or more tragic, than an action through which one achieves redemption and the effects of damnation at the same time. In his earlier exploits while climbing, Barry had shown good judgment and coolness under pressure, but in the end he loses his self-control and, with that, his instinct for self-preservation. Aristotle once asked, "Tragedy or epic—which is the nobler form?" Does it make a difference if one can combine, in film, both forms? CS

Bibliography

Cocks, Geoffrey, James Diedrick, and Glenn Perusek, eds. *Depth of Field: Stanley Kubrick, Film, and the Uses of History*. Madison: University of Wisconsin Press, 2006.

Kagan, Norman. *The Cinema of Stanley Kubrick*. New York: Continuum, 1993.

BATTLESTAR GALACTICA (1978)

DIRECTOR: Richard A. Colla, Alan J. Levi (uncredited)
WRITER: Glen A. Larson
PRODUCERS: John Dykstra, Leslie Stevens (Universal Pictures)
CINEMATOGRAPHER: Ben Colman
EDITORS: Robert L. Kimble, Leon Ortiz-Gil, Larry Strong
ART DIRECTION: John E. Chilberg II
COSTUMES: Jean-Pierre Dorléac
MUSIC: Stu Phillips
CAST: Capt. Apollo: Richard Hatch. Lt. Starbuck: Dirk Benedict. Commander Adama: Lorne Greene. Lt. Boomer: Herbert Jefferson Jr. Athena: Maren Jensen. Boxey: Noah Hathaway. Colonel Tigh: Terry Carter. President Adar: Lew Ayres. Baltar: John Colicos. Cassiopeia: Laurette Spang. Serina: Jane Seymour. Sire Uri: Ray Milland. Narrator: Patrick Macnee (uncredited)
AA: None
AAN: None
DVD: Universal Studios, 2003 (theatrical version)
BLU-RAY: Currently unavailable
DURATION: Theatrical version 124 minutes

This science-fiction epic tells of the near genocide of humans living on twelve planetary colonies attacked by the robotic Cylons, despite the latter's offer of a peace treaty brokered by the traitorous human Baltar (John Colicos). Commander Adama (Lorne Greene) leads the survivors' travel in search of a fabled thirteenth colony, Earth. Along the way, Adama's son Apollo (Richard Hatch) falls in love with single mother Serina (Jane Seymour), while the military must deal with not only an alien resort in league with the Cylons, but also with inept—and in some cases corrupt—politicians who have led them to the brink of destruction.

Filmed as an expensive telemovie pilot to the 1978–1980 television show in initial development prior to *Star Wars* (George Lucas, 1977) but given the green light afterward, *Battlestar Galactica* was given a theatrical release in Europe and Canada, aired on U.S. television with the addition of a new ending that spares the life of Baltar so that he could be an ongoing foe, and then edited down for a U.S. theatrical release. For this reason, the TV series version available on DVD is, in fact, the more complete edition, and the widescreen theatrical release is merely matted off footage from the television aspect. Cheesy dialogue; a friendly, fluffy robotic dog (or "daggit") for Serina's son; and an inferior sequel series, *Galactica 1980* (1980), have led many to be dismissive of the original franchise. And yet *Battlestar Galactica* won two Emmys, and its dystopian science-fiction tale has attracted a cult following in subsequent years.

Actor Richard Hatch wrote a number of novels based on the series and produced a short (but high quality) trailer for a proposed sequel, *Battlestar Galactica: The Second Coming* (1999). The program was eventually rebooted in 2003 as a TV miniseries, in which the Cylons develop a humanoid form indistinguishable from humans themselves, and somewhat controversially at the time, Apollo's wisecracking sidekick Starbuck (Dirk Benedict) was recast as a woman, to great effect. The miniseries was followed by a politically and religiously complex television series from 2005–2009 (in which Hatch appears in the role of extremist politician Tom Zarek); telemovies; and a less successful prequel, *Caprica* (2010), which outlines how the Cylons are developed by humans. The tale of the first Cylon war is anticipated as a forthcoming telemovie, *Battlestar Galactica: Blood and Chrome*. DB

BECKET (1964)

DIRECTOR: Peter Glenville
WRITER: Edward Anhalt. Based on the stage play *Becket*, by Jean Anouilh.
PRODUCER: Hal B. Wallis (Paramount Pictures)
CINEMATOGRAPHER: Geoffrey Unsworth
EDITOR: Anne V. Coates
ART DIRECTION: John Bryan, Maurice Carter, Patrick McLaughlin, Robert Cartwright
COSTUMES: Margaret Furse
MUSIC: Lawrence Rosenthal
SOUND MIXER: John Cox
CAST: King Henry II: Peter O'Toole. Thomas Becket: Richard Burton. King Louis VII: John Gielgud. Bishop Gilbert Folliot: Donald Wolfit. Bishop of Winchester: John Phillips. Bishop of York: Frank Pettingell. Bishop of Chichester: Hamilton Dyce. Pope Alexander III: Paolo Stoppa. Empress Matilda: Martita Hunt. Queen Eleanor of Aquitaine: Pamela Brown. Brother John: David Weston. Gwendolen: Siân Phillips. Theobald of Bec, Archbishop of Canterbury: Felix Aylmer. Cardinal Zambelli: Gino Cervi
AA: Best Writing–Screenplay Based on Material from Another Medium (Edward Anhalt)
AAN: Best Picture (Hal B. Wallis), Best Director (Peter Glenville), Best Actor (Peter O'Toole), Best Actor (Richard Burton), Best Supporting Actor (John Gielgud), Best Art Direction (John Bryan, Maurice Carter, Patrick McLaughlin, Robert Cartwright), Best Costume Design (Margaret Furse), Best Editing (Anne V. Coates), Best Music–Original Score (Lawrence Rosenthal), Best Sound (John Cox)
DVD: MPI Home Video, 2007
BLU-RAY: MPI Home Video, 2008
DURATION: 148 minutes

Based on the play *Becket*, or *The Honor of God*, by Jean Anouilh, and first premiering in Paris in 1959, starring Sir Laurence Oliver as Thomas Becket and Anthony Quinn as Henry II, the movie *Becket*, directed by Peter Glenville, won acclaim and did quite well at the box office, tripling its modest (for the time) budget of $3 million. It also earned a double nomination for the Best Actor Academy Award for Peter O'Toole and Richard Burton. The film also features other luminaries of English-speaking and world cinema, with Sir John Gielgud as King Louis VII, Donald Wolfit as Bishop Gilbert Folliot, Pamela Brown as Queen Eleanor of Aquitaine, and Paolo Stoppa as Pope Alexander III. From beginning to end, this movie, despite its dubious historical credentials,[1] is an energetic, highly literate, tightly plotted, powerfully acted epic. Aside from being an epic drama, *Becket* is also a highly personal story about the friendship, antagonism, and fatal collision between two powerful men. These two men represent two different ethnicities; two different psychological makeups; and two different approaches to power, including the power of the church and state. As previously noted, the film also boasts the services of numerous formidable actors, and it was edited by Anne V. Coates, who had also edited *Lawrence of Arabia* two years earlier. The film went on to win ten Academy Award nominations, with one win (Best Screenplay), and both Burton and O'Toole were nominated and lost, neither of them having earned an Oscar despite numerous nominations.

The film begins with a promising friendship between Becket and Henry, two men whose friendship begins with the highest expectations but eventually goes sour. The reasons for this eventual split, traces of which are seen immediately, have to do with the personalities of the two friends, but also, ultimately, with the positions of power that they have come to represent. They begin well as youthful pals[2] but end up as deadly enemies, for there are significant gaps—mental, ethical, and national—that must separate them. At first (after the initial scene where one leans over the tomb of another lying in state, a statue of bronze, and flagellates himself), the two are seen as carefree youths, one of whom is whoring with a local prostitute while the other is standing guard outside, but things soon get serious. One of them is King Henry II, grandson of William the Conqueror, who invaded and subjugated England 100 years earlier, in 1066, at the Battle of Hastings. The other is a Saxon, Thomas Becket, who seems to have caught the eye of Henry as a boon companion, and possibly a man who could rise to power.

In fact, Henry soon makes Becket his chancellor, despite the objection of the Archbishop of Canterbury, Theobald of Bec (Felix Aylmer), who is, of course, Norman. A Saxon, the archbishop claims, has no place in the court of a Norman king. But Becket accepts the honor, and the position of power, thus becoming the king's closest counselor, mostly because of his pragmatic mind, and because he thinks a Saxon should take any advantage he can in the king's court in the interest of his people. When asked why he accepts by Henry, Becket replies that he follows two principles, one of collaboration and one of honor. Henry mocks at the idea that a collaborator can also be honorable; however, Becket accepts the insult, knowing he has made a compromise with his conscience. But when the Archbishop of Canterbury dies, Henry makes Becket the Archbishop of Canterbury, assuming that Becket would remain loyal, in spite of the fact that he sees how Becket struggles with his compromise of conscience—and that he will remain the same.

But Becket is stricken with remorse and he discovers that loyalty to God—and to his own people—is a higher demand on him than loyalty to a king, whom he knows to be shifty, unscrupulous, and power hungry. When a priest is murdered, he condemns the act and excommunicates those who performed it, ignoring the objections of Henry. Becket flees to France, where he meets King Lewis, played by a deliciously cynical John Gielgud, who directs him to the pope, but the latter, a temporizer where power is concerned, refuses to take a stance against the king of England. When Becket returns to England, he again refuses to give Henry his full allegiance, knowing that his days are numbered. Becket is executed, stabbed by knights at his cathedral while conducting mass in a scene reminiscent of the assassination of Julius Caesar. Henry sees to it that Becket is canonized soon afterward and, conscience-stricken but not repentant, goes through his aforementioned penance act of self-flagellation.

One suspects that there was an unsurfaced homosexual urge on the part of Henry, and the performance of O'Toole, capturing the nuances of a half-mad monarch and jealous, isolated man, is extraordinary. Burton is solid and capable of transforming a rather conflicted man, tormented by his conscience, into a believer sacrificing himself for principle. There are tragic overtones here, but also ironies, mainly in O'Toole's portrait of Henry, a man who knew very well the man he was killing was far superior to him, and perhaps realizing that power of a monarch has its limits. Monarchy in England was never an easy matter. This film well demonstrates that point. CS

Notes

1. Jean Anouilh knew that Thomas Becket was not really Saxon, but he left him with this characterization for dramatic tension, and the film followed suit. See http://en.wikipedia.org/wiki/Becket_(1964_film).

2. In reality, Henry was fifteen years younger than Thomas. See http://en.wikipedia.org/wiki/Becket_(1964_film).

Bibliography

Robertson, J. C., and J. B. Sheppard. *Materials for the History of Thomas Becket*, 7 vols. London: 1875–1885. Part of the Rolls Series.

BEN-HUR (1925)

DIRECTOR: Fred Niblo
WRITER: June Mathis, Carey Wilson. Adapted from the novel by General Lew Wallace.
PRODUCER: Louis B. Mayer (MGM)
CINEMATOGRAPHERS: Clyde D Vinna, René Guissart, Percy Hilburn
EDITOR: Lloyd Nosler
COSTUMES: Herman J. Kaufmann
MUSIC: William Axt, Karl Struss, Glenn Kershner
SPECIAL EFFECTS: Ferdinand D. Earle
CONTINUITY: Bess Meredith
SETTINGS: Cedric Gibbons, Horace Jackson
TITLES: Katharine Hillaky, H. H. Caldwell
CAST: Judah Ben-Hur: Ramon Novarro. Messala: Francis X. Bushman. Simondes: Nigel De Brulier. Sheik Ilderim: Mitchell Lewis. Quintus Arrius: Frank Currier. Mary: Betty Bronson. Princess of Hur: Claire McDowell. Joseph: Winter Hall. Tirzah: Kathleen Key. Iras: Carmel Myers. Sandballat: Leo White. Balthazar: Charles Belcher. Amrah: Dale Fuller. Extras include numerous Hollywood actors, including John Barrymore, Douglas Fairbanks, Joan Crawford, Marion Davies, John Gilbert, Dorothy Gish, Lillian Gish, and Mary Pickford.
AA: None
AAN: None
DVD: Restored version with original tints and Technicolor sequences by Turner Entertainment, 2003. Music in the restored version by Carl Davies, played by the Royal Philharmonic Orchestra. Four-disc collector's edition by Warner Home Video, 2006.
BLU-RAY: Warner Home Video, 2011
DURATION: 143 minutes

Ben-Hur was first made into a big-production epic movie in 1925, adapted from the original General Lew Wallace novel *Ben-Hur: A Tale of the Christ*, which had been immensely popular since its publication in 1880, and was turned into a stage play that ran for many years. The story had been filmed in 1907, but the 1925 version was indeed the first super Hollywood epic production—costing nearly $4 million, making it the most expensive film of the silent era. The production was delayed because of accidents during filming in Italy and having to be moved back to Hollywood to be completed. The original tints and Technicolor sequences had been lost but were later found and added to the 1980s Turner Entertainment video edition. The restored version, with Carl Davies's splendid musical score filling the background, is still a breathtakingly visual and audial treat, very much worth watching and an excellent prelude to its more famous sister of 1959.

The 1925 *Ben-Hur*, one of the many religious-themed grand epics to come from Hollywood during that time, features movie heartthrob Ramon Novarro as Judah Ben-Hur and Francis X. Bushman as Messala, two actors who seemed tailor-made for their roles as part of a hero–villain duo. Novarro looked suitably athletic, his short tunic revealing his muscular legs and his face resembling that of a Greek statue head rather than that of a pious Christian, while Bushman, brawny, menacing, eyes shining with malice, sported a fully Roman regalia, his high-flying plume above his helmet lending him the sinister air of a brutal Roman conqueror. The friendship between the two men is cut short in this earlier version of the story, while the 1959 production allows Judah and Messala at least one friendly encounter before becoming mortal enemies.

The 1925 production is, however, more loyal to the Wallace novel than the 1959 version, which takes more liberties and includes lengthy dialogues and certain modernizations in acting styles, inevitable in the modern era. The 1925 version is also more pious and reverential in tone, and with a more powerful religious theme, despite scenes of nudity—bare-breasted girls in a Roman parade and seminude maidens tending to Iras (Carmel Myers), Messala's sensuous Egyptian mistress (who also attempts to seduce Ben-Hur). Iras is entirely absent in the 1959 version.

Of course the silent-era acting seems stilted and jerky today, but the splendid black-and-white photography of the 1925 version also lends an aura of authenticity to the scenes of the Nativity and the Crucifixion, which are more organically blended with the rest of the action than in the later version, where they come as framing devices to the main events. Here, Mary's face, as portrayed by Betty Bronson, is photographed to express a resplendent feeling of serenity and inner beauty, not in the least maudlin and out of place. This makes the Nativity scene a fluent first episode of the continuing story, rather than a prelude to it. The Crucifixion is also shown as a natural flow of the events that preceded, rather than an added necessity to, the main theme, the Ben-Hur–Messala conflict.

The main story follows the same general lines as the later film, with a few variations and, of course, much less detail. Almost as soon as he meets with his old friend Messala, now a tribune of Jerusalem, Prince Ben-Hur is asked to become his Roman ally, and when he declines, he incurs his formal friend's wrath (it's hard to imagine that these two had ever been friends). And when, by accident, he dislodges a tile from his roof (in the 1959 version it's his sister), which falls on a Roman official entering the city, he and his family are arrested, and he is sent to the galleys. In chains, Ben-Hur is driven along a rocky road with a gang of prisoners and, dying of thirst, is given a cup to drink from by an invisible hand. The hand is later seen sawing a piece of wood (to make sure he is a carpenter—and of course Christ). Ben-Hur takes this act of compassion to heart—by now filled with hatred and feelings of revenge. Later, prior to engaging in a sea battle, Arrius (Frank Currier), a Roman consul, orders his chains unlocked before the impending skirmish, and, when his ship is sunk, Ben-Hur saves the consul's life and is adopted by Arrius and taken to Rome, where he excels as an athlete in the chariot races. However, he returns to Judaea to confront Messala and defeats him in the chariot race, where Messala is killed. The scene of the Crucifixion follows, during which Ben-Hur repents and turns into a Christian, while his mother and sister are cured of leprosy, before they and their son and brother are reunited.

Thus, this much shorter early version of the *Ben-Hur* epic achieves a compactness that gives it the unity of a continuous whole, rather than a lengthy movie of necessity broken into several episodes of high-action drama—the naval battle and the chariot race, of course—interspersed with long-drawn-out dialogue scenes. As said, the Christ story merges better here with the feud between two friends turned enemies. In the early version, the "Story of the Christ" predominates, and the Ben-Hur–Messala antagonism seems designed as a device to carry the religious message of the Wallace novel, but the epic episodes of the naval battle, and especially of the chariot race—both magnificently staged—raise this early film to the level of the epic that was to dominate the Hollywood screens for decades to come. CS

BEN-HUR: A TALE OF THE CHRIST (1959)

Director: William Wyler
Writers: Karl Tunberg, Gore Vidal (uncredited), Christopher Fry (uncredited)
Producer: Sam Zimbalist (MGM)
Second Unit Directors: Andrew Marton, Yakima Canutt, Mario Soldati
Assistant Directors: Gus Agostin, Alberto Cardone
Cinematographers: Robert L. Surtees, Harold E. Wellman, Pietro Portalupi
Editors: John D. Dunning, Ralph E. Winters
Art and Set Direction: William A. Horning, Edward A. Carfagno, Hugh Hunt
Costumes: Elizabeth Haffenden
Music: Miklós Rózsa
Sound Editor: Franklin Milton
Special Effects: A. Arnold Gillespie, Lee LeBlanc
Makeup Artist: Charles Parker
Cast: Judah Ben-Hur: Charlton Heston. Messala: Stephen Boyd. Miriam: Martha Scott. Tirzah: Cathy O'Donnell. Esther: Haya Harareet. Simonides: Sam Jaffe. Quintus Arrius: Jack Hawkins. Sheik Ilderim: Hugh Griffith. Pontius Pilate: Frank Thring. Balthazar: Finlay Currie. Drusus: Terence Longdon. Flavia: Marina Berty. Melchior: Reginald Lal Singh. Tiberius: George Relph. Jesus: Claude Heater (uncredited). Mary: Jose Greci (uncredited). Joseph: Lawrence Payne (uncredited)
AA: Best Picture (Sam Zimbalist), Best Director (William Wyler), Best Actor (Charles Heston), Best Supporting Actor (Hugh Griffith), Best Set Decorations (William A. Horning, Edward C. Carfagno, Hugh Hunt), Best Cinematography (Robert L. Surtees), Best Costume Design (Elizabeth Haffenden), Best Special Effects (A. Arnold Gillespie, Lee LeBlanc), Best Editing (John D. Dunning, Ralph E. Winters), Best Music Scoring (Miklós Rózsa), Best Sound (Franklin Milton)
AAN: Best Writing–Screenplay Based on Material from Another Medium (Karl Tunberg)
DVD: Warner Brothers, 2005. Four-disc collector's edition, with commentary by film historian T. Gene Hatcher and comments by Charlton Heston.
Blu-ray: Warner Brothers, 2011
Duration: 212 minutes

Like its predecessor of 1925, *Ben-Hur* came from the same source, Lew Wallace's popular novel. But the newer version surpasses the earlier one in duration (seventy minutes longer); lavish spectacle made possible by the use of color and the wide screen; scenes of confrontation between two former friends that intensify the drama; and the advanced techniques that had come along in the meantime, more suited to the popular tastes of the 1950s. The 1959 production of *Ben-Hur* came at a time when the religious epic film had reached its apex as popular entertainment, and the studio moguls at MGM ventured a hugely expensive project ($17 million), hoping to recoup previous losses by using a story of proven box-office draw. The project was launched with a top-notch director, William Wyler, in his first epic undertaking; a well-known producer in the genre, Sam Zimbalist (who died during production); a cast headed by one of the most popular actors of the day; armies of technicians, set decorators, and costume decorators; and thousands of extras. It was filmed at the Cinecittà studio in Rome, where hundreds of sets were built, and it took nearly two years to complete. This enormous venture paid off. The movie netted several times its cost, won wide international fame, and garnered twelve Oscar nominations and eleven wins—more than any other movie up to that time.

The timing of remaking the popular Wallace novel into a new epic could not have been more propitious. The decade following World War II had seen social upheavals that influenced, among other things, movie audience tastes. During and right after the war, much screen space had been given to war adventure movies, while the advent of television had made inroads in movie attendance, forcing the studios to resort to new formats to lure ticket buyers back to the movie theaters. The first CinemaScope feature, *The Robe* (1953), changed the movie landscape, offering audiences a screen more than twice the width of its height, which could accommodate battles and other action scenes, along with stereophonic sound. Filmmakers like Cecil B. DeMille had already paved the way for historical spectacles, especially those related to the Roman/early Christian era, with such spectacles as *The Ten Commandments* (1923), *The King of Kings* (1927), *The Sign of the Cross* (1932), *Cleopatra* (1934), and *The Crusades* (1935).

Thus, the return to the ever-popular Roman/Judeo-Christian theme proved ripe again, at a time when Hollywood producers faced intense pressure from the ongoing investigations by the House Un-American Activities Committee, which resulted in the blacklisting and exile of many screenwriters of note.[1] Fear forced producers to weed out politically risky topics (or those thought to be so) from Hollywood productions, and the religious theme appeared a safe haven for many filmmakers who wished to avoid controversy by tackling reverential topics, just at the time that the medium had acquired the means of offering rich spectacle suited to the mentality of the times. Coming after a long line of big-screen hits with religious themes, *Ben-Hur* fit in that category perfectly, thus promoting the renaissance of religious epics, which had become fodder for large audiences in prewar decades. By the mid-1960s, however, the religious, pseudo-historical epic had finally run its course.

Ben-Hur follows *The Ten Commandments* (1956) in close chronology and features the same major actor, Charlton Heston, who plays the leading role here as well. *Ben-Hur*, however, is a better-structured epic. Whereas *The Ten Commandments*, broadly following the biblical narrative, has two distinct parts, hardly unified except by an idea (the Lord will grant freedom to His people), *Ben-Hur*, despite its length and sprawl, has unity of action and, with the exception of a few scenes, unity of place (Judea), two qualities that work in its favor. The theme of revenge is clearly the controlling factor that unifies the action of this grand epic.

Judah Ben-Hur is the scion of a noble Jewish family and a leader among his people. He had formed a boyhood friendship with a Roman youth, Messala (Stephen Boyd), who, upon his return to Israel, and now a powerful ranking official, asks for Judah's help to find and uproot potential local rebellious leaders. When Ben-Hur refuses, appalled by his former friend's effrontery and callousness, the two former friends become mortal enemies, especially after Messala orders Judah's and his family's arrest and enslavement. No one ever returns from the galleys, but Judah, having saved the life of a Roman consul, does, and he comes back to Judaea to confront his former friend in a chariot race, in which the latter is killed. Judah subsequently discovers his mother and sister in a leper valley, where they had been thrown after their imprisonment. He carries them home, and they are miraculously healed after Christ's Crucifixion. The film's action is framed by the story of the Nativity, which had occurred earlier, and the Crucifixion, which ends it.

This intimate story of friendship and betrayal is set in the enormous canvas that includes the entrance of the Roman legions into Jerusalem; the trek of a line of condemned men to the galleys; a naval battle; a show of the glitter of aristocratic social life in Rome; an Arab sheik in his entourage; a stunning chariot race filmed in a specially built eighteen-acre stadium near the Cinecittà studio in Rome; and the Crucifixion, shown during a cataclysmic storm, followed by a miracle. The return of the hero to avenge an injustice is, of course, what binds these spectacular sequences.

Lavish sets representing the city of Jerusalem and other locations built at the Cinecittà studio at great expense by MGM provide the spectacle needed to make the action credible and enhance the heroic persona; however, the spectacle does not overwhelm the intimacy of the personal story. Two major reversals in the movie's action shape Judah's fate and turn him from a potentially bitterly tragic into an epic hero: One occurs when he is suddenly thrust from a high social and tribal position into slavery, and the second when a galley slave, as if "by magic" (to use Messala's words), is transformed into the son of a Roman consul, Quintus Arrius (Jack Hawkins). This gives him both the status to challenge a powerful Roman to a chariot race, which he wins, and the authority to search for his mother and sister. He accomplishes both tasks, although his triumph is marred by the discovery that the two women have lived in a colony of lepers. Ben-Hur's greatest emotional moment in the movie is not his victory over Messala, but his impassionate search for his mother and sister, whom he rescues from their appalling conditions and restores them to family life and dignity. The heroic and the religious themes thus interweave.

In the end, Judah has become compassionate, not only to his closest relatives, but to everyone in general. His fight with Messala cleansed him of his hatred while bringing about justice. But when he was being led to slavery, and was in distress, a figure, whose face is never shown, offers him water. After the discovery of the two women, Ben-Hur sees Jesus in his agony carrying the cross, and for a moment he tries to help, offering water and realizing that this is the man who once helped him. In the ensuing storm after the Crucifixion, his mother's and sister's faces are cleansed of their deformities, as the blood mixed in the rainwater symbolically represents the soul's cleansing. The movie implies that Ben-Hur is a convert from a nearly agnostic and embittered Jewish nobleman to a devout and compassionate Christian, although the movie does not state this directly.

Even on the small TV screen, the movie still looks fresh. The confrontations between Messala and Ben-Hur, both with words and in the arena, are powerful, and the revenge theme keeps the story afloat. The several other themes don't work as well—the Arrius–Ben-Hur relationship, for instance, seems contrived. Although Hawkins speaks some impeccable lines ("In his eagerness to save you, your God also saved the Roman fleet"), his role (and this relationship) seems inserted to promote the plot and is hardly believable (a high-ranking Roman does a favor for a galley slave, his pretext being that this man would do well as a gladiator in the Roman circuses). It is also implied that Arrius is an agnostic, having lost faith in any of the Roman gods, but he is impressed by Judah's dogged pursuit of revenge and faith in his God. The action is also slowed by Judah's numerous encounters and lengthy dialogues with Esther (Haya Harareet), his mother and sister, various apostles, and horse trainers; thus the story line becomes diluted, and the length of the film by today's standards seems excessive. The religious theme also seems more of an addition here than in the earlier (1925) version, where it is built into the story.

One may ask why the movie is subtitled *A Tale of the Christ.* Of course in the original novel by Lew Wallace—and in the subsequent plays and early films—the religious theme is part of the main theme, which is the title, preserved here. Ben-Hur, the hero, is to be converted from a Jew to a Christian, learning the lessons of tolerance, forgiveness, and love of thy neighbor, but this conversion seemed tagged on to the main theme: Ben-Hur, although not amoral and definitely a loyal Jew, is not particularly Christian. He is outraged by Messala's proposal to betray his tribe; indignant and embittered after his enslavement; and out for revenge, which becomes an obsession that abides with him until the chariot race when he destroys Messala.

Needless to say, revenge is not a Christian virtue, although practiced by many Christians in the world of fiction—one example being Hamlet. Ben-Hur believes his God will save him, but it is only chance (or a homosexual urge on the part of Arrius?) that does so. Alas, the movie has to stand as it is—as all movies must—and cannot be remade in modern terms.

Still, this epic, slow pace and all, is a powerful, moving story. The basics are there: a friendship goes sour, a son and brother witness the near extinction of their family, and former friends become enemies. And then there's revenge (it works as a theme—it worked for Shakespeare and other Renaissance playwrights), which the audience craves, and which becomes the main factor. The emotional level of the movie remains high, which—to make an inevitable comparison—is not the case with *Gladiator* (2000), a modern epic with a similar theme; however, in *Gladiator*, the high intensity lies in the constant mayhem surrounding the existence of Maximus, also a wronged man. But the similarities end here, and the slow pace of *Ben-Hur* works to its advantage. The intensity of its emotions allows the viewer to follow the hero's reluctant wanderings and his yearning to return and be reunited with his mother and sister. While the hyperkinetic Maximus ventures into one physical feat after another, becoming a fighting and killing machine, Ben-Hur stimulates us to feel his deep affection, his pride, his revulsion at a friend's treachery. Maximus is a stoic killer, perhaps a true gladiator. Ben-Hur is a charioteer—who goes after the love of the sport, but with a purpose. It is at the emotional—not the intellectual or the artistic—level that *Ben-Hur* wins, still drawing us to it.

Seen from a certain point of view, this epic movie could do without this somewhat contrived interweaving of the themes of revenge and piety. *Ben-Hur* could have been a story about a Roman (as *Gladiator*'s hero is) who overcomes adversity and a vicious enemy and becomes triumphant again. But in the 1950s—an era of skepticism brought about by a brutal World War and the Cold War that followed—the religious theme played an important role. From that point of view, *Ben-Hur* seems dated today; however, its action scenes and the core of humanity radiating from the hero's trek and his overcoming of tremendous odds to reach his goal—these are perfect examples of the epic film at its heroic mode.

Seen from an even more remote (chronologically speaking) point of view, the film reveals two ironies, both perhaps unintentionally placed: The first irony, with its political implications, lies in Messala's arrogant tirade as he outlines his proposition of "collaboration" to Judah; the sum of it is that Rome will grant freedom and justice only to those who go along with its grandiose, and imperialist, plans of conquest. There is no world outside the Roman world, and one has a place in the sun only with cooperation. "The emperor looks at you!" he says to, Judah. The second irony, and perhaps the more poignant one, is when the horse trainer, who is an Arab, joins forces with a Jew, in preparation for the chariot race. Jews and Arabs, both Semitic peoples, are united against their common enemy. Whether the screenwriters of *Ben-Hur* meant this irony to resonate in their time (the 1950s), as it certainly resonates in ours (2000s), depends on one's interpretation. Placed in a larger, political frame, seeing *Ben-Hur* today might be worthy for those two ironies only. CS

Note

1. Among others, Carl Foreman, Ring Lardner Jr., and Dalton Trumbo.

Bibliography

Casson, Lionel. *Ships and Seamanship in the Ancient World.* Princeton, NJ: Princeton University Press, 1971.

Hickman, Roger. *Miklós Rózsa's Ben-Hur: A Film Score Guide.* Lanham, MD: Scarecrow Press, 2011.

Wallace, Lew. *Ben-Hur: A Tale of the Christ.* New York: Harper & Brothers, 1908.

BEOWULF (2007)

Director: Robert Zemeckis
Writers: Neil Gaiman, Roger Avary. Based on the epic poem *Beowulf.*
Producers: Steve Starkey, Robert Zemeckis, Jack Rapke (Shangri-La Entertainment, Imagemovers, Paramount Pictures)
Cinematographer: Robert Presley
Editor: Jeremiah O'Driscoll
Art Direction: Norman Newberry, Greg Papalia
Costumes: Gabriella Pescucci
Music: Alan Silvestri
Cast: Beowulf/Golden Man/Dragon: Ray Winstone. Hrothgar: Anthony Hopkins. Wealthow: Robin Wright-Penn. Wiglaf: Brendan Gleeson. Grendel's Mother: Angelina Jolie. Unferth: John Malkovich. Grendel: Crispin Glover. Ursula: Alison Lohman. Hondshew: Costas Mandylor. Yrsa: Leslie Zemeckis. Gitte: Sonje Fortag (as Sonja Fortag)
AA: None
AAN: None
DVD: Paramount Pictures, 2008
Blu-ray: Paramount Pictures, 2007
Duration: DVD, 110 minutes; Blu-ray, 114 minutes

A 3D motion capture computer-animated epic based on the Old English heroic tale composed between the seventh and ninth centuries, but set in sixth-century Scandinavia,[1] *Beowulf* recounts the passing of the era of heroes and monsters and the beginning of Christianity. In the year A.D. 507, the Danish kingdom, ruled by Hrothgar (Anthony Hopkins), is being attacked by the huge and fearsome humanoid monster Grendel (Crispin Glover). Hrothgar himself is too old and out of shape to take on the creature himself, and with his own warriors unable to defeat the beast, the arrival of the great warrior Beowulf (Ray Winstone) from Geatland is a blessing. We quickly learn that Beowulf is not above embellishing his past achievements, and yet naked and unarmed he is indeed able to kill Grendel. He is alarmed to find that he must also kill Grendel's vengeful mother (Angelina Jolie), and it becomes clear that he has not been told the whole story—that Hrothgar was Grendel's father. But Beowulf also succumbs to the seductive promises of the she-demon. Hrothgar rightly suspects that Beowulf is lying about killing her, and he passes the crown to Beowulf before throwing himself off a cliff. Beowulf marries Hrothgar's young widow, Wealthow (Robin Wright-Penn), and yet as we revisit the kingdom many years later, we find an unsettled King Beowulf with a mistress and an estranged wife. Grendel's mother (who is never named) brings an end to their agreement, and Beowulf's dragon son attacks the kingdom. Although past his prime, Beowulf feels honor bound to kill the dragon himself, dying in the ensuing battle. Beowulf's trusted friend Wiglaf (Brendan Gleeson) is left with the kingdom but faces the same temptation of Grendel's mother as the film closes.

Ray Winstone says that he "always wanted to play a Viking" since he saw Kirk Douglas in *The Vikings* (Richard Fleischer, 1958).[2] He was able to take on a rough-hewn heroic mantle as Will Scarlett in the cult British television series *Robin of Sherwood* (1984–1986), and as an Arthurian knight in *King Arthur* (Antoine Fuqua, 2004). But it is only with the assistance of the performance capture technique that the fifty-year-old actor (chosen for his trademark gravel voice) could be transformed into the youthful, buff Scandinavian hero Beowulf, although strangely less attractive than the real, portly Winstone.

Indeed, the actors are much more engaging in the behind-the-scenes footage available on the two-disc special edition director's cut. Despite improvements made to the performance capture technique since Zemeckis's *The Polar Express* (2004), the faces still do not engage, and *New York Times* writer Manohla Dargis observes that the "human characters move with a perceptible drag effect, as if underwater."[3] For its technical advances, we may be forgiven for thinking we had stumbled across an adult version of a Barbie animation. *Variety* notes that the film nonetheless features "majestic crane shots of the frozen Nordic landscape . . . that are especially striking in 3D."[4]

Cowriter Roger Avary (Oscar winner for cowriting the 1994 *Pulp Fiction*, along with director Quentin Tarantino) sought to address what he saw as inherent mysteries and contradictions in the original epic poem, namely, "If Grendel is half-man, half-demon . . . then who is his father? When Beowulf goes into the cave to kill Grendel's mother, why does he emerge with Grendel's head instead of hers? Where's the proof that the mother was killed?"[5] By contrast, and somewhat alarmingly, Zemeckis proclaims that "nothing about the original poem ever appealed to me," and he dismisses it as "boring."[6] There is, surely, plenty of excitement to be found in the poem:

> Then, such was his fury, the leader of the Geats
> threw out his chest and gave a great roar. . . .
> The defender of the barrow bristled with anger
> [and] spouted murderous fire,
> so that flames leaped through the air.[7]

Ray Winstone is just the man to do such a "great roar" justice, but the otherwise excellent cast lost their spark in the animation process. The saccharine end title song "A Hero Comes Home," indicative of a merely serviceable score, compounds the disappointment. *Beowulf* performed respectfully at the international box office. DB

Notes

1. Heather O'Donoghue, "Introduction," in *Beowulf*, translated by Kevin Crossley-Holland (Oxford, UK, and New York: Oxford University Press, 1999), x.
2. "Creating the Ultimate Beowulf," *Beowulf*, directed by Robert Zemeckis (Paramount Pictures, 2008), DVD.
3. Manohla Dargis, "Beowulf," *New York Times*, 16 November 2007, http://movies.nytimes.com/2007/11/16/movies/16beow.html?_r=0 (23 September 2012).
4. Justin Chang, "Beowulf," *Variety*, 11 November 2007, www.variety.com/review/VE1117935372/ (23 September 2012).

5. Roger Avary, "Foreword," in *Beowulf: The Script Book*, edited by Neil Gaiman and Roger Avary (New York: HarperCollins, 2007), 5.

6. "The Origins of Beowulf," *Beowulf*, directed by Robert Zemeckis (Paramount Pictures, 2008), DVD.

7. *Beowulf*, translated by Kevin Crossley-Holland (Oxford, UK, and New York: Oxford University Press, 1999), 84–85.

Bibliography

Avary, Roger. "Foreword." In *Beowulf: The Script Book*, edited by Neil Gaiman and Roger Avary, 5 (New York: HarperCollins, 2007).

Beowulf. Translated by Kevin Crossley-Holland. Oxford, UK, and New York: Oxford University Press, 1999.

Chang, Justin. "Beowulf." *Variety*, 11 November 2007, www.variety.com/review/VE1117935372/ (23 September 2012).

Dargis, Manohla. "Beowulf." *New York Times*, 16 November 2007, http://movies.nytimes.com/2007/11/16/movies/16beow.html?_r=0 (23 September 2012).

O'Donoghue, Heather. "Introduction." In *Beowulf*, translated by Kevin Crossley-Holland, vi–xxvi. Oxford, UK, and New York: Oxford University Press, 1999.

THE BIBLE: IN THE BEGINNING (1966)

Director: John Huston
Writer: Christopher Fry
Producer: Dino De Laurentiis (20th Century Fox)
Cinematographer: Giuseppe Rotunno
Editor: Ralph Kemplen
Art Direction: Mario Chiari
Music: Toshiro Mayuzumi
Cast: Adam: Michael Parks. Eve: Ulla Bergryd. Cain: Richard Harris. Noah: John Huston. Nimrod: Stephen Boyd. Abraham: George C. Scott. Sarah: Ava Gardner. The Three Angels: Peter O'Toole. Hagar: Zoe Sallis. Lot: Gabriele Ferzetti. Lot's Wife: Eleonora Rossi Drago. Abel: Franco Nero. Noah's Wife: Pupella Maggio. Abraham's Steward: Robert Rietty. Shem: Peter Heinze. Ham: Angelo Boscariol
AA: None
AAN: Best Music–Original Music Score (Toshiro Mayuzumi)
DVD: 20th Century Fox, 2004
Blu-ray: 20th Century Fox, 2011
Duration: 174 minutes

> I'm interested in the Bible as a universal myth, as a prop for numerous legends. It's a collective creation of humanity, destined to solve, provisionally and in the form of fables, a number of mysteries too disquieting to contemplate for a nonscientific era.
>
> —John Huston

John Huston's *The Bible: In the Beginning* is a religious epic with a mythological twist. Originally intending to depict the events chronicled in the entire corpus of the Bible, as the title indicates, the action focuses on the first twenty-two books of Genesis from the Old Testament, thus gaining the late subtitle *In the Beginning*. Similarly structured in format to the Greek and Roman genre of didactic epic,[1] this film as epic contains the classical episodes that make up this form; namely, there is a creation account that determines the nature of how the world came into being and how the four elements—earth, air, fire, and water—were separated from the starry firmament, and by whom. It accounts for the creation of living forms in each of those regions, culminating in the special relationship between the creator and humankind, first of man. What follows are accounts of the origin of woman, the nature of evil, hubris, and the destruction of the world by universal water and fire (*kataklysmos/ekpyrosis*). Finally, humans learn the will of the deity, and through these lessons the moral precepts are taught and transmitted. In Huston's epic, the moral lesson (with the exception of a comedic interlude involving the director starring in an animal circus act) is clearly and distinctly *obedience*.[2]

The Bible: In the Beginning opens with a dramatic recitation of the creation narration from Genesis, accompanied by musical and visual effects to demonstrate the emergence of God's creation by fiat; of the primal elements earth, heaven, waters, and light; of the separation of the opposites (day/light, night/darkness; evening/morning; waters above/waters below; earth/sea); of the creation of creatures that reside in the sea and move across the firmament as they fly toward heaven; and of the creation of the creatures of the earth. Then God tells them to be fruitful and multiply each after their own kind, and he blesses them and sees that it is good.

The recitation continues with the following quote regarding the creation of Man: "Let us make Man in Our own image, after Our likeness." Then the narration pauses, and the camera moves to a close-up of a sand pile, where we witness the slow emergence of a human form as sand is blown from the pile. The narration explains the creation of Man by God breathing into Adam's nostrils the breath of life, making man a living soul. Then God brings the beasts and fowl to Adam (Michael Parks) for him to name. Adam sees his reflection in the water, and after grasping at it and being unable to grab hold of it, the narration continues, saying, "And the Lord said, 'It is not good that man should be alone' . . . and God made a Woman and brought her unto the man." Upon seeing Eve (Ulla Bergryd) for the first time, we finally hear dialogue in the film, from Adam: "This is the bone of my bone; the flesh of my flesh." This creation episode concludes with "God saw everything that He made, and he saw that it was very good." On the seventh day, God rested and blessed and sanctified the day. And with these words, the idyllic golden age of didactic myth is complete.

The mythos of the origin of evil begins with a continuation of the narration of the Garden that God had planted and sent Adam and Eve to, telling them to tend and keep the garden, but admonishing them not to eat of the fruit of the tree of Knowledge of Good and Evil, "lest they shall surely die on the day they eat of it." Then God blesses them and tells them to be fruitful and multiply. What follows is first a modestly symbolic "fruitful and multiply" scene, immediately followed by the temptation of Eve by the serpent in an obvious, although clumsy, causal chain. The serpent tells Eve that they will not die, but rather that their eyes shall be opened and they will be as gods, knowing good and evil. Eve takes a bite of the apple. When Eve tells Adam to taste the apple, saying there is no harm, Adam replies, "It is disobedience." She responds, "It will make us wise." And he eats the apple. The narration returns with the admonition from God, the punishment (sorrow in conception and childbirth and subordination to her husband for Eve; a life of labor upon a cursed land followed by a return to dust, that is, mortality for Adam), and expulsion from the garden.

The Cain and Abel story begins with the narrator defining the name Cain as meaning "Possession" and Abel meaning "breath of Life." Abel (Franco Nero) is seen playing a flute, while Cain (Richard Harris) is tilling the ground with his father Adam. Cain kills his brother because God liked Abel's offerings but not Cain's, resulting in Cain's eternal banishment from the earth as a fugitive. God puts a curse on those who would try to slay Cain so that they would receive sevenfold vengeance on them, and he placed a mark on Cain's forehead lest anyone slay him. Cain married and had children, and his seed populated the earth. They were known for their knowledge and craftsmanship in music, brass work, and the "secrets of the ground." But because the knowledge of good and evil was now in all the people of the earth, God grieved because men were following the ways of evil. Thus, he will be planning a method to rid the world of this evil group, in this case, with a flood. Luckily, Eve also gave birth to a good son Seth, and Noah (John Huston) was born of that generation, thus beginning the mythos of the *kataklysmos* (great flood), followed by the repopulation of the earth by new types of people (Tower of Babel).

The Noah segment of the film is a welcome relief from the somber timbre of the rest of this creative work. There is no doubt that Noah's character differs from earlier ones, especially in the jovial and naïve mannerisms with which he fulfills God's commands. His obedience is a joy, and his labor seems to be almost unconscious; however, he is obedient to the letter, and God blesses him and repopulates the earth with his seed, and all the good animals, thus continuing this story. God makes a covenant with Noah with a bow in the clouds (a rainbow). This ends part one of the film.

The second half of the film opens with a declaration of the lineage of Noah's descendants by his three sons, ending with King Nimrod (Stephen Boyd). The purpose of this mythos is to introduce the hubris of Nimrod in his building of the Tower of Babel and God's punishment of him and his people for this prideful action. (The people building the tower sing a song about the bow of Nimrod being the strongest, which serves as the token of their challenge to God.) The Lord comes down to see the tower and realizes that the people are one, with a common language, with no restraint against what they imagine to do. Then Nimrod takes his bow and shoots an arrow into the heavens. God causes the tower to fall, while the voice-over narrates, "Let us confound their language." After the tower falls and Nimrod attempts to regain control, he tries to command the crowd. When Nimrod attempts to speak to his people, they are all speaking in foreign languages and are unable to communicate with him or one another; madness ensues and there is fighting throughout the region. This, we are told, is the origin of Babel, and how the people once again became scattered around the earth for ten more generations until Abraham is born to serve as the next good man who will be the obedient servant of God's will to lead the people.

The next and last mythos of the film chronicles the Abraham story, which is told in full. It begins with Abraham (George C. Scott) obeying God's call and taking his wife Sarah (Ava Gardner) (whom he loved) and Lot (Gabriele Ferzetti), his brother's son, and many other souls from Ur of the Chaldees and into the wilderness on a journey to the unknown. For this, God promises to bless Abraham by making his name great as the father of a great nation. The story and film end with the sacrifice of Isaac and God's covenant to Abraham. In between, we witness the separation between Lot and Abraham, when Lot chooses to move to the city of Sodom and Gomorrah; a complicated subplot between Sarah and Hagar, her Egyptian slave (who is the mother of Abraham's firstborn son, Ishmael, descendant of the Arab people); and destruction by fire (*ekpyrosis*) of Sodom and Gomorrah by God. But in the end, the universal message of this film rings clear in the final scene, when God makes a covenant with Abraham to give him a son named Isaac; when God asks for that son back, Abraham is ready to sacrifice that child. God stops Abraham and rewards him for his unflinching obedience by saving Isaac from being sacrificed.

Produced by Dino De Laurentiis and likely preserved by the award-winning score and the billing of such Hollywood notables as Ava Gardner, Richard Harris, Peter O'Toole, and George C. Scott, the film nonetheless fails on aesthetic grounds on two counts. First, despite the presence of such star quality, for the majority of the film, it is not action, but the almost dithyrambic droning of didactic recitation of biblical narration by director John Huston that one remembers most about the film; and secondly, and paradoxically, the other memory is Huston's comedic cameo as Noah with all the animals. In the end, perhaps the best cinematic decision made regarding the project *The Bible: In the Beginning* was to end it there. MC

Notes

1. See, for example, Hesiod, *Theogony*; Lucretius, *De Rerum Natura*; Ovid, "Metamorphoses"; etc. As Huston writes in *An Open Book*, "Every interviewer during the filming—almost without exception—asked me if I believed in the Bible literally. I usually answered that Genesis represented a transition from Myth, when man, faced with creation and other deep mysteries, invented explanations for the inexplicable; to Legend, when he attributed to his forebears heroic qualities of leadership, valor and wisdom; to History, when, having emerged from Myth and Legend, accounts of real exploits and events of the past were handed down from father to son before the written word" (329).

2. According to Axel Madsen, "John wanted the film to show the power and terror of the Bible as 'universal myth,' the wrath of Jehovah, the fascination with sin. John wanted his audience to be on man's, not God's, side through these tribal tales and fantasies of the origins of life. Eve's crime should seem disproportionately little compared to the punishment the angry godhead imposes on her and her children forever after" (212–13).

Bibliography

Huston, John. *An Open Book*. New York: Alfred A. Knopf, 1980.

Madsen, Axel. *John Huston: A Biography*. Garden City, NY: Doubleday, 1978.

THE BIRTH OF A NATION (1915)

DIRECTOR: D. W. Griffith
WRITERS: D. W. Griffith, Frank E. Woods. Based on the novel and play *The Clansman*, by Thomas F. Dixon Jr.
PRODUCER: D. W. Griffith (Epoch Producing Corporation)
CINEMATOGRAPHER: G. W. Bitzer
EDITORS: D. W. Griffith, Joseph Henabery, James Smith, Rose Smith, Raoul Walsh
COSTUMES: Robert Goldstein (uncredited), Clare West (uncredited)
MUSIC: Joseph Carl Breil, D. W. Griffith
CAST: Elsie Stoneman: Lillian Gish. Flora Cameron: Mae Marsh. Colonel Ben Cameron: Henry Walthall. Margaret Cameron: Miriam Cooper. Lydia Brown: Mary Alden. Hon. Austin Stoneman, Leader of the House: Ralph Lewis. Silas Lynch: George Siegmann. Gus: Walter Long. Tod Stoneman: Robert Harron. Jeff the Blacksmith: Wallace Reid. Abraham Lincoln: Joseph Henabery. Phil Stoneman: Elmer Clifton. Mrs. Cameron: Josephine Crowell. Dr. Cameron: Spottiswoode Aitken. Wade Cameron: George Beranger. Duke Cameron: Maxfield Stanley. Mammy: Jennie Lee. General Ulysses S. Grant: Donald Crisp. General Robert E. Lee: Howard Gaye. Senator Charles Sumner: Sam de Grasse. John Wilkes Booth: Raoul Walsh. Fallen Foe: Eugene Palette
AA: None
AAN: None
DVD: Kino International, 2011
BLU-RAY: Kino Video, 2011
DURATION: 190 minutes

With a running time of more than three hours, D. W. Griffith's 1915 silent historical epic *The Birth of a Nation* was the longest film made in the United States to that date. The film set new standards in film techniques, particularly in the use of extended crosscutting between different points of action, employed to thrilling effect in the final chase sequence of the film. *The Birth of a Nation* was the first film ever screened at the White House,[1] but the picture remains deeply controversial in the canon due to its overtly racist politics, which were objected to even upon the film's release.[2] Griffith remained steadfast in his rejection of criticism against the film's racism, and although he made *Intolerance* (1916) by way of reply, it was not intended as an apology (as is often asserted).[3] Indeed, Griffith begins *The Birth of a Nation* with a plea against censorship: "A plea for the art of the motion picture. We do not fear censorship, for we have no wish to offend with improprieties or obscenities, but we do demand, as a right, the liberty to show the dark side of wrong, that we may illuminate the bright side of virtue."

Griffith was determined to show a (White) Southern perspective on the Civil War, complaining "Only the winning side in a war ever gets to tell its story,"[4] but the film is ultimately disingenuous when it claims, "This is an historical presentation of the Civil War and Reconstruction Period, and is not meant to reflect on any race or people of today." Richard Dyer suggests that *The Birth of a Nation*'s racial politics can best be viewed as displaying a belief in the separation and essential difference of races, to which miscegenation is the greatest threat.[5]

Griffith begins his film by arguing, "The bringing of the African to America planted the first seeds of disunion," as we see images of the slave trade. The story proper begins in pre–Civil War 1860, as we meet the Northern Stoneman family and the Southern Cameron family, who get tragically caught up in the political events that unfold. The Honorable Austin Stoneman (Ralph Lewis) is an abolitionist master of congress (patterned after the antislavery senator Thaddeus Stevens). In his household are daughter Elsie (Lillian Gish); sons Phil (Elmer Clifton) and Tod (Robert Harron); and a biracial ("mulatto" in the film) housekeeper who, it is implied, becomes Stoneman's mistress, "the great leader's weakness that is to blight a nation." In the Cameron household are Dr. and Mrs. Cameron (Spottiswoode Aitken and Josephine Crowell, respectively); their son Ben (Henry Walthall), who is friends with Phil Stoneman; daughters Margaret (Miriam Cooper) and Flora (the delightful Mae Marsh); and two younger sons, Wade (George Beranger) and Duke (Maxfield Stanley). When the Stoneman boys visit the Camerons at their home in Piedmont, Phil and Margaret fall in love, and Tod and Duke strike up a playful friendship. Ben falls in love with a picture of Elsie Stoneman and keeps it with him throughout the film.

As war breaks out, the Stoneman and Cameron boys are soon in uniform, while in Piedmont the Cameron women hide as their home is raided by black Northern militiamen, saved just in time by Confederate troops. Wade and Duke Cameron die in battle, as does Tod Stoneman, as he faces his former chum Duke on the battlefield. As the war nears its end, Ben Cameron, now known as "The Little General," leads an offensive against a Union trench commanded by Phil Stoneman. Although Ben is wounded, he is rescued by Phil and taken to a military hospital. It is here that he finally meets Elsie, who is working as a nurse, and confesses his love for her. When Ben is sentenced to death as a guerilla, Elsie takes his visiting mother to convince Abraham Lincoln (Joseph Henabery) of the error, and Ben is pardoned.

The young Stonemans are present when Lincoln is assassinated at Ford's Theatre by John Wilkes Booth (Raoul Walsh). Ben makes a bittersweet return to his family in Piedmont, and the Cameron family is disheartened to hear of Lincoln's death, proclaiming, "Our best friend is gone. What is to become of us now?" Putting aside Lincoln's lenient attitude toward the South, to "deal with them as though they had never been away," Stoneman assumes power and proceeds to "put the white South under the heel of the black South." He sends his biracial protégé Silas Lynch (George Siegmann) south to make arrangements, but Lynch is only interested in his own advancement, a "traitor to his white patron and a greater traitor to his own people." Stoneman heads to Piedmont with his family to oversee the Reconstruction. While Ben and Elsie rekindle their romance, Margaret cannot forgive the acts of war, rejecting Phil.

Whites become disenfranchised, injustice is allowed by black juries, and the black legislature is shown to be lazy and incompetent. Ben is inspired to take action when he sees white children put on white sheets and pretend to be ghosts, frightening some black children. He gathers supporters and forms the Ku Klux Klan (KKK), a vigilante group whose members disguise themselves in white robes and fight back against "the Black Menace." Elsie breaks off her engagement when she learns of Ben's involvement. When Flora unwisely heads out alone to fetch water, the black Gus (Walter Long) follows her and proposes. Flora rejects him and runs away. When Gus makes chase, the frightened Flora jumps off a cliff to her death to escape his clutches, but not before naming her assailant to her brother Ben. The Klansmen hunt Gus down and lynch him, leaving his body at the house of Lynch, who orders a search of homes for KKK garb.

Dr. Cameron is arrested for having Klan clothing in his home, but he is rescued by his faithful former slaves and Phil Stoneman, who shoots a black man in the process. Phil and the Camerons take refuge in the country home of two Union veterans, former adversaries united by a common black enemy. Elsie approaches Lynch to ask for leniency for her brother, but Lynch takes the opportunity to propose to the shocked Elsie, who is held prisoner. When her father arrives, he is at first pleased by Lynch's intention to marry a white woman, but when she is identified as his daughter, he soon changes his mind. The Klansmen rescue Elsie and Stoneman from Lynch, as well as the Camerons, who are under attack in the cabin. The Klan is victorious; a new (white-dominated), peaceful era is ushered in; and the two young couples (Elsie and Ben, Margaret and Phil) enjoy their double honeymoon.

Manthia Diawara calls *The Birth of a Nation* the "grammar book for Hollywood's representation of black manhood and black womanhood."[6] When Lillian Gish auditioned for the part of Elsie in the scene where she is forcibly prevented from leaving by the amorous Lynch, she recalls, "I was very blonde and fragile looking. The contrast with the dark man evidently pleased Mr. Griffith."[7] Throughout the film, white womanhood is contrasted with dangerous black manhood such that bell hooks suggests that it becomes a "way to perpetuate white supremacy."[8] And by naming the biracial (blackface) perpetrator Lynch, the victim of crime is transformed into the guilty party.[9]

The Birth of a Nation was seen as the American answer to the expansive Italian cinematic epics *Quo Vadis?* (Enrico Guazzoni, 1913) and *Cabiria* (Giovanni Pastrone, 1914), which had redefined the medium. *Variety* wrote, "Every bit of the film was laid, played, and made in America," and the result was such that "*The Birth of a Nation* overshadowed the foreign-film spectacle" and raised the esteem of the motion picture industry on par in quality (and admission fee) with stage productions.[10] *The Birth of a Nation* was instrumental in setting the film techniques that would define the medium and solidify its transition to respectable middle-class entertainment form. DB

Notes

1. Terry Christensen and Peter J. Haas, *Projecting Politics: Political Messages in American Films* (Armonk, NY: M. E. Sharpe, 2005), 64–65.
2. For a detailed discussion of the film's reception in different eras, see Janet Staiger, "*The Birth of a Nation*: Reconsidering Its Reception," in The Birth of a Nation*: D. W. Griffith, Director*, edited by Robert Lang (New Brunswick, NJ: Rutgers University Press, 1994), 195–213. See also Melvyn Stokes, *D. W. Griffith's The Birth of a Nation: A History of "the Most Controversial Motion Picture of All Time"* (New York: Oxford University Press, 2007).
3. Lillian Gish, with Ann Pinchot, *The Movies, Mr. Griffith, and Me* (Englewood Cliffs, NJ: Prentice Hall, 1969), 165, 359.
4. Gish, with Pinchot, *The Movies, Mr. Griffith, and Me*, 136.

5. Rather, he proposes, than necessarily being founded "on racist *hatred*" itself. Richard Dyer, "Into the Light: The Whiteness of the South in *The Birth of a Nation*," in *Dixie Debates: Perspectives on Southern Cultures*, edited by Richard H. King and Helen Taylor (London: Pluto Press, 1996), 167, emphasis mine.

6. Manthia Diawara, "Black American Cinema: The New Realism," in *Black American Cinema*, edited by Manthia Diawara (New York and London: Routledge, 1993), 3.

7. Gish, with Pinchot, *The Movies, Mr. Griffith, and Me*, 133. Richard Dyer notes that the lighting techniques emphasize this racial contrast, particularly during this scene. Dyer, "Into the Light," 174.

8. bell hooks, *Black Looks: Race and Representation* (Boston: South End Press, 1992), 119–20.

9. On this and the use of white actors in blackface, see Saër Maty Bâ, "Diegetic Masculinities: Reading the Black Body in Epic Cinema," in *The Epic Film in World Culture*, edited by Robert Burgoyne (New York: Routledge, 2010), 365, 368–70.

10. "Review: *The Birth of a Nation*," *Variety*, 1915, http://variety.com/1915/film/reviews/the-birth-of-a-nation-1200409250/ (29 June 2013).

Bibliography

Bâ, Saër Maty. "Diegetic Masculinities: Reading the Black Body in Epic Cinema." In *The Epic Film in World Culture*, edited by Robert Burgoyne, 346–74. New York: Routledge, 2010.

Christensen, Terry, and Peter J. Haas. *Projecting Politics: Political Messages in American Films*. Armonk, NY: M. E. Sharpe, 2005.

Diawara, Manthia. "Black American Cinema: The New Realism." In *Black American Cinema*, edited by Manthia Diawara, 3–25. New York and London: Routledge, 1993.

Dyer, Richard. "Into the Light: The Whiteness of the South in *The Birth of a Nation*." In *Dixie Debates: Perspectives on Southern Cultures*, edited by Richard H. King and Helen Taylor, 165–76. London: Pluto Press, 1996.

Gish, Lillian, with Ann Pinchot. *The Movies, Mr. Griffith, and Me*. Englewood Cliffs, NJ: Prentice Hall, 1969.

hooks, bell. *Black Looks: Race and Representation*. Boston: South End Press, 1992.

"Review: *The Birth of a Nation*." *Variety*, 1915, http://variety.com/1915/film/reviews/the-birth-of-a-nation-1200409250/ (29 June 2013).

Staiger, Janet. "*The Birth of a Nation*: Reconsidering Its Reception." In The Birth of a Nation*: D. W. Griffith, Director*, edited by Robert Lang, 195–213. New Brunswick, NJ: Rutgers University Press, 1994.

Stokes, Melvyn. *D. W. Griffith's* The Birth of a Nation*: A History of "the Most Controversial Motion Picture of All Time."* New York: Oxford University Press, 2007.

BLADE RUNNER (1982)

DIRECTOR: Ridley Scott

WRITERS: Hampton Fancher, David Peoples. Loosely based on the novel *Do Androids Dream of Electric Sheep?*, by Philip K. Dick.

PRODUCERS: Michael Deeley (The Ladd Company, Sir Run Run Shaw, Warner Bros.)

CINEMATOGRAPHER: Jordan Cronenweth

EDITOR: Terry Rawlings, Gillian Hutshin (final cut restoration)

ART DIRECTION: Lawrence G. Paull, David L. Snyder, Linda DeScenna

COSTUMES: Michael Kaplan, Charles Knode

MUSIC: Vangelis

SOUND MIXERS: Peter Pennell, Bud Alper, Graham V. Hartstone, Gerry Humphreys

SPECIAL EFFECTS: Douglas Trumbull, Richard Yuricich, David Dryer

MAKEUP ARTIST: Marvin G. Westmore

CAST: Rick Deckard: Harrison Ford. Roy Batty: Rutger Hauer. Rachael: Sean Young. Gaff: Edward James Olmos. Bryant: M. Emmet Walsh. Pris: Daryl Hannah. J. F. Sebastian: William Sanderson. Leon: Brion James. Tyrell: Joe Turkel. Zhora: Joanna Cassidy. Chew: James Hong. Holden: Morgan Paull. Bear: Kevin Thompson. Kaiser: John Edward Allen. Taffey Lewis: Hy Pyke. Cambodian Lady: Kimiro Hiroshige. Sushi Master: Robert Okazaki. Saleslady: Carolyn DeMirjian. Abdul Ben Hassan: Ben Astar

AA: None

AAN: Best Art Direction–Set Decoration (Lawrence G. Paull, David L. Snyder, Linda DeScenna), Best Effects, Visual Effects (Douglas Trumbull, Richard Yuricich, David Dryer)

BAFTA AWARDS: Best Cinematography (Jordan Cronenweth), Best Costume Design (Michael Kaplan, Charles Knode), Best Production Design–Art Direction (Lawrence G. Paull)

BAFTA Award Nominations: Best Film Editing (Terry Rawlings), Best Makeup Artist (Marvin G. Westmore), Best Score (Vangelis), Best Sound (Peter Pennell, Bud Alper, Graham V. Hartstone, Gerry Humphreys), Best Special Visual Effects (Douglas Trumbull, Richard Yuricich, David Dryer)
DVD: Warner Bros., 2007
Blu-ray: Warner Bros., 2012
Duration: 117 minutes

Blade Runner is a science-fiction spectacle epic, a dystopian vision of the near future (2019) in which human genetically engineered copies, or "Replicants," as they are known, are used as slave labor "Off-world." By the end of the film, it remains unclear how many supposed humans are really Replicants and whether this ultimately makes any difference. A commercial and, for the most part, critical disappointment upon its release in 1982, *Blade Runner* has since become revered for both its dazzling effects and its philosophical treatise on what it means to be human.

Following an "Off-world" rebellion, the Nexus 6 model of Replicants is declared illegal on Earth on penalty of "retirement"—a polite euphemism for death—by special "Blade Runner" police operatives. One such Replicant, Leon (Brion James), infiltrates the Tyrell Corporation, which is responsible for his manufacture, but when asked about his mother during the special "Voight-Kampff" test designed to provoke human emotions, he kills the Blade Runner, Holden (Morgan Paull). The reluctant Deckard (Harrison Ford) is brought in to help with the investigation by the enigmatic Gaff (Edward James Olmos), a detective who most often converses in "city speak," an Esperanto language forged out of several languages.[1] Although Deckard has already quit the force, his old boss, Bryant (M. Emmet Walsh), effectively gives him no option but to take another case, tracking down four Nexus 6 Replicants, including the leader, Roy Batty (Rutger Hauer), along with Leon and two females, Pris (Daryl Hannah) and Zhora (Joanna Cassidy).

Heading over to the imposing pyramid-like structure of the Tyrell Corporation, Deckard meets Tyrell himself (Joe Turkel), who asks him to test his own niece, Rachael (Sean Young), an attractive if aloof brunette. Deckard cannot quite see the point in testing a human with technology used to detect Replicants, but he wearily proceeds, only to find that Rachael is, in fact, a Replicant. Having been given memory implants from Tyrell's real niece, Rachael has been unaware of her true identity. Visiting Deckard at his home, she produces an old photograph of herself as a child with her mother as proof of her humanity. Deckard confronts the distraught Rachael with her own childhood memories, having been given access to her confidential file, and Rachael leaves, throwing down the photo.

Meanwhile, Leon and Roy are seeking information to extend their four-year life span, calling upon eye engineer Chew (James Hong) for information. Chew tells them to ask fellow genetic engineer J. F. Sebastian (William Sanderson), who has access to Tyrell himself, and Roy sends his girlfriend Pris to befriend him. Sebastian, who lives with an assembly of his own living doll-like creations, has a problem similar to that of the Replicants: he is aging too quickly (in his case due to a rare glandular condition). Although they do not initially identify themselves as such, Sebastian recognizes Pris and Roy as Replicants but is obviously fond of the creatures he has helped to create and agrees to get Roy in to see Tyrell through the pretext of their ongoing chess game.

Deckard heads to Leon's apartment looking for clues, finding some sort of scale in the bath and a collection of photographs. Using the computer to enhance the images, Deckard identifies an image of one of the Replicants—Zhora—and armed with this, he heads off to find out what the scale belongs to. Like the Replicants themselves, the scale is from an engineered creature—in this case a snake—who Deckard traces back to Taffy's nightclub. Here he finds Zhora performing an (unseen) exotic dance number with the snake. Seeing through Deckard's cover, Zhora first tries to kill him. She is forced to flee when they are interrupted. Deckard makes chase through the dark, rain-soaked streets, finally shooting her in the back as she crashes through store windows. It is not a dignified "retirement," and Deckard heads straight for alcohol. His mood worsens when Bryant informs him that there are still four Replicants to hunt, as Rachael has disappeared.

Deckard spots Rachael on the street only to be attacked by Leon, who casually knocks Deckard's gun away and is about to kill him when Rachel intervenes, shooting Leon in the head with Deckard's gun. Back at Deckard's home, he assures Rachael that he does not intend to hunt her, but he warns that someone else surely will. Although Rachael tries to leave, Deckard pushes her against the wall, demanding that she confess that she actually wants him.

With the help of Sebastian, Roy is able to confront his "father" Tyrell and demands more time to live, only to be told that changes to his design would be fatal in any case. The prodigal son confesses that he has done "questionable things" but, despite receiving Tyrell's forgiveness, Roy cannot forgive Tyrell, killing his creator by gouging his eye sockets.

It is later reported that Sebastian has also been killed, and Deckard heads to his apartment, where he is attacked by Pris. As she backflips to make her final assault, Deckard shoots her through the abdomen, and Pris flails around on the floor before dying. Her body is discovered by Roy, who breaks Deckard's fingers and hunts him through the building, wanting the Blade Runner to know what it is to live in fear. Yet when Deckard is about to fall to his death, Roy unexpectedly saves him. As he cradles a dove in his hands, Roy laments that his memories will soon be lost "like tears in rain," and upon his death the dove flies skyward.[2] Returning to his apartment, Deckard is relieved to find Rachael still alive, and the two depart. On their way out, he finds one of Gaff's origami creations at the doorway—a unicorn, the very creature that Deckard himself had been daydreaming of earlier. Nodding in acknowledgement, he gets into the lift with Rachael.

Director Ridley Scott (who had previous success with *Alien*, 1979) clashed with many members of his production crew, and the actors suffered through rain-drenched night shoots. When the film tested badly, a voice-over narration was recorded and a new, more optimistic ending added, with Deckard and Rachael rather implausibly escaping to the countryside; as Harrison Ford notes, the new ending "looked like it came from another movie."[3] The changes to *Blade Runner* did not save the film at the box office, despite Ford's popularity following *Raiders of the Lost Ark* (Steven Spielberg, 1981). Several versions of *Blade Runner* exist (the original rough cut ran to nearly four hours but has not been seen since), culminating in Scott's "Final Cut" of 2007, when, for the first time, he was given full control (despite its name, the previous "Director's Cut" had his input but was not, in fact, his own project). To coincide with its release, an extensive feature-length documentary was made, recounting the difficult journey from Philip K. Dick's 1968 novel *Do Androids Dream of Electric Sheep?*

to the (presumably) final interpretation of the film.

When taken alongside Gaff's origami unicorn, the inclusion of Deckard's daydream of the unicorn in the later cuts strongly suggests (as Scott's commentary confirms[4]) that Deckard himself is a Replicant. This seemingly simple key to the film belies its complex implications. At first glance, we may assume that Gaff knows Deckard's thoughts because he has seen his file, but Rachael's implanted memories come from an (unseen) human original, presumably still living out her life. Is the original, human Deckard also still alive elsewhere, carrying out his job? The book goes so far as to have an entire alternative police station, with both stations convinced that they are the proper authority. Scott even contemplated making Tyrell a Replicant as well. In a world of copies, can anyone really know who they are? Gaff has seen Deckard's file, but has someone else seen his? Or if the "original" Deckard was killed in the line of duty, might Gaff in fact know about Deckard because he previously worked with him and knew him well? Can we really be sure just how many Deckards there have been? Why train a new Blade Runner when you can simply re-create an experienced one?

That Deckard is a Replicant hunting other Replicants brings home the mockery of "retirement," for killing one's own kind is murder. In his DVD commentary, Scott suggests that during the course of the film, Deckard "rediscovers his own humanity," but, in reality, Deckard begins as a reluctant executioner—he has already quit the force and must be pressed back into service. He does his duty but is clearly disturbed by it from the outset. He is simply resigned to his own fate and that of the Replicants, unable to see an alternative course of action. In a sense, this does not really change. Gaff and Bryant simply choose to let Deckard and Rachael live. As they are the next model of Replicant, it is unclear how long this reprise will last, or where they can conceivably go. Tyrell explains that he chose to experiment with implanted memories to create a Replicant who is easier to control than the Nexus 6, a model clearly capable of developing volatile emotions, even within a limited four-year life span. It is only because of their violent rebelliousness that this inbuilt fail-safe is not left to run its immanent course; by contrast, Deckard fulfills his duties. He need not be executed, because he is, on the whole, obedient.

Although Rachael runs away from the Tyrell Corporation, she is also strangely passive. In the book, she is a more traditional femme fatale, in keeping with the 1940s noir-inspired elements of the detective narrative. Somewhat implausibly, in the novel, sex with Replicants is outlawed—given the track record of new technologies as facilitators of pornography, surely this would be one of the Replicants' first applications. Rachael seduces Blade Runners to render them incapable of carrying out their job, their love affairs bringing them in too close an affinity with their prey. In the film, it is Pris and Zhora who embody a threatening female Replicant sexuality. Conversely, Rachael only acknowledges her attraction to Deckard under dubiously violent circumstances, in which Deckard is the sexual aggressor. Rachael's human-implanted memories ultimately prove insufficient for her to deal with her newly discovered identity. Roy and his cohorts can at least own their memories, and with them their sense of self. Rachael seems, at times, eerily blank because of the traumatic recognition that there is nothing of herself that is truly hers. It is difficult to imagine a Rachael further from the angry femme fatale manipulating the men around her for her people's cause and her own survival.

Blade Runner creates an expansive spectacle of the futuristic city in decay, tangible in its textures and details, the pinnacle of analog effects before the advent of computer effects-driven spectacle films. Despite reviews that claimed that the look of the film overshadowed any emotional impact of its characters,[5] the human/Replicant divide (or lack thereof) resonates more forcefully as we explore cloning technologies in our own time. A sequel is being planned by Scott. DB

Notes

1. This language was created by Olmos himself for the role. See Charles de Lauzirika, "Dangerous Days: Making *Blade Runner*," *Blade Runner: The Final Cut*, directed by Ridley Scott (Warner Bros., 2007), DVD. Olmos once again came up against humanoid biological copies as Admiral William Adama in the television series *Battlestar Galactica* (2004–2009). For more on the production history, see Paul M. Sammon, *Future Noir: The Making of* Blade Runner (New York: HarperPrism, 1996).
2. Although the film omits the messianic religion of Mercerism found in the novel, Roy nonetheless functions here as a sacrificial Christlike figure, complete with a stigmata.
3. De Lauzirika, "Dangerous Days."
4. Ridley Scott, "Commentary," *Blade Runner: The Final Cut*, directed by Ridley Scott (Warner Bros., 2007), DVD.
5. See, for example, Roger Ebert, "*Blade Runner*," *Chicago Sun-Times*, 2 June 1982, www.rogerebert.com/reviews/blade-runner-1982-1 (7 June 2013), and Janet Maslin, "Futuristic *Blade Runner*," *New York Times*, 25 June 1982, www.nytimes.com/1982/06/25/movies/futuristic-blade-runner.html (7 June 2013).

Bibliography

Ebert, Roger. "*Blade Runner*." *Chicago Sun-Times*, 2 June 1982, www.rogerebert.com/reviews/blade-runner-1982-1 (7 June 2013).

Maslin, Janet. "Futuristic *Blade Runner*." *New York Times*, 25 June 1982, www.nytimes.com/1982/06/25/movies/futuristic-blade-runner.html (7 June 2013).

Sammon, Paul M. *Future Noir: The Making of* Blade Runner. New York: HarperPrism, 1996.

THE BLUE MAX (1966)

DIRECTOR: John Guillermin
WRITERS: David Pursall, Jack Seddon, Gerald Hanley. Based on the novel by Jack O. Hunter.
PRODUCER: Christian Ferry (20th Century Fox)
ADAPTATION FROM THE NOVEL: Ben Barzman, Basilio Franchina
CINEMATOGRAPHER: Douglas Slocombe
EDITOR: Max Benedict
MUSIC: Jerry Goldsmith
CAST: Lt. Bruno Stachel: George Peppard. Gen. Count von Klugermann: James Mason. Countess Kaeti von Klugermann: Ursula Andress. Willi von Klugermann: Jeremy Kemp. Col. Otto Heideman: Karl Michael Volger. Hobach: Anton Diffring. Kettering: Harry Towb. Ziegel: Derek Newark. Fabian: Derren Nesbitt. Von Richthofen (aka The Red Baron): Carl Schell
AA: None
AAN: None
DVD: 20th Century Fox, 2003
BLU-RAY: Currently unavailable
DURATION: 156 minutes

War movies of epic scope made in the 1960s (or earlier) invite inevitable comparisons with such movies made today, not only because of the inherent interest abiding in war, but because of the enormous changes in stylistic approach and the different mind-sets of the two eras. One can venture to state that earlier war movies are more watchable (on several levels) than most war movies made in recent times. For instance, *Pearl Harbor* (2001)—at least in the intense bombing scenes—contains in-your-face violence and shock-and-gore close-ups of bomb explosions, not to mention the overwhelming sound track (DTS didn't help here). And the first twenty minutes of *Saving Private Ryan* (1998) cannot be watched without revulsion, even though the film's harrowing realism and violence are organic to the whole. "Truer" to war realism as graphic violence in today's movies may be, it is not aesthetically more satisfying, no more than the violent plays of Lucius Annaeus Seneca[1] were to the Elizabethans, who preferred them to the Greek originals, which related violent episodes taking place backstage through a messenger. Movies, of course, show a greater degree of realism that any stage play (or any other medium) can match. They speak their own language, but excess is a flaw that afflicts all media, something only internal constraints can cure.

The Blue Max has a much quieter, even sluggish, pace, allowing the viewer to relax and enjoy the splendidly photographed aerial dog-fight sequences, for which this movie is noted. Based on the novel by Jack O. Hunter, a pot-boiler with some literary pretension, *The Blue Max* exhibits the standard traits and pitfalls of 1960s melodrama, including action, sex, a stereotypical hero, a sex goddess of the times, and a love-to-hate villain: there is the masculine-looking George Peppard as Bruno Stachel, an amoral overachiever and lover; a sex goddess in Ursula Andress, who plays Kaeti von Klugermann; and James Mason as Count von Klugermann, a Nazi prototype, although this movie takes place with World War I still raging on.

The movie shows a clash of ideologies in a pre-Nazi Germany: the old aristocracy is gone (or going), and so are officers who think of "honor" and "chivalry" as necessary parts of a military man's code of conducting a war. Such an officer is represented by Otto Heideman, ably played by Karl Michael Vogler, who despises Bruno Stachel's ruthless pursuit of decoration (the "Blue Max") and his willingness to put his personal ambition ahead of interests of the fatherland. Stachel's Mephistophelian—and perfectly German—character is matched by the equally cynical Willi von Klugermann (Jeremy Kemp), who is less prone to drink, more of an exhibitionist than Stachel (something that causes his death), and less inclined to avoid the sirenlike sexy "aunt," the young wife of his Uncle Klugermann. As for the latter, James Mason, whose screen villains far outnumber his heroes, portrays a not-so-reluctant cuckold senior officer who is willing to allow his wife freedom to flirt with other officers, although it is questionable whether he actually knows what happens until the end. His goal is to discover and promote a "hero" who can project the image of a daring German officer gunning down scores of opponents.

Although the movie does not attempt to make this historical context plain, it takes place in 1918, only a few months before Germany capitulated. The old order will die, while the aristocrats who had such titles as "Baron" affixed to their names will soon be gone, and a new order will come along, with heroes like the amoral Bruno Stachel, a man of a humble background who would rise to dominance and provide Hitler with his military cliques and social basis. Honorable officers like Heideman, who strove to keep such words as *chivalry* and *honor* would be out, but, oddly, a Klugermann would survive, for he would be able to see that the projected image of a ruthless individual seeking victory at any cost is what Germany would adopt. Klugermann does not hesitate to murder Stachel at film's end, when the latter's image would have been blemished by scandal. A dead hero would prove more useful than a live officer with a marred reputation.

In some ways, this is Mason's movie, for Peppard, endowed with haughty mannerisms, seems too weak an actor (although good for the fights and the sex scenes) to embody the Nazi of the coming generation. Kemp is better at this, but his image is already blurred by the decadence of a dying aristocracy, whose legacy would only surface sporadically in Hitler's entourage. This movie actually says more than it originally intended to say, and, seen from a vantage point of more than three decades, it deserves an asterisk of some note in the aftermath of World War I and

World War II—for both were fought on the same grounds, by the same sides, and both showed the European transitions of codes, from wars to peace, from aristocracy to populism, from class-ridden societies to, hopefully, an egalitarian and peaceful Europe.

It's necessary for a word more on the acting/actors of this movie. Peppard was chosen for his masculine persona and good looks, but he never managed, in this movie or any that followed, to become the screen icon that some of his contemporaries did—Sean Connery as James Bond, Steve McQueen in *The Great Escape* and other adventures, Michael Caine in the Harry Palmer series, or Peter O'Toole in *Lawrence of Arabia* and subsequent roles. In playing the amoral Stachel, Peppard achieved, if not histrionic ability, at least an archetypal mold that defines that generation of officers in the German Army. Somewhat enigmatic, physically attractive and an able fighter, and seemingly in control of his boiling rage, he is perfect as a flight hero determined to win his twenty "kills" required for the Blue Max. Icily cold but occasionally fair when gunning down his opponents, he is also a passionate, although somewhat sulking, lover, when the occasion arises (as it does a couple of times). He is targeted by a lustful female, as Countess Kaeti, here the Circe not of navigators but of airmen, is a collector of brave German officers. He is her prize, as a compensation for the deprivations she presumably suffers by her sexually inept husband. She is a young woman like the protagonist (Haydée Politoff) of *La Collectionneuse*, to borrow the title of Eric Rohmer's film, which, incidentally, appeared in the same year (1966).

The similarities between these two films end here, but the similarity is notable: in the Rohmer film, a young woman amuses herself by "collecting" men of her acquaintance as one would collect trophies. The only (unwritten and unspoken) condition she imposes on them is that they cannot collect *her*. She reserves the right to choose, on all occasions. In the end, only those who reject her win.

Kaeti is not so technical; she also has a more limited pool to choose from, as well as a watchdog husband, even though most of the time he does not watch her. But she has an unmitigated passion for fliers, her sultry looks are amazing, far surpassing those of the Lolita-like Politoff. Andress belonged to the breed of Swedish sexpots who descended from the north in conquest of a generation of males of Europe and the United States during the late 1950s and 1960s: Anita Ekberg (*La Dolce Vita*) and Elke Sommer (*A Shot in the Dark*), not to mention Bibi Andersson and Liv Ullmann, the serious beauties that proliferated in the Bergman cinema. The sexy trio—Ekberg, Sommer, and Andress—was perhaps more responsible than any other group of women for breaking the barriers of sex and nudity imposed for decades by the Hays Code in the United States—although only Andress left her imprint in American movies.

Some critics felt that Andress was totally misplaced in the film,[2] which might, with her absence, have gained the austere masculinity of a *Lawrence of Arabia*, but I argue that Andress was indeed well placed, and she acted that part as no other could. Heroes must be tested, not only against the attacks of enemy planes in the sky and hostile fire, but their mettle is also tried on moral (or immoral) grounds. Stachel's ruthless amorality and Willi's debauched cynicism must become fodder for a prowling seductress like Kaeti, whose presence is a test for the moral fiber of dissolute societies. As the world of chivalry becomes passé in the aging and war-torn Europe of the twentieth century, it is useful to recall that the showing of this transition must not be given in a typical Hollywood fashion, which demands a flawless hero. A flawed hero is also an archetype. Perhaps this movie's neglect might be attributed to that. Bring back *The Blue Max* for study in the classroom. (And give Hunter's novel another try.) CS

Notes

1. Seneca's *Oedipus*, a replica of the Sophocles play, has Jocasta stabbing her womb before the audience, whereas Oedipus blinds himself by tearing out the sockets of his eyes with his fingers—again before Roman spectators. In Thomas Kyd's *The Spanish Tragedy*, an old man bites his tongue out rather than betray a secret.

2. Mike Mayo, *VideoHound's War Movies: Classic Conflict on Film* (Detroit, MI: Visible Ink Press, 1999), 135.

Bibliography

Farmer, James A. "Hollywood's World War I Aviation Films." *Air Classics*, 24, no. 12 (December 1988).

Hunter, Jack D. *The Blue Max*. London: Cassel Wellington House, 2004. Originally published by Frederick Muller, 1965.

Mayo, Mike. *VideoHound's War Movies: Classic Conflict on Film*. Detroit, MI: Visible Ink Press, 1999.

Solomon, Aubrey. *Twentieth Century Fox: A Corporate and Financial History*. Scarecrow Filmmakers Series, No. 20. Lanham, MD: Scarecrow Press, 1989.

THE BOUNTY (1984)

DIRECTOR: Roger Donaldson
WRITER: Robert Bolt. Based on Richard Hough's *Captain Bligh and Mr. Christian*.
PRODUCERS: Dino De Laurentiis, Bernard Williams (Dino De Laurentiis Company, Bounty Productions)
CINEMATOGRAPHER: Arthur Ibbotson
EDITOR: Tony Lawson
MUSIC: Vangelis
CAST: William Bligh: Anthony Hopkins. Fletcher Christian: Mel Gibson. John Fryer: Daniel Day-Lewis. Admiral Hood: Laurence Olivier. Captain Greetham: Edward Fox. William Cole: Bernard Hill. Ned Young: Phil Davis. Charles Churchill: Liam Neeson. King Tynah: Wi Kuki Kaa. Mauatua (Maimiti): Tevaite Vernette. John Adams: Philip Martin Brown. Botanist David Nelso: Simon Chandler. Matthew Quintal: Neil Morrissey. Thomas Ellison: Dexter Fletcher
AA: None
AAN: None
DVD: MGM, 2000
BLU-RAY: Currently unavailable
DURATION: 132 minutes

Twentieth-century audiences had known the story of the *Bounty* mutiny mainly from the novels by Charles Nordhoff and James Norman Hall, on which the 1935 and 1962 versions (both titled *Mutiny on the Bounty*) are based. But *The Bounty*, the third major movie on the subject, drew its materials from Richard Hough's 1972 history-based book *Captain Bligh and Mr. Christian*, which is partly aimed at restoring the reputation of Captain William Bligh, portrayed as a villain in the fictional accounts given in the two previous epics. The intent was to make a narrative consistent with history, although some fictional elements crept in, as we shall see. It could be of interest to mention that David Lean, while living in the South Pacific in the 1970s, attempted to remake the story along the lines provided by the Hough book, mainly to attempt to "rescue him [Bligh] from his Hollywood image as a flogger and a bully."[1] But Lean's project, which would have come in two parts, *The Lawbreakers*, recounting the story of the mutiny, and *The Long Arm*, detailing the search for the mutineers and Bligh's navigational feat to reach the East Indies, fell through, mainly due to the lack of financing and screenwriter Robert Bolt's withdrawal due to illness. Dino De Laurentiis, who had already invested a considerable amount of resources to construct a replica of *The Bounty*, revived the project with a new director, since Lean was doing *A Passage to India* by this time. Bolt, who was recovering from a stroke, also penned the new script, and Anthony Hopkins, Lean's own choice to play Bligh, was assigned the principal role in the new epic. Mel Gibson, at this time on the threshold of becoming a superstar after his triumphs in *Gallipoli* (1981) and *The Year of Living Dangerously* (1983), both directed by Peter Weir, was given the role of Fletcher Christian.

The 1984 *The Bounty* presented the two principal characters in an entirely different light. To begin with, Bligh and Christian knew one another and were already friends before they sailed together, and Bligh actually promoted Christian to be his sailing master over John Fryer (Daniel Day-Lewis), who had held this position, soon after the storm at Cape Horn, telling the Admiralty that the latter had shown himself incompetent and a coward.

In the first half of the movie, Bligh, as given by Hopkins, appears as a mild-mannered English gentleman, a captain who cares for his crew and who relies on Christian to keep the disgruntled and brawling crew members in line. The film begins at the end, with Bligh's appearance before the Admiralty, where he is being court-martialed for having lost the *Bounty* and is defending himself while giving his account of the mutiny. The rest of the story is told in flashbacks, as the action is occasionally broken to return to the questioning board. Bligh's voice-over commentary is heard, but only sparingly, to help the flow of the narrative.

During the first part of the trip, the purpose of which is the same as in the fictional accounts, to procure roots of the breadfruit in Tahiti to transport to Jamaica as food of the slave population, Bligh appears to be in tune with both the crew and his fellow officers, and none of the cruel floggings and other atrocities seen in the previous movies occur. The ship fails to negotiate Cape Horn and has to change route and go around the African Cape of Good Hope, thence bypassing Australia (New Holland, as it was called then), and then sail into the South Pacific and eventually reach Tahiti, after a considerable delay. At the trial, Bligh is reprimanded by Captain Greetham (Edward Fox) for having lost a month, traveling only eighty-one miles in the storm.

The trouble begins in Tahiti. As Bligh tells the court, his crew, deprived of their domestic comforts for so long, had easily succumbed to the seductive environment of the tropical island, the climate, easy life, short labor, and scores of bare-breasted women who welcomed them and had no scruples sleeping with them. Bligh attributes Christian's change to his loss of moral fiber, and thus his authority and dignity as an officer of the Royal Navy. Inevitably, discipline is slackened, and when the return trip resumes, Bligh, angered by the filth and disorder of a neglected ship, reprimands the crew, which has been softened by the easy life of the tropics. But in trying to restore order and discipline on board his ship, he turns into a tyrant, resembling the Bligh of the two previous movies, flogging three men who had attempted to escape and blaming Christian for the laxity and disorder among his men. Resentment begins to boil, and when Bligh indicates that he will again go around Cape Horn in his return route, gaining fame as one who has circumnavigated the globe, the men rebel. This, by the way, is historically inaccurate, since Bligh intended to go back around South Africa, reach Jamaica, and head to England.

Friction develops, and a wild brawl breaks out, a brawl not initiated by Christian, who almost reluctantly takes the leading role, mostly to avoid slaughter on board the ship. After the ship has been taken over, Captain Bligh and those loyal to him in the crew are lowered into the longboat, with barely enough provisions to reach a neighboring island. The movie never shows the

Pandora (in actuality helmed by Captain Edward Edwards, not Bligh) returning to Tahiti. It only shows Bligh's incredibly arduous sea adventure, during which his courage, compassion, and navigational skills are fully displayed, and he and his companions, with only one loss, reach Coupang, on the island of Timor in the Dutch East Indies, and then return to England.

Meanwhile, Christian and the mutineers return to Tahiti, where they are dismissed by a now hostile King Tynah (Wi Kuki Kaa), who fears reprisals from the king and his British Navy. Christian and a few men and women, including his loyal wife, Mauatua (Tevaite Vernette) (Maimiti of the previous versions), sail for an unknown destination, under the threat of a new mutiny by his men, who insist on returning to Tahiti. Christian holds on to his post until they discover Pitcairn Island, mapped on the wrong longitude, thence untraceable by the British Navy, where the mutineers take refuge. The final scenes show the *Bounty* burning, and the few exiles are doomed never to return home. In England, the trial ends with Bligh's honorable acquittal of any guilt and great praise for his gallant return and navigational skills.

The movie was filmed in Moorea, French Polynesia; New Zealand; and London. *The Bounty* offers good all-around acting, excellent photography, and good action scenes, including a spectacular storm sequence. What it lacks, in comparison to its two predecessors, is a consistent dramatic tension between the two main characters—Bligh and Christian. Hopkins at first seems too benign a character to evoke the hatred of the crew, lacking Trevor Howard's sangfroid and Charles Laughton's malice. Following the departure of the *Bounty* from Tahiti, Bligh becomes hysterically irrational, losing his cool when he discovers that some of his coconuts have been pilfered. Incidentally, Fryer, his former sailing master, stays out of the fray, but his icy contempt for the laxity of Christian is shown in his self-satisfied looks. Day-Lewis makes this character even more hateful than Bligh's. As for Gibson, he seems more like a lovelorn youth than a staunch naturalist with a decided look of conviction for his disobedience. He lacks Clark Gable's bravura masculinity and Marlon Brando's mastery of withheld rage.

Moreover, in the most dramatic scene in the story—the mutiny itself—what is shown is a chaotic melee that lacks the aura of inevitability of a clash between villain and hero, which is trumpeted in the other movies from the moment these characters set foot on the ship. Thus, the audience is held at a distance, uninvolved emotionally, despite some heartbreaking scenes—one of which is Christian's girl slashing her head in sorrow when her lover departs. The movie is a good spectacle, mostly loyal to history, but it lacks the dramatic tensions and heartbreaking and tragic resolutions of the previous two. CS

Note

1. Kevin Brownlow, *David Lean: A Biography* (New York: A Wyatt Book for St. Martin's Press, 1996), 601.

Bibliography

Brownlow, Kevin. *David Lean: A Biography*. New York: A Wyatt Book for St. Martin's Press, 1996.
Hough, Richard. *Captain Bligh and Mr. Christian*. London: Hutchinson, 1972.

BRAVEHEART (1995)

Director: Mel Gibson
Writer: Randall Wallace
Producers: Mel Gibson, Alan Ladd Jr., Bruce Davey (20th Century Fox, Icon Productions, Ladd Company)
Cinematographer: John Toll
Editor: Steven Rosenblum
Art Direction: Ken Court, Nathan Crowley, Daniel T. Dorrance, John Lucas, Ned McLoughlin
Costumes: Charles Knode
Music: James Horner
Sound Mixers: Andy Nelson, Scott Millan, Anna Behlmer, Brian Simmons

SPECIAL EFFECTS: Lon Bender, Per Hallberg

MAKEUP ARTISTS: Peter Frampton, Paul Pattison, Lois Burwell

CAST: William Wallace: Mel Gibson. Princess Isabelle: Sophie Marceau. King Edward I (Longshanks): Patrick McGoohan. Murron: Catherine McCormack. Robert the Bruce: Angus McFadyen. Hamish: Brendan Gleeson. Stephen: David O'Hara. The Leper: Ian Bannen. Campbell: James Cosmo. Young William Wallace: James Robinson. Malcolm Wallace: Sean Lawlor. John Wallace: Sandy Nelson. MacClannough: Sean McGinley. Elder Stewart: Alan Tall. Young Hamish: Andrew Weir. Mother MacClannough: Gerda Stevenson. Young Murron: Mhairi Calvey. Argyle Wallace: Brian Cox. Prince Edward: Peter Hanly. Phillip: Stephen Billington. Craig: John Kavanagh. Mornay: Alun Armstrong. Morrison: Tommy Flanagan. Mrs. Morrison: Julie Austin. Bride's Father: Alex Norton. Lord Bottoms: Rupert Vansittart. Smythe: Michael Byrne. MacGregor: Tam White. Stewart: Donal Gibson. Nicolette: Jeanne Marine. Lord Dolecroft: Martin Dunne. Faudron: Jimmy Chisholm. Lochlan: John Murtagh. Young Soldier: David McKay. Veteran: Peter Mullan. Lord Talmadge: Martin Murphy. Cheltham: Gerard McSorley. Balliol: Bernard Horsfall. Governor of York: Richard Leaf. York Captain: Daniel Coll as Daniel Coli. English General: Niall O'Brien. Sean: Liam Carney. Villager: Bill Murdoch. Farmer: Phil Kelly. Chief Assassin: Joe Savino. Royal Magistrate: David Gant. Jailor: Mal Whyte. English Commander: Paul Tucker

AA: Best Cinematography (John Toll), Best Director (Mel Gibson), Best Effects–Sound Effects Editing (Lon Bender, Per Hallberg), Best Makeup (Peter Frampton, Paul Pattison, Lois Burwell), Best Picture (Mel Gibson, Alan Ladd Jr., Bruce Davey)

AAN: Best Costume Design (Charles Knode), Best Film Editing (Steven Rosenblum), Best Music–Original Dramatic Score (James Horner), Best Sound (Andy Nelson, Scott Millan, Anna Behlmer, Brian Simmons), Best Writing–Screenplay Written Directly for the Screen (Randall Wallace)

DVD: Twentieth Century Fox, 2001

BLU-RAY: Paramount Pictures, 2009

DURATION: DVD, 171 minutes; Blu-ray, 178 minutes

Mel Gibson won Best Director and Best Picture Oscars for the epic historical drama *Braveheart*, which chronicles the life of Scottish hero William Wallace, who fought for independence from the occupying English forces in the thirteenth century. Made for $72 million, bringing in more than $210 million worldwide at the box office, and nominated for ten Oscars (including five wins), the film made everyone proud to have even the most remote Scottish heritage in Wallace's universally appealing call for "Freedom!"

The film begins in A.D. 1200, when the king of Scotland dies without an heir. England's King Edward I (known as Longshanks, Patrick McGoohan under a prosthetic nose) claims the throne for himself but convenes a meeting of truce with the Scottish nobles who oppose him, only to slay them all. Witnessing the aftermath is commoner landowner Malcolm Wallace (Sean Lawlor), along with his sons, John (Sandy Nelson) and the young William (James Robinson). Malcolm is killed in a thwarted revenge uprising, and at his funeral, a young girl comforts the orphaned William by presenting him with a thistle flower. Wallace departs to be raised with his uncle Argyle (Brian Cox).

"Many years later," Longshanks marries off his son Edward (Peter Hanly) to Princess Isabelle (Sophie Marceau) of France, but Edward is only interested in his lover Phillip (Stephen Billington), who Longshanks will later unceremoniously push out a window to his death. Leering at his new daughter-in-law, Longshanks decides to solve his problems in Scotland by luring nobles with the promise of *primae noctis*, first night with any common girl on the day of her wedding (although there is no historical evidence of this). The adult William Wallace (Mel Gibson) returns home on the occasion of such a bittersweet wedding, reuniting with his childhood friend Hamish (Brendan Gleeson) and flirting with the girl who gave him the thistle so many years ago, Murron (Catherine McCormack).

The pair marry in secret to avoid the brutal law, and Wallace dreams of a simple, and peaceful, family life, but when an English soldier tries to rape Murron, Wallace finds himself in a fight with the English garrison, and Murron is killed. Wallace and his fellow villagers slay their English oppressors, and as other Scots join them, they move on to take Lanark. Robert, the 17th Earl of Bruce (Angus McFadyen) and the best contender to the Scottish throne, also wants to follow Wallace, but he is dissuaded by his duplicitous, leper father.

A slightly crazed Irishman called Stephen (David O'Hara) saves Wallace from an assassination attempt as tales of Wallace's heroic deeds spread among the common folk. And so it is only at Wallace's behest that the Scots rally at the Battle of Stirling (but without the actual bridge that was central to the real battle). Even the nobles Craig (John Kavanagh), Lochlan (John Murtagh), and Mornay (Alun Armstrong) are impressed by his tactics, pretending to depart as if they are abandoning the battle, only to return and outflank the British. After Wallace is knighted, he goes on to sack York.

At the Battle of Falkirk, Longshanks sends Irish infantry against the Scots, but they instead greet their Celtic brethren and join the fight against the English. The English cavalry is cut off when the Scots archers light tar behind them, but this time the nobles do indeed depart, having been paid off by Longshanks, and the battle is lost. Robert the Bruce is revealed as Longshanks' knight at Falkirk (it is unlikely that he was in fact there[1]), but upon seeing Wallace's stricken face, he helps get him on Phillip's horse to safety. Wallace recovers to slay Lochlan and Mornay in their homes.

The romanticized tales of Wallace's continuing guerilla war reach Princess Isabelle, who, deprived of the love of her husband, feels compelled to warn Wallace on two occasions of Longshanks' plans against him. The pair finally meet and spend a night together, supposedly conceiving Edward III (which, alas, is impossible given that Isabelle was just a child at the time and did not marry Edward II until after Wallace's death).

Robert the Bruce sends word to Wallace for them to meet and unite at Edinburgh, but the other nobles have arranged an ambush without his knowledge. Wallace is publically tortured and executed as Longshanks lies on his deathbed (in reality, Edward died two years after Wallace, but in narrative terms it is more satisfying for the audience to be assured of the villain's death here).

Jumping ahead to 1314, at Bannockburn, Robert the Bruce decides not to have his accession to the Scottish throne endorsed by King Edward II. Rather, he turns to his fellow Scots and declares, "You have bled with Wallace. Now bleed with me!" The film ends as his troops charge against the surprised English, and we are told that despite being outnumbered, they won their freedom.

Screenwriter Randall Wallace notes that the "actual facts of William Wallace's life as established by historians are miniscule."[2] Gibson continues, saying, "But luckily there's also a lot of legend that surrounds the character."[3] Timelines are compressed, rearranged, and simplified—the Scottish succession was much more complicated in this era—and characters combined and invented.[4] And yet the contested nature of history is acknowledged at the beginning of the film, when our unknown narrator (later revealed to be Robert the Bruce, future king of Scotland) proclaims, "I shall tell you the story of William Wallace. Historians from England will say I am a liar. But history is written by those who have hanged heroes." The film also makes a point of how heroes become larger than life, embellished by folk culture as stories are passed on by word of mouth. At the Battle of Stirling, when a disbelieving Scot doubts Wallace's identity, given that he is supposed to be seven feet tall, Wallace retorts, "Yes, I've heard. Kills men by the hundred. And if he were here, he'd consume the English with fireballs from his eyes, and bolts of lightning from his ass." This exchange partly acknowledges that in some cases (but certainly not all), it is difficult to separate fact from fiction for a figure like Wallace, but it is also a tongue-in-cheek reference to the fact that Gibson is considerably shorter than Wallace was said to have been.

All of this was not enough to satisfy the many historians who have criticized the film, or make any difference to the audience and critics who adore its old-fashioned epic spectacle delivered with contemporary effects. Caryn James of the *New York Times* exclaims that the film was "one of the most spectacular entertainments in years," writing, "In vast, perfectly orchestrated scenes, the English send hundreds of arrows raining on the Scots. They in turn charge at the English carrying pointed wooden poles, the better to impale them. Heads are bashed in; swords are run through bodies."[5]

In making *Braveheart*, Gibson says he was inspired by the older epic film tradition, and *Spartacus* (Stanley Kubrick, 1960) in particular,[6] echoing the fight against an oppressive empire and the Christian imagery of its sacrificial heroism.

In 2006, Gibson had a disastrous fall from grace as the result of drunken anti-Semitic remarks made upon his arrest for drunk driving, and he has struggled to resurrect his career ever since. This has also tended to taint his back catalogue, and certainly with its anti-English diatribe, *Braveheart* has been accused of a xenophobic mind-set.

For all its shortcomings, *Braveheart* nonetheless exemplifies Hollywood epic filmmaking methods for building a heroic narrative at its best, and quite extraordinary for a directing novice (despite his acting experience, Gibson had previously only directed the 1993 *The Man Without a Face*). Although he was criticized for using Irish bagpipes rather than Scottish ones, the score by James Horner (who also wrote for Ron Howard's *Apollo 13* in the same year, and who would go on to win two Oscars for James Cameron's 1997 *Titanic*) became a best-selling and perennial favorite. DB

Notes

1. Andrew Fisher, *William Wallace* (Edinburgh, Scotland: John Donald Publishers, 1986), 82, by far the best biography of Wallace, which is still readily available in a 2007 edition.
2. "Mel Gibson's *Braveheart*: A Filmmaker's Passion," *Braveheart*, directed by Mel Gibson (Twentieth Century Fox, 2001), DVD.
3. "Mel Gibson's *Braveheart*."
4. For excellent detailed discussion of the historical diversions made in the film, some of which completely contradict the sources, while others may be seen as "true invention," in other words, not directly contravened by the sources and in a general sense true to the period, see Colin McArthur, "'That's Show Business!' The 'What' and 'Why' of *Braveheart*'s Historical Distortions," in *Brigadoon, Braveheart, and the Scots* (London and New York: I. B. Tauris, 2003), 178–91. See also Arthur Lindley, "The Ahistoricism of Medieval Film," *Screening the Past* 3, 29 May 1998, www.latrobe.edu.au/screeningthepast/firstrelease/fir598/ALfr3a.htm (12 January 2013).

5. Caryn James, "Film Review: *Braveheart*; The Splashy Epic Finds New Life in the 13th Century," *New York Times*, 24 May 1995, www.nytimes.com/1995/05/24/movies/film-review-braveheart-the-splashy-epic-finds-new-life-in-the-13th-century.html (12 January 2013).

6. "Mel Gibson's *Braveheart*."

Bibliography

Fisher, Andrew. *William Wallace*. Edinburgh, Scotland: John Donald Publishers, 1986.

James, Caryn. "Film Review: *Braveheart*; The Splashy Epic Finds New Life in the 13th Century." *New York Times*, 24 May 1995, www.nytimes.com/1995/05/24/movies/film-review-braveheart-the-splashy-epic-finds-new-life-in-the-13th-century.html (12 January 2013).

Lindley, Arthur. "The Ahistoricism of Medieval Film." *Screening the Past* 3, 29 May 1998, www.latrobe.edu.au/screeningthepast/firstrelease/fir598/ALfr3a.htm (12 January 2013).

McArthur, Colin. "'That's Show Business!' The 'What' and 'Why' of *Braveheart*'s Historical Distortions." In *Brigadoon, Braveheart, and the Scots*, 178–91. London and New York: I. B. Tauris, 2003.

THE BRIDGE ON THE RIVER KWAI (1957)

DIRECTOR: David Lean

WRITERS: Carl Foreman, Michael Wilson (with uncredited contributions by David Lean). Pierre Boulle, author of *The Bridge Over the River Kwai*, the novel on which the film is based, was credited in the Oscar ceremonies.

PRODUCER: Sam Spiegel (Horizon/Columbia Pictures)

ASSISTANT DIRECTORS: Gus Agosti, Ted Sturgis

CINEMATOGRAPHER: Jack Hildyard

EDITOR: Peter Taylor

ART DIRECTION: Donald M. Ashton

TECHNICAL ADVISOR: Major General L. E. M. Perowne

MUSIC: Malcolm Arnold

SOUND EDITOR: Winston Ryder

PROPERTY MASTER: Eddie Fowlie

CAST: Col. Nicholson: Alec Guinness. Shears: William Holden. Maj. Warden: Jack Hawkins. Col. Saito: Sessue Hayakawa: Maj. Clipton: James Donald. Lt. Joyce: Geoffrey Horne. Col. Green: Andre Morell. Capt. Reeves: Peter Williams. Maj. Hughes: John Boxer. Grogan: Percy Herbert. Baker: Harold Goodwin. Nurse: Ann Sears. Capt. Kanematsu: Henry Okawa. Lt. Miura: Keiichiro Katsumoto. Yai: M. R. B. Chakrabandhu. Siamese Girls: Vilaiwan Seeboonreaung, Ngamta Suphaphongs, Javanart Punynchoti, Kannikar Dowklee

AA: Best Director (David Lean), Best Picture (Sam Spiegel), Best Actor (Alec Guinness), Best Writing–Screenplay Based on Material from Another Medium (Pierre Boulle, Carl Foreman, Michael Wilson), Best Cinematography (Jack Hildyard), Best Music Score (Malcolm Arnold), Best Film Editing (Peter Taylor)

AAN: Best Supporting Actor (Sessue Hayakawa)

DVD: Columbia Pictures, 2000

BLU-RAY: Columbia Pictures, 2010. Collector's edition.

DURATION: 165 minutes

The Bridge on the River Kwai is the first of five epics made by David Lean, and in one particular way it is different from any of those that followed. In 1955, despite the success of *Summertime*,[1] Lean was low in funds, and it was on the strength of Katharine Hepburn's recommendation to Sam Spiegel that he was offered the job of directing an epic, a form he had never tried before. Lean accepted the assignment, entering a challenging but unknown territory, an undertaking that would involve unforeseen difficulties but that would eventually catapult him to international fame and an Oscar for Best Director. When Hepburn introduced Lean to him, Spiegel had already obtained the rights of Pierre Boulle's novel *The Bridge Over the River Kwai* (*Ponte de la rivière Kwai*) and assigned the writing of the script to Carl Foreman, then blacklisted and living in England and writing under a pseudonym.

Spiegel subsequently submitted Foreman's draft to Lean, already in Ceylon, but when Lean found it objectionable, Spiegel sent another screenwriter, Calder Willingham, whose work Lean thought even less acceptable than Foreman's.[2] Finally, Michael Wilson arrived in Ceylon, and he and Lean worked smoothly together to fashion the final script. Although much of Foreman's original work survives, it was Wilson's work that gave shape to the character of the American Shears, with Lean contributing ideas and dialogue to the final shooting script. The project took nearly a year to finish, and it came to the brink of collapse several times, but in the end, the result was a spectacular hit with critics and audiences.

The Bridge on the River Kwai is an epic whose themes and structure marked a turning point in the evolution of the epic form as defined by Hollywood standards. Hollywood productions, especially those of the 1950s, were sprawling spectacles, aiming to gain back the earlier glitter of Hollywood usurped by the advent of television in the late 1940s. *The Bridge on the River Kwai* marks a transition from those epics to the war/adventure stories that prevailed in the decade after World War II. Although placing more emphasis on nuanced performances than spectacle and action, *The Bridge on the River Kwai* contains enough war adventure elements to appeal to popular audiences. Filmed entirely on location in Sri Lanka (then Ceylon), in a lush tropical jungle, the film takes full advantage of its locale, thus avoiding the artificiality of the usual Hollywood epic sets and appearing more real. *The Bridge on the River Kwai* follows the same story line of Boulle's novel, on which it was based, with mostly the same characters, who act out of motives similar to those of the characters in the novel.

A group of British prisoners undertake to build a bridge that would connect a railway line from Bangkok to Rangoon, a link that would enable the Japanese to invade India. The Boulle novel is loosely based on history, for the Japanese did build bridges along 250 miles of this section of that railway, using hundreds of thousands of captured allied troops—American, Australian, Dutch, and British—forced to surrender after the capitulation of Singapore and the Dutch East Indies in 1942. The scene in the novel is set at one particular camp near the Burmese border, where a group of British prisoners, under Colonel Nicholson (Alec Guinness), are assigned the building of a major bridge over a stream, the Kwai River, to connect the two sections of the railway, one going south from Rangoon, the other north from Bangkok.

One of the most important differences between the film and the novel is found in the change of identity of one of the major characters, Shears (William Holden). While in the novel Shears is a cavalry officer transferred to Force 316 and the leader of the Commando group, in the film, Shears is an American, a mere sailor ("swab jockey, second class") posing as "Commander Shears," whose true identity is later revealed by Major Warden (Jack Hawkins). This arrangement caused a restructuring of the novel plot, for the American Shears is already in the Japanese camp when the British battalion arrives and is, in fact, preparing to escape. After an initial brush with Nicholson, who subscribes to Colonel Saito's (Sessue Hayakawa) slogan "We are an island in the jungle; escape is impossible" and forbids the formation of an "escape committee," Shears soon escapes on his own, accompanied by a British officer, Jennings, and Weaver, an Australian who had been a pal of Shears in the camp and had apparently known of his fake rank.[3] The last two are killed in the attempt, but Shears manages to reach a native village, and from there he sails down a river and into the ocean, where he is picked up by a British rescue plane. We next see him at Mount-Ravinia Hospital in Ceylon, cavorting with a nurse on the beach, unaware that his true identity is known by the British authorities there and that he is soon to be assigned a role in Force 316, whose mission is to destroy the same bridge, now under way, being built by Nicholson and his troops.

Thus, the film plot has an additional twist to deal with, as Shears's escape is documented in brief nondialogue crosscutting, while the Nicholson–Saito feud is going on. The addition of Shears as an American also adds ironic twists, as Shears has a different take on the war effort as a whole. Although he does not know that Nicholson is willingly building the bridge as a monument to British efficiency, Shears does discern similarities between Nicholson and Major Warden (Captain Warden in the book[4]), under whom he serves in his new expedition. The film Shears sees that both men are unbending disciplinarians, both expecting absolute obedience, and both are ready to sacrifice their lives for the cause they believe in.

A few other differences between the novel and film might also be worth mentioning. While in Boulle's novel all the characters are male, Lean adds several native women who are used as "bearers," replacing native males that the Japanese had conscripted in the village where Warden and his group landed. In the film, a guide called Yai (M. R. B. Chakrabandhu) is going to take them to the bridge after an arduous and lengthy trek through the jungle. Yai is the fourth man, as the Warden group lost one of its men, Chapman (not in the novel) who parachuted into a tree. The film presents the same characters as having the same mind-set, two in particular, Nicholson and Warden, whom the American Shears compares when the latter, wounded, asks to remain behind, as he explodes with, "You are like that Colonel Nicholson, crazy with courage, how to die like gentlemen, for what?"

The American Shears in the film is both cynical and pragmatic, having lost faith in the war effort, as his chores as a graveyard man show him proof of its futility. He sees escape as the only alternative to certain death in the prisoners' camp. His sarcastic remarks about a dead man he is burying ("What did he die for?") and his echoing of Saito's "Be happy in your work"[5] show him to be utterly lacking in loyalty to principle, or even of patriotism—at least at first. But the addition of the early opening scenes with Shears allows the action in the film to get into the heart of the matter quickly and move rapidly toward a resolution.

Colonel Saito, the commander of the Japanese camp (Camp #16), seems to have encountered some difficulties in completing his assignment, mainly due to lack of men and equipment; therefore, he is in a hurry to get his project started, and he counts heavily on a new group of British prisoners who arrive marching through the jungle,[6] led by their indomitable commander, Colonel Nicholson. The main conflict arises by the clash of the personalities of these two men. Saito, hard-driving and anxious to finish his job, orders the men/prisoners to work on the project, including their officers. Nicholson, a stickler for military etiquette, even in the middle of a jungle, resists having his officers do manual labor and refuses to obey, citing the regulations of the Geneva Convention regarding prisoners of war. As a consequence, he and his officers are shut in the camp's punishment huts. Nicholson obdurately refuses to succumb to Saito's threats and rejects the latter's attempts to cajole him by offering him a dinner, and the building of the bridge comes to a halt. After a month of delays, Saito desperately gives in and frees Nicholson and exempts his officers from manual duty. Under Nicholson, the British build the bridge, proud to have won the "battle" with the Japanese.

As Nicholson clashes with Saito, a second story line simultaneously develops with the escape of Shears, whose story is briefly documented without dialogue, as the Saito–Nicholson feud goes on. Shears is eventually rescued by a British search party; his true identity is revealed in a lengthy scene between him and Major Warden, the leader of the commando group; and he is assigned a role in the expedition to blow up the bridge. This group includes two other officers, Joyce (Geoffrey Horne), a Canadian, and Chapman, another British officer, along with Shears and Warden himself. Warden, a former professor of linguistics turned demolitions expert, knows well that Shears comes under compulsion after his fake identity has been exposed, but he and Colonel Green (Andre Morell), his ranking officer, consider his presence essential since Shears had escaped from the same camp they are trying to reach. ("You don't realize what a plum you are for us," Green says to Shears.) The plot is now focused on the activities of this group, with crosscuttings into the Nicholson group back at the camp busy building the bridge.

The commando group is flown to Indochina and parachuted into a clearing, where they are joined by a Siamese guide and several women, who undertake to carry supplies and equipment to the campsite through a thick jungle. After much adversity, which includes a skirmish with a Japanese group, Warden is wounded, but they arrive at the camp on time and prepare to blow up the bridge the next morning when a Japanese train carrying a VIP will be crossing it. Tension builds as the two strands of the plot merge, and the two separate activities begin to integrate. The (first-time) viewer wonders which group is going to win out but also vacillates as to which side to root for: a loyal group of commandos that has made a valiant effort on a key war operation, or Nicholson, who inspired his troops to work for a "cause," telling them that building the bridge "in the middle of the jungle" was a victory against tremendous odds.

As the plot spins its twin yarn, the characters in question undergo intense scrutiny by Jack Hildyard's deft camerawork, which reveals as much about their inner struggles as the rather sparse dialogue (more or less, for some, like Saito, deliver laborious orations) that punctuates their adventure. The four major characters—Nicholson, Saito, Warden, and Shears—as is usual in many Lean epics,[7] are paired, acting either in unison for a common course or in antagonism, or simply because of cultural isolation. Here, the Saito–Nicholson feud has its dimensions, while the duo of Shears and Warden drive for a common cause, although this relationship is marred by antithetical personalities. The conflict between Saito and Nicholson is a clash of personalities, as well as two cultures: the proud Saito sees honor (Bushido) in victory and feels that his enemy should be humiliated and dishonored in defeat; the stubborn Nicholson is intent on showing his Western superiority over the inefficient and blundering (if not barbaric[8]) Easterner. Yet, many have found their personalities complementary, as both are unbending, brutal (in their specific ways) in driving the men under them to extremes, and loyal to what they believe is their cause.

A most potent irony of the movie is built on this relationship, as both switch sides, Nicholson building the bridge with Saito aiding him. Their personalities actually become the main forces that propel the plot to its tragic conclusion. Ironies are also built into the Shears–Warden relationship, as when Shears kicks the broken radio in disgust, but producing the opposite effect: the radio comes to life and starts transmitting, and the group learns that a train will be passing the same day the bridge is finished. This information causes them to accelerate their pace, something that has unforeseen consequences, and unexpected results. Such utterances as, "There's always the unexpected," by Warden, become motifs—one of many—giving added depth to both character and theme. What Warden says happens, but it is the reluctant Shears who becomes the unwitting agent for such change, and for another plot twist.

The ending of *The Bridge on the River Kwai* has provoked questions pertaining to whether it is merely an antiwar movie or one with thematic overtones about the futility of human effort. A group of prisoners of war expend all their energies to build a bridge under false pretenses, as their leader tells them that their work was an honorable goal achieved "in the face of great adversity." On the other hand, the movie also describes the efforts of another group of men dedicated to a patriotic mission—to destroy a work that might enable the enemy to win a war against their own country. After the bridge is blown up—ironically by the man who built it—viewers are left with a puzzle in their hands: Who are they to root for? The man who built it, a dreamer of sorts who wants to prove the superiority of his race, or his compatriots, equally heroic, if not more so, who came there to do their duty, which is to defeat all works built by the enemy? The ironies found in the conduct of everyone involved do not eliminate the puzzle, which is further complicated by the last shots of the movie—Clipton's (James Donald) final utterance, "Madness, madness," and the sight of a hawk (as in the beginning of the movie) that flies surveying the ruins of human effort, an image that might also suggest that there is no rhyme or reason in human endeavor. No matter how heroic—all is for nothing. The ambiguities of the ending beg the question, What does this all mean?

Answers concerning interpretation will vary, but in this case, they might also show the thematic richness of this movie. As the tale is spun, one might trace the development of each character, as well as the relationships that develop in the conflicts between them. The conflicts that arise are between antithetical characters within the same group, or certain characters in different groups with irreconcilable goals between them. The first would be Saito versus Nicholson and Shears versus Warden; the second would be Shears versus Nicholson. And the third is Joyce, who is in conflict with himself, unable to answer any warrior's moral quandary: Is not the killing of an enemy just another name for murder? Since a great deal has already been said about these characters, a few points about the relationships between these men will suffice.

Let's momentarily return to Nicholson, who is the focal point of this epic film, and whose initial harsh encounter with Saito develops into a cold tolerance of each of these men toward the other, but it ends with an unexpected note of reconciliation. After a contentious first half, when Nicholson wins the battle of wills, Saito falls out of the action, occasionally seen in brief shots, either standing on a height surveying the progress of the bridge or looking at the prisoners at work through his binoculars. He seems like a nonentity who has accepted defeat, but not entirely fallen out of sight. But Saito is seen sauntering to the same spot where Nicholson stands on the bridge, admiring his work. The two men have been at odds during this torturous exercise, both having contributed to its construction for entirely different reasons. They are quite conscious that they are still mortal enemies. Both, however, are proud of the work that was accomplished under their leadership—even if Saito has been reduced to a passive figure, he still gave his full support to the endeavor.

At this point, Nicholson, leaning against the bridge railing, over the water, looking away from Saito and still holding his swagger stick (albeit a substitute tree twig), opens his mind to his enemy. He has been in the service for twenty-six years, but what has his life amounted to? Has it been worthwhile? Is he going to leave anything behind, or has his life "not made any difference at all"? As he concludes such existential reflections, he turns and drops his swagger stick, which splashes into the water underneath. Is it a reminder that his work is finished, the emblem of his power gone, and that once more he is a prisoner to the Japanese? Or has the memory of his achievement continued to bolster him? To Nicholson, the bridge has become an emblem of his presence on earth and his chance to escape, and all-human thought that his presence on earth has been for nothing. Deluded, he envisions a work that will survive for hundreds of years, and his delusion has transcended military obligations, even the war itself. What does it matter that the Japanese are fighting the British, or the Americans? His bridge is a poem, "Beautiful!" as Saito ecstatically exclaims (but looking at the sunset), meaningful in itself, containing its own reason for being. There is no other reason. For a moment, the bridge unites the two men in a special bond, otherwise impossible in the context of the cruel war.

Notes

1. *Summer Madness* was the title used in England.
2. Howard Maxford, *David Lean* (London: B. T. Batsford, 2000), 231.
3. "Are you going to tell him the truth, commander?" he asks Shears sarcastically as soon as Nicholson has arrived, and to the latter's negative response, he says, "You are neither an officer nor a gentleman," a statement that drops a casual hint of what is going to be revealed to the viewer later.
4. Erroneously referred to as "Major Warden" by Phillips. See Gene D. Phillips, *Beyond the Epic: The Life and Films of David Lean* (Lexington: University of Kentucky Press, 2006), 228.
5. In the Boulle novel, these words are first spoken to the troops by General Yamashita (p. 14), and then repeated by Saito in the camp. In the film, Saito uses the phrase twice, and Shears repeats it sardonically as he sees Joyce flirting with one of the Siamese girls during the jungle march.
6. They marched in whistling an uplifting martial tune, "Colonel Bogey," which became popular with audiences throughout the world.
7. Lawrence and Ali in *Lawrence of Arabia*, Father Collins and Michael in *Ryan's Daughter*, and Mrs. Moore and Fielding in *A Passage to India* are other examples.
8. As pointed out, this word is deliberately obscured by other sounds in the DVD editions of the film.

Bibliography

Boulle, Pierre. *The Bridge Over the River Kwai*. New York: Presidio Press, 2007.

Brownlow, Kevin. *David Lean: A Biography*. New York: A Wyatt Book for St. Martin's Press, 1996.

Maxford, Howard. *David Lean*. London: B.T. Batsford, 2000.

Phillips, Gene D. *Beyond the Epic: The Life and Films of David Lean*. Lexington: University of Kentucky Press, 2006.

THE BROTHERS KARAMAZOV (1958)

Director: Richard Brooks
Writers: Julius J. Epstein, Philip G. Epstein, Richard Brooks. Based on the novel by Fyodor Dostoyevsky.
Producer: Pandro S. Berman (Avon Productions, MGM)
Cinematographer: John Alton
Editor: John D. Donning
Music: Bronislau Kaper
Cast: Dimitri Karamazov: Yul Brynner. Grushenka: Maria Schell. Katerina Ivanovna: Claire Bloom. Fyodor Karamazov: Lee J. Cobb. Ivan Karamazov: Richard Basehart. Alyosha Karamazov: William Shatner. Smerdyakov: Albert Salmi. Grigory: Edgar Stehli. Capt. Snegiryov: David Opatoshu. Ilyusha Snegiryov: Miko Oscard. Capt. Vrublevski: Frank DeKova. Father Zossima: William Vedder (uncredited)
AA: None
AAN: Best Supporting Actor (Lee J. Cobb)
DVD: Warner Bros., 2012
Blu-ray: Currently unavailable
Duration: 145 minutes

Richards Brooks directed *The Brothers Karamazov* while still under contract for MGM, for whom he made some top films, including *Blackboard Jungle* in 1955 and *Cat on a Thin Hot Roof* in 1958, the same year as *The Brothers Karamazov*. The latter did not enjoy the success of the two aforementioned films, but it is still a gritty, well-made film, based on Fyodor Dostoyevsky's great novel, with a scenario by Julius J. Epstein and Philip G. Epstein, two of the coauthors of the script for *Casablanca*. Indeed, some have praised the screenplay,[1] but the film earned only one Oscar nomination[2] and has languished in obscurity, having failed to be revived as a classic in the DVD/Blu-ray era. But its cast features some of the most notable screen stars of that era, including a magnetic Yul Brynner as Dimitri Karamazov; Lee J. Cobb as the depraved and cunning Fyodor Karamazov, the father of the clan; William Shatner in his screen debut as Alyosha Karamazov (he became a star to later generations as Admiral James T. Kirk in the *Star Trek* TV series and film sequels); Maria Schell, an Austrian actress and bombshell of the times, as the seductress Grushenka; and Claire Bloom as Katerina Ivanovna, an aristocratic lady betrothed to Dimitri Karamazov. Richard Basehart is excellent as Ivan Karamazov, and Albert Salmi outstanding as the older Karamazov's bastard son, Smerdyakov. This gritty, fast-paced action movie offers strong performances by the entire ensemble cast, while a good musical score adds to the suspense of the mounting drama, which, from a certain point onward, becomes a "who-done-it" mystery, with a shocking discovery as to the identity of the real murderer.

Of necessity, the film version has been trimmed of the lengthy philosophical diatribes of Ivan Karamazov, which occupy large sections of the book. Almost from the start, one gets the impression that this is going to be Dimitri's story. It begins with Alyosha's arriving at his father's house, during a drunken orgy where the elderly Karamazov is seen cavorting with the blonde, seductive Grushenka, to ask his father for money for his brother Dimitri. After a fit of anger, Karamazov hands Alyosha 5,000 rubles, instead of the 10,000 Dimitri had requested, and Alyosha brings the money to Dimitri, who visits his betrothed Katerina Ivanovna, an aristocratic young lady whose family is impoverished, and hands her the money.

But a few weeks after that, Katerina visits Dimitri in prison, where he is being held for being unable to pay the damages he caused in a saloon brawl. Katerina, who has by now inherited a dowry of 80,000 rubles from her grandmother, returns the money to him. She will support Dimitri, if they marry, but he proudly refuses, saying he has money coming from his father, who has withheld his mother's inheritance from him. In a subsequent meeting with Dimitri, she entrusts him with 3,000 rubles, in a letter, to give to her father, but Dimitri, who meanwhile has met Grushenka and is drawn to her, spends most of the money, lavishing it on her in several wild parties and gambling sessions at her tavern, where she attracts wealthy patrons. Sparks fly between Grushenka and Dimitri, but Grushenka holds back, calculating that his rich father may also want her, or she could become the wife of Captain Vrublevski (Frank DeKova), a gambler who had seduced her years before and to whom she feels beholden. Dimitri, meanwhile, has put an end to his engagement to Katerina, madly in love with the voluptuous Grushenka, torn by jealousy when he discovers that she is also his father's mistress and that his father hoards his money to marry her, thus depriving his sons of their mother's inheritance.

When Ivan arrives on the scene, he is quite appalled by the family squabbles and disgusted by his father's greed, as well as his debauchery. Ivan, an intellectual who works for a Moscow newspaper and is financially independent, is seemingly above the pettiness of his surroundings, but when he meets Katerina, he instantly falls in love with her, but she responds halfheartedly, knowing she still loves Dimitri. Ivan also gains the attention of his half brother Smerdyakov, who lives in his father's house as a cook and lackey and is prone to fits of epilepsy. He has read Ivan's newspaper articles about atheism, morality, and especially his ideas of freedom, which to him mean that if God does not exist, there is no punishment in the afterlife, and one is free to commit any crime. Things come to a head when Dimitri, Ivan, Alyosha—and Smerdyakov—are visited by the holy man, the ascetic Zossima, who was invited to resolve their disputes, but Zossima refuses to offer a judgment and departs, after blessing Dimitri. When Ivan visits Katerina to tell her that he is leaving for Moscow, he discovers that Grushenka is there, but on false pretenses, for she tells those present that she has no intention of letting Dimitri go. Stunned, Katerina, who thought she had gained an ally, turns to Ivan, but he is baffled and disgusted by these intrigues and goes away speechless.

During a brawl, when all brothers are present, Dimitri, enraged, attempts to strangle his father and is ready to hit him with a candlestick, but the others hold him back. Before he lets him go, he says, "Next time I will kill him," a phrase that will haunt him later during his trial. When old Karamazov is found murdered, Dimitri is arrested and tried, and found guilty, mostly on the damning testimony given by Katerina. She tells the jury about a letter Dimitri had written while drunk, in which he says he intends to kill his father if he does not get his money. In truth, Dimitri had kept half of the money she had given him the first time around, and that is the money that was found on him when he was arrested. Despite his emotional plea in self-defense, he is found guilty and condemned to twenty years of hard labor. The main evidence is the weapon used—a pestle that Dimitri hit his servant Grigory (Edgar Stehli) with, and thought he had killed him, but the jury was told that this was the weapon used to kill Karamazov. The truth comes out later, in a meeting, when the astonished Ivan learns from Smerdyakov that he had faked an epileptic fit, that he let Dimitri believe that the old servant he had hit had died. But the servant was alive, and, instead, Fyodor Karamazov was found dead, hit with a poker by Smerdyakov. Ivan prompts Smerdyakov to tell the truth, but soon thereafter, Smerdyakov is found dead, hanged in the basement by his own hand. Ivan's testimony to the court is thought as a last attempt to save his brother. Dimitri is found guilty.

The film ends with an unexpected twist. With the help of Grushenka and Alyosha, Ivan stages an escape for Dimitri and provides him with the means to go away with Grushenka. The escape succeeds, but Dimitri first wants to stop at Captain Snegiryov's (David Opatoshu) home and beg his pardon, trying to ease the suffering of young Ilyusha (Miko Oscard), who is ill because of the shame his father had been subjected to. He tells the boy that he had avoided the duel, knowing his father was a crack shot in the army, and begs the boy's father to release him from commitment to fight. The boy smiles joyously, relieved from his shame, thinking his father could have killed Dimitri but didn't. After that, Dimitri and Grushenka get away.

The novel ends differently. While an escape of Dimitri and Grushenka is being planned, Dostoyevsky's last chapter describes the death of Ilyusha and Alyosha's bond with the boys of the neighborhood. One, Kolya, first influenced by Ivan's ideas of freedom, has now turned his sympathies to the ailing Ilyusha, and he and the other boys cheer at Alyosha—"Karamazov!"—after they return from the funeral. The film omits the following lengthy diatribes by or about Ivan: the entire chapter entitled "Rebellion," in which Ivan rejects God; the poem "The Grand Inquisitor," in which Jesus confronts a representative of the Spanish Inquisition, who tells him that his presence on earth is no longer needed; the Elder Zossima's reply to Ivan's atheistic dogmas; and Alyosha's influence on Grushenka, which leads to her reformation—only hinted in the movie.

The Brothers Karamazov is a film that has curiously been neglected and has sank into oblivion, despite the fact that it has some major stars in it, along with an excellent plot and great performances. Perhaps it is the awesome weight of the novel, widely considered a major fictional work, with strong religious overtones and exceptional character development, that has dragged the film down. This was not the first or the last time the novel was filmed, and not the first or last time that a famous literary work has failed to measure up to standards. Great novels, *Moby Dick*, *Ulysses*, *War and Peace*, to mention just a few, have rarely been given cinematic treatment worthy of their literary predecessors. Any film based on a lengthy and substantial novel must, of necessity, omit characters and curtail essential exposition details that make massive epic novels great works of art. Even epic films of great length—usually not having exceeded four hours—fail to overcome this obstacle. The gap seems to be widening in recent times, when epic-length films have rarely exceed two and a half hours. CS

Notes

1. Leonard Maltin in his various editions of his *Movie Guide*.
2. Actually, two, as Albert Salmi was also nominated for Best Supporting Actor but turned down his nomination.

Bibliography

Dostoyevsky, Fyodor. *The Brothers Karamazov*. Translated from Russian by Richard Peaver and Larissa Volokhonsky. New York: Farrar, Straus and Giroux, 1990.

C

CALIGULA (1979)

DIRECTOR: Tinto Brass. Additional scenes directed and photographed by Giancarlo Lui and Bob Guccione.

WRITER: Gore Vidal. Writers of additional scenes included Bob Guccione (uncredited) and Giancarlo Lui (uncredited). Dialogue of 1984 version by Franco Rossellini.

PRODUCER: Bob Guccione, Franco Rossellini (Penthouse Films International, Felix Cinematografica)

CINEMATOGRAPHER: Silvano Ippoliti

EDITOR: Nino Baragli. Editing of 1984 version by Enzo Micarelli.

ART DIRECTION: Danilo Donati

COSTUMES: Farani Veste

MUSIC: Paul Clemente

CAST: Caligula: Malcolm McDowell. Drusilla: Teresa Ann Savoy. Macro: Guido Mannari. Nerva: John Gielgud. Tiberius: Peter O'Toole. Claudius: Giancarlo Badessi. Gemellus: Bruno Brive. Ennia: Adriana Asti. Charicles: Leopoldo Trieste. Chaerea: Paolo Bonacelli. Longinus: John Steiner. Livia: Mirella Dangelo. Caesonia: Helen Mirren. Mnester: Richard Parets. Subura Singer: Paula Mitchell. Giant: Osiride Pevarello. Proculus: Donato Placido. Agrippina: Lori Wagner (uncredited)

AA: None

AAN: None

DVD: Image Entertainment, 2007

BLU-RAY: Image Entertainment, 2008

DURATION: 56 minutes (unrated version); 102 minutes (rated version); 153 minutes (alternative version); 124 minutes (1984, *Io, Caligula*)

Caligula charts the adulthood of the Roman emperor Gaius Caesar Augustus Germanicaus, known as Caligula (A.D. 12–41), as he comes to power and abuses that power until his assassination brings his short life to an end. The rather messy production details indicate an equally messy production history, which is perhaps ultimately more entertaining than the film itself. *Caligula* was an attempt by *Penthouse* magazine founder Bob Guccione to make an explicit adult film within a feature film narrative with high production values. Guccione fell out with the original scriptwriter, Gore Vidal, who was cut out of the production and took Guccione to court to remove his name from the film's initial title, *Gore Vidal's Caligula.* Guccione was also at odds with his initial director, Tinto Brass. Brass had intended to significantly contribute to the film's editing process, but Guccione absconded with the film even after an Italian court found in Brass's favor.

Guccione wanted a sexy film that he could market and tie in with *Penthouse*, and with the assistance of Giancarlo Lui, he subsequently filmed additional sexually explicit scenes to add to the picture. Thus, a lesbian sex scene featuring the Penthouse Pets is included with no apparent narrative reason except to have a lesbian sex scene featuring Penthouse Pets, and when Caligula (Malcolm McDowell) arranges to supplement his coffers through a state-run brothel held on board a mock galley, it provides an opportunity for more rather tiresome sexual acts to be displayed.[1]

Guccione had to fight to maintain the considerable violence (which has become somewhat commonplace in the genre in subsequent years) and explicit sex, the likes of which the ancient-world epic has yet to see again. While the early Hollywood epics were fairly racy for their time, before the 1934 Motion Picture Production Code enforced censorship, the contemporary epic remains, for the most part, rather coy when it comes to sex. This is a curious trend when one considers that the material that the ancient-world epic often works with has considerable latitude for explicit content. Guccione's project to bring graphic sex to the feature film has been realized in recent years in the art-film sector in such films as *9 Songs* (Michael Winterbottom, 2004) and *Shortbus* (John Cameron Mitchell, 2006), but in the epic genre, *Caligula* remains a historical aberration. Although Helen Mirren suggests that "now you see it on HBO," such explicit sex is not found, even television's *Rome* (2005 and 2007) does not feature such explicit sex.[2]

There are several edits of the film available on DVD for comparison. The theatrical release and uncut versions begin with Caligula playing with his sister Drusilla (Teresa Ann Savoy) in the idyllic countryside. The implied incestuous affair between the pair is soon confirmed when we see them in bed. And yet in these early scenes, Caligula is sincere, young, and happy, a state that he does not recapture.

Caligula is summoned by Emperor Tiberius (Peter O'Toole) to the Isle of Capri to groom him for succession, under the tutelage of Senator Nerva (John Gielgud). The emperor appears to be ravaged by the effects of syphilis, surrounded by his young playthings in the baths. It is clear that Tiberius also considers Caligula an object for his amusement, ordering him to perform a childhood dance.

Tiberius takes Caligula to a multilevel upper chamber displaying slaves engaged in sexual acts and torture (many will be dead by morning). Despite choosing Caligula as his successor, Tiberius offers him a poisoned drink, but it is a test, and the wise Caligula refuses it. The ominous tone intensifies when Nerva commits suicide by slashing his wrists in his bathtub, disillusioned by the current and future emperors.

Tiberius soon goes into decline, but he rallies when Caligula tries to remove the Imperial ring before his death. Caligula's ally Macro (Guido Mannari) comes to his aid and strangles Tiberius, but Tiberius' young grandson Gemellus (Bruno Brive) witnesses the murder, so to protect himself, Caligula adopts him and names him as his heir. Once Caligula is emperor, he wins the support of the people by granting a general amnesty; however, he makes Gemellus expose Macro as the murderer of Tiberius and executes him publically with a bizarre decapitating machine.

Meanwhile, Drusilla extols Caligula to find a wife and produce an heir. Disguised in drag, Caligula looks over the nubile priestesses of Isis as they bathe and undertake lesbian activities. For once going against Drusilla's advice, Caligula chooses the divorcee Caesonia (Helen Mirren), separating her from the group to have sex with her.

Caligula is merely performing his duty, however, for it is still Drusilla that he cares for most, even though he has lost his initial youthful innocence. This is made clear when he arranges to be invited to the wedding of Livia (Mirella Dangelo) and Proculus

(Donato Placido), only to rape them both in an unprovoked act of sadism. During the night, Caligula performs his childhood dance again, as if in a daze, naked in the rain, suggesting that his mind is unstable.

As a fever overtakes Rome, Gemellus is found taking medicine ostensibly to prevent the disease, but Caligula accuses Gemellus of taking an antidote to poison at the emperor's table and uses it as a pretext for sentencing him to death for treason. Caligula subsequently comes down with the deadly fever himself and is comforted by both his horse Incitatus and Drusilla, despite the risk of contagion. Upon his recovery, Caligula demonstrates his return to power by torturing Proculus and having his dead body defiled.

At the wedding of Caligula and Caesonia (at the very moment she gives birth to their daughter), Drusilla falls ill with fever and the assembled party panics. After Drusilla dies, Caligula mourns by wandering the streets of Rome among the poor. When he returns, he orders the senate to announce that he is a god, and they duly obey.

Caligula then undertakes a mock invasion of Britain just outside Rome itself. Upon his return, Caligula confiscates the lands of his perceived enemies and has them arrested. Caesonia advises him to be wary of Chaerea (Paolo Bonacelli), whose disapproval of Caligula's tyranny is becoming obvious.

Her concern is well founded. When Caligula, Caesonia, and their daughter happily rehearse a play, Chaerea and his allied soldiers murder them. The Imperial ring that had earlier been prematurely taken from the dying Tiberius is now taken from the corpse of Caligula to present to Tiberius' nephew Claudius (Giancarlo Badessi).

Today, Caligula's volatile and heinous behavior is often explained as insanity, but the ancient sources for Gaius Caligula are thought to be a mix of "fact and fiction," and indeed it appears that the emperor himself was keen to build a mythology around himself that emphasized that he was not a mere human.[3] Furthermore, the sources on Caligula had political reasons for their negative portrayal of him. For the film, Malcolm McDowell based his performance on the idea that he was an anarchist, "destroying the Roman Empire from the very top."[4] Caligula's behavior certainly appears to have been extreme and deplorable by contemporary standards; Cassius Dio reports his abduction of a bride during her marriage for her presumed defilement, as depicted in the film (Cassius Dio Cocceianus, *Roman History*, LIX 8.7), and the number of deaths under his rule did concern the populous.

As historian Richard Alston argues, his actions were not necessarily a sign of mental illness (nor, for that matter, an anarchic bent), but rather the means through which a young and inexperienced leader attempted to hold power through both fear and a connection with the divine. Although his behavior ultimately proved unwise to his survival, it was nonetheless often cleverly thought out. For example, Caligula announced his intention to make his horse Incitatus a member of a senate, but he was killed before Incitatus was inducted. Alston writes, "If taken seriously, here is a sign of madness, but surely we see here an insult, calculated and witty, aimed at the senate and their pretensions."[5] This was but one of many such insults, and in the film Caligula forces the senators to bleat like sheep. Caius Suetonius recounts that Caligula's favorite saying was, "Let them hate me as long as they fear me" (Caius Suetonius Tranquillus, *The Lives of the Caesars, Gaius Caligula*, 30.1), a line repeated in the film, but in the end they evidently hated him more than they feared him.

With its ancient-world setting, spectacular interior sets, and extensive running time, *Caligula* has the hallmarks of an epic, but without its heroic core. It is an antiepic with an antihero, on a path of self-inflicted, antisocial descent.[6] But there is little, if any, appreciation of the wider historical and political context to Caligula's reign to help ground the audience during his downward journey, and the slow pace stalls the narrative. *Caligula* is strangely almost entirely lacking in exterior establishing shots, creating a confusing and claustrophobic succession of interior sets. Given the context of Caligula's rule, it is perhaps not surprising that the sex scenes are cheerless rather than erotic. While the *New York Times* dismissed the film as "remarkably repulsive,"[7] Guccione has tried to make the most out of rereleasing various versions of his (only) film throughout the years. *Caligula*'s excellent cast may come as a surprise under the circumstances, and we can only wonder what the film might have looked like had the producer not taken it away from both the writer and director. As it stands, it is a rather tedious, messy curio. DB

Notes

1. For more details on the complex production history of *Caligula* and the different versions of the film, see William Hawes, *Caligula and the Fight for Artistic Freedom* (Jefferson, NC, and London: McFarland, 2009).

2. Helen Mirren, "Commentary," *Caligula*, principal direction by Tinto Brass; additional scenes directed and photographed by Bob Guccione and Giancarlo Lui (Image Entertainment, 2007), DVD.

3. Richard Alston, "Gaius Caligula (AD 37–41)," in *Aspects of Roman History, AD 14–117* (New York: Routledge, 1998), 56–76.

4. Malcolm McDowell, "Commentary," *Caligula*, principal direction by Tinto Brass; additional scenes directed and photographed by Bob Guccione and Giancarlo Lui (Image Entertainment, 2007), DVD.

5. Alston, "Gaius Caligula (AD 37–41)," 66.

6. See Constantine Santas, "The Antiepic," in *The Epic in Film: From Myth to Blockbuster* (Lanham, MD: Rowman & Littlefield, 2008), 157–77.

7. Quoted in Ted Loos, "Film; But Is the World Ready for More of *Caligula*?" *New York Times*, 19 September 1999, www.nytimes.com/1999/09/19/movies/film-but-is-the-world-ready-for-more-of-caligula.html (10 March 2012).

Bibliography

Alston, Richard. *Aspects of Roman History, AD 14–117.* New York: Routledge, 1998.

Hawes, William. *Caligula and the Fight for Artistic Freedom.* Jefferson, NC, and London: McFarland, 2009.

Loos, Ted. "Film; But Is the World Ready for More of *Caligula*?" *New York Times*, 19 September 1999, www.nytimes.com/1999/09/19/movies/film-but-is-the-world-ready-for-more-of-caligula.html (10 March 2012).

Santas, Constantine. *The Epic in Film: From Myth to Blockbuster.* Lanham, MD: Rowman & Littlefield, 2008.

CAPTAIN CORELLI'S MANDOLIN (2001)

DIRECTOR: John Madden
WRITER: Shawn Slovo. Based on the novel *Corelli's Mandolin*, by Louis de Bernières.
PRODUCER: Tim Bevan, Eric Fellner, Mark Huffam, Kevin Loader (Universal Pictures, StudioCanal, Miramax Films)
CINEMATOGRAPHER: John Toll
EDITOR: Mick Ausdsley
MUSIC: Stephen Warbeck
CAST: Capt. Antonio Corelli: Nicolas Cage. Pelagia: Penelope Cruz. Dr. Iannis (Pelagia's Father): John Hurt. Mandras: Christian Bale. Drosoula (Mandras' Mother): Irene Pappas. Capt. Günther Weber: David Morrissey. Carlo: Piero Maggiò. Mr. Stamatis: Gerasimos Skiadaressis. Mrs. Stamatis: Aspasia Kralli. Kokolios: Michael Yiannatos. Velisarios: Pietro Sarubbi. Father Arsenios: Dimitris Kaberidis. Eleni: Viki Maragaki. Young Lemoni: Joanna-Daria Adraktas. Older Lemoni: Ira Tavlaridis. Lemoni's Mother: Katerina Didaskalou. Dimitris: Emilios Chilkis
AA: None
AAN: None
DVD: Universal, 2001. With running commentary by John Madden.
BLU-RAY: Currently unavailable
DURATION: 131 minutes

Captain Corelli's Mandolin is based on Louis de Bernières's best-selling 1994 World War II epic *Corelli's Mandolin*, a sprawling novel whose historical background and complexity of themes are impossible to capture in film. Yet, the movie, placed in the context of the book by revisiting the Italian occupation of the Ionian Islands during World War II, allows the viewer a chance to reevaluate, recall, judge, and draw illuminating conclusions from an account of those tragic days. One such question is, Was this account of the occupation accurate historically? Another is, Were these two cultures—Greek and Italian—served by being reminded that the victory of the one and the shame of the other, the results of the Albanian War, had caused these two brotherly cultures irreparable damage? Have the book and the film done justice to history? And did they bring these two cultures closer to their common roots?

Captain Corelli's Mandolin, shot in its entirety on the Greek island of Cephalonia, is a splendidly photographed romantic/war story, both on the personal level and a chapter of the war itself. In his 2001 DVD commentary, John Madden, director of *Shakespeare in Love* (1998), explains that to capture local color, he had to build an entire village for his sets, not wanting to damage private dwellings when, in the war scenes, he had to demolish it. Numerous locals were used for the crowd scenes, and actual locations where War World II battle episodes occurred were researched methodically. The film covers a period of great interest in Modern Greek history; the Italian occupation of the Seven Islands; and the years following the occupation, including the earthquake of 1953, which destroyed the island. That was a period when Greece was invaded and occupied by the Italians and Germans after a valiant and successful war in Albania in 1940–1941.

Against this backdrop, the love story develops: An Italian captain, Antonio Corelli (Nicolas Cage), is quartered at the house of the local doctor, Dr. Iannis (well played by John Hurt), and he soon develops a liaison with the doctor's daughter, Pelagia (Penelope Cruz), already engaged to a Greek fisherman, Mandras (Christian Bale). This forbidden love thrives in the middle of the war and is rekindled after the Italians are massacred by the Germans following the Italian capitulation in 1943. Corelli, who survives the massacre, is treated by Pelagia's father, who also helps him escape to Italy. Years later, after the earthquake of 1953 (which the film shows), he returns and finds Pelagia still loving him, and they are reunited. The story is quite appealing on this romantic level, but the film also offers scenes where the Italians, Germans, and Greeks intermix in social events, flirting or dancing together and sharing such experiences as treating the ill or witnessing the explosion of a mine. More significantly, the film features some of the battles between the united forces of Greek partisans and Italians fighting a losing battle against the Germans, who prevail and subsequently execute the captured Italian soldiers. To understand the film, it is necessary to visit the historical period it covers and also what the book lays out for the film to absorb as material and follow.

The Italian troops invaded the Greek Ionian Islands in May 1941, after the Albanian front collapsed following Hitler's invasion of Greece in April of the same year. Several Italian Army regiments from the Sixth Division, Acqui, stationed at the headquarters in Corfu, occupied the Seven Islands—Corfu, Paxoi, Lefkada, Zakynthos, Kythyra, Cephalonia, and Ithaca—and the occupation forces numbered in the thousands, with approximately one regiment stationed at each island. Small German units were placed on some of the islands (in Cephalonia and Corfu, for instance) to safeguard the German interests in case of an Italian collapse, anticipating what would actually occur two and a half years later.

The de Bernières novel is quite conscious of Italian influences on the islands, and the historical facts it furnishes, although rather generously borrowed from existing sources, are by and large accurate. The novel is quite ambitious: it embraces not only the Venetian past of the islands, but also their entire history since antiquity, especially the history of Cephalonia, one of the most representative cultures of those islands. Dr. Iannis, a major character in the story, is engaged in writing that history, albeit in fictional style, thus enabling the reader, through this dramatic device, to gain some knowledge of what seems a remote part of the world. De Bernières uses other devices to set up the action of the novel against historical facts: one of these is the shifting of point of view through monologue.

In fact, some chapters serve that purpose, interrupting the action to provide the point of view external to the story line but vital to the theme: chapter 2, for instance, entitled "The Duce," reveals the inner thoughts of Mussolini as he was about to start his campaign against Greece. A little later (in chapter 5), we are given, again through monologue/stream of consciousness, the thoughts of Metaxas, the dictator/prime minister of Greece, famous for having said "No" (*oxi*) to Mussolini. Through this device, one relatively early chapter (chapter 14) gives a touching account of Gracci, the honorable Italian ambassador to Athens who had to deliver Mussolini's ultimatum to Metaxas, fully rendering his abhorrence and shame for the treachery of his leader. Several chapters (4, 6, 10, 15, 17) introduce the thoughts of one of the main characters, "L'Omosessuale," or Carlo, who functions as the voice of the Italian soldier that fought the losing war in Albania and, indirectly, the voice of the author.

Although numerous other characters are introduced through this device, there are four basic characters in the story (as in the film): Dr. Iannis; Pelagia, Iannis's daughter; and Captain Antonio Corelli, not introduced until halfway through the novel, all of them having individual voices and representing different points of view. The fourth important character is Mandras, Pelagia's fiancé, whose voice and narrative gives the reader the background of the war in Albania from the Greek point of view. By becoming one of the fighters of the partisan uprising, he furnishes historical data (always through narrative) about the various factions that fought both against the Germans and one another in the subsequent civil war between the nationalists (EDES) and the communists (EAM/ELAS). This is a large canvas for a novel, resulting in a plotline that is hard to hold together, but de Bernières manages this heterogeneous material with admirable skill.

Perhaps the most important episode in the novel is the emotional involvement of Pelagia, a scrupulous and patriotic young woman, with a foreigner, despite her inner conflicts. Captain Corelli is an enemy, who is also humane, civilized, unwilling to occupy a foreign land, and fully conscious of his guilt in participating in the vile act of the Italian occupation. He is a rather ordinary man, whose one ambition is to become a mandolin player, not one who plays in joints for tourists, but one who will one day be a professional concert player playing in an orchestra, "Vivaldi and Hummel, and even Beethoven,"[1] for the mandolin is a dignified musical instrument, according to Corelli, who calls his mandolin "Antonia," a female name matching his own.

Corelli (bearing the name of the famed Italian violinist and composer Archangelo Corelli, 1653–1713) is presented in the novel as the epitome of the civilized man, who is unwillingly entangled in a vicious and barbaric invasion, in many ways more humiliating to the Italians, the conquerors, than the conquered, but proud, Greeks. The humanity of the Italians, as presented by de Bernières in his book, and the cultural affinities between them and the Greeks are the basis for the common bonds that develop between these characters, especially between Corelli and the understanding Dr. Iannis and his romantic and excitable daughter Pelagia. The other Italians, especially the homosexual and heroic Carlo, are also given sympathetically. In fact, as de Bernières observes in his "Author's Notes," the Acqui Division generally behaved "reasonably well" in the Ionian Islands, despite the admitted Italian atrocities elsewhere during the war and occupation.[2] In fact, the entire two-and-a-half-year period that elapsed under the Italians in the Seven Islands was seen as an idyllic interlude, when the worst crimes committed by Italian soldiers involved cavorting on the beaches with the Greek prostitutes, whereas the Germans who followed them were the ones responsible for the murders, pillage, and brutalities that devastated Cephalonia and the other Ionian Islands.

The romanticized picture of the Italian occupation given in the novel is repeated, and even heightened, in the film. The film seeks out the main points of the book and emphasizes the idyllic backdrop of the island and the Greek and Italian cultural affinities. Madden and writer Shawn Slovo explore similarities between the two peoples but do little to avoid the book's pitfalls in giving the actual conditions the war imposed on the local populations, showing Cephalonians in perpetual festive moods, whether dancing or parading the island's Holy Relic of St. Gerasimos, their patron saint. Once or twice, the film attempts to capture the Greek resentment, when Captain Corelli arrives with an Italian contingent as an occupation force in Cephalonia, and the local Greeks, who could not stomach the fact that the Italians they had defeated in Albania were now occupying their hometown, greet him with jeers and demand that they are allowed to capitulate only to the Germans. But Corelli, here presented as noble minded but a bit weak (as in the book), is not upset by the insult to his honor; he is not a fighting man—nor does not consider himself one. He understands cultural ties with the people he is subjecting and behaves as a friend rather than an enemy. He is presented as possessing an infectious spirit of humanity and a zest for life that matches that of the locals. Dr. Iannis speaks out, almost directly to the movie audience, about how the Greek islands and the Greek people have survived despite earthquakes, wars, and centuries of other calamities. Still, the doctor at once recognizes Corelli as a kindred spirit and welcomes him when the latter is quartered in his house, in exchange for medical supplies from the Italians, thus unwittingly encouraging a romance to blossom between him and his daughter Pelagia, already engaged to the local fisherman Mandras. Greeks and Italians sing together, and Pelagia dances a Western dance (tango) with an Italian officer.

Things soon change, however, for the Italians in Italy capitulate to the Allies, Mussolini is overthrown, and, as a result, the occupation forces of the Ionian Islands must withdraw. But they do face German treachery, and in the film (not in the book), they join the Greek partisans, and together they fight the Germans, although in the end they are slaughtered by them, despite the German promise to give them safe passage. In the film, the massacre is a small-scale conflict compared to the massive atrocities described in the book, but

Madden explains in his DVD commentary that he did film the scene in the actual location of the executions, but many more locations like that exist throughout the island. Corelli is almost killed in the massacre of the Italians, but one of the Nazis, Günther Weber (David Morrissey), with whom he had become close, saves him during the coup de grâce, for even a Nazi can become a reformed human.

Like the book, but to a much lesser degree, the film is true enough to fact, but it cannot, of course, give the full picture of the war. As in the book, the movie shows the Italian occupants of the Seven Islands to be friendly and mild-mannered. They do not seem to want to fight a war, reluctantly serving out their term under the Mussolini dictatorship. By contrast, the Germans of the film are ruthless, trigger-happy, unapproachable, cold killers when executing captives or wiping out entire village populations in reprisals. No one in their right mind would seek them out as companions in a dancing contest. The movie softens the image of the Nazi in the Morrissey character, but only momentarily, for the real Nazis soon stand up when they execute a group of Italians who had chosen to join the Greek partisans.

There are some significant differences between book and film, as one would expect. In the book, Mandras, a major character, returns after the liberation a fully indoctrinated Marxist, changed from a gentle youth into a savage who vows revenge. Mandras attempts to rape Pelagia; Pelagia shoots Mandras; Mandras's mother Drosoula (Irene Pappas) arrives to save Pelagia; Drosoula curses Mandras; and Mandras flees, wading into the sea and drowning himself. In the film, he is the one who helps Corelli escape. The most significant generational/chronological difference in the book is that the book allows Pelagia (and the other characters) to age waiting for Corelli, a Penelope waiting for her Odysseus. In the film, they are reunited when still young, but in the book, Corelli arrives in 1993, many decades later, already a famous musician, a Greek citizen who had lived in Athens for a quarter-century, and a lover of Greece. Their reunion now has spiritual dimensions, although it is still a romance. Corelli offers Pelagia a ride on a motorcycle, and they encounter three young girls riding theirs; they see the girls as symbols of generational change, of the perpetual rejuvenation of Greece.

The movie has cut out much of this material, but it still offers a visual feast of Cephalonia, one of the jewels of the Ionian Sea. Madden gives us two lovers separated by war, but their emotional and cultural affinities bring them back together in the end. Whether or not entirely true to history, the film does its honest best to be an informed part of history, despite the shortcomings of films that have to capture, in a bird's-eye view, a complicated story and simultaneously provide a philosophical commentary on that history. The book invites you to forget the cruel and inhuman past. So does the film. The king that was bred in these islands—Odysseus—knew the minds of men and saw their cities. With Homer overseeing the narratives and events, Madden and de Bernières, and perhaps the Italians, and everyone else—with the Greeks in the mix—relive and recapture the past in the present. CS

Notes

1. Louis de Bernières, *Corelli's Mandolin* (New York: Vintage Books, 1994), 185.
2. De Bernières, *Corelli's Mandolin*, 436.

Bibliography

De Bernières, Louis. *Corelli's Mandolin*. New York: Vintage Books, 1994.

Dimaras, K. T. *History of Modern Greek Literature*. Athens: Ikaros, 1975.

Ebert, Roger. "Captain Corelli's Mandolin," *Chicago Sun Times*, 17 August 2001, www.rogerebert.com/

reviews/captain-corellis-mandolin-2001 (19 September 2013).

Rondoyiannis, Panos. *History of the Island of Lefkas.* Athens, Greece: Etairia of Lefkadian Studies, 1982.

Woodhouse, C. M. *The Story of Modern Greece.* London: Faber and Faber, 1968.

THE CARDINAL (1963)

DIRECTOR: Otto Preminger
WRITER: Robert Dozier. Based on the novel by Henry Morton Robinson.
PRODUCER: Otto Preminger (Columbia Pictures)
CINEMATOGRAPHER: Leon Shamroy
EDITOR: Louis R. Loeffler
PRODUCTION DESIGN: Lyle R. Wheeler, Gene Callahan
COSTUMES: Donald Brooks
MUSIC: Jerome Moross
CAST: Stephen Fermoyle: Tom Tryon. Mona/Regina Fermoyle: Carol Lynley. Celia: Dorothy Gish. Florrie: Maggie McNamara. Frank: Bill Hayes. Din: Cameron Prud'Homme. Monsignor Monaghan: Cecil Kellaway. Cornelius J. Deegan: Loring Smith. Benny Rampell: John Saxon. Cardinal Glennon: John Huston. Father Ned Halley: Burgess Meredith. Lalage Menton: Jill Haworth. Cardinal Quarenghi: Raf Vallone. Cardinal Giacobbi: Tullio Carminati. Father Gillis: Ossie Davis. Monsignor Whittle: Chill Wills. Annemarie Lederbohl: Romy Schneider. Seyss-Inquart: Erik Frey
AA: None
AAN: Best Supporting Actor (John Huston), Best Art Direction/Set Decoration–Color (Lyle R. Wheeler, Gene Callahan), Best Cinematography–Color (Leon Shamroy), Best Costume Design–Color (Donald Brooks), Best Director (Otto Preminger), Best Film Editing (Louis R. Loeffler)
GG: Best Motion Picture–Drama, Best Supporting Actor (John Huston)
GGN: Best Film Promoting International Understanding, Best Actor–Drama (Tom Tryon), Best Actress–Drama (Romy Schneider), Best Director–Drama (Otto Preminger)
DVD: Warner Home Video, 2005
BLU-RAY: Currently unavailable
DURATION: 175 minutes

The Cardinal is an award-winning heroic epic adorned in ecclesiastical vestments, adapted from author Henry Morton Robinson's 1950 novel purportedly inspired by the life of Irish American priest-turned-Catholic cardinal Francis Joseph Spellman.[1] Set within the life of a single priest amid a tumultuous cultural era (World War I and World War II) and produced during the reform era of the Catholic Church's Second Vatican Council (the early 1960s), the action of the film nevertheless moves more like a catechism lesson on dogma than a biography, or even an epic, of any significance designed to instill cathartic effect, unless the effect is to reinforce the dogma of obedience to hierarchy at the expense of self, family, culture, country, or, ultimately, faith.

The action of the film follows Joseph Campbell's paradigm of the epic hero monomyth.[2] The hero is a young Irish American priest of humble origins, Stephen Fermoyle (Tom Tryon). We first see him as the film's opening credits run, responding to the call of the bells from the cathedral campanile, as a solitary man walking across the initiatory terrain of his symbolic journey through the atrium, along the colonnades, up the stairs, across the reflecting pond, and toward the entrance of a building. There he meets his mentor in secret chambers, and they exchange good-byes. Then he meets a small group of people, and we learn that he is to be made a cardinal of the Catholic Church. Following, in flashback, the film draws us to the biographical beginnings of this cardinal-to-be, and we only return to the conclusion of this opening scene at the end of the film.

Our first reflection begins with Father Fermoyle's spiritual and secular entry into the priesthood, where we witness first the solemn Latin ritual of his ordination mass, followed by a meeting with his academic mentor in Rome, Cardinal Quarenghi (Raf Vallone), who discusses two important matters with him. First, he compliments him on his last academic paper and wishes him well on his journey to his assignment in the United States. Then he produces a special ring, a copy of the cardinal's ring that he himself wears, and gives it to the young priest, telling him to hold on to it, for when he "becomes a cardinal." Astonished, young Father Fermoyle takes the ring.

The scene cuts to an American seaport, where Father Fermoyle returns home and is greeted by his mother, brother, and two sisters. They soon meet up with his father (who conducts the local trolley), and once together, they banter about the new priest's upcoming future with Monsignor Monaghan (Cecil Kellaway), with whom Stephen will be stationed. They also reflect on his future as cardinal, as predicted since birth, and joke that the monsignor promised not to promote him to bishop the first day, although eventually it has to happen since it's impossible to be cardinal without first being bishop.

The next scene takes place in the parish, where we are introduced to two friends of Father Fermoyle's father. The first is Monsignor Monaghan. When Stephen begins to tutor Benny Rampell (John Saxon), a Jewish youth who agrees to convert to marry Stephen's younger sister, Mona (Carol Lynley), the monsignor walks in on the two of them actively debating about evolution and creation. Visibly concerned, the monsignor questions the priest about the reason for the discussion and says, "Aren't you getting away from the usual instruction?" Stephen tells him that Benny is a tough nut to crack and needs answers, to which the monsignor calmly and emphatically replies, "There's nothing tough about it. What it amounts to in the long run is simply faith." Later, in private, after asking Stephen about what he studied in Rome, the monsignor lets him know, quite frankly, that he has no need or desire for a curate who is a *racehorse*; what he needs is a *milk horse*. In other words, Stephen is not wanted at the parish. Faith, not knowledge, is all one needs to be a good priest, the old pastor tells the young priest.

The other friend from Stephen's father's past is Mr. Cornelius J. Deegan (Loring Smith), a parishioner who is a Papal Knight of Malta and a rags-to-riches millionaire from the neighborhood who donates to the parish in exchange for advertising favors from the pastor. His work is shoddy, however, as we learn later in the film, when a pipe bursts, leaking rusty water on a statue of the Virgin Mary, appearing to make her weep and causing a stir among the ethnic Italian minority in the Irish Catholic Church. When the monsignor begins to intervene, but in a manner showing distain for the raucous crowd rushing to the Church because of the *miracle*, Father Fermoyle steps before the group and, in Italian, leads them in prayer, only adding more fuel to the fire of envy already enflamed with the monsignor. Deegan and Monaghan teach Stephen two lessons in his spiritual development: Deegan about the external forms of the Knights of Malta, and Monaghan about the external forms of the spiritual life. Both old friends of his father, they serve as the impetus for Stephen's heroic call to adventure.

The next scene is an engagement party for Mona and Benny, and both sides of the family are there, but no one is speaking with the Rampells, Benny's parents, despite the fact that as a banker, Mr. Rampell has done business with many of the folks at the party. Benny, dressed in his soldier's uniform, asks Father Fermoyle, "Whose side is God on?" The question is answered when Deegan announces that Benny is soon going to change his last name to a respectable "Catholic name." And then he jests that maybe they should add an "O" in front of it. At that, Benny and his family walk out, and Benny breaks up with Mona, thus beginning the downward plunge of Father Fermoyle's rising star, beginning with his relationship with his beloved little sister, Mona, who admits to adultery and then runs away when Stephen cannot help her.

Stephen is simultaneously moved to a new parish by Cardinal Glennon (John Huston) due to the cardinal's intention to teach him humility and guard him from his penchant for ambition. He is sent to help the ailing Father Halley (Burgess Meredith), who eventually dies, but Stephen cares for him well, even selling his cardinal's ring to pay for the medication to help him. We learn that the cardinal had misjudged Father Halley all his life and treated him cruelly, and Father Halley had accepted the punishment as his failing, despite the fact that it was his illness (multiple sclerosis) that was the true cause of his inability to better perform his pastoral duties. In the end, even though the cardinal and the dying priest reconciled, it troubled Stephen. Later, news comes from Stephen's brother that Mona has been found pregnant and out of wedlock. Stephen rushes to her and gets her immediate medical help, but to little avail, for, due to a medical complication, Stephen (against his brother's and Benny's pleadings) is forced (by Canon Law) to watch Mona die to save the life of her child (a daughter, Regina, also played by Carol Lynley), who is later raised by her grandparents.

His trial over, Stephen gets promoted to be the secretary to the archbishop, and he returns to Rome with the archbishop for the conclave when the pope dies. When the new pope is elected, Cardinal Glennon offers Stephen's name for a post at the Vatican. Stephen refuses the appointment, stating that he wants to leave the priesthood. (And with this act, the hero refuses the call and enters the belly of the whale.) Furious, Glennon tells him that this will inflame anti-American prejudice all over again and then asks him why. After explaining himself, the cardinal gives Father Fermoyle a one-year leave of absence and says that he will hold the position for him in Rome. This begins the initiation of Father Stephen Fermoyle and the intermission of the film.

The second half of the film opens in Vienna, in 1924, and Stephen is a teacher at the International School of Language about to embark on a two-week holiday from classes. Here, we meet a student of his, Miss Annemarie Lederbohl (later von Hartman) (played by Romy Schneider), who has grown fond of her teacher and decides to teach him that there is more to Vienna than his room and books. She takes him for bike rides, out for coffee, and even to a Viennese ball, until she learns he is a priest. Although Stephen struggles with his attraction to the world, and her, he ultimately returns to the cloth and breaks her in the process, for she, although always engaged during their time together, was, in fact, in love with the priest, and not her betrothed. Despite this knowledge, Stephen returns to the Church, and his call, having completed his meeting the goddess, and the woman as temptress.

The next scene, Rome, 1934, provides the occasion for the hero's atonement with the father and apotheosis and refusal to return. It involves Father Fermoyle's insistence on the Vatican's intervention in the local politics of the American South, specifically in aiding a black priest from Georgia whose church has been destroyed by the Ku Klux Klan (KKK). When the Vatican dismisses Stephen's recommendations to help, his sense of responsibility and obligation leads him to finagle a private visit to Georgia to intervene on the priest's behalf and aid him in his political difficulties. The naivety and audacity of Stephen's demeanor nearly costs the priest his life when the KKK whips him and leaves him for dead, but the next morning, a lone unmasked Klansman returns with some healing salve and a truck to heal the priest's wounds, physically and spiritually. The men are convicted based on the Georgian priest's testimony, and Stephen returns to Rome and must account for his diplomatic transgressions against the Holy See, for he is accused of using this action to split public opinion of Catholic Americans on the issue of racism, against the recommendations of the prelates of the American church. Soon thereafter, however, he is made a bishop by the pope—the boon.

The last series of events surround Hitler's annexation of Austria and Father Fermoyle's assignment to stop the Austrian cardinal, Innitzer, from collaborating with Hitler and urge Catholics to support him. Fermoyle is unsuccessful in convincing Innitzer, and it is not until Hitler tells Innitzer of his plans against the Catholics and Austria that the Austrian cardinal sees the light and changes his allegiance; however, by this time it is too late. The city is destroyed and homes ransacked and looted by Hitler's mob. Father Fermoyle escapes through a secret underground passage in the tombs and returns home to find that Annemarie (his former student with whom he has recently reconnected since her husband had committed suicide for being a Jew, causing her, in fear, to seek asylum in his church) has surrendered to the Gestapo and is now in jail. She is being tried for attempting to flee the country with money and assets. When Stephen meets her in jail, he tells her to fight because her life is important and has meaning, because she is an individual with a God-given soul. Annemarie thanks him for his words and he leaves, having ordered an attorney to assist her with her trial.

The final scene returns to the opening scene, and we hear (this time in English) the notification that Bishop Fermoyle will be made cardinal. Stephen thanks everyone and gives a speech. The film ends with him walking out of the church, arm in arm with his mother, niece, and the rest of his family, *master of the two worlds*, as the closing credits run. MC

> Instead of clearing his own heart, the zealot tries to clear the world.
>
> —Joseph Campbell

Notes

1. Frank Miller, "*The Cardinal* (1963)," *Turner Classic Movies Articles*, www.tcm.com/tcmdb/title/70290/The-Cardinal/articles.html (12 September 2013).

2. Some characteristics of the monomyth include birth prophesy of a future pedigree; a call to adventure and refusal of the call; helpers bearing an amulet; crossing the threshold; initiation, including trials and tests, meeting the goddess of the underworld, the woman as temptress, and atonement with the father; apotheosis and final boon; a return home and refusal of the return; a rescue from without and, after a blessing from the god and or goddess, a receipt of the elixir and a crossing of the return threshold; and, finally, a mastering of the two worlds. Joseph Campbell, *The Hero with a Thousand Faces* (Princeton, NJ: Princeton University Press, 1949).

Bibliography

Campbell, Joseph. *The Hero with a Thousand Faces.* Princeton, NJ: Princeton University Press, 1949.

Miller, Frank. "*The Cardinal* (1963)." *Turner Classic Movies Articles*, www.tcm.com/tcmdb/title/70290/The-Cardinal/articles.html (12 September 2013).

CHEYENNE AUTUMN (1964)

Director: John Ford
Writers: James R. Webb, Mari Sandoz, Howard Fast (uncredited)
Producers: John Ford, Bernard Smith (Warner Bros., Ford-Smith Productions)
Cinematographer: William H. Clothier
Editor: Otho Lovering

MUSIC: Alex North

CAST: Capt. Thomas Archer: Richard Widmark. Deborah Wright: Carroll Baker. Little Wolf: Richardo Montalban. Dull Knife: Gilbert Roland. Red Shirt: Sal Mineo. Spanish Woman: Dolores Del Rio. Maj. Braden: George O'Brien. Capt. Oscar Wessels: Karl Malden. Second Lt. Scott: Patrick Wayne. Tall Tree: Victor Jory. Sgt. Stanislaus Wichowski: Mike Mazurki. Wyatt Earp: James Stewart. Karl Shultz: Edward G. Robinson. Doc Holliday: Arthur Kennedy. Maj. Jeff Blair: John Carradine. Genevieve Plantagenet: Elizabeth Allen

AA: None

AAN: Best Supporting Actor (Gilbert Roland)

GG: None

GGN: Best Supporting Actor (Gilbert Roland)

DVD: Warner Home Video, 2006

BLU-RAY: Currently unavailable

DURATION: 154 minutes

Cheyenne Autumn was John Ford's last western, the only true epic in his canon, by any standard. Its length alone, at two hours and thirty-four minutes, qualifies it as such, but the sweeping saga of a tribe of Indians traveling 1,500 miles from their Oklahoma Navajo reservation to "Cave Victory," their original home in Yellowstone, Wyoming/Montana, under harrowing conditions, is indeed a trip of epic proportions. This epic saga is also marked by Ford's revisionist view of Indians, displaced after centuries of persecution by white men advancing to the West, as Indians of many tribes who suffered the ravages of these intrusions—aside from being shown as villains in most western movies—are at long last portrayed as people with dignity, who have the right to move to the land they once owned. Although the film is not free of flaws, it seems to resonate with audiences more today than when it was released, when it was a failure with audiences and critics and was almost totally ignored by the Academy of Motion Picture Arts and Sciences, nominated only in one category, Best Cinematography (William H. Clothier), and for only one Golden Globe, for Best Supporting Actor (Gilbert Roland).

Shot mostly in Monument Valley—Ford's favorite location for many of his previous works—in 70mm Super Panavision, the film captures in full measure the tribe's tragic epic journey north. Although several leading Indian tribal characters are played by Hollywood actors, Ford utilized Navajo tribe men and women to portray the majority of his characters in their perilous trek. Several distinguished Hollywood stars—James Stewart, Edward G. Robinson, Carroll Baker, and Karl Malden—were also added to the mix, some in the comic interlude of the story, and some in key plot positions. Other key roles were also given to Mexican-born Hollywood actors Richardo Montalban, Gilbert Roland, and Dolores Del Rio, and one important role was assigned to the firebrand of the tribe, Sal Mineo (Red Shirt), who was Italian American and had appeared in a variety of roles, most notably *Rebel Without a Cause*, with James Dean. For the most part, the film takes a pro-Indian stance, as the white leads in the story, Richard Widmark and Caroll Baker, were shown as characters sympathetic to the Indian plight.

The film begins with the Cheyenne tribe confined to the reservation camp in Oklahoma, decimated by hunger and illness from 1,000 members to less than 300. Tribe members are marching into the military camp to await officials from Washington to hear their complaints and provide them with more humane treatment. The officials fail to show up. The tribe is led by aging leader Tall Tree (Victor Jory), who is near death, and his two successors, Little Wolf (Richardo Montalban) and Dull Knife

(Gilbert Roland), both of whom consider the official's failure to appear a snub. Angered, they go back to their camp and leave during the night.

Although their departure is not considered illegal, Captain Thomas Archer (Richard Widmark) is ordered by Major Braden (George O'Brien) to pursue them, capture them if they cross a certain point, and bring them back to the reservation. A Quaker schoolteacher, Deborah Wright (Carroll Baker), who is being courted by Archer, goes with the tribe, mostly to attend to the needs of her former schoolchildren. Tall Tree is carried with his tribe but dies on the way, and he passes on the token of leadership, the sacred bundle, to Little Wolf. The group is pursued by Captain Archer, who avoids any confrontation, but soon Major Braden arrives, with artillery, and is provoked by Red Shirt, a pugnacious youth, into a fight, during which he is killed. Archer's unit follows the Indians, who are drifting north under the most adverse conditions, suffering from disease and hunger, but continue on their course.

As the Indians' trek continues, the action shifts to a comic scene in Dodge City, lasting twenty-one minutes, where Wyatt Earp, the famous gunslinging marshal, played by James Stewart, is shown playing a game of cards with his buddies, Doc Holliday (Arthur Kennedy) and Major Jeff Blair (John Carradine). As the three are absorbed in their game, a group of lowlifes tries to draw their attention. Led by Ken Curtis, who has just murdered a starving Indian, the band of men approach an apathetic Earp, who, when Curtis foolishly challenges him, coolly shoots him in the foot, and then, with the help of Genevieve Plantagenet (Elizabeth Allen), a saloon lady, he first knocks him unconscious, hitting him on the head with a mallet, and then "operates" on him, pulling the bullet out and cauterizing the wound with a bottle of whiskey Plantagenet has provided.

Rumors have spread that Indians are about to attack the city, and in the ensuing chaos, a posse is hastily organized, followed by the saloon women, and when a lone Indian is sighted, panic ensues and the wagon with the women is overturned. Plantagenet is carried in her bloomers by Doc Holliday, and Earp now admits that he had known her in Wichita. The scene seems to shatter the tone of the serious and tragic main stream of action, but some commentators[1] have suggested that Ford intended to lampoon the mass hysteria prevailing among the white populations in the West, arousing them to action against a wretched band of refugee Indians trying to get to their homeland under the harshest conditions. One critic, Andrew Sarris, even suggests that this is the only scene in the film worth watching, the rest of the movie being too dull.[2]

After hunger and illness have decimated the Indians, the group splits; one part of it, led by Dull Knife, goes to Fort Robinson, Nebraska, run by an overefficient, German-descended disciplinarian officer, Captain Oscar Wessels (Karl Malden), who at first offers food and shelter. Deborah Wright, nearly having died of starvation, remains with this group, while caring for a sick child, orphaned and wounded during an attack by the cavalry. Wessels, who initially agrees to accommodate the fugitives in relatively humane conditions, hardens when he receives orders to send them back at once to the original camp in Oklahoma. When they refuse to leave, he imprisons them in narrow quarters with no heat or food until they recant. The prisoners, armed and desperate, break out, and in the melee that follows, Wessels is killed. The escaped prisoners continue their trek and eventually arrive at their destination, Cave Victory, where the remainder of the tribe has already taken refuge.

The scene shifts to Washington, where Archer arrives to plead for the poor conditions of the Indians about to be attacked by government forces. He seeks the help of the secretary of the interior, Karl Shultz (Edward G. Robinson), who resists the advice of the military brass who want to eliminate the tribe. Shultz travels West to the Indian camp with Archer, and as a military detachment is about to launch an attack, he asks for negotiations with the chiefs, Little Wolf and Dull Knife, ensuring them that he is there to help them, not make empty promises. He offers them cigars when they ask for tobacco, and the deal is sealed. The Indians are handed a respite and can remain on their land, thanks to the deus ex machina appearance of Secretary Shultz. In a dramatic scene, Red Shirt, the youth who looks for confrontation, passes the sacred bundle from Little Wolf to Dull Knife as a symbol of new leadership and continued peace. Archer is seen reuniting with Wright, who has adopted a young Indian girl she has cared for, and they plan to lead a peaceful agrarian life on the frontier.

Cheyenne Autumn is an epic tale by any standard. It is a story of displacement, genocide, and migration of a people to their homeland, but also one that demonstrates the irrational mass hysteria created by rumor, press misinformation—the Kansas City scenes show that—overreaction, and ignorance. An epic tale is usually the story of a hero who goes through trials, wins against all odds, and finally saves his people, in the process becoming heroic, winning his plaudits, and gaining success in achieving his goals. Here the reverse takes place: a displaced tribe migrates, its chief dies, and the leaders who are his successors, Little Wolf and Dull Knife, are rivals for succession. Red Shirt, a young hothead, surrenders the sacred bundle, and chiefdom, to Dull Knife and departs—to keep the tribe unified. The hero of the Indians is the tribe itself. Their collective spirit and common sufferings during an incredibly difficult trek define them.

But the epic also has a hero on the other side. Thomas Archer (who has been called an "obedient rebel" by commentator Joseph McBride[3]), while performing his duty as a military man, pursuing and even fighting the tribe, is really a humanitarian at heart, fully conscious of the tribe's pride and adherence to purpose. He may be described as a "quiet hero," a thoughtful person, duty-bound but not a fanatic, and who does well in his role, avoiding a needless massacre, understanding the plight of the fugitives—but also their valor—and getting the girl at the end.

In two previous movies involving conflicts with Indians, *Fort Apache* (1948) and *The Searchers* (1956), John Wayne leads the way as hero, especially in the latter film, in which he totally dominates the scene, but John Wayne would have stolen the show in *Cheyenne Autumn.* His screen persona was far too big for the part, and wisely, Ford did not choose him, whether intentionally or not.

Widmark as Archer seems the right choice, being a man sensitive to the issues, a man of discipline and adherence to the rules, but not the fanatic, half-crazed, or cowardly, as is his counterpart, Wessels. But Archer is not a hero who leads. Rather, he is one who follows the course of events. That deprives Ford's epic of a truly significant figure, as the main characters seem to be an ensemble cast. The trek of the Cheyenne to their homeland moves like a documentary, tracing and defining the nature of the white man's mindless pursuit and eradication of a Native American tribe. *Cheyenne Autumn* is a tribute to the tribe, and to Ford for having the stamina to display it. Ford's last western is a form of redemption, a show of intense interest in redeeming the negative image of so many mindless westerns of the previous decades that portrayed Indians as savages murdering innocent white folk living on the frontier, and therefore deserving reprisals. CS

Notes

1. Historian Joseph McBride in his running commentary, *Cheyenne Autumn*, directed by John Ford (Warner Home Video, 2006), DVD.

2. Andrew Sarris, *"You Ain't Heard Nothing Yet": The American Talking Film History and Memory, 1927–1949* (New York: Oxford University Press, 1998), 209.

3. McBride, *Cheyenne Autumn*, DVD.

Bibliography

Baxter, John. *The Cinema of John Ford*. London: Tantivy Press, 1971.

Bogdanovich, Peter. *John Ford*: Berkeley: University of California Press, 1971.

Gallager, Tag. *John Ford: The Man and His Films*. Berkeley and Los Angeles: University of California Press, 1986.

McBride, Joseph. *Searching for John Ford*. Jackson: University Press of Mississippi, 2011.

Sarris, Andrew. *"You Ain't Heard Nothing Yet": The American Talking Film History and Memory, 1927–1949*. New York: Oxford University Press, 1998.

CITIZEN KANE (1941)

DIRECTOR: Orson Welles
WRITERS: Herman J. Mankiewicz, Orson Welles
PRODUCER: Orson Welles (RKO Radio Pictures, Mercury Productions)
CINEMATOGRAPHER: Gregg Toland
EDITOR: Robert Wise
SET/INTERIOR DECORATION: Darrell Silvera, Perry Ferguson, Van Nest Polglase, A. Roland Fields
ART DIRECTION: Van Nest Polglase
COSTUMES: Edward Stevenson
Music Score: Bernard Herrmann
Sound Recording: John Aalberg
Special Effects: Vernon A. Walker
CAST: Charles Forster Kane: Orson Welles. Jedediah Leland: Joseph Cotton. Susan Alexander: Dorothy Comingore. Mr. Bernstein: Everett Sloane. James W. Gettys: Ray Collins. Walter P. Thatcher: George Coulouris. Kane's Mother: Agnes Moorehead. Emily Norton/Kane: Ruth Warrick. Jerry Thompson: William Alland. Raymond: Paul Stewart. Herbert Carter: Erskine Sanford. Kane's Father: Harry Shannon
AA: Best Writing–Original Screenplay (Herman J. Mankiewicz, Orson Welles)
AAN: Best Picture (Mercury), Best Director (Orson Welles), Best Leading Actor (Orson Welles), Best Cinematography–Black-and-White (Gregg Toland), Best Film Editing (Robert Wise), Best Music–Scoring of a Dramatic Picture (Bernard Herrmann), Best Art Direction/Interior Decoration–Black-and-White (Darrell Silvera, Perry Ferguson, Van Nest Polglase, A. Roland Fields), Best Sound Recording (John Aalberg)
DVD: Turner Home Entertainment, 2001. Two-disc special edition.
BLU-RAY: Warner Bros., 2011. 70th Anniversary Ultimate Collector's Edition.
DURATION: 119 minutes

In Xanadu did Kubla Khan
A stately pleasure dome decree:
Where Alph, the sacred river, ran
Through caverns measureless to man
Down to a sunless sea.

—Samuel Taylor Coleridge,
"Kubla Khan," 1797

Given our title, *The Encyclopedia of Epic Films*, and the related discussions of the genre in the present volume, one question is immediately begged: Is *Citizen Kane* an epic? One can add, Is it an epic tragedy? The two genres have distinct properties, but the epic form has often mixed with other forms, as we have seen.[1]

We must qualify these questions by stating that here we do not examine the film *Citizen Kane* in its usual socio/biographical context; that is, by concerning ourselves with whether it is an accurate representation of the life of William Randolph Hearst, on which it is supposed to be based, nor are we interested in the effects that such a link between subject matter and fictional representation had on the career of its director, although these questions may become relevant if one views *Citizen Kane* as a whole filmic structure. Our questions are only concerned with the formal properties of the film, with how it is to be regarded as a genre, and what bearing raising questions about epic and tragedy in film can have on this film's interpretation. It is important to draw this distinction, for a tragic epic has the added dimension of catastrophe, which isolates it from the euphoric and massive audience response accorded the triumphant hero of the mainstream epic, thus deepening, and delimiting, its appeal, demanding stricter aesthetic criteria.

First, is *Citizen Kane* an epic? Normally, and considering the definitions of the epic we use in this book, *Citizen Kane* obviously lacks some of the most important elements of the epic—length and spectacle. At two hours (119 minutes), it is not considered short, but neither is it regarded as lengthy—certainly not by the standards of length for the epic form that were subsequently established by Hollywood in the decades of the 1950s and 1960s (and that continue to a lesser degree today). But what it lacks in length—and sprawl—it contains/has in grandness—one would even say grandiosity—of theme: it is a biography—albeit to a large degree fictional—of one of the most colorful and prominent Americans of the twentieth century, of an individual high on the social scale, which the movie examines in its broader possible social contexts; therefore, *Citizen Kane* can be regarded as "large" (if not long) as a subject for a movie.

Furthermore, Charles Kane (played by Orson Welles) is, in many ways, an archetypal hero, for he certainly represents (and incorporates) American values: his drive for power and prominence and his desire to be representative of his people, as per his declared intentions (in his published "Declaration of Principles") to better their lot and defend their rights and privileges. If wealth and power are the signs of status of a man with great leadership abilities, Kane (and hidden behind him the persona of William Randolph Hearst) has these in abundance and wishes to use them for the benefit of the lowly crowd. He runs for governor of New York; blasts a corrupt opponent, James W. Gettys (Ray Collins); and even entertains notions of running for president. The film entirely lacks action/adventure, which would be an epic façade for its weighty subject, but, given its tone and seriousness, these superfluities can be dispensed with, for an epic, as its premises imply, should value largeness of theme above the spectacular element.[2] *Citizen Kane* has the sweep and grandeur of human achievement and failure, and the film relates these in a manner that strikes a chord in the collective psyche.

More than anything, Kane is representative of the "nobleman," the "hero" of America, the man (and often the woman) who sets out from poor origins, as Kane's parents were poor, to conquer the world, to smooth out its hard edges, to polish it according to his own standards, even to bend it to his will, for any hero rendering services to his tribe is also a dictator of sorts. Rulers often rise to the top with ruthless means, leveling the ground and often toppling their rivals to gain prominence: Kane buys out the staff/personnel of the *Observer*, a rival newspaper, for his own, the *Inquirer*, because he will tolerate no antagonists. The niece of a president becomes his first wife for prestige, and Susan Alexander (Dorothy Comingore), a poor girl, is his second spouse, for in his ambition he envisions her as an operatic singer on the grand scale. His friends must stay in line, for no one must match or oppose him. The hero—like the mythical Kubla Khan alluded to in the name of his castle—must build his palace on a scale suitable only to great leaders (and rulers) of the past. In Xanadu, he must have his "dome of pleasure," and his parties must be legendary.[3] Like all mythical heroes, Kane rises out of the pack, holding his vassals in liege, and even, symbolically, becomes the head of the knights of the "oblong" table—witness the famous deep focus scene showing the seating at the table of his colleagues during a party for the *Inquirer*. Kane is, or is the equivalent of, the mythical epic hero, a leader of the world whose ambitions, drive for power, and stated (if not actual) benevolence have no end.

From the aforementioned epic premise, it becomes easier to formally declare *Citizen Kane* a tragedy, as well as an epic, for its epic sweep also contains the beginning of its hero's tragic fall. Tragedy by no means precludes the epic hero, for both types feature a noble person who either is of noble descent or acquires nobility through his own efforts. Classical literature features Hamlet and Oedipus in the first category, but in modern America, where the democratic system allows a man and woman of humble origins to rise to the top, a hero does not need the accoutrements of inherited nobility, although inherited wealth will do. One can find examples in Herman Melville's Captain Ahab (*Moby-Dick*), William Faulkner's Thomas Sutpen (*Absalom! Absalom!*), or the illusionary edifice of wealth and power built by the likes of Jay Gatsby and, in the dream world only, Willie Loman. These are tragic heroes, and film has tried, but not always succeeded, in rendering them as strongly as their literary models have.

But *Citizen Kane* has succeeded in giving perhaps the most complete prototype of a screen tragic hero who is also of epic dimension as any film has. Tragedy requires its hero or heroes to fall, and in the play, or other similar narrative form, to end in catastrophe. Aristotle liked Euripides in this sense, for his plays' endings were the most tragic: in *Electra*, for instance, two children murder their mother, and in *Medea*, a mother kills her children. Tragedy also requires a reversal of fortune, although not necessarily a tight plot, even though these are by no means uncommon in modern film—as in Ingmar Bergman's *The Virgin Spring* (1960), for instance.

Tragedy is carefully woven into the visual, discursive, and narrative forms of *Citizen Kane*. The tragic element has a cumulative effect from the opening "March of Time" sequence, with its rather chilling tributes, to the building of Xanadu, a name that implies splendor and vastness, but also the illusion of a dream—a point illustrated in great detail in the film. The search for "Rosebud," a word that becomes the verbal and physical node of the movie, implies the futility of searches that try to ascertain why a goal was not attained. This is also the catalyst of the action, for a reporter, Jerry Thompson (William Alland), embarks on a quest for the truth—a surrogate for the search of the hero, whose secret remains encased in his head when he dies.

We never know why Kane is unhappy, at least we don't get anything but a clue—the word itself—about his inner struggle to find happiness or fulfillment as a human being. His good intentions and joie de vivre come through in the party (and dance) given in his honor at the beginning of the film, but also, to a certain measure, his amorality, or blindness, in buying the services of a rival newspaper, as if such things as stealing another's employees don't matter. In attacking Gettys, he is unable to fathom the mechanics of blackmail, which is a failure of foresight, a result of arrogance and self-will that leads to destruction.

Kane's greatest flaw, however, is his attempt to manipulate others to fall in line with his schemes. "I am Charles Foster Kane," he bawls out to the music instructor, who tries in vain to explain to him that singing takes discipline, training, and, above all, talent. He humiliates Susan Alexander by exposing her vocal ineptitude before large crowds and ends up being the only one who continues applauding her performance, a vulgar imposition of his crude, unrefined taste on an audience—just because he has money.

This is a large-dimensioned man, a man of power, good intentions, and, one might say, honorable motives to be of service to others, but he is unable to grasp his inner failure to connect with the communal spirit—which is exactly what a true hero should be able to do. Whether before he dies, he understands the magnitude of his failure, or whether his holding of the glass ball that depicts his loss of youth brings him to complete understanding remains an open question. As Thompson finally says to the gathered reporters, Rosebud is just a piece of the puzzle, and it by itself does not explain everything that went through Kane's head, but it is a hint of "anagnorisis," something every true tragic hero must undergo to qualify as great, failed through a mistake, and pitiable.

Citizen Kane has consistently appeared in American Film Institute's top 100 movies listing as the number one movie of all time, and the film has also made it to the top of the listings in the *Sight & Sound* polls of critics and influential directors, only being replaced this year (2013) by Alfred Hitchcock's *Vertigo* (1958). Its innovative techniques, deep-focus photography, montages, camera movement, power shots, and sound mixing, among many other characteristics, have left their indelible mark on moviemaking, paving the way for film innovations for decades to come. Despite all this, the film failed to secure Orson Welles a permanent place in Hollywood, and he subsequently made only sporadic appearances as a director and actor of note. But his legacy remains firm, and his place in film may be comparable to that of Sophocles and Shakespeare in drama, for he, like them, portrayed a man of great stature felled not only by fate, but by his own blindness. Charles Kane could not understand that those around him could be used as the pawns of his grandiose schemes, pieces of his puzzle, of which he was a pawn himself. Nor could anyone solve the mystery of his rise and fall. Ironically, Rosebud, the snow sled of his childhood, is seen burning only by the viewer. CS

Notes

1. In addition to the introduction in this volume, see Constantine Santas, "The Classic Epic Form," in *The Epic in Film: From Myth to Blockbuster* (Lanham, MD: Rowman & Littlefield, 2008), 23–34.
2. In his *Poetics*, Book 2, Aristotle describes spectacle as the "least artistic" element, being the product of the "machinist" rather than the poet, in his definition of tragedy, which consists of six parts: plot, character, thought, diction, music, and spectacle. When he turned to comparing the two genres, he did not change that order.
3. In subsequent decades, the Playboy Mansions of Hugh Heffner served a similar purpose, an archetype of pleasure, as did William Randolph Hearst's palace in Northern California, although in different contexts.

Bibliography

Callow, Simon. *Orson Welles: The Road to Xanadu.* London: Johnathon Cape, 1995.

Carringer, Robert L. *The Making of Citizen Kane.* Berkeley and Los Angeles: University of California Press, 1985.

———. "The Scripts of *Citizen Kane*." *Critical Inquiry* 5 (1978): 369–400. Subsequently reprinted in Gottesman, *Perspectives on Citizen Kane*, 1996.

Cook, David A. *A History of Narrative Film*, 2nd ed. New York: W. W. Norton & Company, 1991.

———. *Orson Welles and the Modern Sound Film: A History of Narrative Film.* W. W. Norton & Company, 2004.

Gottesman, Ronald. *Perspectives on Citizen Kane.* New York: G. K. Hall & Co., 1996.

———, ed. *Focus on Citizen Kane*. Englewood Cliffs, NJ: Prentice Hall, 1971.
Kael, Pauline, ed. *The Citizen Kane Book*. Boston: Little, Brown and Company, 1971. Contains Kael's controversial and much-derided article "Raising Kane," as well as the full script by Mankiewicz and Welles.
Naremore, James, ed. *Orson Welles's Citizen Kane: A Casebook in Criticism*. Oxford, UK: Oxford University Press, 2004.
Nasaw, David. *The Chief: The Life of William Randolph Hearst*. New York: Houghton Mifflin, 2000.
Rippy, Marguerite H. *Orson Welles and the Unfinished RKO Projects: A Postmodern Perspective*. Carbondale: Southern Illinois University Press, 2009.
Santas, Constantine. *The Epic in Film: From Myth to Blockbuster*. Lanham, MD: Rowman & Littlefield, 2008.

CLASH OF THE TITANS (1981)

Director: Desmond Davis
Writer: Beverley Cross
Producers: Charles H. Schneer, Ray Harryhausen (Titan Productions, MGM)
Associate Producer: John Palmer
Cinematographer: Ted Moore
Editor: Timothy Gee
Art Direction: Don Picton, Peter Howitt, Giorgio Desideri, Fernando Gonzalez
Costumes: Emma Porteous
Music: Lawrence Rosenthal
Cast: Zeus: Laurence Olivier. Hera: Claire Bloom. Thetis: Maggie Smith. Aphrodite: Ursula Andress. Poseidon: Jack Gwillim. Athena: Susan Fleetwood. Hephaestus: Pat Roach. Perseus: Harry Hamlin. Andromeda: Judi Bowker. Ammon: Burgess Meredith. Cassiopeia: Siân Phillips. Stygian Witches: Flora Robson, Anna Manahan, Freda Jackson. Thallo: Tim Pigott-Smith. Calibos: Neil McCarthy. Acrisius: Donald Houston. Danae: Vida Taylor. Huntsman: Harry Jones
AA: None
AAN: None
DVD: Turner Entertainment and Warner Bros., 2002
Blu-ray: Warner Bros., 2010
Duration: 155 minutes

This ancient-world epic based on the Greek myth of Perseus was the last showcase for the famed stop-motion animation of Ray Harryhausen, after which he went into retirement. The film begins as King Acrisius of Argos (Donald Houston) condemns his daughter Danae (Vida Taylor) and her illegitimate son Perseus to the sea and certain death. Perseus is actually the son of the god Zeus (Laurence Olivier), and from Mount Olympus Zeus commands that Poseidon (Jack Gwillim) free the Titan Kraken and destroy Acrisius and his kingdom with a flood. Danae and Perseus are helped to safety, and the boy (played by Harry Hamlin) grows to be an expert horseman.

On Olympus, the goddess Thetis (Maggie Smith) begs forgiveness on the part of her own son, Calibos (Neil McCarthy), who has enraged Zeus by hunting all but one of his flying horses. Zeus makes Calibos an outcast monster, and the distressed Thetis proclaims that his intended bride Andromeda (Judi Bowker) must forsake all other suitors. But Thetis is also jealous of Zeus' treatment of Perseus and sets him down in the kingdom of Phonecia. Zeus is angry and orders that Perseus be sent weapons from the gods: an almighty sword, a shield, and a helmet that renders its wearer invisible.

The poet and playwright Ammon (played with verve by Burgess Meredith) helps Perseus but cannot dissuade him from going to the city of Joppa unarmed. There Perseus learns that suitors for Andromeda must answer a constantly changing riddle to win her hand and rule the kingdom or be faced with death by fire. Perseus cannot resist using the helmet of invisibility to see the beautiful Andromeda for himself. Upon doing so, he witnesses a giant vulture take her soul away in a cage. Smitten, he proclaims that he has found his destiny.

Following the advice of Ammon, Perseus tames the last of the flying horses, Pegasus, and discovers that Calibos controls the soul of Andromeda and through her sets the riddles. With his newfound knowledge, Perseus is able to answer the next riddle and wins Andromeda's hand in marriage. At the ceremony, Andromeda's mother Cassiopeia (Siân Phillips, known for her role as Livia in the BBC TV series *I, Claudius*, 1976) unwisely declares her daughter more beautiful than Thetis. The goddess angrily declares that Andromeda must be sacrificed as a virgin to the Kraken to make up for the insult.

Although Perseus loses his magical helmet, Athena (Susan Fleetwood) sends as a guide the golden mechanical owl Bubo (the *New York Times* interpreted it as an ancient-world version of R2-D2 from George Lucas' 1977 *Star Wars*, but Bubo was actually designed prior to that film).[1] Perseus sets out to seek the advice of the cannibalistic Stygian witches, who advise him to obtain the head of Medusa, a monstrous woman who can turn all living creatures into stone with her gaze. He departs on his quest without Andromeda and, paying Charon the ferryman, makes his way to the edge of the underworld to Medusa's lair. There he and his men defeat the two-headed dog Dioskilos before descending into Medusa's home. Although Medusa kills Perseus' companions, Perseus himself is able to defeat her by watching her in the reflection of his shield.

During the night, Calibos releases the toxic blood of Medusa's head, from which giant scorpions are born. Perseus kills the scorpions and Calibos himself, and when Bubo releases Pegasus from Calibos' lair, they are able to return to Argos, just as Zeus orders the release of the Kraken. Perseus succeeds in using the severed head to turn the Kraken to stone. The film ends with the marriage of Perseus and Andromeda and the constellations of stars named in their honor.

The extent to which Harryhausen can be seen as a coauthor of the entire film is evident in the way the script was written. Writer Beverley Cross, who also penned the script for *Jason and the Argonauts* (Don Chaffey, 1963) approached Harryhausen and producer Charles H. Schneer with the concept for the film. After researching the Perseus story (which can be found in *The Library* of Apollodorus 2.4.1), Harryhausen found that the "creatures were incorporated . . . in the original legends, so [he] designed certain scenes and he wrote them into the script. Beverley had to tie them all together, along with [Harryhausen's] drawings and concepts . . . so that the whole picture made sense."[2]

Because Harryhausen rightly notes that the myths themselves could be "quite fragmented" across many versions, he felt justified in making alterations.[3] In particular, Harryhausen wanted to depart from traditional depictions of Medusa, which he considered simply not monstrous enough to be sufficiently scary, so rather than merely adorning her head with snakes, he gave her a snake body on her lower half as well. The scene was to appear to be lit by fire, a difficult effect to achieve using stop-motion animation, and the multiple snakes on Medusa's head made for painstaking work.[4]

Harryhausen and Schneer relocated to Europe specifically to enable them to easily use non-American location shoots that were not as familiar to audiences, and *Clash of the Titans* was filmed in England, Malta, Italy, and Spain, with interiors shot at Pinewood Studios.[5] The exterior of Medusa's lair was filmed at the temples of Paestum in southern Italy, which were previously featured as the home of the blind seer in *Jason and the Argonauts*, and for which the crew was permitted to climb over the real ruins.

Clash of the Titans was a commercial success, but the film received a mixed critical reception, for while many appreciated its revival of "grand and glorious romantic adventure," *Variety* dismissed it as a "bore," much to the chagrin of Harryhausen.[6] Although it lacks the pace of *Jason and the Argonauts*, *Clash of the Titans* nonetheless remains a sentimental favorite among Harryhausen fans as an end to an era. Indeed, while stop-motion animation has been replaced by digital effects, Harryhausen's work inspired countless later special effects creators and filmmakers, including Steven Spielberg, James Cameron, and George Lucas.[7] In 2010, a 3D remake of the film was made, directed by Louis Leterrier, bringing the story to a new generation of viewers and using the next generation of computer effects, but harking back to Harryhausen's innovations nonetheless. The original film's suspenseful encounter with Harryhausen's Medusa cannot be matched by its more hectic and photo-realistic remake. DB

Notes

1. Vincent Canby, "*Clash of the Titans* with Olivier as Zeus," *New York Times*, 12 June 1981, http://movies.nytimes.com/movie/review?res=9501EED61138F931A25755C0A967948260&scp=9&sq=%22clash%20of%20the%20titans%22&st=cse (8 January 2012); Ray Harryhausen and Tony Dalton, *Ray Harryhausen: An Animated Life* (New York: Billboard Books, 2004), 270.
2. Jonathan F. Strailey, "A Conversation with Ray Harryhausen," *Clash of the Titans*, directed by Desmond Davis (Turner Entertainment and Warner Bros., 2002), DVD.
3. Strailey, "A Conversation with Ray Harryhausen."
4. Harryhausen and Dalton, *Ray Harryhausen*, 271–75.
5. Strailey, "A Conversation with Ray Harryhausen."
6. "*Clash of the Titans*," *Variety*, 31 December 1980, www.variety.com/review/VE1117789943/ (8 January 2012); Harryhausen and Dalton, *Ray Harryhausen*, 280.
7. Strailey, "A Conversation with Ray Harryhausen."

Bibliography

Canby, Vincent. "*Clash of the Titans* with Olivier as Zeus." *New York Times*, 12 June 1981, http://movies.nytimes.com/movie/review?res=9501EED61138F931A25755C0A967948260&scp=9&sq=%22clash%20of%20the%20titans%22&st=cse (8 January 2012).

"*Clash of the Titans*." *Variety*, 31 December 1980, www.variety.com/review/VE1117789943/ (8 January 2012).

Harryhausen, Ray, and Tony Dalton. *Ray Harryhausen: An Animated Life*. New York: Billboard Books, 2004.

CLASH OF THE TITANS (2010)

DIRECTOR: Louis Leterrier

WRITERS: Travis Beacham, Phil Hay, Matt Manfredi. Based on the motion picture *Clash of the Titans* (1981), directed by Desmond Davis and written by Beverley Cross.

PRODUCERS: Basil Iwanyk, Kevin De La Noy (Thunder Road Film/Zanuck Company, Legendary Pictures, Warner Bros.)

ASSOCIATE PRODUCERS: Karl McMillan, Brenda Berrisford

CINEMATOGRAPHER: Peter Menzies Jr.

EDITORS: Martin Walsh, Vincent Tabaillon

ART DIRECTION: Troy Sizemore, Gary Freeman, Ross Bradshaw, James Foster, Christopher Lowe, Patricio Farrell, Peter James

COSTUMES: Lindy Hemming

MUSIC: Ramin Djawadi

SPECIAL EFFECTS: Nick Davis

CAST: Perseus: Sam Worthington. Zeus: Liam Neeson. Hades: Ralph Fiennes. Calibos/Acrisius: Jason Flemyng. Io: Gemma Arterton. Andromeda: Alexa Davalos. Danae: Tine Stapelfeldt. Draco: Mads Mikkelsen. Apollo: Luke Evans. Athena: Izabella Miko. Solon: Liam Cunningham. Ixas: Hans Matheson. Ozal: Ashraf Barhom. Kucuk: Mouloud Achour. Sheikh Sulieman: Ian Whyte. Eusebios: Nicholas Hoult. Kepheus: Vincent Regan. Cassiopeia: Polly Walker. Aged Cassiopeia: Katherine Loeppky. Prokopion: Luke Treadaway. Spyros: Pete Postlethwaite. Marmara: Elizabeth McGovern. Tekla: Sinead Michael. Pemphredo: Ross Mullan. Enyo: Robin Berry. Deino: Graham Hughes. Phaedrus: Martin McCann. Belo: Rory McCann. Peshet: Kaya Scodelario. Hermes: Alexander Siddig. Ares: Tamer Hassan. Poseidon: Danny Huston. Ammon: William Houston. Captain: Jamie Sives. Hera: Nina Young. Hestia: Jane March. Artemis: Nathalie Cox. Aphrodite: Agyness Deyn. Hephaestus: Paul Kynman. Medusa: Natalia Vodianova. Demeter: Charlotte Comer

AA: None

AAN: None

DVD: Legendary Pictures, Warner Bros., 2010
BLU-RAY: Legendary Pictures, Warner Bros., 2010
DURATION: 102 minutes

Clash of the Titans is a mythological ancient-world epic based on the Greek story of Perseus (Apollodorus, *The Library*, 2.4.1), a remake and reworking of the 1981 Desmond Davis film of the same name. When a fisherman (Pete Postlethwaite, in one of his last films) finds a baby boy and his dead mother at sea, he takes the baby in and raises him. The boy, Perseus (Sam Worthington), grows to manhood but watches his innocent adoptive family perish when Hades (Ralph Fiennes), god of the underworld, exacts revenge for the desecration of a statue of Zeus. Rescued yet again and taken to Argos, Perseus is drawn into a dispute between the humans and the gods. Upon learning that he is, in fact, the son of the god Zeus (Liam Neeson), Perseus nonetheless sides with the humans, and yet becomes Zeus' means of preventing the uprising of Hades from the underworld.

Perseus undertakes a treacherous mission to obtain the head of Medusa (Natalia Vodianova) and defeat the monstrous Kraken, whom the gods have sent to destroy the people of Argos for their insubordination. Perseus and his aids battle the deformed Calibos (Jason Flemyng) (actually the stricken King Acrisius, who had put Perseus and his mother to sea to meet their death); gigantic scorpions who spring from the Hades-infected blood of Calibos; the flying Harpies; and the gigantic Kraken itself. Perseus' helpers mostly perish, but Perseus himself prevails, turning the Kraken to stone with the severed head of Medusa. Cherishing his humanity, Perseus refuses his father's offer to join the gods, but Zeus nonetheless returns to him the revived Io (Gemma Arterton) to keep him company on Earth.

The Greeks continually refashioned their myths, and so, too, film adaptations of myths and the technology used to depict them are refashioned for each generation. Those audience members who grew up with the stop-motion animation of Ray Harryhausen used in the original *Clash of the Titans* will undoubtedly yearn for the charm of yesteryear and despair at the frenetic pace of the remake. For a new generation, Harryhausen's effects may now appear as curiosities of another age, surpassed by the realism of the digital effects on display in the 2010 film. And yet, of course, the one proceeds from the other. The remake pays homage to its superior predecessor by following Harryhausen's reimagining of the Medusa with a serpentine body and incongruously including the comical mechanical owl sent by Athena in the original film (perhaps reminding us that the original was also intended to be just a fun romp).

Clash of the Titans features engaging but regrettably brief appearances by Pete Postlethwaite and Polly Walker (Atia from *Rome*, 2005–2007). Sam Worthington—known from *Avatar* (James Cameron, 2009)—does his best to give an air of heroic importance but does not quite convince. Part of the problem is Perseus' claim that he does not wish to be like the flawed gods, and yet he calls Medusa a "bitch" even after hearing that her monstrous state has been inflicted upon her by the gods as punishment for her own rape. Indeed, the young women in the film—Medusa, Io, Andromeda, and Danae—are all punished for the misdeeds of others. The gods of Greek myth reflected all the vices of their human counterparts, so while the gods in *Clash of the Titans* are deemed unworthy of worship, the humans and their half-human hero also fail to inspire.

The 2010 film left critics cold, both for its content and poor 3D,[1] but it was a commercial success, spawning its own sequel, *Wrath of the Titans* (Jonathan Liebesman, 2012), in which Perseus descends into the underworld to rescue Zeus and save humanity from an uprising of the Titans and the underworld gods. DB

Note

1. See, for example, Manohla Dargis, "*Clash of the Titans* (Remake) (2010): Beware of Greeks Bearing Buzz Cuts," *New York Times*, 1 April 2010, http://movies.nytimes.com/2010/04/02/movies/02clash.html?scp=1&sq=%22clash%20of%20the%20titans%22&st=cse (8 January 2012).

Bibliography

Dargis, Manohla. "*Clash of the Titans* (Remake) (2010): Beware of Greeks Bearing Buzz Cuts." *New York Times*, 1 April 2010, http://movies.nytimes.com/2010/04/02/movies/02clash.html?scp=1&sq=%22clash%20of%20the%20titans%22&st=cse (8 January 2012).

CLEOPATRA (1934)

DIRECTOR: Cecil B. DeMille
WRITERS: Waldemar Young, Vincent Lawrence, Bartlett Cormack (adaptation of historical material)
PRODUCER: Cecil B. DeMille (Paramount Pictures)
ASSISTANT DIRECTOR: Cullen Tate
CINEMATOGRAPHER: Victor Milner
EDITOR: Anne Bauchens (uncredited)
MUSIC: Rudolph G. Kopp, Milan Roder (uncredited)
SOUND EDITOR: Franklin Hansen
CAST: Cleopatra: Claudette Colbert. Caesar: Warren William. Mark Antony: Henry Wilcoxon. King Herod: Joseph Schildkraut. Octavian: Ian Keith. Calpurnia: Gertrude Michael. Enobarbus: C. Aubrey Smith. Apollodorus: Irving Pichel. Brutus: Arthur Hohl. Casca: Edwin Maxwell. Cassius: Ian Maclaren. Charmion: Eleanor Phelps. Potyhinos: Leonard Mudie. Iras: Grace Durkin
AA: Best Cinematography (Victor Milner)
AAN: Best Picture (Paramount Pictures), Best Assistant Director (Cullen Tate), Best Editing (Anne Bauchens), Best Sound (Franklin Hansen)
DVD: Universal, 2006
BLU-RAY: Eureka Entertainment, 2012
DURATION: 103 minutes

Cecil B. DeMille certainly knew how to make spectacular epics in his time, spanning several decades during the silent era and then from the 1930s to the 1950s. His first grand epic, *The Ten Commandments*, filmed in 1923 (and then again in 1956), set a trend for spectacles that Hollywood adopted for years to come, almost all crowd pleasers, thus ensuring DeMille's eminence in the development of American cinema. His most flavorful spectacles were drawn from Roman and biblical themes, in which DeMille added spice with sex scenes, lavish sets, and scores of chorus girls passing as dancers and royal escorts. In the 1930s, he made *The Sign of the Cross* (1932), *Cleopatra* (1934), and *The Crusades* (1935), the last two with Henry Wilcoxon, a heartthrob in those days who, in his later years, became a credible character actor. Wilcoxon looked a more virile action hero than Richard Burton, the Mark Antony in the 1963 *Cleopatra*, who was a more accomplished actor, having played Hamlet (in the Old Vic) and also Alexander the Great, but who lacked credibility as a hard-boiled and battle-scarred warrior, something Wilcoxon had.

Comparisons with the 1963 epic are inevitable, especially since Cleopatra was played by two of the most glamorous stars in the Hollywood firmament—Elizabeth Taylor and Claudette Colbert, although three decades apart. Both were known for their femininity, beauty, and acting talents, and both were willing to display their physical attributes, Colbert just before the Hays Code took full effect, Taylor just as the code was beginning to fade. DeMille was banking on a generous dose of nudity—or seminudity—in his religious epics, deftly mixing piety and desire, making the audience gasp at the plethora of crowds of young women in diaphanous robes (or disrobes) dancing and cavorting before the eyes of dazzled, and sex-starved, Roman legionaries.

The American audiences were also starved, but for different reasons. In the middle of the throes of the Great Depression, they were ready for the gist of the Hollywood mills. They wanted rich spectacles to divert them from their economic woes, and, of course, clever men like DeMille (and many others) obliged. They gave them the spectacles they craved in such extravaganzas as *Ben-Hur* (the early version has topless girls escorting Ben-Hur to Rome); *The Ten Commandments*; and sea adventures and Elizabethan costume dramas with dashing heroes the likes of Errol Flynn, Douglas Fairbanks Jr., and many others. Spectacle was the order of the day, and epics, especially, filled a need of audiences who wanted clashing swords, chariots drawn by horses hard-breathing to victory, and tantalizing women waiting at the end of the line to reward the winners. Some epics were (and are) tragic stories, but the epic form, being larger than life, can accommodate any story line, whether history or fantasy, to suit its ends. Audiences didn't mind, as long as the spectacle was worth its ticket price.

DeMille's *Cleopatra* added to all of that. It featured a love affair between two of the most notorious and ill-fated lovers of history and had history itself and stage drama examples to draw from—Shakespeare's *Julius Caesar* and *Antony and Cleopatra*, not to mention George Bernard Shaw's play *Caesar and Cleopatra*, which was to be filmed more than a decade later.[1] The plot evolves as a slightly decadent and spoiled queen has an affair, first with a mighty Roman general, Caesar, who flush from his victory over his rival Pompey, embarks on his conquest of Egypt, whose riches and large territories would fulfill his dreams of world conquest. Here Caesar is played with élan by Warren William, a genial-looking gentleman who adds a note of distinction among the otherwise average actors who surrounded him—and her. A general bows to her charms, making her his rich acquisition—rich in both real estate and luscious body parts—until a second general, and soon also lover, Antony, arrives following Caesar's assassination, only to surrender his manhood, betraying his homeland for the Egyptian seductress. Amid wild orgiastic dances and the clash of battle, the viewer sees one general assassinated, and the one that follows him, Antony, although a rugged warrior and passionate lover, vacillates between his loyalty to Rome and the charms of the queen. No doubt in love, he loses a crucial naval battle and then plunges a blade into his stomach. Cleopatra, now having lost everything and threatened by the prospect of being hauled to Rome, in chains, and Octavian's (Ian Keith) spoil of war, besieged by all sides, holds an asp, letting it bite her in the breast.

Cleopatra seems almost totally apolitical and barely historical, for it, like its literary counterparts, Shakespeare's *Antony and Cleopatra* and Shaw's *Caesar and Cleopatra*, aims at the drama of lovers and the spectacle around her rather than true history. An epic rarely places history ahead of drama, and this one is no different. The movie has no serious intentions aside from pure entertainment, of which DeMille was master. Some historical events occasionally punctuate its plotline, for instance, the arrival of King Herod (Joseph Schildkraut), who slyly recommends that alliance with Rome is Cleopatra's best course, although that would mean the abandonment of Antony to his enemies. In addition, Enobarbus (C. Aubrey Smith), one of the few generals left to Antony to fight Octavian, but who also leaves him in the end, tells him that he cannot betray his homeland for the sake of a woman.

Is this movie as serious a drama as many have proclaimed it to be? The answer is yes and no. It is because of the undoubted talent of Colbert to project Cleopatra as a woman of stature, beauty, grandeur, and tragic quality. Colbert is equal to the task, both in showing her sexual appeal and being credible as a heroine who plays the end game with dignity, but the movie also has an air of Hollywood product that does not allow it to climb the pedestal of a great classic. There is too much bad dialogue, for one thing—in contrast with the brilliant dialogue of Mankiewicz in the 1963 *Cleopatra.* The dialogue here occasionally sounds stilted, and the accent ranges between impeccable Oxford enunciation and street Hollywood parlance. Furthermore, the movie does not have the dimensions of a true epic—something that did not develop until the 1950s, when the wide screen came into usage. Aside from the magnificent sequences in Cleopatra's barge, a "floating bordello," as some have called it, most scenes are lumped together, and the viewer is lost as to which exact historical event is taking place. Length, after all, has a reason to be the main epic ingredient. It can be both an advantage and a fatal flaw, but without it, an epic will not be the spectacle we expect today, after many decades of trial and error in the Hollywood canon. DeMille is owed credit, however, as he was one of the first (the other being D. W. Griffith) to tackle this magnificent genre, which has enthralled audiences now for more than a century. CS

Note

1. Screenwriters Waldemar Young and Vincent Lawrence borrowed historical materials from Bartlett Cormac, an American actor, playwright, and screenwriter.

Bibliography

Earley, Steven C. "The Epic/Spectacular." In *An Introduction to American Movies*, 146–61. New York: New American Library, 1978.

CLEOPATRA (1963)

Director: Joseph L. Mankiewicz

Writers: Sidney Buchman, Ranald MacDougall, Joseph L. Mankiewicz, Ben Hecht

Producers: Walter Wagner, Darryl F. Zanuck (uncredited), Robert Mamoulian (uncredited) (20th Century Fox, MCL Films, Walwa Films)

Cinematographer: Leon Shamroy, Jack Hildyard (uncredited)

Editors: Dorothy Spencer, Elmo Williams (uncredited)

Art Direction: John DeCuir, Jack Martin Smith, Hilyard M. Brown, Paul S. Fox, Ray Blumenthal, Elven Webb, Maurice Pelling, Boris Juraga, Walter M. Scott, Ray Moyer

Costumes: Irene Sharaff, Vittorio Nino Novarese, Renié

Music: Alex North, Peter Lavathes (uncredited)

Sound Mixers: James Corcoran, Fred Hynes

Special Effects: Emil Kosa Jr.

Cast: Cleopatra: Elizabeth Taylor. Mark Antony: Richard Burton. Caesar: Rex Harrison. Octavian: Roddy McDowall. Rufio: Martin Landau. Casca: Carroll O'Connor. Brutus: Kenneth Haigh. Flavius: George Cole. High Priestess: Pamela Brown. Apollodorus: Cesare Danova. Eiras: Francesca Annis. Ptolemy: Richard O'Sullivan. Sosigenes: Hume Cronyn. Pothinus: Grégoire Aslan. Agrippa: Andrew Keir. Calpurnia. Gwen Watford. Ramos: Martin Benson. Octavia: Jean Marsh

AA: Best Cinematography (Leon Shamroy), Best Art Direction (John DeCuir, Jack Martin Smith, Hilyard M. Brown, Paul S. Fox, Ray Blumenthal, Elven Webb, Maurice Pelling, Boris Juraga, Walter M. Scott, Ray Moyer), Best Costume Design (Irene Sharaff, Vittorio Nino Novarese, Renié), Best Visual Effects (Emil Kosa Jr.)

AAN: Best Picture, Best Actor (Rex Harrison), Best Film Editing (Dorothy Spencer), Best Original Score (Alex North), Best Sound Mixing (James Corcoran, Fred Hynes)

DVD: 20th Century Fox Film Corporation, 2001; 20th Century Fox Film Corporation, 2006. The 2006 edition is a three-disc five-star collection with "Special Features," including a running commentary by Chris Mankiewicz, Tom Mankiewicz, Martin Landau, and Jack Brodsky.

Blu-ray: 20th Century Fox, 2012. Two-disc 50th anniversary edition.

Duration: 248 minutes (320 for director's cut)

Before being undertaken by 20th Century Fox in 1963, *Cleopatra* had been filmed several times, as a silent movie, with Theda Bara as Cleopatra in 1917, and, in the sound era, as an epic movie in 1934, directed by Cecil B. DeMille, with Claudette Colbert as Cleopatra. Although lavish for its time, the DeMille production did not reach the scope and ambition of the 1963 epic, which was designed to rival or surpass in glitter such extravaganzas as *Ben-Hur* and *The Ten Commandments*, made during the preceding decade. Nevertheless, *Cleopatra* remained in the tradition of the 1950s epic sagas, which broached Judeo-Christian or Roman themes, although here the emphasis was placed on producing a grand spectacle with literary pretensions rather than the run-of-the-mill adventure epic where a hero usually triumphs at the end. With a woman's name in the title and an actress in the lead who commanded enormous reputation for beauty and talent, the movie also diverged from the suffocating masculinity of the epics the previous decade had consciously embraced. With a few exceptions, for example, *Gone with the Wind* (1939), *Caesar and Cleopatra* (Gabriel Pascal, 1946), and *Samson and Delilah* (Cecil B. DeMille, 1948), epic moviemaking had largely been a masculine trend established by Hollywood from the outset, as heroes in action sequences, for instance, chariot races or naval battles, demanded virile males in the leads, while most females played decorative roles—dancers, servants, or love interests, at best.

The choice of Elizabeth Taylor in the leading role could not have been more appealing to audiences of that era. A child actress who had progressed into adult roles and already won a Best Actress Academy Award for *Butterfield 8* (1960), in 1963 Taylor was still was at the peak of her career, and it came as no surprise that she would be selected to play one of the most notorious female figures in history—a heroine already immortalized in Shakespeare's *Antony and Cleopatra*. Still, when this epic movie was released, it flopped with both audiences and critics, who balked at its size, slow pace, and loose plotline. The scandal caused by the love affair between its two main leads—Taylor and Burton—did not help matters, dragging down its reputation. Decades later, however, *Cleopatra* has regained some momentum with audiences, who generally regard it as one of the most memorable epics of its era, worthy of renewed attention.

Cleopatra was mounted as an expensive project, meant to save the sinking fortunes of 20th Century Fox, whose executives went to great expense to build colossal and elaborate sets, including an entire fleet for the final Battle of Actium. But with delays, caused mainly by a serious illness of Taylor that threatened her life, and the transfer of the entire project from England to Rome, the cost of the movie escalated, and the production came to a standstill until its protagonist recovered. A new start was necessitated, which, among other things, required the rebuilding of the huge sets in Rome and the rewriting of the entire script by Joseph L. Mankiewicz. The movie ran over budget (with a cost of more than $40 million), but its makers still had ambitions that this would be the epic to end all epics. Aside from its glamorous star, *Cleopatra* was made with exemplary attention to detail in costume and set designs, which received Oscars and set high standards for epic spectacles; however, it netted only $26 million after its initial release, and although it eventually recovered its losses and even made a small profit, it was considered a colossal flop both at the box office and with critical opinion in general. Its failure may be attributed to external factors along the lines of those previously mentioned, delays, change of venue, and so forth, but also to purely aesthetic reasons.

Of the most obvious of these reasons one could mention a few. First, the length. *Cleopatra* is a two-part movie spanning more than four hours, requiring an intermission, thus taxing the patience of audiences, given the fact that it is a largely uneventful and rather talky tale, considering its ambition and scope. The Caesar/Cleopatra episode is rather rambling, offering only sporadic action and failing to engage the interest of viewers used to epic pace and quick plot progression, in spite of the climactic spectacle of Cleopatra's entrance into Rome. Rex Harrison appears as an imposing leader whose mission is to place Cleopatra on the Egyptian throne and defeat her brother and his cohorts, all in Rome's interest. Cleopatra, a feisty raconteur in their numerous exchanges, takes a backseat to his initiatives, only winning his heart, although this affair looks tepid compared to what is to follow. Caesar, an epileptic burdened by larger conflicts—the possibility of Rome sinking into another civil strife, being one—treats Cleopatra as a pawn of Rome's designs, even though he grew to have a fatherly affection for her. Larger than life, Harrison barely fits the image of an epic hero, who must, above all, exhibit the dash and charisma of a lover and fighter. A lukewarm lover, and nary a fighter, and despite his imposing stature, Harrison as Caesar fails to win the empathy of the audience, who must wait for the second part of the movie, where passion and political intrigue combine to move the top-heavy structure forward.

The second part of the movie gains momentum with the entrance of Mark Antony. Soon after Caesar's assassination, in a scene shown as one of Cleopatra's magic rituals, a triumvirate replaces him—Octavian (Roddy McDowall), ruler of Rome; Lepidus, who was to govern Spain and the West; and Antony, who was to govern the East, including Egypt, of course. Antony goes to Egypt to secure the now-queen Cleopatra's large territorial possessions, including much of the Middle East and Ethiopia.

Another reason for the lackluster performance at the box office relates to the original intentions of 20th Century Fox president Spyros Skouras to create an epic where great spectacle and star glamour would be sufficient enough to carry the day. In the late 1950s, the 20th Century Fox studio had experienced several flops at the box office, and *Cleopatra* would provide a way out of that fix. The financial strains were accentuated by the mixed motives of its makers—the changes of producers during production and the differing aims of the two directors involved in the making of the movie. Spyros Skouras was succeeded by Darryl F. Zanuck, and Rouben Mamoulian, the original director, was replaced by Joseph L. Mankiewicz, who, aside from being a distinguished director, was a writer of note. He envisioned a literate epic rather than the blockbuster moneymaker that the studio expected. The aforementioned delays contributed to rewriting the script, causing further expense, a change of leading actors, and a growing public unease about the scandalous Taylor–Burton romance.

The historical background of *Cleopatra* merits some discussion, for it seems that its makers counted on historical authenticity to carry the plot for them. Opening credits state that the story is based on the histories of Plutarch and Suetonius and other Roman historians, and on a modern historical work, *The Life and Times of Cleopatra*, by Italian historian C. M. Franzero, for the major events of the era. Thus, by and large, the basic events of the story are accurately connected to history of the Roman Empire around the latter part of the first century B.C., when Julius Caesar was fighting a divisive war, eventually defeating Pompey at Pharsalus and becoming a life dictator of Rome.

Following this victory, Caesar went to Egypt to secure what was thought to be a rich Roman colony to aid Cleopatra, then fighting a war of succession with her younger brother Ptolemy, a teenage boy, who was then the king. Caesar helped Cleopatra defeat him and his cohorts and become a queen of Egypt. He lingered on in Egypt for a year or two, and his liaison with Cleopatra produced a son, Caesarion, but during his absence, trouble was brewing in Rome, and Caesar had to hurry back. Cleopatra followed him with her young son, triumphantly entering Rome on a chariot drawn by hundreds of slaves. Antony had already been in Egypt, met Cleopatra, saw her in Rome when she visited there, and become her admirer. After Caesar's assassination, he went back to Egypt, and his new meeting with the queen resulted in a torrid romance. While Antony remained in Egypt for far too long, his enemies in Rome plotted against him, and his split with Octavian eventually brought about the famous naval battle at Actium, where Antony and Cleopatra were defeated and subsequently put an end to their lives.

As previously mentioned, the failure of *Cleopatra* as a dramatic structure may be attributed to the vicissitudes of that production. Mankiewicz was under pressure by the producers to finish the movie on schedule, which affected his creative decisions. His idea was that *Cleopatra* should be presented in two parts: the first would be based on George Bernard Shaw's play *Caesar and Cleopatra*, filmed earlier with Claude Raines and Vivien Leigh, while the second part would be based on Shakespeare's *Antony and Cleopatra*. There would be two films, each shown six months apart and each about three hours long. That idea was rejected by Zanuck, who, as did the 20th Century Fox studio in general, wanted *Cleopatra* as one giant movie, already the most expensive movie in history, to be released as soon as possible, in the hopes that it would recover the huge outlays that went into making it. As it turned out, *Cleopatra*, released in June 1963, did poorly (as already mentioned), although it garnered nine Oscar nominations, of which it won four.

Admired today for its elaborate sets, literate dialogue, and excellent acting (by Harrison, Taylor, Landau, McDowall, and many others), the film still suffers from its structural break and the omission of several filmed sequences due to its great length. Perhaps sectioning *Cleopatra* into two parts might have worked, but in different ways. The Shaw play was not intended as film, and the earlier production was static, obviously a staged movie, while the Shakespeare play would have necessitated Shakespearean dialogue, which would be difficult to comprehend (and tolerate) by modern audiences.

Finally, the failure of *Cleopatra* can be attributed to the fact that it was made for financial rather than artistic reasons; it was to rescue the failing studio of 20th Century Fox, and its producers were looking for a moneymaker. Joseph L Mankiewicz, who had also amassed a considerable reputation for a string of screen successes that had not only commercial but literary value (he was the screenwriter of *Citizen Kane*, for instance), was constantly hampered such by delays as change in locale, wrangling among producers, and Taylor's near-fatal illness. These conflicting aims and distractions had an impact on his concept, vision, and handling of the meager plot of the story.

Although this was one of the most glorious eras of the Roman Empire, and it is inherently interesting, the *Cleopatra* that appeared in the final cut (which did not make Mankiewicz happy) is limpid in pacing, dragging on rather than being propelled by its inner dynamics. While glorious sets and costumes and what was advertised as "spectacle" are some of the highest achievements of Hollywood in that sense, the Cleopatra story is fragmented and episodic, and it does not engage even the most patient of reviewers. Luckily—for it is still worth seeing—the DVD edition, a splendid restoration done in 1995, allows the modern viewer to enjoy it in several sittings. As mere spectacle, *Cleopatra* excels, but spectacle alone is not a substitute for a tightly told tale, which some epics do achieve, no matter how magnificent the costumes and settings.

Plot-making is the essence of the epic—and the same rule that applies to other dramas is, in this respect, applicable here, too. Although this grand epic may be considered a flop for the aforementioned—and perhaps many other—reasons, the glamorous presence of Elizabeth Taylor redeems it, to some extent. The film demonstrates that an actress can have the same pull, for an audience of her time and of succeeding ages, as one who can stand her ground amid the plethora of male superstars that populated the epics of that—or any other—period. Her descent from the Sphinx statue during her entrance in Rome is still a magnificent spectacle. Her vitalizing presence and dignity as an actress may have saved the movie from oblivion. Even if one only considers this as a historical relic in the history of great epics of her time, Elizabeth Taylor stood her ground as a female epic persona, the only actress of her time that could have brought the aims of this grand spectacle to fruition. CS

Bibliography

Bradford, Ernie Dusgate Selby. *Cleopatra.* New York: Penguin, 2000.

Burstein, Stanley M. *The Reign of Cleopatra.* Westport, CT: Greenwood, 2004.

Plutarch. *Eight Great Lives.* Edited with an introduction by C. A. Robinson Jr. New York: Holt, Reinhart and Winston, 1960.

CLOSE ENCOUNTERS OF THE THIRD KIND (1977)

Director: Steven Spielberg
Writer: Steven Spielberg
Producers: Julia Phillips, Michael Phillips (Columbia Pictures, EFI Films, Julia Phillips and Michael Phillips Productions)
Cinematographer: Vilmos Zsigmond
Editor: Michael Kahn
Art Direction: Joe Alves, Daniel A. Lomino, Phil Abramson
Music: John Williams
Sound Editor: Frank E. Warner
Sound Mixers: Robert Knudson, Robert Glass, Don MacDougall, Gene S. Cantamessa
Special Effects: Roy Arbogast, Douglas Trumbull, Matthew Yuricich, Gregory Jein, Richard Yuricich
Cast: Roy Neary: Richard Dreyfuss. Claude Lacombe: François Truffaut. Ronnie Neary: Teri Garr. Jillian Guiler: Melinda Dillon. David Laughlin: Bob Balaban. Barry Guiler: Cary Guffey. Maj. "Wild Bill" Walsh: Warren J. Kemmerling. Larry Butler: Josef Sommer
AA: Best Cinematography (Vilmos Zsigmond), Special Achievement Award (for sound effects editing) (Frank E. Warner)
AAN: Best Supporting Actress (Melinda Dillon), Best Art Direction–Set Decoration (Joe Alves, Daniel A. Lomino, Phil Abramson), Best Director (Steven Spielberg), Best Effects–Visual Effects (Roy Arbogast, Douglas Trumbull, Matthew Yuricich, Gregory Jein, Richard Yuricich), Best Film Editing (Michael Kahn), Best Music–Original Score (John Williams), Best Sound (Robert Knudson, Robert Glass, Don MacDougall, Gene S. Cantamessa)
DVD: Sony Pictures Home Entertainment, 2007
Blu-ray: Sony Pictures Home Entertainment, 2011
Duration: 137 minutes

Using his original screenplay, Steven Spielberg directed *Close Encounters of the Third Kind* at a cost of $20 million. The film's worldwide gross was nearly $300 million, and it cemented Spielberg's reputation by earning him an Academy Award nomination for Best Director. The film prefigures his future science-fiction films, namely *E.T. the Extra-Terrestrial* (1982), *Jurassic Park* (1993), and *A.I.: Artificial Intelligence* (2001), which also have at their core a childlike wonder and imagination.

Many critics have commented on the film being a religious film, even comparing some scenes to the gospels. According to Andrew Gordon,

> There has always been a strain of the evangelical in science-fiction literature and film, which accounts for its occasional cult followings; after all, outer space is naturally confused with Heaven, and the sense of wonder at the heart of much science fiction and fantasy is akin to religious awe.[1]

The film opens on Land Rovers driving through the Sonora Desert in Mexico during a sandstorm. Men leave the vehicles and are joined by Mexican policemen. Among them are Claude Lacombe (François Truffaut), a French scientist, and David Laughlin (Bob Balaban), Lacombe's interpreter and a cartographer by trade. They find several World War II planes that arrived overnight, missing since 1945 off the Florida coast, but without pilots or crews. They ask a local man about the planes. His face burned, he tells them the sun came out during the night and sang to him.

The film moves to the Indianapolis traffic control center, where several planes report seeing a bright object moving quickly through the sky. None decide to file an official report. In Muncie, Indiana, that night, Barry Guiler (Cary Guffey), a young boy sleeping in his bedroom, awakens to his toys operating on their own. He wanders downstairs, where he finds an open refrigerator, food spilled on the floor, and the front door open. His mother, Jillian (Melinda Dillon), wakes and sees Barry outside laughing and chasing something.

That same night, Roy Neary's (Richard Dreyfuss) employer calls him back to work on transmission lines because power has gone out. Stopped on the highway while looking at a map, Neary waves a car to go by him. Still lost at a railroad crossing, he pulls down a map from behind the visor. He waves another vehicle to go around him, but it moves above his truck. Crickets stop chirping, mailboxes along the highway shake, and his lights fail. The spaceship hovers above his truck, and objects inside float as if gravity has suddenly quit working. He watches as the ship moves across the sky, following the highway. He follows the UFO as its sightings are reported on the radio. Neary arrives at a turn on the highway high on a hill. He almost hits Barry, who is running in the middle of the road, but Jillian pulls him off the pavement. Other people have gathered there to wait for the UFOs, which fly by with several police cars chasing them.

Neary goes home and wakes his wife, Ronnie (Teri Garr), and the kids. Based on a night Steven Spielberg's father woke his family to see a meteor shower, Neary takes them to where he saw the UFOs.[2] Upset, his wife says, "Don't you think I'm taking this really well?" They kiss and he looks into the sky.

The next day, newspapers report that UFOs were sighted over five counties. Neary studies objects that remind him of something he cannot name. His employer fires him over the phone for not repairing the line. He drives to the UFO site, this time with a camera. Other people are there, too, including people playing cards and Jillian and Barry. She and Neary have facial sunburns. Barry forms a mound out of mud similar to what Neary sees in his mind. Lights in the sky move close to them, but they are only helicopters.

Meanwhile, in Northern India, hundreds of people sing five notes that were implanted in their minds. Scientists record the song. Lacombe asks what direction the sound came from. They all point to the sky. While there, Lacombe designs a sign language equivalent to the musical notes. The Goldstone radio telescope receives a repeating sequence of numbers from the "neighborhood." Laughlin recognizes them as longitudes and latitudes. They quickly find the location in eastern Wyoming.

At Jillian's house, Barry plays five notes on a xylophone, while Jillian draws a hill from the image in her mind. Barry moves to the window and watches clouds move mysteriously. Jillian locks the door, but a bright light shines from the sky, through the keyhole, down the fireplace, and from a floor vent. The vent screws turn from underneath, so she blocks it with a table. Barry crawls outside through a dog door. Jillian attempts to pull him back, but he is pulled out from the other side. With Barry gone, she chases the light as it moves above the field.

At a secret government location, leaders plan something so scary that it "will clear 300 miles of every Christian soul" in eastern Wyoming. They load trucks disguised as Piggly Wiggly and Baskin Robbins delivery vehicles.

In the next scene, the Neary family is having dinner at the kitchen table. Roy stacks mashed potatoes high on his plate and sculpts them. He cries when he sees his family watching, worrying. Later, he sculpts a clay hill in the center of his train track. Frustrated, he runs outside and yells to the sky, "What is it?" The following morning, he tells his wife and kids that everything is fine and attempts to pull down the clay mound. Only the top gives way, revealing a flat-topped mountain. Inspired, he pulls up plants from around the house and pushes them inside through the kitchen window. Frightened by his actions, Ronnie decides to take the kids to her sister's house. Roy sculpts a six-foot-high mountain from dirt shoveled into his living room. While he talks to Ronnie on the phone to coax her into coming back home, television news reports an evacuation from the Devil's Tower area of eastern Wyoming because of an accidental release of nerve gas. The report shows Devil's Tower, the first national monument in the United States, which Neary recognizes as the image in his mind that he has been trying to re-create. Jillian also sees the report and compares it to her paintings.

Neary drives to Devil's Tower. Traffic is heading out of the area to avoid the nerve gas. Neary buys three gas masks and two birds in a cage to test for gas. He meets Jillian, and they drive cross country to avoid roadblocks. Jillian says that the police dragged the river for Barry and asked, ironically, if she "had seen any strangers in the neighborhood." They drive closer to Devil's Tower and see dead animals, but his birds do not die. Although he says the whole thing is a "put on," they both put on their gas masks. They are stopped by men in white coveralls and gas masks and are separated.

Lacombe and Laughlin interview Neary. Lacombe asks if he is an artist and whether he has migraines or any recent burns on his body. "Have you recently had a close encounter with something very unusual?" asks Lacombe. Neary does not answer and receives no satisfying answers to his questions. He is put in a helicopter with other UFO witnesses. As Lacombe tries to argue with Major "Wild Bill" Walsh (Warren J. Kemmerling) to let the people stay because "they were invited," Neary, Jillian, and a man named Larry Butler (Josef Sommer) escape from the helicopter. The rest are helicoptered away. After they are gone, Wild Bill, Lacombe, and Laughlin remove their masks. Wild Bill receives call from a superior who orders him to use sleep aerosol to keep the three escapees from reaching the tower.

As night falls, soldiers search for them but quickly abandon the effort. Instead, the military dusts the area with a sleep aerosol. Larry, worn out by the climb, is sprayed. In a moment reminiscent of *North by Northwest* (1959), Jillian pulls Neary up the face of a rock. On the other side of the tower, an arena is ready for pending arrivals. Several ships spin out of the sky and move closer to the landing area. The scientists play the five tones, and the ships respond musically and then leave. In these scenes, Spielberg used breakthrough technology of digital motion controls that matched the miniatures of dozens of spacecraft to the live action.[3] A cloud moves close to the tower and encircles it. Neary and Jillian move down the mountain toward the arena. He decides to go to the landing area, but she will not go without Barry. They kiss. The ships leave, but a massive ship, larger than Devil's Tower itself, arrives.

Neary stands in the arena as the huge ship hovers above the assembled people. Jillian moves down to the arena. The tones played by the ship break windows. One scientist says, "It seems they are trying to teach us a basic tonal vocabulary." A ramp is lowered from the ship, and a door opens. The missing pilots walk down the ramp. As they are identified, they are crossed off lists of missing persons. Others follow, including civilians, children, and Barry.

Lacombe sees Neary and asks what he wants. Lacombe talks to others about Neary's idea. An alien creature descends from the ship. It is humanoid in appearance, with elongated arms and legs. Soon, small, child-like aliens exit the ship. Men and women in red jumpsuits receive a prayer service and line up to board the ship. Neary joins them, but the aliens pull him out of line, touch him, and guide him to the ramp. An alien greets Lacombe, and they exchange hand gestures. The ship rises and exits the atmosphere.

After the popularity of John Williams's score for Spielberg's film *Jaws*, the two teamed up again for *Close Encounters of the Third Kind*. His score was reminiscent of 1950s science-fiction films, and it had to fit the emotional core of the film, which "required reconciling stylistic imperatives and idioms."[4] The film is about language: "[V]erbal, visual, electronic, and musical—communication and its limitations, language and its possibilities."[5] The possibilities, Spielberg says, are unlimited. JMW

Notes

1. Andrew Gordon, "*Close Encounters*: The Gospel According to Stephen Spielberg," *Literature Film Quarterly* 8, no. 3 (1980): 156.

2. Steven Spielberg, "The Making of *Close Encounters of the Third Kind*," directed by Steven Spielberg (Sony Pictures Home Entertainment, 2007), DVD.

3. Spielberg, "The Making of *Close Encounters of the Third Kind*."

4. Timothy E. Scheurer, "John Williams and Film Music since 1971," *Popular Music and Society* 21, no. 1 (1997): 61.

5. Charlene Engel, "Language and the Music of the Spheres: Steven Spielberg's *Close Encounters of the Third Kind*," *Literature/Film Quarterly* 24, no. 4 (1996): 376.

Bibliography

Engel, Charlene. "Language and the Music of the Spheres: Steven Spielberg's *Close Encounters of the Third Kind*." *Literature/Film Quarterly* 24, no. 4 (1996): 376–84.

Gordon, Andrew. "*Close Encounters*: The Gospel According to Stephen Spielberg." *Literature/Film Quarterly* 8, no. 3 (1980): 156–64.

Scheurer, Timothy E. "John Williams and Film Music since 1971." *Popular Music and Society* 21, no. 1 (1997): 59–72.

COLD MOUNTAIN (2003)

DIRECTOR: Anthony Minghella

WRITER: Anthony Minghella. Based on the novel by Charles Frazier.

PRODUCERS: Steve E. Andrews, Albert Berger, Timothy Bricknell, William Horberg, Bob Osher, Sydney Pollack, Iain Smith, Bob Weinstein, Harvey Weinstein, Ron Yerxa (Miramax, Mirage Enterprises, Bona Fide Productions)

DIRECTOR: Anthony Minghella

WRITER: Anthony Minghella. Based on the novel by Charles Frazier.

PRODUCERS: Steve E. Andrews, Albert Berger, Timothy Bricknell, William Horberg, Bob Osher, Sydney Pollack, Iain Smith, Bob Weinstein, Harvey Weinstein, Ron Yerxa (Miramax, Mirage Enterprises, Bona Fide Productions)

CINEMATOGRAPHER: John Seale

EDITOR: Walter Murch

MUSIC: Gabriel Yared

CAST: Inman: Jude Law. Ada Monroe: Nicole Kidman. Ruby Thewes: Renée Zellweger. Maddy: Eileen Atkins. Stobrod Thewes: Brendan Gleeson. Reverend Veasey: Philip Seymour Hoffman. Sara: Natalie Portman. Junior: Giovanni Ribisi. Lila: Melora Walters. Reverend Monroe: Donald Sutherland. Teague: Ray Winstone. Swimmer: Jay Tavare. Oakley:

Lucas Black. Sally Swanger: Kathy Baker. Esco: James Gammon. Bosie: Charlie Hunnam. Pangle: Ethan Suplee. Georgia: Jack White. Ferry Girl: Jena Malone
AA: Best Supporting Actress (Renée Zellweger)
AAN: Best Leading Actor (Jude Law), Best Cinematography (John Seale), Best Film Editing (Walter Murch), Best Music–Original Score (Gabriel Yared), Best Music–Original Song (T-Bone Burnett and Elvis Costello for "Scarlet Tide" and Sting for "You Will Be My Ain True Love")
DVD: Miramax, 2003
Blu-ray: Miramax, 2003
Duration: 154 minutes

Anthony Minghella's first career plan was to complete a dissertation on Samuel Becket and become an academic, but he abandoned it and became a television script editor and moved to playwriting and screenwriting, which won him an Emmy and a BAFTA Award.[1] As Jim Knowlson writes, his film *Truly, Madly, Deeply*

> put Minghella on the map in world cinema (winning a BAFTA Award and a Writers' Guild Award). *The English Patient*, with Minghella's script based on Michael Ondaatje's almost unfilmable novel, had the greatest commercial success, winning nine Oscars, including Best Picture of 1996.[2]

Minghella convinced novelist Charles Frazier, who won the Pulitzer Prize for his novel *Cold Mountain*, that he could bring the novel to life, because

> boiled down to its bones, the book makes an irresistible case for adaptation to the screen: an honorable man, a journey, a purpose, a series of obstacles, someone waiting with forbearance, and Cold Mountain itself, a place that becomes more than a place, becomes a goal, stands in for a time and way of life [that] have been lost.[3]

The film begins with one of the battles during the Siege of Petersburg, which Minghella planned would be "sufficiently pungent"[4] to set the stage as a Civil War film. Although it is the Confederates who are victorious by the conclusion of the Battle of the Crater, it begins with a clear Northern advantage because Union engineers tunnel below the Confederate troops to place explosives. Above them, Inman (Jude Law), a member of the Confederate Army, studies a photo of Ada Monroe (Nicole Kidman), his fiancée. He keeps her tintype and letters in his worn copy of William Bartram's *Travels*, which she gave him. Others from his hometown of Cold Mountain serve with him, including his Indian friend Swimmer (Jay Tavare) and Oakley (Lucas Black), who is probably too young to fight. The ground suddenly rises around Inman and his friends and swallows him. Hundreds of Union soldiers run toward them. The explosion creates a large ditch that the Union soldiers cannot cross, and Southern soldiers have a "turkey shoot." Inman shoots several men and rescues Oakley, but he is disgusted by the war and ashamed that men have become pieces of meat.

After the battle, hundreds of dead are piled along the road, their clothes removed so others can wear them. Another resident of the Cold Mountain area, Stobrod Thewes (Brendan Gleeson), plays the violin, at Inman's request, to comfort Oakley as he dies. In a later skirmish, Swimmer is killed and Inman seriously wounded. He is taken to a house that has been converted into a hospital. He has a serious throat wound and can barely speak. While recovering, a letter is delivered to him that causes him to throw off his blanket, jump out the window, and return home.

In a flashback to his hometown of Cold Mountain, North Carolina,[5] Inman, a self-aware and self-reflective man who works as a carpenter, assists in building a church for the new minister, Reverend Monroe (Donald Sutherland). His daughter, Ada, is shy of others when she arrives from Charlestown. Impressed by her beauty, Inman pressures Sally Swanger (Kathy Baker), a mutual friend, to introduce them. Sally suggests that Ada ask him to clear a field for Sally. Ada arranges it, and, as he plows, in a "courtship without words,"[6] she plays her piano for him after it is delivered to her new home on a wagon.

Soaked from an evening rain, Inman stands on her porch watching a reception being held for the new minister. Reverend Monroe thanks everyone for the welcome and the new chapel. The only person hostile to the Monroe family is Teague (Ray Winstone), who wanted the property Monroe purchased. Ada takes a tray of root beer outside, ostensibly for their slaves, but actually to see Inman.

After services in the new church, Ada, Inman, and Reverend Monroe take a walk. The minister says he "will not preach war" in his church, to which Inman replies, "I imagine God is weary of being called down on both sides of an argument." Inman gives Monroe his father's sheet music. His father is dead, and his mother died when he was born. Ada opens the music, and inside is a gift of a tintype photo for her. At a later church service, news arrives that the war has begun, and Teague is now Home Guard for the county, as he is too old to fight. Recognizing Teague as a threat to Ada, Inman says she might be safer in Charleston. Before he leaves, Ada visits his apartment. She gives him Bartram's *Travels* and a tintype of herself. They kiss; it is passionate because it must hold them through the war. Inman joins the troops leaving town.

Reverend Monroe sits under the shade of a large tree in front of their house reminiscing, regretting raising Ada as a companion and not a young woman. He asks her to play a song. She does not realize that he dies while she is playing. After his death, she is too embarrassed to keep asking Sally for help because her father's investments lost their value. Teague harasses her each time he meets her, saying she knows Inman is not coming back. Even the rooster scares her. Forced to dig in snow-covered fields looking for food, she writes to Inman and asks him to stop marching and return. She sends the letter in winter, and he gets it in late summer. This is the letter that causes him to desert, which was the "result of a profound war-weariness brought to the point of desperation by Ada's frantic plea."[7]

Ada agrees to have dinner with Sally and her husband Esco (James Gammon), who says she should look down their well with a mirror to see the future. As they hold on to her, she leans back, with the mirror reflecting down into the well water. In the inky blackness she sees a man walking and crows flying. She writes Inman that "yesterday, I saw you walking back to me."

Minghella reveals his "unusual understanding of, sympathy for, and affinity with women"[8] in the relationship of Ada and Ruby Thewes (Renée Zellweger), who arrives at Black Cove Farm because Sally suggested that she might help Ada with the farm. As soon as she arrives she sees all the work that needs to be done. She impresses Ada by killing the rooster and cooking it. Ruby wakes Ada early every day and often disturbs her reading. She says, "We got our own story. It's called 'Black Cove Farm: Catastrophe.'" She had to take care of her family because her father "lived to rest" and was "born tired." Ruby believes he died in the Battle of Petersburg. As Rudy and Ada build a fence, Ruby quizzes her about herbs. Ada admits that everything she has been taught is useless. She can arrange cut flowers but not grow them. She sells her piano to pay for food and seed.

Teague, Bosie (Charlie Hunnam), and Bosie's men suspect Esco's family of harboring deserters. Esco threatens them with a rifle to keep them off his land, but they stab him with a sword. They torture Sally by crushing her hands between the wood of a fence, forcing her two sons, who have been hiding, to attempt to rescue her. Both are shot dead. Teague and Bosie lack basic human compassion. Throughout the film, Minghella shows that love and compassion dignify humans, but "when compassion is removed we retreat into just being another species of the animal kingdom."[9] Ada and Ruby rescue Sally. Later, they catch Ruby's father, Stobrod, taking corn from the crib. Upset at how he has treated her in the past, Ada feeds him outside. He says his "new fiddle [is] full of tunes" about her. He asks them for a coat for his banjo partner Pangle (Ethan Suplee). At their Christmas party, Ada, Ruby, and Sally dance to music played by Stobrod, Pangle, and Georgia (Jack White).[10] Sally, Ada, and Ruby walk back to their homes while the men hide in the woods from the Home Guard.

As Inman walks toward home, he sees a man, Reverend Veasey (Philip Seymour Hoffman), prepare to drop a slave woman, who is pregnant with his baby, into a river. Inman forces him to take her back to town to her bed. Inman makes him write a note and ties him up alongside the city street. On the road, Inman tries to buy eggs from a group of escaped slaves heading north, but he cannot make himself heard. They hear the Home Guard ride toward them, and Inman runs into a cornfield. Crossing through water and marsh to lose the Home Guard's dogs, he finds Reverend Veasey, who escaped his flock but at the loss of his hair. Although he does not want to travel with him, there is only one ferry across a river they must cross. The ferry girl (Jena Malone) says that the normal fare of five dollars is not sufficient for men on the run, so Inman offers her thirty confederate dollars. As they cross, she is shot, and Veasey and Inman paddle frantically across the water.

On the other side, Veasey finds a logging saw along the trail, which they put to use when they meet Junior (Giovanni Ribisi), a man attempting to pull a dead cow out of a creek because it is poisoning his water. They cut the cow with the saw and are invited to dinner and drink his home-brewed alcohol. The house is filled with Junior's family and Circe-like women who spend the meal seducing Veasey and Inman. They successfully reduce Veasey to a sexual pig, while Inman, Odysseus-like, resists Junior's wife, Lila (Melora Walters). Junior turns them in to the Home Guard, and they are chained to other deserters. While marching along a road, they see Union soldiers ride up. They need to hide, but Inman refuses to be "shot again for something I don't believe in." The chained men run, and the Confederate soldiers chase them with bayonets, afraid to fire and draw attention from the Union soldiers. Most of the men are killed, including Reverend Veasey. Inman survives but is chained to the men.

Inman is found by Maddy (Eileen Atkins), a shepherdess, who takes him to her gypsy-style wagon. He warns her that he may bring her trouble, as he is a deserter, but she does not fear the soldiers. "What are they going to do?" she says. She kills a goat for their dinner and nurses him back to health for several days. She delivers a Naturalist moral for the story: "See, I think there's a plan. There's a design for each and every one of us. You look at nature. Bird flies somewhere, picks up a seed, shits the seed out, plant grows. Bird's got a job, shit's got a job, seed's got a job. And *you've* got a job."

Later, Inman arrives, hungry and worn, at a cabin. The owner, Sara (Natalie Portman), is alone with her baby. Although she resists at first, she allows him to enter the cabin, feeds him, and allows him to sleep in a storage room. She gives him her dead husband's clothes and boots. Sara invites Inman to her bed for comfort, but he refuses sex because he loves someone else.[11] The next morning, three union soldiers arrive, wanting food. Sara forces Inman to hide behind the house. The men tie her to a tree and set her baby on the ground. She begs for her baby's life and offers them her only hog. One drags her inside the cabin to rape her. Another comes in a few minutes later and is knocked out by Inman, the first man already dead. Inman points a gun at the remaining soldier and orders him to take off his boots and shirt and leave; Sara raises a rifle and shoots him. Inman then leaves Sara. As he gets closer to home, Inman walks through mountain snow; the journey has also been a "progression beyond himself."[12]

Stobrod, Pangle, and Georgia find a frozen deer and cook it over their fire. Georgia gets sick because of the rancid meat. While he is in the bushes, the other two are approached by Captain Teague and his men, who are looking for three men living in a local cave. Pangle foolishly admits it. Teague asks them to play a song, which Stobrod hopes will soften their hearts, but it brings out the worst in Teague and Bosie. Georgia watches from the bushes while Teague makes them stand to be shot. Pangle believes they are posing for a tintype.

Georgia tells Ada and Ruby what has happened and hides in a barn while they go to recover Stobrod and Pangle's bodies. They find Pangle covered with snow, Stobrod's fiddle in the bushes, and Stobrod at the bottom of the hill, still breathing. They dig the bullet out of his back and take him to an old Cherokee cabin. Ada looks for food and shoots a turkey. She sees a man walking up the road toward her and threatens him. He turns away, but she realizes it is Inman. He is a diminished man, she more robust than when they parted. She introduces Inman to Ruby. Ada says, "I thought I was seeing him fall. Instead, I was seeing him come back to me."

Inman is afraid that the war has changed him. He laments, "If I had goodness, it's gone." That night he plans to sleep alone because he and Ada are not married. Having heard that it is possible to marry by saying "I marry you" three times, Ada says it. He does not turn his back when she removes her dress.

Knowing that Ruby has big plans for the farm, Inman asks her permission to live at Black Cove. Teague and his men arrive after Georgia told them, with some persuasion, where they were. Ruby shoots Teague when he raises a gun to kill Stobrod. Ada knocks Teague off his horse and hits him with her rifle. Inman kills Teague with his own rifle and then chases Bosie, who draws and shoots. Inman returns fire. Ada sees crows fly out of the forest. Inman is hit; he is stunned, and his "world spin[s] while he's still," as if he is within a Zoetrope. Ada reaches for him while he is on the ground and says, "I love you."

Years later, Ada celebrates Easter under her oak tree at Black Cove with her extended family, her red-haired daughter Grace, Ruby and her husband Georgia, Sally, and Stobrod. Inman's life is complete: he lived, mated, and died, but in the middle, he completed a spiritual odyssey.[13] Ada's narration completes the film: "What we have lost will never be returned to us. The land will not heal. Too much blood. The heart will not heal. All we can do is make peace with the past and try to learn from it." JMW

Notes

1. Jim Knowlson, "In Memoriam: Anthony Minghella, CBE, D. Litt. (Hon) (1954–2008)," *Journal of Beckett Studies* 18, nos. 1/2 (2008/2009): 166.

2. Knowlson, "In Memoriam," 169.

3. Anthony Minghella, "Director's Commentary," *Cold Mountain*, directed by Anthony Minghella (Miramax, 2003), DVD.

4. Minghella, "Director's Commentary."

5. The town was built for the film in Transylvania, Romania, because it allowed the filmmakers to place it

in "untrammeled forest." Minghella, "Director's Commentary."

6. Minghella, "Director's Commentary."

7. Edward Buscombe, "The Homecoming," *Sight and Sound* 14, no. 2 (2004): 32.

8. Knowlson, "In Memoriam," 167.

9. Timothy Bricknell, ed., *Minghella on Minghella* (London: Faber and Faber, 2005), 169.

10. The film's sound track was so popular that it generated three popular albums.

11. Minghella says that the "triumph and tragedy of his life is that he meets Ada. Sara is the person Inman should have met at the beginning of the film." Minghella, "Director's Commentary."

12. Minghella, "Director's Commentary."

13. Minghella "had a deep interest in spiritual odysseys and a concern with conscience, guilt, remorse, and atonement." Knowlson, "In Memoriam," 167.

Bibliography

Bricknell, Timothy, ed. *Minghella on Minghella*. London: Faber and Faber, 2005.

Buscombe, Edward. "The Homecoming." *Sight and Sound* 14, no. 2 (2004): 32.

Knowlson, Jim. "In Memoriam: Anthony Minghella, CBE, D. Litt. (Hon) (1954–2008)." *Journal of Beckett Studies* 18, nos. 1/2 (2008/2009): 165.

Myers, Robert M. "It's What People Say We're Fighting For: Representing the Lost Cause in Cold Mountain." In *Why We Fought: America's Wars in Film and History*, edited by Peter C. Rollins and John E. O'Connor, 121–36. Lexington: University Press of Kentucky, 2008.

Young, Josh. "Love among the Ruins: Shooting of A. Minghella's Cold Mountain." *Entertainment Weekly*, 19 December 2003, 28–36.

THE COUNT OF MONTE CRISTO (1934)

DIRECTOR: Rowland V. Lee
WRITERS: Philip Dunne, Dan Totheroh, Rowland V. Lee. Adapted from the 1844 novel by Alexandre Dumas.
PRODUCER: Edward Small (Edward Small Productions, United Artists)
CINEMATOGRAPHER: J. Peverell Marley
EDITOR: Grant Whytock
MUSIC: Alfred Newman
CAST: Edmond Dantes: Robert Donat. Mercedes: Elissa Landi. De Villefort Jr.: Louis Calhern. Fernand Mondego: Sidney Blackmer. Danglars: Raymond Walburn. Abbe Faria: O. P. Heggie. Valentine de Villefort: Irene Hervey. Mme. De Rosas: Georgia Caine. Morrel: Walter Walker. De Villefort Sr.: Lawrence Grant. Jacopo: Luis Alberni. Albert: Douglas Walton. Clothilde: Juliette Compton. Fouquet: Clarence Wilson. Haydee: Eleanor Phelps. Louise XVIII: Ferdinand Munier. Napoleon: Paul Irving
AA: None
AAN: None
DVD: Hen's Tooth Video, 2012
BLU-RAY: Currently unavailable
DURATION: 113 minutes

The 1934 film adaptation of Alexandre Dumas's 1844 classic novel *The Count of Monte Cristo*, although neither the first nor last to have been produced, has certainly become among the most critically acclaimed. Chosen as one of the National Board of Review's Top Ten Films of 1934,[1] this was, in part, due to the superb performance by British actor Robert Donat in the title role. Donat, who five years later went on to win an Academy Award for his role in *Goodbye Mr. Chips*, was praised by the *New York Times*, and the film itself was acclaimed as a "walloping melodrama of revenge."[2] The basic plot is about the struggles and triumphs of a young, loyal sailor carrying out the last wishes of his captain only to face false imprisonment, betrayal, and revenge, before eventually gaining knowledge and, at last, justice. Although replete with epic elements, including dramatic sea voyages, war intrigue, and a heroic journey involving escapes, reversals, transformations, and catharsis, it is the spectacle for which it is best remembered.

After a brief historical textual overlay, *The Count of Monte Cristo* opens with Emperor Napoleon (Paul Irving), now exiled on Elba, standing on a promontory overlooking the sea. A soldier approaches him to tell him of the arrival of a boat, the *Pharaon.* He reports to Napoleon that he had delivered the letter to Captain Leclere, who had said that the king was prepared for war, to which Napoleon replies, "So is the Emperor."

The scene immediately cuts to a fierce storm at sea, during which Captain Leclere is fatally ill in the cabin and two men, Dantes (Robert Donat) and Danglars (Raymond Walburn), are arguing on deck. Dantes wants to throw the shipment overboard to steady the ship; Danglars thinks the captain would have been able to steady the ship without losing precious cargo. A man comes on deck and calls out for Dantes, saying that the captain needs to speak with him, and both men go inside to his quarters. The captain asks to speak to Dantes alone, but Danglars waits outside and overhears everything that is said. The captain tells Dantes that he is ill and dying and is therefore giving Dantes his last order as captain. Then he removes a letter from under his chest and hands it to Dantes, stating that the recipient will be waiting to receive this letter from the captain of the *Pharaon.* Dantes sees that the letter is not addressed and asks to whom he shall deliver it. The captain tells him that the man will make himself known by one word: "Elba." Then the captain dies.

The next scene is the port in Marseilles, followed quickly by a solemn procession led by a cleric. There are women wailing and soldiers following as there is about to be a beheading of ten loyalists to the emperor. A scene cuts to an inside room, where there are three men who, hearing the clamor, mistakenly attribute it to the fact that the *Pharaon* has been sighted and is coming to harbor. One gentleman remarks that the followers of Napoleon will soon be able to raise their heads again. Then he is asked if he will meet Leclere himself, to which he responds no, adding that he will remain in hiding until after sunset.

The scene again shifts to two women on their way to meet the ship: a mother, Mademoiselle De Rosas (Georgia Caine), and her daughter Mercedes (Elissa Landi), who is on her way to meet her beloved, Dantes. It is clear that Mademoiselle De Rosas does not approve of this relationship, and we later see her addressing Mr. Fernand Mondego (Sidney Blackmer), admonishing him for not pursuing his attraction for her daughter more aggressively. Meeting Dantes as he steps off the *Pharaon* at the port is Mr. Morrel (Walter Walker), owner of the shipping company, who briefly discusses the letter with Dantes and then promotes Dantes to captain after hearing of Leclere's death. The scene immediately shifts to a romantic encounter and embrace between Mercedes and Dantes, followed by an abrupt intercession by Mondego spurred on by Mercedes' mother. When questioned about why she loves Dantes, despite the fact that he has no money, or family, Mercedes replies to Mondego, "There are only two things that matter: a man and a woman."

The next scene begins the conspiracy that forms the action of the rest of this epic. Mondego reports to de Villefort (Louis Calhern), the King's magistrate, that according to Danglars, Dantes is carrying a treasonous letter. With this, an arrest warrant is issued for Dantes.

In the next scene, Dantes and Mercedes are alone, romantically seated under a tree. She asks him, "What brings you here?" He replies, "I seek a golden treasure valuable above price." She tells him, "It is not so easy to obtain, pirate, without a formal proposal." They climb up the tree, and there he proposes and she accepts.

Mr. Morrel arranges an engagement party for Dantes and Mercedes, during which time the stranger requesting the letter comes calling for Dantes. When Dantes passes the letter, the gentleman who receives it is arrested but is soon permitted safe passage as he turns out to be the father of de Villefort, the magistrate. After questioning Dantes as to the extent of his knowledge regarding the letter and his father's acquaintance, de Villefort asks Dantes if anyone witnessed who ordered the ship to stop at Elba. Danglars lies and says it was the first mate, Dantes, and Dantes is thus ordered to the dreaded prison Chateau D'If without trial.

Dantes arrives at Chateau d'If with a note to the guard instructing that he is to be there indefinitely. Meanwhile, the letter is decoded, reading that Napoleon has escaped from Elba and is about to attack. De Villefort meets the king, who is playing chess, and tells him of the plans, but he is rebuked, at which time the king's messenger tells him that Napoleon had arrived in France and was greeted with open arms. Upon hearing this, the king praises de Villefort and calls for war. In the next scene, we see the prison guard fraudulently signing a declaration of death on Edmond Dantes.

Napoleon is defeated at Waterloo; Mercedes marries Mondego as her mother's dying wish, despite still pining for Dantes, whom she believes (wrongly) to be dead; and Dantes continues languishing in his cell at Chateau D'If. Then, in his eighth year of imprisonment, he is visited by a fellow prisoner who, trying to escape, chisels his way right through to Dantes' cell. This man, Abbe Faria (O. P. Heggie), who had been imprisoned for twenty years by the time he and Dantes meet, is no usual human, and together they plan a route of escape while the good abbe educates Dantes on subjects ranging from mathematics to philosophy as they work. The abbe is known in the prison as the "mad abbe": "They call me mad, because I speak the truth," he tells Dantes, as he shows him around his prison cell, which resembles a Renaissance library in ruins. The abbe tells Dantes that he is the heir to the Spada family fortune since he was the librarian and tutor to the Duke of Spada, and before he died, the duke left him the location of the lost treasure. The abbe wanted to use the treasure to help ease the suffering of humanity, but the duke's enemies wanted it for themselves, so they tortured the abbe to force him to confess the treasure's location, which he refused to expose, and that is how he landed in the prison.

After an arduous task and only months from succeeding in escaping, the abbe is killed by a cave-in. The dying monk tells Dantes to take a piece of parchment. Then Faria tells Dantes that he is making him his sole heir, saying, "I leave my mind behind in your possession. . . . Use it as an instrument for justice." When Abbe Faria dies, Dantes uses his wits to disguise himself as the corpse of the old monk by sealing himself inside the death sack and getting "buried" by being thrown off the cliff into the dangerous waters off the coastline of the Chateau d'If.

Dantes is picked up and befriended by the crew members of a pirate ship, on which he assumes a new identity: Sinbad. He discovers the Spada treasure on the Isle of Monte Cristo and returns to France with a newfound fortune, and a new mission: to discover what has become of the people who had betrayed him.

Buying the title of count, and with his loyal pirate friends as his stewards, one by one the Count of Monte Cristo begins to take Providence into his own hands, settling accounts with those whom he believes have betrayed justice, as evidenced by his unjust treatment during his time of suffering in prison. After befriending Albert (Douglas Walton), the young son of Mercedes and Fernand Mondego, by faking a kidnapping and then rescuing him, the count ingratiates himself within the social web that he eventually ensnares. Mercedes, Danglars, and Mondego each suffer their own fate as the count rebukes Mercedes for her perceived betrayal of his love; bankrupts and drives Danglars mad for his avarice and greed; and publicly humiliates Mondego for his ambition, causing him to commit suicide. Albert challenges the count to a duel to avenge his father's suicide, and Mercedes comes to see him, asking him to spare the life of her son, believing that the count has devised the plan to kill him. Taken aback at her misconception, he tries to explain that he is not acting out of revenge, but merely justice. Then Mercedes asks the count to claim Albert as "his own," which he does, and he promises not to kill him. She also tells the count that Valentine de Villefort (Irene Hervey), daughter of the count's next victim, is his Albert's beloved. In the duel between Albert and the count, both lives are spared, but Dantes is once again arrested by the king's attorney, de Villefort.

In the final scenes, Dantes receives his day in court and is able to defend himself against his charges and expose his accusers, including de Villefort, before the law by evoking the wisdom that he learned during his years of training with the Abbe Faria. The final scene finds Albert and Valentine stumbling upon the same tree where Dantes and Mercedes were once betrothed, searching for that couple. The camera pans skyward, where the now count and countess are once again seated together hidden in the treetop enveloped in an embrace. MMC

> What a long road you have to travel . . . pray it will take time . . . so that when you emerge into the light, it will not be as a revengeful Horseman of the Apocalypse but as an avenging angel doing the work of God.
>
> —Abbe Faria

Notes

1. "National Board of Review, USA, Awards for 1934," *IMDb*, 20 December 1934, www.imdb.com/event/ev0000464/1934 (25 April 2013).
2. Rob Nixon, "*The Count of Monte Cristo* (1934)," *Turner Classic Movies Articles*, www.tcm.com/this-month/article/337147%7C0/The-Count-of-Monte-Cristo.html (25 March 2013).

Bibliography

"National Board of Review, USA, Awards for 1934." *IMDb*, 20 December 1934, www.imdb.com/event/ev0000464/1934 (25 April 2013).

Nixon, Rob. "*The Count of Monte Cristo* (1934)." *Turner Classic Movies Articles*, www.tcm.com/this-month/article/337147%7C0/The-Count-of-Monte-Cristo.html (25 March 2013).

THE COUNT OF MONTE CRISTO (2002)

DIRECTOR: Kevin Reynolds
WRITER: Jay Wolpert. Adapted from the 1844 novel by Alexandre Dumas.
PRODUCERS: Gary Barber, Roger Birnbaum (Touchstone Pictures)
CINEMATOGRAPHER: Andrew Dunn
EDITOR: Stephen Semel, Christopher Womack
MUSIC: Ed Shearmur
CAST: Edmond Dantes: Jim Caviezel. Mercedes: Dagmara Dominczyk. De Villefort: James Frain. Fernand Mondego:
DIRECTOR: Kevin Reynolds
WRITER: Jay Wolpert. Adapted from the 1844 novel by Alexandre Dumas.
PRODUCERS: Gary Barber, Roger Birnbaum (Touchstone Pictures)
CINEMATOGRAPHER: Andrew Dunn
EDITOR: Stephen Semel, Christopher Womack
MUSIC: Ed Shearmur
CAST: Edmond Dantes: Jim Caviezel. Mercedes: Dagmara Dominczyk. De Villefort: James Frain. Fernand Mondego: Guy Pearce. Armand Dorleac: Michael Wincott. Danglars: Albie Woodington. Abbe Faria: Richard Harris. Jacopo: Luis Guzmán. Maurice: Christopher Adamson. Luigi Vampa: J. B. Blanc. Napoleon: Alex Norton. Old Man Dantes: Barry Cassin. Albert Mondego: Henry Cavill. Morrel: Patrick Godfrey. Col. de Villefort: Freddie Jones
AA: None

AAN: None
VHS: Walt Disney Video, 2003
DVD: Buena Vista Home Video, 2002
BLU-RAY: Touchstone Home Entertainment, 2011
DURATION: 131 minutes

> Treason is all a matter of dates.
>
> —Colonel de Villefort (Clarion)

This epic film, written by Jay Wolpert, is based on themes, characters, and episodes from the 1844 novel *The Count of Monte Cristo*, by Alexandre Dumas. It follows a parade of adaptations of this classical work,[1] and while deviating from the book in some significant ways, essential elements of the Dumas novel remain to establish the film's basic integrity, namely, both tell the tale of a man falsely accused and imprisoned who discovers a hidden treasure and uses it, thereby exacting revenge and, ultimately, justice. The most substantial deviation is the introduction of an early friendship and then betrayal between protagonist Edmond Dantes (Jim Caviezel) and Fernand Mondego (Guy Pearce). It serves as the catalyst for this film's primary epic action.

The film opens with a textual overlay that sets up the historical context of this action: It is 1814, and the French emperor Napoleon (Alex Norton) is exiled on the island of Elba, where he is being held captive by British soldiers. A small rowboat lands on the island, and Edmond Dantes, second mate of the ship *Pharaon*, and Fernand Mondego, come ashore seeking aid for their ailing captain, despite an admonition by Mondego to Dantes that he has overstepped his official duty as second mate by doing so. Dantes responds that the captain is in need of medical attention and that they have no other choice. They are immediately met by English dragoons, and Dantes attracts their attention, to the dismay of Mondego, causing an exciting swashbuckling sword fight (as the opening credits run), until they come face-to-face with Napoleon himself. They report that their captain is ill; the captain is bought ashore to get help, and Mondego and Dantes retreat to their quarters. As these two friends are sitting together drinking a bottle of Napoleon's wine, what transpires between them appears to be insignificant banter between two young friends, but, in fact, it determines the course of action for the rest of the film.

Napoleon enters the room and asks to speak with Dantes alone. He asks Dantes about a chess piece that he saw Dantes throw to Mondego. Dantes tells Napoleon that he and Mondego have a game they have played together since childhood, "King of the Moment," where they pass that piece back and forth. Napoleon replies, "In life, we're all *either* kings or pawns." Napoleon praises Dantes' fidelity to his captain and tells him that loyal friends are rare. Then he asks Dantes to deliver a "sentimental" letter to an old friend in Marseilles. When Dantes reacts, Napoleon reassures him and tells him it is totally innocent; he also tells him it is the price he demands for the use of his physician. Dantes agrees to deliver the letter to Monsieur Clarion. Napoleon also tells him to reveal the details to no one, and Dantes agrees. Unfortunately, Mondego witnesses the transfer of the letter.

Later that evening, Napoleon enters Dantes' room to tell the men to leave the island and that their captain is dead. As their boat rows away, Napoleon, overlooking from the promontory, summarizes, saying, "Kings and pawns, Marchand. Emperors . . . and fools." This recurring theme, complete with the chess piece to serve as the token of recognition, forms the stratagem upon which the rest of the plot is executed. As natural friends, Mondego and Dantes are pitted against one another in an epic game of kings and pawns.

The next scene takes place in the port of Marseilles, where first mate Danglars (Albie Woodington) learns that Mr. Morrel (Patrick Godfrey), the owner of the *Pharaon*, has passed him over to be the new captain of the *Pharaon* in favor of second mate Dantes, much to his dismay. Dantes' beloved, Mercedes (Dagmara Dominczyk), is waiting on the shore, and Mondego meets her there, telling her that Dantes is probably in trouble, so the two of them leave to meet up with him later. When Dantes finally catches up with them and announces that he's been made captain, Mondego, who is obviously jealous, not only for the promotion, but for Mercedes' attention as well, denies him the "king's piece" and walks away. Then Mercedes and Dantes share a romantic interlude where they become betrothed to one another using thread as a ring.

In the following scene, Mondego and Danglars plot against Dantes, and while Mercedes and Dantes are having dinner at the home of Dantes' father, Dantes is arrested and taken away. At the magistrate, Monsieur de Villefort's (James Frain) office, Dantes is told that he is being accused of treason and asked about his contact with Napoleon, which he admits to and reports that Mondego would vouch for him. Then he is asked about the letter, and he produces it and confesses what he knows. When asked if he knows about the contents, he reports that he does not know how to read. The magistrate deems him foolish and innocent and is about to let him go until he realizes that Dantes knows the name of the letter's recipient, Clarion, who happens to be the magistrate's father, at which time the magistrate burns the letter and pretends to offer him a ride home. Instead, he sends him directly to the prison, Chateau d'If. Dantes escapes the guards and ends up at the home of Mondego asking for help, but Mondego confesses that he read the letter and that it was he and Danglars who turned him in. A spectacular sword battle ensues, proving Mondego to be the better fighter. When the beaten and betrayed Dantes finally asks why, Mondego replies, "Because you're the son of a clerk, and I'm not supposed to want to be you." Then Mondego passes the king's piece to Dantes and turns him in to the authorities, telling him to "remember better days."

At Chateau d'If, the warden shows Dantes to his room, sarcastically passing by an etching on the wall that reads, "God will give me justice," and claiming that there is no God. On the day that Dantes' case is to be heard, news has reached the city that Napoleon is marching on Paris, having escaped Elba, and de Villefort and Mondego concoct a scheme to keep Dantes in jail by claiming that he committed murder during his arrest.

Meanwhile, Dantes languishes in jail until he meets Abbe Faria (Richard Harris), an extraordinary fellow prisoner who literally forges through the ground into Dantes' cell as he is attempting to escape. Faria makes a deal with Dantes. In exchange for Dantes' assistance in helping the abbe escape, the abbe will provide Dantes with knowledge, that is, extraordinary knowledge, beginning with reading, writing, philosophy, mathematics, economics, physics, and even fencing, until one day, with the help of the abbe, Dantes figures out the conspiracy of how he, an innocent man, ended up in prison and who sent him there and why.

Shortly thereafter, only months away from gaining freedom, the abbe is injured by a tunnel cave-in, and Dantes tries to save him. Then the priest makes a confession to Dantes and tells him about a secret treasure that he had lied about when he told officials that he didn't know of its whereabouts. He gives Dantes a map and counsels him on how to use his mind and the treasure, but only for good. Dantes says that he will surely use it for revenge. The priest offers him some final advice and dies.

Dantes escapes by posing as the corpse of the abbe, and he is thrown into the sea. He survives the fall, is befriended by pirates, takes on a new name and identity (*Zatarra*), discovers the treasure of Monte Cristo, and plots his revenge with the treasure by becoming the Count of Monte Cristo.

One by one, each of the players on Dantes' checklist becomes embroiled in a snare devised by the new Count of Monte Cristo, and one by one they fall by the hand of their own frailties. It begins when the count is invited to a birthday party by the house of Mondego in thanks for the count's valor in saving their son from a kidnapping. This kidnapping, which is, in reality, a rouse concocted by the count himself, gains him access into and favor in the house of the now-wed Fernand and Mercedes Mondego through their son Albert (Henry Cavill), as well as access to de Villefort, who has also been invited to the party. Upon meeting the count, Mercedes immediately recognizes him. At the party, Mondego and de Villefort concoct a plan to steal the count's shipment of gold coming into the port of Marseilles. After the party, Mercedes sneaks into the count's carriage to meet him, but the count throws her out, telling her that she never loved him, for she married Mondego only one month after his imprisonment.

In another scene, Danglars, who now owns the *Pharaon*, is seen stealing two containers of gold from the count's ship and placing them on the *Pharaon* while he is making the illegal transport for Mondego, stating that Mondego will never notice. The ship is suddenly surrounded by officials, and Danglars is put under arrest for stealing goods from a merchant ship. The Count of Monte Cristo, seemingly innocently passing by, appears and tells Danglars that this issue can be easily resolved if the soldiers are allowed to search the *Pharaon*. Danglars believes that Mondego set him up, but he says that he will not hang for Mondego, and he begins to battle with the Count of Monte Cristo, until the count has him dangling by a rope off the side of the ship. When Danglars asks him who he is, he identifies himself as Edmond Dantes and lets the rope go.

The count next finds de Villefort and identifies himself as Dantes. He forces a confession out of him regarding why he sent Dantes to prison and how de Villefort conspired with Mondego to kill his loyalist father, after which time de Villefort commits suicide.

On his way back, Dantes meets Mercedes again, and she shows him the thread ring. She begs him to rid himself of the hate he has inside for God's sake. Dantes asks if he can ever escape God, and she tells him no because he is everywhere, even in a kiss, and they reunite.

The next morning, she is asked to pack her and her son's things and join the Count of Monte Cristo/Dantes. When she returns to her former home, she is greeted by her husband Mondego, who tells her that he's bankrupt and about to be arrested for theft and murder. He wants her and Albert to leave with him, but she refuses, telling him that Albert is not his son, but the son of Edmond Dantes. Mondego leaves to claim his treasure, but he finds the boxes empty, except for the king's piece. When he looks up, Dantes is there, and he tells Mondego, "Kings to you, Fernand." The two begin to battle; Albert appears to fight Dantes. Mercedes intervenes and tells Albert of his true origin, and there is a final sword fight, during which Dantes kills Mondego.

With the game over, the final scene takes place three months later at Chateau d'If. Dantes, standing on the hilltop overlooking the sea, plants his sword in the earth and vows to the priest and God that all that was used for vengeance will now be used for good. Checkmate. MC

Note

1. Earlier adaptations of note include the 1975 David Greene feature starring Richard Chamberlain and the 1934 Rowland V. Lee film featuring Robert Donat (also reviewed in this volume).

THE CRUSADES (1935)

Director: Cecil B. DeMille
Writers: Harold Lamb, Waldemar Young, Dudley Nichols, Jeanie Macpherson (uncredited), Howard Higgin (uncredited), Charles Brackett (uncredited)
Producer: Cecil B. DeMille (Paramount Pictures)
Cinematographer: Victor Milner
Editor: Anne Bauchens (uncredited), Cordell Fray (uncredited)
Music: Rudolph Kopp
Cast: Berengaria, Princess of Navarre: Loretta Young. Richard, King of England: Henry Wilcoxon. Saladin, Sultan of Islam: Ian Keith. The Hermit: C. Aubrey Smith. Princess Alice of France: Katherine DeMille. Conrad, Marquis of Montferrat: Joseph Schildkraut. Blondel (Troubadour): Alan Hale. Philip the Second, King of France: C. Henry Gordon. Sancho, King of Navarre: George Barbier. The Blacksmith (Hercules): Montagu Love. John, Prince of England: Ramsay Hill. Robert, Earl of Leicester: Lumsden Hare. Alan, Richard's Squire: Maurice Murphy. Hugo, Duke of Burgundy: William Farnum. Frederick, Duke of the Germans: Hobart Bosworth. Karakush: Pedro de Cordoba. Monk: Mischa Auer. Leopold, Duke of Austria: Albert Conti. Sverre, the Norse King: Sven-Hugo Borg. Michael, Prince of Russia: Paul Sotoff. William, King of Sicily: Fred Malatesta. Nicholas, Count of Hungary: Hans von Twardowski. Duenna/Tina: Anna Demetrio. Soldier: Perry Askam. Marshal of France: Vallejo Gantner. Christian Slave Girl: Ann Sheridan (uncredited)
AA: None
AAN: Best Cinematography (Victor Milner)
DVD: Universal Studios, 2006. Part of the *Cecil B. DeMille Collection*, with *Cleopatra* (1934), *Four Frightened People* (1934), *The Sign of the Cross* (1932), and *Union Pacific* (1939).
Blu-ray: Currently unavailable
Duration: 126 minutes

An obviously thrilled Andre Sennwald had the following to say about Cecil B. DeMille's *The Crusades* in his 1935 review of the film for the *New York Times*:

> Mr. DeMille provides two hours of tempestuous extravaganza. On his clamorous screen you will discover the most impressive mass excitement that the screen has offered in years. Once you have granted him his right to exaggerate . . . you are his prisoner until the show has ended. Mr. DeMille has no peer in the world when it comes to bringing the panoplied splendor of the past into torrential life upon the screen. . . . At its best *The Crusades* possesses the true quality of a screen epic. It is rich in the kind of excitement that pulls an audience irresistibly to the edge of its seat.[1]

In subsequent years, *The Crusades* has been frequently overlooked in the expansive repertoire of Cecil B. DeMille epics, and yet the film is a delightful, if historically inaccurate, story of Richard the Lion-Heart of England as he joins the Third Crusade of 1189–1192, to recapture the Holy Lands (although the film condenses elements of the other crusades as well). Victor Milner was quite rightly nominated for an Academy Award for Best Cinematography.

The film was made just after Hollywood's Motion Picture Production Code of moral representations in film started being enforced in 1934, before which DeMille had skirted very close to industry and public standards with such films as *The Sign of the Cross* (1932), but had always managed to argue that the sex and violence served an overall moral message. The enforcement of the code made this approach more difficult, so choosing the Christian Crusades was a pragmatic choice for the famed director. He still manages to introduce elements of a sex comedy, with Richard's sometimes farcical attempts to get Berengaria, Princess of Navarre, into bed—rendered respectable by the fact that she is his wife, and suitably chaste by deferring the consummation until the end and offscreen.

The film begins in 1187, when the Saracens retake Jerusalem. But in England, King Richard (played by DeMille favorite Henry Wilcoxon) is seeking to avoid another marriage, this time to Princess Alice of France (Katherine DeMille, Cecil's daughter). Despite Alice's beauty, Richard wishes to retain an independent England and clearly wants no ties with Philip the Second, King of France (C. Henry Gordon). When a hermit travels through Europe to urge a Crusade—partly, it must be said, to avenge Saracens who have sold Christian women into slavery (including an uncredited Ann Sheridan)—Richard hears him proclaim that all other pledges will be purged. Richard does not believe in God but sees a way out of his French entanglement and leads the English on the Crusade. His brother John (Ramsay Hill) sees the opportunity to seize the crown in his absence, and Conrad, Marquis of Montferrat (Joseph Schildkraut) offers to arrange Richard's death in exchange for being made king of Jerusalem.

Alice takes the cross, too, much to Richard's consternation, but, in any case, he is forced to marry Berengaria, Princess of Navarre (Loretta Young) in exchange for food and supplies when his people nearly starve. Richard does not attend the marriage, sending his sword in his place with minstrel Blondel (comic relief in the form of the reliable character actor Alan Hale, best known today for his role as Little John in Michael Curtiz and William Keighley's 1938 *The Adventures of Robin Hood*). His bride is incensed, but Richard is soon repentant when he sees a beautiful woman watching the Crusaders leave and is alarmed to discover it is his new wife. Despite her protestations, Richard demands that she join him on the Crusade.

Arriving at Acre, the assembled kings and nobles of Europe are addressed by Saladin, the Sultan of Islam (Ian Keith), who asks them to depart in peace, but Richard, despite his complete lack of religious imperative, is bent on war. Berengaria may despise Richard, but she and Saladin find an instant attraction that is even evident to the jealous Richard—all the more reason to attack. Meanwhile, news arrives that Prince John has proclaimed himself king in Richard's absence, a claim that Philip of France is all too ready to support in light of Richard's insult to Alice. Philip's ally, the Marquis of Montferrat, suggests to Berengaria that she should sacrifice herself for the sake of Richard. The English queen has grown to love her king, even though they have vowed to keep their marriage chaste until Richard's sword lies on the tomb of Christ in Jerusalem. Berengaria walks out to meet the Saracen archers, but her injured body is discovered by Saladin himself, who takes her with him to Jerusalem, seeking reinforcements.

Richard conquers Acre in an extended night siege that forms the most spectacular set piece of the film, with some impressive camera cranes and intricate editing. In victory, Richard seeks his wife and not the remains of the true cross that so inspire his fellow Crusaders (their reactions to the cross is one of DeMille's many carefully constructed, and beautifully lit, black-and-white tableaus). In the meantime, the Marquis of Montferrat visits Saladin and offers to arrange the assassination of Richard in exchange for the rule of Jerusalem under Saladin. Saladin is disgusted by such disloyalty and has him killed, but he sends men to rescue Richard when Berengaria offers her love as reward. When Richard is brought to him, the king is distraught to discover his wife's pledge to another man, and he breaks his sword. Although Richard is still bent on war, Berengaria declares, "What if we call Him Allah or God, shall men fight because they travel different roads to Him?" She persuades Richard and Saladin to make peace and open Jerusalem to both Muslims and Christians. Despite the new agreement, Richard is despondent and departs to do something completely new to him: pray, in complete humility, for the forgiveness of God and the return of his wife. Saladin, an honorable man, releases Berengaria from her promise, and she takes Richard's broken sword into Jerusalem so that the pair may be as husband and wife with the blessing of God.

The Crusades was criticized upon its release for lacking any convincing religious piety, particularly when its hero, Richard the Lion-Heart, "frankly accepts the call to arms for selfish reasons."[2] Yet, this highly flawed warlord Richard is a more believable character as a result (despite the fanciful retelling of history), and, if anything, he highlights the truly held beliefs of those around him, while also undermining any sense of Christian superiority over the "infidel" foes. Indeed, the *New York Times* proclaimed, "It is Saladin, in fact, who emerges as the real hero of the photoplay. In the courtly performance of Ian Keith, his suave and generous behavior to the Christians is in startling contrast to the lumberjack whooping of Richard and the chicanery of the allied chieftains."[3] Less equitable is the depiction of the crimes of the Saracens as they retake Jerusalem at the beginning of the film, contradicting the historical records, which suggest that they were far more reserved than the Christians had been when they originally seized the city, but also sitting oddly against the noble behavior of Saladin in the remainder of the film.[4] This is despite DeMille's aim to "bring out that the Saracens were not barbarians, but a highly cultivated people."[5]

Although seemingly successful with $1.5 million in box-office grosses, this was, in fact, only $100,000 more than the film had cost to make. The extensive publicity (which emphasized the expansive sets, costumes, extras, and DeMille's fervor in bringing the spectacle to the screen) actually resulted in an overall loss,[6] a perennial danger faced by epic filmmaking. DB

Notes

1. Andre Sennwald, "Cecil B. DeMille Presents His Latest Spectacle, *The Crusades*, at the Astor Theatre," *New York Times*, 22 August 1935, http://movies.nytimes.com/movie/review?res=9A01E2D6113DE53ABC4A51DFBE66838E629EDE (12 August 2012).
2. "*The Crusades*," *Variety*, 1935, www.variety.com/review/VE1117790164/ (12 August 2012).
3. Sennwald, "Cecil B. DeMille Presents His Latest Spectacle."
4. John Aberth, *A Knight at the Movies: Medieval History on Film* (New York and London: Routledge, 2003), 87–88.
5. Cecil B. DeMille, *The Autobiography of Cecil B. DeMille*, edited by Donald Hayne (London: W. H. Allen, 1960), 313.
6. Simon Louvish, *Cecil B. DeMille and the Golden Calf* (London: Faber and Faber, 2007), 339.

Bibliography

Aberth, John. *A Knight at the Movies: Medieval History on Film*. New York and London: Routledge, 2003.

"*The Crusades*." *Variety*, 1935, www.variety.com/review/VE1117790164/ (12 August 2012).

DeMille, Cecil B. *The Autobiography of Cecil B. DeMille*. Edited by Donald Hayne. London: W. H. Allen, 1960.

Louvish, Simon. *Cecil B. DeMille and the Golden Calf*. London: Faber and Faber, 2007.

Sennwald, Andre. "Cecil B. DeMille Presents His Latest Spectacle, *The Crusades*, at the Astor Theatre." *New York Times*, 22 August 1935, http://movies.nytimes.com/movie/review?res=9A01E2D6113DE53ABC4A51DFBE66838E629EDE (12 August 2012).

THE CURIOUS CASE OF BENJAMIN BUTTON (2008)

DIRECTOR: David Fincher
WRITERS: Eric Roth, Robin Swicord. Based on the short story by F. Scott Fitzgerald.
PRODUCERS: Kathleen Kennedy, Frank Marshall, Ceán Chaffin (Paramount Pictures)
CINEMATOGRAPHER: Claudio Miranda
EDITORS: Kirk Baxter, Angus Wall
ART DIRECTION: Donald Graham Burt, Victor J. Zolfo, Tom Reta
COSTUMES: Jacqueline West
MUSIC: Alexandre Desplat
SOUND MIXERS: David Parker, Michael Semanick, Ren Klyce, Mark Weingarten
SPECIAL EFFECTS: Eric Barba, Steve Preeg, Burt Dalton, Craig Barron
MAKEUP ARTIST: Greg Cannom
CAST: Benjamin Button: Brad Pitt. Daisy Fuller: Cate Blanchett. Caroline: Julia Ormond. Dorothy Baker: Faune A. Chambers. Mr. Gateau: Elias Koteas. Blanche Devereux: Donna Duplantier. Martin Gateau: Jacob Tolano (as Wood). Teddy Roosevelt: Ed Metzger. Thomas Button: Jason Flemyng. Caroline Button: Joeanna Sayler. Queenie: Taraji P. Henson. Tizzy: Mahershala Ali. Benjamin (1928–1931): Peter Donald Badalamenti. Ngunda Oti: Rampai Mohadi. Filamena Gilea: Troi Bechet. Grandma Fuller: Phyllis Somerville. Daisy, Age 7: Elle Fanning. Mr. Daws: Ted Manson. Mrs. Maple: Edith Ivey. Benjamin (1932–1934): Robert Towers. Captain Mike: Jared Harris. Benjamin (1935–1937): Tom Everett. Daisy's Nurse: Sonya Leslie. Daisy, Age 10: Madisen Beaty. Prentiss Mayes: Don Creech. Vic Brody: Christopher DesRoches (as Christopher Maxwell). Rick Brody: Joshua DesRoches. John Grimm: Richmond Arquette. Pleasant Curtis: Josh Stewart. Elizabeth Abbott: Tilda Swinton. Walter Abbott: David Ross Paterson. Young Elizabeth Abbott: Taren Cunningham. Queenie's Daughter, Age 14: Devyn A. Tyler. Caroline, Age 12: Katta Hules. Queenie's Daughter, Age 40: Deneen D. Tyler. Benjamin, Age 12 (1991): Spencer Daniels. Benjamin, Age 8 (1995): Chandler Canterbury. Benjamin, Age 6 (1997): Charles Henry Wyson
AA: Best Art Direction (Donald Graham Burt, Victor J. Zolfo), Best Makeup (Greg Cannom), Best Visual Effects (Eric Barba, Steve Preeg, Burt Dalton, Craig Barron)
AAN: Best Picture (Kathleen Kennedy, Frank Marshall, Ceán Chaffin), Best Director (David Fincher), Best Leading Actor (Brad Pitt), Best Supporting Actress (Taraji P. Henson), Best Writing–Adapted Screenplay (Eric Roth, Robin Swicord), Best Film Editing (Kirk Baxter, Angus Wall), Best Cinematography (Claudio Miranda), Best Costume Design (Jacqueline West), Best Music Written for Motion Pictures–Original Score (Alexandre Desplat), Best Sound Mixing (David Parker, Michael Semanick, Ren Klyce, Mark Weingarten)
DVD: Paramount Pictures, 2009. Two-disc Criterion Collection.
BLU-RAY: Paramount Pictures, 2009
DURATION: 166 minutes

> A man should spend his life or, rather, does spend his life in being born. His life is his birth throes.
>
> —Samuel Butler

The Curious Case of Benjamin Button is an epic Americana folktale loosely based on a short story of the same title written by American author F. Scott Fitzgerald and published in 1922, the same year he began penning his famous novel *The Great Gatsby*. Originally acquired for film rights as early as the 1980s by producer Ray Stark, and passing through the hands of several notable directors and screenwriters before successfully landing with David Fincher and Eric Roth, the film adds a cultural layer of romance and magical realism to Fitzgerald's quirky little satire about the anachronistic life of Benjamin Button, who is born an old man and ages backward.

Little of the nuanced story line of Fitzgerald's piece appears in the film at first glance. In fact, aside from the title, the film's plot seems to have been spawned less from Fitzgerald and more from screenwriter Eric Roth's award-winning film *Forrest Gump* (1994). Although both the film and short story chronicle the life of our lead character, Benjamin, born "under unusual circumstances," and both stress the perspective of the human spirit struggling to embody a world anachronistic to its organic tendencies, they do so in different ways and, in fact, appear to part ways. That is, until the curious tokens of a backward-moving clock and blind watchmaker at the beginning of the film set this epic drama on its course, and suddenly, the two stories flow seamlessly together. With the deepest echoes of the epic form—recognitions and reversals—resounding between these two works, the denouement of the film, like the short story, emerges as a masterfully crafted American critique about our collective and perpetual obsessions with memorializing our cultural footprints, identities, and origins, while paradoxically expressing our universal and personal longings for human meaning through our epic search for love.

Set entirely within the walls of a Louisiana hospital in the throes of historic Hurricane Katrina, the dominant impression of *The Curious Case of Benjamin Button* is the immanence of time. The epic plot of this film, cleverly constructed as a frame narrative, achieves the effect of historical recollection through a conversation between a dying woman, Daisy (Cate Blanchett), speaking with her daughter, Caroline (Julia Ormond), and recalling her life passage through the artifice of a retrieved diary that belonged to the lead character, Benjamin (Brad Pitt), who provides the voice-over of the narration for the action of the film.

Through the technique of recollection, we learn that Benjamin, deceased, wrote the diary as a last will and testament and that Daisy received it at one point in her life but had never read it until now. The film is a live reading by Caroline of Benjamin's life to Daisy, with the occasional parenthetical overlay of commentary by Daisy to enhance the diary's narrative. This third-person/first-person reconstruction provides the locus of immediacy through memory necessary for the telling of Benjamin's life, and it simultaneously explores the deeper philosophical issue of time's significance and meaning as the unfolding of this curious epic about the nature of human time begins. Appropriately, the first two memories recollected from Daisy's journey back in her memory of time, in the script, are about the famous 1928 Okeechobee Hurricane and then about a famous day in 1918. These two events frame the epic narrative and give the coordinates for the story line as it begins to unfold.

In 1918, Daisy recalls, a blind watchmaker invents and presents to the city (in the presence of Teddy Roosevelt, played by Ed Metzger) a marvelous clock for the train station. Intentional in design, the clock's hands move backward. The clockmaker explains that he constructed it that way when he learned that his son had been killed in the war, hoping that this invention can somehow reverse time and bring home the young men who died fighting. We learn that Benjamin is born in that year; we also learn that the war ends that night. Significantly, screenwriter Roth introduces this story as a parallel metaphor to complement the anachronistic chronological life of Benjamin. But why include the blind watchmaker? Is Roth offering an epistemological foundation for his farcical tale of magical realism?[1]

Fitzgerald opens his short story differently, although with his own ironic bent: "As long ago as 1860 it was the proper thing to be born at home. At present, so I am told, the high gods of medicine have decreed that the first cries of the young shall be uttered upon the anesthetic air of a hospital, preferably a fashionable one." He then asks his modern readers to consider whether Benjamin's astonishing history of being born old and aging backward is due to the anachronism that he was born (in 1860) in a hospital and not at home, as was customary at that time.

Why, in 1922, did Fitzgerald choose to set his story in antebellum Baltimore? Cleverly veiled in sardonic tone, this piece uncovers Fitzgerald's sublimations regarding the newly emerging progressive reforms designed to insinuate science and technology into maternal healthcare and their effects on his domestic circumstances.[2]

Fitzgerald's beginning heralds a larger, more serious didactic intertext within his little fantasy story line, and its significance is anything but overlooked in this film. Rather, it is here that Roth shines in Fitzgerald's zeitgeist. Roth's Benjamin Button is born as a deformed newborn whose abhorrent looks cause his father to attempt to commit infanticide by throwing him into the river, but upon reflection, he abandons him on the steps of a nursing home. (Redemption only comes later when Benjamin returns that same father back to the loving remembrance of the river where his parents first met and fell in love.) Fitzgerald's Benjamin Button is born a fully grown, precocious old man who speaks with his father and smokes cigars; his father keeps him forever destined to lead an absurd normal life, forced to comply with societal expectations of his chronological age despite his obvious circumstances. Benjamin Button as a father in Ross's story is merely a character in a diary whom daughter Caroline learns about almost by happenstance; they truly meet as the capricious eye of Hurricane Katrina begins her malevolent dance of destruction. And these distinctions as played out in the script share a paradoxical similarity; they expose the changing cultural mores through which humans define those unities that they call their life, and they also dramatize the ways through which we come know them in time. And then we don't. But for the duration of time in which we share an experience, we all thrive in recollection and memory. And we love. These are the parameters of our human condition and our legacy.

Fitzgerald lived during the most paradoxical and aggressive age of human hope toward conquering God and Nature. It ended in the hubristic fall of the eugenics era but saw the rise of genetics and the great advances of technology, through the Jazz Age and the American Dream. By setting his film during the historic age of Fitzgerald's great works, Roth weaves many memory points from the biography of Fitzgerald, as well as his famous characters, into *The Curious Case of Benjamin Button*, including much of the political intrigue of the time, albeit at times less obvious to the casual observer. For example, Daisy and Caroline are names that appear in Fitzgerald's famous work *The Great Gatsby*; Daisy's profession as a dancer in the film parallels that of Fitzgerald's wife, Zelda. And Captain Mike (Jared Harris) and his hummingbird, ever present as a symbol in *The Curious Case of Benjamin Button*, the film, betrays a macabre cultural recollection of the 1934 Nazi Operation Hummingbird

("Night of the Long Knives"), which was the historical culmination of the bourgeois philosophizing of Fitzgerald's *Great Gatsby* character Tom Buchanan.

At the end of the film, viewers are spared the probable fate of Caroline and Daisy at the immanent call of Katrina and the devastation we know she delivered. Instead, we remain suspended in time within the flutter of the wings of the hummingbird that magically appears outside Daisy's window to bring Benjamin's presence to that moment, as the inimitable dance of Nature hurls at once all the dreamers, including those dreams of a bold, blind watchmaker, where they all end up: upon that mysterious, ineffable river. MMC

> So we beat on, boats against the current,
> borne back ceaselessly into the past.
>
> —F. Scott Fitzgerald

Notes

1. See, for example, Richard Dawkins, *The Blind Watchmaker* (New York: Norton, 1986), in which the author references his twist on the 1802 teleological argument for the existence of God rendered by William Paley (the watchmaker argument).

2. The piece was written during a significant time in Fitzgerald's personal life. Fitzgerald's daughter was born in October 1921, in a hospital (he had been born at home), and his wife became pregnant again the following March but aborted that pregnancy.

Bibliography

Bruccoli, Matthew J., ed. *The Short Stories of F. Scott Fitzgerald.* New York: Scribner, 1989.

Butler, Samuel. *The Note-Books of Samuel Butler.* Edited by David Fifield. Coventry, UK: A. C. Fifield, 1912.

Chagollan, Steve. "F. Scott Fitzgerald Gets a Second Act After All." *New York Times*, 21 August 2005, www.nytimes.com/2005/08/21/movies/21chag.html?pagewanted=all&_r=0 (15 September 2013).

Dawkins, Richard. *The Blind Watchmaker.* New York: Norton, 1986.

West, James L. W., ed. *F. Scott Fitzgerald: A Short Autobiography.* New York: Scribner, 2011.

D

DANCES WITH WOLVES (1990)

Director: Kevin Costner
Writer: Michael Blake. Based on his novel.
Producer: Kevin Costner, Jake Eberts, Jim Wilson (Tig Productions, Majestic Films International)
Cinematographer: Dean Semler
Editors: William Hoy, Chip Masamitsu, Stephen Potter, Neil Travis
Art Direction: Jeffrey Beecroft, Lisa Dean
Costumes: Elsa Zamparelli
Music: John Barry
Sound Mixers: Russell Williams II, Jeffrey Perkins, Bill W. Benton, Gregory H. Watkins
Cast: Lt. John J. Dunbar: Kevin Costner. Stands with a Fist: Mary McDonnell. Kicking Bird: Graham Greene. Wind in His Hair: Rodney A. Grant. Maj. Fambrough: Maury Chaykin. Timmons: Robert Pastorelli. Ten Bears: Floyd "Red Crow" Westerman. Otter: Michael Spears. Smiles a Lot: Nathan Lee Chasing His Horse. Stone Calf: Jimmy Herman. Black Shawl: Tantoo Cardinal
AA: Best Director (Kevin Costner), Best Cinematography (Dean Semler), Best Film Editing (Neil Travis), Best Music–Original Score (John Barry), Best Picture (Jim Wilson, Kevin Costner), Best Sound (Russell Williams II, Jeffrey Perkins, Bill W. Benton, Gregory H. Watkins), Best Writing–Screenplay Based on Material from Another Medium (Michael Blake)
AAN: Best Leading Actor (Kevin Costner), Best Supporting Actor (Graham Greene), Best Supporting Actress (Mary McDonnell), Best Art Direction–Set Decoration (Jeffrey Beecroft, Lisa Dean), Best Costume Design (Elsa Zamparelli)
DVD: MGM, 2011
Blu-ray: MGM, 2011
Duration: 181 minutes

Grossing more than $180 million at the box office and winning seven Academy Awards, *Dances with Wolves* is a visually stunning film that is often compared to the golden age of westerns, especially the films of John Ford.[1] The story follows Lieutenant John J. Dunbar's journey of dying from one culture and being reborn in an alien culture. The film offers viewers many examples of the "noble savage," virtuous Indians and their enemy, the vicious Whites.[2] Costner was honored with a Hunka Ceremony by the Rosebud Sioux Tribal Nation for his sensitive portrayal of Native Americans.[3] While they applauded the use of native actors speaking Lakota, some Native Americans were concerned that the film did nothing to challenge the myth of Native Americans being a "dead culture."[4]

The film opens with a Union surgeon cutting a boot off of Lieutenant Dunbar's foot, but he stops short of surgery because he is too tired. Dunbar awakens, realizes why he is on the table, looks at the other men with amputated limbs, sees his boot on a stack of empty boots, and decides he would rather die than be amputated. He puts his boot back on. He reenters the Tennessee battlefield, where Federal troops have faced Southern troops on the other side of the field for two days. Dunbar sees an opportunity to die quickly and rides out in front of the Southern troops to be shot. He rides at them and then parallel to them. Although they shoot, none hit him, and his own troops cheer. The Southern troops call him back for more. He complies and rides in front of them, leaning backward and lifting his arms as they fire. Inspired by Dunbar's courage, Federal troops cross the field. Dunbar's commanding officer finds him on the ground with one boot in the stirrup, but he has not been hit by any bullets. The commander orders his own surgeon to be brought in to attend to him and promises that Dunbar will keep his foot.

Dunbar, now a hero, is rewarded with a horse, Cisco. Given any assignment he wants, he moves west to Ft. Hayes, Kansas, an "island surrounded by a never-ending sea of prairie." He meets the company commander, Major Fambrough (Maury Chaykin), the "riddle-plying Sphinx, [who] appears like a threshold guardian of the doorway to the Western plains."[5] He mocks Dunbar because he admits that he is there at his own request. Dunbar wants to "see the frontier before it's gone." Fambrough says he is sending him on a "knight's errand." Before he leaves, Fambrough says, "I just pissed in my pants and nobody can do anything about it." As Dunbar rides out of the fort with Timmons (Robert Pastorelli), a mule trader, Fambrough commits suicide. Riding across the prairie, they find a bleached skeleton. Timmons, an obnoxious, disgusting man, says, "Somebody back East say, 'why don't she write?'" Dunbar writes in his journal, "Were it not for my companion, I would be having the time of my life. The foulest man I have ever met." They arrive at the fort without seeing buffalo.

After they unload the wagon at his isolated outpost, Ft. Sedgwick, Dunbar gives Timmons a case of canned goods from his provisions. Dunbar writes, "The country is everything I dreamed it would be. There can be no place like this on earth." He explores the area, finding the remains of a wagon and a dead buck in the water. Timmons is killed on the prairie by Pawnees, and they take his scalp.

After thirty days, Dunbar's only visitor is a wolf he names Two Socks. As he washes in a pond, Kicking Bird (Graham Greene), a Sioux holy man, rides up. Kicking Bird is frightened by Dunbar's sudden appearance and his lack of fear although he is naked. After his visitor leaves, Dunbar buries his excess ordinance and plans a defense in case more Native Americans return. He waits for troops to join him and relieve him.

At the Lakota camp, Kicking Bird reports what he has seen. Wind in His Hair (Rodney A. Grant) says *wasi'chu* (whites) do not ride or shoot well. Although they are said to flourish, he believes it impossible. Kicking Bird counters, "Make no mistake, the whites are coming." He states Dunbar may be a "person with whom treaty may be struck." All Lakota dialogue is spoken in their own language (complete with subtitles) rather than in English. Much of the film was shot in South Dakota, where many of the Native American actors live on reservations.[6]

Although Ten Bears (Floyd "Red Crow" Westerman), the tribe's leader, says that they should discuss it more, some of the boys in the tribe decide to visit the *wasi'chu*. Dunbar hears them arrive, but he knocks himself out as he runs out of his cabin. Otter (Michael Spears) takes Cisco, but Cisco pulls him off his horse and returns to Dunbar. The next morning, his forehead bloodied, Dunbar sees Two Socks on the ridge, disturbed by Lakota riding to the fort. Wind in His Hair yells, "I am Wind in His Hair. Do you see that I am not afraid of you?" He takes Cisco as he leaves, but Cisco pulls him off his horse as well and returns to Dunbar.

Dunbar rides to visit the Indians carrying the U.S. flag. He finds a woman sitting next to a tree. Her hands are bloody because she has cut herself with a knife. Although she is dressed in native clothes, she appears to be white. She faints. Dunbar wraps her arm in the flag and carries her to the Sioux camp. Although Wind in His Hair takes her from Dunbar, he says, "You are not welcome here." Dunbar leaves, but Ten Bears sends Kicking Bird and Wind in His Hair to visit Dunbar at Ft. Sedgwick. Dunbar welcomes them and attempts to ask why there are no buffalo by behaving as one. Dunbar's efforts puzzle Wind in His Hair, who says, "His mind is gone." Kicking Bird realizes that it is an imitation of buffalo, *tatanka*. Dunbar makes them coffee and presents of coffee and sugar.

Back at camp, Kicking Bird asks Stands With a Fist (Mary McDonnell), the woman Dunbar found on the prairie, to remember English, although she last spoke it as a child. Stands With a Fist joined the tribe after her family was killed by the Pawnee.

Dunbar is invited to the Lakota village. They smoke a pipe, and Stands With a Fist attempts to translate. Back at his fort, Dunbar feels a herd of buffalo rumble past. He rides out to the village to alert them. He and the tribe find hundreds of buffalo slaughtered for their skins and tongues. They catch up to the herd and take several buffalo. One wounded buffalo runs toward Smiles a Lot (Nathan Lee Chasing His Horse), who is knocked off his horse. Dunbar saves him by shooting the buffalo. That night the tribe celebrates. Dunbar and Wind in His Hair exchange clothes. Dunbar wears Wind in His Hair's quill chest shield and vest. Back at the fort, he reflects that, "It seems every day ends with a miracle. Until this afternoon, I've never felt lonely." That night, he dances around a fire as Two Socks watches. A few days later, as he leaves to visit the village, Two Socks follows and they play.

In autumn, the tribe gives Dunbar his own lodge. Kicking Bird wants to know how many whites will come. Dunbar tells him it is limited to wagons going west but knows it will be many more. Although Dunbar volunteers to join in a war party against the Pawnee, Kicking Bird asks that he remain behind to watch his family, calling him "Dances With Wolves," his new name. He later states, "I never knew who John Dunbar was. I heard my Sioux name called, and I knew who I was." Dunbar's attraction to the tribe is rooted in the fact that it is "characterized by warrior hierarchy, able and powerful leadership, and strong but obedient and loyal women. Furthermore, it is a culture in which an ethic of honor predominates."[7]

Dunbar speaks with Stands With a Fist, who explains her past and teaches him the Lakota language. When he asks why she is not married, she leaves. Stone Calf (Jimmy Herman) explains that she is in mourning because her husband was killed. Black Shawl (Tantoo Cardinal) tells her that they are "proud of the medicine you are making." Back at the fort, Dances With Wolves writes that he loves Stands With a Fist. He finds her walking in the river. They return to his lodge and make love.

Dances With Wolves provides weapons from his cache when the Pawnees attack.

During the skirmish, he is knocked down by a Pawnee warrior but is able to shoot him with his pistol. Stone Calf is killed by a Pawnee man. The Pawnee are all killed, and the village celebrates that night. Soon thereafter, Dances With Wolves marries Stands With a Fist. He admits to Kicking Bird that many more *wasi'chu* will arrive, as many as the stars. They tell Ten Bears, but he is unconcerned because they drove out the Spanish, the Mexicans, and the Texans. He recognizes that they will keep coming but says, "Our country is all we have, and I will keep fighting for it." They strike camp and move to the winter grounds. Realizing he left his book at Ft. Sedgwick, Dances With Wolves rides back.

There, he realizes that the army has sent more troops and added buildings to his fort. Assuming he is an Indian, the troops kill his horse. He is beaten and chained as a traitor. A major (Wayne Grace) questions him about "hostiles," but Dances With Wolves says there are none. In frustration, he states in Lakota, "I am Dances With Wolves. I have nothing to say to you. You are not worth talking to." Taken on a wagon to be hanged, Dances With Wolves is horrified when the men shoot at Two Socks and kill him. Warriors from the village attack and kill the troops as they cross a river.

They arrive at winter camp, and Dances With Wolves is reunited with Stands With a Fist. As he sits with Kicking Bird and Ten Bears, he remains quiet. He does not regret killing the soldiers, but he knows they will hunt for him, which is bad for the tribe. He decides to leave, although Ten Bear states, "The man they are looking for no longer exists." Kicking Bird gives him a gift saying, "We come far, you and me. I'll not forget you." Dances With Wolves gives him a ceremonial pipe he carved. Smiles a Lot brings him a gift and runs off. It is his book. Riding from the village, Dances With Wolves and Stands With a Fist see Wind in His Hair at the top of the canyon. Wind in His Hair yells, "Do you see that I am your friend? Do you see that I will always be your friend?"

The film ends with a title card that claims, "The great horse culture of the plains was gone and the American frontier was soon to pass into history." The frontier may have passed, but, ironically, the living culture of the plains provided for many of the actors who spoke the living language of their ancestors. JMW

Notes

1. The comparison is not always favorable: "At least once every decade Hollywood offers its apologies to Native Americans for past offenses by announcing 'a major motion picture' that is positive and accurate in its portrayal of Native Americans. When that film appears on the screen, however, it's usually just another reworking of an established Native American subgenre disguised in the popular liberal convention of the moment." Dan Georgakas, "*Dances with Wolves*," *Cineaste* 18, no. 2 (1991): 51.

2. John Carroll, "*Dances with Wolves* and the End of the Western," *IPA Review* 44, no. 3 (1991): 47.

3. "Rosebud Sioux to Honor Costner," *Star Tribune*, 14 October 1990, F8.

4. "Kevin Costner's *Dances with Wolves* does nothing to challenge this myth. He pushes the liberal notion of our noble humanity to the point where I cringe with embarrassment for the man and for the movie." Beth Cuthand, "The Good, the Bad, and the Sentimental," *Black Film Review* 6, no. 3 (1991): 21.

5. Amanda Smith and Thomas Loe, "Mythic Descent in *Dances with Wolves*," *Literature/Film Quarterly* 20, no. 3 (1992): 200.

6. "Costner gives the audience a sense of the grandeur of the frontier, without wallowing in it. His camera takes in the enormous Western landscape, showing humankind's relation to nature in occasional vast panorama shots. These long shots, especially an extended scene showing a buffalo hunt, are as beautiful as any photography in film . . . it is a film meant to be seen on the big screen." Michael MacCambridge, "Costner's Gamble Pays Off in *Dances with Wolves*," *Austin American Statesman*, 21 November 1990, D5.

7. Carroll, "*Dances with Wolves* and the End of the Western," 47.

Bibliography

Carroll, John. "*Dances with Wolves* and the End of the Western." *IPA Review* 44, no. 3 (1991): 47–49.

Cuthand, Beth. "The Good, the Bad, and the Sentimental." *Black Film Review* 6, no. 3 (1991): 21–22.
Georgakas, Dan. "*Dances with Wolves.*" *Cineaste* 18, no. 2 (1991): 51–53.
MacCambridge, Michael. "Costner's Gamble Pays Off in *Dances with Wolves.*" *Austin American Statesman*, 21 November 1990, D5.
"Rosebud Sioux to Honor Costner." *Star Tribune*, 14 October 1990, F8.
Seals, David. "The New Custerism." *Nation*, 13 May 1991, 634–39.
Smith, Amanda, and Thomas Loe. "Mythic Descent in *Dances with Wolves.*" *Literature/Film Quarterly* 20, no. 3 (1992): 199–204.

DAVID AND BATHSHEBA (1951)

DIRECTOR: Henry King
WRITER: Philip Dunne
PRODUCER: Darryl F. Zanuck (20th Century Fox)
CINEMATOGRAPHER: Leon Shamroy
EDITOR: Barbara McLean
ART DIRECTION: Lyle R. Wheeler, George W. Davis, Thomas Little, Paul S. Fox
COSTUMES: Charles Le Maire, Edward Stevenson
MUSIC: Alfred Newman
CAST: King David: Gregory Peck. Bathsheba: Susan Hayward. Nathan: Raymond Massey. Uriah: Kieron Moore. Abishai: James Robertson Justice. Michal: Jayne Meadows. Ira: John Sutton. Joab: Dennis Hoey
AA: None
AAN: Best Art Direction–Set Decoration–Color (Lyle R. Wheeler, George W. Davis, Thomas Little, Paul S. Fox), Best Cinematography–Color (Leon Shamroy), Best Costume Design–Color (Charles Le Maire, Edward Stevenson), Best Music–Scoring of a Dramatic or Comedy Picture (Alfred Newman), Best Writing–Story and Screenplay (Philip Dunne)
DVD: 20th Century Fox, 2006
BLU-RAY: Soul Media, 2011
DURATION: 115 minutes

Gregory Peck stars as Israel's King David in this biblical epic, which focuses on his adulterous affair with Bathsheba (Susan Hayward), the wife of his loyal Hittite soldier Uriah (Kieron Moore). Although nominated for five Academy Awards, the film lacks pace and action, but it was praised for this very restraint given the religious subject matter. Reviewing the film for the *New York Times*, A. H. Weiler writes, "Hollywood, which has essayed biblical themes before, has, in this instance, largely eschewed the synthetic pageantry and flamboyant spectacles of the past," instead giving us David "as a whole man—human, regal, lusty, poetic . . . and pious."[1]

At the beginning of the film, King David appears to be at the height of his reign, but personal difficulties are soon presented in the form of his first wife, Michal (Jayne Meadows), who resents his subsequent marriages. For his part, David resents that Michal chose not to join him in exile and remarried in his absence. Meanwhile, David's sons bicker for wealth, attention, and even the succession itself.

When David spies a voluptuous female neighbor bathing, he is entranced, but he is disappointed to find that she is Bathsheba, the wife of one of his soldiers, Uriah. He nonetheless invites her to dinner and, upon ascertaining that she is caught in a loveless marriage, tries to seduce her. Bathsheba is initially unwilling, but once he makes it clear that he has no intention of ordering her to sleep with him, she confesses that she bathed specifically so that he could see her.

As their affair intensifies, David begins to neglect his official duties and fails to heed the warnings of the prophet Nathan (Raymond Massey). David witnesses some ominous events that he refuses to acknowledge as omens—an adulterous wife is stoned to death, and a soldier dies for daring to lay unconsecrated hands on the Ark of the Covenant, which David has brought to the city. David is indignant at God's sense of vengeance, given that the soldier only sought to prevent the Ark from falling. David continually seeks pragmatic reasons for the events surrounding him, and while ostensibly respectful of Nathan, it is clear that he has no real faith left in God. Such cynical pragmatism is at times endearing (helped by Peck's delivery), for he applies it to his own legend as well, commenting that Goliath, the giant he slew as a boy, seems to get bigger every year.

When Bathsheba falls pregnant, David recalls her husband from the battlefield in the hope that the child can be passed off as legitimate, not realizing that Uriah has sworn to forsake the comforts of home until they are victorious in their campaign. Faced with the prospect of Bathsheba suffering death by stoning, he orders that Uriah's death be arranged in battle, leaving the path clear to marry Bathsheba himself. This great sin brings drought and famine to the land, and the new prince dies in infancy. When Michal and his own son Absolom publically accuse David and Bathsheba of adultery, David's first impulse is to flee, but the palace is surrounded. David, remembering the faith he once held as a boy, attends the tabernacle to lay before the Ark and beg God's forgiveness, not for himself, but for his people and his wife. We are shown his past—being chosen by Samuel and defeating Goliath—before David lays his hands on the Ark, expecting to die for the sake of his people. Instead, he is spared, and the rains fall once more. David returns to Bathsheba, but she looks upon him as a man changed.

Peck was a favorite lead for versatile director Henry King, who features him in a range of genres in *Twelve O'Clock High* (1949), *The Gunfighter* (1950), *The Snows of Kilimanjaro* (1952, in which Peck reteams with Susan Hayward), and *The Bravados* (1958). Screenwriter Philip Dunne would return to Christian themes in *The Robe* (Henry Koster, 1953), famous for being the first CinemaScope film and a phenomenal commercial and critical success. But it is Peck's rendition of the twenty-third psalm (and not Dunne's script) that reviews singled out as one of the highlights of *David and Bathsheba*.[2] DB

Notes

1. A. H. Weiler, "Film from the Bible: Gregory Peck Scores in *David and Bathsheba* Theme Tepid Bath," *New York Times*, 19 August 1951, 89.
2. A. H. Weiler, "Film from the Bible," 89; "Review: *David and Bathsheba*," *Variety*, 1951, http://variety.com/1950/film/reviews/david-and-bathsheba-1200416988/ (6 June 2013).

Bibliography

"Review: *David and Bathsheba*." *Variety*, 1951, http://variety.com/1950/film/reviews/david-and-bathsheba-1200416988/ (6 June 2013).

Weiler, A. H. "Film from the Bible: Gregory Peck Scores in 'David and Bathsheba' Theme Tepid Bath." *New York Times*, 19 Aug 1951, 89.

THE DAY OF THE LOCUST (1975)

Director: John Schlesinger
Writer: Waldo Salt. Based on the novel by Nathanael West.
Producers: Jerome Hellman, Sheldon Schrager (Paramount Pictures, Long Road)
Cinematographer: Conrad L. Hall
Editor: Jim Clark
Costumes: Ann Roth
Music: John Barry
Cast: Homer Simpson: Donald Sutherland. Faye Greener: Karen Black. Harry Greener: Burgess Meredith. Tod Hackett: William Atherton. Big Sister: Geraldine Page. Claude Estee: Richard A. Dysart. Mrs. Odlesh: Jane Hoffman. Adore Loomis: Jackie Earle Haley. Earle Shoop: Bo Hopkins. Claude Estee: Richard A. Dysart. Audrey Jennings: Natalie Schafer. Abe Kusich: Billy Barty. Miguel: Pepe Serna. Big Sister: Geraldine Page

AA: None
AAN: Best Supporting Actor (Burgess Meredith), Best Cinematography (Conrad L. Hall)
BAFTA Awards: Best Costume Design (Ann Roth)
DVD: Paramount Pictures, 2004
Blu-ray: Currently unavailable
Duration: 144 minutes

Directed by John Schlesinger and based on Nathanael West's novel, *The Day of the Locust* is a biting attack on Hollywood and the culture of pretending, which leaves the viewing public feeling cheated. West's novel and Schlesinger's film dismiss the claim artists in West's time made that they could fill the era's loss of faith in formal religion and government authority after the end of World War I.

The film opens with Tod Hackett (William Atherton) renting an apartment at the San Bernardino Arms (often called the "San Berdoo" by the characters). He is immediately attracted to Faye Greener (Karen Black), an actress, who is on the lawn painting her toenails. Inside an empty apartment, Mrs. Odlesh (Jane Hoffman), the landlady, points out a large crack in an interior wall that runs from floor to ceiling. It is partially covered by a needlepoint. He slips a red flower into a hole in the crack. "We call it our earthquake cottage," she says. He rents the apartment, and the next day he arrives for his first day of work as an assistant to an art director at Paramount Studios. Back at the San Bernardino Arms, Tod places found objects and drawings in a collage on the cracked wall. Images used in his collage are shown surrealistically as transitions between scenes, and they heavily influence his vision at the end of the film. Tod is disturbed from his work with Adore Loomis (Jackie Earle Haley), a boy too old to be a child star, hence a Hollywood grotesque, who draws a woman's mouth in lipstick on his window. Throughout the film, Adore is shown singing and tap dancing suggestively.

Tod calls from his office about a used convertible as people, hungry for the romance and happiness that Hollywood films promise, watch stars enter the Paramount lot. He and Faye drive to a theater in Glendale to see her in a speaking role. They meet Earle Shoop (Bo Hopkins), a cowboy and actor, and he and Faye kiss during the film. When she offers to kiss Tod, he says, "Later." The film disappoints Faye because most of her role has been cut. They leave, ignoring a newsreel of Hitler's rise to power. In the lobby, Faye sees a lobby card with a photo of her. She wants it, so Earle breaks the glass and runs. Tod grabs the photo while Earle and Faye run from the theater manager.

Faye takes Tod up on his offer to make her a drink, and she signs the lobby card for him. He says he thinks that he is in love with her. "Just hold me," she says. Back at the studio, Tod sees Adore's mother (Gloria LeRoy) hitting him so he knows how to cry the next time a director tells him to cry. Tod approaches Claude Estee (Richard A. Dysart) for a project and is put on a film about Waterloo. Tod uses toy soldiers, historical paintings, and occasionally Faye and her friend, Mary Dove, as models. After one of their sessions, Tod asks Faye about their relationship. She replies, "I like you a lot . . . [but] I can only marry someone wealthy and criminally handsome." She tries to leave, but he brusquely pulls her close and kisses her. Tod is later taken by Estee to Audrey Jennings's (Natalie Schafer) brothel, where they watch a stag film. Tod notices that Faye's friend Mary works there.

At his apartment, Tod meets two other Hollywood grotesques. One is Abe Kusich (Billy Barty), who is a tough guy, a gambler, and a dwarf, and the other is Faye's elderly father, Harry Greener (Burgess Meredith). Tod offers him a ride up the hill toward Pinyon Canyon, where he plans to sell shoe polish. Even though he no longer has a career in show business, Harry is always performing, dancing from house to house. The sound track swells when his hopes are high and slows as he becomes exhausted, coughs repeatedly, and sweats profusely.

At Homer Simpson's (Donald Sutherland) house, Harry laughs and dances in spite of his pain. The more pain he is in, the harder he performs, finally collapsing on Homer's couch. Faye, concerned about Harry when he does not arrive home on time, finds him when she sees his product case outside. Homer, a retired hotel accountant, is uncomfortable being near her and holds his hands behind his back, and even breaks a glass of milk as he is holding it. His use of his hands is symbolic of his repressed sexual desires. His life is empty, and he is uncomfortable living alone.

Tod and Faye drive into the country to meet Earle. Earle's buddy Miguel (Pepe Serna) shows them their fighting gamecocks. Earle serves fried quail on newspaper with the ironic headline "Four Power Peace Pact Signed." While they are eating, in a scene without dialogue, the sexual tension rises between Miguel and Faye. Earle and Tod become increasingly violent. Earle hits Miguel with a large stick, and while they fight, Tod tries to pull Faye to the ground. She hits him, and he rips off her dress. She climbs the hill to his car. He calms down and gives her the dress and the keys to his car.

Tod visits Harry, who is still having difficulty breathing. Harry chats with a visiting Eskimo couple and elderly twins, so Tod goes into Faye's room. She picks up the phone and says she is on the phone with Audrey Jennings, but she is actually calling Central Casting. Surprised by her announcement, Tod apologizes for his actions. Homer knocks at the door of the house but is too nervous to come in and leaves flowers at the door. He sees a dollar bill on the ground. As he reaches for it, the bill moves away on a string pulled by Adore. Homer becomes more embarrassed and runs off.

In a scene invented for the film, Homer and Faye take Harry to a religious tent revival for healing. Likely based on a famous evangelist, Aimee Semple McPherson, Big Sister's (Geraldine Page) sermon is overtly theatrical and erotic. Harry is put into a wheelchair and taken to the stage. The film intercuts shots of the people onstage, money being given by the crowd, and Big Sister's large staff counting money at adding machines. Big Sister lifts Harry out of the wheelchair. He falls, stands, and bows slightly, believing that he is back on vaudeville. Harry dies that night while Faye sings "Jeepers Creepers" and looks at a pimple on her nose in the mirror.

The next day, Mrs. Odlesh visits Faye, who is mourning with Mary, and offers to take care of funeral arrangements. When Odlesh leaves, Faye asks Mary to get her into Audrey's because she cannot afford burial. At the funeral, Tod is drunk and forces Faye to speak to him. Instead of consoling her in her loss, he warns about contracting syphilis in her new job. While Faye cries at her father's casket, many of the mourners leave to see a celebrity's car that is arriving.

Homer and Faye come to a business arrangement. He is to help her with her career while she lives at his house. He brings breakfast to Faye in her bedroom. Adore comes to the door and mimics Harry, mocking his death. This upsets Faye, but not enough to keep her from asking Homer to open a charge account for her. Homer arrives home late one night to find Faye digging through a trunk in his room, breaking an agreement to keep out of one another's belongings. After an argument, they cry and Faye puts his thick hands around her. They dance clumsily; she cries as he holds his hand awkwardly to her breast.

Filming begins on the Waterloo set although construction on part of the battleground, a hill, is incomplete. The "Danger Keep Off Set" signs are not yet placed on the hill. They stop construction on the hill, so there is quiet on the set. Tod watches a cast of hundreds, Faye and Earle among them, reenact the battle as the cameras roll. The battle moves onto the hill; it collapses and dozens are hurt.

In another scene added for the film, Tod meets studio executives in the studio barbershop, which John Schlesinger says was a

> delicious extension that Waldo Salt and I had great pleasure in putting in. After all, Waldo had no happy memories of Hollywood, because he was blacklisted, so I suppose anything that came close to a kind of truth about passing the buck, which is typical of a studio system, was something we felt justified in including.[1]

Hackett eventually finds Faye, who is safe, and they kiss. She says she quit working for Audrey. He agrees to go to a show with Homer and Faye. Tod dances with her and asks her to come over to his house. When she refuses, he says "pretend you work for Audrey."

Tod and Estee go to Homer's house to see a cockfight. Earle and Miguel have moved into Homer's house and brought their birds. The challenger does not show, so Kusich borrows one of Earle's birds so there is a fight. The film cuts between the birds and Faye, who is dressing to impress Estee. Homer, upset with his treatment by the others, stands outside to watch the party through a window. Faye sees him, calls him a spy, and throws a vase out the window. Later that night, Homer catches Faye in bed with Miguel. Earle fights Miguel, and Faye leaves.

Tod drives to a film premier. Homer, lost, carries his suitcases past the mob outside the theater. Tod tries to pull him in his car, but Homer yells "thief!" Homer sits at bus stop nearby, cracking his fingers. Adore mocks him by dancing and singing "Jeepers Creepers." Adore throws a rock, hitting Homer in the forehead. Like Faye and Hollywood itself, Adore, a performer, teases the cheated. Head bleeding, Homer catches Adore and jumps on him several times. For the first time, Homer feels joy, seemingly not realizing he is killing the boy. Hundreds of people from the premier audience see the commotion and swarm Homer, lifting him up and then dragging him. The mob becomes out of control; a woman is raped, and Faye is dragged away by men. The crowd overturns cars with celebrities inside. One is set on fire. Electrical poles, palm trees, and tents for the film opening burn. A newspaper with the headline "Roosevelt Pleads to Nation to Continue Fight for Tolerance" is ablaze. Tod sees the people from his drawings move zombie-like toward him. He sees an earthquake open up his house—the wall splits apart, and the Waterloo set explodes. The next day at the San Berdoo, Faye comes into Tod's empty apartment. The flower was left in the wall, but his drawings are gone.

While many critics consider Schlesinger's *Midnight Cowboy* (1969) and *Sunday Bloody Sunday* (1971) to be better films, *The Day of the Locust* deserves more than its current "cult following."[2] JMW

Notes

1. Ian Buruma, *Conversations with John Schlesinger* (Westminster, MD: Random House Trade Paperbacks, 2006), 123.
2. Buruma, *Conversations with John Schlesinger*, 98.

Bibliography

Buruma, Ian. *Conversations with John Schlesinger*. Westminster, MD: Random House Trade Paperbacks, 2006.

DEMETRIUS AND THE GLADIATORS (1954)

DIRECTOR: Delmer Daves
WRITER: Philip Dunne. Based on a character created by Lloyd C. Douglas in *The Robe*.
PRODUCER: Frank Ross (20th Century Fox)
CINEMATOGRAPHER: Milton Krasner
EDITOR: Dorothy Spencer, Robert Fritch
ART DIRECTION: Lyle Wheeler, George W. Davis
COSTUMES: Charles Le Maire
MUSIC: Franz Waxman. Themes from *The Robe*, by Alfred Newman.
CAST: Demetrius: Victor Mature. Messalina: Susan Hayward. Peter: Michael Rennie. Lucia: Debra Paget. Paula: Anne Bancroft. Caligula: Jay Robinson. Claudius: Barry Jones. Glycon: William Marshall. Dardanius: Richard Egan. Strabo: Ernest Borgnine. Cassius Chaerea: Charles Evans. Kaeso: Everett Glass. Macro: Karl Davis. Albus: Jeff York. Slave Girl: Carmen De Lavallade. Varus: John Cliff
AA: None
AAN: None
DVD: 20th Century Fox, 2007
BLU-RAY: Twilight Time, 2012
DURATION: 96 minutes

The Roman-era Christian epic *Demetrius and the Gladiators* is a sequel to the first, highly successful CinemaScope picture, *The Robe* (Henry Koster, 1953), which is based on the popular Lloyd C. Douglas novel of the same name. Often seen as the lesser of the two films (the *New York Times* writes, "This one is no more like *The Robe* than either of them is like . . . Roman history"[1]), *Demetrius and the Gladiators* stands up well with the passage of time as it benefits from a greater use of action than its predecessor to make the most of the CinemaScope expanse. The *New York Times* review deems this somewhat inappropriate for the religious core of the film, saying, "They obviously figured that religion may get the people to church, but it takes something more in the way of action to get them into the theater. And so they have millinered this saga along straight Cecil B. Devotional lines, which means stitching on equal cuttings of spectacle, action, sex, and reverence."[2]

The film begins by presenting the closing moments of *The Robe*, as Marcellus and Diana are sent to their death and martyrdom by Caligula (Jay Robinson) for their Christian faith and refusal to acknowledge Caligula's superior authority. Jesus' robe is sent to Peter (Michael Rennie) for safekeeping, but Caligula becomes obsessed with obtaining it, crediting it with magical powers. Meanwhile, Demetrius (Victor Mature), the former slave of Marcellus, comes to the defense of his friend Lucia (Debra Paget) when soldiers searching for the robe are unduly rough with her. He is taken into custody and sentenced to train as a gladiator in an establishment owned by Caligula's uncle, Claudius (Barry Jones), and his wife, Messalina (Susan Hayward). Demetrius tries to escape, as killing other men contradicts his Christian faith. In doing so, he catches the eye of the promiscuous Messalina. As punishment for his attempted escape, Demetrius is sent into the arena without the usual preparations, seemingly a death sentence.

At the revelry granted to the gladiators the night before they must fight, the other gladiators gamble to win the match against him, for they know as a Christian he will not fight back. Gladiator Dardanius (Richard Egan) wins the right and cannot help picking a fight with Demetrius, but the Nubian Glycon (William Marshall, excellent in this small role) intervenes. Watching the encounter, Messalina orders that the two new allies face one another in the arena. Before the fight, Glycon advises Demetrius to put on a good show with the hope of granting them both the favor and mercy of the crowd, but the audience senses their respect for one another, and they are forced to fight in earnest. Demetrius prevails (perhaps somewhat improbably given Glycon's experience), but the crowd asks Glycon to be spared, for he is a long-standing champion and crowd favorite, due for his freedom. Caligula wants him dead, but Demetrius requests that he reverse his decision. Caligula agrees to free Glycon but orders Demetrius' own immediate death. At Messalina's suggestion, he instead pits Demetrius against tigers as a far more entertaining option, but Demetrius is able to slay them.

Messalina arranges for him to be nursed back to health, and she appoints Demetrius as her personal guard. Meanwhile, Messalina's attempt to arrange for Caligula's assassination fails, and, protecting herself, she proclaims Caligula to be a god. When Demetrius rejects Messalina's sexual advances, she returns him to the gladiator school.

Lucia learns of Demetrius' whereabouts and convinces one of the prostitutes to allow her to infiltrate a gladiatorial party, but the jealous Messalina notices her, and after she has Demetrius removed from the party, Lucia is left to the abuse of the other men. Dardanius is about to rape her when she appears to suddenly drop dead, either from shock or injury. Enraged with grief, Demetrius abandons his prohibition against murder and slays Dardanius and the other perpetrators in the arena, a momentous achievement that sends the audience into a frenzy. Claudius requests that Demetrius be granted his freedom for his unprecedented performance, but Caligula first demands that the gladiator relinquish his faith. In effect, he has already done so through his acts in the arena, and disillusioned that his God would allow the horrific debasement of the innocent Lucia, Demetrius willingly acknowledges Caligula's superior authority.

Demetrius is made tribune and becomes a celebrity more highly esteemed than the emperor himself, and Messalina takes him as her lover. Peter visits them, expressing his sadness that Demetrius has lost his way. Even Glycon disapproves of Demetrius' new life and is instead moved by Peter's calm counsel. Demetrius is unsettled, and Messalina runs to Caligula to tell him that Peter is a threat. Caligula himself is already incensed by public protests against him, and he unwisely threatens to crucify his own guards if they cannot stop the rebels, a sign of his increasing instability.

When Demetrius is ordered to find the robe, he is startled to find Lucia, alive but seemingly in a stupor, clutching at the garment. Demetrius breaks down and prays for her recovery, upon which Lucia wakes, thankfully not remembering what had befallen her. His faith revived, Demetrius nonetheless takes the robe to Caligula to avoid needless bloodshed. Believing that it is the robe itself that has the power to achieve the deeds attributed to Jesus, Caligula kills a prisoner and tries to bring him back to life. He is infuriated when he fails, but Demetrius is equally outraged at the senseless murder. He tries to attack Caligula, giving the jealous Caligula the pretext he needs to send Demetrius back to the arena.

Glycon takes the robe, and Messalina implores Demetrius to fight, even offering to become Christian herself. The guards rally against Caligula's plan to publically destroy the popular Demetrius, and when Demetrius refuses to defend himself, the guards assassinate Caligula. Claudius is proclaimed the new emperor and reveals that his apparent stupidity was simply an act of self-preservation. Messalina, surprised that Claudius wants her to be at his side, promises fidelity to her husband. Addressing Demetrius and Glycon, in particular, Claudius grants the Christians the right to practice their faith as long as they do not undertake acts against the state. At the closing of the film, Glycon, Demetrius, and Peter depart to tell the good news to their fellow Christians.

Variety argues that the film tells a "compelling screen story," although given his limited range, they perhaps overstate the case that Victor Mature won "top acting honors for his splendidly projected Demetrius."[3] Jay Robinson is an entertainingly erratic Caligula, while the handsome and buff Richard Egan (who would go on to play the lead role of King Leonidas in the underrated 1961 Rudolph Maté film *The 300 Spartans*) makes a suitably obnoxious gladiatorial opponent for Demetrius. Susan Hayward is rather hammy, as is the film, but both are enjoyable for that very reason.

There is a rousing score by Franz Waxman, who previously won Oscars for his work on *Sunset Boulevard* (Billy Wilder, 1950) and *A Place in the Sun* (George Stevens, 1951). Director Delmer Daves enjoyed a varied career as a writer, director, and producer. He co-penned the screenplay for *Love Affair* (Leo McCarey, 1939, remade as *An Affair to Remember* in 1957), and his directorial efforts include *Destination Tokyo* (1943), *Dark Passage* (1947), and *3:10 to Yuma* (1957), which was nominated for a BAFTA Award for Best Film from Any Source, but, in a strong field, lost to *Bridge on the River Kwai* (David Lean, 1957). DB

Notes

1. Bosley Crowther, "Demetrius Returns; Victor Mature in Title Role at the Roxy *Tanganyika* Offered on Bill at Palace," *New York Times*, 19 June 1954, http://movies.nytimes.com/movie/review?res=9F04E4DC1438E23BBC4152DFB066838F649EDE&scp=2&sq=demetrius%20and%20the%20gladiators&st=cse (11 February 2012).
2. Crowther, "Demetrius Returns."
3. "*Demetrius and the Gladiators*," *Variety*, 1954, www.variety.com/review/VE1117790349/ (11 February 2012).

Bibliography

Crowther, Bosley. "Demetrius Returns; Victor Mature in Title Role at the Roxy *Tanganyika* Offered on Bill at Palace." *New York Times*, 19 June 1954, http://movies.nytimes.com/movie/review?res=9F04E4DC1438E23BBC4152DFB066838F649EDE&scp=2&sq=demetrius%20and%20the%20gladiators&st=cse (11 February 2012).

"*Demetrius and the Gladiators*." *Variety*, 1954, www.variety.com/review/VE1117790349/ (11 February 2012).

DOCTOR ZHIVAGO (1965)

DIRECTOR: David Lean
WRITER: Robert Bolt. Based on the Nobel Prize–winning novel by Boris Pasternak.
PRODUCER: Carlo Ponti (MGM)
CINEMATOGRAPHER: Freddie Young
EDITOR: Norman Savage
ART DIRECTION: John Box, Terence Marsh
SET DECORATION: Dario Simoni
COSTUMES: Phyllis Dalton
MUSIC: Maurice Jarre
SOUND MIXERS: A. W. Watkins, Frank Milton
CAST: Yuri Zhivago: Omar Sharif. Tonya: Geraldine Chaplin. Pasha Antipova/Strelnikov: Tom Courtenay. Lara Antipova: Julie Christie. Yevgraf Zhivago: Alec Guinness. Victor Komarovsky: Rod Steiger. The Girl/Tonya Komarovskaya: Rita Tushingham. Alexander Gromeko: Ralph Richardson. Anna Gromeko: Siobhan McKenna. Lara's Mother: Adrienne Corri. Professor Kurt: Geoffrey Keen. Shasha: Jeffrey Rockland. Katya: Lucy Westmore. Razin: Noel William. Liberius: Gerrard Tichy. Kostoyed: Klaus Kinski. Young Yuri: Tarek Sharif
AA: Best Writing–Screenplay Based on Material from Another Medium (Robert Bolt), Best Cinematography–Color (Freddie Young), Best Music–Original Score (Maurice Jarre), Best Art Direction–Set Decoration–Color (John Box, Terence Marsh, Dario Simoni), Best Costume Design–Color (Phyllis Dalton)
AAN: Best Picture (Carlo Ponti), Best Supporting Actor (Tom Courtenay), Best Director (David Lean), Best Film Editing (Norman Savage), Best Sound (A. W. Watkins, Frank Milton)
DVD: Warner Bros., 2001. Two-disc edition.
BLU-RAY: Warner Bros., 2010. Two-disc edition, with illustrated booklet and various commentaries by principal actors and several filmmakers.
DURATION: 180 minutes (200 for restored version, 2010)

Of the five epic movies that David Lean made between 1957 and 1984, *Doctor Zhivago* was the most popular. The film grossed more money (approximately $200 million worldwide) than all the others combined and garnered ten Oscar nominations, as many as *Lawrence of Arabia*, but it had only five nods. Many critics balked, but Richard Schickel wrote a laudatory essay in *Time*, and filmmaker John Schlesinger, who directed Julie Christie in *Darling* (1965), commended Lean for his successful handling of a new star.[1] After a dismal reception at the theaters, Lean, assisted by Norman Savage, set out reediting the film, which gradually drew more patrons and eventually broke records at the box office, becoming one of the most popular movies of all time.

Lean worked with a number of gifted crew members, including art designer John Box, noted cinematographer Freddie Young, and screenwriter Robert Bolt, and the cast included stalwart Lean regular Alec Guinness and the newcomer from *Lawrence of Arabia*, Omar Sharif. The film was shot in Spain, where Box built a simulacrum of Moscow streets, and in Finland, for the snow-covered steppes in the winter sequences. The rights to the novel by Boris Pasternak had been obtained by the Italian publisher Carlo Ponti, who, with ample financial backing by MGM, asked Lean to direct the picture. Pasternak had gained fame as a man who stood up to the Soviet Union at the height of the Cold War, and his novel *Doctor Zhivago* became a favorite with audiences both as a love story and as a tale of a free man and an artist who is pitted against a soulless, oppressive regime.

Despite certain similarities with Lean's other epics, *Doctor Zhivago* has its own special appeal: it is the product of a story set in the past but with contemporary (of the time it was made) repercussions. The Cold War was at its height in 1965, and although the love story in the film manages to hold the central interest, audiences were also treated to the social transformations brought about by the upheaval that was the Soviet Revolution in 1917. Aristocrats fell (witness the Gromeko family) and fled to the countryside from Moscow, revolutionaries sprang from the ranks of the working class, spies became ranking Bolsheviks, and the ensuing commissariat was determined to wipe out sentiment ("The personal life is dead in Russia; history killed it," says Strelnikov, played by Tom Courtenay), while temporizers like Komarovsky (Rod Steiger) shifted sides without a tint of shame.

The wide canvas undertaken by the film is brilliantly done, sometimes at the expense of structural coherence; however, the dramatic intensity of nearly every sequence saves this long epic from the onus of sentimentality. This is partly achieved by poetic rhythms abounding in the story, and by cinematic legerdemain, which shows highly dramatic scenes in reaction shots, as in the sequences when a squad of Cossacks attacks demonstrators at a peaceful parade. Instead of showing the massacre, Lean has Zhivago (Omar Sharif) witness the scene from his balcony, his eyes reflecting the terror of what he sees in the street below.

Doctor Zhivago presented its writer and director with unusual challenges, for it came from a literary work of great fame but one that was structurally and historically too complex to transform into a workable script. It also presented enormous technical challenges for the film crews. Lean's two previous epics were filmed on location, or on locations closely resembling the locations represented, but at the time, *Doctor Zhivago* was deemed difficult and/or impossible to film in the Soviet Union. It was a huge undertaking, requiring special sets, unusual art design, and general technical excellence at every level. It also required a cast with such special talents as to bring to life Pasternak's original—something that took a great deal of imagination and a long search before the actors and actresses in question were secured. Aside from Sharif playing the leading role of Yuri Zhivago, a newcomer, Julie Christie, plays Lara, his lover, while the young Geraldine Chaplin was chosen to play his wife, Tonya. Rod Steiger, the only American actor, plays Komarovsky, the tormentor of Lara and Yuri and an exemplar of a man capable of surviving the winds of change.

Bolt spent a year writing the script, first in London, and then in Madrid, where he and Lean labored on the final product. The screenplay numbered 250 pages, and some modern filmmakers still treat it as a yardstick of screenwriting.[2] Bolt envisioned a script that would encompass essential elements of Pasternak's novel without compromising the demands of practical filmmaking.

In its original release, the film ran 197 minutes,[3] nearly three and a half hours. The opening and concluding scenes are told by Zhivago's half-brother, Yevgraf (Alec Guinness), seeking his niece, Yuri's and Lara's daughter, and subsequently telling the story of Yuri and Lara through flashbacks. The story is told from the end, to the beginning, middle, and back to the end. Yevgraf's voice tells the tale of two ill-fated lovers caught in a web of circumstances, united by chance and separated by force. Yevgraf, although not a poet himself, is an admirer of Yuri's poetry, and he shows a volume of Yuri's poems to the young girl he is investigating, hoping she is his brother's child. This volume of poems, with the photographs of the two lovers in it,[4] is dedicated to Lara, and it serves a double purpose: it tells the tale of the lovers and also serves as a guidepost of exposition throughout the story.

Doctor Zhivago is an "imagistic" narrative, full of significant visual images: the dry branch that hits against the window in a gale after Yuri experiences his mother's burial; the balalaika, carried from person to person until it becomes a means for identification; the sunflowers at the parting scene between Yuri and Lara. The tumultuous events of the Soviet Revolution are seen through the eyes of a poet, who is shown writing poems but who never reads them to us. His facial expressions while he is writing change, and it is at such moments that Maurice Jarre's "Lara's Theme" intrudes upon our attention. Zhivago is often described as "passive." His eyes reflect the reality around him that we ourselves see, and what we see are images sprung out of the pages of Pasternak. He also remains the center of our attention, although he is not active in the usual manner of an epic hero, who undertakes an arduous task, and the story does not end until it is completed.

In *Doctor Zhivago*, Yuri Zhivago, the doctor/poet, does nothing heroic outside of trying to protect his family during the turbulent years of the Soviet Revolution. In that, he mirrors the author's life and attitudes, which parallel the historical events of the era in which he lived. Pasternak initially sympathized with the Soviet Revolution, but his sympathies changed throughout the years, and he himself was never involved politically. He did, however, belong to the Soviet Writer's Union, which was established 1932, with the aim of revitalizing the "stagnation" of literature, which was caused by "rivalries between the various literary factions."[5]

Following the purges in 1937, Pasternak chose to remain in Russia, while his parents had immigrated to Germany, but their Jewish origin forced them to escape to Britain after Hitler had taken over in 1933. Pasternak had hoped that his writings—he had published several books of poetry and prose and translated the works of Shakespeare (*Hamlet* being one of them) for the Constantin Stanislavski Moscow Theatre[6]—might influence the communist regime to soften its attitude toward the arts, but as the years went on, his hopes were almost completely crushed, although he never openly rebelled.

During the postwar years, he was ready to undertake the writing of an epic novel in the tradition of the great literary novels of the nineteenth century, but the work was not finished until the end of the Stalinist era, which occurred with the death of Stalin in 1953. It took him ten years (1946–1956) to write it, and when it was finished, he was not permitted to publish it in the Soviet Union, since it was considered critical of the regime. But the manuscript was smuggled out of Russia in 1956 and translated by an Italian publisher,[7] and it quickly became an international best-seller. It was regarded not only as a great story, but a provocation against the Soviet regime, and when Pasternak was awarded the Nobel Prize in 1958, he was initially elated by this honor, yet he refused to go to Sweden to accept the prize when he was told by the Soviet regime that if he did so he would not be permitted to return to Russia.

Today, the movie can be viewed from three different historical perspectives: the time of the story itself, spanning five decades, beginning in 1905, with the funeral of Yuri's mother, to the mid-1950s, when Yevgraf interviews Tonya II; the time the movie was released (1965), at the height of the Cold War, when its relevance was undisputed; and today (2013), after a new, restored Blu-ray version with extras was released in 2010, making the movie available to modern audiences in pristine condition. In fact, the film seems to have regained popularity in the 2000s. Gene D. Phillips reports that the film has received more recognition in recent years, noting that, along with *Gone with the Wind*, *Doctor Zhivago* is cited as among the ten best love stories of all time by the American Film Institute.[8] Lean's reputation has received a boost from both viewers and a new generation of filmmakers,[9] who continue to value and reappraise Lean film art. Lean always enjoyed the support of filmmakers more so than that of his critics, and a group of his contemporaries, Fred Zinnemann, William Wyler, and John Ford, to name a few, gave him support, while a later generation, including Steven Spielberg, Martin Scorsese, and John Milius, has honored him in a variety of ways, so it is appropriate that some filmmakers today[10] also see him as a director, one of a kind, whose work has endured the test of time.

None of the aforementioned critics and commentators, however, consider Lean a political writer. This is possibly because Lean focused primarily on the specifics of his film art, being preoccupied with a good script, photographing techniques, imagery, performances, and, above all, the editing of his works, ensuring clarity of narrative. But while *Doctor Zhivago* is admittedly a love story, it is also an indictment of a totalitarian power, which, in the mid-twentieth century, kept a large part of the world under sway, suppressing rebellions from native peoples and threatening the West with nuclear war. Lean's hero is shown as a man pondering the pros and cons of the Soviet Revolution, or at least reacting to some of its representatives with true abhorrence.

One of the scenes, in which Zhivago is reluctantly a witness, is the slaughter of young school children of a military academy, cut down mercilessly by machine-gun fire in an unforgettable scene—among the blooming, yellow, ripening wheat—a scene whose message is reinforced by the astonishing imagery. In fact, Zhivago's life, shown from beginning to end, is an indictment of cruelty, of man being inhumane to man. In this, the message that comes from observing his actions closely—which both the novel and film do—is consistent with what happens to almost every character that surrounds his life: Lara is horrified by the lovers' ill fate when she says that this is a horrible time to live in; Zhivago's wife endures the indignities of their fate uncomplainingly; and Zhivago's uncle, Alexander Gromeko (Ralph Richardson), is appalled by the execution of the tsar and his family. Meanwhile, two other secondary, but strong, characters, Strelnikov and Komarovsky, show two different approaches to the adversity of violent change. Strelnikov kills himself, after fighting for a revolution that he believes will be a more just regime for his country, while Komarovsky, an amoral manipulator, survives by "adjusting" to change.

The message of *Doctor Zhivago* may be that political stress may determine the fate of innocent humans, who are, by nature, pacifist and do not necessarily take up arms to right wrongs. The Red rebels that abduct Zhivago state that when the revolution prevails, all men will be judged politically. Such an attitude is the credo of dictatorships, whether by totalitarian states, or individual dictators, whose emergence dotted the history of the twentieth century and plunged the world into chaos and unspeakable acts of inhumanity. CS

Notes

1. Gene D. Phillips, *Beyond the Epic: The Life and Films of David Lean* (Lexington: University Press of Kentucky, 2006), 354–56.

2. Kathleen Kennedy, "A Celebration," *Doctor Zhivago*, directed by David Lean (Warner Bros., 2010), Blu-ray.

3. It runs 200 minutes in the restored 2001 DVD version and the 2010 Blu-ray edition.

4. *Doctor Zhivago*, directed by David Lean (Warner Bros., 2001), DVD.

5. Boris Pasternak, *Doctor Zhivago*, translated by Richard Peaver and Larissa Volokhonsky (New York: Pantheon, 2010), xvi.

6. See "Pasternak," in "Special Features," *Doctor Zhivago*, directed by David Lean (Warner Bros., 2001), DVD. Also on the 2010 Blu-ray edition.

7. Giangiacomo Feltrinelli of Milan. Kevin Brownlow, *David Lean: A Biography* (New York: A Wyatt Book for St. Martin's Press, 1996), 498.

8. Phillips, *Beyond the Epic*, 360.

9. In the "Special Features" section of the 2010 Blu-ray edition, several contemporary producers/directors/writers, including Nicholas Mayer, Gary Ross, Mikael Solomon, Martin Campbell, and Taylor Hakford, give high praise for *Doctor Zhivago*, showing a renewed interest in Lean and his epics.

10. See note 9.

Bibliography

Brownlow, Kevin. *David Lean: A Biography*. New York: A Wyatt Book for St. Martin's Press, 1996.

Pasternak, Boris. *Dr. Zhivago*. Translated by Richard Peaver and Larissa Volokhonsky. New York: Pantheon, 2010.

Phillips, Gene D. *Beyond the Epic: The Life and Films of David Lean*. Lexington: University Press of Kentucky, 2006.

Santas, Constantine. *The Epic Films of David Lean*. Lanham, MD: Scarecrow Press, 2011.

THE DUELLISTS (1977)

Director: Ridley Scott
Writer: Gerald Vaughan-Hughes. Based on "The Duel" (1908), a short story by Joseph Conrad.
Producer: David Puttman (Paramount Pictures)
Cinematographer: Frank Tidy
Editor: Pamela Power
Art Direction: Bryan Graves
Costumes: Tom Rand
Music: Howard Blake
Cast: Gabriel Feraud: Harvey Keitel. Armand D'Hubert: Keith Carradine. Joseph, Chief of Police: Albert Finney. Dr. Jacquin: Tom Conti. Feraud's Mistress: Gay Hamilton. Laura, D'Hubert's Girlfriend: Diana Quick. Adele, D'Hubert's Wife: Cristina Raines. Bonapartist Agent: Edward Fox
AA: None
AAN: None
DVD: Paramount Pictures, 2002. Collector's edition.
Blu-ray: Shout Factory, 2010
Duration: 100 minutes

Made in 1977, Ridley Scott's *The Duellists* is a pot-boiler, belonging to the action/psychological thriller genre, but of epic dimension, featuring a prolonged series of episodes between two antagonists, both antiheroes, who clash until one is finally defeated. Scott may come under the heading of the generational trio of Spielberg, Scorsese, and Coppola, a group of talented American directors to which he may be attached chronologically. Scott started his career inconspicuously by doing commercials in England until *The Duellists*, which was noticed and received an award at the Cannes Film Festival. When several known directors (among them Jack Clayton and Peter Yates) declined to do *Alien*, considering it a Grade-B horror movie, Scott was asked to do it, and he immediately accepted. *Blade Runner* (1982) followed, and then a string of notable movies in the United States, including *Thelma and Louise* (1992), *Gladiator* (2000), *Black Hawk Down* (2002), *Kingdom of Heaven* (2005), and *Prometheus* (2012), among others.

Most of these movies are true epics, with one signal characteristic that sets them apart from today's run-of-the-mill action/epic movies: Scott's epics are visually dazzling, action-packed, and violent to the extreme, but always propelled by a central moral question, usually in the form of a conflict between one person and another, between one person and a group, or even between groups. For example, a man carries a grudge against another, and there follow a series of clashes. In *Thelma and Louise*, a sort of gender epic, two women run from the law, in a desperate flight to freedom, doomed from the start. *Gladiator*'s hero is motivated by revenge. Balian, in *Kingdom of Heaven* (2005), fights to establish peace on earth. In *Prometheus*, a woman scientist takes part in a space voyage to find her Maker. And so forth. As with the films of David Lean, a director whom Scott resembles in visual style, Scott's epics are epics of both action and thought.

The Duellists was Scott's first movie, made on a tiny budget of only $900,000, a paltry sum considering that it is a period piece. It is based on the true story of two Frenchmen who dueled during a period of thirty years during the Napoleonic Wars. In his DVD commentary, Scott admits that the limited budget forced him to extemporize, filming outdoors to avoid studio expenses, parts in France, most in England and Scotland, and taking advantage of natural light as much as possible. The entire movie is almost shot in a haze, or in a half-light, since it was filmed in the fall and winter months, when daylight is limited to a few hours.[1] He also comments that he was consciously imitating Stanley Kubrick's *Barry Lyndon*, which had appeared a few years earlier (1975) and had set standards for filming on location using natural light and making use of period painting to reproduce authentic costumes.

Scott secured competent actors for the various parts—Harvey Keitel and Keith Carradine for the leads and several others to fit minor but nonetheless important roles. Keitel, who had already become a fixture in Martin Scorsese films, seemed to Scott to be the right character to play an athletic, brooding, uncommunicative, and vindictive man, not a pasteboard villain one sees in Hollywood swashbuckling movies. Carradine also had the required qualities: he was handsome, wholesome looking, athletic, and, above all, he was someone who had been in the military of a bygone era. Scott also obtained the services of distinguished English actors for minor roles, including Edward Fox as a retired French officer, Albert Finney as the mean chief of police, and Tom Conti as a lute-playing guru, friend, and surgeon. As a group, with the three women in minor roles—Gay Hamilton as Feraud's girlfriend, Diana Quick as D'Hubert's nursing mistress, and Cristina Raines as D'Hubert's wife—the ensemble cast works and the characters are believable as both historical and modern, something that Scott evidently wanted to achieve.

For an action movie, *The Duellists* seems a bit too slow, too artsy in its design and pace, in this sense imitating the style of *Barry Lyndon*, which is slow-paced, and even borrowing some of its actors.[2] Its script, written by Gerald Vaughan-Hughes, is based on "The Duel" (1908), a short story by Joseph Conrad, the Polish/English literary master, whose works have often been transferred to the screen.[3] The film's narrative style borrows from the story a certain "stream of consciousness" quality, a contemporary tone that contrasts with its period trappings, and considerable psychological depth.

Two French hussars, enlisted in the army of Napoleon as lower officers, clash over what at first seems a relatively trivial cause, gradually becoming involved in a feud that would last for several decades. One of the men, Gabriel Feraud (Keitel), an expert swordsman, is seen fighting a rival in a sword duel early in the film's action, but the man he wounds is a nephew of the mayor of Strasburg, and soon an irate general dispatches one of his officers who knows Feraud to arrest him. The officer, Armand D'Hubert (Carradine), considers this an act of duty, but a surly Feraud finds the latter's attitude condescending and refuses to surrender. The two end up fighting on the spot, despite D'Hubert's surprise and reluctance. Feraud, obviously of low-class background, resents being arrested by a man whom he considers inferior in dueling skills, and even a coward. Feraud is short and stocky but huskier, limber, more athletic, and more aggressive than D'Hubert, who is a dutiful officer, proud of his position, but who thinks fighting for an insufficient cause is an absurdity. Nevertheless, he fights, for his duty as an officer demands that he defend his honor, but he does not give the matter much thought after the first duel, for he considers the episode forgotten.

However, he is soon challenged again, and this time, suffering from a cold, receives a serious wound, from which he recuperates with the aid of his girlfriend, Laura (Diana Quick). But Feraud, not content with a draw, once more obtrudes on his life and challenges him again. This fight, more ferocious than the first two, becomes an ugly wrestling match from which the two opponents are separated by their witnesses before they massacre one another. More fights ensue, one on horseback, during which Feraud is almost decapitated, although his wound only helps nurse his hatred.

Meanwhile, the Napoleonic Wars are coming to an end (all this history is more or less kept as background), and the two men are shown on a chance encounter during the French Army's retreat in the Russian winter. Nearly frozen to death, the two are ready to fight once again, but their attempt is foiled by an attack from Cossacks, which necessitates their spending their bullets to fend off that danger. Their momentary common purpose does not unite them, however, and Feraud promises that the next fight will be with pistols. He slanders D'Hubert when he refuses to join Napoleon, who had just returned from Elba. After the latter's defeat, D'Hubert, limping from his wounds, visits the chief of police in Paris (Finney), asking that Feraud's name be crossed from the list of those about to be executed for treason for having sided with Napoleon; he also asks that Feraud never know who intervened to save his life. Then he retires to the country, where he sister arranges a match for him with a neighboring beauty, and he settles down to a life of peace.

But Feraud once more intrudes upon his presence, sending two ruffians as his seconds to another duel, this one with pistols. D'Hubert proposes a hide-and-seek fight in the surrounding thickets, an area familiar to him, the duelists being allowed two shots apiece. Feraud is the first to shoot, missing his opponent, twice. He expects, and begs (proudly), to be killed. D'Hubert, however, chooses not to shoot—sparing his enemy's life. He returns to his wife, offering her an orange when she asks him where he had been. In the meantime, Feraud is seen slowly walking up a slope, while, offscreen, the voice of D'Hubert is heard, telling the viewer what his last words to Feraud had been: "From now on, I dictate the terms of our feud; you no longer have any right to obtrude on my affairs, for I consider you dead." Feraud reaches the edge of a cliff, glumly looking at the sunrise. His look indicates that he is mulling over his final defeat.

Told in six episodes, each marking a period from the beginning of the Napoleonic era (1802) to the end (1816), the film achieves an even, rhythmical pace that works to its advantage, for the audience expects that the two opponents are bound to meet again and again. Tension is built as these two contrasting (and in some ways similar) personalities become the hunter and hunted. Feraud appears a dark demon gratuitously stalking a reluctant opponent, whose unwillingness to accept the challenge, calling it "absurd," is equally puzzling. Feraud's spite, resentment, and inability to sympathize are matched by D'Hubert's puzzlement, defenselessness, inertia, and fear. D'Hubert realizes soon enough, however, that reconciliation is not possible, and that only two choices remain to him: one is to follow the advice of his philosopher/doctor, Dr. Jacquin (Conti), and flee, and the other is to stand and fight when cornered.

Feraud's pursuit of him through the years seems an inexplicable obsession, but it is perhaps a synecdoche for war itself: if one opponent is bent on destroying the other, the pursued must be equally hardened and cruel. Reason collapses in the face of hatred. Hatred is irrational but is often disguised as reason; Feraud maintains that his opponent is a coward, a lackey to those of higher rank for the sake of promotion, and one who avoids a real fighter. A coward deserves no quarter. Feraud sees no other way for reconciliation; he will not understand such a thing. He only needs to challenge an opponent, especially one who he thinks he is inferior in stamina or fighting ability.

In every other respect, Feraud is a loyal officer, rising to a rank equal to D'Hubert's and achieving reputation as a duelist; in fact, both do, for their duels become legendary. Of the two, D'Hubert is more human, involved twice in relations with women, thus appearing humanized and normal. He is fully aware of the duel's absurdity and considers it an anachronism. D'Hubert is more of a twentieth-century character, while Feraud adheres to a code of honor, already outdated in his own time. But he, too, is modern. Spite, insecurity, desire for dominance, these are modern remnants of an earlier era, but refined and honed by analysis, as in Fyodor Dostoyevsky's underground heroes.[4]

Feraud could, in contemporary terms, be described as suffering from acute paranoia, for he fails from the very start of their relationship to realize that D'Hubert was simply doing his duty in arresting him and had no personal grudge or intention of humiliating him. Once the feud starts, however, reason is lost on both, because D'Hubert is gradually hardened as well by dueling, receiving professional lessons in swordsmanship and achieving notoriety as a swordsman. He is unwillingly caught up in a spiral of self-demeaning actions that are profoundly corrupting and tragic. But D'Hubert possesses powers of reconciliation that Feraud lacks. He offers Feraud a drink when the two have joined forces to vanquish the Cossacks (which Feraud refuses) and intervenes to save Feraud's life after the latter had been blacklisted following Napoleon's defeat. He is fully conscious that a reasonable, civilized man could rise above a petty hatred perpetuated throughout a lifetime. His fear of a fight, shown in the earlier episodes, has given place to assurance, and even righteous anger, when he finally realizes that he can be the winner in a pistol fight.

His final confrontation with Feraud also shows his contempt for him. He dismisses the proposal of the two ruffians sent to represent Feraud, asserting that no rational man would accept to participate in such a farce. Possessed of a happy family life, he now discards the last vestiges of the duel's earlier glamour, and with that he is ready to end the feud, this time his way. He dares his opponent to fight in the woods, of which he is more familiar; when he wins, he stops short of killing him. By depriving Feraud of an honorable death in a duel, he also deprives him of his honor. In his climb to the edge of the cliff, bathed in rising sunlight, Feraud realizes that he has lost, for his reason for fighting no longer exists; neither does honor carried to absurdity. An epic? Perhaps a minor one. And it already exhibits Scott's virtuosity in the genre: visual splendor, plenty of action, attractive leads, and provocation with thought. CS

Notes

1. Ridley Scott, "Commentary," in "Special Features," *The Duellists, Collector's Edition*, directed by Ridley Scott (Paramount Pictures, 2002), DVD.
2. Gay Hamilton, who was Redmond Barry's inamorata in Stanley Kubrick's *Barry Lyndon*, appears here as Keitel's girlfriend.
3. *Heart of Darkness* (1899) (as Coppola's *Apocalypse Now*) and *Lord Jim* (1900) are two examples. *Nostromo* (1904) was also filmed for television, and David Lean was to begin making a film based on the book, but he died before work on the project could commence.
4. A reference to Dostoyevsky's character in *Notes from Underground*, who confesses his spite against those who have hurt him.

Bibliography

Conrad, Joseph. *The Duel*. Brooklyn, NY: Brooklyn House Publishing, 2001.

E

THE EGYPTIAN (1954)

DIRECTOR: Michael Curtiz
WRITERS: Philip Dunne, Casey Robinson. From the novel by Mika Waltari.
PRODUCER: Darryl F. Zanuck (20th Century Fox)
CINEMATOGRAPHER: Leon Shamroy
EDITOR: Barbara McLean
ART DIRECTION: Lyle R. Wheeler, George W. Davis
COSTUMES: Charles Le Maire
MUSIC: Alfred Newman, Bernard Herrmann
CAST: Merit: Jean Simmons. Horemheb: Victor Mature. Baketamon: Gene Tierney. Akhnaton: Michael Wilding. Nefer: Bella Darvi. Kaptah: Peter Ustinov. Sinuhe: Edmund Purdom. Taia: Judith Evelyn. Mekere: Henry Daniell. Grave Robber: John Carradine. Senmut: Carl Benton Reid. Thoth: Tommy Rettig. Queen Nefertiti: Anitra Stevens
AA: None
AAN: Best Cinematography–Color (Leon Shamroy)
GG: Most Promising Newcomer–Female (Bella Darvi)
DVD: 20th Century Fox, 2011
BLU-RAY: Twilight Time, 2011
DURATION: DVD, 134 minutes; Blu-ray, 139 minutes

This fabulously melodramatic CinemaScope epic is set in eighteenth-dynasty Egypt, presenting the pharaoh Akhnaton (played by Michael Wilding), who came to the throne around 1353 B.C.E., as both blessed and cursed by his monotheistic belief in the sun god Aten. The film depicts Akhnaton as a type of martyred prophet prefiguring the teachings of Christ centuries later. Yet, the story actually revolves around the seemingly lowly Sinuhe, an unwanted infant cast adrift on the Nile in a basket. It is the penitent adult Sinuhe (Edmund Purdom) who narrates the film in flashback.

Twentieth Century Fox wanted another widescreen epic success to follow *The Robe* (Henry Koster, 1953), the first film released in CinemaScope and a phenomenal box-office triumph for Fox. Thus it comes as no surprise to see many of the same crew credited for *The Egyptian*, as well as cast members Jean Simmons and Victor Mature, in smaller but effective roles here. Akhnaton was the father of his more famous son Tutankhamun, whose spectacular remains were discovered in 1922, but there had been more recent archaeological finds that lead to a resurgence in interest in Egypt and helped raise interest in the film[1] (which even begins with a brief travelogue of the wondrous ruins to be found in contemporary Egypt).

An aging physician who tends to the needs of the poor rescues the infant Sinuhe from the River Nile, raising him as his own. Sinuhe earns himself a place in the School of

Life and, following in his father's footsteps, also becomes a surgeon to the poor. At the school, he forges an unlikely friendship with an ambitious soldier, Horemheb (Mature), who takes it upon himself to look after the dangerously inquisitive Sinuhe. While out hunting, Horemheb prevents a lion from attacking the pharaoh, although he does not know his sovereign's identity. When Sinuhe dares to lay hands on Akhnaton in an effort to help with his "holy sickness" (seemingly epilepsy), both Horemheb and Sinuhe are arrested; however, the pharaoh is lenient, believing in love and forgiveness as part of his exclusive religious observance to the sun god Aten. Akhnaton appoints Sinuhe royal physician, rewarding Horemheb with a place among the palace guards previously denied to him by his lowly birth.

Meanwhile, Merit (Jean Simmons), a beautiful tavern maiden, suffers from her unrequited love for Sinuhe, but he has been bewitched by the exotic charms of a Babylonian, Nefer (Bella Darvi). Nefer is an expert manipulator of men, and to the dismay of his friends, Sinuhe gives her all of his worldly possessions, including his house and surgeon's tools. Driven mad by his unconsummated desire, Sinuhe even gives her the deeds to his parents' home and their tombs, robbing them of eternal life. With nothing left to give her, Nefer rejects the dismayed Sinuhe, who realizes his folly too late.

When Sinuhe's parents commit suicide, Sinuhe seeks to at least have their bodies embalmed and restore them a place in the afterlife, working alongside the damned to pay for it. His disappearance from society is ill-timed, for the pharaoh's daughter dies when Sinuhe cannot be found to attend to her. Sinuhe is forced to flee with his loyal and wily servant Kaptah (Peter Ustinov, bringing some much-needed comic relief to the proceedings) as a tearful Merit bids him farewell.

Years later, Sinuhe returns to Egypt to warn of a Hittite invasion with their new iron swords. Sinuhe and Kaptah find a land divided by Akhnaton's religion, and his refusal to wage war on religious grounds has lost him the respect of the military. Sinuhe discovers that he has a son by Merit, but his joy is short-lived when Merit is killed at the temple of the sun god Aten in a plot by his old friend Horemheb and the princess Baketamon (Gene Tierney) to stamp out the religion and seize power. Kaptah departs with Sinuhe's son to protect him from the purge.

Baketamon urges Sinuhe to kill both the pharaoh and Horemheb and assume the throne himself with her at his side, for he is revealed to be the pharaoh's half brother, cast adrift by her own jealous mother. Yet, Akhnaton knows he is ill and, in fact, asks Sinuhe to help him die. Perhaps surprisingly, Sinuhe eventually agrees. The pharaoh's vision of a better world nonetheless touches Sinuhe, and he leaves Egypt to Baketamon and Horemheb, going into exile to contemplate his many crimes and Akhnaton's words of hope.

The film is based on the novel *The Egyptian*, by Mika Waltari, which, in turn, is roughly based on a Middle Kingdom Egyptian story, *Tale of Sinuhe*, adding in the historical figures Horemheb and Akhnaton, whose controversial monotheism is well attested.[2] Although the novel *The Egyptian* was a best-seller, *Variety* notes that it was rather "scholarly" and a brave choice for a film adaptation given that it is a "long way off the standard spectacle beat."[3]

But with "around $4.2 million . . . splurged on bringing ancient Egypt to life again . . . the results justify the expense"[4] (20th Century Fox records put the figure at $3.9 million[5]). Art direction is superb, with $85,000 spent on the throne room alone, and many of the designs were based on their ancient originals.[6] In the midst of such attention to detail, producer Darryl F. Zanuck was also keen for a timely completion, being aware that MGM, Warner Bros., and Paramount were all planning Egyptian films of their own (*The Valley of the Kings* [Robert Pirosh, 1954], *Land of the Pharaohs* [Howard Hawks, 1955], and *The Ten Commandments* [Cecil B. DeMille, 1956], respectively,[7] the latter of which is said to have reused some of the sets from *The Egyptian*).[8] The collaborative score of Alfred Newman and Bernard Herrmann was one of the benefits of this haste, but *Variety*'s enthusiasm for the film was not shared by most critics. Domestically, *The Egyptian* took in $4.25 million, which paled next to *The Robe*'s $17.5 million in the previous year.[9]

Edmund Purdom as Sinuhe, brought in to replace Marlon Brando when the latter went cold on the project,[10] is rather flat in the role, although to be fair he is in any case the naïve straight man to the more charismatic characters around him. Gene Tierney as Baketamon should be merely another villainess to mirror Nefer (who eventually loses both her fortune and her health), and yet she is utterly bewitching in the small role. Rather somber in tone, *The Egyptian* is often considered a disappointing film, yet Sinuhe's despondency when he discovers the bodies of his parents is as touching as it is melodramatic, and the film is gorgeous to listen to and behold. DB

Notes

1. Jon Solomon, *The Ancient World in the Cinema* (New Haven, CT, and London: Yale University Press, 2001), 250.
2. Lloyd Llewellyn-Jones, "Hollywood's Ancient World," in *A Companion to Ancient History*, edited by Andrew Erskine (Chichester, UK, and Malden, MA: Wiley-Blackwell, 2009), 577. See also Dominic Montserrat, *Akhenaten: History, Fantasy, and Ancient Egypt* (New York: Routledge, 2000).
3. "*The Egyptian*," *Variety*, 1954, www.variety.com/review/VE1117790657/ (8 December 2012).
4. "*The Egyptian*."
5. Aubrey Solomon, *Twentieth Century Fox: A Corporate and Financial History* (Metuchen, NJ, and London: Scarecrow Press, 1988), 248.
6. Solomon, *The Ancient World in the Cinema*, 243.
7. Jeffrey Richards, *Hollywood's Ancient Worlds* (London: Continuum, 2008), 142.
8. David Huckvale, *Ancient Egypt in the Popular Imagination* (Jefferson, NC: McFarland, 2012), 28.
9. Solomon, *Twentieth Century Fox*, 225.
10. Solomon, *Twentieth Century Fox*, 93.

Bibliography

"*The Egyptian*." *Variety*, 1954, www.variety.com/review/VE1117790657/ (8 December 2012).

Huckvale, David. *Ancient Egypt in the Popular Imagination*. Jefferson, NC: McFarland, 2012.

Llewellyn-Jones, Lloyd. "Hollywood's Ancient World." In *A Companion to Ancient History*, edited by Andrew Erskine, 564–79. Chichester, UK, and Malden, MA: Wiley-Blackwell, 2009.

Montserrat, Dominic. *Akhenaten: History, Fantasy, and Ancient Egypt*. New York: Routledge, 2000.

Richards, Jeffrey. *Hollywood's Ancient Worlds*. London: Continuum, 2008.

Solomon, Aubrey. *Twentieth Century Fox: A Corporate and Financial History*. Metuchen, NJ, and London: Scarecrow Press, 1988.

Solomon, Jon. *The Ancient World in the Cinema*. New Haven, CT, and London: Yale University Press, 2001.

EL CID (1961)

Director: Anthony Mann
Writers: Fredric M. Frank, Philip Yordan, Ben Barzman (uncredited)
Producer: Samuel Bronston (Samuel Bronston Productions, Dear Film Productions)
Second Unit Director: Yakima Canutt
Cinematographer: Robert Krasker
Editor: Robert Lawrence
Production Design: Veniero Colasanti, John Moore
Costumes: Veniero Colasanti, John Moore
Music: Miklós Rózsa
Cast: El Cid Rodrigo Diaz de Bivar: Charlton Heston. Chimene: Sophia Loren. Count Ordóñez: Raf Vallone. Princess Urraca: Genevieve Page. Prince Alfonso: John Fraser. Prince Sancho: Gary Raymond. Arias: Hurd Hatfield. Fanez: Massimo Serato. Al Kadir: Frank

Thring. Don Diego: Michael Hordern. Count Gormaz: Andrew Cruickshank. Moutamin: Douglas Wilmer. Priest Don Pedro: Tullio Carminati. King Ferdinand: Ralph Truman. Don Martín: Christopher Rhodes. Bermúdez: Carlo Giustini. King Ramiro: Gérard Tichy. Dolfos: Fausto Tozzi. Mother Superior: Barbara Everest. Nun: Katina Noble. Soldier: Nelio Bernardi. Soldier: Franco Fantasia. Ben Yussuf: Herbert Lom

AA: None

AAN: Best Art Direction–Set Decoration–Color (Veniero Colasanti, John Moore), Best Music–Original Song (Miklós Rózsa and Paul Francis Webster for "Love Theme from El Cid [The Falcon and the Dove]"), Best Music–Scoring of a Dramatic or Comedy Picture (Miklós Rózsa)

GG: Special Merit Award (Samuel Bronston)

GGN: Best Motion Picture–Drama, Best Motion Picture Director (Anthony Mann), Best Motion Picture Score (Miklós Rózsa)

DVD: The Miriam Collection, 2008

Blu-ray: Starz/Anchor Bay (Region B), 2011

Duration: 188 minutes

A historical epic based partly on the real figure Rodrigo Diaz de Bivar (Charlton Heston), known as El Cid, and partly on the legend that emerged around him even in his lifetime. El Cid was the hero of Spain who saved the nation from the invading African Moors in the eleventh century, "when men were men and women were Sophia Lorens."[1] If the invaders' leader, Ben Yussuf (Herbert Lom), is a one-dimensional villain ("Kill! Burn!"), the film tempers this by depicting the friendship between Rodrigo and his captured Moorish emir Moutamin (Douglas Wilmer). Moutamin, among others, attacks a Christian village and burns down its church. Rodrigo inadvertently gets drawn into the battle while on his way to be married to Chimene (as she is known here, played by Sophia Loren, but Jimena in history). When Rodrigo takes the prisoners home with him, he finds the peasants ready for revenge. Rodrigo proclaims that killing the emirs will bring only retribution upon them all, and to the alarm of the king's officer, Count Ordóñez (Raf Vallone), he frees the emirs on condition that they swear not to attack the kingdom again. Moutamin is impressed with Rodrigo's honor and mercy, giving him the title of El Cid (originally al-Sayyid, meaning Lord)[2] and proclaiming his eternal friendship.

But there is a heavy cost of this hopeful step toward peaceful relations between Christians and Moors. Rodrigo is accused of treason, and it is his future father-in-law and king's champion Count Gormaz (Andrew Cruickshank) who angrily makes the case to King Ferdinand (Ralph Truman). When Rodrigo's father, Don Diego (Michael Hordern), calls Gormaz a liar, Gormaz shames him by slapping him with his glove. Rodrigo, his fate not yet determined, confronts Gormaz and is forced into a sword fight to restore his family's honor. Rodrigo prevails, but in killing Gormaz, he loses Chimene.

With the king's champion dead, the neighboring King Ramiro (Gerard Tichy) takes the opportunity to challenge the ownership of the city of Calahorra. Rodrigo offers to fight their champion, Don Martín (Christopher Rhodes), in an impressive joust and sword fight that is desperately scrappy and intense, convincing the audience of the sheer hard work involved. (The scene was filmed by second unit director Yakima Canutt, who had worked on William Wyler's 1959 *Ben Hur*.[3]) Rodrigo prevails and is proclaimed king's champion, but when he is sent with Prince Sancho (Gary Raymond) to overcome Moorish vassals who are refusing to pay tribute, he does not realize that Ordóñez has arranged an ambush to have Rodrigo killed in return for Chimene's love. Moutamin comes to Rodrigo's aid, and Rodrigo convinces Sancho to show mercy and let Ordóñez live.

Upon their return, the king forces Chimene to marry Rodrigo, much to the evident jealously of Princess Urraca (Genevieve Page, in the "most provocative performance among the supporting players"[4]). But Chimene retreats to a monastery, having made clear that she will not consummate the marriage.

When King Ferdinand dies, brothers Prince Sancho and Prince Alfonso (John Fraser) argue over the crown. Sancho tries to imprison his brother, but Rodrigo comes to his rescue. Alfonso finds refuge at Princess Urraca's castle, and she arranges for Sancho to be assassinated. Alfonso is crowned king, but Rodrigo refuses to kneel to him until Alfonso swears an oath that he had no knowledge of or part in his brother's death. Alfonso proclaims his innocence but exiles Rodrigo for his effrontery. Chimene reconciles with Rodrigo and joins him in exile, but their plans for a simple family life together are shattered when a crowd gathers calling Rodrigo to lead them. So ends the first half of the film before intermission.

With Ben Yussuf on the move, the battle-scarred Rodrigo takes the crucial city of Valencia (represented here by the walled city of Peñíscola), offering its people bread and inciting them to turn against their corrupt emir Al Kadir (Frank Thring). But when offered the crown by Moutamin, Rodrigo refuses and proclaims his loyalty to King Alfonso. This is despite the fact that the king imprisons Rodrigo's family, which now includes twin daughters he has barely seen. Yussuf's forces arrive at Valencia, and Rodrigo is injured with an arrow in his chest. He refuses to have it removed, for he is determined to lead the army the following day and would not be able to do so if recovering from surgery. Reconciled with King Alfonso and reunited with his family, Rodrigo dies before the final battle; however, he still is able to lead the forces to victory, his corpse strapped onto his horse as it tramples the stunned Yussuf.

Bosley Crowther of the *New York Times* proclaims that the "spectacle is terrific. Only the human drama is stiff and dull in this narrative."[5] Even Charlton Heston, who was very fond of the production, admitted that some scenes were "overwritten,"[6] something that certainly hampers the pacing of the first half of the film. The uncredited, blacklisted Ben Barzman, working primarily from Pierre Corneille's play *Le Cid*, had to toil at breakneck speed to write the script, even as shooting commenced.[7] Despite these difficulties, the film was a tremendous success.

El Cid was primarily shot on location in Spain, with access to the country's castles by virtue of the producer's close relationship with the Franco regime. The number of extras used for the siege of Valencia—3,000 members of the Spanish Army and 1,100 mounted police[8]—would have been prohibitively expensive in the United States, and epic productions were increasingly moving overseas to take advantage of both cheaper labor and good locations.[9]

In any case, director Anthony Mann argued that actors "become more real" on location, whereas in the studio they have to fake a relationship with their surroundings, which the audience can feel.[10] Mann had been brought in to work on the project on the strength of his westerns, and *El Cid* provided him with a chance to prove his mettle with the epic after being replaced by Stanley Kubrick on *Spartacus* (1960). His shot compositions for *El Cid* frequently emphasize an appreciation of space by highlighting the foreground and extreme edges of the screen, for example, Rodrigo's arrival at the burning church, his bloodied sword cutting into the frame.[11] The effect is certainly dramatic, yet it is perhaps ironic that

Mann's compositions often draw attention to themselves as beautiful but artificial impositions on the landscape.

As is often the case, historical figures, events, and names have been simplified or omitted from the film. Much of the information about El Cid comes from legends that emerged long after his death, for instance, the love–hate relationship between Chimene and Rodrigo[12] (an antagonism shared by its lead actors at the time). Historian Richard Fletcher goes so far as to dismiss the real Rodrigo as a mere mercenary, but M. J. Trow argues that then, as now, people liked the idea of a hero, such that even in his own life, inaccurate stories about El Cid were in circulation.[13] The film continues this tradition, but more significantly has been the means by which, however much bathed in the heroic sheen of the film epic, the world outside Spain knows of *El Cid* at all. DB

Notes

1. Bosley Crowther, "Screen: Spectacle of *El Cid* Opens: Epic about a Spanish Hero at the Warner," *New York Times*, 15 December 1961, http://movies.nytimes.com/movie/review?res=9B05E0D6143AE13ABC4D52DFB467838A679EDE (25 May 2012).

2. M. J. Trow, *El Cid: The Making of a Legend* (Phoenix Mill, UK: Sutton Publishing, 2007), 99.

3. Charlton Heston, *In the Arena: The Autobiography* (London: HarperCollins, 1995), 257.

4. "*El Cid*," *Variety*, 1961, www.variety.com/review/VE1117790665/ (25 March 2013).

5. Bosley Crowther, "Screen: Spectacle of *El Cid* Opens."

6. Heston, *In the Arena*, 249.

7. Norma Barzman, *The Red and the Blacklist: The Intimate Memoir of a Hollywood Expatriate* (New York: Tunder's Mouth Press/Nation Books, 2003), 307.

8. "Hollywood Conquers Spain: The Making of *El Cid*," *El Cid*, directed by Anthony Mann (The Miriam Collection, 2008), DVD.

9. Sheldon Hall and Steve Neale, *Epics, Spectacles, and Blockbusters* (Detroit, MI: Wayne State University Press, 2010), 178.

10. "Behind the Camera: Anthony Mann and *El Cid*," *El Cid*, directed by Anthony Mann (The Miriam Collection, 2008), DVD.

11. See Steve Neale, "The Art of the Palpable: Composition and Staging in the Widescreen Films of Anthony Mann," in *Widescreen Worldwide*, edited by John Belton, Sheldon Hall, and Steve Neale (New Barnet, UK: John Libbey, 2010), in which Neale also notes this tendency in his analysis of Mann's widescreen techniques.

12. Trow, *El Cid*, 83–85.

13. Trow, *El Cid*, 103, 212. See Trow for a detailed discussion of the historical and literary sources on El Cid.

Bibliography

Barzman, Norma. *The Red and the Blacklist: The Intimate Memoir of a Hollywood Expatriate*. New York: Tunder's Mouth Press/Nation Books, 2003.

Crowther, Bosley. "Screen: Spectacle of *El Cid* Opens: Epic about a Spanish Hero at the Warner." *New York Times*, 15 December 1961, http://movies.nytimes.com/movie/review?res=9B05E0D6143AE13ABC4D52DFB467838A679EDE (25 May 2012).

"*El Cid*," *Variety*, 1961, www.variety.com/review/VE1117790665/ (25 March 2013).

Hall, Sheldon, and Steve Neale, *Epics, Spectacles, and Blockbusters*. Detroit, MI: Wayne State University Press, 2010.

Heston, Charlton. *In the Arena: The Autobiography*. London: HarperCollins, 1995.

Neale, Steve. "The Art of the Palpable: Composition and Staging in the Widescreen Films of Anthony Mann." In *Widescreen Worldwide*, edited by John Belton, Sheldon Hall, and Steve Neale, 91–106. New Barnet, UK: John Libbey, 2010.

Trow, M. J. *El Cid: The Making of a Legend*. Phoenix Mill, UK: Sutton Publishing, 2007.

ELMER GANTRY (1960)

DIRECTOR: Richard Brooks
WRITER: Richard Brooks. Based on the novel by Sinclair Lewis.
PRODUCER: Bernard Smith (Elmer Gantry Productions)
CINEMATOGRAPHER: John Alton
EDITOR: Marjorie Fowler
MUSIC: André Previn
CAST: Elmer Gantry: Burt Lancaster. Sister Sharon Falconer: Jean Simmons. Jim Lefferts: Arthur Kennedy. William L. Morgan: Dean Jagger. Lulu Bains: Shirley Jones. Sister Rachel: Patti Page. George F. Babbitt: Edward Andrews. Reverend Garrison: Hugh Marlowe
AA: Best Leading Actor (Burt Lancaster), Best Supporting Actress (Shirley Jones), Best Writing–Screenplay Based on

Material from Another Medium (Richard Brooks)
AAN: Best Music–Scoring of a Dramatic or Comedy Picture (André Previn), Best Picture (Bernard Smith)
DVD: MGM, 2001
BLU-RAY: Currently unavailable
DURATION: 146 minutes

Both the film and the novel[1] follow the rise of Elmer Gantry from a loutish vacuum salesman to popular minister who lifts revivalist Sister Sharon Falconer's ministry from the country circuit to her own big-city tabernacle. Large crowds in almost every scene attend such dramatic events as the busting of speakeasies and brothels, nighttime midtown sermons, and a concluding conflagration. Burt Lancaster, at the peak of his career, leads the film in its epic dramatization of the lurid, outlandish behavior of politicians, businessmen, and even average people involved in the unholy trinity of sex, money, and religion, represented respectively by Gantry, George Babbitt, and Sister Falconer.

The film's trailer explicitly highlights this trinity when Lancaster, holding a Bible says, "Elmer Gantry is an all-American boy: He's interested in money, sex, and religion." The film itself, before the credits, warns of the controversy surrounding the book and the film and suggests that the point of the film is to be a corrective to those who "abuse the faith of the people!"—a not-so-subtle jab at industry censors who deemed the novel "unsuitable for the screen." The film then warns viewers to "prevent impressionable children from seeing it." As if to prove these statements, a graphic of a tilted, highly stylized cross covers the screen during the credits, suggesting distress, like an inverted American flag, and then transforms into a traditional, upright wooden cross that casts a long, dramatic shadow.

The film opens with a close-up of the first pages of the Sinclair Lewis novel the film is based on: "Elmer Gantry was drunk. He was eloquently drunk, lovingly and pugnaciously drunk." The scene cuts to a miniature Nativity Crèche and then pulls back to the bar top of a speakeasy during prohibition, and then to Gantry, who is telling risqué jokes to a group of fellow traveling salesmen. As he picks up drinks from the bartender, he stops to admire a woman sitting at the bar wearing a red dress appropriate for the location and the holiday season. Gantry's other impulse, to be a minister of the Lord, is revealed when a woman from the Salvation Army asks for donations. A salesman answers her by saying, "Religion don't belong in any speakeasy." Gantry shows his disagreement by answering, "Jesus wouldn't be afraid to walk in here or any speakeasy to preach the gospel. . . . Jesus had love in both fists. And what is love? Love is the mornin' and the evenin' star that shines on the cradle of the babe." His speech attracts the woman's interest more than that of the salesman, who leaves quickly after the sermon and his loss of funds to the Salvation Army. The young woman stays with him in the hotel overnight. Although Gantry claims that the speech is about "divine love, not carnal love" the effect is the same. He doesn't have money to pay for drinks or tip the bellhop, but he has fully integrated sex and religion into his life.

Gantry leaves town by jumping on the boxcar of a train. While he sleeps inside the boxcar, some hobos steal his shoes and attempt to take his bags. He pushes them off, throws his packages off the train, smiles broadly, and jumps off the train. After Gantry jumps from the train, he walks, shoeless, past a billboard along the tracks. The advertisement reads: "Sister Falconer can save you." This introduces us to a future character, and is a reference to a William Butler Yeats poem, "The Second Coming," which says that the "falcon cannot hear the falconer." Mankind, even members of the ministry, no longer hears God. Down the track, gospel music attracts Gantry to a black church near the railroad. The parishioners are suspicious of him when he walks in, but when he joins their song in a clear, strong baritone voice, the church joyously accepts him.

Smiling, gregarious, and with a hairdo similar to those found in Coen brothers films, Gantry attends the Sister Sharon Falconer tent revival. Falconer arrives, dressed like a milkmaid, a character out of a pastoral novel. She extols the virtues of farming and milking to the parishioners, which, she relates, were made by a bountiful, generous God. The camera moves from below her as she makes her appeal, and then above her as she concludes, showing that she makes the connection between money and God. Jean Simmons portrays the attractive religious inamorata that Gantry falls for as soon as he sees her.

The next day, Falconer moves like a celebrity through the crowd, in dark sunglasses, her long brunette hair tucked into a hat. She refuses an overture from Gantry; he says he is a minister without a church. Gantry uses Sister Rachel's (Patti Page) attraction to him as an entrée to get closer to Sister Falconer with his "Love is the mornin' and evenin' star" speech.

At the "West Iowa" railroad station, Gantry slips onto the train, joins Sister Rachel in her seat, and then uses journalist Jim Lefferts (Arthur Kennedy) to draw Bill Morgan (Dean Jagger), Falconer's manager, away from Falconer. Claiming that he met Falconer two years prior in Cato, Missouri, Gantry tells the story of finding Lulu Bains (Shirley Jones, in her standout, Oscar-worthy performance), his betrothed, naked, behind the altar, "locked in the arms of her lover, a cardsharp." She says he is "amusing" and "smells like a real man."

Gantry pitches an idea to Falconer about finding religion through the Gideon Bible. He makes the connection between religion and commerce, saying, "I didn't make that sale, Lord. You did." He uses his speech about love in the sermon. Afterward, when Falconer congratulates him on moving so many to convert, he kisses her. Disturbed, she says, "The big difference between you and me is that I believe. I really believe." Lefferts, reporting for the *Zenith Times Dispatch*, watches from the dark shadows of the tent, and, after Falconer leaves, he tells Gantry, "Every circus needs a clown. Who knows, you may turn out to be the funniest clown of them all. And the most successful." Gantry invites further circus comparisons when he uses a chimp at the next revival meeting to criticize the theory of evolution and, by implication, Lefferts. The film makes quick cuts between Gantry and Falconer's styles of preaching. Gantry's sermon apparently causes a man to begin barking like a dog. Morgan tells Falconer that Gantry was expelled from a seminary when he was caught seducing the deacon's daughter (Bains) in the church. Gantry saves his position in her ministry when he arrives with the "ticket to the big time" for the revival to work in Zenith, the next big step in her career.

George Babbitt (Edward Andrews), a businessman and real estate magnate, works with a group of ministers to bring Falconer to Zenith. Reverend Garrison, played by Hugh Marlowe, objects when the businessmen want to vote to give Falconer a guarantee of funds. He asks, "Vote to do what? Marry the church to a three-ring circus?" Babbitt says, "Christianity is a growing concern," and carries the argument. With two ministers not voting, they agree to close down the churches in favor of the tent revival.

Clowns are a prominent feature of Zenith's parade for the revival when it arrives. The city audience is raucous and hostile. Morgan tells Gantry, "You certainly promoted us into Zenith, you certainly filled tents, but with what?" Once she arrives, Falconer stands quietly, looking around the tent roof, eventually winning over the audience, even Lefferts. She says, "You may not believe in God, but God believes in you."

After their first night is a success, Falconer calls Gantry "darling" and kisses him on the cheek. When Gantry tries to kiss her back, she says, "God sent you to me as his instrument not as my lover." He begins to see her divided personality: Falcon and Katie Jones from Shanty Town. At times she wants to throw off the Sister Falconer persona and get away, but he pulls her into the darkness under a boardwalk. Lefferts's report literally becomes fish wrap in the next scene.

The film cuts to a brothel, where one of the women reads Lefferts's article out loud. Another, Lulu Bains, shows that she knows Gantry when she gives the same speech that Gantry had given Rachel earlier. Later, Bains listens to Gantry on the radio. Then she goes to a boxing ring to hear him preach. The next night, Gantry and a crowd of righteous followers march to drive out bootleggers and brothels. Gantry recognizes Bains and, because of his guilt for having driven her to this place, asks the police not to arrest her. Lulu invites him to her apartment.

She is ready to capture the moment with hidden photographers. The photos captured are delivered to Morgan with the request that Sister Falconer deliver the money to Lulu's busted-up brothel. Lulu refuses the money after all, and the *Zenith Telegraph*, Lefferts's opposition paper, runs the photos. Afterward, Lulu comes to the much-diminished revival to gloat, but when the audience pelts Gantry with eggs and riots, she is horrified by what she has caused. Lulu runs out of the tent with Gantry in slow pursuit. Lulu arrives home, where her boyfriend, upset at losing the money, beats her. Gantry arrives, throws the man out of Lulu's place, and apologizes to Lulu, saying he is sorry for everything he has done to her. Without Gantry knowing, she recants her previous story to Lefferts, who publishes it.

Lefferts's report causes the next revival meeting, held in Falconer's new tabernacle, to overflow with happy, zealous parishioners. Outside the tent, Falconer sees a shooting star and takes it as a sign from God. For the first time, Falconer attempts a faith healing. It works. A carelessly tossed cigarette smolders near paint cans and then erupts into flames. Gantry tries to rescue Falconer from the fire, but she resists, saying, "Trust in the Lord." The crowd pushes Gantry away from Falconer as they run. Falconer perishes in the flames, then the fire consumes the Waters of the Jordan Tabernacle. The next day, all that is found of Falconer is her Bible. Although this could be a sign of her apotheosis, Sister Falconer is just a falcon. She does not hear the falconer.

At the end of the film, Gantry is strong, still evangelizing to the gathered crowd, but he gives it up as a "childish thing" and leaves alone. While it seems that Gantry will permanently leave the ministry, he will certainly be attracted to sex, religion, and money in the future. As one character says, "I've been converted five times." JMW

Note

1. Sinclair Lewis, *Elmer Gantry: A Novel* (London: J. Cape, 1927).

Bibliography

Daniel, Douglass K. *Tough as Nails: The Life and Films of Richard Brooks.* Madison: University of Wisconsin Press, 2011.

Lewis, Sinclair. *Elmer Gantry: A Novel.* London: J. Cape, 1927.

EXCALIBUR (1981)

Director: John Boorman
Writers: Rospo Pallenberg, John Boorman. Adapted from Thomas Malory's *Le Morte d'Arthur.*
Producer: John Boorman (Orion, Warner Bros.)
Associate Producer: Michael Dryhurst
Cinematographer: Alex Thomson
Editors: John Merritt, Donn Cambern (uncredited)
Art Direction: Tim Hutchinson
Costumes: Bob Ringwood
Music: Trevor Jones
Cast: King Arthur: Nigel Terry. Morgana: Helen Mirren. Lancelot: Nicholas Clay. Guinevere: Cherie Lunghi. Perceval: Paul Geoffrey. Merlin: Nicol Williamson. Mordred: Robert Addie. Uther Pendragon: Gabriel Byrne. Uryens: Keith Buckley. Igrayne: Katrine Boorman. Gawain: Liam Neeson. Cornwall: Corin Redgrave. Kay: Niall O'Brien. Leondegrance: Patrick Stewart. Sir Ector: Clive Swift. Lot: Ciarán Hinds (as Ciarin Hinds). Sadok: Liam O'Callaghan. Astamor: Michael Muldoon. Boy Mordred: Charley Boorman. Mordred's Lieutenant: Gerard Mannix Flynn (as Mannix Flynn). Mador: Garrett Keogh. Ulfus: Emmet Bergin. Young Morgana: Barbara Byrne. Lady in Waiting: Brid Brennan. Aged Morgana: Kay McLaren. Abbot: Eamon A. Kelly (as Eamonn Kelly)
AA: None
AAN: Best Cinematography (Alex Thomson)
BAFTA Award Nomination: Best Costume Design (Bob Ringwood)
Cannes Film Festival Award: Best Artistic Contribution (John Boorman)
Cannes Film Festival Award Nomination: Palme d'Or (John Boorman)
DVD: Warner Bros., 2000
Blu-ray: Warner Bros., 2011
Duration: DVD, 135 minutes; Blu-ray, 141 minutes

Excalibur is the story of King Arthur from conception to death during the Dark Ages, ostensibly adapted from Thomas Malory's *Le Morte d'Arthur* but drawing on other Arthurian material and adding new elements as well. *Variety* writes, "*Excalibur* is exquisite, a near-perfect blend of action, romance, fantasy, and philosophy, finely acted and beautifully filmed."[1] Despite its flaws, the film is one of the most imaginative and evocative renditions of the Arthurian myth.

The adventure begins with Arthur's father, Uther Pendragon (a young Gabriel Byrne), who forges an alliance to unify Britain with the help of Merlin (Nicol Williamson) and the magical sword Excalibur, but Uther breaks this alliance by using Merlin's magic to obtain another man's wife, Igrayne (played by the director John Boorman's daughter, Katrine), under the watchful eye of her daughter Morgana (Barbara Byrne, with the adult Morgana played by Helen Mirren). Merlin's price for arranging the union is Uther and Igrayne's son Arthur, whom Merlin fosters out; however, the larger cost is the peace of the kingdom and the future vengeance of Morgana. When Uther is defeated, he places Excalibur in a stone to prevent its misuse (this prehistory to Excalibur is an invention of the film), and in the subsequent years, knights joust for the right to attempt to withdraw it and become king.

As a young man, Arthur misplaces his brother's sword and innocently removes Excalibur from the stone. Leondegrance (Patrick Stewart, before his success later in the decade in television's *Star Trek: The Next Generation* [1987–1994]) swears his allegiance, but the other knights are not inclined to follow a mere whelp until, at the close of battle, the magic of Excalibur and Arthur's own humility persuade them otherwise. King Arthur and his knights set about bringing the land under one rule, but they are thwarted by a stubborn and seemingly undefeatable foreign knight, Sir Lancelot (Nicholas Clay). Arthur himself is nearly bested but calls upon the magic of Excalibur to help him. Lancelot is defeated, but the sword breaks and Arthur realizes that he should not misuse it for mere vanity. The Lady of the Lake returns it to him restored, and Lancelot becomes the king's champion.

Arthur marries Leondegrance's daughter, Guinevere (Royal Shakespeare Company and television actor Cherie Lunghi), but Lancelot and Guinevere fall in love, such that Lancelot cannot bring himself to stay at the newly built Camelot or sit at the round table with the king he feels he betrays in his heart. Arthur's half sister Morgana, who learns magic under Merlin's tutelage, notices the attraction and entices the drunken Sir Gawain (a young Liam Neeson) into accusing the queen of adultery. When Lancelot is late to the joust to defend their honor, the young Perceval (Paul Geoffrey) offers to become her champion and is knighted, but Lancelot arrives and prevails in the joust, so the queen is declared innocent.

And yet afterward, Guinevere joins Lancelot for a tryst. The jealous Arthur discovers them and leaves Excalibur with them to show that he knows of their treachery. With the royal house in disarray, a famine befalls the land, Lancelot puts himself into exile, and Guinevere retires to a convent. Morgana imprisons Merlin and uses the same magical trickery that was used on her hapless mother to seduce Arthur and bear him a son, raising him in seclusion in preparation for seizing power. An ailing Arthur recognizes that they have all lost their way and announces that the knights can restore the kingdom if they find the Grail. The knights set out on their quest but are thwarted by Morgana and her son Mordred (played as a boy by the director's son, Charley Boorman, who is well known to today's audiences for his motorbike journeys with Ewan McGregor in television's *Long Way Round*, 2004. The adult Mordred is Robert Addie, who would return as a medieval villain in television's *Robin of Sherwood* [1984–1986]).

Despite being plagued by fear and cowardice, Sir Perceval manages to solve the riddle of the Grail, remembering what they have all forgotten: that the king and the land are one. The Grail restores Arthur's health, but they must still face Mordred's forces. Although confined, Merlin is able to defeat Morgana, who is killed by her own son when her magic can no longer conceal her aging and leaves her unrecognizable. Arthur reconciles with both Guinevere and Lancelot, but he is forced to kill his own son and is mortally wounded. He insists that Perceval return Excalibur to the Lady of the Lake, and Arthur is taken to sea on a magical boat. Has he died, or has he been taken to the Otherworld to return one day?

Despite the medieval armor, *Excalibur* resonates with older pre-Christian, Celtic elements. Arthurian scholar Richard White notes that when the Grail and Grail castle are introduced to the Arthurian story for the first time in Chrétien de Troyes's twelfth-century unfinished *Perceval* (*Story of the Grail*), it is without the "Christian associations [that] they are later to acquire. In fact, they probably derive originally from Celtic mythology."[2] Merlin and Morgana call upon pre-Christian spirits of nature, but Merlin himself wearily observes that the one (Christian) God is replacing them.

With its sudden shifts in time to encompass Arthur's entire life (which Vincent Canby of the *New York Times* rightly criticizes for creating an uneven, episodic feel[3]), it is the droll Merlin who is, in fact, the central figure of the film and observer of the heroic (and not so heroic) conquests of those around him. Morgana may be the ostensible villain (she was originally a positive figure in Arthurian tales), but her anger at her parents' treatment by Merlin and Uther is surely justified, such that perhaps it is really Merlin who should be brought to task for his misuse of magic, as he himself acknowledges at one point.

Playing Arthur is Nigel Terry, a veteran of the stage whose big-screen debut was the 1968 Anthony Harvey film *The Lion in Winter*, alongside Peter O'Toole and Katharine Hepburn. Terry and Lunghi (Guinevere) would team up again as romantic partners in another medieval adventure for television's *Covington Cross* (1992).

Director John Boorman was nominated for Academy Awards for *Deliverance* (1972) and *Hope and Glory* (1987), and he won the best director award at the Cannes Film Festival for *The General* (1998). His lush, dreamy fantasy rendition of the Arthurian myth in *Excalibur* captures the mysticism of the Arthurian tales, condensing and changing them in the process. Malory's tales were written in the fifteenth century, using contemporary trimmings to depict the past and condensing earlier French stories of Arthur (for example, the round table comes to us from Wace's *Brut* of 1155, and Camelot is first mentioned in Chrétien de Troyes's *Lancelot* of the twelfth century).[4] It is perhaps not especially useful, therefore, to become overly concerned with the liberties that Arthurian films like *Excalibur* take with such a malleable tradition.

Talking on the set of *Excalibur*, Boorman explained, "If there was ever an Arthur . . . he's sited in about the sixth century. But the date is the least important thing really. I think of the story, the history, as a myth. The film has to do with mythical truth, not historical truth."[5] In the 1970s, Boorman had been working on an adaptation of J. R. R. Tolkien's *The Lord of the Rings*, which never made it into production. He instead applied this work on a quasi-medieval fantasy world to *Excalibur*: "That was my recompense."[6] So the Arthurian world he creates is one of the imagination and not of the past, per se, emphasized by the use of "green gels" in lighting the forest scenes for a "sense of otherworldliness."[7] For all its faults, it is nonetheless this otherworldly atmosphere and imagery of *Excalibur* that stays with the viewer, along with the music of Richard Wagner and Carl Orff, before they had suffered from overuse. DB

Notes

1. "*Excalibur*," *Variety*, 1981, www.variety.com/review/VE1117790761?refcatid=31 (6 August 2012).
2. Richard White, *King Arthur in History and Legend* (New York: Routledge, 1997), xxii.
3. Vincent Canby, "Boorman's *Excalibur*," *New York Times*, 10 April 1981, http://movies.nytimes.com/movie/review?res=9505EFD61138F933A25757C0A967948260 (6 August 2012).
4. White, *King Arthur in History and Legend*, xvii, xix.
5. Harlan Kennedy, "John Boorman–In Interview," *American Film*, March 1981, http://americancinemapapers.homestead.com/files/EXCALIBUR.htm (25 August 2012).
6. Stephen Lemons, "John Boorman," *Salon.com*, 3 April 2001, www.salon.com/2001/04/02/boorman/singleton/ (6 August 2012).
7. Kennedy, "John Boorman."

Bibliography

Canby, Vincent. "Boorman's *Excalibur*." *New York Times*, 10 April 1981, http://movies.nytimes.com/movie/review?res=9505EFD61138F933A25757C0A967948260 (6 August 2012).

"*Excalibur*." *Variety*, 1981, www.variety.com/review/VE1117790761?refcatid=31 (6 August 2012).

Kennedy, Harlan. "John Boorman–In Interview." *American Film*, March 1981, http://americancinemapapers.homestead.com/files/EXCALIBUR.htm (25 August 2012).

Lemons, Stephen. "John Boorman." *Salon.com*, 3 April 2001, http://www.salon.com/2001/04/02/boorman/singleton/ (6 August 2012).

White, Richard. *King Arthur in History and Legend*. New York: Routledge, 1997.

F

THE FALL OF THE ROMAN EMPIRE (1964)

Director: Anthony Mann
Writers: Ben Barzman, Basilio Franchina, Philip Yordan
Producer: Samuel Bronston (Samuel Bronston Productions)
Cinematographer: Robert Krasker
Editor: Robert Lawrence
Production Design: Veniero Colasanti, John Moore
Set Decoration: Veniero Colasanti, John Moore
Costumes: Veniero Colasanti, John Moore
Music: Dimitri Tiomkin
Special Effects: Alex Weldon
Cast: Livius: Stephen Boyd. Lucilla: Sophia Loren. Marcus Aurelius: Alec Guinness. Timonides: James Mason. Commodus: Christopher Plummer. Verulus: Anthony Quayle. Ballomar: John Ireland. Sohamus: Omar Sharif. Cleander: Mel Ferrer. Julianus: Eric Porter. Senator: Finlay Currie. Ballomar: John Ireland
AA: None
AAN: Best Music–Original Score (Dimitri Tiomkin)
DVD: Universal Pictures, 2004; Genius Products, 2008
Blu-ray: Spirit Media, 2009
Duration: 188 minutes

Extravagantly financed and mounted by Samuel Bronston, and directed by the vigorous hand of Anthony Mann, who had also directed the successful *El Cid* a few years earlier, *The Fall of the Roman Empire* tanked at the box office and nearly ruined the fortunes of Samuel Bronston Productions. The reasons for that failure are not hard to imagine and even speak for themselves: audiences had grown weary of lengthy epics where the word/idea *Roman* had been used in the title or implied as the subject of an epic story, as had been the case for decades, since the 1930s, in super productions with big names of leads or directors. In the postwar revival of the epic form, and since the late 1940s, in particular, epics with biblical/Roman themes had flooded the screens, either presenting the evil Romans throwing Christians to the lions (witness *Quo Vadis* in 1951) or persecuting them in many other ways (*The Robe*, 1952; *Demetrius and the Gladiators*, 1953; and many others of similar ilk, including those with lesser box-office grosses).

Then came several big super epics, *The Ten Commandments* (1956) and especially *Ben-Hur* (1959), which cleaned out the Oscars with eleven wins, an event unprecedented until that time. *Spartacus* followed in 1960, featuring such megastars as Kirk Douglas (he was offered the role of Livius in *The Fall of the Roman Empire* but declined), Jean Simmons, Laurence Olivier, Tony Curtis, Charles Laughton, and Peter Ustinov. The years 1963 and 1964 proved very unlucky for the spectacular Roman-themed epic, with the equally extravagant

Cleopatra and *The Fall of the Roman Empire* both flopping with audiences and critics and getting slaughtered at the box office. Put simply, the period of the Hollywood big-budget epic with pseudo-historical and essentially reverent themes was over.

Nevertheless, most of the epics of that era survive in the modern era, thanks mainly to the reissuing of those grandiose works on VHS, the short-lived laser disc, and, in the last decade or so, DVD and Blu-ray, which spurred the revival of those megaworks, distinct for their lengthy running times, expense, extravagance, and spectacle. These would be impossible to make today, when the epic has changed, essentially being transformed by computer-generated imagery (CGI) technology, which radically reduces the expense (in most cases), offering hyperaction spectacles and also reducing duration, a necessity for the multiplex theaters. But younger generations, and older ones alike, motivated by a spurt of nostalgia for the works of an extinct era, still like to see them, especially when home theater entertainment has become accessible to the average viewer.

The Fall of the Roman Empire offers many of the aforementioned ingredients. It has colossal and historically accurate sets,[1] built at great expense, showing Rome as the rich capital of an empire whose life spanned hundreds of years, along with scenes of battles with thousands of real folks fighting one another without the benefit of CGI wizardry. *The Fall of the Roman Empire* builds dramatic tension—slowly, one has to admit—centered on conspiracies and murder, as the action progresses from the first part, when the emperor, Marcus Aurelius (Alec Guinness), a philosopher and writer of note, is aging and helplessly attempting to reconcile the many tribes/nationalities of his empire, inspiring them to the ideals of unity and peace. But his ambitious and humane—and one might say democratic—plan is foiled by his son, Commodus (Christopher Plummer), an unstable youth[2] (preceded in notoriety by Nero and Caligula) who is determined to make Rome the center of a hedonistic empire that would only care for glitter and glory, making this possible by doubling the taxes paid by the various Roman provinces in the East, while crushing any opposition to the northern "barbaric" tribes, who had trusted Aurelius and lived in peace. The dying Aurelius understands his son's juvenile mind-set and choses his trusted general Livius (Stephen Boyd) as his successor. The latter, having been a friend of Commodus as a youth, and rather driven by modesty, or motives that remain a bit unclear, declines the title, hoping that Commodus will act wisely. His one ambition is to serve the empire as a soldier, and, being in love with Commodus' sister, Lucilla (Sophia Loren), he hopes that one day he can marry her.

But as soon as Commodus is crowned emperor by the Roman Senate, he calls in delegations from the Eastern provinces of the empire and demands the doubling of levies, something Livius, following the wishes of the Marcus Aurelius, objects to. This act stirs rebellion in the East, and Livius is sent to crush it. Meanwhile, Commodus has given his sister Lucilla in marriage to the Armenian king Sohamus (Omar Sharif), fearing that she and Livius would conspire against him. Meanwhile, the northern Germanic tribes rebel, and Timonides (James Mason), a converted Greek teacher beloved by Aurelius for his wisdom and erudition and a friend and companion of Livius, is sent to pacify them. But he suffers painful torture at the hands of Ballomar (John Ireland), a rebellious northern chieftain, without complaining, thus gaining the admiration of the northerners, some of whom he convinces to found a peaceful colony within the confines of the empire.

The action moves quickly after that, as the epic gains some momentum. Livius comes back a winner from the East, but Commodus places him under arrest. Timonides, who has brought the northern tribes with him and leaves them in a peaceful camp, is brutally murdered, and Commodus stages a grandiose public assembly, in which he emerges like a god out of a tower with folding doors, frees Livius, and invites him to a duel. The two of them fight in the arena, and Commodus is killed. Livius refuses to stay in Rome, and he and Lucilla leave the city for a life of peace elsewhere.

This lengthy epic is broken into two parts. The first is dominated by Emperor Aurelius, as complications from his weakening health and hold of power begin to weaken him, even as he desperately tries to win the day by offering a universal peace among the vast territories of the Roman Empire. Alec Guinness plays him as noble-minded man of vision, one who knows that the empire has to embrace and accept—and honor—its vast provinces in the East and North. He foresees doom if his son succeeds him and choses Livius as his successor, a man reluctant to wear the mantle of an emperor, knowing the conniving minds of those surrounding Commodus, the blind servant Cleander (played superbly by Mel Ferrer) being one. It is Cleander who plots the death of Aurelius, cutting an apple with a poisoned knife, knowing by touch which side has the poison, and offering the poisoned half to the emperor, while he eats the other.

The second part of the movie is generally livelier and moves at a faster pace, and we get the full picture of Commodus and his juvenile antics, matching those of Charles Laughton as Nero in *The Sign of the Cross* (1935) and Peter Ustinov as the same character in *Quo Vadis* (1951), perhaps besting the image of the same emperor (Commodus) by Joaquin Phoenix in Ridley Scott's 2000 *Gladiator*. There are parallels between the last two epics, as both bend history for dramatic purposes. Both show Commodus dying in the arena, when, in fact, Commodus was strangled in his bed by his mistress, Marcia. Neither Maximus in *Gladiator* nor Livius in the *The Fall of the Roman Empire* are historical characters. Lucilla did not marry an Armenian king, but she was assassinated by her brother in his second year as emperor for having plotted against him.[3] Marcus Aurelius died fighting the northern tribes, the cause of his death not having been determined. The addition of Livius, however, makes the drama more interesting, having added conflicts that would not have existed without him. As given by Christopher Plummer, Commodus is not only a clown and jester (with Plummer cleverly hamming up his part), but a deeply troubled young man who envies his father's wisdom, Oedipally, and actually tries to kill him. At the same time, he seems fixed on Livius's rejection of him as both a lover and general under his command, in a not so suppressed homosexual urge, when his lover rejects him both on principle and for the sake of a woman. The last scene of the duel in the arena shows them in a prolonged embrace, as Livius holds on to his dead enemy, having stabbed him, and will not let him go. If one does not expect a history lesson from *The Fall of the Roman Empire*, one could still enjoy its intense dramatic scenes (especially during the second part), the magnificent sets (not to forget the misty landscapes of the northern frontiers), and an entertaining "window" to real history.[4] CS

Notes

1. Commentary by Neal M. Rosendorf, Ph.D., historian and biographer of Samuel Bronston. "Special Features," *The Fall of the Roman Empire*, directed by Anthony Mann (Genius Products, 2008), DVD.
2. See the commentary by Dr. Ronald Mellor, professor of Roman history at the University of California, Los Angeles. "Special Features," *The Fall of the Roman Empire*, directed by Anthony Mann (Genius Products, 2008), DVD.

3. See the commentary by Dr. Peter Heather, professor of medieval philosophy at King's College, London. "Special Features," *The Fall of the Roman Empire*, directed by Anthony Mann (Genius Products, 2008), DVD.

4. Commentary by Neal M. Rosendorf, "Special Features," *The Fall of the Roman Empire*, directed by Anthony Mann (Genius Products, 2008), DVD.

Bibliography

Basinger, Jeanine. *Anthony Mann*. Middletown, CT: Wesleyan University Press, 2007.

Darby, William. *Anthony Mann: The Life and Films*. Jefferson, NC: McFarland, 2009.

A FAREWELL TO ARMS (1957)

DIRECTOR: Charles Vidor
WRITER: Ben Hecht. Based on the novel by Ernest Hemingway and the play by Laurence Stallings.
PRODUCER: David O. Selznick (Selznick Studio)
CINEMATOGRAPHER: Piero Portalupi, Oswald Morris
EDITOR: John M. Foley, Gerard J. Wilson
MUSIC: Mario Nascimbene
CAST: Lt. Frederick Henry: Rock Hudson. Catherine Barkley: Jennifer Jones. Maj. Alessandro Rinaldi: Vittorio De Sica. Dr. Emerich: Oscar Homolka. Miss Van Campen: Mercedes McCambridge. Helen Ferguson: Elaine Stritch. Bonello: Kurt Kasznar. Passini: Leopoldo Trieste. Aymo: Franco Interlenghi. Maj. Stampi: José Nieto. Father Galli: Alberto Sordi
AA: None
AAN: Best Supporting Actor (Vittorio De Sica)
DVD: 20th Century Fox, 2005
BLU-RAY: Currently unavailable
DURATION: 152 minutes

More than fifty adaptations into film and television have been made of Ernest Hemingway's work,[1] most changing the ending of his stories so they conclude happily. This film is the second adaptation of his novel *A Farewell to Arms*, the first produced in 1932. Twenty-five years after it was released, Hemingway wrote a friend saying that the book had survived the film.

Shot in CinemaScope and DeLuxe Color in "authentic locales," *a Farewell to Arms* was advertised as "a theatrical event of the 1st magnitude," with a cast of "many thousands." It was emphasized that it was Ernest Hemingway's "unique and finest love story of the twentieth century." The film contrasts the drama and violence of World War I to the love affair of a young American ambulance corps lieutenant and a British nurse. The opening of the film oscillates between scenes of bombed city streets and snow-covered mountains, emphasizing that "Hemingway's romantic tragedy of World War I," as it was advertised, was not about war alone. Ironically, it suggests that a modern love story, one that rejects Victorian morals, is as great an offense against society as is war.

Frederick Henry, an American who fails to be hired as a war correspondent and not wanting to kill anyone, joins the Red Cross and works in the Italian ambulance corps. Henry returns to Orsino after being away on leave. The girls in the Villa Rosa brothel yell from the second story window that they have missed him. His staff welcomes him back, including friendly Bonello (Kurt Kasznar) and the child-like pair of Passini (Leopoldo Trieste) and Aymo (Franco Interlenghi). Henry reports to Major Stampi (José Nieto), who says that they will open a road through the snow and soon be on the move. He visits friends Father Galli (Alberto Sordi) and the surgeon Major Alessandro Rinaldi (Vittorio De Sica). Father Galli is a man of heaven: believer of God, rivers, and trout. Rinaldi, often called "Rini," is of the earth: friend of men and alcohol and a lover of women. Rini tells Henry the war has improved because British women work in a new hospital near Orsino, especially Catherine Barkley, a twenty-one-year-old girl who works in the Voluntary Aid Detachment (VAD), in spite of her "uncooperative" attitude.

Rinaldi introduces Henry to Catherine, portrayed by Jennifer Jones, David O. Selznick's thirty-eight-year-old wife. Catherine carries a leather-bound stick that belonged to her fiancé, but he was killed at the Somme. She did not marry him before he left because it would have made it worse for him in battle. She often massages the stick while speaking. Rinaldi warns Henry that if he dates her three times he will have to marry her, saying it is a British law.

Henry drives to a British hospital at night to convince Catherine to go on a date with him, but people in the VAD are not permitted to leave the grounds in the evening. They go to a courtyard, where he attempts to seduce her, and she slaps him when he does not relent. He convinces her that they do not have time to get to know one another because he leaves for the front in the morning. A storm forces them inside an empty room. Laughing and sobbing, Catherine says, "I'm afraid of the rain because sometimes I see myself dead in it." The music adds a discordant two-note refrain to suggest her sad memory of her dead lover. Succumbing to Henry's advances, she imagines that Henry is her lover returned.

Henry drives an ambulance in the parade of soldiers and vehicles leaving town in the midst of hundreds of adults and children crying. He sees Catherine pushing her way through the crowd. He kisses her and promises to return. Henry follows hundreds of vehicles and alpine troops carrying large weapons as they slowly move along back roads through the mountains. Henry drops Rinaldi off at a field hospital. On the way to the front, Henry drives past strange and poignant sights, men entering a cave with a sign over the entrance that says "Villa Rosa," a cannon and man being lifted by rope up a cliff face through fog and snow, and a blessing service for soldiers in the middle of a snowstorm.

Once they arrive at their destination, Henry visits the front. The Italians bombard the enemy on a ridge, while the Germans shoot at the Italian supply depot. A fusillade of bombs drops around Henry, forcing him to take a cable car downhill to his men, but he is wounded in both legs and Passini is killed. He is driven back down the mountain on the lower bunk of his own ambulance. On the bunk above, a man bleeds profusely, blood streaming downward onto Henry. At the field hospital, while Henry sleeps, Father Galli prays, telling him he hopes "God brings you to your river." Once stabilized, the doctors want to send Henry to an American hospital in Milan, but Henry wants to go to Orsino. "It's not geography," Rinaldi explains. "It is Miss Barkley."

The new American hospital is staffed by numerous incompetent people, and Henry is their first patient. The ambulance driver taking him to Milan drives so dangerously that Henry falls off the bunk and lands on the floor. They pull him out of the ambulance by his wounded leg. While competent, Miss Van Campen (Mercedes McCambridge), the superintendent, is too Victorian for Henry, refusing to allow wine in the room. He spits an oral thermometer onto the floor to show his disgust. Miss Van Campen says to her coworker, Miss Ferguson (Elaine Stritch), "Turn him over, Miss Ferguson. Let's see if he can break it that way."

Catherine is transferred to the same hospital where Henry is staying, happy she is able to nurse him back to health. The first night, he pushes her to have sex in the room. The next morning, she says they will "have a strange life." After surgery, Henry is shirtless and lying facedown on his bed, and Catherine is massaging him. He wants to marry her, but she refuses because "wives are not allowed at the front." She says he's her only religion.

The two live as if the war does not exist. They visit the local sites, including renting a boat and swimming in the lake. While at the horse races, Catherine tells Henry she is pregnant. At the same time, an announcer says troops have reached the summit of San Gabriella and San Marco. When Miss Van Campen discovers their affair, she says he is ready for active duty "this very night." When he leaves for duty, Catherine tells him not to worry about her delivering the baby, whom he calls "young Catherine."

Henry arrives back in Orsino. During the months of his absence, the front has moved closer to the city. From their perch, the women at the Villa Rosa watch the explosions at the edge of the city. Major Stampi says that the Germans will arrive soon now that the Russians have a "separate peace" with them. Henry drives an ambulance up the mountain road and out of Orsino but is ordered to return. Orsino's buildings are on fire, and hundreds of people are streaming out of the city. Although exhausted, the doctor wants to stay with his wounded, but his division orders him to retreat. Father Galli's "boss" orders him to stay. Galli leads the men in song until the building is blown up.

Henry drives Rinaldi in the ambulance among the fleeing masses on the road. Bonello leaves the truck when he kills a man who refuses to get off of the ambulance and sits down in a field. The truck loses a wheel, stranding them. Henry and Rinaldi are forced to walk, while Aymo rides with the girls from the Villa Rosa. The mud road is littered with the dead and jettisoned belongings. Rini is feverish from seeing the horrors around him, and he calls himself a coward for leaving Orsino. He is arrested by the battle police and subjected to a trial by court-martial. Judging him a German infiltrator, a spy, and a confessed deserter, he is shot. They also rule Henry a spy, but he escapes and jumps off a railroad bridge into a river. Henry strips a dead man for his clothes and jumps a train to Milan. At the Milan train station, Miss Van Campen and Miss Ferguson are assisting wounded soldiers. When she sees Henry, Miss Van Campen calls the police so they can capture him as a deserter.

At Catherine's hotel, Henry tells her, "I'm through with the war. I've made a separate peace." The newspaper has a photo of him as a deserter, so they hide at a lake villa. Catherine convinces him to escape to Switzerland by boat at night. As he rows, a storm rises. He wants to turn back to protect her and the baby, but she refuses. She is unconcerned about the rain. They avoid a patrol boat by pulling into the rushes.

In Switzerland, they stay at a mountain chalet, where a doctor examines Catherine and finds that she and the baby are fine. She refuses to marry Henry until she is thin again. When spring arrives, her labor pains start, so they go to the hospital. Dr. Emerich (Oscar Homolka) moves her into surgery for a caesarian section and she delivers a boy, but the child soon dies. While at the bar, Henry says, "Maybe it's better that way than to wind up dead on a muddy road. This is the price you pay for sleeping together." Catherine dies from a hemorrhage, and Henry leaves the hospital; the sun rises, the rain disappears: it is a new day. The film ends with flashbacks of what Catherine said in the past, including "We're going to have a strange life, but it's the only life I want." Henry knows Catherine was braver than any soldier, including himself.

The closing scene of *A Farewell to Arms* is an improvement over the 1932 version, which ends happily with Catherine and Frederic celebrating the armistice together. Knowing Hemingway's distaste for the

1932 film, David O. Selznick wrote to Charles Vidor, the director, and said,

> For us to try to convert [the ending] into a scene of blubbering schmaltz may, I fear, lead us into the most severe kind of criticism from Hemingway, from critics, from lovers of the book, and from those millions of people who expect *A Farewell to Arms* to have the unique qualities of Hemingway.

Bosley Crowther, a film critic for the *New York Times*, argues that the new film, although closer to the novel, differs from it structurally and "largely accounts, we feel sure, for a sense of deficiency and inconsequence that emerges from the over-long film."[2] Hemingway himself never saw the ending of the film. He walked out after thirty-five minutes.[3] JMW

Notes

1. Jamie Barlow, "'They Have Rewritten It All': Film Adaptations of *A Farewell to Arms*," *Hemingway Review* 31, no. 1 (2011): 24.
2. Quoted in Barlow, "'They Have Rewritten It All,'" 26.
3. A. E. Hotchner, *Papa Hemingway* (New York: Random House, 1966), 30.

Bibliography

Barlow, Jamie. "'They Have Rewritten It All': Film Adaptations of *A Farewell to Arms*." *Hemingway Review* 31, no. 1 (2011): 14–24.

Hotchner, A. E. *Papa Hemingway*. New York: Random House, 1966.

Laurence, Frank M. "Death in the Matinée: The Film Endings of Hemingway's Fiction." *Literature/Film Quarterly* 2, no. 1 (1974): 44–51.

Leff, Leonard J. "The Breening of America." *PMLA* 106, no. 3 (1991): 432–45.

———. "A Thunderous Reception: Broadway, Hollywood, and *A Farewell to Arms*." *Hemingway Review* 15, no. 2 (1996): 33–51.

FIRST KNIGHT (1995)

DIRECTOR: Jerry Zucker
WRITERS: Lorne Cameron, David Hoselton, William Nicholson
PRODUCERS: Jerry Zucker, Hunt Lowry (Columbia Pictures)
CINEMATOGRAPHER: Adam Greenberg
EDITOR: Walter Murch
ART DIRECTION: Bob Laing, Michael White, Stephen Scott, Giles Masters
COSTUMES: Nanà Cecchi
MUSIC: Jerry Goldsmith
CAST: King Arthur: Sean Connery. Lancelot: Richard Gere. Guinevere: Julia Ormond. Prince Malagant: Ben Cross. Agravaine: Liam Cunningham. Sir Kay: Christopher Villiers. Sir Patrise: Valentine Pelka. Sir Mador: Colin McCormack. Ralf: Ralph Ineson. Oswald: John Gielgud. Peter: Stuart Bunce. Elise: Jane Robbins. Petronella: Jean Marie Coffey. Mark: Paul Kynman. Sir Sagramore: Tom Lucy. Sir Tor: John Blakey. Sir Gawaine: Robert Gwyn Davin. Sir Carados: Sean Blowers. Sir Gaheris: Alexis Denisof. Sir Amant: Daniel Naprous. Sir Gareth: Jonathan Cake. Jacob: Paul Bentall. Gauntlet Man: Jonty Miller. Mark's Wife: Rose Keegan. Challenger: Mark Ryan. Young Lancelot: Ryan Todd
AA: None
AAN: None
DVD: Sony Pictures Home Entertainment, 1997
BLU-RAY: Columbia Pictures, 2008
DURATION: DVD, 129 minutes; Blu-ray, 133 minutes

First Knight is an Arthurian epic focusing on the love triangle between King Arthur (Sean Connery), his new wife Guinevere (Julia Ormond), and the newly knighted Sir Lancelot (Richard Gere). There is no Merlin and no Morgan, for this interpretation does away with the magical backdrop to many of the Arthurian tales, although in the place of Merlin the elderly Oswald (John Gielgud) stands in as a type of sage advisor to Guinevere, who is in need of his assistance as the heir of Leonesse, which is being besieged by Prince Malagant (Ben Cross). Malagant is a former member of Arthur's famed round table but is dismissive of Arthur's dream of equality and justice. One of the reasons Guinevere accepts the proposal of Arthur to partly secure the defense of her lands and people, but she truly admires and loves him, despite being many years his junior.

This happy engagement is sent into turmoil when Guinevere is nearly abducted by Malagant's men en route to her betrothed, only to be rescued by the dashing Lancelot, a commoner and loner who makes money from his swordplay. Although heroic, Lancelot is also brash and shockingly flirtatious. When Malagant later succeeds in making away with Guinevere from Camelot itself, it is Lancelot who is able to rescue her, and Guinevere's own attraction to him becomes evident. Despite the protestations of his knights and Guinevere herself, Arthur rewards Lancelot by making him a fellow knight. Although Lancelot initially accepts with the less-than-honorable intention of wooing Guinevere, he comes to respect the community that Arthur is trying to establish. But when Lancelot proclaims his intention to leave forever to resist temptation, Guinevere kisses him farewell, only to be discovered by Arthur. The two are tried for treason, and Malagant seizes the opportunity to attack Camelot. Arthur is mortally wounded as he exhorts his people to resist, and Lancelot slays Malagant in the ensuing battle. On his deathbed, Arthur forgives the betrayal of his wife and friend, leaving Camelot to them.

First Knight was condemned by many for the casting of Gere as Lancelot, with little effort given to fix his accent.[1] Gere and his fellow cast members are saddled with some truly terrible lines: Lancelot tells Guinevere, "I can tell when a woman wants me. I can see it in her eyes," while upon discovering the would-be lovers kissing, Arthur can only yell at God, "Why? Why? Why?"

The film was also highly criticized for its overall aesthetic and costume choices, creating a dubious image of the Middle Ages. Janet Maslin writes for the *New York Times* that Sean Connery as Arthur is "debonair enough to survive asymmetrical velour outfits," many of which "would be just right for the Starship Enterprise."[2] Writing about *First Knight*, John Aberth proclaims, "so dismissive is the director of history that he is rumored to have blurted out to a reviewer that he didn't give a 'fuck' about the Middle Ages."[3]

Yet, scholar (and author of *The Name of the Rose*) Umberto Eco argues that the Middle Ages are, in fact, always used as a "*pretext*," with "no real interest in the historical background; the Middle Ages are taken as a sort of mythological stage on which to place contemporary characters."[4] It is with this perspective in mind that Jacqueline Jenkins sees Gere's Lancelot as embodying the "central tenets of the American Dream,"[5] in that his success relies not on old world, aristocratic inheritance, but rather his natural abilities.

Despite the very contemporary take on the legend, resonances with the original tale nonetheless remain. French writer Chrétien de Troyes, writing *Lancelot, the Knight of the Cart* (*Lancelot, le Chevalier de la Charrette*) in the twelfth century, worked from earlier themes in the Arthurian tale but introduced Lancelot as a new hero, of sorts. Lancelot endures constant humiliation in his service to the queen, and the tale sets the virtues of marriage in conflict with the courtly love between a lady and her defending knight.[6] For all its faults, *First Knight* shares with de Troyes the focus on otherwise honorable people caught between duty and desire, the individual and the society (more honorable in the film, in fact, as the original story allows them the transgression of adultery).[7] Lancelot, although steadfast in his devotion to Guinevere in *Lancelot, the Knight of the Cart*, is not above some shocking behavior, which is to say that almost in spite of itself, *First Knight* manages to capture some of the spirit of the first Lancelot story, and Jerry Goldsmith's score helps lift an unintentionally amusing endeavor to an entertaining romp. DB

Notes

1. See, for example, Todd McCarthy, "*First Knight*," *Variety*, 25 June 1995, www.variety.com/review/VE1117904221/ (3 September 2012).

2. Janet Maslin, "*First Knight* (1995): The Tale of Camelot, Now Color Coordinated," *New York Times*, 7 July 1995, http://movies.nytimes.com/movie/review?res=990CEFDC1631F934A35754C0A963958260 (3 September 2012).

3. John Aberth, *A Knight at the Movies: Medieval History on Film* (New York and London: Routledge, 2003), 17.

4. Umberto Eco, "The Return of the Middle Ages," in *Faith in Fakes: Travels in Hyperreality*, edited by John Radziewicz and translated by William Weaver (London: Secker & Warburg, 1986), 68.

5. Jacqueline Jenkins, "First Knights and Common Men: Masculinity in American Arthurian Film," in *King Arthur on Film: New Essays on Arthurian Cinema*, edited by Kevin J. Harty (Jefferson, NC: McFarland, 1999), 84–86.

6. Chrétien de Troyes, *Lancelot, the Knight of the Cart*, translated by Ruth Harwood Cline (Athens: University of Georgia Press, 1990).

7. See, for example, Caroline Jewers, "Hard Day's Knights: *First Knight*, *A Knight's Tale*, and *Black Knight*," in *The Medieval Hero on Screen: Representations from Beowulf to Buffy*, edited by Martha W. Driver and Sid Ray (Jefferson, NC, and London: McFarland, 2004), 194–98.

Bibliography

Aberth, John. *A Knight at the Movies: Medieval History on Film*. New York and London: Routledge, 2003.

de Troyes, Chrétien. *Lancelot, the Knight of the Cart*. Translated by Ruth Harwood Cline. Athens: University of Georgia Press, 1990.

Eco, Umberto. "The Return of the Middle Ages." In *Faith in Fakes: Travels in Hyperreality*, edited by John Radziewicz and translated by William Weaver, 59–85. London: Secker & Warburg, 1986.

Jenkins, Jacqueline. "First Knights and Common Men: Masculinity in American Arthurian Film." In *King Arthur on Film: New Essays on Arthurian Cinema*, edited by Kevin J. Harty, 81–95. Jefferson, NC: McFarland, 1999.

Jewers, Caroline. "Hard Day's Knights: *First Knight*, *A Knight's Tale*, and *Black Knight*." In *The Medieval Hero on Screen: Representations from Beowulf to Buffy*, edited by Martha W. Driver and Sid Ray, 192–210. Jefferson, NC, and London: McFarland, 2004.

Maslin, Janet. "*First Knight* (1995): The Tale of Camelot, Now Color Coordinated." *New York Times*, 7 July 1995, http://movies.nytimes.com/movie/review?res=990CEFDC1631F934A35754C0A963958260 (3 September 2012).

McCarthy, Todd. "*First Knight*." *Variety*, 25 June 1995, www.variety.com/review/VE1117904221/ (3 September 2012).

FLIGHT OF THE PHOENIX (1965)

DIRECTOR: Robert Aldrich
WRITER: Lukas Heller. Based on the novel by Elleston Trevor.
PRODUCER: Robert Aldrich (Associates and Aldrich Company)
CINEMATOGRAPHER: Joseph Biroc
EDITOR: Michael Luciano
MUSIC: DeVol
CAST: Frank Towns: James Stewart. Lew Moran: Richard Attenborough. Capt. Harris: Peter Finch. Heinrich Dorfmann: Hardy Krüger. Trucker Cobb: Ernest Borgnine. Sgt. Watson: Ronald Fraser. "Ratbags" Crow: Ian Bannen. Dr. Renaud: Christian Marquand. Standish: Dan Duryea. Mike Bellamy: George Kennedy. Carlos: Alex Montoya. Tasso: Peter Bravos. Gabriel: Gabriele Tinti. Bill: William Aldrich. Farida: Barrie Chase
AA: None
AAN: Best Supporting Actor (Ian Bannen), Best Film Editing (Michael Luciano)
DVD: 20th Century Fox, 2003
BLU-RAY: Currently unavailable
DURATION: 147 minutes

Filmed on location near Yuma, Arizona, and Pilot Knob, California, and at 20th Century Fox Studios, Los Angeles, the film's conflict moves from each man's battle for life in the desert to a battle of dominance between men of the slide rule against men of exploit and adventure. The fourteen men, from Germany, the United States, Great Britain, France, Scotland, Italy, and Mexico, eventually find a way to work together toward a common goal. As director Walter Hill says about Robert Aldrich's films, the best "have a great interior tension—torn by a wide separation between intellect and emotion."[1] Aldrich himself says that one of the recurring themes of his films is that "since it's impossible to 'win' everything in life, whether you're a football player, a soldier, or a politician, your interior self-esteem comes out of how hard you *try* to win—the degree of your struggle. . . . I'm concerned with man's efforts to prevail against impossible odds."[2]

Just after noon on 17 March, a Sunday, an Arabco plane takes off from a desert oil field runway, flying to Benghazi over open desert. The American Frank Towns (James Stewart) is the pilot of the Fairchild C-82 Packet "Skytruck," a twin-engine, twin-boom cargo plane with an inoperable voltage regulator and a bad radio. Lew Moran (Richard Attenborough), the British alcoholic navigator, complains that Arabco's planes always have problems. He reports to Towns that the number four control pulley is binding. Towns turns the controls over to Moran so he can make the repair.

They have twelve passengers. First there is the proper Captain Harris of the British Army (Peter Finch) and his sergeant, Watson (Ronald Fraser). Then there's Heinrich Dorfmann (Hardy Krüger), a fascistic German engineer who was visiting his brother in the fields, and Dr. Renaud (Christian Marquand), a French physician. And then there are several men who work for Arabco. These include Trucker Cobb (Ernest Borgnine), an American who suffered a mental breakdown on the oil fields; "Ratbags" Crow (Ian Bannen), a hostile and hilarious Scot; Mike Bellamy (George Kennedy); Standish (Dan Duryea), the company accountant; Carlos from Mexico (Alex Montoya) and his pet monkey; Tasso (Peter Bravos), a mandolin player; Gabriel from Italy (Gabriele Tinti); and Bill from the United States (William Aldrich).

While at the controls, Moran sees a sandstorm rising. Towns takes over, and, because of the storm, they need an alternate landing strip. They check the chart, looking for the best alternate strip, but Towns boasts, "We're bigger than a local sandstorm." Moran takes a drink from a flask while Towns eulogizes the changes in flying. He comments that pilots used to be treated better and that "flying used to be fun," adding, "You could take pride in just getting there." The sandstorm grows, and they raise their elevation.

Sand causes the right engine to flame out. Towns decides to land the plane before the other engine stalls, but then it does. To be able to take off again, he is forced to land "wheels down," although there is no airstrip. As he lands, cargo breaks loose and several men are hurt. On the ground, Towns rushes the passengers off the plane in case it would explode, but three men are trapped inside. Tasso and Bill are found dead, and Gabriel's leg has been crushed.

The storm clears, and the plane is alone in a wide expanse of desert. About 130 miles off course and without a radio to communicate their position, it will be impossible for rescuers to find them. They bury the two men. When asked to say something at their graves, Towns responds, "Like what, Sorry?" Captain Harris organizes the men and orders Watson to gather flares and create a water rationing plan. Watson detests Harris, having been in the army since he was a boy.

Towns notes in the plane's log for 17 March that the cause of the crash was "pilot error." The doctor gives liquor to Gabriel to dull his pain, while Moran looks on, saving the morphine for when the pain gets worse. The next day the men begin water rationing, at one pint of water per person per day, which would extend supplies to ten or eleven days with no exertion. That night, they huddle inside the plane from the cold outdoors. Towns gives Cobb's handheld radio to Gabriel for comfort. The radio plays "The Phoenix Love Theme (Senza Fine)," sung by Connie Francis.

On 21 March, Captain Harris decides to march out so he can contact rescuers, but Towns finds the idea ridiculous and is concerned that they will die and be added to the list of dead. Navigating the desert is difficult because the surrounding Jebel Haroudj Mountains are composed of magnetic rock. Harris says that they will navigate by the stars, aided by their British military training.

Cobb and Carlos plan to go with Harris, but Cobb is not allowed. He had been removed by Dr. Renaud from his job as chief rigger because of mental exhaustion. Cobb hits Harris in frustration. Captain Harris expects Sergeant Watson to march across the desert, but Watson fakes an injury to avoid going. Carlos gives Bellamy his monkey, Chucho, and the pair leaves. Watson reveals that he has faked his injury when he reports to Towns that Cobb followed Harris. Towns goes after Cobb and finds him dead.

Heinrich Dorfmann, an aircraft designer and misanthrope, believes that Towns has "gone after a lunatic who has no practical value." Dorfmann shows Towns and Moran an idea about building a plane from the components of the wrecked plane. Because the Fairchild C-82 has two engines and two booms, he plans a new aerodynamically sound structure of one boom and engine. They would need to clear the port engine, install skids, and put the men on the wings. He estimates that the project will take twelve days. Moran supports the idea because it gives them hope, and watching one another die would be harder than building a plane in the desert. Towns agrees to the plan. They work at night, using tools that were in the cargo hold and a hand-powered generator to power the lights. Winches and levers give them mechanical assistance when moving large pieces of the plane.

Dorfmann's contempt for others and his grandiose ego are shown in relief when Towns uncovers that someone has been stealing water. Discovered, Dorfmann says, "I didn't steal it. I took it." When Towns asked why he did not ask him for the water, Dorfmann replies, "Because you wouldn't have given it to me." Towns answers, "You're damn right I wouldn't."

As the men remove the starboard wing and pull it over the top of the plane with a winch, Watson sees light coming over the dunes and walks to it. He finds Captain Harris lying facedown in the sand but leaves him there. Later in the evening, Dorfmann finds Harris and brings him into camp. Later they find Gabriel dead, having bled to death after cutting open a vein.

Moran and Towns reveal simmering hostilities between them when Moran questions Towns's reluctance to take orders from Dorfmann; his status as pilot and trailblazer will not allow it. Towns blames Moran for the crash, saying, "If you hadn't made a career out of being a drunk, you wouldn't have been a second-rate navigator in a fifth-rate outfit, and if you hadn't stayed in your bunk to kill that last bottle you might have checked that engineers report on the radio and we might not be here." A few minutes later, after they cool down, Towns says, "Come on you drunken bum. Let's get back to work." Wearing harnesses, they pull the port engine and wing away from the fuselage. They pull the starboard wing over the fuselage and attach it to the port engine bay. Standish paints "Phoenix" on the plane after the mythological bird.

Harris finds Razzia, a nomadic raiding party, encamped for the night on the other side of a dune. He decides to investigate and speak to the group but does not allow Towns to accompany him. Harris orders Watson to go with him and, when he refuses, puts him under open arrest. Dr. Renaud speaks Arabic and wants to go. Towns watches the two speak to the Arabs surreptitiously, needing to be in charge, but Moran convinces him not to get involved because of his importance as their pilot. The next morning, Towns and Moran find that the nomads are gone, leaving behind the bodies of Harris and Renaud, throats slashed, and a lame camel. Towns empties his revolver into it. Watson is happy that Harris is dead. Towns hits him and throws Harris's ID tags at him. In the only appearance of a woman in the film, Watson sits in the sun and sees Farida (Barrie Chase), an Arab dancer he saw in Benghazi, dancing in a mirage. She disappears.

Towns wants to test the engine, but because there are only seven cartridges for the Coffman starter, the device used for ignition of the engine, Dorfmann disagrees, commenting, "You make stupidity a virtue." Dorfmann stops the project until Towns submits to his authority. On the last day of the plane's transformation, Towns finds a catalog for a company that builds model planes. Dorfmann explains that his company's biggest plane, a glider, has a two-meter wingspan, but he designs powered planes. Stunned, Towns hands the catalog to Moran. Pressed, Dorfmann says, "We make nothing but model airplanes. The principles are the same." Moran suggests that he not mention to the others that he is a toy-plane designer. Dorfmann explains that a toy plane is "something you wind up."

The next morning, Towns tests the engine in the completed plane. Dorfmann tells him to keep vibration to a minimum to keep the plane from breaking apart. After using four of the seven cartridges, the engine barely turns. Towns decides to use one cartridge just to blow out the cylinders, in spite of Dorfmann's objections. The sixth cartridge finally ignites the engine. After they celebrate, the men use harnesses to pull the plane to the edge of a downward slope. They climb a ladder, take their positions behind small windscreens, and grab handholds. After difficulty pulling up, they fly over their old campsite and eventually over an oil field by an oasis. They land and stumble down the hill to the water. They quickly reconcile, having accomplished their collective survival.

Made during a time of Cold War tensions, including the building of the Berlin Wall, the film focuses on a small, international cohort of men who prove that the world community can work together again. Like building a full-sized plane from model airplane plans, *The Flight of the Phoenix* shows civilization rising from the ashes of world war. JMW

Notes

1. Walter Hill, "Anarchic Instincts Both Onscreen and Off, Robert Aldrich Battled against a Corrupt and Broken System," *Film Comment* 49. no. 1 (2013): 57.
2. Quoted in John Wakeman, ed., "Aldrich, Robert," *World Film Directors: 1945–1985*, vol. 2 (New York: H. W. Wilson, 1987).

Bibliography

Hill, Walter. "Anarchic Instincts Both Onscreen and Off, Robert Aldrich Battled against a Corrupt and Broken System." *Film Comment* 49, no. 1 (2013): 57.

Milne, Tom. "Robert Aldrich (1962–1978)." In *Robert Aldrich*, edited by Richard Combs, 23–36. London: British Film Institute, 1978.

Wakeman, John, ed. "Aldrich, Robert." *World Film Directors: 1945–1985*, vol. 2. New York: H. W. Wilson, 1987.

FORT APACHE (1948)

Director: John Ford
Writers: James Warner Bellah, Frank S. Nugent
Producers: John Ford, Merian C. Cooper (Argosy Pictures)
Cinematographer: Archie Stout
Editor: Jack Murray
Music: Licaid Hugeman
Cast: Capt. Kirby York: John Wayne. Lt. Col. Owen Thursday: Henry Fonda. Philadelphia Thursday: Shirley Temple. Sgt. Beaufort: Pedro Armendáriz. Second Lt. Michael Shannon O'Rourke: John Agar. Sgt. Michael O'Rourke: Ward Bond. Cochise: Miguel Incan. Silas Meacham: Grant Wuthers. Capt. Sam Collingwood: George O'Brien. Sgt. Festus Mulcahy:

Victor McLaglen. Mary O'Rourke: Irene Rich. Sgt. Quincannon: Dick Foran
AA: Best Director (John Ford), Best Cinematography (Archie Stout)
AAN: None
DVD: RKO Radio Pictures, 2006
Blu-ray: Warner Home Video, 2012
Duration: 125 minutes

Fort Apache is a classic western filmed by John Ford as a part of trilogy that includes subsequent same-themed films—conflicts between frontier settlers and Native Americans—including *She Wore a Yellow Ribbon* (1949) and *Rio Grande* (1950), all featuring John Wayne. *Fort Apache* may also be viewed, along with *The Searchers* (1956) and *Cheyenne Autumn* (1964), as part of another trilogy of films related to Ford's preoccupation with Native American Indians, usually treated as villains in the western film culture in commercial cinema. From *Fort Apache* in 1948 to *Cheyenne Autumn*, Ford's last western in 1964, the director took on the Indian cause, "shifting," according to Andrew Sarris, "his sensibilities from the shadowy world of Dudley Nichols to the sunlit world of Frank S. Nugent, from socially conscious allegory [as in *The Grapes of Wrath*] to crowd-pleasing adventure, and from the lies of art to the half-truths of legend."[1]

The critical establishment in general dismissed Ford's preoccupation with the western genre as subpar popular entertainment, and the genre itself did not fare any better. It was not until after Ford's death in 1973 that Ford's opus in that genre drew critical praise and such films as the "cavalry trilogy" and *The Searchers* were acknowledged as cinematic masterpieces. It was in that span of time that Ford highlighted the conflicts between the white man and Indian Native Americans, making them the central themes in his films and treating them with more depth than in the numerous films in the popular genre.

In the first film, *Fort Apache*, John Wayne plays Captain Kirby York, who knows the Indian ethos and is sympathetic to their plight; in *The Searchers*, Wayne is Ethan Edwards, presented as an Indian hater who seeks revenge on the Comanche tribe leader who abducted his niece; and in *Cheyenne Autumn*, the story is almost entirely centered on the people of the Cheyenne Indian tribe, who leave their reservation in Oklahoma to undertake an enormously lengthy trip, under the most trying circumstances, to reach their homeland in Wyoming and Montana. In these three movies in particular, all of which are epics by definition, Ford seems to treat Indians in different ways: as noble fighters for their rights, marauding hordes plaguing white homesteads on the frontier, and victims of corrupt and bigoted crowds inside the white society. Whichever view seems to be favored in the three films (and others in the Ford canon), there is no doubt that Ford took a profound interest in these conflicts.

In *Fort Apache*, Ford shows the Indians as a peace-minded tribe, the Apaches (in reality the Sioux), but the center of the conflict is the white camp, a military outpost about to change guard, as Lieutenant Colonel Owen Thursday (Henry Fonda), formerly a general in the Civil War and a West Point graduate, arrives to take command and reorganize what he thinks is a loosely run unit—militarily speaking. Up to this point, the Fort Apache outpost has been run by Captain York (Wayne), who has maintained good relations with Indian chief Cochise (Miguel Incan), who trusts him as a man of his word. Colonel Thursday and Captain York, who have experience in dealing with Indians, collide where military tactics and military etiquette are concerned, Thursday being a stickler for discipline, dress, military comportment, and other such things. He is also class conscious, and he will not allow his daughter, Philadelphia (Shirley Temple), to associate, let alone marry, the son of a noncommissioned officer, young Michael O'Rourke (John Agar).

But the most important part of this story is the collision of the two personalities York and Thursday; York knows the Indian Territory, being familiar with the tribes, and seeks an honorable peace treaty between them and the U.S. Army. Thursday vehemently rejects such a proposition and rushes into a battle against the warnings of York, who objects to his rash decisions. Thursday calls York a coward and dismisses him from the field of battle, promising to court-martial him for insubordination. Charging headlong into a trap, he causes his entire detachment to be decimated, but he himself is spared. When York comes to his rescue, Thursday orders him to take him to the spot where a few of his men are still fighting, but this time the charging Apaches kill them all. Thursday completely fails to comprehend Indian warfare or have any sense of reality when it comes to dealing with the frontier. He pays dearly for his mistake, but York, who becomes his successor, describes his valor to journalists from the East, withholding details that would have marred his image.

York is now lieutenant colonel, after reaching a peace agreement with Cochise, who trusts him. Thursday is said to be a fictional substitute for General George Armstrong Custer, who perished under similar circumstances in the battle against the Sioux, led by Sitting Bull and Crazy Horse at the Little Bighorn River a few years earlier. Ford had wanted to make a semihistorical movie but did not want to be tied down by the restrictions of factual history.[2]

Fort Apache features the magnificent locations of Monument Valley, as is usual with Ford movies, and the backdrop adds to the epic character of the conflict. In the end, Thursday is honored as a hero, and York himself, despite his differences with Thursday, calls him so. Meanwhile, Thursday's daughter, Philadelphia, has married the young O'Rourke (John Agar was Shirley Temple's husband), and they have a baby. Wayne gives a heartfelt eulogy standing in front of Thursday's portrait and somewhat jingoistically extols the struggles and sacrifices of the heroes of the West, regardless of their individual idiosyncrasies. After all, Thursday was not a coward—just a bullheaded man who wanted things as they are taught in the military academy. He represents the East fighting in the unknown and rugged territories of the West. The movie is as much about knowing how to fight a war as it is about being brave and training for it. York's experience, his conciliatory spirit, his readiness to obey a man he knew was sending troops to their death, these aspects argue in his favor. When it comes to savvy and know-how, he is unsurpassed.

The irony is that York had to obey a man superior to him in rank, but inexperienced in the territory of the West and unfamiliar with the way the Indian tribes conceive honor—or their resentment at seeing their country being invaded. York is familiar with this, but he is peremptorily silenced when he attempts to offer an opinion or take action that would be appropriate to the circumstances. There is tragedy and irony in the collision of these two giants of the screen, which is partly the reason why *Fort Apache* is perhaps one of the premier classics among westerns. The issues it touches on are large—justice to the conquered but unconquerable and vengeful Indian tribes, who will negotiate with someone who sees their point of view, but who will also fight, and if need be exterminate, anyone who is ready to offend their sense of honor and dignity as a nation.

The two types of military approach featured here, embodied in these two leaders, are also indicative of lack of a deeper understanding when the advancing American civilization encountered Native Americans. It is an issue that Ford treated with relative objectivity, for he, too, seemed unable to see the magnitude of the problems—in today's terms. He was, however, a deep and searching psychologist of the mentality of the Western Frontier. To his credit, he splits the conflict in two dominating personas of the screen and thus is able to analyze the problem to a certain degree. York sought justice, while Thursday sought victory, but Ford was a product of his time, and at least he gave us a point of view in his main hero, John Wayne, provoking thought. Circa 1948, the typical western movie was cowboys and Indians, with Indians getting the wrong end of the stick. *Fort Apache* is a thoughtful western; another one—*The Searchers*—was to follow a few years later. In that film, the point of this terrible conflict of conscience becomes even more poignant. CS

Notes

1. Andrew Sarris, *"You Ain't Heard Nothing Yet": The American Talking Film History and Memory, 1927–1949* (New York: Oxford University Press, 1998), 207.
2. See "Running Commentary" by Ford historian Joseph McBride in "Special Features," *Cheyenne Autumn*, directed by John Ford (Warner Home Video, 2006), DVD.

Bibliography

McBride, Joseph. *Searching for John Ford.* Jackson: University Press of Mississippi, 2001.

Sarris, Andrew. *"You Ain't Heard Nothing Yet": The American Talking Film History and Memory, 1927–1949.* New York: Oxford University Press, 1998.

THE FOUR HORSEMEN OF THE APOCALYPSE (1921)

DIRECTOR: Rex Ingram
WRITER: June Mathis. Based on Vicente Blasco Ibañez's novel *Los cuatro jinetes del Apocalipsis*.
PRODUCER: Metro Pictures
CINEMATOGRAPHER: John F. Seitz
EDITOR: Grant Whytock
ART DIRECTION: Joseph Calder, Amos Myers
CAST: Julio Desnoyers: Rudolph Valentino. Marguerite Laurier: Alice Terry. Madariaga: Pomeroy Cannon. Marcelo Desnoyers: Josef Swickard. Doña Luisa: Bridgetta Clark. Chichí Desnoyers: Virginia Warwick. Karl von Hartrott: Alan Hale. Elena: Mabel Van Buren. Argensola: Bowditch M. Turner. Senator Lacour: Mark Fenton. Etienne Laurier: John Sainpolis. Tchernoff: Nigel de Brulier. Otto von Hartrott: Stuart Holmes
DVD: Available on demand
BLU-RAY: Currently unavailable
DURATION: 132 minutes

Based on Vicente Blasco Ibañez's popular war novel about World War I, *Los cuatro jinetes del Apocalipsis* (*The Four Horsemen of the Apocalypse*), and filmed soon after the war, the silent film was also a major hit, rescuing the ailing Metro Pictures Corporation and making the careers of everyone involved, especially June Mathis, Rudolph Valentino, and the film's director, Rex Ingram. An antiwar film, with a "subtle . . . anti-German sentiment," Ingram created an epic film, stunning in its realism and the number of actors involved, yet having moments of humor and the fantastic. Ingram would go on to direct other successful films, including *The Prisoner of Zenda* (1922), *Scaramouche* (1923), and *Mare Nostrum* (1926).

The film begins as the seeds of war are being sown in Europe, while people in the New World have the luxury of peace and wide-open spaces. Madariaga (Pomeroy Cannon), "the Centaur," a "capricious and despotic" man, achieves great success on the Argentinian plains, taking advantage of its boundless space. From a high hill, he oversees his thousands of head of cattle and sheep. Although the wealthiest person in the area, he lives in a primitive abode with his two daughters and their husbands. His daughter Luisa (Bridgetta Clark) married a Frenchman, Marcelo Desnoyers (Josef Swickard). She was childless for seven years until they receive the good news that she is pregnant. Madariaga hopes that it's a boy and wants to name him Julio, saying, "I need one of my own breed." The younger daughter, Elena (Mabel Van Buren), marries Karl von Hartrott (Alan Hale), a German who is concerned that if the Desnoyers's child is a boy, their small sons, who march in militaristic play using sticks for rifles, will not receive an inheritance. One of the boys even calls Madariaga "Napoleon." When it is announced that the child is a boy, Madariaga celebrates by inviting his workers to "share the joy" and throws them coins from a large chest.

Twenty years later, Madariaga is still enjoying the nightlife and its pleasures, visiting cantinas with his handsome and libertine grandson, Julio (Rudolph Valentino). Julio sees a beautiful woman dancing the tango; he takes her from her partner and dances with her. When the man tries to take her back, Julio hits him on the head with a stick. Madariaga approves. The band and audience are awed by Julio and his partner's tango, including several characters, among them a bearded man with a pipe and a drunk who imagines that he sees a fish in his glass and faints. After Julio and the woman sit down, Madariaga, who is drunk, falls out of his chair. The woman laughs, and Julio, horrified by the fall, drops her to help the old man get back up. Madariaga then realizes that bars are only for the young, and he turns to Julio's younger sister Chichí (Virginia Warwick) for amusement, teaching her how to dance the seductive tango. Her mother stops the training and sends Chichí to her room. She chastises Madariaga because he has already trained her son to be a libertine. He tells Marcelo that, "Youth must have its fling." A polar opposite, von Hartrott raised his three sons to have respect for the Fatherland, but Madariaga calls them "glass-eyed carrot-topped boys." The sons study together, and one text they study admonishes, "Man shall be trained for war, and women for the recreation of the warrior. All else is folly."

Madariaga is later found dead on the ground by his horse, by a stream. His will is read to the family and splits his money between Luisa and Elena. While von Hartrott is happy, Julio is upset; the news "shatters" his ideals, but his pet monkey comforts him by patting his hand. Von Hartrott decides to take his family back to Germany, saying that his first allegiance is to the Fatherland. The boys march out of the room in unison with their father.

Marcelo is disturbed, but his wife says that Karl is right and that they should move back to Paris. Marcelo resists because he had secretly run away from trouble after he was involved in "socialistic student body revolts." When Julio pleads to go, he relents.

In Paris, "discontent [creeps] into the hearts of the Desnoyers family." Marcelo purchases a chateau in the Marne area of France and obsessively attends Parisian auctions to fill it. Julio paints women in the nude, which Marcelo calls debauchery. At Julio's studio, Argensola (Bowditch M. Turner), his secretary, brings him the bills from collectors threatening to go straight to his father. He suggests that Julio ask his mother for money instead. When Julio does, she gives him a piece of a necklace his father gave her. Marcelo shows his friends Senator Lacour (Mark Fenton) and Etienne Laurier (John Sainpolis) a golden bath tub he has purchased. Not impressed, Laurier says his only prize possession is his wife. When Mrs. Marguerite Laurier (Alice Terry) arrives, she and Julio are immediately attracted to one another. She recognizes him from the Tango Palace, where Julio gives lessons. As her husband enters the room, she drops her hanky. Julio picks it up and kisses her hand. After the Lauriers leave, Lacour says that Marguerite's heart is too young for an old man like Etienne Laurier.

Marcelo invites von Hartrott's family to Villeblanche, the site of his chateau. Marcelo has changed since his socialistic days, his chateau having become a treasure palace. Von Hartrott is unimpressed with Marcelo's chateau and his collection, saying he treasures his sons more than objects.

The tango sweeps Paris. Julio has many pupils, but he now dances exclusively with Marguerite. Realizing that they are the center of attention, she says that they will have to meet somewhere else. He suggests meeting in his studio, saying she will be safe. In a famous clip, when she asks if he promises, he looks slyly away and then says "yes," but means "no." The time they spend together becomes their only happiness. Argensola shows him a report of Ferdinand of Austria's assassination, but Julio ignores it as he awaits Marguerite's return. Julio, the secret lover, the romantic, has conquered Marguerite. Argensola takes the paper to Tchernoff (Nigel de Brulier), a seer who lives upstairs from Julio's studio. He says that the news is the "brand that will set the world ablaze."

By July, a maelstrom threatens to engulf Europe. A newspaper reports that the Russians are mobilizing. Tchernoff predicts war and worries about separating families because of their mixed German and French backgrounds. Marcelo comes back to Paris, where Etienne Laurier brings him an anonymous note he has received about Julio and Marguerite. They go to Julio's studio. Marguerite hides behind a curtain while they are there, but Etienne finds her gloves and compact. He lets the compact fall to the floor, and she gasps from behind the curtain. Discovered, she faints when Etienne challenges Julio to a duel. Marcelo convinces him that there should be no scandal, so he agrees to a divorce.

The French military mobilize, and hundreds cheer the soldiers, including Etienne, as they march to war. Meanwhile, above the street, Argensola, Tchernoff, and Julio drink. Tchernoff describes the book of Revelation and shows them a bound collection of Albrecht Durer's illustrations of the Apocalypse. The film replicates the drawings, putting hellish scenes into motion, especially the four horsemen themselves. These men, who will "scatter desolation throughout the world," are highlighted as they exit the underworld: Conquest, a helmeted soldier, and War, swinging his sword and outfitted in armor, are nearly normal in appearance, but Pestilence, "carrying the [empty] scales of famine," is gaunt faced, and Death, who is in "relentless pursuit" and whose face is skull-like, carries a scythe. Tchernoff points at them as they actually ride out of a dark cloud high in the sky.

Marguerite becomes a nurse, saying that it is wrong to love Julio when there is so much sorrow around them. She says Julio is fortunate in that he is a foreigner and does not have to go to war. As men march outside his apartment, Julio's monkey marches in sympathy.

Despite hundreds of refugees on the road leaving Villeblanche and avoiding the oncoming German troops, Marcelo walks back to his chateau. A slim French defense tries to hold off the oncoming army. Sharpshooters shoot at the oncoming Germans, but the "hot hurricane of death" retaliates, bombing the city as the four horsemen ride in the sky. In perhaps the most powerful scene of the film, several men and women are lined up in front of a firing squad for fighting against the Germans. Some are still resistant; one young man proclaims it a great honor to die for his country.

The Germans break open the chateau's gates. Marcelo tries to protect his antiques but to no avail. The general of the Uhlan regiment arrives and Marcelo must entertain him, but instead he sits on the stairs and mourns his loss. His nephew, Otto von Hartrott (Stuart Holmes), now a captain, is one of the occupiers. Marcelo appeals to him, but his answer is, "What else do you expect? This is war." The Germans take the gold tub out of the house as war booty, and Otto prevents Marcelo from interfering.

By the healing waters of Lourdes, Etienne, blinded by the war, is nursed by Marguerite, but he does not know it is her. Julio arrives, claiming that she pretended to love him. She tries to comfort him, saying, "You are a man—you could never understand a woman's desire for atonement!" Realizing that he has been a coward, he decides to join the French military and kisses the hem of her uniform before he leaves.

At the chateau, the Germans "[hold] their revels with all the destructive glory of war." The men dress in women's lingerie, dance on the tables, drink out of their boots, and abuse the staff. Marcelo is thrown into the dungeon. Otto tells him that he will probably be shot at daylight. The Germans plan to go to Paris but are forced to fall back because the French "[are] reclaiming their own." The chateau is made a hospital and filled with the dead and dying. Marcelo, released from the dungeon, is forced to dig a ditch by the German soldiers, but they are soon forced out of the area. As they leave, Marcelo sees that his chateau has been destroyed, the towers and arches blasted by artillery. The four horsemen are still riding.

Marcelo returns to his Paris home. Julio arrives, but Marcelo does not recognize him, as he is in uniform, but he is pleased that his son is defending his country "even when it's not [his]." He also warns him that, "Men of your own blood are fighting on the other side," but he tells him to not spare them.

The fortunes of war turn when the Old World cries for help and the New World arrives, especially the thousands of American soldiers marching toward the front. Both Marcelo and his son happen to be at a Salvation Army unit at the same time. Marcelo is dressed in Argentinian clothes, and for the first time, Julio, no longer the suave romantic, is worn, grimy, selfless, and brave. Shells drop nearby, and Marcelo rides away in a car. Julio is sent to the front. On both sides men in trenches attempt to cross the field through the mud, smoke, and rain. Many die from explosions, left on barbed wire or face-first in the mud. A flare illuminates two men in the darkness, and two of Madariaga's grandsons face one another as enemies. Julio and his cousin Heinrich recognize one another just before two shells land on them. Death, sitting on his horse, watches the scene. Marguerite nurses Etienne to health, but she pulls away when he touches her. Her heart belongs to Julio. Marguerite plans to leave him, but Julio's spirit materializes and indicates that she should stay with Etienne.

The ending sums up war's toll. Von Hartrott loses his sons, and his wife says that they would still be alive had they not left the Argentinian plains. On one hillside of many hillsides with thousands of crosses, Marcelo cries over Julio's grave. Tchernoff, also there mourning all the loss, tells him that he knew Julio and all the dead. The four horsemen ride back into the sky. Peace has come, but they will return until, as Tchernoff says, love reigns. JMW

Bibliography

Oehling, Richard A. "Germans in Hollywood Films: The Changing Image, 1914–1939." *Film and History: An Interdisciplinary Journal of Film and Television Studies* 3, no. 2 (1973): 1–26.

Pratt, George C. *Spellbound in Darkness: A History of the Silent Film.* Greenwich: New York Graphic Society, 1973.

G

GALLIPOLI (1981)

DIRECTOR: Peter Weir
WRITERS: Peter Weir, David Williamson
PRODUCERS: Robert Stigwood, Patricia Lovell (Associated R & R Films)
CINEMATOGRAPHER: Russell Boyd
EDITOR: William M. Anderson
ART DIRECTION: Herbert Pinter, Wendy Stites
COSTUMES: Terry Ryan, Wendy Stites
MUSIC: Brian May
SOUND EDITORS: Don Connolly, Greg Bell, Peter Fenton
CAST: Archy Hamilton: Mark Lee. Jack: Bill Kerr. Les McCann: Harold Hopkins. Zac: Charles Yunupingu. Stockman: Heath Harris. Wallace Hamilton: Ron Graham. Rose Hamilton: Gerda Nicolson. Frank Dunne: Mel Gibson. Billy: Robert Grubb. Barney: Tim McKenzie. Snowy: David Argue. Railway Foreman: Brian Anderson. Athletics Official #1: Reg Evans. Athletics Official #2: Jack Giddy. Announcer: Dane Peterson. Recruiting Officer: Paul Linkson. Waitress: Jenny Lovell. Billy Snakeskin: Steve Dodd. Camel Driver: Harold Baigent. Mary: Robyn Galwey. Lionel: Don Quin. Laura: Phyllis Burford. Gran: Marjorie Irving. Frank's Father: John Murphy. Maj. Barton: Bill Hunter. Mrs. Barton: Diane Chamberlain. Lt. Gray: Peter Ford. Army Doctor: Ian Govett. Sgt. Sayers: Geoff Parry. English Officer #1: Clive Bennington. English Officer #2: Giles Holland-Martin. Egyptian Shopkeeper: Moshe Kedem. Col. Robinson: John Morris. NCO at Ball: Don Barker. Soldier on Beach: Kiwi White. Sniper: Paul Sonkkila. Observer: Peter Lawless. Sentry: Saltbush Baldock. Artillery Officer: Les Dayman. Sgt. Major: Stan Green. Col. White: Max Wearing. Gen. Gardner: Graham Dow. Radio Officer: Peter R. House
AA: None
AAN: None
GG: None
GGN: Best Foreign Film
AUSTRALIAN FILM INSTITUTE AWARDS: Best Director (Peter Weir), Best Film (Robert Stigwood, Patricia Lovell), Best Cinematography (Russell Boyd), Best Editing (William M. Anderson), Best Sound (Don Connolly, Greg Bell, Peter Fenton), Best Leading Actor (Mel Gibson), Best Supporting Actor (Bill Hunter), Best Screenplay–Original or Adapted (David Williamson)
AUSTRALIAN FILM INSTITUTE AWARDS NOMINATIONS: Best Costume Design (Terry Ryan, Wendy Stites), Best Production Design (Herbert Pinter, Wendy Stites), Best Leading Actor (Mark Lee), Best Supporting Actor (Bill Kerr)
DVD: 20th Century Fox, 2005
BLU-RAY: Currently unavailable
DURATION: 107 minutes

Director Peter Weir is best known internationally for his Oscar-nominated Hollywood films *Witness* (1985), *Dead Poets Society* (1989), *The Truman Show* (1998), and *Master and Commander: The Far Side of the World* (2003), but the director had originally been one of the key figures in the revival of the Australian film industry (often referred to as the Australian Film Renaissance or the Australian New Wave) of the 1970s to the mid-1980s with the benefit of new government funding. Weir's *Picnic at Hanging Rock* (1975) and *Gallipoli* (1981) remain national favorites from this era,[1] and the latter, along with George Miller's cult classic *Mad Max* (1979, also starring Mel Gibson), was among the earliest Australian films to have mainstream distribution in the United States. *Gallipoli* tells a tragic loss of life at the Battle of the Nek, part of the Gallipoli campaign in Turkey during World War I, seen through the very personal lens of young men from rural Australia (indeed we see little of the larger historical forces at work). The use of Jean Michel Jarre's electronic music reminds us that this is a nation looking back at its past, reconstructing and simplifying history into myth.[2]

Eighteen-year-old Archy Hamilton (Mark Lee) is a local sprinting champion living on a rural property in Western Australia in 1915. Amid his training he longs to sign up to fight in the war, inspired by patriotic duty, loyalty to the motherland, a vague understanding of a wrong that needs righting, and, perhaps, imaginings of heroic adventure. Also racing at a regional track event is larrikin Frank Dunne (Mel Gibson), who forms a bond with Archy despite losing the race to him and, along with it, all his money. When Archy is turned down for enlistment in the Light Horse Regiment for being under age, Frank suggests that he join him and travel to the city of Perth, where his age will not be known. With the help of some artificial aging from Frank, Archy is accepted in the Light Horse. Although Frank sees the war as a foreign concern, he tries to enlist as well in comradery with Archy. Unfortunately, he cannot ride a horse, so he signs up for the infantry with some of his old mates, Billy (Robert Grubb), Barney (Tim McKenzie), and Snowy (David Argue).

In training at Cairo, the men lightheartedly experience the local sights, haggling for bogus ancient souvenirs, making fun of the British officers, and enjoying local prostitutes (Snowy alone expresses his disgust, wanting to save himself for his wedding night). When Frank and Archy meet up again, Frank is able to transfer to the Light Horse, as the unit is being sent without their horses to the rocky Gallipoli peninsula on the Turkish east coast. His transfer is met with a somber reception by his friends, who resent having their close-knit group broken up.

The arrival at what would later become known as Anzac Cove in Turkey reveals a somewhat shambolic enclave of ANZAC (Australian/New Zealand) forces dug into the sand and beset by Turkish shelling. Frank is reunited with his infantry mates, but in the aftermath of the (unseen) Battle of Lone Pine, he learns from a shell-shocked Billy that Barney is dead and Snowy is badly injured. Frank and Archy are themselves due to go over the trenches at the Battle of the Nek, intended (in the film at least) to be a diversion to allow British troops to land safely. Artillery bombardment that was supposed to allow the Light Horse to traverse the open ground between the trenches stops early due to unsynchronized watches, but the men are ordered over even though the Turks have recovered their firing positions.

Two waves of men are shot down by Turkish machine-gun fire before communications fail, and Frank, volunteered by Archy as a communications runner in his stead, is sent to request a stay. Colonel Robinson (John Morris) declines, having been given inaccurate information about the offensive, so Frank is sent over his head to General Gardner (Graham Dow), who, having heard that the English have not only landed safely but are sitting around drinking tea, agrees that the attack should be reconsidered. Frank does his best to sprint back with the news but does not arrive in time, as Archy goes over the top and is caught midstride by machine-gun fire.

During the charge against Turkish troops at the Battle of the Nek, 234 Australian Light Horsemen were killed in a period lasting only forty-five minutes, the move intended as a diversion to ensure the success of an Allied attack farther north.[3] Certainly the Gallipoli campaign as a whole was in support of a British naval operation to take the Dardanelles Strait and Constantinople, but the film's change to make the Nek offensive itself in support of the British illustrates *Gallipoli*'s thematic concern with a shift in national consciousness whereby the "innocence of obedience to the mother country was erased by the experience of World War I."[4] The British in the film would be laughable (and indeed all non-Australians are depicted in uncomfortably broad stereotypes) were it not for their callous disregard for Australian life, such that the Turks become almost irrelevant as the supposed enemy. The freeze-frame of Archy Hamilton's handsome, blond embodiment of Australian youth is the end of the film, the end of his life, and the end of one national identity as a new one is forged. From tragedy comes a national myth, one focused on the bonds of "mateship" and a new sense of independence that has been personified by the (now archetypal) cynical larrikin figure Frank all along.

Australians observe a national holiday for Anzac Day, 25 April, the date of the first Gallipoli landing. Young school children bake Anzac biscuits (long-lasting cookies that were shipped to soldiers from home). Older students watch Weir's *Gallipoli*. The film thereby continues to be a means by which an idealistic, heroic Australian legend is maintained (as well as representing a much-mourned golden era of Australian filmmaking). DB

Notes

1. A retrospective of the era was screened at New York's Lincoln Center in January 2013. Mike Hale, "When Australia Soared on Film: 'The Last New Wave,'" *New York Times*, 23 January 2013, www.nytimes.com/2013/01/24/movies/the-last-new-wave-70s-australian-film-at-lincoln-center.html?_r=0 (16 May 2013). For more on the Australian film industry during this period, see Susan Dermody and Elizabeth Jacka, *The Screening of Australia* (Sydney: Currency Press, 1987).
2. For an insightful critique of the film's mythologizing published in the year following the film's release, see Amanda Lohrey, "Gallipoli: Male Innocence as a Marketable Commodity," *Island Magazine* 9/10 (1982): 29–34.
3. "Gallipoli and the Anzacs: The Nek," *Australian Government, Department of Veterans' Affairs*, www.anzacsite.gov.au/2visiting/walk_12nek.html (16 May 2013). From start to finish, the Gallipoli campaign claimed 26,111 Australian casualties, including 8,141 deaths. "Gallipoli," *Australian War Memorial*, www.awm.gov.au/encyclopedia/gallipoli (16 May 2013).
4. Jonathan Rayner, *The Films of Peter Weir*, 2nd ed. (London and New York: Continuum, 2003), 119.

Bibliography

Dermody, Susan, and Elizabeth Jacka. *The Screening of Australia*. Sydney: Currency Press, 1987.

"Gallipoli." *Australian War Memorial*, www.awm.gov.au/encyclopedia/gallipoli (16 May 2013).

"Gallipoli and the Anzacs: The Nek." *Australian Government, Department of Veterans' Affairs*, www.anzacsite.gov.au/2visiting/walk_12nek.html (16 May 2013).

Hale, Mike. "When Australia Soared on Film: 'The Last New Wave.'" *New York Times*, 23 January 2013, www.nytimes.com/2013/01/24/movies/the-last-new-wave-70s-australian-film-at-lincoln-center.html?_r=0 (16 May 2013).

Lohrey, Amanda. "Gallipoli: Male Innocence as a Marketable Commodity." *Island Magazine* 9/10 (1982): 29–34.

Rayner, Jonathan. *The Films of Peter Weir*, 2nd ed. London and New York: Continuum, 2003.

GANDHI (1982)

DIRECTOR: Richard Attenborough
WRITER: John Briley
PRODUCER: Richard Attenborough (Goldcrest Films, Columbia Pictures)
CINEMATOGRAPHERS: Billy Williams, Ronnie Taylor
EDITOR: John Bloom
ART DIRECTION: Stuart Craig, Robert W. Laing, Michael Seirton
COSTUMES: John Mollo, Bhanu Athaiya
MUSIC: Ravi Shankar, George Fenton
SOUND EDITORS: Gerry Humphreys, Robin O'Donoghue, Jonathan Bates, Simon Kaye
MAKEUP ARTIST: Tom Smith
CAST: Mohandas Karamchand Gandhi: Ben Kingsley. Kasturba Gandhi: Rohini Hattangadi. Nathuram Godse: Harsh Nayyar. Pandit Jawaharlal Nehru: Roshan Seth. Sardar Vallabhbhai Patel: Saeed Jaffrey. Maulana Azad: Virendra Razdan. Acharia Kripalani: Anang Desai. Margaret Bourke-White: Candice Bergen. Brig. Gen. Reginald Dyer: Edward Fox. 1st Baron Irwin: John Gilgud. Judge R. S. Broomfield: Trevor Howard. 3rd Baron Chelmsford: John Mills. Commentator: Shane Rimmer. Vince Walker: Martin Sheen. Rev. Charles Freer Andrews: Ian Charleston. Gen. Jan Smuts: Athol Fugard. Dr. Herman Kallenbach: Gunther Maria Halmer. Mirabehn (Madeleine Slade): Geraldine James. Muhammad Ali Jinnah: Alyque Padamsee. Khan: Amrish Puri. Khan Abdul Ghaffar Khan (Frontier Gandhi): Dilsher Singh. Senior Officer Fields: Ian Banner. Colins: Richard Griffiths. Kinnoch: Nigel Hawthorne. Nahari: Om Puri. Sgt. Putnam: Bernard Hill. Colin: Daniel Day-Lewis. American Lt.: John Ratzenberger. Mahadev Desai: Pankaj Mohan. Pyarelal: Pankaj Kapoor
AA: Best Picture (Richard Attenborough), Best Director (Richard Attenborough), Best Original Screenplay (John Briley), Best Film Editing (John Bloom), Best Leading Actor (Ben Kingsley), Best Art Direction (Stuart Craig, Robert W. Laing, Michael Seirton), Best Cinematography (Billy Williams, Ronnie Taylor), Best Costume Design (John Mollo, Bhanu Athaiya)
AAN: Best Makeup (Tom Smith), Best Original Score (Ravi Shankar, George Fenton), Best Sound (Gerry Humphreys, Robin O'Donoghue, Jonathan Bates, Simon Kaye)
DVD: Columbia Pictures, 2001. Twenty-fifth anniversary edition, Columbia Pictures, 2007.
BLU-RAY: Columbia Pictures, 2009. Twenty-fifth anniversary edition.
DURATION: 191 minutes

All beings at birth are subject to delusion . . . arising from the pairs of opposites, desire, and aversion. . . . But those men of meritorious deeds in whom sin has come to an end . . . are released from the illusion of opposites . . . (and) know me even at the time of death.

—Antonio de Nicolas, *The Bhagavad Gita*

This captivating film, purportedly twenty years in the making, is director/producer Sir Richard Attenborough's portrayal of Mohandas Karamchand Gandhi, the twentieth-century lawyer and humanitarian activist who led India to independence from British rule. John Briley scripted the award-winning original work by mining primary sources of Gandhi's writings as a guide, and actor Ben Kingsley earned the Academy Award for Best Leading Actor, evoking an almost eerie resemblance to the historical figure, not only in physical appearance, but also demeanor, venturing further to wonder if not in élan itself. Although biographical and semihistorical in subject matter, the structure of the film primarily follows a didactic epic form about an unusual revolutionary, whose eternal message, in

Briley's interpretation, is that the "most fundamental drama of all (is): the war in our hearts between love and hate,"[1] that is, the universal epic struggle between the forces of eros and eris. For the historical Gandhi, this battle, self-actualized, became the fountainhead for his lifelong public duty to the ancient Indian principle of ahimsa (nonviolence) and satyagraha (persistence toward Truth), with a deeper cultural and personal intent of achieving moksha (liberation) in all its manifestations.

Gandhi is structured through frame narratives using flashback, textual overlay, and edifying dialogue to shape its epic context. The opening credit sequence features a serene seaside fishing village passing from sunset to sunrise, symbolizing the eternal flow of the cycle of return (samsara), followed by a textual overlay quote that frames the film's didactic theme: "No man's life can be encompassed in one telling. There is no way to give each year its allotted weight, to include each event, each person who helped to shape a lifetime. What can be done is to be faithful in spirit to the record, and to try to find one's way to the heart of the man."[2]

Immediately after this quote fades, the village scene cuts and we are on a city street. The camera pans to a close-up of a man who turns his head, and we come face-to-face with the person who will become Gandhi's killer, although we do not yet know it. We follow (through the perspective of Gandhi's eventual killer) pilgrims making their way to see the aging and frail Gandhi, and then we witness the point-blank assassination. The scene again cuts to the enormous funeral procession of the corpse of Gandhi as the voice-overs of television commentators quote reactions from celebrities about the news of the leader's death, ending this opening sequence.

The film then flashes back to the early adulthood of Gandhi, specifically to a life-changing moment when he is removed and unceremoniously evicted from his first-class compartment on a train in South Africa, simply because he is Indian. In this scene, the well-attired, young attorney Gandhi is on his way to South Africa, seated in his first-class compartment, reading, when the conductor of the train (at the provocation of a European traveler who notices Gandhi seated in first class) begins questioning how a "coolie" got into the compartment. Shocked, Gandhi replies that he'd purchased a ticket and that he was an attorney. The conductor replies that there are no "colored" attorneys in South Africa, implying that Gandhi was lying, causing Gandhi to produce evidence of his status as attorney. The European angrily retorts by telling the conductor to throw Gandhi out nonetheless; the conductor tells Gandhi that he must move to third class or he will be thrown off the train. Gandhi, in anger and fear, reacts, saying, "I always go first class! I have traveled all over England and I've never."[3] The next scene features Gandhi's luggage being thrown off the platform at the station and him being thrown off the train.

This experience, chronicled in his autobiographical work *The Story of My Experiments with Truth*,[4] sets the stage for Gandhi's internal transformation and public rise, first in South Africa, as spokesperson for the Indian Congress Party of South Africa, initiating a protest rally and burning of mandatory identity passes imposed on Indians living there, and then, following more stringent fingerprinting legislation as a result of this action, instigating nonviolent protests resulting in the large-scale imprisonment of Gandhi and thousands of others before the eventual repeal of the legislation. The lessons learned from these historic moments, portrayed in this film, trace the footprints leading to the birth of his famous doctrine of satyagraha (persistence toward Truth): "Because they may torture my body, may break my bones, even kill me. . . . They will then have my dead body—not my obedience."[5] Although incubated in South Africa, it is on his native soil in India that the birth of Gandhi the epic hero takes place, as the leader of the independence of his people through the doctrines of nonviolence (ahimsa) and "persistence toward Truth" (satyagraha).

This film is the epic of the biography of these ideas as they flow through the character of Gandhi. It showcases several historical moments in India that evoked the call to ahimsa and satyagraha, marking the major sequences of this film, for example, the Jallianwalla Bagh Amritsar Massacre; however, there are significant scenes that also bear the weight of this work for its *epic* quality—those whose placement in the film add depth and formulaic stature to the work as they parallel the personal transformations of Gandhi, the man, with the corresponding effects upon those he influences as he emerges from the status of local agitator to spiritual mahatma.[6]

For example, in an opening scene featuring one of Gandhi's first encounters with *New York Times* reporter Vince Walker (Martin Sheen), when Gandhi is boasting about cultural unity in his South African community ashram, there is a private confrontation between Kasturba (Rohini Hattangadi), Gandhi's wife, and Gandhi in the corridor when he asks her to perform a task that only untouchables do; in this scene, he learns the true value of bhakti (devotion) from the example of his wife as his pure mirror, and publicly it leads to his stand for the elimination of untouchability in Hindu culture. His encounters with English clergyman and friend Charlie Andrews (Ian Charleston) from South Africa help refine his understanding of satyagraha after a chance encounter on a street in South Africa causes him to reevaluate the Christian meaning of "turn the other cheek" to a group of menacing youths threatening him as he walks along the road. And most importantly, he transcends the everyday and finds spiritual release after he returns to his hometown, when he performs the renewal of his wedding vows at the Pranami Temple in Porbandar, and when he is called to the bedside of a dying Kasturba and does not "take a walk," but stays with her until she leaves the earth. In each of these cases, his Truth was found, whether from Hindu, Christian, Muslim, or Humanistic sources. And this became the catalyst for his path to great personal liberation: moksha.

Correspondingly, Gandhi experiences his spiritual persona rising against a tide of public human effort mixed with suffering in such scenes as the historical Dandi March and the brutal witness of satyagraha at the Dharsana Salt Works, until emancipation from outside forces once again brings fighting, this time civil, between Muslims and Hindus, stopped only by a personal hunger strike by Gandhi himself performed as a desperate weapon of human reconciliation. In the film, we learn of Gandhi's final resolution to this matter moments before he is assassinated: "I am simply going to prove to Muslims there (in Pakistan), and Hindus here (in India), that the only devils in the world are those running around in our own hearts—and that's where all our battles ought to be fought."[7]

There are two death scenes in the film, the opening scene portraying the funeral of Gandhi's body, and the closing scene, his cremation. Between these two "deaths," we learn about the life of this man through the eyes of an "everyman" who ended up killing him, but unlike the West, where biography and history mark the parameters of a life, the Indian horizon marks the spaces of time against a landscape of eternity, and likewise, the perspective of Truth lies in the capacity to apprehend truths and never that one truth of that one man. Thus was the plight of the hero of this tale: in the end, his truth proved no more than that of a Westerner in Eastern form in the telling of this epic from a Western perspective. And this is the epic story portrayed in this film, despite the proclamation of liberation upon his death in the film's script; however, wrapped within the Western garb of biographical and historical perspective belies an ancient Indian epos[8] that has yet to be explored, although Gandhi himself sought its deep message, as evidenced in this final quote, and perhaps this film succeeds in answering its call through the fidelity to the life of that man, in spite of the intended didactic message promoted in the film. And that message is found only in the bookends of this film, namely in the funeral sequences, for it is only there that we may discover whether Gandhi was indeed able to achieve his goal of moksha through Truth. Whether Gandhi became liberated and achieved moksha is not for us to know, nor is it for his assassin to know. *He Ram.* MC

Notes

1. John Briley, *Gandhi: The Screenplay* (New York: Grove Press, 1982), 11.
2. Briley, *Gandhi,* 15.
3. Briley, *Gandhi,* 23.
4. In this work, dubbed an autobiography, Gandhi describes his purpose for writing and his personal teleology, stating, "It is not my purpose to attempt a real autobiography. I simply want to tell the story of my numerous experiments with the truth (*satya*)." And his personal goal in life, according to his "non-autobiography," is moksha (liberation), and his plan to achieve it is through the understanding of this truth (*satya*). "What I want to achieve is to attain . . . moksha." "Truth is the sovereign principle . . . truth is God." Introduction, *The Story of My Experiments with Truth* (Ahmedabad, India: Navajivan, 1927–1929).
5. Briley, *Gandhi,* 46.
6. Literally, "great soul." This is the translation of a Sanskrit word for a person who has attained great wisdom but has chosen not to achieve moksha and remain in liberation, but to be sustained on earth to continue to help humankind. See *The Bhagavad Gita,* chapter 7.
7. Briley, *Gandhi,* 177. For the philosophical reference to the meaning behind this profound realization, see the translation of *The Bhagavad Gita* by Antonio de Nicolas (York Beach, ME: Nicolas Hays, 1990, 2004), 107: "And I am seated in the hearts of all; from me are memory, wisdom, and their loss" (15:15). " He who, undeluded thus knows me, as the supreme *purusha.* He is all knowing and worships me with his whole being. . . . Thus has this most secret teaching been disclosed by me, Blameless One; Being Enlightened to this . . . one will be a man possessed by understanding and will have done his work" (15:18–19).
8. Oh God! *He Ram.* These were reportedly Gandhi's last words, although the veracity of this is disputed. This controversy continues the debate as to the true nature of this great leader's spiritual tradition, and this film, although a marvelous Western-styled biopic, adds yet another layer of confusion. In short, the epic itself, that is, this film about Gandhi *the human person,* itself betrays the essence of the message and teaching of Gandhi, the spiritual leader. Furthermore, it seems to lend credence to his assassin's perspective, not in fact, but through Western (mis-) interpretations of the deepest, most complex Hindu spiritual realities.

Bibliography

Briley, John. *Gandhi: The Screenplay.* New York: Grove Press, 1982.

Burns, James MacGregor. *Leadership.* New York: Harper & Row, 1978.

de Nicolas, Antonio, trans. *The Bhagavad Gita.* York Beach, ME: Nicolas Hays, 1990, 2004.

Gandhi, Mohandas Karamchand. *The Story of My Experiments with Truth.* Ahmedabad, India: Navajivan, 1927–1929). See www.columbia.edu/itc/mealac/pritchett/00litlinks/gandhi/index.html (20 February 2013).

GETTYSBURG (1993)

DIRECTOR: Ronald F. Maxwell
WRITER: Ronald F. Maxwell. Based on *The Killer Angels,* by Michael Shaara.
PRODUCER: Robert Katz, Moctesuma Esparza (TriStar Pictures, Esparza/Katz Productions, Turner Pictures)
CINEMATOGRAPHER: Kees Van Oostrum
EDITOR: Corky Ehlers
MUSIC: Randy Edelman
CAST: Lt. Gen. James Longstreet: Tom Berenger. Gen. Robert E. Lee: Martin

Sheen. Maj. Gen. George E. Pickett: Stephen Lang. Brig. Gen. Lewis "Lo" A. Armistead: Richard Jordan. Col. Joshua Lawrence Chamberlain: Jeff Daniels. Brig. Gen. John Buford: Sam Elliott. Lt. Thomas D. Chamberlain: C. Thomas Howell. Sgt. "Buster" Kilrain: Kevin Conway. Henry Thomas Harrison: Cooper Huckabee. Maj. Gen. J. E. B. Stuart: Joseph Fuqua. Maj. Gen. George Meade: Richard Anderson. Capt. Brewer: Dwier Brown. Maj. Gen. Henry Heth: Warren Burton. Lt. Col. Arthur Fremantle: James Lancaster. Brig. Gen. Richard B. Garnett: Andrew Prine. Brig. Gen. James L. Kemper: Royce D. Applegate. Maj. Gen. Isaac R. Trimble: Morgan Sheppard. Lt. Gen. Dick Ewell: Tim Scott. Maj. Gen. Winfield Scott Hancock: Brian Mallon. Maj. Gen. John F. Reynolds: John Rothman. Brig. Gen. J. Johnston Pettigrew: George Lazenby

AA: None

AAN: None

DVD: Turner Home Entertainment, 2004

Blu-ray: Warner Home Video, 2011

Duration: 254 minutes

Michael Shaara's Pulitzer Prize–winning novel *The Killer Angels* sold 2.5 million copies and set a mini industry into motion. Inspired by the book, Ken Burns created his miniseries *The Civil War* (1990). With Robert F. Maxwell as director, Ted Turner planned to turn the book into a television miniseries for one of his cable properties; however, he was so pleased with the results that he gave it a short theatrical release prior to beginning broadcast on television. Released as *Gettysburg*, the film focuses on the three days of the epic battle that had combined losses from both armies exceeding 53,000. Filmed on location where possible, the film had a cast of thousands; one estimate claims 5,000 extras, mostly Civil War reenactors. The film's bloodlessness was due, in part, to its planned release on television, which caused some viewers to question the film's veracity.[1] "The battles fought (with the exception of Little Round Table) lack the necessary, veracious savagery,"[2] and, as with the other 700 Civil War–related films that have been made, the film has historical faults.[3] The film's "real fireworks are in the acting rather than its visual design."[4]

The film begins on 30 June 1863, after General Robert E. Lee (Martin Sheen) and his Confederate troops slip across the Potomac and into Pennsylvania in an attempt to draw Union troops into a battle that, Lee hopes, will end the war. It is the third summer of the war, which few thought would last more than a few months. Lieutenant General James Longstreet's (Tom Berenger) actor-turned-spy, Henry Thomas Harrison (Cooper Huckabee), spots the Union Cavalry 7th Corps, with their 80,000 men, and reports this information to Longstreet. Although Lee is bemused that they are moving on the word of an actor, he gives the order to move at sunrise. He is also concerned that instead of sending him reports, Major General J. E. B. Stuart (Joseph Fuqua) is out getting his name in Northern newspapers.

On the Union side, Colonel Joshua Lawrence Chamberlain (Jeff Daniels) receives a message from Major General George Meade (Richard Anderson) that he will receive 120 mutineers from the 2nd Maine who still owe one year of military service on their contracts. Because the unit they served with disbanded, they refuse to fight. His unit, the 20th Maine, has about 200 men. Captain Brewer (Dwier Brown) presents the prisoners to Colonel Chamberlain, saying, "No one will say nothing if you shoot them." Instead, Chamberlain treats them fairly. The general's younger brother, Lieutenant Thomas D. Chamberlain (C. Thomas Howell), confirms his own thinking, declaring, "You can't shoot them.

You'd never be able to go to Maine again." In an inspiring speech, Chamberlain says the following to them:

> All of us volunteered. We are here for something new. We are an army out to set other men free. America should be free ground. No man has to bow. Here we judge you by what you do. Not by what your father does. What we're fighting for in the end is for each other. If we lose this fight, we lose the war. If you choose to fight, I'd be personally grateful.

All but six men join him in the fight. The 20th Maine marches to Little Round Top, where Chamberlain will command. At the Lutheran Theological Seminary, Brigadier General John Buford (Sam Elliott) foresees the battle and decides to keep the rebel army "stacked up" on the road so they cannot take the high ground.

On 1 July, the first day of the battle, General Lee asks that Longstreet stay behind the line, because, he says to him, "You have a bad habit of moving too far forward." Longstreet responds, "Can't lead from behind." Major General Henry Heth (Warren Burton) makes a tactical mistake by attacking Buford's troops. He believes that it is only a militia but then realizes they are dismounted cavalry.

Lieutenant Chamberlain asks some captured rebel troops why they are fighting. The answer is that they are fighting for their rights. One says he "doesn't fight for 'darkies' one way or the other." The Chamberlains assist an escaped slave, whom they have no dialogue with. A professor, Chamberlain explains to Sergeant "Buster" Kilrain (Kevin Conway) that he sees beyond race to the man. He looks for a "divine spark" and quotes Hamlet's soliloquy, saying, "What a piece of work is a man. How noble in reason, how infinite in faculty. In form and moving how express and admirable. In action how like an Angel." Kilrain counters that if men are angels, "they must be killer angels." He calls him an idealist and says that men have no more "value than a dead dog." Kilrain has his own idealism, however. He adds, "What matters is justice. Which is why I'm here. I'll be treated as I deserve. Not as my father deserved."

Longstreet introduces British officer Lieutenant Colonel Arthur Fremantle (James Lancaster) of the Coldstream guards, and the "eyes and ears of Queen Victoria," to Major General George E. Pickett (Stephen Lang), Brigadier General Lewis "Lo" Armistead (Richard Jordan), Brigadier General Richard B. Garnett (Andrew Prine), and Brigadier General James L. Kemper (Royce D. Applegate). They ask him what he is going to do about the Union blockade of the Confederate states. Kemper argues that the South should not consent to federal rule: "The government of my home is home. It won't be ruled by some president." Lee sends a scouting party to look for General Stuart. Major General Isaac R. Trimble (Morgan Sheppard) arrives and requests that Lee give him another assignment because he feels that Lieutenant General Dick Ewell (Tim Scott) is a "disgrace" because he "would not take the hill." He asks for men to take the hill himself. Lee refuses, saying, "That won't be necessary. You will be of great service, and I thank you."

On the Union side, General Buford meets with Major General Winfield Scott Hancock (Brian Mallon), who is upset about the death of his friend Major General John F. Reynolds (John Rothman). Hancock and Reynolds were friends with General Armistead. Hancock muses about his friends who are fighting on the other side at Gettysburg. "I'd like to see him again, but not like this," he says of Armistead.

On the morning of 2 July, Lee orders an attack on Little Round Top. Lee warns, "We must attack. We can't allow the Federal Army to cut us off from home." Colonel Fremantle tells a story about coming to the South through Texas because of the blockade. He says Texas is a "marvelous place full of Indians and desperadoes." He recognizes that the men fighting are "just transplanted Englishmen. Same god. Same language. Different dreams." While he would like them to be allies, he realizes that his country would never ally with a government that allowed slavery. Longstreet relates to Lee his days of fighting in Mexico with some of the very men who "are waiting for us now. The boys in blue don't quite seem the enemy." Lee responds, "We can only do our duty. To be a good commander you must be willing to command to death of what you love."

At the summit of Little Round Top, Chamberlain prepares for battle and asks his brother to keep his distance for the sake of their mother. Chamberlain explains to his men that they "cannot withdraw in any condition. You must defend this place to the last." Chamberlain's main concerns are that their ammunition is limited to about sixty rounds per man and that they will be flanked. As they fight, he orders ammunition taken from the wounded. Kilrain is wounded, but he keeps shooting, using a tree to bolster his rifle. Finally running out of ammunition, Chamberlain orders an attack using fixed bayonets. They move down the hill "like a swinging door." As he runs down the hill, Chamberlain faces a Confederate officer's pistol, but it is also out of bullets. After the battle, Kilrain tells Chamberlain, "I wanted to tell ya just in case. I never served with a better man." His troops are relieved at Little Round Top and moved to Big Round Top.

Longstreet sends Harrison to spy on the locations of Federal troops and then visits General Lee. That night, Longstreet speaks to General Armistead, who tries to convince him and others that Darwin's theory of evolution is correct. In a moving speech, Armistead talks about his loss of friends because of the division of the country, especially General Winfield Hancock. He reveals, "Winn was like a brother to me. Remember? Towards the end of the evening, things got a little rough. We both began to . . . well, there were a lot of tears. I went over to Hancock. I took him by the shoulder. I said, 'Winn, so help me, if I ever raise my hand against you, may God strike me dead.' Ain't seen him since." He leaves a package to be delivered to Winn's wife, Almira Hancock, in case of his death.

Just past midnight on 3 July, General Stuart arrives at Lee's office. Lee chastises him for not reporting on the enemy's movements. "Perhaps I did not make myself clear. Your cavalry are the eyes of this army. It must never happen again," Lee demands. Stuart offers to resign, which Lee refuses. He recognizes that Stuart is more interested in the pretense of honor and protocol than following orders.

Lee orders Longstreet to "split the federal line" at its center, but Longstreet is concerned that his diminished troops require rest. Longstreet "believes this attack will fail." The troops must walk across an open field for the distance of a mile, and the Federal troops are behind a stone wall "like . . . at Fredericksburg." In spite of his questioning of orders, Lee says, "there is no one I trust more." Longstreet tells his artillery to keep Union artillery silent. Lee visits Brigadier General J. Johnston Pettigrew (George Lazenby), who offers him a copy of his book. Lee responds, "I won't have time to read that today." He tells the assembled men, "I do believe this attack will decide the fate of our country. All the men who died in the past are with you here today." Harrison reveals to Longstreet that he wants to join the attack. Longstreet warns him that, "I don't believe my boys will reach that wall."

Chamberlain's troops are ordered to rest in the safest location available: "Smack dab in the center" of the Union line. Chamberlain reports to Hancock, who congratulates him, stating, "You ordered a bayonet charge. We need fighting men in the army. Well done." Hancock asks for a literary comparison to his situation with his friend General Armistead on the other side. "What would you do Chamberlain? What do the books tell you to do?" Chamberlain has no answer. Hancock is convinced that Southern troops are too tired to attack. Shortly thereafter, Chamberlain is shot and the Southern artillery begins its fusillade.

On the other side of the field, General Armistead speaks to his troops, saying, "All Virginia is here on this day. . . . Let no man forget that you're from old Virginia. For your lands. For your home. For your sweethearts. For your wives. For Virginia." Thousands of men follow him into battle. General Hancock is shot, but he refuses to be pulled off the field until the engagement is over. His friend General Armistead is shot soon after that. Hearing that Hancock was shot, he asks Thomas Chamberlain to "tell General Hancock that General Armistead sends his regrets. How very sorry I am."

Night begins to fall, and General Lee recognizes the failure, admitting, "It's my fault. No. I thought we were invincible. It is all my fault. It is entirely my fault." Lee tells Pickett that he may reform in a defensive position, but Pickett responds, "General Lee, I have no division." He plans to cross back into Virginia and keep fighting. "We will do better another time." He is thankful that the men do not "die for us."

As Richard Alleva says in "It's All in the Acting,"

> as a writer and director of dialogue scenes, Maxwell is much more incisive and self-demanding than he is as a film tactician of carnage and glory. Not with the thunder of cannons does this movie reverberate, but with the voices of men in tents and meadows lifted in argument, complaint, and condolence.[5]

JMW

Notes

1. Unlike the actual battle, "amidst all the action and spectacle of *Gettysburg*, not a single body part in sight is separated from its companions. There are no exploding skulls. Bodies do not instantly become headless, legless, armless torsos. . . . There is some blood spatter. But even that is nothing on the scale required, nothing like the astonishing volume that a human body contains, quarts and quarts of the stuff, flooding from veins, spurting from arteries, flaying and splashing all over the place." Philip Beidler, "Ted Turner et al. at Gettysburg; Or, Reenactors in the Attic," *Virginia Quarterly Review* 75, no. 3 (1999): 497–98.
2. Richard Alleva, "It's All in the Acting: Maxwell's *Gettysburg*," *Commonweal* 120, no. 20 (1993): 28.
3. Bruce Chadwick, "Actor against Actor," *American Heritage* 55, no. 4 (2004): 64.
4. Alleva, "It's All in the Acting," 28.
5. Alleva, "It's All in the Acting," 28.

Bibliography

Alleva, Richard. "It's All in the Acting: Maxwell's *Gettysburg*." *Commonweal* 120, no. 20 (1993): 28.

Beidler, Philip. "Ted Turner et al. at Gettysburg; Or, Reenactors in the Attic." *Virginia Quarterly Review* 75, no. 3 (1999): 488–503.

Chadwick, Bruce. "Actor against Actor." *American Heritage* 55, no. 4 (2004): 64–66.

Hiltbrand, David. "Picks and Pans." *People* 40, no. 14 (1993): 11.

GIANT (1956)

DIRECTOR: George Stevens
WRITERS: Fred Guiol, Ivan Moffat. Adapted from Edna Ferber's novel *Giant*.
PRODUCERS: George Stevens, Henry Ginsberg (Warner Bros.)
ASSISTANT DIRECTOR: Joe Rickards
PRODUCTION MANAGER: Tom Andre
CINEMATOGRAPHER: William C. Mellor
EDITORS: William Hornbeck, Phil Anderson, Fred Bohanan
ART DIRECTION: Boris Leven, Ralph S. Hurst

Set Decoration: Boris Leven, Ralph S. Hurst
Costumes: Marjorie Best, Moss Mabry
Music: Dimitri Tiomkin
Cast: Jordan "Bick" Benedict Jr.: Rock Hudson. Leslie Benedict: Elizabeth Taylor. Jett Rink: James Dean. Luz Benedict I: Mercedes McCambridge. Luz Benedict II: Carroll Baker. Vashti Snythe: Jane Withers. Bob Dace: Earl Holliman. Jordan "Jordy" Benedict: Dennis Hopper. Angel Obregon II: Sal Mineo. Uncle Bawley: Chill Wills. Sir David Karfey: Rod Taylor. Judy Benedict: Fran Bennett. Juana Guerra Benedict: Elsa Gárdenas
AA: Best Director (George Stevens)
AAN: Best Leading Actor (Rock Hudson), Best Leading Actor (James Dean), Best Supporting Actress (Mercedes McCambridge), Best Art Direction–Set Decoration (Boris Leven, Ralph S. Hurst), Best Costume Design (Marjorie Best, Moss Mabry), Best Film Editing (William Hornbeck, Phil Anderson, Fred Bohanan), Best Music–Scoring of a Dramatic or Comedy Picture (Dimitri Tiomkin), Best Picture (George Stevens, Henry Ginsberg), Best Writing–Best Screenplay Adapted (Fred Guiol, Ivan Moffat)
DVD: Warner Brothers, 2005. Two-disc special edition with feature-length commentary by Stephen Farber, Ivan Moffat, and George Stevens Jr.
Blu-ray: Warner Brothers, 2013
Duration: 201 minutes

Giant is an emblematic, leisurely, down-to-earth, lengthy saga, a contrast to the fraught-with-spectacle Hollywood epics of its era. It is a story of character, family conflicts, class struggles, and the manners and mores of the South, and Texas, in particular, rather than one of action and adventure. Masterfully drawn from the novel by Edna Ferber and directed by George Stevens, who had already excelled as a director of a comedy, *Alice Adams* (1935), a regional drama, *A Place in the Sun* (1951), and the idyllic western *Shane* (1953), *Giant* offers a cast of three rising stars of the time, Elizabeth Taylor at the age of twenty-three, James Dean, also twenty-three years old at the time (he died in a car crash as soon as the shooting was completed), and Rock Hudson at the age of twenty-eight. In its second part, the movie also introduces a set of lesser-known actors, some of whom would soon become recognizable names: Carroll Baker, Jane Withers, Earl Holliman, Dennis Hopper, and Sal Mineo (who had costarred with Dean in *Rebel Without a Cause*), among others. *Giant* is a movie that makes strong statements about racism, the rights of ownership, and the status of women in a patriarchal society, while putting to the test the American/Texan of the "go-getter" motto and the values (or disvalues) associated with it.

Hudson plays Jordan "Bick" Benedict, the tall, handsome scion of a Texas cattle rancher family, the Benedicts. He is wealthy, proud, and class-conscious, regarding everyone outside his race and clan as unworthy of notice. The film opens with Bick's trip East to Maryland's Green Acres, to buy a stallion, War Wind, and there he meets Leslie (Taylor), the daughter of a wealthy horse breeder and a young woman whose stunning good looks barely conceal an independence of disposition that does not quite fit his notions of compliant womanhood. Leslie marries this tall Texan out of physical attraction and travels with him to Reata, as Bick's Texas ranch is known. There she becomes known as "Miss Leslie" to his friends and relatives. Leslie easily sees through Bick and challenges him in some ways, while being compliant in others.

The duo is complemented by Jett Rink (Dean), an upstart peon working at Reata who falls in love with Miss Leslie, although he knows full well she is beyond his reach. Like Gatsby (of the book), to whom he bears an uncanny resemblance as a character, he dreams an impossible dream—becoming a wealthy man of status to win an incomparable Southern belle. Catlike, he is crouching in wait, until mere chance serves him a lucky stroke. He is the favorite of Luz (Mercedes McCambridge), Bick's elder sister, who becomes the fourth major character early in the film. Unable to bear the onus of surrendering the management of Reata to a newcomer, and in a fit of jealousy and revenge, Luz savagely spurs War Wind, Leslie's black stallion, while riding back to Reata. She is thrown off and soon dies from a head injury. Ironically, she has bequeathed a strip of land to Jett, who stubbornly holds on to it, despite a generous offer from Bick, who wants to own every piece of land in the vast ranch area. Jett becomes instantly wealthy when he discovers oil on the property.

The three major characters adhere to their point of view as the story evolves: The tall, handsome Bick is proud of his inheritance of a vast land area, boastfully declaring it to be larger than half a million acres to Leslie's father—and he wants a wife to share his goals to continue his inheritance, and to produce him a son similar in mind and ambition to him and his progenitors. Meanwhile, Leslie takes an interest in the small community of Mexican hands that work for her husband. She is appalled by their living conditions and lack of medical care. Despite her husband's objections, she visits the ranch's impoverished community, helps them as she can, and even takes an interest in the loner youth, Jett Rink, seemingly idle, a trodden-under wretch who is treated as "white trash" by his master. While Leslie has no notions of infidelity, Jett idolizes her, pins a paper clip of her picture on his wall, and even prepares "tea" for her during a visit to his hut. Of the three, Dean's character is the most complex and the most intriguing. Seething with hatred against his masters (a hatred that takes him time to conceptualize), he plays down his dislike of his master Bick, fearing a reprisal, but he gives vent to his resentment when "black gold" gushes from one of his pumps, and during a gathering at the ranch he punches his former boss on Thanksgiving Day in front of his friends and relatives. He suddenly becomes important in the Texas scheme of things, and as one of Bick's guests wryly puts it to Bick, "You should have shot him a long time ago. Now he is too rich to kill."

As the film moves into its second generation, all three major players develop and grow into human beings, scarcely resembling their earlier selves. While Bick becomes mellower, shedding some of his prejudices, Leslie adapts to life around her, learning to appreciate her husband's inner strength and real growth. On the other hand, Jett fails to measure up to the social status that his wealth has enabled him to acquire. Of the three, Jett is by a wide margin the most ambiguous—almost an antihero—for he is an outcast, an outsider who is unable to fit into his society even when he becomes wealthy. Unhappy as he is with his lowly status, he becomes even unhappier, spiteful, resentful, and vindictive (and a drunk) when he grows older and wealthy. He is the founder of Jetexas, an oil empire, but he does not enjoy his wealth or wish to create a family and merge into the community that bred him. Rather, he prefers to dominate, show off, and do things only on his own terms.

As the movie shifts to its second part, Jett, now older and a tycoon, is attracted to young Luz, Bick's and Leslie's daughter, and she to him, and, despite their age differences, the match might have been acceptable, had it not been for his sudden and almost inexplicable collapse during a gala event when he was about to be honored by the governor of Texas. Just before that, he had gotten into a fight with "Jordy," Bick's son (played by Hopper), because a hair salon owned by Rink had insulted Jordy's Mexican wife, Juana, refusing to render her services. This leads to a confrontation between an enraged Jordy and Jett, who floors him with a punch. Bick challenges Jett to a fight after that, and the latter, being totally drunk, is barely able to raise his hands. Bick refuses to hit him, saying only, "You are not worth hitting . . . you are all through," and then he walks away. Alone at his table, all guests gone, Jett delivers his "speech," which Luz hears through a crack in the door, and she learns that he was always in love with her mother and wanted to court her daughter as a "replacement." He had almost gone as far as proposing to her that same evening, but she held back, and that accounted for his final failure.

Jett Rink's character is unfinished, like the short life of Dean himself; he is deprived of his natural rights by being poor, insignificant, and marginalized by his rich neighbors and employers; therefore, he is half-grown as a human being, although passionate and driven. He reads "self-improvement" books, as Gatsby does, and the similarity between the two characters is uncanny; Jett dreams of possessing the rich, established, high-society girl, but he has no idea how to go about getting her. By the time he courts Leslie's daughter, he is rich but emotionally spent and a victim of his addiction to alcohol. In this role, Dean is superb, for his instincts as a "method" actor allow him to express his inner world, not through speech, but through body language. While still poor, Jett's movements show him as if readying himself to spring at a victim, as a panther would to catch its prey. When his pump starts gushing oil, he plants his feet on the spot, letting his face get smeared, being symbolically baptized in the liquid gold that has just become his. After Jett humiliates Bick by refusing his offer to buy his land, he struts back, gesturing and punching at the wire fences, swaying his hips and shoulders like a boxer who has just floored his opponent. When he climbs his pump tower and surveys his possessions, he is the giant who has conquered his opponents. He has beaten the cattle rancher with the newfound means of wealth—oil. His is the new order of Texas, thence the name he gives his company: Jetexas.

The movie begs the question, Who is, or what is, the giant? The end of the story might suggest the answer. When the older Benedict and his family, which includes his half-Mexican daughter-in-law, visit a nearby café, the owner is in the process of throwing out a colored old man and his small group. Benedict, bent and frail, stands up to him and gets soundly beaten in a fist fight, but he then wins the admiration of Leslie, for whom her husband's defeat represents a moral victory. The tall Texan is cleansed of his bigotry, and, in Stevens's universal lingo, so is the state. The giant is not any one thing; it could be a country, a state, a whole nation of collective failures, of racial inequality, of male condescension to the opposite sex. *Giant* is the reflection of its characters in a set of mirrors, a metamorphosis of reality.

The title *Giant* is ironic and perhaps emblematic of these developments. It could be attributed to any of the three major characters, for they all grow, but in different ways, or it could represent Texas itself, the vastness of the country, its seemingly infinite resources, its muscle and power, its countryside of endless plains and vistas, its potential for oil wealth. Or the term *giant* could be the Benedict's gothic palatial residence and ranch, the Reata (as Tara is in *Gone with the Wind*), or even Jetexas, the oil company owned by Jett Rink. *Giant* is an ironic title because, whatever it implies, or however literally one applies it to its subjects, it turns out to be the opposite of what one has assumed; it is a reversal of what one has expected it to be all along. A giant can turn out to be something or someone who is very small, or, conversely, a small object (or character) acquiring dimensions one did not see at first. CS

Bibligoraphy

Crowther, Bosley. "Review of *Giant*." *New York Times*, 11 October 1956, http://movies.nytimes.com/movie/review?res=9B07E2D61F38E13BBC4952DFB667838D649EDE (20 September 2013).

Ferber, Edna. *Giant*. New York: Doubleday, 1952.

GLADIATOR (2000)

DIRECTOR: Ridley Scott
WRITER: David Franzoni, John Logan, William Nicholson
PRODUCER: Douglas Wick, David Franzoni, Banko Lustig (DreamWorks, Universal Pictures, Scott Free Productions)
CINEMATOGRAPHER: John Mathieson
EDITOR: Pietro Scalia
ART DIRECTION: Arthur Max, Crispian Sallis
COSTUMES: Janty Yates
MUSIC: Hans Zimmer
SOUND MIXERS: Scott Millan, Bob Beamer, Ken Weston
SPECIAL EFFECTS: Jon Nelson, Neel Corbould, Rob Harvey, Tim Burke
MAKEUP ARTISTS: Paul Egleton, Graham Johnston
CAST: Maximus: Russell Crowe. Commodus: Joaquin Phoenix. Lucilla: Connie Nelson. Marcus Aurelius: Richard Harris. Senator Gracchus: Derek Jacobi. Senator Falco: David Schofield. Juba: Djimon Hounson. General Quintus: Tomas Arana. Maximus' Wife: Giannina Facio. Maximus's Son: Giorgio Cantarini. Antonius Proximo: Oliver Reed
AA: Best Picture (Douglas Wick, David Franzoni, Banko Lustig), Best Leading Actor (Russell Crowe), Best Effects–Visual Effects (Jon Nelson, Neel Corbould, Rob Harvey, Tim Burke), Best Sound (Scott Millan, Bob Beamer, Ken Weston), Best Costume Design (Janty Yates)
AAN: Best Director (Ridley Scott), Best Supporting Actor (Joaquin Phoenix), Best Art Direction–Set Decoration (Arthur Max, Crispian Sallis), Best Cinematography (John Mathieson), Best Film Editing (Pietro Scalia), Best Music–Original Score (Hans Zimmer), Best Writing–Screenplay Written Directly for the Screen (David Franconi, John Logan, William Nicholson)
DVD: Dreamworks Video, 2000. Two-disc Signature Selection.
BLU-RAY: Paramount Pictures, 2009. The Signature Selection.
DURATION: 154 minutes (164 for director's cut)

Directed by Ridley Scott, *Gladiator* won five Oscars and had seven nominations, plus numerous other awards, and it quadrupled its large budget of $103 million, a blockbuster winner at the box office. But critical acceptance was not unanimous, especially when it came to historical accuracy, with the main character invented and a muddled plot attempting to re-create events of the second century A.C.E., which many think marked the beginning of the decline of the Roman Empire. Indeed, the film resembles, to a great extent, *The Fall of the Roman Empire* (1964), directed by Antony Mann, which did poorly at the box office, but it perhaps deserves greater credit as a representation of actual Roman history of the time. Both films, epics on the grand scale, present the era of Marcus Aurelius—one of the last great emperors—at the end of his career, and both, falsely, tell that he was murdered. Commodus, his son and inheritor, is shown as unreliable, caddish, and vindictive, as well as a coward, but Christopher Plummer made him interesting, possessing wit and irony, while the Joaquin character is brutish, ugly, moody, and loutish. *The Fall of the Roman Empire* shows Rome as a place of elegant architecture and light (contrasted with the misty regions of the north), while *Gladiator* is bathed in murky colors, aside from showing constant battle or arena action that is violent, sick, and brutal. It is redeemed somewhat by its spectacular visuals, sure-handed direction, complex montages, and mise-en-scène, so one can hardly reject it as a failure. As an epic, it went with the times, as audiences in the 1990s were generations removed from the audiences of the 1960s, used to rather leisurely spectacle, brighter colors, and occasional humor.

Gladiator is supposedly based on actual Roman history, but it is only marginally historical. Commodus, the Roman emperor, played by Joaquin Phoenix, lived from 161 (A.C.E.) to 192. He was strangled in his bed by his mistress, Marcia,[1] not killed in a gladiatorial duel by Maximus, the former general who had been sold into slavery, turned a gladiator, and returned to Rome to avenge the deaths of his wife and son. He did not strangle Marcus Aurelius, the Roman emperor and Commodus's father, as the movie shows. Aurelius died while fighting German tribes during an expedition to the Danube, although history does not show us the exact manner of his death. Commodus was indeed a corrupt and inept emperor, who dressed as Hercules and wanted to rename Rome after himself, and who preferred gladiator spectacles to running a city ravaged by the plague. There is no real evidence that he had an incestuous desire for his sister, here played with distinction by Connie Nielsen, although he was notorious for other perversions, which the movie mercifully spares us from seeing. Maximus himself (played by Russell Crowe), is a total fabrication, although gladiators like him did exist, and the reality of fighting in the Roman fronts itself was more brutal than a movie can show. Commodus did reign for twelve years (180–192), and he was a corrupt madman, equal to the other two mad emperors, Nero and Caligula—though not as notorious as those two, in part because cinema had up to that time ignored him.[2] The movie shows him as a character beneath contempt, someone with no redeeming qualities whatsoever, an utter villain, richly deserving of his spectacular slaying in a gladiatorial duel with Maximus.

The movie creates a great deal of tension and some suspense, since the viewer expects the thrill given to it by the prospect of Maximus returning to do battle against his archenemy. The viewer's expectations are fulfilled, but, shockingly, Maximus himself dies at the end, as the treacherous Commodus had stabbed him prior to the fight, expecting to have an easy kill. Maximus, however, endures enough pain to kill Commodus before dying.

This is the stuff Hollywood is made of, as it is in some ways reminiscent of *Ben-Hur*, since that movie also shows an innocent man who has been wronged surviving the galleys and returning to search for his mother and sister and avenging their death. He, too, had a worthy (or unworthy) opponent, Messala (Stephen Boyd). There is a confrontation between two adversaries, the climactic chariot race where Messala loses and is killed. Justice prevails. But there is an enormous gap separating the two epics. What separates these two movies is the tension created and the level of violence.

Ben-Hur is four hours in length (*Gladiator* runs two and a half), and it has a leisurely pace, taking long moments for reflection and thoughtful exchanges between characters. It has a religious overtone, and the entire movie is a parallel to the life of Christ. *Ben-Hur* has only two violent episodes—the naval battle and the chariot race—the latter an enduring masterpiece of realistic staging of a large event, spectacle, and great stunt work (although reduced to a minimum since Charlton Heston did most of the charioting). *Gladiator*, on the other hand, features battles, beginning with one that occupies the first fifteen minutes of the movie, along with mutilation, decapitations, slicing of body parts, and unbelievable cruelty—graphically described on all occasions, whether in arid landscapes of the north or in the Roman arena.

Ridley Scott, a director known for his visual style, gives this movie the full treatment, providing some breathtaking vistas of northern landscapes, or Africa. The word violence (*violentia*) is inscribed on the wall outside the Roman Coliseum, which is shown whole, with digital enhancement. The movie, however, goes beyond violence in graphic terms and makes a concept of it. This is not just violence as part of the aesthetic necessity of a movie (if you show gladiators you show how they fight), but violence as part of the moral subtext of the story.

In a way, Maximus in no less of a killer than Commodus—in fact, he commits many more violent acts than the latter. When trained to be a gladiator in the African colony under the tutelage of Oliver Reed, he kills his numerous opponents with lightning speed, wanting to show his mettle and unsurpassed skill as a swordsman and doing so without the slightest remorse. As a general, he was used to routinely killing opponents, since in those days generals fought in the battlefield, unlike today's military leaders of rank who conveniently stay in the rear. Maximus is a killing machine. He has right on his side, but by the time he's finished righting a wrong, he has killed hundreds, with his own hands. His ruthlessness has a stoic resignation to it, but that does not alter the fact of his monstrous deeds. Of course, a gladiator has to do that—Spartacus, in the 1960 production *Spartacus*, did it, too, but those movies used violence sparingly—although more graphically and honestly than epics just preceding it. Maximus attains certain nobility in wanting to rid the world of a murderous monster like Commodus, but being in the killing business himself irreparably tarnishes his image.

While Russell Crowe does a creditable job portraying him and keeping him sympathetic, it is not possible that anyone capable of brutal killings of this magnitude has remained unaffected by them. A compassionate killer is a contradiction in terms. The Rambo movies of the 1980s show us Sylvester Stallone as Rambo returning to Vietnam to save one MIA person, but in the process, he guns down dozens, if not hundreds, of foes. Is he an admirable man—or hero—after that? A good question to ponder. *Gladiator* is as much about our historical/social context as it is about Roman society. It is more American than Roman, or a means of using Roman history for depicting contemporary social phenomena. One could think of Maximus not as a killer, but as what he could have been, a philosopher like Marcus Aurelius (refreshingly played by Richard Harris). Couldn't he go to Africa or Spain, like compatriot Seneca, and write a book about Commodus? That would have probably left a better legacy but not a subject for a moneymaking picture. After all, Roman writers who detailed atrocities—Suetonius, Tacitus, Livius—left us something to think about, but they are not household names. Maximus is (although his name is more ephemeral).

A word or two about other things. The music was irrelevantly good; it was inspiring, but not capable of inspiring passion for this paltry movie. There were also some great performances, wasted for the most part, by veteran actors, with Derek Jacobi as the Roman senator Gracchus, who looks surprised by all the killing, and, Richard Harris, aforementioned, as Marcus Aurelius, with a bust of Plato shown in the background as he is being strangled. Finally there is Oliver Reed, in his last role, playing a cagey gladiator trainer; today he would have been a circus master, a better job. Both Plato and Marcus Aurelius must be turning in their graves. CS

Notes

1. According to other sources, he died being strangled in his bath by a wrestler, Narcicius.

2. With the exception, of course, of Christopher Plummer, who played him with unusual gusto, and some humor, in the 1964 Anthony Mann spectacle *The Fall of the Roman Empire.*

Bibliography

Ebert, Roger. "*Gladiator* Review." *Chicago Sun-Times*, 21 February 2000, www.rogerebert.com/reviews/gladiator-2000 (19 September 2013).

Landau, Diana, Walter Parkes, and Ridley Scott. *Gladiator: The Making of the Ridley Scott Epic.* New York: Newmarket Press, 2000.

Schwartz, Richard. *The Films of Ridley Scott.* Westport, CT: Praeger, 2002.

THE GODFATHER (1972)

DIRECTOR: Francis Ford Coppola

WRITERS: Mario Puzo, Francis Ford Coppola. Based on the novel by Mario Puzo.

PRODUCER: Albert S. Ruddy (Paramount Pictures, Alfran Productions)

CINEMATOGRAPHER: Gordon Willis

EDITOR: William Reynolds, Peter Zinner

COSTUMES: Anna Hill Johnstone

MUSIC: Nino Rota

SOUND EDITORS: Charles Grenzbach, Richard Portman, Christopher Newman

CAST: Don Vito Corleone: Marlon Brando. Michael Corleone: Al Pacino. Santino "Sonny" Corleone: James Caan. Sandra Corleone: Julie Gregg. Tom Hagen: Robert Duvall. Johnny Fontane: Al Martino. Kay Adams: Diane Keaton. Jack Wolz: John Marley. Virgil "The Turk" Sollozzo: Al Lettieri. Bruno Tattaglia: Tony Giorgio. Sgt. McClusky: Sterling Hayden. Peter Clemenza: Richard S. Castellano. Salvatore Tessio: Abe Vigoda. Amerigo Bonasera: Salvatore Corsitto. Barzini: Richard Conte. Connie: Talia Shire. Carlo: Gianni Russo. Alfredo "Fredo" Corleone: John Cazale. Mama Corleone: Morgana King. Luca Brazi: Lenny Montaine. Moe Green: Alex Rocco. Apollonia: Simonetta Stefaneli. Fabrizio: Angelo Infanti. Luca Brasi: Lenny Montana. Paulie Gatto: John Martino. Moe Greene: Alex Rocco. Enzo the Baker: Gabriele Torrei (uncredited)

AA: Best Picture (Albert S. Ruddy), Best Leading Actor (Marlon Brando), Best Writing–Screenplay Based on Material from Another Medium (Mario Puzo, Francis Ford Coppola)

AAN: Best Director (Francis Ford Coppola), Best Supporting Actor (James Caan), Best Supporting Actor (Robert Duvall), Best Supporting Actor (Al Pacino), Best Costume Design (Anna Hill Johnstone), Best Film Editing (William Reynolds, Peter Zinner), Best Music–Original Dramatic Score (Nino Rota), Best Sound (Charles Grenzbach, Richard Portman, Christopher Newman)

DVD: Paramount Pictures, 2008

BLU-RAY: Paramount Pictures, 2008

DURATION: 175 minutes

The Godfather is an epic crime drama that meticulously details the challenges faced by the Corleone Italian American crime dynasty. Based on the novel by Mario Puzo and supported by a large and excellent cast, the film sets the mood by beginning on Don Vito Corleone's (Marlon Brando) daughter Connie's (Talia Shire) wedding day by contrasting scenes of her dancing and singing while he has business to perform. The opening dialogue, spoken by one of his suppliants, sets up the film's themes of vengeance and justice, as well as the ways of the old world of Sicily and the new world of the United States. He pleads for Corleone's vengeance. As godfather, Corleone is a man of power, but he declines to be vengeful, as he is interested in only quick and measured justice. Brando's Oscar-winning performance is realistic, fresh, and powerful yet poignant.

Popular crooner Johnny Fontane (Al Martino) comes to sing at the reception, wowing the wedding party, but his personal agenda is to petition Don Corleone. He implores Corleone to convince Hollywood director Jack Wolz (John Marley) to give him the lead in a new film. Fontane cries during the discussion, and Don Corleone reveals his impatience with weak-willed men by slapping Johnny.

The one wedding guest Don Corleone desires to see does not seek him out. His son Michael (Al Pacino) is a returning war hero who is more interested in going to college than into the family business. As he tells his girlfriend, Kay Adams (Diane Keaton), who has accompanied him to the wedding, about the family business and its methods, he says, "That's my family, Kay. That's not me." The rest of the film shows Michael's transition from war hero to mob boss. Pacino's film debut has been only three years prior, and he had only been in two previous movies. His portrayal of Michael reveals the slow, steel-hard growth of a crime boss. By the end of the film, Michael is the godfather.

Don Corleone sends his consigliore, Tom Hagen (Robert Duvall), to California to convince Jack Wolz to let Johnny Fontane star in his film. After initially being rebuffed, Tom is invited to Wolz's home, where he shows him his $600,000 horse, Kartoom. At dinner, Wolz berates Hagen about why he cannot let Fontane star in his movie, in spite of being perfect for the role. According to Wolz, Fontane destroyed one of his aspiring ingénues and removed her as his sexual plaything. Hagen is told to leave and immediately flies to New Jersey to tell the don the bad news. The next morning, Wolz awakens to finds the head of his prize horse in bed. Wolz decides to hire Fontane.

The family meets with Virgil "The Turk" Sollozzo (Al Lettieri), who wants them to finance the importation of heroin. He tries to hide the assistance he receives from the Tattaglia family, but Hagen reveals it. While Hagen sees the opportunity as a positive, defensive move, and Sonny (James Caan) just sees it as a moneymaker, Don Corleone turns down the offer. He refuses to get involved in moving drugs. He suspects that there is more to the Sollozzo and Tattaglia alliance. Don Corleone sends Luca Brasi (Lenny Montana) to the Tattaglias to see what he can find out. Bruno Tattaglia (Tony Giorgio) kills Brasi. Then, across town, Don Corleone is gunned down at a fruit stand. His normal driver, Paulie (John Martino), called in sick. Don Corleone's son Fredo (John Cazale), inept with a gun, fails to protect his father, and Don Vito is hit several times. In the confusion, Michael finds out from the papers that his father has been shot. Little is known about his condition; however, Don Vito lives. Michael sends Kay to her parents for her safety. He goes to the hospital and finds it abandoned by cops and the family. Enzo the Baker (Gabriele Torrei) stands with him at the hospital stairs as the Sollozzo gang drives by to give the appearance that they have the numbers to protect the don. The ruse doesn't last long, as the police drive up and Sgt. McClusky (Sterling Hayden) harasses Michael. Michael is nearly dragged away when Tom Hagen drives up and challenges their authority. Before he leaves, McClusky punches Michael in the face.

While his father is in the hospital, Sonny controls the family. His reign is marked by violent, eye-for-eye reactions and hotheadedness. Sonny has Peter Clemenza (Richard S. Castellano) bring Paulie in, and he brings in extra men in case of an all-out war. Clemenza, one of the two family caporegimes, takes Paulie outside of town and has him killed for setting up the assassination attempt. Clemenza tells his assistant: "Leave the gun. Take the cannoli."

Tom is picked up off the street by Sollozzo's men. They tell Tom to present to Sonny the same deal offered to Don Vito. Sollozzo tells him, "I don't like violence, Tom. I'm a businessman. Blood is a big expense." Sonny refuses the offer when Tom delivers it. In response to the refusal, Sollozzo sends Brasi's bulletproof vest with fish wrapped within it. Clemenza explains that it means that Brasi now "sleeps with the fishes."

Michael volunteers to meet Sollozzo and McClusky. As a civilian in the fight, he is seen as objective and businesslike. The family arranges to have a pistol in the bathroom so that Michael will not get caught with it when being frisked. McClusky and Sollozzo pick Michael up and pat him down in the car. After a quick turn on a bridge to dodge any Corleone tail, they stop at the restaurant with the planted gun. At the halfway point, the nadir of the film, Michael kills the police captain and Sollozzo. Michael is confident and fearless. In the moments before he pulls the trigger, the camera stays focused on his face as if expecting him to reveal fear, hesitation, and a change of heart, but he does not waver and does not realize that he is on his way to becoming the new godfather.

What follows is Michael's exile in Sicily away from Kay and his family. In danger of retaliation even in Sicily, he is protected by two body guards and a don in Sicily; however, for Michael, it is an intermission in the war. Nino Rota's romantic "Love Theme from *The Godfather*" plays. Even among the U.S. soldiers who are leaving the country they liberated, Michael looks and behaves more like a Sicilian than an American. Much of the time it is a pastoral life spent in quietude. While exploring the countryside around his family's home, he meets his future wife. As in all of Michael's scenes, he shows his fearlessness even when discussing the woman who "struck him with a thunderbolt" with her father.

Connie calls Sonny when she is beaten by her husband. Sonny finds him and beats him in the middle of the street. When Connie calls him again for his help, Sonny drives out to rescue her but gets caught by an enemy family at a toll booth. Michael's rhapsody in the countryside is also at risk. He is told to move to another location. When his wife decides to drive them and turns the key, a car bomb intended for Michael explodes, killing her.

Tom drinks quietly, preparing to deliver the latest, sorrowful news when Don Vito, bandaged and still healing, comes into the room. Corleone is visibly hurt by the news, and after visiting Amerigo Bonasera's (Salvatore Corsitto) mortuary to ensure that Sonny will look his best at his funeral, he sets up a meeting between the five families. Don Corleone promises a truce, saying that he will forego any vengeance he is entitled to and that he will not fight the integration of the drug trade into the mob business, but for this he requires Michael's safe return. After his safe return and being home for more than a year, Michael meets Kay again and tells her that he has moved into the family business, saying, "In five years the family will be completely legitimate." His intent is to move the family from olive oil into casinos.

Michael visits Las Vegas, where his brother Fredo has been learning the casino industry. There, Fredo escorts Michael and a few others into a casino room where Johnny Fontane, a small band, and a number of girls are waiting for him. Michael insists that the band and girls leave. Michael gives Fontane a contract to sign. He will perform at their casino once it is theirs and convince his famous friends to perform as well. While Fontane seems uncomfortable about signing, he knows he must. Moe Greene (Alex Rocco), the casino's owner, arrives. Michael tells him that they are buying him out. He responds, "The Corleone family wants to buy me out. I buy you out. You don't buy me out." Fredo defends Greene to Michael, although Greene obviously treats him with contempt. Michael tells Greene to name his price, and once Greene leaves, he tells Fredo to never take sides with anyone against the family again.

Later, after they make the request, Michael refuses to give the caporegimes, Clemenza and Tessio, the freedom to start their own families. Don Vito tells Michael that the person who sets up a meeting with the Tattaglias will be the traitor and the meeting a pretext for assignation. He also reveals that he had hoped Michael could have an honest, albeit powerful, position, like a governor or senator. In a poignant scene, and lacking the violence and fury of the other deaths in the film, Don Vito dies from a heart attack in his garden while playing with his grandson. After Don Vito's funeral, Salvatore Tessio (Abe Vigoda) is revealed as the traitor.

The last moments of the film show Michael's mastery of the family business. In a series of parallel, intercut scenes, while Michael becomes the godfather of Connie's child, his men assassinate Barzini, the traitor Tessio, Moe Greene, and the lawyer. After the baptism, Michael visits Carlo (Gianni Russo). Michael tells him that he has to pay for setting up his brother Sonny and that he is being sent to Las Vegas; ostensibly, on the way to the airport, Carlo is killed in the car.

Connie accuses Michael of killing Carlo. She is pulled away from him, but Kay follows him and asks if it is true. He allows her to ask this one question about business, telling her that it is not true. Relieved, she walks into another room. Michael's caporegimes congratulate him on his success. From a distance, Kay realizes that Michael has lied to her. The door closes and the steel-hardened Michael has officially become the new godfather. The family business is family, and business is personal. The Corleone's estate is sold and the family continues to move west as American opportunities open up there.

The Godfather has become an American classic, often appearing in the number-two spot in the American Film Institute's top 100 movies listing, after Orson Welles's *Citizen Kane*. It has held this position for decades and left a significant legacy with the American epic gangster film. JMW

Bibliography

Cavallero, Jonathan J. *Hollywood's Italian American Filmmakers: Capra, Scorsese, Savoca, Coppola, and Tarantino*. Urbana: University of Illinois Press, 2011.

Hill, Rodney. *The Francis Ford Coppola Encyclopedia*. Lanham, MD: Rowman & Littlefield, 2010.

Puzo, Mario. *The Godfather*. New York: Putnam, 1969.

THE GODFATHER PART II (1974)

Director: Francis Ford Coppola
Writers: Francis Ford Coppola, Mario Puzo. Based on the novel by Mario Puzo.
Producers: Francis Ford Coppola, Gray Frederickson, Fred Roos (Paramount Pictures, The Coppola Company)
Cinematographer: Gordon Willis
Editors: Barry Malkin, Richard Marks, Peter Zinner
Art Direction: Dean Tavoularis, Angelo P. Graham, George R. Nelson
Costumes: Theadora Van Runkle
Music: Nino Rota, Carmine Coppola
Cast: Michael Corleone: Al Pacino. Tom Hagen: Robert Duvall. Kay: Diane Keaton. Vito Corleone: Robert De Niro. Alfredo "Fredo" Corleone: John Cazale. Connie Corleone: Talia Shire. Hyman Roth: Lee Strasberg. Frankie Pentangeli: Michael V. Gazzo. Francesco "Don Cheech" Ciccio: Giuseppe Sillato. Senator Patrick Geary: G. D. Spradlin. Johnny Ola: Dominic Chianese. Don Fanucci: Gaston Moschi. Peter Clemenza: Bruno Kirby. Bussetta: Amerigo Tot. Al Neri: Richard Bright

AA: Best Supporting Actor (Robert De Niro), Best Art Direction–Set Decoration (Dean Tavoularis, Angelo P. Graham, George R. Nelson), Best Director (Francis Ford Coppola), Best Music–Original Dramatic Score (Nino Rota, Carmine Coppola), Best Picture (Francis Ford Coppola, Gray Frederickson, Fred Roos), Best Writing–Screenplay Adapted From Other Material (Francis Ford Coppola, Mario Puzo)
AAN: Best Leading Actor (Al Pacino), Best Supporting Actor (Michael V. Gazzo), Best Supporting Actor (Lee Strasberg), Best Supporting Actress (Talia Shire), Best Costume Design (Theadora Van Runkle)
BAFTA Award: Best Actor (Al Pacino)
DVD: Paramount Pictures, 2008. The Coppola Restoration.
Blu-ray: Paramount Pictures, 2010. The Coppola Restoration.
Duration: 200 minutes

This sequel to the successful *Godfather* crime drama tells the story of two godfathers, twenty years of the father, Vito (Robert De Niro), and ten years of the son, Michael (Al Pacino). The film's parallel structure moves between and compares the rise of the family and its business under Vito and its descent under Michael. Vito Andolini is born in Italy, immigrates to the United States, and begins a family and a family business. After Vito's death, Michael moves the family to Nevada, and the dynasty falls apart. What should be the crowning achievement to Vito's success instead fails under Michael's leadership. The powerful contrasts are one reason that this was the first motion picture sequel to win the Academy Award for Best Picture.

The film opens with Michael Corleone receiving a kiss on the hand as the new godfather. It then moves to an empty chair, a presence and an absence of the former godfather, a chair that will be difficult for Michael to fill. The film cuts to 1901, the year during which nine-year-old Vito's father, Antonio Andolini, was murdered for an insult to local mafia chieftain Francesco "Don Cheech" Ciccio (Giuseppe Sillato). At Andolini's funeral procession in a dry creek bed, shots are fired. Paolo, his brother, is shot, leaving Vito the only male heir. His mother takes him to Don Ciccio, who sits in a big chair in front of his house. She wants Vito protected and claims that Vito is dimwitted and weak. Ciccio remains convinced that he will seek revenge. She draws a knife, and Vito runs away. Ciccio's men shoot her. Friends hide Vito in a mule basket and transport him in dim twilight and fog to avoid detection by two of Ciccio's men. He eventually arrives in the United States at Ellis Island. Coppola uses a long tracking shot of hundreds of stoic immigrants from throughout Europe. An immigration officer puts Vito's last name as Corleone—the town in Italy where he is from. Vito is found to have small pox and is quarantined alone in a small room in the shadow of the Statue of Liberty and the land of opportunity.

The film jumps from 1901 to 1958, to Vito's grandson Anthony Corleone's first Holy Communion being held on his family's estate on Lake Tahoe, Nevada. In a scene reminiscent of the wedding scene in the first *Godfather* film, hundreds attend the celebration next to the lake, dancing in a pavilion. Connie (Talia Shire), arriving a week later than planned, must wait in line to see her brother. Senator Patrick Geary (G. D. Spradlin) speaks to the party. He thanks the Corleones for the "magnificent check" to a university. In his office, Michael introduces his lawyer Tom to Geary. Senator Geary wants to speak to Michael one-on-one, but Michael says it would insult Tom. The senator knows the Corleones want the Tropicana. Geary needs a payment for the new hotel. "I intend to squeeze," he says. "You try to pass yourselves off as decent Americans. . . . I despise your masquerade. The dishonest way you pose yourself." Michael says, "We're both part of the same hypocrisy but don't think it applies to my family." Michael tells him to put up the license fee himself. Geary laughs and walks out. In contrast to the tension inside, behind Michael as he sits behind the desk speaking to Senator Geary, behind a plate glass window, people walk between the trees. The mottled pattern of the glass is reminiscent of a Manet painting, reinforcing the theme of hidden hypocrisies.

Michael tells Tom to wait outside when Johnny Ola (Dominic Chianese) arrives. Tom only handles certain parts of the family business, he says. This is a change and possible insult to Tom when viewed in comparison to the scene with Senator Geary, but Michael has secret plans, even from Tom. Ola works with Hyman Roth (Lee Strasberg), who has interests in casinos in Nevada and Cuba.

A sign that Michael's family leadership moves from its roots, he hires a band that does not know Italian standards. Frankie Pentangeli (Michael V. Gazzo) asks them to play an Italian song, and instead they play "Pop Goes the Weasel." Michael refuses Pentangeli's call for assistance with the Rosatos because they work with Roth. "Your father never trusted Hyman Roth," Pentangeli says.

Kay is pregnant again, and she reminds Michael that seven years ago he said he would be "completely legit" in five years. Emphasizing the distance between Michael and his family, Michael finds on his bed Anthony's drawing of him in a limousine with boxes to be checked off indicating whether he likes it. Machine-gun fire comes through the windows into the room. What was an idyllic home on the lake is revealed to be a prison: in the darkness and rain, lights come on, revealing men with machine guns. Kay stares at Michael while she holds his child.

The film cuts to Vito Corleone in 1917, when he is attending a stage performance with a backdrop of the Statue of Liberty. Don Fanucci (Gaston Moschin), the "Black Hand," stands and blocks his view. After the play, Fanucci threatens the girl who was on the stage. Vito is intrigued, but he doesn't intervene. Later, a neighbor asks him to hide guns. This is Vito's introduction to Peter Clemenza (Bruno Kirby). Vito loses his job at a deli when Fanucci insists that his neighbor receive a job. Vito seems to take the loss graciously. Vito talks to Clemenza, who says he knows how to return the favor holding the guns. With Vito following, Clemenza breaks into a house and steals a rug. They install it in Vito's apartment and put his son Sonny on top of it. Vito's new criminal career is intimately tied to his family. Later, when Fanucci finds out that Vito, Salvatore Tessio (Abe Vigoda), and Clemenza have been working jobs, Fanucci tells Vito to pay him a cut of what they stole. Vito says that he'll take less, and his partners agree to let him try to offer $50, not $200. "I'll make him an offer he won't refuse," Vito says.

During the Feast of San Rocco, Vito follows Fanucci from the rooftop and meets him on the stairs outside his apartment. Vito shoots him twice. The towel he uses as a silencer catches fire, and the film cuts to fireworks in the street. He shoots Fanucci in the head, takes his money, and throws the guns down some chimney pipes. Back at home, sitting on the stoop in front of his house watching the festival, Vito holds his youngest son. "Michael, your father loves you very much," he says. In a later scene, Vito returns to Sicily and visits Don Ciccio, pretending that he's bringing him a gift from the United States. Because Ciccio is now much older and nearly deaf, Vito has to yell into his ear that he is the son of Antonio Andolini. Vito cuts Ciccio, leaving him dead where his mother had previously tried to kill him. For Don Vito, the family business is family.

Michael takes a train to Miami and then drives to Hyman Roth's house. Roth lives in a modest, sparsely furnished house and is watching a football game when Michael arrives. Roth lives an ordinary suburban life, watching football and eating tuna fish. Roth agrees that Michael can kill Pentangeli. "He's small potatoes," Roth says.

Michael goes to Frankie Pentangeli's house, which is decorated for Christmas. Pentangeli has Vito's old office. A stuffed chair where Vito's large desk had been symbolizes the changes that have taken place since Vito was godfather. "I want you to help me take my revenge," Michael says. Roth tried to have him killed, but he does not know who the traitor is. When Pentangeli goes to meet the Rosato brothers to make a deal with them, he is garroted. The traitor is revealed to the audience when Michael's brother Fredo (John Cazale), sleeping in his bed, receives a call from Johnny Ola. Ola says Pentangeli is taking the deal and will meet with the Rosato brothers. Fredo quickly gets off the phone without answering his questions. Even his wife doesn't know.

Tom Hagen (Robert Duvall) is called in to assist Senator Geary at a brothel (operated by Fredo) when Geary finds that the prostitute he was in bed with is dead. Tom tells him that he should call his office and say he's staying with Michael at Lake Tahoe. The Corleones engineered the leverage they now have over him.

In Havana, the president of Cuba holds a meeting with representatives from General Fruit, UT&T, Pan American Mining, and South American Sugar. Hyman Roth and Michael Corleone also attend. The president passes around a solid gold telephone that UT&T gave him. He assures them that the rebels will be pushed out. "We will tolerate no guerillas in the casinos or the swimming pools," he dictates. On the way to Roth's sixty-seventh birthday party, Michael sees a man blow himself up for Fidel Castro and begins to doubt that the government will hold. An ill man, Roth promises to turn his Havana interests over to Michael upon this death.

Fredo lies to Michael about knowing Johnny Ola. Fredo says he was upset because he was passed over when Michael became don. Michael needs him to show Senator Geary a good time in Havana when he arrives. Michael tells him, "It was Roth who tried to kill me in my home." He adds that Roth won't live to see the New Year. Michael meets with Roth again and asks who gave the go-ahead to kill Frankie Pentangeli. Roth tells the story of his affection for Vito and for Moe Greene. "He was a great man. Someone put a bullet through his eye," he says. Roth did not ask who gave the order because it had nothing to do with business.

Fredo takes Geary and others to a Havana club, where he accidently reveals that Ola told him about the place. Michael realizes that Fredo is the traitor and has his bodyguard, Bussetta (Amerigo Tot), kill Ola. Roth becomes ill and is taken to the hospital. Bussetta follows him, but soldiers kill him before he can kill Roth. As Michael and Fredo try to escape the chaos of the government's collapse, Michael kisses Fredo. He says, "I know it was you, Fredo. You broke my heart." Michael asks him to leave Havana with him, but Fredo refuses.

Tom reveals to Michael that Kay had a miscarriage and lost the baby. "Was it a boy?" is Michael's only question. Tom says Fredo got out of Havana and went to New York City. Michael wants Fredo to know that he can come back. Michael comes home to a dark, quiet house. Kay is sewing, bent over the machine when he comes in. Michael doesn't talk to her. After being held in the house and having the miscarriage, he can't speak to her. His mother, who lives at the house, tells him, "You can never lose your family," she says. "Times are changing," he replies.

Michael Corleone is brought before a senate hearing on mob activities, using Tom Hagen as his lawyer. When Michael is on the stand, a senator accuses him of killing Sergeant McClusky and Virgil "The Turk" Sollozzo. Senator Geary, one of the committee members, says that Italian Americans are patriots of the United States. He pays part of his debt to the Corleone family. In a surprise appearance, Frankie Pentangeli plans to testify against the Corleones. He changes his mind when his brother Vicenzo enters the hearing room. Pentangeli is taken to prison.

Fredo tells Michael that he did not know that his work with Ola would lead to the hit. Seeing him as a threat, Michael cuts Fredo out of his life but promises not to let anything happen to him while their mother is alive. Michael talks to Kay, who says she is leaving him. She says to him, "You're blind, Michael. . . . It wasn't a miscarriage—it was an abortion—like our marriage, it was unholy and evil. . . . It was a son, and I had it killed because this must all end." Later, at their mother's funeral, Fredo stands by her casket with Connie. She asks Michael to let Fredo back in the family. Michael hugs Fredo, looking at Al Neri (Richard Bright), who understands his command. Kay tries to enter the house, but Connie tells her to leave. In a repeated motif throughout the three films, Kay waits for Michael in a doorway. He shuts the door on her.

Michael wants Roth, who is returning from a failed attempt to emigrate to Israel, met at the airport. Michael says, "If history has taught us anything it's that it's possible to kill anyone." Tom sees Frankie Pentangeli at the prison. Tom tells him that the families of Roman traitors who committed suicide were taken care of. This sets up the film's ending, which is similar to the original film. Roth arrives at the Miami airport, and, in a scene reminiscent of the Jack Ruby assassination, the assassin is killed. Pentangeli cuts his wrists in a prison tub. Al Neri kills Fredo in a fishing boat as he says a "Hail Mary," his technique for ensuring a good catch. The film flashes back to all the Corleone siblings sitting together at the dining room table. Michael announces that he joined the military because of the Pearl Harbor attack. "Country isn't your blood," Sonny reminds him. The film concludes with the image of Michael's darkly shadowed face and his memories of a lost family. JMW

Bibliography

Cavallero, Jonathan J. *Hollywood's Italian American Filmmakers: Capra, Scorsese, Savoca, Coppola, and Tarantino.* Urbana: University of Illinois Press, 2011.

Hill, Rodney. *The Francis Ford Coppola Encyclopedia.* Lanham, MD: Rowman & Littlefield, 2010.

THE GODFATHER PART III (1990)

DIRECTOR: Francis Ford Coppola

WRITERS: Francis Ford Coppola, Mario Puzo

PRODUCERS: Francis Ford Coppola, Gray Frederickson, Fred Fuchs, Nicholas Gage (Paramount Pictures, Zoetrope Studios)

CINEMATOGRAPHER: Gordon Willis

EDITORS: Lisa Fruchtman, Barry Malkin, Walter Murch

ART DIRECTION: Dean Tavoularis, Gary Fettis

MUSIC: Carmine Coppola

CAST: Michael Corleone: Al Pacino. Kay Adams Michelson: Diane Keaton. Connie Corleone Rizzi: Talia Shire. Vincent Mancini: Andy Garcia. Don Altobello: Eli Wallach. Joey Zasa: Joe Mantegna. Mary Corleone: Sofia Coppola. Anthony "Tony" Vio Corleone:

Franc D'Ambrosio. Grace Hamilton: Bridget Fonda. B. J. Harrison: George Hamilton. Lionele Tommasino: Vittorio Duse. Cardinal Lamberto: Raf Vallone. Licio Lucchesi: Enzo Robutti. Frederick Keinszig: Helmut Berger. Al Neri: Richard Bright. Calo: Franco Citti

AA: None

AAN: Best Picture (Francis Ford Coppola), Best Supporting Actor (Andy Garcia), Best Art Direction–Set Decoration (Dean Tavoularis, Gary Fettis), Best Cinematography (Gordon Willis), Best Director (Francis Ford Coppola), Best Film Editing (Lisa Fruchtman, Barry Malkin, Walter Murch), Best Music–Original Song (Carmine Coppola and John Bettis for "Promise Me You'll Remember")

DVD: Paramount Pictures, 2008. The Coppola Restoration.

BLU-RAY: Paramount Pictures, 2008. The Coppola Restoration (includes all three films).

DURATION: 162 minutes

This film is the denouement of Don Michael Corleone's career as godfather, detailing the end of a mobster's life, which is ignominious and fruitless. His motivations turn from crime to a legitimacy, personal peace, redemption, and recovery of his family. Instead, he finds corruption all around him, as he says late in the film, "The higher I go, the more crooked it becomes." Not designed as the nostalgic and dramatic mafia film the first two films had been, and unfortunately advertised as the third film in the trilogy, director Francis Ford Coppola saw it as an epilogue to the other two.[1] The film succeeds when viewed with this in mind.

The film opens in Lake Tahoe, Nevada, where the once beautiful Corleone house is in ruins. The sun rises on an empty house, symbolic of Michael's life and what he wants to recover. Michael, now living in New York, has donated millions to the Catholic Church, for which he will receive the Church's highest honor, the Commander of the Order of St. Sebastian. In a letter, Michael asks his children to come to the ceremony and to try to persuade their mother, whom he had shut out of his life, to attend.

At the Basilica of Saint Patrick's Old Cathedral in New York, Michael has a flashback to his brother Fredo's death. Some of his family believes his story that Fredo drowned. His memories of his old life fuel his desire for peace in his life. His adult children, Mary (Sofia Coppola) and Tony (Franc D'Ambrosio), sit up front. Joey Zasa (Joe Mantegna), who now runs the Corleone business, sits at the back of the ceremony.

At the party where guests celebrate the papal award, Vincent Mancini (Andy Garcia), Sonny Corleone's illegitimate son, arrives and is immediately asked to leave but is then allowed to stay. Mary is attracted to Vincent and reminds him that they met when she was eight and he fifteen. Kay attends with her new husband and son Tony. Reporter Grace Hamilton (Bridget Fonda) asks the Corleone lawyer about their connection to the mob and organized crime in Nevada.

Kay wants to speak to Michael about their son, who wants to be in music, but Michael insists that he finish his law degree. Kay says, "Tony knows you killed Fredo." "I did what I could to protect you from the horrors of this world," Michael replies. Kay responds, "But you became my horror." Michael sits in dark corner and says he'll let Tony go.

As in the first two films, in spite of not being don, Michael still sees people during important parties. Don Altobello (Eli Wallach) comes to pay his respects. He says he wants to attach his name to Michael's foundation for $1 million. Zasa comes to give

Michael an award, which seems to mock the Church's honor. Zasa wants Vincent to stop being a "stone in my shoe." He continues, saying, "He thinks he's related to you—a bastard." Michael tells Vincent to make his peace with Zasa, but Vincent bites Zasa's ear. When a family portrait is taken, Michael asks Vincent to join the group photo. Later, Zasa sends two assassins to Vincent's apartment, where Grace is in bed with him. One pulls a knife on her, but Vincent kills both.

A bishop speaks to Michael about problems with the Vatican bank. Michael is willing to help by depositing $500 million in Vatican Immobiliare, but the pope would have to approve Michael's leadership. B. J. Harrison (George Hamilton), Michael's lawyer, says Michael is the new Rockefeller, a great philanthropist. It could become a European multinational corporation. The bishop asks for $600 million, and Michael agrees. Other investors resist the idea of a former mobster leading the Vatican's company. Because the pope's condition is grave, the vote must be ratified soon.

The investors' concern was not without merit. At New York's China Bowl restaurant, Altobello tells Michael that some of his former mob associates want to be part of Immobiliare. Michael will not allow it, wanting it to be a legitimate business. Michael says he will call a meeting so there are no debts or grudges to keep the peace.

Vincent shows Mary around the family's old neighborhood. While they speak, a woman asks him to get rid of Joe Zasa because of his drug sales. Mary asks Vincent, "Did Michael kill his own brother?" Vincent says "no." During a later visit, Vinnie shows her how to roll gnocchi, and they express their love for one another.

Michael and Vincent travel to the meeting in Atlantic City in a helicopter. Michael dissolves their business relationships when he pays out their shares in checks. Zasa says his family took all the risks and made Corleone rich. When Zasa leaves, Altobello follows him. There is a hit on the building from a helicopter, and most of the mob bosses die. Vincent pulls Michael out and steals a car, barely escaping with their lives.

Recovering in his kitchen, Michael says, "Just when I thought I was out. They pull me back in." An allusion to *Oedipus Rex*, Michael says, "The true enemy has not shown his face." Michael's true enemy is himself. Michael has a diabetic attack and then a stroke, and then he drops into a coma. Seeing herself in charge, Connie gives Vincent permission to kill Zasa.

Reminiscent of the festival scene in *The Godfather Part II*, when Vito Corleone kills a mob boss, Vincent follows Connie's orders. Zasa talks to the press during a street celebration of the Feast of San Gennaro, but he is disturbed by one of Vincent's men, who is sitting on a car that is being raffled. Vincent, dressed as a policeman, rides up on a horse and shoots Zasa. Afterward, from his hospital bed, Michael says "I command this family. It was not what I wanted." Michael tells Vincent to leave his daughter. "It's too dangerous. When they come they'll come at what you love." Altobello tells Michael to retire, saying, "Treachery is everywhere."

When there is too much trouble at home, Michael retreats to Sicily. Don Lionele Tommasino (Vittorio Duse) welcomes him and they talk about Altobello, who gave the order for the massacre. Cardinal Lamberto (Raf Vallone) is influential and may be able to help. "Politics and crime are the same thing," Tommasino says. At a gathering honoring Michael, Tony sings the film's love theme. As he sings, Michael remembers his first wedding. Later, Michael tells Mary and son about his first wife. He tells Mary that she cannot see Vincent anymore, but she refuses. Mary looks at photos of Michael's first wife, paralleling the two characters and their fates.

Michael tells Vincent to sell his soul to Altobello, so Vincent meets with Altobello, who welcomes him and introduces him to Don Licio Lucchesi (Enzo Robutti). Lucchesi is the power behind Altobello, who tells him, "You understand guns. Finance is a gun."

Michael comes closest to a rehealed family when Kay arrives by train. He, Mary, and Connie meet her at the station. Later, Michael gives Anthony the drawing shown in *The Godfather Part II* that he had drawn of his dad in a car. Michael drives Kay through the countryside, pausing to watch a wedding in Corleone. He asks for Kay's forgiveness, telling her he had a different destiny planned. Every night he dreams about his lost wife and children, but Michael's plans go awry when news arrives that Tommasino is dead, Cardinal Lamberto has been elected as pope, and Frederick Keinszig (Helmut Berger) is missing, apparently with money from Immobiliare. Kay is shown through a doorway—and she walks farther into the room. As in the previous films, doorways separate Kay and Michael, emphasizing their distance.

At Tommasino's casket, Michael prays, asking for a chance to redeem himself. Vincent reports that Lucchesi controls everything and that he has sent an assassin after Michael. Vincent agrees to give up Mary, and in return he becomes "Vincent Corleone" and the new godfather.

At Anthony's performance in the *Cavalleria rusticana*, Vincent ends his relationship with Mary, telling her to love someone else. The assassin slips into the audience with priests. Connie gives Altobello a cannoli, which he makes her taste before he eats it. In a series of parallel cuts comparing the opera and the mob, in an orgy of death reminiscent of the earlier *Godfather* films, Calo (Franco Citti) kills Lucchesi with his own glasses, Al Neri kills the archbishop, the pope dies from a poisoned drink, and Altobello dies from eating the poisoned cannoli. Attempting to leave the theater, Michael and Mary are shot on the steps of the establishment. Mary dies immediately.

The film cuts to many years later, when Michael's hair is gray. He is sitting alone on a chair in a barren yard. He fondly remembers dancing with Mary and Kay. He dies alone and falls out of the chair. Michael's ambitions, as detailed in *The Godfather* and The *Godfather Part II*, sacrifice his family. He is unable to buy forgiveness and never achieves his desired peace. The film's structure is similar to that of the other two, but, as mentioned earlier, it is unfortunately advertised as the third part of a trilogy instead of a coda; Michael's fall is more important than Vincent's rise as godfather. JMW

Note

1. "Commentary," *The Godfather Part III*, directed by Francis Ford Coppola (Paramount Pictures, 2008), DVD. According to Coppola's commentary, the title of the film was intended to be *The Death of Michael Corleone.*

Bibliography

Cavallero, Jonathan J. *Hollywood's Italian American Filmmakers: Capra, Scorsese, Savoca, Coppola, and Tarantino.* Urbana: University of Illinois Press, 2011.

Hill, Rodney. *The Francis Ford Coppola Encyclopedia.* Lanham, MD: Rowman & Littlefield, 2010.

GONE WITH THE WIND (1939)

Directors: Victor Fleming, George Cukor, Sam Wood

Writers: Sidney Howard, Oliver H. P. Garrett, Ben Hecht, John William Van Druten, Jo Swerling, David O. Selznick. Based on the novel by Margaret Mitchell.

Producer: David O. Selznick (Selznick International Pictures, MGM)

Cinematographer: Ernest Haller, Ray Rennahan, Lee Garmes

Editor: Hall C. Kern, James E. Newcom

Production Design: Willam Cameron Menzies

Art Direction: Lyne Wheeler

Set Decoration: Howard Bristol

Costumes: Walter Plunkett

Directors: Victor Fleming, George Cukor, Sam Wood

Writers: Sidney Howard, Oliver H. P. Garrett, Ben Hecht, John William

Van Druten, Jo Swerling, David O. Selznick. Based on the novel by Margaret Mitchell.
PRODUCER: David O. Selznick (Selznick International Pictures, MGM)
CINEMATOGRAPHER: Ernest Haller, Ray Rennahan, Lee Garmes
EDITOR: Hall C. Kern, James E. Newcom
PRODUCTION DESIGN: Willam Cameron Menzies
ART DIRECTION: Lyne Wheeler
SET DECORATION: Howard Bristol
COSTUMES: Walter Plunkett
MUSIC: Max Steiner
SPECIAL EFFECTS: R. D. Musgrave, Lee Zavitz
VISUAL EFFECTS: Jack Cosgrove
CAST: Rhett Butler: Clark Cable. Scarlett O'Hara: Vivien Leigh. Melanie Wilkes: Olivia de Havilland. Ashley Wilkes: Leslie Howard. Gerald O'Hara: Thomas Mitchell. Ellen O'Hara: Barbara O'Neil. Suellen O'Hara: Evelyn Keyes. Carreen O'Hara: Anne Rutherford. Mammy: Hattie McDaniel. Pork: Oscar Polk. Prissy: Butterfly McQueen. John Wilkes: Howard C. Hickman. Doctor Meade: Harry Davenport. Frank Kennedy: Carroll Nye. Belle Watling: Ona Munson. Charles Hamilton: Rand Brooks
AA: Best Picture (Selznick International Pictures, MGM), Best Director (Victor Fleming), Best Leading Actress (Vivien Leigh), Best Supporting Actress (Hattie McDaniel), Best Cinematography–Color (Ernest Haller, Ray Rennahan, Lee Garmes), Best Art Direction (Lyne Wheeler), Best Film Editing (Hall C. Kern, James E. Newcom), Best Writing–Screenplay (Sidney Howard)
AAN: Best Leading Actor (Clark Gable), Best Supporting Actress (Olivia de Havilland), Best Sound Recording (Thomas T. Moulton), Best Music–Original Score (Max Steiner), Best Special Effects (Jack Cosgrove)
DVD: Warner Home Video, 2009. Seventieth Anniversary Ultimate Collector's Edition
BLU-RAY: Warner Home Video, 2010. The Scarlett Edition.
DURATION: 238 minutes

Gone with the Wind is the definitive American epic, the first big epic production of American cinema (aside from, of course, *The Birth of a Nation*, popular but disgraced by history for its racist theme), telling a story that is entirely American, on American soil, about a crucial period in American history, the defeat of the South and its aftermath during the Civil War (1860–1865). It took producer David O. Selznick several years to mount this enormous production after securing the rights to film the novel from author Margaret Mitchell for a rather meager amount of $50,000 (Selznick later gave Mitchell another $50,000[1]). While the role of Rhett Butler was given to Clark Gable by popular consensus,[2] hundreds of actresses were considered for the title role of Scarlett O'Hara, among them Bette Davis, Katharine Hepburn, Paulette Godard, and Jean Arthur. But the role eventually went to Vivien Leigh, an English actress, still untested in Hollywood, but ultimately proving the right choice.

In addition to Sidney Howard, who produced a first draft of a screenplay that would last five and a half hours, several other prominent writers in Hollywood worked on the script, which was eventually trimmed down to just under four hours (238 minutes) by Selznick, who took over much of the writing of the shooting script.[3] The movie was originally to be directed by George Cukor, who started and was doing a credible job but quit suddenly after he felt he was losing control of direction. He was replaced by Victor Fleming, who appeared in the credits, but who quit and was replaced by Sam Wood. Fleming came back toward the end of the production. The film premiered in Atlanta on 15 December 1939, at Lowe's Theater, with the presence of all the major stars and much pomp and ceremony. It was subsequently shown in New York's Radio City Music Hall and Los Angeles, and it became a sensation in the United States and worldwide. The movie was rereleased several times on the screen and on television, and it was restored and reissued in 1989. It continues to attract large audiences with DVD and Blu-ray editions.

The story is told from the Southern point of view and centers on a great romance that both flourishes and dims during the tumultuous events of that era. It is told with splendor, was filmed at an unprecedented expense ($3.9 million), is based on an enormously popular novel, and features some of the brightest movie stars of that era as protagonists. Even today, it stands as a monument of American moviemaking. *Gone with the Wind* broke records at the Academy Awards (winning eight of thirteen nominations) and in box-office receipts (earning more than $77 million), and it held the record for profits for nearly thirty-five years, when it was topped by Francis Ford Coppola's *The Godfather* (1972), another American epic of a different kind. The total profits from showings, sales, and video rentals are estimated at $2 billion in today's money.

Gone with the Wind is both a romance and a chronicle of the destruction of the Civil War, but it is not an epic that shows battles, rather the effects of those battles—the famous crane shot of countless wounded and dying in Atlanta's square—and the devastation caused by war. The film depicts the burning of Atlanta, the subsequent anarchy during retreat, the depopulation of the South, and the hunger and exploitation that followed. *Gone with the Wind* mostly concerns itself with showing a society that used to live in a hypnotic state of delusions, dreaming that things would go along as they always were—the rich plantation owners would continue their wealthy lifestyles, the Southern belles would continue to be courted by wealthy suitors, and the black slaves, owned by these benign (in the movie) owners, would continue their loyalty—something the film attempts to demonstrate. The black servants of these owners are loyal, loving, and caring for their masters, and they deem themselves lucky to be so well treated. They, too, live in a delusion, and the crumbling of this world is so sudden and so appalling that they seem to bemoan the bad luck of their owners, rather than their own plight. And when a new world emerges out of the ruins, people in it begin the labor of rebuilding with a renewed sense of pride, without quite understanding that the old society has been wiped out and that the winds of change have brought both good and evil.

This long epic comes in two parts. The first, about 105 minutes in length, is a sweeping saga of that war, which begins with a note of optimism on the part of the wealthy plantation owners surrounding Tara, a magnificent mansion owned by the proud but mild-mannered Gerald O'Hara (Thomas Mitchell), whose daughter Scarlett is the center of attention of many neighboring beaus, scions of aristocratic families who band together, confident of the win. Among them is Rhett Butler, a rich adventurer from Charleston and possibly a fugitive of the law who talks of the harsh realities of facing an enemy armed with big guns and a navy, a message that repels his hosts. But he is strongly attracted to the tempestuous Scarlett, even as he witnesses her brush with Ashley Wilkes (Leslie Howard), of the neighboring Twelve Oaks, who tells her in no uncertain terms that he will marry his cousin Melanie (Olivia de Havilland), better suited to him by temperament. Butler's sarcastic overtures infuriate the egotistical and spoiled Scarlett, who vows never to have anything to do with him. But the tide turns when her hasty marriage out of revenge to Melanie's brother, Charles Hamilton (Rand Brooks), ends with the latter's death soon after the start of the war, and the freshly widowed Scarlett dances with Rhett at a ball intended to raise funds for the fighting army.

From that point onward, her romance with Rhett progresses by fits and starts, complicating and involving the lives of other people. When Scarlett travels to

Atlanta to visit Melanie, who is having a baby, while Ashley is in the army, she comes face-to-face with the tragedy of defeat, as she—and the viewer—witnesses the horrid conditions at the hospital—rows of wounded men lying unattended to and dying in the town square, while crowds flee in panic. Scarlett has gone to town to implore Dr. Meade to help her deliver Melanie's baby, but he is too busy tending to the wounded and dying and tells her to do it herself. Taking charge, Scarlett delivers the child and then sends word to Rhett, who is found in a brothel run by Belle Watling (Ona Munson), a madam with a "golden heart" and one of the most colorful characters in the movie. She helps him find a horse and cart, which Rhett uses to drive the three women and the infant through the streets of Atlanta, passing close to an ammunition depot about to explode. In possibly the most spectacular scene in the film, the viewer is treated to the extraordinarily staged burning of Atlanta, a signal moment of epic spectacle in the history of the movies. Remorseful for not having joined the army, Rhett leaves them at a certain point, and Scarlett drives the cart to Tara, where she finds her mother dead, her father gone mad, and Tara in ruins.

The second part of the movie starts by showing a resolute Scarlett having taken charge of the plantation, where some of the remaining servants and her two sisters still live and all do fieldwork just to survive. Scarlett shows her mettle when she shoots a deserter who attempts to rape her, and she buries him with the help of the ill but courageous Melanie. What follows is a succession of events of personal relations, and the war is left to the background, although not forgotten. Needing money to pay taxes, Scarlett finds Rhett, who is broke and in prison, and then marries (her second marriage) Frank Kennedy (Carroll Nye), a former neighbor who is courting one of her sisters and who has just started a lumber business that is thriving, as reconstruction has begun. Scarlett takes control of the establishment and prospers, but she is still unhappy, for when Ashley returns from the war, he makes it clear to her that he will be faithful to his wife. The knowledge that she has been rejected embitters Scarlett, and she never forgives Ashley—and neither does she forget him—and her feelings of resentment do not allow her to appreciate married life with Rhett, who proposes again and this time is accepted.

But Scarlett's stubborn persistence on holding on to the illusion of loving another man poisons their relationship and, directly or indirectly, becomes the cause of her ruined marriage and the loss of both her children with Rhett, one yet unborn. Whether Scarlett knows her own heart—as the dying Melanie tells her that she really loves Rhett—remains something of a mystery. The romance is doomed, and it is only possible to imagine that this woman, whose indomitable spirit helps her survive her fatal flaws, will rise again out of the ashes of her self-imposed destruction. In the end, Scarlett is like the South: flaws or not, it is a place with individuals in it that hold on to their own values—or disvalues—and rise, in new clothes, in a new political and social landscape, but with their old self. The film suggests that, despite changes brought about by violent events, illusions are hard to get rid of. They may be gone with the wind, and a new country may have emerged from the ashes of the old, but the willful, stubborn nature of old ways is still there—glitter and ruin merging into the image of modernity.

Scarlett is the embodiment of these values. She projects the image of an undying, stubborn force that will allow her to resurface, as she does wearing green curtains for a dress to impress Rhett and borrow the money she needs to pay the taxes to keep her old home. It is her undefeatable spirit that keeps Scarlett from being a despicable person. Her endless little tricks, evasions, quick dodges, and alluring smiles tend to keep her on course. It's the me, me, me that holds the center. A weaker and gentler person like Melanie dies; a fumbling and anachronistic Ashley is buried under irresolution; and Rhett, disgusted with the endless tricks and evasions of a worthless belle, finally leaves Scarlett. He, too, survives, for he has seen the very devil ("I was raised in hell," Scarlett tells him at one point).

Rhett is ultimately a decent man, and his amorality is a façade for his swagger. He helps, feels sorry, and has pity for the downtrodden, although he remains cynical about the South's chances. He sees change, but he also has paternal and family feelings, and he hopes that one day domestic bliss can be attained. He wants to possess a lively woman with an independent spirit and a little of the devil in her. He loves Scarlett, but his tolerance of her has limits—finally. Rhett knows that she will always be the same, and he leaves her with his famous, "Frankly, my dear, I don't give a damn." At this point, he doesn't. In actuality, he admits defeat. He cannot tame this stubborn, headstrong, egotistical woman who wants it all but does not appreciate it when she has it. There is no end to this dialectic.

The film, wisely, does not offer closure—or what appears to be a resolution isn't. *Casablanca*, also a story of separated lovers, offers a more satisfactory (and unsatisfactory) ending: Rick lets Ilsa go, but we know they both love one another. He concedes her to another man, for he knows she really belongs with the better man. Rhett is truly disgusted. He has loved a woman for what looks like a lifetime, and yet she is ungrateful, underhanded, and ready to go back to Ashley, or to have things go her own way. She will not relent and will not let things go. And she knows, as she vowed earlier when starving and uprooting and eating a carrot from the soil of Tara, that she will not be hungry again. The South flourishes, too. It has a better climate than the North, better beaches, old palatial homes, and rich history, and it is still cajoled and pampered by tourist waves attracted by both its humidity and lushness. Scarlett O'Hara is the immortal spirit of the South—old or new (or both), like it or not. As she says in her last monologue, sitting on the stairs, "I will go back to Tara." She will be a success, she will wait, and one day he, Rhett, will return to her. But the viewer knows better.

The film was a huge national and international success, but it was torn to shreds by revisionist critics. "Glossy, sentimental, chuckle-headed," Richard Schickel wrote in 1973, adding that the film lacks compelling imagery, that it is "not art," and that it lacks dialogue that "forever implants itself in the viewer's mind."[4] Writing in the same year, Andrew Sarris also dismisses the film as an empty spectacle, although he credits the "film's popular mandate around the world as the single most beloved entertainment ever produced." He adds that, "Selznick's flair for old-fashioned full-bodied narrative even as we pay lip service to the most anemic forms of celebration in the modern cinema." But Sarris, the ultimate admirer of Vivien Leigh, gives praise where praise is due: "Ultimately, there is Vivien Leigh's smile on the screen like a sliver of sunlight piercing the heart."[5] That last remark may also be the answer to the paradox of *Gone with the Wind*, which endures to this day, still gaining viewers, still seen in pristine condition by modern digital technology, still shown in classes.[6]

The question of whether it is art is now a moot point. There has never been a clear demarcation of what is or is not film art, and many art movies have been eclipsed just as much as any other film genre. Epics continue to be made of mixed art credentials—witness *Schindler's List* (1993), *Troy* (2004), and *Lincoln* (2012). But no other epic has reached the popular apotheosis of *Gone with the Wind*, and one ultimately has to answer for its durability.

One answer offered here is that *Gone with the Wind* is Vivien Leigh's movie all the way. She appears in practically every scene in the movie, from beginning to end. She is tied to three of the most important lines in the story: her unfulfilled love for Ashley; her marriage to Rhett, which tragically fails; and her root connection with Tara. The last is the most essential connection. It is Tara (the South) that breeds Scarlett. It is for Tara that Scarlett works at the low end of the story, when she nearly starves and tries by any means to preserve her home, and it is at Tara where she dreams of returning and renewing her life, and possibly her love. All other characters are defeated, dying or withdrawing into their own failed worlds. Everything around Scarlett is gone with the wind, but Tara will remain, and so will Scarlett, the Earth Goddess, the eternal signature of life. CS

Notes

1. Susan Sackett, *Box Office Hits: Hollywood's Most Successful Movies* (New York: Billboard Books, 1990).
2. Gable was under contract to MGM, but Selznick managed to secure his services through his personal ties with Louis M. Mayer, who negotiated distribution rights and a share of the profits. See Scott Siegel and Barbara Siegel, *The Encyclopedia of Hollywood* (New York: Facts on File, 1990), 280.
3. See "Special Features, *The Making of* Gone with the Wind," *Gone with the Wind*, directed by Victor Fleming (Warner Home Video, 2009), DVD.
4. Richard Schickel, "Glossy, Sentimental, Chuckle-Headed," *Atlantic Monthly* (Digital Edition), March 1973, www.theatlantic.com/past/docs/issues/73mar/schick.htm (19 September 2013).
5. Andrew Sarris, "The Moviest of All Movies," *Atlantic Monthly* (Digital Edition), March 1973, www.theatlantic.com/past/docs/issues/73mar/sarris.htm (19 September 2013).
6. I taught it in my class, "The Epic in Film," in the spring of 2007, and my students preferred it to any other epic shown. Many wrote papers about and made presentations on it.

Bibliography

Bridges, Herb. *Gone with the Wind: The Three-Day Premiere in Atlanta.* Macon, GA: Mercer University Press, 1999.

Cameron, Judy, and Paul J. Christman. *The Art of* Gone with the Wind*: The Making of a Legend.* New York: Prentice Hall, 1989.

Sackett, Susan. *Box Office Hits: Hollywood's Most Successful Movies.* New York: Billboard Books, 1990.

Sarris, Andrew. "The Moviest of All Movies." *Atlantic Monthly* (Digital Edition), March 1973, www.theatlantic.com/past/docs/issues/73mar/sarris.htm (19 September 2013).

Schickel, Richard. "Glossy, Sentimental, Chuckle-Headed." *Atlantic Monthly* (Digital Edition), March 1973, www.theatlantic.com/past/docs/issues/73mar/schick.htm (19 September 2013).

Siegel, Scott, and Barbara Siegel. *The Encyclopedia of Hollywood.* New York: Facts on File, 1990.

Vertrees, Alan David. *Selznick's Vision:* Gone with the Wind *and Hollywood Filmmaking.* Arlington: University of Texas Press, 1997.

THE GOOD, THE BAD AND THE UGLY (1966)

DIRECTOR: Sergio Leone
WRITERS: Agenore Incrocci, Furio Scarpelli, Luciano Vincenzoni, Sergio Leone
PRODUCER: Alberto Grimaldi (Produzioni Europee Associati, Arturo González Producciones)
CINEMATOGRAPHER: Tonino Delli Colli
EDITOR: Eugenio Alabiso, Nino Baragli
MUSIC: Ennio Morricone
CAST: Tuco: Eli Wallach. Blondie: Clint Eastwood. Sentenza/Angel Eyes: Lee Van Cleef. Jackson/Bill Carson: Antonio Casale. Baker: Livio Lorenzon. Maria: Rada Rassimov. Pablo Ramirez: Luigi Pistilli. Corp. Wallace: Mario Brega. Union Captain: Aldo Giuffrè. Thomas "Shorty" Larson: José Terrón (uncredited)
AA: None
AAN: None
DVD: MGM, 2004. Extended cut.
BLU-RAY: MGM, 2009. Extended cut.
DURATION: 181 minutes

In the genre largely created by Sergio Leone, at first mocked but then honored with the term *spaghetti westerns* because they were often filmed in Italy and Spain, rather than the American West, one finds a new—and raw (for its time)—version of the western. Most of *The Good, the Bad and the Ugly* film was shot in Almira, Spain, except for the Branston Bridge sequence, which was filmed in northern Spain. Because most of the dialogue is not recorded on the set and dubbed later, some of the syncing between the voices and their lips can be distracting, but the popularity of the genre influenced American filmmakers, especially in their use of violence, for example, Sam Peckinpah's *The Wild Bunch* (1969). Released in Italy as *Il buono il brutto e il cattivo, The Good, The Bad and the Ugly* was planned as the third installment in the "Dollars" trilogy, which includes *A Fistful of Dollars* (1964) and *For a Few Dollars More* (1965). A recent American restoration added scenes that had only been released in the original Italian version. All three films star Clint Eastwood as the "man with no name." The final film is a story of violent men searching for a fortune in gold. The men are minor criminals when compared to the slaughter of war and POW camps. Although the film defines Blondie (Eastwood), Angel Eyes (Lee Van Cleef), and Tuco (Eli Wallach) as one of the three types, ironically, there is little difference between them. All are casually brutal, which makes Leone's point.

Three men enter a town, which is quiet except for the wind, to capture Tuco, a wanted man. The camera alternates between extreme close-ups of the men's faces to wide-angle shots of the dusty main street, while punctuated by Ennio Morricone's dramatic and memorable score. They race into a bar and begin shooting. Tuco jumps out the window and runs off, having left all three men apparently dead. A film card names him "THE UGLY."

The film switches to Angel Eyes, a man hired to find a man named Jackson (played by Antonio Casale), who walks into a home where the family is getting ready for dinner. The mother takes the boy out of the room, leaving the father alone. Angel Eyes sits down and serves himself, using their simple wood spoons and pottery dishes. Ten minutes into the film, Angel Eyes speaks the film's first words to the father—Baker (Livio Lorenzon) paid him $500 to get Jackson's alias. The man tells him it is Bill Carson (also played by Antonio Casale) but says he does not know the location of the case of coins and gives him $1,000 to not kill him and instead kill Baker. In a characteristic Leone moment, the film slowly builds to a scene of violence. Angel Eyes kills him, takes the money, and shoots an older boy on the way out. He visits Baker and gives him the name he needs. Baker pays him the $500, but Angel Eyes tells him that the man paid him a thousand to kill him. He does and reveals himself as slightly more of a sociopath than most other characters in the film. The screen announces that he is "THE BAD."

Tuco is caught by three men. Blondie walks up behind him, shoots the three, and prevents Tuco from grabbing a pistol. He ties him to a horse via lead rope, drops him at the sheriff's office, and collects the $2,000 reward. Tuco is tied to a gallows in the middle of the street and charges are read against him. Blondie, hiding in the livery stable, shoots the rope as Tuco drops and shoots the hats off several men. They split the money but argue about the percentage. Tuco says he takes the bigger risk and deserves a bigger cut. The next time Blondie rescues Tuco from the gallows, he leaves him alone in the desert, still tied up. Laconic and methodical, Blondie is "THE GOOD."

Angel Eyes gets a report from Thomas "Shorty" Larson (José Terrón), a legless Southern soldier, about an armed unit escorting a cash box of gold coins that met a Yankee ambush. Only three of them survived—Stevens (Antonio Casas), Baker, and Jackson—but the gold disappeared. Jackson, a man with one eye, was acquitted at a hearing, disappeared, and became Bill Carson and then reenlisted. His girl Maria (Rada Rassimov) lives in Santa Ana. Angel Eyes visits Maria and beats her to get information about Carson. She tells him he is with the Third Cavalry with General Sibley heading to Santa Fe. Angel Eyes arrives at a destroyed fort where a soldier is cooking used corncobs. He says the Third has left for Glorietta, but he believes they are at Batterville, a Yankee prison camp.

Tuco makes it back into town and gets water out of the well. He then goes into a store and steals guns, the owner's alcohol, a sombrero, and $200. In a short scene originally cut from the American version, Tuco visits a grotto, where he cons his old gang into helping him take revenge against Blondie. They arrive at a hotel where Blondie is cleaning his pistols in a second-floor room. The gang moves quietly upstairs using Colonel Canby's arriving troops to mask their movements. Blondie loads his weapon when he hears them outside the door. When they open the door, he shoots three of them, but Tuco is at his window. Tuco gives Blondie a rope with a noose to put over a beam, but a cannon ball hits the hotel. Tuco falls through the floor, and Blondie disappears. Tuco hunts the countryside for him, following his campsites and smoldering cigars. Blondie is lined up for a shot to save Tuco's replacement from hanging when Tuco finds him and gets the drop on him. He shoots Blondie's canteen and his hat off and forces him to walk 100 miles through the desert. In one of the most striking and absurd visuals of the film, Tuco uses a pink umbrella to protect himself from the sun as he rides, while the heat wears on Blondie. Tuco draws to deliver the coup de grâce, but his attention is diverted by a runaway CSA hospital wagon drawn by six horses. Of the CSA headquarters soldiers inside, five are dead, and the one alive, Bill Carson, has an eye patch. He tells Tuco that the $200,000 in gold is in a cemetery on Sad Hill, but Blondie hears his last words while Tuco is getting water. Each has one part of the necessary information. Tuco and Blondie take the carriage and horses and pose as Carson. All three men know about the gold.

Tuco and Blondie drive to Mission San Antonio. Blondie recovers and Tuco talks to Pablo Ramirez (Luigi Pistilli), his brother. It is revealed that Tuco had two choices when growing up, live a life of crime or dedicate himself to the church. Tuco tells Pablo, "You became a priest because you were too much a coward to do what I do." They leave the mission, but the deviousness of appearances fools them when mounted soldiers in gray turn out to be soldiers in dust-covered blue. The duo is taken to a POW camp filled with hundreds of men. Angel Eyes serves as sergeant. His commanding officer, nearly on his deathbed, says that the POWs should receive good treatment and not be tortured, robbed, or killed. Instead, Angel Eyes tells his men to lay low outside the fort. Angel Eyes invites Tuco to eat with him and asks why he goes by the name of Bill Carson. When he does not answer, Angel Eyes orders music played, and then he and Corporal Wallace (Mario Brega) beat Tuco. Leone makes a direct reference to Nazi concentration camps that played music during torture. Tuco is beaten as long as the song is played. The beauty of the music is contrasted against the brutality of the beating. Tuco tells Angel Eyes the gold's location. Blondie is brought in and given clothes. Angel Eyes recognizes that Blondie is more cunning than Tuco and more dangerous.

Corporal Wallace takes Tuco to a train station. On the way, Tuco pushes Wallace off the train. He kills him and attempts to break the chain detaining him with a rock but is forced to place Wallace's body between the tracks and the chain over the rails. A passing train cuts the chain. Tuco throws off the Confederate uniform and jumps onto the train. Angel Eyes and Blondie arrive in a town being bombarded by advancing troops. Tuco is there, too. Hundreds of civilians are leaving ahead of the bombing. Tuco finds an empty hotel, and a man secretly follows him in, one of the men Tuco left for dead at the beginning of the film. Tuco gets in a bath filled with water but shoots the man when he draws on him. Meanwhile, Blondie walks alone away from Angel Eyes, who sends a man to follow, but Blondie kills him. Blondie and Tuco meet and walk the street together. A man on the second floor shoots at Tuco, misses, and is killed by Tuco. A bomb drops in the street, but through the smoke and dust they shoot two more of Angel Eyes' men.

On the road to the cemetery, they are captured by Union soldiers and taken to Branston Bridge, where an alcoholic Union captain (Aldo Giuffrè) and his troops are protecting it. Hundreds of troops on both sides of the bridge are in World War I–style trenches and endure two attacks a day. Both sides have orders to keep the bridge intact. During one of the battles, even Blondie is moved to say, "I've never seen so many men wasted so badly." Tuco and Blondie realize that if they blow the bridge, both sides will go somewhere else to fight. While they set charges on the bridge, they exchange what they know about the location of the gold.

After they destroy the bridge, Tuco and Blondie cross the river, where they find hundreds of Confederate soldiers dead. A dying soldier is comforted by Blondie, but Tuco rides off. Blondie fires a cannon to knock him off his horse, and Tuco rolls into a grave marker: they have arrived at Sad Hill. Thousands of graves reflect the depth of war's horror. Most are recent, but they surround older graves. Tuco starts at the center, rushing from grave to grave looking for the correct name in a dizzying scene that reveals his frustration and confusion. He finds Arch Stanton's grave and digs at it with a headboard from another grave. Blondie arrives wearing a serape and a sheepskin vest; he is the "man with no name" from the previous two Leone films. Blondie throws Tuco a shovel, but Angel Eyes shows up with another shovel and forces Blondie to dig.

They have a three-way face-off at the center of the circle, which Leone slowly builds to a climax with increasing closeness on the character's faces and eyes. Angel Eyes is killed; he falls into a grave. Tuco finds that his pistol has no rounds. Blondie tells him that there are "two kinds of people. Those with loaded guns and those who dig. You dig." The gold is actually in the unknown grave next to Arch Stanton. Tuco pulls sacks of gold out of the grave, four for each. Blondie sets a noose up and says, "Seems like old times." Tuco stands on a shaky cross, his neck in the noose, and Blondie, from a long distance, shoots the rope. Tuco falls and hits his head against a bag of gold. Blondie rides off into the distance. JMW

Bibliography

Fenin, George, and William K. Everson. *The Western: From Silents to the Seventies.* New York: Grossman, 1973.

Frayling, Christopher. *Spaghetti Westerns: Cowboys and Europeans from Karl May to Sergio Leone.* London: I. B. Tauris, 2006.

GOODFELLAS (1990)

Director: Martin Scorsese
Writer: Nicholas Pileggi, Martin Scorsese. Based on the book *Wiseguy*, by Nicholas Pileggi.
Producer: Barbara De Fina, Bruce S. Pustin, Irwin Winkler (Warner Bros.)
Cinematography: Michael Ballhaus
Editor: Thelma Schoonmaker
Music: Christopher Brooks
Cast: James "Jimmy" Conway: Robert De Niro. Henry Hill: Ray Liotta. Tommy DeVito: Joe Pesci. Karen Hill: Lorraine Bracco. Paul "Paulie" Cicero: Paul Sorvino. Frankie Carbone: Frank Sivero. Billy Batts: Frank Vincent. Sonny Bunz: Tony Darrow. Morris "Morrie" Kessler: Chuck Low. Tommy's Mother: Catherine Scorsese. Spider: Michael Imperioli. Janice Rossi: Gina Mastrogiacomo. Sandy: Debi Mazar. Stacks Edwards: Samuel L. Jackson
AA: Best Supporting Actor (Joe Pesci)
AAN: Best Supporting Actress (Lorraine Bracco), Best Director (Martin Scorsese), Best Film Editing (Thelma Schoonmaker), Best Picture (Irwin Winkler), Best Writing–Screenplay Based on Material from Another Medium (Nicholas Pileggi, Martin Scorsese)
DVD: Warner Home Video, 2004 (two-disc special edition); Warner Home Video, 2007
Blu-ray: Warner Home Video, 2007

An account of real-life mobster Henry Hill (1943–2012) and based on the nonfiction book *Wiseguy* by crime reporter Nicholas Pileggi, Martin Scorsese directed this gangster memoir, which is often ranked with the *Godfather* films as the best gangster-epic film ever made. But where *The Godfather* is romantic and nostalgic, Scorsese's film, while stylish, is rough and uncivilized and "rooted in . . . cultural accuracy,"[1] giving it "documentary power."[2] The documentary power is drawn from the artfully selected sets and costuming, as well as the film's music, set in the twenty-five-year period of the film.

The film opens in New York in 1970. A dark sedan drives down the highway, the camera focusing on its trunk and the noise coming from inside. The car stops and three men step out. They open the trunk, surprised that the person inside, Billy Batts (Frank Vincent), is still alive. Tommy (Joe Pesci) stabs him and Jimmy (Robert De Niro) shoots him. Henry (Ray Liotta) narrates, giving the story of his "ordinary life" in the mob. The film flashes back to Henry's boyhood in 1955. He watches members of the mob across the street from his house standing at the cab stand. "As long as I can remember, I always wanted to be a gangster," he says. He begins parking Cadillacs for the mob and feels as if he belongs and that he is treated like a grown up. His conservative Irish father beats him when he finds out he missed school for a month; the mob retaliates by beating the postman to prevent him from delivering Henry's grades to his house in the future. At thirteen, Henry is making more money than most adults.

Henry works for Paul "Paulie" Cicero (Paul Sorvino). Through Paulie, Henry meets Jimmy "the Gent" Conway and Tommy DeVito. Described as one of the most feared men in the city, the film shows Jimmy being supportive of Henry. Jimmy loves stealing from trucks, especially cigarettes, paying off the drivers not to say anything and to get tips from them on future deliveries. When Henry is arrested for selling cigarettes outside of a manufacturing plant, Jimmy congratulates him but warns him to "never rat on your friends, always keep quiet."

Tommy has a barely suppressed and irrational temper, which is shown in a famous scene that begins with the camera following Henry's point of view as he enters a bar, introducing members of Paulie's gang to the viewers. Tommy tells a story to men around a table, causing them to laugh, but when one of men at the table calls Tommy "funny," he responds threateningly. "How am I funny? What's so funny about me?" Sonny Bunz (Tony Darrow), the restaurant owner, comes to the table to collect a debt owed by Tommy. Tommy breaks a bottle over his head. Then Henry says, "You really are a funny guy." Bunz makes a deal with Paulie on Tommy's debts, but Paulie runs up bills on the restaurant's credit until nothing is left of the business and then burns it.

The point of view moves from Henry Hill to Karen (Lorraine Bracco), his girlfriend, who is a well-dressed and proper woman attracted to the violence of the mob.[3] Karen could not stand him on their first date, but she was intrigued, so Henry takes her to the Copacabana to make up. The camera follows them in a long tracking shot as they enter, moving past people lined up at the door and through the kitchen. The staff sets a table for them in front of the stage where Henny Youngman is entertaining the crowd. Impressed by the service he receives, she asks what he does for living. Henry tells her that he is in construction. Later, Karen calls Henry from a phone booth because a neighbor attempted to rape her. Henry pistol whips the man and gives Karen the gun to hide. "I admit it. It turned me on," she says. They marry soon thereafter, and at the wedding, the most common gift is an envelope of cash. After the wedding, Karen attends a makeup house party with mob wives. In spite of their money, the women are tackily dressed and have ill-behaved children. When the police serve her a warrant to search her home, Karen is polite, offering them coffee because she sees it as normal.

Henry grows overconfident, believing no one goes to jail unless they want to. When Henry, Jimmy, and Tommy need money, they rob the Idlewild Airport. They plan a big score coming from Air France, estimating the eventual take to be around $500,000. After the robbery, they pay Paulie his tribute. Jimmy takes Henry with him to get Morris "Morrie" Kessler (Chuck Low) to pay him. As they are convincing him to pay up, Morrie's hairpiece comes off. Jimmy sees an advertisement for Morrie's wigs saying that "they do not come off."

In 1970, at the Suite Lounge, a bar purchased by Henry Hill, Billy Batts, fresh out of prison, greets Tommy with a hug, reminds him of his days as a shoeshine boy, and then calls Tommy "shoeshine." He says he is only kidding and toasts him. After the drink, he says, "You go home and get your fucking shine box." As Donovan's song "Atlantis" plays, Tommy and Jimmy brutally beat Billy and place him in the trunk of the car. This is where the film began, the beginning of the downfall of these three men. Because Batts is a "made man" from another organization, they need Paulie's permission before they can kill him. They must cover up the murder from the police and the mob. They pick up a shovel at Tommy's mother's (played by Catherine Scorsese) house, but she insists that they stay for dinner. Six months after Batts is killed, Paulie interrogates Henry about him, but he swears he knows nothing about it. At a card game, Tommy becomes more irrational, hassling Spider (Michael Imperioli), a young man who serves them drinks, and then shoots him in the foot, calling it an accident. At a later card game, Spider has a large bandage on his foot, and Tommy kills Spider without provocation.

Henry and Karen have two kids, but Henry spends much of his time with his girlfriend, Janice Rossi (Gina Mastrogiacomo), even setting her up in an apartment around the corner from the Suite Lounge. As Janice shows her apartment to her girlfriends,

Henry is attracted to Sandy (Debi Mazar). When he does not come home for two weeks, Karen goes to Janice's door and beats on the door buzzers telling her to get her own man. When Henry finally arrives, she holds a gun on him but realizes she cannot leave him or hurt him. Paulie and Tommy visit Henry at her apartment, giving Henry the ultimatum that he return home. Paulie sends Henry and Jimmy to Tampa to collect money from a gambler. They succeed but are caught by the FBI, arrested, and serve time. While in jail, Henry sells drugs and becomes an addict. Karen visits him in prison and notices Janice's name in the sign-in book. She complains that no one from the gang is helping her.

Four years later, Henry leaves jail. Karen meets him by the car and takes him to their one-room apartment; disturbed by the poverty, he moves them out. Paulie warns him to stay away from drugs. Henry promises to tell Paulie if anyone is dealing drugs. He moves in with Sandy. Tommy and Jimmy help him move drugs that he gets from Pittsburgh. They receive a tip from Morrie about a Lufthansa flight that they later rob. They celebrate the take of $6 million, and in spite of Jimmy's warnings not to splash the money around, several guys show up flashing big purchases, including minks and cars for their women. Even Henry takes expensive jewelry and an envelope of cash home to Karen. Morrie pushes Jimmy for money for giving him the tip. Tommy kills Stacks Edwards (Samuel L. Jackson) because he did not get rid of the truck in which the cops found his fingerprints on the wheel. Jimmy cuts every link he has with the robbery. He would rather kill than pay them. Morrie is killed with a needle to the neck, Fat Louie Cafora and his wife are found in their new pink Cadillac, two men are found in a Dumpster, and one man is found frozen in a meat truck.

Paulie gives Tommy the news that he will be made. Jimmy and Henry are ineligible because they are not 100 percent Italian, but they all felt that they were being made. The day that he is to be made, Tommy is led to an empty room and shot in the head. This is in retaliation for the death of Billy Batts.

By 1980, Henry is so addicted to drugs that Jimmy says his drug use is "turning his mind into mush." The day he is arrested, he attempts to drop off some guns for Jimmy, pick his brother up from the hospital, and ready drugs for delivery. A helicopter follows overhead as he drives. Judy, his delivery agent, makes a call from his phone, even though he told her not to do so. The police arrest him and bust up his operation. Karen flushes heroin down their toilet before the police find it, although Henry needs it for the cash. Henry goes to Paulie for help, but upset that Henry was dealing drugs, Paulie gives him the cash he is carrying and turns his back on him.

Henry meets Jimmy at a diner to discuss his legal case. Jimmy asks Henry to go to Florida to kill someone, but because he is convinced Jimmy is planning to have him and Karen killed, he joins the Federal Witness Protection Program. After Jimmy and Paulie are arrested and jailed, Henry misses the old life. Speaking directly to the audience, he says, "I'm an average nobody. I get to live the rest of my life like a schnook." Sid Vicious's cover of Frank Sinatra's "My Way" plays over the titles. JMW

Notes

1. Raffaele Donato and Martin Scorsese, "Docufictions: An Interview with Martin Scorsese on Documentary Film," *Film History* 19, no. 2 (2007): 202.

2. Donato and Scorsese, "Docufictions," 202.

3. In his book *Scorsese*, Roger Ebert writes that *Goodfellas* is "unusual in giving good screen time to the women, who are usually unseen in gangster movies." Roger Ebert, *Scorsese* (Chicago: University of Chicago Press, 2009), 283.

Bibliography

Donato, Raffaele, and Martin Scorsese. "Docufictions: An Interview with Martin Scorsese on Documentary Film." *Film History* 19, no. 2 (2007): 199–207.

Ebert, Roger. *Scorsese.* Chicago: University of Chicago Press, 2009.

THE GREATEST SHOW ON EARTH (1952)

DIRECTOR: Cecil B. DeMille
WRITERS: Fredric M. Frank, Barré Lyndon, Theodore St. John, Fredric M. Frank, Theodore St. John, Frank Cavett
PRODUCER: Cecil B. DeMille (Paramount Pictures)
ASSOCIATE PRODUCER: Henry Wilcoxon
CINEMATOGRAPHERS: George Barnes, J. Peverell Marley
EDITOR: Anne Bauchens
ART DIRECTION: Hal Pereira, Walter Tyler
COSTUMES: Edith Head, Dorothy Jeakins, Miles White
MUSIC: Victor Young
CAST: Holly: Betty Hutton. Great Sebastian: Cornel Wilde. Brad Braden: Charlton Heston. Phyllis: Dorothy Lamour. Angel: Gloria Grahame. FBI Agent Gregory: Henry Wilcoxon. Klaus: Lyle Bettger. Mr. Henderson: Lawrence Tierney. Harry: John Kellogg. Assistant Manager: John Ridgely. Circus Doctor: Frank Wilcox. Ringmaster: Robert Carson (as Bob Carson). Buttons' Mother: Lillian Albertson. Birdie: Julia Faye. Buttons the Clown: James Stewart. Themselves: Emmett Kelly, Cucciola, Antoinette Concello, John Ringling North, Tuffy Genders, Lou Jacobs, The Alzanas, Trisco, The Flying Artonys, Lilo Juston, The Chaludis, The Idnavis, The Realles, The Fredonias, Luciana and Friedel, Buzzy Potts, Ernie Burch, Felix Adler, Paul Jerome, Miss Patricia, Eddie Kohl, Tiebor's Sea Lions, Mroczkowski's Liberty Horses, The Zoppes, Bones Brown, Fay Alexander, The Flying Concellos, Lola Dobritch, The Hemadas, Christy and Gorilla, Tonito, The Bokaras, Prince Paul, Jimmy Armstrong, Paul Horompo, Paul Jung, Charley Bell, Gilbert Reichert, C. H. Lindsey, Peterson's Dogs, Rix's Bears, Arthur Burson, La Norma, Jeanne Sleeter, Bill Snyder, The Flying Comets, Veronica Martell, Miss Loni, The Romigs, Rusty Parent, The Maxellos, Martha Hunter, Truzzi, Eugene Scott, James Barnes, Merle Evans, Frank McClosky, Mike Petrillo, Peter Grace, Bob Reynolds, George Werner. Narrator (voice): Cecil B. DeMille (uncredited). Spectator: Bing Crosby (uncredited). Hopalong Cassidy: William Boyd (uncredited). Spectator: Bob Hope (uncredited)
AA: Best Picture (Cecil B. DeMille), Best Writing–Motion Picture Story (Fredric M. Frank, Theodore St. John, Frank Cavett)
AAN: Best Costume Design–Color (Edith Head, Dorothy Jeakins, Miles White), Best Director (Cecil B. DeMille), Best Film Editing (Anne Bauchens)
GG: Best Cinematography–Color (George Barnes, J. Peverell Marley), Best Director (Cecil B. DeMille), Best Motion Picture–Drama
DVD: Paramount Pictures, 2004
BLU-RAY: Currently unavailable
DURATION: 152 minutes

The first film that director Steven Spielberg saw as a young boy,[1] *The Greatest Show on Earth* follows a circus troupe on tour, combining the shows themselves with backstage dramas. It was the biggest commercial success of the year and won two Academy Awards, for Best Picture and Best Writing, but not without controversy. *High Noon* (Fred Zinnemann, 1952) had been widely tipped to win the Best Picture Oscar, but its blacklisted screenwriter, Carl Foreman, had intentionally made the western an allegory of an industry deeply divided by the House Un-American Activities Committee and its quest to uncover communists.

This division is thought to have split the vote.[2] But it is also likely that the industry was rewarding DeMille for the return of a successful, big-budget spectacle epic in an otherwise depressed period for the film industry, following up on the success of his *Samson and Delilah* (1949). When DeMille won the Irving G. Thalberg Memorial Award at the Oscars in 1953, presenter Bob Hope quipped, "Mr. DeMille has brought something new to the movies. They're called customers"[3] (Hope himself and Bing Crosby briefly appear in the audience in *The Greatest Show on Earth*).

DeMille spent a season traveling with the Ringling Bros.–Barnum and Bailey circus, and many sequences were subsequently shot on location, mixing the real circus performers and audience with the actors. As Charlton Heston recalls, this was by no means an easy feat in the days when the Technicolor camera was "as big as a refridgerator."[4]

Trapeze artist Holly (Betty Hutton) is in love with the hard-nosed circus manager Brad Braden (Heston), who appears indifferent to her affections. He has a circus to run and is having trouble keeping swindlers from setting up fixed-gambling rackets, bankrolled by circus rivals. Holly is incensed when Brad brings in the charismatic Great Sebastian (Cornel Wilde) to displace her from the central ring. Sebastian has a reputation as a ladies' man and makes a play for Holly. The two flirt by recklessly competing with one another in the ring. When Holly taunts Sebastian for using a net, he dispenses with it just before performing a new and particularly dangerous trick, falling to the ground and ending up with a paralyzed arm. Holly feels responsible and finally reciprocates his love, but although she convinces Sebastian to stay on selling balloons for the circus, he refuses to marry her while incapacitated. Later, however, Brad is able to goad Sebastian into moving his seemingly ruined hand, bringing hope for recovery and life with Holly.

Meanwhile, elephant wrangler Angel (Gloria Grahame) takes the opportunity to make a play for Brad herself, but she also has to deflect the advances of the jealous elephant handler Klaus (Lyle Bettger). Playing the troupe's unofficial agony aunt to these romantic entanglements is Buttons the Clown (an excellent James Stewart), a sad and lonely figure who is harboring a secret that Holly inadvertently stumbles upon: he is a fugitive doctor wanted for the mercy killing of his terminally ill wife.

But it is the spurned Klaus who has true murder on his mind, and Brad only narrowly prevents him from getting an elephant to crush Angel to death in the middle of a show (Grahame really did have the elephant foot hovering over her head for this scene). The angry Klaus teams up with crooks to stop the circus train and rob its coffers, but as a second circus train approaches at full speed, he realizes that Angel could be killed in the collision, and he himself dies in the attempt to stop the locomotive. The accident scene rivals the circus acts themselves as the central spectacle of the film. Angel escapes unharmed, but Brad is pinned down by the wreckage and badly hurt. With the troupe's doctor unconscious, Holly implores Buttons to stay and help, despite the presence of an FBI agent looking for him. Buttons decides to sacrifice his freedom to save Brad, winning the respect of the agent, who is obliged to arrest him. Faced with near death, Brad comes to his senses and finally declares his love for Holly, but for once she is the one focused on keeping the circus going, gathering up their remaining equipment for an open-air show for a nearby town. The show must go on.

DeMille was beset by floral arrangements from actresses eager to gain roles in the film, but, in fact, he chose Betty Hutton (fresh from her success in George Sidney's 1950 *Annie Get Your Gun*), Gloria Grahame, and Dorothy Lamour for their willingness to perform their circus stunts themselves.[5] DeMille gave Charlton Heston his fourth screen role not on the basis of his previous performance in *Dark City* (William Dieterle, 1950, which DeMille hadn't liked), but rather because Heston had given him a friendly wave on the Paramount lot despite having only met him briefly once before. DeMille simply liked the look of him based on that wave.[6] It was the turning point in Heston's career.

Looking back, it seems remarkable that this was the only film for which DeMille personally received an Oscar (and for Best Film, not Best Director), because it is certainly not the film for which he is most often remembered nor the one that holds up best with the passing of time. His two versions of *The Ten Commandments*—one silent in 1923 and one in the sound era in 1956—are testament to a long, remarkable career producing epic films. DeMille certainly uses his own talent for big-screen spectacle in *The Greatest Show on Earth*, but the narrative is slight, the narration is somewhat overwrought, and the film perhaps survives best as a time capsule of circus culture (one of DeMille's few forays into contemporary life) and the revival of the epic in a difficult period for the industry. DB

Notes

1. Steve Poster, "The Man behind Close Encounters of the Third Kind," in *Steven Spielberg Interviews*, edited by Lester D. Friedman and Brent Notbohm (Jackson: University Press of Mississippi, 2000), 57.
2. Lawrence Christon, "The Greatest Show on Earth: The First Oscar Telecast Had It All: Politics, Controversy, and No-shows," *Variety*, 9 March 2003, www.variety.com/article/VR1117881949 (29 July 2012).
3. Charlton Heston, *In the Arena: The Autobiography* (London: HarperCollins, 1995), 104. On the commercial difficulties in the postwar U.S. film industry and their impact on the epic, see Sheldon Hall and Steve Neale, *Epics, Spectacles, and Blockbusters* (Detroit, MI: Wayne State University Press, 2010), 135–39.
4. Heston, *In the Arena*, 104.
5. Cecil B. DeMille, *The Autobiography of Cecil B. DeMille*, edited by Donald Hayne (London: W. H. Allen, 1960): 370–71.
6. Heston, *In the Arena*, 102–3.

Bibliography

Christon, Lawrence. "The Greatest Show on Earth: The First Oscar Telecast Had It All: Politics, Controversy, and No-shows." *Variety*, 9 March 2003, www.variety.com/article/VR1117881949 (29 July 2012).

DeMille, Cecil B. *The Autobiography of Cecil B. DeMille*. Edited by Donald Hayne. London: W. H. Allen, 1960.

Hall, Sheldon, and Steve Neale. *Epics, Spectacles, and Blockbusters*. Detroit, MI: Wayne State University Press, 2010.

Heston, Charlton. *In the Arena: The Autobiography*. London: HarperCollins, 1995.

Poster, Steve. "The Man behind Close Encounters of the Third Kind." In *Steven Spielberg Interviews*, edited by Lester D. Friedman and Brent Notbohm, 55–69. Jackson: University Press of Mississippi, 2000.

GRAPES OF WRATH (1940)

DIRECTOR: John Ford
WRITER: Nunnally Johnson. Based on the novel by John Steinbeck.
PRODUCER: Darryl F. Zanuck (20th Century Fox)
CINEMATOGRAPHER: Gregg Toland
EDITOR: Robert L. Simpson
ART DIRECTION: Richard Day, Mark-Lee Kirk
COSTUMES: Gwen Wakeling
MUSIC: Alfred Newman
SOUND: Edmund H. Hansen
CAST: Tom Joad: Henry Fonda. Ma Joad: Jane Darwell. Casy: John Carradine. Grandpa: Charley Grapewin. Rosasharn: Dorris Bowdon. Pa Joad: Russell Simpson. Al: O. Z. Whitehead. Muley: John Qualen. Connie: Eddie Quillan. Grandma: Zeffie Tilbury. Noah: Frank Sully. Uncle John: Frank Darien. Winfield: Darryl Hickman. Ruth Joad: Shirley Mills. Thomas: Roger Imhof.

Caretaker: Grant Mitchell. Wilkie: Charles D. Brown. Davis: John Arledge. Policeman: Ward Bond. Bert: Harry Tyler. Bill: William Pawley. Joe: Charles Tannen. Inspection Officer: Selmar Jackson. Leader: Charles Middleton. Proprietor: Eddie Waller. Floyd: Paul Guilfoyle. Frank: David Hughes. City Man: Cliff Clark. Bookkeeper: Joseph Sawyer. Tim: Frank Faylen. Agent: Adrian Morris. Muley's Son: Hollis Jewell. Spencer: Robert Homans. Driver: Irving Bacon. Mae: Kitty McHugh

AA: Best Director (John Ford), Best Supporting Actress (Jane Darwell)

AAN: Best Picture (20th Century Fox), Best Leading Actor (Henry Fonda), Best Film Editing (Robert L. Simpson), Best Sound–Recording (Edmund H. Hansen), Best Writing–Screenplay (Nunnally Johnson)

DVD: 20th Century Fox, 2008

Blu-ray: 20th Century Fox, 2012

Duration: DVD, 123 minutes; Blu-ray, 130 minutes

John Ford's cinematic rendition of John Steinbeck's controversial Pulitzer Prize–winning 1939 best-seller *The Grapes of Wrath* depicts the suffering of rural families through the Dust Bowl during the Great Depression. Reviews made it clear that the predicament faced by farmers, and the communities into which they fled (which are not depicted favorably, but nor are they provided with any potential solutions), were still pressing issues upon the film's release. A reviewer for *Variety* writes, "It is a shocking visualization of a state of affairs demanding generous humanitarian attention . . . its success may lead other producers to explore the rich field of contemporary life [that] films long have neglected and ignored."[1]

Tom Joad (Henry Fonda) is on parole for a murder that he committed in self-defense, but he returns to find his family home deserted. Along the way, he meets disillusioned former preacher Casy (John Carradine) and neighbor Muley (John Qualen), who is hiding out after having been forced off his own land in favor of more efficient Caterpillar tractors. Tom finds his family at his uncle's home, preparing to leave for California, where they have been led to believe ample well-paid work awaits them. Loading as many of their belongings as they can into a jalopy, Casy and the Joad family hit the road. Grandpa (Charley Grapewin) and Grandma (Zeffie Tilbury) die on the difficult journey. Money is tight, but they find people sympathetic to their plight along the way.

Despite being warned that California is not all that it is made out to be, the Joad family presses on, but they are disheartened when they finally arrive at a disheveled camp full of starving families. Although an offer of work arrives, a camp member argues about pay and is threatened with arrest by the sheriff. When he flees, the sheriff fires at him, accidentally shooting an innocent woman. An appalled Tom hits the sheriff to prevent him from chasing the accused man. Casy stays behind to confess to the crime and divert attention away from Tom, only to later be released. Meanwhile, Tom's pregnant sister, Rosasharn (Dorris Bowdon), is distraught when her husband walks out on them, and although it is not directly shown in the film, their baby does not survive.

The Joad family leaves the camp and arrives at a farm for work. Although alarmed by the barricades and armed guards around the farm, they have little choice but to accept work. The family picks peaches but barely makes enough to eat and is still hungry at the end of their dinner. Tom sneaks out of the farm and finds Casy camped nearby. Casy has found a new purpose—to help run a labor strike to force a fair wage from the farm. When the camp is busted, Casy is killed and Tom, in turn, kills one of their attackers, receiving an incriminating blow to the face in the process. The Joad family smuggles him off the farm and makes for the road again, at one point being turned back by locals angry at the influx of interstaters when jobs are already scarce.

The Joads arrive at a government-run camp that is utopian in comparison to what they have experienced so far. There is plumbing, social gatherings, and although overseen by a government official, the camp rules are set and enforced by the inhabitants themselves. But Tom receives a tip-off that their Saturday dance will be infiltrated to create an altercation, giving the local sheriff an excuse to enter the camp and take over. The camp dwellers foil the attempt, but the sheriff returns looking for Tom. Tom departs into the night, telling his distressed mother that he will continue to fight injustice as best he can. The Joad family heads off with the promise of work, and despite their many misfortunes, Ma (Jane Darwell in her Oscar-winning performance) reflects that common folk like them will endure and prevail. It is survival itself that is rendered heroic in the Joad family's odyssey across the Oklahoma Dust Bowl and through the desert to reach the supposed promised land of California.

Dramatic chiaroscuro lighting from cinematographer Gregg Toland lends unease to the silhouetted tree branches in the rural landscapes and oppressiveness to the film's tightly composed conversations, the disquieting effect aided by Alfred Newman's appropriately sparse score. Vivian Sobchack suggests that the emphasis on studio sets is surprising given the subject matter, divorcing the Joads from the expansive landscape from which they are being removed. This, she argues, places visual emphasis on the endurance of family[2] that Ma Joad stresses in her closing speech.

We are in a mythic landscape in *The Grapes of Wrath*, a landscape of anxious American dreams, and in this we can see the connection with the westerns for which John Ford is primarily known (among them *Stagecoach* in 1939, *The Man Who Shot Liberty Valence* in 1962, and *The Searchers* in 1956). Ford charts an equally fraught westward journey in *The Grapes of Wrath* and picked up his third Best Director Oscar for his efforts.[3] Nunnally Johnson's Oscar-nominated screenplay was praised for cutting back the novel's dialogue to its "bare bones," making it "terser, more moving in picture than in book."[4] It was surely a risk on the part of Darryl F. Zanuck to bring such a controversial novel to the screen. Both book and film were widely criticized from both sides of the political spectrum, but this did not hamper (and probably contributed to) their success. The tale has subsequently become part of the American lexicon. DB

Notes

1. "Review: *The Grapes of Wrath*," *Variety*, 1940, http://variety.com/1940/film/reviews/the-grapes-of-wrath-1200412937/ (8 June 2013).
2. Vivian Sobchack, "*The Grapes of Wrath*: Thematic Emphasis through Visual Style," *American Quarterly* 31, no. 5 (1979): 603–6, 611.
3. For more on Ford, see Scott Eymann, *Print the Legend: The Life and Times of John Ford* (New York: Simon & Schuster, 1999).
4. "The New Pictures," *Time*, 12 February 1940, 72.

Bibliography

Eymann, Scott. *Print the Legend: The Life and Times of John Ford*. New York: Simon & Schuster, 1999.

"The New Pictures." *Time*, 12 February 1940, 72.

"Review: *The Grapes of Wrath*," *Variety*, 1940, http://variety.com/1940/film/reviews/the-grapes-of-wrath-1200412937/ (8 June 2013).

Sobchack, Vivian. "*The Grapes of Wrath*: Thematic Emphasis through Visual Style." *American Quarterly* 31, no. 5 (1979): 596–615.

THE GREAT ESCAPE (1963)

DIRECTOR: John Sturges
WRITERS: James Clavell, W. R. Burnett. Based on book by Paul Brickhill.
PRODUCERS: John Sturges, James Clavell (Mirisch)
CINEMATOGRAPHER: Daniel L. Fapp
EDITOR: Ferris Webster
MUSIC: Elmer Bernstein
CAST: Hilts "The Cooler King": Steve McQueen. Hendley "The Scrounger": James Garner. Bartlett "Big X": Richard Attenborough. Ramsey "The SBO": James Donald. Danny "Tunnel King": Charles Bronson. Blythe "The Forger": Donald Pleasence. Sedgwick "The Manufacturer": James Coburn. Haynes "Diversions": Lawrence Montaigne. Griffith "Tailor": Robert Desmond. Von Luger "The Kommandant": Hannes Messemer. Ashley-Pitt "Dispersal": David McCallum. MacDonald "Mac" "Intelligence": Gordon Jackson. Willie "Tunnel King": John Leyton. Ives "The Mole": Angus Lennie. Cavendish "The Surveyor": Nigel Stock. Werner "The Ferret": Robert Graf. Stratwitch: Harry Riebauer. Kuhn: Hans Reiser. Goff: Jud Taylor
AA: None
AAN: Best Film Editing (Ferris Webster)
DVD: MGM, 1998
BLU-RAY: MGM, 2013
DURATION: 172 minutes

The Great Escape, based on the actual escape attempt of 600 Allied prisoners during World War II from an escape-proof prison camp, was directed by John Sturges, and it was the last great film in the prisoner of war genre, a "postwar phenomenon" that began in 1946.[1] It was a huge success despite its downbeat ending and made the lead actors international stars. The film's "cocky"[2] score, written by Elmer Bernstein, was so popular in England that it became the theme music for British World Cup teams. Although the genre's popularity subsided, the film's epic themes of heroism and sacrifice continued in homages, for example, the animated film *Chicken Run* (2000).

Shot in Germany, *The Great Escape* opens on a caravan of military vehicles, dozens of trucks and cars, and their motorcycle escorts, delivering the most successful escapees from other camps to a new "escape-proof" camp. The camp's senior British officer (SBO), Group Captain Ramsay (James Donald), is brought to the commandant, Luftwaffe colonel Von Luger (Hannes Messemer), who says that he is "no common jailer." He has detailed notes on each prisoner. Describing the plan of the camp, he declares, "We have, in effect, put all our rotten eggs in one basket," and, as if he has Mark Twain's quote in mind, says, "and we intend to watch this basket carefully." Ramsay reminds him that it is the POW's duty to "harass the enemy to the best of our abilities," but Von Luger says they should "sit out the war as comfortably as possible."

The trucks are unloaded and hundreds of men flow into the prison yard behind fences. Many of them immediately test the perimeters and plan escapes. The men are a mix of Allied soldiers from England, Australia, Ireland, Scotland, Canada, and the United States; Sturges says, "They're a microcosm of the Allies, men who voluntarily formed the most professional army ever put together to wipe out the Nazis."[3] Flight Lieutenant Danny Velinski (Charles Bronson) and Flight Lieutenant Willie Dickes (John Leyton) quickly plan an escape by joining Russian loggers who are leaving the camp after thinning pine trees. Willie asks other POWs, including Flying Officer Sedgwick (James Coburn), to cause a commotion to cover their escape. Because they are professionals, he is offered a menu of choices, including the "mad prisoner" and "choir practice," but they decide on "knuckles." As the men "fight" and distract the guards, Danny trades cigarettes for a Russian man's coat, and Willie jumps in back of a truck loaded with tree branches. Sedgwick joins Danny as they exit, but a guard recognizes them and pulls them from the line. Stratwitch (Harry Riebauer) uses a pitchfork to probe the truck beds through the branches, discovering Flying Officer "Archie" Ives "The Mole" (Angus Lennie), Willie, and others.

Captain Virgil Hilts (Steve McQueen) walks up to the "wire of death," a line that, when crossed, would cause tower guards to fire at him with machine guns. He studies the view from towers and realizes that there is a blind spot between towers. He tests his theory by throwing a baseball between the two towers and then crosses the line and stands with his back against the fence. They shoot at him, but Von Luger arrives. After first denying it, Hilts admits he was planning to escape and gives up his wire cutters. Von Luger, insulted by Hilts's behavior, asks, "Are all American officers so ill-mannered?" Hilts answers, "About 90 percent." Ives is also sent to the cooler for blowing a "raspberry" at Von Luger. Hilts and Ives talk through their cell doors. Hilts went to college for chemical engineering and raced motorcycles in competitions. Ives previously attempted escape by going over the wire four times and by tunnel seven times. Hilts throws his baseball at the opposite wall and catches it while considering his next escape plan.

The Germans arrive with another prisoner, Royal Air Force squadron leader Roger Bartlett (Richard Attenborough), a man most of the men in the yard know as "Big X." Gestapo agent Kuhn (Hans Reiser) and an SS officer deliver him to Von Luger's office and request that he receive strict confinement. Von Luger refuses because Allied Air Force POWs are the responsibility of the Luftwaffe and their officers. As they leave, they warn Bartlett, "If you escape again and are caught, you will be shot." Big X reports to Ramsay, who says that almost their entire "X" organization is now at the camp. Big X plans to "cause a stink tying up thousands of troops" by freeing 250 men. Although Ramsay is concerned about men's lives, and that the SS would take over the camp in retaliation, Big X says there is no difference between the Luftwaffe and the SS, that all are the enemy.

Big X calls a meeting that night. Von Luger has asked them to devote themselves to cultural pursuits, and they will, while they dig. To accomplish his plan, he orders that three tunnels be dug: Tom, starting in hut 104, heading east; Dick, starting in hut 104, tunneling north from the kitchen; and Harry, beginning in 105 and running east, parallel to Tom. He orders identification papers and civilian clothes for everyone. Big X assigns each man in the room a specific task for his crew: Cavendish "The Surveyor," Hendley "The Scrounger," Danny and Willie "Tunnel Kings," Blythe "The Forger," Sedgwick "The Manufacturer," Ashley-Pitt "Dispersal," MacDonald (Mac) "Intelligence," Haynes "Diversions," and Griffith "Tailor."

Blythe[4] (Donald Pleasence) asks Hendley (James Garner) for a 35 mm camera with a focal plane shutter, and Danny asks for two picks. Hendley takes steel rods from a Nazi truck for one of Danny's picks. Temporarily moving a wood-burning stove, which hides the entrance to the new tunnel, Danny begins his seventeenth tunnel by timing his hits with hammering outside. In another hut, Danny digs below a shower drain, which they hide with a grate when a guard inspects the room.

After nearly two weeks in the cooler, Ives and Hilts are released. Hilts visits the blind spot and reports to Mac (Gordon Jackson) and Big X that he and Ives plan to burrow out like moles just under the surface of the dirt. Ives cannot wait for the planned big escape, as he is "wire happy." Although, Mac says, "It's so stupid it's positively brilliant," the two men are caught and returned to the cooler. Ives hesitates at the door, but a guard pushes him inside.

Ashley-Pitt, or "Dispersal," realizes that the dirt removed from the tunnel has a different appearance from surface dirt. He solves the problem by distributing the dirt from sleeve-shaped bags placed under men's pant legs and released with a string. Properly equipped, Hendley marches men around the compound, and, when he orders them to "look sharp," they drop the dirt.

To obtain example documents for Blythe, Hendley befriends Werner "The Ferret" (Robert Graf). Inviting him into his room, Hendley offers him real coffee and reveals his extensive larder, collected from all the men in the camp, to tempt Werner. He is interested in the marmalade and chocolate, recognizes the commander's butter, and leaves quickly, but not before Hendley steals his wallet. Later, Werner visits Hendley looking for it, but clearly being forced to trade for it, Hendley asks him for a camera for "snapshots."

The camp is busy with "cultural events." Cavendish (Nigel Stock) conducts choir practice that covers Sedgwick's work on a tunnel air handler. Blythe gives a birding lecture to more than a dozen men, until a German officer leaves the building and they resume forging documents. Griffith (Robert Desmond) shows Big X how his crew transforms military uniforms into civilian clothes. Time passes, and Ives and Hilts are released. Seventeen days remain before the new moon, the planned night for the big escape. Big X and Mac ask Hilts to escape; gather information on local roads, police stations, and railway stations; and return.

Big X visits Danny, Willie, and Sedgwick, who move dirt from the tunnel on a wagon and pulley system. The tunnel collapses again, and he decides to close Dick and Harry to focus on Tom and orders it to be reinforced with wood. To accomplish this, Hendley, Sedgwick, and others remove wood slats from behind bookcases, under beds, and in the rafters, which groan ominously because Ashley-Pitt has dirt hidden there. A few days later, Tom reaches the woods.

Hilts, Hendley, and Goff (Jud Taylor) build a still and make alcohol from hoarded potatoes. The three Americans dress as a drum and fife corps to celebrate Independence Day, offering free drinks with the warning not to smoke while drinking. Big X finds the drink "shattering," but Mac says, "It's rather good." While they are outside, Stratwitch and Werner search hut 105 and find Tom's entrance when spilled coffee seeps below the stove. Ives, disturbed by the loss of the tunnel and afraid he will never escape, walks across the warning line and climbs the fence. Although Hilts stops a guard from shooting him, a tower guard shoots him. Upset by Ives's death, Hilts tells Big X and Mac that he will retrieve their information. That night he cuts the fence, escapes, and is caught and returned the next day. He signals to Big X that he successfully reconnoitered the area but then is taken to the cooler.

Blythe loses his vision from progressive myopia. Although he attempts to hide his condition, his roommate Hendley knows. Big X comes to their room and says that Blythe will not be on the escape list because he is a hazard to others. Blythe attempts to prove him wrong by picking up a pin he planted. Hendley suggests that Big X is a hazard because he has been marked by the Gestapo. He takes responsibility for Blythe, saying, "He's not blind if he's going with me, and he's going with me."

A tunnel collapses on Danny, and Danny refuses to go through it again. That night, Hilts is released from the cooler. He opens the end of the tunnel to the surface and realizes it is twenty feet short of the woods. Big X and Max decide that they must risk the escape that night, as the documents are dated. Hilts suggests that they exit the tunnel each time the fence guard walks toward the far end of the compound. An air raid causes the camp to cut the lights, allowing many men, including Danny and Willie, to escape. A guard smoking outside the fence hears an escapee fall as he exits and catches one with his flashlight. The next morning, seventy-six men are missing from camp.

While many of the men, including Mac, Big X, Ashley-Pitt, Hendley, and Blythe, board a train, others attempt other routes. Sedgwick steals a bicycle and rides through countryside, until he finds an empty train car and rides it in to German-occupied France. At a French café, where the waiters are members of the French Resistance, some German officers are killed mob-style by a passing car. Sedgwick asks for their help to get to Spain, and he is eventually delivered there by the French underground.

Hilts takes a German soldier's motorcycle by using a trip wire and then takes his clothes. He arrives at the Swiss border, but there are two barbed-wire fence barriers, and he is surrounded by motorcycles on one side and men on foot on the other. He jumps his motorcycle over the first, shorter, fence, but as he attempts the second jump, he is shot and lands in the wire of the second fence. Patting his motorcycle like a good horse, he stands and smiles at his captors.

Cavendish is picked up by a large commercial truck as he hitchhikes, but instead of finding freedom, he is delivered to the authorities and they threaten to shoot him as a spy. He is led to a room with several of the other escapees, including Haynes (Lawrence Montaigne). Willie and Danny take a rowboat downstream to a major port and climb onto a ship.

Hendley and Blythe jump off the train when SS officers ask for passports. After hiking, they find a German flight trainer. With Hendley at the controls, they lift off, heading toward the Alps, but they develop engine trouble, crash into a ditch, and the plane catches fire. Hendley is hurt and orders Blythe to move away from the plane, not realizing that Blythe is standing on a hill above Nazi soldiers, who shoot him. As he dies, he thanks Hendley for getting him out.

Mac, Big X, and Ashley-Pitt exit the train at a station where Kuhn recognizes Big X. Ashley-Pitt kills him before he can stop Big X and then runs, but German soldiers shoot him. Later, Mac and Big X line up at a bus and are stopped by police checking passports. After clearing Mac for boarding, an officer says, "Good luck" in English. Mac says "Thank you" in English in spite of training others not to fall for this trick. They run but both are caught quickly. Big X runs across rooftops; he is caught when he is walking along a street. Traveling in a truck with other escapees, they are ordered to get out and stretch their legs. "I've never been happier," Big X says, until he sees a guard mount a machine gun on a tripod and fire at them.

Back at the camp, Ramsey is ordered to Von Luger's office. He reports that fifty of Ramsey's officers were shot while escaping. Eleven men have been returned, including Hendley. Von Luger is replaced as Hilts arrives. The POWs gather around him as he is escorted to the cooler. Inside, Hilts throws a ball against the wall and catches it. Although the Americans are largely unaffected, Bartlett's plan is "presented as a vainglorious latter-day Charge of the Light Brigade: 'magnificent but it's not war.'"[5] JMW

Notes

1. Nicholas J. Cull, "Great Escapes: 'Englishness' and the Prisoner of War Genre," *Film History* 14 (2002): 283.

2. Cull, "Great Escapes," 282.

3. Glenn Lovell, *Escape Artist: The Life and Films of John Sturges* (Madison: University of Wisconsin Press, 2008), 224.

4. In Lovell's *Escape Artist*, actor Donald Pleasence, who had been held in a Baltic prison camp during the war, says, "It was an exact reproduction of a prisoner-of-war camp, and just as frightening" (228).

5. Cull, "Great Escapes," 291.

Bibliography

Cull, Nicholas J. "Great Escapes: 'Englishness' and the Prisoner of War Genre." *Film History* 14 (2002): 282–95.

Lovell, Glenn. *Escape Artist: The Life and Films of John Sturges*. Madison: University of Wisconsin Press, 2008.

THE GREATEST STORY EVER TOLD (1965)

DIRECTORS: George Stevens, David Lean (uncredited)

WRITERS: George Stevens, James Lee Barrett

PRODUCERS: George Stevens, Frank I. Davies, George Stevens Jr., Antonio Vellani (George Stevens Productions)

CINEMATOGRAPHER: Loyal Griggs, William C. Mellor

EDITORS: Harold F. Kress, Argyle Nelson Jr., Frank O'Neil

ART DIRECTION: Richard Day, William C. Creber, David S. Hall

SET DECORATION: Ray Moyer, Fred M. MacLean, Norman Rockett

COSTUMES: Vittorio Nino Novarese, Marjorie Best

MUSIC: Alfred Newman

SPECIAL EFFECTS: Johnny Borgese, Daniel Hays

Visual Effects: A. Arnold Gillespie, Robert R. Hoag, J. McMillan Johnson

CAST: Jesus: Max von Sydow. Herod the Great: Claude Rains. Herod Antipas: José Ferrer. John the Baptist: Charlton Heston. Caiaphas: Martin Landau. Pontius Pilate: Telly Savalas. Virgin Mary: Dorothy McGuire. Barabbas: Richard Conte. James the Younger: Michael Anderson Jr. Veronica: Carroll Baker. Judas: David McCallum. Mary Magdalene: Joanna Dunham. Mary of Bethany: Janet Margolis. Claudia: Angela Landsbury. Martha: Ina Balin. "Dark Hermit" (Satan): Donald Pleasance. Matthew: Roddy McDowall. Joseph of Arimathea: Joseph Schildkraut. "Old Aram": Ed Wynn. Roman Centurion: John Wayne. Angel at the Tomb: Pat Boone. Sorak: Victor Buono

AA: None

AAN: Best Direction–Set Decoration–Color (Richard Day, William C. Creber, David S. Hall, Ray Moyer, Fred M. MacLean, Norman Rockett), Best Cinematography (Loyal Griggs, William C. Mellor), Best Costume Design (Vittorio Nino Novarese, Marjorie Best), Best Effects–Special Visual Effects (J. McMillan Johnson), Best Music–Substantially Original Score (Alfred Newman)

DVD: MGM Home Entertainment, 2001

BLU-RAY: MGM Home Entertainment, 2011

DURATION: 260 minutes. Released in the United Kingdom at 198 minutes and the United States at 140 minutes.

The Greatest Story Ever Told is the longest and most expensive of the epics mounted up to that point (1965) that deal with the life of Jesus. It boasts a great and proven director, George Stevens, and a cast of international note, among them Max von Sydow, who had distinguished himself brilliantly in several films by Ingmar Bergman, including *The Seventh Seal* (1955) and *The Virgin Spring* (1960). In his last role, the seventy-three-year-old Claude Rains plays Herod the Great (in a sequence directed with no credit by David Lean), who gave the order to massacre the Jewish children after the visit of the three wise men. José Ferrer plays his successor, Herod Antipas, and Charlton Heston, by now a distinguished veteran of Biblical epics (and a Best Actor Oscar winner for *Ben-Hur*), is John the Baptist. Many other luminaries of film and television—Martin Landau, Angela Landsbury, David McCallum, Carroll Baker, Richard Conte, and Telly Savalas—and a host of others played the various roles demanded by the length and complexity of the story, each adding a piece in the large canvas the movie attempts, to capture the color, historical detail, and dynamics of one of the greatest epochs in the history of humankind. And yet, *The Greatest Story Ever Told* did poorly with both audiences and critics, with only five Academy Award nominations and no wins.

This lukewarm reception can be partly attributed to the length and slow pace of the movie and the fact that the story does not contain a worthy antagonist to give it dramatic tension. Von Sydow is excellent, or as good as one could imagine Jesus to have been, but his antagonists are a succession of persons of the ruling classes, of the Jewish priests who feared him, or the Romans who viewed him as a rabble-rouser who would foment a rebellion. Cecil B. DeMille, now dead, who had mastered the art of the biblical epic throughout the years, always made sure that the Christians suffered at the hands of the evil Romans—as did Nero in *The Sign of the Cross* or the Jews in Egypt, who are tormented by Rameses and saved by Charlton Heston/Moses. Heston had a worthy and appropriately vicious Messala to battle, and destroy, in *Ben-Hur*. There was a certain amount of piety required by the themes of religious epics, but also enough wickedness, usually existing in one person—or group—to generate dramatic tension. The aim of *The Greatest Story Ever Told* is to exult the divinity and the message brought to humanity by the Son of God. The movie turns out to be an almost continuous sermon, appropriate for the pulpit, but not a drama in which two polar forces face one another in a deadly battle—as, for instance, Milton's great epic poem *Paradise Lost*, which lacks neither piety nor grandeur—or offer battles in Heaven between the good and the rebellious angels.

The Greatest Story Ever Told was shot in California, Arizona, and Utah, Stevens wanting an American Western–type landscape, which he thought would appeal to American audiences. The epic, which originally ran for four hours and twenty minutes, premiered in February 1965, and was advertised as having been shot in Cinerama, but it was actually done in 70mm Super Panavision, which gave it an aura of the largeness of its concept. But the reviews were mixed, at best. While some reviewers in *Variety* and the *Hollywood Reporter* called it "powerful" and "an important film," Bosley Crowther was unhappy with the "jarring" effect the "familiar faces in the so-called cameo roles" had on the viewer.[1] And Shana Alexander of *Life Magazine* writes, "The pace was so stupefying that I felt not uplifted—but sandbagged."[2] The film also has pompous opening titles, even advertising a "creative cooperation with the poet Carl Sandburg," which seemed dubious to many.[3] The film was cut repeatedly for various releases in the United States and abroad, but that did not enhance its appeal with moviegoing audiences. It only seemed to make a fragment of its initial investment and took two years to mount and release. To this day, it does not match its Hollywood predecessors in the genre, and it has never recovered.

The movie is not without its high points, however. The dignity and stature of an actor like Max von Sydow gives Jesus the authority he needs from a great actor. Although static in most scenes, as when he preaches to large gatherings, his movements through the crowds, dazzled by his appearances, are fluid and photographed mostly in long shots, as the movie avoids too many close-ups, something that works to its advantage. One can also mention several other actors who excel in their roles, most notably Claude Rains as Herod the Great, who drops dead after learning that the Messiah announced by the three wise men, whose prophesy had threatened his kingdom, has been massacred along with the rest of the Jewish children. The scene showing Jesus in the desert, tempted by the devil by being offered power, is given in shadows, the face of the "Dark Hermit" (Donald Pleasance) barely recognizable, with only his eyes glimmering with malice, giving away the mask of the tempter. Telly Savalas is only average as Pontius Pilate, but Martin Landau knows how to play detestable characters since his Leonard in Hitchcock's memorable *North by Northwest* (1959). But in the first half of the movie, the power and holy gruffness in appearance belong to the half-mad (in the movie) John the Baptist, as given by a muscular and bearded Charlton Heston, transformed into the man of the wilderness who has no fear of the decadent Herod Atticus, or his corrupt wife and daughter.

Unfortunately, the large cast of recognizable actors is restricted to minor appearances, so that even in a movie as long as this, they don't have a chance to develop, and only surround Jesus, as do his followers in the crowd. That works to the epic's disadvantage, at least at the time it was released. Today, modern audiences have no memories of Pat Boone, Victor Buono, David McCallum, or Telly Savalas, and they are more inclined to accept the movie in its own terms, as a grand spectacle that tells the story of Jesus, staged in the Hollywood tradition, in a manner no longer possible in the era of digital effects. The film has also brought about a revival of Fulton Oursler's novel by the same title, originally published in 1949[4] but reprinted in recent times, and for those who find the story moving and appropriately faithful to the gospels, the two works continue their appeal. CS

Notes

1. Bosley Crowther, "Review of *The Greatest Story Ever Told*," *New York Times*, 16 February 1965, http://movies.nytimes.com/movie/review?res=9402E1D8143CE733A25755C1A9649C946491D6CF (20 September 2013).
2. Quoted in Marilyn Ann Moss, *Giant: George Stevens, a Life on Film* (Madison: University of Wisconsin Press, 2004), 287.
3. The movie's opening credits include "Screenplay by James Lee Barrett and George Stevens, based on the Books of the Old and New Testaments, other ancient writings, the writings of Fulton Oursler and Henry Denker, and in creative association with Carl Sandburg." See Harry Medved and Michael Medved, *Hollywood Hall of Shame: The Most Expensive Flops in Movie History* (New York: Perigree Books, 1984), 136.
4. Bosley Crowther, "*The Greatest Story Ever Told*," *New York Times*, 16 February 1965, http://movies.nytimes.com/movie/20845/The-Greatest-Story-Ever-Told/overview (26 December 2008).

Bibliography

Crowther, Bosley. "*The Greatest Story Ever Told*." *New York Times*, 16 February 1965, http://movies.nytimes.com/movie/20845/The-Greatest-Story-Ever-Told/overview (26 December 2008).

———. "Review of *The Greatest Story Ever Told*." *New York Times*, 16 February 1965, http://movies.nytimes.com/movie/review?res=9402E1D8143CE733A25755C1A9649C946491D6CF (20 September 2013).

Medved, Harry, and Michael Medved. *Hollywood Hall of Shame: The Most Expensive Flops in Movie History*. New York: Perigree Books, 1984.

Moss, Marilyn Ann. *Giant: George Stevens, a Life on Film*. Madison: University of Wisconsin Press, 2004.

Oursler, Fulton. *The Greatest Story Ever Told*. New York: Bantam Doubleday Dell Publishing Group, 1989.

GREED (1924)

Director: Erich von Stroheim

Writers: June Mathis, Erich von Stroheim. Based on the novel *McTeague*, by Frank Norris.

Producer: Louis B. Mayer (MGM) (Turner Classic Movies reconstruction produced by Rick Schmidlin)

Cinematographer: Ben F. Reynolds, William H. Daniels

Editor: Joseph W. Farnham (Turner Classic Movies reconstruction edited by Glenn Morgan)

SETTINGS: Cedric Gibbons
CAST: McTeague: Gibson Gowland. Trina Sieppe: Zasu Pitts. Marcus Schouler: Jean Hersholt. Maria Miranda Macapa: Dale Fuller. Mother McTeague: Tempe Pigott. "Mommer" Sieppe: Silvia Ashton. "Popper" Sieppe: Chester Conklin. Selina Sieppe: Joan Standing. Dr. "Painless" Potter: Erich von Ritzau. Miss Anastasia Baker: Fanny Midgley. Charles Grannis: Frank Hayes. Zerkow: Cesare Gravina. Rudolph Oelbermann: Max Tyron. Cribbens: James F. Fulton
DVD: Currently unavailable
BLU-RAY: Currently unavailable
DURATION: Online versions, 103 minutes; Turner Classic Movies reconstruction, 240 minutes

Adapted from the 1899 novel *McTeague*, by Frank Norris, Erich von Stroheim ambitiously filmed nearly every scene and the actual San Francisco–area locations in *Greed* as described in the novel. The original nine-and-a-half-hour (forty-two reels) silent film premiered on 4 December 1924, to twelve men. After the cuts required by the studio, it was a little more than two hours in length. MGM considered *Greed* a failure at the box office and wrote it off as a loss for tax reasons. Most of the material cut from the film has been lost. The Turner Classic Movies reconstruction added optical pans and zooms of still photos of many of the lost scenes. While the reconstruction is more of an academic exercise than a film, it restores lost story lines and characters, and it allows the main characters enough screen time to develop characters of startling psychological intensity, as Stroheim had intended.

Frank Norris (1870–1902), one of American literature's foremost Naturalist writers, emphasized the idea that mankind's fate is predetermined by society, genes, the environment, and his baser instincts. This dark vision of mankind as cruel, miserly, and deceitful offers no heroes. McTeague himself is a large, strong man, a voracious eater, poorly educated, and a slave to his hormones, although he has an occasional appreciation for beauty.

The film opens on the Big Dipper Gold Mine in Placer County, California, in 1908. John McTeague (Gibson Gowland), a young, strong man built for mining, pushes an ore cart into the light. He finds a hurt bird on the track outside. Handling it tenderly, he kisses the bird's beak and carries him along. His boss slaps the bird out of his hand. McTeague throws him down the hill and into a creek.

Hoping to earn some of the area's gold, Dr. "Painless" Potter (Erich von Ritzau) drives his carriage up to Mike's Saloon; a large gold tooth hangs from the carriage's awning. He hands out advertising pamphlets to the bar's patrons. That night, outside of Mike's, Potter exhibits his dental technique to a large crowd. While McTeague watches intently and enjoys the spectacle, his mother imagines him as a dentist. Because she works as a cook and his father drinks and carouses at Mike's, she needs him to move out. Soon thereafter, the father has a heart attack and dies. Worried about the future, his mother arranges an apprenticeship for McTeague with Potter. McTeague is soon practicing dentistry on stage with Dr. Potter, and he impresses a crowd by pulling a man's tooth with his bare hands. McTeague opens his own San Francisco practice on the second floor of a Polk Street building after his mother dies and leaves him $250. He buys a golden bird and a cage at a pet shop and hangs it near his dental chair.

Greed has two secondary story lines involving characters from McTeague's neighborhood. One involves Miss Anastasia Baker (Fanny Midgley), a retired dressmaker, and Charles Grannis (Frank Hayes), who owns a dog hospital and binds books at night. Other lodgers believe that they are in love, even though they have never spoken to one another. They live in two apartments that had formally been one, a thin wall separating them. They hear one another's every movement and listen with great interest.

The other secondary story line is that of Maria Miranda Macapa (Dale Fuller), a Mexican woman who cleans rooms in McTeague's building. She earns money by collecting junk and selling it to Zerkow (Cesare Gravina), the junk man, who lives in a rundown place in a nearby alley. She also sells him gold fillings she steals from McTeague. Although Maria tells everyone she meets about her father's set of hundreds of gold dishes, Zerkow is the only person who believes it. Together they imagine handling piles of gold; in these scenes the film is hand-tinted in gold.

Marcus Schouler (Jean Hersholt), the doctor's only friend, unintentionally introduces McTeague to his future wife, Trina Sieppe (Zasu Pitts). Marcus is a coarse man: he picks his nose, is often jealous, and imagines himself as a cowboy. He works as Charles Grannis's assistant at his nearby dog hospital. Marcus plans to marry Trina and often has dinner with her and her family across the bay near the B Street train station. Trina makes money carving wooden animals for sale at her uncle's (Rudolph Oelbermann, played by Max Tyron) store. One Sunday, Marcus pushes Trina on a swing and she falls, breaking her tooth. She blames Marcus, but he promises his buddy, Doc McTeague, will fix it. At the office, Maria asks if they want to buy a lottery ticket. Marcus does not have any money to buy a ticket, so he tells her the lottery "is against the law!" After Maria says the butcher won $20, Trina buys one. When Trina is in his chair, "for the first time in his life McTeague felt an inkling of ambition to please a woman." It is a complicated and painful break; during her next visit, McTeague gives her ether and kisses her while she is under its effects. After she awakens, he asks her to marry him, but she refuses.

He and Marcus go to a restaurant, where McTeague admits that he has fallen in love with Trina. Marcus decides to let him have her, and they shake hands. They take a train to the Sieppe's for a picnic on Washington's birthday. When they arrive, the Sieppe family is adorned with flags; the boys are carrying wooden rifles; and Father Sieppe, wearing medals and dressed like a Rough Rider, marches the family down the railroad track to Schutzen Park. They need "four bits" for admittance, but McTeague only has a dime, so Marcus buys the tickets. They spend the day riding the carousel, shooting at a shooting gallery, and picnicking on the grass.

Spring rains keep them from having more Sundays together for a couple months, but McTeague is eventually able to visit. Trina meets him at the station and they shake hands and walk along a sewer line by the river. He plays the concertina for her while dark clouds build. Driving rain forces them to run for protection under a building. He asks her to marry him again, but she is horrified by the idea. He kisses her and becomes aggressive. She pushes him back, but they shake hands and she invites him to come back. Trina talks to her mother while she is setting a mousetrap. Her mother says that she is not in love with Marcus, so she must be in love with the doctor. The mousetrap in her mother's hand springs closed, horrifying them.

The next night she tells McTeague that she acted badly but does not love him enough to marry him. McTeague, Trina, and her family go to a show in the city. After the show, the family walks to McTeague's apartment to stay the night. A strange man stops them in the hallway. He is from the lottery and tells her that her lottery ticket is a winner, of $5,000. A title card warns, "Dangers Gather as the Treasures Rise." That night, Marcus introduces Charles Grannis and Miss Baker. Marcus takes McTeague to sleep at the vet's office while Trina sleeps in McTeague's apartment. Marcus thinks to himself that he was a fool to give her up because of the money. Soon after that, Trina invests the winnings in her uncle's business.

At a bar, Marcus, still feeling the loss of the lottery winnings, makes McTeague pay him the money he spent at the carnival and then charges him for staying at the dog hospital. Marcus drunkenly tries to stand, knocking McTeague's pipe out of his hand. He pulls a switchblade, throws it, and it hits the wall near McTeague's head. McTeague is calm until he picks up his broken pipe. Trina tells him later that Marcus is a coward for throwing the knife, saying that Marcus has no right to the money. "It's mine—mine. I mean it's ours, dear," she says.

Their wedding has many guests, including Marcus, the Sieppe family, and most of the people from McTeague's building, but as McTeague puts the ring on her finger, the camera's high angle reveals a large funeral procession on the street below. The casket passes as the minister congratulates the new couple. McTeague gives Trina a bird as a wedding gift and ignores Marcus as he gives her a gold watch. To increase the tension, Stroheim includes multiple angles in the scene. The wedding feast is tense and rushed because the Sieppe family is moving to Los Angeles the next day. Trina's mother wonders when she will see Trina again; she kisses McTeague, telling him to be good to her. In the bedroom, Trina imagines that she is one McTeague's caged birds. He kisses her, and the camera moves to a quick shot of one bird kissing the other. She stands on his toes, rises on tiptoe to reach his lips, and then sits on the bed to cry. The camera retreats out of the room while McTeague closes the curtain.

In the days after the wedding, both Grannis and Baker are happy they met and finally speak. Miss Baker visits Grannis in his room for the first time. In the only instance where greed does not supersede love, after Grannis sells his book binder for $5,000, he and Baker marry and build a doorway connecting their apartments.

Three years pass, and outside a church, Trina inspects flowers from a street seller. Her miserliness now a disease, she opens a clutch full of money to pay for them, but she pretends she has no small change. McTeague pulls a couple coins out of his coin purse. They visit a house they are interested in renting, but Trina says they cannot afford it. She refuses to touch the $5,000 or the $100 in savings at the bottom of her trunk. The house rents for $35 a month. After a Polk Street Improvement Club parade and festival attended by a huge crowd and Marcus as the parade marshal, McTeague tells her that he has rented the house. She still refuses to help pay when he offers to pay half. "You're worse than old Zerkow!" he says. She eventually gives him some money and then admires her hoarded coins while sitting on their bed.

Zerkow asks Maria to marry him, and she agrees because she wants to share in his wealth, but he is interested in her father's gold plates. "Do you think [they] still exist?" he asks. "Perhaps [they are] buried," she tells him. Maria imagines a graveyard filled with gold objects and Zerkow digging them up. Later, Maria gives birth to a sickly child that dies within two weeks. She is so distraught that Zerkow has to take the child's coffin from her. Zerkow pushes Maria to tell him where the gold is, but she does not know what he is talking about. When he puts a knife to her throat, Maria escapes to Marcus's apartment across the alley.

McTeague wants to go to a picnic with friends. Although she says they cannot afford it, Trina agrees to pay half. Their friends see Marcus at the park, so they attempt to have Marcus and McTeague make up and shake hands. When both refuse, a tournament is suggested. Marcus and McTeague win their matches and then wrestle one another. Marcus twists his head and bites through the dentist's earlobe. Bleeding and wanting to kill him, McTeague breaks Marcus's arm.

That fall, Trina reads a letter from her mother asking for $50. McTeague thinks that they should send it and says she gets stingier every day. She offers to pay half if he does. When he does, she adds it to her stash.

Marcus visits; he is leaving to raise cattle with an "English duck" and needs to borrow money. A cat slips into the apartment and watches the birds in the cage. The cat's face is superimposed over Marcus's as he watches the McTeagues. A letter arrives from the Board of Dental Examiners of California. Because McTeague is practicing dentistry without a diploma from a dental college, he is prohibited from practicing dentistry. When he is forced to auction off his equipment, Trina attempts to convince him to sell the concertina and the birdcage, but he refuses. Grannis buys their wedding portrait at the auction and gives it to them. Although she says she did not plan to sell it, Trina reveals that she would sacrifice their marriage for money. After the auction, she plays with the proceeds and hides the money in her trunk. A short scene shows hands crushing two people, a title card declaring, "And Then the Grind Began."

McTeague loses his job and arrives home early. Trina insists that he leave immediately to find employment even though he has not eaten. She takes his separation pay but refuses to give him a nickel for carfare, saying, "A big fellow like you . . . 'fraid of a little walk!" A friend recognizes him on the street and offers to buy him drinks. While he is gone, Trina polishes her money but hides it when she hears McTeague come in. After he threatens to strike her, he falls asleep, and she wonders where he got the money to buy whiskey.

Trina visits Maria at Zerkow's house but finds Maria's body, her throat slashed. There are hundreds of people, police officers, and police cars in the street. The police find Zerkow's body in the bay clutching a "sack full of rusty tin dishes," but these events do not cause Trina to reflect on her own greed. Trina dreams of Maria's ghost asking her to buy a lottery ticket. McTeague wakes her, having run low on bar money. She does not acquiesce until he pinches her and bites her fingers. He wants more and threatens to bite her again. She asks if he still loves her. He says "sure I do," pushes her down on the bed, and then leaves.

Moving further into self-imposed poverty, Trina rents the room where Zerkow killed Maria because it is cheaper than what they are currently paying. McTeague decides to sell a gold tooth he used as a window display to a dentist for five dollars. Back at home, he gives Trina a dollar to buy a steak. At the meat market, she buys rancid meat for fifteen cents and gives him fifty cents back in change. Planning to leave her permanently, McTeague takes his fishing pole, his sole source of income, and his birds, pretending he wants to sell them. After he is gone, Trina counts her money: $450. "No one shall ever get you," she says. When McTeague does not return that night, she searches area bars for him, holding her unhealed hand. Back at the room, she finds her money stolen. She thinks to herself that she would let McTeague keep half if he returned.

Not long after that, a doctor has to amputate two of Trina's fingers because they are gangrenous. She can no longer carve toys, so she takes a job scrubbing floors at a school. She retrieves her investment from her uncle, spreads it on her bed, and lies down with it. McTeague, penniless again, learns that she has the money, so he visits her, but she will not give him a penny. Revealing the depth of his intellect, he says, "Well, then—gi'me a dollar. . . . I wouldn't let a dog go hungry." She shows him her amputated fingers and says, "Not . . . If he'd bitten you?"

In his wandering about town, McTeague rescues a mover from under a fallen piano and gets a job at a music store. McTeague finds his concertina there. They had purchased it from a junk shop. That night he breaks into Trina's room at the school. Although she fights him, he kills her and takes her money.

McTeague, "straight as a homeing [sic] pigeon and following a blind and unreasoned instinct," returns to the Big Dipper Gold Mine to hide in solitude, but working inside the mine during the day and sleeping at night, the constant darkness increases his fear. He leaves two days before the police visit the mine. Calling himself Carter, McTeague goes prospecting in Death Valley with a man named Cribbens (James F. Fulton). They find a rich claim they call "Last Chance." Meanwhile, Marcus sees a reward of $100 posted for John "Doc" McTeague and joins a posse.

In the desert, McTeague is jittery, sensing impending danger; he takes Cribbens's rifle and rides alone into the harsh environment. He shoots at nothing until he is out of bullets. McTeague and his mule drink out of the only watering hole they find. The posse does not follow him into the desert because there is not enough water. Marcus rides alone, taking the sheriff's handcuffs, but his horse dies. He catches McTeague, but his mule runs away with the $5,000. Marcus shoots the mule, killing it, but the bullet also hits the only water canteen he has with him. McTeague takes the gun and beats Marcus with it until he is dead. During the fight, Marcus cuffed himself to McTeague, and so McTeague is now cuffed to a dead man in the desert. He takes the bird from the cage, kisses it, and releases it from his bloody hands. It falls onto the empty canteen, dead. JMW

Bibliography

Lennig, Arthur. *Stroheim*. Lexington: University Press of Kentucky, 2000.

THE GUNS OF NAVARONE (1961)

Director: J. Lee Thompson
Writer: Carl Foreman. Adapted from Alistair MacLean's *The Guns of Navarone*, 1957.
Producers: Geoffrey Drake, Gregory Peck, Carl Foreman (Columbia Pictures, Highroad Productions)
Cinematographer: Oswald Morris
Editor: Allan Osbiston
Costumes: Monty Berman, Olga Lehman
Music: Dimitri Tiomkin
Sound: John Cox
Special Effects: Bill Warrington, Chris Greenham
Cast: Capt. Mallory: Gregory Peck. Cpl. Miller: David Niven. Maj. Franklin: Anthony Quayle. Col. Andrea Stavros: Anthony Quinn. Pvt. Pappadimos: James Darren. Maria: Irene Pappas. Anna: Gia Scala. CPO Brown: Stanley Baker. Jensen: James Robertson Justice. Barnsby: Richard Harris. Lt. Muesel: Walter Gotel. Hauptmann Sessler: George Mikell. Commodore James Jensen: James Robertson Justice
AA: Best Effects–Special Effects (Bill Warrington, Chris Greenham)
AAN: Best Picture (Carol Foreman), Best Director (J. Lee Thompson), Best Writing–Screenplay Based on Material from Another Medium (Carl Foreman), Best Film Editing (Allan Osbiston), Best Music–Scoring of a Dramatic Comedy or Picture (Dmitri Tiomkin), Best Sound (John Cox)

DVD: Columbia, 2000
Blu-ray: Sony Pictures, 2011
Duration: 157 minutes

This popular war epic came on the heels of the blockbuster epic *The Bridge on the River Kwai* (1957), also distributed by Columbia Pictures, and to some extent aspiring to imitate it, for it, too, features an expedition of Allied commandoes aiming to blow up a facility crucial to war operations. *The Guns of Navarone* was written and produced by Carl Foreman (also one of the writers of *The Bridge on the River Kwai*), with the cooperation of Alistair McLean, on whose novel the script was based. The film's exterior scenes were photographed on location on the island of Rhodes (Navarone in the film), but interior and "rear projection" scenes, including the "gun cave" sequences, were filmed at Pinewood Studios and Shepperton Studios in England. The movie was a critical and box-office hit, grossing $18 million, a considerable profit for its time, while garnering several Oscar nominations, with one win.

The Guns of Navarone is one of numerous war epics made within decades of the actual historical event it describes, and, although fictional, it is more or less representative of the reality of World War II in that corner of the Mediterranean. The Germans were entrenched in the Greek islands of Crete and Rhodes and were successful in blocking Allied operations by crushing the local resistance with atrocities, and by guarding the straits between Greece and Turkey with big guns. Allied naval forces would have to attempt to pass through those straits, an operation that would endanger the lives of more than 2,000 troops, trapped on the island of Kiros, from where they would have to be evacuated within days or be destroyed by German air raids. A group of Allied commandoes undertakes to blow up the guns so that the naval fleet carrying the Allied troops can safely pass. The commandoes are sent to their certain deaths by the Allied headquarters in Cairo, for the mission to blow up two big guns fortified inside an impregnable cave guarding the straits is considered virtually impossible, but an attempt must be made.

Aside from the requisite big-action scenes, the movie also stresses moral conflicts, including intrigue and betrayal, developing as the story progresses, while the spectacular climax gave this film its irresistible draw during an era before computer-generated imagery explosions became common. Thanks to DVD and Blu-ray restored versions, with enhanced visual and audio effects, this war epic continues to appeal to today's viewers, despite its length and relatively slow pacing. In his DVD commentary, director J. Lee Thompson notes that had he been making the film today, he would have trimmed many lengthy sequences—like the rock-climbing episode and several dialogue-laden interior scenes, for instance, to tighten the plot. He also notes that in making this movie, he meant to stress the moral issues the commandoes were constantly facing, more so than mere action seen in the customary "action flick," then or now.[1]

To achieve this end, the producers chose actors who would mesh into a believable group of characters for such a mission, but who could also be sensitive to the sufferings they caused to the locals and one another. Gregory Peck, then forty-six years of age and already an established major star, plays a world-renowned New Zealand mountain climber, Captain Mallory, who is enlisted to help the commandoes climb Navarone from its most inaccessible side, a perpendicular cliff at the southern tip of the island. Mallory, who takes over the operation after the leader, Major

Franklin (Anthony Quayle), is seriously injured during the climb, gives a credible performance as a man riddled with moral dilemmas while pursuing a perilous, if not suicidal, mission. Mallory's assistant, Corporal Miller (David Niven), is presented as a genius with explosives, but also as a man revolted by Mallory's decision to leave the wounded Franklin to the Germans and his compromising morality to the mission. But in a crunch, he can be a detective who unravels a plot inside the group and finds ways to circumvent the treachery. He also possesses a sense of humor as a defense against the harshness of the mission and the inhumanities imposed on the group.

This rest of the ensemble cast includes several other luminaries in the constellation of 1960s cinema, a mixed lot as it turns out. Stanley Baker, a distinguished British actor, plays an expert engineer who had fought during the Spanish Civil War and a known knife killer, CPO Brown (the "butcher of Barcelona"), and James Darren, as Private Pappadimos, is the son of a Greek immigrant who is famed for his knife work and killing instincts. He has a sister on the island named Maria (Irene Pappas), who slaps him in the face when she sees him in the middle of a dangerous operation, saying, "Why didn't you write any letters?" As Maria, Pappas plays a redoubtable female rebel with a friend in the underground, Anna, played by Gia Scala, an Italian beauty of the 1960s, here a young Greek woman who claims to have been tortured by the Germans and has lost her speech. She is actually working for the Germans to avoid being tortured.[2] The cast is rounded out by a brooding Anthony Quinn in his pre-Zorba days, playing a Greek former colonel, Andreas Stavros. Stavros had been conducting guerilla operations in Crete. It appears that he has a grudge against Mallory, blaming him for his wife and children's deaths at the hands of the Germans. He has vowed to kill him after the war.

This type of war epic requires characters that present themselves as the good guys working for the Allied forces, since they are attempting to destroy the Germans, but in such an operation, the heroic type has to do some dirty things, and, if he is a decent fellow, he may suffer a conflict of interests. Knowing that had he left the injured Major Franklin to the Germans and that they would administer scopolamine to him, forcing secrets out of him and thus imperiling the mission, Mallory refuses to carry him along, while Andreas Stavros, an embittered warrior, recommends "putting a bullet into him." "Better for him, better for us," he states. Mallory, now in charge, responds that he will resort to that means "when and if that is necessary." But this is an operation that must be completed—a mission that cannot fail, since on it hang the lives of thousands. The typical war dilemmas require that as much brutality, if not more, as that of the enemy must be used if the mission is to succeed. Such moments occur several times as the action of this movie evolves. Mallory, who blames some of his blunders on his "Anglo-Saxon decency," realizes that he has to drop it, since compassion cannot win a war at crucial moments. Choices have to be made, and the good man loses ground to the ruthless warrior. Major Franklin is eventually left behind when the Germans capture the group during a village wedding. Another episode involves Anna, who states that she had been tortured by the Germans and now serves as their informant. When she is uncovered as a traitor, Mallory, the leader of the group, is challenged by Miller and is ready to shoot her, when Maria, quicker, shoots her former friend.

The movie shows that war will turn humans into beasts. But war epics, essentially melodramas, require a happy ending. Miller is successful in blowing up the guns, along with the entire mountainside and the Germans inside it; the victory is complete. Two in the company are dead, one is wounded and left captive, a girl is dead, and villages are being burned, while countless German troops are being killed (for a good cause, of course), but Miller and Mallory congratulate one another, and Stavros has plans for Maria—later.

War adventures in the 1960s were not awesome tragedies—as *Saving Private Ryan* was in the 1990s—and the war is fodder for the entertainment industry. War is presented as a game—as it is in all war movies—with ugly moments, but in this film, the viewer of today still gets a kick during the two-plus hours of entertainment, with fine Greek landscapes and Greek peasants dancing the *kalamatianos*, personable actors to look at, and perhaps a glimpse into what happened not so long ago. If a war movie has to travel the trodden path, this one does it with panache, with some ambition to illustrate moral conflicts, fine acting, as much realism as is needed, engrossing action sequences, and a moment or two of unintended humor—as when the elegant Miller, always as lively as in uttering a bon mot, leads the Germans to a dead rat he planted at the base of the guns as a decoy. CS

Notes

1. "Commentary" by J. Lee Thompson, *The Guns of Navarone*, directed by J. Lee Thompson (Sony Pictures, 2011), Blu-ray.
2. In his "Commentary," Thompson states that Scala, who had worked with him on his previous film, was very "eccentric" and difficult to work with, but a good actress. She unfortunately committed suicide soon after the movie was completed.

Bibliography

MacLean, Alistair. *The Guns of Navarone.* London and Boston: HarperCollins, 1957.

Mecomber, Mrs. "Aboard the USS *Slater* in Albany, NY." *NewYorkTraveler.net*, 2 August 2010, http://newyorktraveler.net/aboard-the-uss-slater-in-albany-ny (20 September 2013).

Steinberg, Cobbett. *Film Facts.* New York: Facts on File, 1980.

H

***HAWAII* (1966)**

DIRECTOR: George Roy Hill
WRITERS: Dalton Trumbo, Daniel Taradash. Based on the novel by James Michener.
PRODUCERS: Walter Mirisch, Lewis J. Rachmil (Mirisch Corporation)
CINEMATOGRAPHER: Russell Harlan
EDITOR: Stuart Gilmore
COSTUMES: Dorothy Jeakins
MUSIC: Elmer Bernstein
SOUND: Gordon Sawyer
SPECIAL EFFECTS: Paul Byrd, Daniel Hays
VISUAL EFFECTS: Marshall M. Borden, Linwood G. Dunn, James B. Gordon, Albert Simpson
CAST: Jerusha Bromley: Julie Andrews. Rev. Abner Hale: Max von Sydow. Capt. Rafer Hoxworth: Richard Harris. Dr. John Whipple: Gene Hackman. Charles Bromley: Carroll O'Connor. Keoki Kanakoa: Manu Tupou. Malama Kanakoa: Jocelyne Lagarde. Rev. Dr. Thorne: Torin Thatcher. Capt. Janders: George Rose. Mason: Michael Constantine. Kelolo: Ted Nobriga. Noelani: Elizabeth Logue. Iliki: Lokelani S. Chicarell. Rev. Abraham Hewlett: Lou Antonio. Micah Hale, 4 Years: Robert Oakley. Micah Hale, 7 Years: Henrik von Sydow. Micah Hale, 12 Years: Clas S. von Sydow. Micah Hale, 18 Years: Bertil Werjefelt. Rev. Immanuel Quigley: John Cullum
AA: None
AAN: Best Supporting Actress (Jocelyne Lagarde), Best Cinematography–Color (Russell Harlan), Best Costume Design–Color (Dorothy Jeakins), Best Effects–Special Visual Effects (Linwood G. Dunn), Best Music–Original Music Score (Elmer Bernstein), Best Music–Original Song (Elmer Bernstein and Mack David for "My Wishing Doll"), Best Sound (Gordon Sawyer)
DVD: MGM, 2005
BLU-RAY: Currently unavailable
DURATION: DVD, 161 minutes; VHS, 189 minutes

In 1959, the Mirisch Corporation purchased the screen rights to James Michener's epic historical novel *Hawaii*, which sold more than 4 million copies, for $600,000.[1] Five years later, when George Roy Hill was hired to replace director Fred Zinnemann, production had still not begun, chiefly because of the problem of turning Michener's 937 pages into a workable screenplay. They decided to narrow the screenplay to two story lines from the massive book, the history of the Hawaiian natives and the arrival of willful Congregationalist missionaries. Advertised as monumental filmmaking, it took "two oceans, three continents, five years in preparation, [and] two years in production" for Michener's "beautiful, fierce vision of paradise [to be] brought to life."[2] Some critics, including Louise Sweeney from the *Christian Science Monitor*, said that, "It's [an] overwhelming sermon of a movie [that] often entertains but rarely inspires."[3]

The film opens with Hawaiian native Keoki Kanakoa's (Manu Tupou) lecture on the history of Hawaii to potential missionaries. In the distant past, King Kanakoa said that the gods were changing, and he took his people from Bora Bora so they could continue to honor the gentle god Kane. They were led to Hawaii by Mano the Shark, "who guided his children through secret pathways of the sea when they were lost." He tells his Yale audience that they lived thirty generations in peace, "until you came and the gods were changing again. . . . Weapons, tall ships, books, and numbers caused Hawaiians not to doubt the greatness of your Christian god."

In the audience, Reverend Abner Hale (Max von Sydow) and Dr. John Whipple (Gene Hackman) decide to go to Hawaii. They visit Reverend Dr. Thorne (Torin Thatcher), who respects Dr. Whipple more than Hale because Hale is too proud. Reverend Hale receives a letter that he has been accepted as long as he gets married. They suggest that he meet Jerusha Bromley (Julie Andrews) at Walpole, New Hampshire, a town re-created for the film.[4]

Jerusha still misses her last suitor, Captain Rafer Hoxworth (Richard Harris), a New Bedford whaler, whom she has not seen for two years. Her father, Charles Bromley (Carroll O'Connor), says she may send Hale away if she wishes. Reverends Hale and Thorne arrive at Charles Bromley's house. Thorne is given a package of letters intended for Jerusha from Captain Hoxworth, but he does not deliver them. During the visit, Hale becomes ill and is forced to stay at the Bromley residence. While Thorne says the family should leave what happens between Abner and Jerusha in the hands of the Lord, he moves the letters from one pocket to another. Because of his poor social skills, her mother finds Hale "dreadful." Jerusha surprises Abner by accepting his awkward proposal of marriage and his plan to move to Hawaii.

When they are aboard the sailing vessel *Thetis* in Boston, Reverend Thorne preaches to the assembled missionaries that they have "two divine missions: to bring the heathen to the lord and civilize him." He adds, "You are to spend yourselves in Christ so generously that in later years it may be said of you 'They came to a nation in darkness. They left it in light.'"

Their passage around Cape Horn was filmed off the coast of Norway, 150 miles north of the Arctic Circle.[5] Hale irritates Captain Janders (George Rose) by preaching to the crew and claiming that Janders's novels, written by Smollet, Defoe, and Voltaire, are "profane and damnable." Hale converts Mason, one of the sailors (Michael Constantine), but after a gam with another ship, Mason gets drunk and Hale takes back his Bible. Jerusha calls Hale a bully, saying she is as "good of a judge of God's will as you." Jerusha gives Mason her own Bible.

The passage is arduous; only Hale is well enough to eat with the crew. Hale forces Jerusha to eat bananas. Avoiding the Roaring Forties off of Cape Horn, Janders navigates the ship through the Strait of Magellan. At the west exit, the strong south winds push them dangerously close to large rocks called the "Four Evangelists." Keoki is sent up the mast to loosen the ties on the top gaff sail. After he sets the block, the sailors haul the sail, but the line breaks and the block hits Keoki on the head. He falls to the deck and lands on Hale. Mason climbs the mast, and Hale calls for God to help him. Mason attaches the block, and the boat sails closer to the wind, avoiding the oncoming Evangelists. In the South Pacific, Jerusha comes to their berth after a bath and perfumes herself with lilac. Although she says sex is one of the purposes of marriage, Abner feels depraved because she takes his mind off God. They have sex, but the next day he regrets it.

The ship arrives at Lahaina, the capital of the island of Maui, Hawaii, where the naked islanders flock to the boat via outrigger canoes and swimming to meet the repressed pilgrims. Keoki slips off his dress suit and swims to meet his mother's royal barge. Played by Tahitian Jocelyne Lagarde, she is Queen Malama, the *Alii Nui* of all the islands. Kelolo, Keoki's father, is the king's deputy at Lahaina. Hale is stunned by Keoki's transformation and says he must refer to him as "reverend" in spite of their agreement that they are brothers in Christ. Because of her size, Malama is brought aboard on a sling. A woman missionary faints when they realize that the *Alii Nui* can have several husbands and is married to her brother.

Hale interferes with the *Alii Nui*'s wishes several times before the ship is moved from anchor. She asks Jerusha to teach her to write, but Abner says Malama must first know God. She slaps Hale when he says that he will not permit them to be separated. She insists so that *haoles* (whites) will not steal her island. Later, Kelolo shows Hale the family shrine called a *heiau*. The center stone was brought from Bora Bora. Hale calls it idolatry and attempts to tear it down. Keoki does not allow him to touch it but admits that it is an "abomination" that cannot be destroyed until they learn to be Christians. Hale meets Noelani (Elizabeth Logue), Keoki's sister and his future wife. Hale is horrified because "any lustful union is a damnable sin."

Malama discovers that Jerusha is pregnant. Before Dr. Whipple leaves for Oahu, he says that Jerusha should use the native midwives to help, but that he will return before the baby is born. Jerusha and Abner move into a grass hut, where a young woman, Iliki (Lokelani S. Chicarell), has been left for them by Malama. Hale considers her placed in their care by the hands of God.

Three weeks later, Abner still has not met with Malama to ask for land for his church. When Jerusha explains to her that it is for a church, Malama gives Abner land on a windswept plateau. When warned by the elders that he should keep every side of the church open for the winds, he says "nonsense."

Malama brings her letter to President Monroe for Hale to read, perhaps as a test of what the words actually say. Hale calls it a remarkable accomplishment. To celebrate, she says that will give them land, but they refuse, saying they want nothing for themselves. This is a turning point for Malama, who decides that she wants to learn about their God. When Hale offers to start the next day, she says, "We begin now!" Hale begins by attempting to convince her that she is evil, corrupt, and sinful. He says, "To find grace you must be humble," but she responds, saying, "Maybe you proud, too." Hale also tells her that unless she ends her incestuous marriage, she will not receive grace.

The island population is caught between the extremes of American culture, the Puritan-like missionaries, and licentious sailors when Captain Hoxworth's ship arrives. The islanders swim out to greet it, leaving behind their clothes, and a party is held that night with dancing and drinking. Hale finds Iliki and pulls her away and rescues Noelani from men planning to rape her. Captain Hoxworth sees Jerusha and calls himself a "god-abandoned fool" for losing her to Reverend Hale. Hale and Jerusha ask Malama to make laws that will keep the girls from swimming out to the ships for their own protection.

Reverend Abraham Hewlett (Lou Antonio) arrives at the island with his dead wife.

She died while in childbirth on the way. They hoped to find the doctor at Lahaina. Jerusha and Hale are frightened that Jerusha's delivery may have the same outcome. In preparation, Hale memorizes a book about childbirth. "You will live," he promises. When Jerusha begins having contractions, Abner refuses to let native midwives help her with the pain and bleeding. After a difficult delivery because the baby was in breech position, she is exhausted, gray, and dismal. Hale names the boy Micah (played by several different actors) and tells Jerusha, "I love you more than I love God," but the next day he asks her to forget what he said because it was blasphemy.

Malama creates the new laws, and Kelolo will enforce them. The natives are to serve God and love Jesus. Sailors are required to go back to their ships at night. Captain Hoxworth and three other captains tell Malama that there will be trouble if they cannot stay overnight. That night they return, and fighting breaks out in the street. Captain Hoxworth sees Jerusha, and they kiss. He is horrified about her relationship with Hale, saying, "He has made an old woman of you." She is tempted to leave with him but runs toward the church when it catches fire. She and the natives fight the fire by tamping it down and dousing it with water. Her dress catches fire, but Kelolo saves her. Malama sends the sailors back to their ships. For Jerusha and Hoxworth, the moment is gone. On his way back to the ship, Captain Hoxworth sees Iliki and offers her passage. Hale storms aboard the ship looking for Iliki, but Hoxworth throws him into the water, where a shark cuts his leg. Hale is pulled out of the water, and Dr. Whipple treats him. As he heals, he tells Jerusha that he cannot love her and God, but Jerusha responds that "God is to be worshipped. A wife to be loved."

After he is restored to health, Hale is called to an annual meeting in Honolulu, where they discuss Reverend Hewlett, who has been "bedding with a native woman since his wife died." Hewlett is removed from the ministry. Leaving the room, he says, "You love them as converts and despise them as people. . . . I gladly depart from a ministry in which love has no place." Whipple resigns before he can be censored for having performed Hewlett's wedding ceremony.

Back at Maui, at Malama's behest, Kelolo announces to Hale that he is evil, corrupt, and sinful, but Hale says that their incestual marriage still prevents grace. Malama is caught between her love for Kelolo and her love of Jesus. In an open-air classroom, Hale finds Keoki teaching the story of how Hawaiians moved from Bora Bora following Mano the Shark. Although Keoki compares the story to the migration of Abraham in the Bible, Hale tells him to dismiss the class. Even though Keoki brought him to the islands, Hale has no plans to ordain him. Keoki warns that his mother is dying and then the whistling winds will arrive. Dr. Whipple examines her and finds no direct cause for her impending death. On her deathbed, Malama renounces her marriage, so Hale baptizes her "Ruth Malama Keokoa." Malama admonishes her people that after she dies, they should not cut their skin, strike out their teeth, or pluck out their eyes. She whispers something to Kelolo and dies. Afterward, the whistling winds blow Hale's church apart.

Later, Hale visits Malama's grave and straightens up her disturbed gravesite. He hears music coming from the forest, and like Nathaniel Hawthorne's Goodman Brown finding evil in the forest, Hale arrives in the middle of Keoki and Noelani's traditional Hawaiian marriage. Hale exclaims, "Your mother will curse you from her grave." They say that they have removed her from her grave and are following her final instructions. Having broken his teeth and poked out one of his eyes, Kelolo paddles his outrigger to Bora Bora, following Mano, and taking Malama's heart.

Hale calls on God to bring them plagues and destroy them. The next *Alii Nui* arrives, but the child is deformed. Keoki drowns the baby. During his sermon, Hale is gleeful that God has punished them. Jerusha is horrified; defiant, she stands and leaves with their children. Hale says his only regret is not having the opportunity to save the child's soul. Jerusha regrets not being able to save its life.

Dr. Whipple is called to examine Micah, but when he sees Jerusha, he says she is working herself to death. Whipple discovers that Micah has the measles. Because the illness is deadly to all Hawaiians, he quarantines the island and separates the children from the adults. Hundreds of affected islanders lie along the beach at night to cool down, although they will catch pneumonia. After Keoki dies in the water, Whipple exclaims, "Fifty years ago, this was a true paradise. . . . We may see the last Hawaiian lowered into his grave." Thereafter, Jerusha refuses to call herself a Christian because the Hawaiians were "filled with Christian sweetness." They were annihilated by "disease, despair, our lack of love, our inability to find them beautiful. Our contempt for their ways, our lust for their land, our greed, our arrogance." After Abner says his ministry is at an end, Jerusha tells him to give them his love and "win them to a merciful God."

Captain Hoxworth arrives, bringing Jerusha a house he built in New Bedford and took down in pieces so that she will not have to live in their "pig sty." A changed person, Hale sadly shows him her grave, saying "of her bones, Hawaii was built."

Years later, Hale battles with sugar planters and assembles public protests to protect Hawaiian land. Reverend Immanuel Quigley (John Cullum) reports that each mission needs to be self-supporting, so they will be investing in sugar mills and operating them. Hale objects, declaring, "We are taking the land of the people we came to save." He refuses his appointment to a church in Connecticut because his ministry in Hawaii has not ended but agrees that his children should attend school there.

On the pier, Hale shakes hands with his three children, Lucy, David, and Micah (now 18), before they leave for New England. Reverend Quigley says that Hale should come back as well because his friends are there. Hale responds, "In this place, I have known God, Jerusha Bromley, and Ruth. Beyond that, a man needs no friends."

Reverend Thorne's prayer to the missionaries before they left New England was that they "spend [themselves] in Christ so generously that in later years it may be said [that] 'They came to a nation in darkness. They left it in light.'" The film shows that the reverse is actually true. At the end of her life, Queen Malama attempted a middle path that would honor native traditions and the new ways introduced by the missionaries. Unfortunately for the island people, it fails. Jerusha correctly identifies the missionaries' failings: contempt of the natives, lust for land, greed, and arrogance. It is for these reasons that Kelolo moves the *heiau* stone back to Bora Bora. For the second time, a god of violence forces the gentle god Kane to flee.

The shorter, 161-minute version of the film does not alter Hale's character; however, it substantially reduces Jerusha's role in Hale's growth. It cuts many of the scenes that emphasize her mature and loving Christianity and her opposition to Hale's adolescent, overzealous practices. If the 189-minute film is eventually released on Blu-Ray, Jerusha will be restored to her full power. JMW

Notes

1. "The Making of *Hawaii*," *Hawaii*, directed by George Roy Hill (MGM, 2005), DVD.
2. "Shouts and Muumuus," *Time*, 21 October 1966, 136.
3. Louise Sweeney, "*Hawaii* almost Outdoes Island as Spectacle: Ready to Sail," *Christian Science Monitor*, 17 October 1966, 6.
4. "The Making of *Hawaii*."
5. "The Making of *Hawaii*."

Bibliography

"Shouts and Muumuus." *Time*, 21 October 1966, 136.
Sweeney, Louise. "*Hawaii* almost Outdoes Island as Spectacle: Ready to Sail." *Christian Science Monitor*, 17 October 1966, 6.

HELL'S ANGELS (1930)

DIRECTOR: Howard Hughes
WRITERS: Marshall Neilan, Joseph Moncure March, Howard Estabrook, Harry Behn
PRODUCERS: Howard Hughes (The Caddo Company)
CINEMATOGRAPHERS: Elmer Dyer, Tony Gaudio, Harry Perry, E. Burton Steene, Dewey Wrigley, Harry Zech
EDITORS: Douglass Biggs, Frank Lawrence, Perry Hollingsworth
MUSIC: Hugo Riesenfeld
CAST: Monte Rutledge: Ben Lyon. Roy Rutledge: James Hall. Helen: Jean Harlow. Karl Armstedt: John Darrow. Baron von Kranz: Lucien Prival. Lt. von Bruen: Frank Clarke. Baroness Von Kranz: Jane Winton. Lady Randolph: Evelyn Hall. Zeppelin commander: Carl von Haartman. Capt. Redfield: Douglas Gilmore. RFC Squadron Commander: Wyndham Standing. Rittmeister von Richthofen: Wilhelm von Brincken
AA: None
AAN: Best Cinematography (Tony Gaudio, Harry Perry)
DVD: Universal Studios, 2004
BLU-RAY: Currently unavailable
DURATION: 127 minutes

Howard Hughes brought unique talents to *Hell's Angels*. As director, prior to *Hell's Angels*, he helmed several financially and critically successful films, including *Everybody's Acting* (1927) and *Two Arabian Knights* (1928), which won Hughes an Academy Award for Best Director of a Comedy. His films *The Racket* (1928) and *The Front Page* (1931) were also nominated for Academy Awards. As an aviator he set world speed records, including a flight around the world; designed airplanes; and owned a major airline. Originally planned as a silent feature, *Hell's Angels* contains some of the most dramatic footage of aeronautical scenes ever shot, including many from the planes' cockpits. Hughes brought more than fifty World War I planes into service and re-created an Allied base and a German airfield for the film. Because the movie's plot is made up of scenes that are loosely tied together, the main interest of the film lies in its dramatic and large-scale aerial scenes.

The nominal story of the film begins when two brothers, Roy and Monte Rutledge (James Hall and Ben Lyon, respectively), visit Germany during Octoberfest with their fellow Oxfordian, a German citizen, Karl Armstedt (John Darrow). Roy, a serious, idealistic, and romantic man, misses his girlfriend Helen (Jean Harlow), even as he enjoys the country. Monte, a womanizer and coward who leads a dissolute life, arrives with a woman whom he quickly abandons for a tryst with Baroness Von Kranz (Jane Winton) at her home. Baron von Kranz (Lucien Prival) arrives unexpectedly and challenges him to a duel. Monte packs for England, and although Roy tells him he cannot walk out on a duel, he leaves anyway. Roy takes his place with Armstedt acting as his second. Filmed in silhouette with a purple-tinted sky, they stand and fire. Roy is hit, but it is too dark for von Kranz to see that he has taken his revenge on the wrong man.

Back at Oxford, Roy has survived the duel with only a flesh wound on his upper arm. He attempts to have Monte meet Helen, but Monte is convinced that any girlfriend of Roy's would be fat and ugly. In actuality, Helen is a curly, blonde-haired beauty. News arrives that Germany has declared war on France. Karl Armstedt soon receives a special-delivery letter requiring him to report to the German 18th Army Corps within three days. He loves England but cannot refuse. Roy enlists in the Royal Flying Corps (RFC). Monte calls him a fool for joining, but he foolishly believes that he can kiss a girl selling kisses (Marian Marsh) at a streetside enlistment station with no consequence. He pays for the kiss by having to enlist in the RFC, where he serves with his brother.

In the only sequence shot in color, Roy, in his constant desire to be honorable, serves on a committee for Lady Randolph's (Evelyn Hall) Charity Ball. Monte meets Helen at the ball in Randolph's beautiful mansion. They are immediately attracted to one another. While Roy does committee work, Monte and Helen sit outside and drink together. She kisses Monte and asks him to take her home.

At her home, Helen asks Roy up for a drink and a cigarette. She changes into a revealing robe. She says Roy's idolization of her "makes her feel guilty" because he is "frightfully high-minded." She wants to be free. Although he says he should leave, they kiss and he stays. After they have sex, Monte says he feels "rotten," so she kicks him out. Monte arrives at the barracks and lies to Roy about where he has been, claiming that he stopped at a bar after he dropped Helen off. He tries to warn Roy about her, but Roy says, "You don't know anything about decent women."

In a blue-tinted night scene, a Zeppelin dirigible, with Armstedt serving on board, flies through the clouds over London. Their objective is London's Trafalgar Square. They halt the engines and lower Armstedt's observation car so he can direct the bombing. He aims the bombs over the water and reports the objective as completely destroyed.

Although Monte says he is too tired when their squadron is called for duty, he and Roy chase the Zeppelin through clouds and fog in one of four biplanes. Needing to climb to an altitude the planes cannot reach, the dirigible releases its water ballast. The Zeppelin commander (Carl von Haartman) decides that the observer's car is holding them down. Because winching it up would take too long, they cut the wires and Armstedt drops to his death. They jettison everything they do not need and still fail to gain enough altitude and speed. Because the ship must not fall into enemy hands, more than a dozen men walk through the bomb bay doors and into the clouds. The Rutledges' plane is shot down, and they crash into a farmer's field. The remaining plane flies into the Zeppelin, ripping it in half. The dirigible explodes and falls near Monte and Roy, who are forced to run from the conflagration.

While the boys are serving in France, Helen is also there working at Lady Randolph's canteen. As she is being harassed by Captain Redfield (Douglas Gilmore), Roy and Monte enter. Redfield pokes fun at Roy, who has only been at the front for three weeks. Later, at the airbase, Harry, a fellow pilot, has not returned from a mission he went on in Monte's stead. Although he is called "yellow" by the others, when Monte is called up for action, he claims that he is ill and says it is a "politician's war." The squadron commander (Wyndham Standing) calls him a disgrace to the squadron, which has been ordered to destroy the German's central munitions dump at Spraug to assist the Seventh Brigade in a coming ground assault. Two men are needed to fly a captured Gotha G.V., a long-range heavy bomber, to bomb the depot. The Rutledges volunteer, although they know the chance of returning is low.

Six hours before their flight, Roy tries to visit Helen, but she is off duty. Monte and Roy visit Grosson's, a local pub that is filled with soldiers. Roy finds Helen in a side room with a soldier. She says to Roy, "I wouldn't belong to you if you were the last man on earth. You make me sick." At Café Jacques, Monte finds a girl. Roy, still upset, says that Helen "wasn't like this before." An hour before they need to be in the air, Monte is drunk and refuses to leave. Because they do not want to be shot for desertion, they take the German plane, which weighs 20,000 pounds, carrying dozens of hand-loaded bombs in its undercarriage, into the night sky.

That morning, leaving from Rittmeister von Richthofen's (Wilhelm von Brincken) flying circus headquarters, Lieutenant von Bruen (Frank Clarke) leads dozens of German planes into the sky in a "V" formation for the day's mission. As they fly over the Spraug Munitions Depot, von Bruen notices the Gotha circling below. Monte drops the bombs, and the resulting explosions are filmed from numerous angles. Fire spreads and munitions self-immolate. The mission is a success, but von Bruen and his formation retaliate, leaving behind von Richthofen, who watches the battle from above. The RFC arrives, and an intense air battle of fifty planes commences. A number of close-ups reveal the destruction caused by the bullets as they strike the planes, shred engines, and perforate the pilots. When Roy's steering control is hit, he refuses to land. After they shoot down more German planes, von Richthofen attacks the Gotha, causing it to catch fire, drop into a deep nosedive, and crash near German troops.

Roy and Monte are taken to a German commander, General von Kranz, the same man who challenged Monte to a duel. Von Kranz asks if the attack on the depot was to prepare for another attack. They will be shot as spies if they do not answer. They do not answer and are taken to a cell. A firing squad lines up in front of their barred window and shoots a British soldier. Monte says he cannot face death and will tell the general what he wants to know. Roy says he will go instead because the general has "got it in for you."

Roy is brought to the general and says he is willing to talk on one condition. Claiming his "friend" will call him a traitor, he needs to kill him. When the general objects that "one does not kill a friend," Roy claims that Monte stole his girlfriend. Knowing this to be in Monte's character, he gives Roy a pistol with one bullet. In the cell, Roy gives Monte another chance, but Monte bangs on the cell door saying he will tell everything he knows. Roy shoots him and is led to the firing squad. "I'll be with you in just a minute, Monte," he says. Moments later, there are explosions in the distance. The film's point of view switches to the Seventh Brigade as they begin their charge.

While the film may be construed as showing war as futile because it ends with the death of the brothers, it shows Roy's sacrifice as being noble and honorable. The film also predicts the rising importance of air dominance in future wars. JMW

Bibliography

Wetta, Frank J., and Martin A. Novelli. "Good Bombing, Bad Bombing: Hollywood, Air Warfare, and Morality in World War I and World War II." *OAH Magazine of History* 22, no. 4 (2008): 25–29.

Wildenberg, Thomas. "A Visionary Ahead of His Time: Howard Hughes and the U.S. Air Force: Part I, the Air Corps Design Competition." *Air Power History* 54, no. 3 (2007): 30–39.

———. "A Visionary Ahead of His Time: Howard Hughes and the U.S. Air Force: Part II, the Hughes D-2 and the XF-11." *Air Power History* 55, no. 1 (2008): 16–27.

HERCULES (LE FATICHE DI ERCOLE) (ENGLISH-DUBBED VERSION 1959, ORIGINAL ITALIAN VERSION 1958)

DIRECTOR: Pietro Francisci
WRITERS: Ennio De Concini, Pietro Francisci, Gaio Fratini
PRODUCER: Federico Teti (O.S.C.A.R. Film, Galatea)
EXECUTIVE PRODUCER: Ferruccio de Martino
CINEMATOGRAPHER: Mario Bava
EDITOR: Mario Serandrei
SET DECORATION: Flavio Mogherini
COSTUMES: Giulio Coltellacci
MUSIC: Enzo Masetti
CAST: Hercules: Steve Reeves. Iole: Sylvia Koscina. Jason: Fabrizio Mioni. King Pelias: Ivo Garrani. Eurysteus: Arturo Dominici. Iphitus: Mimmo Palmara. The Sybil: Lidia Alfonsi. Queen Antea: Gianna Maria Canale. Chironi: Afro Poli. Aesculapius: Gian Paolo Rosmino (as G. P. Rosmino). Ulysses: Gabriele Antonini. Amazon: Gina Rovere
AA: None
AAN: None
DVD: Image Entertainment, 2006 (with *Mole Men against the Son of Hercules*); Image Entertainment, 2009 (in the *Hercules Collection*); Good Times Video, 2001; Mill Creek Entertainment, 2006 (as part of the *Warriors 50-Movie Pack Collection*)
BLU-RAY: Currently unavailable
DURATION: 104 minutes

In ancient mythological Greece, the immortal Hercules saves Princess Iole of Jolco when her horse-drawn chariot veers out of control. Hercules is on his way to her kingdom to assist her father, King Pelias, in the training of Prince Iphitus. Iole tells Hercules of the death of her uncle, Aeson, the original king of Jolco, and the disappearance of the magical Golden Fleece. Both events are blamed on Chironi, a friend of Hercules, upon his disappearance with Aeson's son Jason, Iole's cousin. Gossip in Jolco suggests that King Pelias might really have arranged the murder, and Pelias's advisor Eurysteus warns Pelias that Hercules is bound to discover the truth. The oracle Sybil cautions Pelias to beware of a man wearing one sandal, but Hercules arrives wearing two. He proceeds to train with the men, but while he initially gains the admiration of many—including a young Ulysses—they are also fearful of his superhuman strength.

Prince Iphitus is resentful of Hercules, particularly after losing a discus competition to him. When Hercules leaves to kill a lion that has been savaging local children, the prince follows to join him but is killed by the beast. Hercules duly, if comically, defeats the stuffed lion. Pelias uses the death of his son as an excuse to send Hercules to kill the Cretan Bull as redemption. Iole also blames Hercules for Iphitus's death, and hurt by her rejection (and of forever being an outsider among humans), Hercules asks the gods to make him mortal so that he can experience true human love and family. His wish is granted, and he sets forth on his mission.

Hercules kills the Cretan Bull and, along the way, finds Jason and a dying Chironi, who refuses to tell Jason the truth about his father's death. Hercules takes Jason back to Jolco to claim the throne, but Jason loses a sandal on the way and Pelias recalls Sybil's prophecy that such a man will cause his downfall. Pelias demands that Jason go on a long voyage to find the Golden Fleece and prove his claim. Hercules joins Jason to assist him on his quest.

On their voyage, the crew is captured by the Amazons, female warriors ruled by Queen Antea, who falls in love with Jason. Upon hearing that the men are to be put to death, Ulysses drugs the Amazons and the men they are entertaining, allowing the remaining crew to rescue their shipmates. At their next destination, the men are set upon by primitive inhabitants, and Jason kills a dragon that is defending the Golden Fleece. On the underside of the fleece, Jason finds his father's last words naming his brother Pelias as his murderer.

One of the crew members is actually Pelias's advisor Eurysteus, and upon their return to Jolco he takes the fleece to Pelias. Hercules is imprisoned, and when Jason confronts the king, a fight breaks out. Hercules escapes, kills Eurysteus, and stops the king's cavalry. Meanwhile, Pelias confesses his crime to Iole and commits suicide, telling her to go to Hercules. After Jason is safely on the throne, Hercules and Iole depart together.

Hercules, also known as *The Labors of Hercules*, was a commercial box-office success as a result of an intensive $1 million advertising campaign by Joseph E. Levine, who claimed to have made up to $18 million from his $120,000 purchase of the U.S. rights to an Italian film known as *La Fatiche di Ercole*.[1] The Italian cycle of muscleman films was then able to benefit from the success of *Hercules*. Most were often only vaguely connected to a genuine mythological tradition at the outset, but, in any case, this was completely undermined when the hero's name was switched around at will to suit different foreign markets.[2]

The story depicted in *Hercules* is mostly based on the tale of Jason and the Argonauts, but Hercules had a few battles with lions in Greek myth, one of which was part of his twelve labors, as was an encounter with the Cretan Bull and the Amazons.[3] The labors were originally punishment for killing his wife and children while temporarily insane at the hands of the Goddess Hera. In the mythic tradition, yet another fit of madness causes Hercules to murder Iphitus, with whom he was actually on good terms.[4] It is worth bearing in mind that the Greeks themselves developed multiple (and sometimes contradictory) versions of their heroic myths, including those of Hercules. In any case, by the time we come to *Hercules Against the Moon Men* (*Maciste e la regina di Samar*, Giacomo Gentilomo, 1964), it should be clear that the Italian peplum film is not the place to worry about authenticity.

Often poorly acted and poorly dubbed, critics of the time frequently dismissed the Hercules muscleman films, but this scarcely mattered to an eager public.[5] Today, *Hercules* is a delightfully camp pleasure, perhaps best known for former Mr. Universe Steve Reeves in the lead role. Reeves previously had a small part in the offbeat MGM musical *Athena* (directed by Richard Thorpe, 1954) and reprised the role of Hercules in the sequel *Hercules Unchained* (*Ercole e la regina di Lidia*, 1959, also directed by Pietro Francisci). Reeves's limited acting skills are part of the hammy charm of *Hercules*, but needless to say it is his body that is the main spectacle of the film.[6]

The ancient-world epics being produced in the United States during this period were grander in scope and cost. By comparison, *Hercules* may not seem particularly epic in tone, yet we cannot exclude this film and ones like it, as they were an integral part of the public consciousness of the ancient world on the big screen in the 1950s and 1960s.[7] DB

Notes

1. Anthony T. McKenna, "Joseph E. Levine: Showmanship, Reputation, and Industrial Practice, 1945–1977" (Ph.D. diss., University of Nottingham, 2008), 99, http://etheses.nottingham.ac.uk/549/1/Complete_Thesis.pdf (14 January 2012); Jon Solomon, *The Ancient World in the Cinema* (New Haven, CT: Yale University Press, 2001), 117.

2. Solomon, *The Ancient World in the Cinema*, 317.

3. See, for example, Apollodorus, *The Library*, 2.4.10, 2.5.1, 2.5.7, 2.5.9; Apollonius of Rhodes, *The*

Argonautica. For those unfamiliar with (but interested in) classical sources, Tufts University has some useful full-text English translations available online through the Perseus Digital Library, www.perseus.tufts.edu/hopper/.

4. See, for example, Homer, *The Odyssey* 21.14, and Apollodorus, *The Library* 2.6.1.

5. Richard Nason, "Screen: Weak *Hercules*; Italian-Made Spectacle Opens at 135 Theatres," *New York Times*, 23 July 1959, http://movies.nytimes.com/movie/review?res=9D01EEDB1F3CE63BBC4B51DFB1668382649EDE&scp=3&sq=hercules%20steve%20reeves&st=cse (8 January 2012). On the reception of the Italian peplum films in the U.S. popular press, see Mark Jancovich, "'An Italian-Made Spectacle Film Dubbed in English': Cultural Distinctions, National Cinema, and the Critical Reception of the Postwar Historical Epic," in *The Epic Film in World Culture*, edited by Robert Burgoyne (New York and London: Routledge, 2011), 161–75.

6. On the bodybuilders in the peplum film and their role in contemporary Italian and U.S. culture, see Richard Dyer, "White Man's Muscles," in *White* (London and New York: Routledge, 1997), 145–83.

7. For a study of the peplum film with an annotated filmography, see Patrick Lucanio, *With Fire and Sword: Italian Spectacles on American Screens, 1958–1968* (Metuchen, NJ, and London: Scarecrow Press, 1994).

Bibliography

Dyer, Richard. "White Man's Muscles." In *White*, 145–83. London and New York: Routledge, 1997.

Jancovich, Mark. "'An Italian-Made Spectacle Film Dubbed in English': Cultural Distinctions, National Cinema, and the Critical Reception of the Postwar Historical Epic." In *The Epic Film in World Culture*, edited by Robert Burgoyne, 161–75. New York and London: Routledge, 2011.

Lucanio, Patrick. *With Fire and Sword: Italian Spectacles on American Screens, 1958–1968*. Metuchen, NJ, and London: Scarecrow Press, 1994.

McKenna, Anthony T. "Joseph E. Levine: Showmanship, Reputation, and Industrial Practice, 1945–1977." Ph.D. diss., University of Nottingham, 2008, http://etheses.nottingham.ac.uk/549/1/Complete_Thesis.pdf (14 January 2012).

Nason, Richard. "Screen: Weak *Hercules*; Italian-Made Spectacle Opens at 135 Theatres." *New York Times*, 23 July 1959, http://movies.nytimes.com/movie/review?res=9D01EEDB1F3CE63BBC4B51DFB1668382649EDE&scp=3&sq=hercules%20steve%20reeves&st=cse (8 January 2012).

Solomon, Jon. *The Ancient World in the Cinema*. New Haven, CT: Yale University Press, 2001.

HOTEL RWANDA (2004)

DIRECTOR: Terry George
WRITERS: Keir Pearson, Terry George
PRODUCERS: Robert Cicutto, Izadore Gordon (United Artists, Lions Gate Films)
CINEMATOGRAPHER: Robert Fraise
EDITOR: Naomi Geraghty
ART DIRECTION: Emma MacDevitt
SET DECORATION: Estelle Ballack
COSTUMES: Ruy Filipe
MUSIC: Rupert Gregson-Williams, Andreas Guerra
CAST: Paul Rusesabagina: Don Cheadle. Tatiana Rusesabagina: Sophie Okonedo. Hakeem Kae-Kazim: George Rutaganda. Gregoire: Tony Kgoroge. Neil McCarthy: Jean Jacques. Odette: Lebo Mashile. Col. Oliver: Nick Nolte. General Bizimungu: Fana Mokoena. Elys Rusesabagina: Mosa Kaiser. Diane Rusesabagina: Mathambo Peterson. Chloe: Naxolo Maqashalabala. Jean Batiste: Thulani Nyembe. Hutu Captain: Simo Moguwaza. Priest: Roberto Citran. Jack Daglish: Joaquin Phoenix
AA: None
AAN: Best Leading Actor (Don Cheadle), Best Supporting Actress (Sophie Okonedo), Best Writing–Original Screenplay (Keir Pearson, Terry George)
DVD: MGM, 2005. Includes the documentary "A Message for Peace: Making *Hotel Rwanda*."
BLU-RAY: MGM, 2011
DURATION: 122 minutes

Hotel Rwanda is a historical epic drama, for it describes one man's odyssey in saving other people's lives in the context of a historical event, a movie almost as heroic and gripping as *Schindler's List* was in its day. In Steven Spielberg's *Schindler's List*, a man saves 1,100 Jews from Hitler's Holocaust camps by employing them in his pottery factory; in *Hotel Rwanda*, a man saves about an equal number of people (1,200) by providing shelter for them in his hotel during a brutal, genocidal war between tribes in Rwanda in 1994 that left more than 1 million people dead. In both cases, a man rises from the levels of amorality (Schindler) or ordinariness (Rusesabagina) to heroic status, saving lives for no reason other than that his humanity dictated his actions. Although Schindler's ostensible reason is making money, the real reason for his compassion rises out of his feelings of revulsion and disgust in seeing a civilized country, his Germany, reach an unprecedented level of barbarity, while Rusesabagina starts out wanting to lead his family to safety and, in the process, assumes a role that seems too large for any human in his condition—saving from slaughter a group of people that have gathered at his hotel. In today's movie landscape, its mythical/fictional world, as in real life, it is difficult to ascribe nobility to any action, but this story is based solidly on fact, and the survivors are still alive to tell their own individual tales.

The Rwandan Civil War started after the Belgians left the country, as they did in the Congo. A minority, the Tutsis, supposedly favored by them, was overwhelmed by the Hutu militias that had been organizing themselves to take over. A war of genocide aimed at exterminating the Tutsis erupted; it turned out to be a systematic extermination of populations regardless of any ethical considerations or age differentiation, or regard for international law. This was an unfortunate time for the Rwanda victims. The Gulf War had just ended a few years back; the landing at Somalia had been a disaster for U.S. troops; and the Clinton administration, embroiled as it was in too many complex problems at home, failed to take immediate action—and actually never did. The United Nations (UN) had peacekeeping (not "peace-enforcing") forces on the ground, but the units were too small to be able to impose order and prevent a catastrophe. The Tutsis were practically left to themselves, helpless victims of brutal executioners, and their only hope for survival was flight. Not everyone made it to the border. The Hutu militia, under General Bizimungu, showed no mercy. Rather than simply shooting their victims, they bought a large number of machetes from China and used these to hack their victims to pieces—women and children included. Their purpose was total extermination of the Tutsi tribe, a minority favored by the Belgians, who had, in their time, committed atrocities themselves.

The film presents a single event as a synecdoche of the entire war, and by concentrating on the heroic deeds of one man, it achieves a unique perspective and narrative lucidity that makes the events it describes even more horrifying and unacceptable to the appalled viewer. This movie avoids the gore of violent movies of this genre (something for which it was criticized) and focuses instead on the deeds and feats of a resourceful individual. It is through his actions that one of the most catastrophic and inhumane events in African history is portrayed.

From the beginning, one man is in charge of the guests at his hotel. The people are being threatened with extinction at the same time that the man is trying to safeguard his own wife and several children. The events narrated in the film are based on the personal recollections of Paul Rusesabagina, who was an assistant manager of Hotel De Milles Collins in Kigali, the Rwandan capital, in April 1994. Rusesabagina (played by Don Cheadle) is himself Hutu, but his wife is Tutsi, as are most of his guests. When the Hutu forces arrive, the hotel is ordered to be evacuated, but Rusesabagina knows that they are going to their deaths and pleads with the Hutu general Bizimungu (Fana Mokoena) to spare their lives. When the latter orders him to shoot his own family, Rusesabagina offers him money, as much money as he has at the hotel (100,000 francs). The general accepts the bribe and lets them go, but he and his family, along with a crowd of guests, eventually return to the hotel, having nowhere else to go.

Showing infinite resourcefulness under excruciating circumstances,[1] Rusesabagina resorts to any method available to him at the moment, bribing officials with money or booze, appealing to the UN and other European leaders, hiding as many people as he can, feeding the refugees, transporting refugees to what he thinks are safe places, and finally saving most of the displaced peoples' lives. At such moments, any human seems powerless against the forces of evil he confronts, which include the inexcusable and unexplainable indifference of the UN (and the United States) to the plight of millions, a shameful chapter in its history. The atrocities committed are momentous and almost similar to those committed by the Nazis, although the film spares us from gruesome sights of executions, only showing the victims—but the point is made.

Instead, the film shows us Rusesabagina's desperate attempts to do the best he can under harrowing circumstances, and in the process we enjoy the brilliant performance of Don Cheadle, who could not have embraced this role with more zeal and credibility—portraying a man on the edge of destruction, who nevertheless seems unphased by any setback he meets. His resourcefulness and ready wit even win the admiration of his captors, and he manages to escape perils against which an ordinary man would have no chance. Cheadle in action is a marvel to watch. He singlehandedly drives this movie. The humanitarian aspect of the film—its weight and message—is admirable, as it tells us about the failures of our civilization. But this movie is about a man's courage, his inventiveness, his wit, and his refusal to let his circumstances get the better of him. His is not an exercise in vanity—and this is not the usual Hollywood hero, who relies on glamour and slick superhuman feats (martial arts and so forth) to help him dazzle an audience.

To be specific, Cheadle is the opposite of Tom Cruise, who in his entire career has never managed to give a performance that even comes close to Cheadle's gutsy reactions under savage pressure. Not to disparage Cruise, but he is the archetype of a different kind of audience—those who go to the movies to seek thrills and glamour—and looks—provided by charismatic actors. Cheadle is the common man who becomes transformed from an ordinary assistant hotel manager into a hero, a man whose notions of style at the beginning of the story, when he brags about his cigars, somewhat degrade his image, but one whose moral stature escalates quickly as the movie's action progresses. He not only saves captive innocents from destruction, he points the way to correcting moral flaws inherent in war and conflict, flaws shared by humanity, not just one faction (and fraction) of it.

The movie's message is complex, but it is almost entirely related to what Cheadle, impersonating the hero in true moral dimension, shows us of how we fail to acknowledge failure or admit our flaws, thinking of "others" as being evil, while we pronounce ourselves the good ones who save them. Doubtless, our culture has produced altruists—like the Red Cross nurse who fights an equal battle, allying herself with Rusesabagina and his folks—but on the whole it has displayed little appetite for saving victims or getting involved when our immediate interests are not at stake. Rwanda is a poor country, with no diamonds and no oil or other exploitable products. We left it to its fate and turned our backs to its endangered people when they were being slaughtered by fanatical bands of rebels. Yes, it was civil war, but we could have done more to save the victims.

Critics were almost unanimous in praising the movie and its message. Michael Rechtshaffen said, "The actor impressively carries the entire picture, delivering the kind of note-perfect performance that's absolutely deserving of Oscar consideration."[2] Roger Ebert, piling up praise, as did many other critics, called the movie a "riveting drama," adding, "The film works not because the screen is filled with meaningless special effects, formless action, and vast digital armies, but because Cheadle, Nolte, and the filmmakers are interested in how two men choose to function in an impossible situation. Because we sympathize with these men, we are moved by the film."[3]

By centering on Cheadle's performance, we acknowledge the fact that one actor—with the givens of direction and writing—can shape and form an archetype and mold it, simultaneously, into an image of protest, inspiration, and deeply felt involvement—mental and moral strength, a savior of sorts—something Arnold Schwarzenegger and Tom Cruise cannot provide. It is the muscled hero versus the principled and conscientious man of action who has few resources but who, through his own wit, stamina, and determination, cares for his neighbor—and even for people he has never seen—as much as he does for his own immediate family. Here the art of the movie does not show artistic achievement of photographic marvels, distracting us from admiring human behavior. No magnificent landscapes of Africa are provided, as in *Out of Africa* or similar movies. This business at hand—for the writer, director, and actors—is far too urgent for all that. Here a lesson is taught to humanity, and blame is assigned for one of its great humanitarian failures. We ought to listen. CS

Notes

1. Roger Ebert called him an "expert in situational ethics." Quoted in Jeff Shannon, "*Hotel Rwanda*," *Amazon.com Editorial Reviews*, www.amazon.com/Hotel-Rwanda-Don-Cheadle/dp/B0007R4T3U (21 September 2013).
2. Michael Rechtshaffen, "*Hotel Rwanda*," *Hollywood Reporter*, 22 December 2004, www.hollywoodreporter.com/thr/reviews/review_display.jsp?vnu_content_id=1000628945 (21 September 2013).
3. Roger Ebert, "*Hotel Rwanda*," *Chicago Sun-Times*, 21 December 2004, www.rogerebert.com/reviews/hotel-rwanda-2004 (21 September 2013).

Bibliography

Ebert, Roger. "*Hotel Rwanda*." *Chicago Sun-Times*, 21 December 2004, www.rogerebert.com/reviews/hotel-rwanda-2004 (21 September 2013).

Lovgren, Stefan. "*Hotel Rwanda* Portrays Hero Who Fought Genocide." *National Geographic News*, 9 December 2004, http://news.nationalgeographic.com/news/2004/12/1209_041209_hotel_rwanda.html (21 September 2013).

Rechtshaffen, Michael. "*Hotel Rwanda*." *Hollywood Reporter*, 22 December 2004, www.hollywoodreporter.com/thr/reviews/review_display.jsp?vnu_content_id=1000628945 (21 September 2013).

"Rwanda: How the Genocide Happened." *BBC News*, 18 December 2008, http://news.bbc.co.uk/2/hi/1288230.stm (21 September 2013).

Shannon, Jeff. "*Hotel Rwanda*." *Amazon.com Editorial Reviews*, www.amazon.com/Hotel-Rwanda-Don-Cheadle/dp/B0007R4T3U (21 September 2013).

"United Nations Welcomes Establishment of International Fund for Rwanda." *UN.org*, 4 April 2005, http://www.un.org/News/Press/docs/2005/iha1031.doc.htm (21 September 2013).

HOW THE WEST WAS WON (1962)

Directors: Henry Hathaway: "The Rivers," "The Plains," "The Outlaws." John Ford: "The Civil War." George Marshall: "The Railroad." Richard Thorpe: "Historical Sequences" (uncredited)

Writer: James R. Webb

Producer: Bernard Smith (Cinerama)

Cinematographers: William H. Daniels, Milton R. Krasner, Charles Lang, Joseph LaShelle

Editor: Harold F. Kress

Art Direction: George W. Davis, William Ferrari, Addison Hehr

SET DECORATION: Henry Grace, Don Greenwood Jr., Jack Mills
COSTUMES: Walter Plunkett
MUSIC: Alfred Newman, Ken Darby
SOUND: Franklin Milton
MAKEUP ARTISTS: Sydney Guilarof, William Tuttle, Jay Sebring
CAST: Zebulon Prescott: Karl Malden. Eve Prescott: Carroll Baker. Lilith Prescott: Debbie Reynolds. Rebecca Prescott: Agnes Moorehead. Linus Rawlings: James Stewart. Julie Rawlings: Carolyn Jones. Zeb Rawlings: George Peppard. Cleve Van Valen: Gregory Peck. Roger Morgan: Robert Preston. Jethro Stuart: Henry Fonda. Mike King: Richard Widmark. Gen. William T. Sherman: John Wayne. Gen. Ulysses S. Grant: Harry Morgan. Col. Jeb Hawkins: Walter Brennan. Charlie Gant: Eli Wallach. Marshall Lou Ramsey: Lee J. Cobb. Dora Hawkins: Brigid Bazlen. Cpl. Peterson: Andy Devine. Agatha Clegg: Thelma Ritter. Narrator: Spencer Tracy
AA: Best Writing–Story and Screenplay Written Directly for the Screen (James R. Webb), Best Film Editing (Harold F. Kress), Best Sound (Franklin Milton)
AAN: Best Picture (Bernard Smith), Best Art Direction–Set Decoration (George W. Davis, William Ferrari, Addison Hehr, Henry Grace, Don Greenwood Jr., Jack Mills), Best Cinematography (William H. Daniels, Milton R. Krasner, Charles Lang, Joseph LaShelle), Best Costume Design (Walter Plunkett), Best Music–Substantially Original Score (Alfred Newman, Ken Darby)
DVD: MGM, 2008
BLU-RAY: Warner Bros., 2008
DURATION: 162 minutes

In 1952, when Hollywood studios were stumped by the rise of television and theater ticket buyers stayed home to see programs on their little TVs, movie moguls resorted to ways and means to lure back their lost customers. One method—and the main one—was to offer audiences greater spectacles in color and on wide-screens. This would accommodate the showing of casts of thousands; great epic battles of history, especially of the biblical/Roman variety, and great vistas of mountains, plains, deserts, and natural wonders—things impossible to do on TV. Thus came about such wondrous large screens as CinemaScope, VistaVision, Panavision, and a variety of others, which did exactly that. Audiences came back, although the battle between big screen and television went on for decades and actually never ended. One of the most intriguing of these wide-screen wonders was Cinerama, a three-strip process that required three projectors that filmed the wide vistas in three different planes, seamed together electronically in the laboratory, and later projected on a very long (up to 100 feet) curved screen that gave the impression of a three-dimensional spectacle of stunning clarity, while several speakers produced stereophonic sound, a total novelty at the time. Large theaters were built throughout the United States and around the world,[1] veritable palaces, with uniformed ushers and theater managers personally welcoming patrons, who were dressed as if going to an official event, sitting in luxurious seats and waiting for the velvet curtains to be drawn before the start of the grand spectacle. However, the new medium had its shortcomings. While the Cinerama process was well fitted for large expanses, mountainous areas, plains, and rivers, it could never offer intimate scenes between characters. It could not use close-ups, and action was photographed from a distance, thence it was impossible to photograph normal screen activity of an intimate nature. Because of this drawback, it was used for travelogues, geographical marvels, and other such spectacular shows, similar to those shown in IMAX theaters in our own time. What you usually see are groupings of people, mass gatherings, moving crowds, natural wonders, and adventures in the wilderness, with plenty of action. In those uncommon intimate scenes, one or two characters in the screen seem remote or isolated, with empty spaces to the right and left.

In the span of a decade (1952–1962), only two feature pictures were made, *The Wonderful World of the Brothers Grimm* and *How the West Was Won*, both completed in 1962 and shown within months of one another. The latter used three major directors, John Ford, Henry Hathaway, George Marshall, and several others with second units, as well as a large cast with numerous major stars, few of whom survived from beginning to end, and dozens of minor characters, many uncredited. The story spans several decades, from the 1840s to the 1880s. It covers the early movement west of small units, mostly families going down rivers on rafts; the larger movement in the Plains; the Civil War; the Pony Express; the building of the big railways Union Pacific and Central Pacific; the battle with the Arapaho Indians to make room for the passage of the railways; a spectacular buffalo stampede; and the spread of the outlaws and the battle of the law to wipe them out so that peaceful communities could live in peace.

The restored version of *How the West Was Won*, made in 2000, offers an aspect ratio wider than that of CinemaScope, which varies between 1.66:1 to 2.66:1,[2] with Cinerama expanding to 2.89:1, thus leaving today's viewer, even with a large TV, looking at a long strip of film on the screen, barely identifying the main characters, let alone crowds, which appear as small dots on the screen. The seams that used to join the three strips seem to have been eliminated, but one can often still see them when they are not entirely matched due to different shades of lighting.

The first episode, "The Rivers," set around 1840, recounts the family of Zebulon Prescott (Karl Malden), a preacher, who is seen traveling on a raft, starting on the Erie Canal and traveling down Ohio River to reach Illinois, at that time considered Western country. On the way they encounter a mountain man, a trapper, Linus Rawlings, who is going east, to Pittsburg, to sell his furs, which are loaded on his canoe. James Stewart is long-haired and aging but still gets the attention of Carroll Baker, Eve here, looking dazzling in the wilderness, her sobriquet fitting her. Linus, aghast but attracted, says no for the time being but promises to return. He is forced to, as he runs into a pirate gang run by the grizzled and ever-pressed Walter Brennan, Colonel Jeb Hawkins, whose young daughter Dora (Brigid Bazlen) takes him on a tour of a cave to show him a "varmint" and then pushes him into a well. He survives and rejoins the Prescott family as they themselves have wandered into the pirates' den, and together they demolish and burn the establishment. Prescott buries the villains, his prayer to God being, "Accept them, Lord, whether you want them or not." But their luck does not hold. They are soon caught in the river's rapids, and their raft, carrying all their possessions, is split apart by the current. Both Prescott parents die. Linus, unable to live without Eve, returns and marries her, and they settle at a homestead near where her parents died.

Meanwhile, the irrepressible Debbie Reynolds, Lilith, the older daughter of the Prescotts, has moved to St. Louis, where she is now a dancer. She attracts the attention of two men, one of whom is a gambler, Cleve Van Valen, played by Gregory Peck, and the other a wagon master, Roger Morgan (Robert Preston), who is leading a large wagon train westward. Morgan proposes twice, and Lilith rejects him both times, but she is attracted to Cleve. Lilith tells him that she is determined to get to California, where she has been told she has inherited a gold mine, so he joins her in the wagon train and they are both headed west. Lilith makes a new friend there, Agatha Clegg, played by Thelma Ritter, a grouchy and elderly woman starved for a husband, something she will never find. After surviving an Indian attack, Cleve and Lilith get to the gold mine, but when Lilith finds out that it is just an abandoned shack, Cleve leaves her, however, when he later sees her in a riverboat, dancing again, his luck has turned, he proposes again, and this time she accepts.

The scene changes again, now ten years later, as the Civil War rages. Linus has enlisted in the Union Army, but he is killed, and his son Zeb (George Peppard), living with his elderly mother, Eve, now past middle age, wants to enlist, too, so he leaves her and his young brother behind. We next him in the Battle of Shiloh, a bloody affair. Zeb strikes up a friendship with a confederate deserter, but he stabs him to death when the latter tries to shoot General William T. Sherman and General Ulysses S. Grant—played by John Wayne and Harry Morgan, respectively—while conferring on the fortunes of war. In the lengthy canvas scene of Cinerama, the viewer hardly sees Wayne, who usually fills the screen with his presence, except as a figure lost with the others, in the dark, since the sequence was filmed at night. This is the only appearance of the Duke, not an impressive one, whether one believes that he could or could not play General Sherman. Not much can be said of Harry Morgan, who has to be identified by name by the commentator.

When the war ends and Zeb returns home, he finds his mother dead of sorrow for the death of Linus. He leaves his farm to his brother and joins the army again, becomes a cavalry officer, and is dispatched to help the men working on the railroad tracks of the Central Pacific Railroad. The operation is being headed by Mike King (Richard Widmark), who is forced to negotiate with the Arapaho Indians for the passage of the railroad through their territory. The man who speaks their language is Jethro Stuart (Henry Fonda), an old friend of Linus who connected with Jeb, but neither of them can make the stubborn and unprincipled King respect the natives' rights. When King ignores those rights, the Arapahos turn a huge herd of buffalos loose. The massive animals stampede through the camp and destroy everything in their path, including many of the families of the working men.

Jeb becomes a U.S. marshal and a law man. He marries and is raising a family when his "Aunt" Lilith, now widowed and broke, invites him to travel with her to a ranch in Gold City, Arizona, which is all that remains of her fortune, and live there in peace. But when they arrive in Gold City, Jeb sees an old enemy, a gunslinger named Charlie Gant (Eli Wallach), along with his gang, making threats, since Zeb killed his brother. The local marshal, Lou Ramsey (Lee J. Cobb), refuses to have anything to do with the outlaws, not wanting to disturb his peaceful town, but when he has proof that Gant intends to rob a train carrying a load of gold, he joins forces with Zeb. As the gang boards the train, a gunfight ensues. Here, in one of the most spectacular scenes of a train wreck ever seen, Gant and his gang are killed, the train derails and crashes, its logs falling off, filling the wide-screen with wreckage, while the stereophonic sound roars. Lilith stays on with her new family to live the rest of her life in peace, the only member of the cast surviving from the beginning to the end of the Cinerama spectacular.

The voice of Spencer Tracy steadily accompanies the five sequences, tying the narrative together, while the music of Alfred Newman, playing variations of the "Green Leaves" melody, ties the themes of Western pioneering to the broad visual on the screen. The viewer is treated to modern overviews of Los Angeles and San Francisco, the two great centers of the West, built with the sweat and toil of those common folk venturing into the Western wilderness, lost and found, like the surviving lines of Linus Rawlings and the Prescotts. CS

Notes

1. Sixty throughout the United Sates and 200 around the world, according to David Stohmaier, director of Cinerama, in the running commentary for *How the West Was Won*, directed by Henry Hathaway, John Ford, George Marshall, and Richard Thorpe (MGM, 2008), DVD.

2. Frank E. Beaver, *Dictionary of Film Terms* (New York: McGraw-Hill, 1983), 52.

Bibliography

Beaver, Frank E. *Dictionary of Film Terms*. New York: McGraw-Hill, 1983.

L'Amour, Louis. *How the West Was Won*. New York: Bantam Books, 1988.

THE HUNT FOR RED OCTOBER (1990)

DIRECTOR: John McTiernan
WRITERS: Larry Ferguson, Donald Stewart. Based on the novel by Tom Clancy.
PRODUCERS: Larry DeWaay, Mace Neufeld, Jerry Sherlock (Paramount Pictures, Mace Neufeld Productions)
CINEMATOGRAPHER: Jan De Bont
EDITOR: Dennis Virkler, John Wright
MUSIC: Basil Poledouris
SOUND EDITORS: Cecelia Hall, George Watters II
SOUND MIXERS: Richard Bryce Goodman, Richad Overton, Kevin F. Cleary, Don J. Bassman
CAST: Marko Ramius: Sean Connery. Jack Ryan: Alec Baldwin. Bart Mancuso: Scott Glenn. Capt. Vasili Borodin: Sam Neil. Adm. Greer: James Earl Jones. Andrei Lysenko: Josh Ackland. Skip Tyler: Jeffrey Jones. Capt. Viktor Tupolev: Stellan Skarsgård. Dr. Yevgeniy Petrov: Tim Curry. Capt. Vasili Borodin: Sam Neill. Adm. Yuri Padorin: Peter Zinner. Petty Officer Jones: Courtney B. Vance. Jeffery Pelt: Richard Jordan. Adm. Painter: Fred Dalton Thompson. Capt. Davenport: Daniel Davis
AA: Best Effects–Sound Effects Editing (Cecelia Hall, George Watters II)
AAN: Best Film Editing (Dennis Virkler, John Wright), Best Sound (Richard Bryce Goodman, Richad Overton, Kevin F. Cleary, Don J. Bassman)
DVD: Paramount Pictures, 2003
BLU-RAY: Paramount Pictures, 2008
DURATION: 134 minutes

After directing the highly successful film *Die Hard* (1988), John McTiernan wanted to make a realistic film where the people in the military and the intelligence community were treated as "decent people."[1] Based on Tom Clancy's novel of the same name, *The Hunt for Red October* popularized the "techno-espionage thriller," and one reviewer said that McTiernan achieved his goals and created a "thriller that treated its audience as adults and had as much respect for the characters in its story."[2]

The Hunt for Red October is the story of two men working against all odds to keep the Cold War from becoming hot: a Soviet sub commander, Marko Ramius (Sean Connery), and an American CIA researcher, Jack Ryan (Alec Baldwin). Ramius plans to take the Soviet Union's newest sub, the *Red October*, a sub built as a first-strike weapon, to the U.S. government and defect with his crew. The film opens as he heads his sub into the North Atlantic. Meanwhile, Ryan, an academic who studies submarines for the CIA living in London with his British wife and daughter, leaves Heathrow Airport for a meeting with Admiral Greer (James Earl Jones) in Washington, DC. Ryan has intelligence photos of *Red October*, which worries them because it is longer and wider than the standard Typhoon-class sub. At the meeting, Greer tells Ryan that satellites have caught the *Red October* leaving the Polyarny Inlet that morning, so Ryan immediately leaves to visit a shipyard that builds nuclear submarines[3] to speak with a sub builder, Skip Tyler (Jeffrey Jones), who is building a Deep Submergence Rescue Vehicle (DSRVs), which is rigged with a generic docking collar. Inspecting Ryan's photos, Tyler suspects that the *Red October* has a new propulsion system, a "magnetohydrodynamic drive," often called a "caterpillar" drive. The new system would allow a sub to move through the water quickly and quietly, merely sounding like whales or "magma displacement."

Ramius meets with the Soviet political officer in his stateroom to open their orders. The scene begins in Russian, but McTiernan moves to English by using a technique first used in *Judgment at Nuremberg* (1961): the political officer speaks in Russian while the camera zooms in on his mouth and speaks English when the camera zooms out. Ramius's orders are for *Red October* to rendezvous with Captain Viktor Tupolev's (Stellan Skarsgård) submarine the *Konovolov*, which will "hunt" them so they can test their systems. The officer insists on announcing the plans to the crew, but Ramius kills him, making it look like an accident. He burns the orders and substitutes his own. The captain retains the political officer's missile key despite the objections of Dr. Yevgeniy Petrov (Tim Curry). The cook's assistant witnesses the exchange.

Ramius announces their orders to the crew and the great advantage their ship will have over the *Konovolov*, and the Americans. He orders the silent caterpillar drive engaged. Inspired by Ramius's speech, the sailors sing. To show secret conversations between Ramius and Captain Vasili Borodin (Sam Neill), McTiernan uses a wide-angle lens.[4] Unbeknownst to the crew, Ramius's letter to Admiral Yuri Padorin (Peter Zinner), chairman of the Red Fleet and Ramius's wife's uncle, to let him know of his intention to defect arrives in Padorin's office. Padorin and the Soviet premier order their Atlantic fleet sortied.

The USS *Dallas*, a Los Angeles–class attack sub, commanded by Bart Mancuso (Scott Glenn), follows the *Red October* and hears it go silent, except for the sound of magma displacement and the singing crew. Petty Officer Jones (Courtney B. Vance), a sonar technician, investigates the sound.

Admiral Greer arranges a briefing for Jeffery Pelt (Richard Jordan), the president's national security advisor (NSA), and the Joint Chiefs of Staff, to be given by Ryan. As he begins, Ryan is shown in extreme close-up, highlighting his separation from the other attendees. No longer merely an object of academic study, the *Red October*—named after the October Revolution in 1917, and roughly the same size as a World War II aircraft carrier—is determined to be a first-strike weapon, and with fifty-eight nuclear subs heading to the Atlantic, it could be a prelude to war. The NSA reports that the Soviet fleet has orders to sink the *Red October*. Afraid the Soviets have a "madman on their hands," Ryan realizes that Ramius is going to defect because there are no subs in the Pacific; it is the first anniversary of his wife's death, he has no children, and he is Lithuanian. He was also able to handpick his crew. Having four days until the *Red October* is in a position to fire missiles, Pelt gives Ryan three days to contact Ramius and assist him, otherwise they must destroy him. Pelt advises Ryan to contact the commanders in the Atlantic directly, avoiding regular channels. Unlike other war films, the main goal of the film is to avoid war.

The *Red October*'s conspiring officers dine in secret, and Ramius tells them about his letter to Padorin, explaining that when Cortez arrived in the New World, he burned his ships to motivate his men. Their main worry is the Americans, not the Russians. Meanwhile, Tupolev receives his new orders seven hours late. He must push the reactor to 105 percent to catch up to and destroy the *Red October.*

The *Red October* arrives at Red Route One, a common passage used by Soviet subs, and Ramius speeds through the canyon, putting the ship and crew through its paces. McTiernan uses a gimbaled set to show the sub's turns through the canyon. Ramius removes an officer from the deck when he interferes with his mental calculations at the right moment to turn the boat. The caterpillar drive is suddenly no longer being cooled by the cryogenic plant, so they are forced to use normal propulsion.

Ryan takes a rough helicopter ride to the aircraft carrier. Regretting it, he says, "The next time you get a bright idea, put it in a memo." There he has to convince Admiral Painter (Fred Dalton Thompson) and Captain Davenport (Daniel Davis) to assist him. They ask more questions than he can answer. Ryan's fear of turbulence is revealed in a discussion of serious injuries he incurred in a helicopter accident during the Vietnam War. Ryan later realizes Ramius already has a plan and that faking a nuclear accident would be the most likely way to cause the crew to abandon the boat. The Soviet ambassador, Andrei Lysenko (Josh Ackland), admits to Jeffery Pelt that they have alerted the fleet in the Atlantic, but he says that it is a massive rescue operation for a lost submarine. He does not accept Pelt's offer for a joint rescue mission.

A Soviet antisubmarine aircraft south of Iceland drops sonar buoys, causing the *Red October* to go to battle stations. When the aircraft drops its torpedoes, the *Red October* launches countermeasures, which fail. To avoid the torpedo and narrowly missing the canyon wall, Ramius orders the sub to turn and reverse the starboard shaft, making it turn quicker. A fitting inside the boat breaks and Borodin closes a valve, a traditional film technique in World War II films, but it is otherwise unnecessary.[5] After the caterpillar is repaired, Ramius and Borodin discuss living in the United States. Ramius pulls a "Crazy Ivan" to see if anyone is following. To avoid detection, the *Dallas* shuts down and "makes like a hole in the water."

On board the *Dallas,* Bart Mancuso and his crew discuss the recorded sounds using thoughtful analysis. The *Dallas* gets a message to meet Ryan on the surface. Ryan, who is in a helicopter, pushes the crew to use their reserve fuel so he can reach the sub. Ryan has to drop into the water before they run out. The *Dallas* uses an escape trunk to pull him out of the water, as he has only four minutes of survival time in the icy water.

The Soviet ambassador speaks to Pelt, this time with the desire to have the United States fire on the *Red October* to destroy it. The *Dallas* receives notice from the National Command Authority that they are authorized to use any necessary force against the *Red October.* Mancuso's boat once again catches the *Red October.* Ryan has to convince Mancuso that Ramius is actually trying to defect, not attack the United States. Ryan tries to find a way that will not violate orders. Mancuso calls the chief to the conn with his sidearm in case he needs to protect the ship from Ryan; however, he orders the boat "all back full" as their presence is revealed. He opens the outer doors for the torpedoes and is ready to fire. In response, the *Red October* floods its tubes and plots a solution but leaves doors closed. The *Red October* goes shallow, and the *Dallas* follows. Via Mancuso's Morse code and Ramius's "ping" responses, the *Dallas* determines that Ramius intends to defect and they plan the handover, during which Ramius will "scuttle" the ship in the Laurentian Abyss. When they arrive, the reactor and ventilation "fail," forcing the crew off the ship and into life rafts. An American Seahawk helicopter drops a torpedo, which is blown up by Admiral Greer on the *Reuben James.* He instructs the sailors that they heard it hit the hull, not "self-destruct," as it did.

Ryan, Mancuso, Jones, and others take the *Mystic*, a DSRV, from the *Dallas* to the *Red October.* Mancuso carries a pistol, so Ryan fears he that will be a cowboy, but he accepts one from him in case Ramius changes his mind about defecting. In the *Red October*'s control room, the officers face one another. To break the ice, in spite of being a nonsmoker, Ryan signals to the *Red October*'s engineer that he wants a cigarette. The ice is broken when Ryan turns "green" attempting to smoke it. Ramius calls Mancuso a buckaroo, but Ramius turns the ship over to him and asks for asylum. They are alerted to the *Konolav*'s presence when one of its torpedoes misses them. Short of crew, Ramius puts Ryan on the steering. Ramius orders him to turn straight into the torpedo. The *Red October* hits the torpedo and breaks apart because the safeties were still set at that distance. Borodin is suddenly killed by a bullet, and Ramius and Ryan follow the saboteur into engineering. Mancuso gives Ramius his weapon. Ryan finds that the saboteur is a cook, and, although he hesitates, he shoots him.

Aboard the *Konolav*, Captain Tupolev sets the torpedo's safeties to off, moves behind the *Red October*, and launches a torpedo. Unable to attack a Soviet ship without orders, the *Dallas* moves in front of the torpedo, leading it away. They release countermeasures and surface near the Soviet crew, but the torpedo remains active and is drawn to the *Konolav* and destroys it. Seeing the explosion erupt to the surface, the Soviet crew believes that it was the *Red October.*

Pelt meets the Russian ambassador, telling him that the wreckage is too deep to search and that arrangements have been made for the crew, but the ambassador, hat in hand, admits that they have lost another sub. The submarine is hidden in a river in Maine. Ramius quotes Columbus,[6] and Ryan welcomes Ramius to the New World. In the last scene of the film, he is sleeping on a plane heading to London, in spite of his fear of flying, with a stuffed animal, a brother for his daughter.

The Hunt for Red October is an anti-cowboy military film; it focuses on the coolheaded determination needed for such events. Indeed, in attempting to stop a weapon capable of killing millions, only two men are killed. Both killings are done with consideration and caution: one each by Marko Ramius and Jack Ryan. JMW

Notes

1. John McTiernan, "Director's Commentary," *The Hunt for Red October*, directed by John McTiernan (Paramount Pictures, 2003), DVD.
2. David Brooks, "Review: *The Hunt for Red October*," *Wall Street Journal*, 1 March 1990, 14.
3. McTiernan, "Director's Commentary."
4. McTiernan, "Director's Commentary."
5. McTiernan, "Director's Commentary."
6. The Columbus quote was created by the screenwriters. McTiernan, "Director's Commentary."

Bibliography

Brooks, David. "Review: *The Hunt for Red October.*" *Wall Street Journal*, 1 March 1990, 14.

Walsch, Frances M. *Intelligence in Contemporary Media.* New York: Novinka, 2011.

I

INTOLERANCE (1916)

DIRECTOR: D. W. Griffith
WRITER: D. W. Griffith
PRODUCER: D. W. Griffith (Triangle Film Corporation, Wark Producing Corporation)
ASSISTANT DIRECTORS: Arhtur Berthelon, Allan Dwan, Erich von Stroheim, W. Christy Cabanne, Tod Browning, Jack Conway, George Nicholls, Llyod Ingraham
CINEMATOGRAPHER: G. W. Bitzer
EDITOR: D. W. Griffith (uncredited), James Smith (uncredited), Rose Smith (uncredited)
ART DIRECTION: Walter L. Hall
COSTUMES: D. W. Griffith (uncredited), Clare West (uncredited)
MUSIC: D. W. Griffith, Joseph Carl Breil, Carl Davis
CAST: The Woman Who Rocks the Cradle/Eternal Mother: Lillian Gish
The Modern Story: The Dear One: Mae Marsh. The Boy: Robert Harron. The Dear One's Father: Fred Turner. Arthur Jenkins: Sam De Grasse. Mary Jenkins: Vera Lewis. The Uplifters and Reformers: Mary Alden, Eleanor Washington, Pearl Elmore, Lucille Browne, Mrs. Arthur Mackley. The Friendless One: Miriam Cooper. The Musketeer of the Slums: Walter Long. A Crook: Tod Browning
The Judean Story: The Nazarene: Howard Gaye. Mary: Lillian Langdon. Mary Magdalene: Olga Grey. First Pharisee: Gunther von Ritzau. Second Pharisee: Erich von Stroheim. The Bride of Cana: Bessie Love. The Bride's Father: William Brown. The Bridegroom: George Walsh. Wedding Guest: W. S. Van Dyke
The French Story: Brown Eyes: Margery Wilson. Prosper Latour: Eugene Pallette. Brown Eyes's Father: Spottiswoode Aitken. Brown Eyes's Mother: Ruth Handforth. The Mercenary: A. D. Sears. Charles IX: Frank Bennett. Duc d'Anjou: Maxfield Stanley. Catherine de Medici: Josephine Crowell. Marguerite de Valois: Constance Talmadge. Henry of Navarre: W. E. Lawrence. Adm. Coligny: Joseph Henabery. Page: Chandler House
The Babylonian Story: Mountain Girl: Constance Talmadge. The Rhapsode: Elmer Clifton. Prince Belshazzar: Alfred Paget. The Princess Beloved: Seena Owen. King Nabonidus: Carl Stockdale. High Priest of Bel: Tully Marshall. Cyrus: George Siegmann (uncredited). Extra: Douglas Fairbanks (uncredited)
AA: None
AAN: None
DVD: Eureka Video, 2000
BLU-RAY: Currently unavailable
DURATION: 177 minutes

Continuing on from the monumental success of *The Birth of a Nation* (1915), D. W. Griffith lost all his money on the extravagant $485,000 *Intolerance* (subtitled *Love's Struggle Throughout the Ages*), the "cost of forty ordinary films."[1] The movie was intended as a response to the criticisms of racism made against the earlier film (but was by no means an apology, for Griffith did not agree with the assessments[2]). *Intolerance*, a silent-film epic tale of love and intolerance throughout four different time periods, may not have been successful upon its release, but it has since become regarded a cinema classic,[3] setting the template for future historical epics in its scope and visual grandeur. Among the bit players are a number of figures who would later rise to prominence, including Tod Browning (*Dracula*, 1931), W. S. Van Dyke (*The Thin Man*, 1934; *Marie Antoinette* 1938), and Douglas Fairbanks (*The Thief of Bagdad*, 1924).

The four stories are intercut with one another, connected by the image of the eternal mother (Lillian Gish) rocking her cradle. The most extravagant of the tales portrays the sixth century B.C.E. defeat of the city of Babylon at the hands of Cyrus the Persian. Although Griffith goes to great pains to point out the historical sources for his story, he departs from them by having Cyrus (George Siegmann) besiege the great walls of Babylon. Although Cyrus's initial campaign is not successful, he finds help from within. The High Priest of Bel (Tully Marshall) is incensed by the toleration of other deities within the city and decides to plot against King Nabonidus of Babylon (Carl Stockdale) and his son Prince Belshazzar (Alfred Paget), letting Cyrus into the city. The scheme is discovered by a young and spirited Mountain Girl (Constance Talmadge, charming in the role), who is enchanted with Belshazzar after he saves her from humiliation at the marriage market. But she is unable to convince the prince in time, as Cyrus enters the city. The brave Mountain Girl is killed defending the city in battle, while Belshazzar and his betrothed take their own lives to escape the humiliation of capture.

The other most prominent story tells a contemporary cautionary tale outlining the ill effects of charity when it is based on intolerance. When a mill owner cuts his workers' wages by 10 percent (ironically to fund his sister's charity, the Jenkins Foundation), the workers go on strike, only to be defeated. The Dear One (Mae Marsh) lives in poverty, and The Boy (Robert Harron) turns to crime, while The Friendless One (Miriam Cooper) becomes the mistress to the crime boss, known as The Musketeer of the Slums (Walter Long). When The Dear One and The Boy fall in love and marry, The Boy announces his intentions to turn straight, but he is framed by The Musketeer and sent to prison. Meanwhile, The Dear One loses their baby to the Jenkins Foundation after she is discovered drinking whiskey for her cold and is taken for a drunken mother. The Musketeer offers to help, but his intentions are not honorable, and The Boy returns just in time to prevent his wife's rape. The Friendless One, jealous of her rival, shoots The Musketeer through an open window, and The Boy is convicted of the crime. He is saved from the gallows just in time when The Friendless One finally confesses, and the couple gets their baby back.

The final two stories are given much shorter treatment. The French tale tells of the St. Bartholomew's Day Massacre of the Protestant Huguenots by the Roman Catholics in 1572. The Protestant Henry of Navarre (W. E. Lawrence) arrives in Paris to wed Margaret, sister to King Charles IX (Frank Bennett), but Charles' mother, Catherine de Medici (Josephine Crowell), is unhappy with the influx of Huguenots and conspires to convince him to have them slain. Caught up in these events is the innocent Brown Eyes (Margery Wilson), a Huguenot who (it is inferred) is raped and killed in the purge before her betrothed can rescue her.

The Biblical section, the shortest section of the film, recounts Jesus' role at the wedding at Cana, where he turns water into wine, and the saving of Mary Magdalene (Olga Grey) as the woman taken into adultery (although she is not so named in the Bible), where he impels only, "He that is without sin among you, let him first cast a stone at her" in punishment of her adultery. The intolerance of the Pharisees is also highlighted, and finally we see the Crucifixion itself. The film as a whole ends as angels appear in the sky, ushering in a new era of peace, during which time armies lay down their weapons and fields of flowers replace prison walls.

The shortness of the biblical and French stories renders them less effective and leads to an unevenness in the final intercut film, which was originally intended as two four-hour screenings but was reduced when exhibitors protested.[4] Commenting in 1919, *Variety* wrote, "The public wasn't entirely crazy about D. W. Griffith's massive production *Intolerance* when he presented it [in 1916]. At that time there was too much interest in the greatest drama of the time—the war."[5] The year 1919 saw the release of the modern tale separately as *The Mother and the Law*, and the spectacular Babylonian tale as *The Fall of Babylon*, the title taken from two paintings that influenced Griffith's vision of Babylon.[6] Both films were expanded with additional material and new endings, with the Mountain Girl surviving to take her suitor (the Rhapsode) home for a new life back in the mountains.[7] Musical stage acts were well-received additions.[8]

The enormous Babylonian sets, which were 200 feet high, drew inspiration from paintings, but also archaeological finds, although, as Jon Solomon notes, "Griffith combined Persian, Assyrian, Sumerian, and Babylonian ingredients into one Irano/Mesopotamian stew,"[9] the kind of iconographic hodgepodge that would continue to characterize Hollywood's forays into the ancient world epic for decades to come. Beyond the beauty, detail, and scope of its visual spectacle, Griffith's *Intolerance* would also set new standards in film techniques, among them the precursor of the camera crane (Griffith placed the camera on an elevator platform on tracks[10]). Not such a bad legacy for a "failed" film. DB

Notes

1. Jeffrey Richards, *Hollywood's Ancient Worlds* (London: Continuum, 2008), 31.
2. Lillian Gish, with Ann Pinchot, *The Movies, Mr. Griffith, and Me* (Englewood Cliffs, NJ: Prentice Hall, 1969), 165, 359. Gish writes extensively on the making and reception of *Intolerance.*
3. The film may not have succeeded at the box office, but *Variety* predicted its eventual status: "*Intolerance* reflects much credit to the wizard director, for it required no small amount of genuine art to consistently blend actors, horses, monkeys, geese, doves, acrobats, and ballets into a composite presentation of a film classic." "Review: *Intolerance*," *Variety*, 1916, http://variety.com/1915/film/reviews/intolerance-1117792001/ (15 June 2013).
4. Gish, with Pinchot, *The Movies, Mr. Griffith, and Me*, 179.
5. "Review: *The Fall of Babylon*," *Variety*, 1919, http://variety.com/1918/film/reviews/the-fall-of-babylon-1200409306/ (15 June 2013).
6. Richards, *Hollywood's Ancient Worlds*, 29.
7. Edward Wagenknecht and Anthony Slide, *The Films of D. W. Griffith* (New York: Crown, 1975), 88–89.
8. Variety, "Review: The Fall of Babylon."
9. Jon Solomon, *The Ancient World in the Cinema* (New Haven, CT, and London: Yale University Press, 2001), 235.
10. Gish, with Pinchot, *The Movies, Mr. Griffith, and Me*, 175.

Bibliography

Gish, Lillian, with Ann Pinchot. *The Movies, Mr. Griffith, and Me*. Englewood Cliffs, NJ: Prentice Hall, 1969.

"Review: *The Fall of Babylon*," *Variety*, 1919, http://variety.com/1918/film/reviews/the-fall-of-babylon-1200409306/ (15 June 2013).

"Review: *Intolerance*," *Variety*, 1916, http://variety.com/1915/film/reviews/intolerance-1117792001/ (15 June 2013).

Richards, Jeffrey. *Hollywood's Ancient Worlds*. London: Continuum, 2008.

Solomon, Jon. *The Ancient World in the Cinema*. New Haven, CT, and London: Yale University Press, 2001.

Wagenknecht, Edward, and Anthony Slide. *The Films of D. W. Griffith*. New York: Crown, 1975.

J

JASON AND THE ARGONAUTS (1963)

DIRECTOR: Don Chaffey
WRITERS: Jan Read, Beverley Cross. Based on *The Argonautica*, by Apollonius of Rhodius.
PRODUCER: Charles H. Schneer (Columbia Pictures)
ASSOCIATE PRODUCER: Ray Harryhausen
CINEMATOGRAPHER: Wilkie Cooper
EDITOR: Maurice Rootes
ART DIRECTION: Herbert Smith, Jack Maxsted, Tony Sarzi Braga
MUSIC: Bernard Herrmann
VISUAL EFFECTS: Ray Harryhausen
CAST: Jason: Todd Armstrong. Medea: Nancy Kovack. Acastus: Gary Raymond. Argus: Laurence Naismith. Zeus: Niall MacGinnis. Hermes: Michael Gwynn. Pelias: Douglas Wilmer. King Aeëtes: Jack Gwillim. Hera: Honor Blackman. Hylas: John Cairney. Phineas: Patrick Troughton. Phalerus: Andrew Faulds. Hercules: Nigel Green
AA: None
AAN: None
DVD: Columbia Pictures, 1999
BLU-RAY: Sony Pictures Home Entertainment, 2010
DURATION: 100 minutes

In this much-loved ancient-world epic (Tom Hanks declared it the "best film ever made"[1]), Jason of Greek myth searches for the famed Golden Fleece to secure his rightful place on the throne of Thessaly and bring peace to his kingdom. The story is based on *The Argonautica*, by Apollonius of Rhodius, but the real author of the film is recognized to be Ray Harryhausen, whose stop-motion animation of Jason's various monstrous foes and aids forms the showpieces of the film.

At the beginning of the film, Pelias (Douglas Wilmer) attacks Thessaly and overthrows King Aristo, but Pelias causes the wrath of Hera (Honor Blackman) when he kills Aristo's daughter in the goddesses' temple. A disguised Hera tells him that a man with one sandal, Aristo's son Jason (Todd Armstrong), will overthrow him, but she also warns him: "Kill Jason, and you kill yourself."

Twenty years later, Hera conspires for Jason to rescue Pelias from drowning. Although Jason loses his sandal in the water and thereby reveals his identity to Pelias, Jason himself does not know the king and unwittingly tells him of his plans to take back the throne. He first intends to bring back the famed Golden Fleece so that it may restore the prosperity and faith of his people. Yet, Jason confesses to a disguised Hermes (Michael Gwynn) that he does not himself believe in the gods, so Hermes takes him to Mount Olympus. Hera tells Jason that Zeus (Niall MacGinnis) has permitted her to help him but five times and says that he will find the fleece in Colchis, "at the end of the world."

Back in Greece, Jason relies on his countrymen's pride to find a crew, holding competitive games so that they may secure a place on his voyage. Unknown to Jason, Pelias' son Acastus (Gary Raymond) succeeds in joining the voyage, with the intent of undermining the mission.

Talking through a figurehead on Argus' (Laurence Naismith) ship, Hera directs Jason to the Isle of Bronze but cautions him that his men must take only food and water and nothing else. Once on the island, Hercules (Nigel Green) takes a huge brooch pin from a treasury under a massive statue of Talos the Titan, despite the protests of his friend Hylas (John Cairney). Talos comes alive to avenge the desecration, the first of Harryhausen's great creatures to appear in the film, creaking with metal upon metal. Although the men try to escape by sea, Talos straddles the straights like the Colossus of Rhodes and shakes the men from their boat. Jason is forced to ask for Hera's assistance again and learns to attack Talos at his heels, making him bleed his vital ichor and die. Unseen by the other men, Hylas is crushed by the falling Talos. Hercules is crestfallen, remaining on the island to search for his friend. An older actor (the charismatic Nigel Green) was chosen to play Hercules specifically to differentiate the film from the popular Italian muscleman films and give more resonance to his somber departure from the quest.[2]

Acastus uses Hercules' departure as an opportunity to whip up rebellion among the men, and Jason calls upon Hera to show her favor to the crew. Following her advice, the Argonauts set sail to Phrygia to seek the guidance of the blind Phineas (Patrick Troughton). Phineas demands that Jason first rid him of the Harpies that have been sent by Zeus to plague him for his sins. As the Harpies are drawn into the temple ruins with food, Jason's men quietly cover the building with nets, capturing the Harpies and caging them for Phineas. The grateful Phineas tells them to go through the Clashing Rocks to get to Colchis, but as Jason can no longer call on Hera, Phineas gives him a talisman of Triton to help them.

Although Jason and his men witness another ship being crushed by the rocks, Jason decides to proceed. Seemingly about to face their own destruction, Jason curses the gods and throws his Triton amulet away, but Hera summons the massive Triton himself to hold the rocks open for the Argo. Jason is able to rescue one crewmember from the crushed ship—the beautiful Medea (Nancy Kovack).

Approaching Colchis, Acastus secretly makes his way onshore to warn King Aeëtes (Jack Gwillim) of Jason's plan to take the fleece. Although Jason and his men are initially welcomed by the king, it is simply a pretext to capture them. Medea, however, has fallen in love with Jason and frees them.

Acastus tries to obtain the Golden Fleece himself but is fatally wounded by the seven-headed Hydra who defends it. Jason defeats the Hydra, and his men take the fleece, but they are pursued by King Aeëtes, who uses the teeth of the dead Hydra to bring forth skeleton warriors. During the battle, an injured Medea is revived by the fleece and taken by Argus to the safety of the ship. Jason leads the skeletons over a cliff and swims to the safety of his ship.

At the close of the film, the gods watch the triumphant Jason as he kisses Medea, but they warn them to enjoy their moment of happiness, for the gods' game with Jason will continue another day, a mere hint of the tragedy that will befall the pair when Jason forsakes Medea and she kills their children (Euripides, *Medea*; Apollodorus, *The Library*, 1.9.28).

The film ends somewhat abruptly and does not show Jason's triumphant return to Thessaly or the overthrow of Pelias. But as a whole, it is nonetheless memorable for Jason's encounters with Harryhausen's creatures; a suitably adventurous-sounding score from Bernard Herrmann that emphasizes brass and percussion; and the depiction of the capricious Greek gods interfering with the affairs of humans as if they were mere chess pieces in their game.

Harryhausen's special effects spectacles were planned first, and the script was then written around them. The skeleton warriors became his favorite, having first used a single skeleton in *The 7th Voyage of Sinbad* (Nathan Juran, 1958). Scenes in *Jason and the Argonauts* featuring all seven skeletons were so laborious that Harryhausen was able to complete only thirteen frames a day, or less than one second of finished film, and the entire sequence took four and a half months to complete.[3]

During its time, *Jason and the Argonauts* received a mixed critical reception. *Variety* gave it an enthusiastic review, praising its "spectacular mythological landscape and characters," but the *New York Times* declared that it was "no worse, but certainly no better, than most of its kind."[4] *Variety*'s opinion prevailed with the audience and the industry. In 1991, Ray Harryhausen was awarded with a special Oscar, the Gordon E. Sawyer Award, which honors "an individual in the motion picture industry whose technological contributions have brought credit to the industry,"[5] presented by his lifelong friend, science-fiction writer Ray Bradbury. DB

Notes

1. Richard Schickel, "The Harryhausen Chronicles," *Jason and the Argonauts*, directed by Don Chaffey (Columbia Pictures, 1999), DVD.
2. Ray Harryhausen and Tony Dalton, *Ray Harryhausen: An Animated Life* (New York: Billboard Books, 2004), 152.
3. Harryhausen and Dalton, *Ray Harryhausen*, 151–52, 169–74. See also Ray Harryhausen, *Ray Harryhausen's Fantasy Scrapbook: Models, Artwork, and Memories from 65 Years of Filmmaking* (London: Aurum Press, 2012), as well as Ray Harryhausen and Tony Dalton, *The Art of Ray Harryhausen* (London: Aurum Press, 2005).
4. "*Jason and the Argonauts*," *Variety*, 1963, www.variety.com/review/VE1117792120/ (8 January 2012); "Jason and Argonauts Seek Golden Fleece at Loew's State," *New York Times*, 8 August 1963, http://movies.nytimes.com/movie/review?res=9506E7DE1431E73BBC4053DFBE668388679EDE&scp=5&sq=%22jason%20and%20the%20argonauts%22%20review&st=cse (8 January 2012).
5. Academy of Motion Picture Arts and Sciences, "Gordon E. Sawyer Award," *Oscars.org*, www.oscars.org/awards/academyawards/about/awards/sawyer.html (22 December 2011).

Bibliography

Harryhausen, Ray. *Ray Harryhausen's Fantasy Scrapbook: Models, Artwork, and Memories from 65 Years of Filmmaking*. London: Aurum Press, 2012.

Harryhausen, Ray and Tony Dalton. *The Art of Ray Harryhausen*. London: Aurum Press, 2005.

———. *Ray Harryhausen: An Animated Life*. New York: Billboard Books, 2004.

"*Jason and the Argonauts*." *Variety*, 1963, www.variety.com/review/VE1117792120/ (8 January 2012).

"Jason and Argonauts Seek Golden Fleece at Loew's State." Movie Review, *New York Times*, 8 August 1963, http://movies.nytimes.com/movie/review?res=9506E7DE1431E73BBC4053DFBE668388679EDE&scp=5&sq=%22jason%20and%20the%20argonauts%22%20review&st=cse (8 January 2012).

JOURNEY TO THE CENTER OF THE EARTH (1959)

DIRECTOR: Henry Levin
WRITERS: Walter Reisch, Charles Brackett. Based on the novel by Jules Verne.
PRODUCERS: Charles Brackett (Cooga Mooga Film Productions, Joseph M. Schenck Enterprises, 20th Century Fox)
CINEMATOGRAPHER: Leo Tover
EDITOR: Stuart Gilmore, Jack W. Holmes
ART DIRECTION: Lyle R. Wheeler, Franz Bachelin, Herman A. Blumenthal
SET DECORATION: Walter M. Scott, Joseph Kish
COSTUMES: David Folkes
MUSIC: Bernard Herrmann
SPECIAL EFFECTS: L. B. Abbott, James B. Gordon, Carl W. Faulkner

CAST: Alexander "Alec" McEwen: Pat Boone. Prof. Oliver Lindenbrook: James Mason. Carla Göteborg: Arlene Dahl. Jenny Lindenbrook: Diane Baker. Count Arne Saknussem: Thayer David. Hans: Peter Ronson. Groom: Robert Adler. Dean: Alan Napier. Prof. Bayle: Alex Finlayson. Paisley: Ben Wright
AA: None
AAN: Best Art Direction–Set Decoration–Color (Lyle R. Wheeler, Franz Bachelin, Herman A. Blumenthal, Walter M. Scott, Joseph Kish), Best Effects–Special Effects (L. B. Abbott, James B. Gordon, Carl W. Faulkner), Best Sound (Carl W. Faulkner)
DVD: 20th Century Fox, 2003
BLU-RAY: Twilight Time, 2012
DURATION: 124 minutes

"Twentieth Century Fox Now Brings to the Screen, on a Scale Tremendous beyond Belief, the Story of an Unprecedented Expedition to Regions Never Explored Before!"[1] So proclaims the original theatrical trailer for *Journey to the Center of the Earth*, based on the 1864 novel by Jules Verne. This CinemaScope film version of the adventure epic is set in the year 1880, when the recently knighted Professor Oliver Lindenbrook of Edinburgh (James Mason) is leading an expedition to the center of the Earth. Key sequences from the film are echoed in Steven Spielberg's *Raiders of the Lost Ark* (1981), namely a secret location revealed by a shaft of sunlight at a designated time and date, and an escape from a large, rolling boulder within a cavern. *Journey to the Center of the Earth* boasts excellent set designs and special effects for its time (for which it gained Academy Award nominations) and memorable giant subterranean creatures, and the movie has remained a delight for many generations of young viewers.

Joining Lindenbrook on the perilous downward journey is his student Alec (pop singer Pat Boone, who sings along the way); a robust Icelandic guide named Hans (Peter Ronson); Hans' interpreter, Carla Göteborg (Arlene Dahl); and Hans' endearing duck Gertrude. Gertrude and Carla are new additions to the tale, the former providing comic relief and cuteness for young viewers, and the latter adding sexual friction with James Mason and the visual appeal of Arlene Dahl's phenomenal figure. Left behind to wait for the team is Lindenbrook's niece and Alec's fiancée Jenny (Diane Baker, who would go on to a distinguished career in television and may be familiar to today's viewers as House's mother in *House*, 2004–2012).

The film version of *Journey to the Center of the Earth* also deviates from the novel by adding rivals for Lindenbrook's goal. The first is Carla's husband, who races ahead of them to Iceland when Lindenbrook (foolishly, as it turns out) asks his opinion of a mysterious inscription hidden beneath volcanic rock. Count Arne Saknussem (Thayer David) claims to have made it to the center of the Earth and provides instructions to repeat his journey. But Göteborg's advantage is soon lost when he is murdered by Count Saknussem, the explorer's descendant, who feels that he has a right to his ancestor's legacy and is willing to go to extraordinary lengths to ensure his exclusive success. Confronted with her late husband's diary, which seems to confirm Lindenbrook's accusations against him, Göteborg's widow allows the team to use his expedition equipment on the condition that she join them, much to Lindenbrook's consternation.

Following Count Saknussem's instructions, Lindenbrook (and secretly also Count Saknussem) wait for the designated day when a shaft of sunlight shines through a mountain crevice and points out a hidden entrance within a volcano, through which they can gain access to the center of the Earth. So begins the descent and the beginning of many strange underground terrains—luminescent rocks, multicolor crystals, giant mushroom trees, and sinking salt sands among them. Although Carla hears the footsteps of Saknussem in the night, Lindenbrook dismisses her as merely a nervous woman. Saknussem presses on and leads the group astray, covering up the markings of his ancestor and making new ones in their stead. Lindenbrook and his team discover the treachery and Carla is vindicated; however, when Alec becomes separated from the others, Saknussem finds the young man and demands his assistance. Alec refuses and Saknussem, true to form, shoots him from behind, injuring his arm. The sound alerts the others to their location, and Saknussem is overpowered. Despite his crimes, no one in the party can bring themselves to execute him, so he becomes a reluctant and dangerous addition to the expedition.

In a memorable sequence of the film, Lindenbrook's team discovers an underground sea and must build a raft to traverse it, but the shore is home to "Monstrous, Flesh-Eating Dimetrodons!" (as the trailer tells us, actually fabulously accessorized iguanas playing the part of dinosaurs), and the travelers barely make it to sea. It is here that they find the most central point of the Earth, but they have little chance to rejoice in the finding before they crash ashore in a violent storm. Poor, faithful little Gertrude the duck becomes a meal to Saknussem (cue tears in younger audience members), and Hans, evidently able to forgive murder and attempted murder, is thrown into his own murderous rage for the death of his beloved pet. The others hold him back, but luckily Saknussem gets his just deserts at last and is killed in a landslide. The remaining explorers discover the lost city of Atlantis, where the bones of Arne Saknussem point the way out through a shaft leading to the open air. Escaping an attack by a giant chameleon (one wonders what these poor creatures normally snack on), the team must blast an obstructing rock from the shaft, prompting a volcanic eruption in the process. But fear not, the lucky crew is carried to safety in an Atlantian altar conveniently made of asbestos. They return home to glory, Alec to marriage with his sweetheart Jenny, while the feisty Carla manages to maneuver a somewhat bewildered Lindenbrook into a proposal of his own.

While we now think of Jules Verne as one of the forefathers of the science-fiction genre (along with H. G. Wells), the term was not used in his lifetime,[2] and his *Voyage au centre de la terre* was one of his series of *voyages extraordinaires* (extraordinary journeys), which would go on to include *Twenty Thousand Leagues under the Sea* (1870) and *Around the World in Eighty Days* (1873). The novel expounds the heroic, if sometimes obsessive, search for scientific truth within its speculative adventure narrative, even as demurs to a measure of human limitation. As Lidenbrook (as he is in the novel) tells the timid Axel, "Science, my boy, is made up of mistakes, but of mistakes [that] lead to the discovery of truth."[3] The film makes considerable changes to the novel but is still able to capture its sense of wonder. Bernard Herrmann's score, with its suitably ominous use of organ in the overture, emphasizes the otherworldly nature of the underground realm.

Axel becomes Alec in the film version, where, unlike the novel, he volunteers for the journey rather than being pressed into it. In the novel, it is a young Gräuben who waits for him at home, and, disconcertingly for Axel at least, Gräuben is rather more brave than he. With an interest and ability in science ahead of her time, she would gladly join them if she were not a woman. Writing on the novel and film, science-fiction author David Brin argues, "What seems firm is that science fictional women tend to be bolder than their eras, and science fictional men seem to like it that way."[4]

Bosley Crowther of the *New York Times* is dismissive of the film, saying, "Even those horrible giant lizards are grotesque without being good. Their only service is to frighten little children, who should be the best customers for this foolish film."[5] But *Variety* counters: "The actors neither take themselves nor the picture seriously, which is all on the plus side."[6]

Many adaptations of Jules Verne's work appeared during this same decade as it came out of copyright. British actor James Mason had starred as Captain Nemo in a film version of Verne's *20,000 Leagues Under the Sea* (Richard Fleischer, 1954), alongside Kirk Douglas. The film won two Academy Awards, one for art direction/set decoration and one for special effects. Mason was known for his delectable, sonorous voice. He is best remembered for *Lolita* (Stanley Kubrick, 1962); *North by Northwest* (Alfred Hitchcock, 1959); and *A Star Is Born* (George Cukor, 1954), alongside Judy Garland, for which he was nominated for an Academy Award.

Director Henry Levin would go on to make his mark in the 1960s with some lightweight sex comedies that included *Come Fly with Me* (1963) and *Honeymoon Hotel* (1964), although it is the treatment of the darker theme of rape in *Where the Boys Are* (1960) that makes it more than just the average teen flick of the time.

There have been numerous versions of *Journey to the Center of the Earth* made for television, while on the big screen, a 3D family feature film was released in 2008, directed by Eric Brevig and starring Brendan Fraser. This version is based on the idea that Verne's story might actually have been based on a real expedition. The film performed respectably at the box office, but *Variety* said that it "emphasizes . . . how technology ends up dictating content," with outstanding effects, not much plot, but at least some humor.[7] DB

Notes

1. "Theatrical Trailer," *Journey to the Center of the Earth*, directed by Henry Levin (20th Century Fox, 2003), DVD.
2. David Brin, "Introduction," in *Journey to the Center of the Earth*, written by Jules Verne (New York: Modern Library, 2003), xi.
3. Jules Verne, *Journey to the Center of the Earth* (New York: Modern Library, 2003), 134.
4. Brin, "Introduction," xv.
5. Bosley Crowther, "*Journey to the Center of the Earth*; Verne Fable Opens at the Paramount," *New York Times*, 17 December 1959, http://movies.nytimes.com/movie/review?res=9E07E3DE173AEF3BBC4F52DFB4678382649EDE (7 July 2012).
6. "*Journey to the Center of the Earth*," *Variety*, 1959, www.variety.com/review/VE1117792196/ (7 July 2012).
7. John Anderson, "*Journey to the Center of the Earth*," *Variety*, 29 June 2008, www.variety.com/review/VE1117937550/ (5 July 2012).

Bibliography

Anderson, John. "*Journey to the Center of the Earth*." *Variety*, 29 June 2008, www.variety.com/review/VE1117937550/ (5 July 2012).

Brin, David. "Introduction." In *Journey to the Center of the Earth*, written by Jules Verne, xi–xv. New York: Modern Library, 2003.

Crowther, Bosley. "*Journey to the Center of the Earth*; Verne Fable Opens at the Paramount." *New York Times*, 17 December 1959, http://movies.nytimes.com/movie/review?res=9E07E3DE173AEF3BBC4F52DFB4678382649EDE (7 July 2012).

"*Journey to the Center of the Earth*," *Variety*, 1959, http://www.variety.com/review/VE1117792196/ (7 July 2012).

JUDGMENT AT NUREMBERG (1961)

DIRECTOR: Stanley Kramer
WRITER: Abby Mann
PRODUCERS: Stanley Kramer, Phillip Langner (Roxlom Films)
CINEMATOGRAPHER: Ernest Laszlo
EDITOR: Frederic Knudtson
PRODUCTION DESIGN: Rudolph Sternad
SET DECORATION: George Milo
COSTUMES: Jean Louis
MUSIC: Ernest Gold
CAST: Chief Judge Dan Haywood: Spencer Tracy. Dr. Ernst Janning: Burt Lancaster. Col. Tad Lawson: Richard Widmark. Mrs. Bertholt: Marlene Dietrich. Hans Rolfe: Maximilian Schell. Irene Hoffman: Judy Garland. Rudolph Peterson: Montgomery Clift. Judge Emil Hahn: Werner

Klemperer. Brig. Gen. Matt Merrin: Alan Baxter
AA: Best Leading Actor (Maximilian Schell), Best Writing–Screenplay Based on Material from Another Medium (Abby Mann)
AAN: Best Leading Actor (Spencer Tracy), Best Supporting Actor (Montgomery Clift), Best Supporting Actress (Judy Garland), Best Art Direction–Set Direction–Black-and-White (Rudolph Sternad, George Milo), Best Cinematography–Black-and-White (Ernest Laszlo), Best Costume Design–Black-and-White (Jean Louis), Best Director (Stanley Kramer), Best Film Editing (Frederic Knudtson), Best Picture (Stanley Kramer)
DVD: MGM, 2004
BLU-RAY: Currently unavailable
DURATION: 186 minutes

An epic film of law and the judiciary and a classic postwar film, *Judgment at Nuremberg* is also a microcosm of the war, a clash of cultures, a film that questions legality and justice on both sides. The movie opens with the Allied Forces at the end of World War II blasting one of the most recognizable symbols of Nazi power: the swastika at Nuremberg's Nazi party rally grounds. Spencer Tracy plays the unassuming Maine judge Dan Haywood, who takes the position as chief judge when no one else would at a Nuremberg war crimes trial of mid-level members of the German government. He arrives in Nuremberg amid the rubble of bombed-out buildings. "I didn't know it was so bad," he comments. Haywood's driver is too ambitious and too angry for him, and he asks him to quit honking at pedestrians and passing cars. Haywood stays at a house once owned by a wealthy family, the Bertholts, and he finds that the state of Maine could stay in one room.

Stanley Kramer reproduces the actual courtroom for historical accuracy; the Allied judges face the Nazi judges, adding tension that Kramer makes full use of by compressing space with telephoto lenses, making the arguments personal and claustrophobic. Judges judge other judges. In a different world, the roles could be reversed. It is a mirror that Kramer attempts to cause the film's audience to reflect upon.

Colonel Tad Lawson (Richard Widmark) lays out the case against the Nazi judges for their part in the Holocaust. They committed crimes in the name of the law. He says what passed for justice during the Third Reich was murder, brutalities, and atrocities. Race became part of law, more people were put to death with the death penalty, and sexual sterilization became a matter of course. Lawson brings in two examples of the miscarriage of justice in Nazi courtrooms: Rudolph Peterson (Montgomery Clift) and Irene Hoffman (Judy Garland).

In defense of the four judges, Hans Rolfe (Maximilian Schell) puts the world on trial, claiming that Americans profited from Hitler and that Dr. Ernst Janning's (Burt Lancaster) guilt is the world's guilt. Schell's performance is riveting and dynamic. Rolfe makes Peterson the object of the trial by focusing on Peterson's family's mental competence and Peterson's own mental capacity. He makes the case that Peterson deserved sterilization because he is mentally incompetent. The judges followed the law in the heredity health court. Although Lawson tries to move the discussion from Peterson's own mental competence to the legality of sterilization, he is unsuccessful. Rolfe then repeats many of the legal maneuvers that were used when he seems to retry the famous Feldenstein case. This case became a show trial for the Nazis. Irene Hoffman, an Aryan who broke the law by having sex with a non-Aryan (Feldenstein), was imprisoned. Feldenstein was put to death in the original trial. Lawson shows that while Janning was known to have dedicated his life to justice, he had prejudged the trial, knowing the decision was more propaganda than it was justice.

Colonel Lawson puts himself on the stand so that he can show film of concentration camps. This is the first Hollywood film to use actual film from the camps, and it dedicates seven minutes to showing gruesome scenes of starving prisoners, bulldozers moving bodies like cord wood into mass graves, and lampshades made from human skin. Later, at the prison, Judge Emil Hahn (Werner Klemperer) turns to another man in the prison and says, "They say we killed millions of people. How could it be possible?" The man answers, "It's possible. It all depends on the facilities. . . . It's not the killing that's the problem. It's disposing of the bodies. That's the problem." Hahn and others have been deliberately oblivious to how members of their own country have been disappearing.

Throughout the trial, an intense Janning sits in stony silence. To learn more about him, Judge Haywood orders Janning's book about the Weimar Constitution. Janning is aristocratic, solid, and square-shouldered, the judicial and intellectual equivalent of an Adolf Eichmann. He eventually takes the stand and condemns himself, his fellow judges, and the people of Germany in a long monologue. He reveals that brilliant lawyers and academics are prey to calls for patriotism like any other person when their country is in danger, but it becomes misguided when they violate their own consciences. He says, "What was going to be a passing phase had become the way of life. . . . Once more it is being done for love of country. It is not easy to tell the truth, but if there is to be any salvation for Germany, we who know our guilt must admit it . . . whatever the pain and humiliation."

The film is punctuated by scenes of Haywood's exploration of the city of Nuremberg and meeting its people. He visits the open-air market and the Nazi stadium rally grounds, among other locations. The sound track has echoes of music and songs sung by Nazis. During the trial, Haywood meets Mrs. Bertholt (Marlene Dietrich), the woman who used to own the home he is staying in. She is living in a hovel with boards on the windows. In spite of her severe drop in status, she still participates in and organizes cultural events. Part of the reason for her fall was because her husband Karl had been convicted in a trial for his participation in the Malmedy Massacre, during which eighty-four U.S. POWs were killed. Haywood walks with Mrs. Berthold. She says she did not know about the concentration camps. As a sign of her civilized behavior, she translates "Lili Marlene," a German love song set in World War I, for him.

The movie clearly shows that the Holocaust had not risen from a particular evil that only Germans were susceptible to. Both Lawson and Haywood receive pressure to ease off the defendants. Brigadier General Matt Merrin (Alan Baxter) attempts to have Lawson soften the prosecution's goals by stating that the situation in Germany is tentative. The Cold War is coming. Berlin is being sectioned off from the west by the Russians. The U.S. military is trying to figure out how to deliver coal and food to Berlin, and they need the help of the German people, which would not happen with stiff sentences. Lawson responds by saying, "What was the war about? What was it about?" Haywood receives his share of pressure as well. A U.S. senator advises him not to upset the new Germany, an important ally, and another judge asks about the judge's political affiliation. Mrs. Bertholt, who gives him the present German stance, says, "We must forget if we want to go on living." The irony is that someone has to remember, and it has to be the law and incorruptible. Haywood gives the four judges life sentences. Turning a blind eye to injustice even to one person will corrupt a democracy. JMW

Bibliography

Stevens, George. *Conversations with the Great Moviemakers of Hollywood's Golden Age at the American Film Institute.* New York: Knopf, 2006.

K

KHARTOUM (1966)

Directors: Basil Dearden, Eliot Elisofon (introductory scenes)
Writer: Robert Ardrey
Producer: Julian Blaustein
Cinematographer: Ted Scaife
Editor: Fergus McDonell
Art Direction: John Howell
Set Decoration: John Bodimeade
Music: Frank Cordell
Special Effects: Richard Parker
Makeup Artists: Bill Lodge, Tom Smith
Cast: General Charles Gordon: Charlton Heston. Muhammad Ahmad/Mahdi: Laurence Olivier. Prime Minister William Ewart Gladstone: Ralph Richardson. Foreign Secretary Granville Leveson-Gower: Michael Hordern. Col. J. D. H. Stewart: Richard Johnson. Jobei Pasha: Zia Mohyeddin. Sir Evelyn Baring (Ruler of Egypt): Alexander Knox. Maj. Kitchener: Peter Arne. Khalifa Abdullah: Douglas Wilmer. William Hicks: Edward Underdown
AAN: Best Writing–Story and Screenplay Written Directly for the Screen (Robert Ardrey)
DVD: MGM, 2002
Blu-ray: Currently unavailable
Duration: 136 minutes; DVD, 126 minutes

Khartoum is based on a historical episode: the fall of Khartoum, capital of Sudan, to the Arab leader Mahdi, when Gladstone was prime minister of the British Empire, in 1884. Shot mostly on location in Egypt for the battle scenes and exteriors, the rest of the movie was filmed at Pinewood Studios, in England. *Khartoum* can legitimately be called the last grand epic of the 1950s and 1960s, when the spectacular epics dominated the big screen. It can be considered the "last" in the sense that it offers the typical Hollywood formula: good versus bad guys, when the hero wins, if not the battle, at least glory. And the values (or disvalues) are those distinctive of the great epic era: valor in battle, bravery beyond belief, generosity toward the defeated, and cowardice of those who refuse to help the great hero win his battle. Add spectacle and you will have the full Hollywood formula of the epic, alive since the early days of filmmaking. *Khartoum*, however, is dominated by an austere masculinity, the business of men at war, and the subject matter narrows, focusing entirely on the defeat of one of the greatest military heroes of the late Victorian era.

Khartoum "leaps" over *Lawrence of Arabia* by four years (the latter was made in 1962), thus hanging on to the older Hollywood formula, whereas *Lawrence of Arabia* has already introduced the antihero, or at least the enigmatic Englishman (both are Englishmen) whose actions are not as clear-cut and analyzable as General Charles Gordon's. The two actors who embody these personalities also are diametrically different. Peter O'Toole portrays a handsome megalomaniac whose unbelievable exploits are countered by acts of barbarism and brutality; his self-worship is matched by his deep insecurity, and his love of the Arabs seems to have been a façade for self-deification. By contrast, Gordon is selfless, compassionate to the people he has adopted—the Sudanese—and loyal to the end to the city he has undertaken to defend against enormous odds. He is also a devout Christian, holding the Bible under his arm, and a hero known for his compassion, having distinguished himself in freeing slaves in Egypt and China. Charlton Heston plays him down to a "t," despite the fact that (as in the case of Laurence) Gordon was of medium height and Heston about a foot taller. A perceived weakness in his persona is his adopted English accent, which clashes with his previous performances in great epics, depriving him of his sonorous voice, for which he was famous in his previous efforts. His persona, already honed by such mega epics as *The Ten Commandments*, *Ben-Hur*, and *El Cid*, fits the type of hero dedicated to a noble cause and committed to a battle for justice and humanity.

Gordon is also fighting against a fanatic Muslim, Mahdi, a character entirely fascinating and intriguing, as presented by the talented Laurence Olivier. The latter commands an army of believers like himself. He takes his commands (he says) directly from Prophet Mohammad and aims to conquer the world that belongs to Muslims, from Morocco, to Sudan, to Istanbul, and he brags that a mere British general guarding Khartoum, then belonging to the British, was not going to stop him. Mahdi has, however, heard of Gordon and his bravery, and he consents to meeting him face-to-face,[1] twice, advising him to save his life and the lives of those who would die defending a hopeless cause. Gordon, of course, refuses to abandon his people. He urges the civilian population to evacuate and stands and fights to the last, reminding viewers of such historical figures as Leonidas at Thermopylae and General Custer at Little Bighorn. As already mentioned, this role fits Heston's image perfectly. Although looking somewhat worn out and prematurely aging (Heston was only forty-eight then), he stands his ground, loses valiantly, and, godlike, appears at the top of the stairs of his palace yard, impressing the crowd, but speared to death by a fanatic. A statue is raised in Khartoum, where he is still worshipped as a great hero—as he is today in England.

The movie, while splendidly photographed in Ultra Panavision, and spectacular in landscape vistas and battle scenes, failed to generate the interest that its predecessors in the genre had. One reason may be the relative limpness of the usually vigorous Heston (he appeared rejuvenated two years later as Taylor in *The Planet of the Apes*), and also perhaps because of a certain fakeness in the portrait of Mahdi in the usually reliably chameleonic Olivier. The makeup appears disingenuous, his accent seems somewhat forced to sound "too" Arabic, and his general demeanor is that of a rather run-of-the-mill tribal rebel, rather than the magnificent historical figure he is trying to portray. Another reason is that the Hollywood epic as we knew it, with its values, for instance, bravery, patriotism, and good guys versus the bad, had begun to look too worn out, and audiences, at the height of the Vietnam War, had grown antagonistic to sympathetic heroes thrown in their way, in defiance of reality. On the other hand, many Hollywood movies had switched to showing cowards with twisted psyches or megalomaniacs and fanatics. After all, audiences had seen the likes of Norman Bates and Dr. Strangelove, not to mention the other Lawrence (of Arabia), on the screen. The epic was changing; it was time to turn to the antihero. But for that, let us switch to the discussion of such a changing heroic image, a slicker, more complex, and less sympathetic one, suffering profound changes at this point in history.

The epic, budgeted at $6 million, was a failure at the box office and had a generally poor reception by critics and audiences, some complaining about its admittedly slow pace during the first part of the movie (which comes with an overture and intermission) and its historical inaccuracies. There is no record of Gordon and Mahdi ever meeting; or of Gordon being speared on the steps of his headquarters; or of Gordon being beheaded, with his head on a stick, shown to Mahdi, who turns away in revulsion.[2] The close relationship of Mahdi and Gordon, especially during the second meeting between them, when Mahdi implores Gordon to leave Khartoum, implies Mahdi's homosexual attraction to Gordon—but to him only, for the puritanical Gordon would not even tolerate this idea. Despite all the criticism, the last few scenes of the epic are truly engrossing, and even moving, personal, and intimate, as the canons explode and innocent people are massacred. Not a *Lawrence of Arabia*, *Khartoum* is an epic that modern audiences can rediscover and appreciate. The battles, the armies, the Nile, and the desert stretches are all real. Today, computer-generated imagery would have replaced all of that. The rediscovered epic, made during the golden age of epic-making, even in its declining days, comes back to life, as a species that vanished in practice but lives in memory. CS

Notes

1. This meeting never took place; they only corresponded briefly, and their meeting has not been documented. See "Facts from the Vault" inside the DVD cover, *Khartoum*, directed by Basil Dearden (MGM, 2002).

2. The DVD version censors that scene, and we only see the stick, but not the head on top of it.

Bibliography

Caillou, Alan. *Khartoum*. New York: Signet Books, 1966.

KING ARTHUR (2004)

DIRECTOR: Antoine Fuqua
WRITER: David Franzoni
PRODUCER: Jerry Bruckheimer (Touchstone Pictures, Jerry Bruckheimer Films)
CINEMATOGRAPHER: Slawomir Idziak
EDITORS: Conrad Buff, Jamie Pearson
ART DIRECTION: Anna Rackard, Yann Biquand, Colman Corish, Conor Dennison
COSTUMES: Penny Rose
MUSIC: Hans Zimmer
CAST: Arthur (Lucius Artorius Castus): Clive Owen. Lancelot: Ioan Gruffudd. Tristan: Mads Mikkelsen. Gawain: Joel Edgerton. Galahad: Hugh Dancy. Bors: Ray Winstone. Dagonet: Ray Stevenson. Guinevere: Keira Knightley. Merlin: Stephen Dillane. Cerdic: Stellan Skarsgård. Cynric: Til Schweiger. Jols: Sean Gilder. Horton: Pat Kinevane. Bishop Germanius: Ivano Marescotti. Marius Honorius: Ken Stott. Alecto: Lorenzo De Angelis. Fulcinia: Stefania Orsola Garello. British Scout: Alan Devine. Ganis: Charlie Creed-Miles. Lucan: Johnny Brennan. Merlin's Lieutenant: David Murray. Arthur's Mother: Maria Gladkowska. Young Arthur: Shane Murray-Corcoran. Young Lancelot: Elliot Henderson-Boyle. Lancelot's Father: Clive Russell. Lancelot's Mother: Stephanie Putson. Pelagius: Owen Teale (uncredited)
AA: None
AAN: None
DVD: Buena Vista, 2004
BLU-RAY: Buena Vista, 2007
DURATION: 136 minutes

King Arthur is a reimagining of the Arthurian myth as a legend based on a real historical figure. The film proclaims: "Historians agree that the classical fifteenth-century tale of King Arthur and his knights rose from a real hero who lives a thousand years earlier in a period often called the Dark Ages. Recently discovered archaeological evidence sheds light on his true identity." Alas, historians do not agree that there was definitely a real Arthur, and among those who do, there is considerable disagreement about his identity. One theory first proposed in 1925, by Kemp Malone, is that he was Lucius Artorius Castus, a Roman general of the second century A.D. in charge of defending Hadrian's Wall against northern incursion, and that perhaps heroic stories about him had simply been updated to the Saxon conflicts of the sixth century, when we have our first mention of Arthur.[1] Subsequently, in 1978, C. Scott Littleton and Ann C. Thomas suggested that while there were pre-Christian Celtic elements in Arthurian legend, many similarities could be found with the traditional stories of a people called the Sarmatians (from what today would be around Georgia), who were pressed into the Roman legion in the second century A.D. and served under Artorius in northern Britain. Whether archaeological evidence proves their presence for "several centuries" afterward is contested.[2] Nonetheless, screenwriter David Franzoni (who previously worked on Ridley Scott's *Gladiator*, 2000) turned to this theory when trying to imagine a more realistic human and political perspective on Arthur.[3]

After the Sarmatian story is established at the beginning of *King Arthur*, the young Lancelot (Elliot Henderson-Boyle, with the older Lancelot played by Ioan Gruffudd) is taken from his home village in A.D. 452, and given a good luck token by a young girl—despite his later testy flirtation with Guinevere, it is this young love that haunts his memory through the film. Lancelot joins other Sarmatians in Britain and eventually comes under the leadership of the "ancestrally named" Lucius Artorius Castus, or Arthur (Clive Owen), referring to Littleton and Thomas's speculation that the name may have been passed down from the original second-century man. The knights come to the defense of Bishop Germanius (Ivano Marescotti), who is attacked by Woads on his journey to Hadrian's Wall. The audience's sympathies are cleverly divided in this scene—we are positioned with the knights but, post-*Braveheart* (Mel Gibson, 1995), are surely conditioned to also sympathize with the blue-painted Scots defending their own land. The knights believe that Bishop Germanius has come to give them their release papers after fifteen years of service, after which there are only six knights left. He has in fact come to demand of them another, seemingly suicidal, mission, to go north of the wall into hostile Woad territory and rescue Roman nobleman Marius (Ken Stott) and his son Alecto (Lorenzo De Angelis), the favorite godson of the pope. They are in danger from the Saxons, who are invading to take advantage of the immanent withdrawal of the Romans from Britain (just what Marius and his family are doing so far in hostile territory is never explained).

Marius is not amenable to rescue, having set up a wealthy estate with terrified subjugated peasants working for him. Although Arthur is Christian himself, he is horrified to find that Marius has entombed alive a number of heathens and supposed troublemakers under a dubious Christian pretext. A young boy and a Woad woman, Guinevere (Keira Knightley, sporting an improbably plum English accent), are the only survivors. Despite the protestations of his rather more practical men, Arthur takes these survivors and the peasants along with him. Marius is killed when he tries to take over, and his son informs Arthur that his former tutor and friend Pelagius (Owen Teale) has been executed in Rome for preaching the equality of men.

Once encamped, Guinevere leads Arthur into the woods seemingly for a romantic tryst, but, in fact, to meet Merlin (Stephen Dillane), the leader of the Woads. Merlin has been tracking them in his lands and has made it clear that he has spared their lives, yet Arthur still cannot trust him, for the Woads killed his mother in a raid. Merlin and Guinevere point out that his mother was also a Woad, but they cannot yet convince him to stay to lead their people's defense against the Saxons. While making their mountain retreat, Guinevere and the knights are able to fend off the Saxons temporarily on a frozen lake, when Dagonet (Ray Stevenson of TV's *Rome*, 2005–2007) sacrifices himself to split the ice and plunge the Saxons to a cold death. This innovative encounter, enhanced with computer-generated imagery, is surely the visual highlight of the film.

The survivors make a somber return to the wall, and even Arthur is totally disillusioned by both Rome and the Church. Guinevere makes love to Arthur as the Saxons arrive outside the wall, and the ever-honorable Arthur realizes that he cannot turn away from his mother's people. Although his men initially depart with their freedom papers, they all turn back to help Arthur and the Woads defend the wall against the Saxons. Even Bors (the reliable and charismatic Ray Winstone), who has a lover and eleven young children to think of, joins the battle. Guinevere proves herself a capable warrior, but despite their best efforts, Lancelot and Tristan (Mads Mikkelsen) die in battle. Arthur is able to kill Cerdic (Stellan Skarsgård), leader of the Saxons; the famed Battle of Badon Hill is won; and the Saxons are temporarily held at bay. At the wedding of Guinevere and Arthur, Merlin proclaims Arthur their king, much to the evident bemusement of his men, and the voice of Lancelot proclaims the immortality of the fallen through the tales of Arthur and his knights.

This ending was added to the film when the climactic funeral scene was deemed too sober by test audiences, although in presenting the original "alternate" ending, director Antoine Fuqua suggests that the darker tone was perhaps the more interesting of the two.[4] Fuqua's original vision for the film was also seemingly darker, but there was studio pressure to get a family-friendly rating. Some material has been reinstated for the DVD director's cut. Screenwriter Franzoni also wanted to avoid the "polite version of Arthur. If someone's a great warrior, that means they're also a great killer."[5] This is, in fact, in keeping with the earliest historical evidence for Arthur and Badon Hill, such as that written by Nennius in the early ninth century, in which Arthur is described not as a king but as a mighty "war-leader."[6] Nennius is also the beginning of Arthur the legend, given that he asserts that Arthur slayed 960 men on his own at Badon Hill and attributes magical qualities to Arthur's dog and the grave of Arthur's son.

Franzoni's original conception was to have a more conflicted relationship between the knights, drawing comparisons with soldiers conscripted into the Vietnam War.[7] The film's early camaraderie was added by another writer (*Variety* reviewer Todd McCarthy makes a comparison with John Sturges's *The Magnificent Seven* of 1960[8]), but certainly an element of dissent remains with Lancelot, who is the closest of the Sarmatians to Arthur and yet far more pragmatic than his leader. It is his relationship with Arthur that is the key to the love triangle in this version, as Lancelot clearly resents the influence Guinevere has on Arthur and the path she sets him on. Ioan Gruffudd makes a smoldering and self-deprecating Lancelot, but while reviews praised the performance of Keira Knightley as Guinevere, her attraction to Arthur is never really convincing, such that the audience may be inclined to agree with Lancelot's perception of her as manipulating Arthur for the sake of her people. The snarling Saxon leader Cerdic provides Arthur with a delightfully wicked foe, even if such characterization provides a somewhat conveniently simplistic moral landscape.

King Arthur brings to life a seldom-depicted moment in history, even as it mythologizes Arthur and his knights in its own way. This may not be the Arthurian tale that audiences expected, but it is all the more engaging for that very reason, and a solid ensemble cast makes *King Arthur* a better film than was appreciated upon its release. DB

Notes

1. Kemp Malone, "Artorius," *Modern Philology* 22, no. 4 (1925): 367–74.

2. C. Scott Littleton and Ann C. Thomas, "The Sarmatian Connection: New Light on the Origin of the Arthurian and Holy Grail Legends," *Journal of American Folklore* 91, no. 359 (1978): 513–27. This argument is further developed in C. Scott Littleton and Linda A. Malcor, *From Scythia to Camelot: A Radical Reassessment of the Legends of King Arthur, the Knights of the Round Table, and the Holy Grail* (New York: Garland, 1994). Refuting the ethnic survival of the Sarmatians in the subsequent centuries is Tom Shippey, "Fuqua's King Arthur: More Myth Making in America," *Exemplaria* 19, no. 2 (2007): 312.

3. John Matthews, "An Interview with David Franzoni," *Arthuriana* 14, no. 3 (2004): 116.

4. Antoine Fuqua, "Commentary," *King Arthur*, directed by Antoine Fuqua (Buena Vista, 2004), DVD.

5. Matthews, "An Interview with David Franzoni," 118.

6. The battle is also recorded in "The Annals of Wales" from the tenth century, and Gildas's "The Ruin of Britain," c. 548, although the latter gives credit for the victory to Ambrosius Aurelianus and not Arthur. Richard White, *King Arthur in Legend and History* (New York: Routledge, 1997), 3–6. The timelines are somewhat off in the film, given that the Roman withdrawal from Britain is usually dated to about A.D. 410, whereas the Battle of Badon Hill is dated by the annals as A.D. 516.

7. Matthews, "An Interview with David Franzoni," 118.

8. Todd McCarthy, "*King Arthur*," *Variety*, 5 July 2004, www.variety.com/review/VE1117924277/ (6 September 2012).

Bibliography

Littleton, C. Scott, and Ann C. Thomas. "The Sarmatian Connection: New Light on the Origin of the Arthurian and Holy Grail Legends." *Journal of American Folklore* 91, no. 359 (1978): 513–27.

Littleton, C. Scott, and Linda A. Malcor. *From Scythia to Camelot: A Radical Reassessment of the Legends of King Arthur, the Knights of the Round Table, and the Holy Grail.* New York: Garland, 1994.

Malone, Kemp. "Artorius." *Modern Philology* 22, no. 4 (1925): 367–74.

Matthews, John. "An Interview with David Franzoni." *Arthuriana* 14, no. 3 (2004): 115–20.

McCarthy, Todd. "*King Arthur*," *Variety*, 5 July 2004, www.variety.com/review/VE1117924277/ (6 September 2012).

Shippey, Tom. "Fuqua's King Arthur: More Myth-Making in America." *Exemplaria* 19, no. 2 (2007): 310–26.

White, Richard. *King Arthur in Legend and History.* New York: Routledge, 1997.

KING KONG (1933)

DIRECTORS: Merian C. Cooper (uncredited), Ernest B. Schoedsack (uncredited)
WRITERS: James Creelman, Ruth Rose. Based on an idea conceived by Edgar Wallace and Merian C. Cooper.
PRODUCER: David O. Selznick (RKO Radio Pictures)
CINEMATOGRAPHERS: Eddie Linden, Vernon Walker, J. O. Taylor
EDITOR: Ted Cheesman
CHIEF TECHNICIAN: Willis O'Brien
MUSIC: Max Steiner
CAST: Ann Darrow: Fay Wray. Carl Denham: Robert Armstrong. John "Jack" Driscoll: Bruce Cabot. Capt. Englehorn: Frank Reicher. Charles Weston: Sam Hardy. Native Chief: Noble Johnson. Witch King: Steve Clemente (as Steve Clemento). Second Mate Briggs: James Flavin. King Kong: King Kong. Pilot of Plane That Kills Kong: Merian C. Cooper (uncredited). Machine Gunner on Plane That Kills Kong: Ernest B. Schoedsack (uncredited)
AA: None
AAN: None
DVD: Turner Entertainment, 2005
BLU-RAY: Currently unavailable
DURATION: 104 minutes

It may be difficult to imagine a time when the great ape King Kong was not emblazoned on the collective consciousness of popular culture. In addition to its undoubted cultural influence, this adventure epic has continued to inspire subsequent filmmakers and special effects technicians. Director Merian C. Cooper recalls that they had to invent eleven new film processes to make *King Kong*'s many spectacles possible.[1] What they did not have to create were two of the lead characters, for the film tells the story of filmmaker and explorer Carl Denham (Robert Armstrong), based on Cooper himself. At the beginning of the movie, Denham has gruffly bowed to public pressure to include a pretty face in his next exotic nature film. Walking the streets of New York, he finds Ann Darrow (Fay Wray), out of work, hungry, and pretty. After she is reassured that the job is strictly business, Ann sails away with Denham, Captain Englehorn (Frank Reicher), and first mate John "Jack" Driscoll (Bruce Cabot), who thinks women are a "nuisance" but perhaps protests too much. Driscoll is based on fellow director Ernest B. Schoedsack, who had earlier gone on ethnographic filmmaking adventures with Cooper, making similar complaints about taking a woman with them for the shooting of *Grass: A Nation's Battle for Life* (1925).[2]

Captain Englehorn cannot understand why Denham is leading them to the middle of nowhere until Denham reveals to them a secret map of an uncharted island, where the inhabitants have inherited a huge wall built to keep out a legendary fearsome beast, Kong. Arriving at the island, they interrupt an indigenous ceremony, and the Native Chief (Noble Johnson), upon seeing Ann, tries to barter for her. As the party retreats to their ship, Jack awkwardly confesses to Ann that he loves her. His euphoria soon turns to panic when Ann is kidnapped by the black villagers, who offer her up to a gigantic ape, Kong, as his new bride. The men form a rescue party and bravely venture behind the wall into a forgotten jungle world where they must battle huge dinosaurs in the course of their pursuit. When they catch up with Kong, he kills everyone except Jack and Denham, and Denham goes back for reinforcements and after he is cut off by a ravine.

Meanwhile, Kong curiously peels off Ann's clothes, smelling her and tickling her as she writhes and screams. (This scene was soon cut by censors for being too "salacious," a move that amused Cooper given that in screenings he attended, audiences laughed rather than were shocked.[3]) But when Ann is threatened by a variety of monstrous creatures, it is Kong who defends her in spectacular fight sequences. Jack takes the opportunity of one such distraction to rescue Ann, but Kong follows them back to the village. Denham may not have managed to get his footage but quickly decides on a more profitable product—Kong himself. Using gas bombs, he subdues the beast and takes him back to New York.

Denham's stage show is a sellout, presenting a downcast and restrained Kong. When Jack puts his arm around Ann and photographers set off their flashbulbs in rapid fire, Kong seems to think that Ann is in danger and breaks free. Wreaking havoc across the city in search of Ann, he finally takes her from the window of a high-rise when Jack is knocked out trying to defend her. Kong climbs the Empire State Building clutching the screaming Ann but puts her down to defend himself when fighter planes are sent in to shoot at him. As his injuries mount, Kong falls to his death, and Jack climbs up to comfort Ann. Denham looks at Kong's body and declares, "It wasn't the airplanes. It was beauty [that] killed the beast."

King Kong mobilizes a number of racial stereotypes that are articulated along gendered, sexualized lines, such that despite its engrossing spectacular qualities, the film may make for uncomfortable viewing today. James A. Snead argues that "in *all* Hollywood film portrayals of blacks . . . the political is never far from the sexual . . . and nowhere is this more plainly to be seen than in *King Kong*."[4] Upon seeing Ann, the Native Chief exclaims, "Look at the golden woman!" and he immediately wants her as the new bride of Kong, offering to exchange six of his own women to obtain her. What is assumed here is not only the power of men to exchange or withhold their women, but also the inherent superiority of the white woman's beauty. Damon Young therefore argues that the cinematic conventions through which women are codified as visual objects are "inseparable from the racism of those same operations"[5]—none of the black female offerings would seem to have had this effect on Kong.

Through Kong's blackness, he, too, is visually coded along racist lines in affinity with the "natives" who serve him and dance dressed as him, sharing an intrigue with the white woman such that interracial desire is paired with interspecies desire. Desiring a white woman is naturalized, but acting upon that desire is, by definition here, monstrous except in the case of a white man. And yet while Kong disrobes Ann and is clearly seen as a threat to her, he spends most of his time defending her from attack from other creatures, to the extent the audience may find themselves in the (admittedly ambivalent) position of backing Kong. Thus, Steven Jay Schneider argues that Kong complicates any simple binary analysis of the interracial match.[6]

Of course, the most famous film creature of all time has been ripe for analysis along a myriad of other lines, including, but not limited to, "Kong as Christ . . . Kong as commodity, Kong as rapist . . . Kong as Third World . . . Kong as myth,"[7] Kong as special effects marvel. Within the film, Kong is the "eighth wonder of the world" as a monstrous animal specimen, standing in contrast with civilized human refinement and bringing the destructive force of the untamed natural world into the heart of modernity. While Kong may seem to be the embodiment of beastliness taken to an extreme, it is perhaps more fruitful to regard him as a mythic liminal (in-between) figure, who confronts and mediates our cultural extremes, symbolically dealt with by killing him off. In the narrative, human technology wins over bestial might, but for the audience, Kong cuts across these binaries because he is a technological wonder in himself, showcasing the extraordinary stop-motion animation of Willis O'Brien.[8] In 1933, *Variety* wrote, "While not believing it, audiences will wonder how it's done. If they wonder they'll talk, and that talk plus the curiosity the advertising should incite ought to draw business all over. *Kong* mystifies as well as it horrifies."[9] DB

Notes

1. Merian C. Cooper, "Commentary," *King Kong*, directed by Merian C. Cooper and Ernest B. Schoedsack (Turner Entertainment, 2005), DVD.
2. Kevin Brownlow and Christopher Bird, "I'm King Kong! The Exploits of Merian C. Cooper," *King Kong*, directed by Merian C. Cooper and Ernest B. Schoedsack (Turner Entertainment, 2005), DVD.
3. Cooper, "Commentary."
4. James A. Snead, "Spectatorship and Capture in *King Kong*," in *Representing Blackness: Issues in Film and Video*, edited by Valerie Smith (New Brunswick, NJ: Rutgers University Press, 1997), 30.
5. Damon Young, "Ironic Identities and Earnest Desires: King Kong and the Desire to Be Looked At," Conference Proceedings, Thinking Gender: The NEXT Generation, University of Leeds, 21–22 June 2006, www.gender-studies.leeds.ac.uk/assets/files/epapers/epaper26-damon-young.pdf (25 June 2013), 6.
6. Steven Jay Schneider, "Mixed-Blood Couples: Monsters and Miscegenation in U.S. Horror Cinema," in *The Gothic Other: Racial and Social Constructions in the Literary Imagination*, edited by Ruth Bienstock Anolik and Douglas L. Howard (Jefferson, NC, and London: McFarland, 2004), 75–76.

7. Noel Carroll, "King Kong: Ape and Essence," in *Planks of Reason: Essays on the Horror Film*, edited by Barry Keith Grant and Christopher Sharrett (Metuchen, NJ, and London: Scarecrow Press, 1984), 215–16.

8. Whom stop-motion animator Ray Harryhausen (perhaps best known for his work on Don Chaffey's 1963 *Jason and the Argonauts*) calls the "grandfather" of the craft in the United States. Ray Harryhausen, "Commentary," *King Kong*, directed by Merian C. Cooper and Ernest B. Schoedsack (Turner Entertainment, 2005), DVD.

9. "Review: *King Kong*," *Variety*, 6 March 1933, http://variety.com/1933/film/reviews/king-kong-2-1200410783/ (8 July 2013).

Bibliography

Carroll, Noel. "King Kong: Ape and Essence." In *Planks of Reason: Essays on the Horror Film*, edited by Barry Keith Grant and Christopher Sharrett, 215–44. Metuchen, NJ, and London: Scarecrow Press, 1984.

"Review: *King Kong*." *Variety*, 6 March 1933, http://variety.com/1933/film/reviews/king-kong-2-1200410783/ (8 July 2013).

Schneider, Steven Jay. "Mixed-Blood Couples: Monsters and Miscegenation in U.S. Horror Cinema." In *The Gothic Other: Racial and Social Constructions in the Literary Imagination*, edited by Ruth Bienstock Anolik and Douglas L. Howard, 72–89. Jefferson, NC, and London: McFarland, 2004.

Snead, James A. "Spectatorship and Capture in *King Kong*." In *Representing Blackness: Issues in Film and Video*, edited by Valerie Smith, 25–45. New Brunswick, NJ: Rutgers University Press, 1997.

Young, Damon. "Ironic Identities and Earnest Desires: King Kong and the Desire to Be Looked At." Conference Proceedings, Thinking Gender: The NEXT Generation, University of Leeds, 21–22 June 2006, www.gender-studies.leeds.ac.uk/assets/files/epapers/epaper26-damon-young.pdf (25 June 2013).

KING KONG (2005)

Director: Peter Jackson
Writers: Fran Walsh, Philippa Boyens, Peter Jackson. Based on a story by Edgar Wallace and Merian C. Cooper.
Producers: Jan Blenkin, Carolynne Cunningham, Fran Walsh, Peter Jackson (Universal Pictures, Wingnuts Films)
Cinematographer: Andrew Lesnie
Editors: Jamie Selkirk, with Jabez Olssen
Production Design: Grant Major
Art Direction: Dan Hennah, Simon Bright, Joe Bleakley
Set Decoration: Dan Hennah, Simon Bright
Costumes: Terry Ryan
Music: James Newton Howard
Sound Editors: Mike Hopkins, Ethan Van der Ryn
Sound Mixers: Christopher Boyes, Michael Semanick, Michael Hedges, Hammond Peek
Visual Effects: Joe Letteri, Brian Van't Hul, Christian Rivers, Richard Taylor
Cast: Ann Darrow: Naomi Watts. Carl Denham: Jack Black. Jack Driscoll: Adrien Brody. Capt. Englehorn: Thomas Kretschmann. Preston: Colin Hanks. Kong/Lumpy: Andy Serkis. Hayes: Evan Parke. Jimmy: Jamie Bell. Choy: Lobo Chan. Herb: John Sumner. Mike: Craig Hall. Bruce Baxter: Kyle Chandler. Manny: William Johnson. Harry: Mark Hadlow. Maude: Geraldine Brophy. Taps: David Dennis (as David Denis). Weston: David Pittu. Zelman: Pip Mushin. Gunner: Peter Jackson
AA: Best Sound Editing (Mike Hopkins, Ethan Van der Ryn), Best Sound Mixing (Christopher Boyes, Michael Semanick, Michael Hedges, Hammond Peek), Best Visual Effects (Joe Letteri, Brian Van't Hul, Christian Rivers, Richard Taylor)
AAN: Best Art Direction (Grant Major, Dan Hennah, Simon Bright)
GGN: Best Director–Motion Picture (Peter Jackson), Best Original Score–Motion Picture (James Newton Howard)
DVD: Universal Studios, 2006
Blu-ray: Universal Studios, 2009
Duration: 179 minutes (201 for extended cut)

Following the success of the *Lord of the Rings* trilogy (2001–2003), director Peter Jackson was able to revive a project that had previously been cancelled—a remake of *King Kong* (Merian C. Cooper and Ernest B. Schoedsack, 1933). Hoping to engage with fans throughout the process, Jackson uploaded detailed production and postproduction video diaries on a fan website (subsequently released on DVD). Upon its release, Roger Ebert of the *Chicago Sun-Times* declared the film "one of the great modern epics."[1]

In New York City, 1933, Al Johnson's "I'm Sitting on Top of the World" plays while we see starving citizens and, prophetically, the suffering of caged animals at the zoo. The ironic music serves to emphasize the Depression-era conditions rather than distance us from them. Ann Darrow (Naomi Watts) at least has a job, but she and her rarely paid colleagues are nonetheless dependent on soup kitchens. When the vaudeville theater closes down, she briefly considers going into burlesque, but it is here that she is spotted by filmmaker Carl Denham (Jack Black). Denham is himself in a jam. His leading lady has pulled out of his latest film venture, and his financial backers want to sell off his existing footage as stock. Ann is swayed to join his on-location shoot in "Singapore" when she learns that the screenplay is being written by Jack Driscoll (Adrien Brody), a playwright whose work she admires.

When Driscoll turns up on the ship with an incomplete script, Denham conspires to keep him on board. Despite an initial misunderstanding, Ann and Jack begin to fall in love. Denham reveals that their real destination is the legendary Skull Island, rumored to be home to a strange and ferocious beast. Captain Englehorn (Thomas Kretschmann) and his crew are none too pleased with this development, and they are right to be concerned. The ship crashes into the island's rocky outcrops, and when Denham takes a party ashore, they are attacked by the local inhabitants. Although one crewmember dies, Englehorn arrives to defend the survivors. As they try to make repairs to their ship, Ann is abducted and strung up as an offering to a gigantic ape—Kong. The first mate, Hayes (Evan Parke), leads the rescue party to the other side of an enormous protective wall and into the jungle. The action intercuts between Ann's predicament with Kong and the rescue party's encounters with various creatures on the island, among them dinosaurs and massive (suitably disgusting) insects.

When Ann sees a pit of human skeletons adorned with the same necklace as she has been given, she fears the worst. Although she manages to amuse Kong when she displays her vaudeville skills for him, he has a tantrum when she stops. Kong nonetheless saves her from becoming a snack for some latter-day Tyrannosaurus Rex (the premise being that the dinosaurs have had time to evolve) in an extended fight sequence. The injured Kong departs, but a thankful Ann runs after him, realizing that her survival on the island may depend on him. They watch the sunset together, and Ann falls asleep in his hand, only to be rescued by Jack. Denham callously stalls their rescue from the other side of the wall, waiting with chloroform to capture Kong. Ann is horrified by this development but is powerless to prevent it.

Back in New York, she refuses to be part of Denham's stage show, where a chained and dejected Kong becomes enraged when a replacement blonde is brought in. He breaks free and wreaks destruction upon the city in his search for Ann. But it is Ann who finds Kong, and although they enjoy a quiet moment together, the ape is soon pursued, fleeing to the top of the Empire State Building, where Ann follows him. Ann's screams in this version are not from fear of the beast, but in protest at the planes that have been sent to kill him. Upon his death, Jack arrives to comfort Ann, while Denham contemplates the fallen beast.

Cynthia Marie Erb argues that there is a significant shift in tone from the original to Jackson's film, with the latter's focus on the melancholy of Kong.[2] Certainly, as played by Andy Serkis, with the assistance of motion-capture technology, this Kong is the most human-seeming, and his relationship with Ann speaks to an empathic connection across species. As Barbara Creed notes, in Jackson's film, Kong seems to want a companion, not a sexual conquest. This contrasts with the erotic undertones of the original, in which a scene depicting Kong disrobing and smelling Ann was soon cut by the censors. Watts's Ann entertains him and plays with him.[3] Following Kong's demise, this animal–human relationship is quickly replaced by the heterosexual (human) relationship between Jack and Ann, but it is the former that carries the greatest emotional weight.

Juxtaposed with this new Ann, Denham emerges more forcefully as the villain of the piece, yet this is undercut by the casting of Jack Black and the comic elements of the role. Tone is a tricky issue throughout the film. Are the Skull Island "natives" so excessive as to add ironic distance to the stereotypes they invoke, or do they simply reinforce them?[4] Does the addition of a heroic black first mate (Evan Parke) "offset the jungle stereotypes," as Jonathan Rosenbaum (ironically) suggests?[5] Jackson's *King Kong* is a film about making a film, and a film about remaking a 1933 cinema classic, but this is not 1933, so for all its charms, this film leaves a bitter aftertaste. DB

Notes

1. Roger Ebert, "*King Kong* (2005)," *Chicago Sun-Times*, 12 December 2005, www.rogerebert.com/reviews/king-kong-2005 (25 June 2013).
2. Cynthia Marie Erb, *Tracking King Kong: A Hollywood Icon in World Culture* (Detroit, MI: Wayne State University Press, 2009), 210.
3. Barbara Creed, *Darwin's Screens: Evolutionary Aesthetics, Time, and Sexual Display in the Cinema* (Carlton, Australia: Melbourne University Press, 2009), 180, 190.
4. For an in-depth discussion, see Damon Young, "Ironic Identities and Earnest Desires: King Kong and the Desire to Be Looked At," Conference Proceedings, Thinking Gender: The NEXT Generation, University of Leeds, 21–22 June 2006, www.gender-studies.leeds.ac.uk/assets/files/epapers/epaper26-damon-young.pdf (25 June 2013), 6–7.
5. Jonathan Rosenbaum, "*King Kong*," *Chicago Reader*, 9 December 2005, www.chicagoreader.com/chicago/king-kong/Film?oid=1149986 (25 June 2013).

Bibliography

Creed, Barbara. *Darwin's Screens: Evolutionary Aesthetics, Time, and Sexual Display in the Cinema.* Carlton, Australia: Melbourne University Press, 2009.

Ebert, Roger. "*King Kong* (2005)." *Chicago Sun-Times*, 12 December 2005, www.rogerebert.com/reviews/king-kong-2005 (25 June 2013).

Erb, Cynthia Marie. *Tracking King Kong: A Hollywood Icon in World Culture.* Detroit, MI: Wayne State University Press, 2009.

Rosenbaum, Jonathan. "*King Kong*." *Chicago Reader*, 9 December 2005, www.chicagoreader.com/chicago/king-kong/Film?oid=1149986 (25 June 2013).

Young, Damon. "Ironic Identities and Earnest Desires: King Kong and the Desire to Be Looked At." Conference Proceedings, Thinking Gender: The NEXT Generation, University of Leeds, 21–22 June 2006, www.gender-studies.leeds.ac.uk/assets/files/epapers/epaper26-damon-young.pdf (25 June 2013).

THE KING OF KINGS (1927)

DIRECTOR: Cecil B. DeMille
WRITER: Jeanie Macpherson
PRODUCER: Cecil B. DeMille (DeMille Pictures Corporation)
ASSISTANT DIRECTOR: Frank Urson
CINEMATOGRAPHER: J. Peverell Marley
EDITORS: Anne Bauchens (uncredited), Harold McLernon (uncredited)
ART DIRECTION: Mitchell Leisen
COSTUMES: Earl Luck
FILM PRODUCTION: William J. Cowen, Roy Burns
TECHNICAL ENGINEERING: Paul Sprunck
CAST: Jesus: H. B. Warner. Mary: Dorothy Cumming. Mary Magdelene: Jacqueline Logan. Judas Iscariot: Joseph Schildkraut. Caiaphas: Rudolph Schildkraut. Pontius Pilate; Victor Varconi. Peter:

Ernest Torrence. James: James Nell. John: Joseph Striker. Matthew: Robert Edeson. Thomas: Sidney D'Albrook. Andrew: David Imboden. Philip: Charles Belcher. Bartholomew: Clayton Packard. Simon: Robert Ellsworth. James, the Less: Charles Requa. Thaddues: John T. Prince. Barabbas: George Siegmann. Mark: Micky Moore. Martha: Julia Faye. Lazarus: Kenneth Thomson
AA: None
AAN: None
DVD: Criterion, 2004. The Criterion Collection (special edition two-disc set featuring both cuts of the film).
Blu-ray: Currently unavailable
Duration: 1927 version, 155 minutes; 1928 version, 112 minutes

Cecil B. DeMille's *The King of Kings*, the silent-era blockbuster epic about the life of Jesus, all but defines the genre of religious epic. Presented almost entirely in black and white, except for the Resurrection scene (and the beginning scene in the longer cut), the epic qualities of the film are textbook, with spectacular and exotic scenes weaving the figures of the Passion within mostly familiar canonical text, although occasionally straying with extracanonical story lines for added intrigue and dramatic effect.

The epic backstory that frames the narrative of the Passion of Jesus is not the humble infancy narratives of the gospels, as expected. Instead, the racy and opulently portrayed action of DeMille's *The King of Kings* opens in medias res, at the banquet hall of the courtesan Mary Magdalene (Jacqueline Logan), who is lamenting the absence of her apparent lover, Judas Iscariot (Joseph Schildkraut). When she learns that he has gone off with a carpenter from Nazareth, she decides to win him back. Two of her male companions bet against the prospect, wagering a bag of gold and Cleopatra's ring that Mary Magdalene is no match for the wonder-worker. Laughing, Mary sets off on a winged chariot driven by Nubian Zebras in search for Judas.

Immediately following that scene, we are brought back to the Gospel (Mark 2:1–2) and introduced to the home of Jesus (H. B. Warner) at Capernaum, where we witness perhaps one of the most touching scenes in the film: a blind child seeking healing from Jesus. There we also meet the child Mark (Micky Moore), who is healed by Jesus and who is later to become one of the writers of the gospels. And we meet Judas Iscariot for the first time. He is described as ambitious and one who "joined the Disciples in the belief that Jesus would be the nation's King, and reward him with honor and high office." Judas is preaching to the crowd outside of Jesus' home telling them that Jesus will throw off the yoke of Rome and give them back their land. Meanwhile, the people outside are lame, blind, and seeking Jesus' power to heal them. Also in the scene are "Pharisee, Scribe, and Temple Guard—spies of the High Priest," Caiaphas (Rudolph Schildkraut). They are described as being driven by the "fury of religious hatred." We meet Peter (Ernest Torrence), "giant Disciple, a fisherman, quick of temper, but soft of heart," who protects Mark from the Pharisees who tell him Jesus is not from God. Finally we are led into the house, where we meet Jesus, Mary (his mother, played by Dorothy Cumming), and the other disciples. It is here that Mark finds the blind boy and shows him the way to the "Great Physician" to be healed. Then the Shofar heralds the Sabbath, but Jesus heals the child anyway, at his mother's request, giving the enemies reason to accuse him. With the healing of the blind boy, we witness the face of Jesus for the first time on the screen. Judas, observing the miracle, remarks to Peter that Jesus would be king straightaway if he would shun the poor and heal the rich.

The next scene portrays Mary Magdalene entering Capernaum in search of Judas and finding him at the home of Jesus. There, we experience Jesus exorcizing her of the seven deadly sins[1] and becoming transformed into his docile disciple, kneeling at his feet.

After this scene, the film turns attention to the more traditional themes leading to the Passion, beginning with the attempts by High Priest Caiaphas to rid himself of the wonder-worker, this time because he sees Jesus as a "menace to his rich profits from the temple." After portrayals of such traditional scenes, including the raising of Lazarus (Kenneth Thomson), the stoning of the adulteress, and the turning of the tables in the temple, there is a scene where Caiaphas meets Judas on the steps of the temple. Judas, holding a crown in his hand, is warned by Caiaphas, who says, "Hearken thou *King Maker*! Thou shalt pay with thy life for this—and thy Master, and thy fellow knaves likewise." Immediately following, as Jesus steps out of the temple, holding a lost baby lamb found milling about, a victim of the recent temple melee, the throng of followers, donning and waving palm branches, rushes out to meet him, and we realize that Judas had intended the crown for this moment. Jesus tells them, "Do ye not understand, My Kingdom is not of this world," as Judas, holding the crown, hears him from behind a wall. They turn to Judas; he drops the crown. They kneel before Jesus, and he blesses them praying the "Our Father" prayer.

Judas then betrays Jesus to Caiaphas for thirty pieces of silver, as there was no hope left for his plans of an earthly kingdom. He swears to deliver the enemy to Jesus at his secret place of prayer, which he does.

The scenes depicted of the Passion drama include the Last Supper, the betrayal in the garden of Gethsemane, Peter's denial, the meeting with Pontius Pilate (Victor Varconi), and the presentation to the people of the choice between Barabbas (George Siegmann) and Jesus. (In the presentation scene, Jesus is put on display beside Barabbas as a mock king wearing the thorn of crowns and a purple mantle as his royal robe.) After Jesus' conviction, we see a broken and distraught Judas presenting Caiaphas with the pouch of coins, attempting to return it, but being rebuked. He drops the bag, spilling the coins to the ground, and picks up the rope that was tying the bag shut. Seeing Jesus about to pick up his cross, Judas turns away in horror, covering his eyes.

The solemn "Way of the Cross" scene presents the cathartic climax of the film, and it certainly delivers. There is an introduction of a subplot of the two thieves that adds interest to the expected conclusion to the canonical story. (For example, we meet the mother of one of the thieves.) At the moment of Jesus' death, we witness the sky opening up with lightning strikes and the wind hurling about while an earthquake breaks open the land and collapses people and trees into the cavernous gaps. Among the visions we recognize is the image of Judas, dangling from a tree by a rope, being swallowed into the earth. A soldier pierces his side, while another proclaims, "Truly, this man was the son of God!" And the temple veil is rent from top to bottom, causing Caiaphas to confess his guilt upon the altar. And the people prayed for the light to return, for the land was covered in darkness. At last, the light returns, and a dove appears, flying around the cross where the corpse of Jesus is still located, closing the scene.

The Resurrection scene begins by describing that the tomb of Jesus was sealed by priests and guarded by Roman soldiers, but it is explained that "after three days of Death . . . He had promised to rise." Returning to color film, the opening action after the introduction appears vibrant, as the soldiers hear noises and leave the tomb area just in time to witness the miracle of the resurrected Jesus moving the boulder aside as the sun begins to rise. Lilies and doves appear everywhere, as Mary, his mother, and Mary Magdalene appear at the tomb and, noticing the empty tomb, Mary Magdalene begins weeping. She is approached by Jesus, who asks her why she is crying. She tells him that someone has taken her Lord away and she doesn't know where. He tells her to stop crying; she looks up and recognizes him and tries to hug him, but he tells her not to touch him for he has not "yet ascended" to his father. But he gives her a message to tell the others, that he ascends to his God and her God. And with that news, she proclaims, "He is risen!" and the film returns to black and white.

The last scene depicts the apostles, together and shut inside when the resurrected Jesus appears to them in a vision, saying, "Behold my hands and my feet that it is I, myself. Handle me, and see: for a spirit hath not flesh and bones—as ye see me have" (Luke 24:39). He speaks to Peter and embraces Mark, but Thomas (Sidney D'Albrook) has to touch his wounds to believe. And Jesus tells them, "And these signs shall follow them that believe: in My Name, they shall speak with new tongues—they shall lay hands on the sick, and they shall recover." And finally, "Go ye therefore, and teach all nations—and preach the gospel to every creature" (Mark 16:15).

The final image has the figure of the risen Jesus superimposed over a modern city with the words, "Lo, I am with you always" inscribed across the screen. And with this, DeMille's epic comes to a close.

It is said that Cecil B. DeMille painstakingly sought interfaith support for this endeavor, soliciting clergy as advisors and maintaining a spiritual decorum on the set.[2] He even blamed the Roman politicians as the cause of Jesus' demise in a speech he gave to his cast on the evening of the script reading in 1926, claiming that it was Rome that truly feared "that the ideals of Jesus, accepted by the people, would sweep away the power of Rome."[3] Despite his efforts, however, not everyone received the film as intended. Jewish groups claimed that it perpetuated the myth of Jews as Christ killers, requiring the director to make a series of changes and some apologies. Even writer John Steinbeck purportedly proffered a pithy resolution when asked about his position on the issue, remarking, "Saw the picture, loved the book."[4] Nevertheless, it is this film that DeMille credits with making his studio possible, and the film was remade in 1961 by director Nicholas Ray. MC

Notes

1. Of course, this scene is Luke 8:2, although the demons are not specifically mentioned.
2. Excerpt from Robert S. Birchard, "*The King of Kings*," in *Cecil B. DeMille's Hollywood* (Lexington: University Press of Kentucky, 2004), from DVD insert, p. 16, *The King of Kings*, directed by Cecil B. DeMille (Criterion, 2004), DVD.
3. Birchard, quoted in DVD insert, p. 16, *The King of Kings*.
4. Quoted in Felicia Feaster, "*The King of Kings* (1927)," *Turner Classic Movies Articles*, www.tcm.com/this-month/article/72479%7C62585/The-King-of-Kings.html (23 May 2013).

Bibliography

Birchard, Robert S. *Cecil B. DeMille's Hollywood*. Lexington: University Press of Kentucky, 2004.

Feaster, Felicia. "*The King of Kings* (1927)." *Turner Classic Movies Articles*, www.tcm.com/this-month/article/72479%7C62585/The-King-of-Kings.html (23 May 2013).

KING OF KINGS (1961)

Director: Nicholas Ray
Writer: Philip Yordan
Producer: Samuel Bronston (MGM)
Cinematographer: Miguel Berenguer, Milton R. Krasner, Franz Planer
Editor: Harold F. Kress
Music: Miklós Rósza
Cast: Jesus: Jeffrey Hunter. Herod: Grégoire Aslan. Mary: Siobhan McKenna. Joseph: Gérard Tichy. Pontius Pilate:

Hurd Hatfield. Lucius: Ron Randell. Claudia: Viveca Lindfors. Herodias: Rita Gam. Mary Magdelene: Carmen Sevilla. Salome: Brigid Bazelon. Barabbas: Harry Guardino. Judas: Rip Torn. Herod Antipas: Frank Thring. Caiaphas: Guy Rolfe. Peter: Royal Dano. John the Baptist: Robert Ryan. Balthazar: Edric Conner. Nicodemus: Maurice Marsac
AA: None
AAN: None
GGN: Nest Motion Picture Score (Miklós Rósza)
VHS: MGM, 1995
DVD: Warner Home Video, 2009
BLU-RAY: Warner Bros., 2011
DURATION: 168 minutes (171 for DVD)

King of Kings is a religious, didactic epic depicting the biblical accounts of the life of Jesus against the backdrop of the fulfillment of the Jewish Messianic prophecy.[1] Beginning with the sacking of Jerusalem by Pompey in 63 B.C. and the elevation to the throne of Herod the Great as the "false King of the Jews," the epic continues within a historical backdrop and political intertext, with the Nativity narrative and biographical outline of the life, death, and presage of Jesus and his mission. Producer Samuel Bronston spared no cost or effort in verisimilitude of costume design, purportedly commissioning craftspeople from throughout Spain (where the film was shot) to painstakingly reproduce period jewelry and dress in authentic textiles.[2] New to the canonical accounts is the addition of the elevated role of the biblical criminal Barabbas, who serves here as zealous freedom fighter in contrast to the docile Jesus. The epic qualities that buttress the film, other than subject matter, are length and spectacle, especially the musical score, which was nominated for a Golden Globe.

The film garnered mixed reception from critics, and although occasionally scathing, the overall respect for the production has improved throughout time, perhaps for differing reasons. For example, a 1961 *Time* article reportedly spewed the following list of superlatives regarding the film: "corniest, ickiest, phoniest, and most monstrously vulgar of all the big Bible stories told in the last decade."[3] Conversely, in a 2003 retrospective about director Nicolas Ray, author Anthony Lane has this to say about *King of Kings*: "The film has nothing to tell us about the redemption of sin, but there are moments when it redeems the kitsch of a derided genre."[4] A mellow kitsch depicts the film today; blasphemy was what it was called in the old days. Today, the issue is the medium; then, perhaps it was more the message.

The King of Kings begins with a majestic musical overture followed by an opening scene depicting the siege of the Temple of Jerusalem in 63 B.C. by Pompey and his Roman troops. The film presents the didactic intertext of the action through the medium of narration with commentary (written by Ray Bradbury and delivered by Orson Welles, both uncredited) interspersed within the dialogue. In the opening scenes, we learn of the slaughter of the high priests of Jerusalem by Pompey; of the preservation of the Torah; and of Herod the Great's rise to power. Finally, we learn of the promise that "God would send the Messiah to deliver them (the Jews) forth."

The scene cuts and the narration and action change to the Nativity of Jesus, followed by the presentation of gifts by the three wise men. When Herod (Grégoire Aslan) hears of this, he orders all male children in Bethlehem to be put to the sword. The Roman soldier Lucius (Ron Randell), who is ordered to this task, at first refuses because he exclaims that Romans do not murder children; nevertheless, the slaughter of innocents begins. Mary (Siobhan McKenna) and Joseph (Gérard Tichy) flee to Egypt, and Jesus' life is spared. Immediately following, we witness the death of

Herod at the hand of his son, Herod Antipas (Frank Thring). The narration continues twelve years later, with Jesus (Jeffrey Hunter), Mary, and Joseph returning to Nazareth.

The second arena of action begins in the next scene. The narrator skips ahead twenty years in time and introduces Pontius Pilate (Hurd Hatfield) as the new governor of Judea, and Barabbas (Harry Guardino), a leader of 10,000 rebel Jews who is wanted as a criminal and killer. We also meet Pilate's wife and learn that it is her father who gave Judea to Pilate as their wedding gift, and he hardly seems delighted to have it. When Herod comes out to meet Pilate to take him to Jerusalem, he comes across John the Baptist (Robert Ryan) baptizing people in the Jordan River. Herod makes reference to "one more messiah." Herodias (Rita Gam), Herod's wife, and Salome (Brigid Bazelon), Herod's stepdaughter, are also there, and Herodias claims that John the Baptist speaks ill of her.

The action then moves to a dramatic spectacle scene depicting a legion of Roman soldiers pitted against the Jewish rebels, who are called to battle at the sound of a shofar. Barabbas escapes. and Pilate orders him to be captured.

The next scene is the baptism of Jesus by John the Baptist. Here we see, for the first time, the face of the character of Jesus as a grown man. There is no narration. The eyes of the two men simply meet. Next come scenes of his forty days in the desert, followed by his selection of apostles.

The rest of the film's first half chronicles the biblical account of the life of Jesus as recounted in the Synoptic Gospels, including a deeply symbolic and artistically crafted interpretation of the beheading of John the Baptist and a spectacular theatrical pageant depicting the "Sermon on the Mount," with the exception of a subplot involving the apostle Judas (Rip Torn) and the outlaw Barabbas conspiring, which presents a deviation and twist to the canonical texts.

The second part of the film includes a majestic entr'acte reprising the title theme of the work, followed by a biblical recounting of the Jesus narrative, including his entrance into Jerusalem for the Passover, his arrival on a donkey, and the waving of palm branches marking his entrance to the city by the people. This spectacle scene proves to herald the denouement of the film, for here, Judas, mastermind of the plot to conspire with Barabbas, witnesses the plan of Barabbas as he watches while Jesus enters the temple with the throng. In a stunning presentation of juxtapositions of mise-en-scène, we experience a mystical Jesus serenely soaring upward toward the temple entrance amid a crowd of followers immediately interrupted by a militant cry, "Long live Judea!" heralded by Barabbas. Suddenly, the throng breaks out in cheers, rebels break jars in releasing weapons, and there is pandemonium in the city as the rebels break through the walls and enter Jerusalem, inciting the Roman troops to intervene in a stunning and ruthlessly cold and savage scene. Barabbas is injured in the battle, and Judas comes to visit the despondent rebels, telling them that Jesus can overtake Herod and then he (Judas) will force Jesus' hand.

The conclusion of the film more or less follows the canonical through the Crucifixion, with a few variations from tradition. For example, the Last Supper is staged at a table configured in a Y shape; Judas' betrayal is explained; and at the court of Pilate, Jesus refuses to speak, so Lucius is appointed to speak in Jesus' defense. Pilate claims he lacks jurisdiction over Jesus and sends him to Herod Antipas, who fears he is John the Baptist brought back to life. He asks Jesus to perform a miracle, and when Jesus doesn't respond, he sends him back to Pilate, who gets angry and tells his wife that his crime is that he is different and he refuses to behave as the others do, and that if he can influence even Caesar's daughter, he is dangerous. And *this*, then, is the reason why Jesus is beaten, crowned with thorns, and prepared for crucifixion.

In the following scene, Lucius enters the prison to release Barabbas. Barabbas says that he and Jesus both wanted freedom, although their methods of achieving it differed. Lucius disagrees, telling Barabbas that the freedom Jesus spoke of was not the same freedom he killed for, and he then tells Barabbas that Jesus was already carrying his cross, in Barabbas' place.

Both Judas and Barabbas witness Jesus' procession with his cross toward his death. They eventually meet along the path. Barabbas asks Judas why Jesus is dying in his place, as he never did anything for Jesus. Then, in a symbolic and significant scene, the camera moves to the mound where Jesus is on the cross, dying. An unknown man places a ladder[5] on the back of the cross and unobtrusively nails to the top of the cross a wooden sign with the letters INRI engraved on it (Jesus of Nazareth; King of the Jews). Returning to the scene of Judas and Barabbas, who have just witnessed the event, we see Judas turn to Barabbas (who is seemingly unaware of what has just happened), stare at him for a moment, and then look down. He notices a blood-soaked rock on the ground, obviously stained by Jesus as he passed. Judas turns around, picks up the rock, and slowly walks away, leaving Barabbas alone on the hill.

Upon the death of Jesus, the sky darkens and Lucius says, "He is truly the Christ." Barabbas finds Judas, who has hung himself from a tree; Jesus is taken from the cross and placed in a sepulcher.

The next scene depicts a woman awakening at the tomb where Jesus was buried and finding the tomb empty. She runs after a man and asks him," Sir, have you hidden him? Tell me where and I will take him away." Jesus turns around, and he calls her by name, stating, "Magdelene . . . go to my disciples. Tell them I ascend to my Father and your Father. To my God and your God." As he walks away, she exclaims, "He is arisen."

The scene then shifts to the disciples on the seashore with their nets spread across the sand. The narration continues, describing Christ's sightings at Emmaus and Jerusalem, and then the action continues with Christ's final sighting on the shore of Galilee, where his voice is heard telling the apostles to preach the Gospel as his shadow moves slowly toward the sea, superimposing itself on the net spread out on the sand, forming a cross.

In 1960, during the filming of this production, there was a rare hurricane in Spain that literally destroyed the elaborate and massive set construction of the "Temple of Judea." Producer Bronston, recounting the event, recalls the moment when he was called to the set and witnessed the demise of the last column. "Rebuild it," he said. And they did.[6] Kitsch notwithstanding, the epic still stands. MC

Notes

1. This film is billed as a remake of the earlier silent film of the same title, directed by Cecil B. DeMille in 1927, although the narrative and emphasis differ substantially, with the DeMille piece focusing more on the adult life of Jesus, while this film traces the historical development of the Messianic prophecy through the figures of Jesus and Barabbas.

2. Robert Siegel, "Holiday Edition: The Making of MGM's *King of Kings*," *Blu-ray.com*, 24 December 2011, www.blu-ray.com/news/?id=7939 (25 May 2013).

3. Quoted in Pierre Greenfield, "Out of the Past: *King of Kings*," *Parallax View.org*, 24 June 2010, http://parallax-view.org/2010/06/24/out-of-the-past-king-of-kings/ (8 May 2013).

4. Anthony Lane, "Only the Lonely: A Nicholas Ray Retrospective," *New Yorker*, 24 March 2003, www.newyorker.com/archive/2003/03/24/030324crci_cinema (25 May 2013).

5. The ladder may be a token here for Jacob's ladder, a significant symbol of God's redemption of his people. "Behold, I am with you and will keep you wherever you go, and will bring you back to this land. For I will not leave you until I have done what I have promised you" (Genesis 28:15). For a parallel selection, see also John 1:51.

6. Siegel, "Holiday Edition: The Making of MGM's *King of Kings*."

Bibliography

Greenfield, Pierre. "Out of the Past: *King of Kings*." *Parallax View.org*, 24 June 2010, http://parallax-view.org/2010/06/24/out-of-the-past-king-of-kings/ (8 May 2013).

Lane, Anthony. "Only the Lonely: A Nicholas Ray Retrospective." *New Yorker*, 24 March 2003, www.newyorker.com/archive/2003/03/24/030324crci_cinema (25 May 2013).

Siegel, Robert. "Holiday Edition: The Making of MGM's *The King of Kings*." *Blu-ray.com*, 24 December 2011, www.blu-ray.com/news/?id=7939 (25 May 2013).

KINGDOM OF HEAVEN (2005)

Director: Ridley Scott
Writer: William Monahan
Producer: Ridley Scott (20th Century Fox)
Cinematographer: John Mathieson
Editors: Dody Dom, Chisako Yokoyama (director's cut)
Music: Harry Gregson-Williams
Visual Effects: Wesley Sewell
Cast: Balian, Baron of Ibelin: Orlando Bloom. Godfrey of Ibelin: Liam Neeson. Raymond, Count of Tiberias: Jeremy Irons. Princess Sibylla: Eva Green. Guy de Lusignan: Marton Csokas. Reynald de Chatillon: Brendan Gleeson. Saladin: Ghasson Massoud. Priest: Michael Sheen. King Richard: Iain Glen. Almaric: Velibor Topic. Templar Master: Ulrich Thomsen
AA: None
AAN: None
DVD: 20th Century Fox, 2006. Four-disc director's cut.
Blu-ray: 20th Century Fox, 2006
Duration: 144 minutes (194 for director's cut)

Ridley Scott made *Kingdom of Heaven* in the tradition of the grand epic, borrowing its subject matter from a major historical period—the Crusades—showcasing memorable battle sequences, impressive sets, an ensemble of capable actors, and literally a cast of thousands. It was filmed in northern Spain for the winter sequences; in Seville and other Spanish locations for interiors; and in Morocco desert locations, where a giant set representing Jerusalem was built. The Moroccan army provided many of the extras so that the battles look real, although, of course, computer-generated imagery was used to enhance the special effects. In its initial release, the movie did poorly at the box office in the United Sates, but it had better luck in Europe and throughout the rest of the world. It garnered no Oscar nominations and was generally viewed as one of Scott's lesser efforts; however, upon the release of the four-disc "director's cut" in 2006, which runs half an hour longer, going from 144 minutes in the original to 194, the film gained momentum with home theater audiences, even though critics in general remain skeptical about its historical accuracy. Scott and his screenwriter, William Monahan, claim that the book is based on solid research, but character traits were altered at times to accommodate dramatic purposes. The various DVD versions may produce some confusion, but the final director's cut is what is being examined here.[1]

Unlike most epics that preceded it, whether in the heyday of epic films (the 1940s through the 1960s) or in the modern era, *Kingdom of Heaven* is conceived not as a battle of good versus evil, but rather as a pilgrimage of an individual who sets out to change the nature of the conflict. As the title suggests, Balian (Orlando Bloom), the main character in the film, intends to establish a Kingdom of Heaven, which, in the film's dialogue, translates to "kingdom of conscience." As in most Ridley Scott films, his hero is motivated by an inner drive to make crucial decisions when faced with individual dilemmas, here the turning point of a war. This epic can be viewed as a reflection of the conflicts of a historical period, a romance/action adventure (erroneously in my opinion), a clash of ideologies between East and West, a raid for land and riches, or a genuine pilgrimage to discover a moral imperative more so than to merely conquer.

The Crusades started at the end of the eleventh century (around 1095) under the authority of the papacy (Pope Urban II), and their ostensible purpose was to recover the Holy Sepulcher from the Muslims, who were then expanding to the West. There were eight Crusades in all, but the most important were the first three, when Jerusalem was taken and the Kingdom of Jerusalem, which included the principality of Antioch and the countships of Edessa and Tripoli, was established and then lost again to the Muslims. The film concentrates on the Second Crusade, which started in 1147, and ended in 1186, with the retaking of Jerusalem by the Muslim Saracen leader Saladin (played by Ghasson Massoud). It is only the last two years of this period with which the film occupies itself. The major characters in the film are based on historical figures, with the exception of Balian of Ibelin, a young French blacksmith who feels the urge to travel to the Holy Land when his father, a knight, Godfrey of Ibelin (Liam Neeson), returns from the war and teaches his son how to fight. Godfrey is ambushed by his brother while en route to the Mediterranean and dies at Messina, commissioning his son to continue his trip to Jerusalem. Balian is shipwrecked, but he reaches his destination after an arduous trip through the desert.

There he finds two camps vying for supremacy. The legitimate one is that of King Baldwin IV (played by an uncredited Ed Norton), who is supported by the barons of the kingdom, the Templars, and the Count of Tiberias (Jeremy Irons), a defender and courtier of the King Baldwin, who is dying of leprosy. His legitimate heir is his sister's son, Baldwin V, who is still a child. The king's sister, Sibylla (Eva Green), is married to the arrogant and foppish Guy de Lusignan (Marton Csokas), whose cohorts are a group of reckless local lords led by two extremely ambitious men, Reynald de Chatillon (Brendan Gleeson) and Gerard de Rideford (aka Templar Master, played by Ulrich Thomsen). When the king dies, and soon thereafter his young son, Reynald and Gerard stage the coronation of Lusignan, who, spurred on by the others, undertakes an ill-advised campaign against Saladin after they ambush a caravan of peaceful Muslims and kill Saladin's sister.

In the meantime, Balian has established a friendship with Tiberias and also drawn the attention of Sibylla; he eventually becomes her lover. Both he and Tiberias object to the expedition against Saladin, and Balian warns that it would not be wise to take the army, and all the knights, with them on a journey across the desert without the water of the city. Indeed, Lusignan's army, exhausted from heat and thirst, becomes easy prey for the forces of Saladin, which destroy it and take its leaders captive. Reynald is slaughtered in a graphic beheading scene, but Lusignan is kept as hostage. Meanwhile, Balian senses that Saladin is going to attack Jerusalem, now without defenders, for Tiberias, seeing defeat as certain, has fled to Cyprus. Balian rounds up the male population, gives them a rousing speech, and "confers" knighthood upon them. His strategy proves brilliant, for when Saladin attacks with all his war machines and even manages to bore a hole in the wall, he is repulsed and forced to ask for terms. Balian accepts to surrender the city, and Saladin ensures him that the city's entire population will be escorted to the sea. A massive exodus of the Christian population streaming out of Jerusalem is shown, and that, to Balian, is the "Kingdom of Heaven" established on earth—with a peace pact. Balian and Sibylla are now free to enjoy one another's love and their new life.

Kingdom of Heaven is not a particularly religious movie, as were some of the older epics, for instance, *Ben-Hur, The Ten Commandments*, or DeMille's *The Crusades.* Those movies took a rather lofty, sanctimonious Christian (or biblical) point of view. The Romans repressed the Jews and Christians (or the Arabs in *Ben-Hur*); the Jews suffered at the hands of the Egyptian Pharaohs; and, earlier, in DeMille's *The Crusades*, Saladin is presented as an evil man and infidel. *Kingdom of Heaven* is a movie bent on showing parallels between older cultures and their wars, and their parallels with similar clashes today. Wars happen for a variety of reasons, one of which is the search for wealth, many times undertaken by the West with expeditions to the East, as modern politics play out. The Crusades were launched ostensibly to recover the Holy Land, and there was truth in that, but the result is that the West, in the process, obtained many of Eastern products—spices, sugar, silk, dyes for clothes, and, a bit later, gunpowder—all items introduced to the West following the Crusades.

Spiritually, it is hard to see that any of the individuals populating this film were saved, except, of course, for Balian, who steadfastly remains idealistic, or at least humanistic in the broadest sense, for it is he who represents knighthood in its ideal form, as it was conceived in the Middle Ages, as its philosophers and poets—Dante, Ariosto, and others—conceived him. He is only a blacksmith, but also the son of a knight, and right from the start, he displays his virtues—concern for the downtrodden being the primary Christian virtue—and, in addition, he exhibits bravery in battle, war savvy, and a strategic mind. Balian's search is spiritual, but his mission changes as the circumstances he encounters allow. He, too, fights with fury when he must, but his larger purpose is to save the people of Jerusalem rather than defeat Saladin. In essence, he is an embattled Christ figure.

Many viewers (and reviewers) attributed the relatively lukewarm reception of this film to Orlando Bloom's performance as Balian, claiming that he does not possess the charisma and screen presence of Russell Crowe in Scott's earlier grand epic *Gladiator.* This comparison is unfair, and if one places the two actors in the context of the films they were in, Bloom actually gains the advantage. Crowe was more muscular, more vindictive, and, when trained as a fighting machine in the Roman arena, as much of a killer as anyone else there. He had no particularly distinguishing spiritual qualities or goals—aside from revenge. Bloom's Balian, on the other hand, gains on that point. He is a man in search of a soul and, in terms of cultural progression from antiquity to more modern times, a man with the distinct spiritual qualities of the Middle Ages, as his father, Godfrey, tells him upon his departure from France. He had heard of compassion, meekness (he possesses a certain self-effacement, in contrast to the brassiness of a sword hero), and the obligation of a knight to help the helpless. This is all written in his face, which projects his inner world, emblematic of the transfiguration of a humble blacksmith into a warrior who is incorruptible and untainted by the flatulent, arrogant, ignorant, and brutal predecessors who were supposed to be doing what he actually comes to achieve.

The film also shows the tragically masked leper king, wise in mellow-toned voice, like a figure from Homeric Hades, foreseeing the decaying and betrayal of his kingdom by those who had usurped power in his name. And Jeremy Irons as Tiberias is excellent, a man who can read the decrees of fate but is too weak to stand up to the pretenders, and, knowing the collapse of the kingdom, at least as he perceives it, flees to safety, refusing to stand up and fight. Finally, Saladin, played with distinction by Ghassan Massoud, is a man above internal conflict, menacing and terrible in his revenge but serenely pragmatic and honorable, yielding to necessity and allowing the determined Christian population to flee to safety rather than sacrifice his own army in a futile fight. Saladin represents the Eastern cultures, which in the bygone of Hollywood movies, were represented as the "evil" side the West had to conquer and drive away.

This is an epic, and a film about war, but in a film one can always read between the lines, and Ridley Scott is known for his attempts to treat serious sociopolitical and religious matters (and other subjects) in subtext fashion. Whether one accepts points of view that may tamper with history is another question, but a movie—and an epic one to boot—need not always present absolutely accurate historical truth to be effective. The movie/epic can be seen as a trope for contemporaneity. And as such, it will remain controversial, for this is a statement of opinion, tackling political and religious views that continue to afflict and torment the relations between East and West. The version of the Crusades given in *Kingdom of Heaven* is presented as a metaphor for this conflict.

Above all, the film aims to depict the ugly reality of the war, and in that sense it gives a grim view of all participants, for it was a violent, blood-soaked period of history that produced those events. Swords were prepared that could cut the human body in half with one blow (Godfrey, who is reputed to have done so, is teaching his son Balian how to do the same thing). Other weapons, for example, maces, were prepared to crush a human skull without spilling a drop of blood (which was sin!). Other weapons, of mass destruction—arrows, for instance, or axes—were developed to destroy the human body with unbelievable efficiency, and one wonders if the automatic weapons of today could do more damage (at least they kill more quickly and efficiently). Seen in that light, the movie must be viewed as a moral statement of man's inhumanity to man, which continues today in one way or another, rather than as a discourse as to which side was right, which culture superior. CS

Note

1. See disc three in the "extended director's cut," where Monahan discusses his research on the Crusades era. Both he and Scott decided to base the action of the movie on three key concepts—the development of Balian's character into the main player, responsible for the surrender of Jerusalem; the interest created in the plot by the significance of the leper king Baldwin; and the siege of Jerusalem. The original uncut version of this movie was nearly four hours in length, at 222 minutes, trimmed to 144 minutes for theatrical exhibition in 2005. The four-disc DVD version of 2006 runs 195 minutes, while the Blu-ray version also runs 194 minutes.

Bibliography

Ebert, Roger. "*Kingdom of Heaven.*" *Chicago Sun-Times*, 2 May 2005, www.rogerebert.com/reviews/kingdom-of-heaven-2005 (23 September 2013).

Hamilton, Bernard. *The Leper King and His Heirs: Baldwin IV and the Crusader Kingdom of Jerusalem.* Cambridge, UK, and New York: Cambridge University Press, 2005.

Scott, Ridley. *Kingdom of Heaven: The Making of the Ridley Scott Epic.* New York: Newmarket Press, 2005.

L

LADY JANE (1986)

DIRECTOR: Trevor Nunn
WRITERS: David Edgar, Chris Bryant
PRODUCER: Peter Snell (Paramount Pictures)
ASSOCIATE PRODUCER: Ted Lloyd
CINEMATOGRAPHERS: Derek V. Browne, Douglas Slocombe
EDITOR: Anne V. Coates
ART DIRECTION: Fred Carter, Martyn Hebert
COSTUMES: Sue Blane, David Perry
MUSIC: Stephen Oliver
CAST: Lady Jane Grey: Helena Bonham Carter. Guilford Dudley: Cary Elwes. John Dudley, Duke of Northumberland: John Wood. Dr. Feckenham: Michael Hordern. Mrs. Ellen: Jill Bennett. Princess Mary: Jane Lapotaire. Frances Grey, Duchess of Suffolk: Sara Kestelman. Henry Grey, Duke of Suffolk: Patrick Stewart. King Edward VI: Warren Saire. Sir John Bridges: Joss Ackland. Sir John Gates: Ian Hogg. Renard, the Spanish Ambassador: Lee Montague. Marquess of Winchester: Richard Vernon. Archbishop Cranmer: David Waller. Earl of Arundel: Richard Johnson. Thomas: Pip Torrens. Dr. Owen: Matthew Guinness. Robert Dudley: Guy Henry. John Dudley: Andrew Bicknell. Peasant Leader: Clyde Pollitt. Executioner: Morgan Sheppard. Lady Anne Wharton: Zelah Clarke. Katherine Grey: Laura Clipsham. Housekeeper: Janet Henfrey. Under Treasurer: Brian Poyser. Herald: Philip Voss. Steward: Robert Putt. Tavern Keeper: Stewart Harwood. Brothel Keeper: Carole Hayman. Soldier: Richard Moore. Porter: Michael Goldie. Dressmaker: Denyse Alexander. Jeweller: Gabor Vernon. Singer: Robert Martin Oliver. Singing Maid: Nicky Croydon. Manservant: John Abbott. Wedding Dancers: Jeannette Fox, Alison Woodgate, Philippa Luce, Eliza Kern, Krzysia Bialeska, Cryss Jean Healey. Lady Warwick: Adèle Anderson. Lady Robert Dudley: Anna Gilbert
AA: None
AAN: None
DVD: Paramount Pictures, 2003
BLU-RAY: Currently unavailable
DURATION: 136 minutes

Lady Jane was Helena Bonham Carter's first big-screen release, followed shortly by the more successful *A Room with a View* (directed by James Ivory in 1985 but released in 1986, just one month after *Lady Jane*). Lady Jane (Carter) was both the legitimate and nominated heir to Edward VI (Warren Saire), son of Henry VIII. After Edward's death on 6 July 1553, Jane was officially proclaimed queen on 10 July, before being deposed just nine days later, on 19 July, in favor of Queen Mary, and beheaded the following year on 12 February. The historical epic recounts her later tragic teenage years, embellishing the facts with a heady romance and an idealistic social reform agenda.

Lady Jane's parents, the Duke and Duchess of Suffolk (Patrick Stewart and Sara Kestelman), had hoped to match Jane with King Edward himself, with whom she is well matched in scholarly temperament. John Dudley, Duke of Northumberland (John Wood), reveals that the king is dying, a fact that he and his fellow councilors wish to be kept secret given the contested succession. For a while, Mary (Jane Lapotaire) and Elizabeth had been declared illegitimate and therefore ineligible to inherit the crown, but Henry VIII had taken the extraordinary step of declaring that he had the royal right to declare them his successors anyway, leaving Princess Mary and the country with the expectation that she would be queen. This would mean a return to Catholicism and, as Dudley points out to Jane's mother, the potential loss of lands and possessions they had gained from the Old Church under protestant reformation. Jane has not only been brought up in the reformed church, but she is devout and intelligent, evident in her religious debate with Doctor Feckenham (Michael Hordern).

With the prospect of Mary's succession looming, Dudley and Grey's parents conspire to put Jane on the throne with Dudley's youngest son Guilford (Cary Elwes, most fondly remembered for Rob Reiner's 1987 *The Princess Bride*) as her husband and future king. The young Jane is appalled at the idea of marriage and has to be literally beaten into submission by her mother, but it is the gentle request of her friend the king that finally brings her around. Guilford, for his part, is shown to be a drunken gambler who has to be dragged from a whorehouse to be sobered up to meet his betrothed. Despite this inauspicious beginning, the pair discover that they are both disenchanted by the corruption of the adult world around them, and they fall in love.

Meanwhile, Guilford's father instructs Edward's doctors to keep him alive—but in terrible pain—with arsenic and bullies Edward into signing a declaration that Jane should succeed the throne, before finally allowing him to die. Jane is distressed to be declared queen and is suspicious of her husband's ambitions but finally agrees that she may be able to do some good as ruler. She sets about on social reforms, but her idealism and political inexperience are such that she seems not to fully appreciate the threat that Mary poses. Jane's defending force soon is defeated, and her council abandons her.

When Mary becomes queen, she shows mercy to the young Jane until the Duke of Suffolk, overcome by guilt for his treatment of his daughter and fearful of Mary's planned marriage to Philip of Spain, raises forces to reinstate Jane and prevent a Spanish king. Although he is unsuccessful, Mary's marriage cannot proceed until she has quelled the threat posed by Jane, either through conversion or death. Jane and Guilford refuse to convert (although his sly father does so willingly), and they are beheaded.

In reality, Queen Jane was astounded to find that her husband had ambitions to be king and that he had knowledge of Edward's document proclaiming her heir, while Jane herself had remained ignorant.[1] Guilford's mother even told him to stop sleeping with Jane until she agreed to make him king. But Guilford's father, John, Duke of Northumberland, is the traditional villain of the tale. In fact, Edward had already made a plan for the succession, written in his own hand, which excluded Mary and Elizabeth and nominated any future sons of the Duchess of Suffolk as the first heir, and secondly any sons of Jane. This was later crossed out and amended to nominate Jane herself. Whether the alteration was at the behest of the duke is impossible to say, but certainly the film's depiction of Edward's deathbed protestations at removing his half sister Mary from the succession would seem to be inaccurate.

Despite the liberties always taken with historical material, the film bases many of its scenes on historical documents. More importantly for its success as a film experience, Helena Bonham Carter and Cary Elwes are engaging as young lovers, even if reviewers found that the film veered into Franco Zeffirelli territory, echoing his *Romeo and Juliet* (1968) and *Endless Love* (1981), Tudor style.[2] Director Trevor Nunn, best known for his career in theater (including directing the original Broadway productions of *Cats* and *Les Misérables*), was somewhat reserved in his film direction in this instance, with *Variety* commenting that he had unfortunately "brought little of his tremendous theatrical flair to the screen here."[3] The performances are nonetheless excellent, particularly from the strong supporting cast. DB

Notes

1. Eric Ives, *Lady Jane Grey: A Tudor Mystery* (Chichester, West Sussex, UK, and Malden, MA: Wiley-Blackwell, 2009), 189.
2. Janet Muslin, "Screen: *Lady Jane*," *New York Times*, 7 February 1986, www.nytimes.com/1986/02/07/movies/screen-lady-jane.html (9 September 2012).
3. "*Lady Jane*," *Variety*, 1986, www.variety.com/review/VE1117792419/ (9 September 2012).

Bibliography

Ives, Eric. *Lady Jane Grey: A Tudor Mystery*. Chichester, West Sussex, UK, and Malden, MA: Wiley-Blackwell, 2009.

"*Lady Jane*." *Variety*, 1986, www.variety.com/review/VE1117792419/ (9 September 2012).

Muslin, Janet. "Screen: *Lady Jane*." *New York Times*, 7 February 1986, www.nytimes.com/1986/02/07/movies/screen-lady-jane.html (9 September 2012).

LAND OF THE PHARAOHS (1955)

DIRECTOR: Howard Hawks
WRITERS: William Faulkner, Harry Kurnitz, Harold Jack Bloom
PRODUCER: Howard Hawks (Warner Bros.)
CINEMATOGRAPHER: Lee Garnes, Russell Harlan
EDITOR: Vladimir Sagovsky
MUSIC: Dimitri Tiomkin
CAST: Pharaoh Khufu: Jack Hawkins. Princess Nellifer: Joan Collins. Hamar: Alexis Minotis. Vashtar: James Robertson Justice. Senta: Dewy Martin. Capt. Treneh: Sydney Chaplin. Mikka: James Hayter. Nailla: Kerima. Xenon: Piero Giagnoni. Mabuna: Bud Thompson
AA: None
AAN: None
DVD: Warner Bros., 2007. With running commentary by Peter Bogdanovich and Howard Hawks.
BLU-RAY: Currently unavailable
DURATION: 106 minutes

Land of the Pharaohs is Howard Hawks's only epic,[1] made at a time when the epic genre was at its height and released a year before Cecil B. DeMille's blockbuster *The Ten Commandments* (1956) and a few years before *Ben-Hur* (1959). Hawks himself regarded it his least successful movie,[2] squeezed in between the highly successful *Gentlemen Prefer Blondes* (1954), and his classic western *Rio Bravo*, with John Wayne in 1958. Audiences failed to show up, and critics dismissed his epic as inane, far below the standards set by most of the cinematic works of this great American director. *Land of the Pharaohs*, which was made at a considerable cost—nearly $3 million—barely made a profit; however, the movie was popular in France, where critics and audiences ranked it higher than the standard epics of the time and found it superior in intelligence, plot, and acting. Peter Bogdanovich, who made the aforementioned remark in his audio running commentary of the movie, also shares the common view that the epic was, by and large, a failure, and he documents his remarks by comments made by Hawks after the film's release. This epic, however, is by no means forgotten, and aside from the fact that it is still popular with modern audiences, it merits positive nods for plot ingenuity, spectacular sets, and noteworthy acting, despite the lack of superstar leads.

Land of the Pharaohs does share some of the characteristics of the epics of the time, but also some distinct differences. It features "casts of thousands," as every standard grand epic does, but it avoids massive army confrontations, and it generally lacks the action and suspense that one finds in the epics of its era. It does have pomp and glitter in the costumes of the time it represents and massive and spectacular sets, as well as a carefully and skillfully laid out plot design that makes for compelling viewing. Neophyte Joan Collins stars in her first major role as Princess Nellifer, and a stalwart Jack Hawkins, known mostly in his later roles in such epics as *The Bridge on the River Kwai*, *Ben-Hur*, and *Lawrence of Arabia*, plays Pharaoh Khufu, obsessed with building a pyramid[3] in which he will be entombed with his treasures for his second life—and eternity. To achieve his goal, he raids neighboring countries to accumulate enough riches, and as the story starts, he is coming back with treasure after winning a narrow victory over a neighboring tribe. He brings back as a hostage Vashtar (James Robertson Justice), leader of his people and an expert architect, to whom he assigns the task of building his tomb after the latter negotiates freedom for his people when the tomb is completed. These negotiations and other matters of importance are handled by Hamar, Khufu's high priest, played expertly by Alexis Minotis, who oversees both ceremonial aspects of the pharaoh and carries out his orders.

To secure his goal, to accumulate the greatest riches on earth, which will enable him to live a happy afterlife, Khufu exacts tribute from his empire, and envoys arrive from his colonies to offer him required treasure. One of these is Princess Nellifer, the envoy of Cyprus, who only brings herself as her people's tribute, for, as he tells him provocatively, they are too poor to pay what he demands. If her offer is not accepted, then tribute will be sent to him. She only has a loyal servant, Mabuna (Bud Thompson), with her. When she is about to be seized as insubordinate, she resists, and both she and Mabuna are lashed for their impudence. But Khufu cannot resist Nellifer's sexual attractions, and she soon seduces him into making her his second wife and showing her the hidden chamber, where the most prized treasures intended for his tomb are hidden. When she asks for a necklace of precious stones, he refuses and prohibits her from entering this chamber again.

Nellifer now seduces his captain, Treneh (Sydney Chaplin), and with the aid of Mabuna, they scheme to assassinate Queen Nailla (Kerima) and her son Xenon (Piero Giagnoni) with the use of a cobra. As the snake slithers toward Nailla's young son, Xenon, who plays a flute Nellifer had given him, Nailla falls on the snake to save her son and dies instead. Nellifer is now ready to carry out her plan to assassinate Khufu and become the empress, since the queen is dead. Nellifer dispatches Mabuna, her slave, to assassinate Khufu, knowing where the latter has gone to find treasure, but in the ensuing struggle, Mabuna is killed and Khufu wounded. Despite his injuries, he rides back to his capital, and there he confronts Treneh, killing him but being mortally wounded himself. As he dies, he sees the precious necklace Nellifer is wearing and immediately knows that she has been the schemer. Confident that she will inherit the throne, Nellifer accompanies Hamar and the mute priests who will be entombed with the dead king, for she is obliged by law to see his internment. Hamar, who has guessed her schemes, has the mechanism of the tomb activated, and a large rock is released, knocking the levers that hold the sand and blocking out the passage. Nellifer realizes that she has been tricked and begs for her life, but it is too late. No one can escape from the tomb Vashtar had built. He and his son Senta (Dewy Martin) and the rest of his tribe are now free to go back to their land.

Despite the general opinion that this was an inferior work by Hawks's standards—he had never before tackled a biblical epic—*Land of the Pharaohs* is an intriguing movie, with clever dialogue, good performances by all parties involved, and a neat plot with unexpected twists and turns and a satisfying denouement. Although Khufu, the pharaoh, is seen by commentator Peter Bogdanovich as a man obsessed with his "second life," and thus indifferent to the countless sufferings he imposed on his people to build his tomb, Hawkins plays Khufu with dignity, and the director ascribes to him a sense of fairness. The villain is the plotting and greedy Nellifer, who gets "her just deserts" at the end for her plots and murderous scheming. Alexis Minotis is perhaps the most skillful of all the actors, showing his loyalty to his king, a shrewd understanding of the enslaved architect and his people, and he is cunning enough to plumb the depths of Nellifer's connivance and trips her up in her own game. He is a good and wise counselor to his master, and he delivers justice for his own immolation in the depths of the pyramid, making certain his own death restores order to what looks like an irrational wish. Thus, Hawks manages to convey a delicate balance between sheer spectacle, an intriguing plot, and excellent performances to direct not one of the colossi epics of the times, but one of sufficient intrigue and glitter, and, above all, one that shows man's vanity and greed, but also a sense of moral balance, for a sense of justice prevails when the honest worker is rewarded and the connivers punished. CS

Notes

1. If one does not count *Red River* (1948), a western, and some war movies made in the 1940s, which have epic elements.
2. "Commentary," *Land of the Pharaohs*, directed by Howard Hawks (Warner Bros., 2007), DVD.
3. The Pyramid of Khufu, of "Cheops," as it later came to be known.

Bibliography

Weiler, A. H. "*Land of the Pharaohs* Is Standard Saga." *New York Times*, 27 July 1955, http://movies.nytimes.com/movie/review?res=9805E2DB103AE53BBC4F51DFB166838E649EDE (23 September 2013).

THE LAST EMPEROR (1987)

DIRECTOR: Bernardo Bertolucci
WRITERS: Mark Peploe, Bernardo Bertolucci
PRODUCER: Jeremy Thomas (Recorded Picture Company, Hemdale Film, Yanco Films Limited)
CINEMATOGRAPHER: Vittorio Storaro
EDITOR: Gabriella Cristiani
ART DIRECTION: Ferdinando Scarfiotti, Bruno Cesari, Osvaldo Desideri
COSTUMES: James Acheson
MUSIC: Ryuichi Sakamoto, David Byrne, Cong Su
SOUND MIXERS: Bill Rowe, Ivan Sharrock
CAST: Pu Yi, Adult: John Lone. Pu Yi, 3 Years: Richard Vuu. Pu Yi, 8 Years: Tijger Tsou. Pu Yi, 15 Years: Wu Tao. Wanong: Joan Chen. Reginald Johnston: Peter O'Toole. Detention Camp Governor: Ying Ruocheng. Chen Pao-chen: Victor Wong. Big Li: Dennis Dun. Amakasu: Ryuichi Sakamoto. Eastern Jewel: Maggie Han. Interrogator: Ric Young. Wen Hsiu: Wu Jun Mei. Chang: Cary Hiroyuki Tagawa. Ar Mo: Jade Go. Yoshioka: Fumihiko Ikeda. Pu Chieh, Adult: Guang Fan. Pu Chieh, 7 Years: Henry Kyi. Pu Chieh, 14 Years: Alvin Riley. Lord Chamberlain: Jiang Xi Ren
AA: Best Picture (Jeremy Thomas), Best Director (Bernardo Bertolucci), Best Art Direction–Set Decoration (Ferdinando Scarfiotti, Bruno Cesari, Osvaldo Desideri), Best Cinematography (Vittorio Storaro), Best Costume Design (James Acheson), Best Film Editing (Gabriella

Cristiani), Best Music–Original Score (Ryuichi Sakamoto, David Byrne, Cong Su), Best Sound (Bill Rowe, Ivan Sharrock), Best Writing–Screenplay Based on Material from Another Medium (Mark Peploe, Bernardo Bertolucci)
DVD: Criterion, 2008. The Criterion Collection.
BLU-RAY: Criterion, 2009
DURATION: 160 minutes

> Once upon a time, I . . . dreamt I was a butterfly . . . conscious only of my happiness as a butterfly. Soon I awakened, and there I was, myself again. Now I do not know whether I was then a man dreaming I was a butterfly, or whether I am now a butterfly, dreaming I am a man.
>
> —Zhuangzi (Chuang-tsu), fourth century B.C.E., translated by Antonio de Nicolas

The Last Emperor is an epic film inspired by the autobiography of Pu Yi, the last emperor of China and the final ruler of the Qing Dynasty who ascended to the throne in 1908, at the age of three, and abdicated in 1917 (reigning again briefly as emperor of Manchukuo in a puppet regime in 1934–1935). Following his removal, he was captured first by the Soviets and then later repatriated to China, where he spent a decade in the Fushun War Criminals Management Center (a Maoist labor reformatory), before being pardoned and released. His post reformatory occupations included serving at the Peking Botanical Gardens and later as a literary editor. While the action of this film chronicles the autobiography of Pu Yi, the epos of it is far from a biopic; rather, it chronicles the effects of the philosophical wars, within and without, bred from an eternally mercurial culture on the nature of one self-proclaimed anachronistic[1] man who would be emperor, but for an omen. Alternatively, this is an epic about the cricket and the butterfly.

The film begins in medias res in 1950, at a train station on the Manchurian border, with political prisoner Pu Yi (played by numerous actors) returning to China from the Soviet Union, along with other political prisoners. He is distinguished from the others only because he is wearing eyeglasses. There is a commanding voice instructing prisoners to keep moving and keep silent. A group of prisoners recognize Pu Yi as their deposed emperor and bow. He flees for the restroom, where he catches his reflection in the sooty mirror. Then, amid the monochromatic background of the scene, we hear someone screaming to open the door and we observe a red stream flowing from the sink, as a banging on the bathroom door breaks visual attention and draws the audience into a flashback from 1908: the day that Pu Yi was removed from his mother's arms, taken out of his home, and carried to the Forbidden City to become emperor.

The flashback continues through the coronation process as the child, accompanied by his father and wet nurse, continuously cries and objects, wanting to go home. When he fidgets during the actual coronation and his father tells him, "Don't worry, it will be over soon," a cleric admonishes the father. (In his autobiography, Pu Yi recalls that some believed his father's words were a bad omen of his reign.) After the ceremony, the child runs out the door, flapping his arms like wings, chasing the arc of the flowing yellow banner from the imperial flag. Once outside, he witnesses his vast military, and the toddler of three begins to romp through the ranks, until he becomes intrigued by the sound of a cricket and is determined to hunt it down. He finds it in the pocket of a soldier, who pulls a box out of his pocket and presents the cricket in the box to the young leader.

Flashing back to the present, we see Pu Yi on the floor, a man's voice screaming at him, "You are a criminal. You must be judged." Pu Yi replies, "I am the lord of ten thousand years." The man picks up a razor blade, looks at him and says, "If you really wanted to die, you would have succeeded." Pu Yi says, "They'll kill me anyway." The man replies, "Whatever happens, whether you'll be kept alive or killed, you will be judged, anyway."

Then, as Pu Yi turns to put his broken glasses back on, we have another flashback and meet a pet turtle face-to-face, as Pu Yi, the child, sits with his eunuch companions, who are trying to teach him about his new home as they sit with him before a wooden model of the Forbidden City. When they tell him he has to take a bath, the giggling child erupts in protest until they placate him with song. In the bath he asks, "Is it true that I can do anything I want?" They respond, "Of course your majesty. You are the lord of ten thousand years." Then, proclaiming, "I am the son of Heaven!" Pu Yi, seeing his wet nurse, runs to her screaming, "I want to go home!" Then his wet nurse tells him a significant story: "Once upon a time there was a great tree and a great wind, and they were always fighting. But when wind came back it was angrier and stronger than ever." And then we witness the backstory of Ar Mo (Jade Go), the wet nurse, of how she was forcefully separated from her father and newborn to become the wet nurse of the emperor.

The film continues, chronicling Pu Yi's years at the detention center up to his death by alternating action and flashback, a method that serves two important functions, both philosophical and historical, although they eventually coincide as the surprising denouement of the film emerges. During significant shifts in the consciousness of Pu Yi, we simultaneously watch as his biography slowly creeps through the present; through flashback, however, the interior landscape of Pu Yi slowly begins to emerge, despite what we witness outside (on-screen) through the mundane visuals and dialogue of his ten-year internment and the time that follows. For example, in the next scene, at the concentration camp where he is being kept, he is briefly separated from his brother (who is not only his lifelong companion, but also almost his servant, as he performs even the simplest tasks for him, for instance, tying his shoes and reminding him to brush his teeth). The action immediately moves to a flashback of Pu Yi's first meeting with his brother. He is jealous of the fact that his brother is permitted to live at home with his mother, while he is not. When he sees his mother again, he sternly tells her that he does not remember her. Pu Yi shows his brother the high consorts who claim that they are his mothers, "but they are not," he protests. Then we see him being consoled and nursed by Ar Mo with the high consort witnessing disapprovingly. The next scene flashes forward, and Pu Yi's brother, Pu Chieh (also played by various actors), is brought into the emperor's detention room to be his roommate. Noticing the bandages on Pu Yi's hands, Pu Chieh embraces and consoles him.

Another reason for the use of flashback is to provide important historical background to explain the psychological transformation occurring in Pu Yi. For example, when Pu Yi arrives at the camp, he is forced to read about the history of the Chinese people, specifically the revisionist story of his own abdication in 1912. As Pu Yi stoically and rebelliously reads, his brother weeps. The flashback provides the reason, for Pu Yi learned of his impending situation from his younger brother, who was the first to boast to him that he was no longer emperor. In the scene, the brothers are learning calligraphy, but Pu Yi is not interested in his studies, while Pu Chieh is studying diligently. Pu Yi sees that his brother is wearing "imperial yellow," a color that only the emperor is permitted to wear. His brother tells him the color is common now, and anyway he is no longer emperor. Pu Yi calls his brother a liar, but his brother was telling the truth. He discovers the truth, calling his entire staff liars. Then he asks for Ar Mo. She is whisked away against her will. He is told he is too old to have a wet nurse because it is not healthy. He replies, "She is not my wet nurse. She is my butterfly." Then he leaves, screaming her name through the empty streets of the Forbidden City, until the scene cuts back to the concentration camp again.

The governor of the camp (played by Ying Ruocheng, who forces the detainees to write their life stories to confess their pride) is reading *Inside the Forbidden City*, by Reginald Fleming Johnston. Through this artifice, we are brought through the next flashback, and we learn that Johnston (Peter O'Toole) was Pu Yi's tutor and was largely responsible for the emperor's fascination with all things Western, despite his early traditional upbringing. Johnston teaches Pu Yi that a gentleman "means what he says and says what he means." Pu Yi says that he is not a gentleman then because he's not allowed to do that, for everyone is always telling him what to say. During the years with Mr. Johnston, Pu Yi learns to ride a bike. Johnston also introduces him to George Washington, the "revolutionary president." His constant yearning to leave the palace comes to a head when his mother dies. He makes a frenzied attempt to leave, and when he is unable to, he smashes his pet mouse against the walls of the palace gates and then lands on the roof of the palace, causing Johnston to organize a human rope to save his life. Johnston convinces Pu Yi that the best way for him to escape is marriage, and so Pu Yi marries, twice. It was only in 1924, with his expulsion apparent, and as he was given an hour to pack his belongings and flee, that the unwilling emperor admits, "I always thought I hated it; now I am afraid to leave."

As a guest of the Japanese embassy and later in Tianjin, Pu Yi enjoys his days as a Western playboy with his two wives, but that time is short-lived, with the loss of one wife due to her divorcing him and the arrival of a Japanese spy, Eastern Jewel (Maggie Han), who coerces him into action against the Chinese Republic by telling him that their traditional homeland in Manchuria has been desecrated and that the Imperial tombs of the Manchurian people have been robbed and the body of the empress dowager hacked to pieces and her pearl necklace given away as a wedding present. Johnston left in 1931. Pu Yi asks him if he believes a man can become emperor again. His reply is yes, and shortly thereafter, in 1932, the Japanese establish Pu Yi as the emperor of the puppet state of Manchukuo, although he believes that he is indeed a head of a sovereign region. When his wife becomes pregnant by another "Manchurian" man (Pu Yi's driver) and knowledge of her infidelity becomes public, Pu Yi is forced to sign away the kingdom of Manchuria. His driver commits suicide, and his wife, an opium addict, leaves after the child is born dead.

After three years in the concentration camp, Pu Yi is still unable to care for himself. His evaluators admonish him, saying, "Stop hiding behind your private story." Pu Yi replies, "People do not change. I let it happen." What follows is the attack on Shanghai, the attack on Pearl Harbor, and Pu Yi's surrender to the Americans (although he is ultimately intercepted by the Russians and captured). In his final scene with his wife, who returns as he is fleeing, she spits in his face. Crying, he leaves her and flees.

Back in the camp, Pu Yi is tilling a garden, and the guard reproaches him for signing every accusation made against him. Calmly pruning flowers, Pu Yi takes responsibility for it all. The guard tells him, "You are only responsible for what *you do*. Is that so terrible to be useful?" In a turning point, the next scene is Pu Yi's graduation from camp, and having been deemed remolded after a decade, he is pardoned and released.

The final scenes portray Pu Yi tending to a greenhouse garden; riding a bicycle home from work; and witnessing a Maoist parade, in which his old teacher from the camp is now being held a prisoner by the Red Guard youth. He finally returns to the abandoned Forbidden City, now a museum, and slowly makes the journey back up the steps to the throne room and almost to the throne, but for the shout of a young boy who tells him to step away from the throne. The emperor tells him who he is and that he can prove it. Then, reaching his arm behind the throne, Pu Yi pulls out the small box and hands it to the young boy, who opens it to find the cricket of the emperor's youth. As the boy looks up to find Pu Yi, he finds that he has disappeared. The closing scene has a crowd of tourists entering the city, the tour guide noting that the emperor died in 1967. "Between a man and a butterfly . . . is called the transformation of material things." MC

Note

1. Henry Pu Yi, *The Last Manchu: The Autobiography of Henry Pu Yi, Last Emperor of China* (New York: Skyhorse, 2010).

Bibliography

Pu Yi, Henry. *The Last Manchu: The Autobiography of Henry Pu Yi, Last Emperor of China.* New York: Skyhorse, 2010.

THE LAST KING OF SCOTLAND (2006)

Director: Kevin Macdonald
Writers: Peter Morgan, Jeremy Brock. Based on the novel by Giles Foden.
Producers: Lisa Bryer, Andrea Calderwood, Charles Steel (Fox Searchlight Pictures, DNA Films, FilmFour)
Cinematographer: Anthony Dod Mantle
Editor: Justine Wright
Music: Alex Heffes
Cast: Idi Amin: Forest Whitaker. Dr. Nicholas Garrigan: James McAvoy. Kay Amin: Kerry Washington. Sarah Merrit: Gillian Anderson. Stone: Simon McBurney. Dr. Garrigan Senior: David Ashton. Mrs. Garrigan: Barbara Rafferty. Dr. Merrit: Adam Kotz. Sarah Merrit: Gillian Anderson. Jonah Wasswa: Stephen Rwangyezi. Perkins: Chris Wilson. Dr. Thomas Junju: David Oyelowo. Masanga: Abby Mukiibi Nkaaga
AA: Best Leading Actor (Forest Whitaker)
DVD: 20th Century Fox, 2007
Blu-ray: 20th Century Fox, 2006
Duration: 123 minutes

Inspired by real events and introducing a fictional character, Nicholas Garrigan (James McAvoy), who becomes involved in African and international intrigue, *The Last King of Scotland* depicts the rise of Idi Amin, an infamous, violent leader brilliantly played by Forest Whitaker. As Peter Bradshaw states in a review published by the *Guardian*, "Whitaker treats the audience to a full-throated, technically accomplished cadenza of pure acting exuberance that you feel ashamed for enjoying quite so much."[1] However, because the film is limited to Garrigan's perceptions, it obscures the deaths of more than 300,000 people during Amin's regime.[2] Garrigan goes to Uganda for adventure, including sexual adventure, so he is easily reduced to various, although parallel, symbols, for example, "a young imperialist," the "British government," "Faust," and "white colonialism."[3]

Based on Giles Foden's 1998 Whitbread Prize–winning novel of the same name, the film opens in 1970 with students happily running from college to jump into a lake, celebrating their graduation. Among them is a new medical doctor, Nicholas Garrigan. That night, while at dinner with his parents, the senior Dr. Garrigan (David Ashton) and wife toast to the two practicing together. To avoid this eventuality, in his bedroom, Nicholas spins a globe. Rejecting Canada, the second randomly chosen country is Uganda.

Garrigan arrives in the country at the end of General Idi Amin's coup, which removed Milton Obote from power. On the way to a Ugandan health clinic, he sees Amin's men on the road in military vehicles. At the clinic, Garrigan works with Dr. Merrit (Adam Kotz) and his wife Sarah (Gillian Anderson), where they care for local children. Although he says he is there to "make a difference," Sarah correctly states that he is an "unlikely candidate for this type of work."

Garrigan convinces Sarah to see Amin speak. Amin is greeted by thousands of well-wishers, including warriors in traditional dress. Amin announces that his government will be one of "action not words," including building new schools, roads, and houses. Garrigan joins the crowd's excitement, but Sarah is suspicious, seeing little difference between Amin and Obote. On the way back to the clinic, their road is blocked by Amin's soldiers. Amin's car has hit a cow, and Amin requires a hand splint. Garrigan assists Amin but is irritated by the wounded, bellowing cow. When no one helps it, Garrigan grabs a nearby pistol and kills it. Amin's soldiers point their weapons at Garrigan because he took Amin's gun, but Amin is intrigued by Garrigan because of his quick temper and because he is Scottish. They make an immediate connection because both hate the British and love all things Scottish. That night, Garrigan invites Sarah for a drink. She is intrigued but refuses.

Next morning, Garrigan is awakened by Jonah Wasswa (Stephen Rwangyezi), the Ugandan minister of health, to take him to Amin in the presidential limo. Amin asks him to serve Uganda, offering to make him his personal physician. Garrigan refuses, saying he is committed to serving at the clinic. Amin promises to return him home after the evening's state dinner and even pays local tailors to fit him for a new suit. That night, Amin introduces him to his wives, including Kay (Kerry Washington), to whom Garrigan is attracted. Garrigan does not return to the clinic, instead becoming Amin's close confidant.

Garrigan is introduced to international intrigue by Stone (Simon McBurney), a slippery British agent, and the British high commissioner, Perkins (Chris Wilson), who wants Garrigan to assist them. Amin's statements and actions concern them, especially such claims that, "Africans only understand a firm hand." Garrigan is contemptuous saying, "Bloody English."

In the middle of the night, Garrigan is called to help Amin, who is convinced someone poisoned him in an assassination attempt. After an examination, Garrigan presses against Amin's stomach to release built-up intestinal gas. Amin is embarrassed, but Garrigan promises everything that passes between them is confidential. Becoming an important confidant, Amin gives him assignments outside of his expertise, including judging bids for a major high-rise. Amin calls Garrigan and Wasswa his "two closest advisors."

When he is not treating the president or his family, Garrigan assists at the local hospital. He meets with Amin's previous personal physician, Dr. Thomas Junju (David Oyelowo). They hear explosions and gunfire near Makindye Prison, where Obote's people are being held. Garrigan is called to see Kay's son Mackenzie, who is not allowed to leave her home because he is epileptic. Kay will not allow Garrigan to take Mackenzie to the hospital for treatment because he is an embarrassment to Amin. The next day, Amin brings Garrigan a "small gift" for helping his son: a convertible Mercedes. Amin asks him to drive him to the airport because he is flying to Libya. When Garrigan challenges him about hiding his son, Amin says, "You have touched me and I will reconsider. I respect your honesty." Rebel soldiers ambush the car, and Garrigan speeds away, running over a solder. Realizing that someone has revealed his travel plans, Amin puts Masanga (Abby Mukiibi Nkaaga) in charge of his security. At a bar at the local Holiday Inn, Garrigan sees Wasswa speaking to a foreigner. He mentions this to Amin when he delivers papers for him to sign.

Later, Garrigan sees Kay and Mackenzie, who is healthier, at one of Amin's pool parties. Stone arrives and mentions privately that people who speak out against the regime disappear and that Wasswa is also missing. When asked, Amin explains that Wasswa fled to Tanzania because he embezzled funds. Garrigan realizes his culpability and attempts to resign. Amin is friendly, then threatening, but he eventually convinces him to stay. They go to a party, where Amin ropes his finance minister and women dance topless around a fire. Garrigan and Kay slip away and have sex. She warns him that he needs to leave the county because Amin does not trust anybody. Garrigan returns to his apartment, which has been ransacked, his passport taken and replaced with a Ugandan passport. He stops at Stone's home to request help to escape. Stone tells him that Amin wiped out the Acholi and Langi tribes because of their opposition to to the regime and that locals call Garrigan Amin's "white monkey." Stone says he must earn his passage. Garrigan realizes that Stone is requiring him to kill Amin.

Amin, in his paranoia, expels all Asians from the country, even from the hospitals. Garrigan argues with Amin's soldiers that it is a human rights violation to do so. He visits Amin to tell him that it will damage his reputation, but Amin dismisses him as just a doctor. Hundreds of people leave the country, among them Sarah, who Garrigan sees riding on a bus.

Kay calls Garrigan; she is pregnant with his child and needs an abortion. Amin plans to kill them both. Unable to use the hospital, he gathers instruments to operate at her house. Amin forces him to come to his office. He says his head is exploding. News reports claim that he is a cannibal, and he blames Garrigan for not persuading him to keep the Asians in the country. He then threatens to expel journalists. Garrigan advises him not to throw them out and to instead meet with them face-to-face so that he can charm them. Requiring Garrigan's support, Amin insists that he attend the press conference. Amin does charm them, saying that the British hate him because they are jealous, so he created the "Save Britain Fund."

After the news conference, Garrigan is finally able to go to Kay. He discovers that she has gone to the village, where he finds her surrounded by wailing women. She has been dismembered, her dead body lying on an operating table. One of the wailers tells him, "This is what happens when you betray your president." Angry, he visits Amin, who is watching porn films. Amin explains his actions, stating, "I made an example of her because she betrayed me." Garrigan offers him some headache pills. Amin forgets them, so Garrigan holds on to the bottle.

Amin takes Garrigan to the Entebbe International Airport to assist the 250 hostages taken by the Popular Front for the Liberation of Palestine in exchange for prisoners held by Israel. Amin announces that there they will have the best care because his personal doctor is available to them. Dr. Junju is assisting. When leaving Masanga's car, Garrigan accidentally leaves the pills in the vehicle. Masanga is suspicious of the contents and gives a child soldier one of the pills as a test. Garrigan sees this and forces the child to spit it out, revealing that it is indeed poison.

Masanga and his men drag Garrigan through the airport and beat him inside a closed store. Amin arrives and questions him, saying, "Is there one thing that you have done that is good? 'I will go to Africa and play the white man with the natives.' We are not a game. We are real. I think your death will be the first real thing that has happened to you." They insert meat hooks into his chest and pull him up to the ceiling with ropes. Dr. Junju watches from the side. He faints.

The Israeli government agrees to negotiate as a first step toward an agreement, and all non-Israeli hostages are released. Masanga orders Garrigan lowered. Junju bandages him while they are gone and slips him into the group of freed hostages as they board a plane. Junju says, "Go home and tell the truth about Amin. They will believe you. You are a white man." Garrigan has a window seat on the plane as it rises over the city. Amin's men take Junju to the back room and shoot him. The film ends with documentary footage of Amin in a news conference and jubilant crowds celebrating after he is thrown from power. He dies in exile in Saudi Arabia.

Garrigan believed that his education and status as a European would give him special abilities to help the Ugandan people, but instead, he never comes to understand Uganda, Ugandans, or Amin. Reflecting on Garrigan as a character, director Kevin Macdonald states,

> Nicholas Garrigan . . . is a deeply ambiguous character. And I relate to that ambiguity: At that age you make decisions not always for the right reasons, you want to have a good time, and you're oblivious to the pain you're causing. He's also a representative of colonial power and of the privileged white interloper. I see his trajectory as a Faust story of a man who sells his soul for fame, comfort, and luxury.[4]

This focus on an imaginary, passive, and ambiguous character, however, reduces the film to a "synecdochical treatment of [Amin's] reign of terror," which is "profoundly inadequate to the task of revealing his brutality."[5] JMW

Notes

1. Quoted in Lesley Marx, "*The Last King of Scotland* and the Politics of Adaptation," *Black Camera* 3, no. 1 (2011): 69.
2. Duane Dudek, "Historic Friction: Filmmaker Goes against Grain of Truth to Dramatize Life of Idi Amin," *Milwaukee Journal Sentinel*, 13 October 2006, www.jsonline.com/entertainment/movies/29191764.html (24 September 2013).
3. Marx, "*The Last King of Scotland* and the Politics of Adaptation," 65.
4. Ali Jaafar, "Warped Love Story," *Sight and Sound* 17, no. 2 (2007): 35.
5. Marx, "*The Last King of Scotland* and the Politics of Adaptation," 69.

Bibliography

Dudek, Duane. "Historic Friction: Filmmaker Goes against Grain of Truth to Dramatize Life of Idi Amin." *Milwaukee Journal Sentinel*, 13 October 2006, www.jsonline.com/entertainment/movies/29191764.html (24 September 2013).

Jaafar, Ali. "Warped Love Story." *Sight and Sound* 17, no. 2 (2007): 35.

Marx, Lesley. "*The Last King of Scotland* and the Politics of Adaptation." *Black Camera* 3, no. 1 (2011): 54–74.

THE LAST SAMURAI (2003)

Director: Edward Zwick
Writers: John Logan, Marshall Herskovitz, Edward Zwick
Producers: Michael Doven, Tom Egelman, Marshall Herskovitz, Scott Krope, Paula Wagner (Warner Bros., Bedford Falls Company, Cruise/Wagner Productions)
Cinematographer: David James
Editor: Victor Du Bois, Steven Rosenblum
Production Design: Lilly Kilvert
Art Direction: Christopher Burian-Mohr, Jess Gonchor, Kim Sinclair
Set Decoration: Gretchen Rau
Costumes: Ngila Dickson
Music: Hans Zimmer
Sound Mixers: Andy Nelson, Anna Behlmer, Jeff Wexler
Cast: Capt. Nathan Algren: Tom Cruise. Katsumoto: Ken Watanabe. Nakao: Shun Sugata. Nobutada: Shin Koymada.

Gen. Hasegawa: Togo Ikawa. Emperor Meiji: Shichikosuke Nakamura. Omura: Masato Harada. Ujio: Hiroyuki Sanada. Col. Bagley: Tony Goldwin. Simon Graham: Timothy Spall. Taka: Koyuki Kato. Col. Bagley: Tony Goldwyn. Zebulon Gant: Billy Connolly. Winchester Rep: William Atherton

AA: None

AAN: Best Supporting Actor (Ken Watanabe), Best Art Direction–Set Decoration (Lilly Kilvert, Gretchen Rau), Best Costume Design (Ngila Dickson), Best Sound Mixing (Andy Nelson, Anna Behlmer, Jeff Wexler)

Award of the Japanese Academy: Best Foreign Film

DVD: Warner Home Video, 2004

Blu-ray: Warner Home Video, 2006

Duration: 154 minutes

When asked whether *The Last Samurai* is history or Hollywood, director Edward Zwick, who coauthored the script with John Logan and Marshall Herskovitz, preferred to call his epic "Historywood," implying that it is more like Hollywood fiction than history. As epic-makers often do, he would have audiences believe that his story is based on solid historical facts, with additions of the necessary epic trimmings, namely action and size, for the contemporary market is thirsting for more and bigger spectacle. From his and his collaborators' comments,[1] we learn that although Tom Cruise's character, Captain Nathan Algren, is a fabrication, the story this epic tells is more or less a reproduction of a historical period, the opening of the Japanese empire to the west, particularly post–Civil War America, which attempted to expand the influence of its newborn industrial might into other countries and, in doing so, affected other cultures not yet Westernized, for its own interests. Forced by the circumstances of history to change and modernize its antiquated military system, Japan, an isolated country for centuries, was opening up its borders, ironically seeking the help of its future rival to do so.

The action of the epic begins on 4 July 1876, the anniversary of the first centennial of American independence, but a difficult time for the United States, which had suffered one of its greatest defeats on 25 June of that same year, when General George Armstrong Custer and his 7th Regiment had been massacred by the Sioux Indians at Little Bighorn in Montana. But the United States was enjoying a tremendous advantage, for technology had helped improve the Civil War weaponry, and the country could now compete with the European powers for dominance in the East. The process had already begun more than twenty years earlier, when Matthew C. Perry, under orders by President Fillmore, arrived in Japan in 1853, with a powerful fleet, demanding that the country be opened up to Western visitors or be destroyed. Convulsions inside Japan produced the demotion of the shogun, the prime minister of the emperor, and the assignments of the training of troops to Americans and other Westerners. The class of the samurai—warriors at the service of feudal lords that had ruled Japan for centuries—was to be abolished, by force if necessary, and replaced by modern armies modeled after those of Western powers.

It is more or less within this historical context that *The Last Samurai* is set, but its director and his collaborators saw it not merely as an action piece or a semi-historical document, but as a complex tale attempting to embrace a multiplicity of themes—cultural contrasts and the values of military/heroic conduct—and, perhaps above all, as a vehicle for highlighting personal tragedies resulting from the savagery of war. It is also a Romantic tale, set in an exotic land,[2] where a Western hero ventures, becomes immersed in that culture, learns its ways, fights for their cause, and, finally, loves one of its women, the widow of the man he killed in self-defense.

Zwick is quite conscious of earlier epic-makers, Akira Kurosawa and David Lean, in particular, who traversed the path of cultural confrontations and created epics distinguished for their thought, historical context, and entertaining action. Zwick admiringly mentions such epics of past eras as *The Guns of Navarone*, *The Great Escape*, *Lawrence of Arabia*, and *The Bridge on the River Kwai*, war epics that place their protagonists in foreign lands, where they have either been captured and imprisoned, or where they have undertaken perilous missions—escapes or commando raids—that require exceptional courage, daring, and superhuman effort. In the same breath, he also mentions the works of Kurosawa, a much-admired Japanese auteur in the West, as both an imitator of Western epics (the works of John Ford, for instance), and also as one whose works in turn inspired Western epics.[3]

The Last Samurai seems to be a blend of many of these past masters' techniques and methods, and the film's makers seem to have consciously tried to imitate and continue the genre of the war epic that specializes in mixing cultures. War, in particular, is fertile ground for stories, with international casts whose manners, battle methods, mentality, and codes of honor are bound to conflict with one another, and where the opportunities for cultural clashes are most available, even inevitable.

The epic of cultural contrasts is even more relevant today than when it first started in the days of Kurosawa and Lean, for, as some commentators have pointed out,[4] the troubles of a military force occupying a foreign country may be attributed to the inability of the occupier to translate the meaning of his motives into a language clear to the natives. In *The Last Samurai*, Captain Nathan Algren (Cruise) has to reexamine his own purpose in fighting a Japanese samurai, about whom he initially knew nothing. He embarks on a mission with an extremely limited vision of the culture he is attempting to invade and Westernize, contemptuous of their awkward efforts to learn and adjust to his Western—and supposedly superior—methods. When he begins training the Japanese troops, he views them as an inferior race, a disorganized group of laughable clowns who cannot even shoot straight when the target (himself) is not moving. But Algren, a serious and generous man, is capable of learning after his bitter defeat at the hands of a samurai warrior he thought he could easily defeat.

As he is held captive in the land of the samurai, being restored to health by them rather than being tortured, he begins to have second thoughts, gradually recognizing that they have extraordinary human qualities that he never suspected: they have compassion for a defeated but honorable enemy, they possess a dignity unimaginable in warriors (usually thought of as gruff, bloodthirsty monsters), and they are dedicated to a sense of personal honor—Bushido—an idea that takes him awhile to grasp but that he eventually embraces. The movie is about his awakening and transformation. At first surprised, he gradually adapts to their manners and language until he becomes their most dedicated supporter, practically merging and identifying with their culture; a disaffected man from the internal wars in his own country, he recovers his inner strength and code of honor, an American equivalent to Bushido, a conviction that values independence, valor in battle, and humanity that accepts neither defeat nor shame.

Thus, the mystique of the Japanese samurai and the valor of the U.S. soldier fighting in a foreign land do not produce a cultural clash, but rather an unusual merging of the two cultures. Without being condescending, director Zwick and scriptwriter Logan borrow the exceptional qualities of the Japanese warrior and invest them in an American warrior. Zwick achieves this by creating a double archetype, a feat almost (but not quite) accomplished by David Lean in *Lawrence of Arabia*, where an Arab, Sherif Ali, embodying native qualities, becomes the shadow of the uncompromising Lawrence, who gradually learns from his "barbarian" friend qualities only latent in himself, for instance, compassion for a defeated enemy and real friendship.

Similarly, in *The Last Samurai*, Captain Algren meets Katsumoto (Ken Watanabe), the leader of the samurai tribe that has rebelled against the emperor, and whom he initially fights and is defeated by. Impressed by Algren's brave stance, Katsumoto takes him to his mountain haunts, has him restored to health, and seeks to understand him—to learn his enemy's methods. In the process, he gains respect for his enemy, and the two begin to approach one another's mentality and background. Katsumoto—much like the leader of an Indian tribe in the American West—is the last remnant of a disappearing culture. He comprehends his coming end, but his sense of honor, Bushido, will not allow him to surrender his weapons and accept the new order of compromising bureaucrats that now surround the emperor. In the centuries-long tradition, he and his tribe of fighters have developed a civilization of proud men who give up their lives for a cause, but who can think of no way of changing it. Their qualities—the control of mind and body and their fighting skills—have become outdated, but they prefer to die rather than change. Algren, who has seen the extinction of a similar culture, the American Indian tribes, discovers, to his own astonishment, that the Japanese warrior is not what has been presented to him—a stubborn rebel, but a man (and woman) of principle, living isolated lives of superior strength, admiring qualities of the warrior tribe now outdated by Western technology. The sword is being replaced by gunpowder. Nothing can reverse this trend, and the Japanese samurai culture, nurtured for many centuries, will go extinct, and with it the sense of honorable conduct, perfected to the form of an art.

In this sense, both Katsumoto and Algren are heroes—and archetypes—of a bygone era. The two fit together well, becoming the medium of merging cultures, one of them being the model to whose ideas the other adapts, and from whom he learns. It is a story of extinction, showing a race of heroes with admirable qualities and personal traits that, admirable as they may be, do not fit the current society. Today, precision weapons wipe out an enemy without the benefit, or need, of a personal showdown. An enemy is killed, but nothing is shown of his or her character. The killed enemy becomes an abstraction, a "terrorist," a term that precludes any sympathy, let alone admiration, for the fallen.

But our era still yearns for those qualities that distinguished the fighter, more adept with simple weapons, more vulnerable and a victim to technology, but, at least in past ages and cultures, more capable of expressing the human qualities that have disappeared with him. Samurais are gone, but myths about them—as for American Western heroes—still endure. They may be just that—myths—for we have no way of knowing exactly what transpired under war circumstances in those days, and humanity has a tendency to invest its heroes with superhuman qualities they may or may not have. An American star, Tom Cruise, embodies an American adventurer who learns the ways of the East. Similarly, a Japanese star, Ken Watanabe, embodies the qualities of the samurai, now in eclipse, but enlarged by poetic—or epic moviemaking—imagination. CS

Notes

1. "Special Features," *The Last Samurai*, directed by Edward Zwick (Warner Bros., 2004), DVD. For further information on the selection of the cast, historical backgrounds, choice of locations, and so forth, see John Logan, *Tom Cruise: The Last Samurai* (New York: Roundtable Press/Time, 2003).

2. *The Last Samurai* was filmed on three continents, New Zealand, where most of the external action sequences were filmed, Japan, and Burbank Studios in California.

3. "Special Features."

4. Chris Matthews, MSNBC commentator, interview, Spring 2004.

Bibliography

Logan, John. *Tom Cruise: The Last Samurai.* New York: Roundtable Press/Time, 2003.

LAWRENCE OF ARABIA (1962)

DIRECTOR: David Lean
WRITERS: Robert Bolt, Michael Wilson
PRODUCER: Sam Spiegel (Columbia Pictures, Horizon Pictures)
ASSISTANT DIRECTOR: Roy Stevens
CINEMATOGRAPHER: Freddie A. Young
EDITOR: Anne V. Coates
PRODUCTION DESIGN: John Box
ART DIRECTION: John Stall
SET DECORATION: Dario Simoni
COSTUMES: Phyllis Dalton
MUSIC: Maurice Jarre
SOUND EDITORS: Winston Ryder
SOUND DUBBING: John Cox
SPECIAL EFFECTS: Cliff Richardson
GENERAL FACTOTUM: Eddie Fowlie
CAST: T. E. Lawrence: Peter O'Toole. Sherif Ali: Omar Sharif. Prince Feisal: Alec Guinness. Auda Abu Tayi: Anthony Quinn. Gen. Allenby: Jack Hawkins. Col. Brighton: Anthony Quayle. Turkish Bey: José Ferrer. Mr. Dryden: Claude Rains. Jackson Bentley: Arthur Kennedy. Gen. Murray: Donald Wolfit. Gasim: I. S. Johar. Majid: Gamil Ratib. Tafas: Zia Mohyeddin
AA: Best Picture (Sam Spiegel), Best Director (David Lean), Best Cinematography (Freddie A. Young), Best Editing (Anne V. Coates), Best Music–Substantially Original Score (Maurice Jarre), Best Sound (John Cox), Best Art Direction–Set Decoration–Color (John Box)
AAN: Best Leading Actor (Peter O'Toole), Best Supporting Actor (Omar Sharif), Best Writing–Screenplay Based on Material from Another Medium (Robert Bolt)
DVD: Columbia Pictures, 1999
BLU-RAY: Sony Pictures Home Entertainment, 2012
DURATION: 222 minutes

Lawrence of Arabia, David Lean's second epic film, is loosely based on an actual historical figure, T. E. Lawrence, the legendary English officer who led the Arabs in their liberation struggle during World War I. The makers of the film drew their basic sources for making the epic as much from the numerous biographies written about Lawrence, as well as his autobiography, *Seven Pillars of Wisdom* (1926), as they did from the accounts of the man by several individuals who knew the director personally. One of them was Lowell Thomas, an American journalist[1] whose documentary films and lectures made Lawrence a celebrity in England and the United States in the 1920s.[2]

Lawrence achieved the status of a mythical hero of the desert, a liberator of an oppressed people, and a man whose military genius endowed him with the glitter of Pompey or Alexander.[3] A leader in the Arab Revolt of 1916–1918, whose life and accomplishments were acknowledged in a number of fields, including archeology, engineering, and literature, Lawrence remained an enigma to his many admirers before his death in a motorcycle accident in 1935, and long after that, to this day. *Lawrence of Arabia* added to the mystique of his life and his accomplishments, especially since the film was (and is) much admired for its dynamic cast, unequaled photography of desert vistas, and brilliant script that combined the talents of the then-blacklisted Michael Wilson, coauthor of Lean's *The Bridge on the River Kwai*, and Robert Bolt, who had won acclaim with his play *A Man for all Seasons. Lawrence of Arabia* won numerous awards, including Oscars for Best Picture and Best Director, and sparked much interest, with several books being written about it. In addition, restoration of the film during Lean's time (1988) and a recently released (2012) Blu-ray edition based on the original negative of the film, with numerous illuminating extras on the details of the production, have renewed interested in perhaps the most intriguing epic film of the twentieth century.

Before the Lean production, several attempts had been made to film Lawrence's story during the 1950s, notably by Alexander Korda, the Hungarian/English movie mogul and director, but they were thwarted either by financial exigencies or by Lawrence's living brother, Professor Arnold W. Lawrence, who was his brother's literary executor and had refused to sell the rights to *Seven Pillars of Wisdom* to cinema producers.[4] Eager to make another blockbuster epic with Lean after the success of *The Bridge on the River Kwai*, Sam Spiegel finally obtained the rights from Professor Lawrence, and Michael Wilson, who had collaborated on the script of *The Bridge on the River Kwai*, was assigned to write the new script. Wilson worked on the project for more than a year, producing several drafts between September 1959 and January 1961, when he left the project. His script did not suit Lean's tastes, and Robert Bolt was subsequently asked to take over the project. He rewrote the screenplay in its entirety, although the structural outlines of Wilson's script were retained in the final draft.[5] Today's video versions of the film assign credit for the screenplay to both authors.

Spiegel and Lean obtained permission from King Hussein of Jordan to film *Lawrence of Arabia* in the Jordanian desert, with considerable help in logistical matters. Several known actors were considered for the lead—among them Marlon Brando and Albert Finney—but Lean finally settled on an unknown, Irish stage actor Peter O'Toole, and the project was launched in the fall of 1960. It took nearly two years to complete in Jordan, Morocco, and Spain. Aside from the difficulties resulting from the logistics of moving actors and equipment to three different locations, Lean and his collaborators faced the problem of transferring to the screen one of the most enigmatic historical figures of the twentieth century.

Thomas Edward Lawrence was born in North Wales in 1888, the illegitimate son of Sir Thomas Chapman, 7th Baronet from Westmeath, Ireland, who eloped with his daughter's governess, Sara Maden, and adopted the name of Mr. Lawrence for the rest of his life. Young Thomas Edward was the second of five illegitimate sons, and this fact may, according to some of his biographers,[6] have accounted for his unusual personality. Lawrence attended Oxford and traveled to the Middle East on scholarships to research the influence of the Crusaders on modern architecture, receiving a first-place prize in modern history for his efforts. During his youth, he toured the Middle East, mostly on foot, making Arab friends and learning their language. At the outbreak of World War I in 1914, when England allied with France against Germany and Turkey, Lawrence was dispatched to Cairo, Egypt, as an intelligence officer to work for the Bureau of Arab Affairs. He was assigned a position as a liaison officer to Prince Feisal, brother of Abdullah and Ali, the sons of Hussein Ibn Ali, emir of Mecca. He later took part in numerous military operations, blowing up Turkish trains and taking the city of Aqaba allied with Auda Abu Tayi, sheik of Hawaitat, and other Arab tribes in the area. In 1918, under orders from General Edward Allenby, he led an army of Arabs that he coordinated with the British forces in their attack and capture of Damascus. He subsequently served in diplomatic missions, acting as an adviser of Arab affairs in the Colonial Office. In 1922, he enlisted in the Royal Air Force under the name of John Ross, and later in the Royal Tank Corps as T. E. Shaw, a name he legally adopted in 1927. In 1935, he retired to a country cottage and died in a motorcycle accident. He was buried at St. Nicholas Church, Moreton, Dorset,[7] drawing praise from such luminaries as Winston Churchill, who called him "one of the greatest beings of our time."[8] Despite his achievements, he remained an enigmatic figure, and even some of the details in his own descriptions—his capture and alleged rape by the Turks at Deraa, for instance, have been doubted.[9] *Seven Pillars of Wisdom*, his own account of the two-year Arab campaign, proved him a literary master and historian and ranking him among the greatest writers in English literature.

Out of a medley of historical data, literary sources, and journalistic accounts, David Lean, Michael Wilson, and Robert Bolt fashioned a screenplay based on his Arab campaign, the period during which Lawrence displayed his military genius. Both Wilson and Bolt used *Seven Pillars of Wisdom* as their basic source, but when Bolt took over the project entirely, according to a Lean biographer, "he chose to alter history for dramatic purposes."[10] His script, following the basic outlines of Wilson's earlier one, shows departures from the historical accounts, which can be briefly noted as follows: (a) Lawrence's expedition against Aqaba is shown as the first major event in the film, omitting an entire sequence of events described in *Seven Pillars of Wisdom* and in *Revolt in the Desert* (1919).[11] The historical Lawrence was indeed sent from Cairo to scout Feisal's "intentions" at the beginning of the war, but his mission included several phases before the decision to attack the Aqaba Turkish stronghold.

The opening chapters in *Seven Pillars of Wisdom* (books one through three, chapters I through XXXVII, nearly one-third of the book) describe Lawrence's first meeting with Feisal; his return to Cairo; and his rejoining Feisal with British support, which led to the successful defense of Yenbo, a British naval stronghold, and the recapturing of an important Turkish outpost, Wejh, after which the Turkish operations became defensive. The plan to attack Aqaba had first been instigated as a joint effort with Anglo-French naval forces,[12] led by French Colonel Bremond and Sir Archibald Murray, in charge of British operations in the Arab campaign. It was to be a frontal attack with a large navy force and troops descending on Aqaba from the rugged western terrain. Lawrence, who saw this as a repeat of the disaster the Allied forces had suffered at Gallipoli earlier, proposed an attack on Aqaba from the interior northeast side, with select Arab troops coming out of the Nefud Desert, a move that the Turks could not have anticipated. By that time, Lawrence was a seasoned veteran of the Arab campaign, knowledgeable of the language, geography, and history of the Middle East, and not the enthusiastic but untested novice we first see in the film.

The expedition against Aqaba, a key first episode in the film, is only one chapter in Lawrence's own account of the war, and it was instigated by the joint agreement between Feisal and Auda Abu Tayi, not inspired in a vision sequence during Lawrence's first night at Feisal's camp. The numerous British officers deployed in the field during the two-year war mentioned in *Seven Pillars of Wisdom* are condensed into one, Colonel Brighton (Anthony Quayle), while the chief of the Arab Bureau, Dryden (Claude Rains), is a combination of both General Clayton, the chief of intelligence in Egypt, and Ronald Storrs, Oriental secretary of the residency in Egypt.[13] In the film, Lawrence is ignorant of the Sykes–Picot Agreement until the later stages of the campaign, while the historical Lawrence, who had met Sir Mark Sykes,[14] was fully cognizant of this development, and the guilt felt for having misled his Arab friends resulted from keeping it a secret. Two of Lawrence's Arab collaborators in the campaign, Sherif Ali ibn el Hussein of the Harith tribe (Omar Sharif) and Auda Abu Tayi of the Hawaitat (Anthony Quinn) have been reshaped to fit their roles in the film's sequences; the historical Auda, for instance, had already joined forces with Feisal in planning the expedition against Aqaba when the historical Lawrence was already on the scene, while the film shows him meeting Lawrence at the Hawaitat well after they had crossed the Nefud;[15] and the historical Ali, a powerful ally of Feisal in *Seven Pillars of Wisdom*, is entirely absent from the Aqaba expedition and is not the central character who becomes Lawrence's friend and intimate companion in the film. Aside from his physical differences from the hero of Lawrence as rendered by Peter O'Toole (being much shorter, for instance), the Lawrence of *Seven Pillars of Wisdom* is, in crucial ways, an entirely different character from the film hero.

Throughout his narrative, the historical Lawrence presents himself as a rather self-effacing character, by and large respectful of his superiors and having a high regard for General Allenby, although he was far from naïve about the latter's intentions. The film presents Allenby (Jack Hawkins) impressively, showing his firm grasp of the new front, his quick assessment of Lawrence, and his decisive actions, but it also presents him as a manipulator of Lawrence, "totally unscrupulous," as Dryden sardonically describes him. In *Lawrence of Arabia*, Peter O'Toole, under the guiding hand of Lean and as given in Bolt's script, is at first shown as a vain braggart, playing tricks on his colleagues ("The trick is not to mind that it hurts," he tells a fellow officer who burnt his finger trying to snuff out a match), initially contemptuous of the Arabs, disrespectful of his superiors (as to some degree was Lawrence while in Cairo), and subject to abrupt shifts of mood, although later proven a valiant hero and brilliant strategist. The film also describes him as a rather unstable, "half-mad" (Dryden) individual, and even a bloodthirsty monster. The crucial event of his metamorphosis in the film is the episode at Deraa, after Lawrence is lashed and possibly raped (although the scene is only suggestive of what might have happened) by the Turks. Despite Ali's protests, he returns to Allenby (by this time in Jerusalem) and asks to be released from his duties. When Allenby persuades him to stay on the campaign, Lawrence gives orders to "take no prisoners" (in fairness, neither did the Turks, who had wiped out an entire village), an order that leads to the massacre of a retreating Turkish column. Although this event is recorded in *Seven Pillars of Wisdom*, the main attention of the author is given to the drive to Damascus, during which Lawrence shows no signs of disobedience or any extraordinary change in personality. Lean, on the other hand, makes much of this change, and Lawrence is stained, at least in the eyes of Ali, who is the last of his Arab friends to leave him in tears, never to see him again.

Thus, Lean/Bolt make the history of Lawrence not so much a chronicle of the Arab campaign—as *Seven Pillars of Wisdom* does—but a story of personal relations, the rise and fall of a hero who is, in many ways, an unstable man, or at least a "flawed" character. Lean's Lawrence is the central interest of the film, while in *Seven Pillars of Wisdom*, he is the narrator who modestly recounts in his slow-paced style a multifaceted and weighty event, the Arab campaign. In the book, the war is the main subject; in the film, the war becomes the vehicle for the hero's adventures, and a tale of a tragic rise and fall, fully reminiscent of Greek tragedy.

These changes in the film facilitate a sequential narrative that mostly describes Lawrence as a man in conflict, while action takes a backseat to character development. The structure of the film is based on that idea. Thus, coherence is achieved in a screenplay that uses a flashback technique that first shows the death and funeral of Lawrence followed by the two years of the actual Arab campaign. The film's action scenes are relatively sparse, and they by and large describe events that actually took place. Historically speaking, Lawrence's campaign in Arabia is given fairly accurately in its broadest outlines, but Bolt strove to present the psychological portrait of a complex hero with the freedom of a literary artist; his is a tight, literate script, a play based on history rather than an exact reproduction of history.

David Lean collaborated with him enthusiastically at first, although some accidental interruptions caused further delays and some friction between them, especially in shaping the second part of the film.[16] Always an independent thinker when adapting material either from literary sources or history, Lean molded and shaped this material to comply with aesthetic criteria, important to cinema, rather than following a historical line suggested by a biography. Aesthetic principles required such things as determining the length (nearly four hours) to adequately cover the subject matter; choosing the right actor to play the leading role; and selecting the most suitable locations, in the Jordanian desert, not far from where the actual events took place.[17] To these practical considerations one has to add the director's predilections and individual style; the multiple ironies created by the conflicts in the drama; and the numerous subthemes that emerge in attempting to film the life of a complex historical figure at a crucial time in history in this part of the world, still in turmoil today.

The aforementioned points are not given here to ignore the film's technical excellence. The celebrated cut of Lawrence blowing out a match followed by the instant appearance of a sunrise in the desert; the mirage sequence, when Ali materializes out shimmering blue-hued desert flats, as if floating in the air; Lawrence's rescue of Gasim out of the "sun's anvil"; donning the Arab silk garb after Ali admiringly tells him, "Indeed nothing is written unless a man writes it"—these and numerous other memorable images make *Lawrence of Arabia* the unforgettable epic that it has become, half a century after it was made. It was a collaborative effort, but Lean led the way in fashioning a landmark of cinematic art. CS

Notes

1. In the film he appears as Jackson Bentley, excellently played by the American actor Arthur Kennedy.
2. Kevin Brownlow, *David Lean: A Biography* (New York: A Wyatt Book for St. Martin's Press, 1996), 408.
3. In the "Deleted Balcony Scene," appearing on disc three of the Blu-ray edition of *Lawrence of Arabia*, General Allenby describes Lawrence as a "poet general," comparing him to Xenophon, Hannibal, and Nelson, to the astonishment of Lawrence. *Lawrence of Arabia*, directed by David Lean (Sony Pictures Home Entertainment, 2012).
4. Brownlow, *David Lean*, 406.
5. For an extensive analysis of this subject, see Joe Dmohowski, "Unfinished Business: Michael Wilson's *Seven Pillars of Wisdom* Screenplay," *Film History* 27, no. 1 (2012): 56–73.
6. Several biographies of Lawrence exist, one by a friend of Lawrence, the poet Robert Graves, *Lawrence and the Arabs* (London: J. Cape, 1927).

7. In Lean's film, Lawrence is buried at St. Paul Cathedral, London.

8. "The Legend of Lawrence," quoted in the original 1962 souvenir booklet. *Lawrence of Arabia,* directed by David Lean (Columbia Pictures, 1999), DVD.

9. See the documentary *Lawrence of Arabia: The Battle for the Arab World,* directed by James Hawes (PBS Gold, 2003), DVD. "Commentary," by director James Hawes, is an excellent source of materials, including a documentary film of the historical Lawrence.

10. Brownlow, *David Lean,* 430.

11. T. E. Lawrence, *Revolt in the Desert* (New York: Garden Publishing Company, 1926). *Revolt in the Desert* is a condensed version of Lawrence's campaign that may be a quicker (and no less accurate) guide to a reader interested in comparing essential features of the campaign with the events given in the film.

12. T. E. Lawrence, *Seven Pillars of Wisdom* (New York: Anchor Books, 1991), 167. Originally printed in New York by G. H. Doran, 1926.

13. Lawrence, *Seven Pillars of Wisdom,* 57. Gene D. Phillips claims that Dryden was based on David Hogarth, the deputy director of the Arab Bureau. *Beyond the Epic: The Life and Films of David Lean* (Lexington: University Press of Kentucky, 2006), 275.

14. Michael Korda, *Hero: The Life and Legend of Lawrence of Arabia* (New York: HarperCollins, 2010), 81–82.

15. Phillips states that Auda of the film crossed the Nefud Desert with Lawrence's group. *Beyond the Epic,* 308.

16. In September 1961, when Bolt was jailed after a massive rally in Trafalgar Square against the use of the atomic bomb, he was freed after the intervention of Spiegel, but the jailing caused inevitable delays in the completion of the script. Phillips, *Beyond the Epic,* 276.

17. Portions of the film were also shot in Morocco and Spain, before a few interior scenes were filmed at England's Shepperton Studios.

Bibliography

Brownlow, Kevin. *David Lean: A Biography.* New York: A Wyatt Book for St. Martin's Press, 1996.

Catton, Steven C. *Lawrence of Arabia: A Film's Anthropology.* Berkeley and Los Angeles: University of California Press, 1999.

Dmohowski, Joe. "Unfinished Business: Michael Wilson's *Seven Pillars of Wisdom* Screenplay." *Film History* 27, no. 1 (2012): 56–73.

Graves, Robert. *Lawrence and the Arabs.* London: J. Cape, 1927.

Korda, Michael. *Hero: The Life and Legend of Lawrence of Arabia.* New York: HarperCollins, 2010.

Lawrence, T. E. *Revolt in the Desert.* New York: Garden Publishing Company, 1926.

———. *Seven Pillars of Wisdom.* New York: Anchor Books, 1991.

Morris, Robert L., and Lawrence Raskin. *Lawrence of Arabia.* Foreword by Martin Scorsese. New York: Anchor Books/Doubleday, 1992.

Phillips, Gene D. *Beyond the Epic: The Life and Films of David Lean.* Lexington: University Press of Kentucky, 2006.

Santas, Constantine. *The Epics of David Lean.* Lanham, MD: Scarecrow Press, 2011.

Turner, Adrian. *The Making of David Lean's Lawrence of Arabia.* London: Dragon's World, 1994.

LETTERS FROM IWO JIMA (2006)

DIRECTOR: Clint Eastwood

WRITER: Iris Yamashita. From a story by Iris Yamashita and Paul Haggis based on *Picture Letters from the Commander in Chief,* by Tadamichi Kuribayashi and Tsuyoko Yoshido (editor).

PRODUCERS: Clint Eastwood, Paul Haggis, Robert Lorenz, Tim Moore, Steven Spielberg (DreamWorks SKG, Warner Bros., Malpaso Productions)

CINEMATOGRAPHER: Tom Stern

EDITORS: Joel Cox, Gary D. Roach

MUSIC: Kyle Eastwood, Michael Stevens

SOUND EDITORS: Alan Robert Murray, Bob Asman

CAST: Gen. Kuribayashi: Ken Watanabe. Pvt. Saigo: Kazunari Ninomiya. Baron Nishi: Tsuyoshi Ihara. Shimizu: Ryo Kase. Lt. Ito: Shidou Nakamura. Hanako: Nae. Capt. Tanida: Bando Takumi. Kashiwara: Takashi Yamaguchi. Adm. Ohsugi: Nobumasa Sakagami. Col. Adachi: Toshi Toda. Nozaki: Yuki Matsuzaki. Adm. Ichimaru: Masashi Nagadoi. Lt. Col. Oiso: Hiro Abe. Maj. Gen. Hayashi: Ken Kensei. Lt. Okubo: Eijiro Ozaki. Lieutenant Fujita: Hiroshi Watanabe

AA: Best Sound Editing (Alan Robert Murray, Bob Asman)

AAN: Best Director (Clint Eastwood), Best Picture (Clint Eastwood, Robert Lorenz, Steven Spielberg), Best Writing–Original Screenplay (Iris Yamashita, Paul Haggis)

DVD: Warner Home Video, 2007. Two-disc special edition.

BLU-RAY: Warner Home Video, 2007

DURATION: 141 minutes

Letters from Iwo Jima is told from the perspective of Japanese soldiers who defended Iwo Jima from the U.S. military in an attempt to prevent them from moving into Japan, 750 miles to the north. During the six-week battle, 20,129 Japanese were killed, and "of the 70,000-strong invading force, 6,821 died and almost 22,000 were wounded."[1] This is Clint Eastwood's second film about the battle on Iwo Jima. The first, *Flags of Our Fathers* (2006), focuses on the lives of the Americans who raised the flag on Mt. Suribachi. Cinematographer Tom Stern says, "*Flags* looks out while *Letters* is a descent, an internal story; this reflects the mindsets of the two armies."[2] Onda Taeko, writing for *Yomiuri Online*, says about the Japanese opening of *Letters from Iwo Jima*, "Today the person who had the power to tell us the Japanese experience during the war was Clint Eastwood, an American."[3] *Letters from Iwo Jima* highlights the humanity of the Japanese soldiers on Iwo Jima and the interference caused by tradition and outdated, illogical regulations when fighting in modern warfare. Eastwood's two films "illustrate the complete cost of waging war, and it's a high price paid by both sides."[4]

Most of the film was shot in California, for cave interiors, and Iceland for black-sand beaches.[5] The illusion of being on Iwo Jima was "cemented" by filming on the island "with Ken Watanabe for a series of sequences in which General Kuribayashi walks the beaches, climbs Mount Suribachi, and devises his defense."[6] The film palette uses muted colors, nearly monochrome, except for occasional bursts of color that highlight the red rising sun in the Japanese flags, the gold in officer insignia, and the orange flames in explosions. The effect is similar to the hand-tinted scenes from such early black-and-white films as *Greed*, used to emphasize the desire for money. *Letters from Iwo Jima*'s color scheme highlights government bureaucracy and the war's violence.

The film opens on a Japanese memorial on Iwo Jima's Mt. Suribachi ("Sulphur Island"), a bowl-shaped volcanic hill overlooking the beach and island, in 2005. A black obsidian Japanese memorial overlooks the beach and ocean, and the camera moves to pillbox emplacements, guns, turrets, and battlements and then follows archeologists as they dig inside the miles of tunnels left by Japanese soldiers.

Throughout the film, characters narrate letters they write and letters they receive. Flashing back to 1944, newly conscripted Private Saigo (Kazunari Ninomiya), who looks too young to be a soldier, is writing to his wife, Hanako (Nae). He writes that he and the other soldiers dig on the beach all day, and he wonders if he is digging his own grave. Captain Tanida (Bando Takumi), an overly ambitious and traditional officer, catches Saigo telling Kashiwara (Takashi Yamaguchi), "Damn this island. Let the Americans have it."

General Kuribayashi (Watanabe), the new commander of 109th Division of the Imperial Japanese Army flies over the island and narrates his letter to his wife, apologizing that he did not complete his work on their kitchen. He lands at the airfield, and Admiral Ohsugi (Nobumasa Sakagami) and other officers welcome him. Kuribayashi wants to walk to headquarters and see the island. He arrives at the beach as Saigo and Kashiwara are being beaten by Captain Tanida. He asks him, "Do you have an excess of soldiers? . . . A good captain uses his brain, not just his whip." Kuribayashi tells Tanida to cease digging immediately and to give them proper breaks. Later, as hundreds of his soldiers march through town, Kuribayashi discovers tanks that are out of commission and have been waiting for parts for a month. He orders civilians evacuated from the island.

Lieutenant Ito (Shidou Nakamura) reports to the general and his staff about recent air-force losses at Saipan. They cannot expect air support. Kuribayashi discovers that the army is under the command of Colonel Adachi (Toshi Toda) because navy regulations say that until the Americans land, their planning is kept separate. Although some of the staff disagrees, Kuribayashi orders that artillery be moved to higher ground and that they make Suribachi fortifications their priority.

Some of the officers believe that Kuribayashi has private sympathies toward the United States. While their fears are unfounded, he flashes back to experiences there. He writes a letter from the United States and discusses how surprised he is that it is filled with cars. At a reception for him given by the U.S. military, Kuribayashi is given a pearl-handled 1911 Colt 45, which he wears on his hip. Another officer with experiences in the United States is Lieutenant Colonel Nishi (Tsuyoshi Ihara), a baron and Olympic gold medalist in horse jumping who went to the Los Angeles Olympics. He leads the 26th Tank Regiment. Nishi reports that the military has kept news from Kuribayashi, that most of the combined fleet was destroyed at Mariana. Little striking power will be available for them from the air or sea. He realizes Imperial headquarters is deceiving its officers. General Kuribayashi orders a major change in strategy. They will abandon beach defenses and fight from caves they dig so that they can fight to the end.

Saigo and his friend Nozaki (Yuki Matsuzaki) meet Shimizu (Ryo Kase), a new troop, but Saigo will not allow him to sleep where his good friend Kashiwara slept before he died of "honorable dysentery." Nozaki is suspicious of Shimizu because he was a member of the Kempeitai (military police). Unconvinced, Saigo asks, "What would he spy on. Your letters?" Forced to eat weed soup because they are conserving food supplies, Saigo remembers the bakery he and his wife ran in Ohmiya. The Kempeitai took what they wanted in the bakery. Next, they took all of the baking equipment for the metal. They eventually took Saigo. In a later conversation, Shimizu reveals that he was discharged from the Kempeitai after being in the service for five days because he refused the order to kill a family's barking dog. He pretended to kill it, and once discovered, his superior killed it and discharged him for insubordination.

Kuribayashi replaces Admiral Ohsugi with Admiral Ichimaru (Masashi Nagadoi). Ohsugi wants to fight to the death and die honorably. Kuribayashi tells him, "Tunnel digging may be futile. Maybe the stand on Iwo will be futile. Maybe the whole war is futile. But will you give up then? We will defend this island until we are dead! If our children can live safely for one more day it would be worth the one more day that we defend this island!"

The U.S. Air Force arrives, bombarding the airfield and gunnery positions day and night. A report says that the American fleet left Saipan. General Kuribayashi talks over the radio to the troops spread throughout island caves: "Time has come to show your true colors. Fight with honor. You are not allowed to die until you kill ten soldiers. I will always be in front of you." As the men prepare for battle, they wrap their torsos in *sen'ninhari*, "thousand-stitch belts," or a "sash with 1,000 red knots made by 1,000 women and touted as 'bullet-proof.'"[7]

Kuribayashi holds firing until the beach is covered with thousands of Americans. U.S. soldiers use flamethrowers on the pillboxes and quickly destroy them. Captain Tanida sends Saigo to Colonel Adachi to request another machine gun after one is destroyed. Saigo overhears Adachi radio request for reinforcements. There are none available, and he is told to hold out. Adachi then requests permission to lead a suicide mission. General Kuribayashi tells him, "You must hold them off. Join forces in the north caves." Adachi gives Saigo a note to take to his commander that recommends that they commit suicide. Saigo reports what he heard, but Tanida says it is the coward's way. Six of his men kill themselves by grenade, and Tanida shoots himself. Saigo and Shimizu run to join the troops in the northern caves and continue fighting.

There, Lieutenant Colonel Oiso (Hiro Abe) orders them to rendezvous at the east cave, and from there they will go to Motoyama with no cover for two kilometers. At Motoyama, Lieutenant Ito tells Saigo and Shimizu that, "It was your duty to stay in your position until death. You should have died with your fellow troop members." He orders them on their knees and raises his sword. They are saved by General Kuribayashi, who is there to use the transmitter. He declares, "I don't want you to kill my soldiers needlessly." He leaves orders to fight from the caves, but after he is gone Ito orders the men to follow Major General Hayashi (Ken Kensei) into an attack to take back Mt. Suribachi. Ito calls Kuribayashi a "weak American sympathizer."

The men are met with an overwhelming American response, so Ito goes to Lieutenant Colonel Nishi to request help from his troops. Nishi reminds him that Kuribayashi countermanded Hayashi's order, but Ito plans to do it. Hayashi's order costs a thousand men their lives. After the loss, Ito refuses to go back to the caves, so he releases his men to Nishi's command. Planning to throw himself under an enemy tank with a land mine, Ito lies down with some dead soldiers and waits. At the end of the film, a group of U.S. soldiers finds Ito sleeping in a cave by himself.

Saigo is with Nishi's men when a wounded American soldier is dragged into their cave. Nishi forces them to treat him. He talks to him and finds out that he is from California and is named Sam. Later, when Nishi checks on Sam, he has died. For his men, Nishi translates a letter Sam had from his mother. In an attack on the cave, Nishi is blinded. He orders Lieutenant Okubo (Eijiro Ozaki) to take charge of the men and to guide them north. He tells them, "Do your best. Do what's right." They leave under darkness, and Nishi shoots himself.

Shimizu thinks about Sam's letter. He says, "I was taught they were savages. His mother's words were the same as my mother's." He decides to surrender. Saigo feigns agreement and lets Shimizu leave by himself. A guard wants to leave with Shimizu, but an officer shoots him. Shimizu surrenders to U.S. soldiers who give him water, but he is left with two soldiers who "don't want to be sitting ducks," so they kill him.

Okubo's men, including Saigo, find Shimizu dead, with a white flag in his hand. Saigo weeps over him. They have to run through crossfire and not shoot because they have no bullets to spare. They arrive at General Kuribayashi's headquarters. Kuribayashi says that Saigo looks familiar and says, "You almost lost your head." Saigo reminds him, "that was the second time you saved me. The first time was when you landed on the island."

Saigo writes a letter to his wife detailing how they have had no water or food for five days. A message arrives from headquarters that they are unable to send reinforcements to Iwo Jima. Kuribayashi receives a radio transmission from his hometown of Nagano of children singing to bolster him and his troops: "We shall fight with pride and honor at any price. Our proud island Iwo Jima." When his remaining men are ready for a last attack, he orders Saigo to stay and burn everything, saying, "Everything happens in threes."

Kuribayashi speaks to the assembled troops outside, stating, "Although Japan has lost. . . . Be proud to die for your country. I will always be in front of you." They move quietly into an American encampment and attack. Instead of burning everything as ordered, Saigo saves some papers by putting them in a bag and burying it. Kuribayashi is hurt in the engagement, and Lieutenant Fujita (Hiroshi Watanabe) drags him away. Kuribayashi orders Fujita to cut his head off. Fujita pulls his sword but is shot by a U.S. soldier. Saigo finds him, and Kuribayashi asks one more favor: "Bury me so that no one can find me." Kuribayashi shoots himself. Saigo buries him with the shovel he used to bury the bag. American soldiers arrive, and one finds Kuribayashi's revolver. Saigo gets angry when he sees the revolver in the soldier's waistband. Saigo is knocked down and taken away on a stretcher. He lies in an outdoor infirmary as the red sun sets on the empire.

Moving forward to 2005, archeologists have found the bag Saigo buried, filled with undelivered letters. The film ultimately reveals a military in which, unfortunately for the men, "conviction supplants reason, and compromise represents a betrayal of integrity."[8] JMW

Notes

1. Emiko Ohnuki-Tierney, "Letters to the Past: Iwo Jima and Japanese Memory," *Media Development* 54 no. 4 (2007): 17.
2. Quoted in David E. Williams, "A Line in the Sand," *American Cinematographer* 88, no. 3 (2007): 32.
3. Quoted in Ohnuki-Tierney, "Letters to the Past," 19.
4. Williams, "A Line in the Sand," 39.
5. Williams, "A Line in the Sand," 32.
6. Williams, "A Line in the Sand," 38.
7. Ohnuki-Tierney, "Letters to the Past," 18.
8. Richard A. Blake, "Life among the Dead: A Powerful Antiwar Statement," *America*, 19 February 2007, http://americamagazine.org/issue/603/film-review/life-among-dead (25 September 2013).

Bibliography

Blake, Richard A. "Life among the Dead: A Powerful Antiwar Statement." *America*, 19 February 2007, http://americamagazine.org/issue/603/film-review/life-among-dead (25 September 2013).

Cardullo, Bert. "Why We Fight, or Men, War, the Movies, and Metaphor." *Midwest Quarterly* 52, no. 3 (2011): 239–55.

Ohnuki-Tierney, Emiko. "Letters to the Past: Iwo Jima and Japanese Memory." *Media Development* 54 no. 4 (2007): 17.

Williams, David E. "A Line in the Sand." *American Cinematographer* 88, no. 3 (2007): 28–32.

THE LIFE AND DEATH OF COLONEL BLIMP (1943)

DIRECTOR: Michael Powell
WRITER: Emeric Pressburger
PRODUCERS: Michael Powell, Emeric Pressburger, Richard Vernon (Rank Organization, The Archers, Independent Producers)
CINEMATOGRAPHERS: Georges Perinal, Jack Cadriff
EDITOR: John Seabourne Sr.
COSTUMES: Joseph Buto, Matilda Etches
MUSIC: Allan Gray
SOUND: C. C. Desmond Dew
CAST: Col. Clive Wynne-Candy: Roger Livesey. Theo Kretchmar-Schuldorff: Anton Walbrook. Edith Hunter/Barbara Wynn/Angela "Johnny" Cannon: Deborah Kerr. Frau von Kaltenek: Ursula Jeans. Spud Wilson: James McKechnie. Kaunitz: David Ward. Col. Betteridge: Roland Culver. Col. Goodhead: Eric Maturin. The Nun: Yvonne André. The Matron: Marjorie Gresley. The Bishop: Felix Aylmer. Stuffy Graves: Neville Mapp. Hoppy: David Hutcheson. Café Orchestra Leader: Dennis Arundell. Von Schönborn, President of Tribunal: A. E. Matthews. Period Blimp: Spencer Trevor. Baby-Face Fitzroy: Frith Banbury. Frau von Kalteneck: Ursula Jeans. Col. Burg: Theodore Zichy. Nurse Erna: Jane Milligan. The Texan: Capt. W. Barrett, U.S. Army. The Sergeant: Cpl. Thomas Palmer, U.S. Army
AA: None
AAN: None
DVD: Criterion, 2002. The Criterion Collection. Restored version by the British Film Institute, with an audio commentary by Michael Powell and Martin Scorsese.
BLU-RAY: Criterion, 2013
DURATION: 163 minutes

Michael Powell and Emeric Pressburger (an Austrian émigré), who were known as "The Archers," produced some of their most important films under the financial sponsorship of J. Arthur Rank, a tycoon who was responsible for the revival of English cinema during the 1940s, when some of their most noteworthy films were produced. Among these are *One of Our Aircraft Is Missing* (1942), *A Matter and Life and Death* (1946), *The Black Narcissus* (1957), and *The Red Shoes* (1948), movies that built a solid reputation for their creators and promoted English cinema abroad. *The Life and Death of Colonel Blimp* is their only epic-length production, covering three generations and three wars, the Boer War, World War I, and World War II, and featuring three basic characters, two men and a woman in three impersonations. It is not an epic of combat or other war action, but of the evolution of an idea, while the war stays in the background. The main question the movie seems to propagate is: Is war to be fought honorably, "by the book," as Martin Scorsese remarks in his 2002 DVD commentary,[1] or is the enemy to be exterminated by all means, foul or fair, as the Nazis were doing?

The concept for *The Life and Death of Colonel Blimp* was derived from a famous English cartoonist, David Low, whose cartoon character "Blimp" (or a "Captive Blimp") was an archetype of "stupidity," not the particular stupidity of one colonel, or of the political right or left, but "Stupidity has no frontiers, domestic or foreign, partly, professional or social," Low himself writes.[2] *The Life and Death of Colonel Blimp* manages to demonstrate that point by showing how the nuts and bolts of the human brain can produce the mental eczemas that we can call stupid human actions. The movie operates on several levels, the personal (falling in love with the same look-alike woman three times), the military (not knowing which one of its members suffers from mental retardation and which one is brilliant), and the national (for an entire nation can be duped by the murderous Nazis, whom they falsely thought to be "gentlemen" fighting an honorable war—if such a thing exists).

In his DVD commentary, made when he was an old man, Powell notes that his selection of the subject was influenced by David Lean, who, while editing his film *One of Our Aircraft Is Missing*, made an observation about a deleted scene that showed two British officers of two different generations arguing about the abandonment of old "gentlemanly" values by a ruthless enemy—the Germans—who had bombed and used poison gas against civilian populations during World War I.[3] Lean maintained that a movie could be made that would show the two different sets of values during modern warfare, the old versus the new. The idea seems to have been heeded, thus becoming the genesis of *The Life and Death of Colonel Blimp*.

With these two ideas—Powell's archetype and Lean's remark—combined, Powell and Pressburger created their main character, the aristocratic British officer Clive Wynne-Candy (Roger Livesey), and portrayed him in three different stages of his life, presumably while these changes in war ethics were occurring. Clive is first seen as an overweight old man reposing in a Turkish bath and being "arrested" by an eager lieutenant, Spud Wilson (James McKechnie), who wants to teach the old general how to distrust an enemy who lacks any sense of honorable rules. Leader of the Home Guard, Clive was conducting an exercise coded "War Starts at Midnight," but the surprise arrest is supposed to teach the older generation of soldiers a lesson. Spud and the general, who is completely outraged, scuffle and fall into a pool, and the next shot shows the general emerging from a similar pool forty years earlier, in 1902, when Clive was a young officer fresh from the Boer War, where he had distinguished himself.

As he emerges from a similar bath, Clive is seen as a dashing young officer in

Berlin, developing a liaison with a young English woman who accompanies him to a fashionable café where uniformed military men are mixing. In a scuffle with a belligerent German, Kaunitz (David Ward), who does not like an aria from *Mignon* that Clive has asked the orchestra to play, Kaunitz spits on him. Clive floors the German with a right swing. To settle the dispute, Clive has to fight a duel with Theo Kretchmar-Schuldorff (Anton Walbrook), another German officer totally unknown to him. Both Clive and Theo are wounded in the duel, and Theo, who does not speak English, manages to announce that he has won the heart of Clive's girl, a young English woman named Edith Hunter (Deborah Kerr). Hunter is living in Germany and teaching English to the Germans, intending to learn German and then go back to the English and teach German to them. Recuperating at the same hospital, the two men become friends, and Clive graciously accepts Theo's confession that he loves Edith. Clive leaves for England, hardly suspecting that he himself has fallen in love with the girl.

The next phase of the story shows us Clive, now a senior officer, in 1918, fighting in World War I, with Germany about to surrender, and Theo, a prisoner of war in England. Clive has met a young nurse, Barbara Wynn (Kerr in her second reincarnation), who remarkably resembles Edith. Although twenty years her senior, he marries her, and they live happily until the third part of the story, in which we see Clive again, now a superannuated general, head of the Home Guard, at the beginning of World War II. Now bald, fat, and mustachioed, Clive is about to give a radio speech that the government thinks will undermine the morale of the British Army—and the people of England fighting for their lives. Incidentally, Clive has developed a fatherly relationship with a much younger woman, Angela "Johnny" Cannon (who looks remarkably like both Edith and Barbara), who is his chauffer.

The older Clive is still unable to understand that times have changed, that the old rules of honorable conduct while fighting a war are in the past, and that the young officers consider him a blundering old man whose ideas are dangerous and should not be broadcast. That Clive fails to understand—that the rules of engagement are now different and that wars are not fought between gentlemen—raises the question, What is stupidity? Is it naïveté, or just simply sticking to one's principles? We are left with the alternatives of making up our minds. Apparently, many in England, including Winston Churchill himself—a commentator alleges—did not understand this point. And yet it was Churchill himself who sent the letter proposing the banning of the film, fearing that any allegations to officer incompetence might dishearten his troops. Of course, we don't know that Churchill meant that, or that the film said—in a very subtle way—that Churchill, too, was stupid. Thus, the ironies in the film interweave, and the question of what stupidity is remains open-ended. Clive is an honorable soldier who has fought victorious wars for his country, and he should be treated with respect, and also be allowed to speak his mind, no matter what he says, because, after all, he is in a democracy and fighting for his democratic rights against Hitler.

But for all that, Clive still misses the point that Nazism is a ruthless war machine playing a war game under false pretenses. This is a lesson that Theo, now in England and an exile from Nazism, has come to understand perfectly well, and we know that he has come to understand this when we hear him narrating his individual story to an official who is trying to determine whether he should be offered refuge in England, or whether he is a spy. In these dangerous times, who could tell the difference?

Theo has no choice but to seek the help of his old friend Clive, who comes to his rescue, and it is during the meeting of the two men, after so much time has passed, that we learn his part of the story.

Yes, he had married Edith Hunter, and had sons with her, but when Hitler came to power in 1933, their sons became Nazis. Edith died, presumably of a broken heart, and none of her sons came to her funeral. Walbrook delivers those lines with unusual depth of emotion, but also with great acumen. He warns Clive that this is not 1902, not even 1918, when an honor code among adversaries prevailed and rules of conduct at war were observed. Now, he tells him, you are fighting an enemy without any sense of morality, who is determined to exterminate you with all means possible, with no regard for any rule of ethics. Nazism is a new brand of warfare—extermination of an enemy with any means possible. Clive listens, not quite comprehending the magnitude of what Theo has stated, and he remains entrenched in his old notions, apparently not capable of change or perceiving the new reality. It is as if the "Brave New World" is passing him by. He joins the Home Guard with other senior officers who have been discarded by the new war machine as irrelevant, and he is even arrested, still perceived as a threat to security by the most eager Spud Wilson. But when released, and sitting on a bench, dejected, Theo and Johnny approach him and, seemingly reconciled to the new reality, he relents. In the end, Clive, Theo, Johnny, and her boyfriend, Spud, who had arrested Clive, all go to dinner together. War, nationality, the gender gap, and brawling all pile up, but friendship prevails in the end. Clive sheds his dejection and joins them.

The Life and Death of Colonel Blimp understandably caused a furor, for the authorities did not think it was appropriate to portray a German who knows what is true, while a British officer, stuck in his antiquated ideas, seems uncomprehending, if not downright stupid. "Blimp" is the word created in a cartoon to indicate precisely that idea—that people can be stupid in any sphere of existence. The Churchill letters had the opposite effect on Powell, who stated that his country is still a democracy, and ideas, no matter what and under what conditions, should be allowed to circulate. But the issue was finally settled by the influence of J. Arthur Rank, who had enough pull (180,000 pounds) to get his expensive (for the time) film released. The controversy brought unusual success at the box office, despite that fact that some critics complained that the film is both slow and "dull."

Entire sections were cut out, more than twenty minutes of the movie, and even when it was distributed in the United States, it took many years before it was fully restored, in 1988, when Criterion invited Michael Powell himself—then still alive (but speaking in slurred speech)—to give his reminiscences. Among those who made comments where several other scholars, and part of the DVD commentary is given by Martin Scorsese, who praises the film and states that it influenced his own work. Today the film is considered a rare specimen of cinematic art, for it combines the visual artistry of Powell and the verbal genius of Pressburger, a rare feat, for intelligent scripts don't quite go hand in hand with visually stunning cinematic enterprises.

The film is also a romance—albeit of an unusual kind—a war adventure with minimal action and a commentary on perception of war reality. It is the dialectic, not the art, that makes this memorable. Politically incorrect on all counts, the film attempts to insult anyone in power, whether a prime minister or a lower-echelon army officer. Ironically, the cleverest person in it is a woman—the same woman playing three roles.

Edith is more intelligent than the two gentlemen she dates and the one she later marries. Edith was an English woman who had taken refuge in Germany because women of her time were treated as legal concubines—or illegal ones if they had to be, or were damned to poverty and slave labor. Her counterpart, Barbara Wynn, twenty years later, marries an honorable officer and is content to be his wife, but she also dies for a reason that remains unaccounted for. And her final counterpart, Angela, refuses to be called by her Christian name because that is the last thing she wants to be. Call her "Johnny," the streetwise female urchin who has learned to endure bombing by Hitler and bullying by her male superiors in the army. She knows how to play tricks, hiding under a table so she won't be arrested and running away from a crowd of uniformed men when she must. English women served in the army in World War II, just as honorably as men (just as American women went to work in factories to ensure victory). The film gives a woman the last word. She is the one who knows and understands change. In the world of two sexes, she is not afflicted by her counterpart's stupidity. That, unfortunately, remains the privilege of the male sex—at least in the view of this film. CS

Notes

1. Martin Scorsese, "Commentary," *The Life and Death of Colonel Blimp*, directed by Michael Powell (Criterion, 2002), DVD.
2. David Low, "Was Colonel Blimp Right?" *London Evening Standard*, 14 October 1942, 6.
3. Michael Powell, "Commentary," *The Life and Death of Colonel Blimp*, directed by Michael Powell (Criterion, 2002), DVD.

Bibliography

Christie, Ian. *The Life and Death of Colonel Blimp (Script) by Michael Powell and Emeric Pressburger*. London: Faber and Faber, 1994.

Kennedy, A. L. *The Life and Death of Colonel Blimp*. London: BFI Film Classics, 1997.

Low, David. "Was Colonel Blimp Right?" *London Evening Standard*, 14 October 1942, 6.

Powell, Michael. *A Life in Movies: An Autobiography*. London: Heinemann, 1996.

LINCOLN (2012)

DIRECTOR: Steven Spielberg
WRITER: Tony Kushner. Based on *Team of Rivals: The Political Genius of Abraham Lincoln*, by Doris Kearns Goodwin.
PRODUCERS: Steven Spielberg, Kathleen Kennedy (DreamWorks SKG, 20th Century Fox Film Corporation, Reliance Entertainment)
CINEMATOGRAPHER: Janusz Kaminski
EDITOR: Michael Kahn
PRODUCTION DESIGN: Rick Carter, Jim Erickson
COSTUMES: Joanna Johnston
MUSIC: John Williams
SOUND MIXERS: Andy Nelson, Gary Rydstrom, Ron Judkins
CAST: Abraham Lincoln: Daniel Day-Lewis. Mary Todd Lincoln: Sally Field. Elizabeth Keckley: Gloria Reuben. Robert "Robbie" Todd Lincoln: Joseph Gordon-Levitt. Tad Lincoln: Gulliver McGrath. William H. Seward: David Strathairn. Preston Blair: Hal Holbrook. Thaddeus Stevens: Tommy Lee Jones. Fernando Wood: Lee Pace. George H. Pendleton: Peter McRobbie. Speaker of the House Schuyler Colfax: Bill Raymond. Francis Preston Blair: Hal Holbrook. Ulysses S. Grant: Jared Harris. Robert E. Lee: Christopher Boyer. Edwin Stanton: Bruce McGill
AA: Best Leading Actor (Daniel Day-Lewis), Best Production Design (Rick Carter, Jim Erickson)
AAN: Best Director (Steven Spielberg), Best Picture (Steven Spielberg, Kathleen Kennedy), Best Cinematography (Janusz Kaminski), Best Writing–Adapted Screenplay (Tony Kushner), Best Costume Design (Joanna Johnston), Best Film Editing (Michael Kahn), Best Music Written for Motion Pictures–Original Score (John Williams), Best Sound Mixing (Andy Nelson, Gary Rydstrom, Ron Judkins), Best Supporting Actor (Tommy Lee Jones), Best Supporting Actress (Sally Field)
DVD: DreamWorks, 2013

Blu-ray: DreamWorks, 2013. Two-disc DVD and Blu-ray combo pack.
Duration: 150 minutes

Lincoln was somewhat of a cause célèbre in the cinematic world of 2012, and it was nominated for twelve Oscars, of which it won only two—Daniel Day-Lewis for Best Leading Actor as Abraham Lincoln being one.[1] The film stirred debate among historians, but on the whole it had a favorable critical reception and was recommended as a national treasure by President Barack Obama, who praised it for its portraiture of one of America's greatest presidents. It is based on the historical work *Team of Rivals: The Political Genius of Abraham Lincoln*, by Doris Kearns Goodwin, and the screenplay was written by Tony Kushner, who also wrote Spielberg's *Munich* in 2005. After receiving a 550-page treatment by Kushner, enough material to make a TV miniseries, Spielberg and his coproducer, Kathleen Kennedy, decided to focus on the last four months of Lincoln's life, when, as the Civil War was winding down, Lincoln focused his energies on passing the Thirteenth Amendment to the U.S. Constitution, which would free the slaves.

Most of the action of the movie concentrates on the month of January 1865, when the lame duck congress was still in session. Sixty-four defeated Democrats were still in it, and Lincoln hoped that twenty of them would vote his way, since the election was behind them and they could be brought over if promised a position in the new cabinet or some work in their individual states. It was a clever tactical maneuver, although at times, with Lincoln's cabinet holding a rather gloomy view of its prospects of winning, it looked like a futile move. Nevertheless, Lincoln, at the risk of being called a dictator or tyrant by the opposition,[2] was determined that a document would be on his desk to sign by 1 February.

The president knew that this was the right time to pass the measure, before the South capitulated, after which the slavery question would likely remain unsettled. The Emancipation Proclamation, which had passed two years before, would be viewed as a "War Act," granted by the Constitution to a wartime president, and it would be voided once the war was over and the freed slaves would be reclaimed by their owners. Although Lincoln could count on the majority of House Republicans, an amendment to the Constitution would require a two-thirds majority, so he was forced to expend his political capital and oratorical skills to secure the needed votes. As Spielberg explains, the movie focuses on this period, 9 January to 31 January 1865, the most essential phase of Lincoln's late career, so the film had to dispense with most scenes of his daily life, save some that were considered essential to this goal.[3] Thus, the film remains essentially plotless, following a narrow line of related episodes of confrontation between Lincoln and his inner circle, and the larger scenes of tumultuous clashes in Congress.

The story opens with Lincoln visiting the battlefield, the first shots showing soldiers killing and mauling one another in the mud fields of battle. Later, the president is shown interviewing two black soldiers, who question him about what is going to happen to them next: Promotion to officer rank? Elevation in status? The vote? When? Lincoln seems stoical, although obviously pained, as he takes in a measure at the casualties of the war. It is January 1865, months after his election to a second term. Back home, he is eager to get the votes by hook or by crook, even if he has to "influence" some citizens from Southern states to put pressure on their representatives, alluding to state benefits from the federal government after the war. Pressure is being exerted on those who would vote against the amendment to abstain, but pressure is also being placed on Lincoln by his loyal cabinet members, especially Edwin Stanton (Bruce McGill), his secretary of state, who points out that he should wrap up the war, rest on his laurels, and let things take their course, instead of antagonizing the Democratic (and some Republican) members of Congress. This tension is compounded by the complaints of his wife Mary Todd (Sally Field), who is showing signs of emotional distress, and his son Robert ("Robbie," played by Joseph Gordon-Levitt), just back from Harvard and wanting to enlist.

But Lincoln seems relentless, and he presses on, especially when told that he only needs thirteen votes for the two-thirds majority, since seven would go along or abstain; however, his efforts seem to be stymied by some in the ranks of his own party, although mostly by two formidable opposing Democrats, Fernando Wood of New York (Lee Pace), the firebrand and antislavery orator, and George H. Pendleton of Ohio (Peter McRobbie), both of whom deliver telling but bigoted speeches against the freedom of the slaves. Among the most fervent abolitionists is Thaddeus Stevens (Tommy Lee Jones), who fears that the president might abandon his commitment, not only to win the war, but to grant total freedom, including the right to vote, to the black slaves. Lincoln responds to Stevens that the Reconstruction should be achieved in stages, preserving the Southern way of life and treating the Confederate states as equals after their surrender. This ambivalence is well presented in the performance of Daniel Day-Lewis, whose Lincoln is a man of measured response, calm in the face of the huge problems facing him. His Lincoln is tall, lanky, prematurely aged, terse, and wily, bent under his huge burdens but stubbornly adhering to his principles. He often makes light of the resistance of those around him, with the exception of a few, one of whom is his army general, Ulysses S. Grant (Jared Harris).

The film gains momentum and oratorical intensity as soon the action shifts to the chamber of the U.S. House of Representatives, where the question of the Thirteenth Amendment is debated. As mentioned, the House had already passed the Emancipation Proclamation, and the amendment had already passed the Senate. After Lincoln and his surrogates put pressure on the wavering representatives to vote for or abstain, the amendment passes by a mere two votes. The movie wraps up quickly after that verdict, with the surrender of the South at Appomattox, Virginia, on April 3, a short scene in which Robert E. Lee (Christopher Boyer), on his horse and in his gray Confederate uniform, is seen being greeted by Grant and senior officers, all of whom lift their hats; in response, Lee also lifts his, a salute on both sides. Not one word is spoken during this brief, strikingly visual scene. The ending comes as Tad (Gulliver McGrath), Lincoln's younger son, is attending a play, which is interrupted with the announcement that the president has been shot. In the early hours of 15 April, Lincoln is shown dead on his bed, surrounded by members of his immediate circle.

Lincoln is photographed mostly in dark shadows and muted exterior scenes, presenting Lincoln as a pithy, unyielding individual committed to a cause while facing resistance from his closest advisers and cabinet members. Daniel Day-Lewis speaks his lines softly, in a low thin voice, which rises to intensity during moments of passion. Lincoln is also shown as a foxy, manipulative individual, who might seem opportunistic in different hands, but the aim of the movie is to present not just him and his maneuverings, but to explain as fully as time allows the cause for which he fights—and gives his life. One could categorize the film as a "didactic" epic, for it is clearly meant to show such values as equality, a word repeated—and distorted—by several of those who use it. "God made blacks unequal," roars Fernando Wood, to a frenzied applause by a minority. Lincoln is clever and surprisingly erudite, citing Euclid's theorem that "if two objects are equal to a third, they are equal between themselves." This terse saying could mean the following: if A (a white man) and B (a black man) are equal to C (a human being), then A and B are also equal. Lincoln sought to win his cause with popular stories—and he had plenty of those up his sleeve—and common sense, not by raising his voice and pounding the table, which he sometimes did, but by the power of persuasion, his most winning asset. CS

Notes

1. Liam Neeson, who had previously worked with Spielberg on *Schindler's List* (1993), was offered the role of Lincoln but withdrew, and Lincoln was then given to Daniel Day-Lewis.
2. Fernando Wood, a democratic congressman from New York known for his inflammatory antislavery ranting in Congress, did call him that plus a few other derogatory names during the Congress sessions.
3. See "Extra Features," *Lincoln*, directed by Steven Spielberg (DreamWorks, 2013), DVD and Blu-ray.

Bibliography

Goodwin, Doris Kearns. *Team of Rivals: The Political Genius of Abraham Lincoln*. New York: Simon & Schuster, 2005.

Taylor, Philip M. *Steven Spielberg: The Man, His Movies, and Their Meaning*, new ed. New York: Continuum, 1994.

LORD JIM (1965)

DIRECTOR: Richard Brooks

WRITER: Richard Brooks. Based on the novel by Joseph Conrad.

PRODUCER: Richard Brooks (Columbia Pictures)

CINEMATOGRAPHER: Freddie A. Young

EDITOR: Alan Osbiston

ART DIRECTION: Geoffrey Drake

COSTUMES: Phyllis Dalton

MUSIC: Bronislau Kaper

CAST: Lord Jim: Peter O'Toole. Cornelius: Curt Jürgens. Marlow: Jack Hawkins. Gentleman Brown: James Mason. The General: Eli Wallace. Stein: Paul Lukas. Schomberg: Akim Tamiroff. The Girl/Jewel: Daliah Lavi. Waris: Juzo Itami. Chief Du-Ramin: Tatsuo Saito. Brierly: Andrew Keir. Robinson: Jack MacGowran. Malay: Eric Young. Capt. Chester: Noel Purcell. Captain of Patna: Walter Gotell. Moslem Leader: Rafiq Anwar

AA: None

AAN: None

BAFTA AWARD NOMINATIONS: Best Art Direction (Geoffrey Drake), Best Cinematography–Color (Freddie A. Young)

DVD: Columbia Pictures, 2004

BLU-RAY: Currently unavailable

DURATION: 154 minutes

Richard Brooks's *Lord Jim* follows the same line of action as Joseph Conrad's novel, which is based on an actual event, a rumor that a steamship, *Jeddah*, had foundered off the coast of Malaysia carrying nearly 1,000 Muslim pilgrims to Mecca, in August 1880. The report also held that the ship's European captain and his crew had abandoned the steamer at the most critical hour, jumping to safety into a lifeboat. *Jeddah*, however, survived and reached port, and during a subsequent hearing before an examining board, the captain and his officers were disgraced and stripped of their naval certificates. Conrad had traveled as a merchant seaman several times to the South China Sea between 1883 and 1887, and his story took its lead from those events.

Brooks wrote the script for the film himself, following Conrad's tale consistently and photographing it in the Malaysian archipelago and at Shepperton Studios in England. His cast is made up of remarkably gifted actors, led by Peter O'Toole as Jim, and his crew included Freddie A. Young as cinematographer—both veterans of David Lean's *Lawrence of Arabia*, which had triumphed a few years earlier. The acting is laced with solid performances by many veterans of the screen; the dialogue follows similar utterances as in the novel, while a rousing musical score by Bronislau Kaper gives this movie added flair. By all counts—a famous literary source, directorial savvy, capable acting, an adventure story in the South Seas—this should have been a notable film in an era when the epic cycle was still at its peak. Yet, when the film was released in 1965, it flopped with both audiences and critics, earned no Academy Award nominations, and has practically sunk into oblivion, the following decades having not treated it kindly. While the film may deserve better treatment, it still gets limited attention from modern viewers outside a limited following among select audiences. With all these drawbacks, it still maintains a certain epic grandeur.

As Conrad tells us, *Lord Jim* is the story of a man with prominent masculine qualities[1]—tall, handsome, and seemingly brave—and, of course, he is in the naval business. But, as per most Conrad heroes, he is handicapped by a fatal flaw, in this case fear, which leads to an act of cowardice that the hero tries to redeem through painful self-torment and heroic acts of daring and bravery. After confessing his cowardice, Jim takes the advice of a friend who defended him at his trial to disappear from the face of the earth, and he goes underground, hiding in obscurity for the rest of his life.

After his introduction into the naval business by an older seaman named Marlow,[2] who had initiated his career, Jim, having suffered a serious leg injury, takes a job as chief mate on the SS *Patna*, a vessel carrying 1,000 Muslim pilgrims to Mecca, their place of worship. But during a storm, as the steamship is about to founder, Jim, in a moment of panic, jumps into the lifeboat, abandoning the ship and its passengers to what seems certain death. However, as with *Jeddah*, the *Patna* survives and is hauled to harbor by a passing French ship. As in the novel, an inquiry is held, but only Jim appears. He confesses his guilt and is subsequently disgraced and loses himself into the motley crowds in various harbors in Malaysia, doing numerous humiliating jobs as expiation for his cowardice.

He is eventually assigned a dangerous mission by a philanthropist entrepreneur, Stein (Paul Lukas), to go upstream to Patusan, carrying dangerous explosives on a boat to aid a tribe being subjected to a local thug, The General (Eli Wallace), who plans to execute a large number of prisoners. Betrayed by a native spy, one of his two companions on the boat, Jim manages to carry out his mission, reaching Patusan and helping the locals organize a successful rebellion, defeating The General, liberating the tribe, and becoming their hero. A romance develops between Jim and Jewel, "The Girl" (Daliah Lavi), a woman of mixed parentage, and Jim is rewarded with the title "Tuan Jim," Lord Jim, honored as the tribe's savior. But later Jim fails to detect the treachery of a duplicitous and notorious criminal, "Gentleman Brown" (James Mason), who arrives on the initiative of Cornelius (Curt Jürgens), who had escaped death when The General was killed. Brown negotiates a false truce and subsequently launches a night attack on the village with a group of looters to steal its jewels. When Waris (Juzo Itami), the son of the chief, is killed, Jim feels responsible, and although he is given the night before the funeral to flee, he remains and is shot by the youth's father during a funeral ceremony the next day.

Still, this intense drama did not meet audience expectations, and while it is hard to pinpoint the reason for its failure, one cannot avoid some speculation about what caused it. For one, Jim's hero status provokes some comparison with that of *Lawrence of Arabia*, since the same actor plays both roles, and with what seems to be similar intensity. What makes an epic hero is the manner in which he is perceived by an audience, who wants (or at least is used to) a winner, even in spite of flaws in a hero's makeup. And *Lawrence of Arabia* starts with Lawrence's death and funeral, which is actually an encomium, and proceeds to show an inspired youth who dashes headlong into danger, winning victories and building his image grade by grade as he treks through the desert, and reaching his apotheosis in the scene where he is seen nimbly stepping atop a blown-up Turkish train. Such images carry the viewer along, and Lawrence gains a mythical stature never quite eradicated by his eventual defeat at Damascus. *Lord Jim*, on the other hand, starts with a hero's act of cowardice, which brands him as an antihero who fails from the outset, the rest of the movie action designed to allow him to redeem himself. His self-effacing removal from society to a lonely "paradise," where his actions show him to be courageous, do not entirely restore him to an audience's esteem, even though he gains dignity by his heroic death at the end.

Another reason for the film's difficulties may be attributed to the way the story is structured. Beginning with the voice of Marlow, which follows Jim's actions through the first third of the story, the narrative loses steam when the voice ceases and the story stumbles along, episodically, to its final phase at Patusan. With the loss of Marlow's voice, so evocative at the beginning, the viewer is thus deprived of this narrator's perspective. Despite gripping adventure sequences, the plotline never actually recovers the fluency and clarity it had at the beginning. One could mention the plethora of villains encountered by Jim in the latter part of the action, all played by veteran actors—The General by Eli Wallace, Cornelius by Curt Jürgens, the shifty Gentleman Brown by a brilliant James Mason, and the shady Schomberg by Akim Tamiroff—an aspect that does not help Jim's image with the viewer. They are presented in the film in a tapestry of murkily haphazard underground men whose business seems to be the demeaning of humanity. Jim does defeat some but does not dominate them, as Lawrence does in *Lawrence of Arabia*, and thus, they, as a whole, "steal the show." Finally, the locals, having raised Jim to the status of their "Lord," lose their faith in him, seeing him as another Western intruder in their land, one who has done more damage than good in their isolated but would-be-happy land, in fact, more damage than the thugs who had plagued it.

One can also argue that Jim is still a hero, despite all this. They at least bury him with honor, setting his remains to burn on a pyre equal to one of their own. With all its flaws, *Lord Jim* is still an eminently watchable movie—one that begs a modern viewer's notice, especially the viewer who is also a reader of Conrad's undying masterpiece. CS

Notes

1. Conrad describes him as follows: "He was an inch, perhaps two, under six feet, powerfully built, and he advanced straight at you with a slight stoop of the shoulders, head forward, and a fixed from-under stare [that] made you think of a charging bull." Joseph Conrad, *Lord Jim*, edited by Thomas C. Moser (New York: W. W. Norton, 1968), 3.

2. Marlow is also the narrator of two other Conrad stories, *Heart of Darkness* and *Youth*.

Bibliography

Conrad, Joseph. *Lord Jim*. Edited by Thomas C. Mosler. New York: W. W. Norton, 1968.

Daniel, Douglass K. *Tough as Nails: The Life and Films of Richard Brooks*. Madison: University of Wisconsin Press, 2011.

LOST HORIZON (1937)

DIRECTOR: Frank Capra
WRITERS: Robert Riskin, Sidney Buchman (uncredited), Herbert J. Biberman (uncredited). Based on the novel by James Hilton.
PRODUCER: Frank Capra (uncredited) (Columbia Pictures)
ASSISTANT DIRECTOR: Charles C. Coleman
CINEMATOGRAPHER: Joseph Walker
EDITORS: Gene Havlick, Gene Milford
ART DIRECTION: Stephen Goossón
COSTUMES: Ernst Dryden
MUSIC: Morris Stoloff, Dimitri Tiomkin
SOUND: John P. Livadary
CAST: Robert Conway: Ronald Colman. Sondra: Jane Wyatt. Lovett: Edward Everett Horton. George Conway: John Howard. Barnard: Thomas Mitchell. Maria: Margo. Gloria: Isabel Jewell. Chang: H. B. Warner. High Lama: Sam Jaffe. Lord Gainsford: Hugh Buckler (uncredited). Prime Minister: David Torrence (uncredited)
AA: Best Art Direction (Stephen Goossón), Best Film Editing (Gene Havlick, Gene Milford)
AAN: Best Picture (Columbia), Best Supporting Actor (H. B. Warner), Best Assistant Director (Charles C. Coleman), Best Music–Score (Morris Stoloff, Dimitri Tiomkin), Best Sound–Recording (John P. Livadary)
DVD: Sony Pictures Home Entertainment, 2005
BLU-RAY: Currently unavailable
DURATION: 134 minutes

"In these days of war and rumors of wars—haven't you ever dreamed of a place where there was peace?" So begins the film version of James Hilton's 1933 novel *Lost Horizon*, which tells of an idyllic Tibetan community and lamasery of Shangri-La, whose occupants live in seclusion and wait for the time when the world may need to turn to another, more harmonious, way of life. Nominated for an Oscar for Best Picture (among others), it won Best Art Direction and Best Film Editing. The legacy of the book and film is evident in the longevity of the concept of Shangri-La itself. Frank S. Nugent (writing for the *New York Times*) called the $2 million production a "grand adventure film, magnificently staged, beautifully photographed, and capitally played . . . there is no denying the opulence of the production."[1]

The film begins in the Chinese city of Baskul, where diplomat Robert Conway (Ronald Colman) has been sent to evacuate Westerners from a burgeoning local revolution. When the power goes out amid general chaos, Conway and his brother George (John Howard) set fire to a hangar so that the final evacuation plane can land (a spectacle not included in the novel). Unknown to the final evacuees, however, their pilot has been overpowered and replaced by an imposter.

Along with the Conway brothers is paleontologist Lovett (camp comic relief in the form of the delightful Edward Everett Horton); failed businessman on the lam Barnard (Thomas Mitchell); and the terminally ill Gloria (Isabel Jewell), a young woman whose heavy makeup and sassy attitude were taken at the time to deem her of "dubious respectability."[2] Although Robert is due to return to acclaim and promotion back in England, he drinks too heavily on the plane and his weariness with the political world soon becomes evident. He asks whether his brother's official report says "we saved ninety white people? Hooray for us. Did you say we left 10,000 natives down there to be annihilated? No. No, you wouldn't say that. They don't count." It is clear that Robert longs for a more equitable way of life but cannot envisage how he could possibly help to bring it about with mere diplomacy.[3]

The passengers soon realize that they are being taken in the wrong direction, but they are powerless to intervene with their mysterious new pilot. The plane refuels only to crash-land high in the Tibetan mountains, killing the pilot, but the passengers are rescued by the inhabitants of a nearby lamasery, called Shangri-La. Nestled between mountains, their fertile valley is shielded from snow but also from all communication. Robert finds himself unexpectedly relieved to be cut off from the rest of the world, especially when he finds himself falling for Sondra (Jane Wyatt), the local school teacher who was fostered in Shangri-La when her explorer parents died.

The simple, carefree existence of Shangri-La begins to have its effects on the other visitors, who gradually begin to relax and shed the emotional baggage from their previous lives. Barnard confesses that he is a wanted swindler, but he regains his self-esteem and purpose by planning an irrigation and plumbing scheme for the locals. Supporting him is Gloria, who sheds her makeup and, seemingly by implication, becomes morally redeemed herself. For his part, Lovett ("Lovey" to Barnard) undertakes to teach the local children geology. Only George is impatient to return home and becomes increasingly frustrated with their apparent host, the enigmatic Chang (H. B. Warner). And yet a beautiful young woman called Maria (Margo) nonetheless sets her sights on him.

Beyond his own bourgeoning love affair, Robert finds an even stronger lure to remain—to take over Shangri-La itself. He discovers that the High Lama (Sam Jaffe, brought back to reshoot the role after an unsuccessful replacement by Walter Connolly) is actually the 200-year-old founder of the lamasery, the unique conditions of the Valley of the Blue Moon and a life of moderation extending the natural life expectancy of all its inhabitants. The High Lama dies, secure in the knowledge that he has finally found the right man to succeed him. George understandably thinks the story is the words of a madman, and when it becomes clear that they were, in reality, kidnapped at the behest of the High Lama, he bribes porters to help them escape. Robert tries to talk George out of taking Maria with him, having been told she is actually an old woman who will revert to her true age in the outside world; however, Maria tells him she was kidnapped, too, and Robert reluctantly admits that her story makes more sense than those of the other inhabitants. Upon their escape, Maria does in fact become an elderly woman and dies, and George, fleeing in horror from the sight (and its implications), falls to his death. Although he is rescued, Robert relinquishes his old life in search of Shangri-La, and the film ends as his journey back finally meets with success.

Although Robert Conway laments the racial inequalities of the world he is leaving behind, those same inequalities are replicated in Shangri-La itself, a fantasy of benevolent colonialism with white Europeans still in control and the indigenous population doing all the menial labor. Why would the High Lama need to search for an outsider to take over his role when Chang seems perfectly capable of doing so? In the absence of illness, a rule of (white) moderation is apparently sufficient to bring about utopia, although Maria, alone of all the inhabitants, finds it stifling. We see so little of Maria, however, that her critique of this seemingly idyllic world fails to resonate.

Throughout the years, sections of the film had been trimmed and the original nitrate was deteriorating, but a search initiated in the 1970s found a full-length sound track and all but seven minutes of footage, which was replaced with production stills for the 1986 restoration[4] (a further digital restoration was undertaken in 1998). Even the reconstituted film does not represent director Frank Capra's original vision for a much lengthier fantasy epic (his first cut was six hours long), but he was curtailed by the more pragmatic wishes of Columbia boss Harry Cohn.[5] As it was, the film was the most expensive picture Columbia had ever attempted. Capra achieved heightened realism by shooting at the Los Angeles Ice and Cold Storage Warehouse, which enabled him to capture the cold breath of his actors and use (artificially produced) snow, but it also wreaked havoc on the equipment and slowed filming. Capra shot many scenes with multiple cameras, considerably increasing the cost of exposed film. *Lost Horizon* would take "more than five years to earn back its costs," and relations between Capra and the studio soured,[6] despite his previous success in raising Columbia's prestige with the Oscar-winning *It Happened One Night* (1934) and *Mr. Deeds Goes to Town* (1936). *Lost Horizon*'s set designs and special effects still impress today, and although the film's ideological support of colonialism dates the work, the abstract concept of Shangri-La is one that can still captivate the viewer.

In 1954, Columbia planned a remake of *Lost Horizon* as a musical, but it did not eventuate,[7] although a Broadway musical, *Shangri-La*, did emerge two years later (*Time* writes, "there is possibly something more than just comic about using a Broadway musical to portray serenity and moderation"[8]). A TV movie was produced in 1960, and a big-screen musical version finally came about in 1973, with music by Burt Bacharach. It was a flop. DB

Notes

1. Frank S. Nugent, "Columbia's Film of Hilton's *Lost Horizon* Opens at the Globe," *New York Times*, 4 March 1937, 27.

2. Nugent, "Columbia's Film of Hilton's *Lost Horizon* Opens at the Globe." In the novel, Conway is joined by swindler businessman Barnard, but also by Christian missionary Roberta Brinklow and Conway's restless junior colleague Captain Charles Mallinson, whose basic character is much the same as the film's George. Maria and Sondra are based on only one such figure in the book.

3. This speech was cut later in 1937, when the film was trimmed down for small-town circulation, and it was omitted in the 1942 wartime reissue. Only a 16 mm print remained for the restoration but has since gone missing. Charles Champlin and Robert Gitt, "Commentary," *Lost Horizon*, directed by Frank Capra (Sony Pictures Home Entertainment, 2005), DVD. Joseph McBride, *Frank Capra: The Catastrophe of Success* (New York: Simon & Schuster, 1992), 356.

4. Stephen Farber, "Cuts in Film: *Lost Horizon* Restored," *New York Times*, 3 September 1986, C19.

5. For more production details, see John Paul Rosas, "Photo Documentary with Narration by Historian Kendall Miller," Columbia TriStar, 1999, *Lost Horizon*, directed by Frank Capra (Sony Pictures Home Entertainment, 2005), DVD. See also McBride, *Frank Capra*, 351–66, 370, and Frank Capra, *The Name above the Title: An Autobiography* (New York: Da Capo, 1997), originally published in New York: Macmillan, 1971.

6. McBride, *Frank Capra*, 351, 363–65.

7. "Musical Version of *Lost Horizon*," *New York Times*, 10 August 1954, 15.

8. "New Musical in Manhattan," *Time*, 25 June 1956, 88.

Bibliography

Capra, Frank. *The Name above the Title: An Autobiography*. New York: Da Capo, 1997. Originally published in New York: Macmillan, 1971.

Farber, Stephen. "Cuts in Film: *Lost Horizon* Restored." *New York Times*, 3 September 1986, C19.

McBride, Joseph. *Frank Capra: The Catastrophe of Success*. New York: Simon & Schuster, 1992.

"Musical Version of *Lost Horizon*." *New York Times*, 10 August 1954, 15.

"New Musical in Manhattan." *Time*, 25 June 1956, 88.

Nugent, Frank S. "Columbia's Film of Hilton's *Lost Horizon* Opens at the Globe." *New York Times*, 4 March 1937, 27.

LOST HORIZON (1973)

DIRECTOR: Charles Jarrott
WRITER: Larry Kramer. Based on the novel by James Hilton.
PRODUCER: Ross Hunter (Columbia Pictures)
CINEMATOGRAPHER: Robert Surtees
EDITOR: Maury Winetrobe
PRODUCTION DESIGN: Preston Ames
COSTUMES: Jean Louis
MUSIC: Burt Bacharach, Hal David

CHOREOGRAPHER: Hermes Pan
CAST: Richard Conway: Peter Finch. Catherine: Liv Ullmann. Sally Hughes: Sally Kellerman. Sam Cornelius: George Kennedy. George Conway: Michael York. Maria: Olivia Hussey. Harry Lovett: Bobby Van. Brother To-Lenn: James Shigeta. High Lama: Charles Boyer. Chang: John Gielgud
AA: None
AAN: None
DVD: SPE, 2011
BLU-RAY: Twilight Time, 2012
DURATION: 150 minutes

James Hilton's 1933 novel *Lost Horizon* had been made into an expensive Hollywood film in 1937, directed by Frank Capra; a not especially successful Broadway musical in 1956; and a made-for-television movie (*Shangri-La*, George Schaefer, 1960). Finally, it was made into this Burt Bacharach musical oddity of 1973, which was an expensive failure at the box office.

Diplomat Richard Conway (Peter Finch) is among the last to leave during an evacuation of Westerners from an upheaval in China, but, along with his brother George (Michael York), jaded journalist Sally Hughes (Sally Kellerman), failed comedian Harry Lovett (Bobby Van), and disgraced businessman Sam Cornelius (George Kennedy), he has, in fact, been kidnapped, and the group finds themselves in the remote but idyllic Tibetan community of Shangri-La, cut off from the outside world. The brothers each fall in love, while Sally, Sam, and Harry find renewed interest in life, but all is not well. George finds the seclusion creepy rather than serene, and he arranges an escape with his love interest, Maria (Olivia Hussey), who longs to see the outside world he speaks so passionately about. Richard argues with him, for not only has the aging High Lama (Charles Boyer) asked him to take over the running of Shangri-La, he has also been told that Maria is, in reality, very old and will die upon leaving her home. Maria convinces Richard that the stories are mere fantasy designed to keep them all prisoners, and Richard reluctantly leaves with them. But the remarkable stories are true, and upon seeing his lover's sudden aging and death, George cannot cope and flees, falling (or perhaps flinging himself) down a precipice to his death. Richard is rescued but returns to Shangri-La, his story an inspiration to those left behind who would also like to believe in Shangri-La.

With its isolationist politics and white, imperialist rule, *Lost Horizon* seems to belong to another time, forgivable in 1937 but less so in 1973. Burt Bacharach and Hal David's music is also not at its best, although the song "Living Together, Growing Together" met with moderate chart success. Vincent Canby of the *New York Times* calls the film "hilarious," but for unintentional reasons, including the poor choreography by Hermes Pan, who in his former glory arranged dances for Fred Astaire and Ginger Rogers, as well as a number of musical classics, but here has to settle for Sally Kellerman's farcical attempts "to keep time."[1] It is at this camp level of enjoyment that viewers have returned to the film, but at 150 minutes long, the film overstays its welcome. DB

Note

1. Vincent Canby, "Ross Hunter's Version of *Lost Horizon* Opens," *New York Times*, 15 March 1973, 58.

Bibliography

Canby, Vincent. "Ross Hunter's Version of *Lost Horizon* Opens." *New York Times*, 15 March 1973, 58.

M

***MALCOLM X* (1992)**

DIRECTOR: Spike Lee
WRITERS: Arnold Perl, Spike Lee. From *The Autobiography of Malcolm X*, by Alex Haley and Malcolm X.
PRODUCERS: Jon Kilik, Preston Holmes, Monty Ross, Spike Lee (Largo International N.V., JVC Entertainment Networks, 40 Acres and a Mule Filmworks)
CINEMATOGRAPHER: Ernest Dickerson
EDITOR: Barry Alexander Brown
COSTUMES: Ruth E. Carter
MUSIC: Terence Blanchard
CAST: Malcolm X: Denzel Washington. Dr. Betty Shabazz: Angela Bassett. Baines: Albert Hall. Elijah Muhammad: Al Freeman Jr. West Indian Archie: Delroy Lindo. Shorty: Spike Lee. Sophia: Kate Vernon. Laura: Theresa Randle. Billie Holliday: Nicky Howard. Rudy: Roger Guenveur Smith. Judge: William Kuntzler. Chaplain Gill: Christopher Plummer. Brother Earl: James McDaniel. Speaker #1: Bobby Seale. Speaker #2: Reverend Al Sharpton. Brother Johnson: Steve White. Capt. Green: Peter Boyle. FBI Agent: John Sayles. Thomas Hayer: Giancarlo Esposito. Euology Performer (voice): Ozzie Davis
AA: Best Costume Design (Ruth E. Carter)
AAN: Best Leading Actor (Denzel Washington)
DVD: Warner Home Video, 2005
BLU-RAY: Warner Home Video, 2012
DURATION: 202 minutes

On a mission to portray Malcolm X's life from a black director's point of view, Spike Lee campaigned the film's producers to direct, asking Norman Jewison to step aside. Once at the helm, he realized that Warner Brothers' funding for the film was inadequate, partly because the company did not want the film to be more than three hours long. Lee argued, "[T]his is an epic film. You go through five, six decades. This man had so many transformations and metamorphoses. You don't do that in a two-hour film."[1] To follow Malcolm's life and his influence required shooting in New York, Egypt, and South Africa, including hundreds of extras. Substantiating his arguments was an early screenplay draft written by poet James Baldwin that would have been "nearly four and a half hours of screen time." Like Lee, "Baldwin dedicates the first half of the scenario to Malcolm's life before his prison term and conversion to Islam."[2] Although Lee studied *The Godfather* as a model because it was an epic film made on a small budget,[3] he was forced to seek funds from friends to complete the film, including Bill Cosby, Oprah Winfrey, Janet Jackson, Prince, Magic Johnson, and Michael Jordan.

To prepare for his tour de force portrayal of Malcolm X, Denzel Washington studied the role for a year. Martin Scorsese says, "Denzel's performance is one of the best of American movies."[4] The opening one-take sequence starts with a crane shot and moves to a handheld Steadicam; the camera follows Malcolm Little and his friend Shorty as they move through the city in their zoot suits. Malcolm goes to a barbershop, where Shorty conks his hair. That night they go to a dance, which is Lee's homage to musicals from the 1930s, especially Vincente Minelli's films.[5] The Lionel Hampton orchestra plays while dozens of energetic teens dance. A beautiful white woman, Sophia (Kate Vernon), introduces herself to Malcolm. She convinces him to take his girlfriend Laura (Theresa Randle) home and return to her. Malcolm is suspicious of Sophia's motivations, but they become lovers.

Throughout the film are flashback sequences to Malcolm's family life in Omaha, Nebraska. His father preached Garveyism, a demand for Black power, and the Ku Klux Klan retaliated by burning his family home, beating him, and leaving him to die tied to train tracks. Their family was left destitute when his life insurance was not paid; the children were sent to other family members when their mother was put into an insane asylum. Malcolm and Shorty play cops and robbers, dressed in their zoot suits, and Malcolm pretends to drop dead in a park, a foreshadowing moment for Malcolm's life that is also reminiscent of his father's fate and an homage to Billy Wilder's *Ace in the Hole.*[6]

Malcolm often goes to Harlem, including celebrating the victory of the "Brown Bomber," Joe Louis, in his heavyweight championship bout with Billy Conn with thousands of others. Malcolm begins working for West Indian Archie (Delroy Lindo) by running numbers for his gambling operation, selling drugs, and pimping prostitutes. Archie teaches him how to look smooth and handle himself. Malcolm decides to place a bet with Archie for $600. He wins, but Archie refuses to pay. As Malcolm and Sophia listen to Billie Holliday (Nicky Howard) singing at a bar, Archie and two men arrive and order him into the alleyway. Malcolm runs from them, apparently escaping death.

Malcolm plans robberies with his own gang, which includes Shorty, their girlfriends, and Rudy (Roger Guenveur Smith). Malcolm is overconfident, unafraid, even describing himself as an animal, but also paranoid. To show Rudy who is in charge, he pulls a gun, points it at Rudy's temple, and plays Russian roulette. He and Shorty break into a house, and Malcolm recklessly takes a ring off a sleeping man's finger. After several successful robberies, Shorty conks Malcolm's hair in his house. The police break in an arrest them.

They are sentenced to ten years of hard labor for breaking and entering by a judge played by civil rights attorney William Kuntzler. Malcolm serves time at the Charlestown State Prison and is thrown into solitary confinement because he refuses to give the guard his prisoner number. He eventually breaks down and says the number. Out of solitary, Malcolm meets Baines (Albert Hall), who brings him a "fix" of nutmeg mixed into water to ease him off his addiction. Baines chastises him for his conked hair, saying, "Why not look like what you are? The white man sees you and laughs. He laughs because he knows you are not white." Pressing harder, Baines asks, "Who are you?" And so begins Malcolm Little's conversion to the Nation of Islam.

Baines preaches that black men must have respect for themselves. He meets Malcolm in the prison library, where they compare the definition of the words *black* and *white.* Malcolm begins his study of the dictionary, eventually copying each word's definition. He challenges the prison's minister, Chaplain Gill (Christopher Plummer), during church service about Jesus' skin color, saying Jesus was not a pale face. In a jail cell, Baines tells him to bend his knees to pray, and Malcolm does. Later, Malcolm receives a letter from the leader of the Nation of Islam; filmed with a motion-controlled camera, the Honorable Elijah Muhammed (Al Freeman Jr.) appears to Malcolm in a vision bathed in golden light and tells him, "The world belongs to us—the black man." Malcolm undergoes a physical transformation that reflects his inner transformation: his hair close-cropped and no longer conked, facial hair, and glasses.

Once Malcolm is released from prison, Baines introduces him to the Honorable Elijah Muhammed at his office in Chicago. Because of his immense respect, Malcolm refuses to tower over Elijah by not standing erectly and not looking him directly in the eyes. He is introduced to Brother Earl (James McDaniel) and becomes a leader of the Nation. He preaches in Harlem, competing for attention with other speakers, played by Bobby Seale, cofounder of the Black Panthers, and the Reverend Al Sharpton. Malcolm wrestles with his past when Shorty attends one of his services, but Shorty is unconvinced what he does is not a scam. Malcolm visits West Indian Archie, who had a massive stroke that has affected his speech. Ironically, Malcolm thanks Archie for saving his life, although Archie claims that he was not going to shoot him in the alley.

Malcolm's audiences grow because of his inspiring rhetorical skills, for example, the sharply drawn chiasmus, "We didn't land on Plymouth Rock. Plymouth Rock landed on us." At one gathering he meets Dr. Betty Shabazz (Angela Bassett), a Muslim who lectures on hygiene and diet. They later marry and have four daughters. Although the number of days he spends away from home frustrates her, Betty believes in his mission. Spike Lee interviewed Dr. Shabazz and had her assistance in the making of the film.

Malcolm receives word that Brother Johnson (Steve White) has been attacked by police. When some question his ability to put theory into practice, Malcolm visits the police station, with several others from the Nation, where Johnson is being held and demands to see him. Once they point out that the street is lined with Muslim men, they are let in to see Johnson, finding him battered and bleeding. Malcolm demands that Johnson is taken to the hospital, and, marching like a military platoon, he leads the brothers to the hospital. The cop on the beat, Captain Green (Peter Boyle), says, "That's too much power for one man to have."

Malcolm changes his name to Malcolm X, because it removes his slave name and replaces it with a symbol representing the unknown. He pledges himself to Elijah even if it costs him his life. He is assigned to build temples throughout the nation. He speaks to a crowd in Harlem, many of whom hold signs that say, "We must have justice." He preaches, "Alcohol and prostitution pacify us. . . . You've been had. You've been hoodwinked." Although he brings his own flair to what he says, the film shows that he parrots Elijah's words.

Baines reports to Elijah that many of the Nation's ministers express concern that the message is becoming Malcolm, not the ministry. At a lecture at Columbia University, Malcolm tells the audience of white students and faculty that he used to live like an animal in the same neighborhood. In a scene with 10,000 extras playing members of the Nation of Islam, Malcolm speaks with Elijah and dozens of ministers in attendance.

Betty reports to Malcolm that Elijah has fathered illegitimate children with several women. She is afraid what will happen if he causes trouble in the Nation. He promises that the church will provide for her. Malcolm meets the women and their children and discusses the problem with

Elijah, who uses scripture to justify himself. He speaks to Baines and questions their morality. Baines hopes to allay him by saying, "One hand washes the other." Reminding him of the words Baines told him in prison, he says, "God's word is not no hustle."

Responding to reporters' questions about the assassination of President John F. Kennedy, Malcolm says that Kennedy's chickens came home to roost. There is a horrified reaction to his words nationwide, and Elijah challenges his comments and, distancing himself from him, puts him on leave. Baines closes a curtain between Malcolm and Elijah when the meeting is over, symbolizing the beginning of a permanent rift. Betty begins receiving harassing phone calls, probably from members of the Nation.

Malcolm travels to Egypt to begin a hajj, a journey to Mecca that all Muslims are required to perform. In Cairo, while visiting the pyramids and the Great Sphinx, Malcolm is constantly observed by men with cameras. Malcolm takes seven circuits around the Kaaba, and on his hajj realizes that whites can be Muslims, too. Filming this footage, Spike Lee's crew became the first to use 35mm motion-picture film during a hajj. When he arrives in the United States, Malcolm desires to find a "common solution to common problems." He creates a secular political group, the Organization of Afro-American Unity (OAAU), which is named after the Organization of African Unity (OAU) and the Muslim Mosque, Inc., which "adhered to the more orthodox tenets of Sunni Islam."[7]

The night before Malcolm's final speech, a Harlem Y dance is being held in the Audubon Ballroom, where he will speak. Preparing to kill him, assassins case the place and load their guns. Malcolm is writing his speech in a hotel room, where a hidden microphone overhears his conversation with Betty. An FBI agent (played by director John Sayles) says, "Compared to King this guy's a monk."

Malcolm and Betty take separate cars to the Audubon Ballroom. Knowing he will be assassinated, Malcolm calls it a "time for martyrs," but the camera shows his fear and concern by moving him on a dolly with the camera, or by rotating around his face. Malcolm does not allow Brother Earl to protect him so he is not hurt. When Malcolm begins speaking to the crowd, someone yells, "Get your hand out of my pocket" as a diversionary tactic. The assassins stand and kill Malcolm with pistols and a shotgun, causing bedlam. One of the assassins, Thomas Hayer (Giancarlo Esposito) is shot and grabbed by some of the audience members. After it is over, police stroll in, revealing no interest in bringing the assassins to justice.

After the shooting, archival photographs and footage of Malcolm are used, and Ozzie Davis narrates the eulogy he gave at the funeral. The film ends with several shots revealing Malcolm's influence on contemporary society: crowds in Soweto, South Africa, fighting against apartheid; crowds in Harlem on Malcolm X Street; and Nelson Mandela repeating a portion of one of Malcolm's speeches to South African schoolchildren shortly after he was released from prison.

Some critics complained that the film drops Malcolm's half sister Ella, as well as his brothers, from the story, especially in light of their remaining with the Nation after Malcolm left it,[8] but "in the end, Spike made a classic Hollywood narrative in a classic Hollywood style . . . a seamless rendering of a Bildungsroman narrative."[9] *Malcolm X* is a film of transformation: Malcolm's personal transformation, through self-education and adherence to religion, as well as the transformations he affected for civil rights in the United States and around the world. JMW

Notes

1. "By Any Means Necessary: The Making of *Malcolm X*," *Malcolm X*, directed by Spike Lee (Warner Home Video, 2005), DVD.
2. Keith Corson, "Bringing Malcolm to the Masses: The Long Journey from Page to Screen," *Souls: A Critical Journal of Black Politics, Culture, and Society* 12, no. 1 (2010): 74.
3. "Commentary," *Malcolm X*, directed by Spike Lee (Warner Home Video, 2005), DVD.
4. "By Any Means Necessary."
5. "Commentary."
6. "Commentary."
7. August Meier and John Bracey, "*Malcolm X*," *Journal of American History* 80, no. 3 (1993): 1,198
8. Meier and Bracey, "*Malcolm X*," 1,197
9. Corson, "Bringing Malcolm to the Masses," 85.

Bibliography

Corson, Keith. "Bringing Malcolm to the Masses: The Long Journey from Page to Screen." *Souls: A Critical Journal of Black Politics, Culture, and Society* 12, no. 1 (2010): 70–88.

Meier, August, and John Bracey. "*Malcolm X*." *Journal of American History* 80, no. 3 (1993): 1,197–99.

MARIE ANTOINETTE (1938)

DIRECTORS: W. S. Van Dyke II, Julien Duvivier (uncredited)

WRITERS: Claudine West, Donald Ogden Stewart, Ernest Vajda. F. Scott Fitzgerald (uncredited), Talbot Jennings (uncredited). Based, in part, on the book by Stefan Zweig.

PRODUCERS: Hunt Stromberg, Irving Thalberg (uncredited) (MGM)

CINEMATOGRAPHERS: William Daniels, George J. Folsey (uncredited), Leonard Smith (uncredited)

EDITOR: Robert J. Kern

ART DIRECTION: Cedric Gibbons

COSTUMES: Adrian, Gile Steele

MUSIC: Herbert Stothart

CAST: Marie Antoinette: Norma Shearer. Count Axel de Fersen: Tyrone Power. King Louis XV: John Barrymore. King Louis XVI: Robert Morley. Princesse de Lamballe: Anita Louise. Duke d'Orléans: Joseph Schildkraut. Madame du Barry: Gladys George. Count de Mercey: Henry Stephenson. Countess de Noailles: Cora Witherspoon. Prince de Rohan: Barnett Parker. Comte d'Artois: Reginald Gardiner. La Motte: Henry Daniell. Toulan: Leonard Penn. Comte de Provence: Albert Van Dekker. Empress Maria Theresa: Alma Kruger. Drouet: Joseph Calleia. Robespierre: George Meeker. The Dauphin: Scotty Beckett. Princesse Thérèse: Marilyn Knowlden

AA: None

AAN: Best Supporting Actor (Robert Morley), Best Leading Actress (Norma Shearer), Best Art Direction (Cedric Gibbons), Best Music–Original Score (Herbert Stothart)

VENICE FILM FESTIVAL AWARD: Volpi Cup Best Actress (Norma Shearer)

VENICE FILM FESTIVAL NOMINATION: Mussolini Cup Best Film (W. S. Van Dyke)

DVD: Turner Entertainment, Warner Entertainment, 2006

BLU-RAY: Currently unavailable

DURATION: 157 minutes

"Four years in preparation! 152 speaking parts! 5,500 extra players! 98 massive sets! Twenty years of tumultuous drama crowded into two hours of roaring screen thrills."[1] So proclaimed the official MGM trailer for *Marie Antoinette*, a historical epic based on the life of the ill-fated queen of France with the popular star Norma Shearer in the title role, initially a production planned by her late husband, Irving Thalberg. It is a pity, of course, that such an expensive reproduction of Versailles should be in black and white (the original director, Sidney Franklin, requested to shoot the film in Technicolor but was turned down due to spiraling costs[2]). And yet the women's gowns, created by Adrian, bring the screen alive with textures—satin, sequined embroidery, velvet, and fur—lit to perfection by cinematographer William Daniels and his uncredited colleagues. The film is partly based on the 1933 biography written by Stefan Zweig,[3] a sympathetic portrait of the queen as an inexperienced maiden led astray.

We first meet the supposedly teenaged Marie Antoinette as she learns of her betrothal to the Dauphin of France (Scotty Beckett). Her excitement at being the future queen of France is soon dampened when she meets her fiancé, the flabby and bumbling Louis (Robert Morley). Once alone, Louis bluntly tells her, "They'll never be an heir because of me." By their second wedding anniversary, Marie Antoinette is a social recluse, her barren state leaving her open to the vicious barbs of the king's mistress, Madame du Barry (Gladys George). The camp and powdered Duke d'Orléans (Joseph Schildkraut), who makes no secret of his dislike for du Barry, seems to come to her rescue, launching her onto the social scene without her husband. So follows of barrage of wild and extravagant parties, and it is during a particularly reckless and expensive gambling session that Marie Antoinette meets the Swedish count, Axel de Fersen (Tyrone Power). Although she makes a play for him, he humiliates her with his rejection, despite an evident attraction.

Marie Antoinette's wanton behavior attracts the condemnation of her mother's ambassador in Versailles, Count de Mercey (Henry Stephenson), who demands that she make peace with du Barry. The fabulously garish du Barry cannot help but relish her public triumph, and Marie Antoinette foolishly retaliates. The king (John Barrymore) informs her that she is to be sent back to Austria and her marriage annulled, and d'Orléans withdraws his friendship in the face of this turn of events.

But Marie Antoinette finds unexpected support elsewhere, when the Dauphin finally stands up to his father and demands that he keep his wife, while Count Axel offers his friendship and respectful love. He kisses her nonetheless, and the film cuts to the coming dawn; back in the era of Hollywood's Motion Picture Production Code of morals, surely many viewers at the time interpreted this as suggestive of a sexual encounter. Marie Antoinette returns to the palace to discover that the king is dying, as her husband proclaims that they can at last be husband and wife. Upon the king's death, the new monarchs feel trapped by their new position, and Axel departs for the United States to avoid bringing disgrace upon the new queen.

After the intermission, we see the rather public birth of the royal couple's second child. Despite this happy occasion, the splendor of Versailles is contrasted with the poverty of the peasants, who begin to openly object to the monarchy, throwing stones at Marie Antoinette's carriage. The Duke d'Orléans is suspected of stirring up much of the trouble and indeed is so bold as to demand Louis' abdication when Marie Antoinette is innocently caught up in a conspiracy to steal a diamond necklace. Marie Antoinette unwisely takes the matter to court, for d'Orléans has control of the judges, who find against her. The peasants, emboldened by the court's decision, start an uprising, and Orléans removes his wig and wipes off his makeup, abandoning his assumed role as Versailles fop to reveal his true aspirations.

Before long, Louis, Marie Antoinette, and the children are held hostage at Versailles, and an escape plan hatched by Count Axel is thwarted when the monarch is recognized by a village priest. In prison, the couple reveals if not a passionate love, then at least a respectful one, and on his final night, Louis puts on a brave face for his children. The guards come to take the Dauphin away on the day of his father's death, his distraught mother bidding him farewell to the orchestral strains of the French lullaby "Fais dodo." Axel surrenders himself so that he might support the queen one last time before her death, and it is a shockingly aged and drawn Marie Antoinette who is sent to the guillotine.

It is quite an undertaking for an otherwise glamorous star of this era (indeed *Time* calls her MGM's "fussiest star"[4]) to allow herself to be filmed in this way. Even though Shearer does not really convince in the teenage years (she was in her early thirties at the time), the role would garner her sixth nomination for Best Actress at the Academy Awards. She lost out to Bette Davis in *Jezebel* (William Wyler, 1938) but did win the Volpi Cup at the Venice Film Festival.

Time Magazine writes, "Even for Hollywood's most extravagant moments, the scale on which this picture was produced remains gargantuan." Indeed, the audience may have been forgiven for thinking that the "picture is far superior to the revolution from which it was derived, and . . . if there are any disparities between them, they can be charged off to the fault of the latter, as the mishaps of a dress rehearsal."[5] But the extravagant $2.9 million production actually ended up a loss. Costs were always a concern, and the original director, Stanley Franklin, who had been developing the film in preproduction for more than a year, was effectively forced off the project by MGM's cofounder, Louis B. Mayer, for refusing a tight filming schedule. Mayer complained, "When a producer tells me he has a prestige picture, I know we're going to lose money."[6] Shearer's previous film, the Thalberg-produced *Romeo and Juliet* (George Cukor, 1936), had also lost money, and after Thalberg's death in 1936, Mayer started to rein in costs at the studio, grumbling to Robert Morley during the filming of *Marie Antoinette*, "God how I hate epics."[7] Despite his reservations about the genre, the relationship between the royal couple is beautifully dealt with, even if the melodramatic treatment may be out of style today, and the film only sketchily hints at the politics of the era outside Versailles. DB

Notes

1. "Trailer," *Marie Antoinette*, directed by W. S. Van Dyke II (Turner Entertainment, Warner Entertainment, 2006), DVD.
2. Scott Eyman, *Lion of Hollywood: The Life and Legend of Louis B. Mayer* (New York: Simon & Schuster, 2005), 255.
3. Stefan Zweig, *Marie Antoinette: The Portrait of an Average Woman*, translated by Eden Paul and Cedar Paul (New York: Cedar Press, 1933), available in reprint. The style of writing is quite dated, however. For a more accessible account, including translations of some of the pamphlets of the time, see Chantal Thomas, *The Wicked Queen: The Origins of the Myth of Marie Antoinette* (New York: Zone Books, 1999).
4. "The New Pictures," *Time*, 22 August 1938, 47.
5. "The New Pictures," 47.
6. Eyman, *Lion of Hollywood*, 225–26.
7. Eyman, *Lion of Hollywood*, 257.

Bibliography

Eyman, Scott. *Lion of Hollywood: The Life and Legend of Louis B. Mayer*. New York: Simon & Schuster, 2005.

"The New Pictures." *Time*, 22 August 1938, 47–48.

Thomas, Chantal. *The Wicked Queen: The Origins of the Myth of Marie Antoinette*. New York: Zone Books, 1999.

Zweig, Stefan. *Marie Antoinette: The Portrait of an Average Woman*. Translated by Eden Paul and Cedar Paul. New York: Cedar Press, 1933.

MARIE ANTOINETTE (2006)

Director: Sofia Coppola
Writer: Sofia Coppola. Based on the book *Marie Antoinette: The Journey*, by Antonia Fraser.
Producers: Ross Katz, Sofia Coppola (Columbia Pictures, Pricel and Tohokushinsha, American Zoetrope)
Cinematographer: Lance Acord
Editor: Sarah Flack
Production Design: K. K. Barrett
Art Direction: Anne Seibel, Pierre du Boisberranger
Costumes: Milena Canonero
Music: Brian Reitzell
Cast: Marie Antoinette: Kirsten Dunst. Louis XVI: Jason Schwartzman. Comt-

esse de Noailles: Judy Davis. Louis XV: Rip Torn. Duchesse de Polignac: Rose Byrne. Comtesse du Barry: Asia Argento. Aunt Victoire: Molly Shannon. Aunt Sophie: Shirley Henderson. Emperor Joseph: Danny Huston. Empress Maria Theresa: Marianne Faithfull. Princesse Lamballe: Mary Nighy. Comte Louis de Provence: Sebastian Armesto. Count Axel de Fersen: Jamie Dornan. Duchesse de Char: Aurore Clément. Vergennes: Guillaume Gallienne. Léonard: James Lance. Comte Charles d'Artois: Al Weaver. Raumont: Tom Hardy. Ambassador Mercy: Steve Coogan

AA: Best Costume Design (Milena Canonero)

Cannes Film Festival Award: Cinema Prize of the French National Education System (Sofia Coppola)

Cannes Film Festival Nomination: Palme d'Or (Sofia Coppola)

DVD: Sony Pictures, 2007

Blu-ray: Region B, Pathe Distribution, 2012

Duration: DVD, 118 minutes; Blu-ray, 123 minutes

The screening of Sofia Coppola's *Marie Antoinette* at Cannes was notoriously accompanied by "lusty boos and smatterings of applause,"[1] and her take on the infamous queen continues to divide audiences. Coppola's vision of Versailles, where the movie was filmed on location, is deliberately anachronistic in look and sound—a brightly lit riot of costumes, mixed accents, and pop music—and its focus is personal, rather than political. Or more precisely, it is the politics of high school, as Coppola herself suggests.[2] She presents the insular, bitchy world of Versailles that the young queen must navigate, where rumblings of peasants are distant rumors far removed from court life and are never presented directly.

The film opens to the guitar-laden strains of "Natural's Not in It," by Gang of Four, whose lyrics suggests a "new purchase" is just what is needed to fill hours of leisure time. While being fitted with bright pink shoes and reclining in her undergarments, Marie Antoinette casually licks some icing from one of many cakes and smiles directly at the audience. We are at once challenged by both what we expect—and do not expect—from a film about Marie Antoinette.

But it is an earlier, teenaged Marie Antoinette with whom we begin the story proper. Embracing her mother, the queen of Austria (played by rock legend Marianne Faithfull), Marie Antoinette departs for her marriage to the French heir. Upon her arrival at the French border, she weeps as her dog is taken from her, and she is stripped naked to be adorned afresh in French attire. She receives a rather disdainful reception at the court of Versailles and is dismayed by the complex rituals surrounding her new life. When Marie Antoinette complains about the overcomplicated rules for dressing in the morning, exclaiming "This is ridiculous!" Comtesse de Noailles (Judy Davis) replies haughtily, "This, Madame, is Versailles!" as if that were all the explanation necessary. The pointlessness of the ceremonies of Versailles, the overload of protocol and excessive consumption—of food, of clothes—soon becomes images of a society in decadent decay.

Comtesse du Barry (Asia Argento), the mistress to King Louis XV (Rip Torn), is amused to hear that nothing happens on the royal couple's wedding night, and Marie Antoinette's position at court—and the Franco–Austrian alliance—is continually in peril as the marriage remains unconsummated for an astounding seven years. It is Marie Antoinette herself who is made to feel the burden of this failure. When Louis's sister-in-law gives birth, Marie Antoinette walks through the passages of Versailles, overhearing the whispers against her, only to finally crumble in the privacy of her own rooms. This scene cuts directly into a montage set to Bow Wow Wow's "I Want Candy" as Marie Antoinette indulges in patisseries, champagne, and clothes, including the much-commented upon inclusion of a pair of Converse Hi Top sneakers. The juxtaposition of these scenes makes the latter sequence not so much the embodiment of spoilt excess usually associated with Marie Antoinette, but rather of despair and frustration channeled into material goods. The use of upbeat pop at this moment in the narrative is, therefore, highly ironic, the alienation of being a young woman echoing Coppola's earlier films, *The Virgin Suicides* (1999, also featuring Dunst), and 2003's *Lost in Translation* (which won an Oscar for Coppola for Best Writing–Original Screenplay).

Upon the death of Louis XV, his son (Sofia Coppola's cousin Jason Schwartzman) prays, "Dear God, guide us and protect us, we are too young to reign." The couple is shown to be naïve in matters of state, finances, and the practicalities of sex. The marriage is finally consummated, and Marie Antoinette, in full public view of the court, gives birth to a daughter.

The queen finds companionship with Duchesse de Polignac (Rose Byrne), and passion with the Swedish count, Axel de Fersen (Jamie Dornan). She also finds a certain degree of freedom from court oppression in her fantasy of farm life at Le Petit Trianon, a freedom underscored by the queen's abandonment of corsetry and looser, handheld camera work.

This idyllic period soon comes to a somber close, as Marie Antoinette loses the support of the aristocrats and suffers the loss of a baby. Following the storming of the Bastille (which is reported but not shown), an angry mob arrives at Versailles, while Louis and Marie Antoinette solemnly continue the seemingly pointless rituals of an extravagant dinner. The royal family departs on a beautiful Versailles morning, and we are shown the still quiet of a disheveled room in Versailles after the mob has finished with it.

Marie Antoinette's ultimate fate is not shown in the film, but, of course, Coppola can assume this knowledge on the part of the audience. Narrative closure may occur offscreen, but the film is nonetheless framed by Marie Antoinette's arrival and departure at Versailles.

Her nineteen years at Versailles are suggested and compressed in such a way that the audience does not have a clear sense of time (there are no date titles to be found here). In short, this is not a conventional historical film, and to judge it unfavorably on this basis is to miss the point of the movie. There are indeed languorous sequences in which not much of importance seems to happen in terms of conventional plotting (cause and effect), and between frenetic montage sequences set to pop music, some shots seem to be held longer than might seem necessary. As dawn breaks on Marie Antoinette's eighteenth birthday to the sound of birdsong, and the wind rustles through the trees and grass at Le Petit Trianon, it is a sense of transient time itself that is captured.[3]

The historical epic presents the past as the tangible present, which we can see, touch, smell, and taste, a sensory immersion made possible by the accumulation of physical objects in a film.[4] The Converse-infiltrated world of *Marie Antoinette* takes this tendency to its logical extreme, constantly reminding us that we are looking back on the past and literally reconstructing it through the filter of the present day. As Roger Ebert writes in his review for the *Chicago Sun-Times*, "Marie seems to think she is a teenager living in the present, which of course she is—and the contemporary pop references invite the audience to share her present with ours."[5] In this way, *Marie Antoinette* is more honest in its approach to history than the regular historical epic, demanding of its audience an aware and questioning stance in relation to the world it presents.[6] Sophia Coppola herself states that her aim "was not to make a big historical epic" in the conventional sense,[7] and yet she manages to capture and comment upon the nature of time all the more forcefully.

The use of contemporary, post-punk and New Romantic pop music throughout the film—juxtaposed with eighteenth-century Baroque music—continuously reminds the viewer of this dialogue between the past and the present. This is not simply a case of "now" and "then," given that the pop songs are sourced from several decades and therefore come with their own range of cultural and personal associations. Coppola was particularly inspired by the New Romantics of the early 1980s and their romanticized vision of the eighteenth century.[8] A teenager herself in the 1980s, Coppola's Versailles becomes a teen world of competing cliques aesthetically modeled on New Romantic music videos, complete with an Adam Ant substitute in the form of Count Axel de Fersen. For Coppola, as for all of us, the past comes already imagined.

And yet somewhat surprisingly, the infamous French queen has not been put on celluloid very often. There is a German silent film (*Marie Antoinette: Das Leben einer Königin*, Rudolf Meinert, 1922), and the French *Marie Antoinette reine de France* (*Shadow of the Guillotine*, Jean Delannoy, 1956, currently only available on DVD in the original French), which was nominated for the Palme d'Or at Cannes. The 1938 black-and-white epic Hollywood production *Marie Antoinette* (W. S. Van Dyke II, 1938), starring Norma Shearer, takes a personal approach to her life, but brief cutaways to the uprising peasants and political upheavals are not well integrated into the story. Coppola's *Marie Antoinette* dispenses with this outside world entirely, heightening the heady but stifling atmosphere of Versailles. Since Coppola's rendition, Benoît Jacquot's *Les adieux a la reine* (*Farewell, My Queen*, 2012), won three César Awards in France, having been nominated for ten. DB

Notes

1. Manohla Dargis, "Under the Spell of Royal Rituals," *New York Times*, 25 May 2006, www.nytimes.com/2006/05/25/movies/25fest.html?_r=0 (15 February 2013).
2. Eleanor Coppola, "The Making of *Marie Antoinette*," *Marie Antoinette*, directed by Sofia Coppola (Sony Pictures, 2007), DVD.
3. Thus Heidi Brevik-Zender suggests that *Marie Antoinette* embodies Walter Benjamin's notion of "now-time," while for Anna Rogers, it is suggestive of Deleuze's "time-image." Heidi Brevik-Zender, "Let Them Wear Manolos: Fashion, Walter Benjamin, and Sofia Coppola's *Marie Antoinette*," *Camera Obscura* 26, no. 3 (2011): 1–33; Anna Rogers, "Sofia Coppola," *Senses of Cinema*, November 2007, http://sensesofcinema.com/2007/great-directors/sofia-coppola/#24 (9 March 2013).
4. On the phenomenology of the epic, see Vivian Sobchack, "'Surge and Splendor': A Phenomenology of the Hollywood Historical Epic," in *Film Genre Reader II*, edited by Barry Keith Grant (Austin: University of Texas Press, 1995), 280–307.
5. Roger Ebert, "*Marie Antoinette*," *Chicago Sun-Times*, 20 October 2006, http://rogerebert.suntimes.com/apps/pbcs.dll/article?AID=/20061019/REVIEWS/610190303/1023 (9 March 2013).
6. Similarly, Greta Austin argues that ironic historical films (for example, *Monty Python and the Holy Grail*, Terry Gilliam and Terry Jones, 1975) have particular value in reminding us that the past "can only be imagined, inadequately, by us today." Greta Austin, "Were the Peasants Really So Clean? The Middle Ages in Film," *Film History* 14 no. 2 (2002): 136–41.
7. Coppola, "The Making of *Marie Antoinette*."
8. Coppola, "The Making of *Marie Antoinette*."

Bibliography

Austin, Greta. "Were the Peasants Really So Clean? The Middle Ages in Film." *Film History* 14, no. 2 (2002): 136–41.

Brevik-Zender, Heidi. "Let Them Wear Manolos: Fashion, Walter Benjamin, and Sofia Coppola's *Marie Antoinette*." *Camera Obscura* 26, no. 3 (2011): 1–33.

Dargis, Manohla. "Under the Spell of Royal Rituals." *New York Times*, 25 May 2006, www.nytimes.com/2006/05/25/movies/25fest.html?_r=0 (15 February 2013).

Ebert, Roger. "*Marie Antoinette*." *Chicago Sun-Times*, 20 October 2006, http://rogerebert.suntimes.com/apps/pbcs.dll/article?AID=/20061019/REVIEWS/610190303/1023 (9 March 2013).

Rogers, Anna. "Sofia Coppola." *Senses of Cinema*, November 2007, http://sensesofcinema.com/2007/great-directors/sofia-coppola/#24 (9 March 2013).
Sobchack, Vivian. "'Surge and Splendor': A Phenomenology of the Hollywood Historical Epic." In *Film Genre Reader II*, edited by Barry Keith Grant, 280–307. Austin: University of Texas Press, 1995.

MASTER AND COMMANDER: THE FAR SIDE OF THE WORLD (2003)

DIRECTOR: Peter Weir
WRITERS: Peter Weir, John Collee. Based on the novel by Patrick O'Brian.
PRODUCERS: Samuel Gordon Jr., Peter Weir, Duncan Henderson (20th Century Fox Film Studios, Miramax Films, Universal Pictures)
CINEMATOGRAPHER: Russell Boyd
EDITOR: Lee Smith
PRODUCTION DESIGN: William Sandell
ART DIRECTION: Bruce Crone, Mark W. Mansbridge, Marco Nero, Héctor Romero
SET DECORATION: Robert Gould
COSTUMES: Wendy Stites
MUSIC: Ivan Davis, Christopher Gordon, Richard Tognetti
SOUND EDITOR: Richard King
SOUND MIXERS: Paul Massey, Doug Hemphill, Art Rochester
VISUAL EFFECTS: Daniel Sudick, Stefen Fangmeier, Nathan McGuinness, Robert Stromberg
MAKEUP ARTISTS: Edouard F. Henriques, Yolanda Toussieng
CAST: Capt. Jack Aubrey: Russell Crowe. Dr. Stephen Maturin: Paul Bettany. 1st Lt. Thomas Pullings: James D'Arcy. 2nd Lt. William Mowett: Edward Woodall. Capt. Howard: Chris Larkin. Midshipman Blakeney: Mark Pirkis. Master Allen: Robert Pugh. Carpenter Lamb: Tony Dolan. Boatswain Hollar: Ian Mercer. Coxswain Barrett Bonden: Billy Boyd. Carpenter Mate Nagle: Bryan Dick
AA: Best Cinematography (Russell Boyd), Best Sound Editing (Richard King)
AAN: Best Picture (Samuel Gordon Jr., Peter Weir, Duncan Henderson), Best Director (Peter Weir), Best Art Direction–Set Decoration (William Sandell, Robert Gould), Best Sound Mixing (Paul Massey, Doug Hemphill, Art Rochester), Best Costume Design (Wendy Stites), Best Film Editing (Lee Smith), Best Visual Effects (Daniel Sudick, Stefen Fangmeier, Nathan McGuinness, Robert Stromberg), Best Makeup (Edouard F. Henriques, Yolanda Toussieng)
DVD: Miramax, 2004
BLU-RAY: 20th Century Fox, 2008
DURATION: 138 minutes

Master and Commander: The Far Side of the World is a period piece of epic dimensions, based on the novel of Patrick O'Brian, a best-selling English author and historian whose works center on the naval battles during the Napoleonic Wars, mostly fought in the year 1805. The film features Russell Crowe playing a hero of the British Navy, Captain "Lucky" Jack Aubrey, who is chasing a phantom French ship called the *Acheron* through the South Seas. The film required a large budget of more than $100 million, mostly to cover expenses of buying the original ship that was preserved in England, and reconstructing an exact replica of the warship HMS *Surprise*, to be used as a duplicate in sea battles. Weir was a well-known Australian auteur who had started his career with several highly interesting art movies in Australia. He was subsequently attracted to Hollywood, where he made a series of mainstream blockbusters that solidified his career as a director of taste and erudition. One of his characteristics is his tendency to elaborate on interestingly placed personas that have more than one side. These sides are sometimes contradictory, but Weir manages to balance them out so that they do not appear as unresolved conflicts.

At first, Crowe as Captain Aubrey appears to be a cross between Captain Bligh (*Mutiny on the Bounty*, 1935) and Fletcher

Christian, a ruthless disciplinarian with the charisma of a matinee idol, but that impression is soon dispelled, for Aubrey turns out altogether likeable, a born leader of men, a patriot dedicated to duty, intent on his mission, a hero in the best sense, a sensitive man placed in a situation where the slightest appearance of weakness is a fatal flaw. Conscious that his dilapidated ship and motley crew are no match for the superb French frigate he is pursuing with orders to destroy, he knows he must use cunning to overcome a superior adversary who usually attacks during a fog and slips away, only to shadow him. As the line between mutiny and obedience hangs in the balance, Aubrey has to play the mental game as well, leading his men by implanting in them the belief that he is invincible and fair, but also a stickler for discipline; above all, he abhors weakness in his officers. He is a disciple of Horatio Nelson, having served under him in his youth, and that in the British naval ethos defines the archetypal nineteenth-century naval officer, a leader of the high seas whose men had to endure life in cramped quarters, eating rotten food and being subjected to primitive medical conditions.

A naval story breeds a special kind of hero, for in his absolute ruler's small universe he is nothing short of a god. He is worshipped, feared, and hated, all at the same time. But he must not be despised. Any failure of principle, any deviation from the course he has carved, even the slightest hesitation in his set course of action, will be seen as a weakness, and at once his tightly knit unit will break apart. Aubrey draws from his inner strength, and he will hold back compassion to reprimand a wavering midshipman and dole out corporal punishment on a man who fails to salute him.

There is a larger point in the conception of this archetypal hero, however. This is not a case between villain and hero, as in the Bligh/Christian of *Mutiny on the Bounty*, where a completely villainous captain sadistically punishes the mutinous officer, nor is he the vile and evil Claggart of *Billy Budd*, whose victim is a hated innocent, incapable of striking back (but one who eventually does). Rather, we hear the reasoned voice of his friend, Dr. Stephen Maturin (Paul Bettany), putting to the test the principle of absolute authority, which the naval captain is obliged to uphold. This argument reminds of the Ahab–Starbuck conflict in *Moby Dick*, where the first mate advances the argument that it is a sin to take revenge against one of God's creatures—as the perverted logic of Ahab dictates.[1] For a moment, Aubrey sounds and behaves exactly like Ahab; he seems to ignore the ship's poor condition, his men's suffering, and the futility of a pursuit of a superior enemy.

Aubrey and Maturin clash when the HMS *Surprise* is headed for the Galapagos Islands, where Maturin makes an argument in favor of observing rare animal species while there. Aubrey stubbornly rejects the notion that any act in the advancement of science is more important than his war mission. A classic argument ensues: the conduct of war is more important than any other pursuit—more urgent than science or humanity, or any other peaceful pursuit. Aubrey is not without an understanding of the arts; he is a considerably talented musician and plays duets with Maturin during their spare moments,[2] but as pointed out, his naval/military discipline is of the utmost importance to him. Does any of the crew, he argues, want to live in London, which is occupied by the French? Do they want to be subjects of Napoleon? In the end, his persistence in following his mission—to find, destroy, sink, or burn the *Acheron*—defines the mind-set of this naval hero, who is one of a specimen of the utter patriot, not of the unenlightened militarist, but of the military men of the Age of Enlightenment. Such men could handle the violin as well as the saber; they could lose an arm (Aubrey just gets scratches) and dismiss this as a minor deformity; they could watch the greatest cruelty on their ship—a battle on a ship is indiscriminate slaughter—without wincing; they could empathize but stay calm and cool under the greatest pressure. These are not inconsiderable virtues, evident in the military, navy, or other institutions, today.

Peter Weir is an Easterner/Westerner director with polish, whose concept of the master and commander is that of a totally civilized human under extreme stress, one who will not lose his humanity in the midst of the most inhuman conflict that war has placed on the concept of man fighting for his nation—or a cause. But a warrior with tastes, one who at least has a glimpse of the world of art and science, is better than one without them. CS

Notes

1. The comparison ends here. Aubrey is devoted to his mission, while Ahab is totally consumed by his hatred of a whale and is seen as rebelling against nature more so than against an enemy.
2. Weir is famous for inserting classic music into the majority of his movies. In this case, we hear classic music from compositions of Johann Sebastian Bach, Wolfgang Amadeus Mozart, Ralph Vaughn Williams, and Luigi Boccherini, among others.

Bibliography

O'Brian, Patrick. *Master and Commander: The Far Side of the World.* New York: J. B. Lippincott, 1969.

McGregor, Tom. *The Making of Master and Commander.* New York: W. W. Norton, 2003.

THE MISSION (1986)

Director: Roland Joffé
Writer: Leon Robert Bolt
Producers: Fernando Ghia, David Puttnam (Warner Bros.)
Cinematographer: Chris Menges
Editor: Jim Clark
Production Design: Stuart Craig
Set Decoration: Jack Stephens
Costumes: Enrico Sabbatini
Music: Ennio Morricone
Cast: Capt. Rodrigo Mendoza: Robert De Niro. Father Gabriel: Jeremy Irons. Altamirano: Ray McAnally. Felipe Mendoza: Aidan Quinn. Carlotta: Cherrie Lunghi. Hontar: Ronald Pickup. Cabeza: Chuck Low. Father Fielding: Liam Neeson. Indian Boy: Bercelio Moya. Witch Doctor: Sigisfredo Ismare. Indian Chief: Asuncion Ontiveros. Sebastian: Daniel Berrigan
AA: Best Cinematography (Chris Menges)
AAN: Best Art Direction–Set Decoration (Stuart Craig, Jack Stephens), Best Costume Design (Enrico Sabbatini), Best Director (Roland Joffé), Best Film Editing (Jim Clark), Best Music–Original Score (Ennio Morricone), Best Picture (Fernando Ghia and David Puttnam)
DVD: Warner Home Video, 2003
Blu-ray: Warner Home Video, 2010
Duration: 125 minutes

The Mission is an award-winning cultural epic cleverly garbed in clerical clothes. Set within the idyllic and paradisiac geography of the eighteenth-century South American landscape, but about the treacherous and tumultuous politics of eighteenth-century Europe, the film exposes how victims and martyrs are borne in the name of culture and religion, and how politics and religion make strange bedfellows, but, most importantly, how casuistry without action, above all, is the greatest evil of all.

The Mission opens with a textual overlay that informs the viewer that this film is based on historical events that occurred around 1750, near the "borderlands of Argentina, Paraguay, and Brazil." What immediately follows is the presentation of a Cardinal dictating to his secretary a letter to the pope. He is reporting on the conclusion of events that he had been sent to deal with in the New World, and his assessment goes through several significant revisions. This opening structure signals that the nature of this film is didactic in intent.

The first version of his assessment is a quixotic phrase: "The Indians are once more free to be enslaved by the Spanish and Portuguese settlers." This line is quickly revised, and he replaces it with, "Your Holiness I write to you in this year of our Lord 1758 . . . from the great mission of San Miguel. These missions have protected the Indians from the depredations of the settlers . . . and have earned much resentment because of it." He adds, "The noble souls of these Indians incline toward music. It was from these missions the Jesuit fathers carried the word of God to those Indians still existing in their natural state, and received in return, martyrdom."

In the next scene, we see Indians carrying a man tied to a cross. They throw him into the river. The crucified man awakens when his body reaches the water, and the rapids drag him down into a cascading backward free fall into the sacred Iguazu Falls, plunging him downward, purportedly to his death. The Cardinal continues, saying, "The death of this priest was to form the first link in the chain of which I now find myself a part . . . little in this world unfolds as we predict. How could the Indians have supposed that the death of that unsung priest would bring among them a man whose life was to become intertwined with their own?" Thus, before the opening credits fade, we learn from the Cardinal's dictation the varied and entangled strategic missions woven into this cultural epic, soon to be unraveled through the action of the film, and also of the players who are to serve as their tokens. What is left ambiguous, even to the end, however, is toward that end.

The action begins at the site of the martyred priest's settlement. We meet Father Gabriel (Jeremy Irons), the superior who is responsible for sending the martyred priest to this site, and Father Fielding (Liam Neeson), field companion to the martyred priest. As Father Fielding completes the prayers upon the makeshift memorial site by the seaside, Father Gabriel leaves the shore and heads into the mountains alone. There is a dramatic and adventurous scene demonstrating the athletic skill of Father Gabriel, as he traverses the landscape of the jungle through rapids, steep mountains, up the waterfall, and into deep brush, until he comes upon a clearing, at which point he sits down and, somewhat paradoxically, pulls out an oboe and begins to play. He piques the interest of a group of local inhabitants who at first approach with hostility and then later welcome him by the hand into their community. Once there, he introduces the village to images of the Virgin Mary and the infant Jesus, and he teaches music.

The film switches back to narrative and continues with the Cardinal's dictation: "With an orchestra, the Jesuits could have subdued the whole continent. So it was that the Indians of the Guarani were finally brought to account to the everlasting mercy of God . . . and of the short-lived mercy of man." The action then moves directly to a battle scene in which a band of slave traders, led by Captain Rodrigo Mendoza (Robert De Niro), is in the process of capturing Guarani Indians to sell them. Father Gabriel confronts Mendoza and tells him that the Jesuits are building a mission on this territory and that these people are becoming Christians.

Captain Mendoza is the star of the next scene as he rides back into town with his latest acquisition of slaves. While there, he notifies his business partner, Cabeza (Chuck Low), about the presence of the Jesuit missionaries and their intentions of opening a new mission, San Carlos. He also learns that his betrothed is in love with his younger brother, Felipe (Aidan Quinn). As a result, he fights his brother in a duel and kills him with a dagger in a fit of anger and betrayal. The captain lands in solitary confinement, languishing.

After six months, Father Gabriel visits Mendoza at the request of the prison, and they exact a bargain from one another: "You killed your brother and it was a duel and the law can't touch you," says Father Gabriel to Mendoza. And then he tells Mendoza that he knows he loved his brother but that he is a coward who is running away from the world. When Mendoza tells Father Gabriel that he believes there is no redemption for him, he asks Mendoza to dare to choose his own penance. Mendoza replies, "Do you dare to see it fail?" And with that, Mendoza joins Gabriel on the expedition back to the settlement at the top of the mountain, dragging the burden of his earthly belongings with him along the trail in a manner resembling the Sisyphean effort of a transport mule.

Finally, after a seemingly endless trek through the jungle, redemption comes to Mendoza in one of the most powerful scenes in the film. An exhausted Mendoza, almost unable to move, falls to his knees with the weight of his belongings when a member of the Guarani tribe approaches him carrying a dagger. Broken, Mendoza lowers his head in supplication, as the Indian shows him the dagger blade, and then from behind him, slowly cuts the rope binding Mendoza to his "cargo." As the armor-laden parcel free-falls down the ravine and into the river, Mendoza falls prostrate and breaks into tears. He is first consoled by Father Gabriel and later by the entire Guarani tribe, who laugh—with him—at his new freedom. A new man, Mendoza is ordained a Jesuit, and he, Fielding, and Gabriel set up the Mission of San Carlos with the community of the Guarani Indians.

The next scene opens at a meeting with Cabeza, Hontar (Ronald Pickup), and the Cardinal. The reason for the Cardinal's mission? "Between ourselves, Your Eminence, the Jesuits are too powerful here," says Cabeza. He cryptically explains that he trusts that there will be no dispute between the Vatican, Spain, and Portugal about what ought to be done regarding the Jesuit missions. The Cardinal replies that he had once been a Jesuit himself.

The next day during the hearing before the Cardinal, we learn of the details surrounding the controversy: In the Treaty of Madrid, Spain and Portugal divided certain lands in the New World, lands that belonged to the Guarani people. Spain had outlawed slavery, but Portugal had not, and the Guarani were part of a lucrative slave trade. The region above the falls, where the Mission of San Carlos was, used to belong to Spain, but it was transferred to Portugal in the treaty, thus now belonging to Portugal; however, the mission, as property of the Church, was under papal jurisdiction of Rome, explaining the purpose of the Cardinal's visit. (The Jesuits, opposed to slavery, are nevertheless under the strict obedience of the pope.) In short, Portugal (and Spain) wanted the Guarani as slaves in the New World; they threatened by holding the Jesuits ransom in Europe.

During the testimony before the Cardinal, Father Gabriel explains that to survive, the Guarani have to run from slave traders. When Cabeza proclaims that there is no slave trading occurring in Spanish territories, Mendoza shouts out, "That is a lie!" As a cleric, he is ordered by the Cardinal and his superior to repent in public, although he knows that he is speaking the truth. This affront causes deep consternation in him, despite his dedication to fidelity and benevolence. In addition, his action further fuels the case against the Jesuits, since it was used by the state as an example of "Jesuit contempt."

Then the Cardinal and Father Gabriel have a man-to-man talk during which Father

Gabriel tells the Cardinal the truth about the politics: the Spanish have slaves, and they buy them from the Portuguese; they want the missions closed because the missions are the only safe havens left for the Guarani. The Cardinal tells Father Gabriel the truth about the politics, stating, "Do you know what is at stake here? . . . The very existence of the Jesuit order, both here and in Europe."

The Cardinal journeys with Father Gabriel to all the mission sites but decides that the Guarani must leave the missions. The Guarani protest and refuse to leave, threatening to fight. The Cardinal orders the Jesuits not to fight or they will be excommunicated. In the next scene, the Cardinal confesses to Father Gabriel that he knew all along that this would be his decision, but he came to see the missions simply to convince the Jesuits not to resist the transfer of the mission territories for the benefit of the Jesuit Order in Europe.

What happens next marks the denouement of *The Mission*, although in the end, as promised, little unfolds as predicted. The call to battle begins when a young Guarani boy finds Mendoza's sword in the water (baggage long discarded but not forgotten). He polishes the sword and presents it to Mendoza, who, putting aside his breviary, picks it up. Father Fielding also joins the battle, but Father Gabriel resists, proclaiming the law of charity and love above all others. While Mendoza and Father Fielding die fighting alongside the Guarani men, Gabriel serves Mass in the village for the benefit of the women and children. The soldiers approach the village and open fire, killing aimlessly, while Father Gabriel leads a procession holding the Body of Christ until he, too, is gunned down.

The next scene takes place back in the city, where the Cardinal, Cabeza, and Hontar are seated at the table speaking about the events at the mission. The Cardinal asks if it was all necessary. Cabeza tells him, "I did what I had to do, given the legitimate purpose, which you sanctioned." Hontar replies, "You had no alternative, your Eminence. We must work in the world." The Cardinal laments," No . . . thus have we made the world. Thus have I made it."

The final scene shows the Guarani children retrieving items from the waters of the river—a violin, a candelabrum—as the voice over of the Cardinal closes with, "So, your Holiness, now your priests are dead and I am left alive. But in truth, it is I who am dead, and they who live . . . the spirit of the dead will survive in the memory of the living." MC

> The light shines in the darkness and the darkness has not overcome it.—John 1:5

Bibliography

Kennedy, T. Frank, S.J. "An Integrated Perspective." In *The Jesuit Tradition in Education and Missions: A 450-Year Perspective*, edited by Christopher Chapple, 201–25. Scranton, PA: University of Scranton Press, 1993.

MR. SMITH GOES TO WASHINGTON (1939)

Director: Frank Capra
Writers: Sidney Buchman, Lewis R. Foster
Producer: Frank Capra (uncredited) (Columbia)
Cinematographer: Joseph Walker
Editors: Gene Havlick, Al Clark
Art Direction: Lionel Banks
Costumes: Robert Kalloch
Music: Dimitri Tiomkin
Sound: John P. Livadary
Cast: Clarissa Saunders: Jean Arthur. Jefferson Smith: James Stewart. Sen. Joseph Paine: Claude Rains. Jim Taylor: Edward Arnold. Gov. Hopper: Guy Kibbee. Diz Moore: Thomas Mitchell. Chick McGann: Eugene Pallette. Ma Smith: Beulah Bondi. Senate Majority Leader: H. B. Warner. President of the Senate: Harry Carey. Susan Paine: Astrid Allwyn. Mrs. Hopper: Ruth Donnelly. Sen. MacPherson:

Grant Mitchell. Sen. Monroe: Porter Hall. Senate Minority Leader: Pierre Watkin. Nosey: Charles Lane. Bill Griffith: William Demarest. Carl Cook: Dick Elliott. The Hopper Boys: Billy Watson, Delmar Watson, John Russell, Harry Watson, Garry Watson (as Gary Watson), Larry Simms (as Baby Dumpling). Radio Broadcaster (Himself): H. V. Kaltenborn

AA: Best Writing–Original Story (Lewis R. Foster)

AAN: Best Picture (Columbia), Best Director (Frank Capra), Best Leading Actor (James Stewart), Best Supporting Actor (Harry Carey), Best Supporting Actor (Claude Rains), Best Art Direction (Lionel Banks), Best Film Editing (Gene Havlick, Al Clark), Best Music–Scoring (Dimitri Tiomkin), Best Sound–Recording (John P. Livadary), Best Writing–Screenplay (Sidney Buchman)

DVD: Sony Pictures Home Entertainment, 2005

Blu-ray: Currently unavailable

Duration: 125 minutes

Director Frank Capra, who had won Academy Awards for *It Happened One Night* (1934), *Mr. Deeds Goes to Town* (1936), and *You Can't Take It with You* (1938), finished his contract with Columbia with the controversial but commercially successful *Mr. Smith Goes to Washington*, a comedy-drama that tells the tale of a simple, idealistic young man's efforts to expose corruption in the U.S. Senate. While Columbia had been known for pumping out inexpensive B films, Capra's prestige pictures of the 1930s helped to place the studio among the eight major players in Hollywood. The film cost $2 million, partly courtesy of its meticulously researched, detailed sets, but this is not a spectacle-based epic. It is, however, a heroic film that strives to place its everyman within the nation's epic history—embodied first in the Washington monuments that he tours with awe, and then in Mr. Smith himself as he struggles to defend an ideal of nation and democracy.

When U.S. senator Sam Foley dies, Governor Hopper (Guy Kibbee) is called upon to nominate a replacement, but Hopper is under the thumb of corrupt media businessman and political boss, Jim Taylor (Edward Arnold), who wants him to put a malleable stooge into the position. Hopper is also under pressure from committees, while at home, the governor's children want him to choose Jefferson Smith (James Stewart), leader of the Boy Rangers. The anxious and befuddled Hopper flips a coin, only to find that it lands next to an article about Smith. He decides that Smith is the best compromise and that being idealistic and naïve about politics should render him easily manipulated. In Washington, it soon becomes clear that Smith is out of his league, but he is heartened to be mentored by his father's old friend, Senator Joseph Paine (Claude Rains).

Unfortunately, Paine is also corrupt, colluding with Taylor to profit from a dam-building project. Wanting to make sure that Smith is suitably distracted, Paine encourages him to draft a bill for a national boys' camp. An excited Smith comes up with scheme whereby boys throughout the nation can fund the camp by sending in spare coins. Unfortunately, Smith nominates for the camp land that is part of Paine and Taylor's graft dam plan, and Paine brings in the considerable charms of his daughter Susan (Astrid Allwyn) to keep Smith away from the Senate when their bill is being read.

Smith's secretary, Clarissa Saunders (Jean Arthur), is at first appalled to be left babysitting Smith, but she gradually becomes impressed by his morals and tells him to look into Paine's bill. When Smith starts to ask some inconvenient questions, Taylor tries to buy his silence by promising to set him up politically for life. The horrified Smith rejects the offer but is disillusioned when Paine finally admits that twenty years earlier he had made such an arrangement with Taylor himself. Smith ignores Paine's plea not to raise objections to the dam scheme, only to be accused of having bought up the land for the boys' camp himself, with a view to personally profiting from the pocket money of the youth of the United States. Smith is shocked to witness the falsified evidence against him, including testimony from Paine himself, but as a dejected Smith sits on his bags at the Lincoln Memorial,[1] Saunders arrives and convinces him to remain and fight using a scheme she has devised.

Smith turns up at the Senate, and before the vote can be taken to expel him, he stands and asks to be recognized. Smith then proceeds to remove food from his pockets, and it becomes immediately clear that he intends to begin a filibuster, a measure whereby a member refuses to yield the floor to delay or prevent a vote. Saunders coaches Smith from the gallery (and also eventually sends a message to confess that she is in love with him), so that he demands the presence of a quorum and refuses to yield except for questions or other points of order that will not require that he give up the floor. When Saunders learns that Taylor is controlling the press coverage of the filibuster in Smith's home state, she enlists the Boy Rangers to print off favorable pamphlets, but the boys are intercepted and even hurt by Taylor's men. With no accurate news coverage reaching his state, telegrams are brought in to the Senate to show that Smith has no support from the people. Although Smith refuses to give in, the exhaustion from talking on his feet for hours on end[2] finally gets the better of him, and he collapses on the Senate floor. In the face of Smith's heroic fight for justice, Paine can take the shame no longer and confesses that it is he who is guilty of fraud, not Smith.

With the cynical hindsight of the twenty-first century, *Mr. Smith Goes to Washington* may sound like patriotic hokum, but Smith's success—and with it the fate of democracy—is, in fact, rather tenuous. In the face of overwhelming media control of public opinion, it is only Paine's last-minute change of heart that saves both Smith and the integrity of the Senate.[3] And although Smith himself is presented as the hero of the day, it is really Saunders whose knowledge and astuteness enables him to undertake his marathon filibuster. This suggests that some mediation is necessary after all between small-town values and big-city pragmatism.

It is not that democracy wins by a hairsbreadth (and therefore could just as easily have fallen the other way) that offended in 1939, but the very notion that there could be corruption in the Senate in the first place. Audience members walked out of the Washington premiere hosted by the National Press Club, and senators expressed their outrage in the press.[4] Even the State Department declared that *Mr. Smith Goes to Washington* would damage the image of democracy at a fragile time, given that war had broken out in Europe just two weeks before the premiere.[5] Capra himself had questioned filming a political satire when the "black cloud of war hung over the chancelleries of the world,"[6] but a visit to the Lincoln Memorial revitalized him (just as it does Jefferson Smith in the film), and he left convinced that the "more uncertain the people of the world . . . the more they need a ringing statement of America's democratic ideals."[7] For Capra, then, the film was not an attack on democracy, but rather its reinvigoration, and the healthy box-office returns suggested that the audience was willing to share his view (or that controversy was good for business regardless).[8] In the midst of the political ballyhoo surrounding the film, the *New York Times* declared, "*Mr. Smith* is one of the best shows of the year. More fun, even, than the Senate itself."[9] DB

Notes

1. Charles J. Maland argues that it is this characteristic moment of "abyss" in Capra's films that make them ultimately more complex than the utopian fantasies they are sometimes taken for. Charles J. Maland, "Capra and the Abyss: Self-Interest versus the Common Good in Depression America," in *Frank Capra: Authorship and the Studio System*, edited by Robert Sklar and Vito Zagarrio (Philadelphia, PA: Temple University Press, 1998), 95–129.

2. Spare a thought for poor Jimmy Stewart, who did not have to act hoarse for these scenes, as his throat was swabbed with mercury to produce the desired irritation. Frank Capra, *The Name above the Title: An Autobiography* (New York: Da Capo, 1997), 276, originally published in New York: Macmillan, 1971.

3. Indeed, Michael P. Rogin and Kathleen Moran suggest that, "Far from assuming a virtuous traditional public opinion that simply needs to be aroused, these films worry that the public is largely 'created' by modern media and are reachable only through the questionable techniques of mass media itself." Michael P. Rogin and Kathleen Moran, "Mr. Capra Goes to Washington," *Representations* 84, no. 1 (2003): 219.

4. Capra, *The Name above the Title*, 282–93.

5. Rogin and Moran, "Mr. Capra Goes to Washington," 214–15.

6. Capra, *The Name above the Title*, 259.

7. Capra, *The Name above the Title*, 260.

8. For a detailed examination of the reception of the film, see Eric Smoodin, "'Compulsory' Viewing for Every Citizen: *Mr. Smith* and the Rhetoric of Reception," *Cinema Journal* 35, no. 2 (1996): 3–23.

9. Frank S. Nugent, "The Screen in Review; Frank Capra's *Mr. Smith Goes to Washington*," *New York Times*, 20 October 1939, http://movies.nytimes.com/movie/review?res=9403EED8143EE23ABC4851DFB6678382629EDE (2 July 2013).

Bibliography

Capra, Frank. *The Name above the Title: An Autobiography*. New York: Da Capo, 1997. Originally published in New York: Macmillan, 1971.

Maland, Charles J. "Capra and the Abyss: Self-Interest versus the Common Good in Depression America." In *Frank Capra: Authorship and the Studio System*, edited by Robert Sklar and Vito Zagarrio, 95–129. Philadelphia, PA: Temple University Press, 1998.

Nugent, Frank S. "The Screen in Review; Frank Capra's *Mr. Smith Goes to Washington*." *New York Times*, 20 October 1939, http://movies.nytimes.com/movie/review?res=9403EED8143EE23ABC4851DFB6678382629EDE (2 July 2013).

Rogin, Michael P., and Kathleen Moran. "Mr. Capra Goes to Washington." *Representations* 84, no. 1 (2003): 213–48.

Smoodin, Eric. "'Compulsory' Viewing for Every Citizen: *Mr. Smith* and the Rhetoric of Reception." *Cinema Journal* 35, no. 2 (1996): 3–23.

MUTINY ON THE BOUNTY (1935)

DIRECTOR: Frank Lloyd

WRITERS: Talbot Jennings, Jules Furthman, Carey Wilson. Based on the novel by Charles Nordhoff and James Norman Hall.

PRODUCERS: Frank Lloyd, Irving Thalberg (MGM)

CINEMATOGRAPHER: Arthur Edeson

EDITOR: Margaret Booth

MUSIC: Herbert Stothart, Nat W. Finston (uncredited)

CAST: Capt. William Bligh: Charles Laughton. First Mate Fletcher Christian: Clark Gable. Midshipman Roger Byam: Franchot Tone. Chief Hitihiti: William Bambridge. Tehani: Movita. Maimiti: Mamo Clark. Quintal: Byron Russell. Tommy Ellison: Eddie Quillan. Burkitt: Donald Crisp. Coleman: Percy Waram. Maggs: Ian Wolfe. Mr. Fryer: De Witt Jennings. Sir Joseph Banks: Henry Stephenson. Mrs. Byam: Spring Byington

AA: Best Picture (MGM)

AAN: Best Director (Frank Lloyd), Best Leading Actor (Charles Laughton), Best Leading Actor (Clark Gable), Best Leading Actor (Franchot Tone), Best Writing–Screenplay (Talbot Jennings, Jules Furthman, Carey Wilson), Best Music–Score (Herbert Stothart, Nat W. Finston), Best Film Editing (Margaret Booth)

DVD: Warner Home Video, 2004

BLU-RAY: Warner Home Video, 2010

DURATION: 132 minutes

Mutiny on the Bounty is one of several epic films based on the 1932 Charles Nordhoff and James Norman Hall novel loosely recounting a historical incident in the late eighteenth-century English naval chronicles, the mutiny on HMS *Bounty*. These films tell, with minor variations of both the novel and the historical event, the story of the munity that occurred in the South Seas, while the *Bounty* was on a mission to transport breadfruit seedlings to the West Indies as a source of nutrition for the slave population. An Australian film, *In the Wake of the Bounty* (1933), with Errol Flynn, came first, followed by *The Mutiny on the Bounty* versions in 1935 and 1962, and *The Bounty*, in 1988, with Anthony Hopkins as Bligh and Mel Gibson as Christian. (All of them above portray William Bligh, the captain of the *Bounty*, as a reckless villain, while history shows him as a great navigational hero and a man of compassion.)

The 1935 film stars Charles Laughton as Captain William Bligh, Clark Gable as first mate Fletcher Christian, and Franchot Tone as midshipman Roger Byam, one of the three principal players in the cast. In the Nordhoff/Hall novel, Byam is actually the narrator of the story, which is told from a first-person point of view. In the film, Byam is a friend of Christian and remains so until the mutiny, refusing to take part in it, but he is held on board the *Bounty* with a few others due to lack of space in the longboat that carries away Bligh and the men who remain loyal to him. When the *Bounty* returns to Tahiti, where the mutinous crew took refuge for several years, Byam stays with them, renewing his friendship with Christian and the native girl Tehani (Movita), while Christian marries Maimiti (Mamo Clark), Chief Hitihiti's (William Bambridge) daughter. The small community of exiles lives a Rousseaulike natural existence of song and dance, until a British man-of-war is sighted. Byam and the several men who had not participated in the mutiny choose to return to London, while Christian and the mutineers, along with a small crowd of natives, take off for an unknown destination.

Byam does not know that the *Pandora*, the British frigate, is captained by Bligh, who seizes him and his companions and puts them in irons, dismissing Byam's claim that he and the men with him did not take part in the mutiny. In London, during his trial, Byam delivers a fiery speech before the examining board, exposing the cruelties that were the real cause of the mutiny. While the rest of the men are hanged, Byam is pardoned on a plea to the king by Sir Joseph Banks (Henry Stephenson), a powerful friend of the family, and he soon returns to sea as midshipman on another man-of-war.

Meanwhile, the plot follows two other strands. After the mutiny, when on the longboat with his followers, Bligh decides to head for Timor, in the Dutch East Indies, despite the distance of 3,500 miles, from where he would gain swift passage to England. He achieves that goal by clever navigation, judicious management of the meager supplies on the boat, and dogged determination and stamina. In this section of the story, he shows an entirely different side of himself, being fair to his mates, winning against tremendous odds, and showing compassion, bravery, and steadfastness, traits missing when he was captaining the *Bounty*. But as soon as he shows up on the frigate *Pandora* in Tahiti, he reverts to his previous self, pursuing Christian and the *Bounty* with irrational hatred, to the point of wrecking his ship on the reefs and having to reach Australia in the ship's boats with his prisoners and crew. Upon his return to England, he becomes the chief witness in the ensuing trial, making sure Byam and those with him are condemned to hang.

On the other hand, Christian and the mutineers, knowing their fate is sealed if captured, sail on until they reach Pitcairn Island, a bare rock without a port and wrongly mapped, where Christian gives orders to sink and burn the *Bounty* to avoid detection. There they remain for the rest of their lives. History records that the group degenerated into anarchy, weakened by inbreeding, murder, and rape until all but two vanished. Many years later, parts of the wreckage of the *Bounty* were found, and also a small community, descendants of the *Bounty* and the Tahiti natives. Those people still live there.[1]

Most of the action of the film is centered on the friction between Bligh and Christian and the inevitable clash of wills between them that leads Christian to the mutiny. Laughton's Bligh is a self-styled villain lacking any trait of human compassion and who uses fear as a tool for "efficiency." He flogs a man already dead and punishes Byam by ordering him to climb aloft during a storm for only a minor infraction. His cruelties to the crew continue to be a constant provocation to Christian, who steadfastly remains loyal despite his captain's atrocities, but his patience eventually wears out and he seizes the ship when Bligh orders a dying man on deck to witness a flogging.

Mutiny is the worst crime on the high seas, from which there is no return, and Christian and those following him are doomed to a life of permanent exile. Gable's Christian is shown as a man who faces a moral dilemma, trapped between his loyalty to his superior and his outrage at witnessing inhuman treatment of his mates. Bligh, described as the "devil" and envious of his mate's charisma and popularity with the crew, summons every inch of energy to reach England to pursue the "mutinous dog," as he calls Christian. While Christian can be seen as a tragic hero, making a decision that seals his doom (although he wins the audience's admiration), Bligh is shown as utterly bereft of human compassion, legally a winner, but rebuffed by an admiral as the trial ends in his favor. Byam, on the other hand, is exonerated, starts a new career as a midshipman, and becomes a catalyst for fairer treatment for those who serve ships.

The film won the Academy Award for Best Picture in 1935, along with several nominations, among them Best Actor for Laughton, Gable, and Tone. As Fletcher Christian, Gable reluctantly had to shave off his mischievous mustache, showing himself as capable of playing a serious role of a man torn between human compassion and duty. Gable's personality was perfectly suited to the occasion, for he is shown as brave, human, just, and protective of his men, but also incapable of withholding his impulse to munity, which brought down many other men aside from himself. As Bligh, Laughton, heavy-browed to emphasize his menacing looks, is believable as a monster without any moral dimension. Laughton admirably manages to evoke the contempt of audiences, rendering the image of a "perfect" villain, who masks his brutality as loyalty. One of the admirals sees through him and, while congratulating him for his heroic navigation skills, withholds any praise for the outcome. Bligh fails to win anyone's heart, rendering a potentially tragic contours story to sea adventure as melodrama.

This sea adventure has generally been regarded as the superior of both its predecessor with Errol Flynn and to the two films that followed. It has energy, good performances, and black-and-white photography that emphasizes the starkness of life on board a ship, but also the perfect pairing of "good" versus "evil" personalities. Much of its success lies in this rather simplistic, but always effective, formula. CS

Note

1. For a description of the community descended from the original fugitives of the *Bounty*, living on Pitcairn Island at the time the film was made, see "Special

Features," "Pitcairn Island Today," 1935, *Mutiny on the Bounty*, directed by Frank Lloyd (Warner Home Video, 2004), DVD.

Bibliography

Alexander, Caroline. *The Bounty: The True Story of the Mutiny on the Bounty*. New York: Viking Penguin, 2003.

Brownlow, Kevin. *David Lean: A Biography*. New York: A Wyatt Book for St. Martin's Press, 1996.

Hough, Richard. *Captain Bligh and Mr. Christian*. London: Hutchinson, 1972.

MUTINY ON THE BOUNTY (1962)

DIRECTOR: Lewis Milestone
WRITER: Charles Lederer. Adapted from the novel by Charles Nordhoff and James Norman Hall.
PRODUCER: Aaron Rosenberg (uncredited) (MGM)
CINEMATOGRAPHER: Robert Surtees
EDITOR: John McSweeney Jr.
ART DIRECTION: George W. Davis, J. McMillan Johnson
SET DECORATION: Henry Grace, Hugh Hunt
MUSIC: Bronislau Kaper, Paul Francis Webster
SPECIAL EFFECTS: A. Arnold Gillespie, Milo B. Lory
CAST: First Mate Fletcher Christian: Marlon Brando. Capt. William Bligh: Trevor Howard. Seaman John Mills: Richard Harris. Seaman Alexander Smith: Hugh Griffith. Horticulturalist William Brown: Richard Haydn. Seaman Matthew Quintal: Percy Herbert. Samuel Mack: Ashley Cowan. Sailing Master John Fryar: Eddie Byrne. Minarii: Frank Silvera. Princess Maimiti: Tarita Teriipia
AA: None
AAN: Best Picture (Aaron Rosenberg), Best Art Direction–Set Decoration–Color (George W. Davis, J. McMillan Johnson, Henry Grace, Hugh Hunt), Best Cinematography–Color (Robert Surtees), Best Effects–Special Effects (A. Arnold Gillespie, Milo B. Lory), Best Film Editing (John McSweeney Jr.), Best Music–Substantially Original Score (Bronislau Kaper), Best Music–Original Song (Bronislau Kaper, Paul Francis Webster for "Follow Me")
DVD: Warner Home Video, 2006. Two-disc special edition.
BLU-RAY: Warner Home Video, 2011
DURATION: 178 minutes (185 for UK edition)

The 1962 version of *Mutiny on the Bounty* is an epic adventure that fits the mold of the big spectacles of the time, with an excellent cast, flawless direction by Lewis Milestone (who replaced Carol Reed, an initial choice), a rousing musical score by Bronislau Kaper, and location scenes filmed in the South Pacific in widescreen Ultra Panavision 70mm. Slow-paced but gaining momentum as the sea yarn evolves, *Mutiny on the Bounty*, like its predecessors, is based on the novel by Charles Nordhoff and James Norman Hall. It recounts an incident that took place on the South Seas in the late 1780s, the mutiny on the HMS *Bounty*, instigated by the first mate, Fletcher Christian (Marlon Brando), against the ship's captain, William Bligh (Trevor Howard).

Made earlier in several different versions,[1] notably in 1935, with Charles Laughton and Clark Gable, now considered a classic, the 1962 version flopped with both critics and audiences, despite its several Oscar nominations. Its lukewarm reception is usually attributed to Brando's alleged miscasting as a British officer; the fact that it went over budget, eventually costing $19 million; and the unfortunate circumstance that 1962 was also the year of the release of *Lawrence of Arabia*, which won the most important Oscar honors. But in modern times, the epics of the 1950s and 1960s, which looked like an extinct species for many decades, are being reevaluated and issued on DVD and Blu-ray versions, giving older viewers a chance to revisit old favorites, while younger audiences can also taste the glitter and splendor of the older epics. It is worth noting that Marlon Brando, who had been offered the role of T. E. Lawrence in *Lawrence of Arabia* and had turned it down, evoked critical venom as Fletcher Christian, sporting an English accent and practically altering his screen persona. Today, however, many viewers look at him as the perfect foil to the "villainous" Trevor Howard, who excels as Captain Bligh.

The story of the *Bounty* evolves in a linear manner, as the voice of William Brown (Richard Haydn), the horticulturalist on board, is heard introducing the purpose of the voyage and occasionally picking up the thread of the narrative. The *Bounty*, with a crew of about thirty to thirty-five seamen, three officers, Fletcher Christian as the first mate, and William Bligh as the captain, is sailing to Tahiti under orders from the Royal Admiralty to carry roots of breadfruit to transplant in Jamaica to feed the slave population there. The year is 1787, during the reign of King George III, and the ship, a three-mast frigate,[2] must sail to its destination via the only two routes available to it. It can go west, around Cape Horn, and face the adverse winds and storms that plague that part of the planet, or sail east, around the Cape of Good Hope, which takes longer but is safer. Captain Bligh, stubborn and unyielding, chooses the first route, but the storms almost sink the *Bounty*. Declaring failure, he chooses the second route, and the ship arrives in Tahiti after a considerable delay.

Christian, as played by Brando, is first shown as a foppish English aristocrat who arrives to the ship late with two elegant ladies by his side. He is a last-minute choice for the voyage but soon shows that he is quite capable of performing the duties of a Royal Navy officer. Bligh, who had previously traveled with Captain Cook states that this is also his "first captainship," and he is eager to steer a ship practically around the globe to fulfill his mission. Despite his inexperience, Christian sees through Bligh immediately, and knows he will have to deal with an unyielding, even sadistic, disciplinarian who will impose the harshest punishment even for a minor infraction. The first instance of Bligh's cruelty is when Seaman John Mills, played by Richard Harris, is to receive two dozen lashes for just a word or two he said that the captain thought offensive.

Trevor Howard makes a credible Bligh—perhaps not as colorful as his predecessor Laughton in the 1935 version, but in some ways even meaner. His motto is "instill fear" into the men; remind them of the repercussions that come with any sign of disobedience. While he deplores the laxity of morals in Tahiti, he allows his men to mix with the local women (even urging them to do so to keep the local chief's favor). He shows his true colors when he places three seamen, Quintal (Byron Russell), Smith (Hugh Griffith), and Mills, in irons for trying to desert and stay in Tahiti, and he then cuts the water rations of the crew in half to preserve the 1,000 plants that the ship is carrying—far too many—to show his excessive zeal and excuse his tardiness when they reach port. He has the water ladle with the cup hung high up on a mast, so anyone who wants a drink must climb up to reach it. When a man attempting to do so falls to his death, another man attacks the captain, and, as a consequence, he is "keel-hauled," that is, tied to a rope and dragged along the ship. He dies after being mauled by a shark.

Despite disagreeing with the captain's practices, Christian remains firmly loyal, but when Bligh refuses water to a seaman who had drank seawater and is dying of thirst and near death, he hits Bligh with the handle of the ladle and then threatens him with death if he makes another move to resist. Bligh is allowed to leave the ship with two of his officers and several members of the crew in a longboat, sailing east, nearly 4,000 miles, to Timor. He manages to arrive back in England, although we are not shown how. The next time we see him, we find him standing before an examining board of the Admiralty in England, where he is acquitted of wrongdoing but is severely chastised by the admiral for his lack of compassion. His mission is proclaimed a "failure."

Christian and the rest of the rebels return to Tahiti, but fearing reprisals by the Royal Navy, they flee again, and, seeing a naval ship approaching, they turn at night and reach Pitcairn Island, which is charted 175 miles off its location on the maps. They take refuge there. The island is rich in vegetation, breadfruit, and game, an island paradise. Men and women from Tahiti are with them in the new colony, including Princess Maimiti (Tarita Teripia). But Christian has a change of heart. He asks the three men who had aided him in the mutiny—Mills, Smith, and Quintal—to consider returning to London. His conscience torments him, for he is well aware of his treason and cannot live with the knowledge that he would be unable to defend himself for his actions—at the risk of hanging. He gives the three men the night to think his proposal over. But the *Bounty* catches fire during the night and is seen burning. Christian and the others rush to the ship to try to extinguish the fire; however, it is too late. In the process, Christian suffers fatal burns and is brought back to the island, but Brown sees that he is near death. Maimiti mourns at his side as he dies. Mills and the other two men, he is told, set fire to the ship, not wanting to return to England to hang.

Viewers inevitably compare Clark Gable's Christian, of the 1935 production, to that of Marlon Brando, who was criticized as being miscast and deemed responsible for the failure of the 1962 version of *Mutiny on the Bounty*. Brando managed to mimic the British accent well enough (something he had done in *Julius Caesar* as Mark Antony a few years earlier), but his persona seemed incompatible with that established in his previous films, as a low-class, inarticulate bumbler. Here he deconstructs the image of Christian established earlier by Gable, making him a more deliberate than an impulsive person, slowly reacting, camouflaging his rage, but letting it show in his body language, which is perfectly in tune with his method acting. His answers are crisp, often verging on the sarcastic, but when he explodes, he reminds of the image of Brando one knows from his other roles. Brando's performance is the key to the dynamics of the story, matching Trevor Howard's Bligh, whose perfectly controlled demeanor makes him if not somewhat sympathetic, at least entirely believable as the cold-blooded master of the *Bounty*.

The tragic end of this epic sea adventure tale is also a tale of moral dilemmas. Christian's munity is a result of an unyielding man's, his captain's, cruel, inhuman treatment of the crew, depriving them of drinking water after a series of other inhuman acts of cruelty. Christian is also reproached by Mills, who clearly guesses that the first mate is becoming less and less inclined to endure the savage mistreatment of his men, having had doubts about the captain's sanity. He has resisted the impulse to rebel several times, and he is under stress. Finally, when a cup of water is denied to a dying man, he takes control of the ship and ousts the captain, but he then falls into fits of depression. He is torn between his duty as an officer, which he knows he should never trespass, and his duty to humanity. He does what he does not simply out of outrage, but in the interests of a suffering crew. Christian's dilemma is whether one should be more loyal to human mistreatment or to his sworn duty as an officer. His death is also the result of another dilemma—that the two are inseparable. He wants to vindicate himself—although the latter would endanger the lives of the men who followed him. From that there is no escape. That would be the opposite of the first dilemma: vindicating himself at the expense of several of the men who were loyal to him. The fire comes almost as a merciful end to his moral torments. It releases him from having to face yet another dilemma—but one that would have been honorable. CS

Notes

1. First as a silent film in Australia, in 1915, and later as *In the Wake of the Bounty*, with Errol Flynn, in 1933, also in Australia.

2. For the 1962 version of the film, a much larger ship, about 118 feet in length (the earlier one had been about ninety feet), was built, mainly to accommodate the technical crew and the heavier equipment of the Ultra Panavision 70mm cameras.

Bibliography

Alexander, Caroline. *The* Bounty*: The True Story of the Mutiny on the* Bounty. New York: Viking Penguin, 2003.

N

THE NAME OF THE ROSE (1986)

DIRECTOR: Jean-Jacques Annaud
DIRECTORS: Andrew Birkin, Gérard Brach, Howard Franklin, Alain Godard. Based on the novel by Umberto Eco.
PRODUCERS: Bernd Eichinger, Bernd Schaefers (Constantin)
ASSOCIATE PRODUCERS: Pierre Hebey, Herman Weigel
CINEMATOGRAPHER: Tonino Delli Colli
EDITOR: Jane Seitz
ART DIRECTION: Giorgio Giovannini, Rainer Schaper
COSTUMES: Gabriella Pescucci
MUSIC: James Horner
MAKEUP ARTIST: Hasso von Hugo
CAST: William of Baskerville: Sean Connery. Adso of Melk: Christian Slater. Remigio da Varagine: Helmut Qualtinger. Severinus: Elya Baskin. The Abbot: Michael Lonsdale. Malachia: Volker Prechtel. Jorge de Burgos: Feodor Chaliapin Jr. Ubertino da Casale: William Hickey. Berengar: Michael Habeck. Venantius: Urs Althaus. The Girl: Valentina Vargas. Salvatore: Ron Perlman. Michele da Cesena: Leopoldo Trieste. Jerome of Kaffa: Franco Valobra. Hugh of Newcastle: Vernon Dobtcheff. Pietro d'Assisi: Donald O'Brien (as Donal O'Brian). Cuthbert of Winchester: Andrew Birkin. Bernardo Gui: F. Murray Abraham. Cardinal Bertrand: Lucien Bodard. Jean d'Anneaux: Peter Berling. Bishop of Alborea: Pete Lancaster. Voice of Adso as an Old Man: Dwight Weist
AA: None
AAN: None
BAFTA AWARDS: Best Actor (Sean Connery), Best Makeup Artist (Hasso von Hugo)
CÉSAR AWARDS: Best Foreign Film (Jean-Jacques Annaud)
DVD: Warner Home Video, 2004
BLU-RAY: Warner Home Video, 2011
DURATION: DVD, 126 minutes; Blu-ray, 131 minutes

The Name of the Rose was adapted from the surprise 1980 best-selling novel of the same name, originally penned in Italian by academic Umberto Eco. The book is a murder mystery set at an abbey in northern Italy in 1327, purportedly based on a real missing manuscript. For director Jean-Jacques Annaud, the film version of the tale would be perhaps both his biggest failure and his biggest success, for while the film received savage reviews in the United States and performed relatively poorly there, it became the film for which he is most highly regarded in Europe.

The beginning of the film is marked by the arrival at an unnamed Benedictine abbey of the Franciscan brother William of Baskerville (Sean Connery), whose name evokes both Sherlock Holmes and the English Franciscan philosopher William of Ockham, and thereby alerts us to the film's combination of detective plot and medievalism. Brother William is accompanied by the novice Adso (Christian Slater in an early film role), a character who retrospectively narrates the events as he recalls them in his advancing years. They are one of many parties arriving for a papal debate, but Brother William notices a fresh grave, and the Abbot (Michael Lonsdale) confides that a young illustrator, Brother d'Anneaux (Peter Berling), seems to have fallen to his death, seemingly from a window that cannot open, and many suspect evil forces are at work. But when he is asked to informally investigate, Brother William deduces that the monk must have thrown himself from another part of the abbey and his body fallen down the slope. Not long after the conference begins, a Greek translator, Venantius (Urs Althaus), is found dead, upturned in a pot of animal blood. His tongue and finger are mysteriously darkened.

When William and Adso visit the scriptorium where the monks write and illustrate, they find that the illustrator's work contains surprising humor, but they are prevented from examining the work of the translator by the assistant librarian, Berengar (Michael Habeck), and are not granted permission to enter the library itself. Returning to the scriptorium later, William finds a mysterious note from Venantius with directions in invisible ink. They are startled by someone else in the library (in fact, Berengar), and making chase, Adso unexpectedly finds himself at the receiving end of the affections of a peasant girl, with whom he makes love. The following day, Berengar is found dead in his bathtub, also with a blackened tongue and finger.

William's investigations lead him to believe that Berengar had persuaded the young illustrator Brother d'Anneaux to sleep with him in exchange for access to a rare book, but guilt over their encounter prompted d'Anneaux to take his own life. His friend Venantius and Berengar seem to have been killed for reading the same forbidden book. Prompted by the escalating fears of the assembled monks, the Abbot calls for an inquisition. Investigator Bernardo Gui (F. Murray Abraham, fresh from his Oscar-winning success in Milos Forman's 1984 *Amadeus*) arrives, much to William's consternation, for they were fellow inquisitors before Gui had William thrown in jail for disagreeing with him.

William is aided by the herbalist Severinus (Elya Baskin), who locates the secret book but also dies before he is able to give it to William. Meanwhile, Gui discovers the hunchback monk and former heretic Salvatore (Ron Perlman) undertaking some sort of black magic. Gui also accuses Adso's peasant girl of witchcraft, but although she is discovered with Salvatore, it seems more likely under the circumstances that she has simply been prostituting herself for food. Remigio (Helmut Qualtinger) is also arrested, primarily because he was also a member of the same heretical cult as Salvatore. William gets himself into trouble yet again by refusing to support Gui's dubious findings, but William and Adso manage to escape from the guards when the sudden death of the librarian causes panic.

The pair finds their way into a secret room within the labyrinthine library, where the aging and blind Jorge de Burgos (Feodor Chaliapin Jr.) is in possession of the book at the heart of the events: Aristotle's second book of poetics devoted to the merits of humor. De Burgos views the book as dangerously undermining proper decorum and faith. Having poisoned its pages, he is assured that those who read it will die, but William has come prepared with a glove. De Burgos snatches the book away and inadvertently starts a fire when he knocks over a candle upon his departure.

As the library goes up in flames, the peasant girl is rescued from the stake by her people, while Salvatore and Remigio burn helplessly. Gui attempts to flee, fearing that he has lost control of the situation, but the peasants upend his wagon and send him to his death. William and Adso escape the fire, and as they depart the abbey the next day, Adso bids farewell to the peasant girl, whom he still fondly remembers years later as an old man.

The film announces at the outset that it is a "palimpsest of Umberto Eco's novel." A *palimpsest* is the term used for manuscripts that have had writing scraped away so that they can be reused and written over, under which the older writing can often still be faintly seen. This was customary practice in the Middle Ages setting of the tale, when the parchment or vellum was prepared from animal skin and was relatively hardy but expensive. In other words, the film writes over the novel, a new version through which glimpses of the older version can still be seen.[1] This type of playfulness with words and how meaning is produced can be seen throughout the novel and is hinted at in the film.

In his academic writing, Eco is known for his work on semiotics, the study of signs, being anything that stands in for something else, for example, a word, a gesture, or an image. In the novel, Brother William, in effect, stands in for Eco himself, in his fascination (and ultimate frustration) with signs: "I have never doubted the truth of signs. . . . What I did not understand was the relation between signs. . . . I should have known well that there is no order in the universe"[2] Indeed, in his *Postscript to the Name of the Rose*, Eco notes that the "ingenuous reader may not even realize that this is a mystery in which very little is discovered and the detective is defeated,"[3] which is not the case in the film version.

In his review of *The Name of the Rose*, Vincent Canby of the *New York Times* suggests that the novel upon which the film is based was more "like a professor's joke," with "lengthy asides (some of which are in untranslated Latin) and incidental footnotes to history." He adds, "These cover everything from the political maneuvering within the Avignon papacy, the fight for the Holy Roman Empire and the church's merciless suppression of heresies (Waldensian, Albigensian, and Catharist, among others), to the invention of eyeglasses and gunpowder."[4] The film version cannot include the many details and digressions of life and thought in the Middle Ages, but it is able to relish the concrete visual details that can so strongly suggest the medieval.

The Name of the Rose is a European coproduction filmed partly at the twelfth-century Eberbach Monastery in Germany; on soundstages at Rome's Cinecittà Studios; and partly at an elaborate, full-scale set constructed outside of Rome. Indeed, it is truly alarming to learn of the lengths that director Jean-Jacques Annaud went to in an effort to create the material world of the monks: custom handmade manuscripts written and illustrated by monks who today ordinarily work on restoration of the original pieces; pottery copied from manuscript pictures and made in the traditional, historically correct manner; replica furniture made from solid hardwood; and undyed (and smelly) goat wool robes. Annaud argues, "If you don't go through those details, the audience would not know why it doesn't look right, but they will feel it."[5]

This is not to say that the film is entirely accurate (for example, the inquisitor Gui was a real figure, but the circumstances of his death are unknown, and even Annaud is annoyed by the film's inclusion of a very Renaissance sculpture of the Virgin Mary[6]), and the film's idea of the period conforms to film stereotypes of medieval life as "dirty, dangerous, sexy, ignorant, passionate, doomed, and so on." But as

William F. Woods notes, these stereotypes are precisely the means by which lay viewers access the medieval.[7] *The Name of the Rose* may lack the scope and action of other historical epics, and its Gothic aesthetic can become oppressive, but it succeeds in (quite literally) building an ominous vision of the past as a material world for its actors and audience to experience. DB

Notes

1. Lynn Christine Miller, "*The Name of the Rose*: Adaptation as Palimpsest," *Text and Performance Quarterly* 7, no. 2 (1987): 78.
2. Umberto Eco, *The Name of the Rose* (London: Vintage Books, 2004), 484. See also Helen T. Bennett, "Sign and De-Sign: Medieval and Modern Semiotics in Umberto Eco's *The Name of the Rose*," in *Naming the Rose: Essays on Eco's* The Name of the Rose, edited by M. Thomas Inge (Jackson and London: University Press of Mississippi, 1988), 119–29.
3. Umberto Eco, *Postscript to the Name of the Rose*, translated by William Weaver (San Diego, CA: Harcourt Brace Jovanovich, 1984), 54.
4. Vincent Canby, "Film: Medieval Mystery in *Name of the Rose*," *New York Times*, 24 September 1986, http://movies.nytimes.com/movie/review?res=9A0DE0DE153AF937A1575AC0A960948260 (25 May 2012). The sections that remain untranslated in the novel are translated in Adele J. Haft, Jane G. White, and Robert J. White, *The Key to* The Name of the Rose (Harrington Park, NJ: Ampersand Associates, 1987).
5. Julie Cohen and David Dessites, "Photo Video Journey with Jean-Jacques Annaud," *The Name of the Rose*, directed by Jean-Jacques Annaud (Warner Home Video, 2004), DVD.
6. Greta Austin, "Were the Peasants Really So Clean? The Middle Ages in Film," *Film History* 14, no. 2 (2002): 137.
7. William F. Woods, "Authenticating Realism in Medieval Film," in *The Medieval Hero on Screen: Representations from Beowulf to Buffy*, edited by Martha W. Driver and Sid Ray (Jefferson, NC: McFarland, 2004), 48.

Bibliography

Austin, Greta. "Were the Peasants Really So Clean? The Middle Ages in Film." *Film History* 14, no. 2 (2002): 136–41.

Bennett, Helen T. "Sign and De-Sign: Medieval and Modern Semiotics in Umberto Eco's *The Name of the Rose*." In *Naming the Rose: Essays on Eco's* The Name of the Rose, edited by M. Thomas Inge, 119–29. Jackson and London: University Press of Mississippi, 1988.

Canby, Vincent. "Film: Medieval Mystery in *Name of the Rose*," *New York Times*, 24 September 1986, http://movies.nytimes.com/movie/review?res=9A0DE0DE153AF937A1575AC0A960948260 (25 May 2012).

Eco, Umberto. *The Name of the Rose*. London: Vintage Books, 2004. Originally published as *Il nome della rosa*. Milano, Italy: Bompiani, 1980.

———. *Postscript to the Name of the Rose*. Translated by William Weaver. San Diego, CA: Harcourt Brace Jovanovich, 1984.

Haft, Adele J., Jane G. White, and Robert J. White. *The Key to* The Name of the Rose. Harrington Park, NJ: Ampersand Associates, 1987.

Miller, Lynn Christine. "*The Name of the Rose*: Adaptation as Palimpsest." *Text and Performance Quarterly* 7, no. 2 (1987): 77–78.

Woods, William F. "Authenticating Realism in Medieval Film." In *The Medieval Hero on Screen: Representations from Beowulf to Buffy*, edited Martha W. Driver and Sid Ray, 38–52. Jefferson, NC: McFarland, 2004.

NASHVILLE (1975)

DIRECTOR: Robert Altman
WRITER: Joan Tewkesbury
PRODUCER: Robert Altman (ABC Entertainment, American Broadcasting Company, Paramount Pictures)
CINEMATOGRAPHER: Paul Lohmann
EDITOR: Dennis M. Hill, Sidney Levin
COSTUMES: Jules Melillo
MUSIC: Arlene Barnett, Jonnie Barnett, Karen Black, Ronee Blakley, Gary Bussey, Juan Grizzle, Allan F. Nicholls, Dave Peel, Joe Raposo
CAST: Tom Frank: Keith Carradine. Connie White: Karen Black. Barbara Jean: Ronee Blakely. L. A. Joan: Shelley Duvall. Barnett: Allen Garfield. Linnea Reese: Lily Tomlin. Opal: Geraldine Chaplin. Tricycle Man: Jeff Goldblum. Hal Phillip Walker: Thomas Hal Phillips. Haven Hamilton: Henry Gibson. Frog: Richard Baskin. Mr. Green: Keenan Wynn. John Triplette: Michael Murphy. Pfc. Glenn Kelly: Scott Glenn. Tommy Brown: Timothy Brown. Albuquerque:

Barbara Harris. Sueleen Gay: Gwen Welles. Delbert Reese: Ned Beatty. Elliott Gould: Elliott Gould. Bud Hamilton: David Peel. Lady Pearl: Barbara Baxley. Mary: Cristina Raines. Bill: Allan F. Nicholls. Kenny Fraiser: David Hayward. Wade: Bob Doqui

AA: Best Music–Original Song (Keith Carradine for "I'm Easy")

AAN: Best Supporting Actress (Ronee Blakely), Best Supporting Actress (Lily Tomlin), Best Director (Robert Altman), Best Picture (Robert Altman)

DVD: Paramount Pictures, 2000

BLU-RAY: Criterion, 2013

DURATION: 159 minutes

Robert Altman calls the scenes in his film *Nashville* a "microcosm of the Hollywood syndrome."[1] Far from being critical of the city of Nashville and country music, his "objective was just to take country-western culture and the Populist kind of culture and . . . reflect American sensibilities and politics."[2] The film is "recognized as a masterpiece in its treatment of the spectacularization of American culture through an ostensible examination of the country music industry."[3]

A panorama of Nashville, it was filmed on location with no stage work. Altman's intent was to set up "events"[4] and film them live, including miking the actors to avoid rerecording the audio in a studio. Altman felt that the errors and mistakes that the camera picked up are "what the movie is about."[5] His overlapping sound tracks, with multiple babble where we are accustomed to the artifice of one character speaking at a time, typify Altman's subversion of familiar devices. Altman's "cinema technique is characterized by devices that unsettle the viewer."[6]

Altman uses three "connecting tissues" to move from event to event: Opal (Geraldine Chaplin), a BBC reporter; the rider of a three-wheeled motorcycle, "Tricycle Man" (Jeff Goldblum); as well as a campaign vehicle with large speakers on top with recorded campaign messages from independent presidential candidate Hal Phillip Walker (Thomas Hal Phillips). His messages, written to be things politicians do not say, were written and voiced by Thomas Howell.

Nashville is a musical in which all music was recorded live, similar to concert footage. The film's diegetic music plays for about an hour of the film, the songs often written by the actors themselves. The film moves to Haven Hamilton (Henry Gibson) recording a song in a studio that celebrates the centennial: "We must have been doing something right to last 200 hundred years." He finds "Frog" (Richard Baskin, the film's musical director) less than adequate and throws him out of the recording studio. Irritated, Hamilton says, "You get a haircut. You don't belong in Nashville." In another studio, Opal watches Linnea Reese (Lily Tomlin) sing with a gospel choir.

Most of the cast is in attendance when country-western star Barbara Jean's (Ronee Blakely) airplane arrives at the airport. The Tennessee Twirlers throw batons, and enthusiastic campaigners interfere with Barbara Jean and her fans as she exits the plane and speaks to the assembled crowd. Mr. Green (Keenan Wynn) arrives at the airport to pick up his niece, Martha. She tells that him she has changed her name to "L. A. Joan" (Shelley Duvall). Hamilton arrives at the airport in an open Jeep. Tom Frank (Keith Carradine), a rising rock star with the band Bill, Mary, and Tom also arrives by plane. Patterned on Loretta Lynn, Barbara Jean goes inside the airport to greet her fans but faints on her way into the building.

Once Barbara Jean is taken to the hospital, the audience races away from the parking lot, causing a crash, and vehicles pile up on the highway. Opal says, "It's America. All those cars smashing into each other." At the hospital, several people crowd into Barbara Jean's room and vie for her attention, including her husband and manager Barnett (Allen Garfield) and Hal Phillip Walker's political operative, John Triplette (Michael Murphy). When the others leave, Private First Class Glenn Kelly (Scott Glenn) watches over her because his mother had once saved her life.

At a bar, Hamilton and several others listen to the bands. Tommy Brown (Timothy Brown), a black country singer, is accused of being an "Oreo" by a man in attendance. Albuquerque (Barbara Harris) talks to Frog about cutting a demo album. The audience finds Sueleen Gay's (Gwen Welles) off-pitch singing difficult to listen to, but a bartender calls Triplette to say that he has found a girl who is "provocative."

Tom calls Linnea and tries to set up a date with her, having previously met her, but she is having dinner with her family. He calls later while he is in bed with Opal. Linnea's husband Delbert (Ned Beatty), a poor father and bumbling politico, listens to the call as he watches a pot of boiling water. She eventually agrees to see Tom perform at a bar.

Haven Hamilton holds a party at his Lincolnesque cabin outside of Nashville, where Triplette attempts to convince him to support his candidate. He finds Hamilton willing when he says, "Walker thinks you'd make a fine governor of this state. Should the time come, he'll be there with his organization." Hamilton invites Triplette to his performance that evening at the Opry. Elliott Gould visits Hamilton. While Hamilton's son Bud (David Peel) sings a song to Opal, she sees Gould and interrupts his conversation. Hamilton tells her, "I will not tolerate rudeness in the presence of a star." Then he adds, "Two stars."

Altman used three cameras to film at the "new" Opry. The event could not be reshot, so it was filmed from several angles. Hamilton performs, and then Connie White (Karen Black) takes stage. Albuquerque attempts to get backstage to make contacts for cutting her song. Hamilton sends his best wishes to Barbara Jean as she listens to the radio in her hospital room. Barbara Jean is upset by Connie White's songs, but Barnett wants to listen to the radio. They argue and he goes to a bar to "hobnob." At the bar, Hamilton's wife, Lady Pearl (Barbara Baxley), discusses the Kennedy assassinations with Opal. Hamilton gives Triplette key information he needs to convince him to appear on the stage with Walker. Connie White and Barbara Jean will not appear on the same stage, but Haven will perform on any stage where Barbara Jean performs.

A panorama of Nashville scenes reveals the characters in various locations. Delbert Reese and his children attend a church where Hamilton is singing in the choir, while Linnea attends a black church and sings with its choir. Barbara Jean sings from her wheelchair at a small church with Private First Class Kelly and Mr. Green in attendance. At a racetrack, Albuquerque sings and dances while cars race around the track. Few can hear her, including Hamilton, Lady Pearl, and Tommy Brown. Mary (Cristina Raines) is in bed with Tom. She tells him she loves him, but he does not respond. The next day, Mary and Bill (Allan F. Nicholls) fight. Triplette visits them to offer them a spot in the gala. Mary says, "We can't vote for him because we're registered Democrats."

When Barbara Jean leaves the hospital, she is followed by dozens of people, some carrying horseshoes of flowers that were in her room. Mr. Green arrives and is told that his wife expired while he was absent.

Kenny Fraiser (David Hayward) walks by Walker's campaign headquarters and then rents a room from Mr. Green. He later calls his mother while L. A. Joan walks around him in her underwear. Not interested in her seduction attempt, he tells her not to touch his fiddle case.

Barbara Jean sings to an audience from a stage built to look like a riverboat. She tells rambling stories, strikes up the band to start a song, and then rambles again. The audience reacts negatively to Barnett taking her off stage. He announces that they can see Barbara Jean for free at the Parthenon in Centennial Park. He is forced to join the political rally. He sets rules with Triplette that she is not to be associated with Walker in any way.

Linnea is sitting at a back table waiting to see Tom perform. When he arrives onstage, he surprises Bill and Mary by saying, "I used to be part of a trio," yet he invites them onstage for a song. Tom plays his song "I'm Easy" (winner of the Academy Award for Best Music–Original Song). Half a dozen women in the audience, having been in bed with him recently, believe he is singing to them. He directs his song to Linnea, and she falls to his seduction.

Meanwhile, Sueleen sings her provocative song to a crowd of male Walker supporters, who expect her to start stripping immediately. She attempts to sing a song by her favorite singer, Barbara Jean, but they push her to "take it off." She wants to leave, and Triplette and Barnett realize that they did not make it clear to her what they required. Triplette tells her she can sing at the Parthenon if she strips. She insists, "I'm going to be as big of a star as Barbara Jean." She strips and leaves the stage, embarrassed and frustrated. Delbert takes her home. She talks to her friend Wade (Bob Doqui) about having to strip. He says, "That's dreadful. You can't sing. I wish you'd give it up. They're going to walk on your soul. They're going to kill you in this town." Unconvinced, she invites him to see her perform at the Parthenon.

In bed, Linnea and Tom, the most narcissistic of womanizers, listen to his song play on a reel-to-reel tape. She teaches him how to sign "I love you." He calls another woman before she leaves the room.

At the Parthenon, Walker's motorcade arrives. Although Barnett objects to the Walker banner on stage, Barbara Jean performs with Hamilton. Each of the film's characters move through the crowd or go onstage. Kenny tries to keep Mr. Green from looking for L. A. Joan in the big crowd. Green is angry that she never paid her any respect. As Barbara Jean sings "My Idaho Home," Kenny unlocks his violin case, removes a gun, and shoots her. Private First Class Kelly grabs him. Barbara Jean is killed, and Hamilton is hit in the shoulder. Hamilton takes the microphone and says, "This is Nashville. They can't do this to us in Nashville. . . . Somebody sing. Sing." He hands the microphone to Albuquerque, and Barbara Jean is carried off. Albuquerque rises to the occasion and sings, "It don't worry me. You may say I ain't free, but it don't worry me." Linnea's gospel choir joins in. Sueleen stands onstage, stunned that her hero has been shot and killed. Wade's words prove to be too true. Private First Class Kelly leaves, disappointed that he failed to save Barbara Jean's life.

As Hassan Melehy states, the "movie's various narratives converge in the surprise of an allegorized retelling of the Kennedy assassination. This cinematic death does anything but heal the trauma, but rather in classically traumatic fashion repeats the event."[7] JMW

Notes

1. Robert Altman, "Audio Commentary," *Nashville*, directed by Robert Altman (Paramount Pictures, 2000), DVD.

2. Altman, "Audio Commentary."

3. Hassan Melehy, "Narratives of Politics and History in the Spectacle of Culture: Robert Altman's *Nashville*." *Scope: An Online Journal of Film and TV*

Studies 13, www.scope.nottingham.ac.uk/article .php?issue=13&id=1097 (27 September 2013).

4. Altman, "Audio Commentary."

5. Altman, "Audio Commentary."

6. Maurice Yacowar, "Actors as Conventions in the Films of Robert Altman," *Cinema Journal* 20, no. 1 (1980): 14.

7. Melehy, "Narratives of Politics and History in the Spectacle of Culture."

Bibliography

Melehy, Hassan. "Narratives of Politics and History in the Spectacle of Culture: Robert Altman's *Nashville*," *Scope: An Online Journal of Film and TV Studies* 13, www.scope.nottingham.ac.uk/article .php?issue=13&id=1097 (27 September 2013).

Yacowar, Maurice. "Actors as Conventions in the Films of Robert Altman." *Cinema Journal* 20, no. 1 (1980): 14–27.

THE NEW WORLD (2005)

DIRECTOR: Terrence Malick
WRITER: Terrence Malick
PRODUCER: Sarah Green (New Line Cinema)
CINEMATOGRAPHER: Emmanuel Lubezki
EDITORS: Richard Chew, Hank Convin, Saar Klein, Mark Yoshikawa
MUSIC: James Horner
CAST: Capt. John Smith: Collin Farrell. Pocahontas: Q'orianka Kilcher. Capt. Newport: Christopher Plummer. John Rolfe: Christian Bale. Chief Powhatan: August Schellenberg. Opechancanough: Wes Studi. Edward Wingfield: David Thewlis. Samuel Argall: Yorick van Wageningen. Ben: Ben Mendelsohn. Tomocomo: Raoul Trujillo. Lewes: Brian F. Byrne. Nonoma: Irene Berard. Thomas Savage: John Savage. King James I/VI: Jonathan Price. Queen Anne: Alexandra W. B. Malick
AA: None
AAN: Best Cinematography (Emmanuel Lubezki)
NATIONAL BOARD OF REVIEW AWARD: Best Performance by a Breakthrough Actress (Q'orianka Kilcher)
DVD: New Line Home Video, 2005. Extended director's cut released in 2008.
BLU-RAY: New Line Home Video, 2009
DURATION: 135 minutes (172 for extended cut)

Terrence Malick produced few films in the four decades preceding *The New World*, among them the critically acclaimed *Badlands* (1973), *Days of Heaven* (1978), and *The Thin Red Line* (1998). *The New World* was produced after a failed attempt to film the life of Che Guevara, and it did poorly at the box office, barely recouping the $30 million investment of producing it; however, it did well in South America, especially in Argentina, where it netted nearly $60 million. Despite it's rough inception, the film has gained in reputation in recent years, as it has been chosen among the fifty best films of the decade.[1] *The New World* is important not so much as a historical document, but as a poetic retelling of the story of Pocahontas and her role in the fortunes of the first colonists in Virginia, starting with the expedition in 1607 and continuing to the death of Pocahontas a few decades later. It is also important because it marks another "comeback" by Terrence Malick, whose prolonged absences from the screen—but unchanged style—have befuddled his critics and audiences.

The film adroitly avoids direct explicitness as to what exactly happens between Pocahontas (played by fourteen-year-old Q'orianka Kilcher) and Captain John Smith (Collin Farrell) and says enough to underscore the fact that she was his savior when his life was threatened and that she also saved the remnants of the colony from starvation the first winter they were there. The film belongs almost entirely to her, showing her as an intelligent child (the actual Pocahontas was no more than twelve when Smith first met her) who grew up to be a young woman of consequence, almost an ambassador between her race and the invading representatives of the English Crown. She is gentle; understanding; loving, as much or more than a Christian, to her fellow men and women; and quick to learn English and adapt to the ways of the colony. She does not marry Smith—at she least does not have a completely clear understanding of what that entails—but when she visits England, invited by the king, she does accept the offer of the character played by Christian Bale, John Rolfe, and becomes his wife and bears him a son, before she dies on their way back to America.

The film shows her as more of a mother figure, despite her extreme youth, than a lover of creatures of the wild, for she exhibits both civilized tendencies, or the ability to adapt and merge with the conquerors, and the ability to provide a new breed for the conquerors of her land. She is a princess who behaves royally, so to speak, for she comprehends that the new people she sees are not mere conquerors of her land and intruders and usurpers of her thrones, as others in her tribe see them, but new friends who could earn their rights to be here through hard labor and battling against enormous odds. She has no biases, something extraordinary for such a young person. She is a pacifist who believes that violence will not solve anything and that people are basically the same no matter whether bred in the wild or in civilized towns. Pocahontas—that name is never mentioned in the film—is the earth mother, the generation that will bring a new age and the fertility goddess of the new land. Sexual but not sexy, she is played with extraordinary grace by Kilcher, whose sexuality, but not any promiscuous tendencies, elevated her to the throne of matriarch of a new race of men and women.

Malick's film is directed more as a poetic, even lyrical, ballad of the adventures of these colonists. It avoids excessive violence, although enough is given (without the obligatory graphic gore) in the several skirmishes between the natives—the Naturals, as they are called—and the desperate colonists. The camera synthesizes shots of wild nature with action nearly in slow motion, achieving a rhythm and flow that avoids abrupt transitions or cuts, as if it were not in a hurry to tell us the story, but to create in us a mood to watch and revel in the beauty unfolding before our eyes. Filmed less than ten miles from the actual locations where these events occurred, near the James River, *The New World* is authentic history viewed through the telescope of time, brought to modernity without being trivialized by the tendency of today's storytellers to deconstruct or be overly specific about events that remain unclear. This is imagined, rather than "real" history, a story told with fidel ity of sentiment rather than tedious footnoting of events. We do not hear the names of those participating in the story, although presumably we know who they are. It is almost like an abstract painting, told photographically rather than as exposition. The music of James Horner gives it an aura of a tone poem, enriched by classic themes from Richard Wagner and Wolfgang Amadeus Mozart.[2] We understand what we see; we know how the New World was created—imaginatively, not historically. Like Walt Whitman, Terrence Malick gives us a wide vista in broad strokes and in the process reveals—in one of the most prosaic scenes of the film—that this was the land of promise, a Garden of Eden, with its knowledge of good and evil waiting to be given to those daring to conquer it.

Pocahontas remains a true princess, the real mother of America, and perhaps one should see her statue (and that of John Smith, her sponsor) in Virginia, near where the events described occurred. This film offers an alternative, for it is a minor paean to her humility, creativeness, and glory. CS

Notes

1. *TimeOut* editors, "The TONY Top 50 Movies of the Decade," *TimeOut*, 25 November 2009, www.timeout.com/newyork/film/the-tony-top-50-movies-of-the-decade (27 September 2013).

2. Wagner's *Das Rheingold*, and Mozart's sections of Piano Concerto No. 23 are played on the sound track, along with the song "Listen to the Wind," composed by Horner and Henry Westenra.

Bibliography

Sterritt, David. "Film, Philosophy, and Terrence Malick." *Undercurrents* 2, www.fipresci.org/undercurrent/issue_0206/sterritt_malick.htm (27 September 2013).

TimeOut editors. "The TONY Top 50 Movies of the Decade." *TimeOut*, 25 November 2009, www.timeout.com/newyork/film/the-tony-top-50-movies-of-the-decade (27 September 2013).

A NIGHT TO REMEMBER (1958)

DIRECTOR: Roy Ward Baker
WRITER: Earl St. John. Based on the book by Walter Lord.
PRODUCER: William MacQuitty (Rank Organization)
CINEMATOGRAPHER: Geoffrey Unsworth
EDITOR: Sidney Hayers
ART DIRECTION: Alex Vetchinsky
MUSIC: William Alwyn
CAST: Second Officer Charles Herbert Lightoller: Kenneth More. Capt. Arthur Rostron: Anthony Bushell. Capt. Edward John Smith: Laurence Naismith. Thomas Andrews: Michael Goodliffe. J. Bruce Ismay: Frank Lawton. Col. Archibald Gracie: James Dyrenforth. First Officer William Murdock: Richard Leech. Wireless Operator John Phillips: Kenneth Griffith. Assistant Wireless Operator Harold Bride: David McCallum. Margaret "Molly" Brown: Tucker McGuire. Charles Joughin, "The Baker": George Rose. Robbie Lucas "Father of Three": John Merivale. Mrs. Liz Lucas: Honor Blackman. Capt. Stanley Lord: Russell Napier
AA: None
AAN: None
GG: Best Foreign Film
DVD: Criterion, 1998
BLU-RAY: Criterion, 2012
DURATION: 132 minutes

While James Cameron's *Titanic* (1997) broke records in box-office revenues[1] and garnered eleven Oscars, equaling the number earned by *Ben-Hur* in 1959, the film that comes closest to the historical truth of the famous sinking of the world's great liner is *A Night to Remember*, made in 1958. Its makers claimed that *A Night to Remember* depicts the events more accurately than other films telling this story, and the 2012 Blu-ray Criterion Collection edition, in a new digital restoration, with a variety of extra materials, helped revive this film as the most accurate depiction of the 1912 sinking that shook the world.[2]

A Night to Remember is as compelling as any docudrama that describes this extraordinary event. It is devoid of the excess baggage that characterizes Cameron's more modern counterpart, *Titanic*, which treats the sinking of the great ship as the backdrop for a romance between stars Leonardo DiCaprio and Kate Winslet, two star-crossed lovers, who put on a glittering Hollywood extravaganza but sideline the main event, which was the drama of the of the naval catastrophe. *A Night to Remember* was filmed in the Pinewood Studios in England, and its producers took unusual steps to achieve authenticity at every level, securing the best story, script writing, direction, camera work, and art direction. Producer William MacQuitty claims that the reproduction of the ship's interiors was accurate in every way and that he had the middle section of the ship built on the lot, on a cement basis that still exists, using 4,000 tons of steel.[3] Actors were recruited from the best Britain had to offer at that time, and despite the absence of big names in the cast, this meticulous production remains the most authentic and compelling of any on the subject, before or since.

The action is lean and to the point, not allowing the story line to be sidetracked by subplots or other minutiae that could interfere with the main story. The episodes are organically connected, having to do with only one thing, the unexpected and shocking conclusion of the large ship's maiden voyage. The touching stories of a young man in the steerage section courting a young woman of a different foreign group despite her mother's objections, of a father who has to give precedence in the rescue boat to his young wife and three children, of a young couple who refuse to separate and prefer to die together, these and other small incidents like them are stories connected to the main idea, thus enhancing the plot and enlivening dramatization. Various themes are interwoven into the plot, all related to the event itself.

In his lengthy commentary, MacQuitty offers the explanation that what attracted him to the sinking of *Titanic* as a film project is what he calls the "end of an era," the tearing down of the artificial walls that separated the "steerage" groups, whose tickets cost only twelve pounds, while the aristocratic class paid a whopping 875 pounds apiece, and that for the privilege of displaying their fine clothes, and thus showing their superiority over the common run of humanity. The film, however, adroitly avoids the onus of social critique, for, although the sinking exposed the arrogance of those who traveled on the ship and the ineptitude of those who managed it, the responsibility for the disaster was shared and collective, and not the result of any particular factor. The arrogance of even thinking that a man-made machine could conquer the forces of nature under any circumstances, that a floating palace, no matter how large, could be "unsinkable," that the belief that nothing is impossible if talented humans set their minds on achieving—that is the underlying theme that the assembled parts of the movie subtly reveal.

This was indeed a collective failure, not just the "luck of the draw," although luck had a hand in it. Human providence, however, especially when the stakes are high, is nothing but a deliberate design to forestall bad luck—especially in an age when technology makes succeeding against all the odds quite attainable. Still, there seems to be a puzzling dilemma in calculating the odds, as the disasters of the shuttles *Challenger* and *Columbia* later in the twentieth century (including the 2003 disaster) demonstrate. How accurately can this be done? In a film made in the 1960s, *Fate Is the Hunter* (Ralph Nelson, 1964), an investigation of a plane crash reveals the cause of the crash as a cup of coffee spilling onto wires next to the pilot's seat, and the cause is removed by making certain that no coffee cups could be placed there again, but the final implication is that no matter how many precautions one takes, plane crashes will always occur—and they have since then. Should we then surrender, fatalistically, to the possibility of another crash (it's only a matter of time), or another sinking?

To its credit, *A Night to Remember* avoids naïveté by carefully assembling all the clues, or as many as possible, to show in some detail the causes of the disaster, and letting them speak for themselves. For one thing, wireless, which had just started being used in large liners, was not fully utilized, was not taken seriously, and the employees working the wireless were at the bottom of the scale in pay. Philips, the wireless operator of the *Titanic*, had been receiving messages of ice ahead but thought that those didn't matter and failed to report them to the captain. The astonished viewer of then and of today sees this as criminal negligence or dereliction of duty.

Captain Smith himself (played very well by Laurence Naismith), although aware of the ice danger ahead, casually inspects the steering section of the bridge and then goes to sleep, only to be awakened when it is too late. Most importantly, the *Californian*, having stopped because of the proximity of ice, ignores the distress signals of the *Titanic*, its captain showing a callous indifference when awakened, which any sensible viewer would find astounding. Of course, bad luck is also a factor: the *Carpathia*, the ship that had received the wireless signals and whose responsible captain was racing to the rescue, was more than four hours away, arriving too late. These ironies—and the complexity of the causes—are admirably captured by the writer and director of *A Night to Remember*, a film of unmatched skill and substance, relating the events with an icy (no pun intended) objectivity that yet warms the heart.

The film also shows heroism of large dimensions: the second officer, Charles Lightoller, played by Kenneth More, the only recognizable name in the cast, is a dedicated, masterful organizer in whose hands the rescue operation succeeds, to save hundreds of lives. But even he interprets the order "women and children first" to mean "women and children only," thus causing many lifeboats, capable of carrying as many as sixty people, to be only partly filled. Many more lives could have been saved. Thomas Andrews (Michael Goodliffe), the designer of *Titanic*, who is aboard, warns the captain early enough of the inevitability of sinking and the shortness of time remaining. The captain himself recovers and directs activities with as much common sense and professionalism as can be possible under the circumstances. The heroic musicians play tunes to the end. There is little panic among passengers, considering the circumstances, and although many more lives could have been saved by filling the lifeboats to capacity, the rescue itself shows the human being overcoming the knowledge and distress of doom, and most die as heroes rather than cowards—all now equalized by the threat of death—and that is something of a plus in the human condition.

In his book *A Night to Remember* (1955), Walter Lord remarks that, "The 46,328-ton *Titanic* sailed under hopelessly outdated safety regulations."[4] It carried only sixteen lifeboats, and not all of them were filled to capacity, thus of the 2,028 passengers, only 750 were saved, most of them of the first or second class, while 1,278, mostly from the steerage class, perished. The wireless operators, overtaxed with sending individual messages from passengers, did not pay enough attention to ice warnings received from the *Californian*, while the officers in the latter ship, only ten miles away, did not heed the SOS signals and rockets fired from *Titanic*. The disaster brought about new, rigorous regulations for navigation: ice warnings were taken seriously, while the United States and Great Britain took precautions for the sailing ships in that part of the Atlantic by establishing ice patrols and Coast Guard vessels to keep an eye on iceberg movements. Today's precautions are in line with developed technology, and wireless operators are on the alert twenty-four hours a day. Above all, the idea that any ship is "unsinkable" was dropped from the naval vocabulary, as man became conscious of the unceasing battle of man versus nature. The *Titanic*'s sinking was an avoidable disaster, a tragic event largely attributed to human hubris. CS

Notes

1. It eventually broke world records, hitting the $1 billion mark and later the $2 billion mark, worldwide.
2. *Titanic* (1953) was a film that preceded it. A German movie called *Titanic* was made in 1943. Some footage from it is used in *A Night to Remember.*
3. William MacQuitty, "The Making of *A Night to Remember*," *A Night to Remember*, directed by Roy Ward Baker (Criterion, 1998), DVD. See also the audio commentary by Don Lynch and Ken Marschall, author and illustrator, respectively, of *Titanic: An Illustrated History.*
4. Walter Lord, *A Night to Remember* (New York: St. Martin's Griffin, 2005), 88. Originally published in New York: Holt, 1955.

Bibliography

Lord, Walter. *A Night to Remember.* New York: St. Martin's Griffin, 2005. Originally published in New York: Holt, 1955.

Lynch, Donald, and Ken Marschall. *Titanic: An Illustrated History.* New York: Hyperion, 1992.

O

ONCE UPON A TIME IN AMERICA (1984)

DIRECTOR: Sergio Leone
WRITERS: Leonardo Benvenuti, Piero De Bernardi, Enrico Medioli, Franco Arcalli, Franco Ferrini, Sergio Leone. Based on the novel *The Hoods*, by Harry Goldberg.
PRODUCERS: Claudio Mancini, Arnon Milchan (Ladd Company, Embassy National Pictures, PSO International)
CINEMATOGRAPHER: Tonino Delli Colli
EDITOR: Nino Baragli
MUSIC: Ennio Morricone
CAST: David "Noodles" Aaronson: Robert De Niro. Maximilian "Max" Bercovicz: James Woods. Deborah Gelly: Elizabeth McGovern. Frankie Manoldi: Joe Pesci. Young Deborah: Jennifer Connelly. Eve: Darlanne Fluegel. Fat Moe Gelly: Larry Rapp. Philip "Cockeye" Stein: William Forsythe. Patrick "Patsy" Goldberg: James Hayden. Sgt. P. Halloran: Bruce Bahrenburg. Young Noodles: Scott Schutzman Tiler. Young Patsy: Brian Bloom. Young Cockeye: Adrian Curran. Dominic: Noah Moazezi. Bugsy: James Russo. Officer "Fartface" Whitey: Richard Foronji. Young Max/David Bailey: Rusty Jacobs. Peggy: Amy Ryder. Young Peggy: Julie Cohen. Al Capuano: Clem Caserta. Young Fat Moe: Mike Monetti. Detroit Joe: Burt Young. Carol: Tuesday Weld. James Conway O'Donnell: Treat Williams. Chicken Joe: Richard Bright. Crowning: Gerard Murphy. Police Chief Vincent Aiello: Danny Aiello. Sharkey: Robert Harper
AA: None
AAN: None
DVD: Warner Home Video, 2011
BLU-RAY: Warner Home Video, 2011
DURATION: 229 minutes

Inspired by the book *The Hoods*, by Harry Goldberg, director Sergio Leone said he spent most of his adult life making this film about Jewish mobsters in the United States. When he first spoke to Arnon Milchan about the story, Leone told it frame by frame and in real time. The outline for the film was 200-plus pages.[1] Milchan says the film "took a year to prepare, eleven months to shoot six days a week, and another year to postproduce." He adds, "It had 152 speaking parts. We rented the Orient Express for one shot. We had one shot in Paris, one shot in Venice [Italy]. Every single costume was handpicked. I remember telling Sergio, 'Who will know the difference?' He said, 'The screen smells and breathes.'"[2] Leone planned every detail of the film, demonstrating to his actors how to play their roles, and even playing Morricone's film score on the set while they were recording the film. "Leone later told *American Film* that the tale [was] 'a perfect and loving hymn to the cinema [and that he] wanted to make that film and no other.'"[3]

The first version of the film previewed in Boston and New York ran 260 minutes, but after a poor response the "film's U.S. distributor, The Ladd Company, pared the film down to 143 minutes."[4] American critics panned the shortened film. As critic Richard Schiekel observes, the film was "easy to cut. Not easy to replace."[5] Leone later released a 227-minute version at Cannes, and upon seeing it, "many critics rereviewed the film, acknowledging that the studio-edited version seemed like a completely different picture. Comparing the two versions, *New Yorker* film critic Pauline Kael wrote, 'I don't think I've ever seen a worse case of mutilation.'"[6] There were three versions released in the United States, two shortened versions and one in which the time sequence is arranged chronologically and makes little sense because the transitional moments no longer match. A fully restored 269-minute version is available only in Italy.

The film covers three time periods, childhood (1923), the period just prior to prohibition (1931–1932), and the modern (1968). The film opens in 1932; an instrumental version of "America the Beautiful" plays as the camera reveals bullet holes, in the shape of a body, in a mattress. Men from Frankie Manoldi's (Joe Pesci) National Syndicate are questioning Eve (Darlanne Fluegel) about the location of her lover, "Noodles" (Robert De Niro), who betrayed his friends. She is shot when she says she does not know. The men visit Fat Moe Gelly (Larry Rapp) in a room behind his restaurant. They bloody him until he tells them that Noodles is at Chun Lo's Chinese Theater. They enter the theater, checking each man in the audience. David "Noodles" Aaronson is behind the theater screen in the opium den. There, an attendant is serving him soup and delivers a newspaper with the report of bootleggers killed by the Feds, friends he betrayed.

A phone next to Noodles rings and does not stop ringing for several minutes as the scene transitions through a lamp flame to a rain-soaked street, where Noodles walks past three men on stretchers—Patrick "Patsy" Goldberg (James Hayden), Philip "Cockeye" Stein (William Forsythe), and Max Bercovicz (James Woods)—although Max's body is burnt beyond recognition. As the phone continues to ring, the film cuts back to Noodles calling Sergeant P. Halloran (Bruce Bahrenburg) to turn in his friends. An attendant at the den warns Noodles that men are hunting for him. He runs to Moe's restaurant, enters the building, and calls the elevator down. The man guarding Moe watches the elevator rise again, but Noodles takes the stairs and shoots the man in the head from behind. Noodles wants to go to Eve, but Moe warns him that they were already there. Noodles takes a key from a tall-case clock and visits a train station locker. Inside is a briefcase filled with newspapers—not what he expected. He rechecks the locker. He walks to the ticket desk and takes the first available train to Buffalo.

In 1968, while an instrumental version of John Lennon and Paul McCartney's "Yesterday" plays, Noodles arrives in New York. Noodles visits Moe and returns the key. Noodles had been summoned by a mysterious invitation, but Moe knows nothing about it. Still in love with Moe's sister, Deborah (Elizabeth McGovern), Noodles is told she is now a big star. Noodles goes to the restroom and opens a peephole above the toilet. He remembers seeing young Deborah practice dancing in the restaurant storeroom.

The film flashes back to young Noodles (Scott Schutzman Tiler) looking through the hole. Young Deborah (Jennifer Connelly in her first film appearance) is determined to transcend her life. She flashes him but then tells her father to spray for cockroaches. He follows her into a busy city street filled with hundreds of people at open-market stalls and dozens of horse-drawn wagons and cars. He follows her asking, "Who are you calling a cockroach?" She says, "Go look at yourself."

The gang, young Patsy (Brian Bloom), young Cockeye (Adrian Curran), and Dominic (Noah Moazezi), arrives; their boss, Bugsy (James Russo), wants them to retaliate against a newsstand vendor who has not paid for protection. They set fire to the newsstand and attempt to pick up their pay at Bugsy's bar. They must choose between their pay or rolling a drunk. They choose the drunk and follow him outside, but Officer "Fartface" Whitey (Richard Foronji) walks onto the street at the same moment. The boys attempt to block his view with a passing wagon filled with furniture, but young Max (Rusty Jacobs), who is sitting on the wagon, pulls the man onto the wagon and takes his watch. Max climbs on top of the furniture into a chair, as if he is on a throne. Throughout the film, Cockeye plays the pan flute, used as diegetic music, which is integrated into Morricone's haunting film score.

Back home, young Noodles avoids his parents by reading Jack London's *Martin Eden* in a bathroom shared by several apartments. Young Peggy (Julie Cohen) enters the unlocked bathroom. She opens her robe for him but refuses to go further, requiring payment of a Charlotte Russe. Later, Noodles finds Max as he is unloading a large-format camera from the wagon. He uses it to take Noodles' photo. Noodles steals the pocket watch out of Max's pocket, but Fartface catches him and confiscates it. A lifelong alliance between Max and Noodles begins. Noodles and Max photograph Fartface having sex with Peggy on a rooftop. Using the negative to blackmail him, he is forced to give them the same deal he gives Bugsy. They take the watch back and begin working for themselves.

During Pesach, Deborah walks through neighborhood celebrants content and happy. Although her father says that she should not "let the goyim in," she allows Noodles to follow her into the storeroom. Clearing apples away so he can sit, although he sits away from her, she reads him the Song of Solomon and compares him unfavorably to the descriptions. He attempts to kiss her but hears Max yelling for him. Deborah says, "Go on. Run. Your mother is calling you." Max splits up money with him from a recent job, but Bugsy and his men arrive. They are brutally beaten; Noodles returns to Deborah, his face bloodied, but she keeps him locked out.

Noodles and the gang move into the bootlegging business when they visit Al Capuano (Clem Caserta) to sell him a system Noodles created to rescue liquor thrown into the bay during Coast Guard searches. The bottles are stored in a crate tied below a buoy but tied above a large bag of salt. As salt dissolves, the crate rises to the surface. Their first attempt proves successful. They row into a foggy harbor and find their buoys. Max and Noodles hug and then fall into the water, but when Noodles surfaces, he does not immediately find Max because he pretends to drown. They take a briefcase to the train station locker. They swear to put 50 percent of their takes into a shared fund. Fat Moe will keep the key to the locker, only giving it back when they are together, not knowing what it unlocks. They are caught on the street by Bugsy. He shoots Dominic, the youngest of the gang, in the back. As Noodles holds him, Dominic says, "Noodles, I slipped." Noodles stabs Bugsy as two mounted policemen ride up. One attempts to stop Noodles, but he is stabbed as well. Arrested, Noodles is taken to a reformatory as Max, Patsy, Cockeye, and young Fat Moe (Mike Monetti) watch from across the street. Noodles serves nine years.

Old Noodles is standing at an expensive mausoleum. Inside are the sarcophagi of his three friends. A key hangs from a plaque that is inscribed, "Erected to their everlasting memory by their friend and brother David Aaronson 'Noodles' 1967." The key opens a locker with a case full of money and a note that reads, "Advance payment for your next job." He walks under a bridge and a Frisbee almost hits him in the head. No explanation for the Frisbee is given or the hand that catches it, but the 269-minute version of the film probably clarifies the transition from this scene to Max taking Noodles' suitcase as he leaves prison in 1931.

Now an adult, Noodles leaves prison with just the suitcase. Max picks him up in a hearse, part of the gang's liquor business, and takes him to a back alley door behind Fat Moe's restaurant. Patsy, Cockeye, and Fat Moe welcome him back and introduce him to the "Scotch heating" plumbing that pipes in liquor. Peggy (Amy Ryder) runs the brothel allied to the speakeasy. He sees Deborah at the bar. She invites him to Broadway, where he can spy on her every night. Max calls him away. Deborah says, "Your mother is calling."

Max introduces Noodles to Frankie Manoldi and Detroit Joe (Burt Young). Joe offers them a heist of diamonds coming from Detroit and planned to be shipped to Holland. While they are robbing the business in masks, Carol (Tuesday Weld), their inside person, tells Noodles that he must hit her. She enjoys being beaten, and Noodles rapes her. They meet Detroit Joe and his men near disused docks. Patsy walks to their car and exchanges stones for payment. He kills Joe by shooting him in the eye through his jeweler's loupe. Max and Cockeye shoot the car with machine guns. One man escapes and runs into a factory. He is shot by Noodles in a blizzard of down. As they drive away, Noodles is angry. He did not know the plan to betray Joe for Frankie Manoldi. Noodles decides that they should go for a swim with the car and drives off a dock.

Their gang begins working for hire for the highest bidder, including unions. They rescue James Conway O'Donnell (Treat Williams), known as Jimmy "Clean Hands," a young labor organizer about to be burned alive by Chicken Joe (Richard Bright), one of mobster Crowning's (Gerard Murphy) men.

Police chief Vincent Aiello (Danny Aiello), who has been bribed to squash union strikes, visits the hospital where his wife delivered their first boy of four children. There, the gang switches the identity tags on some of the babies. Excited to see his baby boy, Aiello opens his baby's diaper and realizes it is a girl. The room's phone rings; it is Noodles calling from Peggy's brothel. He explains that Aiello's son is still in the maternity ward, but if Aiello switches to their side they will let him know which child is his. They plan to give him a random tag number because Patsy lost the actual switch list. They see Carol, who is now at the brothel, and her husband watches through a peephole. Cockeye quips, "Beats the hell out of the movies." The men pull handkerchiefs over their faces. She says one she got to know personally, so they pull down their pants so she can decide who it was. Max is attracted to her and pulls her close. She tries to bring Noodles into the clutch, but he pushes her hand away. He leaves for a date with Deborah, something he has waited for his entire life.

For the special dinner, Noodles has reopened a hotel on the Jersey Shore that had been closed for the season. Deborah admits that he is the only person she has ever cared about but that he would keep her from accomplishing her goals. She asks him to dance to music from a small orchestra. Later they sit on the beach, where he tells her his two most important memories: Dominic's last words and her. He quotes the Song of Solomon and promises, "Nobody's gonna love you the way I'd love you." She surprises him when she says she plans to leave for Hollywood the next day. She kisses him in the car; Noodles brutally rapes her as the car drives to their destination. The next morning, Noodles watches Deborah leave on a train bound for Los Angeles.

Noodles meets the gang. Max is sitting on a pope's throne he purchased. Moe gives Noodles a cup of coffee, which he continues to stir, and he sits quietly. Max explains that while Noodles has been in the opium den stoned and calling for "Deborah," they were working with the union. Even Jimmy "Clean Hands" respects them. Although they had agreed that "broads do not get in the way," Carol is there. When Noodles challenges this, Max kicks her out. Jimmy calls for their help because he was nearly killed by Chicken Joe. The gang kills Chicken Joe, Crowning, and his body guards. The guys celebrate with Jimmy, who has been crippled, in his hospital room. Sharkey (Robert Harper), Jimmy's lawyer and their go-between, suggests that they move into the trucking business because prohibition is ending. Max likes the idea, but Noodles refuses. When Sharkey suggests that Max dump Noodles, Max says he and Noodles should go swimming.

They go swimming in Florida, where Max considers hitting the Federal Reserve Bank in Manhattan. Noodles says, "You're really crazy," which enrages him. Back in New York, Carol asks Noodles to make Max drop the idea because he would be killed in the attempt. If he cannot talk him out of it, then he should betray him, even if it means going to jail. The night before the robbery, they hold a wake for Prohibition at the speakeasy. Max, Cockeye, and Patsy drink to the "demise of Fat Moe's speakeasy." Noodles goes into another room and calls Sgt. Halloran to tip him off about the Federal Reserve robbery. This is the phone call he places at the beginning of the movie. After he hangs up, Max enters. Sensing Noodles' reluctance, he says, "Maybe I should just dump you." Noodles says, "You're really crazy." Max knocks him out.

Returning to 1969, Noodles meets Carol at her retirement home. She says Max wanted to die because he started shooting first. Noodles visits Deborah backstage after watching her star in *Antony and Cleopatra*, the first time they have seen one another since he raped her. He wants to see if she did the right thing in turning him down and ask if he should attend a party he was invited to at the residence of Secretary Bailey. Saying that Bailey was in political trouble, she suggests tearing up the invitation. As he leaves, Deborah introduces him to Secretary Bailey's son, David (Rusty Jacobs, the same actor who plays Young Max), saying "his name's David, just like yours."

Noodles enters Bailey's Long Island mansion and is taken upstairs. Although Bailey is revealed to be a still-living Max, Noodles pretends as if he is Bailey. Noodles' contract is to kill him. Holding the pocket watch, Max says, "I took away your life from you. . . . I left you thirty-five years of grief." Noodles responds, "Many years ago I had a dear friend. I turned him in to save his life." Noodles exits the mansion grounds, where a Mack garbage truck is waiting. A person resembling Max follows him, but the truck drives between them. The man disappears, perhaps into the truck's garbage grinder. Vintage cars from the 1930s drive by carrying flappers on their way to a 1968 costume party[7] as Kate Smith's "God Bless America" plays.

In an interview, James Woods says he does not know if Max jumps into the garbage truck, but "we know he's not going to show up in the future."[8] Noodles is then shown back at the opium den in 1932, behind the screen of the Chinese shadow play, smoking opium. Filmed from above, he looks at the sheer fabric hanging over him, as if it is a movie screen. He closes his eyes, and the film freezes on his ecstatic smile.

The ending reveals that the sequences from 1968 are an opium dream. Noodles regrets Dominic's death, raping Deborah, betraying the gang, and their deaths. He escapes by swimming in an opium haze, which "wipes out memories, strife, mistakes . . . and time."[9] Max has shown his ability to rise after death, and Noodles dreams he rises again. In a note to the screenwriters and production staff, Leone writes, "it is this unrealistic vein that interests me most, the vein of the fable, though a fable for our own times and told in our own terms. And, above all, the aspects of hallucination, or a dream-journey, induced by the opium with which the film begins and ends, like a haven and a refuge."[10] JMW

Notes

1. Arnon Milchan, *Once Upon a Time: Sergio Leone*, directed by Howard Hill (Warner Home Video, 2011), DVD.
2. Jill Kipnis, "Picture This," *Billboard*, 14 June 2003, 61.
3. Kipnis, "Picture This," 61.
4. Quoted in Rachael Bosley, "Wrap Shot," *American Cinematographer* 84, no. 1 (2003): 144.
5. Richard Schiekel, "Film Commentary," *Once Upon a Time in America*, directed by Sergio Leone (Warner Home Video, 2011), DVD.
6. Bosley, "Wrap Shot,"144.
7. Stuart Kaminsky, "Narrative Time in Sergio Leone's *Once Upon a Time in America*," *Studies in the Literary Imagination* 16, no. 1 (1983): 72.
8. James Woods, *Once Upon a Time: Sergio Leone*, directed by Howard Hill (Warner Home Video, 2011), DVD.
9. This is the final line of the script. Kaminsky, "Narrative Time in Sergio Leone's *Once Upon a Time in America*," 67.
10. Kaminsky, "Narrative Time in Sergio Leone's *Once Upon a Time in America*," 70.

Bibliography

Bosley, Rachael K. "Wrap Shot." *American Cinematographer* 84, no. 1 (2003): 144.

Godden, Richard. "Maximizing the Noodles: Class, Memory, and Capital in Sergio Leone's *Once Upon a Time in America*." *Journal of American Studies* 31, no. 3 (1997): 361–84.

Kaminsky, Stuart. "Narrative Time in Sergio Leone's *Once Upon a Time in America*." *Studies in the Literary Imagination* 16, no. 1 (1983): 59–74.

Kipnis, Jill. "Picture This." *Billboard*, 14 June 2003, 61.

ONCE UPON A TIME IN THE WEST (C'ERA UNA VOLTA IN WEST) (1968)

DIRECTOR: Sergio Leone
WRITERS: Bernardo Bertolucci, Sergio Leone, Sergio Donati
PRODUCER: Falvio Morcella (Finanzia San Marco, Paramount Pictures)
CINEMATOGRAPHER: Tonino Delli Colli
EDITOR: Nino Baragli
ART DIRECTION: Carlo Simi
SET DECORATION: Carlo Simi
COSTUMES: Carlo Simi
MUSIC: Ennio Morricone
MAKEUP ARTIST: Alberto De Rossi
CAST: Frank: Henry Fonda. Jill McBain: Claudia Cardinale. Harmonica: Charles Bronson. Cheyenne: Jason Robarts. Morton: Gabriele Ferzetti. Sam: Paolo Stoppa. Stong: Woody Strode. Snaky: Jack Elam. Sheriff: Keenan Wynn. Brett McBain: Frank Wolff. Barman: Lionel Stander. Sam: Paolo Stoppa
AA: None
AAN: None
OTHER AWARDS: Academy of Science Fiction, Fantasy, and Horror Films Saturn Award for Best DVD Classic Film Release; David di Donatello Award for Best Production; Golden Screen Award; National Film Preservation Board's National Film Registry
DVD: Paramount Home Entertainment, 2003. Two-disc special collection.
BLU-RAY: Paramount Home Entertainment, 2011
DURATION: 166 minutes (145 for U.S. release)

Once Upon a Time in the West was Sergio Leone's fourth western, after *A Fistful of Dollars* (1964), *For a Few Dollars*

More (1965), and *The Good, the Bad and the Ugly* (1966), all of which were filmed in their entirety in Spain and Italy, in the early and mid-1960s; however, *Once Upon a Time in the West* was filmed in various locations, mainly in Spain, with mostly second units shot on locations fitted into the main action, in Monument Valley in Arizona, and in Utah, and with interior work done mainly in Cinecittà Studios in Rome. It was released in both Italian and English; financed and distributed by Paramount; and, as a genre, it belongs to the American epic western, although as critic David Thomson observes, "Despite Monument Valley and the stars, we never feel we are in America or with people who think American."[1] Splendidly photographed in mostly arid locales, the film moves at a nearly catatonic pace, with bursts of quick violence that come in surges and rhythms, as if a director conducted it as an opera,[2] where the prolonged shots accompanied by natural sounds—like the creaking doors or the buzz of the cicadas—are the introductory notes before an aria, when the singers hit the "high C" notes.

One of the opening shots shows one of three gunmen sent to kill Harmonica (Charles Bronson), Snaky, played by veteran western actor Jack Elam, who is lying in wait, his face unshaven, while a fly wanders over his stubble. He tries to chase it away by grimacing, too lazy to move his hand, but he fails repeatedly. When the fly finally perches on a swing door next to him, he traps it in the muzzle of his gun, blocking it with his finger so it cannot escape. Snaky lets it buzz inside the barrel and then frees it. A few moments later, after this long-drawn-out wait, a squeaky sound of a harmonica is heard, followed by quick fire, and the three waiting men are dead. The fourth gradually rises up and folds his left arm in a shoulder patch, and the scene ends. He is both being pursued and in pursuit. He is sure to show up again soon.

In this visual movie, the characters talk in sparse dialogue that makes them near mutes. Lengthy close-ups alternate with long shots, showing vistas of arid land, thus giving the movie its epic scope, while telling a rather intimate story of revenge. Revenge is the theme, but it twists into a double plot: One strand remains hidden until the very end, while the other becomes quickly obvious. A peaceful man with a dream, Brett McBain (Frank Wolff), living out in the country near Falstaff, Arizona, in a place he has named Sweetwater, lives with his three children, Patrick, Maureen, and Timmy. He is preparing a feast for someone important who is about to arrive as a guest. While drawing water from the well, he suddenly hears a shot and sees his daughter falling. He rushes to her, but he is shot too, and so is his older boy, who rushes out from the house. The youngest, Timmy, is standing in front of the house when three men approach. One of them asks the tallest, "Should we shoot this one too, Frank?" The tall man, a close-up showing his browned face and blue eyes, responds coldly, "No, he has heard my name." And he shoots the boy.

Stunned, audiences recognize the face of Henry Fonda, an icon in American cinema, a man who had played young Lincoln, Wyatt Earp, Pierre Bezukhov,[3] Manny Balestrero,[4] and even the president of the United States (*Fail Safe*, 1963), a man who was a screen hero, a family man, a saintly and revered persona on the American screen, here playing a sadistic killer, a faint smile on his face, his cheek distorted by chewing tobacco, while killing a child.

This action generates the second revenge theme. To hide his identity, Frank and his gang have planted evidence that the killer was Cheyenne (Jason Robarts), an outlaw, and his gang. Cheyenne is immediately arrested but manages to escape and hide at a trading post between Falstaff and Sweetwater, where Harmonica is also lurking. Meanwhile, a train has arrived, and a young woman of fashion, a straw hat on her head and carrying some baggage, is looking for someone waiting for her (McBain was about to send his older son Patrick to pick her up). Seeing no one, she hires a man, Sam (Paolo Stoppa), to take her to Sweetwater in his horse-drawn wagon. They stop at the trading post, where the barman (Lionel Stander), flattered to see a lady of fashion enter his ramshackle establishment, leers at her. She is Jill McBain (Claudia Cardinale), the woman the McBains were preparing the dinner for, a former prostitute from New Orleans who had married Brett a month earlier. Next we see her at the funeral, where a crowd is gathered to bury the four victims. She is asked to return to Flagstaff but refuses, preferring to stay at her husband's house and live there.

The second theme of revenge is established after that. Cheyenne joins forces with Jill, for he has reason to suspect who did the killing, for which he was blamed. He is also fond of her because he reminds him of his mother as she prepares coffee for him. He and Harmonica become allies, while Jill is threatened and raped by Frank, who had known her in New Orleans. Frank also has problems. He works for a railroad baron, Morton (Gabriele Ferzetti), who uses his own private cars as his headquarters, from where he directs his operations, running a railroad west. His orders to Frank were to intimidate, not kill, McBain, who was in the planning stages of building a station at his place, anticipating that the railroad being built would have to stop there, since it was the only place that could provide water, essential to railroad. But Morton is a cripple, walking on crutches and wearing a neck brace, and Frank had designs of getting rid of him and taking over the station himself. That is actually why he killed the McBain family, not wanting anyone else to lay claim to Sweetwater afterward; however, he had not planned on the arrival of Mrs. McBain, and her coming has interfered with his plans. But being sexually attracted to her, he keeps her alive for the time being.

Morton also suspects Frank of wanting to take over his operations. He has his goons plan to kill him while in town, but Harmonica helps Frank escape, telling an astonished Jill that he reserves the privilege of killing him for himself. Things evolve faster from this point onward. Jill puts her property up for auction, convinced she can't fight the gangs by herself, but Frank and his cohorts prevent anyone from bidding more than $200, while Harmonica sees to it that the auction is not concluded.

In the meantime, Cheyenne raids Morton's wagon, and he and his gang kill everyone inside. Returning to his boss's headquarters, Frank finds them all dead and scattered about outside the wagon, and Morton, heavily wounded, crawling to a water hole to drink some water. Frank leaves him dying there and takes matters into his own hands. The inevitable confrontation between Frank and Harmonica occurs, and the two stand against one another, in a classic western wide shot, where two enemies confront one another, ready to draw. Just before that, Frank wants to know who Harmonica is. The latter laconically replies that the secret will be revealed as one of the two is dying. Quicker, Harmonica shoots Frank in the heart, and as the latter totters in astonishment and falls to the ground, he still has enough breath to ask, "Who are you?" Harmonica places his harmonica in his dying foe's mouth. In a flashback, the viewer sees Frank, much younger, placing a harmonica in a boy's mouth, as the boy holds on his shoulders a man with a noose around his neck. Finally exhausted, the boy drops to the ground, and the man with the noose around his neck also drops to his death.

The boy was Harmonica, the hanged man, his brother.

The revenge is complete, as now both Harmonica and Jill are vindicated. Cheyenne has also played a crucial role, having wiped out Morton's gang, thus freeing the area of its criminal elements, and Jill can now be free to build her station, helping the railroad of progress to continue west. She is very fond of Cheyenne now, and she asks him to stay, but he says he has to go. He and Harmonica ride off to their solitary wandering, but they haven't gone far when Cheyenne stalls. When asked why, he shows Harmonica a wound on his side, a bullet from Morton before he died. Harmonica places the dead body on Cheyenne's horse and rides off, passing through the buzzing activity of a crowd of builders, too busy to pay attention to the men who saved them.

Once Upon a Time in the West is a myth: profiteers, gangs, gunmen, common folk, dirt, sweat, and blood—all are in the mix. In the end, the killers are killed or ride off, and the honest folk stay behind to build a station. Bernardo Bertolucci and Sergio Leone saw to it that a hero was left behind: a woman. And Claudia Cardinale as Jill McBain delivers. A voluptuous beauty gone to honest ways leads the tribe. Plot twists, cruelty, and all, this epic movie works, for it leaves viewers with a sense of hard-earned victory. CS

Notes

1. David Thomson, *A Biographical Dictionary of Film*, 3rd ed. (New York: Alfred A. Knopf, 1996), 138.
2. Leone's "spaghetti westerns" were often likened to operatic compositions.
3. A man of peace in King Vidor's adaptation of the Tolstoy novel *War and Peace* (1957).
4. In Alfred Hitchcock's *The Wrong Man* (1956), a man falsely accused of robbery and incarcerated.

Bibliography

Thomson, David. *A Biographical Dictionary of Film*, 3rd ed. New York: Alfred A. Knopf, 1996.

OUT OF AFRICA (1985)

DIRECTOR: Sydney Pollack

WRITER: Kurt Luedtke. Based on the novel *Out of Africa*, by Isak Dinesen (Karen Blixen's pen name); *Isak Dinesen: The Life of a Storyteller*, by Judith Thurman; and *Silence Will Speak*, by Errol Trzebinski.

PRODUCER: Sydney Pollack, Kim Jorgensen (Mirage Enterprises, Universal Pictures)

CINEMATOGRAPHER: David Watkin

EDITORS: Fredric Steinkamp, William Steinkamp, Pembroke J. Herring, Seldon Kahn

PRODUCTION DESIGN: Stephen B. Grimes

ART DIRECTION: Colin Grimes, Cliff Robinson, Herbert Westbrook

ART DIRECTION: Josie MacAvin

COSTUMES: Milena Canonero

MUSIC: John Barry

SOUND MIXERS: Chris Jenkins, Gary Alexander, Larry Stensvold, Peter Handford

CAST: Karen Blixen: Meryl Streep. Denys Finch Hatton: Robert Redford. Baron Bror Blixen/Hans Blixen: Klaus Maria Brandauer. Berkeley Cole: Michael Kitchen. Elknap: Shane Rimmer. Farah Aden: Malick Bownes. Kamante: Joseph Thiaka. Chief Kinanjui: Stephen Kinyanjui. Lord Delamere: Michael Gough. Felicity: Suzanna Hamilton. Lady Bellfield: Rachel Kempson. Lord Belfield: Graham Crowden. Minister: Benny Young. Sir Joseph Aloysius Byrne: Leslie Philips. Lady Byrne: Annabel Maule. Mariammo: Iman

AA: Best Picture (Sydney Pollack), Best Director (Sydney Pollack), Best Art Direction–Set Decoration (Stephen Grimes, Josie MacAvin), Best Cinematography (David Watkin), Best Writing–Screenplay Based on Material from Another Medium (Kurt Luedtke), Best Music–Original Score (John Barry), Best Sound (Chris Jenkins, Gary Alexander, Larry Stensvold, Peter Handford)

AAN: Best Leading Actress (Meryl Streep), Best Supporting Actor (Klaus Maria Brandauer), Best Costume Design (Milena Canonero), Best Film Editing (Fredric Steinkamp, William Steinkamp, Pembroke J. Herring, Seldon Kahn)
DVD: Universal Home Video, 2000
BLU-RAY: Universal Home Video, 2012. Extras include a running commentary by director Sydney Pollack.
DURATION: 162 minutes

Based mostly on Isak Dinesen's best-selling novel/memoir *Out of Africa*, the film recounts the adventures of Karen Blixen, who in real life had married her cousin from Sweden, Baron Bror Blixen, and gone to Kenya with him to start a new life after a sentimental disappointment in Denmark. Dinesen was, of course, the pen name of Blixen, and the book is a leisurely, episodic narrative, in diary form, that is a scenario of six interrelated episodes that build up to an emotional and heartrending conclusion.[1] The plot is linked by stretches of voice-over by Blixen, speaking directly to the audience, as she begins the story of her adventure in Africa, beginning, intercutting, and concluding the action.

The film was shot almost entirely in Kenya, Africa, with some exteriors in northern England, subbing for the snow-capped locales in Denmark. Special sets were built in what would have been the small town of Nairobi in those early days, in locations where Blixen's story actually occurred, with the use of actors who represent actual members of the Kikuyu tribe, and locals as extras. Although the duration of Blixen's stay in Africa spanned seventeen years, the film gives the impression that the narrative occurs in a much shorter period, since the main characters involved do not seem to age perceptibly. The story begins in 1913, and while World War I raged in Europe, in Kenya it was only a small episode, involving neighboring colonies, and it did not substantially affect the lives of the main characters in the story. Blixen returned to Denmark in 1931, but her novel/memoir did not appear until 1934, and it was not that well known until the production of the movie *Out of Africa* in 1985, when it became a best-seller.

Out of Africa is the story of Blixen's adventures, told from a unique viewpoint, for she writes about what she sees and experiences. Her personality emerges as the story progresses, and the viewer gathers impressions of this woman, who, perhaps unbeknownst to herself, has become a true hero of humanity, a teacher, friend, and ally of the Kikuyu, a tribe of Somalis, to whom she provides employment, medical help, and at least nominal independence for those she had employed before being forced to leave Kenya due to financial failure. Her story is an epic adventure of her inner metamorphosis from a rather innocuous European lady of manners to a hard-boiled, but not hardened, woman who rises above circumstances that would have dragged another of her class down. Although wealthy, she had failed to marry the man she loved, Baron Hans Blixen (Klaus Maria Brandauer), so she settled for his brother Bror (also played by Brandauer), titled but penurious and none too loyal when it came to marital fidelity. He proposed an enterprise of raising cattle in Kenya, but when she arrived there, he had changed plans and told her he had purchased land for a coffee plantation. While he spent his time away on hunting trips, she labored to tend to the farm, but the enterprise eventually failed, and, broke, she had to return to Denmark.

As Karen's marriage to Bror developed into a loveless formality, she started a relationship with Denys Finch Hatton (Robert Redford), an independent spirit, hunter, and sportsman with whom Karen carries on an affair for much of the story. Denys is a sensitive man who plays Mozart on his gramophone. He is kind to those he meets, but he is basically a hermit, not the marrying kind, and he tells Karen so when Bror asks her for a divorce. Denys chides Karen for her sense of possession, telling her that her wish to marry him amounts to a desire for ownership, not much different from her desire to own a farm, a tribe, her school children—Africa. But as director Sydney Pollack explains in his commentary, Karen's affair with Denys provides an important complication to the nearly plotless narrative—the "spine," as he calls it—and also the romantic interest. Denys' closest friend, Berkeley Cole (Michael Kitchen), is equally uncommitted to marriage (he lives with a native, Mariammo). He dies of a tropical fever before the story ends. Denys has a passion for flying, but he is a poor pilot, and he gets himself killed only a few days before Karen leaves after her establishment burns down.

Baroness Karen Blixen, as played by Meryl Streep, is a woman who is noble in every sense of the word. She is tolerant of her husband's philandering and lack of interest in their common enterprise, endures the hardship of running a coffee farm without any help, and has to travel back to Denmark to be cured of syphilis she contracted from Bror. As her affair with Denys fails and her business is destroyed, Karen is obliged to sell her luxurious furniture and return to Denmark. At the last moment, she makes an emotional plea to Sir Joseph Byrne (Leslie Philips), the new governor of Kenya, eliciting a promise that he will allow a piece of land for the Kikuyu tribe, who worked for her and would have nowhere else to go, to live in. Just before she leaves, Bror, now married to Felicity (Suzanna Hamilton), a wealthy and socially ambitious young woman, brings her the news that Denys has died in a plane crash. Karen's final dream of love vanishes, and we see her bidding farewell to her native friend and servant, Farah (Malick Bownes), who takes her to the station. She asks him for a last favor: to call her by her first name. He says, "Karen." Karen had developed a deep emotional bond with her other servants, one of whom, Kamante (Joseph Thiaka)—a boy she had hired as a cook after convincing him to seek medical help for his infected foot, and who lived on, perpetuating her legend)—visited the set at an advanced age when the film was being made.[2]

Karen Blixen is a heroine, and one of unusual dimensions. Her heroic status comes from her inner strength and inner nobility. In the face of her husband's blatant deceptions, she manages to avoid hating him, and they remain friends. Karen displays one characteristic, above all else, that distinguishes her as a heroine of unusual dimension. She is an empire-builder, but one who does not resort to ruthlessness to gain her ends—as is the usual practice of those who seek to build at the expense and exploitation of others, one could say a premise built into capitalistic enterprise. She is a capitalist, yes; otherwise she would not undertake a trip to an unknown country, enduring a marriage to a worthless man and suffering the vagaries of the wilderness and wartime turbulence. Her moves toward acquiring a fortune are made in the spirit of fair play, as she behaves more as a philanthropist than an entrepreneur—taking care of a boy with a lacerated leg, or fragile old people, respecting their traditions, and paying fair wages to her employees. She is the one who would build a school—if not a church—and a new society. She would seek stability in marriage. She would have children and descendants, and she respected an ancient country, using it but not depleting its resources or recklessly destroying it.

Karen is the heroine of the spirit of goodwill and philanthropy—in the broadest sense. It is tragic that her ventures fail. Her husband proves a cad and her lover an attractive but uncommitted escapist, and the colonial environment that comes with acquisition of Kenya and its being annexed to the British Crown contributes to her material downfall. She leaves the country, in compassion and sorrows, but not in defeat. She cares for the natives and secures a portion of the land that "was theirs before it was ours," as she tells the new governor, and she leaves the place with love in her heart for everything that she saw and experienced, but especially for the land.

Building such an image of a woman in a film becomes possible with the dedicated and technically excellent writing and direction by Sydney Pollack and his writers, photographers, and crew, but more than anything else, it was the performance of Meryl Streep that made the portrait of Karen Blixen so compelling. She adopted a heavy foreign accent, which, with a lesser actress, could have been a disastrous cacophony; instead, it is a melody, a rhythm and cadence that matches the visual splendor of the photographed landscapes. Her speech is intriguing, but portions of her voice-over determine rhythm, cadence, and even the pace of the film—especially a film that, for the most part, retains the diary form of its source and does not resort to plot devices.

Voice-over in film is often cumbersome, usually destructive of tone and nuance if not done properly. Here, voice-over, in the strangely unnatural but tonal sounds of Streep's deep voice, becomes the masterstroke of a film that defines a heroine not just by her body language, or her actions, but by her voice. Hers is an imitation of imperfectly spoken English, but here imperfection becomes perfection, just as a noble woman kneeling before the representative of a mighty monarch is an act of compassion, but also real dignity and superiority. Stooping before the boots of unworthiness makes the possessor of power worthy. Even so, it is the governor's wife seeing a noblewoman begging on her knees who gives her word of honor for him. Heroism comes in many forms, but here it is innermost strength and real affection—a merging of acting with reality—that defines its power. CS

Notes

1. Sydney Pollack, "Commentary," *Out of Africa*, directed by Sydney Pollack (Universal Home Video, 2000), DVD; Sydney Pollack, "Commentary," *Out of Africa*, directed by Sydney Pollack (Universal Home Video, 2012), Blu-ray.
2. Pollack, "Commentary."

Bibliography

Dinesen, Iask. *Out of Africa*. New York: Modern Library, 1952.

Thurman, Judith. *Isak Dinesen: The Life of a Storyteller*. New York: St. Martin's Press, 1982.

Trzebinski, Errol. *Silence Will Speak: A Study of the Life of Denys Finch Hatton and His Relationship with Karen Blixen*. Chicago: University of Chicago Press, 1977.

P

A PASSAGE TO INDIA (1984)

DIRECTOR: David Lean
WRITER: David Lean. Based on the novel by E. M. Forster.
PRODUCERS: Richard B. Goodwin, John Brabourne (EMI Films, Home Box Office, Thorn EMI Screen Entertainment)
ASSISTANT DIRECTORS: Patrick Cadell, Christopher Figg
CINEMATOGRAPHER: Ernest Day
EDITOR: David Lean
PRODUCTION DESIGN: John Box, Herbert Westbrook (uncredited)
ART DIRECTION: Cliff Robinson, Leslie Tomkins, Herbert Westbrook, Ram Yedekar
SET DECORATION: Hugh Scaife
COSTUMES: Judy Moorcroft
MUSIC: Maurice Jarre
SOUND: Graham B. Hartstone
PROPERTY MASTER: Eddie Fowlie
CONTINUITY: Maggie Unsworth
CAST: Richard Fielding: James Fox. Adela Quested: Judy Davis. Mrs. Moore: Peggy Ashcroft. Dr. Aziz: Victor Banerjee. Narayan Godbole: Alec Guinness. Ronny Heaslop: Nigel Havers. Mahmud Ali: Art Malik. Mr. Turton: Richard Wilson. Mrs. Turton: Antonia Pemberton. Vakyl Hamidullah: Saeed Jaffrey. Armitrao: Roshan Seth. McBryde: Michael Culver. Maj. Callendar: Clive Swift. Mrs. Callendar: Ann Firbank
AA: Best Supporting Actress (Peggy Ashcroft), Best Music–Original Score (Maurice Jarre)
AAN: Best Picture (Richard B. Goodwin, John Brabourne), Best Leading Actress (Judy Davis), Best Director (David Lean), Best Writing–Screenplay Based on Material from Another Meeting (David Lean), Best Cinematography (Ernest Day), Best Film Editing (David Lean), Best Art Direction–Set Decoration (John Box, Leslie Tomkins, Hugh Scaife), Best Costume Design (Judy Moorcroft), Best Sound (Graham B. Hartstone)
DVD: Columbia, 2005; Columbia, 2008. The 2008 version is a two-disc collector's edition.
BLU-RAY: Columbia, 2010
DURATION: 163 minutes

After a hiatus of nearly fourteen years, following the debacle of *Ryan's Daughter* at the Algonquin Hotel in New York in 1970, David Lean returned to England when producers Richard B. Goodwin and John Brabourne were preparing to film E. M. Forster's *A Passage to India*, more than a decade after the author's death in 1971. Forster, who had for decades held back from allowing his famous novel to be filmed, had stipulated that if permission was to be granted to film it after his death, the Indian author and playwright

Santha Rama Rau, who had already written a successful play in 1962 (a play that Lean admired), was to write the screenplay. After being contacted by Goodwin and Brabourne, who were eager to have Lean do the project, Lean spent more than a year in Delhi writing his own script, politely turning down Rau's screenplay, thinking it too literal and unfilmable.

Lean lost no time surrounding himself with trusted collaborators who had been with him in many of his past endeavors: cinematographer Ernest Day,[1] art director John Box (who had built the sets for *Lawrence of Arabia* and *Doctor Zhivago*), general factotum Eddie Fowlie, continuity person Maggie Unsworth, and composer Maurice Jarre (who had composed the scores for his three previous epics). Lean personally sought spectacular locations in India where the exteriors where to be filmed,[2] thus taking control of all the major aspects of the film, directing, writing the script, and finally doing the editing. Lean wrote the script for *A Passage to India* with the utmost attention to details about sets, locations, dialogue, and photography, describing every single scene and the shots in it—and he shot the movie exactly as it was in the script.[3] Following the screenplay's completion, Lean and his crew scouted locations in India and selected Bangalore,[4] where sets were built by John Box to correspond with what the fictional city of Chandrapore would look like. After six months in India, the cast and crew returned to England to finish the remaining interior scenes, one of which was the staging of Dr. Aziz's trial, which Lean expanded as the climactic event of the movie.

Lean's greatest challenge, it seems, was translating Forster's philosophical novel, with its many "side tracks,"[5] into a visual cinematic work with a streamlined plot, while retaining its "four or five wonderful characters."[6] He kept the basic outline of Forster's plot but eliminated some episodes and a few of the secondary characters, stressing the two most important scenes—the episode at the Marabar Caves, where Aziz is accused by Adela Quested of having attempted to rape her, and the trial of Aziz, which Lean purposely enlarged in scope and dramatic tension, leaving out most of the last section of the book and altering the ending.

The story starts in London, where Adela (Judy Davis) is seen purchasing the tickets for herself and Mrs. Moore (Peggy Ashcroft) on a rainy day. It then cuts to Bombay, with the pomp and circumstance of the viceroy's arrival, which coincides with that of the two women. While on a train to Chandrapore, Forster's fictional city, they are met by Mrs. Turton (Antonia Pemberton), the collector's wife, who invites them for a drink after they had recovered from their travels. It is during this dinner that Adela finds out that the Turtons are snobbish bigots, for they make it clear to her and Mrs. Moore that they—the English—and the Indians live socially apart, although the latter have "all the virtues." At the train station, they are greeted by Ronny (Nigel Havers), Mrs. Moore's son, a stiff official who little resembles the engaging and lively youth Adela had known in England.

While they settle at Ronny's quarters, Adela expresses her wish "to see India." To oblige, Mr. Turton proposes a "bridge party," where all sorts of Indians—Sikhs, Muslims, and "even a Parsee"—can be invited. The bridge party is a mixed success, as the English, to show difference in rank, stay aloof, taking tea at a raised platform, while the Indians are packed together standing and looking, in isolation. But during the party, Adela meets Fielding (James Fox), a college schoolteacher who, sincerely wishing to be courteous to the ladies, invites them to a "tea party," where they will meet an Indian Brahman and professor, Narayan Godbole (Alec Guinness), who will tell her all she wants to know about Hindu philosophy. Adela asks if he also can invite Dr. Aziz (Victor Banerjee), whom Mrs. Moore had accidentally met at the Mosque a few nights before and was impressed by his affable personality. Of course Fielding obliges, and the tea party thus becomes the catalyst of the events to follow.

It is at this point that the first serious complication occurs, when Aziz, overly polite and anxious to please the ladies, invites them to a "picnic at the Marabar Caves, a wonder of India," an invitation that provokes an ominous look from Godbole. Aziz acts without thinking, trying to correct his blunder of inviting them to his house, "a horrible shack," which would put him to shame. The invitation is eagerly accepted, but prior to that, two incidents take place that further complicate the plot. One is that Adela, offended by Ronny's rudeness to the Indians at Fielding's tea party, tells him that she has decided not to marry him, and the other is that she subsequently visits a ruined temple, where she sees erotic statues and is chased away by monkeys as she gazes at them with astonishment.

Lean explains that he added this visually dazzling scene, which offended some viewers and critics, to give some depth to Adela's character, a "stick" in Forster's novel,[7] and make her feel the stirrings of sexual awakening, something that would explain her collapse at the caves. That was Lean's major concern as he wrote his script, feeling that modern audiences would not accept a totally unexplained event in Forster's novel, Aziz's alleged attack on her, and her own inability to account for her accusations that he had been attacked. Another complication is that Fielding, who was to be at the Marabar expedition with Godbole, misses the train because Godbole had miscalculated the length of one of his prayers.[8] Aziz travels with the two ladies by train, and by elephant after leaving the train station, and they arrive at the first cave, where Mrs. Moore, frightened by the echo, collapses in her chair and refuses to go farther, advising Aziz not to take "too many people" with him in climbing to the upper caves. Aziz follows her advice and takes only the guide. As Aziz excuses himself and goes off to light a cigarette, Adela drifts into one of the caves, and when Aziz returns after a few minutes, she is gone. Aziz asks the guide about Adela's whereabouts. The guide nods vaguely and seems not to have seen anything, and Aziz slaps him in anger, but he does see Adela at the lower bottom of the ravine entering Mrs. Callendar's (Ann Firbank) car. He hastily runs down to camp, where Fielding has just arrived. Aziz's recounting of the incident does not produce any explanation, and Mrs. Moore advises, "I think that we should all go back"; however, as soon as they arrive, Aziz is arrested, without a warrant and with no explanation as to why.

Thus ends the first part of the movie. In the second part, the pace quickens, as Fielding, eager to protect his friend, visits McBryde (Michael Culver), the police chief, hoping to explain to him that Aziz is innocent. But McBryde is already preparing his report, believing Aziz is guilty, because, as he tells Fielding, "the psychology is different here," claiming that, "the dark races are attracted to the fairer, but not vice versa," as he repeats during the trial.

The trial, filmed at Shepperton Studios in England, is expertly staged by Lean, who exposes the pretentious claims of the English Raj, which tries to prove a case without other evidence, while also not taking into account the testimony of numerous witnesses. The trial is interrupted by a scene showing Mrs. Moore's death while on board a liner returning to England. At the same time, an enraged Mahmud Ali (Art Malik), a friend of Aziz's who is with the defense, goes into a ranting tirade against the British Raj that disrupts the trial and makes the crowds outside roar, "Mrs. Moore." The trial concludes with a dramatic interrogation of Adela by McBryde, but the result is the opposite of what he expects, for Adela suddenly sputters out, "I made a mistake," adding, "Dr. Aziz never entered the cave."

But after this triumph, Fielding, trying to help Adela through the crowd because her former friends have abandoned her, is seen by Aziz, who misunderstands his gallant gesture and denounces Fielding, saying, "You English are all the same! I will not have anything to do with any of you again." The rift between the two friends seems irreparable at this point, but when Fielding visits Aziz at Kashmir,[9] Aziz melts when he is told that he has married "Mrs. Moore's daughter," and he and Aziz reconcile again. This change of the ending (Forster has Aziz and Fielding parting) has been criticized by many, but Lean chose a benign tone between the parties, and the last scene shows Adela at her rain-streaked window, almost in tears, as she reads Aziz's letter of forgiveness.

A Passage to India went on to garner eleven Oscar nominations, among them Best Director and Best Film Editing, both for Lean, but it won only two, Peggy Ashcroft as Best Supporting Actress and Maurice Jarre for his evocative score.[10] Richard Schickel, who had been president of the National Society of Film Critics at the Algonquin Hotel fifteen years earlier, wrote a laudatory piece in *Time*, whose cover featured Lean and his new epic endeavor. Even Pauline Kael, who had led the attack against Lean at the Algonquin, melted with praise for Lean's new venture in a *New Yorker* article, stating that Lean's work was superior to Forster's original novel.[11] The film restored Lean's reputation as a prime director and gave him the momentum to continue filmmaking by attempting to adapt the Joseph Conrad novel *Nostromo*, but delays and illness prevented him from finishing that final project.[12] CS

Notes

1. Day was subbing for Freddie Young, who was too old to undertake the new venture but had worked under Lean as a cinematographer in previous works.

2. Some of the scouting was first done by his general factotum, Eddie Fowlie, who preceded him in finding and suggesting the multiple locations where the numerous exterior shots were made.

3. According the comments made by Nigel Havers, who played Ronny, Lean had a reading of his script with all the major actors involved before shooting started, "and he didn't change a thing." Nigel Havers, "Commentary" *A Passage to India*, directed by David Lean (Columbia, 2008), DVD, disc 2.

4. Forster's Chandrapore would have been near Patna, on the Ganges, in northern India, near Calcutta, while Bangalore is a large city in southern India, where technical means of filming were more readily available.

5. See Steven Organ, ed., *David Lean Interviews* (Jackson: University of Mississippi Press, 2009), 88.

6. Organ, *David Lean Interviews*, 88.

7. Organ, *David Lean Interviews*, 82.

8. In his DVD commentary, Richard B. Goodwin opines that Godbole had purposely missed the train not wanting to witness an event that he thought would be disastrous. Richard B. Goodwin, "Commentary," *A Passage to India*, directed by David Lean (Columbia, 2008), DVD, disc 1.

9. See Goodwin, "Commentary."

10. As Steven Silverman explains in his DVD commentary for *Ryan's Daughter*, this was the "year of *Amadeus*," which went on to reap most of the major awards. Steven Silverman, *Ryan's Daughter*, directed by David Lean (Warner Home Video, 2006), DVD.

11. See Pauline Kael, *For Keeps: Thirty Years at the Movies* (New York: Plume Press, 1996), 1,045.

12. See Constantine Santas, *The Epic Films of David Lean* (Lanham, MD: Scarecrow Press, 2011), 155–63.

Bibliography

Brownlow, Kevin. *David Lean: A Biography*. New York: A Wyatt Book for St. Martin's Press, 1996.

Day, Ernest. "*A Passage to India*." *American Cinematographer* 66, no. 2 (1985): 58–62.

Forster, E. M. *A Passage to India*. New York: A Harvest/HBJ Book, 1984.

Kael, Pauline. *For Keeps: Thirty Years at the Movies.* New York: Plume Press, 1996.
Organ, Steven, ed. *David Lean Interviews.* Jackson: University of Mississippi Press, 2009.
Santas, Constantine. *The Epic Films of David Lean.* Lanham, MD: Scarecrow Press, 2011.

PATHS OF GLORY (1957)

DIRECTOR: Stanley Kubrick
WRITERS: Stanley Kubrick, Calder Willingham, Jim Thompson. Based on the novel by Humphrey Cobb.
PRODUCERS: James B. Harris, Kirk Douglas (Bryna Productions)
CINEMATOGRAPHER: Georg Krause
EDITOR: Eva Kroll
MUSIC: Gerald Fried
CAST: Col. Dax: Kirk Douglas. Cpl. Philippe Paris: Ralph Meeker. Gen. George Broulard: Adolphe Menjou. Gen. Paul Mireau: George Macready. Lt. Roget: Wayne Morris. Maj. Saint-Auban: Richard Anderson. Pvt. Pierre Arnaud: Joe Turkel. Pvt. Maurice Ferol: Timothy Carey. Pvt. Lejeune: Kem Dibbs. Capt. Nicols: Harold Benedict. Capt. Rousseau: John Stein. Fr. Dupree: Emile Meyer. Sgt. Boulanger: Bert Freed. German Singer: Susanne Christian
AA: None
AAN: None
DVD: MGM, 1999
BLU-RAY: Criterion, 2010
DURATION: 88 minutes

Although it had been banned throughout much of Europe, especially in France, until the 1970s because it questions governmental authority and military decision-making, Winston Churchill praised *Paths of Glory*'s authenticity. The film's central theme is the social stratification of war, the ambition and incompetence of the leadership, and the emphasis of war and leadership on automatism and conformism.[1] Shot in black and white, the film opens in France in 1916. While the narration discusses the heavily fortified line of trenches, where "[s]uccess was measured in yards and hundreds of thousands of lives," Kubrick's use of wide-angle lenses reveals the sumptuous French chateau of General Paul Mireau (George Macready), which he used as his headquarters. Mireau welcomes General George Broulard (Adolphe Menjou), who exclaims, "This is splendid. Superb." Broulard arrives with the request that Mireau's men make an offensive on a key sector the Germans have held for a year called the "Anthill" (originally called the "Pimple" in Cobb's novel[2]) in two days. Mireau objects because his men are in poor shape from previous offensives, until Broulard bribes him with another star and leadership of the 12th Corps.

In scenes Kubrick shot in long single takes, Mireau tours the trenches. He asks each soldier he meets, "Are you ready to kill more Germans?" The first he asks is Private Maurice Ferol (Timothy Carey) of Company A. The next is Corporal Philippe Paris (Ralph Meeker), who is in the midst of cleaning his rifle. Mireau speaks to him in clichés: "Be good to it and it will always be good to you." A bomb explodes nearby. The general ducks but seasoned soldiers do not. The third soldier he meets is shell-shocked (Fred Bell), but Mireau brands him a coward and orders him out of the regiment. Mireau's sycophantic assistant, Major Saint-Auban (Richard Anderson), tells him his tours have had an incalculable effect on the men.

Mireau's next stop is to see Colonel Dax (Kirk Douglas). Arriving just as Dax is washing himself, Mireau calls his dirt dugout a "neat little spot." They discuss the twenty-nine casualties from the previous night, whom Saint-Auban claims gathered together in a "herd instinct" and "lower animal sort of thing." Mireau tells Dax his regiment will take the Anthill, estimating loses at 35 percent. He equates patriots with honesty, and having been a lawyer before the war, he responds to Dax's sharp tongue by quoting Samuel Johnson's words on patriotism as "the last refuge of a scoundrel." Mireau threatens to put him on indefinite furlough, but Dax, unwilling to leave his men, says, "We'll take the Anthill if any soldiers in the world can take it."

That night, Lieutenant Roget (Wayne Morris), an alcoholic company commander, leads a reconnaissance patrol through the wire. Lieutenant Roget, Corporal Paris, and Private Lejeune (Kem Dibbs) crawl out of the trenches, under barbed wire, under black sky and smoke, from bomb crater to bomb crater. Roget orders Lejeune to move out and check ahead, but Paris objects because it is improper to split up night patrols. A flare bursts, lighting up dozens of bodies. Roget becomes more nervous and, assuming Lejeune is dead, throws a grenade and fast-crawls back to his dugout. Paris works his way forward to find Lejeune's smoking body. Back at Roget's dugout, he threatens to report him for endangering lives, being drunk on duty, and showing cowardice in the face of the enemy. Roget replies that as an officer, "It's my word against yours. Whose word do you think they will be willing to accept?" Dax arrives, asks for the report, finds Roget's bottle of liquor, and orders him to finish his report immediately.

Dax reports to his subordinate officers that the attack will start with an artillery barrage for fifteen minutes but not to expect reinforcements until sundown. Dax tours the trenches. His men are ready and nervous as artillery bombards no-man's-land. He exits the trenches and whistles the men forward, and hundreds of men run out of the trenches. Through blast holes, barbed wire, explosions, and machine-gun fire, the men run, and usually die.

From an observation post, Mireau and his officers notice that B Company has not left the trenches and joined the fight. He orders Captain Nicols (Harold Benedict), the artillery spotter, to commence firing on B Company. He resists but calls the battery commander, Captain Rousseau (John Stein), with the orders. Rousseau refuses unless he receives a written order signed by General Mireau. Meanwhile, Colonel Dax goes to the B Company and orders Lieutenant Roget and his men to give it another try. He whistles and a man falls on top of him, preventing him from leaving the trenches again.

After the failed attack, Mireau orders Dax and the 701st back to headquarters, saying, "If those little sweethearts won't face German bullets, they'll face French ones!" In a meeting with Broulard and Dax, Mireau asks for ten men from each company to be tried for cowardice under penalty of death—100 men total. When Dax argues that the attack was impossible, Mireau says the "only proof that it was impossible would be their dead bodies at the bottom of the trenches." Dax offers himself in their place. Ignoring it as not being a "question of officers," Broulard suggests taking one man from each company, a total of three, for the first wave. Dax volunteers to be the advocate for the accused. Afterward, in a scene shot from a high angle, Mireau tells Dax, who is shown in a lower position, that he will break him for his lack of loyalty.

After the men have been selected, Dax meets Private Ferol, Corporal Paris, and Private Arnaud in the dungeonlike guard room and tells them that they are being put on trial for their lives. At the general court-martial, in a palatial room, Mireau sits on a settee, and five judges sit behind a long table. The chief judge of the court-martial (Peter Capell) dispenses with "unnecessary formalities" and refuses to read the indictment. It is clear that the accused have no rights. Private Ferol is called first. He testifies that he was in the first wave and advanced to the middle of no-man's-land, finding himself with only one other soldier. The others were gone. Acting as prosecutor, Major Saint-Auban asks Ferol why he did not take the Anthill alone.

Private Arnaud testifies that he advanced and they reached their own wire, but most of the men died before they got three steps from the trenches. No men in his company went beyond the wire. He was chosen to be "coward" randomly. When Dax tries to read Arnaud's record of heroism to the judges, he is not allowed to do so. In frustration, Dax says, "No one reached the German wire, including myself."

Corporal Paris is brought before the court. They do not believe his story that he was knocked out when another man landed on him. Dax tells the court, "There are times I'm ashamed to be a member of the human race, and this is one of them. . . . The attack was no disgrace to France, but this court-martial is." The court adjourns, and the accused are escorted to back to the guard room.

In the guard room, a duck dinner is brought from General Mireau. Although it is their last meal, they do not eat it. Father Dupree (Emile Meyer) tells them to prepare for the worst because Colonel Dax was unable to reverse the court's decision. Paris gives Dupree a letter to deliver to his wife. Arnaud becomes belligerent at the father's clichéd advice that death comes to all. He hits Dupree. Paris hits Arnaud, and he falls against a column, receiving a skull fracture. A doctor reports that he may not live through the night.

Lieutenant Roget reports to Dax, who asks how he chose Corporal Paris. Refusing to admit he had a personal motive, Dax puts Roget in charge of the firing squad. He carefully details Roget's duties, emphasizing the last step of firing a bullet through each man's head. After Roget leaves, Captain Rousseau arrives at Dax's room.

Dax meets with General Broulard that evening. Broulard admits that the number of casualties suggests that the troops tried, but the "unfair pressures" from newspapers and politicians caused them to have the executions. He states that executions improve morale and maintain discipline. Attempting to use Rousseau's story to stop the executions, Dax reports that General Mireau had ordered the artillery to bomb his own men and says that has sworn affidavits to prove it.

The next morning, a firing squad arrives at that guard room with a stretcher. Corporal Paris breaks down, and Sergeant Boulanger (Bert Freed) says, "It's the last decision you make. Behave like a man." At the firing line, the men are tied to posts, even Private Arnaud in his stretcher. Major Saint-Auban reads the charges against Corporal Paris, Private Ferol, and Private Arnaud. As Lieutenant Roget hands Paris a blindfold, he tells him he is sorry. The drums quit, and the firing squad fires.

Afterward, Broulard and Mireau eat at a small table in the chateau. Mireau says, "It had a certain splendor. They died wonderfully. You couldn't ask for better." Dax arrives at Broulard's request. Broulard turns to Mireau and states, "It came to my attention that you were going to fire on your own men." Mireau denies the charges, saying that he is "the only completely innocent man in this whole affair." Mireau leaves, and Broulard offers Dax Mireau's command, claiming that Dax was after the job from the start. Dax calls him a "degenerate sadistic old man." Broulard asks, "Wherein have I done wrong?" Dax says he pities him because he does not know the answer.

Dax arrives at his office and notices that his men are in a small café next door drinking. The men cheer when the café's proprietor (Jerry Hausner) brings to his small stage a young German singer (Susanne

Christian, who later becomes Mrs. Stanley Kubrick) whom he describes as a "little pearl washed ashore by the tide of war." The men whistle and jeer. Dax stands outside, disturbed. She begins singing, but no one hears her over the cheers and clapping. Her song is "The Faithful Hussar" ("Der Treue Husar"); written in 1825, it tells the story of a faithful soldier rushing to his beloved's deathbed. She cries as she sings it. Even if many of the men do not know the meaning of the words, they hum along, encouraging her, participating in a moment of beauty. Many cry. Dax finally sees one instance where he can be proud of humanity, but at that same moment he receives orders that they are to be immediately moved back to the front. JMW

Notes

1. Jesse Bier, "Cobb and Kubrick: Author and Auteur (*Paths of Glory* as Novel and Film)," *Virginia Quarterly Review* 61, no. 3 (1985): 461, 470.
2. Andrew Kelly, "The Brutality of Military Incompetence: *Paths of Glory*," *Historical Journal of Film, Radio, and Television* 13, no. 2 (1993): 215.

Bibliography

Bier, Jesse. "Cobb and Kubrick: Author and Auteur (*Paths of Glory* as Novel and Film)." *Virginia Quarterly Review* 61, no. 3 (1985): 453–71.

Kelly, Andrew. "The Brutality of Military Incompetence: *Paths of Glory*." *Historical Journal of Film, Radio, and Television* 13, no. 2 (1993): 215–27.

THE PATRIOT (2000)

DIRECTOR: Roland Emmerich
WRITER: Robert Rodat
PRODUCERS: Dean Devlin, Mark Gordon, Gary Levinsohn (Columbia Pictures Corporation, Centropolis Entertainment, Mutual Film Company)
CINEMATOGRAPHER: Caleb Deschanel
EDITOR: David Brenner
MUSIC: John Williams
SOUND MIXERS: Kevin O'Connell, Greg P. Russell, Lee Orloff
CAST: Benjamin Martin: Mel Gibson. Gabriel Martin: Heath Ledger. Charlotte Selton: Joely Richardson. Col. William Tavington: Jason Isaacs. Col. Harry Burwell: Chris Cooper. Thomas Martin: Gregory Smith. Margaret Martin: Mika Boorem. Susan Martin: Skye McCole Bartusiak. Nathan Martin: Trevor Morgan. Samuel Martin: Bryan Chafin. William Martin: Logan Lerman. Anne Howard: Lisa Brenner. Peter Howard: Joey D. Vieira. Mrs. Howard: Mary Jo Deschanel. Rev. Oliver: Rene Auberjonois. Jean Villeneuve: Tchéky Karyo. Gen. Lord Charles Cornwallis: Tom Wilkinson. Capt. Wilkins: Adam Baldwin. John Billings: Leon Rippy
AA: None
AAN: Best Cinematography (Caleb Deschanel), Best Music–Original Score (John Williams), Best Sound (Kevin O'Connell, Greg P. Russell, Lee Orloff)
DVD: Sony Pictures Home Entertainment, 2000
BLU-RAY: Sony Pictures Home Entertainment, 2000
DURATION: 165 minutes

Planned as a blockbuster summer release, *The Patriot*, a Revolutionary War epic, was written by Robert Rodat, of *Saving Private Ryan*, and directed by Roland Emmerich, of *Independence Day* and *Godzilla*. Speaking about the film, Emmerich one said, "I'm always skeptical about historical dramas. But I could see that these were characters I could relate to, and they were engaged in a conflict that had a significant outcome—the creation of the first modern democratic government."[1] There have been relatively few epic films made about the Revolutionary War, because, as William Hallahan, author of *The Day the American Revolution Began*, says, "We're very quick to spot hypocrisy in our current politicians, and these guys, even the nonslaveholders, although great and brilliant men, all have feet of clay."[2]

Mel Gibson's character, Benjamin Martin, was created from three Revolutionary War–era figures: "Thomas Sumter, whose exploits on the battlefield won him the nickname the 'Carolina Gamecock'; Daniel Morgan, the rifleman who stated that he would risk everything for the American cause; and Francis Marion, who was popularly known as the 'Swamp Fox.'"[3] However, he is also a modern man, "devoted to his family, wracked by guilt, and possessed of a Bob Vila-esque interest in furniture making."[4] The film opens with Martin's voice-over narration. He states, "I have long feared my sins would revisit me and the cost is more than I can bear," because of the massacres he had participated in during the French and Indian War. This dark past is hidden from his family because he is a changed man. He lives on a beautiful plantation, nearly an Arcadian paradise, with his seven children and his servants, but no slaves. A generous, loving father, he lightly chastises his two youngest boys when they swim instead of working the fields, and he teaches the constellations to his daughters. He cultivates patience through his hobby of carpentry by attempting to build a reproduction of a British spindle-backed rocking chair. When it breaks when he sits in it, he throws the pieces across the room. His anger and violence lurk just below the surface. He visits his wife's grave, the woman who changed him. A letter arrives from Charlestown requesting his presence at a meeting. He takes his family along, dropping his youngest children with his sister-in-law, Charlotte Selton (Joely Richardson), asking her to "[k]eep an eye on the heathens."

While people in the streets agitate for war, Colonel Burwell (Chris Cooper) addresses the colonial assembly, asking that South Carolina be the ninth colony to support the Continental Army. Although Martin and Burwell are friends, having served together during the French and Indian War, Martin argues against fighting the British, saying that 3,000 tyrants a mile away can be as bad as a tyrant 3,000 miles away. He also wants to protect his children. He declares, "Wars are not fought only by childless men. I will not fight. I will not cast a vote to send others in my stead." The assembly votes to pass the levy to support the Continental Army, and the crowd celebrates. Martin's eldest son Gabriel (Heath Ledger) is embarrassed and enlists, saying, "When I have a family of my own I won't hide behind them." While away, Gabriel writes home that the troops live with "defeat and privation" and their losses are "grievous," and he plans to return south to fight with General Gates.

One night, the Martin family hears distant gunfire; Benjamin recognizes the sound of "six pounders" from artillery. Martin tells his family to "stay in close." While they eat dinner, Gabriel enters, wounded and bleeding. As they bandage him, he reports that General Gates marched them straight at the Redcoats and lost. The Green Dragoons rode in and killed 200 men. The battle moves onto Martin's fields; the household cares for the wounded from both sides. Although a British officer thanks them for their care, Colonel William Tavington (Jason Isaacs), leader of the British Dragoons, discovers that Gabriel is carrying a report for American troops and decides to hang him. Martin asks him to reconsider, but Tavington calls it "rules of war." One of Martin's other sons, Thomas (Gregory Smith), attempts to save his older brother, but he is shot in the back by Tavington. He orders the livestock destroyed, Martin's home burnt, and the wounded American soldiers killed. Martin runs inside his burning house to retrieve his guns and hatchet from the French and Indian War. Telling his other children to hide in the fields, he takes the boys with him into the woods to find the British. They catch up to the men. "Aim small miss small," the boys say, repeating the lessons that their father taught them while hunting. Martin fires, moves, fires again, confusing the soldiers as he shoots them, while the boys shoot from another location. One of the last remaining soldiers holds a knife against Gabriel's throat. Martin kills him with a hatchet throw and then cuts him beyond death.[5] The British who escape report that one man attacked them, and they call him a ghost.

Martin hides his family at Charlotte's country home. Gabriel plans to join General Gates at Hillsborough, saying it is his duty. Martin argues, "Your duty is to your family. Thomas is dead. How many more will die before you heed my word?" Gabriel rejoins the fight and finds a tattered flag in the dirt. Another soldier calls it a "lost cause," a "tacit correlation between the colonists' struggle for independence and the lost cause of the Southern confederacy,"[6] an indication of how "perseverance in the face of defeat" and other aspects of Southern "Lost Cause ideology have become embedded in popular culture."[7]

Burwell is now in command, and Martin reports to him, willing to join the fight. Burwell plans to keep Cornwallis (Tom Wilkinson) in the South until the French arrive in six months, and he makes Martin colonel. As colonel, Martin's first action is to transfer his son under his command. Although he objects, Gabriel takes his new role. His first task is to go to a church to recruit militia members. He announces that the South Carolina militia is being called up. Many men object to this call, but Anne Howard (Lisa Brenner), Gabriel's school friend, inspired by Gabriel's words, chastises them. Several stand and join, including Anne's father, Peter (Joey D. Vieira), and the church's minister, Reverend Oliver (Rene Auberjonois). Gabriel asks Howard if he can have permission to write Anne. Meanwhile, Benjamin visits a bar for recruits. Testing the waters, inside he yells, "God save King George." Many of the men draw weapons. Knowing he has come to the right place, he signs several men.

At their marsh hideout by a burned-out church, Jean Villeneuve (Tchéky Karyo) trains the new recruits. They adopt guerilla tactics against the British. They stop a wagon carrying alcohol, correspondence from Cornwallis, and two great danes, gifts from the king meant for Cornwallis. In camp, Gabriel repairs the frayed flag with a needle and thread. Martin reads Cornwallis's journal and finds his weakness.

General Lord Charles Cornwallis meets with Colonel Tavington to discuss their difficulty in finding the militia. He blames the militia's growth on Tavington, because of his brutality. Tavington responds that he advances himself through victory.

Wearing British uniforms, Martin and a small crew bomb a British ship in the harbor loaded with a supply of arms and munitions. Gabriel calls on Anne and stays overnight in her room. Her family allows this because they have sewn him into a "bundling bag." Peter donates supplies to the militia.

The militia attacks a British wagon, claiming it for the Continental Army, but a British soldier signals for help and dragoons ride up from all sides. Many members of the militia are taken prisoner. Back at camp, Gabriel asks his father about Ft. Wilderness. He says that they found all the settlers who had sought refuge at Ft. Charles from French and Indian raiders dead. Martin recalls the events, revealing, "We caught up with them at Ft. Wilderness. We took our time. Cut them apart slowly piece by piece. I can see their faces. I can still hear their screams." He still asks God's forgiveness.

Martin rides into the British Ft. Caroline carrying a white flag, with Cornwallis's great danes following. He is invited into General Cornwallis's outer office, where he sits in a spindle-backed rocking chair. It does not break. Inside the office, he identifies himself only as a colonel in the Continental Army. He agrees to return Cornwallis's personal items from the wagon but promises, "As long as your soldiers attack civilians I will have soldiers kill officers." He proposes a prisoner exchange and asks for his men back, revealing that he has British officers held prisoner at the top of the ridge. With a telescope, Cornwallis sees the men and agrees to the exchange. As Martin leaves the fort with his men, Tavington objects to Cornwallis's order that he cannot be touched. Tavington and Martin face one another. Martin promises to kill him "soon." He whistles for the dogs, and they follow him. The British officers held for ransom are revealed to be mannequins. Cornwallis orders Tavington to capture Martin. Tavington receives a promise for land in Ohio as payment for capturing the colonel, in spite of his brutal tactics.

Tavington approaches Captain Wilkins (Adam Baldwin), who knows Martin, to assist. Wilkins realizes that Martin is probably hiding his family at his wife's sister's plantation. At her plantation during the night, one of the boys watches as the dragoons ride up the road. He wakes Charlotte; she gathers the children and hides them in a cellar below the kitchen. They run from the house as troops shoot the servants and set fire to the house.

One of Martin's men, John Billings (Leon Rippy), finds his family dead outside his burnt home. Reverend Oliver says it is a time for mourning, not vengeance, but John shoots himself. In reaction, Martin gives the men a week's furlough to attend to their own families. Charlotte, Gabriel, Martin, and the rest of the family hide in a Gullah village with former slaves next to the ocean. While they fish, Martin explains that Gabriel's mother changed him after the French and Indian War. Anne arrives in a wagon with her family. She and Gabriel are married by Reverend Oliver. During the wedding celebration, Martin gives Anne his wife's blue North Star necklace, a symbol of her constant nature. After the party, Martin sits with Charlotte on the beach and they kiss.

Anne and her family return to Pembroke. Tavington rides into the town's church while the community is gathered there and accuses them of aiding Martin and his rebels. He promises to forgive their treason if he is given information about Martin. One man reports that Peter Howard sends them supplies through the black swamp to an old mission. Tavington orders Wilkins to burn the church, saying, "honor is found in the ends not the means." They burn the church with everyone inside. This scene caused many critics and historians to question the film's accuracy. According to Steve Vineberg of the *Chronicle of Higher Education*,

> The *Patriot* is the ultimate bad-faith movie. It subjects us to two and a half hours of atrocities on the pretext that it's presenting a slice of American history. Its trumped-up dramatization of the Revolutionary War, however, is about as convincing as the hucksterish vision of World War II that Hollywood manufactured in the 1940s . . . just Nazis in red coats.[8]

Martin's militia finds the remnants of the burning church with a lock and chain on the burnt front door and the North Star necklace in the embers. They bury the remains. Gabriel rides off to find Tavington and his dragoons. Tavington kills Reverend Oliver and Gabriel with a sword. By the time Benjamin arrives, Tavington is gone, and he is unable to save his son.

Colonel Burwell visits Martin. Gabriel's body lies on a cot. Martin says, "I have long feared that my sins would return to visit me. And the cost is more than I can bear." Burwell says that the army has a chance now that Greene and Morgan are down from Virginia, but Martin says, "I have run my course." After Burwell and his troops ride off, Martin finds Gabriel's repaired flag; inspired, he rides with the flag to catch up to Burwell and Villeneuve and joins them at the lead. Preparing for a battle the next day, Martin suggests that, based on Cornwallis's captured letters, Cornwallis has no fear of militias. Martin believes that he should and convinces his men to fire from the front line. He melts one of Thomas' toy British soldiers and forms it into a shot.

The next day, Cornwallis's men and the militia march toward one another. During the battle, Tavington sees Martin and charges through the British lines toward his militia. Martin grabs a flag from a retreating soldier and yells at the men to hold the line. Cornwallis orders his artillery to focus on center to drive them back. Martin spears a horse with the flag staff, loads his pistol and cocks it, and shoots Tavington in the shoulder as artillery rounds drop around them. Tavington attacks with his sword, cutting Martin's tomahawk in two and slicing him in the back. While Martin is on his knees, Tavington says, "It appears you are not the better man." Martin ducks and stabs him in the stomach. "You're right. My sons were better men." He kills him. Cornwallis sounds the retreat. The Americans have won the battle.

Martin writes to Charlotte that the war has turned. Cornwallis is surrounded, and the French have arrived. Cornwallis eventually surrenders. The militia disbands. Burwell names his new son Gabriel, Villeneuve gives his adieu, and Martin takes his family to his house, which is being rebuilt. Charlotte carries a baby in her arms.

Although some critics found the film "long and soupy, the lines uttered, formulaic, and unconvincing,"[9] the greatest disappointment is that the first genre-defining Revolutionary War film still remains elusive. JMW

Notes

1. Quoted in Jamie Malanowski, "The Revolutionary War Is Lost on Hollywood," New *York Times*, 2 July 2000, www.nytimes.com/2000/07/02/movies/film-the-revolutionary-war-is-lost-on-hollywood.html?n=Top%2fReference%2fTimes%20Topics%2fPeople%2fG%2fGibson%2c%20Mel (30 September 2013).
2. Quoted in Malanowski, "The Revolutionary War Is Lost on Hollywood."
3. Donald E. Pease, *The New American Exceptionalism* (Minneapolis: University of Minnesota Press, 2009), 135.
4. Malanowski, "The Revolutionary War Is Lost on Hollywood."
5. "Gibson's character seems to be a reprise of his role as a crazed Scottish fighter against the British in *Braveheart* (1987)." Peter C. Rollins and John E. O'Connor, eds., *Why We Fought: America's Wars in Film and History* (Lexington: University Press of Kentucky, 2008), 56.
6. Pease, *The New American Exceptionalism*, 37.
7. Rollins and O'Connor, *Why We Fought*, 129.
8. Steve Vineberg, "*The Perfect Storm* Is Just Soggy, but *The Patriot* Is a Betrayal," *Chronicle of Higher Education* 46, no. 47 (2000): B11.
9. Malanowski, "The Revolutionary War Is Lost on Hollywood."

Bibliography

Malanowski, Jamie. "The Revolutionary War Is Lost on Hollywood." *New York Times*, 2 July 2000, www.nytimes.com/2000/07/02/movies/film-the-revolutionary-war-is-lost-on-hollywood.html?n=Top%2fReference%2fTimes%20Topics%2fPeople%2fG%2fGibson%2c%20Mel (30 September 2013).

Pease, Donald E. *The New American Exceptionalism*. Minneapolis: University of Minnesota Press, 2009.

Rollins, Peter C., and John E. O'Connor, eds. *Why We Fought: America's Wars in Film and History*. Lexington: University Press of Kentucky, 2008.

Vineberg, Steve. "*The Perfect Storm* Is Just Soggy, but *The Patriot* Is a Betrayal." *Chronicle of Higher Education* 46, no. 47 (2000): B11.

PEARL HARBOR (2001)

DIRECTOR: Michael Bay
WRITER: Randall Wallace
PRODUCERS: Michael Bay, Jerry Bruckheimer (Touchstone Pictures, Jerry Bruckheimer Films)
CINEMATOGRAPHER: John Schwartzman
EDITOR: Roger Barton, Mark Goldblatt, Chris Lebenzon, Steven Rosenblum
MUSIC: Hans Zimmer
SOUND EDITORS: Christopher Boyes, George Watters II
SOUND MIXERS: Greg P. Russell, Peter J. Devlin, Kevin O'Connell
VISUAL EFFECTS: Eric Brevig, John Frazier, Edward Hirsh, Ben Snow
CAST: Capt. Rafe McCawley: Ben Affleck. Capt. Danny Walker: Josh Hartnett. Nurse Lt. Evelyn Johnson: Kate Beckinsale. Lt. Col. James Doolittle: Alec Baldwin. Young Rafe McCawley: Jesse James. Young Danny Walker: Reiley McClendon. Danny's Father: William Fichtner. Admiral Husband E. Kimmel: Colm Feore. Petty Officer Doris Miller: Cuba Gooding Jr. Capt. Thurman: Dan Aykroyd. Lt. Red Winkle: Ewen Bremner. Nurse Betty Bayer: Jaime King. Maj. Jackson: Leland Orser. President Franklin Delano Roosevelt: Jon Voight
AA: Best Sound Editing (Christopher Boyes, George Watters II)
AN: Best Effects–Visual Effects (Eric Brevig, John Frazier, Edward Hirsh, Ben Snow), Best Music–Original Song (Diane Warren for "There You'll Be"), Best Sound (Greg P. Russell, Peter J. Devlin, Kevin O'Connell)
DVD: Touchstone, 2001
BLU-RAY: Buena Vista Home Entertainment, 2006
DURATION: 183 minutes

Michael Bay followed the blockbuster successes of *The Rock* (1996) and *Armageddon* (1998) with *Pearl Harbor*. Its central topic, the Japanese sneak attack on Pearl Harbor, Oahu, Hawaii, on 7 December 1941, nearly qualifies as a subgenre of the epic war film. Several other films deal with the attack, including *Air Force* (1943), *From Here to Eternity* (1953), *In Harm's Way* (1965), and *Tora! Tora! Tora!* (1970). Most critics agree that the film attempted to "turn a historic defeat into a flag-waving spectacular."[1] The filmmakers took great pains to make the attack, which is a forty minute spectacle in the center of the film, accurate, but it does not "compensate for the inadequacies of the film as a whole."[2]

The film opens in 1923, with Rafe McCawley (Jesse James) and Danny Walker (Reiley McClendon), young boys living in Tennessee, as they play with Danny's father's crop-dusting equipment. After his father returns from a flight, they hop aboard his biplane. Rafe accidently starts the plane, and they fly for a few hundred feet. Danny's father (William Fichtner) arrives and pulls him home. A bitter man, he calls Danny a "no account boy" and beats him. To protect Danny, Rafe hits Danny's father with a board, saying, "I will bust you up you dirty German." Danny tells him he is his best friend, but he follows his father home.

The film jumps forward to 1941. McCawley (Ben Affleck) and Walker (Josh Hartnett) are now training in Army Air Corps P-40s. Rafe challenges Danny to play "chicken." They narrowly pass one another and are brought in front of their commander, Lieutenant Colonel James Doolittle (Alec Baldwin). Doolittle is upset, but McCawley reminds him of himself fifteen years earlier. Doolittle says McCawley's request to be transferred to the British Royal Air Force's Eagle Squadron, which accepts American pilots, has been approved.

Several navy nurses are traveling to New York by train. Among them, Nurse

Lieutenant Evelyn Johnson (Kate Beckinsale) is telling her colleagues about meeting McCawley four weeks earlier. He was afraid of failing his eye exam because of reading problems caused by dyslexia. She passes him, but because he switched files in an attempt to pass the test, she overmedicates him. He faints, breaking his nose. That night he brings her a bottle of champagne to thank her. McCawley and his friends greet the women at the train as it arrives. Her friends meet his, and they all attend a Swing dance. McCawley and Johnson leave the party and take a police boat for a joy ride past the Queen Mary. He tells her he is going to England to fight in the war. He asks that she not see him off, but when she does, he knows she loves him. The news reports that the German Luftwaffe is attacking London.

Although President Franklin Delano Roosevelt (Jon Voight) is concerned that the United States is pretending that war does not exist, Admiral Husband Kimmel (Colm Feore), stationed at Pearl Harbor, receives a message to transfer twelve destroyers to the Atlantic. Meanwhile, in Japan, they are planning a massive single attack on Pearl Harbor. They consider this move inevitable because the United States has cut off their oil. To prepare for the attack, they float model ships in a small pool. They also modify torpedoes to allow for Pearl Harbor's shallow water.

Johnson and her friends, now serving at Pearl Harbor, find the hospital there little more than a place to treat the sunburns of handsome pilots. Rafe's experiences are quite different, as pilots are often killed in the line of duty. Their mission is to shoot down bombers heading to England. Rafe is hit and crashes into the ocean.

On one of the ships, a black cook, Petty Officer Doris Miller (Cuba Gooding Jr.), and a large racist white man fight. While Johnson is bandaging Miller after winning the contest, Walker delivers news that McCawley is dead. That night, Walker and his friends remember McCawley with drinks. Walker is told that McCawley volunteered.

The Japanese set up teams of radio operators to send out messages that the Americans will intercept. They list each potential target in the Pacific, including Hawaii. These messages are decoded in Washington, D.C., by Captain Thurman (Dan Aykroyd), who realizes that they are flooding the radio because something big is happening.

At a viewing of Charlie Chaplin's *The Great Dictator*, Johnson sees a newsreel about U.S. peace talks with the Japanese government. Outside, she sees Walker. They have been avoiding one another. Over coffee, Walker tells her stories of his childhood with McCawley. They happen to see their friend, Lieutenant Red Winkle (Ewen Bremner), propose to one of the nurses, Betty Bayer (Jaime King). That night, Walker visits Johnson at her house. Although she resists him, she decides it is time to move on and puts McCawley's letters in a box.

In Washington, Thurman and others observe that the Japanese fleet is operating under radio silence, and two entire carrier divisions have disappeared, probably by entering the "vacant sea," an area between normal shipping lanes. Thurman believes that they are planning an attack on Pearl Harbor. At Pearl, a Japanese spy takes photos of the harbor by taking flight tours, and the military works with untested radar that cannot reveal whether objects are birds or planes.

McCawley sends word that he is alive. He survived the crash and recovered in German-occupied France. He arrives at Pearl Harbor and visits Evelyn. She says, "You died. So did I." He feels betrayed since she and Walker are now together.

Walker and McCawley fight at a bar. The military police arrive to break them up.

Japanese pilots, believing that the future of the empire hinges on the attack, fly their planes off the deck of aircraft carriers. At Pearl Harbor, they drop torpedoes into the water, sinking many ships, including the USS *Arizona*. Miller moves onto the deck of his battleship, the USS *West Virginia*, and takes over an antiaircraft gun after the operator is killed. He shoots down several planes.

The USS *Oklahoma* slowly heels over. Men slide off its deck, and the ship capsizes. Many men are trapped inside and sent to watery graves. To achieve these effects, the filmmakers "constructed an intricate thirty-foot-long model of the *Arizona*. A crew reconstructed the bow section of the *Oklahoma* on a giant gimbal that allowed the ship to roll over."[3]

McCawley, Walker, and others drive to a small mechanic runway where the planes have not been destroyed. The Zeros follow as they move to the smaller airfields as well. McCawley and Walker ask for cover fire as they enter the P-40s. In the air, they fly close to the ground, each with Zeros in close pursuit. They "play some chicken" and force several Zeros to crash into one another.

At the hospital, the doctors and nurses fill every syringe they have with morphine to treat the incoming wounded. Although the hospital is in chaos, Johnson is clear-headed and marks each patient injected with morphine with an "M" in red lipstick. She also uses a stocking for a tourniquet. By keeping her fingers plugged on his artery, Johnson keeps Major Jackson (Leland Orser) alive. Johnson is ordered outside to manage triage, allowing only those who can be saved into the hospital. Among the incoming dead is Betty.

The Japanese achieve a tremendous victory, only losing twenty-nine planes out of 350. President Roosevelt receives the report that an entire fleet was lost at anchor. In front of cameras and radio microphones, he delivers the news that 3,000 lives have been lost and that the United States is now at war. His military brass later report that the Japanese could penetrate as far as Chicago, but the United States could not get planes to Japan. Roosevelt leaves the room by standing from his wheelchair and saying, "Do not tell me it can't be done."

Preferring to avoid a downbeat ending, the film moves to the U.S. retaliation on Japan and "Doolittle's Raid." McCawley and Walker are called to serve with Doolittle. As McCawley is packing to leave, Johnson arrives. She says, "You're acting like I didn't love you. Loving you kept me alive." She plans to stay with Walker because she is pregnant. After reporting to Doolittle, they are promoted to captain and will receive the Silver Star. Their new assignment will require that they go without knowing their assignment. The men are lined up in a hangar and told that they must learn how to take off in 467 feet and fly thirty feet above the ground. They plan to bomb Tokyo with B-25 Mitchell bombers that take off from aircraft carriers. Doolittle dramatically lightens their planes to achieve this goal. Lacking the fuel to return to the ship, they will land in China.

Johnson convinces Major Jackson to allow her to work in the command post so she knows what happens during Doolittle's Raid. He allows her to work there and pretend to type. On board the aircraft carrier, Doolittle realizes that the Japanese patrol boats will soon discover them. Although they are 624 miles from their target, he decides to launch as soon as they further strip the planes and load extra cans of fuel. Once over Japan, they drop bombs on factories, but antiaircraft guns fire. The planes rise to 800 feet to get into the clouds and avoid the flak. Their extra fuel spent, they finally see the coast of China. Forced to glide in, they ditch in a paddy field, where they are pinned down by Japanese troops. Walker is captured and tied to a yoke, but McCawley shoots his captors. Others shoot at McCawley, but Walker hits them with the yoke and is shot. As Walker is dying, McCawley tells him, "You're going to be a father. I wasn't supposed to tell you." Walker says, "No you are." The raid offers the least accurate moments in the film.

> In reality, the raid damaged little but Japanese pride, but here vast factories erupt in flames. The aftermath, as Doolittle's planes ditch in China, degenerates into an absurd shoot-'em-up, something of a "Gunfight in the OK Rice Paddy." The dignified Japanese seen in the body of the film here revert to the crude wartime stereotype.[4]

Doolittle, McCawley, and the others arrive at Pearl Harbor. Johnson sees Danny's casket being taken off the plane. The narration states, "Before the Doolittle raid, America knew nothing but defeat. After it, nothing but victory. . . . W.W. II began at Pearl Harbor." The film ends with Rafe and Evelyn playing with their little boy, Danny, in a garden by an airport. Rafe honors Danny's father's memory by flying him in a biplane.

While the film dramatically reproduces the destruction of the fleet in Pearl Harbor, it also reproduces the "propagandistic contours of the standard World War II narrative, replete with themes of national heroism, individual courage, and military triumph."[5] JMW

Notes

1. Nicholas J. Cull, "*Pearl Harbor*," *American Historical Review* 106, no. 5 (2001): 1,916.
2. Frank Wetta, "*Pearl Harbor*," *Journal of Military History* 65, no. 4 (2001): 1,140.
3. Christopher Probst, "One Nation, Under Siege: Cinematographer John Schwartzman, ASC, and Director Michael Bay Set a Classic Romance amid America's Darkest Days in *Pearl Harbor*," *American Cinematographer*, May 2001, 40.
4. Cull, "*Pearl Harbor*," 1,917.
5. Carl Boggs, "*Pearl Harbor*: How Film Conquers History," *New Political Science* 28, no. 4 (2006): 451.

Bibliography

Boggs, Carl. "*Pearl Harbor*: How Film Conquers History." *New Political Science* 28, no. 4 (2006): 451–66.

Cull, Nicholas J. "*Pearl Harbor*." *American Historical Review* 106, no. 5 (2001): 1,916–17.

Probst, Christopher. "One Nation, Under Siege: Cinematographer John Schwartzman, ASC, and Director Michael Bay Set a Classic Romance amid America's Darkest Days in *Pearl Harbor*." *American Cinematographer*, May 2001, 40.

Wetta, Frank. "*Pearl Harbor*." *Journal of Military History* 65, no. 4 (2001): 1,138–40.

THE PIANIST (2002)

Director: Roman Polanski

Writer: Ronald Harwood. Based on *Death of a City*, by Wladyslaw Szpilman.

Producers: Robert Benmussa, Roman Polanski, Alain Sarde (R. P. Productions, Heritage Films)

Cinematographer: Pawel Edelman

Editor: Hervé de Luze

Costumes: Anna B. Sheppard

Music: Wojciech Kilar

Cast: Wladyslaw Szpilman: Adrien Brody. Dorota: Emilia Fox. Jurek: Michal Zebrowski. Henryk Szpilman: Ed Stoppard. Wladyslaw's Mother: Maureen Lipman. Wladyslaw's Father: Frank Finlay. Halina Szpilman: Jessica Kate Meyer. Regina Szpilman: Julia Rayner. Yehuda: Paul Bradley. Itzak Heller: Roy Smiles. Janina: Ruth Platt. Majorek: Daniel Caltagirone. Marek: Krzysztof Pieczynski. Janina's husband: Ronan Vibert. Gebczynski: Krzysztof Pieczynski. Antek Szalas: Andrew Tiernan. Dorota's Husband: Valentine Pelka. Dr. Luczak: Tom Strauss. Capt. Wilm Hosenfeld: Thomas Kretschmann. Lednicki: Cezary Kosinski

AA: Best Leading Actor (Adrien Brody), Best Director (Roman Polanski), Best

Writing–Adapted Screenplay (Ronald Harwood)
AAN: Best Cinematography (Pawel Edelman), Best Costume Design (Anna B. Sheppard), Best Film Editing (Hervé de Luze), Best Picture (Robert Benmussa, Roman Polanski, Alain Sarde)
BAFTA Awards: Best Film (Robert Benmussa, Roman Polanski, Alain Sarde), David Lean Award for Direction (Roman Polanski)
Cannes Film Festival Award: Palme d'Or (Roman Polanski)
DVD: Universal Studios, 2006
Blu-ray: Studio Canal, 2002
Duration: 150 minutes

Roman Polanski called *The Pianist* the "most important film of [his] life." Based on the autobiography of pianist Wladyslaw Szpilman, *Death of a City* (published in English as *The Pianist: The Extraordinary True Story of One Man's Survival in Warsaw, 1939–1945*), the film also evokes Polanski's experiences as a child in Krakow, Poland, during World War II, and the loss of his mother in a concentration camp. The film won the Palme d'Or for best feature at the Cannes Film Festival. Stuart Klawans of the *Nation* calls the film a "study of character and history that knows irony to be a part of life and not the purpose of art."[1]

The film opens in Warsaw, in 1939, with archival black-and-white footage. It then shows Szpilman (played by Adrien Brody) playing Frederic Chopin's Nocturne in C-Sharp Minor (Op. Posth.) for Warsaw Radio while explosions rock the street outside. An explosion breaks windows, and pieces of the ceiling fall. An engineer in the booth signals Szpilman to stop playing. He does not, but another explosion convinces him to join the mass of people exiting the building. Dorota (Emilia Fox), his friend Jurek's sister, stops him and introduces herself. She loves his playing and wants to meet him. Pointing out the obvious, Jurek (Michal Zebrowski) says it is not the best time. Szpilman asks, "Where have you been hiding her?" He chases after them as a window explodes near them on the street level.

Szpilman arrives at his family home. His older brother Henryk (Ed Stoppard) tunes the radio, while his father (Frank Finlay), mother (Maureen Lipman), and two sisters, Regina (Julia Rayner) and Halina (Jessica Kate Meyer), decide what to pack and what to leave behind because the Polish government moved to Lublin and all able-bodied men must leave the city. Szpilman resists, saying, "I'm not going anywhere. If I'm going to die, I'm going to die in my own home." When a broadcast reports that the British government has declared war on Nazi Germany, and that France would soon make a similar declaration, they stay and celebrate that Poland will no longer be alone.

The celebration is short-lived, as Nazi troops march into Warsaw and quickly emplace repressive laws against Jews. Because Jewish families have been ordered to own no more than 2,000 zlotys, they must hide 3,000. Not interested in the family's argument where to hide it, Szpilman calls Jurek to see Dorota. They meet; she recently finished her studies in the cello. He takes her to the Paradiso for coffee, but a sign says "No Jews." Because Jews are not allowed in the park or on public benches, they are forced to stand and talk. Jews are later required to wear a Star of David on their sleeves.

All Jews are ordered to be moved into a Jewish "quarter," the ghetto. Henryk immediately recognizes that the area is far too small to hold 400,000 people. The family has only twenty zlotys left, so they decide to sell their piano. A buyer offers 2,000 zlotys, far below what it is worth. As they walk with other Jews toward their district, Szpilman sees Dorota standing on the sidewalk and speaks to her. "I didn't want to come. I couldn't stop myself. It's too absurd," she says. At their new residence, they see workmen blocking off their street. When completed, it is topped with barbed wire and broken glass. In a makeshift street market, while the elderly die around them and vendors sell food from wire cages, Szpilman and Henryk attempt to raise money by selling family books.

To earn money, Szpilman plays the Café Capri. He wants to do something important, so he visits Yehuda (Paul Bradley), who prints Socialist newspapers. Yehuda says he is too well known to assist. On the way home, Szpilman sees a small boy attempting to enter the ghetto by crawling under the wall while someone beats him from the other side. Szpilman tries to help, but he dies in his arms.

At dinner, his mother says she will not allow depressing conversation so they can enjoy their meal together. Henryk tells a story of Germans allowing a surgeon to operate on a Jew: as he makes his first incision, the SS burst in and shoot the patient, and then the doctor and everyone else. He says, "Isn't that a laugh? You've lost your sense of humor?" Outside, German troops drive up to the building across the street and enter a fourth-floor apartment. Inside is a family eating at a dining-room table, like the Szpilman family. The German soldiers push a man in a wheelchair to the balcony and drop him onto the street. They take others down the stairs and shoot them. One tries to climb a wall, but he is shot. As the Nazis drive away, they drive over the bodies they left in the street.

As Szpilman plays for the Café Capri, his sister interrupts him with news that Henryk has been taken by the Nazis. He asks Itzak Heller (Roy Smiles), a Jewish collaborator, to help. Szpilman calls him an important man. Henryk is later thrown out onto the street, and he asks Wladyslaw why he had to interfere. Wladyslaw calls him "mad." They get news that the ghetto will be closed and the people sent to labor camps in the east.

On 15 March 1942 the Jews are moved out of the ghetto, along with their belongings. They are eventually moved into an *Umschlagplatz*, a collection area. One of the guards says, "You're going to work. You'll be better off than in this stinking ghetto." While they wait, one man says, "We let them take us like sheep to slaughter." A boy sells caramel pieces for twenty zlotys, an outrageous price, but Wladyslaw's father buys one and cuts it into six pieces for his family. As they board a train, Heller pulls Szpilman from the line, although he challenges him. Szpilman walks back to the ghetto, which is empty except for the dead in the street and luggage left behind. He goes to the Café Capri. He hides with another man below the floor.

Szpilman, now a slave laborer, and other men are marched outside the ghetto to demolish a wall. There, food is plentiful, and people are well dressed. He sees his friend Janina (Ruth Platt) but realizes that she would be hanged for helping a Jew. A couple men get bread when the soldiers are not looking. They are marched back. A man pulls some from the line and tells them to lie down, and he shoots them in the back of the head.

At a construction site, Szpilman sees Majorek (Daniel Caltagirone), who says that Jews who have been forced onto the trains have never been seen again. "They're exterminating us," he declares. He says that they intend to fight. Later, Szpilman drops some bricks off of his hod and is viciously whipped by a soldier. Majorek finds a job better suited for him in supply, and he arranges to have pistols delivered inside sacks of potatoes. They throw them over the wall and into the ghetto before they are searched on the way back in. In time, Szpilman asks Majorek to help him escape. Majorek says, "It's easy to get out. It's how you survive once you're there." The arrangements made, Szpilman slips away from a work group after they leave the ghetto. He follows Janina to her apartment. Szpilman eats and soaks in a tub. Her husband takes him to Marek's (Krzysztof Pieczynski) house. The next day, Marek takes him to an apartment near the ghetto wall. He tells him to leave the curtains open during the day, and Janina will bring him more food. He gives Szpilman a slip of paper to use in an emergency and locks him in as he leaves.

The nadir of his experience during the Holocaust is the time he spends alone. From his room he sees the resistance begin in the ghetto. His door eventually opens, and it is Janina with food. She says that the Jews are now fighting back and that the rest of the Poles will rise. The next time he sees her, she arrives with her husband (Ronan Vibert), and they tell him to gather his things and leave with them because their weapons have been discovered. He decides to stay. Before leaving, Janina's husband says, "Jump from the window if they storm the place."

Szpilman hears Germans marching up the stairs, so he opens the window and clears a path to it. Then the footsteps descend the stairs. Time passes, and he has only crumbs of food left. He accidently breaks some dishes trying to find more, alerting his neighbors to his presence. They knock on his door saying, "Open up or we'll call the police." He leaves and is questioned by a woman in the hallway. He runs while she yells, "He's a Jew! Stop the Jew!"

On the snowy street, he pulls the emergency information out of his shoe and walks to the address. At the door, he says, "Mr. Gebczynski sent me." Dorota answers the door. Her brother Jurek is dead. She is married now and pregnant. He sleeps on their sofa and wakes to Dorota playing the cello.

Gebczynski (Krzysztof Pieczynski) takes him to an apartment door. "You're in a very German area. Safest place to be, right in the lion's den." Inside is a piano he cannot play because he must be silent. Locked inside, he begins to play's Chopin's Andante Spianato and Grande Polonaise, Op. 22, without touching the keys.[2] On another day, his door is unlocked, and Gebczynski delivers food with Antek Szalas (Andrew Tiernan), his new helper. Szalas was a technician at Warsaw Radio. They say that the Allies are bombing Germany and that it is the beginning of the end.

Time passes. Szpilman's quiet, isolated life has affected him. Now gaunt and bearded, he watches the hospital across the street. Szalas arrives, delivering sausage and bread, much later than promised. He had problems buying the food because of lack of money, so Szpilman gives him his watch to sell. The Allies have landed in France.

Dorota and her husband (Valentine Pelka) come to let Szpilman know that they are leaving the city, but they find Szpilman seriously ill. Szalas collected money to feed Szpilman but kept it for himself and left Szpilman to die. Dr. Luczak (Tom Strauss) examines him and arranges for medicine. The Polish attack German installations, including the hospital across the street, which causes the Germans to retaliate and burn much of the city. A woman is shot in the street, and soldiers surround Szpilman's building. A tank arrives. It raises its turret and fires, hitting the apartment next door. Szpilman leaves his apartment through an exploded wall and hides on the roof. Soldiers shoot at him from another building, so he drops to the balcony of an apartment. He hides behind garbage cans overnight and moves into the now-abandoned hospital.

The following day, the Germans pile bodies in the street and eat lunch as the bodies burn. Then they set fire to the hospital and other buildings with flamethrowers. Szpilman leaves the hospital and sees his city in ruins. Finally finding an intact house, he discovers a can of pickles, but before he can open it, a vehicle approaches. Soldiers enter the building, and Szpilman hides in the attic. He hears Moonlight Sonata being played on a piano. That night, he returns downstairs to open the can with fireplace tools. Captain Wilm Hosenfeld (Thomas Kretschmann) discovers him and asks him several questions, the last being what he does for a living. "I was a pianist," Szpilman answers. Hosenfeld leads him to the piano and tells him to play something. Terrified, cold, and hungry, fingers stiff, Szpilman, the world-class concert pianist, plays Chopin's Ballade No. 1 in G-Minor, Op. 23. After he finishes, Hosenfeld asks him to show him where he hides. The next day, the house becomes a military headquarters, with Hosenfeld in charge. He takes food and a can opener to the attic. He reports that the Russians are across the river. Hosenfeld gives him his winter coat.

The Germans soon abandon the building, and the Russians enter the city. Szpilman goes onto the street, and the soldiers nearly mistake him for a German soldier. Szpilman's friend Lednicki (Cezary Kosinski), returning to Warsaw, sees Germans held behind wire fences. He calls them murderers and assassins. "You took my violin. You took my soul," he yells. One soldier asks if he knows Szpilman, "I was helping him," Lednicki replies. Szpilman and Lednicki return to the place, but the soldiers are gone.

The film closes with Szpilman at the piano with an orchestra in front of a large crowd. He is playing Chopin's Nocturne in C-Sharp Minor, the song he left uncompleted at Warsaw Radio in 1939.

The film reproduces the tone of Szpilman's autobiography by accurately portraying his detachment. "He never complains—no self-pity. There's no indication that he's using his enormous will to do anything but survive."[3] JMW

Notes

1. Stuart Klawans, "Polanski's Holocaust," *Nation*, 6 January 2003, www.thenation.com/article/polanskis-holocaust (30 September 2013).

2. "One of very few works in Chopin's oeuvre not for solo piano. It elegantly communicates Szpilman's unconscious reliance upon his intimate relationship with the piano and the vast repertoire of music stored in his memory as a musical-hallucinatory coping mechanism." Alexander Stein, "Music and Trauma in Polanski's *The Pianist* (2002)," *Psychoanalytic Inquiry* 27, no. 4 (2007): 450.

3. Adam Tolbert, "*The Pianist*: Interview with Ronald Harwood," *Creative Screenwriting* 9, no. 6 (2002): 33.

Bibliography

Klawans, Stuart. "Polanski's Holocaust." *Nation*, 6 January 2003, www.thenation.com/article/polanskis-holocaust (30 September 2013).

Portugese, Catherine. "*The Pianist*." *American Historical Review* 108, no. 2 (2003): 622.

Stein, Alexander. "Music and Trauma in Polanski's *The Pianist* (2002)." *Psychoanalytic Inquiry* 27, no. 4 (2007): 440–54.

Tolbert, Adam. "*The Pianist*: Interview with Ronald Harwood." *Creative Screenwriting* 9, no. 6 (2002): 33.

THE POSEIDON ADVENTURE (1972)

DIRECTOR: Ronald Neame
WRITERS: Stirling Silliphant, Wendell Mayes. Based on the novel by Paul Gallico.
PRODUCER: Irwin Allen (20th Century Fox, Kent Productions)
CINEMATOGRAPHER: Harold E. Stine
EDITOR: Harold F. Kress
ART DIRECTION: William J. Creber
SET DECORATION: Raphael Bretton
COSTUMES: Paul Zastupnevich
MUSIC: John Williams
SOUND MIXERS: Theodore Soderberg, Herman Lewis
VISUAL EFFECTS: L. B. Abbott, A. D. Flowers
CAST: Rev. Scott: Gene Hackman. Rogo: Ernest Borgnine. James Martin: Red Buttons. Nonnie: Carol Lynley. Acres:

Roddy McDowall. Linda Rogo: Stella Stevens. Belle Rosen: Shelley Winters. Manny Rosen: Jack Albertson. Susan: Pamela Sue Martin. Chaplain: Arthur O'Connell. Robin: Eric Shea. Linarcos: Fred Sadoff. Nurse: Sheila Mathews (also known as Sheila Allen). Doctor: Jan Arvan. Purser: Byron Webster. Chief Engineer: John Crawford. M. C.: Bob Hastings. Mr. Tinkham: Erik Nelson. The Captain: Leslie Nielsen

AA: Best Music–Original Song (Al Kasha, Joel Hirschhorn for "The Morning After"), Special Achievement Award–Visual Effects (L. B. Abbott, A. D. Flowers)

AAN: Best Supporting Actress (Shelley Winters), Best Art Direction–Set Decoration (William J. Creber, Raphael Bretton), Best Cinematography (Harold E. Stine), Best Costume Design (Paul Zastupnevich), Best Film Editing (Harold F. Kress), Best Music–Original Dramatic Score (John Williams), Best Sound (Theodore Soderberg, Herman Lewis)

DVD: 20th Century Fox, 2006

BLU-RAY: 20th Century Fox, 2012

DURATION: 112 minutes

Based on the 1969 best-selling novel of the same name by Paul Gallico, *The Poseidon Adventure* recounts the efforts of passengers aboard an aging luxury liner to escape when the vessel becomes capsized in a storm. Following the success of *Airport* (George Seaton, 1970), the decade ushered in a slate of disaster films, of which the Oscar-winning *The Poseidon Adventure*, *The Towering Inferno* (John Guillermin, 1974), and *Earthquake* (Mark Robson, 1974) are the most renowned. Like *Airport*, *The Poseidon Adventure* concerns the danger of travel, but as Stephen Keane suggests, at the heart of the disaster film cycle is the power and danger of the natural elements, even if human greed, hubris, and pure folly play a central part in how those elements take effect.[1] Certainly many films before *Airport* contained natural disasters, or the spectacle of destruction, but in the disaster movie, the disaster itself provides the central predicament that traps its cross-section of characters.

In *The Poseidon Adventure*, the passengers are led by the charismatic Reverend Scott, played by Gene Hackman, the biggest star attraction of the film following his success in *The French Connection* (William Friedkin, 1971), for which he would go on to win an Academy Award for Best Actor. Scott is being sent to Africa by the Church by way of reprimand for his unorthodox methods, but Scott himself relishes the chance to exercise more freedom there. He sermonizes to the passengers that they must not pray to God to help them, but rather to that part of God within themselves so that they may help themselves, and he puts this approach into action when disaster strikes.

Joining him on board are a policeman named Rogo (Ernest Borgnine), accompanied by his former prostitute wife Linda (Stella Stevens); a lonely bachelor haberdasher and jogger, James Martin (Red Buttons); a young band led by Nonnie (Carol Lynley), on their way to a music festival; a teenage girl named Susan (Pamela Sue Martin), along with her kid brother Robin (Eric Shea); and Belle and Manny Rosen (Shelley Winters and Jack Albertson, respectively), on their way to Israel to meet their new grandson. Borgnine, Buttons, Winters, and Albertson were all former Academy Award winners, the use of aging stars a key method of the disaster film to enable viewers to more easily keep track of so many characters.

On the bridge, the captain (Leslie Nielsen before his switch to comedy) is forced by company representative Linarcos (Fred Sadoff) to go full speed ahead instead of taking on ballast to steady the ship. The captain is incensed, insisting that the ship is top-heavy, old, and unsafe. During the New Year's Eve party, the captain is called back to the bridge with news of an earthquake in Crete, which sends a tidal wave toward the ship and capsizes it. In the most spectacular sequence of the film, the ballroom overturns, and guests slide, smash, and fall from tables to their doom, crashing into glass and being crushed by moving furniture. These sequences were partly achieved with the assistance of a tilting set.[2]

Reverend Scott soon springs into action, pushing up the fallen Christmas tree to act as a ladder to an upper deck (or rather, an inverted lower deck), where an injured waiter (Acres, played by Roddy McDowall) secures it. The ship's chaplain (Arthur O'Connell) stays to assist and comfort those who are too injured or frightened to join Scott in his escape plan, and who (foolishly as it turns out) trust the purser's (Byron Webster) command that they wait to be rescued. The purser and most of the guests are soon dead as water floods the ballroom.

The small band of survivors then proceeds to the perilous journey of climbing higher into the ship to avoid the flooding water. Acres falls to his death in a flooded vertical air shaft, despite Rogo's valiant attempts to save him, and Rogo is indignant when Scott admonishes him. The group comes across more survivors being led toward the bow by the ship's doctor, and Rogo tries to convince the group to join them; however, persuaded by Robin's knowledge of the ship, Scott is adamant that they need to find the engine room. Scott searches for the route and then returns, just in time to take the small group with him, including the momentarily lost Robin.

Alas, the way to the engine has been flooded, and when Scott gets trapped underwater, former underwater swimming champion Belle dives in to save him. Belle and Scott secure a rope for the others to follow (the actors performed these underwater sequences themselves), but Belle suffers a heart attack and dies. Manny is understandably heartbroken but agrees to continue so he can see his grandson, as Belle wanted.

In the engine room, Scott leads the survivors across a catwalk to the propeller-room door, where Robin (who had been studying the liner) has told them that the ship's plating is at its thinnest. But another explosion causes Linda to fall to her death, and Rogo attacks Scott with a barrage of insults. Scott, Rogo, Manny, Martin, Susan, and Robin are unable to get to the propeller room, as ruptures caused by the explosions release scalding steam over the entrance. In a final act of heroism, Scott leaps onto the valve wheel and closes off the steam. (In his commentary, director Ronald Neame admits that the viewer does not know what exactly is being turned by the wheel, and it is unclear what is happening until the steam suddenly stops.[3]) Scott yells at God, "You want another life? Then take me!" and unable get back from the wheel, he falls into water and fire to his death. Martin must convince Rogo to stop complaining and start leading. Rogo takes over the leader's mantle and gets the five survivors to the propeller room, from which they are rescued by helicopter (a grander ending had been planned, but the budget ran out).

The powers that be are certainly in a testing mood, whether it is Scott's God, or Poseidon, the god of the sea from Greek mythology, after which the liner is named, who, appropriately for this story, was also the god of storms and earthquakes. Scott's course of action is indeed the right one, and he is able to save lives, but Scott suffers from failings that even Greek mythology recognized as dangerous: hubris and lack of respect for the gods (Odysseus is condemned to an extended and perilous homeward sea journey in Homer's *The Odyssey* partly because of these faults). The ship's chaplain is Scott's friend, but he sees that the weak and injured need help and may not always be capable of helping themselves. Scott sacrifices his life, either as punishment or redemption, but he leaves this mortal coil an angry man, still at war with his maker. In the end, it is not necessarily the strongest—or the most famous—who survive on the Poseidon. Yet, in his commentary, director Neame agrees with Scott's position that "God is too busy running the universe" so "we have to take care of ourselves."[4]

It has been argued that *The Poseidon Adventure* reflects a certain apathy of the era, embodied in the "morose lyrics and [a] dreary pace" of the film's Academy Award–winning song "The Morning After"[5]; however, songwriter Al Kasha recalls that he and Joel Hirschhorn (who only had twenty-four hours to complete the song) intended it to be a "song of hope."[6] Indeed, the film appeals to the idea that even the most ordinary and perhaps not especially brave among us has the ability to rise to the occasion in exceptional circumstances, so it is heroism rather than merely the spectacle of disaster that propels the narrative in *The Poseidon Adventure.*

While the film was aimed at young viewers, by contrast, the novel is a darker, adult tale in which the disaster strips people of their humanity. Author Paul Gallico had sailed on the *Queen Mary* in 1937, and during a storm the liner had turned on its side momentarily before righting itself. This incident became the inspiration for the novel, and the film used the actual retired *Queen Mary* (docked at Long Beach, California, as a hotel), as well as replicating its rooms for studio-set work.[7] The otherwise heroic efforts of the novel's protagonists are undermined when many who stay behind are, in fact, also rescued, and sacrifices made along the way seem pointless. Human weakness is exposed at the heart of violence, racism, and homophobia, but disturbingly, we are asked to relate to characters who forgive rape and domestic violence.[8] The novel's prevailing feeling of despair and human failure seeps into the feature film but is overridden by heroic success.

Despite being a phenomenal commercial success, making nearly $100 million at the box office, the project was nearly cancelled at the last minute. Twentieth Century Fox executives balked at the $5 million budget, concerned that a big special-effects epic would not appeal to audiences favoring small, character-driven titles in the late 1960s and early 1970s. Producer Irwin Allen, who had considerable television success with such programs as *Lost in Space* (1965–1968), was able to convince them otherwise and secured half of the financing privately. Allen's next film was *The Towering Inferno*, cementing his reputation as the "master of disaster."[9]

In retrospect, Neame felt that he should have asked some of the actors to tone down their performances a little, but even reviewers at the time could see that the over-the-top quality of the project is part of its very appeal.[10] The film has since become a cult classic, and Neame was regularly hosted on the *Queen Mary* by its fan club. John Williams's score was used sparingly by Neame, but Williams would soon work on his most memorable music for *Jaws* (Steven Spielberg, 1975) and *Star Wars* (George Lucas, 1977).

In 2006, *The Poseidon Adventure* was remade with a $160 million budget simply as *Poseidon* (Wolfgang Petersen, who also directed *Das Boot*, 1981, and *The Perfect Storm*, 2000). The film was nominated for an Academy Award for Best Visual Effects. DB

Notes

1. Stephen Keane, *Disaster Movies: The Cinema of Catastrophe* (London and New York: Wallflower, 2006), 17.
2. Ronald Neame, "Commentary," *The Poseidon Adventure*, directed by Ronald Neame (20th Century Fox, 2006), DVD.
3. Neame, "Commentary."
4. Neame, "Commentary."
5. William Graebner, "America's Poseidon Adventure: A Nation in Existential Despair," in *America in the Seventies*, edited by Beth Bailey and David Farber (Lawrence: University Press of Kansas, 2004), 160.
6. "The Morning After Story," *The Poseidon Adventure*, directed by Ronald Neame (20th Century Fox, 2006), DVD.
7. "RMS *Queen Mary*," *The Poseidon Adventure*, directed by Ronald Neame (20th Century Fox, 2006), DVD.
8. Paul Gallico, *The Poseidon Adventure* (London: Arrow Books, 1969, 2006).
9. Michele Farinola and Mimi Freedman, "Backstory: *The Poseidon Adventure*," 2000, *The Poseidon Adventure*, directed by Ronald Neame (20th Century Fox, 2006), DVD.
10. See Roger Ebert, "*The Poseidon Adventure*," *Chicago Sun-Times*, 21 December 1972, http://rogerebert.suntimes.com/apps/pbcs.dll/article?AID=/19721221/REVIEWS/212210301/1023 (10 June 2012).

Bibliography

Ebert, Roger. "*The Poseidon Adventure*." *Chicago Sun-Times*, 21 December 1972, http://rogerebert.suntimes.com/apps/pbcs.dll/article?AID=/19721221/REVIEWS/212210301/1023 (10 June 2012).

Gallico, Paul. *The Poseidon Adventure*. London: Arrow Books, 1969, 2006.

Graebner, William. "America's Poseidon Adventure: A Nation in Existential Despair." In *America in the Seventies*, edited by Beth Bailey and David Farber, 157–80. Lawrence: University Press of Kansas, 2004.

Keane, Stephen. *Disaster Movies: The Cinema of Catastrophe*. London and New York: Wallflower, 2006.

PROMETHEUS (2012)

DIRECTOR: Ridley Scott
WRITERS: Jon Spaiths, Damon Lindelof
PRODUCERS: Ridley Scott, David Giler, Walter Hill (20th Century Fox)
CINEMATOGRAPHER: Dariusz Wolski
EDITOR: Pietro Scalia
MUSIC: Marc Streitenfeld
CAST: Dr. Elizabeth Shaw: Noomi Rapace. Meredith Vickers: Charlize Theron. David: Michael Fassbender. Charlie Holloway: Logan Marshall-Green. Peter Wayland: Guy Pearce. Janek: Idris Elba. Fifield: Sean Harris. Millburn: Rafe Spall. Ford: Kate Dickie. Chance: Emun Eliott. Ravel: Benedict Wong. Elizabeth Shaw's Father: Patrick Wilson. Last Engineer: Ian Whyte. Sacrifice Engineer: Daniel James
AA: None
AAN: None
DVD: 20th Century Fox, 2012
BLU-RAY: 20th Century Fox, 2012. DVD/Blu-ray combo.
DURATION: 124 minutes

Prometheus, a big-budget science-fiction film of epic proportions, was released in 2012, and was well received nationally and internationally, but it earned only modest critical approval and practically no major awards, despite its ambitious themes. Ridley Scott had produced highly regarded science fiction in earlier decades, *Alien* in 1973, and *Blade Runner* in 1983, both of which have to do with artificial intelligence androids that attack humanity, either during expeditions to explore the cosmos or by invading the Earth and threating the human race. *Prometheus* is based mainly on the Greek myth of a Titan who attempted to give mankind knowledge (the gift of fire) and was punished by the gods, who feared mankind would eventually usurp their power.

A group of scientists undertake to visit the moon of a remote planet, where evidence discovered by noted scientists has shown that a civilization similar to ours may have been responsible for the genesis of our human species on Earth. The inhabitants of that moon are called "Engineers," having been responsible for the creation of mankind. The year of the expedition is late twenty-first century, the action spanning the years between 2089 and 2093, but two years elapse while the spaceship *Prometheus* travels from Earth to that planet, during which most of the crew are in cryogenic stasis, awakened only upon the arrival of the ship at its destination. The project is being funded by a multibillionaire, Peter Wayland (Guy Pearce), CEO of the Wayland Corporation, and it is to be captained by an expert space navigator, Janek (Idris Elba), and overseen by the mission's supervisor, Meredith Vickers (Charlize Theron). An android, David (Michael Fassbender), is in charge of the spaceship's operations and acts as helper and general factotum during the expedition.

The action begins as the viewer sees a sculptured android standing on the edge of a cataract, a large discuslike object hovering above him, departing and leaving him there. He drinks a potion from a cup and disintegrates rapidly, and his remains fall into the cascading current. We see his DNA spirals disintegrate and then reintegrate, suggesting a mutation of his species. The scene changes to the present, showing a group of archeologists headed by Dr. Elizabeth Shaw (Noomi Rapace) and her partner, Charlie Holloway (Logan Marshall-Green), who, in a Scottish cave in the Isle of Skye, discover images millennia old that resemble those of various ancient civilizations on Earth. They conclude that these are signs of the origins of the cosmos from alien visitors, whom they call "Engineers," who brought their DNA to Earth, thus creating mankind.

Immediately after that, there is a scene of a funeral, where a young Elizabeth—Ellie—asks her father where the dead go. His answer is that it depends on one's beliefs—some to Heaven, others to Paradise. That is the belief acquired at a young age by Elizabeth—that the human being has been created by some superior being in the universe, and her later scientific career becomes dedicated to the mission of discovering who our creator(s) are.

We next find ourselves flying in a spaceship, *Prometheus*, where the robot David is seen watching a scene from the film *Lawrence of Arabia*, hearing Peter O'Toole saying after snuffing out a match, "Certainly it hurts. The trick is not minding that it hurts." As *Prometheus* is approaching its destination, Janek is preparing to land, while David brings the crew out of its stasis. Vickers explains to them that they have arrived at their destination, and she gives them instructions that they are not to make contact with any creatures they find. Her talk is followed by a "show," in which a holograph of Peter Wayland, who had initiated the expedition and who is now dead, is explaining his intentions for their mission. His purpose was to discover the mysteries of life and death. He makes allusions to Prometheus, the Titan who challenged the gods and was expelled from Olympus. His prediction seems to doom the expedition, since he, like Prometheus—and the name of his ship—attempted to displace the gods, learn their secrets, and spread the information to mankind. The original Titan is brave and arrogant, but also the giver of secrets hitherto withheld from the always curious human minds. Wayland's "son" is David, the android he created, possibly containing his own DNA, and like him—and his hero, Lawrence of Arabia—David is undaunted by danger or pain. The fact that he does not have a soul, and is "doomed" to immortality, makes him even more daring, but jealous of humans, whose souls can possibly live on.

The crew of *Prometheus* consists of a motley crowd. Some went for purely monetary reasons, others for scientific curiosity, while one, Elizabeth Shaw, was spurred by her religious feelings, accepting this as an "invitation" to meet their makers. This is contrary to Darwinian evolution, one biologist, Millburn (Rafe Spall), observes, a feeling that is seconded by Holloway, who maintains that the future expedition is based on a hunch, rather than on clear scientific evidence. Dr. Shaw, however, believes that the creation is based on the action of a cosmic "deity," and by discovering the Engineers, the expedition could discover this deity and find out the reason for the creation of human beings.

The crew returns to the spacecraft when a tremendous storm threatens, but two crew members, Millburn and Fifield (Sean Harris), get stranded in the cave, and they are soon attacked by a snakelike creature that breaks Millburn's arm and then chokes him to death, while Fifield's helmet is melted by a gelatinous liquid and he falls into the puddle and apparently dies. He later reappears, mutated, and attacks and kills several crew members, before he is killed. David has discovered a cylinder in the cave while disobeying Vickers's orders to "copy" his findings, and he brings the liquid contained in it back to the ship. He finds out that the liquid contains the DNA of the Engineers, and that it matches that of the humans. He offers Holloway a drink in which he mixes the liquid. Soon thereafter, Holloway has sex with Shaw, and he impregnates her with the contaminated liquid, despite the fact that she is sterile. When David informs her that she is three months pregnant, Shaw rushes to an automated operating machine and performs a caesarean on herself. She drags out a monstrous, squidlike creature and annihilates it (she thinks). Holloway is brought back to the ship, sickened, but Vickers refuses to let him in and burns him to death using a flamethrower.

Meanwhile, David reveals to the crew that Wayland is still alive; he has been brought out of cryonic stasis and is preparing to join the expedition. Wayland explains that his purpose is to defeat death. The next morning, just before he leaves with the group, Vickers addresses Wayland as "father," raising suspicion that she, too, is an android. Wayland explores the countless bottlelike tubes found in the cave, containing some virulent "weapon of mass destruction," according to Janek weapons intended to destroy the Earth. Engineers in stasis exist in the cave, and when David wakes one of them that looks exactly like the one that jumped from the cataract in the first scene, the latter kills Wayland and decapitates David, whose head remains alive. Shaw escapes and runs out to warn Vickers and Janek, telling them that a large horseshoelike vehicle is about to take off to destroy the Earth. The humanlike monster that killed Wayland pursues Vickers and Shaw, and Shaw releases her alien offspring with its tentacles (for it has not died), and it attacks the humanlike Engineer and chokes him. A horseshoelike (juggernaut) spacecraft of the Engineers attempts to leave and travel to Earth to destroy it. Janek rams the spacecraft *Prometheus* into it and destroys it, but he gets killed, along with the rest of the crew. Vickers is crushed under it as it falls to the ground, but David tells Shaw how to escape, and she embarks on another ship, and travels by herself into space, still wanting to find out who created the Engineers. We see Shaw's offspring regenerating, its belly opening to turn into a prehistoric-looking monster, opening its jaws, a sign that Shaw will either be pursued or that the Earth has yet to be attacked.

Reactions from audiences, critics, and reviewers have offered myriad interpretations of this cinematic epic tale,[1] but a few of the most notable will suffice here. The name of the ship *Prometheus* suggests the most obvious: as Wayland explains in his speech to the crew, the Titan Prometheus, attempting to bring civilization to mankind, knowledge that is privileged only to the gods, is punished by being expelled from Olympus. Like Prometheus, Wayland implies that mankind is repulsed by the gods when attempting to unravel the secrets of the universe, or to improve its lot; as a consequence, it is condemned to servitude, blindness, and death. But that does not mean that new efforts to unravel the mysteries of man's origins should be abandoned.

Two roads are open: one is scientific progress, which provides the means with which to travel to other worlds found in space; the other is to assert a religious belief that whoever created us cannot abandon us to blindness and death. The two most important characters, therefore, in this tale are representatives of those two views. One is the robot David, who possesses mental capacities that exceed those of humans—in memory and the ability to interpret and synthesize knowledge—thus he has the capability to explain facts that come into his purview. The other is a scientist, Dr. Shaw, who acquires faith in her youth through her father's beliefs in a happy world in the hereafter, and she thus believes that whoever created us cannot and will not abandon us to our fate. She represents belief in God, and she wears a cross around her neck. The others in the crew represent either hired scientists (the biologists Millburn and the geologist Fifield) or functionaries that run and administer the ship. The owner of the corporation, Wayland, thought dead but kept alive in stasis, has brought Shaw along, since he is superstitious and thinks she could come in handy on the chance that the Engineers are indeed divine and have created mankind out of love.

Both David and Shaw are open to an interpretation of the motives. Shaw is daring; can withstand pain and shock; and ventures to launch another expedition, not giving up on her search for the motives of the creators. She believes that the Engineers obviously created us, but who created them? The interpretation of David is more ambiguous. As a creature of man's scientific ingenuity, he has inherited man's features: he is handsome, vain, and athletic (he shoots balls into a basket while riding a bicycle), and he even has feelings and emotions, showing a partiality for Shaw and poisoning her boyfriend. Although only a disembodied head at the end, he will accompany Shaw on her next expedition. He has unparalleled intellectual ingenuity, deconstructing ancient tongues, and he is thus able to understand aliens.

David ponders a phrase he hears from a film he likes, *Lawrence of Arabia*: "The trick, William Potter, is not minding that it hurts." He combs his hair vainly as he watches blond Peter O'Toole, impeccably coiffed (O'Toole's real hair was dark), and combs his own hair to look like him. This may be the most important clue to his personality: In *Lawrence of Arabia* (based on Lawrence's autobiography, *Seven Pillars of Wisdom*, 1926), Lawrence is a split personality: He comes into the Arab conflict as a power to reshape their map and give them their freedom. But he cannot entirely get rid of his entrenched loyalty to an Englishman. David, who is awake during the two-and-a-half-hour trip on *Prometheus*, unlike the others, who are in stasis, has had time to ponder and acquire additional human characteristics, but also to develop his ego as a new force to be reckoned with. If the universe is to be explored, he is the one to give directions, to lead, and to conquer. In this sense, he is both a Promethean and a Nietzschean Superman, figures that many poets and scientists—and science-fiction writers—have envisioned: Aeschylus, Goethe (his Homunculus in *Faust, Part Two*), Mary Shelley in *Frankenstein*, and, of course, to make the list short, Stanley Kubrick in giving us HAL in *2001: A Space Odyssey*. In fact, David is very much like HAL: both are machinelike androids. HAL has a red eye that sees and hears everything, and David, a humanoid, lives and behaves in a perfectly human manner, obedient, if not obsequious, but cryptic in his thoughts and devious in his actions.

This humanoid, then, is Prometheus. David has absorbed what he can from his makers and is a perfect imitator, but he develops ambitions to reach beyond and exceed their accomplishments. But, as Prometheus, he is punished: decapitated, although alive, he is still chained for his transgression—as his live head is placed in a bag and carried along by Dr. Elizabeth Shaw. She will run the show from now on. The Titan helped the human; now the human will take the Titan along for the ride, which supersedes all other concerns but one: the search for our creators will go on. CS

Note

1. Ben Walters, "*Prometheus*: What Was That About? Ten Key Questions," *Guardian*, 8 June 2012, www.guardian.co.uk/film/2012/jun/08/prometheus-ten-key-questions (30 September 2013).

Bibliography

Walters, Ben. "*Prometheus*: What Was That About? Ten Key Questions." *Guardian*, 8 June 2012, www.guardian.co.uk/film/2012/jun/08/prometheus-ten-key-questions (30 September 2013).

Q

QUO VADIS (1951)

DIRECTOR: Mervyn LeRoy
WRITERS: S. N. Behrman, Sonya Levien, John Lee Mahin. Based on the novel *Quo Vadis: A Tale of the Time of Nero* (1895), by Henryk Sienkiewicz.
PRODUCER: Sam Zimbalist (MGM)
CINEMATOGRAPHER: Robert Surtees, William V. Skall
EDITOR: Ralph E. Winters
ART DIRECTION: William A. Horning, Cedric Gibbons, Edward C. Carfagno
SET DECORATION: Hugh Hunt
COSTUMES: Herschel McCoy
MUSIC: Miklós Rózsa
CAST: Marcus Vinicius: Robert Taylor. Callina/Lygia: Deborah Kerr. Nero: Peter Ustinov. Aulus Plautius: Felix Aylmer. Pomponia: Nora Swinburne. Petronius: Leo Genn. Poppaea: Patricia Laffan. Peter: Finlay Curry. Ursus: Buddy Baer. Seneca: Nicholas Hannen. Phaon: D. A. Clark-Smith. Lucan: Alfredo Varelli. Terpnos: Geoffrey Dunn. Acte: Rosalie Crutchley. Nazarius: Thomas Miles. Eunice: Marina Berti. Tigellinus: Ralf Truman. Chilo: John Rudduck. Croton: Arthur Walge. Galba: Pietro Torri. Paul: Abraham Sofaer
AA: None
AAN: Best Picture (Sam Zimbalist), Best Supporting Actor (Leo Genn), Best Supporting Actor (Peter Ustinov), Best Art Direction–Set Decoration–Color (William A. Horning, Cedric Gibbons, Edward C. Carfagno, Hugh Hunt), Best Cinematography (Robert Surtees, William V. Skall), Best Costume Design–Color (Herschel McCoy), Best Film Editing (Ralph E. Winters), Best Music–Scoring of a Dramatic or Comedy Picture (Miklós Rózsa).
DVD: Warner Home Video, 2008. Two-disc special edition, with running commentary by F. X. Feeny.
BLU-RAY: Warner Home Video, 2009
DURATION: 174 minutes

Although religious epics had routinely been made since the early days of cinema, nothing was comparable in scope, spectacle, large cast, and budget to *Quo Vadis*, the first of the grand epics to be produced by MGM during the 1950s. Pompously announced as "colossal," and "industry's greatest spectacle ever," and supposed to have been even greater than *Gone with the Wind*, *Quo Vadis* was made just before the advent of the CinemaScope wide-screen (*The Robe* followed two years later), and it was filmed entirely on location in Rome and at Cinecittà Studios at a cost of $7 million, a staggering sum in those days. While featuring only one recognizable American star, Robert Taylor, *Quo Vadis* was studded with talented British actors of the stage and screen, including Peter Ustinov, Leo Genn, and Deborah Kerr, an actress who subsequently excelled on the American screen.

Ustinov, then only twenty-eight and a newcomer to the screen, gave the role of the mad emperor a polish unprecedented since the days of Charles Laughton, who had played Nero in *The Sign of the Cross* a couple of decades earlier. These two epics, made two decades apart, had similar story lines—the persecution of early Christians by the Romans—but *Quo Vadis* boasted color and a greater spectacle, far more elaborate sets, expensive costumes, thousands of extras in its crowd scenes, and even sixty-five lions imported from neighboring European countries for the man-eating scenes in the arena.

Based on the best-selling 1895 novel by Polish author Henryk Sienkiewicz, a recipient of a Nobel Prize for Literature in 1905, *Quo Vadis* (*Where Are You Going?*) was turned into a successful play by Wilson Barrett called *The Sign of the Cross*, which was later adapted into several popular films: *Quo Vadis* in 1912 and 1926, and *The Sign of the Cross* in 1932, also featuring a Roman legionnaire falling in love with a Christian girl. Directed by Mervyn LeRoy, whose credits included *Little Caesar* (1930), *Gold Diggers* (1933), and *Madame Curie* (1943), the 1951 version of *Quo Vadis* again drew its plot from Sienkiewicz's novel, which was based on historical facts drawn mainly from the Roman historians Suetonius and Tacitus describing the last years of Nero's life, between A.D. 64 and 68, when the notorious Roman emperor allegedly burned the city to be inspired to write an epic song.

Although several characters (among them Marcus and Lygia) are fictitious, the film makes allusions to facts of history—Nero's murder of his mother, Agrippina, and his wife, Octavia; his accusations against and torture of Christians; and, more specifically, his relationships with Seneca and Petronius, two Roman authors with whom Nero had close ties and who influenced his life. Seneca makes only a shadowy appearance in the film, but Petronius, nicknamed the "Arbiter of Taste," is skillfully portrayed by Leo Genn as a polished, opportunistic flatterer who curries favor with the tyrant to safeguard his and his family's interests. The film also makes much of Nero's lunacy, mainly thanks to a "no-holds-barred" performance by Peter Ustinov, whose unsettling portrayal of Nero as practically the Antichrist must have struck home, especially at a time when Hitler's crimes were still a fresh memory.

Compared with grand epics that would follow in the 1950s, *Quo Vadis* offers little action and, instead, concentrates on the romance between Marcus (Taylor) and Lygia (Kerr), the Nero–Petronius relationship, and the burning of Rome and the chaotic scenes that followed, concluding with a spectacle in the arena, where Christians are tortured or devoured by lions. The main plotline, however, is laced with a number of subplots, divided evenly between events surrounding the Roman court of Nero and the activities in the Christian camp. This makes for a rather static epic, but much color is added by clever dialogue, subtle characterizations, and a marked, if mostly indirect, moral angle showcasing in broad strokes Christian love against the inhumanities of tyranny.

The story begins with Nero's manic depressive mood after he has failed to produce a song and Petronius' half-mocking advice to him that he needs inspiration worthy of him. Meanwhile, Marcus, a military tribune, has arrived in Rome, victorious after a lengthy campaign in Britain. He is welcomed by both Nero and those surrounding him, including Nero's new consort, Poppaea (Patricia Laffan), who lusts after him, and Tigellinus (Ralf Truman), head of the Pretorian Guard, obviously envious of Marcus's triumphs. Marcus visits his "uncle" Petronius, who recommends some diversion by offering his exotic-looking Spanish slave, Eunice (Marina Berti), unaware that she is in love with him. Marcus also visits an old retired warrior, Aulus Plautius (Felix Aylmer), and notices his protégé, Callina (Kerr), who prefers to be called Lygia—as Poland, her native country, was known in Roman times. Marcus is so impressed by Lygia's beauty and grace that he instantly falls in love with her. He, of course, is unaware of the fact that Aulus, his wife Pomponia (Nora Swinburne), and the giant Ursus (Buddy Baer), Lygia's guardian since her childhood, are all Christians. During one of his visits to Rome, Marcus also meets Paul (Abraham Sofaer), who presents himself as a "philosopher," a fact that raises some suspicions in Marcus's mind.

After her reluctance to join him at a party, Marcus has Lygia seized by guards and escorted to the palace quarters, where, attired in splendor, she catches jealous Poppaea's eye, and even Nero's. Petronius subtly suggests to Marcus that "she is too narrow in hips," and thus Marcus can retain her as his "hostage," by the emperor's orders. The party is lavish entertainment, including a wrestling match, during which Croton (Arthur Walge), the top gladiator of Rome, strangles an opponent to death.

Puzzled by Lygia's rejection, Marcus suspects that she belongs to a secret sect, and he commissions Chilo (John Ruddock), a spy for hire, to find out where they meet. Accompanied by Croton, the three attend a secret Christian gathering, during which Peter (Finlay Curry), newly arrived in Rome, speaks of Christ, whom he had known in person, and bestows his blessing on the local converts. Marcus, Croton, and Chilo follow Lygia and her small group, which includes Pomponia and Ursus. The latter, suspecting that they are being followed, sends them home and remains behind. In a brief violent scene, he dispatches Marcus easily, and while Chilo slides out of sight, he wrestles with Croton, breaking his neck and lifting his body over his head and tossing it down a steep stone staircase. Then he carries the unconscious Marcus to Aulus's place, where his wounds are tended by Lygia herself. Marcus's passion for her intensifies, and he proposes marriage to her, freeing her from his bondage to him at the same time. After some hesitation, she accepts but then balks at the idea of living a Roman life of luxury, in spite of the fact that Marcus assures her that a statue of Christ will be included in the mix of other gods in his garden. Still failing to comprehend her divided loyalties, Marcus leaves in a rage, breaking a cross on her wall in half.

Meanwhile, Poppaea plans Marcus's undoing, suspecting his ties to the Christian girl she saw at the party. When the court, including Petronius and a dejected Marcus, moves to Antium, a luxury resort, Nero reveals to his entourage a model for a new city, Neropolis, designed by his architect Phaon (D. A. Clark-Smith) to replace Rome, which, to everyone's astonishment, he intends to destroy. Petronius, now realizing that mere flattery will not appease a madman, begins to express himself more directly. Marcus leaves the group abruptly and rushes to Rome, realizing from Tigellinus's remarks that the Christian quarters are already burning. He arrives in time to save Lygia and her company from the mob, but a large section of the city is already in flames.

As revolt is in the air, Poppaea suggests to a frightened and clueless Nero that he can use the Christians as scapegoats for setting the fire in Rome and punish them. The final act of the drama shows Marcus being arrested and thrown in the same prison where Christians are awaiting death in the arena. A vast crowd applauds when Christians are crucified and burned alive, but there is a change of heart when Ursus, the giant who loyally protects his ward Lygia during the climactic scene, battles a bull, wrestles the beast to the ground, and snaps its neck, a feat that provokes the crowd to ask for clemency, which Nero denies. Marcus breaks his bonds and jumps into the arena, and he and his military friends overwhelm the Pretorian Guard. The crowds are now in open rebellion, and a vengeful mob rushes into the palace to kill Nero, who strangles Poppaea, and then, aided by Acte (Rosalie Crutchley), his former lover and slave, commits suicide. Meanwhile, the crowd cheers a triumphant General Galba (Pietro Torri), who enters Rome with his legions as its liberator from the bizarre and monstrous tyrant. Marcus, Lygia, Nazarius (Thomas Miles), and Ursus are seen driving away to a new life with their possessions in a cart.

The two threads of the epic drama have thus fully developed. Many Christians die as martyrs, and Peter, having returned to Rome, has been crucified upside down, but the Christian ethos of love and peace becomes the main message of the movie with the conversion of Marcus from a rugged military Roman to a man of peace. The corrupt court of Nero has dissolved, reinforcing the moral that the evils of tyranny will eventually backfire. Even Petronius, a cynic and court-flatterer, has a change of heart. Having received a message from Nero inquiring "about his health" and knowing that the end is coming, he stages a "last supper," with his loyal friends surrounding him, having them witness his own death, and having just enough time to dictate a letter to his former master revealing his abhorrence of his monstrosities and mocking his boring songs. He frees his loving slave Eunice, but she, unable to part from him, slashes her own wrists and dies by his side. In this, possibly the most poignant scene in the movie, Petronius sounds almost Christian, as does Eunice when she tells him that she expects to be with him in the next life.

Magnificently staged, although not critically acclaimed, *Quo Vadis* is still one of the most spectacular and intriguing epics of the era, setting the tone for a string of Roman/Christian epics to follow, a trend that defined the mind-set of an era worn by a monstrous war but heartened by the overthrow of the Axis powers. The epics offered spectacle, showed up the perils of tyranny, and counteracted the emergence of television, but the moral uplift they offered was at the heart of their popular acceptance. Society craved good heroes defeating evil. Simplistic as that formula might sound, it became the main vehicle that carried the grand epic forward for at least another decade. CS

Bibliography

Sienkiewicz, Henryk. *Quo Vadis: A Tale of the Time of Nero*, 1st American ed. Translated by S. A. Biniom. Philadelphia, PA: Henry Artemus, 1895.

R

THE REMAINS OF THE DAY (1993)

DIRECTOR: James Ivory
WRITER: Ruth Prawer Jhabvala. Based on the novel by Kazuo Ishiguro.
PRODUCERS: John Calley, Ismail Merchant, Mike Nichols (Merchant Ivory Productions, Columbia Pictures Corporation)
CINEMATOGRAPHER: Tony Pierce-Roberts
EDITOR: Andrew Marcus
PRODUCTION DESIGN: Luciana Arrighi
ART DIRECTION: John Ralph
SET DECORATION: Ian Whittaker
COSTUMES: Jenny Beavan, John Bright
MUSIC: Richard Robbins
CAST: James Stevens: Anthony Hopkins. Miss Sally Kenton: Emma Thompson. Lord Darlington: James Fox. Jack Lewis: Christopher Reeve. Reginald Cardinal: Hugh Grant. William Stevens: Peter Vaughan. Thomas Benn: Tim Pigott-Smith. Dupont D'Ivry: Michael Lonsdale. Elsa: Emma Lewis. Irma: Joanna Joseph. Lizzie: Lena Headey. Charlie: Ben Chaplin. Prime Minister: Frank Shelley. German Ambassador: Wolf Kahler. Viscount Bigge: Jeffry Wickham
AA: None
AAN: Best Leading Actor (Anthony Hopkins), Best Leading Actress (Emma Thompson), Best Art Direction–Set Decoration (Luciana Arrighi, Ian Whittaker), Best Costume Design (Jenny Beavan, John Bright), Best Director (James Ivory), Best Music–Original Score (Richard Robbins), Best Picture (John Calley, Ismail Merchant, Mike Nichols), Best Writing–Screenplay Based on Material Previously Produced or Published (Ruth Prawer Jhabvala)
DVD: Columbia Pictures Home Entertainment, 2001
BLU-RAY: Currently unavailable
DURATION: 134 minutes

The film team of James Ivory and Ismail Merchant has been successful with a number of films produced, including several Henry James adaptations and E. M. Forster's *Howards End*. Their films are often described as "Merchant-Ivory" films, a term that has earned its own dictionary definition: "A so-called 'heritage film' that is typically a rich visual dramatization of an Edwardian novel but [that] replaces its original irony with a lovingly nostalgic recreation of the past."[1]

Based on the Kazuo Ishiguro's Booker Prize–winning novel (1989), the original screenplay was written by Harold Pinter when it was to be directed by Mike Nichols. After the directing duties went to James Ivory, some dialogue from Pinter's work remained in the script, but he insisted that his name be removed from the credits.[2] Ishiguro says that the main question he sought when writing the book was, "What would we do if caught up in the appeasement era?"[3]

The film opens with cars driving through the present-day English countryside and arriving at the sale of Lord Darlington's (James Fox) estate following his death. An American millionaire, former congressman Jack Lewis (Christopher Reeve) purchases many of the pieces in an attempt to keep them on his new property. The house had been filled with a staff the size of a "small army" but is now empty. The estate's long-standing head butler Stevens (Anthony Hopkins) reads a letter from his former lead housekeeper, Miss Sally Kenton (Emma Thompson), who says her marriage to Thomas Benn (Tim Pigott-Smith) is over. She does not know what is in her future, but she wants to be useful again. Stevens tells Lewis that the staff plan needs to be revised because Lewis's wife will be moving into the house. Lewis offers one of his cars, a Daimler, so Stevens can drive to England's West Country to visit Kenton in an attempt to pursue her to return.

Stevens recalls that the last time Lord Darlington enjoyed greeting his neighbors was during a fox hunt. That was the same day he told Miss Kenton that her staff was allowed no gentlemen callers. He found it a "major irritation" that there are those people "going from house to house looking for romance."

The film flashes back to Stevens reporting to Lord Darlington that he plans to hire a new butler named Stevens, his father. Stevens silently watches Kenton as she picks flowers and delivers them to him, although he regards his room as his "private place of work," preferring to "keep things as they are." Once William Stevens (Peter Vaughan) is on duty, Miss Kenton addresses him as "William," as she would any under servant, but Stevens insists that she address him as Mr. Stevens.

The senior Stevens has a bout of pain on the stairs as he sweeps. He enters a hidden door, leaving the broom and dustpan behind. Kenton shuts the open door. She reports to the younger Stevens, "If you're searching for your dustpan, it's on the landing." She wants him to know what his father has done. Stevens retrieves the broom and dustpan. Kenton finds a ceramic statue that has been misplaced. She tells Stevens and insists on waiting until he sees the error. "Your father is entrusted with more than he can handle. . . . Whatever he once was he no longer has the same abilities."[4]

Lord Darlington tells Stevens that they are expecting an American delegate to his conference, Congressman Lewis from Pennsylvania, a wealthy man who earned money from the cosmetics industry. During a small meeting, the senior Stevens falls and drops a tray of silver. Darlington asks Stevens to remove his father from duty around conference delegates, who will arrive in two weeks. He has created the conference because he saw how the Versailles Treaty had gone too far, even causing a German friend to commit suicide. Darlington says, "I've felt it my duty to put out a hand to help Germany." Stevens puts his father on lighter duty.

Darlington's godson, Reginald Cardinal (Hugh Grant) will be secretary to the conference. Cardinal is wary of the Nazis, their dictatorship, and their treatment of Jews. Cardinal plans to marry. Because he never had the "talk" with Cardinal, Darlington asks Stevens to have the "birds and bees" discussion with him. Darlington says, "Someone has to tell him. In a way, it would be easier if you did it. . . . Give him the basic facts and be done with it." Stevens approaches Cardinal, who is secretly smoking in the garden. He claims a friendship they have not had but is called away before saying anything beyond "All living creatures would be relevant to our discussion."

Congressman Lewis and French delegate Dupont D'Ivry (Michael Lonsdale) arrive early. D'Ivry has sore feet from wearing tight shoes. Lewis interferes with his footbath by attempting to discuss the upcoming conference because "things are moving in a direction that you would not approve of." At the conference's first meeting, the thirty men in attendance listen to Darlington: "It's in our own interest to have a free, equal, and strong Germany, to assist Germany in her virile struggle." In another attempt to discuss the issues privately, Lewis explains to D'Ivry that he wants to "restrain the Germans." D'Ivry responds, saying, "Germany wants peace as much as we do. She needs peace."

While Stevens attends to the conference, the senior Stevens becomes seriously ill and is put to bed. After the doctor examines his father, Stevens visits him for a moment. In their only intimate moment, his father says he has fallen out of love with his wife, Stevens's mother. He adds, "I loved her once. I found her carrying on. A good son. Proud of you." Stevens does not react and quickly returns to his work.

During a conference dinner, D'Ivry says that he has been impressed by talk of peace and will do his "utmost to change attitudes [toward] our former foe." Unimpressed, Lewis stands and declares, "The United States does not want war. Neither do we care for peace at any price." He raises his glass to the "classic English gentleman of the old school," calls them amateurs, and toasts the professionals. Darlington responds by saying, "What you call amateurism is what I call honor." "Professional" to Darlington means "greed and power." Kenton reports to Stevens that his father passed away and requests permission to close his eyes. Stevens explains, "My father wanted me to continue my work. I can't let him down." The doctor reports he died painlessly from a severe stroke.

Two young German women, Elsa (Emma Lewis) and Irma (Joanna Joseph), are hired for the estate. Darlington is happy for the opportunity to practice his German. Visiting German dignitaries discuss the Fascist racial laws as "sanitary measures" and how German workers are "kept in line." While having a late-night drink, Benn presses Stevens's unquestioning belief in Darlington's "higher moral standing." Benn points out that Miss Kenton is a "good looking woman," to which Stevens replies, "I'd be lost without her."

Lord Darlington reads an anti-Semitic book that convinces him that he must fire Elsa and Irma for the "well-being" of his guests. Although Stevens is surprised by the decision because they work "extremely well," he agrees to let them go. Miss Kenton refuses to let them go because it would "be wrong and a sin." Although she threatens to quit, she remains, stating, "I'm not leaving. I've nowhere to go. I have no family. I'm a coward. I'm frightened of leaving and that's the truth. All I see out in the world is loneliness, and it frightens me. That's all my high principles are worth, Mr. Stevens. I'm ashamed of myself." Stevens's only response is that she is "extremely important to [the] house."

Lord Darlington later regrets his decision to let the Jewish maids go. He laments, "One would like to do something for them. It was wrong what occurred." Stevens asks Kenton if she knows how to contact them. He says, "You were as distressed as I was about it." Flabbergasted by this statement, she asks, "Why do you always have to hide what you feel?" At a later time, she believes she catches Stevens watching a pretty servant. "Can it be that our Mr. Stevens is flesh and blood after all?" she asks. She says he has a guilty smile. Visiting him in his study, she sees him hide his book from her. Believing it to be "racy," she asks why he is shy about it. Revealing her attraction to him, she corners him and removes the book from his hands. "Oh dear, it's just a sentimental love story," she says. He claims to read these books to "develop [his] command and knowledge of the English language" and further his education. One suspects that he was dreaming of her as he reads the romance. There are, as Kazuo Ishiguro says, "two ways to waste your life: emotionally and politically."[5] Stevens excels at both.

Miss Kenton sees her own life as empty when the new girl, Lizzie (Lena Headey), gives her notice because she plans to marry Charlie (Ben Chaplin), the head footman. That night, her irritation causes Stevens to say that they should "communicate only during the day." The next day, Miss Kenton visits Benn in a pub. Benn says, "If I don't like something, I want to be in a position to say 'stuff it.'" He suggests that the two of them open a small boardinghouse. He calls her by her first name. They kiss, but she becomes uncomfortable and leaves.

The next week, Cardinal arrives unexpectedly and asks to stay in a room. Stevens tells Miss Kenton that he will expect his usual room. She plans to see Benn that evening. He has asked her to marry him. She tells Stevens, "I'm thinking about it. I thought you should know." Stevens responds, "I trust you'll have a most pleasant evening." Lord Darlington tells Cardinal to make himself "scarce" because his visitors are confidential and Cardinal is a "newshound." Cardinal watches from the room upstairs as they arrive. Among others, he sees the prime minister (Frank Shelley) arrive. The German ambassador (Wolf Kahler) asks his assistant to note the paintings Darlington owns "for later." He later claims to Darlington that "the führer is a man of peace"; however, they would not allow a country like Czechoslovakia "to thumb its nose at the 1,000-year German Reich." Miss Kenton returns but is stopped from entering by security. She tells Stevens that she has agreed to marry Benn and would like an early release from her duties.

Cardinal asks Stevens to have a drink with him. He came to observe the conference and wants to know what they are talking about. Stevens says, "It's not my place to be curious about such matters." Cardinal says that the Germans are using British "high and noble motives and twist them to their own foul ends." Stevens responds, stating, "His Lordship is working to bring peace in our time." Cardinal responds, "Are you as deluded as he is?" Stevens excuses himself, goes to the wine cellar, and passes Miss Kenton's room. He overhears her crying and interrupts by telling her about an area of the house that had not been dusted.

The film then flashes forward again. On the way to visit Mrs. Benn (Kenton) in the West Country, Stevens's Daimler runs out of fuel and will not restart. At a pub, he is taken for a gentleman. He claims that his main "concern [is] . . . foreign policy." He continues, "Not that I ever held a high office. . . . It was my good fortune to have consorted with many men of influence." He stays in a room where the pub owner's son once slept. He died at Dunkirk.

The next day, Viscount Bigge (Jeffry Wickham) offers to drive him to his car. On the way, he recognizes Stevens as a manservant. Bigge asks about Lord Darlington, who "tried to make a deal with Hitler." He adds, "He sued a newspaper. . . . Lucky he wasn't tried for treason." At first Stevens denies working for Darlington. When asked if he trusted him, Stevens responds that he did. Bigge asks, "If a mistake was to be made, wouldn't you rather have made your own?" Stevens says, "In a very small way, I did make my own small mistake."

On her way to meet Stevens, Mrs. Benn is stopped by her husband, although they are separated. He brings news that their daughter Catherine is expecting and that the house is empty without her. Arriving late for tea, she finds Stevens rereading her letter as he waits. They have not seen each other for more than twenty years. They discuss Darlington. Stevens says "his heart was broken" and that Cardinal was killed in the war. She is considering returning to service, but it would have to be near where her grandchild will be born.

They walk along the boardwalk with other "out of season" visitors. Mrs. Benn reveals to Stevens that she left the Darlington estate to annoy him. She states, "There are times when I think what a mistake I've made of my life." They wait together for her bus at a bus stop. Once she is on the back of the bus, they shake hands. The scene ends with the image of their hands slipping apart as the bus leaves.

Back at Darlington Hall, Stevens and his staff mount the paintings Mr. Lewis has purchased on the walls. Lewis mentions the Darlington conference. He remembers delivering his opinion but not what he said. Stevens says he was too busy to listen.

The film follows the "life of an emotionally and sexually repressed butler as it dovetails with that of his employer, a well-meaning but wrongheaded aristo-twit who, in the mid-1930s, secretly works to appease Hitler, avoid war, and preserve England's rigid social hierarchy,"[6] but Ishiguro says, "Most of us were butlers for a time."[7] JMW

Notes

1. "Merchant-Ivory film," *Brewer's Dictionary of Phrase and Fable*. London: Chambers Harrap, 2009.
2. Robert Emmett Long, *James Ivory in Conversation: How Merchant Ivory Makes Its Movies* (Berkeley: University of California Press, 2006), 227.
3. "Blind Loyalty, Hollow Honor: England's Fatal Flaw," *The Remains of the Day*, directed by James Ivory (Columbia Pictures Home Entertainment, 2001), DVD.
4. Preparing for her role, Emma Thompson discussed her character with her grandmother, who had served as a domestic. Long, *James Ivory in Conversation*, 228.
5. "*The Remains of the Day*: The Filmmakers' Journey."
6. Bert Cardullo, "The Servant," *Hudson Review* 47, no. 4 (2005): 617.
7. "Blind Loyalty, Hollow Honor."

Bibliography

Cardullo, Bert. "The Servant." *Hudson Review* 47, no. 4 (2005): 616–22.

Long, Robert Emmett. *James Ivory in Conversation: How Merchant Ivory Makes Its Movies*. Berkeley: University of California Press, 2006.

"Merchant-Ivory film." *Brewer's Dictionary of Phrase and Fable*. London: Chambers Harrap, 2009.

ROB ROY (1995)

DIRECTOR: Michael Caton-Jones
WRITER: Alan Sharp. Based on the historical novel by Sir Walter Scott.
PRODUCERS: Peter Broughan, Richard Jackson (United Artists, Talisman Productions)
CINEMATOGRAPHER: Karl Walter Lindenlaub
EDITOR: Peter Honess
MUSIC: Carter Burwell
CAST: Rob Roy MacGregor: Liam Neeson. Mary: Jessica Lange. Lord James Montrose: John Hurt. Archibald Cunningham: Tim Roth. McDonald: Eric Stoltz. John Campbell, Duke of Argyll: Andrew Keir. Killearn: Brian Cox. Alasdair: Brian McCardie. Tam Sibbald: David Hayman. Guthrie: Gilbert Martin. Betty: Vicki Masson
AA: None
AAN: Best Supporting Actor (Tim Roth)
DVD: MGM, 1997
BLU-RAY: MGM, 2011
DURATION: 139 minutes

Directed by Michael Caton-Jones, *Rob Roy*, a swashbuckling costume drama, is a departure from his earlier films, the likes of *Memphis Belle* (1990) and *Doc Hollywood* (1991). *Rob Roy* depicts a period of decline in Scottish power and culture because of rising English power and the loss of young Scots to the New World. This decline is paralleled by Rob Roy's own fall, caused by his overweening sense of honor. Based on the stories of the historical Rob Roy, as well as Sir Walter Scott's "dense, dialect-heavy volume that makes the movie look effervescent by comparison,"[1] several reviewers called the film a "Scottish Western," but "[i]Instead of Monument Valley it has the Highlands,"[2] and, like westerns, "good men become outlaws over cattle. Rich men carve up God's green earth. Dumb guys pick fights in bars. And back at the ranch, anxious women wait for their kilted cowboys to come down from the hills."[3]

Rob Roy MacGregor (Liam Neeson) and his men are hunting for cattle rustlers in the Scottish hills. The men have stolen more than thirty cattle from Lord James Montrose (John Hurt). Once they find them, Roy plans to talk to them in the morning because he knows one of them, Tam Sibbald (David Hayman). When Roy approaches them to reclaim the cattle, Sibbald attacks. Roy knifes him and tells the others to put down their weapons. His men retrieve their swords and take the cattle. Roy and his men bring the cattle into his village of Craigrostan. Most of the 200 people living on his 300 acres are old, sick, or very young. Most young men move to the United States; even his friend McDonald (Eric Stoltz) desires to emigrate to Virginia. Roy washes himself in the lake; checks on his children in their beds; and has sex with his wife, Mary. The next day, Roy tells his wife about his plan to borrow 1,000 pounds from Lord Montrose to buy and sell cattle. He lectures his children on honor being "man's gift to himself." After the children return to the house, Mary seduces him on the hillside.

At Montrose's estate, the nobility bet on a sword fight between two men. Lord Montrose introduces Archibald Cunningham (Tim Roth) to John Campbell, Duke of Argyll (Andre Keir), who says he is "another one of your likely lads." Argyll's man Guthrie (Gilbert Martin) challenges Cunningham to a sword fight to the first cut, which Cunningham wins. Guthrie is prevented from stabbing him in the back by Argyll. Later, Betty (Vicki Masson), one of Montrose's maids, leaves Cunningham's bed and is harassed by Montrose's factor, Killearn (Brian Cox). Killearn speaks to Cunningham about the debts he owes to local tradesmen. Although he has no funds to leave or pay them off, he says, "I cannot wait to be out of the damnable place."

Montrose speaks to Cunningham about his debts and Killearn's report that he has been "saddling his servant wenches." Because Cunningham is penniless, Montrose is afraid he will join Argyll. After Cunningham leaves, Roy makes his request of a loan of 1,000 pounds for three months. They agree on terms, using his land as collateral. Killearn brings the contract to a tavern. Guthrie arrives and tells Roy that he heard he "back stabbed Tam Sibbald." Roy challenges him to "the first cut" and cuts his own hand on Guthrie's blade, saying, "Well done. Some other time when we're both sober." Contract still unsigned, Roy tells McDonald to stay with Killearn until it is.

Betty asks Cunningham to take her away with him. He responds saying, "I am but a bastard abroad seeking my fortune in the favors of great men." She tells him she is pregnant. She overhears Killearn tell Cunningham about an idea he had for him to get out of debt. The following day, Killearn forces McDonald to wait as he takes debt payments from villagers. At the end of the day, Killearn lies to McDonald that Montrose is traveling and that he left without signing the note. Instead of the agreed letter of credit, McDonald receives a bag with 1,000 pounds in coin.

Roy tells the village that his plan is to pay men to buy and drive 300 cattle. He announces a celebration of their forthcoming success. As hundreds dance and musicians play, McDonald rides home alone in the dark. Cunningham rides up behind him. McDonald rides faster but is knocked from his horse by a rope tied between trees. McDonald stumbles away and hides the coins in a tree, but Cunningham follows, kills him, and finds the coins. Cunningham dumps his body in a lake. McDonald's horse arrives at Craigrostan without a rider.

Although others, including his younger brother Alasdair (Brian McCardie), believe that McDonald took the money and sailed to the United States, Roy believes something else happened and searches for him. Mary stresses to him the importance of renegotiating the terms of the contract with Montrose as soon as possible.

Argyll visits Montrose; he is angry that Montrose sullies his reputation by calling him a "Jacobite," a person who desires the return of the Catholic Stewarts to the throne. Roy visits Montrose. He is willing to renegotiate as long as Roy agrees to lie about Argyll being a Jacobite. Roy's honor offended, he says, "What you ask is below men." Montrose tells him that his land is forfeit and calls out the watch. "You have slept your last peaceful night," Montrose says, threatening him. At home, Roy tells Mary of his refusal to bear false witness. They argue. He asks, "Would you lie against my conscience?" She responds, "You revel in it. The great man against all." He decides to sleep in the woods alone.

Cunningham is ordered to return Roy "broken but not dead." Roth earned his Academy Award nomination by playing Cunningham "as nasty as they come, a thin and girlish sword fighter who can carve up all the beefy hackers foolish enough to challenge him, and a clever and sadistic enemy to those he must hunt down."[4]

Roy sleeps in the hills while Mary and the children stay at home. The next morning, Cunningham and his men attack the Roy home from boats. Cunningham forces Mary inside the house and rapes her to further antagonize Roy. His men burn their crops and outbuildings. Although he has promised to protect Mary, Alasdair sleeps in a field. After he is finished assaulting the family and destroying their property, Cunningham sets fire to the house roof. While it burns, Mary recovers, arranging her clothes and hair. After the men have remounted their boats, Alasdair runs to the water saying he will avenge her. She makes him swear that he will not tell Roy: "If I can bear it to be done, you can bear to be silent."

Montrose realizes that Cunningham is involved. He tells him, "You have a rare grasp of the conspirator's mind." Betty stops Cunningham as he leaves. She was fired because she is pregnant. He refuses to help her, saying, "It will not be the first bastard born in Scotland."

Meeting with his men around a fire, Roy tells them that they must not fight Montrose in an open battle; however, he promises his honor will be satisfied. Roy moves his family to another house. Betty arrives and tells Mary that she overheard Killearn speaking to Cunningham about the easiest 1,000 pounds he would ever earn. Although she has a "bastard's bastard in [her]," she says she still loves him. Mary responds, "Love is never a sin. Only the lack of it." Mary tells Roy about Betty's condition and her story, advising that he take the case to the Duke of Argyll, but he has a different idea.

At the tavern, Killearn tells Guthrie to find Roy, but Roy walks in at that very moment. Roy challenges Killearn, but Guthrie defends him. Roy quickly dispatches Guthrie and takes Killearn to face his accuser. Alasdair finds Betty dead by hanging herself. Mary is forced to challenge Killearn herself. When she does, Killearn says she walked away from her burning house "like a queen." He realizes that Cunningham's rape resulted in pregnancy, so he tells her she must tell Montrose that Cunningham stole the money alone or he will tell Roy. Outraged, she draws her knife and cuts his neck. He runs to the lake, where Alasdair kills him.

Frustrated that Killearn was abducted, Montrose tells Cunningham, "You and Killearn have hands in matters not in sight." Cunningham burns houses searching for Roy, while Roy and his men watch from a hill. They decide to retreat rather than challenge a much larger force. After the others have retreated, Alasdair fires at Cunningham's men, hitting one. Alasdair is shot, and Roy carries him up the hill. As Alasdair dies, he tells him about Mary's rape. Caught, Roy is tied to Cunningham's horse and led back to town. On the way, Cunningham questions him about Killearn, promising that he will not be hurt. Roy says, "You're a thief and a murderer and violator of women."

They deliver Roy to Lord Montrose at Glen Orchy Bridge. Roy tells him what he knows about Cunningham, but Montrose says that they are "desperate words from a desperate man" and orders him hung from the bridge. Roy grabs a rope and ties it around Cunningham's neck. He then swings off the bridge holding on to it. Cunningham's men fire as he drifts downstream and down several waterfalls. He avoids capture by hiding in the stomach of a dead cow.

Mary visits the Duke of Argyll and relates the story of Roy's loan and his refusal to bear false witness against Argyll. She tells him, "Though I love his honor, it is but a moon-casting shadow to the love I bear him." Argyll lends her a house where the family can stay. Roy arrives. She admits she is pregnant and does not know who the father is. Roy visits Argyll about challenging Cunningham to a duel. Argyll is convinced that Cunningham would kill him, but he agrees to the contest. Cunningham also agrees to the fight.

At the estate, Montrose and Argyll bet that if Roy wins, Montrose will "acquit him of all he owes," and if he loses, Argyll will pay the debt of 1,000 pounds. During the fight, Cunningham cuts Roy several times without Roy landing a single blow. Worn down and bleeding, Roy drags the tip of his blade on the ground. Cunningham presses the tip of his blade to Roy's throat, but Roy prevents it from entering his flesh by grabbing the blade in one hand and killing him with his claymore, which is in the other. Cunningham dead, Argyll tells Montrose that he will hold him to their bargain. Roy goes home to heal with his family.

The first half hour of the film shows Roy and his wife celebrating the sexual freedom they have as a loving couple. The remaining time seems intent on making them pay for these "transgressions." Roy returns home, viewers imagine, with hopes of renewing their activities. Rob Roy is famous for his heroics, "but the film doesn't convey much sense of why he should matter to modern viewers, who may know less about Rob Roy the folk hero than Rob Roy the drink."[5] JMW

Notes

1. Janet Maslin, "Film Review: *Rob Roy*," *New York Times*, 7 April 1995, 1.
2. Andy Pawelczak, "*Rob Roy*," *Films in Review*, July–August 1995, 60.
3. Brian D. Johnson, "*Rob Roy*," *Maclean's*, 10 April 1995, 50.
4. Jay Stone, "*Rob Roy* an Unsatisfying Swashbuckler," *Ottawa Citizen*, 13 April 1995, E6.
5. Maslin, "Film Review: *Rob Roy*," 1.

Bibliography

Johnson, Brian D. "*Rob Roy*." *Maclean's*, 10 April 1995, 50.

Maslin, Janet. "Film Review: *Rob Roy*." *New York Times*, 7 April 1995, 1.

Pawelczak, Andy. "*Rob Roy*." *Films in Review*, July–August 1995, 60.

Stone, Jay. "*Rob Roy* an Unsatisfying Swashbuckler." *Ottawa Citizen*, 13 April 1995, E6.

THE ROBE (1953)

DIRECTOR: Henry Koster
WRITERS: Albert Maltz, Philip Dunne. Adaptation by Gina Kaus from the novel by Lloyd C. Douglas.
PRODUCER: Frank Ross (20th Century Fox)
CINEMATOGRAPHER: Leon Shamroy
EDITOR: Barbara McLean
ART DIRECTION: Lyle R. Wheeler, George W. Davis
SET DECORATION: Paul S. Fox, Walter M. Scott
COSTUMES: Charles Le Maire, Emile Santiago
MUSIC: Alfred Newman
CAST: Marcellus Gallio: Richard Burton. Diana: Jean Simmons. Demetrius: Victor Mature. Peter: Michael Rennie. Caligula: Jay Robinson. Justus: Dean Jagger. Sen. Gallio: Torin Thatcher. Pontius Pilate: Richard Boone. Miriam: Betta St. John. Paulus: Jeff Morrow. Emperor Tiberius: Ernest Thesiger. Junia: Dawn Addams. Abidor: Leon Askin. Rebecca: Helen Beverley. Quintus: Frank Pulaski
AA: Best Art Direction–Set Decoration–Color (Lyle R. Wheeler, George W. Davis, Walter M. Scott, Paul S. Fox), Best Costume Design–Color (Charles Le Maire, Emile Santiago)
AAN: Best Leading Actor (Richard Burton), Best Cinematography–Color (Leon Shamroy), Best Picture (Frank Ross)
GG: Best Motion Picture–Drama
DVD: 20th Century Fox, 2007
BLU-RAY: 20th Century Fox, 2009
DURATION: 128 minutes

The Robe is a Roman-era Christian epic based on the highly successful 1943 novel of the same name by Lloyd C. Douglas, which depicts the gradual conversion of a Roman tribune to Christianity after he carries out the Crucifixion of Jesus. Picking up two Academy Awards, it is best known as the first CinemaScope film to have been released, ushering in a wave of big-screen epics in the years that followed. Sheldon Hall and Steve Neale note that *The Robe* had originally been a wartime project cancelled due to shortages, but although it was ready for shooting in 1952, in the old, narrower format, the film "was delayed for the sets to be redesigned and rebuilt" for CinemaScope, "adding $500,000 to the eventual $4.1 million budget."[1] It was a huge financial success, "second only to *Gone with the Wind* (Victor Fleming, 1939) in *Variety*'s annually updated chart."[2]

Writing for the *New York Times*, Bosley Crowther notes the promise and limitations of the new CinemaScope format, writing, "The shape of the screen—wide and narrow—makes for occasional oppressiveness. A sense of the image being pressed down and drawn out inevitably occurs. Close-ups, too, become oppressive. However, the system seems fully flexible, and some exciting employments of it may be anticipated confidently."[3]

That *The Robe* was conceived as a cinematic event is emphasized even in the opening titles, which take place on a backdrop of rich red velvet theatrical curtains, opened to reveal a Roman arena, its gladiators saluting Emperor Tiberius (Ernest Thesiger). The voice of Tribune Marcellus Gallio (Richard Burton) introduces us to Rome, with its "finest fighting machine in history." As Marcellus enters the slave market, he prevents the escape of an educated Greek slave, whom he will encounter again soon. The handsome Marcellus is soon revealed to be an arrogant womanizer, who is gently chastised when he is reunited with his childhood friend Diana (Jean Simmons), now a beautiful woman intended for the emperor's heir Caligula (Jay Robinson). Caligula's arrival makes clear a long-standing animosity between the two men, heightened when Caligula buys twin slave girls from under Marcellus. In a petty and foolish response, Marcellus in turn outbids Caligula for the Greek slave. Marcellus allows a Greek, called Demetrius (Victor Mature), to be unbound, and Demetrius honorably reports to the Gallio household, even though he could have escaped. Yet, when the house steward tells Demetrius that to "be a slave in this household is an honor," Demetrius retorts, "to be a slave anywhere is to be a dog."

Upon his return, Marcellus is reprimanded by his father, Senator Gallio (Torin Thatcher), who is frustrated by his son's immaturity. As he predicts, Caligula retaliates and sends Marcellus to the garrison in Jerusalem, the "scum of the army," in a rebellious land. When Diana bids farewell to Marcellus, he extracts from her a declaration of love and suddenly realizes that he feels likewise. Diana promises to seek the intervention of Tiberius on their behalf.

Marcellus and Demetrius arrive in Jerusalem at Passover, and while Marcellus is told of the local prophecy of the Messiah, Demetrius witnesses the arrival of Jesus, seen only in the distance. Demetrius is a changed man, and he feels compelled to follow the stranger, but he follows his duty to serve Marcellus, until the tribune makes arrangements for Jesus to be arrested for stirring up the people. Demetrius departs to try to warn Jesus, only to be informed by a repentant Judas that it is too late (complete with melodramatic thunderclap).

Demetrius pleads with a hungover Marcellus to intercede on Jesus' behalf, but Marcellus has no interest in the matter. Pontius Pilate (Richard Boone) calls for Marcellus to inform him that Emperor Tiberius has recalled him to Capri, but before he departs, Pilate orders him to crucify three criminals, including the "fanatic." As the criminals carry their crosses, Demetrius tries to stop Jesus from being whipped, but Demetrius is himself knocked unconscious as a result. He awakens to an ominous daytime darkness and ascends the mount to see the crucified Jesus. Meanwhile, the Romans play dice, and Marcellus wins Jesus' robe. Although seemingly oblivious to the fate of the men he has killed, when Marcellus puts on the robe in the middle of a storm, he descends to his knees and begs for it to be taken off. Is he beset by madness or guilt, or is this divine retribution? Demetrius calls him a murdering animal and curses him before leaving with the robe.

On the voyage back to Capri, Marcellus is plagued by nightmares and visions of Christ, and the members of his crew suspect that he is mad. On Capri, Diana stops Marcellus from throwing himself off the rocks. Witnessing Marcellus suffering another attack, the kindly Emperor Tiberius instructs him to find the bewitched robe and destroy it, while collecting the names of the treasonous disciples. Indeed, Tiberius prophesizes that such a movement calling for freedom will surely bring about the end of the empire one day.

Marcellus journeys back to Palestine in search of Demetrius with the help of a Syrian merchant guide, Abidor (Leon Askin). Posing (unconvincingly) as a merchant himself, Marcellus is welcomed into a small village, where he finds followers of Jesus who had known him personally. Although he finds their simple honesty puzzling, he is moved by them, almost against his will. Abidor tells him that Pilate is paying for information about Christians, but Marcellus sends him away. And yet when the paralyzed Miriam (Betta St. John) tells him of Jesus' wish that they build their world on love and charity, Marcellus responds that "worlds are built on force."

Marcellus finds Demetrius visiting in the village with Peter the fisherman (Michael Rennie), and he demands that Demetrius burn the robe. He refuses, but when Marcellus tries to dispose of it himself, he finds that he cannot. Instead, to his surprise, he finds that his fear departs him. Marcellus meets Peter as the villagers assemble, but the village elder, Justus (Dean Jagger), is murdered in cold blood by Roman soldiers who have surrounded them. Marcellus attempts to intercede only to be informed that Tiberius is dead and Caligula now rules. After undertaking single combat with centurion Paulus to resolve the dispute (in what *Variety* singles out as a "highlight" of the film),[4] Marcellus prevails and orders the troops to retreat.

Despite the violent means by which Marcellus comes to the villagers' defense, he nonetheless refuses to take his opponent's life, signaling the change in his moral code. When Peter asks him to join them in spreading the word of Jesus, Marcellus confesses that he crucified the Messiah. Marcellus is astonished when Peter forgives him for such a crime.

Later in Rome, Caligula commands Diana's presence to inform her that her beloved Marcellus is in the city. He is incensed that Diana would still prefer her Christian fugitive over the emperor himself. Caligula cruelly shows Diana the captured Demetrius being tortured to obtain the location of the Christians, and he takes pleasure in her distress; however, upon departing, Diana discovers that Marcellus' family steward is himself a Christian, and he takes her to meet Marcellus in their underground hideout. Marcellus tells Diana the story of the man who wore the robe. Although Diana is moved by his story of justice and charity, she declares, "[T]he world just isn't like that."

Caligula is infuriated when Demetrius is rescued from under the Praetorian Guard at the palace dungeon by Marcellus and his fellow Christians. He sends guards to search the Gallio house. They find nothing, and the injured Demetrius and the Christians come out of hiding once the guards depart. When the Gallio family physician is unable to help Demetrius, Peter arrives and restores him. Having been disowned by his father, Marcellus tries to get Demetrius out of Rome, only to be pursued. (The *Variety* review notes of this "standout" chase sequence that the "four charging white steeds [go] head-on into the camera" to create a "most effective 3-D illusion."[5]) Sacrificing himself, Marcellus remains to delay the Romans, while Demetrius and his fellow Christians escape. The two men bid farewell to one another as friends and equals.

Visiting the captured Marcellus, Diana declares her ongoing love but remains pragmatic about the futility of his faith, although she does want to be able to think as he does. When Caligula takes the unexpected step of giving Marcellus a trial, Marcellus renews his pledge of loyalty to Caligula but refuses to renounce Jesus. The emperor's followers duly sentence him to death. To Caligula's dismay, Diana asks to join Marcellus, overcome by disgust for Caligula and having a newfound faith in the Christian God. Giving the robe to the Gallio's steward, Diana and Marcellus calmly climb the steps of the palace to their death, but they are seen ascending the clouds into heaven.

While the trailer for the film proclaims that it has both "faith and spectacle," the film was criticized for emphasizing the latter at the expense of its spiritual story. Despite these reservations, the *New York Times* also comments that "it is notable that Christ is seen only as a wide-robed figure on a distant hill and a tormented, indistinguishable victim burdened beneath the heavy cross. In this respect, the picture has dignity and restraint."[6] In comparison to other ancient-world epics, *The Robe* is actually short on spectacle events as such, and the dramatic scoring to its religious plot may feel overwrought to today's audiences.

Richard Burton and Jean Simmons are beautifully engaging as the reunited childhood sweethearts. Their story is, of course, a fictional one set against the historical background, which itself is tampered with. Tiberius is curiously reasonable here—Suetonius relates that during his retirement on Capri, the emperor engaged in depraved acts, including pedophilia (Caius Suetonius Tranquillus, *The Lives of the Caesars*, Tiberius, 43–45). Peter O'Toole's depiction of the aging Tiberius as a syphilitic lecher in *Caligula* (Tinto Brass, Giancarlo Lui, Bob Guccione, 1979) is probably closer to the mark, but understandably inappropriate for 1953. Jay Robinson's camp, hammy, and shrill Caligula is a delight, although in the film he is prematurely objectionable; in reality, the people were glad to be rid of Tiberius and had initially welcomed Caligula.[7] He lost this support in fewer than six months after coming to power and was assassinated in less than four years, an event depicted in the sequel to *The Robe*, *Demetrius and the Gladiators* (Delmer Daves, 1954). The sequel follows the fortunes of Demetrius as he becomes a gladiator and struggles with a loss of faith in the face of Roman barbarity.

The Robe's phenomenal success and the CinemaScope format itself helped the revival of the epic in the following years. *The Robe* was nominated for Best Picture but lost to *From Here to Eternity* (Fred Zinnemann, 1953). Richard Burton had received an Academy Award nomination the previous year for his role in another Henry Coster film, *My Cousin Rachel* (1952), and he was nominated again for his lead in *The Robe*, losing out to William Holden in *Stalag 17* (Billy Wilder, 1953).

The DVD and Blu-ray editions of *The Robe* have added a coscript writer credit for Albert Maltz, one of the "Hollywood Ten" who was sent to prison for refusing to answer questions or name names to the House Un-American Activities Committee. Film critic Jeffrey Richards suggests that Maltz may be responsible for a telling sequence in the film that diverts from the book. Tiberius demands that Marcellus find out the names of the Christian followers while on his mission to find the robe, in doing so linking ancient Imperial tyranny with contemporary McCarthyism.[8] Indeed, the Roman-era biblically inspired epic need not rely on its religious message for its ongoing appeal, for at a more fundamental level, its narrative is one of freedom and resistance against oppression. DB.

Notes

1. Sheldon Hall and Steve Neale, *Epics, Spectacles, and Blockbusters* (Detroit, MI: Wayne State University Press, 2010), 136, 147.
2. Hall and Neale, *Epics, Spectacles, and Blockbusters*, 148.
3. Bosley Crowther, "The Screen: *The Robe* Shown in CinemaScope; Movie Based on Douglas's Novel Stars Richard Burton, Jean Simmons, Victor Mature. Much-Heralded Film Process Gives Viewers a Smashing Display of Spectacle," *New York Times*, 17 September 1953, http://movies.nytimes.com/movie/review?res=9D06E0D71339E23BBC4F52DFBF668388649EDE&scp=3&sq=robe%20richard%20burton%20henry%20koster&st=cse (10 March 2012).
4. "*The Robe*," *Variety*, 1953, www.variety.com/review/VE1117794512/ (10 March 2012).
5. "*The Robe*."
6. Crowther, "The Screen: *The Robe*."
7. Richard Alston, "Gaius Caligula (AD 37–41)," in *Aspects of Roman History, AD 14–117* (New York: Routledge, 1998), 56.
8. Jeffrey Richards, *Hollywood's Ancient Worlds* (London: Continuum, 2008), 67–68.

Bibliography

Alston, Richard. "Gaius Caligula (AD 37–41)." In *Aspects of Roman History, AD 14–117*, 42–57. New York: Routledge, 1998.

Crowther, Bosley. "The Screen: *The Robe* Shown in CinemaScope; Movie Based on Douglas's Novel Stars Richard Burton, Jean Simmons, Victor Mature. Much-Heralded Film Process Gives Viewers a Smashing Display of Spectacle." *New York Times*, 17 September 1953, http://movies.nytimes.com/movie/review?res=9D06E0D71339E23BBC4F52DFBF668388649EDE&scp=3&sq=robe%20richard%20burton%20henry%20koster&st=cse (10 March 2012).

Hall, Sheldon, and Steve Neale. *Epics, Spectacles, and Blockbusters*. Detroit, MI: Wayne State University Press, 2010.

Richards, Jeffrey. *Hollywood's Ancient Worlds*. London: Continuum, 2008.

"*The Robe*." *Variety*, 1953, www.variety.com/review/VE1117794512/ (10 March 2012).

ROBIN HOOD (2010)

DIRECTOR: Ridley Scott

WRITER: Brian Helgeland. From a story by Brian Helgeland, Ethan Reiff, and Cyrus Voris.

PRODUCERS: Brian Grazer, Ridley Scott, Russell Crowe (Imagine Entertainment, Universal Pictures)

CINEMATOGRAPHER: John Mathieson

EDITOR: Pietro Scalia

PRODUCTION DESIGN: Arthur Max

ART DIRECTION: John King, David Allday, Raymond Chan, Karen Wakefield

SET DECORATION: Sonja Klaus

COSTUMES: Janty Yates

MUSIC: Marc Streitenfeld

CAST: Robin Longstride: Russell Crowe. Marion Loxley: Cate Blanchett. Sir Walter Loxley: Max von Sydow. William Marshal: William Hurt. Godfrey: Mark Strong. Prince John: Oscar Isaac. King Richard the Lionheart: Danny Huston. Eleanor of Aquitaine: Eileen Atkins. Friar Tuck: Mark Addy. Sheriff of Nottingham: Matthew Macfadyen. Little John: Kevin Durand. Will Scarlet: Scott Grimes. Allan A'Dayle: Alan Doyle. Sir Robert Loxley: Douglas Hodge. Isabella of Angoulême: Léa Seydoux. King Philip of France: Jonathan Zaccai. Baron Baldwin: Robert Pugh. Baron Fitzrobert: Gerard McSorley. Belvedere: Velibor Topic. Loop: Ciaran Flynn. Father Tancred: Simon McBurney. Village Mother: Denise Gough. Farmer Paul: John Nicholas. Capt. of the Royal Barge: Thomas Arnold. Royal Equery: Pip Carter. Stone Mason Longstride: Mark Lewis Jones. Jimoen: Bronson Webb. Adhemar: Denis Menochet. Church Deacon: Jamie Beamish. Exchequer: John Atterbury. Sheriff's Thug: Luke Evans. Gaffer Tom: Roy Holder. Baron Baldwin's Grandson: Mark David. Margaret Walter's Maid: Ruby Bentall. Sentinel: Ned Dennehy. Slovenly French Cook: Nicolas Simon. Walter's Cook: Lisa Millett. Messenger: Stuart Martin. Princess Isabel of Gloucester: Jessica Raine. Ragged Messenger: Steve Evets. Ruffian: Eric Rulliat. King Philip's Aide: Abraham Belaga. Young Robin: Jack Downham. Sentry: Richard Riddell. French Capt.: David Bertrand. Groom: Arthur Darvill. Lady-in-Waiting: Giannina Facio. Woman at Bog: Hannah Barrie. Soldier Boy: Lee Battle. Soldier #2: Nicky Bell. Little John's Wench: Andrea Ware. Tom the Pig Man: John O'Toole. Northerner: Ralph Inneson. French Informant: Zuriel De Peslouan. Distinctive Man: Jake Curran. French Flagship Captain: Samuel Dupuy. Justiciar: Nick Lucas. Cardinal Roger: Alan Charlesworth. French Boy: Lothaire Gerard. Laughing French Soldier: Mat Laroche. Equerry: Chris Jared. Feral Children: Joseph Hamilton, James Hamilton, James Burrows, Danny Clarke, Tom Blyth

AA: None

AAN: None

ART DIRECTOR'S GUILD AWARD NOMINATION: Excellence in Production Design–Feature Film–Period or Fantasy Film (Arthur Max)

DVD: Universal Studios, 2010

BLU-RAY: Universal Studios, 2010

DURATION: 149 minutes

Director Ridley Scott and lead actor Russell Crowe, who found critical and commercial success in 2000 with *Gladiator* (which won five Academy Awards, including Best Picture and Best Leading Actor for Crowe), teamed up again for a $200 million epic treatment of the Robin Hood backstory.

This film eschews the traditional tale of run-ins between Robin's charitable band of outlaws and the Sheriff of Nottingham, instead creating an origin tale that ends when the "legend begins." Indeed, *Variety*'s Justin Chang complains in his review that the film "feels too long, yet incomplete, and the events it leaves offscreen (for what, the sequel?) are precisely those that make the tale worth retelling."[1] But this narrative choice is, in fact, one of the film's strengths, because writer Brian Helgeland is able to construct a new story about Robin with some unanticipated turns, which, given the weight of the Robin Hood legacy, is no small feat.

Scott's reimagined tale begins in France, where we meet our future hero Robin Longstride (Crowe) as an able archer returning home from the Crusades with King Richard the Lionheart (Danny Huston) in the year A.D. 1199. But Robin ends up in the stocks, ostensibly for brawling, but really for telling the king that their God has abandoned them for the massacre of captive Muslim men, women, and children. After Richard himself dies in battle, Robin escapes with his companions Will Scarlett (Scott Grimes), Little John (Kevin Durand), and Allan A'Dayle (Alan Doyle). They head toward the coast; however, they interrupt the wily Sir Godfrey (Mark Strong) and his mercenaries killing off the king's knights, a thwarted assassination attempt on Richard arranged by Philip Augustus, king of France. Godfrey escapes, and the dying Sir Robert Loxley (Douglas Hodge) asks Robin to take his father's sword back to Nottingham for him. Robin and his men assume the identities of the dead knights, taking the king's boat to England and returning his crown. Before making good on their escape for fear of being exposed, they are spotted by Godfrey, who understandably wants to erase all witnesses to his treachery.

The petulant new king, John (Oscar Isaac), is angry that the treasury has been depleted by his brother's campaign, and he assigns Godfrey to exact new taxes from the people. He does not realize, however, that Godfrey's men are French soldiers using the tax collection as a cover to slaughter the people and cause political instability in the country to precede a French invasion.

Good to his word, Robin goes north to Nottingham to return Loxley's sword, inadvertently announcing the knight's death rather abruptly to his wife Marion (a feisty Cate Blanchett, who is evidently not a maid in this version). There is a motto on the sword that stirs old memories in Robin, and the elderly and blind Sir Walter Loxley (the ever-reliable Max von Sydow) seems to recognize Robin's name. Loxley conspires to keep Longstride in Nottingham, offering him payment of the valuable sword in exchange for posing as his dead son, partly to protect Marion and their lands from the greedy and lascivious Sheriff of Nottingham (Matthew Macfadyen, sadly not given much to do here).

Marion is initially shocked by her father-in-law's insistence that Robin impersonate her husband. She is embarrassed to undress him for bathing and annoyed to have him in her bedchamber. Yet, Robin is moved by her difficulties on the land: the last of her seed grains have been stolen by local youths living in Sherwood Forest, and the deer now belong to the king. When Friar Tuck (Mark Addy) arranges, under orders, to send the last of the local church's seeds to York, Robin threatens to expose his honey and mead-making business to the authorities. The pragmatic Tuck joins forces with Robin, Will, John, and Allan to lay an ambush, pretending to be the Sherwood outlaws and taking the grain back to sow Marion's fields. But Robin is surprised to find that Marion has befriended the errant forest gang who stole her seed in the first place.

The elderly Loxley has another motive for keeping Robin in Nottingham, aside from helping his beloved daughter-in-law, who is clearly far from helpless. When the king's former advisor, William Marshal (William Hurt), visits his old friend Loxley, the two men reveal that Robin is the son of an old companion of theirs, slain for daring to demand that a charter of rights be brought into law to protect the people. As the northerners buckle under Godfrey's attacks and make plans to join forces against King John, Loxley hopes that Robin will be able to take up his father's mantle. For his part, Marshal is, in effect, a loyal and adept spy of the realm, and despite his falling out with King John, he makes sure that news of Godfrey's treason and the impending French invasion reaches the king.

Facing a large-scale (fictional) French invasion, John has little choice but to agree to a future charter of rights in return for a united defense of the realm with the assistance of the rebelling northerners. After Loxley is cruelly murdered by Godfrey, Robin declares his love to Marion and heads south to meet the French forces. He is alarmed to find that Marion has followed, disguised as a knight in armor (much as Robin had done earlier), with her Sherwood gang in tow. Robin duly kills Godfrey with a long-range arrow, and the English prevail, but while the dismayed King Philip Augustus turns back to France, King John seems equally displeased that his men are praising Robin for leading the victory instead of him.

King John reneges on his promise to enshrine the rights of the people in law and instead proclaims his full royal power as bestowed by God, denouncing Robin as an outlaw for impersonating a knight and stirring up dissent. In Nottingham, the sheriff declares that anyone who assists Robin will be executed, but when he cannot affix the notice to a tree for want of a hammer and nail, Robin's arrow does the job for him. The fugitive returns to the forest with Marion and his fellow outlaws, and the film ends with a striking, painterly end-credit sequence.

The real King John was indeed pressed into signing a charter of liberties—the Magna Carta—in 1215. And while Richard is normally the returning hero-king of Robin Hood films, his ambiguous depiction here follows the more somber critique of the Crusades found in *Robin and Marian* (Richard Lester, 1976) and Scott's own 2005 *Kingdom of Heaven* (which ends with Richard's departure to the Holy Lands). Crowe's Robin is haunted by the slaughter of Muslim prisoners, attested to by both Muslim and Christian historical sources, which was against the conventions of warfare even in this period.[2] But as for Robin Hood himself, there is no evidence that such a man existed in the time of either Richard (1189–1199) or John (1199–1216). His origins appear to lie in the Middle Ages; however, there is no consensus as to whether there was a single, original man, or if the tales grew from an amalgam of many real outlaw figures, or indeed simply arose as oral folktales.[3] And yet despite these foggy origins, the mythic power of Robin Hood is quite separate to the search for a real Robin.

So, too, the cinema epic rarely strives for historical accuracy in itself, but rather a sensory experience of history. As with Antoine Fuqua's *King Arthur* (2004), Scott's *Robin Hood* abandons its more florid cinematic forbears in favor of gritty quasi-historical realism, which is nonetheless of compelling visual beauty thanks to the cinematography of John Mathieson (who also worked on Scott's *Gladiator* and *Kingdom of Heaven*). It may be a rather sober rendition, but it is difficult to imagine that 2010 audiences would really expect from Crowe or Scott the merriment of Errol Flynn in *The Adventures of Robin Hood* (Michael Curtiz and William Keighley, 1938). Scott's *Robin Hood* dovetails the film with its two major battle scenes, indicative of the way that the story has been opened up beyond the usual Nottingham setting to make the most of the epic potential of the tale and contemporary digital effects, but also providing a "brief, brutal seminar in twelfth-century military tactics, complete with massed archers, wall climbers, and vats of boiling oil."[4] Yet, this is not so much the medieval rather than medievalism, by which the medieval is reinterpreted by subsequent eras, for the final beach invasion has no basis in history, and Marion's arrival at the battlefield stretches credibility somewhat.

Box-office returns were healthy internationally, but the film failed to attract the praise or awards of Crowe and Scott's earlier collaboration. DB

Notes

1. Justin Chang, "*Robin Hood*," *Variety*, 9 May 2010, www.variety.com/review/VE1117942702/ (28 April 2012).
2. John Aberth, *A Knight at the Movies: Medieval History on Film* (New York and London: Routledge, 2003), 72–73.
3. Aberth, *A Knight at the Movies*, 150–55, 163; Stephen Knight, *Robin Hood: A Complete Study of the English Outlaw* (Oxford, UK, and Cambridge, MA: Blackwell, 1994), 24, 262–88.
4. A. O. Scott, "*Robin Hood* (2010)," *New York Times*, 13 May 2010, http://movies.nytimes.com/2010/05/14/movies/14robin.html (24 April 2012).

Bibliography

Aberth, John. *A Knight at the Movies: Medieval History on Film*. New York and London: Routledge, 2003.

Chang, Justin. "*Robin Hood*." *Variety*, 9 May 2010, www.variety.com/review/VE1117942702/ (28 April 2012).

Knight, Stephen. *Robin Hood: A Complete Study of the English Outlaw*. Oxford, UK, and Cambridge, MA: Blackwell, 1994.

Scott, A. O. "*Robin Hood* (2010)." *New York Times*, 13 May 2010, http://movies.nytimes.com/2010/05/14/movies/14robin.html (24 April 2012).

ROBIN HOOD: PRINCE OF THIEVES (1991)

Director: Kevin Reynolds
Writers: Pen Densham, John Watson
Producers: Pen Densham, John Watson (Morgan Creek Productions, Warner Bros.)
Cinematographer: Douglas Milsome
Editor: Peter Boyle
Art Direction: Fred Carter
Costumes: John Bloomfield
Music: Michael Kamen
Cast: Robin Hood: Kevin Costner. Azeem: Morgan Freeman. Marian Dubois: Mary Elizabeth Mastrantonio. Will Scarlett: Christian Slater. Sheriff George of Nottingham: Alan Rickman. Mortianna: Geraldine McEwan. Friar Tuck: Micheal McShane. Lord Locksley: Brian Blessed. Guy of Gisborne: Michael Wincott. Little John: Nick Brimble. Fanny: Soo Drouet. Wulf: Daniel Newman. Bull: Daniel Peacock. Duncan: Walter Sparrow. Bishop of Hereford: Harold Innocent. Much the Miller's Son: Jack Wild. Kenneth of Cowfall: Michael Goldie. Peter Dubois: Liam Halligan. Interrogator: Marc Zuber. Old Woman: Merelina Kendall. Sarah: Imogen Bain. Farmer: Jimmy Gardner. Villager: Bobby Parr. Courier: John Francis. Red-Headed Baron: John Hallam. Gray-Bearded Baron: Douglas Blackwell. Celtic Chieftain: Pat Roach. Ox: Andy Hockley. Broth: John Dallimore. Kneelock: Derek Deadman. Hal: Howard Lew Lewis. Scribe: John Tordoff. Sergeant: Andrew Lawden. Lady in Coach: Susannah Corbett. Small Girl: Sarah Alexandra. Soldier: Christopher Adamson. Executioner: Richard Strange. King Richard: Sean Connery (uncredited)
AA: None
AAN: Best Music–Original Song (Michael Kamen, Bryan Adams, Robert John

Lange for "[Everything I Do] I Do It for You")
BAFTA Award: Best Supporting Actor (Alan Rickman)
BAFTA Award Nomination: Best Costume Design (John Bloomfield)
GGN: Best Original Score–Motion Picture (Michael Kamen), Best Original Song–Motion Picture (Michael Kamen, Bryan Adams, Robert John Lange for "[Everything I Do] I Do It for You")
Grammy Award: Best Song Written Specifically for a Motion Picture or for Television (Michael Kamen, Bryan Adams, Robert John Lange for "[Everything I Do] I Do It for You")
Grammy Award Nomination: Best Instrumental Composition Written for a Motion Picture or for Television (Michael Kamen)
DVD: Warner Home Video, 2003
Blu-ray: Warner Home Video, 2009
Duration: 149 minutes (extended version)

This $48 million reimagining of the Robin Hood legend was panned by critics, but that did not stop the film from making worldwide grosses of more than $390 million. Kevin Costner's stardom was at its height. His 1990 *Dances with Wolves* won Academy Awards for Best Director and Best Picture at the March 1991 Oscars ceremony, and *Robin Hood: Prince of Thieves*[1] was released the following June, but *Variety* wrote, "The best that can be said for Costner's performance is that it is pleasant. At worst, it can be argued whether it is more properly described as wooden or cardboard."[2] Costner retains his American accent, as does Christian Slater as Will Scarlett, while Mary Elizabeth Mastrantonio's accent as Marian is changeable throughout, all of which is most distracting. Yet, Morgan Freeman as Robin's Moorish companion Azeem and Alan Rickman as the Sheriff of Nottingham add gravitas and humor, respectively. Although some reviews found Rickman's performance overbearing[3] (and indeed he refused to come on board the project until he was promised full rein[4]), it is a delightful pleasure.

The adventure begins in 1194, not in Nottingham, but rather in a dungeon in Jerusalem, where Robin of Locksley (Costner) has been imprisoned while on the Third Crusade with King Richard. In his escape, he is unable to free his fellow "infidels," but he is able to help a Moorish prisoner, Azeem (Freeman), who pledges to stay by Robin's side until he can repay the debt. Robin has no choice but to take Azeem with him back to England, where they help a youngster who is being chased by the sneering Sir Guy of Gisborne (Michael Wincott). Robin finds his home in ruins, with only the blinded Duncan (Walter Sparrow) remaining. Robin's father, Lord Locksley (the fabulous Brian Blessed, alas seen only briefly here), has been killed by order of the Sheriff of Nottingham (Rickman) under the pretext of trumped-up charges of Satanic worship, so that the sheriff can seize Locksley's land. In fact, it is soon revealed that it is the sheriff himself who worships the dark arts under the tutelage of the witch Mortianna (Geraldine McEwan). Robin is beset by guilt, for his father had not wanted him to join the "foolish" Crusades.

Robin seeks out his childhood companion, Lady Marian Dubois (Mastrantonio), to return her late brother's ring to her, having sworn to protect her in his stead. Unfortunately, Marian remembers Robin as a childhood bully and attacks him while she is disguised in armor. As cousin to the absent King Richard, she feels that she is already adequately protected by her status. Marian does not believe the charges made against Robin's father, and Robin soon realizes that the Bishop of Hereford (Harold Innocent) was party to their falsification.

Pursued by those who have taken his lands, Robin is forced to flee into Sherwood

Forest, where he encounters a ragged group of outlaws headed by Little John (Nick Brimble). As a noble, an American film star, and the hero of the film's title, it is inevitable that Robin seeks to take over leadership himself, much to the irritation of Will Scarlett (Slater). With Robin's training, the outlaws raid convoys passing through the forest and redistribute the stolen taxes back to the poor. Among their victims are Friar Tuck (Micheal McShane), who decides to join them, and Marian, who has reassessed her opinion of Robin (particularly after seeing him bathe naked) but returns home nonetheless.

In desperation, the sheriff hires Celtic mercenaries to attack the outlaws' camp. Among the survivors is Will Scarlett, who reveals that he is Robin's half brother, cast aside when the young Robin could not accept his widower father taking a new woman. Will is ostensibly working for the sheriff, but as he actually wants to believe in Robin's cause, the two brothers are reconciled.

Meanwhile, the witch Mortianna reveals herself to be the sheriff's real mother, and she encourages her son to secure the throne for himself by marrying a royal. The sheriff promises that he will spare the lives of the rebels' children if Marian will marry him. When he schedules some of the insurgents to be hanged on their wedding day, Robin and the survivors of the raid are able to rescue them. As the people flee, Azeem exhorts them to join Robin in a rebellion against the sheriff, and the peasants find the courage to fight. Although the bishop completes a hasty marriage, Robin slays the sheriff and prevents him from raping Marian. Azeem is finally able to repay his debt to Robin when he prevents his death at the hands of Mortianna, and Friar Tuck disposes of the corrupt bishop. The film closes with the marriage of Robin and Marian, interrupted only momentarily by the arrival of King Richard himself (Sean Connery in an uncredited performance).

The film is particularly remembered for the song "(Everything I Do) I Do It for You," which was nominated for an Academy Award and spent eight weeks at number one on the U.S. Billboard charts. An orchestral version of the tune became Maid Marian's theme in the film. In an otherwise uneven score,[5] Michael Kamen's excellent fanfare for the film's overture has subsequently also become very well known (even if its source is not always remembered), for it has been widely used in other contexts, including sporting events.

It is difficult for subsequent Robin Hood films to escape from the legacy of Errol Flynn in *The Adventures of Robin Hood* (Michael Curtiz, William Keighley, 1938), even if it is also hard to imagine our hero donning green tights again with any credibility. Vincent Canby writes in his *New York Times* review: "The movie's dour production design is . . . a downer. The dominant colors are brown, black, olive, mouse-gray, which may serve realism but not the spirit of the fable. This 'Robin Hood' has a dreary and haunted look."[6] Ridley Scott's 2010 even grittier rendition of the tale in *Robin Hood* was criticized along similar lines. In short, critics have been resistant to updating either the story or the look of the Robin Hood myth, even though this is precisely how myths have always worked. Certainly, Robin Hood has rather murky historical origins, and Marian was relatively late in the continual additions to his tradition.

Pen Densham and John Watson's Robin does not merely strive for fairness and justice for their own sake. He has a more personal stake—to regain his land and restore his late father's honor. As

Robin is forced into friendship with one of the "infidels" he left England to slay, he begins to understand his father's condemnation of the Crusades. But John Aberth takes the writers and filmmakers to task for failing to acknowledge how many of the film's reinventions had, in fact, been taken from the British television series *Robin of Sherwood* (1984–1986), among them the introduction of a Saracen among the merry men and the use of black magic.[7] The similarities did not escape the notice of series creator Richard Carpenter, who although understandably aggrieved, nonetheless—and rather generously under the circumstances—noted that "each version" of Robin Hood "seems to take something from the previous version."[8] *Robin of Sherwood* was nominated for a BAFTA TV Award for Best Children's Programme (Entertainment/Drama), and it won for Best Original Television Music by Clannad. In subsequent decades, it has attracted a cult following in the United Kingdom and the United States, with regular fan conventions.

For their part, writers Densham and Watson, in their DVD commentary for *Robin Hood: Prince of Thieves*, claim an independent inspiration for the character of Azeem in their script, which was written on spec. By the time the project came to its director, Kevin Reynolds was forced to make the film under a crippling deadline in competition with 20th Century Fox, who was making a rival film. This was John Irvin's *Robin Hood*, starring Patrick Bergin and Uma Thurman, but it was shown on U.S. television instead of being given a theatrical release in light of the phenomenal publicity and hype surrounding the Costner vehicle. Although seldom remembered as a result, it has much to commend it over its rival. In particular, while Mary Elizabeth Mastrantonio is given very little to do and is not especially engaging in *Prince of Thieves*, Thurman as Marian is given a convincing heroic path of her own, and her romance with Robin is more compelling as a result. DB

Notes

1. The film's subtitle, *Prince of Thieves*, is the name of the Alexandre Dumas's Robin Hood novel, published posthumously in 1872, although the film is not based on that work.
2. "*Robin Hood: Prince of Thieves*," *Variety*, 1991, www.variety.com/review/VE1117794519/ (23 May 2012).
3. Vincent Canby, "A Polite Robin Hood in a Legend Recast," *New York Times*, 14 June 1991, http://movies.nytimes.com/movie/review?res=9D0CE1DF113CF937A25755C0A967958260 (23 May 2012).
4. Pen Densham and John Watson, "Commentary," *Robin Hood: Prince of Thieves*, directed by Kevin Reynolds (Warner Home Video, 2003), DVD.
5. Christian Clemmensen, "*Robin Hood: Prince of Thieves*," *Filmtracks: Modern Soundtrack Reviews*, 24 September 1996, www.filmtracks.com/titles/robin_hood.html (17 June 2012).
6. Vincent Canby, "A Polite Robin Hood in a Legend Recast."
7. John Aberth, *A Knight at the Movies: Medieval History on Film* (New York and London: Routledge, 2003), 188.
8. Richard Carpenter and Ian Sharp, "Commentary," *Robin of Sherwood*, directed by Ian Sharp (Acorn Media, 2008), DVD. Carpenter and Sharp have much to say on these overlaps, with Sharp quipping "that's why the film was called *Prince of Thieves*."

Bibliography

Aberth, John. *A Knight at the Movies: Medieval History on Film*. New York and London: Routledge, 2003.

Canby, Vincent. "A Polite Robin Hood in a Legend Recast." *New York Times*, 14 June 1991, http://movies.nytimes.com/movie/review?res=9D0CE1DF113CF937A25755C0A967958260 (23 May 2012).

Clemmensen, Christian. "*Robin Hood: Prince of Thieves*." *Filmtracks: Modern Soundtrack Reviews*, 24 September 1996, www.filmtracks.com/titles/robin_hood.html (17 June 2012).

"*Robin Hood: Prince of Thieves*." *Variety*, 1991, www.variety.com/review/VE1117794519/ (23 May 2012).

RYAN'S DAUGHTER (1970)

DIRECTOR: David Lean
WRITER: Robert Bolt
PRODUCER: Anthony Havelock-Allen (MGM)
ASSISTANT DIRECTORS: Pedro Vidal, Michael Stevenson
SECOND UNIT DIRECTORS: Roy Stevens, Charles Frend
CINEMATOGRAPHER: Freddie Young
EDITOR: Norman Savage
PRODUCTION DESIGN: Stephen Grimes
ART DIRECTION: Roy Walker
COSTUMES: Jocelyn Richards
MUSIC: Maurice Jarre
SOUND MIXERS: John Bramall, Gordon K. McCallum
PROPERTY MASTER: Eddie Fowlie
CAST: Charles Shaughnessy: Robert Mitchum. Rose "Rosy" Ryan/Shaughnessy: Sarah Miles. Maj. Randolph Doryan: Christopher Jones. Fr. Hugh Collins: Trevor Howard. Michael: John Mills. Thomas Ryan: Leo McKern. Tim O'Leary: Barry Foster. McCardle: Archie O'Sullivan. Mrs. McCardle: Marie Kean. Maureen Cassidy: Evin Crowley. Corporal: Barry Jackson. Driver: Douglas Sheldon. Paddy: Philip O'Flynn. Capt. Smith: Gerald Sim. Private: Des Keogh. Maureen's Boyfriend: Donald Neligan. Constable O'Connor: Brian O'Higgins. Bernard: Niall O'Brien
AA: Best Supporting Actor (John Mills), Best Cinematography (Freddie Young)
AAN: Best Leading Actress (Sarah Miles), Best Sound (John Bramall, Gordon K. McCallum)
DVD: Warner Home Video, 2006. Two-disc special edition, digitally remastered and restored 65mm version of the film.
BLU-RAY: Currently unavailable
DURATION: 206 minutes

The idea for *Ryan's Daughter* originated with Robert Bolt, who had collaborated with David Lean on *Lawrence of Arabia* (1962) and *Doctor Zhivago* (1965), both of which brought in box-office treasure and twelve Oscars. Lean was taking a year or two off after his labors, and was living in Italy, when he received a letter from Bolt asking him if he would be amenable to doing a new project of Gustave Flaubert's masterpiece *Madame Bovary*. Lean was initially cool to the idea, but he gradually started rethinking the proposal, provided that the story was modernized and filmed in a place outside of France. They thought of India, and several other locations, but they eventually settled for Western Ireland, the Dingle Peninsula, where Lean, with the help of his loyal factotum, Eddie Fowlie, found a spectacular beach that suited their purposes. Although the central idea of Flaubert's novel was retained—a young woman dissatisfied with her husband takes a lover—Lean wanted a parallel story to evolve next to it so that the plot would be raised to epic level. Consequently, the time frame was set to 1916, when the Irish Rebellion, "the Troubles," as it came to be known, was at its peak. War was raging in Europe, and the Irish rebels, led by the national hero Tim O'Leary, had sided with the Germans, and a big load of arms and ammunition was expected to be dropped near the location of Kirarry, a village where the action takes place.

The main story is that of Rose (Rosy) Ryan, the local publican's daughter, who was in love, or fancied she was, with the local schoolteacher, Charles Shaughnessy, played by Robert Mitchum. Lean and Bolt wanted a strong actor to play, against type, a timid, self-effacing schoolteacher, an actor with screen charisma, known for his tough roles in the past, who would be believable when he becomes a tower of strength in the second part of the movie. "If you took a weak man for the part," says Lean, "it would be boring."[1] Robert Mitchum was chosen for the part, after Marlon

Brando and Paul Scofield declined. For the part of Rosy Ryan/Shaughnessy, Lean chose Sarah Miles, who was Bolt's wife at the time, and for her lover, Major Randolph Doryan, the young American actor Christopher Jones, whose voice was dubbed, as Lean discovered, much to his dismay, that Jones could not handle an English accent.

The secondary parts were given to outstanding actors, some of whom had worked with Lean before. John Mills, known for several roles in Lean's English period, plays the "village idiot," Michael, and he won an Oscar for his efforts. Trevor Howard, also in two previous Lean films of his early period, was assigned the role of the local priest, Father Hugh Collins (the role was offered to Alec Guinness, who turned it down). And Thomas Ryan, the publican, was given to Leo McKern. Barry Foster was chosen for the role of Tim O'Leary, the Irish revolutionary leader. The noticeable thing is that each of these men have, either directly or indirectly, a role in Rose's fortunes as the plot evolves. Structurally, the movie is so well put together that these connections with Rosy seem logical and even inevitable.

The story begins with Rosy seen roaming the beaches, holding an expensive black-laced umbrella over her head, anxiously awaiting the arrival of Charles, who had been at a teachers' convention in Dublin. She is chided by Father Collins for aimless "mooning about," but she shakes him off rather insolently, and soon she and the teacher meet. Charles seems surprised and pleased to see her coming to welcoming him, and the two engage in a pleasant chat, during which it is obvious that she is smitten with her teacher, while he seems to suspect nothing. The wind blows Charles' hat off of his head, and while running after it, Rosy's is blown away, too, and they both run after them, exchanging hats, a hint of their future union. Charles scrambles up the dunes, "to pay [his] respects to his wife," and soon we see him kneeling before her tomb. Rosy continues her rambling, placing her bare foot on Charles' footsteps in the sand, until a wave washes them away.

Meanwhile, Charles joins a group of locals at Ryan's pub, where the bigoted food store owner McCardle (Archie O'Sullivan) questions him rudely about his visit to Dublin, seconded by Ryan, both of whom reprimand him about his indifference to the cause—not visiting Sackville Street, which was bombed by the British for their hideouts of the rebels. Here we witness the low esteem that Charles is held to by the locals, especially McCardle, who whispers to the others after Charles is gone that "teaching children makes a man childish." Only the priest comes to Charles' defense, politely inquiring about what he has heard there.

Upon his return to the schoolhouse, Charles finds Rosy there, guessing at once why she has come. She says, "I came because I have something to say," and soon adds, "I love you." Here again we see Charles' low esteem of himself. He keeps saying that "teachers are a poor lot," and that she is "mistaking a penny mirror for the sun." He tells her that he only taught her about Byron, Beethoven, and Captain Blood, but that he is not one of them. Again, Rosy defiantly responds with, "You are always building a low pit for yourself, instead of standing on a heap of pride." When finally she says, "You don't want me then?" Charles melts, for he really cannot resist this desirable young woman who is literally throwing herself at his feet. They soon get married, in a memorable "bacchanalian" scene, which Lean describes in great detail.

At this point, a secondary plot is introduced, as Tim O'Leary and a friend, Paddy (Philip O'Flynn), are seen driving a horse-drawn cart. A constable on a bicycle passes by and recognizes them. O'Leary instantly makes a decision and shoots the constable, who drops from the bicycle, dragging himself on the ground muttering, "Jesus." O'Leary runs to him and shoots him again, making sure he is dead. The two rebels are next seen driving the cart with the constable's body, shoving the whole thing down a mine shaft a short distance away. They continue their way on foot to Limerick, and soon reappear driving a lorry. They stop to have a look at Ryan, who is preparing for his daughter's wedding, and O'Leary comes to a conclusion after he sees him, saying, "the locals are no good," and that they have to bring some "good lads" from Dublin. They are obviously preparing to receive a load of weapons and ammunition from a German cargo ship, to be dropped in rafts near that beach. This is the only time that O'Leary appears in the first part of the movie, but the double plot has already been established.

The marriage of Charles and Rosy seems doomed from the beginning. Despite his manly appearance, Charles is a tepid lover, for he tends to treat Rosy as a delicate art object—as the bust of Beethoven on his mantle shows—added to his collection, rather than as a young woman who wants sexual satisfaction as a normal part of wedded life. One day Rosy is seen running in tears along the beach, where she has another encounter with Father Collins, always a paternal figure to her (more so than her actual father), who asks if she has health, enough money to live, and a good husband. When she asserts that she does and then claims, "There is something more!" the priest angrily slaps her in the face and then cautions her, saying, "Don't nourish your wishes, Rosy. You can't help having them, but don't nourish them!"

His words seem prophetic. There is a cut to a swampy spot, where a tall, wedge-like rock signifies the bus stop. Michael is seen in the swampy area picking wild flowers as the bus stops and a man steps out of it. The camera zooms in closer, as Michael sees the profile of the young man in uniform standing there, waiting and moving toward his baggage to retrieve his cigarette case. A military vehicle soon arrives, with a fussy driver, who apologizes and explains that he had to change a tire. Michael runs after them, begging for a ride, and the young officer calls, "Get in." They pass by the schoolhouse, where the officer, Major Doryan, notices a woman's red garment, blowing in the wind to dry. They pass through the village and are stared at by the hostile villagers. They arrive at the camp, where a voluble Captain Smith (Gerald Sim) welcomes his younger superior officer with ostensibly obsequious gesturing. In a rather long-drawn-out scene, he paints him a picture of the village life, his light duties—"more like police work"—and that there is "no local strumpet, married or virgin." He recommends that he bring his wife here, as he sees her picture on the table, not realizing that she is dead. He also imparts an important fact: that the "publican" by the name of Ryan is the informer, adding, "We slip him a fiver now and then." This is indeed an important piece of information that will become a key factor in the plot later in the film.

One hour into the film, Lean decided to bring the lovers together as soon as possible. In an exquisite ground shot, Doryan is seen dragging his right foot—for he is a war hero and an invalid—along the pavement of the village street, where the local hussy, Maureen Cassidy (Evin Crowley), and her female friend are watching him as he is drawing near. Seeking to attract his attention, Maureen calls him "peg leg," which instantaneously draws a reaction from Doryan in the form of a prolonged stare that sends the two hussies scampering inside the house. The door of the pub opens, and Doryan, looking unnerved, goes in. There is a cut to Rosy, who is sitting at a side table reading, looking surprised at the young man, who rings the bar bell. "I didn't know you were serving," he says politely, and she responds with, "I was just minding." As he is drinking his whiskey and smoking a cigarette, Rosy steals a look at him. At the same time, Michael, who is sitting at a corner, begins pounding his foot on the wooden wall, and Doryan goes into a fit of the shakes—something Captain Smith had described to him a day or two earlier. His seizure continues as a flashback shows him crawling into a shelter while bombs are exploding outside. Terrified, Michael rushes out, and Rosy secures the door behind him. Then she approaches the prostrate Doryan and touches his hand. They exchange a glance and begin to kiss wildly. The remainder of the first part is an arrangement of an assignation of the two lovers in the forest, near a tower, where they make love, in scenes that were criticized by some for their blatant eroticism.

Part two, after an intermission, begins with Charles with his school class on the beach, on a nature walk, looking for "cuttlefish." Already suspicious about his wife's going off to ride "Princess," the mare her father bought her, with the British officer, Charles begins to trace footsteps in the sand. One of them is clearly the officer's, whose right foot left signs of dragging. In a dream sequence, Charles "sees" the couple, attired in Victorian splendor, walking toward him, in a dazzlingly photographed scene, while strains of Beethoven's 5th Symphony are heard on the sound track, the same music Charles plays on his phonograph. Next, the two lovers are seen on a height—at "Brandon"—Doryan resting on the grass, while Rosy sees Michael walking away, limping, evidently having discovered some traces of their lovemaking in a cave and having found a button from Doryan's uniform there.

This sequence concludes with a "pantomime," where Michael, dressed as the major, with a fake VC on his chest, appears at a village gathering, causing a big ruckus. He is interrupted by the priest, who asks him to "take the foolish things off," but Michael resists. When Rosy appears on horse, returning from her assignation with Doryan, Michael smiles at her, grabs her horse reins, and refuses to let her pass. She begs him, and he does let her go, but he salutes her militarily, as the crowd, as witnessed by McCardle and Ryan, breaks into mocking laughter. Ashamed, Ryan rushes into his tavern. The secret is now out, and from that point onward, Rosy suffers the jeers and insults of the villagers, especially the vicious Mrs. McCardle (Marie Kean), the owner of the shop, who refuses to sell to Rosy, taunting her as a "British officer's whore" as she exists the store.

Two things converge at this point to radically change the story. One is the great storm, photographed at life's peril, and the other is the reappearance of Tim O'Leary, this time with his fellow rebels, to recover weapons and ammunition to be dropped nearby during the night. As the storm rages on, and as Ryan is trying to push a group of drunken village codgers out of his tavern, he sees O'Leary at the door to his upstairs quarters. It takes him a minute or so to recognize him, but when he does, he tips his eyebrow in a military salute. O'Leary demands that he round up a dozen or so able-bodied villagers to help him salvage the loads of weapons that have been dropped on the beach, and Ryan has no alternative but to comply. But before the group exits near morning, Ryan is told to "cut the wire," the telephone connection with the military barracks in Constable O'Connor's (Brian O'Higgins) house. He does so "under duress," as he tells O'Connor, but before he does, he rings camp and tells them of O'Leary's presence and the ongoing operation. This is a key turn of events, as will be shown later.

Meanwhile, the storm is in full force, and O'Leary and his companions are seen on the beach trying to locate the crafts loaded with weapons. After a futile search, and as daylight comes, Ryan, feeling some guilt for his betrayal, implores them to get out while they can. At this moment, the entire village, led by Father Collins, descends on the beach, cheering O'Leary and eager to help him retrieve the weapons. Men, women, and children search and find guns and ammunition, and they gather what they find, which is plenty to fill O'Leary's lorry, which is stuck in the sand; however, the crowd helps to free it, and O'Leary and his companions start out, to the enthusiastic cheers of the crowd. But as they turn the corner, they see Doryan in front of them, in the middle of the road, while a detachment of his troopers around him have their finger on the triggers of machine guns. O'Leary attempts to escape, but he is shot by Doryan, and he and his companions are captured. Charles and Rosy are present, but that does not prevent the villagers from accusing her of being the "informer." They seize her in front of her husband, who has been subdued by the crowd in the schoolyard, and cut her hair and strip her. Father Collins arrives in the nick of time and prevents any further violence.

By this time, Charles has witnessed a nocturnal assignation of his wife, who goes out in her slip to meet her lover. He takes off in the middle of the night, and it is not until two days later that Father Collins finds him sitting on a rock in the farther crags of the beach, thinking out his situation and making decisions. After he returns home, Charles has a talk with Rosy, telling her that he can no longer stand the situation and that he is going to leave her. He is polite in saying this, and he offers half of his little fortune of 200 pounds to her. She admits her guilt, saying, "It's busted Charles. I busted it."

The story concludes with Doryan's suicide, and with Charles and Rosy leaving town for Dublin. They have to "run the gauntlet," walking through the village street to take the bus, being jeered by the crowd. The villagers whistle at them and chant "informer." As the bus arrives, Rosy kisses Michael's wet cheeks, while Father Collins asks Charles if they are going to part. Interpreting his mute look as "yes," Collins responds with, "I doubt it, and that's my parting gift to you."

Before exiting the village, Rosy stops to bid farewell to her father, who rives momentarily when she tells him she will write to him. In a later shot, we see Ryan holding a drink, a look of guilt in his face. No one in the village, including Charles or Rosy, knows or suspects that he is the informer.

Despite its splendid photography and well-knit story, *Ryan's Daughter* ran into a wall of critical wrath when it was released, despite the fact that it won two Oscars[2] and ran for two years in London and eventually made a profit.[3] Its poor critical reception in general, especially by the National Society of New York critics at the Algonquin Hotel a few days after its premiere in 1970,[4] was so bitterly disappointing to Lean (and his collaborators) that he stayed away from trying another venture for some time and even thought of quitting filmmaking altogether.[5] Although *Ryan's Daughter* garnered sporadic praise for individual performances[6]—Sarah Miles was nominated for an Oscar, while John Mills and Freddie Young won—the poor critical reception of *Ryan's Daughter* had a shattering effect on Lean, and it took nearly fourteen years of indecision and wrecked projects before he attempted what turned out to be his last film, *A Passage to India*, which partially restored his marred reputation with both the public and critics.

Today, *Ryan's Daughter* can be seen in a different light, partly because of what seems a revival of interest in Lean films as new publications have come to light,[7] and also thanks to video editions of the movie,[8] which have helped the public reacquaint itself with the film, particularly the 2006 thirty-fifth anniversary DVD reissue in a new digital transfer from the restored 65mm original print. The two-disc anniversary set contains a running commentary by surviving members of the cast and crew. The second disc also contains comments by directors and film historians, who express their views in the "Making of *Ryan's Daughter*" feature,[9] providing an opportunity for younger viewers to reassess the classic Lean movie and reach their own conclusions about its success or failure. Of particular interest is the participation of Richard Schickel,[10] who speaks out about the Algonquin meeting and his role in it, asserting[11] that he merely passed the general opinion of those critics present in that meeting on to Lean, who left the room amid Pauline Keal's jeers. The commentators on this DVD edition include Sarah Miles, Eddie Fowlie, Sandra Lean, Petrine Day Mitchum, and Lean biographer Stephen M. Silverman, to name a few, most offering laudatory remarks,[12] but the details that emerge from these reminiscences should prove useful to those seeking to gauge the critical dispute or gather source materials about this lengthy production.

Regardless of what one thinks of the rejection of this film by critics in 1970, or others since then,[13] *Ryan's Daughter* constitutes a set piece on the canvas painted by the five Lean epics, adding a unique and irreplaceable part to it. Today, mostly because of the restored version of the movie with the 2006 DVD edition, the movie has found a younger generation of viewers that has led to a renewed interest in Lean's most unappreciated work. CS

Notes

1. Steven Organ, ed., *David Lean Interviews* (Jackson: University of Mississippi Press, 2009), 35.
2. The later *A Passage to India* also won two Academy Awards but had eleven nominations.
3. See the commentary in "The Making of *Ryan's Daughter*," *Ryan's Daughter*, directed by David Lean (Warner Home Video, 2006), DVD.
4. See the introduction to this book.
5. Sandra Lean, *David Lean: An Intimate Portrait* (New York: Universe Publishing, 2001), 52.
6. For a list of praise given to others, see Michael Tanner, *Troubled Epic: On Location with* Ryan's Daughter (Malta: Collins Press, 2007), 180–81.
7. Worth mentioning at this point are Gene D. Phillips, *Beyond the Epic: The Life and Films of David Lean* (Lexington: University of Kentucky Press, 2006), and Michael Tanner, *Troubled Epic*.
8. See Matthew Kennedy, "David Lean's Problem Child: Gorgeous but Flawed *Ryan's Daughter* on DVD," *Bright Lights Film Journal*, 5 December 2006, http://brightlightsfilm.com/52/ryans.php#.Uks_HGD8ms (1 October 2013).
9. These include Lady Sandra Lean, Lean's sixth and last wife; Sarah Miles; Petrine Day Mitchum, daughter of Robert Mitchum; assistant director Michael Stevenson; second unit director Roy Stevens; art director Roy Walker; assistant editor Tony Lawson; location manager Eddie Fowlie; director John Boorman; director Hugh Hudson; Lean biographer Stephen M. Silverman; and film historian Richard Schickel. Most of these individuals participate in the running commentary on both discs, and they each also appear in the section entitled "The Making of *Ryan's Daughter*" on the second disc. *Ryan's Daughter*, directed by David Lean (Warner Home Video, 2006), DVD.
10. Referred to in both the "Commentary" and "The Making of *Ryan's Daughter*" features, *Ryan's Daughter*, directed by David Lean (Warner Home Video, 2006), DVD.
11. On the occasion of the reissue of *Ryan's Daughter* on the 2006 DVD, in which a number of former Lean collaborators and other commentators, named in note 7, pay belated tribute to Lean's achievements.
12. Of interest are Hugh Hudson's opening remarks that "Lean is a cinematic novelist," who opens with a description of dark clouds at dawn, connecting this imagery to the events that follow. John Boorman is the

only one who attributes the failure of *Ryan's Daughter* to its sprawling structure, into which a "small story" was placed. "People sensed that," he concludes.

13. The negative critical reaction to *Ryan's Daughter*, along with a few laudatory comments made at the time, is described in great detail in Kevin Brownlow, *David Lean: A Biography* (New York: A Wyatt Book for St. Martin's Press, 1996), 584–88.

Bibliography

Brownlow, Kevin. *David Lean: A Biography*. New York: A Wyatt Book for St. Martin's Press, 1996.

Kennedy, Matthew. "David Lean's Problem Child: Gorgeous but Flawed *Ryan's Daughter* on DVD." *Bright Lights Film Journal*, 5 December 2006, http://brightlightsfilm.com/52/ryans.php#.Uks_HGz8ms (1 October 2013).

Lean, Sandra. *David Lean: An Intimate Portrait*. New York: Universe Publishing, 2001.

Organ, Steven, ed. *David Lean Interviews*. Jackson: University of Mississippi Press, 2009.

Phillips, Gene D. *Beyond the Epic: The Life and Films of David Lean*. Lexington: University of Kentucky Press, 2006.

Santas, Constantine. *The Epic Films of David Lean*. Lanham, MD: Scarecrow Press, 2011.

Tanner, Michael. *Troubled Epic: On Location with* Ryan's Daughter. Malta: Collins Press, 2007.

S

SAMSON AND DELILAH (1949)

DIRECTOR: Cecil B. DeMille
WRITERS: Jesse Lasky Jr., Fredric M. Frank, Harold Lamb, Vladimir Jabotinsky. Based on the novel *Judge and Fool*, by Vladimir Jabotinsky (uncredited), based on the history of Samson and Delilah in the Bible, Judges 13–16.
PRODUCER: Cecil B. DeMille (Paramount Pictures)
CINEMATOGRAPHER: George Barnes
EDITOR: Anne Bauchens
ART DIRECTION: Hans Dreier, Walter H. Tyler, John Meehan (uncredited)
SET DECORATION: Sam Comer, Ray Moyer, Maurice Goodman (uncredited)
COSTUMES: Edith Head, Gile Steele, Dorothy Jeakins, Gwen Wakeling, Eloise Jensson
MUSIC: Victor Young
SPECIAL EFFECTS: Barney Wolff (uncredited)
VISUAL EFFECTS: Farciot Edouart, Devereaux Jennings, Gordon Jennings, W. Wallace Kelley, Paul K. Lerpae, Jan Domela (uncredited), Cliff Shirpser (uncredited)
CAST: Delilah: Hedy Lamarr. Samson: Victor Mature. The Saran of Gaza: George Sanders. Semadar: Angela Lansbury. Prince Ahtur: Henry Wilcoxon. Miriam: Olive Deering. Hazelelponit: Fay Holden. Haisham: Julia Faye. Saul: Russ Tamblyn (as Russell Tamblyn). Tubal: William Farnum. Teresh: Lane Chandler. Targil: Moroni Olsen. Storyteller: Francis J. McDonald. Garmiskar: William Davis. Lesh Lakish: John Miljan. Fat Philistine Merchant Wearing No Robe: Arthur Q. Bryan. Spectator: Kasey Rogers (as Laura Elliot). Lord of Ashdod: Victor Varconi. Lord of Gath: John Parrish. Lord of Ekron: Frank Wilcox. Lord of Ashkelon: Russell Hicks. First Priest of Dagon: Boyd Davis. Lord Sharif: Fritz Leiber. Leader of Philistine Soldiers: Mike Mazurki. Merchant Prince: Davison Clark. Wounded Messenger: George Reeves. Bar Simon: Pedro de Cordoba. Village Barber: Frank Reicher. Prince: Colin Tapley. Narrator: Cecil B. DeMille (uncredited)
AA: Best Art Direction–Set Decoration–Color (Hans Dreier, Walter H. Tyler, Sam Comer, Ray Moyer), Best Costume Design–Color (Edith Head, Gile Steele, Dorothy Jeakins, Gwen Wakeling, Eloise Jensson)
AAN: Best Cinematography–Color (George Barnes), Best Effects–Special Effects (Cecil B. DeMille Productions), Best Music–Scoring of a Dramatic or Comedy Picture (Victor Young)
GGN: Best Cinematography–Color (George Barnes)
VHS: Paramount Pictures, 1995
DVD: Official release not currently available
BLU-RAY: Currently unavailable
DURATION: 126 minutes

Samson and Delilah was Cecil B. DeMille's first film based on a biblical story since *The King of Kings* (1927), and, more broadly, he had not delivered a Christian religious tale since *The Sign of the Cross* (1932) and *The Crusades* (1935). It did not seem the most auspicious time to revive the religious epic, given that the industry was experiencing an overall decline at the box office during the postwar years. Studio executives were reticent to fund the project until DeMille showed them a sketch of a "big, brawny athlete . . . and a ravishingly attractive young girl."[1] He got his money. *Samson and Delilah* was Paramount's highest-grossing film to date, and it garnered the biggest box-office take of all films in 1950, with its $3,097,563 budget bringing in $11 million domestically.[2] Writing in 1949 for the *New York Times*, Bosley Crowther says of the film:

> There are more flowing garments in this picture, more chariots, more temples, more peacock plumes, more animals, more pillows, more spear-carriers, more beards, and more sex than ever before. At least, that's the sizable impression which Mr. DeMille has achieved by bringing together the Old Testament and Technicolor for the first time.[3]

Although the film seems a little awkward to today's eyes, as the first color biblical epic, *Samson and Delilah* would revitalize the film industry for more than a decade.

The story is taken from chapters 13 through 16 of the book of Judges of the Bible, where the angel of God proclaims to his mother that Samson will help the Israelites against their Philistine oppressors. As Samson's story in the Bible is only about three pages long, DeMille expanded the tale by turning to Vladimir Jabotinsky's 1930 novel *Judge and Fool*, in which Samson's later love interest, Delilah, becomes the younger sister of his wife (an unnamed figure in the Bible), making sibling rivalry and jealousy driving forces in the film. Samson begins as a somewhat selfish hero, suffering not so much a fall from grace as its discovery, a trajectory also offered to Delilah rather than the unrepentant figure of the Bible.

Samson (played by Victor Mature) is the strongest man among a conquered people, the Danites, who are ruled by the oppressive Philistines. Samson rejects the interests of his fellow Israelite Miriam (Olive Deering), having been smitten by the Philistine Semadar (Angela Lansbury). Spurred on by her sister Delilah (Hedy Lamarr), Samson preempts a royal lion hunt and instead kills the lion with his bare hands (what is intended as a spectacular highlight of the film unfortunately does not play well today thanks to a poorly matched body double, Mature's dubious efforts with a stuffed lion, and below-standard editing between the two Samsons. DeMille found Mature so skittish on set that he is said to have lambasted him for being "100 percent yellow"[4]).

Samson wins the admiration of the Philistines' leader, the Saran of Gaza (a fabulously cynical George Sanders), who grants him permission to choose a Philistine bride. Samson chooses Semadar, much to the chagrin of both Delilah and Semadar's betrothed Prince Ahtur (DeMille regular Henry Wilcoxon). The Philistines are also unhappy with the match. With the goading of Delilah, Semadar turns against Samson and gets out of him the answer to the riddle he has sent the guests (in the Bible it is the guests themselves who convince Samson's bride to help them). When Samson departs to pay the price of the riddle, Semadar is married to Prince Ahtur instead. Samson returns, and the wedding ends in violence, resulting in Semadar's death. Samson is devastated, and understandably refuses to marry Delilah in her place.

Samson takes out his vengeance against the Philistines with raids of violence, and the Saran tries to turn Samson's own people against him by enforcing crippling taxes upon the Danites until they offer him up for capture. Samson presents himself to Ahtur only to humiliate him by savaging his troops, armed only with the jawbone of an ass. Back at the Philistine court, Delilah has become the mistress of the Saran but offers to capture Samson for an exorbitant price. She claims the desire for revenge, but the Saran sees through her pretense and knows that she desires Samson.

Samson does indeed fall for Delilah's charms, and she learns the secret to his superhuman strength: his long hair. Delilah asks Samson to run away with her to Egypt, but when Miriam brings news of his father's death and that his mother has been "chained to a post and whipped," he immediately forgets Delilah and gets ready to depart to help his people. Delilah is enraged once more, and drugging Samson, she cuts his hair and delivers him to Saran, demanding that he be kept alive but in humiliating servitude.

Delilah's triumph is short-lived, however, for when the Saran shows the now blinded Samson turning the millstone, she is overcome with pity and remorse. When she goes to aid in his escape, his rage unleashes his recovered strength. Forgiving Delilah and thanking his God, Samson stays to exact his revenge on the Philistines. Binding him with a whip to keep up their pretense in front of the Saran, Delilah leads him to the pillars of their temple of Dagon, which Samson pushes over, causing the destruction of the temple and crushing himself, Delilah, and many of the Philistines to death. In that the Philistines remain in power, Samson does not fulfill his potential to help his people, but hope for them remains in the figure of young Saul (Russ Tamblyn), who will later become their leader.

DeMille would later perfect his skills with the color biblical epic *The Ten Commandments* (1956), and by comparison, *Samson and Delilah* is rather set-bound and relies on the final temple destruction before we really get the benefit of an expansive spectacle and a cast of thousands. There are inconsistencies in the plot; although Hedy Lamarr makes a beautiful Delilah, there seems no good reason why Samson suddenly relents to her affections when he has been at best disinterested and at worst disgusted by her throughout the film. And having learned that Samson's strength lies in his hair, why would the Philistines allow it to regrow? Admittedly this also features in the Bible, presumably meaning that Delilah did not reveal her knowledge to her people.

DeMille suffered some harsh criticism of the film, but the $1 million spent in advertising and promotional gimmicks—which included Kellogg's "Samson-sized Cornflakes"—turned out to be a good investment.[5] It was the phenomenal commercial success of *Samson and Delilah* that ushered in the new wave of ancient-world epics throughout the 1950s and into the 1960s. The film won Oscars for Best Art Direction–Set Decoration (unfortunately these cannot be truly appreciated given the lack of a high-quality official DVD or Blu-ray transfer at the time of writing) and Best Costume Design for color film (indeed the female leads are eclipsed by their wardrobe). And yet it is the performance of George Sanders as Saran that is the most mesmerizing aspect of the film, as he makes the most charming of villains. DB

Notes

1. Cecil B. DeMille, *The Autobiography of Cecil B. DeMille*, edited by Donald Hayne (London: W. H. Allen, 1960), 364–65.
2. Sheldon Hall and Steve Neale, *Epics, Spectacles, and Blockbusters* (Detroit, MI: Wayne State University Press, 2010), 137.
3. Bosley Crowther, "The Screen: Lavish De Mille Film Arrives; *Samson and Delilah* Has Its Premiere at Two Theatres, Rivoli and Paramount," *New York Times*, 22 December 1949, http://movies.nytimes.com/movie/review?res=9906E5DD133CE53ABC4A51DFB4678382659EDE (12 August 2012).

4. Charles Higham, *Cecil B. DeMille* (New York: Da Capo, 1973), 287. DeMille's own account in his autobiography is far more diplomatic.

5. Jon Solomon, *The Ancient World in the Cinema* (New Haven, CT, and London: Yale University Press, 2001), 165.

Bibliography

Crowther, Bosley. "The Screen: Lavish De Mille Film Arrives; *Samson and Delilah* Has Its Premiere at Two Theatres, Rivoli and Paramount." *New York Times*, 22 December 1949, http://movies.nytimes.com/movie/review?res=9906E5DD133CE53ABC4A51DFB4678382659EDE (12 August 2012).

DeMille, Cecil B. *The Autobiography of Cecil B. DeMille*. Edited by Donald Hayne. London: W. H. Allen, 1960.

Hall, Sheldon, and Steve Neale. *Epics, Spectacles, and Blockbusters*. Detroit, MI: Wayne State University Press, 2010.

Higham, Charles. *Cecil B. DeMille*. New York: Da Capo, 1973.

Solomon, Jon. *The Ancient World in the Cinema*. New Haven, CT, and London: Yale University Press, 2001.

SCARAMOUCHE (1952)

DIRECTOR: George Sidney
WRITERS: Ronald Millar, George Froeschel. Based on the novel by Rafael Sabatini.
PRODUCER: Carey Wilson (MGM)
CINEMATOGRAPHERS: Charles Rosher, Robert Surtees
EDITOR: James Newcome
ART DIRECTION: Cedric Gibbons, Hans Peters
SET DECORATION: Edwin B. Willis, Richard Pefferle
COSTUMES: Gile Steele, Frank Roberts, Tomme McCoig
MUSIC: Victor Young
CAST: André Moreau: Stewart Granger. Noel, Marquis de Maynes: Mel Ferrer. Lenore: Eleanor Parker. Aline de Gavrillac: Janet Leigh. Philippe de Valmorin (Marcus Brutus): Richard Anderson. Queen Marie Antoinette: Nina Foch. Georges de Valmorin: Lewis Stone. Doutreval: John Dehner. Perigore: Richard Hale. The Drinker Scaramouche: Henry Corden. Chevalier de Chabrillaine: Henry Wilcoxon. Gaston Binet: Robert Coote
AA: None
AAN: None
DVD: Warner Home Video, 2003
BLU-RAY: Currently unavailable
DURATION: 115 minutes

When it opened worldwide in movie theaters in 1952, *Scaramouche* became one of the most popular swashbuckling movies ever, and it made Stewart Granger a big Hollywood star. In the two previous decades, Tyrone Power and Errol Flynn had been the most popular swashbuckling heroes, and before them Ramon Novarro and Douglas Fairbanks Sr. in the silent era. Power dominated in the early 1940s with such swashbuckler hits as *The Mark of Zorro* (1940) and *Blood and Sand* (1941), with Rita Hayworth. Flynn, who had started earlier and did quite a few action movies, excelled in *Captain Blood* (1935), *The Adventures of Robin Hood* (1938), and *The Sea Hawk* (1940), ever fencing with his nemesis, Basil Rathbone, both excellent fencers. These swashbucklers, and many others, were melodramas, mostly costumers, laced with flamboyant male leaders, glamorous leading ladies, and villainous opponents who matched the leads in wit and fencing skills, coveting the lady in question but failing to win her, as she was always the hero's prize. Swashbucklers fell short of epic length and massive casts, but they contained epic elements, including elaborate sets, adventures on land or the high seas, and heroes who, aside from romancing the lady, worked for some tribal or national cause, fighting injustice and setting things right. Examples are Zorro, an aristocrat who worked to free the masses, and Robin Hood, the medieval legendary hero who fought a pretender and helped restore Richard I to the throne of England.

Scaramouche is based on Rafael Sabatini's 1921 novel[1] by the same name (subtitled *A Romance of the French Revolution*), which had been filmed earlier (1923) with Ramon Navarro as Andre Moreau and Lewis Stone, who had also been in the previous production as the villain Marquis de la tour d'Azyr, in the silent era. The 1952 film was shot in splendid Technicolor by Charles Rosher, with lavish sets and costumes matching those of the bygone era, as well as a rousing musical score by Victor Young. The cast that includes Nina Foch as Queen Marie Antoinette; Janet Leigh as the ingénue young lady Aline de Gavrillac; Eleanor Parker as the troupe performer Lenore; and Mel Ferrer as the wicked Noel, Marquis de Maynes. Parker as Lenore is Granger's love interest throughout much of the story, although a parallel romance develops, as Moreau is also attracted to Aline, whom he originally thinks is his sister. Granger as the amoral adventurer Moreau for once takes life seriously when his close friend, Marcus Brutus (Richard Anderson), an alias for Philippe de Valmorin, is killed in a duel with de Maynes, the best swordsman in France and a cousin of the queen. The Sabatini novel, condensed to fit into a near-two-hour limit to suit show schedules, is not an epic in the classic Roman/religious genre prevalent at the time. Yet, it contains epic elements, for it features an amoral hero who turns patriotic at a time when hostility to the monarchy was fueling enmities within the ranks of the aristocracy. But much of the novel's action described in the revolutionary ranks is omitted, and the plot centers on the antagonism between Moreau and de Maynes, which culminates in a flamboyant and meticulously staged final duel.

The choice of leads alternated, as the original intent was to stage a musical, with Gene Kelly as Moreau, Ava Gardner as Lenore, and Elizabeth Taylor as Aline. When it was decided that the movie would be a swashbuckling adventure, Kelly dropped out, and with him Gardner and Taylor. Stewart Granger accepted the role, providing that he would be the lead; in fact, he would play both Moreau and de Maynes (as a year later he would play a double role in *The Prisoner of Zenda*), but Ferrer was given the role of latter, and the choice proved fortuitous, for Ferrer would match, or even surpass, Granger in fencing skills, but not in screen presence. Granger, whose actual name was James Lebland Stewart (he had it changed so as to not be identified with the American actor by the same name), came from England, where he had been a matinee idol and had played several roles, some quite popular, in such movies as *Caravan* (1946), *Captain Boycott* (1947), and *Blanche Fury* (1948). Coming to Hollywood, he became a big star when he was paired with Deborah Kerr in *King Solomon's Mines* (1951), and again in *The Prisoner of Zenda* (1953). He was married to Jean Simmons, with whom he made several movies, among them *Young Bess* (1951) and *Moonfleet* (1955). Tall, athletic, and skilled in fencing, Granger took the part offered by MGM and seemed to fit his role as the suitor of young Janet Leigh and a worthy opponent of the coldhearted Noel, Marquis de Maynes.

Mel Ferrer, a ballet dancer turned actor, learned to fence and, with Granger, subjected himself to weeks of rehearsals to stage the several fights—especially the last one—with his on-screen opponent. The two were perfectly matched as hero and villain, and their personal rivalry soon becomes the main motif of the action. The viewer falls under the spell of Granger's passion for revenge and Ferrer's lofty disdain for his opponent. The action, filmed inside a theater lobby, on the stairs and balcony, is like a Ping-Pong match, intense and absorbing, where the final smashing serve crushes an opponent. Any music score is entirely omitted, the only sound being the clashing of steel swords, accelerating as the two foes tiptoe on a balcony, jump over staircases, slash the velvet off seats, and demolish nearly every prop, offering an unforgettable sight of suspense and action. The entire seven-minute duel took place without doubles, and the actors, especially the heavier Granger, suffered numerous injuries during the eight-week rehearsals; however, it remains the longest—and possibly the best—fencing dual in film history without doubles or digital special effects. One could actually claim that the duel is the star of the film.

The story takes off when Moreau witnesses the death of his friend Philippe, who, as Marcus Brutus, had been distributing pamphlets highlighting the motto, "*liberté, egalité, fraternité*," some of which had reached the queen's quarters. At a casual meeting at an inn near the Gavrillac Estate, where Moreau had met Aline de Gavrillac, Philippe provokes de Maynes and is easily stabbed to death after a valiant effort to defend his honor. Moreau challenges de Maynes but, seeing that he is outmatched, escapes, but not before vowing to meet his enemy again as an accomplished fencer and run him through in the same manner as his friend was.

Meanwhile, two women have come into Moreau's life. One is Lenore, his steady paramour, whom he abducts as she is about to marry a rich man, and the other is Aline de Gavrillac, whom he casually meets after a road accident. He begins flirting with her until, in the course of the conversation, he learns that she is his half sister. Pursued by de Maynes's troops, he joins a commedia dell'arte troupe, in which Lenore is the principal performer, and gains his new identity, replacing an actor named Scaramouche (Henry Corden), known for his scarred face. Scaramouche is also a member of the revolutionary group, and he knows who de Maynes's fencing teacher is. His performances with Lenore attract attention, and he and the troupe move to Paris, where they give performances to high-class audiences in plush theaters. By this time, he has been asked to become a member of the National Assembly, encouraged to do so to stop de Maynes, who systematically challenges liberal members to duels, eliminating them. True to form, Moreau, in turn, starts challenging opponents and kills or wounds them in duels, while de Maynes, through the machinations of Lenore and Aline, who both conspire to keep Moreau alive, is always absent on some mission in the queen's service. Finally, Moreau/Scaramouche notices that de Maynes is present at one of his performances, and before the latter has time to slip away, he confronts him and wins the battle but refrains from killing his opponent.

Moments later, he learns from de Valmorin père that his father was actually the older Marquis de Maynes, Noel's father. His birth had been an indiscretion of the older aristocrat, a well-kept secret until now; therefore, Andre immediately figures out that Noel is his half brother, and that is the reason why he could not kill him. The thought flashes through his mind that Aline is not his sister. Thus, he is free to marry her. But Lenore has the last laugh. As the wedding procession goes by beneath her window, she tosses a rose to the groom, a trick toy that spurts blank ink in his face—something she had learned during the shows. She then turns to meet her new suitor, a small man with a grin on his face, who is slipping his hand into his waistcoat—none other than a neophyte Napoleon Bonaparte.

With this note of silliness, the adventure ends, but lightheartedness had been the tone of the movie, which turns half serious only at crucial moments. No one minds, of course, as long as the hero gets comeuppance, and with the right girl to boot. CS

Note

1. Other Sabatini novels that have been filmed include *The Sea Hawk*, filmed in 1940, with Errol Flynn in the lead, and *Captain Blood*, filmed in 1936, also with Flynn, both directed by Michael Curtiz.

Bibliography

Sabatini, Rafael. *Scaramouche*. New York: Houghton Mifflin, 1921, 1949.

SCHINDLER'S LIST (1993)

Director: Steven Spielberg
Writers: Thomas Keneally, Steven Zaillian. Based on the novel by Thomas Keneally.
Producers: Branko Lustig, Gerald R. Mollen, Steven Spielberg (Universal Pictures, Amblin Entertainment)
Cinematographer: Janusz Kaminski
Editor: Michael Kahn
Production Design: Allan Starsky
Art Direction: Ewa Braun
Costumes: Anna B. Sheppard
Music: John Williams
Sound Mixers: Andy Nelson, Steve Pederson, Scott Millan, Ron Judkins
Makeup Artists: Christina Smith, Matthew W. Mungle, Judith A. Cory
Cast: Oskar Schindler: Liam Neeson. Itzhak Stern: Ben Kingsley. Amon Goeth: Ralph Fiennes. Emilie Schindler: Caroline Goodall. Helen Hirsch: Embeth Davidtz. Poldek Pfefferberg: Jonathan Sagall. Marcel Goldberg: Mark Ivanir. Julian Scherner: Andrzej Seweryn. Albert Hujar: Norbert Weiser. Danka Dresner: Anna Mucha
AA: Best Director (Steven Spielberg), Best Picture (Branko Lustig, Gerald R. Mollen, Steven Spielberg), Best Cinematography (Janusz Kaminski), Best Art Direction–Set Decoration (Allan Starsky, Ewa Braun), Best Film Editing (Michael Kahn), Best Music–Original Score (John Williams), Best Writing–Screenplay Based on Material Previously Produced or Published (Steven Zaillian)
AAN: Best Leading Actor (Liam Neeson), Best Supporting Actor (Ralph Fiennes), Best Costume Design (Anna B. Sheppard), Best Makeup (Christina Smith, Matthew W. Mungle, Judith A. Cory), Best Sound (Andy Nelson, Steve Pederson, Scott Millan, Ron Judkins)
DVD: Universal Studios, 2004
Blu-ray: Universal Studios, 2013. Twentieth anniversary edition.
Duration: 196 minutes

Schindler's List is one of the greatest historical epics ever made, and a turning point in the career of Steven Spielberg, who, up to that time, had been making entertaining blockbusters, starting with *Jaws* in 1975, the *Indiana Jones* franchise in the 1980s, *E.T.* in 1982, and several other megaproductions in those two decades (the 1970s and 1980s), which made him one of the best-known—if not one of the wealthiest—moviemakers of his era. *Schindler's List* catapulted him into the position of one of the greatest directors of all time. Shot in black and white, with only a few spots of color here and there, as well as at the beginning and end of the film, *Schindler's List* tells the story of the Holocaust, the extermination of millions of Jews by the Nazis during World War II.

The epic was also a turning point in the history of the movies. It is a distinct departure from the Hollywood epic in that it deals with a significant historical event without trying to gloss over, distort, or change history for the sake of storytelling, but it is presented in the most authentic way possible, conscientiously depicting the Nazi atrocities in all their horror. Based on Thomas Keneally's meticulously researched novel, *Schindler's List* (or *Schindler's Ark*) hardly deviates from its source. Keneally says in his introduction that he wrote his story "[b]ased on interviews with fifty of

Schindler's survivors from seven nations—Australia, Israel, West Germany, Austria, the United States, Argentina, and Brazil."[1] He visited the sites of the labor camps in Cracow, Płaszów, Auschwitz-Birkenau, and other locations of mass executions and wrote his story in the novel form without falsifying his sources, avoiding any fictionalizing of the events because "it would debase the record."[2]

But *Schindler's List* is also a great movie in its own right. Rapidly paced, splendidly photographed and edited, movingly scored by John Williams, and superbly acted by both major and minor characters, the movie avoids the usual excesses of the epic form,[3] where spectacle is there for its own sake, but its episodes unfold in the clearest terms, letting the horrors in the labor camps speak for themselves. Hundreds of little vignettes are deftly seamed together to follow a thread, the rise to success and great wealth of Oskar Schindler, a Catholic German-Czech industrialist and member of the Nazi Party, who wins the favor of key Nazi officials by bribing them to recruit Jewish prisoners from the camps to build his luxurious pottery factory. At first, Schindler appears a callous opportunist, a drinker, womanizer, and war profiteer, but as his business prospers and he earns enough money to bribe German officials, he changes into a philanthropist and tries to save as many lives of those Jews working for him as he can. In the end, he manages to save 1,100, who survive to tell their tale and Schindler's role in it.

The plot is a chronological sequence of events, beginning with the displacing of the Jewish population at Cracow, Poland, forcing thousands to evacuate their homes and take shelter in the ghetto, in crammed quarters. Schindler (Liam Neeson) negotiates with Itzhak Stern (Ben Kingsley), who represents wealthy Jews in the ghetto, the Jewish Council (*Judenrat*), convincing them to finance his enterprise of a factory to provide the German Army with luxury kitchen items, enameled pottery, and other kitchenware, "essential for the war effort." At this point his motives are purely monetary, but as soon as the ghettos are liquidated and their population led into the labor camps, Stern's task becomes harder, as he must now select those of the prisoners who can be called "essential workers." Among the confusion and mayhem, he gradually begins to trust Schindler and even have some respect—and later affection—for him, seeing that his boss is actually trying to save as many of the prisoners as he can, regardless of their abilities.

The appearance of SS lieutenant Amon Goeth (Ralph Fiennes) changes this configuration. Goeth has been assigned the construction of a new concentration camp at Płaszów, and as the new leader of the camp, he shoots anyone he pleases indiscriminately, making life much harder for Schindler and his factory workers. Goeth needs a maid for his headquarters and residence. As a row of women stand in the freezing cold, he selects the last—and prettiest—a young woman shaking from hunger and cold. When Goeth asks her name, standing a bit apart so that "he won't give her his cold," she tells him, "Helen Hirsch." Moments later, Goeth has a female engineer protesting loudly that the building they are in will collapse right then and there. "An educated Jew? Like Karl Marx?" Goeth says sardonically when she explains that she is a university graduate, before one of his officers shoots her.

As the story is about to reach its midpoint, four main characters emerge, two Jews and two Nazis, whose fortunes interconnect, carrying the plot forward. One of the important relationships in the film is between Schindler and Stern. Schindler, growing concerned but holding on to his workers, is increasingly dependent on

Stern, whose loyalty is unquestioned, but who is insecure and nearly accidentally carted away to the concentration camps. Suspicious at first, Stern learns to trust, and even admire, Schindler, as he witnesses his change of heart after the ghetto population is brutally forced to move into the labor camps. The other key relationship is between Schindler and Goeth, both playing a cat and mouse game, as Goeth suspects Schindler of disloyalty but keeps him afloat for the sake of the huge bribes and other amenities that Schindler is able to provide him with. Schindler, whose reputation as a benevolent factory owner where no Jew is killed, has to play his double role of loyal Nazi and crypto-sympathizer of the Jews he employs.

Goeth also has a personal problem: he really likes, and lusts after, Helen (Embeth Davidtz), whom he keeps as his personal servant and treats her nicely around others, but also beats her brutally, as she tells Schindler in one of their secret talks. Goeth loathes himself for having feelings for Helen, teasing her into a confession of what she thinks of him, but also telling her that a German cannot like a "vermin" and a "rat," names applied to the captive Jews. Fiennes's excellent performance touches on the deep psychosis that tears Goeth apart, a man who, as Schindler tells Helen, would be a "normal" person under ordinary circumstances. Goeth even entertains dreams that he will save Helen for himself, so he can live with her in Vienna after the war, a statement that evokes a "You are mad" from Schindler.

When a group of workers at Schindler's factory is to be carted off to Auschwitz to be incinerated or poisoned at the gas chambers, Schindler plays his last card and offers to buy them all, offering Goeth a huge sum of money—suitcases of banknotes. Goeth accepts, as the war is winding down and a surrender imminent. Schindler also has to bribe the camp commander at Auschwitz with diamonds to secure the safety of his prisoners. But Goeth will not give up Helen. Schindler gambles his last penny for her. Stern has been typing as many names as Schindler can afford to pay for, an exorbitant price for any man, woman, or child, but the end of the war and the unconditional surrender of Germany in 1945 bring everything to a halt. As Schindler's factory workers are present to hear the news on the radio, Nazi guards arrive with an order to shoot all the Jews in the camp. Schindler addresses them, telling them that they have the choice of carrying on with their orders and shooting the prisoners, or they can "go home to their families as men, not as murderers."

Being a war profiteer and a member of the Nazi Party, Schindler is preparing to depart during the night, but he breaks down and cries, guilty that he did not use more of his wealth, his car, his Nazi badge, to save the lives of even a few more prisoners. They have a gift for him: a ring they have fashioned from gold hidden in the dental bridges of their teeth. And Stern gives him a letter absolving him of any war crimes. The next morning, the prisoners wander off until they encounter a mounted Soviet officer, who tells them not to go east, for they hate them there, too. He advises them to seek food in a neighboring town.

The film ends in an epilogue, photographed in color, where surviving members of the Schindler workers, accompanied by the actors who played them, each place a stone on his tomb in Jerusalem. CS

Notes

1. Thomas Keneally, *Schindler's List* (New York: Scribner's Paperback Fiction, 1982, 1993), 9.

2. Keneally, *Schindler's List*, 9.

3. Most of the movie was photographed with handheld cameras, avoiding the use of cranes and other paraphernalia of the traditional epic for the sake of authenticity.

Bibliography

Feinberg, Steven, and Samuel Totten. "Steven Spielberg: A *Social Education* Interview." *Social Education* 59, no. 6 (1995): 365–66.

Keneally, Thomas. *Schindler's List.* New York: Scribner's Paperback Fiction, 1982, 1993.

Schickel, Richard. "Holocaust: Heart of Darkness." *Time*, 13 December 1993, 75–76.

THE SEARCHERS (1956)

DIRECTOR: John Ford
WRITER: Frank S. Nugent. Based on the novel by Alan Le May.
PRODUCERS: Cornelius Vanderbitt Whitney, Merian C. Cooper, Patrick Ford (Warner Bros., C. V. Whitney Pictures)
CINEMATOGRAPHER: Winton C. Hoch
EDITOR: Jack Murray
MUSIC: Max Steiner
CAST: Ethan Edwards: John Wayne. Martin Pawley: Jeffrey Hunter. Aaron Edwards: Walter Coy. Martha Edwards: Dorothy Jordan. Ben Edwards: Robert Lyden. Lucy Edwards: Pippa Scott. Young Debbie: Lana Wood. Adolescent Debbie: Natalie Wood. Lars Jorgensen: John Qualen. Mrs. Jorgensen: Olive Corey. Brad Jorgensen: Harry Carrey Jr. Rev./Capt. Samuel Clayton: Ward Bond. Laurie Jorgensen: Vera Miles. Chief Scar: Henry Brandon. Charlie McCorry: Ken Curtis. Jerem Futterman: Peter Mamakos. Mose Harper: Hank Worden. Antonio Moreno: Emilio Feguerua. Look (Gild Goose Flying in the Night Sky): Beulah Archueletta
AA: None
AAA: None
DVD: Warner Home Video, 2006. Two-disc anniversary edition, with an introduction by Patrick Wayne, running commentary by Peter Bogdanovich, and an appreciation by directors Curtis Hansen, Martin Scorsese, and John Milius.
BLU-RAY: Warner Home Video, 2006
DURATION: 119 minutes

The Searchers was the sixth movie John Wayne made with John Ford (three more were to follow), and their collaboration had, by that time, matured enough to make an acknowledged masterpiece of the American western cinema. The film had modest success at the box office,[1] but it was not well received by critics and received no Oscar distinctions; however, in later decades, critics and public alike have regarded it as an American cinematic masterpiece and a complex study of racial conflicts in the Western front during the post–Civil War era. Although the action takes place in western Texas, the film was actually photographed in Monument Valley—a favorite spot for filming in the Ford canon—in VistaVision, an aspect ratio that allows greater depth of composition than the usual CinemaScope technique, which had prevailed in the 1950s as the main vehicle for epic spectacles.

Some of today's critics assign the movie a very high ranking in the Ford cinematic lore,[2] and the finest work between John Ford and John Wayne, a director–actor collaboration highly regarded in American cinema, and the western genre in particular. The American Film Institute has placed *The Searchers* on its list of the 100 best American movies ever made and ranks it as the number one western. This revival of favorable criticism has been aided by the 2006 Blu-ray edition of this movie, released by Warner Bros., which has sparked renewed viewer interest, as large modern TV screens allow for ample display of the magnificent images of locales in Monument Valley.

As the story begins, we see the image of a mounted man approaching a homestead in western Texas, where he is welcomed by his brother's family. The man is Ethan Edwards (Wayne), who is returning to the house of his brother, Aaron (Walter Coy), after an absence of eight years, five of which he spent in the Civil War, fighting on the Confederate side. Edwards has brought back with him a fortune of Yankee gold dollars, some freshly minted, suggesting that he perhaps gained this treasure unlawfully. He is warmly received by his brother; his wife Martha (Dorothy Jordan); their two daughters, Debbie (Lana Wood), eight, and Lucy (Pippa Scott), old enough to have a boyfriend; and their son Ben (Robert Lyden), still a teenager.

After spending a night at his brother's house, Ethan joins a group headed by Captain Samuel Clayton (Ward Bond) of the Texas Rangers, who is also the community's preacher, to take part in a search for thieves who have stolen cattle from a neighboring homestead. The group includes Martin Pawley (Jeffrey Hunter), a youth with Cherokee blood adopted by the Edwards family who is considered a son. Ethan soon suspects that this is a ruse by the Comanches to get them out of the way so they can attack the homesteaders. Ethan returns to his brother's home only to find it burning; Aaron, Martha, and Ben dead (and Martha possibly raped); and Debbie and Lucy abducted.

After an unsuccessful pursuit of the Indian attackers, headed by Scar (Henry Brandon), the chief of the Nawyecka tribe of the Comanches, Ethan takes off with Martin and Brad Jorgenson (Harry Carrey Jr.), Lucy's fiancé, determined to find and rescue the two girls. When Ethan reveals to him that Lucy has been raped and murdered, Brad, enraged, rushes off to attack the Indians, but shots heard soon thereafter indicate that he has been killed. Paired with Martin, Ethan continues his trek, but during a winter blizzard they become lost. A year later, he returns to Lars Jorgenson's (John Qualen), where new events develop.

Laurie Jorgenson (Vera Miles) begs Martin, her love interest, to stay with her and get married, and Ethan reads a letter sent to him by Jerem Futterman (Peter Mamakos), a trader, saying that he has evidence that can put him on Debbie's trail. Laurie begs Martin to stay and settle down, but Martin tells her he has to go, for he is now certain that Ethan wants to find Debbie to kill her because she has been held by the Comanches to be one of Scar's wives. When Martin joins Ethan, he has already been at Futterman's place, where the latter shows him a piece of cloth that he recognizes as his niece's. Futterman asks for $1000 for a reward, and Ethan gives him $60, promising the rest when he finds his niece. He suspects a trap and takes precautions, and when Futterman and two of his men sneak up on them at night, Ethan shoots them down.

Martin and Ethan, paired until the end of the search—thence the plural title *The Searchers*—continue their trek, which lasts a total of five years. Meanwhile, back home, Laurie is being courted by the ungainly but available Charlie McCorry (Ken Curtis), and, after receiving a letter from Martin and reading the details of his search, including his taking a "squaw" wife, she decides to marry him. The letter becomes a device for condensing the plot, which, as previously mentioned, spans five years. This technique allows the viewer to follow the strand of the two men's odyssey, while an eye is kept on the Jorgensen home.

Martin's Indian wife, Look (Beulah Archueletta), escapes when asked to provide Scar's whereabouts. She is later found dead inside an Indian camp, shot during a cavalry raid. While Laurie decides to marry McCorry, Ethan and Martin push onward, and they eventually learn from a Mexican trader, Antonio Moreno (Emilio

Feguerua), where a man called "Cicatrix," Scar in Mexican, can be found. Moreno takes them to his location, and they fake negotiations with him, but Scar recognizes them and hunts them down; however, they do see Debbie, who shows them the scalps Scar has taken as revenge for the killing of his two sons. Debbie recognizes them, too, and runs down a hill to warn them. She remembers some English but refuses to leave "her people." An enraged Ethan attempts to shoot her, but Martin shields her with his body. Scar and his men attack, and the two barely escape with their lives.

When they return to the Jorgensen ranch, the wedding between McCorry and Laurie is about to take place. Martin and McCorry fight fiercely over who has precedence of the bride, and the wedding is broken. A young army lieutenant arrives to tell them an Indian attack is imminent; he has brought along a tired elderly man, Mose Harper (Hank Worden), a half-wit and who has appeared at key points of the action, always citing the Bible, and who gives them clues as to where Scar is. Captain Clayton calls the Texas Rangers, allowing Ethan and Martin to join him. They attack again, this time with reinforcements from the cavalry. Martin finds Debbie in a hut and kills Scar as a full fight erupts, annihilating the Comanche tribe. Debbie runs away. Ethan catches up to her in a cave and grabs her and lifts her in the air, as if preparing to strangle her. Then he suddenly takes her in his arms and says, "Let's go home, Debbie." They return to Lars Jorgensen's, and Debbie is reunited with her family. Now Laurie can marry Martin, but Ethan does not stay for the wedding. The camera follows him as he slowly struts away and vanishes into the desert.

Wayne as Ethan Edwards is a lonely man who remains distant and unapproachable, emerging from the vastness of the desert. He acts as an avenger and savior of his niece and then disappears where he came from. In his role as Ethan, Wayne is shown as a moody, misanthropic individual, dismissing anyone who does not see things his way—right or wrong—and at the same time establishing an aura of mystery about him that is hard to interpret. What he says is stated briefly and with emotion, but much more is revealed about him through his body language. Perhaps he keeps a secret inside him, guilt or self-loathing. He means to save his niece when he starts his trail, but after learning that she has been captive of the Comanches for a lengthy period of time, his pursuit becomes vengeance—both for her captors and her.

Ford uses body language to reveal character, and the careful viewer will catch a glimpse of something that might otherwise go unnoticed. For instance, when Martha takes Ethan's coat in her hands as the latter is about to go with the Texas Rangers, she caresses it with what seems excessive affection, a detail that does not escape the notice of Captain Clayton, who is standing near her. As a commentator observes,[3] Martha is the first to see Ethan coming, and he, in turn, kisses her tenderly on the forehead. Without dialogue to reveal a secret, this could indicate that Ethan may have been her lover before he left eight years before, and that he may have suspicions that Debbie is actually his own daughter. That would explain his rage against her abductors, his guilt for deceiving his own brother, and also his hatred of Debbie after she has been molested by the Comanche chief. But when on the road, nothing awes him, not the desert, not isolation, or any of his companions. Only Martin stays with him, for reasons that soon become entirely clear to the viewer.

Ethan possesses cunning, avoiding traps and escaping the notice of others, and he has knowledge of the territory, just as the natives do. He is the only one in the Clayton group who knows that Nawyecka, the name of Scar's tribe, means "go-around"; therefore, they need to keep hunting them on the move, rather than pinning them down in a particular spot. He speaks their language well enough to communicate and also commands enough Mexican to get by. He dominates his environment, whether with a group, or by himself, or with Martin. He believes that nothing can beat him, and when wounded, he responds to Martin's wish to see him dead with a standard, oft-used phrase: "That will be the day."

His western odyssey is shared by a companion, Martin Pawley, smaller in size—as is Montgomery Clift in *Red River*—and like Clift, Pawley is used to underscore Wayne's older character. Pawley follows Ethan from start to finish, but his reasons for joining in the search are different; even after years of wandering—some of their adventures compressed in the letter he sends to Laurie—he remains steady in his goal, to find Debbie and bring her back home. Pawley is a lively youth, quarrelsome, fearless, impulsive, ready to pick a fistfight, but on the whole, he is a more balanced individual than Ethan, who is surly, moody, and prone to outbreaks of rage. Free from guilt and with the look of an innocent, at least at the start of their journey, he has what Ethan lacks: a sense of communal living and family unity. In the end he joins in and marries Laurie, while Ethan wanders off in isolation and estrangement.

Another character who defines Ethan from start to finish is Ward Bond, a sidekick to Wayne in this and previous movies, here as Captain/Reverend Samuel Clayton. He is a more well-rounded individual than the lonely Ethan, and a fully functioning member of the small community he is tied to. More than any other character in the movie, Clayton is both a man of action and a community unifier. As a captain of the Texas Rangers, he dispatches his duties, guarding against raids, whether by hostile Indians or otherwise, buries the dead, marries couples, and is ready to place anyone under arrest, including Edwards himself for the killing of Futterman. But more importantly, Clayton displays the moral fiber that Ethan lacks: a fair treatment of the enemy, whoever he is. He guards against Indian attacks, but, unlike Ethan, he is not a racist or a bitter man. During a stand at the river, when the Indians retreat, Clayton tries to stop Ethan from shooting at them as they are trying to retrieve their dead and wounded. On another occasion, when Clayton and his group discover an improvised tomb where a dead Indian is buried under a rock, Ethan shoots the Indian's eyes, to which Clayton responds, "What good did that do you?" Ethan sarcastically points out that a dead Indian without his eyes cannot enter his land of spirit, and that he will wander in the winds forever. While Ethan is entirely consumed by his racial hatred, Clayton, rough-hewn and crusty as he is in his own way, serves the community and keeps its social fabric in place.

As homesteads are set apart, each family is a small community in and of itself, and each serves as a functioning unit for such social events as weddings or refugees returning home, as well as a starting point for operations. There are two homesteads that are primary centers in *The Searchers*. One is the Aaron Edwards homestead, to which the prodigal brother returns but which will be destroyed soon thereafter. The other is the Lars Jorgensen home, where major events unfold, for example, the departure of the Texas Rangers to find Debbie, the would-be marriages(s) of Laurie, and the eventual return of Ethan bringing back Debbie (who is expected to become a member of this family). Other characters also swarm there, including Charlie McCorry, with his guitar and heavy (and real) Colorado accent, a suitor of Laurie, whom he almost wins, his plans ruined by the timely return of Martin Pawley, with whom Laurie is in love. Pawley will settle there as the groom; Debbie will become a member of the family; and an itinerant, aging, and seemingly half-witted, but cunning, Mose Harper, who cites the Bible and provides timely clues in the final search for Debbie, will settle. There, the homeless Mose will find a roof over his head, friends to tend to his old age, and the rocking chair he has craved his entire life.

As for the Indian camps, Ford provides glimpses of several tribes that live in the scattered and vast areas of Monument Valley. As Ethan and Martin travel under the cover of traders, they run into a friendly tribe, where the chief is willing to give away his daughter—the portly Look—in marriage to Martin, who becomes her reluctant mate. Look flees when she learns the true purpose of their wandering but leaves a sign to direct their search. During the raid at Scar's camp, she is found dead, possibly killed by the Yankee cavalry that had raided that tribe.

Ford presents the Indian tribes from an objective point of view, underscoring the racism of both sides. Scar hated the intruders in his land and displayed the number of scalps he had in his possession—for every son he had lost; his vengeance is justified, although no less inhuman. In some ways, he is Ethan's double: both are motivated by vengeance, so the hero/villain equation does not exactly work in usual fashion. The hero is as flawed, as his adversary, and it is hatred that motivates both men. On the whole, however, the movie is Wayne's/Ethan's, so his flaw is drawn in much more graphic detail; Scar is not shown in any act of atrocity, but Ethan is. He is the one who shoots the eyes out of a dead Indian, and he is shown scalping Scar after Martin has killed him—in self-defense.

Magnificently shot in Monument Valley, *The Searchers* has become a landmark—both of a favorite locale of the West and American moviemaking—stressing the struggles of the advancing frontier, the displacement of the natives, and the family tragedies that ensued. "This land will be a happy place to live one day," Mrs. Jorgensen says after her son is killed, counteracting her husband's pessimism. "Maybe our bones will have to be under the earth before that happens," she adds. Ford's tales are told with simplicity, clarity, and steady purpose.

The movement West, especially after the divisive and bloody Civil War, could not be stopped. It was a movement not without conflict, tragedy, displacement, and racism that will need decades—even centuries—before it is overcome, for that is the dynamic of the expanding Republic.

A western movie is a genre created for entertainment that needs the dichotomy of hero versus villain to satisfy an audience. For decades, the Indians were the "heavies." The white man clashed with them—as with the hero running down various desperadoes—and won the battle, and the girl in the process. Ford raises the commonplaceness of the standard formula to a new level. He presents the Indians in their dignity and fighting spirit as they tried to stop the encroachment of the whites upon their land. *The Searchers* is the epitome of his art, trying to show how both sides fought and hated for a long time, before the arrival of peace and coexistence. Perhaps he should be honored as an epic filmmaker for that reason. CS

Notes

1. Its gross domestic income was ranked twentieth in earnings. Peter Bogdanovich, "Running Commentary," *The Searchers*, directed by John Ford (Warner Home Video, 2006), DVD; Peter Bogdanovich, "Run-

ning Commentary," *The Searchers*, directed by John Ford (Warner Home Video, 2006), Blu-ray.

2. David Thomson, *A Biographical Dictionary of Film*, 3rd ed. (New York: Alfred A. Knopf, 1996), 796–97.

3. Bogdanovich, "Running Commentary."

Bibliography

Herzberg, Bob. *Savages and Saints: The Changing Image of American Indians in Westerns*. Jefferson, NC: McFarland, 2008.

Le May, Alan. *The Searchers*. New York: Curtis Publishing Company, 1954.

Pippin, Robert B. *Hollywood Westerns and American Myth: The Importance of Howard Hawks and John Ford*. New Haven, CT: Yale University Press, 2010.

Thomson, David. *A Biographical Dictionary of Film*, 3rd ed. New York: Alfred A. Knopf, 1996.

SEVEN YEARS IN TIBET (1997)

DIRECTOR: Jean-Jacques Annaud
WRITER: Becky Johnston. Based on the book by Heinrich Harrer.
PRODUCERS: Jean-Jacques Annaud, Iain Smith, John H. Williams (TriStar Pictures, Entertainment Film Distributers)
CINEMATOGRAPHER: Robert Fraisse
EDITOR: Noelle Boisson
COSTUMES: Enrico Sabbatini
MUSIC: John Williams
CAST: Heinrich Harrer: Brad Pitt. Peter Aufschnaiter: David Thewlis. Ingrid Harrer: Ingeborga Dapkunaite. Ngawang Jigme: B. D.Wong. Kungo Tsarong: Mako. Regent: Danny Denzongpa. Pema Lhaki: Lhakpa Tsamchoe. The Great Mother: Jetsun Pema. General Chang Jing Wu: Ric Young. Tashi: Ama Ashe Dongtse. Dalai Lama, 14 Years: Jamyang Jamtsho Wangchuk. Dalai Lama, 8 Years: Sonam Wangchuk. Dalai Lama, 4 Years: Dorjee Tsering
AA: None
AAN: None
GGN: Best Original Score–Motion Picture (John Williams)
DVD: TriStar Pictures, 1997
BLU-RAY: TriStar Pictures, 2007
DURATION: 136 minutes

In the mountains the shortest way is from peak to peak, but for that route one must have long legs.

—Friedrich Nietzsche

Writing about *Seven Years in Tibet*, director Jean-Jacques Annaud confesses that his films share a common theme, despite changes in "masks and costumes," and this film is no exception. Can knowledge, enlightenment, or human effort ever amend what heredity dictates?[1] *Seven Years in Tibet* explores this question in a cleverly concealed heroic epic wrapped in a bildungsroman disguise.

Titled after the 1952 autobiographical travel adventure by Heinrich Harrer, famed Austrian mountaineer and tutor to the young Dalai Lama, *Seven Years in Tibet*, upon first glance, chronicles Harrer's physical and spiritual coming-of-age against the emotional and historical landscape of the World War II and the occupation of Tibet by the Chinese People's Liberation Army. Structurally organized in the form of a heroic epic, and unlike the book, the film develops Harrer's interesting personal intertext by weaving significant didactic excerpts from the thesis of Friedrich Nietzsche's *Thus Spoke Zarathustra* as symbols in guiding the narrative of the epic plot of the film to its conclusion. In this manner, Harrer becomes transformed on the screen to the archetypal hero of the stature and persona of Nietzsche's *Zarathustra*, namely the Overman, through a reworking of Harrer's autobiography by screenwriter Becky Johnston, who included elements of his life not found in the book at crucial junctures in the script.

Seven Years in Tibet begins as the credit sequence opens to the drones of monks chanting amid a breathtaking view of mountains. The valley emerges from the clouds as a procession leads to the tent of a young Tibetan boy[2] who is being greeted by visitors bringing him gifts, among them a European-styled music box.[3] The fidgety child becomes enchanted when he hears the haunting melody of Claude Debussy's *Clair de Lune.*[4] As the child reaches out to grab the music box in delight, the melody of *Clair de Lune* seems to take elemental form as the camera pans out across the procession scene, through the lofty terrain of the Himalayas and seemingly all the way to a car in Austria, where the sound cuts to introduce the main character of the film, Heinrich Harrer (Brad Pitt), arguing with his pregnant wife, Ingrid (Ingeborga Dapkunaite).[5] The couple is driving to the train station to deliver Heinrich to his dream assignment: a spot on the prestigious German expedition team to climb the famed Nanga Parbat Mountain in the Himalayas. At the station, Heinrich meets fellow Austrian and expedition leader Peter Aufschnaiter (David Thewlis). They are greeted by the press, and Heinrich is treated as a national hero and given a Nazi flag for the voyage, despite Aufschnaiter being the team leader. The two leave for what was planned to be a four-month expedition that changes their lives forever.

The character differences between the two traveling companions become obvious after a pivotal scene that proves to be a literal cliff-hanger between Heinrich and Peter early in the script. Heinrich is badly injured when he becomes distracted thinking about his son, now a month old, while climbing Nanga Parbat. Bleeding from his injury, he continues on, disguising the extent of the damage. When a rock slide endangers Peter's life and Heinrich is chastised for putting both their lives at risk by daring to take the lead despite being injured, we discover the root character of Heinrich Harrer.[6] He tells Peter, "No, you put your life at risk; *I* saved it, so shut up." And Peter is quick to respond: "Next time you lie about an injury, Heinrich, you're off the team." This tension and antinomy between the heroic and egocentric team member Harrer and the value-laden leader Aufschnaiter are blatantly portrayed throughout the early part of the film, and this relationship forms the foundation for the epic dialectic that comes to general resolve in its second half.[7]

After the team fails to reach the summit of Nanga Parbat, Peter orders everyone back to camp. Disgusted by their lack of will and effort, Heinrich lags behind as the others retreat down the mountain toward the base. On his way back, alone, Heinrich follows a band of pilgrims who are passing around an image of the young Dalai Lama. One of them hands him one of the pictures,[8] "for protection," although he does not acknowledge it, telling the pilgrim that it doesn't mean anything to him.

Upon reaching the camp, Heinrich and the team are arrested by British authorities as prisoners since war has broken out between Germany and Great Britain.[9] This begins a series of imprisonments and escapes[10] that eventually leads Peter and Heinrich to make their way to the forbidden city of Llasa,[11] where they meet the young Dalai Lama, after a series of interesting adventures of epic note. These include separating and coming together again; experiencing a chance encounter with strangers along the road who lead them to a prophecy;[12] entering the city in a disguise; being aided by a god; and ultimately, for Harrer, discovering a lost origin. But lost between the pages of history and the misty horizon of the forbidden city of the Himalayas lies the true story of *what* origin, for the film *Seven Years in Tibet* tells of an epic fraught with many masks, as its opening sequences foreshadow and history uncovered as the film was in production.[13] Is the film about the Dalai Lama? Is it about Harrer's spiritual transformation? Is it an epic about the German search for Shambhala in the Himalayas, and if so, did they find it? Why is this an epic, and what kind of hero is Harrer?

The answer to this question of origins is not an easy one, causing some reviewers to balk at the film's perception of gravity,[14] for truly, where is the denouement of this plot, and what, frankly, is the point? Without Nietzsche, there really isn't one; with him, however, this epic is sublime.

The plot points emphasized in the film but not found in the original work of Harrer's *Seven Years in Tibet* are significant keys to identifying the epic intertext of Nietzsche's Dionysian Overman in the film: Dionysos himself emerges in the mask of his famed character, Zarathustra. Here, as in *Thus Spoke Zarathustra*, the hidden Dionysian philosophy of embodiment is narrated in Harrer's heroic mythos as creative will through assimilation, and the concrete manifestation of eternal recurrence is evident through the personhood of the Dalai Lama and the embodiment of the culture of Tibet. Thus, by recognizing Nietzsche's Spirit of Music embodied in the European music box (introduced in the opening scene) as the intertext, the plot's themes of the will to power through assimilation (through the emphasis on Harrer's relationship with his son, whose fictional name is Rolf—perhaps a reference to William Rolph and his theory of assimilation), and finally eternal return (when Harrer leaves his pregnant real wife (his blood lineage) in search of an eternal marriage (his spiritual lineage), are fulfilled. The quest is accomplished at the end, in a pure Dionysian theosophy, when this spirit returns again to the mountaintop: "Never yet have I found the woman from whom I wanted children, unless it be this woman whom I love: for I love you, O eternity. *For I love you, O eternity!*"[15]

The concluding scenes of the film find Heinrich returning[16] from Tibet, music box in hand, at the door of his former wife's house. Young Rolf refuses to see him, but when Heinrich drops off the music box and leaves the room, the young child picks it up and begins to play with it. Harrer, peering through the door, smiles. The conclusion of the film finds Harrer again on a mountaintop, this time with a Tibetan flag at his side, and only witnessing images of father and son once again aiming toward the summit.[17]

"Creation is the great redemption from suffering . . . through a hundred souls I have already passed on my way, and through a hundred cradles and birth pangs. Many a farewell I have taken; I know the heart-rending last hours. But thus my creative will, my destiny wills it . . . my will wills."[18] MC

Notes

1. Jean-Jacques Annaud, Becky Johnston, and Laurence B. Chollet, *The* Seven Years in Tibet *Screenplay and Story Behind the Film* (New York: Newmarket Press, 1997), 12.
2. Friedrich Nietzsche, *The Portable Nietzsche*, edited by Walter Kaufman and translated by Walter Kaufman (New York: Viking, 1984), 2, 122–23.
3. "What is a saint doing in the forest?" asks Zarathustra. The saint answers, "I make songs and I sing for them." Nietzsche, *The Portable Nietzsche*, 123–24.
4. For the significance of this esoteric reference, one must follow the musical link of the *Clair de Lune* reference to the finale of Camille Saint-Saëns's 1886 Suite and compare it to the end of *Zarathustra*, where the idol once again appears in the form of the "long-eared" ass.
5. Nietzsche, *The Portable Nietzsche*, 181.
6. Nietzsche, *The Portable Nietzsche*, 214.
7. Nietzsche, *The Portable Nietzsche*, 167.
8. Nietzsche, *The Portable Nietzsche*, 135.
9. Nietzsche, *The Portable Nietzsche*, 160.
10. Nietzsche, *The Portable Nietzsche*, 199.
11. Nietzsche, *The Portable Nietzsche*, 214.
12. Nietzsche, *The Portable Nietzsche*, 245.
13. Shortly before the release of the film, an investigation into Harrer's past revealed that perhaps there was more to his mission in Tibet than climbing mountains. Records indicate that he had been a member of the Nazi Party and had enlisted in Hitler's Storm Troopers in 1933 (when they were still illegal in his native Austria), even earning the rank of sergeant in the SS. In 1938, the source says, he had requested permission to marry, "giving proof that he and his fiancée were

Aryans." These facts forced Annaud to rework the film and left Harrer calling his prewar anti-Semitic beliefs the "shame of [his] life." Douglas Martin, "Heinrich Harrer, 93, Explorer of Tibet, Dies," *New York Times*, 10 January 2006, www.nytimes.com/2006/01/10/obituaries/10harrer.html?_r=0 (13 January 2013).

14. Roger Ebert, "*Seven Years in Tibet*," *Chicago Sun-Times*, 10 October 1997, www.rogerebert.com/reviews/seven-years-in-tibet-1997 (13 January 2013).

15. Nietzsche, *The Portable Nietzsche*, 343.

16. Nietzsche, *The Portable Nietzsche*, 295.

17. Nietzsche, *The Portable Nietzsche*, 438.

18. Nietzsche, *The Portable Nietzsche*, 199.

Bibliography

Annaud, Jean-Jacques, Becky Johnston, and Laurence B. Chollet. *The Seven Years in Tibet Screenplay and Story Behind the Film*. New York: Newmarket Press, 1997.

Ebert, Roger. "*Seven Years in Tibet*." *Chicago Sun-Times*, 10 October 1997, www.rogerebert.com/reviews/seven-years-in-tibet-1997 (13 January 2013).

Martin, Douglas. "Heinrich Harrer, 93, Explorer of Tibet, Dies." *New York Times*, 10 January 2006, www.nytimes.com/2006/01/10/obituaries/10harrer.html?_r=0 (13 January 2013).

Nietzsche, Friedrich. *The Portable Nietzsche*. Edited by Walter Kaufman. Translated by Walter Kaufman. New York: Viking, 1984.

THE SIGN OF THE CROSS (1932)

Director: Cecil B. DeMille
Writers: Sidney Buchman, Waldemar Young. Adapted from a play by Wilson Barrett.
Producer: Cecil B. DeMille (Paramount Pictures)
Cinematographer: Karl Struss
Editor: Anne Bauchens
Art Direction: Karl Leisen
Costumes: Karl Leisen
Music: Rudolph G. Kopp, Jay Chernis, Paul Marquardt, Milan Roder
Cast: Marcus Superbus: Fredric March. Mercia: Elissa Landi. Empress Poppaea: Claudette Colbert. Emperor Nero: Charles Laughton. Tigellinus: Ian Keith. Titus: Arthur Hohl. Favius: Harry Beresford. Stephan: Tommy Conlon. Dacia: Vivian Tobin. Servillius: Clarence Burton
AA: None
AAN: Best Cinematography (Karl Struss)
DVD: Universal Studios, 2006. The Cecil B. DeMille Collection. The current version was restored to its original 125-minute length by the UCLA Film Archives, aided by the DeMille Estate and Universal Pictures.
Blu-ray: Currently unavailable
Duration: 125 minutes

Cecil B. DeMille was the first to understand the commercial value of the religious epic, and his productions are held by some as being responsible for the poor reputation that the epic film has attained as shallow spectacle with questionable artistic merit.[1] But DeMille also pioneered the epic film spectacle, bringing it to unmatched levels of popularity and setting forth a tradition that would last for decades. He clearly knew the box-office potential of religious spectacle as much as any filmmaker, and he gave audiences what they craved: martyred heroes and heroines (especially the latter), colorful villains, dissolute emperors loosely based on history, tribal leaders divinely inspired, and, above all, clashes between good and evil, with plenty of miracles artfully photographed with special effects so as to appear awesome biblical events to the faithful. By the time *The Sign of the Cross* was made, DeMille had already filmed *The Ten Commandments* (1923) and *The King of Kings* (1927), both in the silent era, but both enormously popular and path-setting. DeMille was a masterful filmmaker who understood the value of elaborate sets and lavish costumes, but, above all, he knew how to evoke notable performances from his actors. For *The Sign of the Cross* he selected Claudette Colbert to play the decadent Empress Poppaea; a virile and dashing male actor, Fredric March, for the role of Marcus Superbus; Elissa Landi as Marcus's doomed Christian lover Mercia; and

Charles Laughton as one of the two best actors to play Nero in cinematic history—the other being Peter Ustinov in *Quo Vadis*, more than a decade later.

DeMille shrewdly recognized that moviegoers wanted more spectacle than piety, so he threw in suggestive sex (the film provoked the wrath of the Catholic Legion of Decency, which led to the formation of the Hays Code in the early 1930s), scantily clad women dancing, and a masculine military man who attracted the attentions of a lustful empress. *The Sign of the Cross* combines these elements perfectly. Choosing the time of Roman history noted for its moral laxity, the prevalence of the ethos that might is right, and the birth of a new religion, *The Sign of the Cross* takes the audience back to the time of Nero burning Rome to amuse himself and compose a song. In the opening scene, he is seen uttering nonsense verses, falling into a fit of melancholy when one of the strings of his lyre is broken, so his "epic" could not be finished. Christians were an easy target when he wanted someone to blame for the fire, and Nero, on the advice of a corrupt Roman guard, Tigellinus (Ian Keith), raids the Christian quarters, arrests and kills its leaders, and throws the group into prison, later to become a spectacle to Colosseum patrons who feasted on the spectacle of humans being devoured by lions.

Meanwhile, an intrigue is at work. Nero's bravest and most loyal general, the prefect of Rome, Marcus Superbus, has fallen in love with a Christian girl, Mercia, while he is the object desire of his lustful and decadent Empress Poppaea, who tries in vain to seduce him. He begs Nero to save the girl he loves, but the emperor, under the influence of the malicious empress, turns him down. He could save her only if she renounced her faith, something she refuses to do, forcing Marcus to follow her to her death. Naturally, he converts to Christianity just before he dies. Both will be united in heaven. This formula worked before, as well as in succeeding epics, for the crowd craves a hero who, if not victorious in his battle with evil forces, must die for the faith.

The film became notorious for its villains, however. Colbert is shown practically bare-breasted while taking a bubble bath submerged in donkey's milk, about to indulge in a lesbian scene with one of her ladies in waiting, while Nero complains of a "splitting headache" after a night of "delicious debauchery." Later, at the Colosseum, he is seen eating grapes (and other delicacies), giving the thumbs down to the gladiators being carved to death beneath him. This scene was practically duplicated in a later epic, *Spartacus*, with Laurence Olivier, who plays a Roman senator coolly severing the carotid artery of a slave gladiator climbing a wall to reach his captors, while Roman ladies yelling for the "kill" giggle in the background.

Hollywood rarely portrays Romans as good (*The Fall of the Roman Empire* does), and, for purely commercial reasons, it has given modern audiences, especially during the early decades of cinema, an evil empire, forgetting that the Romans produced some good emperors (Augustus, Herodes Atticus, Marcus Aurelius, among others), and also numerous historians, philosophers, and poets (Livy, Tacitus, Cicero, Horace, and Virgil come to mind). The Romans were also responsible for an unprecedented period of peace that lasted almost six centuries, as well as the preservation of the Hellenistic civilization and culture (although, of course, they are also responsible for the conquest of Greece and the plunder of Greek art). CS

Note

1. Steven C. Earley, *An Introduction to American Movies* (New York: New American Library, 1978), 147.

Bibliography

Earley, Steven C. *An Introduction to American Movies.* New York: New American Library, 1978.

SPARTACUS (1960)

DIRECTOR: Stanley Kubrick
WRITER: Dalton Trumbo. Based on the novel by Howard Fast.
PRODUCER: Edward Lewis (Universal Pictures, Bryna Productions)
CINEMATOGRAPHER: Russell Metty
EDITOR: Robert Lawrence
PRODUCTION DESIGN: Alexander Golitzen, Roger Forse (uncredited)
ART DIRECTION: Eric Orbom
SET DECORATION: Russell A. Gausman, Julia Heron
COSTUMES: Valles, Bill Thomas
MUSIC: Alex North
VISUAL EFFECTS: Saul Bass
CAST: Spartacus: Kirk Douglas. Marcus Licinius Crassus: Laurence Olivier. Varinia: Jean Simmons. Gracchus: Charles Laughton. Lentulus Batiatus: Peter Ustinov. Julius Caesar: John Gavin. Helena Glabrus: Nina Foch. Crixus: John Ireland. Tigranes Levantus: Herbert Lom. Marcus Publius Glabrus: John Dall. Marcellus: Charles McGraw. Claudia Marius: Joanna Barnes. David: Harold J. Stone. Draba: Woody Strode. Ramon: Peter Brocco. Gannicus: Paul Lambert. Guard Captain: Robert J. Wilke. Dionysius: Nicholas Dennis. Caius: John Hoyt. Laelius: Frederic Worlock. Antoninus: Tony Curtis
AA: Best Supporting Actor (Peter Ustinov), Best Art Direction–Set Decoration–Color (Alexander Golitzen, Eric Orbom, Russell A. Gausman, Julia Heron), Best Cinematography–Color (Russell Metty), Best Costume Design–Color (Valles, Bill Thomas)
AAN: Best Film Editing (Robert Lawrence), Best Music–Scoring of a Dramatic or Comedy Picture (Alex North)
GG: Best Motion Picture–Drama
GGN: Best Motion Picture Actor–Drama (Laurence Olivier), Best Supporting Actor (Peter Ustinov), Best Supporting Actor (Woody Strode), Best Motion Picture Director (Stanley Kubrick), Best Original Score (Alex North)
BAFTA AWARD NOMINATIONS: Best Film from Any Source (Stanley Kubrick)
DVD: Universal Studios, 2006
BLU-RAY: Universal Studios, 2010
DURATION: 189 minutes

Spartacus is a Cold War ancient-world epic about a Thracian gladiator who leads his fellow gladiators and slaves in an uprising against their Roman owners. The film is based on the 1951 novel by Howard Fast. Ancient-world epics like *Spartacus* were plentiful in the wide-screen era, from the mid-1950s through to mid-1960s, of which *Spartacus* is one of the best examples.

The opening credit sequence featuring Roman statues was designed by the legendary Saul Bass, set to Alex North's rousing score. It is 73 B.C., and the Thracian slave Spartacus (Kirk Douglas) is working the mines of Libya; however, his rebellious spirit is soon made evident when he bites a Roman soldier who tries to punish him for helping a fellow slave who is struggling. The effete and pretentious Roman Batiatus (Peter Ustinov) arrives to select slaves for his gladiatorial school, looking at their teeth as if they were merely horses. He chooses the condemned Spartacus, who is then duly trained in gladiatorial skills under the tutelage of the cruelly efficient Marcellus (Charles McGraw). When the gladiators are given slave women for the night, Spartacus is at once entranced, but Batiatus and Marcellus arrive to watch the two have sex, and the enraged Spartacus declares, "I'm not an animal!" His naked companion, Varinia (Jean Simmons), gently reprimands him, saying, "Neither am I," suggesting that Spartacus himself has unknowingly mirrored the behavior of his captors. Spartacus hands her clothing back to her, much to the disgust of the Romans, and a bond is forged between the two slaves.

Although Spartacus tries to befriend the other gladiators, his efforts are not always reciprocated. A black gladiator (Woody Strode, excellent in his small role as Draba) tells him, "You don't want to know my name. I don't want to know your name. . . . If we [are] matched in the arena together, I'll have to kill you." His warning is fulfilled when two visiting aristocratic Roman women take evident relish in selecting the men for their physical appeal and, then, as if being considerate, suggest that the gladiators should fight to the death wearing "just enough for modesty," given the excessive heat. Spartacus is defeated, but Draba refuses to kill him, instead throwing his trident at the Romans in disgust. When Draba leaps up to attack them, the powerful patrician Crassus (Laurence Olivier) coolly slits his throat. Draba's body is hung upside down at the gladiator school, but rather than acting as the intended warning to the other gladiators to stay in line, it seems to inspire them. Draba's depiction is a deviation from the novel, where he is a broken man whom Spartacus tries to comfort. The film version works better by making Draba a hero for Spartacus to model himself on. Spartacus kills Marcellus, and the other gladiators follow him in rebellion, while Batiatus sensibly makes his escape with Varinia.

The gladiatorial rebels are soon joined by runaway slaves, and their numbers grow, the very young to the very old enjoying the simple pleasures of freedom. Among the new recruits is Antoninus (a role created especially for Tony Curtis), who escapes from Crassus after understanding the full implications of being his "body slave." Crassus explains his desires in a roundabout way, saying he likes "both snails and oysters," but even this oblique reference to bisexuality was deemed too much by censors (the scene was subsequently reinstated in the 1991 restoration). By contrast, Spartacus seems to take a fatherly interest in the young man. He recognizes that as a "singer of songs," Antoninus can galvanize the rebels.

In Rome, the slave uprising is both a practical concern and a political embarrassment, but is also a means by which enemies and political rivals, Senator Gracchus (Charles Laughton) and Senator Crassus, can vie for power. Gracchus is a complex (fictional) figure, pragmatically corrupt when needed and indulgent in his vices, and yet a champion of the republican democracy. In a sly move, Gracchus manipulates Crassus's supporter, Marcus Publius Glabrus (John Dall), into confronting Spartacus, taking Crassus's military support base with him. When Spartacus prevails, Glabrus goes into exile. But Crassus is not to be outdone. Spartacus hires pirate ships to lead the insurgents out of Italy to their freedom. Crassus simply outbids him, and the trapped Spartacus is forced into a hopeless fight. Crassus caps his victory by taking Spartacus's wife and newborn son captive.

In what has become the best-known scene of the film, Crassus offers to spare the life of the rebels if they identify their leader. Spartacus is, of course, willing to identify himself for the sake of his people, but he is prevented from doing so when first Antoninus, and then nearly every male among them, rises and proclaims, "I am Spartacus!"

Crassus attempts to win the affections of Varinia, in part to better understand what she saw in Spartacus, but she is understandably not even remotely interested. Gracchus arranges for Batiatus to sneak away with Varinia and her child and grants them their freedom. Gracchus then commits suicide, thereby robbing Crassus of the satisfaction of revenge.

As all of the rebels are crucified on the road to Rome, only Antoninus and Spartacus remain. Crassus finally recognizes the man whom he had once seen fight and forces the men to fight to the death. Spartacus prevails, sparing Antoninus the agony of crucifixion. As the young man dies, they declare their love for one another as father and son. Crassus has Spartacus crucified, but the film ends with the fleeing Varinia introducing his free infant son, and with him the hope for a future without slavery.

As for the historical Spartacus, Plutarch comments that he had more intelligence and valor than would be expected of someone of his background and circumstance (*Crassus*, 8.2), and indeed that Spartacus's wife had seen omens of his future greatness (*Crassus*, 8.3), suggesting a certain religious quality that also became associated with him. Although there is little evidence as to what the gladiator schools were like during his time, the ancient sources confirm that the gladiators themselves were from different origins, and as most were newly enslaved, they would have been particularly keen to regain their freedom. Slaves were often used to fight in private and political conflicts, the implications of which disturbed Cicero (*Pro Tullio*, 8). As historian Keith R. Bradley notes, "When gladiatorial contests by their very nature thrust slaves into situations where their lives were threatened, revolt may have seemed to many no less hazardous an alternative."[1]

After the initial insurrection, rural slaves were attracted, in part, by Spartacus's practice of dividing the plunder equally. As their numbers grew, the rebels appear not to have been united by a particular goal or destination, and it seems that despite numerous military victories, Spartacus was unable to control his troops adequately for long-term planning.[2] Spartacus was finally defeated by Crassus's forces in 71 B.C., and he died in this battle, although Appian tells us that his body was never found, and 6,000 captives were indeed crucified afterward along the road from Capua to Rome (*The Civil Wars*, 1.14.120). In subsequent centuries, Spartacus became an archetype of the freedom fighter, an image particularly cultivated in France, Italy, and the United States in the eighteenth and nineteenth centuries through art, novels, and plays.[3]

But in the aftermath of the McCarthy era in the United States, Spartacus gained a new cultural resonance. Novelist Howard Fast became interested in Spartacus while in prison for refusing to answer questions to the House Un-American Activities Committee (HUAC) in 1950. His self-published book *Spartacus* became a best-seller. Screenwriter Dalton Trumbo was also jailed for his refusal to comply with HUAC, one of the famed "Hollywood Ten" who did so. The involvement and open screen credits for the blacklisted Fast and Trumbo led to right-wing picket lines at screenings, famously crossed by the new president, John F. Kennedy.[4] In the film itself, as Crassus comes to power, he tells Gracchus, "The enemies of the state are known. Arrests are in progress . . . lists of the disloyal have been compiled." The film's most famous sequence, in which practically all the male dissidents claim their identity as Spartacus, resonates most powerfully against this political background of naming names for an oppressive but powerful regime.

Through the characters of Varinia and the black gladiator Draba, this oppression is further linked with the civil rights movement that would gain traction in the coming decade. On the score of sexual rights, the novel and film have not been judged favorably, for homosexuality and bisexuality become symbols of Roman degeneracy, in contrast with the heterosexual purity of the rebels.[5] In the film, Crassus follows his proposition to Antoninus by proclaiming, "There's only one way to deal with Rome. . . . You must abase yourself before her." And, of course, before Crassus. Taking a different interpretation, Tony Curtis suggests that his character Antoninus rebels against Roman intimidation and lack of respect rather than homosexuality itself.[6]

Indeed, the film's success was partially due to the flexibility of its message. As Jeffrey Richards argues, the film could be read as an "attack on either Fascist or Communist totalitarianism. But, unlike other epics, it could also appeal to Marxists and Zionists."[7] By dovetailing the film with a reference to the eventual demise of Rome through Christianity in the opening voice-over, and ending with the crucifixion of Spartacus (a change to the story that is said to have irritated screenwriter Trumbo), the film could also be read as a Christian allegory. Despite the pickets, both the right and left could find something that appealed.

The power plays on-screen were paralleled by similar power plays offscreen, involving squabbling actors, numerous rewrites, and the firing of initial director Anthony Mann (who went on to make *El Cid* in 1961 and *The Fall of the Roman Empire* in 1964), mostly hinging on Kirk Douglas's desire to control the project, which was made through his own production company, Bryna.[8] Douglas had worked with replacement director Stanley Kubrick on *Paths of Glory* (1957). Curtis recalls that Kubrick was still considered a young upstart at the time and was not respected by many on the set, yet Curtis found that Kubrick knew what he wanted and was meticulous in his direction.[9] Kubrick may be best regarded for his idiosyncratic later films including *2001: A Space Odyssey* (1968), and *A Clockwork Orange* (1971), but when in Hollywood mode here, the result is still memorable.

Although it attracted some contrasting reviews, overall *Spartacus* was a critical success, with a bevy of Academy Awards and nominations—notably not for Best Picture or Best Director, perhaps in light of the political controversy. Despite a healthy box-office return (particularly overseas), high production and distribution costs meant that the film actually failed to make a profit upon its initial release.[10] Such is the danger of the blockbuster epic. In retrospect, what distinguishes *Spartacus* from other epics of this era is the humor of the script (not found in the novel), delivered by an excellent cast, and the relish with which the Romans are delightful in their decadence, such that the seductive power of Rome is clear even as it simultaneously repels. DB

Notes

1. Keith R. Bradley, *Slavery and Rebellion in the Roman World, 140 B.C.–70 B.C.* (Bloomington and Indianapolis: Indiana University Press, 1989), 85–86, 89, 92–93.
2. Bradley, *Slavery and Rebellion in the Roman World*, 96, 98, 100–101.
3. Maria Wyke, *Projecting the Past: Ancient Rome, Cinema, and History* (New York and London: Routledge, 1997), 34–72.
4. Frederick Ahl, "*Spartacus, Exodus*, and Dalton Trumbo: Managing Ideologies of War," in *Spartacus: Film and History*, edited by Martin M. Winkler (Malden, MA: Wiley-Blackwell, 2007), 70–71, 73.
5. Wyke, *Projecting the Past*, 61–62.
6. *The Celluloid Closet*, directed by Rob Epstein and Jeffrey Friedman (Sony Pictures Home Entertainment, 1996), DVD.
7. Jeffrey Richards, *Hollywood's Ancient Worlds* (London: Continuum, 2008), 87.
8. John Baxter, *Stanley Kubrick: A Biography* (London: HarperCollins, 1997) 123–41.
9. Tony Curtis and Barry Paris, *Tony Curtis: The Autobiography* (London: Heinemann, 1993), 180–85.
10. Sheldon Hall and Steve Neale, *Epics, Spectacles, and Blockbusters* (Detroit, MI: Wayne State University Press, 2010), 179.

Bibliography

Ahl, Frederick. "*Spartacus, Exodus*, and Dalton Trumbo: Managing Ideologies of War." In *Spartacus: Film and History*, edited by Martin M. Winkler, 65–86. Malden, MA: Wiley-Blackwell, 2007.

Baxter, John. *Stanley Kubrick: A Biography*. London: HarperCollins, 1997.

Bradley, Keith R. *Slavery and Rebellion in the Roman World, 140 B.C.–70 B.C.* Bloomington and Indianapolis: Indiana University Press, 1989.
Curtis, Tony, and Barry Paris. *Tony Curtis: The Autobiography.* London: Heinemann, 1993.
Hall, Sheldon, and Steve Neale. *Epics, Spectacles, and Blockbusters.* Detroit, MI: Wayne State University Press, 2010.
Richards, Jeffrey. *Hollywood's Ancient Worlds.* London: Continuum, 2008.
Wyke, Maria. *Projecting the Past: Ancient Rome, Cinema, and History.* New York and London: Routledge, 1997.

THE SPY WHO LOVED ME (1977)

Director: Lewis Gilbert
Writers: Christopher Wood, Richard Maibaum. Based on the novel by Ian Fleming.
Producer: Albert R. Broccoli (United Artists)
Cinematographer: Claude Renoir
Editor: John Glenn
Music: Marvin Hamlisch (title song by Carly Simon)
Cast: James Bond: Roger Moore. Anya Amasova: Barbara Bach. Maj. Karl Stromberg: Curt Jürgens. Jaws: Richard Kiel. Sergei: Michael Billington. Miss Moneypenny: Lois Maxwell. Naomi: Caroline Mundo. "Q": Desmond Llewlyn. "M": Bernard Lee
AA: None
AAN: None
DVD: MGM, 2002
Blu-ray: MGM, 2013
Duration: 126 minutes

James Bond movies are epics by way of their very structure (if not in actual length), and their archetypical heroes. The men—the various Bond heroes that have played that role for more than five decades—are cartoonlike characters, with little, if any, depth, but with such defined archetypal qualities as courage, daring, cunning, and athletic abilities. But, above all, they have a clearly set mission—to find and defeat an enemy that threatens the tribe, a nation, a region (usually the Western World), or even the entire world. Their adventures take them to exotic locales, major cities, and their final destination, where a villain has set up an elaborate hideaway equipped with weapons of mass destruction ready to be launched against a particular set of nations—the West during the Cold World, and the globe in more recent times. This formula has been unchanged: the hero, Agent 007, named James Bond, usually alone but at times aided by a female (and instant lover), embarks on a mission to discover and destroy a particular enemy.

This formula includes not only the main hero—Bond—but the villains who play opposite him. While Bond has been played by only six leads in sixty-plus years—Sean Connery, Roger Moore, George Lazenby, Timothy Dalton, Pierce Brosnan, and Daniel Craig—each Bond movie features a new villain, all colorful, strong characters who share several archetypal characteristics of a villain: they are paranoid megalomaniacs, devoid of moral scruples, having amassed fortunes and, in some cases, powerful paramilitary organizations, and all are bent on taking over the world by getting hold of a weapon capable of delivering a telling blow that will allow them to dominate.

Arguably, the success of a Bond movie at the box office may be directly related to the personality of their villain. A blockbuster movie like *Goldfinger* (1964) may be the result of one of the most colorful villains ever, Auric Goldfinger, played with great gusto by the German actor Gert Frobe (whose voice was dubbed because he could not speak English), a mad genius but quite capable of hatching a bold scheme of capturing Fort Knox, exploding an atomic device in it and cornering the gold market for decades. That would make him rich. Of course Bond, played by the redoubtable Sean Connery, although at times a step behind the villain, catches up in time, disarms the device, and saves the world from plunging into financial chaos. Other colorful villains include Adolfo Celi, the eyepatched villain Emilio Largo of *Thunderball* (1965), who steals a nuclear aircraft, obliging Bond to display his powers of diving underwater to discover the sunken craft in the Bahamas. Later villains include Christopher Lee, an actor known for his Dracula persona, here a thug with three nipples and a golden gun who seizes a "Solar Agitator," a solar energy device (at the time of the energy crisis) that would allow its owner to dominate the energy market. In modern times, conveniently shifting thematic subjects, *Tomorrow Never Dies* (1997) features Paris Carver (Teri Hatcher), whose husband threatens to take over the twenty-first century's emerging superdynasty, the communications industry.

Of course, it is always Bond who is the main attraction in a Bond movie, for he is the one who invariably saves the world, but his being matched with a supervillain is crucial in creating the antagonism needed between good and evil, and the actors who play them contribute heavily to that success. Of those, Sean Connery, Roger Moore, and Pierce Brosnan have been the most charismatic, in that order—specifically the first two—Connery and Moore—whose movies enjoyed their heyday during the Cold War, when the threat of nuclear conflict was at its highest, in the 1960s and 1970s, in particular. In the 1980s, and especially in the 1990s and 2000s, when the nuclear threat from the Cold War took a backseat but was replaced by terrorist threats, the Bond movies had to invent villains that were terrorists of some sort or other. Their movies and heroes also had to compete with war and spy thrillers that featured such actors as Bruce Willis, Harrison Ford, and Arnold Schwarzenegger, who matched or surpassed Connery and Moore, the early Bonds, in physical appearance or toughness. The latter lost the humor of the former, but times had changed, too, for in our times spy and terrorist thrillers are taken in dead seriousness, viewed as real threats (especially after 9/11), dropping the comic-strip features that characterized the earlier Bond movies.

Still, it can be said that in the Bond films, the most successful franchise in film history, having lasted five decades (and still going), there is little doubt that the archetypal conflict between hero and villain, between the potential destroyer of mankind and its savior, is the main point of interest. Villains in the Bond movies come in all disguises—gold bullion tycoons, jewel and art collectors, mad Soviet generals, large conglomerate tycoons, mafia dons, and so forth—but they all share one characteristic: a sense of omnipotence, a hunger for power that will make them rulers of the human universe. This is not a concept alien to literature, or to some of the other arts, or to actual life. Literature, especially of the Judeo-Christian tradition, has produced the arch-villain of heavens, the snake who dragged Eve from Eden, and Satan who tempted Job (to use examples from the Bible itself), and the literary tradition offers the same Satan, frozen in a cake of ice in the pit of Hell in Dante's *Inferno*, a symbol of a frozen heart, and Satan again in Milton's *Paradise Lost*, the fallen angel who wants to take revenge on God by destroying his creatures. In modernized guises, we have Mephistopheles in *Doctor Faustus* by Marlow, Mephistopheles in Goethe's *Faust*, and the fascinating (from a purely aesthetic point of view) devil in Dostoyevsky's *The Brothers Karamazov*, the figure that lays forth, in a dream, the premises of modern relativism and destroys the mind of Ivan Karamazov. In history (and real life), the figures of Caligula (also in a play by Camus), Hitler, and Bin Laden come to mind. Many other examples (and a much broader discussion) can be offered, but these will do for our purpose.

The Spy Who Loved Me was made during the Cold War, but also at a time of cooling tensions, as the concept of détente in the Nixon/Kissinger era was being promoted, which had a bearing on the politics that inevitably creep into the Bond plot structures. The villain here, played by the German actor Curt Jürgens, is Karl Stromberg, a tall, barrel-chested, white-haired, imposing figure residing in an underwater city that he calls the *Atlantis*,[1] his headquarters, from where he directs underground operations, employing distinguished scientists to invent a code that will enable him to track the underwater routes and locations of nuclear submarines. His plan is to divert the submarines from their routes and steer them close to a supertanker he has built, called the *Liparus*, the largest in the world (600,000 tons), where the submarines, along with their nuclear weaponry, will be sucked in and kept their until missiles are launched to destroy New York City and Moscow. A nuclear war will be started that will exterminate humankind, and Stromberg will then fulfill his dream of building an underwater civilization, a much superior race of humans in a far richer environment. Of course, Stromberg has no compunction whatsoever in exterminating all those who would betray him or stand in his path.

His first victim—that we see—is his own secretary, whom he suspects of treachery, for a microfilm copy of the tracking system has disappeared. Without hesitation, he presses a button when she is in the elevator, and she drops into a pool of sharks that tear her to pieces. A panel decorated with Botticelli's *La Primavera* falls, concealing the scene, which is witnessed by two terrified scientists who had been employed by Stromberg to invent the tracking mechanism. Stromberg coolly assures them that their pay of $10 million each has been deposited at their Swiss bank, but a few moments later we see him pushing another button blowing up the helicopter carrying the two scientists away. He announces the death of the scientists to the world as "an unfortunate accident," and wryly adds, "Burial was at sea." He gives orders to his hired assassins, the seven-foot, four-inch Jaws (Richard Kiel) and the burly Sergei (Michael Billington), to find the microfilm copy and kill anyone who stands in their path.

Stromberg gives the external appearance of supercool, polished esthete, a man of tastes and elegance, a civilized recluse who is devoted to higher ideals for the ultimate good of humanity. He alone knows what is good for everyone else. He has contempt for the outside world and its leaders, who, in his stated opinion, waste their time exploring space, and thinks that his plan to create an underwater civilization, if executed, will be justified by history. The death of millions, or even billions, of people does not concern him, for he will create a far superior world. He is a paradox, for there is no trace of vulgarity in him, and he gives the impression of an ascetic on a mission to save the world from its wrong path. He is passionate about the sea species he has gathered in his tanks, a world in which he sees "beauty," "ugliness," and "death." The walls of his hermitage are decorated with panels of copies of the greatest paintings—and the music of Mozart and other classical composers is being played while he eliminates those he doesn't like. CS

Note

1. A sunken civilization described in Plato's *Critias* (or *Atlantis*), a subject of much speculation among archeologists and other antiquarians.

Bibliography

Berardinelli, James. "*The Spy Who Loved Me*: A Film Review by James Berardinelli." *ReelViews.net*, 1995, www.reelviews.net/movies/s/spy_who.html (4 October 2013).

Wood, Christopher. *James Bond, The Spy Who Loved Me*. New York: Twentieth-Century Publishers, 2006.

T

300 (2007)

Director: Zack Snyder
Writers: Zack Snyder, Kurt Johnstad, Michael B. Gordon. Based on the novel by Frank Miller, with painted colors by Lynn Varley.
Producers: Gianni Nunnari, Mark Canton, Bernie Goldmann, Jeffrey Silver (Warner Bros., Legendary Pictures, Virtual Studios)
Associate Producers: Wesley Coller, Silenn Thomas, Nathalie Peter-Contesse
Cinematographer: Larry Fong
Editor: William Hoy
Production Design: James D. Bissell
Art Direction: Isabelle Guay, Nicolas Lepage, Jean-Pierre Paquet
Set Decoration: Paul Hotte, Philippe Lord
Costumes: Michael Wilkinson
Music: Tyler Bates
Cast King Leonidas: Gerard Butler. Queen Gorgo: Lena Headey. Theron: Dominic West. Dilios: David Wenham. Captain: Vincent Regan. Stelios: Michael Fassbender. Astinos: Tom Wisdom. Daxos: Andrew Pleavin. Ephialtes: Andrew Tiernan. Xerxes: Rodrigo Santoro. Pleistarchos: Giovani Antonio Cimmino
AA: None
AAN: None
DVD: Warner Home Video, 2007. With running commentary by Zack Snyder, Kurt Johnstad, and Larry Fong.
Blu-ray: Warner Home Video, 2007. With running commentary by Zack Snyder, Kurt Johnstad, and Larry Fong.
Duration: 111 minutes

The film *300* is based on Frank Miller's 1999 graphic novel of the same name,[1] which, in turn, is partly based on the 1961 film *The 300 Spartans* (directed by Rudolph Maté), itself loosely based on a historical battle at Thermopylae in 480 B.C.E., recounted by the Greek historian Herodotus in Book VII of his work *The Histories.* While elements of Herodotus remain in *300,* the movie's hard-bodied heroes and hybrid human beasts owe more to the mythological muscle-man tradition. The film largely follows Miller's graphic novel in aesthetic and plot, but it extends the role of Queen Gorgo (ably performed by Lena Headey) and politics at home in Sparta. Frequent use of slow motion emphasizes the graphic novel origin, and the film is most often noted for its high-contrast visual style and battlefield digital effects.

The film opens with the brutal Spartan upbringing and initiation of King Leonidas (Gerard Butler), during which he kills a wolf by trapping it in a rocky passage. Later, as an adult, with a young son of his own, the king kills a messenger from the Persian king Xerxes (Rodrigo Santoro), who seeks their submission. Leonidas is unable to take his army to war without the support of corrupt priests and politicians. Instead, he takes 300 of his best warriors on a "stroll" with the clear intention of mounting a seemingly suicidal confrontation against the Persians. The Spartans have knowledge of the territory on their side, however, and are able to channel the Persians to a narrow passage, reducing their numbers to a potentially manageable front line. Only a few other Greeks join them in their campaign.

Back in Sparta, the powerful and wily councilman Theron (Dominic West) agrees to help the queen gain support for her husband's campaign, but only in return for sex. She consents, but he is unduly brutal with her. At the council, Theron betrays her, and the queen kills him, inadvertently revealing the Persian gold coins he is harboring, which expose him as a traitor.

On the battlefield, the deformed and rejected Spartan Ephialtes (Andrew Tiernan) tells Xerxes how to circumnavigate the rocky passage. Learning of the betrayal and their imminent defeat, most other Greeks choose to leave, but the Spartans are defiant and stay to face death. The Spartans' sacrificial heroism inspires the rest of the Greeks to join the fight, and the film ends at the beginning of this final victorious battle.

Whether this victory will usher in a new "age of freedom," as the Spartans claim, is dubious given that they put the "imperfect" to death at birth. The remaining "perfect" white, male, and ostensibly heterosexual Spartan heroes, are contrasted against the multiple racial, physical, and sexual identities to be found in the Persian army camp. As is frequently the case in sword-and-sandal epics, the villains seem to be having more fun with their orgies than the monogamous Spartans. The Persians may be presented as the invading foreign hordes, but they appear more accepting of difference than the Spartans, who claim to be upholding freedom. Within the moral shorthand of the film, however, the multiple Persian identities are equated with a loss of identity once enslaved by the bejeweled and painted Xerxes. Yet, while the Spartans dismiss even their Athenian cousins as "philosophers and boy lovers," surely their own buff bodies and camp little leather jocks make for at least a potentially queer eyeful. As Todd McCarthy notes in *Variety*, "Possibly nowhere outside of gay porn have so many broad shoulders, bulging biceps, and ripped torsos been seen onscreen as in *300*."[2]

Such unresolved tensions are often found within the male epic, with its focus on the idealized male body as it enacts a particular brand of male-bonded heroism and sacrifice.[3] *300* has been criticized for being fascist in its politics and aesthetics,[4] and it is specifically the Spartan military who is the savior in the film. If the aim is to rid the world of "mysticism and tyranny" (and not just "tyranny," as in the 1961 film), then the Spartans must also address their own dishonest politicians and priests, by implication replacing them with martial law. Although the graphic novel was written before 9/11, the post–9/11 climate gives resonance to the 2007 film's heroes being under attack in their homeland, even though in *300* it is the Persians who are the superpower. As a result, both sides of the political spectrum have found cause for complaint about the film, although, given its success, *300* is perhaps more usefully to be thought of as providing an outlet for these contemporary cultural conflicts to be played out.[5]

The spectacle of Leonidas' beautiful arrow-filled corpse in its crucifixion pose evokes both Christ and St. Sebastian, and this Spartan sacrifice in the name of freedom is such a heightened moment of narrative and digital spectacle that the audience is expected, by this time, to have forgotten the film's opening scene: baby skulls, their own young put to death by the Spartans to maintain their racial purity. There is, therefore, an underlying uneasiness to the film not present in its more traditionally heroic predecessor *The 300 Spartans.*

300 is director Zack Snyder's biggest commercial success to date. At the time of this writing, a follow up film based on a forthcoming Frank Miller graphic novel is being planned. DB

Notes

1. Frank Miller and Lynn Varley, *300* (Milwaukie, OR: Dark Horse Books, 1998, 1999, 2006).
2. Todd McCarthy, "*300*," *Variety*, 9 March 2007, www.variety.com/review/VE1117932810 (7 January 2012).
3. See Richard Dyer, "White Man's Muscles," in *White* (London and New York: Routledge, 1997), 165, 176; Leon Hunt, "What Are Big Boys Made Of? *Spartacus, El Cid,* and the Male Epic," in *You Tarzan: Masculinity, Movies, and Men*, edited by Pat Kirkham and Janet Thumin (London: Lawrence Wishart, 1993), 65–67, 69–70, 81–82.
4. See, for example, Jeffrey Richards, *Hollywood's Ancient Worlds* (London: Continuum, 2008), 185.
5. See Monica Silveira Cyrino, "'This Is Sparta!' The Reinvention of the Epic in Zack Snyder's *300*," in *The Epic Film in World Culture*, edited by Robert Burgoyne (New York and London: Routledge, 2011), 26–27.

Bibliography

Cyrino, Monica Silveira. "'This Is Sparta!' The Reinvention of the Epic in Zack Snyder's *300*." In *The Epic Film in World Culture*, edited by Robert Burgoyne, 19–38. New York and London: Routledge, 2011.

Dyer, Richard. "White Man's Muscles." In *White*, 145–83. London and New York: Routledge, 1997.

Hunt, Leon. "What Are Big Boys Made Of? *Spartacus, El Cid*, and the Male Epic." In *You Tarzan: Masculinity, Movies, and Men*, edited by Pat Kirkham and Janet Thumin, 65–83. London: Lawrence Wishart, 1993.

McCarthy, Todd. "*300*." *Variety*, 9 March 2007, www.variety.com/review/VE1117932810 (7 January 2012).

Miller, Frank, and Lynn Varley. *300*. Milwaukie, OR: Dark Horse Books, 1998, 1999, 2006.

Richards, Jeffrey. *Hollywood's Ancient Worlds*. London: Continuum, 2008.

THE 300 SPARTANS (1962)

Director: Rudolph Maté
Writer: George St. George. Based on original story material by Ugo Liberatori, Remigio Del Grosso, Giovanni D'Eramo, and Gian Paolo Callegari.
Producers: Rudolph Maté, George St. George (20th Century Fox)
Cinematographer: Geoffrey Unsworth
Editor: Jerome Webb
Art Direction: Arrigo Equini
Costumes: Ginette Devaud
Music: Manos Hadjidakis
Cast: King Leonidas: Richard Egan. Themistocles of Athens: Sir Ralph Richardson. Ellas: Diane Baker. Phylon: Barry Coe. Xerxes: David Farrar. Hydarnes: Donald Houston. Gorgo: Anna Synodinou. Ephialtes: Kieron Moore. Agathon: John Crawford. Pentheus: Robert Brown. First Delegate: Laurence Naismith. Artemisia: Anne Wakefield. Demaratus: Ivan Triesault. Megistias: Charles Fawcett. Myron: Michael Nikolinakos. Xenathon: Sandro Giglio. Toris: Anna Raftopoulou. Samos: Dimos Starenios. Gryllus: George Moutsios. Demophilus of Thespiae: Yorgos Moutsios. Mardonius: N. Papaconstantinou. Artabanus: John G. Contes. Woman at Shield Ceremony: Marietta Flemotomos
AA: None
AAN: None
DVD: 20th Century Fox Home Entertainment, 2008
Blu-ray: Currently unavailable
Duration: 109 minutes

The 300 Spartans is an ancient-world epic based on the story told in Book VII of *The Histories*, by the Greek historian Herodotus, of the real battle between a bare 300 Spartans and the vastly larger invading Persian army, led by King Xerxes, in 480 B.C.E. Xerxes (David Farrar in his last role) is a petulant leader who cannot understand the mentality of a people who would stubbornly oppose his seemingly insurmountable force. As his troops approach Greece, he frees the captive Spartan spy Agathon (John Crawford) so that he may report what he has seen to the Greeks assembling at Corinth, but Agathon does not address the assembly, understanding all too well that they would indeed be scared by the scale of the impending invasion.

The representatives from the Greek city-states argue among themselves but clearly favor a separatist approach. Only the Athenian Themistocles (played with presence by Sir Ralph Richardson) and the Spartan king Leonidas (Richard Egan) advocate for a combined Greek resistance. Themistocles reminds the assembly that the Athenians defeated the Persians at Marathon, alone and outnumbered. Indeed, it is partly to avenge his father's defeat that Xerxes returns. Themistocles argues that the Persians' strength "lies in their unity," so in a show of Greek unity, Themistocles places the Athenian fleet under Spartan control. Outside the assembly, Leonidas tells Themistocles that the narrow pass at Thermopylae is the ideal location for the landing troops to confront the Persians, using the terrain to their advantage.

But back in Sparta, Leonidas struggles to persuade his own council that waging the defense so far from Sparta is in their best combined interests. When the council proclaims that the troops may not depart until after a religious festival, Leonidas marches toward Thermopylae with 300 of his personal guards. While Themistocles is disappointed by their small number, the news that the Spartans will fight inspires the Thespians to join them.

Following the troops is the young Spartan Phylon (Barry Coe) and his intended bride, Ellas (Diane Baker), daughter of Leonidas' second in command, Pentheus (Robert Brown). Phylon is initiated into the Spartan troops, only to be stripped of this honor when Agathon reveals that he saw Phylon's father in the enemy camp, but Ellas convinces Phylon to shadow Leonidas and wait for an opportunity to prove himself worthy. Ellas, however, finds the journey difficult, and Phylon carries her to a goat farm, where they are taken in. The goat herder Samos (Dimos Starenios) tells Phylon of the danger that the Persians could outflank the Greeks if they discover an old goat-herding trail that circumnavigates the pass. Although Samos is sent to warn Leonidas, the farmhand Ephialtes (Kieron Moore) overhears, and after a failed attempt to court Ellas, he departs to find the Persian camp.

Seeing that the Persians are preparing to attack, Leonidas buys his men time to rebuild a defensive wall by mounting a nighttime raid on the Persian camp. Although they fail to assassinate Xerxes as planned, they create the diversionary delay they need. Phylon secretly joins the raiding party and is able to save the life of Pentheus when he is injured. Although Leonidas initially admonishes him, Phylon is welcomed back into the troops. Leonidas will need all the help he can muster, for Queen Gorgo (Anna Synodinou) sends word that additional Spartan troops will not be joining them.

On the battlefield, Xerxes appears to have the advantage in sheer numbers, but Leonidas uses the terrain and superior battle strategies to continually outwit the Persian forces. In an exchange based on Herodotus (*The Histories*, 7.226.1), Xerxes' advisor Hydarnes (Donald Houston) asks to speak with Leonidas, proclaiming, "When we attack today, our arrows will blot out the sun." Leonidas calmly replies, "Then we will fight in the shade."

Disgraced by the Persian failures in battle, Hydarnes falls out of favor, and Xerxes' lover, Queen Artemisia (Anne Wakefield), persuades Xerxes to return home on a religious pretext. Xerxes grows suspicious of Artemisia after hearing gossip that her mother was Greek, but, in any case, he is given reason to stay and fight when Hydarnes brings Ephialtes with news of the goat pass. Artemisia advises that they also send Phylon's father, Gryllus (George Moutsios), as a more dependable guide in case the unknown Ephialtes is really leading them into a trap. Gryllus and Artemisia are working together to undermine Xerxes, and Gryllus sneaks away to warn Leonidas.

Leonidas tells the troops to retreat and sends Phylon home with a message that the Spartans will stay and fight. Demophilus (Yorgos Moutsios) proclaims that the Thespians will also stay and fight. In the course of the final battle, the Spartans become cut off, with the Thespians under attack at the rear, and Leonidas acknowledges that they can no longer defend the pass, but he exhorts his men to attempt to kill Xerxes.

When Leonidas himself is killed, Xerxes offers the remaining men free passage if they surrender his body. Pentheus refuses, for although they will die, "Greece will live." In a haunting end to the battle, Persian arrows do indeed blot out the sun as they descend upon the defiant Spartans. The camera lingers on the body of King Leonidas, lying with a fellow soldier's arm across his chest and another's head resting on his body, united in the stillness of death.

At the close of the film, the narrator proclaims that the Spartans were a "stirring example to free people throughout the world, of what a few brave men can accomplish once they refuse to submit to tyranny." The sacrifice of the Spartans in defense of Greece inspires the rest of the Greeks to join together and defeat the Persians.

As a whole, *The 300 Spartans* stays surprisingly close to the account given by Herodotus. Of the remarkable Artemisia, Herodotus says, "I find it a great marvel that a woman went on the expedition" (7.99). He asserts that "she gave the king the best advice of all his allies" (7.99). And yet at the Battle of Salamis, Artemisia rams an allied ship, and while Xerxes mistakenly believes that she, in fact, destroyed an enemy vessel, Herodotus speculates that it may have been a ruthlessly self-preserving strategy by Artemisia (8.87). In *The 300 Spartans*, Artemisia is an expert manipulator of the vain and childish Xerxes, but her purpose is to loyally aid her mother's people.

But, of course, *The 300 Spartans*, like all historical epics, is as much about the time in which it was produced as the era it depicts. As a Cold War epic, the Spartan–Athenian alliance has been interpreted as representing the North Atlantic Treaty Organization—headed by the American actor Richard Egan as Leonidas and the British Sir Ralph Richardson as Themistocles—against the evil Eastern empire of Persia, standing in for the Soviet Union.[1] In recent years, the same story has reflected a different political climate and a new era of epic filmmaking technologies. *The 300 Spartans* inspired a graphic novel that was the basis for a commercially successful remake, *300* (Zack Snyder, 2007), which, in turn, has revived interest in the otherwise not particularly well-known original film. In *300*, the digital effects themselves are the main spectacle of the film, which was shot primarily on a soundstage and digitally completed thereafter.

The 300 Spartans belongs to an earlier era of the epic, employing a few thousand cast members shot on location, lending atmosphere particularly to the battle scenes (admittedly the interior scenes of Xerxes' camp appear stagey by comparison). There is a palatable sense of place in *The 300 Spartans* that is missing in the remake. Although it received a negative critical reception at the time of its release[2] and does not pursue some of its superfluous plot details and characters, the heroes of *The 300 Spartans* nonetheless have a dignity that is somewhat lacking in the morally compromised Spartans of *300.*

Rudolph Maté had a distinguished career as a cinematographer in Europe and then Hollywood before turning his hand to directing, taking on a number of different genres. DB

Notes

1. Jeffrey Richards, *Hollywood's Ancient Worlds* (London: Continuum, 2008), 138.

2. "*The 300 Spartans*," *Variety*, 1962, www.variety.com/review/VE1117795685/ (8 January 2012); "Richard Egan and Ralph Richardson Star in *300 Spartans*," *New York Times*, 20 September 1962, http://movies.nytimes.com/movie/review?res=9F03E6D81E38E63ABC4851DFBF668389679EDE&scp=2&sq=the%20300%20spartans&st=cse (8 January 2012).

Bibliography

"*The 300 Spartans.*" *Variety*, 1962, www.variety.com/review/VE1117795685/ (8 January 2012).

"Richard Egan and Ralph Richardson Star in *300 Spartans.*" *New York Times*, 20 September 1962, http://movies.nytimes.com/movie/review?res=9F03E6D81E38E63ABC4851DFBF668389679EDE&scp=2&sq=the%20300%20spartans&st=cse (8 January 2012).

Richards, Jeffrey. *Hollywood's Ancient Worlds*. London: Continuum, 2008.

2001: A SPACE ODYSSEY (1968)

Director: Stanley Kubrick
Writers: Stanley Kubrick, Arthur C. Clarke. Based on the short story "The Sentinel," by Arthur Clarke.
Producer: Stanley Kubrick (GMG)
Cinematographers: Geoffrey Unsworth, John Alcott
Production Design: Anthony Masters, Harry Lange, Ernie Archer
Art Direction: John Hoesli
Art Direction: Robert Cartwright (uncredited)
Music: Richard Strauss, Johann Strauss, Aram Khachaturian, Geörgy Ligeti
Special Effects: Wally Weavers, Douglas Trumbull, Con Pederson, Tom Howard
Cast: Dr. David Bowman: Keir Dullea. Dr. Frank Poole: Gary Lockwood. Moon-Watcher: Daniel Richter. Dr. Heywood Floyd: William Sylvester. Dr. Andrei Smyslov: Leonard Rossiter. Mission Controller (voice): Frank Miller. Elena: Margaret Tyzack. Poole's Father: Alan Gifford. Poole's Mother: Ann Gillis. Dr. Ralph Halvorsen: Robert Beatty. Dr. Bill Michaels: Sean Sullivan. HAL 9000 (voice): Douglas Rain
AA: Best Effects–Visual Effects (Wally Weavers, Douglas Trumbull, Con Pederson, Tom Howard)
AAN: Best Director (Stanley Kubrick), Best Art Direction–Set Decoration (Anthony Masters, Harry Lange, Ernie Archer), Best Writing–Story and Screenplay–Written Directly for the Screen (Stanley Kubrick, Arthur C. Clarke)
DVD: Warner Home Video, 2007. Two-disc special edition.
Blu-ray: Warner Home Video, 2007
Duration: 148 minutes

Today, Stanley Kubrick's *2001: A Space Odyssey* still stands out as the one science-fiction epic to have endured for many decades—actually generations—being untarnished by the passage of time and having left in its wake such popular space epics as the *Star Wars* sequences, *Star Trek*, *Alien* and its sequels, and many others of similar ilk of later decades. Its superiority, however, does not lie in its longevity, but in its vision, dazzling sets, visual style, music-score sequences, and, more than anything else, its mystery. The film is a gripping story, despite its leisurely pace, a history of the past and future of mankind and the daring spirit of exploration into space, and its cliff-hanger sequences add intensity to the action. It attempts to give no easy answers to the mystery of man's place in the universe. This is heavy stuff, but Kubrick handles it with superb ease, sliding from epoch to epoch and episode to episode with the deftness of a Michelangelo placing figure after figure into a superb order describing the genesis of man, his relation with the Creator, and his future fate. One can stand in awe gazing at the ceiling of the Sistine Chapel, but one does not depart from it in fright or confusion, just as one can still view *2001* and be awed by the spectacle, the magic of man-made machines floating in space, showing man's voyage into the unknown.

Kubrick took great pains to make a science-fiction movie that was technologically equal to its daring themes. During preparation for filming, in addition to his own extensive reading on the subject, he consulted scientists at academic, military, and industrial institutions in the United States and Great Britain in wide-ranging research that lasted several years. Nuclear scientists, astronomers, geophysicists, and scores of technicians from related fields offered expertise in the form of memos and letters. Harry Lang and Frederick Ordway III of NASA's Marshall Space Flight Center in Huntsville, Alabama, were hired by Kubrick to assist him in designing and constructing the elaborate sets according to the latest available knowledge of the time. Work at the design stage was done at the Polaris Production Center in New York; for construction and filming, crews moved to the MGM British Studios in Borehamwood, England. The original music score is a rousing mix of several classical composers, including Richard Strauss's *Thus Spake Zarathustra*, Johann Strauss's *The Blue Danube*, and György Ligeti's *Atmospherics, Lux Aeterna, and Requiem.*[1]

The film comes in four parts. The first is "The Dawn of Man," which is composed in a series of vignettes showing the early ape man and its leader, the Moon-Watcher (Daniel Richter), in a state of hunger, feeding on the spare vegetation in an arid landscape, competing for water in a small water hole, and fighting another tribe. This state changes when an unexplained phenomenon, the sudden appearance of a black monolith, appears at dawn as they awake, and they surround it with obvious curiosity, and even some kind of worship, as a foreign object. This is the catalyst for action, as the Moon-Watcher toys with the idea of using a bone of a dead animal, first to kill an opponent vying for the same water in the pool, and then to kill an animal and share the flesh with his tribal companions.

As a bone flies in the air, there is an abrupt cut to a space vehicle traveling through space, as the viewer also sees an enormous rotating spaceship, which is soon identified as the Space Station, some distance above the Earth. The lone traveler in the vehicle is identified as Dr. Heywood Floyd (William Sylvester), chairman of the National Council of Astronautics, who soon joins a mixed company in the rotating spaceship, among whom is a Soviet representative, Dr. Andrei Smyslov (Leonard Rossiter), who is curious to know about Heywood's secret mission to Clavius—a substitute name for the moon—as there are rumors of an epidemic there. But Heywood is not free to disclose the nature of his assignment, and after a brief exchange with his young daughter, who is to celebrate her birthday the following day, he departs for Clavius on another spaceship, approaching a base there and touching down into a red-colored vault in a spectacular sequence as the strains of *The Blue Danube* waltz are heard in the background.

At Clavius, Heywood briefs a committee stationed there that he has arrived to inspect a mysterious object that has been discovered forty feet under the surface, planted there 4 million years ago, its existence a total mystery. Speaking with the dry calm of a micromanager, he gives a morale-boosting speech to the group and then boards another ship and arrives at the location of the object, where astronauts in space suits surround the rectangular monolith, which seems to "have been deliberately planted there," as one of the men says to a puzzled Heywood.

After the monolith emits a screeching sound, the action of the film shifts to another sequence, entitled "Mission to Jupiter," eighteen months later. The camera pans slowly to reveal the round head of a lengthy spaceship, with a series of smaller compartments and several transmitting discs outside it, a massive engine compartment, and four atomic jet propulsion engines at the rear. In a strange way, this massive spaceship resembles the one thrust into the air by the man ape at the end of the first section of the narrative, 4 million years earlier. This is the spaceship *Discovery*, which is carrying five astronauts, three in hibernation in casketlike containers, and two, Dr. Frank Poole (Gary Lockwood) and Dr. David Bowman (Keir Dullea), overseeing the ship's functions and communicating with the Earth. A sixth passenger is HAL 9000 (voiced by Douglas Rain), the ship's computer, a large round eye placed in each compartment of the ship to oversee the ship's functions.

Frank Poole is first seen jogging and shadowboxing in a circular lane that allows him to run up and down effortlessly. He soon joins Bowman, who is eating his synthetic meal, evidently without much enthusiasm. They exchange a few banalities and engage in a brief conversation with an agent from Earth, who also talks to HAL, asking how they are enjoying their close relationships. All blandly answer that they are doing well; only HAL expresses some emotion, provoking the interviewer to ask Poole and Bowman whether the computer has real emotions, since he appears to speak about his mission with some pride. They respond that they, too, have noticed his pride and admit that the computer may have emotions, but as to whether he has real feelings, it is impossible to know.

This observation actually becomes the main theme of this section and, in a way, of the entire story. The first appearance of the monolith prompts the ape man to defeat an enemy by using a bone for a tool, thus giving him knowledge that, by the time the discovery of the second monolith occurred, millions of years later, led his descendants to invent more tools, more machines, weapons of destruction, and potentially lethal computers, like HAL. In such later movies as *Alien*, *Aliens*, *Prometheus*, and others, it is called the android, a computerized robot that looks exactly like a human being. This is actually man's own creation—and an image of himself. As in the Bible, God created man in his own image; now, in turn, man creates a creature in his own image. HAL is only a red eye peering into the actions of two men, under whom he serves, easily beating them in chess games, a creature/machine of superior intelligence, one that has never committed an error. HAL boasts about his errorless record since first he was invented in 1992, in Urbana, Illinois.

But when he predicts that a component vital for communication is going to fail in seventy-two hours, the astronauts communicate with their Earth base and are told that the information has been checked by HAL's duplicate on Earth and found to be false. Poole and Bowman begin to suspect that something has gone wrong with HAL. They hide themselves in a pod where they cannot be heard and decide to disconnect HAL. They plan to then run the ship by themselves. But HAL is able to read their lips. He knows their plan, and as soon as Poole ventures outside the ship to replace the supposedly damaged component, he disconnects him and murders him. Bowman can only see the floating Poole in space, and he decides to go outside to rescue his companion; however, when he tries to reenter the ship, HAL blocks his entrance.

This part of the story is the only sequence that suggests the potential of the arising conflict between creator and the creature created, in this case a machine that man has created to aid him in his explorations, but the machine has "acquired" human characteristics, hubris being one of them. HAL has become the evil "creature" that fights his creator. The great irony of the scene is that HAL underestimates the craftiness and determination of Bowman, who musters the ingenuity and courage to calmly use the pod's tool handles to twist open the bolts of the entrance door and then blast himself into the ship. Recovering his helmet, and able to breathe, Bowman—methodically and rather maliciously—ignores the pleas of HAL, who, amazed and humiliated, begs Bowman to spare him, take a "stress pill," calm down, and let things be "normal" again. But it's no use. Bowman enters the compartment where the vital components for HAL are kept and coolly turns them off. HAL, still pleading that he is "losing his mind," starts singing a song taught to him by his instructor in Urbana—"Daisy, Daisy, give me your answer do!"—as his voice deepens and dies down.

As part of the title suggests, this is indeed a "space odyssey," in fact, *The Odyssey*. The essence of Homer's epic, undiminished by time, lives here, at least in its original metaphorical sense. Collectively, this is man's voyage into the unknown, but the man at the helm, although losing his companions, forges on, fighting giant monsters, demons,[2] vengeful gods, witches, and natural disasters. Odysseus summons his wit and will and ultimately triumphs against human or superhuman agents that would daunt an ordinary human. So does Bowman. His double name—David (against Goliath), Bow-man (archer)—gives him the strength to fight a physically superior adversary and aim at his further goal. Following the monolith, now unafraid, he enters the planet Jupiter, racing unimaginable space and arriving at a glittering architectural interior. He is now an old man who sees himself in senescence eating a meal, and then wrinkled and dying in bed, from where he gazes at the monolith planted before him—the immortal entity that brought him there. He evolves into an infant with large, luminous, bright eyes, a child again, back to Earth.

There is no single interpretation for this tale. Countless viewers and critics reacted to it with dozens of interpretations, but never with indifference. Visually told, with spare dialogue, and often with none, the movie dazzles the eyes and enchants the ears, shaking man's sense of security on a small planet but, in its probing way, enabling the viewer to marvel at the immensity of the cosmos, yet an inescapable part of it. CS

Notes

1. Kubrick had originally asked Alex North to compose the score, and North did, but when it came to recording the music, Kubrick changed his mind, leaving North in the lurch. When, unbeknownst, North went to see the movie, he was shocked to find out that his music had been dropped from the film.
2. "Δαίμονας," the original Greek word, means divinities that are both good and evil, trying to foil a hero in reaching his destination, or block and destroy (or save) him at will.

Bibliography

Agel, Jerome, ed. *The Making of Kubrick's 2001*. New York: New American Library, 1970.
Clarke, Arthur. *2001: A Space Odyssey*. New York: W. W. Norton, 1968.
Kagan, Norman. *The Cinema of Stanley Kubrick*. New York: Continuum, 1989.

THE TEN COMMANDMENTS (1923)

DIRECTOR: Cecil B. DeMille
WRITER: Jeanie Macpherson
PRODUCERS: Adolph Zukor, Leslie Lasky (Famous Players-Lasky Corporation)
ASSOCIATE DIRECTOR: Cullen Tate
CINEMATOGRAPHER: Peverel Marley, Archibald Slout, J. F. Westerberg
EDITOR: Anne Bauchens
ART DIRECTION: Paul Iribe
TECHNICAL DIRECTOR: Roy Pomeroy
CAST: "Prologue": Moses: Theodore Roberts. Rameses: Charles de Rochefort. Miriam (Sister of Moses): Estelle Taylor. Wife of Pharaoh: Julia Faye. Son of Pharaoh: Terrence Moore. Aaron: James Neil. Dathan: Lawson Butt. Task Master: Clarence Burton. "Story": Martha McTavish: Edythe Chapman. John McTavish: Richard Dix. Dan McTavish: Rod La Rocque. Mary Leigh: Leatrice Joy. Sally Lung: Nita Naldi. Redding: Robert Edeson. The Doctor: Charles Ogle. The Outcast: Agnes Ayres
AA: None
AAN: None
DVD: Paramount Pictures, 2006. Three-disc fiftieth anniversary collection containing both the 1923 and 1956 versions, with commentary by Katherine Orrison.
BLU-RAY: Paramount Pictures, 2012
DURATION: 136 minutes

Made in1923, *The Ten Commandments* was the first biblical epic directed by Cecil B. DeMille, who by that time had been in Hollywood for ten years, having already directed forty films, and having founded Paramount Studios. From that point onward, DeMille was to mount several epics of biblical/Roman/medieval themes, namely *The King of Kings* (1927, still in silent mode), *The Sign of the Cross* (1932), and *The Crusades* (1935). And following the hiatus of World War II, when epics declined, he again mounted two spectacular epics, *Samson and Delilah* in 1949, and the extravagant 1956 *The Ten Commandments*, a repeat (only in theme) of the silent movie, much lengthier, in color and widescreen, with major stars, a film that has left its imprint on the American psyche, adding to the legend of great American epics of the late 1940s and 1950s.

Yet, the 1923 silent version is not entirely to be forgotten. For one, it started the legend of biblical epics, and with that a tradition of religious epic form that is unique to Hollywood. It is full of pieties, to be certain, much of it due to the Hays Code that came into effect about the time that DeMille started his epic, forcing filmmakers to curtail explicit sex scenes, which abound in early Hollywood (D. W. Griffith presented naked women in *Intolerance*, 1917), and DeMille followed suit in several of his comedies during the postwar years. The religious epic film became a staple in Hollywood productions. It appealed to the mass audiences and went with the times of conservatism during the 1950s, when the House Un-American Activities Committee investigations blacklisted authors and directors and restrained, if not stifled, the development of socially daring films. But DeMille's early start allowed him to dominate the genre, exploit its potential, and establish a tradition that, in many ways, has never been eclipsed in Hollywood (witness *The Passion of the Christ*, Mel Gibson, 2004).

The 1923 version, much shorter than its remake in 1956, at 136 minutes, contains two stories: The first part, named the "Prologue," is the biblical tale of Moses (Theodore Roberts) leading his people from Egypt, parting the Red Sea, receiving the Ten Commandments carved on a rock in a spectacular scene of divine revelation, and then witnessing and scattering an orgy staged by his people, who turn pagan and worship a golden calf. The audience first sees a crowd of enslaved Israelites, men and women, hauling a large statue of a sphinx, being lashed by heartless goons, servants of Pharaoh Rameses (Charles de Rochefort), who arrogantly dismisses the appeal of Moses to let his people go. Nine plagues have struck Egypt, but the pharaoh still refuses. Then Moses invokes God's wrath upon the pagans, issuing a warning to Rameses that every firstborn male Egyptian child would perish.

When the young son of Rameses is struck by a disease and dies, the pharaoh allows the Israelites to depart, and we see the exodus of the crowd—a scene that was hand-color tinted and was to be repeated with far greater splendor in the 1956 version. When the pharaoh pursues the Israelis, having revenge on his mind for the death of his son, Moses saves his people by parting the Red Sea, while the Egyptians drown. Later, while Moses climbs up Mount Sinai to receive the Ten Commandments, the crowd remains behind. Led by his brother Aaron (James Neil) and Dathan the "Lewd" (Lawson Butt), they build a golden calf and worship it as a pagan god, with the obligatory DeMille orgy, much of it photographed in long shots, and far from offensive to modern audiences (but not to the Hays watchdogs), who had already seen much more sex and nudity. For authenticity, the captions shown on the screen in the "Prologue" are quotations from Exodus, documenting and chronicling the authenticity of the story.

The second part of the film abruptly turns into a contemporary morality play that enhances the idea that the Ten Commandments, as given by Moses to the people of Israel, are a moral imperative that the modern world must embrace. Katherine Orrison says in her running commentary that the destruction, both physical and moral, brought about by World War I had caused a loosening of morals, and a movie like *The Ten Commandments* contained a much-needed message.[1] The "Story," therefore, seems like a literal application of the Word of God.

A pious, sincerely religious mother, Martha McTavish (Edythe Chapman), has brought up her two sons in poverty, urging them to follow the path of righteousness. While the older boy, John (Richard Dix), is strongly religious, his brother Dan (Rod La Rocque) points at the holes in his shoe and complains that God and His Commandments are not enough to provide sustenance, and riches. Martha holds a large Bible and displays it on every occasion when she talks to them, but Dan is uneasy and seeks adventure on a rainy night. A street gamin, Mary (Leatrice Joy), hungry and clutching her little dog as the rain pours, tries to steal some food from a half-opened window of the restaurant where Dan is dining. She is chased and takes refuge in the workshop of John, who is a carpenter. She is soon welcomed by Martha, who treats her as a member of the family, and after both brothers court her, she chooses to marry Dan (although she actually loves John), who leaves the family and starts a successful business.

In a hurry to get rich quickly, Dan imports cement from Calcutta, but one of the sacks contains a woman who had escaped from a leper colony. Dan, who is none too loyal to Mary, starts a liaison with Sally Lung (Nita Naldi), a Eurasian, who is lovely but carries the dreaded disease with her. When he learns she is a leper, and to steal a string of pearls he has given her, he shoots her. Dan also steals in his business, as he doctors the mix of cement and sand, and a big church he is building collapses, killing his mother. He goes back to his estranged wife, and Mary, troubled by the ugly turn of events, temporarily protects him as the police pursue him. Dan cruelly tells her that she has contracted leprosy and then tries to flee to Mexico, but he is shipwrecked on a stormy sea. Mary rejoins John, and, appealing to Jesus in a briefly superimposed scene when he heals a leper woman, Mary is healed, too. Dan has violated two commandments, "Thou Shalt not Kill," and "Thou Shalt not Steal." The moral of the story is too obvious to the modern viewer, but the story is told grippingly, with striking visual style possible then because of the fluency of narrative without dialogue that was easily grasped by the audience. Some actually prefer this version to the later, much more elaborate, richer, and longer version of 1956. Whatever one's preferences, the 1923 version of *The Ten Commandments* has its place in the evolution of the epic form and film history. CS

Note

1. Katherine Orrison, "Commentary," *The Ten Commandments*, directed by Cecil B. DeMille (Paramount Pictures, 2006), DVD; Katherine Orrison, "Commentary," *The Ten Commandments*, directed by Cecil B. DeMille (Paramount Pictures, 2012), Blu-ray.

Bibliography

Orrison, Katherine. *Written in Stone: Making Cecil B. DeMille's Epic* The Ten Commandments. New York: Vestal Press, 1999.

THE TEN COMMANDMENTS (1956)

DIRECTOR: Cecil B. DeMille
WRITERS: Aeneas MacKenzie, Jesse L. Lasky Jr., Jack Gariss, Fredric M. Frank. Based on *Pillar of Fire*, by Joseph Holt Ingram; *On Eagle's Wings*, by E. E. Southon; and *Prince of Egypt*, by Dorothy Clarke Wilson. Also based on the Bible, with materials drawn from the Qur'an and the works of Josephus.
PRODUCERS: Cecil B. DeMille, Henry Wilcoxon (Paramount Pictures)
CINEMATOGRAPHER: Loyal Griggs
EDITOR: Anne Bauchens
ART DIRECTION: Hal Pereira, Walter H. Tyler, Albert Nozaki
SET DECORATION: Sam Comer, Ray Moyer
COSTUMES: Edith Head, Ralph Jester, John Jensen, Dorothy Jeakins, Arnold Friberg
MUSIC: Elmer Bernstein
SOUND MIXER: Loren L. Ryder
VISUAL EFFECTS: Farciot Edouart, John P. Fulton, Paul K. Lerpae
CAST: Moses: Charlton Heston. Pharaoh Rameses II: Yul Brynner. Nefretiri: Anne Baxter. Sephora: Yvonne De Carlo. Joshua: John Derek. Lilia: Debra Paget. Dathan: Edward G. Robinson. Pharaoh Sethi I: Sir Cedric Hardwicke. Baka: Vincent Price. Bithiah: Nina Foch. Yoshebel: Martha Scott. Memnet: Judith Anderson. Aaron: John Carradine. Pentaur: Henry Wilcoxon. Infant Moses: Frazer Heston. Jethro: Eduard Franz
AAN: Best Picture (Cecil B. DeMille), Best Cinematography–Color (Loyal Griggs), Best Art Direction–Set Decoration–Color (Hal Pereira, Walter H. Tyler, Albert Nozaki, Sam Comer, Ray Moyer), Best Sound–Recording (Loren L. Ryder), Best Film Editing (Anne Bauchens), Best Costume Design–Color (Edith Head, Ralph Jester, John Jensen, Dorothy Jeakins, Arnold Friberg)
AA: Best Effects–Special Effects (John P. Fulton)
DVD: Paramount Pictures, 2006. Three-disc fiftieth anniversary collection containing both the 1923 and 1956 versions, with commentary by Katherine Orrison.
BLU-RAY: Paramount Pictures, 2011. Two-disc special edition.
DURATION: 219 minutes

Cecil B. DeMille may be regarded as one of the two great filmmakers—the other being D. W. Griffith—who created the epic form in American cinema in the early twentieth century. While Griffith's career was marked by his absence from lengthy epics matching his first two pioneering works, *Birth of a Nation* (1915) and *Intolerance* (1916), DeMille continued to thrive beyond the silent era, producing and directing films in nearly every genre—dramas, westerns, and adventure stories—but, above all, epics, in the 1920s and 1930s, with *The Ten Commandments* (1923), *The King of Kings* (1927), *The Sign of the Cross* (1932), *Cleopatra* (1934), and *The Crusades* (1935). The religious/biblical/Roman epic, which he had practically invented, was continued after the war with such spectacles as *Samson and Delilah* in 1949 and the remake of *The Ten Commandments* in 1956, which proved to be the most massive and lucrative production he ever undertook. This was his last and grandest epic, and one of the most popular movies ever made, excelling in plot design, art direction, impressive sets and costumes, and special effects that pioneered technical innovations for the time. The film also contains splendid photography and a cast of distinguished actors from DeMille's past and present film endeavors. It cost a staggering sum of $13.5 million to make, but the results exceeded $43 million, and estimates of up to $80 million worldwide, while it continued to make giant profits from TV showings after it had left the theaters.

The Ten Commandments was filmed at Paramount Studios and on location in Egypt, after DeMille obtained considerable logistical support from President Gamal Abdel Nasser, an avid fan of DeMille, whose *The Crusades* a couple of decades earlier had impressed him for its fair treatment of Arab leaders, especially Saladin.[1] Crews in Egypt included extras from the Egyptian Army playing Jewish slaves, and location filming of many scenes was deftly matted with shots in the studios. Lavish costumes, carefully researched to match Egyptian models of the period, give the film the glow of historical authenticity combined with Hollywood glitter, something DeMille had practiced for decades. DeMille also hired actors he had known in his previous endeavors—Henry Wilcoxon (also his coproducer) and newcomer Charlton Heston, who had excelled as a circus master in *The Greatest Show on Earth*; he also gave opportunities to actors who had been in trouble under the House Un-American Activities Committee investigations, Edward G. Robinson being one of them. Casts of thousands were thrown into the mix, and some scenes, for example, the Exodus and the parting of the Red Sea, among others, remain ingrained in the American psyche for their majesty and technical excellence.

For decades, the film (along with *The Kings of Kings*) was played on television during Passover and Easter holidays, marking both Jewish and Christian religious events, and it is themed to appeal to the idea of freedom from bondage at a time when actors, directors, and screenwriters had been blacklisted or jailed during the McCarthy era. Like most DeMille spectacles, *The Ten Commandments* is a mixture of entertainment and pious or patriotic themes, offering lavish entertainment, while keeping religion or patriotism as a front. Such intentions do not negate DeMille's sincerity or belief that the Word of God and the idea of freedom from a totalitarian regime go together—or that freedom has been threatened throughout history. His method was to use Roman history or biblical stories to make his point through what he believed was the best medium: cinematic spectacle. Carefully staged and choreographed scenes include courts of decadent oppressors, spiced with seminude dancers brought on the stage on numerous occasions, as, for instance, when Moses returns a conqueror of Ethiopia, with a black wife—not named as such in the film—offering the spoils of victory to the pharaoh. Moses as an Egyptian prince is an accomplished man, displaying his architectural genius when an obelisk, a token built to illustrate Sethi's greatness, is hoisted and an impressive statue of Sethi is shown on the screen in a masterful matte shot.

More than any traditional epic, before or since, *The Ten Commandments* is a tribute to Hollywood's development of the epic form that was invented by DeMille and other Hollywood greats, mostly on DeMille's own terms. There were no limits to the expense, production values, star power, and sprawling spectacles that manage to keep viewers in their seats for hours on end. *The Ten Commandments* embodies all these values. It would be folly to dismiss this epic as a mere Hollywood extravaganza without substance. It is a work that charts its path steadily, employing all the cinematic means available to it to find its way into its audience's consciousness. If not a great work of art, it is a work of great artistry.

The film opens with an announcement by the director himself, who tells his audience that his work embodies the idea of freedom, which today, as in any moment in history, is at peril. DeMille also offers information about the materials he chose for the film, explaining that since the Bible omits the period between Moses' birth and his appearance as a grown man in the pharaoh's court, he had to use facts from other sources, mentioning Philo and Josephus, two historians at the time of Christ whose works helped him fill in some of the missing details. His purpose is to reassure his viewers that the materials used are not casual, but collected with great care, and guided by a purpose—to display the way of God in shaping human life. In a way it is a Miltonic parable: as John Milton states in the first line of *Paradise Lost*, his poem was written to "justify the ways of God to man." Anachronistic as this idea may seem to some today, it worked for the 1950s audiences, serving its purpose of providing entertainment with a moral.

The epic is divided in two parts, the first concentrating on Moses (Heston) as an Egyptian prince and one of the two successors of Sethi I, played with distinction by Sir Cedric Hardwicke, who favors Moses over his legitimate son, Rameses (Yul Brynner). The antagonism between the two successors begins at this point and does not end until the cataclysm that drowns Rameses' forces during the parting of the Red Sea. The tension between the two antagonists drives the action of the story. Heston's Moses as an Egyptian prince galvanizes the viewer with his royal bearing, devotion to his adopted father, and compassion for the slaves, as he saves Yoshebel (Martha Scott), who is about to be crushed to death by a huge stone, unbeknownst that she is his real mother. On the other hand, Brynner's Rameses also evokes a magnetic screen presence: bald-headed and muscular, his eyes dart malice and jealousy at his brother-pretender, who is the favorite to succeed his father as pharaoh.

Anne Baxter as Nefretiri is the apple of discord between the two rivals, but her affections clearly belong to Moses, sparking the jealousy of Rameses, who is waiting for his chance to pounce on Moses, for whom he has barely concealed contempt. The first part ends with Memnet's (Judith Anderson) treachery, when she reveals to Nefretiri that Moses is the son of Hebrew slaves, an act that costs her her life. A piece of cloth, which Memnet had found in the casket when the infant Moses was saved, is the evidence that convinces Moses that he is indeed the son of Hebrew slaves. His subsequent discovery that Yoshebel is his mother is crucial to his decision to mix with the Hebrews, denounce Nefretiri, and confess the truth to Sethi, who, embittered, leaves it up to Rameses to decide what to do with Moses. Instead of killing him, and thus making him a martyr, Rameses takes him to the desert and abandons him to his fate, certain Moses will die wandering in the wilderness.

A subplot develops during part one and runs through the entire film. It involves

Joshua (John Derek), a young stonecutter in the slave camp, who is in love with Lilia (Debra Paget), a slave girl who has also attracted the attention of two others, Baka (Vincent Price), the pharaoh's master builder, and Dathan (Robinson), a Hebrew overseer who learns the identity of Moses as Baka is killed by Moses and reveals the secret to Rameses, in exchange for the rank of the master builder and the possession of Lilia. Lilia is forced to marry him to save Joshua.

The second part shifts the action to Moses and his wanderings, his visit to Mount Sinai, and his return to Egypt as the Deliverer. This part is actually divided into several episodes, all the result of Moses' exile. Against all odds, Moses survives his desert trek, as the viewer hears DeMille's voice quoting from the Bible, explaining the purpose of Moses' ordeal as designed by God. We witness Moses' struggle for survival, his meeting a group of women near a well and his rescuing them from tribal attackers, and his subsequent joining the tribe of Jethro (Eduard Franz), a Bedouin sheik of Midian, and a distant descendant of Ishmael, the bastard son of Abraham, who had been condemned to stray from the tribes of Israel. Jethro has nine daughters, who delight at the sight of this handsome hero and distant cousin of their original heritage, and vie for the right to marry him. Moses chooses Sephora, the eldest, played by the beautiful, blue-eyed Yvonne De Carlo, whose strong presence helps Moses build his confidence and gain his new identity, leading the life of a shepherd and wandering with his new tribe, until he is inspired to visit Mount Sinai, where he hears the voice of God in the burning bush. He then knows that he is the Deliverer.

The story continues with the return of Moses to Egypt, joining his brother Aaron, who helps him in his new mission to free the slaves. In the Bible, Aaron speaks for Moses, as Moses has a stutter, but DeMille chose to allow Moses to do the talking in the movie. Now in a long beard and graying hair, holding the staff Rameses had given him at the beginning of his journey, he performs several tricks with it, turning it into a cobra, but Rameses laughs at him, for some of his magicians can easily duplicate his tricks. He contemptuously demands that Moses perform his tricks to make his slaves build bricks without straw. Moses faces rebellion and provokes a laugh from Dathan, now the master builder, a powerful man and husband of Lilia.

Moses demands that Rameses free the slaves, but when the latter rejects his pleas, Moses bring on the Plagues from God, turning the waters of the Nile red, bringing on a storm that pounds Egypt with hail, and calling the green cloud of death that kills Egypt's firstborn sons, including the son of Rameses. In desperation, Rameses bids Moses to take his people and go away. The spectacular scene of the Exodus follows, one of the most elaborately staged scenes in film history, with memorable tableaus of live action—youngsters pushing a stubborn mule laden with their possessions, camels, horses, geese and other animals, and carriages in which the elderly and disabled are carried. Meanwhile, Nefretiri, who still loves Moses, is rejected by him when he tells her that he now only loves God. A spurned woman—reminding of Poppaea in *The Sign of the Cross* and Delilah in *Samson and Delilah*—Nefretiri vindictively urges a humiliated Rameses to pursue and destroy Moses and his tribe, if he does not want to be "laughed at" by those around him. Rameses orders an attack, and his chariots chase the Hebrews, who by now have reached an impasse at the Red Sea, but Moses bids the waters to part and his tribe escapes. Rameses' forces are drowned as they attempt to cross. Rameses returns to Nefretiri and sits on his throne, admitting, "His God *is* God."

The final chapter is written with the rebellion of Noah's tribe, led by Dathan, who prompts them to build the golden calf while Moses wanders up Mount Sinai to obtain the Word of God. Here another spectacular scene adds to the already overloaded spectacle, as the Word of God is engraved on the two tablets, as a voice—actually in the sound track mix of voices—pronounces each commandment for the viewer to share with Moses. Angered by the rebellion and the sensual paralysis of his people, Moses angrily tosses the tables on the calf, which dissolves in flames. After wandering for forty years in the desert, Moses only has a view of the Holy Land, but it is Joshua who leads the much-tested Hebrews there. CS

Note

1. Katherine Orrison, "Commentary," *The Ten Commandments*, directed by Cecil B. DeMille (Paramount Pictures, 2006), DVD; Katherine Orrison, "Commentary," *The Ten Commandments*, directed by Cecil B. DeMille (Paramount Pictures, 2011), Blu-ray.

Bibliography

Orrison, Katherine. *Written in Stone: Making Cecil B. DeMille's Epic* The Ten Commandments. New York: Vestal Press, 1999.

THE THIN RED LINE (1998)

Director: Terrence Malick
Writer: Terrence Malick. Based on the novel by James Jones.
Producers: Robert Michael Geisler, Grant Hill, John Roberdeau (Fox 2000 Pictures, Geisler-Roberdeau, Phoenix Pictures)
Executive Producer: George Stevens Jr.
Associate Producers: Sheila Davis Lawrence, Michael Stevens
Cinematographer: John Toll
Editor: Leslie Jones, Saar Klein, Billy Weber
Music: Hans Zimmer
Sound Mixers: Andy Nelson, Anna Behlmer, Paul "Salty" Brincat
Cast: Lt. Col. Gordon Tall: Nick Nolte. Pvt. Witt: Jim Caviezel. First Sgt. Edward Welsh: Sean Penn. Capt. James "Bugger" Staros: Elias Koteas. Pvt. Bell: Ben Chaplin. Capt. Charles Bosche: George Clooney. Pfc. Doll: Dash Mihok. Capt. John Gaff: John Cusack. Cpl. Fife: Adrien Brody. Marty: Miranda Otto. Brig. Gen. Quintard: John Travolta. Sgt. Keck: Woody Harrelson. Pvt. Charlie Dale: Arie Verveen. First Lieutenant Band: Paul Gleeson. Pvt. Train: John Dee Smith. Pvt. Weld: Travis Fine. Pvt. Coombs: Matt Doran
AA: None
AAN: Best Cinematography (John Toll), Best Director (Terrence Malick), Best Film Editing (Leslie Jones, Saar Klein, Billy Weber), Best Music–Original Dramatic Score (Hans Zimmer), Best Picture (Robert Michael Geisler, Grant Hill, John Roberdeau), Best Sound (Andy Nelson, Anna Behlmer, Paul "Salty" Brincat), Best Writing–Screenplay Based on Material Previously Produced or Published (Terrence Malick)
Blu-ray: 20th Century Fox, 2002
Blu-Ray: Criterion, 2010
Duration: 99 minutes

Terrence Malick's *The Thin Red Line* is the second film based on James Jones's 1962 novel about World War II; the first was produced in 1964 and directed by Andrew Marton. Some critics found Malick's film a "virtually plotless mélange of nature documentary, metaphysical debate, and bloodletting."[1] Many focused on the large number of topflight Hollywood talent who were cut from the film, especially Adrian Brody's role as Corporal Fife, who was reduced from the main character of the novel to one rarely seen or heard in the film; however, most critics understood the film as Malick's "meditation on thc naturc of war, or the war in nature, [which] echoes philosophical treatises."[2]

The thoughts of the soldiers are presented as fleeting and fragmentary voice-overs, sometimes seeming to give a little more insight into an individual's life than a grave marker; however, their thoughts and insights are additive and intimately human, and they become "stream-of-consciousness poetics."[3] The thoughts of five characters are central to the film and viewers' understanding of it: Private Witt (Jim Caviezel), an AWOL soldier who believes in a Gnostic spark and Emerson's "Transparent Eyeball"; First Sergeant Edward Welsh (Sean Penn), a nihilist who moves toward Witt's position by the end of the film; Lieutenant Colonel Gordon Tall (Nick Nolte), whose career has faltered and who is dedicated to winning the battle for redemption; Private Bell (Ben Chaplin), who often thinks about his wife Marty (Miranda Otto), who is shown in soft-focus flashbacks;[4] and Captain James "Bugger" Staros (Elias Koteas), a lawyer by education and a leader with genuine concern for his men. The voice-overs become a collective unconsciousness. Together with the film's narrative structure, they "divest the battle scenes of the excitement or grandeur typical of the genre."[5]

The film opens with Witt thinking about nature contending with itself, the ocean with the sea, as he watches Melanesian children and their mothers on the beach while natives sing in background. He meditates on his mother's death, how she faced it courageously, and wonders if he will handle his own with the same calm. A U.S. Navy patrol boat arrives with Sergeant Welsh, there to pick up his AWOL soldier. He says, "Witt, you haven't learned a thing. How many times you've been AWOL?" Welsh made a deal for Witt. He will be a stretcher bearer, because "[he'll] never be a real soldier. . . . In this world, a man, himself, is nothing. There is no world but this one." Witt says, "You're wrong. I've been to another world."

Witt is brought back to the ship to join his company, C Company of the 2nd Battalion, 27th Infantry Regiment, 25th Infantry Division. On the ship's deck, Brigadier General Quintard (John Travolta) pushes Tall to take the island. His words are threatening, reminding Tall that he has not risen in rank as quickly as he should have; this is his last opportunity. Although Tall believes that he has been used and that he has degraded himself, he says he wants the island of Guadalcanal "as much as I have to." Below deck, Captain Staros walks among his men. Bell thinks of his wife and wonders to himself, "Why should I be afraid to die?" An alarm rings; the men suit up and move up, out of the ship, into landing craft. They land on the beach but find it deserted. Moving inland, hundreds of men walk through mud and tree roots, where they find two dead U.S. soldiers. They march into the hills, sharing muddy roads with trucks and jeeps. Witt thinks to himself, "Maybe all men have one big soul." He and others on the stretcher brigade stop for water along a river.

At Hill 210, Tall tells Staros, "We're going straight up that hill," so they can take the Japanese bunkers at the top. Staros points out that there is no way to flank the bunker, and his soldiers do not have water, to which Tall replies, "The only time to worry about a soldier is when they stop bitching." The next morning, two batteries of 105s, Tall says to "buck the men up," launch artillery shells that hit the hillside. Hundreds of men move up the grassy hill. Two soldiers approach the bunkers, but both are shot with only one bullet each. Other men move up, but now it is a barrage. They call for stretchers. Tall arrives to see the situation for himself and calls it "magnificent." Witt rejoins the company as a soldier. During these scenes, the camera's movement is often a "sinuous, decentered tracking shot that glides over multiple planes of action, following one character and then shifting to others with just the smallest turns of its roving but precisely defined perspective."[6]

Sergeant Keck (Woody Harrelson) accidently pulls a grenade pin from a grenade on his belt, and it explodes. He exclaims, "I blew my butt off. What a fucking recruit trick to pull." He is attended to by Witt, Bell, and Private First Class Doll (Dash Mihok). Although Witt tells him he is going to be all right, he dies.

Tall calls Staros and tells him to "commit everybody." Because of heavy casualties, Staros says his company alone cannot survive it, and he requests a patrol reconnaissance instead. Tall gives him a direct order, but Staros refuses "to lead them to their deaths." Tall decides to join him on the hill. On his way, Tall thinks, "Shot us in a tomb. Can't lift the lid. A role I never asked for." By the time Tall arrives, the Japanese assault has lessened. Believing Staros to be a coward, Tall says, "We're taking everybody over to that ledge. We need to take it by nightfall." Bell and six other men are sent to the top of the hill. As Bell climbs, he thinks of his wife as she stands in the ocean's surf. He reports that there are five guns in the bunkers. He is joined by Captain Gaff (John Cusack), who is on a flanking mission. Bell calls in a fire mission. After the "fire for effect" is completed, they are able to throw a grenade into one of the bunkers. They quickly take the bunkers; the remaining Japanese soldiers sit against a wall, exhausted, hungry, and praying. More American troops arrive and begin cleaning out underground passages.

Gaff asks Tall for water for the men. Tall replies, "Don't worry about water, Gaff. We can't stop now. If some of the men pass out, why, hell, they'll just have to pass out. They're all tough boys." Tall thinks to himself, "I've eaten untold buckets of shit to get here." He orders three men to find water.

Witt studies a dead Japanese soldier who seems to ask him, "Are you righteous? Kind? Does your confidence lie in this? Know that I was, too." Moving farther inland, they find a Japanese encampment that is strongly defended but quickly lost. Walking among the dead and wounded, a voice says, "This great evil—where does it come from? How did it steal into the world? What seed, what root did it come from? Is this darkness in you, too?" Private Charlie Dale (Arie Verveen) tells a Japanese officer, "I'm going to sink my teeth into your liver." He sits down with the dead and dying, plugging his nose with tobacco to hide the smell.

Tall relieves Staros of his command, turning it over to First Lieutenant Band (Paul Gleeson). Staros says, "I don't like to see my men get killed, sir." Tall responds, "Nature's cruel, Staros." He will recommend that Staros be transferred to the Judge Advocate General's office (JAG) and to receive the Silver Star and a Purple Heart. Tall later announces to the troops that they will be relieved by a reserve battalion and that they have earned a week's rest. That night, they use flamethrowers to destroy the Japanese encampment. Staros's men thank him for fighting for the flanking maneuver and watching out for them and keeping them together." They say, "We're all sorry to see you go." He tells them that he thinks of them as his sons. He thinks to himself, "My dear sons. You'll live inside me now. I'll carry you wherever I go."

Bell thinks of his wife as she is shown on a swing. He thinks to himself, "I want to stay changeless to you. Who lit this flame in us? No war can put it out." He receives a letter from home, a "Dear John" letter. She writes, "I met an air force captain. I want a divorce. It just got too lonely, Jack. Oh, my friend. Help me leave you." Mrs. Bell "is revealed as the 'real enemy' and has confirmed to the soldier the futility of his mission—why fight an enemy seemingly a million miles from home if you have already lost the very thing you are fighting to protect?"[7]

Witt walks through the native village, but now the villagers do not trust him, and the children hide. He thinks to himself, "We were a family—now we're standing against each other." Witt arrives back at the camp, where cases of liquor are being distributed. He sees men jumping into the surf, playing cards, drinking, and smoking, but Bell is sitting alone. Private Train (John Dee Smith) says to himself, "War don't ennoble men. It turns them into dogs. Poisons the soul." Welsh asks Witt why he is such a "troublemaker." Witt says, "You care about me. Why do you always make yourself out like a rock? . . . I still see a spark in you."

Back on duty, the platoon is walking in a river looking for Japanese troops. Private Weld (Travis Fine) discovers that their lines have been cut. Uncomfortable in his new role, Band hesitatingly decides to send someone to check the line. Fife, Witt, and Private Coombs (Matt Doran) are sent. They see Japanese troops coming down river. Coombs is shot and floats downstream as he dies. Witt decides that he needs to stay to hold them off, while Fife reports to the lieutenant. Witt, surrounded by the Japanese, raises his weapon and is shot. Later, Welsh and his men bury Witt, leaving his weapon and helmet atop his gravesite. Ever the Nihilist Walsh asks, "Where's your spark now?"

After Captain Bosche (George Clooney) gives a clumsy self-introductory speech about his role as being a father to his men and Welsh being the mother, Welsh thinks to himself, "You're in a box. They want you dead or in their lie. There's only one thing a man can do—find something that's his, and make an island for himself." The film ends with their ship heading to another battle. An unidentified voice says, "O, my soul, let me be in you now. Look out through my eyes. Look out at the things you made—all things shining."

The Thin Red Line questions the grandiose and jingoist mythos of World War II films by delving into soldiers' most intimate thoughts, revealing fragmentary and often contradictory truths about war. JMW

Notes

1. Stuart Klawans, "In Memory of Movies as Grand but Futile Gestures," *Chronicle of Higher Education* 45, no. 24 (1999): B9.
2. James Morrison, "Reviews: *The Thin Red Line*," *Film Quarterly* 53, no. 1 (1999): 38.
3. Morrison, "Reviews," 37.
4. "From the outset Mrs. Bell is presented as an enigma with contradictory qualities: As the narrative progresses she is, through her voice and her husband's rememberings, his comfort, his confessant, his salvation at times of duress, and ultimately his foe. She oscillates from being adored to being subtly reviled as the implicit cause of her husband's stint in the war." Susie Walsh, "Friendly Fire: Epistolary Voice-Over in Terrence Malick's *The Thin Red Line*," *Film Quarterly* 33, no. 4 (2005): 307.
5. Morrison, "Reviews," 36.
6. Morrison, "Reviews," 37.
7. Walsh, "Friendly Fire," 310.

Bibliography

Jones, James. *The Thin Red Line*. New York: Scribner's, 1962.

Klawans, Stuart. "In Memory of Movies as Grand but Futile Gestures." *Chronicle of Higher Education* 45, no. 24 (1999): B9–B10.

Morrison, James. "Reviews: *The Thin Red Line*." *Film Quarterly* 53, no. 1 (1999): 35–38.

Rijswijk, Ian-Malcolm. "Terrence Malick's *The Thin Red Line*: Some Historical Considerations." *Film and History* 41, no.1 (2011): 26–47.

Rybin, Steven. *Terrence Malick and the Thought of Film*. New York: Lexington Books, 2012.

Walsh, Susie. "Friendly Fire: Epistolary Voice-Over in Terrence Malick's *The Thin Red Line*." *Film Quarterly* 33, no. 4 (2005): 306–12.

TITANIC (1997)

DIRECTOR: James Cameron
WRITER: James Cameron
PRODUCERS: James Cameron, Jon Landau (20th Century Fox, Paramount Pictures, Lightstorm Entertainment)
CINEMATOGRAPHER: Russell Carpenter
EDITORS: Conrad Buff IV, James Cameron, Richard A. Harris
PRODUCTION DESIGN: Peter Lamont
ART DIRECTION: Martin Laing, Charles Dwight Lee
SET DECORATION: Michael Ford
COSTUMES: Deborah Lynn Scott
MUSIC: James Horner
SOUND EDITORS: Tom Bellfort, Christopher Boyes
SOUND MIXERS: Gary Rydstrom, Tom Johnson, Gary Summers, Mark Ulano
VISUAL EFFECTS: Robert Legato, Mark A. Lasoff, Thomas L. Fisher, Michael Kanfer
MAKEUP ARTISTS: Tina Earnshaw, Greg Cannom, Simon Thompson
CAST: Fictional: Jack Dawson: Leonardo DiCaprio. Rose DeWitt Bukater: Kate Winslet. Caledon "Cal" Nathan Hockley: Billy Zane. Ruth DeWitt Bukater: Francis Fisher. Rose Dawson Calvert: Gloria Stuart. Brock Lovett: Bill Paxton. Lizzy Clavert: Susy Amis. Fabrizio De Rossi: Danny Nucci. Spicer Lovejoy: David Warner. Historical: Margaret "Molly" Brown: Kathy Bates. Thomas Andrews: Victor Garber. Capt. Edward J. Smith: Barnard Hill. J. Bruce Ismay: Jonathan Hyde. John Jacob Astor IV: Eric Braeden. Col. Archibald Gracie: Bernard Fox. Benjamin Guggenheim: Michael Ensign. Wallace Hartley: Jonathan Evans. First Officer William Murdoch: Ewan Stewart. Second Officer Charles Lightholler: Jonathan Phillips. Jack Phillips: Gregory Cooke
AA: Best Picture (James Cameron, Jon Landau), Best Director (James Cameron), Best Art Direction–Set Decoration (Peter Lamont, Michael Ford), Best Cinematography (Russell Carpenter), Best Effects–Visual Effects (Robert Legato, Mark A. Lasoff, Thomas L. Fisher, Michael Kanfer), Best Film Editing (Conrad Buff IV, James Cameron, Richard A. Harris), Best Costume Design (Deborah Lynn Scott), Best Sound (Gary Rydstrom, Tom Johnson, Gary Summers, Mark Ulano), Best Effects–Sound Effects Editing (Tom Bellfort, Christopher Boyes), Best Music–Original Dramatic Score (James Horner), Best Music–Original Song (James Horner, Will Jennings for "My Heart Will Go On")
AAN: Best Leading Actress (Kate Winslet), Best Supporting Actress (Gloria Stuart), Best Makeup (Tina Earnshaw, Greg Cannom, Simon Thompson)
DVD: Paramount Pictures, 2005. Three-disc collector's edition.
BLU-RAY: Paramount Pictures, 2012
DURATION: 195 minutes

James Cameron's 1997 *Titanic* stands as the most popular, luxurious, and expensive production of the legendary sinking of the world's largest (at that time) passenger liner and the most written about sea tragedy in the history of navigation. Several screen versions of the sinking preceded Cameron's much talked about epic movie, the 1953 *Titanic*, and, most notably, *A Night to Remember*, in 1958, which is judged as the most accurate retelling of the 1912 naval catastrophe. But Cameron's work won its fame because of newer technology that allowed for the showing of the wreck of the actual ship *Titanic*, discovered at the bottom of the North Atlantic Ocean in 1985, and it became a subject of search for years to come, with Cameron himself diving the three-mile distance to the sea floor to photograph the wreckage several times.[1]

Cameron's story does not focus exclusively on the naval disaster, but rather on a love story between two fictional lovers, a modern Romeo and Juliet romance that occupies the first part of the movie and adds momentum and emotional uplift as the doomed ship carrying thousands of passengers begins to founder in the Atlantic after scraping a floating iceberg. Not all critics were unanimous in praising this addition, but the audiences loved it, and *Titanic* broke box-office records worldwide, while the Academy of Motion Picture Arts and Sciences awarded it eleven Oscars, the most given to a film since *Ben-Hur* in 1959. The film remains popular, and in 2012 it was rereleased in 3D, while a four-disc Blu-ray version, with multiple commentaries and other extra features, does justice to the visual splendor and special sound effects of the movie in its restored HD version.

As Cameron states in his retrospect, as the audience already knows the ending of the story, he wanted to show them what it was like to go through the wrenching experience of witnessing the greatest naval catastrophe in modern history. The addition of the drama of the two lovers is meant to intensify the emotional complexity of the story, adding suspense, as the viewer is forced to root not only for the various passengers and crew undergoing a life and death situation, but for the seemingly doomed couple. He also wanted to highlight the class warfare between those in the steerage class and the first- and second-class passengers. At the same time, Cameron's film exploits the newer technology, mostly the newly emerging (at the time) computer-generated imagery (CGI) technology, which can be used to enhance the special effects and raise realism to a new level. Through newer technology, a compelling love story, and a large and distinguished cast, he brings his audience close to the horror, confusion, and chaos that prevailed in the last hours before the sinking.

To bring his drama/epic to life, Cameron built a full-scale model of *Titanic*—almost as large as the original ship at nearly 800 feet long—at Playas de Rosario, Baja, California, which he used for most of the establishing shots and action of the filming, with CGI images to replicate the ship at various angles. The sets included large, full-scale sections of the decks, dining room and smoking-room sections, and much of the first- and second-class interiors, based on the actual design of the ship and surviving records. Footage of the remains of the sunken *Titanic*, discovered by divers in 1985, was used, and Cameron himself made several underwater trips to the site of the wreck. In 1996, he photographed the sunken ship, and this footage, combined with CGI images simulating parts of the wreck, appears in the opening scenes of the film.

The story begins on the deck of the Russian ship *Akademic Mstislar Keldysh*, where a treasure hunter, Brock Lovett (Bill Paxton), and his crew recover a safe from the sunken wreck, hoping to find a precious stone in it, but instead they find a well-preserved painter's notebook and soon discover the hand-drawn sketch of a nude woman wearing a blue diamond around her neck. The scene shifts to a 100-year-old California woman, who is watching the news on TV and recognizes the diamond in the sketch,[2] for she herself once wore it. She is soon whisked by helicopter to the deck of the *Akademic Mstislar Keldysh*. Once aboard the ship, she is shown a digital reproduction of what happened to *Titanic* on the fateful night of 15 April 1912, how it broke in two sections before sinking to the bottom of the ocean. From this point onward, she needs little prodding to begin telling them her story, which is "somewhat different," as she puts it, from what they think happened to *Titanic*. Her narrative reveals who she is, what actually happened, and how she managed to survive the sinking.

Her fictional story is used by Cameron as a "framing device" to insert a narrator, an old woman who calls herself Rose Dawson Calvert (Gloria Stuart), to tell what unfolded on *Titanic* before, during, and after the ship sank. Her story becomes the main thread of the narrative, the romance of Rose DeWitt Bukater (Kate Winslet) and Jack Dawson (Leonardo DiCaprio), the two star-crossed lovers. This tale, with its own dramatic twists and turns, interweaves with the actual happenings on board the ship during its most crucial hours, and, in a way, it becomes the axis of the plot. It is compelling enough to fill the initial sequences of the story of *Titanic*; for one thing, it lasts for more than ninety minutes before *Titanic* hits the ice, and it concludes with Rose's narrative, where the film ends. The popularity of the film *Titanic* is due to the heartbreaking tragedy of the lovers, which heightens the suspense as their own adventure holds the interest of the viewer, who witnesses countless other tragedies as the greatest ship in the world sinks.

Cameron conceived the idea of adding a romance tale to the main event of the story to connect the much-told story, both in written word[3] and via film and TV productions, with modern audiences and provide a thematic balance to the starkness of the sinking, already known to audiences from previous screen versions. Thus, he created another strand to dovetail with the main story, as well as a set of fictional characters who interact with many of the individuals who were actually on board the liner. He also broadened his tale by adding the theme of class distinctions, the wealthy passengers of the first and second classes and those of mixed nationalities, mostly immigrants, who traveled in steerage, or third class. The clash of cultures portrayed aboard the ship enhances the effects of those distinctions by making one of the lovers, Jack, a poor young man traveling in the steerage section, and the other an impoverished high-society girl engaged to be married to a wealthy young tycoon, Caledon "Cal" Hockley (Billy Zane), who is traveling with her in first class. The drama intensifies as the two plotlines play out during the agonizing hours before the ship meets its fate.

Cameron's script adds a host of fictional characters, who indeed become the main players in the story, although some of the historical characters on board are equally strongly drawn. The tale of two young lovers carries the main plot of the film, which is thematically enlarged to accommodate the class distinctions among the passengers. Jack Dawson is a penniless bohemian painter returning to his native Wisconsin after learning his trade in Paris, and he meets Rose in the most dramatic early scene of the trip, as she attempts to jump into the ocean to commit suicide. He has a pal named Fabrizio (Danny Nucci), with whom he shares the earnings of a poker game to buy a ticket on *Titanic*. Jack becomes a hero early on, when he saves Rose from jumping overboard after a scuffle with her fiancé Cal, and he is rewarded by being invited to dinner in the first-class dining room the following night. There, he meets the cream of aristocracy, mocks their pretended elegance, and provokes suspicion in the mind of Cal and his English valet/henchman Spicer Lovejoy (David Warner), who has the looks of an assassin and relentlessly tracks down Jack and Rose, even as *Titanic* is sinking.

Of the historical characters, a few are worth mentioning. On board *Titanic* is J. Bruce Ismay (Jonathan Hyde), managing director of the White Star Line, and a man who is presented in the movie as arrogant, ignorant ("Who's Freud? Is he a passenger?" he asks after provocative remarks by a rebellious Rose), and pushy, for he appears pressing Captain Smith to increase the speed of the ship to break a record by arriving in New York a day earlier than scheduled. There is no historical evidence that such a thing actually happened, and Ismay is portrayed as a fool and coward who escapes in one of the lifeboats while other luminaries, like John Jacob Astor IV (Eric Braeden), the richest man on the ship, perish. Captain Edward J. Smith (Barnard Hill), in his last voyage before retirement, is shown as being inept, slow to react, and practically catatonic and entirely useless as a leader in the ship's final moments. By contrast, Thomas Andrews (Victor Garber), the ship's builder, stays calm, predicts with accuracy the ship's floating time, and urges incredulous passengers, who believe that *Titanic* is "unsinkable," to enter the lifeboats. Despite these warnings, only 750 passengers enter the lifeboats, as many are not filled to capacity. More than 1,500 of those on board *Titanic* perish. Margaret "Molly" Brown, a newly rich American woman, is among the passengers, and, as given by Kathy Bates, she plays a significant role in Jack and Rose's tale, and also shows exemplary courage during the rescue, thence nicknamed "The Unsinkable Molly Brown."

Cameron's film makes no mention of the *Californian*, a vessel that stood only ten miles from *Titanic* but failed to respond, or of other ships[4] that received SOS messages from *Titanic* but were too far away to get there in time, with the exception of the *Carpathia*, which responded. Unfortunately, it arrived two hours late and could only pick up survivors. The *Carpathia*, which was actually speeding at the time to reach *Titanic*, is shown only briefly after the rescue operations are over and the rescued passengers are aboard. Thus, the story of Jack and Rose becomes the main structural device through which the audience travels to reach the conclusion of the story.

While the scenes showing the foundering of *Titanic* are overwhelming in their power, the viewer's attention is drawn to Jack's fortunes, as Rose returns to the lower decks to save her lover and frees him by axing a chain that ties him to a pole. The two then run from a vicious Cal, who sends bullets flying as he tries to kill them both. Later, while floating in the water after the ship has disappeared from the ocean's surface, Jack gallantly helps Rose onto a floating door, while he freezes to death holding her hand. This is really the pinnacle of the action, while the disaster remains a backdrop. The romance between two lovers resonates with audiences, and the film gains its notoriety thanks to it. The sinking of the world's largest ship and the innumerable tragedies of those who perished are treated in the most realistic manner possible, with passionate interest by Cameron, but his story gains its immense momentum—and fame—by the brief love affair of Jack and Rose, a girl intended for riches and a shiftless painter from Wisconsin. CS

Notes

1. According to Nathaniel Philbrick in his introduction to the fiftieth anniversary edition of Walter Lord's book *A Night to Remember* (1955), numerous tourists and treasure-seekers visited the submerged wreck of *Titanic* at the bottom of the ocean, and one couple even got married at the ship's bow, in tribute to Leonardo DiCaprio and Kate Winslet's "balancing act" on the bow of the ship. See Walter Lord, *A Night to Remember* (New York: St. Martin's Griffin, 2005), xi. Originally published in New York: Holt, 1955.

2. Drawn by James Cameron himself, as he explains in his "Commentary." *Titanic*, directed by James Cameron (Paramount Pictures, 2012), Blu-ray, disc one.

3. Walter Lord's best-selling book *A Night to Remember* (1955) had spurred the making of the film by the same title in 1958, and a subsequent TV production in 1965, both of which deal solely with the sinking of the ship. Cameron knew of the book, and it was his watching the film that brought about his interest in making *Titanic*.

4. One of them was the *Olympic*, a sister ship of *Titanic*, which was 500 miles away at the time. Other

ships got word of the events as they were unfolding and transmitted the information to New York, spreading the news of the catastrophe while the *Titanic* was sinking. See Lord, *A Night to Remember.*

Bibliography

Donnelly, Judy. *Titanic, Lost . . . And Found.* New York: Random House, 2012.

Lord, Walter. *A Night to Remember.* New York: St. Martin's Griffin, 2005. Originally published in New York: Holt, 1955.

THE TOWERING INFERNO (1974)

Directors: John Guillermin, Irwin Allen (action sequences)
Writer: Stirling Silliphant. Based on the *The Tower*, by Richard Martin Stern; *The Glass Inferno*, by Thomas N. Scortia; and *The Glass Inferno*, by Frank M. Robinson.
Producer: Irwin Allen (20th Century Fox, Warner Bros.)
Cinematographers: Fred J. Koenekamp, Joseph F. Biroc (action sequences)
Editors: Harold F. Kress, Carl Kress
Production Design: William J. Creber
Art Direction: Ward Preston
Set Decoration: Raphael Bretton
Costumes: Paul Zastupnevich
Music: John Williams
Sound Mixers: Theodore Soderberg, Herman Lewis
Cast: Chief Michael "Mike" O'Hallorhan: Steve McQueen. Doug Roberts: Paul Newman. Jim Duncan: William Holden. Susan Franklin: Faye Dunaway. Harlee Claiborne: Fred Astaire. Patty: Susan Blakely. Simmons: Richard Chamberlain. Lisolette: Jennifer Jones. Jernigan: O. J. Simpson. Sen. Parker: Robert Vaughn. Bigelow: Robert Wagner. Lorrie: Susan Flannery. Paula Ramsay: Sheila Allen (as Sheila Mathews). Giddings: Normann Burton. Mayor Ramsay: Jack Collins. Kappy: Don Gordon. Scott: Felton Perry. Carlos: Gregory Sierra. Mark Powers: Ernie Orsatti. Angela Allbright: Carlena Gower. Phillip Allbright: Mike Lookinland. Mrs. Allbright: Carol McEvoy
AA: Best Cinematography (Fred J. Koenekamp, Joseph F. Biroc), Best Film Editing (Harold F. Kress, Carl Kress), Best Music–Original Song (Al Kasha, Joel Hirschhorn for "We May Never Love Like This Again")
AAN: Best Supporting Actor (Fred Astaire), Best Art Direction–Set Decoration (William J. Creber, Ward Preston, Raphael Bretton), Best Music–Original Dramatic Score (John Williams), Best Picture (Irwin Allen), Best Sound (Theodore Soderberg, Herman Lewis)
DVD: 20th Century Fox, 2006
Blu-ray: 20th Century Fox, 2009
Duration: DVD, 164 minutes; Blu-ray, 165 minutes

Following the success of producer Irwin Allen's *Poseidon Adventure* (1972), made on a budget of $5 million, Allen's next project, *The Towering Inferno*, was given $11 million, but costs spiraled to $14 million. Two studios came on board as the result of the conflict regarding two similar books that had been optioned by 20th Century Fox and Warner Bros. Allen convinced them that two competing films on the same topic—people trapped in a burning skyscraper—would split the box-office dollar. Although he could not convince them to let him direct the film as a whole, Allen did end up directing the action sequences. Featuring real fire and dangerous stunts, and what would become the ubiquitous all-star cast, headed by Paul Newman and Steve McQueen (who insisted that they each have exactly the same number of words of dialogue),[1] the film remains breathtaking, if perhaps more difficult for audiences to watch in a post–9/11 world.

Charlton Heston, who stars in *Earthquake* (Mark Robson, 1974), defines the disaster film as one that contains a

> disparate group of people, most of them strangers to each other, thrown suddenly into a life-threatening situation, usually (not invariably) a natural disaster. The

> movie explores the disaster as spectacularly as possible and traces the reaction of the various characters to the common danger.[2]

At the beginning of *The Towering Inferno*, we are introduced to our "disparate group" in San Francisco. Each is given a convenient title in the publicity material, including "The Architect," Doug Roberts (Paul Newman), who discovers that shortcuts appear to have been taken in the construction of his latest, and tallest, skyscraper (known as the Glass Tower), particularly with the wiring. He confronts the builder, Jim Duncan (William Holden), and Duncan's shifty son-in-law Simmons (Richard Chamberlain), who is becoming increasingly estranged from his wife.

In his own personal life, Doug has issued somewhat of an ultimatum to his girlfriend, Susan Franklin (Faye Dunaway): move to the country to start a new life and family with him or stay in the city and take a promotion—but without him. The fact that she is called "The Girlfriend" leaves us reasonably confident how this particular plotline will pan out. Meanwhile, aging con man Harlee Claiborne (Fred Astaire) has a wealthy widow in his sights, Lisolette (Jennifer Jones). While everyone prepares to attend the Glass Tower's grand opening, one of its residents, the deaf widow Mrs. Allbright (Carol McEvoy), declines the invitation on behalf of herself and her two children, Angela (Carlena Gower) and Phillip (Mike Lookinland). Publicist Bigelow (Robert Wagner) plans to arrive late at the party so that he can first see his secretary and mistress Lorrie (Susan Flannery, best known in more recent years as the matriarch Stephanie Forrester on *The Bold and the Beautiful*, a character on the air from 1987 to 2012).

When a small fire breaks out in a storage room, it does not seem particularly threatening, but the audience, of course, knows that disaster looms. Although some of the cocktail party's 295 guests are able to make their way to safety, most are soon trapped at the top of the Glass Tower in the Promenade Room on the 135th floor, cut off from escape by the escalating fire. "The Fire Chief," Mike O'Hallorhan (Steve McQueen), arrives to sort out the fire and lament at the folly of human endeavor that would see such a firetrap built in the first place.

As the firefighters are continually thwarted by the building's scale, the audience waits to see who among the guests will survive. Lisolette tries to alert Mrs. Allbright and her family of the danger, and spotting them on the security cameras, Doug and a security guard, Jernigan (O. J. Simpson), come to the rescue. While Jernigan gets Mrs. Allbright out, Doug, Lisolette, and the children are cut off and must make a perilous journey to the Promenade Room, only making their way through a blocked fire door with the help of two firefighters who climb all the way up the building to blast it open.

With the stairways consumed by flames, a rescue helicopter is sent to the roof, but it crashes and explodes into flames when scared and impatient guests rush toward it and force it to swerve in strong winds. As a desperate last attempt to rescue the guests, a breeches buoy is set up with an adjacent building, and a lottery system is set up to use it. Although power is out, Doug rigs the external glass elevator to make a controlled descent with twelve guests on board, including Lisolette and the children. Explosions within the building cause Lisolette to fall to her death, and the elevator hangs perilously from the side of the skyscraper. Mike and his colleague Mark (Ernie Orsatti) help attach the elevator to a helicopter so that it can be flown to safety, but Mark dies in the effort. Meanwhile, cut off in their office tryst, Bigelow dies in an attempt to get help, and Lorrie is forced to make a fatal jump from the flames.

At the top of the building, the remaining men grow restless waiting to be rescued, and Simmons tries to get into the buoy ahead of his turn, causing a chaotic surge toward it. The buoy breaks under the weight and takes them to their doom.

The only option left to the firefighters is to explode the water tanks on top of the building, which will potentially kill some of the guests but provides the best hope of saving at least some of them. Mike and Doug set the timed charges and then join the others in the Promenade Room to tie themselves down as best they can. The ensuing surge of water puts out the fire, but, as predicted, its force also claims lives. The shocked survivors take stock of the loss of life, and the reformed Harlee is left only with Lisolette's cat for comfort. The two heroes of the day, Mike and Doug (or, as far as the audience is concerned, really Steve and Paul), somberly acknowledge one another, as Doug promises that he will ask Mike how to construct a building with firefighters in mind.

In the film version, the fire is accidental but, in effect, the result of deliberate cost-cutting measures and shoddy work. In Richard Martin Stern's novel *The Tower*, these shortcuts are exploited by a saboteur as a protest against his lack of employment.[3] Indeed, many commentators have seen the disaster genre's success throughout the 1970s as a reflection of U.S. cultural unease in the wake of that era's high unemployment, "stagflation" (rising prices combined with economic downturn), crippling gasoline prices following the 1973 Arab oil embargo, the war in Vietnam (with the fall of Saigon in 1975), Watergate (1972–1974), and the Iran hostage crisis (1979–1981).[4] It must be remembered that Irwin Allen laid down the template for the genre in his phenomenally successful *Poseidon Adventure* of 1972; in other words, well before many of these events. It is nonetheless the case that social, political, and economic unrest are ever-present in *The Tower*, and even if they are not explicit in the film version, they form its cultural backdrop.

More directly, it is hardly surprising that the public was alarmed by the safety issues illustrated in the film, although experts at the time noted that, in reality, buildings do not have the obvious design flaws of the Glass Tower.[5] Technical advisor Jack Cavallero from the San Francisco Fire Department nonetheless suggests that the film was a "way to sell a message to the people, a way to get the point across," that fires in high-rise buildings are their most difficult challenge.[6]

Writing for the *New York Times*, Vincent Canby praises the film's special effects and says that although "overwrought and silly in its personal drama," it has "an advantage over most movies of this sort in that it has a really classy cast."[7] But while our leads survive, Canby's suggestion that the characters' "life spans conform roughly to their billing" is not entirely accurate. Part of the pleasure of such disaster films as *The Towering Inferno* is to see who is punished, who is redeemed, and who is simply the victim of the amoral whims of chance or fate, and perhaps the rather ghoulish desire to see our screen stars meet their doom. DB

Notes

1. Michele Farinola, "AMC Backstory: The Towering Inferno," 2001, *The Towering Inferno*, directed by John Guillermin (20th Century Fox, 2006), DVD, disc two.

2. Charlton Heston, *In the Arena* (London: HarperCollins, 1995), 470.

3. Richard Martin Stern, *The Tower* (New York: McKay, 1973).

4. See, for example, Nick Roddick, "Only the Stars Survive: Disaster Movies in the Seventies," in *Performance and Politics in Popular Drama: Aspects of Popular Entertainment in Theatre, Film, and Television, 1800–1976*, edited by D. Brady (Cambridge, UK: Cambridge University Press, 1980), 243–69; Beth Bai-

ley and David Farber, "Introduction," in *America in the Seventies*, edited by Beth Bailey and David Farber (Lawrence: University Press of Kansas, 2004), 1–8.

5. Paul Goldberger, "*Inferno* Dim Threat as Reality," *New York Times*, 4 February 1975, 70.

6. Quoted in Goldberger, "*Inferno* Dim Threat as Reality," 70.

7. Vincent Canby, "*The Towering Inferno* First-Rate Visual Spectacle," *New York Times*, 20 December 1974, 20.

Bibliography

Bailey, Beth, and David Farber. "Introduction." In *America in the Seventies*, edited by Beth Bailey and David Farber, 1–8. Lawrence: University Press of Kansas, 2004.

Canby, Vincent. "*The Towering Inferno* First-Rate Visual Spectacle." *New York Times*, 20 December 1974, 20.

Goldberger, Paul. "*Inferno* Dim Threat as Reality." *New York Times*, 4 February 1975, 70.

Heston, Charlton. *In the Arena*. London: HarperCollins, 1995.

Roddick, Nick. "Only the Stars Survive: Disaster Movies in the Seventies." In *Performance and Politics in Popular Drama: Aspects of Popular Entertainment in Theatre, Film, and Television, 1800–1976*, edited by D. Brady, 243–69. Cambridge, UK: Cambridge University Press, 1980.

Stern, Richard Martin. *The Tower*. New York: McKay, 1973.

TROY (2004)

DIRECTOR: Wolfgang Petersen
WRITER: David Benioff
PRODUCERS: Wolfgang Petersen, Diana Rathbun, Colin Wilson (Warner Bros.)
CINEMATOGRAPHER: Roger Preatt
EDITOR: Peter Honess
COSTUMES: Bob Ringwood
MUSIC: James Horner
CAST: Agamemnon: Brian Cox. Achilles: Brad Pitt. Menelaus: Brendon Gleeson. Helen: Diane Kruger. Priam: Peter O'Toole. Paris: Orlando Bloom. Hector: Eric Bana. Thetis: Julie Christie. Odysseus: Sean Bean. Andromache: Saffron Burrows. Briseis: Rose Byrne. Great Ajax: Tyler Mane. Patroclus: Garreth Hedlund
AA: None
AAN: Best Costume Design (Bob Ringwood)
DVD: Warner Home Video, 2005
BLU-RAY: Warner Home Video, 2007
DURATION: 163 minutes (196 for director's cut)

Wolfgang Petersen's *Troy* both fits and defies the epic classical mold, and it does so with a certain amount of dignity, despite its lack of real depth and shortcomings in plot and design. Inspired[1] by Homer's poem *The Iliad*, *Troy*, a departure from the Roman/biblical epics that dominated cinema in the 1950s and 1960s, shifts the focus of action to the Greek classical world, by and large ignored by Hollywood in terms of significant output. *Troy* aspires to link antiquity with modernity by demonstrating the hegemony of a superpower and the conflicts between heads of state, with their uncertain and destructive outcomes. Filmed on location in Malta and Mexico, the film features spectacular battle sequences, heroic deeds, guile, and romance—an irresistible combination of live action and digital effects for the modern viewer. Added to that is the glow of Hollywood stars, with Brad Pitt as Achilles, Eric Bana as Hector, and Peter O'Toole as Priam, among others, to portray the great war heroes of antiquity, whose feats are sung by Homer and other poets. Achilles, fated to die in battle and gain glory rather than live and be forgotten, as his goddess mother has told him, is the archetype of valor—*arête*, or excellence—a fearless demigod, unbeatable in battle, although still vulnerable, who can be viewed as a surrogate war hero of today.

Despite its technical excellence and some good performances, *Troy* is still a flawed epic for a number of reasons, but here, two, both related to its formal qualities, will be singled out. First, the movie has a loose, episodic plot that stretches over a lengthy period of time: the expedition of the Greeks to take Troy, after Paris (Orlando Bloom) seduces and abducts Helen (Diane Kruger), wife of King Menelaus of Sparta (Brendon Gleeson). The Greeks set up a siege of Troy, and it takes them ten years of hard fighting before they capture it, after using a ruse; it was cunning not valor that won them the day. The movie admittedly draws its materials from *The Iliad*, but also from other sources, some from *The Odyssey*, which describes episodes of the sack of Troy in flashbacks, and some from Virgil's *The Aeneid*, the second book of which describes the sack of Troy in detail. The writers have also accessed other sources, including works on the Trojan War written by other authors during antiquity[2] and historical and archeological data, while some scenes—the lengthy sexual liaison that develops between Achilles and Briseis (Rose Byrne), for instance—are pure inventions.

In spite of its great length, Homer's *The Iliad* has a tight plot, covering only nine weeks (or so) of the ninth year of the war, and its theme is the wrath of Achilles and its effects on the Greeks, who were losing without his fighting power. *Troy* is true to some of this, but its makers chose to broaden the plot by attempting to cover the entire war, and the result seems somewhat improbable, for no one gets visibly older in the ten-year stretch. Thus, the plot turns out to be a chronological sprawl, although the authors cleverly avoid the mention of the duration of the war—cinematically it does not matter—or other factors, for example, the absence of the gods, so prominent in *The Iliad*. In the movie, the gods are only seen as oversized statues, their power invoked (mostly by the Trojans), but their involvement in the actual outcome of the battle is omitted. To modern audiences this may seem an advantage, for this omission frees the filmmakers from the added burden of describing deities from long ago who are past their coin value.

A more serious drawback may be seen in the fact that the plot of *Troy* is not only episodic and somewhat slow moving, but in that it attempts to combine two strands. One is the revenge theme, the Greek campaign against Troy to reclaim Helen, the abducted queen of Sparta—a theme that is generally given as one of the causes of the Trojan War. The other theme developed here is the ambition of the Greek leaders, led by the arrogant and conquest-minded Agamemnon (Brian Cox), whose clash with the proud strongman Achilles is responsible for the early near-defeat of the Greeks, for at a certain point Achilles refuses to fight, and the result is a standstill. When he decides to return to battle, he kills Hector, the leader of the Trojans, after the latter has killed his "cousin" Patroclus (Garreth Hedlund).

The problem here is that the screenwriters of *Troy* could not quite make these two strands of plot cohere smoothly. On balance, the Paris–Helen plot is the weaker one, for the romance is a tepid affair,[3] hardly a motive for a large army to go after the missing woman—at least not in the Hollywood terms outlined here. The first third of the movie suffers from the lack of real sparks between the two lovers, who indulge in sexual acts (more explicit in the director's cut), while the gruff and warlike older folks decide that they cannot outline a credible reason for the war they are about to embark on. Agamemnon is a greedy superpower-monger, Menelaus a cuckolded husband who cheats freely and says a wife is just for "breeding," and Achilles a narcissistic muscleman who needs his mother's, Thetis's (Julie Christie), advice to make up his mind whether to fight for glory and die, or stay home, marry, and be forgotten. Brad Pitt's performance does not make him either more believable as Achilles, who was the tallest (aside from Ajax Major), handsomest, and most ferocious among the Greeks.

Then the movie details, rather sluggishly, the sailing of the Greek fleet to the harbor of Troy, filled with digitally reproduced model ships, the equally improbable "10,000" (here 50,000) Greek troops landing, and the early bloody battles. There is no sense of time, and the ten year period during which the war lasted is given in sporadic episodes, with cross-cutting and telling the stories from both sides—the Trojans making sorties from their fortified city, the Greeks responding in kind, unable to get through and win the day. There are several confrontations, one being between Orlando Bloom's Paris and Brendon Gleeson's Menelaus, between a pretty teenager (not to mention his cowardice) and the menacing and gruff Menelaus. Paris can't seem to muster up the courage to fight and retreats into his brothers' arms. Hector absurdly kills Menelaus, adding insult to inaccuracy, for in the Homeric story, Menelaus not only survives, he returns to his wife with trophies after a seven-year hiatus spent wandering and gathering riches.

On the other hand, the killing of Patroclus by Hector is a well-staged confrontation, as is the duel between Hector and Achilles, during which Hector is killed and dragged around the city, as Homer tells happened. Pitt is athletic as Achilles, but Bana is superior as Hector, and the real hero of the movie. He is a noble hero, a loyal father and husband, and he wins the hearts of the audience with his dignity and true bravery. Troy is finally taken through the ruse of the Trojan Horse, and the story ends with the destruction of Troy and the burning of the body of Achilles in a pyre. When the Greeks enter Troy, they kill every major figure except Paris, an expert archer, who shoots Achilles in the heel (his sensitive spot) and then escapes with Helen, Andromache (Saffron Burrows) and her young son, and a few others through a tunnel. In *The Iliad*, Achilles is already dead, by the same hand, and, of course, Helen is freed and goes back with her husband—as we learn in *The Odyssey*. In the film, Agamemnon is also killed in the final battle, a fact that remains ahistorical, for ancient narrators—including many tragedians—state that Agamemnon returned home and was killed by Clytemnestra, his wife, and her lover Aegisthus.[4]

Thus, the plot of *Troy* becomes a mishmash of themes, drawn from different sources and hardly connecting into an organic whole. By contrast, *The Iliad*, despite its size and many diversionary stories of the gods, is noted for its terse action, quick pace, and powerful central theme—the anger of Achilles, μῆνις (wrath, anger)—a key phrase in its first line, which becomes the catalyst for the main events that unfold. The fighting stops, and the war slips into a dangerous lull, taken advantage of by the Trojans, who rally and nearly defeat the Greeks. Odysseus is sent to Achilles, imploring him to reconsider; the latter sends Patroclus wearing his armor, but Hector easily kills him. Now Achilles is seized by a second "wrath," his desire for revenge against his friend's killer, which reveals a more savage (but, even so, nobler) Achilles, who overwhelms the Trojans, kills many without mercy, and scatters the rest into hiding behind the walls of Troy. The film does stay close to *The Iliad* story here, giving this climactic battle between the two warriors and the dragging of the body of the defeated Hector as the ultimate disgrace of a warrior. The most moving scene in the Homeric epic is showing Priam, the proud king, coming to claim the body of his fallen son from Achilles. *The Iliad* concludes with that episode, its final lines going on to say that nine days were granted by the victor to the Trojans to bury their fallen chief.

In *Troy*, Petersen chose to extend the action of *The Iliad*, presenting the building of the Trojan Horse, the sacking of Troy, the destruction that follows, and the death of most of the war leaders on both sides. In his commentary, he admits that he opted to do so to provide closure to the story. His movie starts with the abduction of Helen and concludes with her escape with Paris, thus allowing the lovers to flee to safety. In his director's cut, which adds more than half an hour to the original theatrical release, the love scenes between Paris and Helen are lengthier and more sexual, and Achilles "grows" into a passionate lover of Briseis, splendidly played by the Australian actress Rose Byrne. It is to save her life that Achilles joins the Greeks inside the Trojan Horse, who slip out of the wooden construction at night and open the gates of Troy. In the ensuing destruction, he searches for her and reaches her as she stabs Agamemnon as he is trying to rape her, and he is shot by Paris in the heel, his sensitive spot. Achilles, given by Pitt with some sensitivity, is thus alienated from the Greeks from start to finish, fighting a war he does not want and falling victim to his fate, but showing some sensitivity along with his skill as a brave (and brutal) fighter. His best scene remains Priam's plea to him, after his duel with Hector.

Petersen recalls that O'Toole, who asked that not a single line of *The Iliad* be altered, is splendid as Priam, rendering dignity to the whole. Recalling the death of his old father, Achilles is moved by the old man's pleas to be given the mutilated body of his son so he can give the proper ritual for a fallen hero, breaking down and crying over the dead body of his enemy. He also frees Briseis, showing his metamorphosis from a savage warrior into a human touched by emotion. To his credit, Pitt rises to the occasion in this scene, changing from a reluctant, sullen, and angry warrior into someone capable of seeing the war from both sides. Add the magnificent portrait of Hector given by Bana and you get a sense that the filmmakers, despite their difficulties with form, were at least conscious of the awesome tragedy of a conflict without a cause—or a cause that was pretense, the abduction of a woman, a disguise of the real reason of conquest and imperial greed. CS

Notes

1. As the opening credits tell, rather than the more usual "Based on," which indicates a closer relationship between an original and the work adapted.
2. See Constantine Santas, "Introduction," in *The Epic in Film: From Myth to Blockbuster* (Lanham, MD: Rowman & Littlefield, 2008), 6–9.
3. In the director's cut version, the scenes between Paris and Helen are more sexually explicit, as are those between Achilles and Briseis.
4. In his DVD commentary in the director's cut edition, Wolfgang Petersen explains some of these plot changes, claiming that the killing of Agamemnon in Troy provides satisfaction to the audience at the end, as Agamemnon, a villain, has just seized and is about to rape Briseis. She stabs him in the neck as Achilles, subsequently killed by Paris, is trying to reach and save her.

Bibliography

Santas, Constantine. "Introduction." In *The Epic in Film: From Myth to Blockbuster*, 6–9. Lanham, MD: Rowman & Littlefield, 2008.

Winkler, Martin M. Troy*: From Homer's Iliad to Hollywood Epic.* New York: Blackwell, 2006.

V

THE VIKINGS (1958)

DIRECTOR: Richard Fleischer
WRITERS: Calder Willingham, Dale Wasserman. Based on the novel *The Viking*, by Edison Marshall.
PRODUCER: Jerry Bresler (Bryna Productions)
CINEMATOGRAPHER: Jack Cardiff
EDITOR: Elmo Williams
PRODUCTION DESIGN: Harper Goff
MUSIC: Mario Nascimbene
CAST: Einar: Kirk Douglas. Eric: Tony Curtis. Ragnar: Ernest Borgnine. Morgana: Janet Leigh. Egbert: James Donald. Fr. Godwin: Alexander Knox. Enid: Maxine Audley. Aella: Frank Thring. Kitala: Eileen Way. Sandpiper: Edric Connor. Bridget: Dandy Nichols. Bjorn: Per Buckhøj. Narrator: Orson Welles (uncredited)
AA: None
AAN: None
SAN SEBASTIÁN INTERNATIONAL FILM FESTIVAL AWARD: Zulueta Prize, Best Actor (Kirk Douglas, tied with James Stewart for *Vertigo*)
DIRECTOR'S GUILD OF AMERICA AWARD NOMINATION: Outstanding Directorial Achievement in Motion Pictures (Richard Fleischer)
DVD: MGM Home Entertainment, 2003
BLU-RAY: Currently unavailable
DURATION: 111 minutes

The names Kirk Douglas and Tony Curtis are most often remembered together for their teaming in Stanley Kubrick's *Spartacus* of 1960, but the pair first costarred in this less well-remembered Viking adventure set in the ninth century, "the best advertisement for beer-drinking since the breweries put wrestling on TV."[1] An uncredited Orson Welles sets the scene in his opening narration, telling the audience, "The Vikings in Europe of the eighth and ninth [centuries] were dedicated to a pagan god of war, Odin. Cramped by the confines of their barren, ice-bound northlands, they exploited their skill as shipbuilders to spread a reign of terror then unequalled in violence and brutality." Based on Edison Marshall's 1952 novel, the film boasted a budget of $4 million.[2] Douglas, who made the film through his production company, Bryna, had chosen director Richard Fleischer on the strength of his work on *20,000 Leagues Under the Sea* (1954). The film was, in Douglas's words, a "tremendous hit," and he named his next son Eric after one of the lead characters.[3]

It is, in fact, Curtis who plays Eric, the bastard son of the Viking conqueror Ragnar (Ernest Borgnine, Academy Award winner for Best Leading Actor in Delbert Mann's *Marty*, 1955) who rapes the queen of Northumbria in England and kills the king. Eric's birth is kept secret from the succeeding King Aella of Northumbria (Frank Thring), and the infant is sent abroad with the pummel stone of the royal sword around his neck as a pendant. But he is captured by Vikings and raised as a slave among his father's people. Eric comes into conflict with Ragnar's heir, Prince Einar (Douglas, who was actually older than his "father," Borgnine), although the young men do not realize that they are, in reality, half brothers. Eric is sentenced to be drowned by the incoming tide for blinding Einar in one eye with his hawk; however, Eric is saved when he calls for Odin's help and the wind turns the tide early (and, unusually for the epic, thereby seems to confirm the existence of a pagan god).

The Vikings kidnap the Welsh princess Morgana (played by Janet Leigh) (a name actually from Arthurian legend added to the tales in the twelfth century by Geoffrey of Monmouth), who has been betrothed to King Aella. Although they intend to ransom her, Einar is taken with both her beauty and reserve. He has willing enough bed partners at home but wants a wholesome woman who would resist such advances, partly for her purity and partly for the pleasure of rape. But Morgana is smart enough to understand his desires, and she refuses to fight him, much to his annoyance. Eric comes to her rescue, and with the help of her handmaiden, they take to the sea in a small boat. Although the Vikings discover the abduction, their pursuit is foiled by fog. While Eric has the benefit of a compass, the Vikings instead collide with one another, and the unlucky Ragnar is pulled aboard Eric's boat and taken to England as a captive.

Although Morgana feels obliged to marry Aella for the sake of her people, she and Eric fall in love. Aella sentences Ragnar to death in a pit of wolves, but with his hands bound and not in possession of a sword, Ragnar believes such a death will deny him an afterlife in Valhalla. Eric severs his bonds and gives him a sword, and the two men (in fact, father and son) exchange a look of mutual respect before Ragnar leaps into the pit to his death. For defying the king, Eric loses a hand (unfortunately the bound limb remains the same length as the uninjured arm, so the effect is unconvincing).

Einar and his men attack the English fort, ostensibly to avenge the death of Ragnar, but really so that Einar can reclaim Morgana. Once he finds her and declares his love for her, she confesses that she loves only Eric. Einar is told of their kinship, but the Viking does not believe it, and yet he does not take the opportunity to kill Eric after a thrilling castle-top encounter. He is instead slain by Eric. Eric, still none the wiser, cannot understand why Einar did not strike him down, and, as he had done with his father, he gives Einar a sword in his dying moments so that he, too, may enter Valhalla. The seedy King Aella is disposed of, and although we presume that Eric will now take the throne with Morgana as his queen, the film ends with the funeral pyre of Einar as it heads out to sea.

The ending thereby emphasizes the flawed heroism of Douglas's Einar. (As costar Tony Curtis recalls, since Douglas "was making the picture, he always made sure he was the most important actor in the movie."[4]) But reviews quite reasonably noted that it was difficult at times to work out who the real hero was supposed to be, Douglas or Curtis.[5] Bosley Crowther of the *New York Times* nonetheless proclaims that "there is plenty of action, and the scenery is occasionally superb—just like a lot of westerns. It's strictly a Norse opera, in two words."[6] *Variety* was more generous, saying, "The Vikings is spectacular, rousing, and colorful," and it praised the performances, along with the authentic location shooting "in the Norse fjord area and various parts of Europe, including the Bavarian

Studios."[7] In fact, Douglas, not one to be crossed, ended the Norway shoot early in favor of the studio when the Norwegians demanded more money.[8]

Ragnar, King Aella, and Eric are all loosely based on historical figures, and when *The Vikings* was made, historical evidence appeared to support its depiction of the Norse. A letter to the real King Ethelred of Northumbria from Alcuin of York in the year 793 (but preserved in a twelfth-century source) laments that "never before has such a terror appeared in Britain as we have now suffered from a pagan race, nor was it thought possible that such an inroad from the sea could be made."[9] But John Aberth notes that many (but not all) historians have reassessed the Vikings and now place "as much emphasis on their peaceful, yet no less impressive, activities as traders, shipbuilders, settlers, and explorers as . . . on their inescapable deeds as conquerors and pirates," and certainly the English were just as warmongering during this time as the Vikings.[10] *The Vikings* captures the feeling of this dangerous period and manages to lend a tragic air to its sometimes brutal heroic code. DB

Notes

1. Bosley Crowther, "*The Vikings* (1958): Norse Opera," *New York Times*, 12 June 1958, http://movies.nytimes.com/movie/review?res=9C05E4DE1F3AE73ABC4A52DFB0668383649EDE (5 July 2012).
2. John Aberth, *A Knight at the Movies: Medieval History on Film* (New York and London: Routledge, 2003), 43.
3. Kirk Douglas, *The Ragman's Son: An Autobiography* (London: Pan Books, 1988), 283, 298.
4. Tony Curtis, with Peter Golenbock, *American Prince: My Autobiography* (New York: Virgin, 2008), 187.
5. Crowther, "*The Vikings* (1958)."
6. Crowther, "*The Vikings* (1958)."
7. "*The Vikings*," *Variety*, 1958, www.variety.com/review/VE1117796117/ (5 July 2012).
8. Douglas, *The Ragman's Son*, 285.
9. Aberth, *A Knight at the Movies*, 30.
10. Aberth, *A Knight at the Movies*, 31. See Aberth for an extended discussion of the historical Vikings of the late eighth to the middle eleventh centuries and their depictions in film.

Bibliography

Aberth, John. *A Knight at the Movies: Medieval History on Film*. New York and London: Routledge, 2003.

Crowther, Bosley. "*The Vikings* (1958): Norse Opera." *New York Times*, 12 June 1958, http://movies.nytimes.com/movie/review?res=9C05E4DE1F3AE73ABC4A52DFB0668383649EDE (5 July 2012).

Curtis, Tony, with Peter Golenbock. *American Prince: My Autobiography*. New York: Virgin, 2008.

Douglas, Kirk. *The Ragman's Son: An Autobiography*. London: Pan Books, 1988.

"*The Vikings*." *Variety*, 1958, www.variety.com/review/VE1117796117/ (5 July 2012).

VIVA ZAPATA! (1952)

DIRECTOR: Elia Kazan
WRITER: John Steinbeck
PRODUCER: Darryl F. Zanuck (20th Century Fox)
CINEMATOGRAPHER: Joe MacDonald
EDITOR: Barbara McLean
ART DIRECTION: Leland Fuller, Lyle R. Wheeler
SET DECORATION: Claude E. Carpenter, Thomas Little
MUSIC: Alex North
CAST: Emiliano Zapata: Marlon Brando. Josefa Zapata: Jean Peters. Eufemio "Mano" Zapata: Anthony Quinn. Fernando Aguirre: Joseph Wiseman. President Porfirio Diaz: Fay Roope. Pablo Gomez: Lou Gilbert. Francisco Indalecio Madero: Harold Gordon. Señora Espejo: Mildred Dunnock. Don Nacio de la Tor: Arnold Moss. Señor Espejo: Florenz Ames. Gen. Victoriano Huerta: Frank Silvera. Pancho Villa: Alan Reed. Hernandez: Henry Silva
AA: Best Supporting Actor (Anthony Quinn)
AAN: Best Leading Actor (Marlon Brando), Best Art Direction–Set Decoration–Black and White (Leland Fuller, Lyle R. Wheeler, Claude E. Carpenter, Thomas Little), Best Music–Scoring of a Dramatic or Comedy Picture (Alex North), Best Writing–Story and Screenplay (John Steinbeck)
DVD: 20th Century Fox, 2013
BLU-RAY: 20th Century Fox, 2013
DURATION: 113 minutes

Elia Kazan had been a successful actor, credited with "creating a technique of acting," and he was "one of the three founders of the . . . Actors Studio,"[1] as a director of theater and a film director. Kazan is also famous for his testimony in front of the House Un-American Activities Committee, where he infamously named former communists in the film industry. Kazan's career has been one of the "most influential, dynamic, and controversial careers in American cinema."[2] Often read to reveal Kazan's true feelings about communism, *Viva Zapata!* is a "microcosm of the upheaval that resulted from clashing ideologies and the economic and social consequences of those collisions."[3] Most critics agree that the film offers a clear indictment of tyranny and support of democracy. Emphasizing the exclamation point in the film's title, 20th Century Fox's advertising exclaimed, "Shout excitement! Cry adventure! Thunder fury!" The story of the "fire and tempest of the man with the heart of a tiger," "the Robin Hood of Mexico," "the man with a circle around his name."[4]

The film opens in Mexico City, Mexico, in 1909, with a delegation of Indians entering the presidential grounds. Entering the gates, they are searched by guards and forced to leave their weapons and take off their hats. Inside the palace, President Porfirio Diaz (Fay Roope) welcomes them, saying, "Good morning my children." He receives a list of their names. After hesitating to tell them the reason for the visit, they tell him that their land has been stolen. A big estate has fenced in their land with barbed wire; sugarcane now grows where they once raised their corn. They have owned the land since the days of Spanish rule. Diaz tells them to verify their facts, verify the boundaries, take the matter to court, and be patient. Emiliano Zapata (Marlon Brando) speaks for the first time and challenges him, replying, "We can't verify the boundaries. Guarded by armed men. . . . Do you know of any land suit that was won by country people? We make our tortillas out of corn not patience. We need your authority to cross that fence." Upset by this challenge to his authority, Diaz circles Zapata's name on the list.

The Indians return home and cut the fence wire. They find their boundary stones, but armed men on horseback ride up, and a man with Gatling gun begins firing. Zapata pulls the gun down with a whip. The men have orders to capture Zapata.

Zapata, his brother Eufemio, or "Mano" (Anthony Quinn), and Pablo Gomez (Lou Gilbert) are hiding in the high desert when a man approaches them from a distance. Although Mano shoots at him to scare him off, the man still advances. It is Fernando Aguirre (Joseph Wiseman). He carries a "writing machine," which he calls his "sword of the mind." He brings them information about a man named Francisco Madero (Harold Gordon), who is challenging the president's tyranny and making preparations for a revolution in Texas. Zapata cannot read and has Gomez read the letter. Aguirre says that Madero wants Zapata to come to Texas. Zapata sends Gomez instead.

Mano and Zapata follow Josefa (Jean Peters), Zapata's love interest, and her mother, Señora Espejo (Mildred Dunnock), into a church. Mano holds her mother's mouth shut as Zapata speaks to Josefa. He wants to ask her father for her hand in marriage. She knows that her father will refuse because Zapata has no land or money. He tells her that he has been offered a position by Don Nacio de la Tor (Arnold Moss) because he is the best judge of horses in the country. Josefa calls him a "conceited monkey." He pretends to threaten to take her by force. She pulls a long, thin needle from her hair that she would use to kill him in the night. Once they leave, she and her mother agree that they like him.

The next day, Zapata inspects the horses at a ranch for Don Nacio. He finds the people so hungry that they will eat the horse's grain. A ranch hand calls them lazy and beats a child eating the grain. Zapata hits the man. Don Nacio tells him that violence is no good. He says, "Are you responsible to everybody? You can't be the conscience of the whole world." He reminds Zapata about his marriage plans and that the "president has drawn a circle around [his] name."

Aguirre and Gomez arrive from Texas. Aguirre says, "Up there the government governs with the consent of the people." Madero wants a message. Zapata, thinking of Josefa, tells him to find someone else. "I have private affairs. I don't want to be the conscience of the world. I don't want to be the conscience of anybody."

Circumstances again intervene when soldiers on horseback are seen leading an Indian with a rope tied around his neck. His crime was crawling through a fence to plant his corn. Zapata tells them to let him go. They gallop away, dragging the man behind.

Zapata visits Josefa's father, Señor Espejo (Florenz Ames), but he is given a "permanent and unchanging 'no'" after asking for Josefa's hand in marriage. He calls him a "man of substance without substance" and refuses to allow his daughter to sit "squatting on the bare earth patting tortillas like an Indian." Upset, Zapata leaves, saying that Espejo will relegate Josefa to a life as "queen of the warehouses and mistress of the receipt book." Soldiers grab him as he exits the house. The people in the square resist by clapping rocks together. Zapata is led away on a rope behind horses. Many Indians follow; some walk in front of the soldiers. The Indians tell the guards, "We're guarding the prisoner." The soldier releases Zapata, and before he can telegraph his superiors, they cut the telegraph lines.

Zapata and his men roll an unpowered draisine loaded with explosives down a canyon railroad track toward a train. It explodes and derails the train. They take powder and dynamite off the train but find no ammunition. At a military outpost, Indian women take bags with powder leaking from the bottoms to the outpost wall. Soldiers fire at them, and one woman lights the powder trail before dying. The walls tumble, and the villagers enter. While Zapata's men feed the people from the food stored there, Zapata sits at a raised table. Women salute him by bringing their children to him. A boy who stopped a Gatling gun is introduced to Zapata. He offers him a pig as reward, but the child wants Zapata's beautiful white horse. He decides to reward the boy with it.

Aguirre brings a paper to Zapata that Gomez reads. Francisco Madero has made Zapata general of the armies of the south. Señor Espejo invites him to dinner. He wears a bandolier. They ask questions of one another and give aphorisms as answers. News arrives that President Diaz has left the country. Josefa shocks her mother by kissing Zapata. Outside, Mano says that he has loved 100 women and does not understand why Zapata loves only one. Zapata and Josefa are married. That night, she finds Zapata out of bed and standing next to a window. He is worried that Madero has educated men around him. "My horse and my rifle won't help him," he says. He asks her to teach him to read. Josefa brings the Bible, and they start at Genesis.

Zapata and his men visit Madero. They ask when the village lands will be given back to the people. Madero says that it must be done under the rule of law. Madero shows Zapata a map with two streams and a house. He offers him the ranch as a common reward for generals. Zapata responds, "I did not fight for a ranch." Aguirre tells him, "The same men who governed before are now in that room. They have his ear." Madero asks Zapata to disband his army. Zapata takes his watch and gives him his rifle to show him how easily property can be taken. "Time is one thing to lawmakers, but to a farmer there's a time to plant and a time to harvest. And you cannot plant at harvest time." He seems to have reached Ecclesiastes 3 in learning to read.

General Victoriano Huerta (Frank Silvera) advises Madero to kill Zapata. Madero says that he does not shoot his own people. Huerta responds, "You'll learn." Privately, Huerta says, "Madero is a mouse, he can be handled. Zapata is a tiger. You have to kill a tiger." Madero visits Zapata's village and convinces them to disarm. Mano reports that his outposts have spotted Huerta with mounted troops. Madero claims that he can stop them. Mano dismounts Huerta's lead scout and dresses in his clothes. He leads Huerta's troops to Zapata's troops; however, Zapata's troops fail because Huerta's troops were prepared for their ambush. Later, Madero is placed under house arrest. He is taken to see Huerta at night, but once he leaves the car, he is assassinated.

Zapata and Mano question a man they suspect of treason, telling him, "244 good farmers with victory in their mouths will never chew it." The man is killed. Gomez is being held because he met with Madero before he was killed. He requests that Zapata kill him himself. Zapata meets Pancho Villa (Alan Reed) at the presidential palace. Villa plans only to be president of his ranch. He asks Zapata, "Can you read?" Zapata nods. "Then you're the president. I just appointed you. There isn't anyone else," Pancho Villa declares. As president, Zapata meets a delegation from Motelos who bring him a petition. After an awkward silence, they accuse Mano of taking the land that was distributed. Zapata tries to dismiss them without dealing with the problem, but one says, "The land can't wait. Stomachs can't wait." Zapata asks his name. He begins to circle the name "Hernandez" (Henry Silva) and recognizes the irony. Aguirre tries to prevent Zapata from leaving with them but is unable to do so.

Zapata arrives at his brother's house. Mano is on a sofa with a woman at his feet. Zapata asks, "Did you take the land from these people?" Mano assents, "I took their wives, too." Mano is killed in a shootout. Zapata decides to take his body home.

Men ride up to Zapata's cabin with news that a federal colonel is joining Zapata and will turn over his troops and ammunition to him. Josefa, afraid he will die if he goes, tries to stop him. If he dies, he says, he knows the people no longer need him. He adds, "Strong people don't need a strong man."

At the garrison, Zapata sees his white horse. A federal officer had killed the boy and taken the horse. The horse senses danger, and federal soldiers fire from above, killing Zapata. His body is dropped into the village plaza to show that the "tiger is dead." The people look at the body. "Who do they think they are fooling? He could be anybody. He's in the mountains. You couldn't find him now. If we need him again, he'll be back." The film ends with a vision of Zapata's white horse on the hill.

Bosley Crowther of the *New York Times* writes, "This ardent portrait of [Zapata] throbs with a rare vitality, and a masterful picture of a nation in revolutionary torment has been got by director Elia Kazan."[5] JMW

Notes

1. John Simon, "Elia Kazan: A Director's Notes," *New Criterion* 28, no. 1 (2009): 19.
2. Dan Georgakas, "Kazan, Kazan," *Cineaste* 36, no. 4 (2011): 4.

3. Jonathan M. Schoenwald, "Rewriting the Revolution: The Origins, Production, and Reception of *Viva Zapata!*" *Film History* 8, no. 2 (1996): 109.

4. "Trailer," *Viva Zapata!* directed by Elia Kazan (20th Century Fox, 2013), DVD.

5. Quoted in Schoenwald, "Rewriting the Revolution," 109.

Bibliography

Georgakas, Dan. "Kazan, Kazan." *Cineaste* 36, no. 4 (2011): 4–9.

Schoenwald, Jonathan M. "Rewriting the Revolution: The Origins, Production, and Reception of *Viva Zapata!*" *Film History* 8, no. 2 (1996): 109–30.

Simon, John. "Elia Kazan: A Director's Notes." *New Criterion* 28, no. 1 (2009): 18–19.

W

WAR AND PEACE (1956)

DIRECTOR: King Vidor
WRITERS: Bridget Boland, Robert Westerby, Mario Camerini, Ennio De Concini, Ivo Perilli, Gian Gaspare Napolitano, Mario Soldati, King Vidor. Based on the novel *Voyna i mir*, by Leo Tolstoy.
PRODUCERS: Dino De Laurentiis, Carlo Ponti (Paramount Pictures, Ponti-De Laurentiis Cinematografica)
CINEMATOGRAPHER: Jack Cardiff
EDITOR: Leo Cattozzo
COSTUMES: Maria De Matteis
MUSIC: Nino Rota
CAST: Natasha Rostova: Audrey Hepburn. Count Pierre Bezukhov: Henry Fonda. Prince Andrei Bolkonsky: Mel Ferrer. Anatole Kugarin: Vittorio Gassman. Helene Kuragina: Anita Ekberg. Maria Bolkonskaya: Anna Maria Ferrero. Sonya Rostova: May Britt. Count Nikolai Rostov: Jeremy Brett. Dolokhov: Helmut Dantine. Napoleon: Herbert Lom. Field Marshal Kutuzov: Oskar Homolka. Platon Karataev: John Mills. Prince Vasili Kugarin: Tullio Carminati. Countess Natalia Rostov: Lea Seidl. Prince Mikhail Andreevich Rostov: Barry Jones. Lisa Bolkonskaya: Milly Vitale. Prince Bolkonsky: Wilfrid Lawson. Denisov: Patrick Clean
AA: None
AAN: Best Director (King Vidor), Best Cinematography–Color (Jack Cardiff), Best Costume Design–Color (Maria De Matteis)
GG: Best Foreign-Language Film
GGN: Best Motion Picture–Drama, Best Motion Picture Actress–Drama (Audrey Hepburn), Best Motion Picture Director (King Vidor), Best Supporting Actor (Oskar Homolka)
DVD: Paramount Pictures, 2002
BLU-RAY: Currently unavailable
DURATION: 208 minutes

Although shunned by critics and audiences of its time, barely making a box-office return for the $6 million it cost to produce, King Vidor's lengthy epic of the famous Tolstoy novel still stands as a lavish production featuring some of the superstars of the time, a spectacular Battle of Borodino, the burning of Moscow, and the retreat and destruction of Napoleon's army. An American/Italian production containing international stars, in both good and mixed performances, *War and Peace* remains a testament to the Hollywood mode of cranking up big spectacles to win back audiences from their addiction to their televisions. Perhaps Sergei Bondarchuk's colossal eight-hour Russian version of the same novel in 1968 dimmed Vidor's epic even further (not to speak of the BBC/Time-Life Series TV version of 1973, directed by John Davis, with Anthony Hopkins), but even so it has not deprived it of the right to be reviewed and revisited. The

1950s Hollywood epics are a unique class of their own in Hollywood history, and they are based on certain cinematic practices—wide-screen, use of megastars, and, above all, spectacle that had no precedent—and they have never been repeated in the same mode, although they have left their mark on epic movie history.

War and Peace was filmed in VistaVision, a wide-screen version that allowed for a frame about three times the size of a normal 35mm frame.[1] Although this film has yet to be issued on Blu-ray, a well-preserved edition was issued on DVD beginning in 2002, for TV screens, that maintains the original width of ratio but reduces the length of the original, thus missing some of the wide images. This becomes important in the late sequences, when Napoleon's army is seen retreating during the Russian winter. As one would expect, the plot has been significantly condensed and some characters entirely omitted, and some sections of Tolstoy's four-volume massive novel, the Masonic rituals described in great detail when Pierre Bezukhov becomes a Freemason, as well as the two epilogues, were left out altogether.

The screenplay, written by seven writers, plus King Vidor, has a certain choppiness of plot and dialogue, especially in the first part of the movie, which deals with family relationships and the display of wealth in Russian society as the Napoleonic Wars approach. It is 1805, but peace still reigns in Russia's most "European" city, St. Petersburg, where Tolstoy's novel opens, at a soirée given by Anna Pavlovna Scherer, an aristocrat associated with the Tsarist Court, in whose chambers the cream of Russian society gathers.

The first seventy pages of the Tolstoy novel, which are mostly in French, are entirely omitted from the film, which opens at the Rostov's, an aristocratic and well-connected, but impoverished, family. Count Nikolai Rostov (Jeremy Brett) and his wife, Countess Natalia Rostov (Lea Seidl), have three young children (four in the Tolstoy novel), Natasha, thirteen; Nikolai, twenty; and the boy Petya, only nine. An orphan cousin, Sonya, fifteen, lives with them and is already in love with Nikolai. They are connected with several other families, but among their most important friends is Pierre Bezukhov (Henry Fonda), the illegitimate son of the very wealthy Count Bezukhov, who soon dies and leaves his favorite son (he had dozens of illegitimate children) all his wealth. Bezukhov is friends with Prince Andrei Bolkonsky (Mel Ferrer), who is unhappily married to Lise, a shallow socialite whom he soon leaves to go to war. Another family of importance is headed by Prince Vasili Kugarin (Tullio Carminati), who has a son, Anatole (Vittorio Gassman), and a daughter, Helene (Anita Ekberg). Anatole is a notorious womanizer who seduces Natasha (Audrey Hepburn) after she has promised to marry Andrei, who has left for the war. His sister Helene contrives a hasty marriage with the now-wealthy Pierre, a marriage that ends in disaster.

Another character of note is Dolokhov (Helmut Dantine), a friend of Anatole's, and just as amoral, reckless, and dangerous. When he openly flirts with Pierre's wife and openly insults Pierre, the latter challenges him to a duel and accidentally almost kills him. After that, Pierre and Helene are separated, but they don't quite leave the scene altogether. Helene helps her brother court Natasha, who naïvely believes he loves her, and she consents to elope with him. Pierre stops her in time, preventing a disastrous complication in her life by revealing to her that Anatole is already married. The first part of the movie ends with the Battle of Austerlitz, in which Andrei, heading a charge, is wounded and accidentally saved by Napoleon himself (Herbert Lom), who is riding by surveying the remains of the defeated Russian army. An armistice comes, and Andrei returns to St. Petersburg, where he witnesses his wife's death during childbirth.

The second part of the movie occupies itself mostly with Napoleon's invasion of Russia, his defeat of the Russian army at the Battle of Borodino, and his occupation of Moscow, which has been left empty of inhabitants and burning after the strategic retreat by Field Marshal Kutuzov (Oskar Homolka), who waits until winter, when Napoleon decides to leave the city, defeated by the lack of action and the Russian winter, a broken man. Pierre has been captured and taken prisoner during the retreat, suffering countless hardships by sheer willpower and a profound understanding of the futility of war. One cannot dismiss this movie as an empty Hollywood spectacle without acknowledging some fidelity to Tolstoy's work, with all the necessary omissions entailed by its sheer size. The line of narrative is clear, and some of the performances are worthwhile and even luminous.

Miscast as Pierre Bezukhov, Henry Fonda still gives an honest performance for a day's work. He looks anything but the Pierre of Tolstoy, loyally given by Bondarchuk, director of the 1968 Russian *War and Peace.* There, Pierre is portly, ungainly, and an object of ridicule among those aristocrats with whom he consorts early in the film. But Fonda's innate honesty as actor comes through, for, if anything, Bezukhov, an embodiment of Tolstoy (as is Konstantin Levin in *Anna Karenina*), is not the typical St. Petersburg aristocrat, intent on either gaining glory fighting or living a decadent life as a pleasure-seeking Russian aristocrat and woman chaser. Pierre seeks truth. At first enamored of Napoleon's glory, he thinks him the savior of the world who will sweep away corrupt governments and cleanse the world of the stigma of modern decadence; however, as the story progresses, Pierre sees the horror and devastation caused by Napoleon's invasion of his country, and he decides not to flee Moscow, as the others have. Instead, he plans to stay and kill Napoleon, but when he has a chance to do so, he stops short, not wanting to take another life. Pierre is not a man of action, but a surveyor of human endeavor—as one man says the gods are in *The Iliad*—but he is also human enough to have sinned, fallen in love, and endured incredible hardships during captivity. In the end, he rejoins society, when, after the death of Andrei, he becomes Natasha's husband.

The brightest star in this production is Audrey Hepburn as Natasha. Her slight frame, elegant posture, burning black eyes, and cheerful manner (for the most part) gave her a freshness and liveliness that few actresses of the time possessed. She is not the sexpot Anita Ekberg, who plays the decadent Helene Kuragina, but her spontaneous charm and Europeanized diction make her a standout character throughout the movie. The rest of the supporting cast, for the most part, consists of well-made choices. Mel Ferrer, trained in ballet dancing, has the elegance of a European star, rather than appearing as a stolid Russian one, and he admirably performs a troubled officer who escapes to war, honestly believing that his country needs him. In Tolstoy's book, his death is the most moving episode of the long story, a brokenhearted and repentant Natasha at his side. He dies a hero, perhaps in vain.

Of the other numerous characters, a few need to be mentioned here. Vittorio Gassman plays Anatole Kugarin with the charm of the devil, easily seducing Natasha with the help of his equally decadent sister Helene, the two vying, and almost betting, to see who will outdo the other in intrigue and deception. Tolstoy spots as the rock-bottom of Russian decadence a society riddled by greed, scandal, mock Europeanization, and aimless drifting into anarchy. The war cleanses them, thanks to the strategic sagacity of Field Marshal Kutuzov, who fights only one big battle before Moscow but wisely leaves an empty city to the vain, self-destructive dictator, allowing him to fall into his own strategic blunders. To make an analogy, Kutuzov is an Odysseus, rather than an Achilles, that role fitting the ambitious and valiant Prince Andrei.

Also worth mentioning is Platon Karataev (played admirably by John Mills), a saintly man dragged along with the prisoners during Napoleon's retreat, a man Pierre knows and admires for his saintly disposition, and whose death by execution at the hands of a French guard he witnesses. Karataev, it might be said, is perhaps the ultimate example of Pierre's redemption. At the end, Pierre no longer believes in divine salvation—he never crosses himself in hours of need, as others do—but he believes in humanity's ability to redeem itself, to free itself from conflicts, provided good men make a stand against those who seek to destroy it. CS

Note

1. Frank Beaver, *Dictionary of Film Terms* (New York: McGraw-Hill, 1983), 301.

Bibliography

Beaver, Frank. *Dictionary of Film Terms.* New York: McGraw-Hill, 1983.

Tolstoy, Leo. *War and Peace: The Maude Translation; Backgrounds and Sources; Essays in Criticism.* Edited by George Gibian. New York: W. W. Norton and Company, 1966.

APPENDIX A: SUPERHERO AND FRANCHISE EPICS

THE AMAZING SPIDER-MAN (2012)

Director: Marc Webb
Writers: James Vanderbilt, Alvin Sargent, Steve Kloves. Based on the Marvel comic book by Stan Lee and Steve Ditko.
Producers: Avi Arad, Laura Ziskin, Matt Tolmach (Columbia Pictures)
Cinematographer: John Schwartzman
Editors: Alan Edward Bell, Michael McCuster, Pietro Scalia
Production Design: J. Michael Riva
Art Direction: Page Buckner, Michael E. Goldman, David F. Klassen, Susan Wexler
Set Decoration: Leslie A. Pope
Costumes: Kim Barrett
Music: James Horner
Cast: Peter Parker/Spider-Man: Andrew Garfield. Gwen Stacy: Emma Stone. The Lizard/Dr. Curt Connors: Rhys Ifans. Capt. Stacy: Denis Leary. Uncle Ben: Martin Sheen. Aunt May: Sally Field. Flash Thompson: Chris Zylka. Dr. Rajit Ratha: Irfan Khan. Richard Parker: Campbell Scott. Mary Parker: Embeth Davitz. Jack's Father: C. Thomas Howell. Jack: Jake Ryan Keiffer. Store Clerk: Michael Barra. Peter Parker, Age 4: Max Charles
AA: None
AAN: None
DVD: Sony Pictures Home Entertainment, 2012
Blu-ray: Sony Pictures Home Entertainment, 2012. Three-disc combo, including Blu-ray, DVD, and digital copy.
Duration: 136 minutes

> It wasn't about the spider at all. It was about the man.
>
> —Matthew K. Manning, *Spider-Man: Inside the World of Your Friendly Neighborhood Hero*

The Amazing Spider-Man is a film about the iconic Marvel superhero that promises to tell a "different side" of the Peter Parker story, and it delivers. In this newly inspired interpretation, we find more than the adventures of the "science nerd bitten by a genetically altered spider"; we see a thoughtful and relevant American epic about a smart, although restless, teenager's search for his origins, purpose, and place in a seemingly chaotic world. Oh, and there is a solid superhero movie somewhere in there, too.

Set in New York City and its neighboring borough, Queens, and filmed in the gritty, urban, pedestrian, crowded halls of Midtown Science High School and the hypersleek, sanitized, glass ceilings of the high-tech superlab Oscorp, this could easily be mistaken for a generic adolescent science-fiction summer thriller with formulaic elements and little else. In fact, this film contains a multitude of formulaic devices, any one of which can prove sufficient fodder to fill an average superhero plot: a giant lizard menacing the city, a mad/genius scientist creating a formula that goes terribly wrong, the threat of contagion being inflicted on the people of a city, a skyscraper burning down in an explosion, a bridge collapsing, a plot to vaccinate veterans with experimental medications without their knowledge or consent. Yet, astonishingly, these events do not provide the primary action of this epic. That comes from something entirely different, and that's what sets this film apart.

Spider-Man creator Stan Lee intended that this superhero's character be developed into someone different from the other superheroes of the comic-book genre,[1] and this film explores that other, *different* side of him. The film opens when Peter is a mere child of four (played by Max Charles), and in the first few minutes of the action we learn a little about his backstory and how he came to be raised by his Uncle Ben (Martin Sheen) and Aunt May (Sally Field). This opening scene sets the stage for the rest of the film, as several props serve as visual memory points (specifically a toy lizard, eyeglasses, an encased spider, and a briefcase[2]) to aid the reader in keeping attuned to the unraveling plotline: Why did his parents leave him? When the teenage Peter (Andrew Garfield) accidentally discovers his father's briefcase, it sparks a memory that leads to a chain of events that produce the action of this epic. In pure Aristotelian style, Peter's use of reasoning, complete with hubristic flaws in judgment, produces the threads that comprise his own web of destiny, leading to his new persona as the amazing Spider-Man. The briefcase leads him to a photo of his father's partner, Dr. Curt Connors (Rhys Ifans), and also to his father's secret formula for human cell regrowth using cross-species genetics. Peter traces Dr. Connors to Oscorp, where he begins his web of deception, ironically entering the lab under an assumed name, but being recognized by his classmate, Gwen Stacy (Emma Stone), who is employed by Dr. Connors. (Peter also has a crush on her.) It is here that he again breaks the rules and, following another clue from the briefcase, enters the spider-laden lab where the infamous arachnid encounter takes place and he acquires unusual strengths.

Having gained an appreciation of his new abilities, Peter begins to show signs of transformation to Aunt May and Uncle Ben: getting into trouble in school, appreciating the feeling of revenge, and arrogance. Although concerned, they give him space. Peter ventures to Dr. Connors's house and introduces himself, during which time he passes off his father's equation as his own. (In this hubristic act, Peter falls victim to the fate of such mythic heroes as Phaethon, and he will soon pay the price.) The turning point of the action occurs when Uncle Ben asks Peter to pick up Aunt May since he had to take time off from work to get Peter out of trouble in school. Peter forgets to do it because he is at the lab testing the equation with Dr. Connors. In a culminating scene, Peter witnesses the death of Uncle Ben due to his *inaction*; we later see the terrifying effects on numerous people, including Dr. Connors, due to his flawed *action*. (Injecting the regrowth serum into his own disabled arm, Dr. Connors becomes deformed and turns into the villain the Lizard, and Spider-Man is forced to battle him while witnessing the devastation he causes, including the near-fatal loss of a young child named Jack and the firsthand terror of a father's grief at the thought of losing his son.) In between, he becomes a *cruzado de la noche* (night crusader), not to seek justice, as Captain Stacy says, but in search of revenge, and he dons a mask, not to seek revenge, as Uncle Ben says, but to hide his humiliation.

But thanks to the lessons learned from the everyday heroes he meets on his journey, for example, Jack's father (who brings himself and his team of brothers to Spider-Man's rescue in his time of need), Captain Stacy (who reminds Spider-Man that he is not alone when he is being taunted by the Lizard during a climactic battle), and ultimately Dr. Connors himself (who holds his arm out as a lifeline to the dying hero and saves him), Peter finds out what it is to be a man—to do the right thing, no matter what. At the end of the day, this film sings the epic tale of the amazing Spider-Man, America's hero. He is the American Everyman: superhero. Latex optional. MC

Notes

1. Speaking about his vision of Spider-Man in the foreword to Steve Saffel's *Spider-Man the Icon: The Life and Times of a Pop Culture Phenomenon*, Lee writes, "I had different aspirations for Peter Parker. I wanted him be frail and nerdy looking, inhibited and shy, scorned by the high school jocks and ignored by the female classmates, at least in the beginning."

2. For the more sophisticated symbol hunter, there is also an elaborate numerical scavenger hunt via posters and numbers that leads to a fascinating esoteric twist to the story's denouement: the number 36. Here is a small clue to get you started: the plot begins to unfold at Oscorp (the address is 3 Columbus Circle [a real place in history]); Peter's father met his mother on 9th Avenue (also known as Columbus Circle), and this is also where he happened to have purchased the infamous briefcase. The posters in the film are also great clues.

Bibliography

Manning, Matthew K. *Spider-Man: Inside the World of Your Friendly Neighborhood Hero.* New York: DK Publishing, 2012.

Saffel, Steve. *Spider-man the Icon: The Life and Times of a Pop Culture Phenomenon.* London: Titan Books, 2007.

ARMAGEDDON (1998)

DIRECTOR: Michael Bay
WRITERS: Tony Gilroy, Shane Salerno, Robert Roy Pool, Jonathan Hensleigh, J. J. Abrams
PRODUCERS: Jerry Bruckheimer, Gale Anne Hurd, Michael Bay (Touchstone Pictures, Jerry Bruckheimer Films, Valhalla Motion Pictures)
CINEMATOGRAPHER: John Schwartzman
EDITORS: Mark Goldblatt, Chris Lebenzon, Glen Scantlebury
PRODUCTION DESIGN: Michael White
ART DIRECTION: Geoff Hubbard, Lawrence A. Hubbs, Bruton Jones
SET DECORATION: Rick Simpson
COSTUMES: Michael Kaplan, Magali Guidasci
MUSIC: Trevor Rabin
SOUND EDITOR: George Watters II
SOUND MIXERS: Kevin O'Connell, Greg P. Russell, Keith A. Wester
VISUAL EFFECTS: Richard R. Hoover, Pat McClung, John Frazier
CAST: Harry Stamper: Bruce Willis. Dan Truman: Billy Bob Thornton. A. J. Frost: Ben Affleck. Grace Stamper: Liv Tyler. Chick: Will Patton. Rockhound: Steve Buscemi. Col. Willie Sharp: William Fichtner. Oscar Choi: Owen Wilson. Bear: Michael Clarke Duncan. Lev Andropov: Peter Stormare. Max: Ken Campbell. Copilot Jennifer Watts: Jessica Steen. Gen. Kimsey: Keith David. Flight Director Clark: Chris Ellis. Narrator: Charlton Heston
AA: None
AAN: Best Effects–Sound Effects Editing (George Watters II), Best Effects–Visual Effects (Richard R. Hoover, Pat McClung, John Frazier), Best Music–Original Song (Diane Warren for "I Don't Want to Miss a Thing"), Best Sound (Kevin O'Connell, Greg P. Russell, Keith A. Wester)
DVD: Buena Vista Home Entertainment, 1999
BLU-RAY: Touchstone Home Entertainment, 2010
DURATION: DVD, 147 minutes; Blu-Ray, 150 minutes

Armageddon is an end of the world science-fiction disaster epic in which an asteroid the size of Texas is hurtling toward Earth, threatening the destruction of every living organism (largely mirroring the plot of Mimi Leder's *Deep Impact*, which was released earlier in 1998). As narrator Charlton Heston (with the combined cultural associations of both the biblical epic and the 1970s disaster film) tells the audience, "it happened before" with the dinosaurs, and "it will happen again." The first warning signs come as meteors destroy the Space Shuttle *Atlantis* while it is in orbit, and meteorites bombard the planet, causing the requisite scenes of destruction. When the approaching asteroid is identified, NASA puts together a plan to drill a hole into it and blow it up with a nuclear bomb, with the blast sending the fragments clear of Earth. To undertake the mission, they call on the help of expert driller Harry Stamper (Bruce Willis) and his team, among them the talented but reckless A. J. Frost (Ben Affleck), who wants to marry Harry's daughter Grace (Liv Tyler), much to his objection. The ragtag bunch is put through intensive astronaut training before launching on shuttles *Freedom* and *Independence* to refuel at the Russian space station, but a fuel leak causes an explosion, and the crew, along with Russian Lev (Peter Stormare), barely escapes alive. One shuttle crash-lands, while the other overshoots the planned landing site, and the drilling proves particularly difficult. After many casualties, the bomb is set in place in the shaft. Harry stays behind to detonate it himself when the remote system is damaged, saying goodbye to his daughter and giving his blessing to A. J. Despite being widely canned by critics for its jingoistic heroics, *Armageddon* was the blockbuster hit of 1998 (being eclipsed by only Steven Spielberg's *Saving Private Ryan* at the domestic box office but exceeding it worldwide). DB

BATMAN (1989)

DIRECTOR: Tim Burton
WRITERS: Bob Kane, Sam Hamm, Warren Skaaren
PRODUCERS: Jon Peters, Peter Guber (Warner Bros.)
CINEMATOGRAPHER: Roger Pratt
EDITOR: Ray Lovejoy
PRODUCTION DESIGN: Anton Furst
ART DIRECTION: Terry Ackland-Snow, Nigel Phelps, Leslie Tomkins
SET DECORATION: Peter Young
COSTUMES: Bob Ringwood, Linda Henrikson
Music: Danny Elfman
CAST: Batman/Bruce Wayne: Michael Keaton. Joker/Jack Napier: Jack Nicholson. Vicki Vale: Kim Basinger. Alexander Knox: Robert Wuhl. Commissioner James Gordon: Pat Hingle. Harvey Dent: Billy Dee Williams. Alfred Pennyworth: Michael Gough. Carl Grissom: Jack Palance. Alicia Hunt: Jerry Hall. Bob the Goon: Tracey Walter. Mayor: Lee Wallace. Lt. Eckhardt: William Hootkins
AA: Best Art Direction–Set Decoration (Anton Furst, Peter Young)
DVD: Warner Bros., 2005
BLU-RAY: Warner Bros., 2010
DURATION: 126 minutes

After Superman heralded the beginning of the comic-book superheroes in 1938, the pantheon soon expanded, and Batman first appeared in *Detective Comics* #27 in May 1939, before headlining his own *Batman* comic in the spring of 1940, which is also when his adversary the Joker was introduced.[1] Tim Burton's film *Batman* follows the Joker's earliest origin story (there are several subsequent versions) from *Detective Comics* #168 (February 1951), in which he obtains his pale skin and ironic smile after falling into a vat of chemicals. The Joker (Jack Nicholson) uses the chemical plant to contaminate the city's household and personal products, causing an outbreak of fatal laughing fits. When the Mayor (Lee Wallace) decides to call off the city's bicentennial celebrations in light of the crisis, the Joker draws the populace out by offering to shower them with $20 million in cash, intending, rather, to continue his poisoning scheme at the occasion. His criminal activities are foiled by Batman, millionaire Bruce Wayne (Michael Keaton), who has taken to costumed vigilantism after witnessing his parents' murder. During the course of the film, he comes to realize that the Joker is responsible for their deaths.

Meanwhile, journalist Vicki Vale (Kim Basinger) tries to track down the truth behind reports of Batman and becomes romantically involved with Wayne. She also attracts the attention of the Joker, and in the film's finale, he drags her to the top of a gothic cathedral (in scenes that echo both Fritz Lang's 1927 *Metropolis* and Alfred Hitchcock's 1958 *Vertigo*), only to be rescued by Batman, and the Joker falls to his death. Director Tim Burton (*Beetlejuice*, 1988) brings what would become his trademark gothic, expressionistic vision to the city of Gotham, the film gaining an Oscar for its sets; however, with Prince's pop music, Keaton's high-waisted jeans, Basinger's big hair and even bigger ball gowns, it is also comically and fabulously 1980s in its styling. So, while at the time the film may well have seemed a "murky, brooding piece" without the "camp of the 1960s *Batman* TV series,"[2] from the retrospective vantage point of twenty-first-century superhero films, this seems like carnivalesque camp fun. *Batman* was a box-office smash. DB

Notes

1. Sheila Benson, "Movie Review: Bat Angst in Basic Black," *Los Angeles Times*, 23 June 1989, http://articles.latimes.com/1989-06-23/entertainment/ca-2570_1_bruce-wayne-kim-basinger-s-vicki-vale-jack-nicholson-s-joker (13 July 2013).
2. Benson, "Movie Review: Bat Angst in Basic Black."

Bibliography

Benson, Sheila. "Movie Review: Bat Angst in Basic Black." *Los Angeles Times*, 23 June 1989, http://articles.latimes.com/1989-06-23/entertainment/ca-2570_1_bruce-wayne-kim-basinger-s-vicki-vale-jack-nicholson-s-joker (13 July 2013).

BATMAN & ROBIN (1997)

DIRECTOR: Joel Schumacher
WRITERS: Bob Kane, Akiva Goldsman
PRODUCER: Peter Macgregor-Scott (Warner Bros.)
CINEMATOGRAPHER: Stephen Goldblatt
EDITOR: Dennis Virkler, Mark Stevens
PRODUCTION DESIGN: Barbara Ling
ART DIRECTION: Richard Holland, Geoff Hubbard
SET DECORATION: Corree Cooper
COSTUMES: Ingrid Ferrin, Robert Turturice
MUSIC: Elliot Goldenthal
CAST: Mr. Freeze/Dr. Victor Fries: Arnold Schwarzenegger. Batman/Bruce Wayne: George Clooney. Robin/Dick Grayson: Chris O'Donnell. Poison Ivy/Dr. Pamela Isley: Uma Thurman. Batgirl/Barbara Wilson: Alicia Silverstone. Alfred Pennyworth: Michael Gough. Commissioner Gordon: Pat Hingle. Dr. Jason Woodrue: John Glover. Julie Madison: Elle MacPherson. Ms. B. Haven: Vivica A. Fox. Nora Fries: Vendela Kirsebom Thomessen. Gossip Gerty: Elizabeth Sanders. Bane: Jeep Swenson
AA: None
AAN: None
DVD: Warner Bros., 2005
BLU-RAY: Warner Bros., 2010
DURATION: DVD, 126 minutes; Blu-ray, 130 minutes

As Batman (now George Clooney) and Robin (Chris O'Donnell) suit up for another adventure with director Joel Schumacher at the helm, we get close-up shots of their rubber-suited buttocks and cod-pieced crotches, brief moments of ridiculously excessive camp delight in an otherwise painfully tedious film. The pair is brought in to fight Mr. Freeze (Arnold Schwarzenegger), formerly Dr. Victor Fries, whose terminally ill wife is in cryogenic suspension, but after a lab accident, Fries/Freeze can only survive at low temperatures, making his way in the world with the help of a special diamond-powered suit. This means that he must embark on a series of diamond heists to survive. Also up against the caped crusaders is Poison Ivy (Uma Thurman), formerly Dr. Pamela Isley. Isley is working on a Wayne-funded research project looking at ways to help nature fight back against human mistreatment. Her henchman is Bane (Jeep Swenson), a chemically pumped muscleman and bondage party escapee. After being attacked by her lab partner, an incident during which she suffers exposure to dangerous chemicals, Isley finds that she has developed an intoxicating breath and a deadly kiss. As Thurman vamps it up with a carefully affected drawl, Poison Ivy's chemically enhanced charms create a rift between Batman and Robin. Meanwhile, Bruce Wayne's butler Alfred (Michael Gough) is dying of the same disease suffered by Freeze's wife. Alfred's orphaned niece Barbara (Alicia Silverstone) turns up, only to discover the household secret and become Batgirl. Poison Ivy and Freeze team up with a plan to freeze the city, paving the way for Poison Ivy to return it to nature. The bat team defeats the villains, but Batman successfully appeals to Freeze's remaining humanity to help save Alfred. Although both Ivy and Freeze are sent to Arkham Asylum, Batman promises Freeze access to laboratory facilities to help save his wife in return for his good deed.

George Clooney smiles at inappropriate moments, either unsure what to make of the meager role or faintly embarrassed by it, and his perfunctory romance with Julie Madison (Elle MacPherson) is dropped from the final wrap-up, one of many irrelevant and messily constructed plot points. *Batman & Robin* had such a hostile critical reception that Warner Bros. put the franchise on the backburner for eight years before its revival by Christopher Nolan. DB

BATMAN BEGINS (2005)

DIRECTOR: Christopher Nolan
WRITERS: Bob Kane, David S. Goyer, Christopher Nolan
PRODUCERS: Larry Franco, Charles Roven, Emma Thomas (Warner Bros., DC Comics, Syncopy/Patalex II Productions)
CINEMATOGRAPHER: Wally Pfister
EDITOR: Lee Smith
PRODUCTION DESIGN: Nathan Crowley
ART DIRECTION: Peter Francis, Paul Kirby, Simon Lamont, Dominic Masters, Alan Tomkins, Susan Whitaker
SET DECORATION: Paki Smith, Simon Wakefield
COSTUMES: Lindy Hemming
MUSIC: Hans Zimmer, James Newton Howard
CAST: Bruce Wayne/Batman: Christian Bale. Alfred: Michael Caine. Henri Ducard: Liam Neeson. Rachel Dawes: Katie Holmes. Jim Gordon: Gary Oldman. Dr. Jonathan Crane/The Scarecrow: Cillian Murphy. Carmine Falcone: Tom Wilkinson. Earle: Rutger Hauer. Ra's Al Ghul: Ken Watanabe. Flass: Mark Boone Junior. Thomas Wayne: Linus Roache. Lucius Fox: Morgan Freeman. Finch: Larry Holden. Judge Faden: Gerard Murphy. Loeb: Colin McFarlane. Martha Wayne: Sara Stewart. Bruce Wayne, Age 8: Gus Lewis

AA: None
AAN: Best Cinematography (Wally Pfister)
DVD: Warner Bros., 2005
BLU-RAY: Warner Bros., 2008
DURATION: 134 minutes

The premise of *Batman Begins* is not only to provide a detailed origin story for the legendary figure, but also to imagine how a mortal human might actually be capable of becoming a one-man crime-fighting machine. Director Christopher Nolan (previously known for his Oscar-nominated independent 2000 feature *Memento*) explains, "I wanted to try to do it in a more realistic fashion than anyone had ever tried to do a superhero film before," while at the same time giving it an old-fashioned epic, mythic treatment.[1] The young Bruce Wayne (Gus Lewis) experiences an early trauma when he falls down a well and is surrounded by bats, leaving him with a lifelong phobia. His sheltered aristocratic life is shattered when his parents are gunned down in front of him in the alleys of Gotham City, after he asks them to leave an opera early. Although the killer is put in jail, the adult Bruce (Christian Bale) seethes with unrealized, vengeful anger and guilt, and is beyond the reach of childhood friend Rachel (Katie Holmes) and faithful butler Alfred (Michael Caine), who raises him after his parents' death. Bruce disappears in Asia, where he is taken in by the mysterious League of Shadows, headed by Ra's Al Ghul (Ken Watanabe) and assisted by Henri Ducard (Liam Neeson), who instructs Bruce in advanced fighting techniques. But Bruce declines an offer to join the brotherhood, returning to Gotham City. Using the experimental products developed by his late father's colleague, Lucius Fox (Morgan Freeman), Bruce assumes the identity of the animal he fears most. Batman takes on Gotham's criminal figures, Carmine Falcone (Tom Wilkinson) and creepy psychiatrist Dr. Jonathan Crane (Cillian Murphy), whose plan to turn Gotham's residents against one another using psychotropic drugs turns out to be masterminded by Ducard. Batman foils the scheme with the help of Rachel and the only honest cop in town, Jim Gordon (Gary Oldman). The film may end with the requisite destructive chase and fight sequences, but the almost-romance is delicately handled, and the performances are excellent. DB

Note

1. Indeed, Nolan even compares Batman to the flawed hero Hercules of Greek mythology. Quoted in Andrew Pulver, "He's Not a God—He's Human," *Guardian*, 15 June 2005, www.guardian.co.uk/film/2005/jun/15/features.features11 (13 July 2013).

Bibliography

Pulver, Andrew. "He's Not a God—He's Human." *Guardian*, 15 June 2005, www.guardian.co.uk/film/2005/jun/15/features.features11 (13 July 2013).

BATMAN FOREVER (1995)

DIRECTOR: Joel Schumacher
WRITERS: Bob Kane, Lee Batchler, Janet Scott Batchler, Akiva Goldsman
PRODUCERS: Tim Burton, Peter Macgregor-Scott (Warner Bros.)
CINEMATOGRAPHER: Stephen Goldblatt
EDITORS: Mark Stevens, Dennis Virkler
PRODUCTION DESIGN: Barbara Ling
ART DIRECTION: Christopher Burian-Mohr, Joseph P. Lucky
SET DECORATION: Cricket Rowland
COSTUMES: Bob Ringwood, Ingrid Ferrin
MUSIC: Elliot Goldenthal
SOUND EDITORS: John Leveque, Bruce Stambler
SOUND MIXERS: Donald O. Mitchell, Frank A. Montaño, Michael Herbick, Petur Hliddal
CAST: Batman/Bruce Wayne: Val Kilmer. Harvey Two-Face/Harvey Dent: Tommy Lee Jones. Riddler/Edward Nygma: Jim Carrey. Dr. Chase Meridian: Nicole

Kidman. Robin/Dick Grayson: Chris O'Donnell. Alfred Pennyworth: Michael Gough. Commissioner Gordon: Pat Hingle. Sugar: Drew Barrymore. Spice: Debi Mazar. Gossip Gerty: Elizabeth Sanders. Dr. Burton: Rene Auberjonois
AA: None
AAN: Best Cinematography (Stephen Goldblatt), Best Effects–Sound Effects Editing (John Leveque, Bruce Stambler), Best Sound (Donald O. Mitchell, Frank A. Montaño, Michael Herbick, Petur Hliddal)
DVD: Warner Bros., 2000
Blu-ray: Warner Bros., 2010
Duration: 122 minutes

Joel Schumacher took over the Batman film franchise (with Tim Burton staying on as producer), upping the camp factor, while musical flurries reminiscent of the 1966–1968 television program in Elliot Goldenthal's score emphasize the return to an earlier style of Batman, even among the still-gothic expanse of Gotham City. Val Kilmer assumes the role of Bruce Wayne, who rejects an experimental project suggested by his idolizing employee, Edward Nygma (Jim Carrey), to make 3D television by manipulating audience members' brainwaves. Edward becomes a successful businessman selling his 3D units, but in his dual identity as the Riddler, he sends Wayne a series of disturbing riddles. Wayne seeks the advice of psychologist Dr. Chase Meridian (Nicole Kidman), who has been brought to Gotham City to help deal with another adversary, Harvey Two-Face (Tommy Lee Jones). Two-Face has a grudge against Batman for failing to protect him from the acid attack that left one side of his face deformed. Although Chase is infatuated with Batman, she goes on a date with Bruce, until Two-Face interrupts the charity circus event with a bomb. While acrobat Dick Grayson (Chris O'Donnell) is able to dispose of it, his family dies. Bruce takes in the traumatized young man, but Dick's curiosity leads him to discover the bat cave, after which he assumes his own superhero identity as Robin. Also making a new double act are the Riddler and Two-Face, and at the launch of a new interactive addition to his television technology, the Riddler is able to extract Bruce's thoughts, revealing his double identity as Batman. Chase is kidnapped and Robin captured in the rescue attempt, but Batman is able to prevail.

While the villains are entertaining, Kidman could do little with some truly terrible lines, and Kilmer's Wayne is repressed to the point of being comatose. It is Wayne's butler Alfred (Michael Gough) who emerges the sleeper character whose story we might rather have been told, given that he claims responsibility for Robin's fetishistic new suit, complete with faux nipples. A mixed critical reception did not hurt the healthy box-office returns. DB

BATMAN RETURNS (1992)

Director: Tim Burton
Writers: Bob Kane, Daniel Waters, Sam Hamm
Producers: Denise Di Novi, Tim Burton (Warner Bros.)
Cinematographer: Stefan Czapsky
Editors: Chris Lebenzon, Bob Badami
Production Design: Bo Welch
Art Direction: Tom Duffield, Rick Heinrichs
Set Decoration: Cheryl Carasick
Costumes: Bob Ringwood, Mary Vogt
Music: Danny Elfman
Visual Effects: Michael Fink, Craig Barron, John Bruno, Dennis Skotak
Makeup Artists: Ve Neill, Ronnie Specter, Stan Winston
Cast: Batman/Bruce Wayne: Michael Keaton. Penguin/Oswald Cobblepot:

Danny DeVito. Catwoman/Selina: Michelle Pfeiffer. Max Shreck: Christopher Walken. Alfred: Michael Gough. Mayor: Michael Murphy. Ice Princess: Cristi Conaway. Chip: Andrew Bryniarski. Commissioner Gordon: Pat Hingle
AA: None
AAN: Best Effects–Visual Effects (Michael Fink, Craig Barron, John Bruno, Dennis Skotak), Best Makeup (Ve Neill, Ronnie Specter, Stan Winston)
DVD: Warner Bros., 2000
Blu-ray: Warner Bros., 2010
Duration: 126 minutes

Tim Burton's second outing for the *Batman* franchise was also a box-office blockbuster, with Batman this time up against multiple foes. The aristocratic Cobblepot family disposes of their deformed and violent infant son in a stream, where the infant travels through the sewers to arrive at the abandoned penguin habitat at Gotham's old zoo. Some thirty-three years later, Gotham City's lauded businessman, Max Shreck (Christopher Walken), is kidnapped and taken to the city sewers, where the Cobblepot infant has become the Penguin (Danny DeVito). The Penguin blackmails Shreck with evidence of his unethical and criminal dealings, forcing him to agree to help the Penguin gain acceptance in the world above. When Shreck returns to work, he finds that his self-conscious secretary Selina (Michelle Pfeiffer) has stumbled upon his nefarious plans to drain Gotham's power supply. Shreck pushes her out of the office window, but she miraculously survives, and upon returning to her lonely pink apartment, the former secretary proceeds to dispose of her little-girl trappings and make herself a cat suit, as the city's alley cats look on.

In a well-orchestrated stunt, the Penguin saves the mayor's (Michael Murphy) baby, and Shreck maneuvers to have the Penguin become the new mayor. In her new secret identity as Catwoman, Selina starts exacting revenge on Shreck by blowing up one of his stores. She is confronted by Batman, and the two have a kinky "vinyl versus rubber" fight that Batman wins. Meanwhile, Selina and Bruce begin an awkward romance but soon discover one another's alternate identities.

Catwoman invites the Penguin to join forces but is momentarily disturbed when he arranges the death of Gotham's beauty queen, framing Batman for the crime. The Penguin turns against his ally when Catwoman rejects his sexual advances, but Catwoman appears to have taken on the mythical nine lives of her namesake. Batman exposes the insincerity of the Penguin to the people, and the Penguin retaliates by equipping his army of penguins with missiles. But Batman diverts them back to the zoo, and the Penguin dies in toxic waste. Catwoman electrocutes Shreck and, despite being shot several times, survives to fight another day. The film's grotesque, circus aesthetics are strangely appealing, and Pfeiffer's acidic Catwoman is delightful; however, the plot is too messy and Batman himself fades into the background as the supposed heroic focus. DB

THE DARK KNIGHT (2008)

Director: Christopher Nolan
Writers: Bob Kane, Jonathan Nolan, Christopher Nolan, David S. Goyer
Producers: Emma Thomas, Charles Roven, Christopher Nolan (Warner Bros., Legendary Pictures, DC Comics, Syncopy)
Cinematographer: Wally Pfister
Editor: Lee Smith
Production Design: Nathan Crowley
Art Direction: Nathan Crowley
Set Decoration: Peter Lando
Costumes: Lindy Hemming
Music: Hans Zimmer, James Newton Howard

Sound Editor: Richard King
Sound Mixers: Lora Hirschberg, Gary Rizzo, Ed Novick
Visual Effects: Nick Davis, Chris Corbould, Timothy Webber, Paul J. Franklin
Makeup Artists: John Caglione Jr., Conor O'Sullivan
Cast: Bruce Wayne: Christian Bale. Joker: Heath Ledger. Harvey Dent: Aaron Eckhart. Alfred: Michael Caine. Rachel: Maggie Gyllenhaal. Gordon: Gary Oldman. Lucius Fox: Morgan Freeman. Ramirez: Monique Gabriela Curnen. Wuertz: Ron Dean. Scarecrow: Cillian Murphy. Lau: Chin Han. Mayor: Nestor Carbonell
AA: Best Sound Editing (Richard King), Best Supporting Actor (Heath Ledger, posthumously)
AAN: Best Art Direction (Nathan Crowley, Peter Lando), Best Cinematography (Wally Pfister), Best Film Editing (Lee Smith), Best Makeup (John Caglione Jr., Conor O'Sullivan), Best Sound Mixing (Lora Hirschberg, Gary Rizzo, Ed Novick), Best Visual Effects (Nick Davis, Chris Corbould, Timothy Webber, Paul J. Franklin)
DVD: Warner Bros., 2009
Blu-ray: Warner Bros., 2008
Duration: 152 minutes

In *The Dark Knight*, director Christopher Nolan and lead Christian Bale team up once again following their 2005 *Batman Begins*, with Maggie Gyllenhaal taking over the role of Rachel from Katie Holmes. Lieutenant Jim Gordon (Gary Oldman) and District Attorney Harvey Dent (Aaron Eckhart), with the after-hours assistance of Batman, finally begin to make real inroads in their fight against crime. The partnership is an uneasy one, however, because Dent is dating Bruce Wayne's former love, Rachel. As the remaining crime syndicate begins to feel the pressure, the criminals reluctantly accept the assistance of the Joker (Heath Ledger), a scarred man in every sense of the word. It soon becomes clear that the Joker is not even interested in money, but rather anarchy, nor is he interested in defeating Batman, but rather revels in their antagonistic relationship. When Dent and Rachel are kidnapped by the Joker, only Dent survives, albeit horrendously burnt and disfigured on one side of his face. Disillusioned and deranged, "Two-Face" Dent sets out to get revenge on Gordon, not the Joker. Batman saves Gordon's family, and Dent dies, but in the interest of maintaining the memory of Dent as a hero for the city of Gotham, Batman takes the blame for his misdeeds.

With a budget of $185 million, the film made more than $1 billion worldwide. *The Dark Knight* garnered two Academy Awards, one of them posthumously awarded to Heath Ledger for his performance as the Joker. As critic David Stratton writes, "*The Dark Knight* will always be remembered for Ledger's unforgettable, genuinely creepy villain."[1] Although Batman himself pales in comparison, as with *Batman Begins*, the film benefits from being more of a psychological thriller than a typical superhero movie. DB

Note

1. David Stratton, "Heath Ledger's Brilliance Gives Batman Film a Better Class of Villain," *Australian*, 11 July 2008, www.theaustralian.com.au/arts/ledger-brilliance-gives-batman-class/story-e6frg8n6-1111116882869 (22 June 2013).

Bibliography

Stratton, David. "Heath Ledger's Brilliance Gives Batman Film a Better Class of Villain." *Australian*, 11 July 2008, www.theaustralian.com.au/arts/ledger-brilliance-gives-batman-class/story-e6frg8n6-1111116882869 (22 June 2013).

THE DARK KNIGHT RISES (2012)

Director: Christopher Nolan
Writers: Bob Kane, Jonathan Nolan, Christopher Nolan, David S. Goyer

Producers: Emma Thomas, Christopher Nolan, Charles Roven (Warner Bros., Legendary Pictures, DC Comics, Syncopy)
Cinematographer: Wally Pfister
Editor: Lee Smith
Production Design: Nathan Crowley, Kevin Kavanaugh
Art Direction: James Hambidge, Naaman Marshall
Set Decoration: Peter Lando
Costumes: Lindy Hemming
Music: Hans Zimmer
Cast: Bruce Wayne: Christian Bale. Commissioner Gordon: Gary Oldman. Bane: Tom Hardy. Blake: Joseph Gordon-Levitt. Selina: Anne Hathaway. Miranda Tate: Marion Cotillard. Fox: Morgan Freeman. Alfred: Michael Caine. Foley: Matthew Modine. Dr. Pavel: Alon Moni Aboutboul. Daggett: Ben Mendelsohn. Stryver: Burn Gorman. Capt. Jones: Daniel Sunjata
AA: None
AAN: None
DVD: Warner Bros., 2012
Blu-ray: Warner Bros., 2013
Duration: 165 minutes

Christopher Nolan's third and (reportedly) final installment to his Batman trilogy will, unfortunately, be forever tainted by the tragic events at the film's midnight screening in Aurora, Colorado, where twelve people were shot dead and seventy injured. Warner Bros. delayed their announcement of box-office takings and made a donation to a charity supporting the victims.

The film begins as Batman has been in hiding for some eight years, after taking the blame for Harvey Dent's murder. Bruce Wayne (Christian Bale) has become a recluse, unable to move on with a life of his own after the death of his childhood sweetheart, Rachel. Cat burglar Selina (Anne Hathaway) robs Wayne of his mother's pearls, her real objective being to get his fingerprints to sell in exchange for a fresh start. When Commissioner Gordon (Gary Oldman) stumbles across the creepy, masked Bane (Tom Hardy) hiding with his henchmen in the sewers of the Gotham City, only rookie cop Blake (Joseph Gordon-Levitt) believes him, seeking out Bruce Wayne to ask for the help of Batman. Bane and his men violently take over the stock exchange, ruining Wayne Enterprises in the process. Although Batman approaches Catwoman (she is not explicitly called this in the film) for help in fighting Bane, she turns him over to protect herself, and Wayne ends up in a foreign underground prison. Meanwhile, Bane turns Wayne Enterprises' shelved nuclear power reactor into a bomb and takes over the city, letting the people of Gotham turn against its wealthy elite.[1] Wayne eventually escapes, only to discover that the real villain is supposed clean energy advocate and love interest Miranda Tate (Marion Cotillard), the daughter of his old foe Ducard. With Catwoman's help, Batman saves the city, staging his own death in the process and "retiring" with Selina. Blake, whose first name is actually Robin, discovers the bat cave and, we assume, his own heroic destiny. Although perhaps too long, the film's reimagining of Catwoman is particularly well done, as we are left genuinely unsure of her next move. DB

Note

1. With its mock trials held by a vengeful populace, Mark Fisher argues that the film's vision of the financial crisis "demonises collective action against capital while asking us to put our hope and faith in a chastened rich." Mark Fisher, "Batman's Political Right Turn," *Guardian*, 23 July 2012, www.guardian.co.uk/commentisfree/2012/jul/22/batman-political-right-turn?INTCMP=SRCH (14 July 2013).

Bibliography

Fisher, Mark. "Batman's Political Right Turn." *Guardian*, 23 July 2012, www.guardian.co.uk/commentisfree/2012/jul/22/batman-political-right-turn?INTCMP=SRCH (14 July 2013).

HARRY POTTER AND THE CHAMBER OF SECRETS (2002)

Director: Chris Columbus
Writer: Steve Kloves. Based on novel by J. K. Rowling.
Producers: Chris Columbus, Michael Barnathan, David Barron, Mark Radcliffe (Heyday Films, 1492 Pictures)
Cinematographer: Roger Pratt
Editor: Peter Honess
Production Design: Stuart Craig
Art Direction: John King, Neil Lamont
Set Decoration: Stephenie McMillan
Costumes: Lindy Hemming
Music: John Williams
Cast: Harry Potter: Daniel Radcliffe. Hermione Granger: Emma Watson. Ron Weasley: Rupert Grint. Professor Albus Dumbledore: Richard Harris. Professor Minerva McGonagall: Maggie Smith. Severus Snape: Alan Rickman. Rubeus Hagrid: Robbie Coltrane. Draco Malfoy: Tom Felton. Neville Longbottom: Matthew Lewis. Ginny Weasley: Bonnie Wright. Uncle Vernon Dursley: Richard Griffiths. Aunt Petunia Dursley: Fiona Shaw. Dudley Dursley: Harry Melling. Professor Gilderoy Lockhart: Kenneth Branagh. Tom Marvolo Riddle: Christian Coulson. Moaning Myrtle: Shirley Henderson. Dobby the House Elf (voice): Toby Jones
AA: None
AAN: None
DVD: Warner Bros., 2003. Complete eight-film collection, Warner Bros., 2011.
Blu-ray: Warner Bros., 2007
Duration: 161 minutes (174 for extended version)

In this second, darker film, Harry (Daniel Radcliffe) returns to Hogwart's, despite the house elf, Dobby's (Toby Jones), best efforts to keep him at home for his second year. Harry has several confrontations with Draco Malfoy (Tom Felton) and his father, who represent the elite, or "pure-bloods," in the wizarding world. Ron's (Rupert Grint) younger sister, Ginny (Bonnie Wright), enters Hogwart's to become the damsel in distress of the film. Voldemort's origin as Tom Riddle (Christian Coulson) is revealed in his diary, which exerts an alarming power over Ginny. The Chamber of Secrets houses a basilisk that Harry, using the Sword of Gryffindor, defeats, saving Ginny and destroying Riddle (or at least this manifestation). Later films reveal that the diary contained a Horcrux, a part of Voldemort's soul anchored to earth. This is the last film in which Richard Harris appears as Dumbledore. By the end of this film, our heroes have once again triumphed over the immediate threat, but Harry and his friends leave Hogwarts under a shadow. However, Dobby becomes a free elf. JMW

HARRY POTTER AND THE DEATHLY HALLOWS: PART 1 (2010)

Director: David Yates
Writer: Steve Kloves. Based on novel by J. K. Rowling.
Producers: David Barron, David Heyman, J. K. Rowling, Lionel Wigram (Warner Bros., Heyday Films)
Cinematographer: Eduardo Serra
Editor: Mark Day
Production Design: Stuart Craig
Art Direction: Andrew Ackland-Snow
Set Decoration: Stephenie McMillan
Costumes: Jany Temime
Music: Alexandre Desplat
Visual Effects: Tim Burke, John Richardson, Christian Manz, Nicolas Aithadi
Makeup Artists: Amanda Knight, Nick Dudman, Lisa Tomblin
Cast: Harry Potter: Daniel Radcliffe. Hermione Granger: Emma Watson. Ron Weasley: Rupert Grint. Uncle Vernon Dursley: Richard Griffiths. Aunt Petunia Dursley: Fiona Shaw. Dudley Dursley: Harry Melling. Professor Albus Dumbledore: Michael Gambon. Fenrir

Greyback: Dave Legeno. Severus Snape: Alan Rickman. Rubeus Hagrid: Robbie Coltrane. Cormac McLaggen: Freddie Stroma. Lavender Brown: Jessie Cave. Draco Malfoy: Tom Felton. Neville Longbottom: Matthew Lewis. Ginny Weasley: Bonnie Wright. James Potter: Adrian Rawlins. Lily Potter: Geraldine Somerville. Remus Lupin: David Thewlis. Dolores Umbridge: Imelda Staunton. Bellatrix Lestrange: Helena Bonham Carter. Wormtail: Timothy Spall. Luna Lovegood: Evanna Lynch. Nymphadora Tonks: Natalia Tena. Minister Rufus Scrimgeour: Bill Nighy. Xenophilius Lovegood: Rhys Ifans. Lord Voldemort: Ralph Fiennes. Kreacher (voice): Simon McBurney. Dobby (voice): Toby Jones

AA: None

AAN: Best Art Direction–Set Decoration (Stuart Craig, Stephenie McMillan), Best Visual Effects (Tim Burke, John Richardson, Christian Manz, Nicolas Aithadi)

BAFTA Award Nominations: Best Special Visual Effects (Tim Burke, John Richardson, Christian Manz, Nicolas Aithadi), Best Makeup/Hair (Amanda Knight, Nick Dudman, Lisa Tomblin)

DVD: Warner Bros., 2011. Complete eight-film collection, Warner Bros., 2011.

Blu-ray: Warner Bros., 2011

Duration: 146 minutes

In this last installment (in two parts) in the series, Harry (Daniel Radcliffe) does not return to Hogwart's at the beginning of the film. Days from his seventeenth birthday, which is the age of wizard adulthood, Harry leaves the Muggle home of his aunt and uncle for the last time, breaking the charm that has protected him from Voldemort (Ralph Fiennes). Voldemort nearly destroys Harry during this transfer; Harry loses Hedwig, his owl, in the battle. While at the Weasley's, Harry, Ron (Rupert Grint), and Hermione (Emma Watson) help with a wedding and plan their Horcrux hunt. Before they leave, they receive three of the four bequests Dumbledore (Michael Gambon) made them: Dumbledore's Deluminator, a copy of *Tales from Beedle the Bard*, and the snitch Harry captured in his first quidditch match. In the midst of a wedding celebration, news arrives that the Ministry has fallen—Harry, Ron, and Hermione are on the run. Thanks to Hermione's magical abilities, they travel with a tent, books, and clothing in one small purse. They run to Sirius's home, which now belongs to Harry, including the house elf, Kreacher (Simon McBurney), who helps them locate the real Horcrux locket. Unfortunately, this refuge is revealed in their efforts, and they begin to travel throughout England, camping in a new place each night.

Dissention builds between the companions as the influence of the Horcrux, paired with little food and no clear plan for finding more, culminates in Ron's abrupt departure. After a disastrous visit to Godric's Hollow, the home of both Harry and Dumbledore, where Harry's wand is destroyed, the Sword of Gryffindor miraculously appears and Ron returns. Ron destroys the locket-Horcrux, overcoming its temptation. In pursuit of the Deathly Hallows, the three pay a visit to Luna's father and hear the "Tale of the Three Brothers" and learn of the three hallows: the Elder Wand, the Resurrection Stone, and the Cloak of Invisibility. Death Eaters, summoned by Mr. Lovegood (Rhys Ifans), nearly catch them.

Since the air battle at the beginning of the film, Voldemort has been curiously absent. Harry receives glimpses of Voldemort seeking something on the continent. Harry becomes convinced that Voldemort seeks the Elder Wand. Shortly after this adventure, Harry, Ron, and Hermione are captured by "Snatchers," who take them to Malfoy Manor, where they realize another

Horcrux lies in the Malfoy vault of Gringot's Bank. Harry manages to reach help, and Dobby comes to him in the dungeons of Malfoy Manor. He helps to battle their way out; in the process, Draco (Tom Felton) and Bellatrix (Helena Bonham Carter) are disarmed, but Dobby, as he takes Harry, Ron, and Hermione to safety, is fatally wounded by Bellatrix's knife. Harry mourns yet another death and buries Dobby. JMW

HARRY POTTER AND THE DEATHLY HALLOWS: PART 2 (2011)

DIRECTOR: David Yates
WRITER: Steve Kloves. Based on novel by J. K. Rowling.
PRODUCERS: David Barron, David Heyman, J. K. Rowling, Lionel Wigram (Warner Bros., Heyday Films, Moving Picture Company)
CINEMATOGRAPHER: Eduardo Serra
EDITOR: Mark Day
PRODUCTION DESIGN: Stuart Craig
ART DIRECTION: Andrew Ackland-Snow, Neil Lamont
SET DECORATION: Stephenie McMillan
COSTUMES: Jany Temime
MUSIC: Alexandre Desplat
SOUND EDITOR: James Mather
SOUND MIXERS: Stuart Wilson, Stuart Hilliker, Mike Dowson, Adam Scrivener
VISUAL EFFECTS: Tim Burke, John Richardson, David Vickery, Greg Butler
MAKEUP ARTISTS: Amanda Knight, Nick Dudman, Lisa Tomblin
CAST: Harry Potter: Daniel Radcliffe. Hermione Granger: Emma Watson. Ron Weasley: Rupert Grint. Professor Albus Dumbledore: Michael Gambon. Fenrir Greyback: Dave Legeno. Severus Snape: Alan Rickman. Griphook/Professor Filius Flitwick: Warwick Davis. Rubeus Hagrid: Robbie Coltrane. Cormac McLaggen: Freddie Stroma. Lavender Brown: Jessie Cave. Draco Malfoy: Tom Felton. Young Petunia Dursley: Ariella Paradise. Neville Longbottom: Matthew Lewis. Ginny Weasley: Bonnie Wright. James Potter: Adrian Rawlins. Young James Potter: Alfie McIlwain. Lily Potter: Geraldine Somerville. Young Lily Potter: Ellie Darcey-Alden. Remus Lupin: David Thewlis. Bellatrix Lestrange: Helena Bonham Carter. Wormtail: Timothy Spall. Luna Lovegood: Evanna Lynch. Nymphadora Tonks: Natalia Tena. Griphook/Professor Filius Flitwick: Warwick Davis. Aberforth Dumbledore: Ciarán Hinds. Lord Voldemort: Ralph Fiennes. Ollivander: John Hurt
AA: None
AAN: Best Art Direction–Set Decoration (Stuart Craig, Stephenie McMillan), Best Makeup (Amanda Knight, Nick Dudman, Lisa Tomblin), Best Visual Effects (Tim Burke, John Richardson, David Vickery, Greg Butler)
BAFTA AWARD: Best Special Visual Effects (Tim Burke, John Richardson, David Vickery, Greg Butler)
BAFTA AWARD NOMINATIONS: Best Production Design (Stuart Craig, Stephenie McMillan), Best Sound (James Mather, Stuart Wilson, Stuart Hilliker, Mike Dowson, Adam Scrivener), Best Makeup/Hair (Amanda Knight, Nick Dudman, Lisa Tomblin)
DVD: Warner Bros., 2011. Complete eight-film collection, Warner Bros., 2011.
BLU-RAY: Warner Bros., 2011
DURATION: 130 minutes

This last film begins where the last one ended, at the grave of Dobby, a "Free Elf"; however, Harry (Daniel Radcliffe) realizes that action must be taken. In his conversations with Griphook (Warwick Davis), the Gringott's goblin, and Ollivander (John Hurt), the wand-maker, Harry realizes that Dumbledore's grave contains the Elder Wand, and he is certain that Voldemort (Ralph Fiennes) is on his way to collect it. But Harry decides to pursue Horcruxes, not Hallows, and convinces Griphook to help them enter the Malfoy vault. With Ron (Rupert Grint) and Hermione (Emma Watson), Harry succeeds in finding the Horcrux in the vault, but he is almost undone by Griphook's treachery. Nonetheless, he and his friends manage to escape on the back of a dragon. On the heels of their escape, Voldemort arrives and, in a fury, kills everyone in Gringott's. The sword of Gryffindor, which Griphook had taken, disappears under his dead hand. At this moment, Voldemort realizes that Harry is hunting his Horcruxes. Through his link with Voldemort, Harry catches a glimpse of Hogwart's. Convinced that the last Horcrux is somewhere in the school, he and his friends "disapparate" to Hogsmeade, the village outside the school. Aberforth (Ciarán Hinds), Dumbledore's brother, rescues them from the Death Eaters patrolling the village, but he also challenges Harry's dedication to Dumbledore. Yet, Aberforth helps them enter Hogwart's, and they find the Room of Requirement filled with rebellious students. Again, with the help of friends, Harry locates the next Horcrux and destroys it.

As he is searching, Voldemort launches his attack on Hogwart's. Snape (Alan Rickman) is expelled from the school, and the instructors mount their defense, a combination of intangible protection spells and explosive charges. In a nod to *Bedknobs and Broomsticks* (1971), the suits of armor throughout the school come to life. Certain that the Elder Wand is not truly his, Voldemort kills Snape. Harry and his friends come to the side of the dying Snape, who instructs Harry to take his memories to the Pensieve. Snape dies gazing into Harry's eyes. In the Pensieve, Harry sees the life story of Snape, which reveals that he loved Lily Evans (Potter) and tried his best to save her from Voldemort. We also learn that Dumbledore is convinced that Harry himself is a Horcrux and needs to die. Harry is left to accept that his death will help destroy Voldemort. Opening the snitch that contains the Resurrection Stone, Harry is comforted by his dead family and friends and goes to confront Voldemort, who strikes him with the killing curse. Harry awakens to find himself in a white space. Dumbledore (Michael Gambon) emerges from the light to congratulate him and tell him that he has a choice: to return or "go on."

Harry chooses to return and finds Voldemort recovering from the death of the Horcrux within Harry. Voldemort and his followers march back to Hogwart's triumphant, carrying Harry's limp body. Led by Neville (Matthew Lewis), Hogwarts still stands against Voldemort, and the last battle begins as Harry reveals that he is still alive. Harry pursues Voldemort while the others pursue the snake, now truly the last Horcrux. Neville draws the Sword of Gryffindor from the Sorting Hat and cuts off the head of the snake. Harry and Voldemort tumble to the courtyard after Harry reveals that he, not Snape, is the true master of the Elder Wand. Their final duel ends with the Elder Wand spinning from Voldemort's hand into Harry's. Voldemort flakes to dust in the wind. Inside the school, the last of the Death Eaters are destroyed. Outside, Ron and Hermione join Harry on a stone bridge, where Harry breaks the Elder Wand and throws it into the abyss. He has dropped the Resurrection Stone in the forest. Only the Cloak remains of the Deathly Hallows. We can assume that Harry will pass it to his son, as it was passed on to Harry. The final scene of the film goes nineteen years into the future, where Harry and his friends are seeing their own children off to Hogwart's. The final frame zooms in on the three friends. JMW

HARRY POTTER AND THE GOBLET OF FIRE (2005)

DIRECTOR: Mike Newell
WRITER: Steve Kloves. Based on novel by J. K. Rowling.
PRODUCER: David Heyman (Warner Bros., Heyday Films)
CINEMATOGRAPHER: Roger Pratt
EDITOR: Mick Audsley
PRODUCTION DESIGN: Stuart Craig
ART DIRECTION: Andrew Ackland-Snow, Neil Lamont
SET DECORATION: Stephenie McMillan
COSTUMES: Jany Temime
MUSIC: Patrick Doyle
VISUAL EFFECTS: Jim Mitchell, John Richardson, Timothy Webber, Tim Alexander
MAKEUP ARTISTS: Amanda Knight, Eithne Fennel, Nick Dudman
CAST: Harry Potter: Daniel Radcliffe. Hermione Granger: Emma Watson. Ron Weasley: Rupert Grint. Professor Albus Dumbledore: Michael Gambon. Professor Minerva McGonagall: Maggie Smith. Severus Snape: Alan Rickman. Rubeus Hagrid: Robbie Coltrane. Draco Malfoy: Tom Felton. Neville Longbottom: Matthew Lewis. Ginny Weasley: Bonnie Wright. James Potter: Adrian Rawlins. Lily Potter: Geraldine Somerville. Frank Bryce: Eric Sykes. Cedric Diggory: Robert Pattinson. Wormtail (Peter Pettigrew): Timothy Spall. Professor Alastor "MadEye" Moody: Brendan Gleeson. Sirius Black: Gary Oldman. Bartemius "Barty" Crouch Junior: David Tennant. Lord Voldemort: Ralph Fiennes
AA: None
AAN: Best Art Direction–Set Decoration (Stuart Craig, Stephenie McMillan)
BAFTA AWARD: Best Production Design (Stuart Craig)
BAFTA AWARD NOMINATIONS: Best Special Visual Effects (Jim Mitchell, John Richardson, Timothy Webber, Tim Alexander), Best Makeup/Hair (Amanda Knight, Eithne Fennel, Nick Dudman)
DURATION: 157 minutes

In his fourth year, Harry (Daniel Radcliffe) faces the challenges of the Triwizard Tournament. Even though he is underage, his name is drawn from the cup to compete with representatives of not only the two rival schools, Durmstang and Beauxbatons Academy of Magic, but also Cedric Diggory (Robert Pattinson), a member of Hufflepuff. Harry is confused and overwhelmed, but he manages to endure the challenges with the help of a number of friends. The final challenge is a maze in which he and Cedric cooperate to a tie, both seizing the cup at the same moment. They are transported to a graveyard, where the partially revived Voldemort (Ralph Fiennes) kills Cedric and uses Harry's blood to complete the revitalization of his own body. In the duel that follows, the twin cores of Voldemort and Harry's wands bring the ghosts of Cedric, James, and Lily out to protect Harry so that he can escape and return to Hogwart's with Cedric's body. Cedric's death is the first innocent death Harry witnesses. It has a profound effect upon him, as does the revelation that Voldemort is alive, a fact that the wizarding community can no longer deny. JMW

HARRY POTTER AND THE HALF-BLOOD PRINCE (2009)

DIRECTOR: David Yates
WRITER: Steve Kloves. Based on novel by J. K. Rowling.
PRODUCERS: David Barron, David Heyman, Lionel Wigram (Warner Bros., Heyday Films)
CINEMATOGRAPHER: Bruno Delbonnel
EDITOR: Mark Day
PRODUCTION DESIGN: Stuart Craig
ART DIRECTION: Andrew Ackland-Snow, Neil Lamont
SET DECORATION: Rosie Goodwin, Stephenie McMillan
COSTUMES: Jany Temime

Music: Nicholas Hooper
Visual Effects: Tim Burke, John Richardson, Tim Alexander, Nicolas Aithadi
Cast: Harry Potter: Daniel Radcliffe. Hermione Granger: Emma Watson. Ron Weasley: Rupert Grint. Professor Albus Dumbledore: Michael Gambon. Fenrir Greyback: Dave Legeno. Professor Minerva McGonagall: Maggie Smith. Severus Snape: Alan Rickman. Rubeus Hagrid: Robbie Coltrane. Cormac McLaggen: Freddie Stroma. Lavender Brown: Jessie Cave. Draco Malfoy: Tom Felton. Neville Longbottom: Matthew Lewis. Ginny Weasley: Bonnie Wright. Lily Potter: Geraldine Somerville. Remus Lupin: David Thewlis. Dolores Umbridge (voice): Imelda Staunton. Bellatrix Lestrange: Helena Bonham Carter. Wormtail: Timothy Spall. Luna Lovegood: Evanna Lynch. Nymphadora Tonks: Natalia Tena. Professor Horace Slughorn: Jim Broadbent. Lord Voldemort: Ralph Fiennes
AA: None
AAN: Best Cinematography (Bruno Delbonnel)
BAFTA Award Nominations: Best Production Design (Stuart Craig, Stephenie McMillan), Best Special Visual Effects (Tim Burke, John Richardson, Tim Alexander, Nicolas Aithadi)
DVD: Warner Bros., 2009. Complete eight-film collection, Warner Bros., 2011.
Blu-ray: Warner Bros., 2009
Duration: 153 minutes

In his sixth year, Harry (Daniel Radcliffe) wrestles not only with the ongoing challenge of Voldemort (Ralph Fiennes), but also with puberty. He feels responsible for Sirius's death, and he is angry and impatient. He also begins a relationship with Ginny Weasley (Bonnie Wright). He begins "private lessons" with Dumbledore (Michael Gambon), using the Pensieve to investigate memories of Voldemort so that Harry will know everything Dumbledore does. Dumbledore begins the year with a mysteriously withered hand, which he refuses to explain. Professor Slughorn (Jim Broadbent) joins the staff at Hogwart's, providing Harry with a supportive potions master; however, more importantly, Slughorn holds a memory vital to the revelation of Voldemort's rise to power. Harry's discovery of the "half-blood prince's" potions book allows him to excel in potions because it contains notes and insights that allow him to surpass even Hermione (Emma Watson). Meanwhile, a series of failed attacks on Dumbledore reveal a threat within Hogwart's. Draco Malfoy (Tom Felton) has been tasked by Voldemort with killing Dumbledore, and he is also working in the Room of Requirement to create a passage from Voldemort's Death Eaters to enter Hogwart's.

Meanwhile, Harry and Dumbledore embark on a journey to find one of Voldemort's Horcruxes, which are pieces of Voldemort's soul encased in objects significant to Voldemort. The diary was the first, and Marvolo Gaunt's ring was the second. Their secret journey takes them to an underground lake with an island at the center, on which a fount of poison must be consumed to reach the Horcrux. Dumbledore refuses to let Harry drink; the headmaster suffers greatly as he sips the potion, but they seize the Horcrux and return home, with Dumbledore ailing. He sends Harry to find Snape (Alan Rickman), but Draco emerges from the shadows and disarms Dumbledore, but he cannot kill him. After motioning to Harry for silence, Snape emerges from the shadows and kills Dumbledore. Snape, Draco and the other Death Eaters flee the school after launching the mark of the Dark Lord into the sky in triumph over Dumbledore's death. In his pursuit of Snape, Harry uses one of the spells he found in his potions textbook. Snape announces that the book is his, saying, "I am the half-blood prince," and he then disappears into the dark. With the death of Dumbledore, Harry realizes that he alone must finish Dumbledore's quest to find and destroy the remaining Horcruxes; it is a terrible blow when he realizes that the locket that he and Dumbledore retrieved is not a Horcrux; however, with Ron (Rupert Grint) and Hermione's help, Harry is determined to succeed. JMW

HARRY POTTER AND THE ORDER OF THE PHOENIX (2007)

Director: David Yates
Writer: Michael Goldenberg. Based on the novel by J. K. Rowling.
Producers: David Barron, David Heyman, Lorne Orleans, Lionel Wigram (Warner Bros., Heyday Films)
Cinematographer: Slawomir Idziak
Editor: Mark Day
Production Design: Stuart Craig
Art Direction: Andrew Ackland-Snow, Neil Lamont
Set Decoration: Stephenie McMillan
Costumes: Jany Temime
Music: Nicholas Hooper
Cast: Harry Potter: Daniel Radcliffe. Hermione Granger: Emma Watson. Ron Weasley: Rupert Grint. Professor Albus Dumbledore: Michael Gambon. Professor Minerva McGonagall: Maggie Smith. Severus Snape: Alan Rickman. Rubeus Hagrid: Robbie Coltrane. Draco Malfoy: Tom Felton. Uncle Vernon Dursley: Richard Griffiths. Aunt Petunia Dursley: Fiona Shaw. Dudley Dursley: Harry Melling. Piers: Jason Boyd. Malcolm: Richard Macklin. Miss Arabella Figg: Kathryn Hunter. Neville Longbottom: Matthew Lewis. Ginny Weasley: Bonnie Wright. James Potter: Adrian Rawlins. Lily Potter: Geraldine Somerville. Remus Lupin: David Thewlis. Dolores Umbridge: Imelda Staunton. Bellatrix Lestrange: Helena Bonham Carter. Luna Lovegood: Evanna Lynch. Nymphadora Tonks: Natalia Tena. Professor Alastor "MadEye" Moody: Brendan Gleeson. Kingsley Shacklebolt: George Harris. Sirius Black: Gary Oldman. Lord Voldemort: Ralph Fiennes
AA: None
AAN: None
BAFTA Award Nominations: Best Production Design (Stuart Craig, Stephenie McMillan), Best Special Visual Effects (Tim Burke, John Richardson, Emma Norton, Chris Shaw)
DVD: Warner Bros., 2007. Complete eight-film collection, Warner Bros., 2011.
Blu-ray: Warner Bros., 2007
Duration: 138 minutes

Harry (Daniel Radcliffe) begins his fifth year still feeling guilty about the death of Cedric. While still in "Muggle" space, he and his cousin Dudley (Harry Melling) are set upon by Dementors. Harry is brought to the headquarters of the Order of the Phoenix, Sirius Black's (Gary Oldman) ancestral home, but, still underage, he is denied permission to join their efforts against Voldemort (Ralph Fiennes). After defending himself at the Ministry of Magic, which is trying to deny the return of Lord Voldemort, Harry returns to Hogwart's. The Ministry, in the form of Dolores Umbridge (Imelda Staunton), dictates the curriculum and general practices of the school, eventually driving Dumbledore (Michael Gambon) out. Frustrated, Harry creates "Dumbledore's Army," training his fellow students to defend themselves from the Dark Arts. Luna Lovegood (Evanna Lynch) becomes part of the gang. Harry feels the growing presence of Voldemort. Snape's (Alan Rickman) efforts to teach him Occlumency, which would block Voldemort's access to Harry, are a colossal failure, both because of Harry's distrust of Snape and his profound connection to Voldemort. Voldemort's efforts to influence Harry trick him into returning to the Ministry of Magic for a significant battle, which results in the death of Black; however, Voldemort's efforts to use Harry fail. Both the prophecy that set these events in motion and Voldemort's confirmed existence are revealed. JMW

HARRY POTTER AND THE PRISONER OF AZKABAN (2004)

DIRECTOR: Alfonso Cuarón
WRITER: Steve Kloves. Based on novel by J. K. Rowling.
PRODUCER: Chris Columbus, David Heyman, Mark Radcliffe (Warner Bros., Heyday Films, 1492 Pictures)
CINEMATOGRAPHER: Michael Seresin
EDITOR: Steven Weisberg
PRODUCTION DESIGN: Stuart Craig
ART DIRECTION: Andrew Ackland-Snow, Neil Lamont
SET DECORATION: Stephenie McMillan
COSTUMES: Jany Temime
MUSIC: John Williams
VISUAL EFFECTS: Tim Burke, Roger Guyett, Bill George, John Richardson
MAKEUP ARTISTS: Amanda Knight, Eithne Fennel, Nick Dudman
CAST: Harry Potter: Daniel Radcliffe. Hermione Granger: Emma Watson. Ron Weasley: Rupert Grint. Professor Albus Dumbledore: Michael Gambon. Professor Minerva McGonagall: Maggie Smith. Severus Snape: Alan Rickman. Rubeus Hagrid: Robbie Coltrane. Draco Malfoy: Tom Felton. Neville Longbottom: Matthew Lewis. Ginny Weasley: Bonnie Wright. Uncle Vernon Dursley: Richard Griffiths. Aunt Petunia Dursley: Fiona Shaw. Dudley Dursley: Harry Melling. Aunt Marge: Pam Ferris. James Potter: Adrian Rawlins. Lily Potter: Geraldine Somerville. Shaun Shunpike: Lee Ingleby. Sirius Black: Gary Oldman. Professor Sybil Trelawney: Emma Thompson. Cornelius Fudge: Robert Hardy. Peter Pettigrew: Timothy Spall. Professor Remus Lupin: David Thewlis
AA: None
AAN: Best Music–Original Score (John Williams), Best Visual Effects (Tim Burke, Roger Guyett, Bill George, John Richardson)
BAFTA AWARD: Audience Award
BAFTA AWARD NOMINATIONS: Alexander Korda Award for Best British Film (Chris Columbus, David Heyman, Mark Radcliffe, Alfonso Cuarón), Best Production Design (Stuart Craig), Best Special Visual Effects (Tim Burke, Roger Guyett, Bill George, John Richardson), Best Makeup/Hair (Amanda Knight, Eithne Fennel, Nick Dudman)
DVD: Warner Bros., 2003. Complete eight-film collection, Warner Bros., 2011.
BLU-RAY: Warner Bros., 2007
DURATION: 161 minutes (174 for extended version)

This third installment in the series, under a new director, Alfonso Cuarón, despite its maturing heroes, is more playful than the earlier films. Harry (Daniel Radcliffe) returns to Hogwart's under the cloud of the escaped Sirius Black (Gary Oldman), once a good friend of Harry's parents. The wizarding world is convinced that Black works in the service of Voldemort and is bent on destroying Harry. Indeed, Black longs to reach Harry, but to reveal the true murderer of James and Lily Potter (Adrian Rawlins and Geraldine Somerville, respectively), and Peter Pettigrew (Timothy Spall). On the train on the way to Hogwart's, Harry meets the mysterious and shabby Remus Lupin (David Thewlis), who helps him recover from his first encounter with Dementors, "soul-sucking fiends." In this film, we learn that Harry's father, Lupin, Pettigrew, and Black were once friends at Hogwart's. At the conclusion of the movie, Pettigrew is revealed as the one who betrayed James and Lily to Voldemort, but he escapes. While Harry loses the mentorship of Lupin because it becomes public knowledge that he is a werewolf, he finds a family connection in his godfather, Sirius Black; however, Sirius must remain in hiding. JMW

HARRY POTTER AND THE SORCERER'S STONE (2001)

DIRECTOR: Chris Columbus
WRITER: Steve Kloves. Based on novel by J. K. Rowling.
PRODUCERS: Chris Columbus, Michael Barnathan, Duncan Henderson, Mark Radcliffe (Warner Bros., Heyday Films, 1492 Pictures)
CINEMATOGRAPHER: John Seale
EDITOR: Richard Francis-Bruce
PRODUCTION DESIGN: Stuart Craig
ART DIRECTION: John King, Neil Lamont
SET DECORATION: Stephenie McMillan
COSTUMES: Judianna Makovsky
MUSIC: John Williams
CAST: Harry Potter: Daniel Radcliffe. Hermione Granger: Emma Watson. Ron Weasley: Rupert Grint. Professor Albus Dumbledore: Richard Harris. Professor Minerva McGonagall: Maggie Smith. Severus Snape: Alan Rickman. Lord Voldemort: Ralph Fiennes. Rubeus Hagrid: Robbie Coltrane. Draco Malfoy: Tom Felton. Neville Longbottom: Matthew Lewis. Ginny Weasley: Bonnie Wright. Uncle Vernon Dursley: Richard Griffiths. Aunt Petunia Dursley: Fiona Shaw. Dudley Dursley: Harry Melling
AA: None
AAN: Best Art Direction–Set Decoration (Stuart Craig, Stephenie McMillan), Best Costume Design (Judianna Makovsky), Best Music–Original Score (John Williams)
DVD: Warner Bros., 2002. Complete eight-film collection, Warner Bros., 2011.
BLU-RAY: Warner Bros., 2007
DURATION: 152 minutes (159 for extended version)

Based on the blockbuster series of books by J. K. Rowling, each film in the epic series of Harry Potter and his friends, witches and wizards in training who fight the steady encroachment of evil into their lives, the lives of their quirky elders, and even the larger "Muggle" world of London and the British countryside, became a blockbuster as well. The books and films have become so identifiable with England that they were featured as part of the opening ceremony at the 2012 Olympic Games in London, with such other British icons as James Bond, Peter Pan, and David Bowie.

In *Harry Potter and the Sorcerer's Stone*, the opening film in the series, we meet eleven-year-old Harry (Daniel Radcliffe), who lives in the cupboard under the stairs of N. 4 Privet Dr. with his Muggle aunt, uncle, and cousin. Despite Uncle Vernon's (Richard Griffiths) best efforts, Harry learns that he is a wizard with an invitation to attend Hogwart's School. After a shopping trip in the magical Diagon Alley, where he and Hagrid (Robbie Coltrane), the half giant, gather his supplies for school, including his wand and Hedwig, his snowy owl, Harry boards the Hogwart's Express. Here he meets Hermione (Emma Watson) and Ron Weasley (Rupert Grint), who will be his companions throughout the epic. Once at school, Harry is "sorted" into Gryffindor House with Ron and Hermione, and he begins his education. He also meets the instructors who will shape his life: his house master, Professor McGonagall (Maggie Smith); the mysterious Snape (Alan Rickman), the potions master; and, of course, Albus Dumbledore (Richard Harris), headmaster of Hogwart's. Harry grapples with his fame as the "Boy Who Lived" as he and his friends unwind the mystery of the Sorcerer's Stone in a race with Voldemort (Ralph Fiennes) to discover it. Voldemort, the murderer of Harry's parents, is the archvillain of this epic. Harry is tied to him in numerous ways, which are revealed throughout the series. The first film ends with the jubilant success of Harry and his friends, winning the house cup for Gryffindor, as well as thwarting Voldemort in his pursuit of immortality. JMW

HULK (2003)

DIRECTOR: Ang Lee
WRITERS: Stan Lee, Jack Kirby, James Schamus, John Turman, Michael France
PRODUCERS: Gale Anne Hurd, Avi Arad, James Schamus, Larry Franco (Universal, Marvel Enterprises, Valhalla Motion Pictures, Good Machine)
CINEMATOGRAPHER: Frederick Elmes
EDITOR: Tim Squyres
PRODUCTION DESIGN: Rick Heinrichs
ART DIRECTION: John Dexter, Greg Papalia
SET DECORATION: Cheryl Carasik
COSTUMES: Marit Allen
MUSIC: Danny Elfman
CAST: Bruce Banner: Eric Bana. Betty Ross: Jennifer Connelly. Ross: Sam Elliott. Glenn Talbot: Josh Lucas. Father (Dr. David Banner): Nick Nolte. Young David Banner: Paul Kersey. Edith Banner: Cara Buono. Young Ross: Todd Tesen. Security Guard: Stan Lee
AA: None
AAN: None
DVD: Universal Studios, 2004
BLU-RAY: Universal Studios, 2008
DURATION: 138 minutes

Ang Lee, who has won Best Director Oscars for *Crouching Tiger, Hidden Dragon* (2000), *Brokeback Mountain* (2005), and *Life of Pi* (2012), turned his hand to the antihero "superhero" the Hulk, who was created by Stan Lee and Jack Kirby at Marvel Comics in 1962, during what is known as the Silver Age of Comic Books. Lee was intrigued by the idea of making a monster a superhero, citing as inspiration the way that Frankenstein's monster is strangely sympathetic, and combining this with the double identity of Dr. Jekyll and Mr. Hyde.[1] The Hulk is, therefore, another cautionary figure against playing God with science, for his superhuman abilities are a curse. In the original comic book, the Hulk begins life as Bruce Banner, becoming the Hulk after he is caught in the blast of his own experimental gamma bomb.[2] Lee's film follows a later, revised origin story in which Banner's scientist father (played by Nick Nolte and called David in the film) experiments on himself and passes on some of his altered DNA to his son, Bruce (Eric Bana). We later learn that David tried to kill the young Bruce but accidentally killed the mother instead, a traumatic memory that Bruce has repressed. Bruce is also a talented scientist who is researching human regeneration with his former girlfriend Betty Ross (Jennifer Connelly). After a laboratory accident, Bruce transforms into a huge, rampaging green beast every time he gets angry. Betty asks her estranged father, General Ross (Sam Elliott), to help Bruce, taking him to a secret desert army base for safe keeping, but entrepreneur Glenn Talbot (Josh Lucas) takes over, hoping to create supersoldiers for the military. The Hulk breaks out of the base, fighting the army in the desert until Betty calms him. Meanwhile, David uses the lab equipment on himself, and father and son fight it out in their monstrous forms. Although the site is bombed, Bruce survives and secretly provides humanitarian aid in the jungle. Reviews were divided, for while many praised Lee's efforts to emphasize the psychological trauma within the story, many found it overly long and ponderous, with unconvincing special effects. DB

Notes

1. Jason Bainbridge, "'Worlds within Worlds': The Role of Superheroes in the Marvel and DC Universes," in *The Contemporary Comic Book Superhero*, edited by Angela Ndalianis (New York: Routledge, 2009), 68.

2. Stan Lee and Jack Kirby, "The Incredible Hulk, #1," 1962, *Essential Incredible Hulk*, vol. 1 (New York: Marvel Comics, 2003).

Bibliography

Bainbridge, Jason. "'Worlds within Worlds': The Role of Superheroes in the Marvel and DC Universes." In *The Contemporary Comic Book Superhero*, edited by Angela Ndalianis, 64–85. New York: Routledge, 2009.

Lee, Stan, and Jack Kirby. "The Incredible Hulk, #1." 1962, *Essential Incredible Hulk*, vol. 1 (New York: Marvel Comics, 2003).

IMMORTALS (2011)

Director: Tarsem Singh Dhandwar
Writers: Charles Parlapanides, Vlas Parlapanides
Producers: Gianni Nunnari, Mark Canton, Ryan Kavanaugh (Universal Pictures, Relativity Media, Virgin Produced)
Cinematographer: Brendan Galvin
Editor: Wyatt Jones, Stuart Levy, David Rosenbloom
Production Design: Tom Foden
Art Direction: Michael Manson, Michele Laliberte, Jean Kazemirchuk, Félix Larivière-Charron
Set Decoration: Jille Azis, Eve Boulonne, Elise de Blois, Marie-Soleil Dénommé
Costumes: Eiko Ishioka
Music: Trevor Morris
Cast: Theseus: Henry Cavill. King Hyperion: Mickey Rourke. Stavros: Stephen Dorff. Phaedra: Freida Pinto. Zeus: Luke Evans. Zeus Disguised as Old Man: John Hurt. Lysander: Joseph Morgan. Aethra: Anne Day-Jones. The Monk: Greg Bryk. Dareios: Alan Van Sprang. Helios: Peter Stebbings. Ares: Daniel Sharman. Athena: Isabel Lucas. Poseidon: Kellan Lutz. Heracles: Steve Byers. Cassander: Stephen McHattie
AA: None
AAN: None
DVD: Universal Sony, 2012
Blu-ray: 20th Century Fox, 2011
Duration: 110 minutes

From the producers of *300* (Zack Snyder, 2007) comes this disappointing 3D foray into Greek myth. Theseus (Henry Cavill) is a mortal stonemason and mere peasant. Yet, he is nurtured and tutored by the god Zeus (Luke Evans), disguised as an old man (John Hurt). Theseus' implausibly located cliff-top village is threatened by the invasion of King Hyperion (Mickey Rourke), who wishes to bring an end to the Olympian gods who ignored his pleas and allowed his family to die. He doesn't mind if most of humanity gets wiped out in the process, because, quite simply, he is the bad guy. Hyperion is searching for a magical bow, hoping to release the Titans from their imprisonment in Mount Tartaros and resume the war between rival immortal beings.

Although Theseus is at first reluctant to take on the heroic mantle, the oracle Phaedra (Freida Pinto) convinces him of his destiny, and, despite his lowly birth, he is able to rally the Greek forces. Hyperion nonetheless succeeds in releasing the Titans, and the Olympian gods, who by law cannot interfere with mere mortal concerns, are finally pressed into the fight. After heavy casualties, Zeus seals the Titans back inside the mountain and takes Theseus with him to Olympus. Back on Earth, Phaedra raises Theseus' son, and Zeus returns to once more take on the role of mentor.

Immortals continues the same visual aesthetic of *300* and even rehashes its battle plan by having the main conflict take place in a narrow passage where the enemy's superior numbers count for little. Rather improbably, it does not occur to Hyperion to simply destroy more of the Greek defensive wall with his magic bow and create a more advantageous battleground for his forces. The problem is not that *Immortals* messes with the rich tapestry of Greek myth, because the Greeks did that themselves, but rather that it turns it into something rather tiresome. The camp flourishes of the gaudy Olympian wardrobe and John Hurt (looking suitably amused) as the elderly version of Zeus provide at least some entertainment value along the way. It performed well internationally but significantly behind the box-office takings of *300*. DB

***INDEPENDENCE DAY* (1996)**

Director: Roland Emmerich
Writers: Dean Devlin, Roland Emmerich
Producer: Dean Devlin (20th Century Fox, Centropolis Entertainment)
Cinematographer: Karl Walter Lindenlaub
Editor: David Brenner
Production Design: Oliver Scholl, Patrick Tatopoulos
Art Direction: Jim Teegarden
Set Decoration: Jim Erickson
Costumes: Joseph Porro
Music: David Arnold
Sound Mixers: Chris Carpenter, Bill W. Benton, Bob Beemer, Jeff Wexler
Visual Effects: Volker Engel, Douglas Smith, Clay Pinney, Joe Viskocil
Cast: Capt. Steven Hiller: Will Smith. President Thomas J. Whitmore: Bill Pullman. David Levinson: Jeff Goldblum. First Lady Marilyn Whitmore: Mary McDonnell. Julius Levinson: Judd Hirsch. Gen. William Grey: Robert Loggia. Russell Casse: Randy Quaid. Constance Spano: Margaret Colin. Albert Nimziki: James Rebhorn. Marty Gilbert: Harvey Fierstein. Maj. Mitchell: Adam Baldwin. Dr. Brackish Okun: Brent Spiner. Capt. Jimmy Wilder: Harry Connick Jr.
AA: Best Effects–Visual Effects (Volker Engel, Douglas Smith, Clay Pinney, Joe Viskocil)
AAN: Best Sound (Chris Carpenter, Bill W. Benton, Bob Beemer, Jeff Wexler)
DVD: 20th Century Fox, 2000
Blu-ray: 20th Century Fox, 2008
Duration: 145 minutes

With its invading aliens of pure evil, *Independence Day* takes a science-fiction B-movie template from the 1950s, mixed with the 1970s disaster epic (a genre that director Roland Emmerich would also draw on for *The Day After Tomorrow*, 2004, and his 2009 film *2012*), and expands the scale with Oscar-winning special effects. Todd McCarthy, writing for *Variety*, argues that the film harnesses the best elements of Cecil B. DeMille, among them the "boldest possible opposition between good and evil . . . ultimate triumph through ingenuity and heroism."[1]

When a number of alien spacecraft arrive on Earth, attempts to communicate fail. David Levinson (Jeff Goldblum), a cable repairman who also happens to be a MIT graduate (and genius), discovers evidence that the aliens intend to attack, warning the president (Bill Pullman) with the help of his former wife and the White House director of communications, Constance Spano (Margaret Colin). After the aliens do indeed attack major cities throughout the world, the president is taken to the infamous Area 51, where they learn of the aliens' intention to wipe out humanity. Using a captured alien vessel, Levinson and Captain Steven Hiller (Will Smith) set out for the alien mother ship to infect it with a computer virus, rendering it vulnerable to a nuclear bomb. The president, bereaved by the loss of his wife, joins the air campaign that follows, but they are only victorious when Vietnam veteran Russell Casse (Randy Quaid) rams one of the alien vessels and reveals a weak spot. As the remnants of the mother ship burn up in the atmosphere like a fireworks display, the 4th of July is celebrated as independence day for the entire world. Made for $75 million, it was not the film's special effects that helped *Independence Day* bring in more than $800 million at the worldwide box office, but rather its charmingly simplistic brand of heroism. DB

Note

1. Todd McCarthy, "Review: *Independence Day*," *Variety*, 1 July 1996, http://variety.com/1996/film/reviews/independence-day-3-1200446236/ (22 June 2013).

Bibliography

McCarthy, Todd. "Review: *Independence Day*." *Variety*, 1 July 1996, http://variety.com/1996/film/reviews/independence-day-3-1200446236/ (22 June 2013).

INDIANA JONES AND THE KINGDOM OF THE CRYSTAL SKULL (2008)

DIRECTOR: Steven Spielberg
WRITERS: David Koepp, George Lucas, Jeff Nathanson, Philip Kaufman
PRODUCERS: Frank Marshall, Flávio R. Tambellini, Kathleen Kennedy, George Lucas (Paramount Pictures, Lucasfilm)
CINEMATOGRAPHER: Janusz Kaminski
EDITOR: Michael Kahn
PRODUCTION DESIGN: Guy Hendrix Dyas
ART DIRECTION: Mark W. Mansbridge
SET DECORATION: Larry Dias
COSTUMES: Mary Zophres
MUSIC: John Williams
CAST: Henry "Indiana" Jones: Harrison Ford. Irina Spalko: Cate Blanchett. Marion Ravenwood: Karen Allen. Mutt Williams: Shia LaBeouf. "Mac" George Michale: Ray Winstone. Professor Oxley: John Hurt. Dean Charles Stanforth: Jim Broadbent. Dovchenko: Igor Jijikine
AA: None
AAN: None
DVD: Paramount Pictures, 2008. Complete four-film collection, Paramount Pictures, 2008.
BLU-RAY: Complete four-film collection, Paramount Pictures, 2012
DURATION: 127 minutes

Coming almost two decades after the original three films in the Indiana Jones franchise had appeared, *Indiana Jones and the Kingdom of the Crystal Skull* now had to compete with the many superhero computer-generated imagery epics coming out by the dozen. For this reason, the Indiana Jones movies have lost some of their luster, and they seem more like a nostalgia enterprise than a new thing on the planet. A stalwart movie hero, Harrison Ford has played more than a dozen other characters in addition to the daredevil Jones of the earlier adventures, from comedies to drama/action movies, and he has grown as an actor of "many guiles," to imitate literature's most enterprising hero, Odysseus of Homer. Throughout his career, he has constantly been in tight spots, and he always manages to evade, get out safely, and, more often than not, get a girl at the end (although he is far from the safest romantic type, but in a pinch he will do).

Indiana Jones and the Kingdom of the Crystal Skull takes him back, not to the 1930s, to the time of Hitler and the Nazis, but to the late 1950s—to justify his aging for once—and this time he is called away from his settling down as a man drawing a pension to act as adventure hero once again. In this installment, Jones has a new female companion, Irina Spalko, played by the "now" girl Cate Blanchett, who aids him in tracking down enemies from the Soviet Union. His adventures keep him in his native land, with a few excursions into Latin America, where, after countless escapes and present-day explosions, he learns a few secrets, one of which is that he has a son, heavily involved in trafficking, but a son nevertheless, Mutt Williams (Shia LaBeouf), who turns out to be Henry Jones III. All ends well, especially when Marion Ravenwood (Karen Allen), aged but still attractive, shows up. The viewer is advised to stay with the first three movies of the franchise, but not totally ignore this one. As with the previous film, *Indiana Jones and the Kingdom of the Crystal Skull* retains its comic-strip character/hero and has a few laughs to offer, being an epic only by osmosis. CS

INDIANA JONES AND THE LAST CRUSADE (1989)

DIRECTOR: Steven Spielberg
WRITERS: Jeffrey Boam, Menno Meyjes, George Lucas, Philip Kaufman
PRODUCERS: Robert Watts. Arthur F. Repola (Paramount Pictures, Lucasfilm)
CINEMATOGRAPHER: Douglas Slocombe
EDITOR: Michael Kahn
PRODUCTION DESIGN: Elliot Scott
ART DIRECTION: Stephen Scott
SET DECORATION: Peter Howitt
COSTUMES: Joanna Johnston, Anthony Powell
MUSIC: John Williams
SOUND EDITORS: Ben Burtt, Richard Hymns
SOUND MIXERS: Ben Burtt, Gary Summers, Shawn Murphy, Tony Dawe
CAST: Henry "Indiana" Jones: Harrison Ford. Professor Henry Jones: Sean Connery. Marcus Brody: Denholm Elliott. Dr. Elsa Schneider: Alison Doody. Sallah: John Rhys-Davies. Professor Walter Donovan: Julian Glover. Young Indy: River Phoenix. Gen. Vogel: Michael Byrne. Kazim: Kevork Malikyan. Young Henry Jones: Alex Hyde-White
AA: Best Effects–Sound Effects Editing (Ben Burtt, Richard Hymns)
AAN: Best Sound (Ben Burtt, Gary Summers, Shawn Murphy, Tony Dawe), Best Music–Original Score (John Williams)
DVD: Paramount Pictures, 2008. Complete four-film collection, Paramount Pictures, 2008.
BLU-RAY: Complete four-film collection, Paramount Pictures, 2012
DURATION: 127 minutes

To complete the 1980s Indiana Jones trilogy, Steven Spielberg and George Lucas once more turned to the theme of fighting the Nazis—something Spielberg would go on to do again on a more serious note with *Schindler's List* (1993). The totemic symbol this time returns to the West as well, with the West's most potent symbol, the Holy Grail, which the Nazis, for some curious reason (their pursuit of the Tabernacle also seems illogical), pursue, perhaps as an emblem of their conquest—and annihilation—of Western civilization as we know it. Three forces actually embark on a quest for the Holy Grail, or Chalice, which, passed on to Joseph of Arimathea by Jesus, was lost and sought again during the time of King Arthur in the twelfth century. It has since been sought by a secret brotherhood centered in Venice; by Professor Henry Jones Sr., who happens to be Indy's father; and by the Nazis and their cohorts, Professor Walter Donovan (Julian Clover), who teaches at Barnett College, where the elder Jones also teaches anthropology, and Dr. Elsa Schneider (Alison Doody), a woman anthropologist who also has anthropological interests but is allied with the Nazis.

For a time, it becomes confusing who is pursuing what and for what reason, but as the various phases of the adventure unfold, it becomes clear that the motives of the various agents interchange, while their personalities remain one-dimensional and cartoonlike.

Dr. Jones, the father, played by Scottish-accent speaking Sean Connery ("It is better to be shafe than shorry!"), is ill-matched to his not-much-younger, virile son Indy (who speaks with a blatantly American accent), but the relationship is comic, so these minor discrepancies don't seem to matter. Professor Jones (Sr.) is an authority on the Grail, and his quest is based on authentic documents; he has devised a diary with a map and instructions, and for that reason he is abducted by the Nazis.

Indy embarks on a pursuit, not of the Grail, but of his father. He ends up in Venice and allies himself with Dr. Schneider, and after a few comic mishaps in a rat-infested tunnel and an obligatory boat chase in the Venice canals (scenes endlessly repeated in the James Bond movies), he soon takes off for Castle Brunwald in Austria, where he finds his father. The two escape in a motorcycle chase; they end up in Hatay and proceed to the Canyon of the Crescent Moon, where the Grail is hidden. Indiana single-handedly defeats the Nazis, who ride into the desert in a monstrous tank, which finally drops and smashes into a canyon (reminding of the truck in Spielberg's *Duel*); the Nazis are practically exterminated, but not Donovan, who, seconded by Schneider, has followed a daring Indy into the crevices of the Crescent Moon. There we learn that Donovan is pursuing the Chalice to attain personal immortality—while Hitler would want it simply to deprive his enemies of it. To force Indy to dare pass the three challenges needed to reach the Grail, he shoots Indy's father, who can only be healed by the Chalice. Through clever guesswork, Indy solves the riddles, crosses a chasm, and finds himself in the chamber, where a knight-hermit has been waiting for him for 700 years. There are many cups there, and Indy must choose the correct one, but Donavan, who has followed him, along with Schneider, picks the wrong one, drinks from the fountain, and turns to ashes in front of a terrified Dr. Schneider. Indy picks the right one—a wooden cup, made by a carpenter—and brings it back and heals his dying father; the earth cracks, and Schneider, trying to reach for the cup, falls into a chasm. Indy, too, tries to reach the Grail, but he is warned by his father that it is not to be had by humans. When asked what he has gained from it—the adventures, the quest—Jones Sr. utters, "Illumination." CS

INDIANA JONES AND THE TEMPLE OF DOOM (1984)

Director: Steven Spielberg
Writers: Willard Huyck, Gloria Katz, George Lucas
Producers: Robert Watts. Kathleen Kennedy (Paramount Pictures, Lucasfilm)
Cinematographer: Douglas Slocombe
Editor: Michael Kahn
Production Design: Elliot Scott
Art Direction: Roger Cain, Alan Cassie
Set Decoration: Peter Howitt
Costumes: Anthony Powell
Music: John Williams
Visual Effects: Dennis Muren, Michael J. McAlister, Lorne Peterson, George Gibbs
Cast: Henry "Indiana" Jones: Harrison Ford. Willie Scott: Kate Capshaw. Short Round: Ke Huy Quan. Mola Ram: Amrish Puri. Chattar Lal: Roshan Seth. Capt. Blumburtt: Philip Stone. Lao Che: Roy Chiao. Wu Han: David Yip. Kao Kan: Ric Young. Chen: Chua Kah Joo
AA: Best Effects–Visual Effects (Dennis Muren, Michael J. McAlister, Lorne Peterson, George Gibbs)
AAN: Best Music–Original Score (John Williams)
DVD: Paramount Pictures, 2008. Complete four-film collection, Paramount Pictures, 2008.
Blu-ray: Complete four-film collection, Paramount Pictures, 2012
Duration: 118 minutes

Although *Indiana Jones and the Temple of Doom* retains most of the comic-strip qualities of *Raiders of the Lost Ark*, it has its own distinct characteristics. For one, it develops a darker, more edgy theme, pitting its hero against a horde of villains who command black magic, with powers to exterminate Western civilization in its totality (if, of course, the hero does not intervene). *Indiana Jones and the Temple of Doom* shifts locales, from the Middle East to India, where Jones is helping an endangered tribe regain its most valuable totem—a magic stone dedicated to the god Shiva—which had been stolen by a rival tribe that had conquered it and enslaved its children. As with *Raiders of the Lost Ark*, where the tribal totem was the Ark, representing not only the Jews, but Christians and Western cultures in general (including the United States), here the totem is an Eastern mystical symbol that empowers the tribe that owns it over its rivals, who, in turn, can dominate and crush all other cultures if they acquire all five of the stones.

As the villain, Mola Ram (played by Indian actor Amrish Puri) says, Moslems, Jews, Christians will be exterminated by the Thuggees, who live at the Pankot Palace, ruled by a corrupt Maharaja, Chattar Lal (Roshan Seth), and already possess three of the Shiva stones. They are embarking on a search for the other two, deep in the cavities of the Temple of Doom, employing the children of the Mayapore, the defeated tribe, whom they keep in chains. Jones (Harrison Ford), who had fled Shanghai after a brawl at a nightclub, arrives at Pankot Palace accompanied by a singer, Willie Scott (Kate Capshaw), and Short Round (Ke Huy Quan), a young boy who is both his mentor and sidekick. With the aid of these two individuals, and after incredible perils, he finds one of the three stolen totem stones and brings it back to the Mayapore people, restoring their power and liberating the slave children.

Still retaining many of the qualities of the "Saturday matinee serial," *Indiana Jones and the Temple of Doom* is a darker story than *Raiders of the Lost Ark*, having the trio of savers tested to the limits of human endurance, although Capshaw, who later became Steven Spielberg's wife, seems to be playing a decorative role, just along for the ride. But like the two other characters, she, too, must ride an elephant, cross a lagoon infested with alligators and snakes, and survive the torments of the palace, which include soup dishes of boiled sheep eyes, stuffed monkey heads, a bug-filled custard pie, and snake bellies bursting with tiny, slithering reptiles. Their descent into the palace's cavities resembles a trip to Hades, where Indy embarks on his quest for the stones; however, he and his two companions are caught and tortured, and they escape riding a runaway contraption on rails through a tunnel. They cross a rope bridge, hang on to a vertical wall as it snaps, and are saved by the cavalry after Indy defeats Mola Ram, who plunges into the lagoon and is eaten by alligators. Thus, the redemption of the Mayapore tribe is achieved, thanks to a hero's intervention, although this was certainly not his tribe. We like to give a helping hand, the movie implies, when just people are oppressed and we the mighty can afford to do so. Because of its violent action (all of this is live-action stunt work, without today's digital photography), *Indiana Jones and the Temple of Doom* received a PG-13 rating, the first of its kind, and Steven Spielberg and George Lucas had to make a special appeal for the classification to be overturned to the Motion Picture Association of America and its president, Jack Valenti. CS

IRON MAN (2008)

Director: Jon Favreau
Writers: Stan Lee, Don Heck, Larry Lieber, Jack Kirby, Mark Fergus, Hawk Ostby, Art Marcum, Matt Holloway
Producers: Avi Arad, Kevin Feige (Paramount Pictures, Marvel Entertainment, Fairview Entertainment)
Cinematographer: Matthew Libatique
Editor: Dan Lebental
Production Design: J. Michael Riva
Art Direction: David F. Klassen, Richard F. Mays, Suzan Wexler
Set Decoration: Lauri Gaffin
Costumes: Laura Jean Shannon, Rebecca Bentjen
Music: Ramin Djawadi
Sound Editors: Frank E. Eulner, Christopher Boyes
Visual Effects: John Nelson, Ben Snow, Daniel Sudick, Shane Mahan
Cast: Tony Stark/Iron Man: Robert Downey Jr. Rhodey: Terrence Howard. Obadiah Stane: Jeff Bridges. Pepper Potts: Gwyneth Paltrow. Christine Everhart: Leslie Bibb. Yinsen: Shaun Toub. Raza: Faran Tahir. Agent Coulson: Clark Gregg. Gen. Gabriel: Bill Smitrovich. Abu Bakaar: Sayed Badreya. Himself: Stan Lee
AA: None
AAN: Best Sound Editing (Frank E. Eulner, Christopher Boyes), Best Visual Effects (John Nelson, Ben Snow, Daniel Sudick, Shane Mahan)
DVD: Paramount Pictures, 2008
Blu-ray: Paramount Pictures, 2011
Duration: 126 minutes

Marvel Comics' Iron Man first appeared in *Tales of Suspense* #39 in 1963, originally conceived as a Vietnam-era hero. Jon Favreau's 2008 film follows the comic book's plot but is updated to fit the post–9/11 world. Wealthy playboy and arms manufacturer Tony Stark (Robert Downey Jr.) is taken prisoner in Afghanistan while visiting to demonstrate his latest developments to the U.S. military. A fellow captive saves Stark's life using a magnet to keep shrapnel from entering his heart. He assists Stark in building an armored suit to escape in, powered by a miniature version of Stark Industries' experimental power source, the Arc Reactor. Stark returns home determined to abandon weapons manufacturing, but he discovers that his right-hand man, Obadiah Stane (an almost unrecognizable Jeff Bridges), has been selling Stark weapons to the terrorists and actually organized his abduction. Obadiah builds his own, more powerful armored suit, and the pair does battle. Obadiah is killed when Stark's loyal assistant, Pepper Potts (Gwyneth Paltrow), causes an explosion by overloading the large Arc Reactor. At a press conference designed to cover up the incident, the narcissistic Stark cannot help revealing his identity as Iron Man. A critical and commercial hit, *Iron Man* benefits from a witty script and charismatic performance by Robert Downey Jr., around whom everyone else more or less plays it straight. The film is critical of the U.S. arms industry, such that dealer Obadiah becomes the bigger villain than the terrorists who use his weapons. But at the same time, in the light of revelations made about U.S. interrogation techniques, David Denby of the *New Yorker* was enraged by scenes in which the terrorists waterboard Tony Stark. He writes, "We cast our sins onto others."[1] Stan Lee, Iron Man's cocreator and writer, makes one of his (now trademark) cameo appearances, clearly basking in the digital effects era of the comic-book feature film. DB

Note

1. David Denby, "Unsafe," *New Yorker*, 5 May 2008, www.newyorker.com/arts/critics/cinema/2008/05/05/080505crci_cinema_denby (7 July 2013).

Bibliography

Denby, David. "Unsafe." *New Yorker*, 5 May 2008, www.newyorker.com/arts/critics/cinema/2008/05/05/080505crci_cinema_denby (7 July 2013).

IRON MAN II (2010)

DIRECTOR: Jan Favreau
WRITERS: Stan Lee, Don Heck, Larry Lieber, Jack Kirby, Justin Theroux
PRODUCER: Kevin Feige (Paramount Pictures, Marvel Studios, Fairview Entertainment)
CINEMATOGRAPHER: Matthew Libatique
EDITORS: Dan Lebental, Richard Pearson
PRODUCTION DESIGN: J. Michael Riva
ART DIRECTION: Page Buckner, Michael E. Goldman, David F. Klassen, Suzan Wexler
SET DECORATION: Lauri Gaffin
COSTUMES: Mary Zophres
MUSIC: John Debney
VISUAL EFFECTS: Janek Sirrs, Ben Snow, Ged Wright, Daniel Sudick
CAST: Tony Stark/Iron Man: Robert Downey Jr. Pepper Potts: Gwyneth Paltrow. Lt. Col. James "Rhodey" Rhodes: Don Cheadle. Natalie Rushman/Natasha Romanoff: Scarlett Johansson. Justin Hammer: Sam Rockwell. Ivan Vanko: Mickey Rourke. Nick Fury: Samuel L. Jackson. Agent Coulson: Clark Gregg. Howard Stark: John Slattery. Senator Stern: Garry Shandling. Jarvis: Paul Bettany. Himself: Stan Lee
AA: None
AAN: Best Visual Effects (Janek Sirrs, Ben Snow, Ged Wright, Daniel Sudick)
DVD: Paramount Pictures, 2010
BLU-RAY: Paramount Pictures, 2010
DURATION: 124 minutes

Tony Stark (Robert Downey Jr.) is jubilant that his Iron Man armored suit has enabled him to single-handedly achieve a worldwide peace treaty, but Senator Stern (Garry Shandling) is applying pressure on Stark to share his technology with the U.S. military. Stark refuses, making fun of rival Justin Hammer (Sam Rockwell) and failed attempts to replicate the suit. Despite his bravado, Stark is slowly being poisoned by the palladium that powers the Arc Reactor, which is keeping shrapnel out of his heart. Losing interest in his company, he makes Pepper Potts (Gwyneth Paltrow) the new CEO. There is, in fact, another functioning suit, built by Russian Ivan Vanko (Mickey Rourke), who seeks revenge against Stark after his father was kicked out of the company by Stark's father for his greed. Vanko attacks Stark at a Formula 1 race, only to be defeated and imprisoned. The opportunistic Hammer breaks him out of jail and sets him up in the lab to create more suits. Meanwhile, Rhodey (Don Cheadle) dons one of Stark's suits himself to quell his friend's irresponsible behavior, later delivering it to the military, where Hammer provides some additional armaments. When Stark is given some of his father's old possessions by spy agency S.H.I.E.L.D., he stumbles upon the disguised plans for a new element and uses it to replace his palladium power source, cleansing his blood. Back at the expo, Hammer's new drone robot warriors are remotely activated by Vanko, and Stark and Rhodey must team up to defeat them. In the aftermath, Stark and Potts finally kiss.

As in the first film, the arms industry and corporate world cannot be trusted, but while the government and military are not corrupt, they also do not have what it takes to save the day. In Iron Man's comic-book world, that honor may belong to special, individual heroes, but *Iron Man II* reveals the inherent risks of such concentrated power. The screenplay and action sequences are not as tightly delivered this time around, and there is perhaps too much material that is merely there to set up future sequels. As with the original, the droll lines from Robert Downey Jr. lift the film aided by the performance by Sam Rockwell as Iron Man's would-be nemesis with an inferiority complex. DB

THE LORD OF THE RINGS: THE FELLOWSHIP OF THE RING (2001)

DIRECTOR: Peter Jackson
WRITERS: Fran Walsh, Philippa Boyens, Peter Jackson. Based on the novel *The Fellowship of the Ring*, by J. R. R. Tolkien.
PRODUCERS: Peter Jackson, Barrie M. Osborne, Fran Walsh, Mark Ordesky, Tim Sanders (New Line Cinema, WingNut Films, Saul Zaentz Company)
CINEMATOGRAPHER: Andrew Lesnie
EDITOR: John Gilbert
PRODUCTION DESIGN: Grant Major
ART DIRECTION: Dan Hennah
SET DECORATION: Dan Hennah
COSTUMES: Ngila Dickson, Richard Taylor
MUSIC: Howard Shore
SOUND MIXERS: Christopher Boyes, Michael Semanick, Gethin Creagh, Hammond Peek
VISUAL EFFECTS: Jim Rygiel, Randall William Cook, Richard Taylor, Mark Stetson
MAKEUP ARTISTS: Peter Owen, Richard Taylor
CAST: Frodo Baggins: Elijah Wood. Gandalf: Ian McKellen. Aragorn: Viggo Mortensen. Boromir: Sean Bean. Meriadoc "Merry" Brandybuck: Dominic Monaghan. Everard Proudfoot: Noel Appleby. Peregrin "Pippin" Took: Billy Boyd. Celeborn: Marton Csokas. Samwise "Sam" Gamgee: Sean Austin. Arwen: Liv Tyler. Galadriel: Cate Blanchett. Gimli: John Rhys-Davies. Saruman: Christopher Lee. Legolas Greenleaf: Orlando Bloom. Lord Elrond: Hugo Weaving. Bilbo Baggins: Ian Holm. Sauron: Sala Baker. Isildur: Harry Sinclair. Gollum/Witch-King (voice): Andy Serkis. Rivendale: Sabine Crossen (uncredited)
AA: Best Cinematography (Andrew Lesnie), Best Makeup (Peter Owen, Richard Taylor), Best Music–Original Score (Howard Shore), Best Effects–Visual Effects (Jim Rygiel, Randall William Cook, Richard Taylor, Mark Stetson)
AAN: Best Picture (Peter Jackson, Barrie M. Osborne, Fran Walsh), Best Supporting Actor (Ian McKellen), Best Director (Peter Jackson), Best Writing–Screenplay Based on Material Previously Produced or Published (Fran Walsh, Philippa Boyens, Peter Jackson), Best Art Direction–Set Decoration (Grant Major, Dan Hennah), Best Costume Design (Ngila Dickson, Richard Taylor), Best Film Editing (John Gilbert), Best Music–Original Song (Enya, Nicky Ryan, Roma Ryan for "May It Be"), Best Sound (Christopher Boyes, Michael Semanick, Gethin Creagh, Hammond Peek)
DVD: New Line Home Video, 2002. Four-disc extended edition, New Line Home Video, 2004.
BLU-RAY: New Line Home Video, 2002. Two-disc combo, including Blu-ray and DVD.
DURATION: 178 minutes

The *Lord of the Rings* trilogy can be seen as three related tales of the battle between good and evil, a worn-out topic among epic-makers, whether in literary works or in film, but in the digital era—then well under way (2001–2003)—this and other franchise epics became a decisive tool in the hands of filmmakers, especially those whose work relied largely on special effects. Peter Jackson, the director of the sequence, was able to give his masterwork the look needed as the translation of an extremely descriptive fantasy novel that had appeared nearly half a century earlier, in three parts. Jackson decided that one film, no matter how lengthy, could not be done, so he chose to do three films to adapt the massive novels of J. R. R. Tolkien, published in the mid-1950s, into a functional screen time.

The three epics were filmed simultaneously during a nearly two-year period, with main locations in New Zealand, and they were released for the screen in three sequential seasons, 2001, 2002, and 2003. The project, seen as one movie, became the longest epic story in the history of cinema, but it was rewarded with worldwide attendance, breaking records and winning numerous awards. The third film, *The Return of the King*, garnered eleven Oscars, including Best Picture for 2003.

The Lord of the Rings trilogy is based on Nordic mythology, which is not particularly Christian. It draws its materials from the Greco-Roman mythology, as had been the case with epics for decades. Tolkien was an Oxford scholar who had written critical works on Nordic mythology, particularly on the Old English epic poem *Beowulf*. Jackson's intent was to show that England had a "prehistory," found not in actual written annals (although *Beowulf* is proof that it existed), but in its legends, the Nordic tribes that fought in old England and the northern countries, including Denmark and Scandinavia.

In the first part of the trilogy, *The Fellowship of the Ring*, we meet the people of Middle-earth, a large region where individuals live in peace and prosperity, unaware of lurking danger. Its inhabitants include the Hobbits, who are tiny people (average height three feet, six inches) living in the Shire, a green valley that looks like a tiny earthly paradise. They live in harmony with nature and are easygoing, cultivating the earth and enjoying peace and prosperity.

One day this little corner of Middle-earth is visited by one of the wizards, Gandalf (Ian McKellen), who finds a very old man living there, Bilbo Baggins (Ian Holm), who is celebrating his 111th birthday. Bilbo possesses the Ring of Power and an old document written in the language of Mordor around the year 3434, during the Second Age. When Gandalf reads the text, he reveals that it was forged by the Dark Lord Sauron (Sala Baker) in the fires of Mount Doom, and taken by Isildur (Harry Sinclair), High King of Condor, from the hand of Sauron. The inscription reads, "One Ring to rule them all." The Ring can bring all the other powers of darkness under him to those who possess it. Gandalf informs Bilbo that the forces of darkness are already in motion and that the search for the Ring is on. Bilbo had found the Ring in Gollum's (Andy Serkis) cave. He has had it in his possession for sixty years, and it has delayed his old age. But as evil is stirring at Mordor, Gandalf reminds him that the Ring has awakened, having heard its master's call.

The Spirit of Evil and the Ring are the same; Sauron has survived and returned; his Orcs have multiplied, and his fortress, Barad-dur, is rebuilt in the land of Mordor. Sauron only needs the Ring to enslave all the lands and cover them with darkness. The Ring itself yearns to return to the hand of its master, Gollum, its first possessor, who knows where it is and will soon find it; therefore, the Ring must be transferred to someone else. As Gandalf cannot have it, being afraid of its power, he agrees to have it transferred to Frodo Baggins (Elijah Wood), one of the Hobbits, a youth who leads an innocent life at the Shire. The latter is persuaded to undertake the journey with his pal Samwise (Sean Austin) to the inn of the Prancing Pony, where the transfer will occur. Meanwhile, Gandalf visits Saruman (Christopher Lee), his fellow wizard and his superior in wit and cunning. Gandalf tries to enlist his powers so that the two of them can fight Sauron, but Saruman proposes that the two join forces with Sauron, Lord of Mordor, who, inside his fortress, sees all. Gandalf tells Saruman that he has abandoned reason for madness, which brings moral strife between the two. Gandalf is temporarily held in bonds and loses power.

At the inn of the Prancing Pony, where the exchange of the Ring is to take place, Aragorn (Viggo Mortensen) appears and warns the group of four friends (Pippin [Billy Boyd] and Merry [Dominic

Monaghan], two other young Hobbits, have joined Frodo and Sam) that the Orcs, the black horsemen to whom Sauron had given the nine Rings of Power, are arriving; they are horrifying and powerful creatures, Ringwraiths, neither living nor dead. During their flight, Frodo is wounded but saved by Arwen (Liv Tyler), princess of the Elves, and she, being pursued by the black horsemen, is saved by a flood. By invoking her powers, she takes him to Rivendale (Sabine Crossen), where Frodo is healed and his friends regroup and are joined by several others.

Gandalf, transformed into a bird, escapes Saruman's stronghold and joins the Council, in which Lord Elrond, of the House of Elrond (Hugo Weaving), presides. His decision is that the Elves are not powerful enough to resist the coming Orcs, but the joint forces must try to prevent the end of the world; therefore, the mission to return the Ring to Mordor and destroy it must go on as planned. The group includes Aragorn; the Ranger, a human who is the son of Arathorn and an Isildur heir (Arwen, who falls in love with him, reveals that to him); and Boromir (Sean Bean), son of Lord Denethor of Minas Tirith, and the one who proposes the use of the Ring for their own power. This view is rejected by the Council, and Boromir concedes to the majority and joins them. The others who join are Legolas (Orlando Bloom), one of the Elves and an expert archer, and Gimli (John Rhys-Davies), a brave and hard-fighting dwarf representing his race. Frodo offers to take the Ring to Mordor, along with his nine companions. Thus, the Fellowship of the Ring is formed.

The nine members of the fellowship include the four young hobbits, Gandalf, Aragorn, Boromir, Legolas, and Gimli. Bilbo, an aged man now living with the Elves, gives Frodo the Ring, which he hangs around his neck—like an albatross. This is the group that forms the Fellowship of the Ring. But soon thereafter, their group leader, Gandalf, in a fight with the monster Balrog, a demon from the ancient world, falls into a chasm and disappears. As the rest go through their arduous trek, they encounter stout resistance by the Orcs, the army of the Dark Lord, but Gimli proposes an alternative route, through the mines of Moria. There they fight a Cyclopslike giant, whom they eventually kill with arrows, but when they escape, they have to do battle with the Dark Horsemen, during which Boromir is mortally wounded and falls. They also go through the Realm of the Lady of the Wood, where a female prophet, Galadriel (Cate Blanchett), momentarily transformed into a monster as she is attracted by the power of the Ring, eventually relents and reveals to Frodo through a mirror some of the horrors he will encounter on his mission.

Among the Elves we have also seen a beautiful young princess, Arwen, who falls in love with Aragorn, but she is warned by her father that she will lose her immortality if she marries him. After the death of Boromir, Frodo decides to cross a lake alone and get to Mount Doom, but he is joined by Sam, who cannot leave his friend alone in his quest and swims to join him, almost drowning but rescued by Frodo. The two will continue their perilous path alone. That is where the first film in the trilogy ends. CS

THE LORD OF THE RINGS: THE RETURN OF THE KING (2003)

Director: Peter Jackson
Writers: Fran Walsh, Philippa Boyens, Peter Jackson. Based on the novel *The Return of the King*, by J. R. R. Tolkien.
Producers: Peter Jackson, Barrie M. Osborne, Fran Walsh (New Line Cinema, WingNut Films, Saul Zaentz Company)
Cinematographer: Andrew Lesnie
Editor: Jamie Selkirk
Production Design: Grant Major

ART DIRECTION: Dan Hennah
SET DECORATION: Dan Hennah, Alan Lee
COSTUMES: Ngila Dickson, Richard Taylor
MUSIC: Howard Shore
SOUND EDITORS: Ethan Van der Ryn, Mike Hopkins
SOUND MIXERS: Christopher Boyes, Michael Semanick, Michael Hedges, Hammond Peek
VISUAL EFFECTS: Jim Rygiel, Randall William Cook, Joe Letteri, Alex Funke
MAKEUP ARTISTS: Peter Owen, Richard Taylor
CAST: Frodo Baggins: Elijah Wood. Everard Proudfoot: Noel Appleby. Madril: John Bach. Sauron/Orc: Sala Baker. Eldarion: Sadwyn Brophy. Grima Wormtongue: Brad Dourif. Gandalf: Ian McKellen. Aragorn: Viggo Mortensen. Boromir: Sean Bean. Meriadoc "Merry" Brandybuck: Dominic Monaghan. Peregrin "Pippin" Took: Billy Boyd. Samwise "Sam" Gamgee: Sean Austin. Arwen: Liv Tyler. Galadriel: Cate Blanchett. Gimli: John Rhys-Davies. Saruman: Christopher Lee. Legolas Greenleaf: Orlando Bloom. Bilbo Baggins: Ian Holm. Gollum/Smeagol: Andy Serkis. Deagol: Thomas Robins. Theoden: Bernard Hill. Gamling: Bruce Hopkins. Isildur: Harry Sinclair. Lord Elrond: Hugo Weaving. Eomer: Karl Urban. Eowyn: Miranda Otto. Rosie Cotton: Sarah McLeod. Eldarion: Sadwyn Brophy. Damrod: Alistair Browning. Celeborn: Marton Csokas. Irolas: Ian Hughes. Witch-King/Gothmog: Lawrence Makoare. Grimbold: Bruce Phillips. Faramir: David Wenham. Denethor: John Noble. The Ring (voice): Alan Howard
AA: Best Picture (Peter Jackson, Barrie M. Osborne, Fran Walsh), Best Director (Peter Jackson), Best Writing–Adapted Screenplay (Fran Walsh, Philippa Boyens, Peter Jackson), Best Film Editing (Jamie Selkirk), Best Art Direction–Set Decoration (Grant Major, Dan Hennah, Alan Lee), Best Costume Design (Ngila Dickson, Richard Taylor), Best Makeup (Richard Taylor, Peter King), Best Music–Original Score (Howard Shore), Best Music–Original Song (Fran Walsh, Howard Shore, Annie Lennox for "Into the West"), Best Sound Mixing (Christopher Boyes, Michael Semanick, Michael Hedges, Hammond Peek), Best Effects–Visual Effects (Jim Rygiel, Randall William Cook, Joe Letteri, Alex Funke)
DVD: New Line Home Entertainment, 2004. Four-disc extended edition, New Line Home Video, 2004.
BLU-RAY: New Line Home Entertainment, 2004. Two-disc combo, including Blu-ray and DVD.
DURATION: 201 minutes

The Return of the King, the third film in the *Lord of the Rings* trilogy, begins with a retrospect, a scene that shows how Gollum (Andy Serkis) obtained the Ring. It appears that he was originally a Hobbit-like creature called Smeagol, and he and his friend Deagol (Thomas Robins) were fishing when his hook caught the Ring. In his struggle to possess the Ring, Smeagol kills Deagol, and from then onward he is a divided creature, for the Ring has an effect on him, transforming him into a hideous creature and giving him a treacherous mind. His Smeagol nature emerges occasionally, and when subdued by Frodo (Elijah Wood) and Sam (Sean Austin), he leads them to their destination, but his evil nature prompts him to gain the Ring for himself, and, with that, absolute power.

Meanwhile, despite the defeat of Saruman, Sauron (Sala Baker) still has overwhelming power, and he soon attacks the last bastion of the lord/kings, Minas Tirith, the city of kings, where Lord Denethor (John Noble) reigns. He is the father of Boromir, who has already died valiantly, and Faramir (David Wenham), who, in vain, tries to persuade him that an attack on Minas Tirith is imminent. Denethor is a dissolute, decadent king, half-mad, who does not believe that danger exists. He continues with his gluttonous ways and is indifferent to what happens. Gandalf (Ian McKellen) appeals to him to fight, but Denethor remains in his mordant state. But the others know that if this last bastion of freedom falls, Sauron will have won. Theoden (Bernard Hill) joins them, and the new band of fellowship includes the old fighters, Aragorn (Viggo Mortensen), who is their natural leader, Legolas (Orlando Bloom), the Elf, always brave and expert with his arrows, Gimli (John Rhys-Davies), the valorous and fearless dwarf wielding his ax, and Eowyn (Miranda Otto), Theéoden's daughter, who is a valiant fighter, and who takes Pippin (Billy Boyd) along on her horse.

The city is defended, but Theoden dies while fighting one of the monsters. The land of Mordor still stands, and it must be attacked as a diversion, so that Frodo can reach the Mount Doom to throw the Ring into the fire. The others soon join in the journey, and they approach the gates of Mordor, with its tower of Barad-dur, where Sauron views everything with his fiery eye. They unite in a colossal fight, in which the vastly superior forces of Sauron are unleashed. The fellowship forces are all but doomed. Frodo, carried up Mount Doom by the loyal Sam, is ready to throw the Ring in when Gollum attacks him. Finally, it is Gollum who falls into the molten lava beneath and perishes, along with the Ring, which boils and melts out of view and is gone forever. The battle is won. The tower collapses; the earth opens and devours the Orcs; and Aragorn, as the legitimate heir of Arathorn, is crowned king. He marries Arwen (Liv Tyler), who decides to become mortal and live a short but happy life. The four Hobbits return home, but Frodo, unable to find peace, for his experiences have forever divided his nature and made him a loner, departs with Gandalf for a long sea voyage, presumably to also to become a wizard one day. Sam, however, remains at home and marries his sweetheart, and we soon see him happily kissing his wife and hugging his two kids. Normalcy has returned to Middle-earth, now a free land.

The epic trilogy works well on the allegorical/archetypal level—possibly the cause for its popularity. The battle between good and evil is the topic more explored by epics than any other film genre, and not much subtlety is needed here to outline it. The epic has generated two basic methods, which have become its lifelines: it has given audiences unparalleled entertainment, and it has appealed to the tribal instincts, mainly those of survival. The tribe is attracted by entrainment—and wizards of the medium, for instance, Cecil B. DeMille, and now Peter Jackson, understand this well—but also by, perhaps less knowingly, the appeal of heroes that aid it, albeit in imaginative ways, in overcoming its fears of annihilation. As in previous ages, the twentieth century (and now the twenty-first) had its share of such fears—wars, plagues (like the Asiatic flu pandemic), and natural disasters, but, above all, man-made conflicts, for example, two major wars and countless minor ones, the fear of terrorism, and so forth, which have left the public consciousness with a false sense of security, often shattered by these events. The villain is not always nature, although it can be, but, for the most part, it is man himself. Count evil dictators and you will have more than the fingers of your two hands.

There are also other fears, and the *Lord of the Rings* (and others epics) explores those, too: as some commentators have stated, the Ring is an artifact that, despite its beauty, has a grip on those who possess it, corrupting them with dreams of power and eventually weakening and destroying them. Perhaps, it is the "machine" itself, so feared by some writers of the nineteenth century, the likes of Thomas Carlyle, who saw industrialization as the way to perdition. In fact, J. R. R. Tolkien may have been a neo-romantic at heart, describing the idyllic existence of the Shire threatened by intrusions of the outside world; the world of the Elves is also threatened with extinction—as was the peaceful existence of the inhabitants of Middle-earth. And the revolt of the trees, which come to the rescue of the kingdom of Rohan, shows nature's revolt against those that would destroy it. The story may even go deeper than the Romantic era, back to *Beowulf*'s medieval Europe, even back to the Garden of Eden, where the Serpent introduced "knowledge" as the beginning of man's travails in the path of civilization. CS

THE LORD OF THE RINGS: THE TWO TOWERS (2002)

DIRECTOR: Peter Jackson
WRITERS: Fran Walsh, Philippa Boyens, Peter Jackson, Stephen Sinclair. Based on the novel *The Two Towers*, by J. R. R. Tolkien.
PRODUCERS: Peter Jackson, Barrie M. Osborne, Fran Walsh, Mark Ordesky (New Line Cinema, WingNut Films, Saul Zaentz Company)
CINEMATOGRAPHER: Andrew Lesnie
EDITOR: Michael Horton
PRODUCTION DESIGN: Grant Major
ART DIRECTION: Dan Hennah
SET DECORATION: Dan Hennah, Alan Lee
COSTUMES: Ngila Dickson, Richard Taylor
MUSIC: Howard Shore
SOUND EDITORS: Ethan Van der Ryn, Mike Hopkins
SOUND MIXERS: Christopher Boyes, Michael Semanick, Michael Hedges, Hammond Peek
VISUAL EFFECTS: Jim Rygiel, Randall William Cook, Joe Letteri, Alex Funke
MAKEUP ARTISTS: Peter Owen, Richard Taylor
CAST: Frodo Baggins: Elijah Wood. Madril: John Bach. Sauron: Sala Baker. Sharku/Snaga: Jed Brophy. Éothain: Sam Comery. Grima Wormtongue: Brad Dourif. Gandalf: Ian McKellen. Aragorn: Viggo Mortensen. Boromir: Sean Bean. Meriadoc "Merry" Brandybuck: Dominic Monaghan. Peregrin "Pippin" Took: Billy Boyd. Samwise "Sam" Gamgee: Sean Austin. Arwen: Liv Tyler. Galadriel: Cate Blanchett. Gimli/Treebeard (voice): John Rhys-Davies. Saruman: Christopher Lee. Legolas Greenleaf: Orlando Bloom. Gollum: Andy Serkis. Theoden: Bernard Hill. Gamling: Bruce Hopkins. Lord Elrond: Hugo Weaving. Théodred, Prince of Rohan: Paris Howe Strewe. Eomer: Karl Urban. Eowyn: Miranda Otto
AA: Best Sound Editing (Ethan Van der Ryn, Mike Hopkins), Best Effects–Visual Effects (Jim Rygiel, Randall William Cook, Joe Letteri, Alex Funke)
AAN: Best Picture (Peter Jackson, Barrie M. Osborne, Fran Walsh), Best Art Direction–Set Decoration (Grant Major, Dan Hennah, Alan Lee), Best Film Editing (Michael Horton), Best Sound (Christopher Boyes, Michael Semanick, Michael Hedges, Hammond Peek)
DVD: New Line Home Entertainment, 2003. Four-disc extended edition, New Line Home Video, 2004.
BLU-RAY: New Line Home Entertainment, 2003
DURATION: 179 minutes

The Two Towers is darker and scarier, concentrating on the human part of the longer story. It is based on a few crucial incidents that advance the narrative beyond its initial phases and introduce new characters and locales, while the initial theme—the impending destruction of the world by the evil forces of the Dark Lord Sauron (Sala

Baker)—remains the same. The initial group of the nine is now broken in three groups. The first includes Frodo (Elijah Wood) and Sam (Sean Austin), who continue their trek to Mount Mordor, although they are soon joined by Gollum (Andy Serkis), a half-human creature (presented in animated form), whom, after being subdued by them, becomes their guide, answering to the name of Sméagol. The second group consists of the other hobbits, Merry (Dominic Monaghan) and Pippin (Billy Boyd), whom, after being captured, wander into the magic Fargora Forest, where they remain until they are rescued by the trees, which, in another magical transformation, come alive. Then there are the three loyal companions: Legolas, the Elf archer (Orlando Bloom); Aragorn, the Ranger (Viggo Mortensen); and Gimli, the Dwarf (John Rhys-Davies).

The three are soon stopped by Eomer (Karl Urban), nephew of King Theoden (Bernard Hill) and third marshall of the Riders of Riddermark. They are taken to the kingdom of Rohan, where a peaceful people, the Edores, live a stoic life of isolation, but who, like everyone else in Middle-earth, are now threatened by Saruman (Christopher Lee), the evil wizard, and Sauron, the Dark Lord. The latter two live in the two towers, Orthanc, the stronghold of Saruman, and Barad-dur, the fortress of Sauron. They are soon to unleash their dark forces, the Urak-hai, against the Edoras fortress. King Theoden, however, has been weakened, reduced to a zombie, thanks to the magic spell of a traitor in his court, Wormtongue (Brad Dourif), who is the secret agent and emissary of Saruman. But Theoden is restored to youth and power as soon as the three heroes arrive, accompanied by Gandalf (Ian McKellen), who has been restored to life and transformed from a "Grey" to a "White" wizard, with increased powers after escaping from the clutches of the monster Balrog. His metamorphosis makes him a stronger and more determined leader, and his effect on the still-weakened Theoden is decisive.

Meanwhile, a second love story develops, for Theoden's beautiful daughter Eowyn (Miranda Otto) cannot conceal her admiration for Aragorn, who cannot easily forget his emotional tie with the Elf princess Arwen (Liv Tyler). The latter is reminded by her father, Elrond (Hugo Weaving), that she must give up Aragorn, who will either be killed in the fight again Sauron's forces, or, if he wins, will marry a mortal woman. If Arwen still chooses to marry him, she will, tragically, lose her immortality.

Another development, a more subtle one (in the context of the mythical tale), is the change in Frodo, who begins to feel the effects of the Ring, the albatross he carries, for it is its corrupting power that weakens his will. Soon, however, the forces of Sauron and Saruman combined attack in a vast siege, using war machines, ramming rods to break the gate open, and great numbers of determined fighters imbued with hatred to destroy the last stronghold of humanity, the kingdom of Rohan. After an all-night battle in the rain, and despite stout resistance, it seems the battle has been lost when aid arrives from two sources. Eomer, the estranged nephew of Theoden, dashes into battle from the side of a hill with his long-speared horsemen, and unexpected help comes from the trees, now transformed into semihumans and carrying Merry and Pippin with them. The evil forces of Sauron have been held back, temporarily, and Saruman has been defeated. CS

RAIDERS OF THE LOST ARK (1981)

Director: Steven Spielberg
Writers: Lawrence Kasdan, George Lucas, Philip Kaufman
Producers: Frank Marshall, Robert Watts (Paramount Pictures)
Cinematographer: Douglas Slocombe
Editor: Michael Kahn
Production Design: Norman Reynolds
Art Direction: Leslie Dilley
Set Decoration: Michael Ford
Costumes: Deborah Nadoolman

MUSIC: John Williams
SOUND EFFECTS EDITORS: Ben Burtt, Richard L. Anderson
SOUND RECORDING: Bill Varney, Steve Maslow, Gregg Landaker, Roy Charman
VISUAL EFFECTS: Richard Edlund, Kit West, Bruce Nicholson, Joe Johnston
CAST: Henry "Indiana" Jones: Harrison Ford. Dr. Marcus Brody: Denholm Elliott. Marion Ravenwood: Karen Allen. Sallah: John Rhys-Davies. Maj. Arnold Toht: Ronald Lacey. Rene Belloq: Paul Freeman. Satipo: Alfred Molina. Col. Dietrich: Wolf Kahler. Gobler: Anthony Higgins. Barranca/Monkey Man: Vic Tablian. Col. Musgrove: Don Fellows. Maj. Eaton: William Hootkins
AA: Best Art Direction–Set Decoration (Norman Reynolds, Leslie Dilley, Michael Ford), Best Sound (Bill Varney, Steve Maslow, Gregg Landaker, Roy Charman), Best Film Editing (Michael Kahn), Best Effects–Visual Effects (Richard Edlund, Kit West, Bruce Nicholson, Joe Johnston), Special Achievement Award for Sound Effects Editing (Ben Burtt, Richard L. Anderson)
AAN: Best Picture (Frank Marshall), Best Director (Steven Spielberg), Best Cinematography (Douglas Slocombe), Best Music–Original Score (John Williams)
DVD: Paramount Pictures, 2003. Complete four-film collection, Paramount Pictures, 2008.
BLU-RAY: Complete four-film collection, Paramount Pictures, 2012
DURATION: 115 minutes

The Indiana Jones franchise, as it is ultimately called, initially consisted of three films made in the 1980s (1981–1989), with the fourth, *Indiana Jones and the Kingdom of the Crystal Skull*, coming nineteen years later, with only two of its original characters (Harrison Ford and Karen Allen—with a photo of Sean Connery) returning to the fourth effort by director Steven Spielberg. It did well enough at the box office, but with Jones getting older and having lost his box-office draw (but not his charisma), the franchise had obviously come to an end. But when the first movie, *Raiders of the Lost Ark*, burst onto the scene in 1981, the country, still in the throes of the Cold War, could appreciate a cartoonlike hero who could single-handedly defeated an assortment of villains in quick succession. This hero, however, is a conscious transfer to older times—the fight against the Nazis—and not the Soviets or other conspirators of the Cold War era, a space already preempted by the Bond movies, but that context works, for the hero of *Raiders of the Lost Ark* does indeed attempt to defeat archetypal "bad guys," as the Nazis were then. The idea was first conceived by George Lucas, already well known for his *Star Wars* trilogy (a comic-strip epic series also of the science-fiction variety), and he and Spielberg, already famous for such blockbuster movie epics as *Close Encounters of the Third Kind* (1977) and *Jaws* (1975), and a master of evoking emotion in audiences likely to be intimidated by oversized and exotic menaces against humanity, collaborated to forge the ultimate fantasy to suit the times.

Critics generally dismissed the allegorical nature of this fantasy and associated *Raiders of the Lost Ark* with Saturday matinee serials, which feature heroes battling scores of villains in successive episodes. Although simplistic in the concept of its hero, the movie is complex in its mythological associations, some derived from the Bible, others from medieval literature, even though, on the surface, the action takes place in the contemporary world, after the Nazis had gained power and were threatening humanity with domination. In a sense, *Raiders of the Lost Ark* can stand on the allegorical level alone, for it is a battle of good against evil, but its solid historical and geographical basis gives it a sense of reality, and almost believability. Thus, the movie works simultaneously on several levels.

Just as any of the previously mentioned comic-strip heroes, the protagonist of the film has a double nature. Outwardly, he is a mild-mannered university professor, a doctor of anthropology who seems less than enchanted—and almost torpid—as an everyday college teacher, bored with the tedium of lecturing anthropology to apathetic students. Underneath, however, he is simmering with the desire for exploration, and when occasion offers, he embarks on various expeditions to collect ancient artifacts, some of which bring him face-to-face with harrowing adventures. Undaunted, he goes on a search for the Tabernacle, the "Ark," which in the Old Testament is described as containing the tablets that Moses obtained directly from God on Mount Sinai. For a moment, the audience is transferred back to *The Ten Commandments*, where Charlton Heston, who represents Moses in that movie, hears the voice of God from the burning bush, and he witnesses flaming arrows engraving the commandments on the tablets. Here the hero is Indiana Jones (Ford), whose main interest is anthropological, while his brush with the Nazis seems incidental, but he soon becomes aware of the Nazis' pursuit of the Ark, for reasons not entirely clear, other than it is the "Fuhrer's" wish. But it also becomes evident that by that act, the Nazis would obtain and keep (or destroy) the Jews' most valuable traditional religious symbol, thus negating one of the most potent religious symbols of the West (while the cross, significantly, becomes the swastika).

While Jones's initial interest in the Ark is purely archeological, he soon becomes aware of the Nazis' intentions and plans to foil them. His hero's archetypal dimensions are rooted in Hercules (physical prowess); Odysseus (mental agility); and a movie actor, Humphrey Bogart—whose tough persona he emulates admirably and precisely down to the fedora hat, adding the bullwhip and leather jacket for good measure. Jones is capable of dealing as many blows as he takes, outlasting, although often barely, his nastiest foes. Using both brawn and brains, Jones, wearing an outmoded fedora hat, reminded audiences of the likes of Humphrey Bogart and the adventure serials with characters who had become comic-strip heroes in the 1930s and 1940s. Harrison Ford as Jones outshines most previous screen heroes, repeatedly eluding unimaginable perils, for example, climbing out of a snake pit and defeating a giant pugilist as he barely escapes decapitation by a moving plane propeller; and he survives being dragged behind a runaway truck, as did Hector after being dragged behind the chariot of Achilles. Jones seems to relish killing dozens of foes in his righteous brawls, doing so without the overtly sarcastic asides of Bond, but, on occasion, not less humorously. When a local swordsman—most of the action happens in Cairo, Egypt—attempts to intimidate him by twirling his saber like a baton in the hands of an expert cheerleader, Jones coolly shoots him on the spot—and all the swordsman's rehearsal tricks are in vain. In terms of sheer heroic daring-do, John Wayne, James Bond, and Clint Eastwood combined could not do better.

Jones is an amalgam of these personas—a summing up of an action hero's qualities that make him a potent and dynamic image for postmodern audiences. The fact that he remains a comic-strip creation is significant, for viewers can get their thrills and laughs without having to think too seriously (or think at all). Daring and foolhardy, physically rugged, mentally nimble, lucky to the point of absurdity, and, most importantly, assisted by an equally hardnosed female partner (Karen Allen as Marion), Indiana Jones combines qualities that make him one of the most exciting screen heroes of the past several decades. Incidentally, the actual name of Jones is Henry Jr.; the name "Indiana" was given him after Steven Spielberg's dog. CS

SPIDER-MAN (2002)

DIRECTOR: Sam Raimi
WRITER: David Koepp. Based on the Marvel comic book by Stan Lee and Steve Ditko.
PRODUCERS: Laura Ziskin, Ian Bryce, Grant Curtis, Avi Arad, Stan Lee (Columbia Pictures)
CINEMATOGRAPHER: Don Burgess
EDITORS: Arthur Coburn, Bob Murawski
PRODUCTION DESIGN: Neil Spisak
ART DIRECTION: Steve Arnold
SET DECORATION: Karen O'Hara
COSTUMES: James Acheson
MUSIC: Danny Elfman
SOUND MIXERS: Kevin O'Connell, Greg P. Russell, Ed Novick
VISUAL EFFECTS: John Dykstra, Scott Stokdyk, Anthony LaMolinara, John Frazier
CAST: Peter Parker/Spider-Man: Tobey Maguire. Mary Jane Watson: Kirsten Dunst. Harry Osborn: James Franco. Norman Osborn/Green Goblin: Willem Dafoe. May Parker: Rosemary Harris. J. Jonah Jameson: J. K. Simmons. Ben Parker: Cliff Robertson. Flash Thompson: Joe Manganiello. Dennis Carradine: Michael Pappajohn. Mendel Stromm: Ron Perkins. Bernard: John Paxton
AA: None
AAN: Best Visual Effects (John Dykstra, Scott Stokdyk, Anthony LaMolinara, John Frazier), Best Sound Mixing (Kevin O'Connell, Greg P. Russell, Ed Novick)
DVD: Sony Pictures Home Entertainment, 2002
BLU-RAY: Sony Pictures Home Entertainment, 2011
DURATION: 121 minutes

Spider-Man is introduced with a narrative by Peter Parker (Tobey Maguire), an unassuming high school suburbanite and science geek who lives with his aunt and uncle and is in love with the literal girl next door. He warns us that the story we are about to see is not for the faint of heart, that he's not an average guy, and that this is not going to be a happy little tale. He isn't lying. The film recounts how Peter's life was forever changed during a school field trip to a science exhibit.

During this early scene, we are introduced to several of the main characters of the *Spider-Man* trilogy. Harry Osborn (James Franco), Peter's best friend, meets Peter and the other students at the exhibit. He arrives with his father in a private limousine. Harry's father, Dr. Norman Osborn (Willem Dafoe), is the owner of Oscorp, a manufacturing company with large government military contracts. We learn that Dr. Osborn is impressed with Peter's intelligence and initiative and perhaps not that impressed with Harry, his own son.

Also at the exhibit is Mary Jane Watson (M. J.) (Kirsten Dunst), Peter's next-door neighbor, and a popular, although shy, girl. Peter has a crush on her but is afraid to approach her. Harry steals Peter's lines and starts a conversation. As the photographer for the school newspaper, Peter eventually gets up the nerve to request a photo of M. J. in front of the exhibit of genetically enhanced super spiders. During the photo shoot, he is stung by one of the spiders. Thus begins the adventure of how Peter Parker transforms into Spider-Man.

Coincidental with his physical changes due to the spider bite (muscles, strength, dexterity, etc.), Peter is bitten by love for M. J., as they speak to one another through the backyard fence, until a boyfriend comes to pick her up in his car. In an attempt to impress the girl with a car of his own, Peter enters a wrestling contest to win money to buy one, lying to his Uncle Ben (Cliff Robertson), who drops him off, by claiming that he is going to the library. Before getting out of the car, Peter's uncle tries to have a heart-to-heart talk with him, for Uncle Ben and Aunt May (Rosemary Harris) have been worried about the recent changes in his behavior (and for good reason). Just before leaving the car, Uncle Ben offers some fatherly advice, to which Peter abruptly retorts, "You're *not* my father." Kindly responding, Uncle Ben tells Peter to always remember that *with great power comes great responsibility*. (This is the theme of the film.)

In the wrestling ring, Peter dons the colorful costume he'd created for the event: the Human Spider. The ring announcer doesn't like it, so he changes the name, much to Peter's dismay, but Peter wins under the new name: the Amazing Spider-Man. The company cheats Peter out of the advertised payoff, and Peter leaves in a fury. But there's a robbery as Peter is leaving, and the robber gets away with the cash. Still miffed, Peter does nothing to stop him. Peter later learns that his uncle has been shot by the same man when he tried to stop the thief from stealing his car. Due to guilt and shame because of his last series of actions involving his uncle, Peter vows to use his powers responsibly by donning his Spider-Man costume and protecting innocent victims like his uncle. He earns money by selling Spider-Man photos (as a freelance photographer) to the local newspaper, the *Daily Bugle*.

A subplot involves Norman Osborn's rise and demise as the Green Goblin. Oscorp has been contracted to produce a performance-enhancing chemical for the U.S. military. When the military threatens to pull the contract because development is taking too long, Osborn sacrifices himself and takes the prototype chemical, which greatly enhances his abilities but also causes him to develop an evil alter ego under duress (he is dubbed the Green Goblin by J. Jonah Jameson [played by J. K. Simmons], editor of the *Daily Bugle*). This villain is the nemesis of Spider-Man. In a pithy exchange between the two, the Green Goblin predicts Spider-Man's future when he makes him an offer and seemingly gives him a choice (which is actually not a choice, as Peter later learns):

> You and I are not so different . . . I chose my path, you chose the path of the hero. And they found you amusing for a while, the people of the city. But one thing they love more than a hero is to see a hero fail, fall, die trying . . . eventually they will hate you . . . those teeming masses exist for the sole purpose of lifting the few exceptional people onto their shoulders. . . . You and me. . . . We're exceptional . . . I'm offering you a choice. Join me. . . . Imagine what we could accomplish together . . . what we could create. Or we could destroy! Cause the deaths of countless innocents in selfish battle again and again and again until we're both dead! Is that what you want?

A series of events culminate in the Green Goblin discovering the identity of Spider-Man and kidnapping M. J. (as vengeance for Peter's perceived betrayal of his friendship with Harry by "loving" M. J. even though Harry was dating her). Luring Spider-Man to the top of the Queensboro Bridge (in a creative nod to a classic scene from the famed comic *Amazing Spider-Man* #121, where Gwen Stacy dies, but this time with the physics correct[1]) and dangling M. J. in one hand and a boxcar full of schoolchildren in another, the Green Goblin drops them both, forcing Spider-Man to make yet another choice. He manages to save them all.

In a final battle, Spider-Man defeats the Green Goblin, but not without a final test, for at the last moment, Osborn is revealed and makes an emotional plea for mercy while simultaneously activating his weapons. Spider-Man jumps to safety, and Osborn/the Green Goblin is killed by his own weapon. When Spider-Man returns the body of Norman to the Osborn home, Harry sees him and from that point onward holds a dark vengeance and hatred for the hero, believing that he killed his father, knowing nothing of his alter ego.

After Norman's funeral, while still at the cemetery, M. J. professes her love for Peter, but, realizing that the people closest to him get hurt, he tells her they can only be friends. The film ends with the following narration by Peter: "Whatever life holds in store for me, I will never forget these words: *with great power comes great responsibility.* This is my gift, my curse. Who am I? I am Spider-Man." MC

Note

1. James Kakalios, *The Physics of Superheroes* (New York: Gotham Books, 2005).

Bibliography

Kakalios, James. *The Physics of Superheroes.* New York: Gotham Books, 2005.

Saffel, Steve. *Spider-Man the Icon: The Life and Times of a Pop Culture Phenomenon.* London: Titan Books, 2007.

SPIDER-MAN 2 (2004)

DIRECTOR: Sam Raimi

WRITERS: Alvin Sargeant, Alfred Gough, Miles Millar, Michael Chabon. Based on the Marvel comic book by Stan Lee and Steve Ditko.

PRODUCERS: Avi Arad, Laura Ziskin, Grant Curtis, Stan Lee, Joseph M. Caracciolo (Columbia Pictures)

CINEMATOGRAPHER: Bill Pope

EDITOR: Bob Murawski

PRODUCTION DESIGN: Neil Spisak

ART DIRECTION: Jeff Knipp, Steven A. Saklad, Thomas Valentine, Thomas P. Wilkins

SET DECORATION: Jay Hart

COSTUMES: James Acheson, Gary Jones

MUSIC: Danny Elfman

SOUND EDITOR: Paul N. J. Ottosson

SOUND MIXERS: Kevin O'Connell, Greg P. Russell, Jeffrey A. Haboush, Joseph Geisinger

VISUAL EFFECTS: John Dykstra, Scott Stokdyk, Anthony LaMolinara, John Frazier

CAST: Peter Parker/Spider-Man: Tobey Maguire. Mary Jane Watson: Kirsten Dunst. Harry Osborn: James Franco. Norman Osborn/Green Goblin: Willem Dafoe. May Parker: Rosemary Harris. J. Jonah Jameson: J. K. Simmons. Ben Parker: Cliff Robertson. Flash Thompson: Joe Manganiello. Dennis Carradine: Michael Pappajohn. Bernard: John Paxton. Dr. Otto Octavius/Dr. Octopus/Doc Oc: Alfred Molina. Rosalie Octavius: Donna Murphy. Mr. Aziz: Aasif Mandvi. Usher: Bruce Campbell

AA: Best Visual Effects (John Dykstra, Scott Stokdyk, Anthony LaMolinara, John Frazier)

AAN: Best Sound Mixing (Kevin O'Connell, Greg P. Russell, Jeffrey A. Haboush, Joseph Geisinger), Best Sound Editing (Paul N. J. Ottosson)

DVD: Sony Pictures Home Entertainment, 2004

BLU-RAY: Sony Pictures Home Entertainment, 2007

DURATION: 128 minutes

Spider-Man 2, set two years after the first film, narrates the struggles of Spider-Man's alter ego, Peter Parker (Tobey Maguire), as he spirals through a series of losses: job (as a pizza delivery boy); girl (M. J., when she becomes engaged to someone else); best friend (Harry Osborn, still enraged at Spider-Man for killing his father); and eventually even his powers, not only as Spider-Man, but even as Peter Parker, science nerd, now attending Columbia University but underperforming due to outside pressures. Uncle Ben's admonition that *with great power comes great responsibility* looms heavily on him, and falsely reasoning that the relegation of power will release him of responsibility, he contemplates relinquishing the Spider-Man persona; however, a chance conversation with friend Harry Osborn (James Franco), now head of research for Oscorp, seems to turn everything around for the better.

Oscorp has hired Peter's academic idol, Dr. Otto Octavius (whose research on fusion comprises the subject of his overdue project at Columbia), and Peter is granted a rare meeting with the renowned nuclear scientist. Octavius (Alfred Molina) twice offers Peter advice during their meeting, which is crucial to the epic plot's denouement. His first remark comes in response to the doctor's misjudgment of Peter's character as being brilliant but lazy, reported to him by Peter's professor, a friend of the scientist. Octavius admonishes Peter, saying, "Being brilliant's not enough, young man. You have to work hard. Intelligence is not a privilege, it's a gift. And you use it for the good of mankind." (This statement will come back to haunt Octavius and prove crucial for Peter to remember.) The second comment has to do with love, as he recounts to Peter, in the presence of his intelligent and devoted wife, the importance of a balanced relationship in one's life. He says, "Love should never be a secret. If you keep something as complicated as love stored up inside, it could make you sick."

Peter is invited to Oscorp's sustained fusion experiment, featuring the research of Dr. Octavius. Assisted by his wife, Octavius dons artificial tentacles attached to his spinal cord (designed as a safety measure with the added protection of a neural inhibitor) and begins the experiment. When his experiment begins to go awry, but he hasn't yet achieved the desired state, Octavius refuses to halt it in time, with disastrous results, including the death of his wife (and true love) and the permanent attachment of the mechanical apparatus to his body, with the impairment of the inhibitor chip creating the villain Dr. Octopus (Doc Oc, as he is dubbed by the *Daily Bugle*).

Lost without the love of his life and determined to rebuild his sustained fusion reactor, but unaware of its dire consequences, Doc Oc battles, and beats, Spider-Man in a series of events, with capers including a bank robbery (where Aunt May is taken hostage) and a technically superb runaway train sequence. He even makes a deal with Harry to exchange Spider-Man for the needed element, Tritium, which only Oscorp can provide. When Harry outlines the plan, Doc Oc kidnaps M. J. and is able to finally capture Spider-Man and produce him to Harry, causing Harry to at last realize the true identity of the superhero.

In a culminating showdown, Spider-Man/Peter is forced to reason with both Harry and Doc Oc (in separate scenes) to resolve the plot. To discover the whereabouts of Doc Oc's waterfront lab so he can save the city and rescue M. J., Spider-Man successfully reasons with Harry that there are "more important things going on than you and me here," ultimately convincing his former best friend to reveal the whereabouts of Doc Oc's lair. Once there, and after doing battle, Spider-Man reveals his identity to Doc Oc, attempting to reach inside the monster to the Dr. Octavius he once was by repeating the doctor's words about the role of intelligence, and it works. In a final act of sacrifice, Dr. Octavius/Doc Oc destroys his own invention by diverting the river, although drowning in the process, his last words an emotional epiphany: "I will not die a monster."

M. J. sees the unmasked Peter and finally understands. Peter confesses his love to M. J. but reiterates that they cannot be together. Meanwhile, at the Osborn estate, Harry sees a vision of his father in a mirror, which asks him to avenge him and choose vengeance of his father's killer over friendship. When Harry smashes the mirror, it reveals the Green Goblin's secret headquarters.

The final scene finds M. J., as a runaway bride, heading to Peter's house.

Standing in his doorway, she tell him, "It's wrong that we should be half alive . . . half of ourselves. I love you. . . . Isn't it about time somebody saved your life?" They kiss, but the police scanner goes off, and so does Spider-Man. MC

Bibliography

Kakalios, James. *The Physics of Superheroes.* New York: Gotham Books, 2005.

Saffel, Steve. *Spider-Man the Icon: The Life and Times of a Pop Culture Phenomenon.* London: Titan Books, 2007.

SPIDER-MAN 3 (2007)

DIRECTOR: Sam Raimi
WRITERS: Sam Raimi, Ivan Raimi, Alvin Sargeant. Based on the Marvel comic book by Stan Lee and Steve Ditko.
PRODUCERS: Avi Arad, Laura Ziskin, Grant Curtis, Stan Lee, Kevin Feige, Joseph M. Caracciolo (Columbia Pictures)
CINEMATOGRAPHER: Bill Pope
EDITOR: Bob Murawski
PRODUCTION DESIGN: J. Michael Riva, Neil Spisak
ART DIRECTION: Christopher Burian- Mohr, David F. Klassen, Dawn Swiderski, Suzan Wexler
SET DECORATION: Leslie A. Pope
COSTUMES: James Acheson, Katina Le Ker
MUSIC: Christopher Young, with themes by Danny Elfman
CAST: Peter Parker/Spider-Man: Tobey Maguire. Mary Jane Watson: Kirsten Dunst. Harry Osborn: James Franco. Norman Osborn/Green Goblin: Willem Dafoe. May Parker: Rosemary Harris. J. Jonah Jameson: J. K. Simmons. Ben Parker: Cliff Robertson. Flash Thompson: Joe Manganiello. Dennis Carradine: Michael Pappajohn. Bernard: John Paxton. Gwen Stacy: Bryce Dallas Howard. Capt. George Stacy: James Cromwell. Eddie Brock Jr./Venom: Topher Grace. Flint Marko/Sandman: Thomas Haden Church. Emma Marko: Theresa Russell. Penny Marko: Perla Haney-Jardine
AA: None
AAN: None
DVD: Sony Pictures Home Entertainment, 2007
BLU-RAY: Sony Pictures Home Entertainment, 2007
DURATION: 139 minutes

In *Spider-Man 3*, Peter Parker (Tobey Maguire) battles his darkest demons: the ones inside. Although by outward appearances everything seems perfect—he's got the girl (now a professional actress with a Broadway role) and public acclaim as Spider-Man—things soon begin to unravel as old villains come to call, instigated by an oozing, black, alien symbiotic mass that eventually envelops him in the dark persona of Black Spider-Man. Through the action of the film, Peter/Spider-Man retraces the haunting memory of his Uncle Ben's tragic death through encounters with the escaped convict Flint Marko (Thomas Haden Church), the recently discovered killer of his uncle, who morphs into the villain Sandman. He relives father figure turned villain Norman Osborn's gruesome death through the death of his beloved friend Harry, who had re-created his father's villainous character, the Green Goblin, to become the New Goblin. Finally, Peter witnesses his own death and transformation by ridding himself of his symbiotic skin, which, unfortunately, lands on his rival, Eddie Brock (Topher Grace), who becomes the powerful Venom. Overcoming the illusions of power and realizing the importance of forgiveness, friendship, and love, Peter learns the heroic virtues that come with free choice, and that there is a big difference between being an Everyman and the son of no man. MC

Bibliography

Kakalios, James. *The Physics of Superheroes.* New York: Gotham Books, 2005.

Saffel, Steve. *Spider-Man the Icon: The Life and Times of a Pop Culture Phenomenon.* London: Titan Books, 2007.

STAR WARS: EPISODE I, THE PHANTOM MENACE **(1999)**

Director: George Lucas
Writer: George Lucas
Producers: Rick McCallum, George Lucas (Lucasfilm)
Cinematographer: David Tattersall
Editors: Ben Burtt, Paul Martin Smith
Production Design: Gavin Bocquet
Art Direction: Phil Harvey, Fred Hole, John King, Rod McLean, Peter Russell
Set Decoration: Peter Walpole
Costumes: Trisha Biggar
Music: John Williams
Sound Editors: Ben Burtt, Tom Bellfort
Sound Mixers: Gary Rydstrom, Tom Johnson, Shawn Murphy, John Midgley
Visual Effects: John Knoll, Dennis Muren, Scott Squires, Rob Coleman
Cast: Qui-Gon Jinn: Liam Neeson. Obi-Wan Kenobi: Ewan McGregor. Queen Amidala/Padmé: Natalie Portman. Anakin Skywalker: Jake Lloyd. Senator Palpatine: Ian McDiarmid. Shmi Skywalker: Pernilla August. Sio Bibble: Oliver Ford Davies. Capt. Panaka: Hugh Quarshie. Jar Jar Binks (voice): Ahmed Best. C-3PO (voice): Anthony Daniels. R2-D2: Kenny Baker. Sabé: Keira Knightley. Finis Valorum: Terence Stamp. Darth Maul: Ray Park. Yoda (voice): Frank Oz
AA: None
AAN: Best Sound (Gary Rydstrom, Tom Johnson, Shawn Murphy, John Midgley), Best Effects–Sound Effects Editing (Ben Burtt, Tom Bellfort), Best Effects–Visual Effects (John Knoll, Dennis Muren, Scott Squires, Rob Coleman)
DVD: 20th Century Fox Home Video, 2007. The Prequel Trilogy (*Episode I, The Phantom Menace; Episode II, Attack of the Clones; Episode III, Revenge of the Sith*), 20th Century Fox Home Video, 2008.
Blu-ray: The Prequel Trilogy (*Episode I, The Phantom Menace; Episode II, Attack of the Clones; Episode III, Revenge of the Sith*), 20th Century Fox Home Video, 2011.
Duration: 136 minutes

Star Wars: Episode I, The Phantom Menace is the first of the three prequels that were released between 1999 and 2005, when George Lucas again took over the direction of three more episodes of the immensely successful *Star Wars*, following a period of twenty-two years since the first trilogy started in 1977, and sixteen years after the last film in that series, *Return of the Jedi*, had come out 1983. In the intervening years, digital technology had advanced considerably, and when *The Phantom Menace* was released to theaters in 1999, the computer-generated imagery special effects were stunningly superior, especially when shown in IMAX theaters, with their wide screens and superior sound effects, which overwhelmed the viewer, who was able to get the impression of the sight and sound similar to that of a 3D production—something that was to come soon enough.

Although this first of the three episodes of the prequel sequence seems to tell the hexalogy of *Star Wars* backward, introducing new characters and names to remember, as well as additional plot complications, the prequels add dimension to the galactic universe of *Star Wars* and complete the cycle of the story, both in terms of winners and losers and the tracing of the heroes and heroines of the larger story, beginning with Anakin Skywalker (Jake Lloyd) as the early hero, his conversion into the villain Darth Vader by the Force, his love for Queen Amidala (Natalie Portman), and his parentage of Luke and Leia, the hero and heroine of the stories already told.

The new trilogy, of course, demanded cast replacements, since so much time had passed since *Return of the Jedi*. Ewan McGregor replaced Alec Guinness as Ben Obi-Wan Kenobi; Harrison Ford as Hans Solo was no longer there; Carrie Fisher's character as Princess Leia had not yet been born; and Anakin Skywalker was a gifted nine-year-old boy who grew up under the guidance of Obi-Wan Kenobi, only to later turn into the dreaded Darth Vader of the Empire and the father of Luke Skywalker (played by Mark Hamill before). The film also introduces two budding actresses, Natalie Portman, who plays the fourteen-year-old Queen Amidala, while Keira Knightley is Sabé, Amidala's her handmaiden and momentarily her decoy. Portman stayed on for all three prequels, making a name for herself and rising to stardom, while Knightley sought other avenues, namely the *Pirates of the Caribbean* sequence (2003–2006). Liam Neeson, the celebrated actor in *Schindler's List* and other mega productions, took over the role of Qui-Gon Jinn, who leads a delegation (including the young Kenobi) sent by the Jedi Knights' supreme leader, Finis Valorum (Terence Stamp), to the Galactic Republic Trade Federation, his mission being to negotiate the easing of taxation on the planet Naboo.

The Trade Federation, however, is dominated by Darth Sidious, of the order of the Sith, perennial enemies of the Jedi, and he sets out to kill the delegation members from Naboo and then invade that planet and subdue it. The queen of Naboo, Amidala, disguised as the handmaiden Padmé, her decoy Sabé posing as the queen, is also captured but soon freed. The delegation, with the queen and her maid, arrive at the settlement of Mos Espa, where they meet a young boy who seems unusually gifted, having created his own droid device, C-3PO (Anthony Daniels), which he later uses to win races and launch a fight with the Federation and its corrupt Senate, dominated by Senator Palpatine (Ian McDiarmid) of Naboo, who proves to be the arch-villain and a traitor to his own people. He is soon elected as the supreme chancellor of the Galactic Republic, allied to the Sith and seeking to control the Force, and, thence, the balance of power in the Republic.

Meanwhile, another sinister character comes on the scene, Darth Maul (Ray Park), the Sith Master, who engages Obi-Wan and Qui-Gon in a mortal battle, but, even if he is killed by Obi-Wan, he manages to mortally wound Qui-Gon. The latter dies and is buried with honors in his native Naboo, and during his funeral, the queen confers an honor to the race of Gungans, who had helped him in his fight. Qui Gon was the nominal leader of the Naboo tribe in *The Phantom Menace*, and his death also meant that Liam Neeson would no longer be part of the sequence. Qui-Gon, however, is the hero of this first prequel, and his legacy remains alive in his surviving partner, Obi-Wan, and his protégé, Anakin, both of whom will continue to perpetrate his fight for right balance of the Force, the dominant factor in the Galactic Republic. CS

STAR WARS: EPISODE II, ATTACK OF THE CLONES (2002)

Director: George Lucas
Writers: Jonathan Hales, George Lucas
Producers: Rick McCallum, George Lucas (Lucasfilm)
Cinematographer: David Tattersall
Editors: Ben Burtt, George Lucas
Production Design: Gavin Bocquet
Art Direction: Ian Gracie, Phil Harvey, Fred Hole, Jonathan Lee, Michelle McGahey, Peter Russell
Set Decoration: Peter Walpole
Costumes: Trisha Biggar
Music: John Williams
Visual Effects: John Knoll, Rob Coleman, Pablo Helman, Ben Snow
Cast: Obi-Wan Kenobi: Ewan McGregor. Padmé Amidala: Natalie Portman. Anakin Skywalker: Hayden Christensen. Count Dooku/Darth Tyranus: Christopher Lee. Mace Windu: Samuel L. Jackson. Supreme Chancellor Palpatine: Ian McDiarmid. Shmi Skywalker: Pernilla August. Jango Fett: Temuera Morrison.

Boba Fett: Daniel Logan. Senator Bail Organa: Jimmy Smits. Sio Bibble: Oliver Ford Davies. Jar Jar Binks/Achk Med-Beq (voice): Ahmed Best. Cliegg Lars: Jack Thompson. C-3PO: Anthony Daniels. R2-D2: Kenny Baker. Yoda (voice): Frank Oz

AA: None

AAN: Best Effects–Visual Effects (John Knoll, Rob Coleman, Pablo Helman, Ben Snow)

DVD: 20th Century Fox Home Video, 2005. The Prequel Trilogy (*Episode I, The Phantom Menace; Episode II, Attack of the Clones; Episode III, Revenge of the Sith*), 20th Century Fox Home Video, 2008.

Blu-ray: The Prequel Trilogy (*Episode I, The Phantom Menace; Episode II, Attack of the Clones; Episode III, Revenge of the Sith*), 20th Century Fox Home Video, 2011.

Duration: 142 minutes

Of the three prequels to *Star Wars, Attack of the Clones* was the weakest in terms of box-office returns, Academy Awards received (none), and critical acceptance. Nevertheless, in terms of its action and plot development of the whole, it provides important links and helps the reader of the hexalogy make sense of the complexities of the saga. At 142 minutes in length, it is also the longest film in the series.

The boy Anakin (Hayden Christensen) has grown into a young man, who, with the help of his mentor, Obi-Wan Kenobi (Ewan McGregor), and the former queen of Naboo, Padmé Amidala (Natalie Portman), now also a beautiful young woman, forms an alliance with the Jedi knight Dooku (Christopher Lee) and prepares a movement that will enable them to attack the Republic, dominated by a corrupt Senate. There is an assassination attempt against the queen using a dart manufactured on the distant planet Kamino. As Anakin escorts Amidala back to her home planet, Naboo, Obi-Wan remains behind to investigate the origin of the poisonous dart and discovers an army of clones, assembled secretly by the Republic, their purpose being to conquer and dominate the Republic. Obi-Wan tracks down Jango (Temuera Morrison), the leader of the clones, following him to a remote, rocky planet called Geonosis, where the droids are assembled, soon to become the real threat of the Republic. Palpatine (Ian McDiarmid) is assigned as their leader, while Darth Sidious, a Sith, is in control of the Republic.

In a fight with the clone army leader Dooku, Anakin loses his right arm, which is later replaced by a prosthetic one. In a secret ceremony, Anakin and Amidala, who in the meantime have fallen in love, marry, with the androids C-3PO (Anthony Daniels) and R2-D2 (Kenny Baker) as witnesses, and Amidala is soon pregnant. This may actually be the most important event of the hexalogy, because it marks their alliance, which produces the future heirs and leaders of the three sequels. Their marriage and the birth of their twin children, Luke and Leia, are the links between all six episodes, as Anakin will change nature, sever relations with Obi-Wan, and become the dreaded Darth Vader, the enemy of the Jedi, eventually being forced to fight his own son. CS

STAR WARS: EPISODE III, REVENGE OF THE SITH (2005)

Director: George Lucas

Writer: George Lucas

Producers: Rick McCallum, George Lucas (Lucasfilm)

Cinematographer: David Tattersall

Editors: Roger Barton, Ben Burtt

Production Design: Gavin Bocquet

Art Direction: Ian Gracie, Phil Harvey, David Lee, Peter Russell

Set Decoration: Richard Roberts

Costumes: Trisha Biggar

MUSIC: John Williams
MAKEUP ARTISTS: Dave Elsey, Nikki Gooley
CAST: Obi-Wan Kenobi: Ewan McGregor. Padmé Amidala: Natalie Portman. Anakin Skywalker: Hayden Christensen. Count Dooku: Christopher Lee. Mace Windu: Samuel L. Jackson. Supreme Chancellor Palpatine: Ian McDiarmid. Queen of Naboo: Keisha Castle-Hughes. Senator Bail Organa: Jimmy Smits. Sio Bibble: Oliver Ford Davies. Jar Jar Binks: Ahmed Best. C-3PO: Anthony Daniels. Ki-Adi-Mundi/Nute Gunray: Silas Carson. R2-D2: Kenny Baker. General Grievous (voice): Matthew Wood. Yoda (voice): Frank Oz
AA: None
AAN: Best Makeup (Dave Elsey, Nikki Gooley)
DVD: 20th Century Fox Home Video, 2005. The Prequel Trilogy (*Episode I, The Phantom Menace; Episode II, Attack of the Clones; Episode III, Revenge of the Sith*), 20th Century Fox Home Video, 2008.
BLU-RAY: The Prequel Trilogy (*Episode I, The Phantom Menace; Episode II, Attack of the Clones; Episode III, Revenge of the Sith*), 20th Century Fox Home Video, 2011.
DURATION: 140 minutes

The third *Star Wars* episode, *Revenge of the Sith,* is the culmination of the two previous episodes, which wrap up the hexalogy of *Star Wars* as it now stands, although another episode is in the planning stages, expected to be out in 2015. *Revenge of the Sith* broke box-office records upon its release, and although it did not fare any better with Academy Awards or critical recognition, it musters a powerful dramatic resolution that brings the battle of this fictional galactic universe, between the forces of good and evil, to a climax, which, with a pause of a generation, was to continue—and has already been concluded—in the original trilogy.

Three years had elapsed since *Attack of the Clones.* A separatist army of clones, led by General Grievous (Matthew Wood), is wreaking havoc on the Republic, and Obi-Wan Kenobi (Ewan McGregor) wages a brave counterattack, but this time without the aid of Anakin Skywalker (Hayden Christensen), who has sided the chancellor of the Galactic Republic, Palpatine (Ian McDiarmid), who has kept his real identity as a Sith concealed. While the battles rage, Anakin learns that Padmé (Natalie Portman) is pregnant, but he fears that his wife will die during childbirth. At the same time, he is turned down by the Jedi Council as a Master and, at this point, resentful and disappointed, believes Palpatine's admonitions that he will become more powerful and able to save his wife and defeat his enemies if he were to accept the dark side of the Force. He is convinced, becomes Palpatine's assistant, and changes his name to Darth Vader, already known to the previous generation of audiences of the first trilogy as the most feared enemy of the Jedi.

This brings about the disapproval of Padmé, who tries to convert him back to his previous loyalties, but Darth Vader refuses and tries to subdue her. Obi-Wan Kenobi interferes; saves Padmé; and then engages in a fierce battle with Darth Vader, whose left arm and legs he dismembers. He then throws him into a volcano and leaves him there as dead. Padmé gives birth to twins Luke and Leia, and in her heart she still believes that Darth Vader can be regenerated.

But Vader is not yet dead. Palpatine finds him alive and brings him to a doctor, who rebuilds his missing limbs using cybernetic materials. Palpatine also informs him that his wife has died in childbirth. Darth Vader is now completely dominated by the dark side of the Force, and he starts planning his revenge, building a Death Star that will destroy Naboo. Padmé is buried with honors, and her twins are adopted by Senator Bail Organa (Jimmy Smits) of the Empire, as the former Galactic Republic is now called. The children are separated. Leia is given to Alderaan, a resident in the Naboo community, while Luke is taken to Tatooine by Obi-Wan as an orphan and given to his uncle and aunt to live as a farmer. Obi-Wan is able to communicate with the spirit of Qui-Gon Jinn, reassuring the former leader that he intends on supervising Luke's upbringing and convincing him that he is of great heritage and under obligation to grow up and defeat the dark side of the Force, now dominating the Empire.

The viewer of the prequels has thus been given additional parts of the larger story that remained unknown until now and is now able to understand the hexalogy in its entirety, and, if of the younger generation, to go back and revisit the sequels. CS

STAR WARS: EPISODE IV, A NEW HOPE (1977)

DIRECTOR: George Lucas
WRITER: George Lucas
PRODUCERS: Gary Kurtz, Rick McCallum, George Lucas (20th Century Fox)
CINEMATOGRAPHER: Gilbert Taylor
EDITORS: Paul Hirsch, Richard Chew, Marcia Lucas
PRODUCTION DESIGN: John Barry
ART DIRECTION: Norman Reynolds, Leslie Dilley
SET DECORATION: Roger Christian
COSTUMES: John Mollo
MUSIC: John Williams
SOUND MIXERS: Don MacDougall, Ray West, Bob Minkler, Derek Ball
SOUND EFFECTS: Ben Burtt
VISUAL EFFECTS: John Stears, John Dykstra, Richard Edlund, Grant McCune, Robert Blalack
CAST: Luke Skywalker: Mark Hamill. Princess Leia Organa: Carrie Fisher. Han Solo: Harrison Ford. Darth Vader: David Prowse. Grand Moff Tarkin: Peter Cushing. Ben Obi-Wan Kenobi: Alec Guinness. R2-D2: Kenny Baker. C-3PO: Anthony Daniels. Owen Lars: Phil Brown. Beru: Shelagh Fraser. Chewbacca: Peter Mayhew. Chief Jawa: Jack Purvis. Boba Fett: Mark Austin. Wedge Antilles: Denis Lawson
AA: Best Art Direction–Set Decoration (John Barry, Norman Reynolds, Leslie Dilley, Roger Christian), Best Costume Design (John Mollo), Best Film Editing (Paul Hirsch, Richard Chew, Marcia Lucas), Best Music–Original Score (John Williams), Best Sound Mixing (Don MacDougall, Ray West, Bob Minkler, Derek Ball), Best Effects–Visual Effects (John Stears, John Dykstra, Richard Edlund, Grant McCune, Robert Blalack), Special Achievement Award–Sound Effects (Ben Burtt)
AAN: Best Supporting Actor (Alec Guinness), Best Director (George Lucas), Best Picture (Gary Kurtz), Best Screenplay–Screenplay Written Directly for the Screen (George Lucas)
DVD: Two-disc enhanced wide-screen edition, 20th Century Fox Home Video, 2006. Star Wars Trilogy (*Episode IV, A New Hope; Episode V, The Empire Strikes Back; Episode VI, Return of the Jedi*), 20th Century Fox Home Video, 2011.
BLU-RAY: Star Wars Trilogy (*Episode IV, A New Hope; Episode V, The Empire Strikes Back; Episode VI, Return of the Jedi*), 20th Century Fox Home Video, 2011.
DURATION: 121 minutes

The Star Wars original trilogy (1977–1983) and the three "prequels" (1999–2005), which arrived on the screen sixteen years later, can be considered one of the greatest cinematic events ever, a popular phenomenon, if you will, for the six movies are tied by common threads of plot, their characters imprinted in the popular imagination for four decades now, and the phenomenon is still alive and thriving, as one more movie with the same general topic has been released since then,[1] and another one entitled *Star Wars: Episode VII* is due out in 2015.[2] The original series, with its prequels, has spawned a television series that is still running, video games, radio programs, and new theatrical releases of the original trilogy, and it has netted numerous Oscars, among many other awards, earning more than $4 billion at the box office.

While the popular acceptance of the Star Wars franchise has been enormous,[3] critical reaction, highly favorable at first, has waned considerably with the arrival of the three prequels. The Star Wars movies have been called "epic space operas," the term *space opera* having replaced *soap opera*, a term used mainly for television melodramas that feature good guys in conflicts with villains, or bad guys, in this case changing from epic heroes to villains in the vast and expanding areas of conflicts not on Earth but in the skies. The typical epic of earlier eras had heroes borrowed from history of historical fiction, going back to mythological tales—Babylonian, Sumerian, Greek, Roman, or medieval—from Eastern to Western and Northern Europe, to the American West, thus creating the popular, archetypal hero, the most popular of heroes, as the history of cinema has shown. Space operas brought in the new heroes, most of whom battle invaders from outer space who are threatening our civilization. Space operas had been made before the 1970s—witness *The Invasion of the Body Snatchers* (Don Siegel, 1956)[4]—but it was not until Stanley Kubrick's *2001: A Space Odyssey* in 1968 that the space science-fiction epic took off in a serious vein. But there is a difference.

Kubrick's *2001* is regarded as something of an art movie that made its mark on the mainstream theater, but it does not offer easy answers. It starts with mystery, the monolith, which sparks man's imagination to enterprise, and it ends with a monolith, still a mystery. The movie gives no clue as to its origin. There is no villain, except for a computer—HAL 9000—which is man-made. This sparked the invention of a series of androids in movies that came later, including *Alien* (1977) and its sequels, and, of course, in *Star Wars*, we have man-made machines at the service of man, who occasionally turn against him. Those are not the main villains, however. The Galaxy, where the action happens, has its own, the Darth Vaders and the like, which spur a series of reactions from the heroes of the skies, fighting the intergalactic wars to save their own.

George Lucas claims that seeing *The Hidden Fortress* (1958) inspired him (in part) to write the script for the Star Wars series,[5] and that statement must not remain unnoticed. For one thing, both movies involve groups of people cast out of their previous authority positions and hiding in remote locations until they can regroup, plan a counterattack, and reclaim their previous authority. To do so they must traverse vast distances (expressed in relative terms); elude or confront numerous natural obstacles or hostile hordes; and, in the process, show bravery, courage, cunning, the ability to conceal their true identities, and the readiness of wit needed to face the adversity that often comes their way. Theirs are difficult, arduous, and exhausting tasks that, more often than not, go beyond the pale of human endurance. And the feats are performed, and the people on the right side, that is, those winning our sympathies, are victorious and achieve their ends. It is a story in which now-archetypal formulas have been repeated since the beginning of time, from Gilgamesh to Odysseus, King Arthur, Robin Hood, Hamlet, Hercules (in movies), and Harry Potter. Audiences delight to see heroes win in the end, especially if their ends coincide with those of the tribe.

Star Wars is a story that takes place in the Galaxy and involves fantastic shapes of planets, asteroids, intergalactic vehicles, robots, weapons (laser beams), and other such paraphernalia, most of which Lucas introduces to the screen in grand manner. Only a certain amount of realism is achievable in such a context and narrative format; the main heroes are human, for instance, and some of the scenes were filmed on location, rather than being composed digitally, as was also the case with the later series.

Star Wars: Episode IV, A New Hope begins the saga of intergalactic wars between two great powers in the Galaxy, the Empire, which stands for a dark force of evil, and the tribe of the Jedi, previously defeated by the Empire and now living on an isolated planet, practically bereft of its previous powers. But they undertake a mission to save Princess Leia (Carrie Fisher), who has been living in the Empire and has dispatched a message with the plans of the Death Star craft, which is the main weapon of the Empire, and through which the Empire is able to strike and destroy entire planets. The message, carried by two androids (or "droids"), R2-D2 (Kenny Baker) and C-3PO (Anthony Daniels), arrives in a pod that lands on the planet where Luke Skywalker (Mark Hamill) lives on a farm with his uncle and aunt. Luke is a restless youth who yearns for adventure rather than school or farming. When the pod carrying the androids lands on his uncle's place, Luke soon discovers that old Obi-Wan Kenobi (Alec Guinness) lives not far from there, and from him he learns the secrets of the Force (although not his actual identity, for he is the son of Darth Vader, or the fact that Princess Leia is his twin sister). To undertake this expedition, they enlist the services of Han Solo (Harrison Ford), a mercenary who possesses the fastest ship in the Galaxy, capable of traveling at the speed of light and maneuvering through asteroids. Their mission is to get to the Death Star and escape with Leia.

The comrades make it to their destination and find Leia, but during a battle with Darth Vader (David Prowse), Obi-Wan Kenobi is killed. The rest escape and safely return to their planet; however, the Empire is not through, and led by Grand Moff Tarkin (Peter Cushing) and Darth Vader, it launches a counterattack. The valiant fighters of the planet manage to explode the Death Star, and Darth Vader flies back to the Empire in defeat. The victors celebrate their accomplishment, receiving their medallions of honor. Of course, with two sequels (in the 1980s) and the later prequels, the story becomes much more complicated, for in the process, we learn the origin of the evil Darth Vader, the father of Luke and Leia, and the transformational power of the Force, which can turn an identity either good or evil.

The first three episodes, which, according to Lucas, were conceived as one story with three chapters, are, of course, and continue to be, the most ingenious in terms of story line, the most inventive, and by far the most popular, although the last three, made in modern times, have gained technologically and sparkle with computer-generated, digitally superior spectacle. But the first episode (now IV) ushered in the digital age (although most scenes were composed in traditional animation) and the vast consequences, commercially and artistically, of the virtual reality image now generated for the big screen. It is a brave new world, now at its peak, and still evolving, with no end in sight. Despite this technological progress, the last three episodes, although "prequels," have not achieved the widespread popularity of the first three, just as the late James Bond sagas, despite their technological/special effects innovations, have lost the gloss and heroic glitter of the first four or five films, made in the 1960s.

Star Wars: Episode IV was filmed on location in Tunisia for the desert scenes, and in Death Valley, California, for the scenes in the canyons, although, of course, the galactic battles and interiors were digitally designed. This gives the early episodes some air of reality, however remote it may be, for the emphasis is on intergalactic wars, and the entire film had to be seen as science-fiction fantasy. But the battle between good and evil is the crux of the matter, and viewers thought they recognized a sort of American western transferred to the skies. Lucas explored a myth, the eternal battle of good (the Force), envied by evil—strangely also motivated by the Force—which is an unrecognizable entity in the universe, and only sages like Obi-Wan Kenobi can recognize and master it to some degree, or transmit it to others through judicious advice. The Force rules the Galaxy, and whoever masters its admonitions will become the eventual ruler—of eternal good and peace. CS

Notes

1. *Star Wars: The Clone Wars* (2008).
2. *Star Wars: Episode VII*, http://en.wikipedia.org/wiki/Star_Wars.
3. A total of 94 percent and 97 percent for the first two, a respectable 79 percent for the third, but dropping to 57 percent with *The Phantom Menace* in 1999, according to *Rotten Tomatoes*, generally reflecting critical attitudes. "*Star Wars*," *Wikipedia*, http://en.wikipedia.org/wiki/Star_Wars.
4. Remade by Philip Kaufman in 1978.
5. George Lucas, "Commentary," *The Hidden Fortress*, directed by Akira Kurosawa (Criterion, 2001), DVD.

Bibliography

Campbell, Joseph. *The Power of Myth*. New York: Anchor Books, 1991.

Henderson, Mary. *Star Wars: The Magic of Myth*. New York: Bantam Books, 1997.

Larsen, Stephen. *Joseph Campbell: A Fire in the Mind*. New York: Inner Traditions, 2002.

STAR WARS: EPISODE V, THE EMPIRE STRIKES BACK (1980)

DIRECTOR: Richard Marquand
WRITERS: Lawrence Kasdan, George Lucas
PRODUCERS: Gary Kurtz, Rick McCallum, George Lucas (Lucasfilm)
CINEMATOGRAPHER: Peter Suschitzky
EDITORS: Paul Hirsch, T. M. Christopher, George Lucas (uncredited), Marcia Lucas (uncredited)
PRODUCTION DESIGN: Norman Reynolds
ART DIRECTION: Leslie Dilley, Harry Lange, Alan Tomkins
SET DECORATION: Michael Ford
COSTUMES: John Mollo
MUSIC: John Williams
SOUND RECORDISTS: Bill Varney, Steve Maslow, Gregg Landaker, Peter Sutton
VISUAL EFFECTS: Brian Johnson, Richard Edlund, Dennis Muren, Bruce Nicholson
CAST: Luke Skywalker: Mark Hamill. Princess Leia Organa: Carrie Fisher. Han Solo: Harrison Ford. Lando Calrissian: Billy Dee Williams. C-3PO: Anthony Daniels. Darth Vader: David Prowse. Chewbacca: Peter Mayhew. R2-D2: Kenny Baker. Yoda (voice): Frank Oz. Ben Obi-Wan Kenobi: Alec Guinness. Boba Fett: Jeremy Bulloch. Chief Ugnaught: Jack Purvis. Adm. Piett: Kenneth Colley
AA: Best Sound (Bill Varney, Steve Maslow, Gregg Landaker, Peter Sutton), Special Achievement Award–Visual Effects (Brian Johnson, Richard Edlund, Dennis Muren, Bruce Nicholson)
AAN: Best Art Direction–Set Decoration (Norman Reynolds, Leslie Dilley, Harry Lange, Alan Tomkins, Michael Ford), Best Music–Original Score (John Williams)
DVD: Wide-screen edition, 20th Century Fox Home Video, 2006. Star Wars Trilogy (*Episode IV, A New Hope*; *Episode V, The Empire Strikes Back*; *Episode VI, Return of the Jedi*), 20th Century Fox Home Video, 2011.
BLU-RAY: Star Wars Trilogy (*Episode IV, A New Hope*; *Episode V, The Empire Strikes Back*; *Episode VI, Return of the Jedi*), 20th Century Fox Home Video, 2011.
DURATION: 124 minutes

Coming on the heels *Episode IV, A New Hope*, *Star Wars: Episode V, The Empire*

Strikes Back could technically be imagined as a sequel, but Lucas prefers to call this and other episodes chapters of the same story. *Star Wars* is a story that, according to Lucas, was conceived in its totality, and although its prototypes were Saturday matinee serials, or westerns and the samurai films of Akira Kurosawa, this was an initial script resembling a vast epic novel with six chapters, in which the tales of his heroes were linked by generations, characters related to one another by kinship or other ties, and the plots are evolving phases of the same story. He chose to start with *Episode IV*, in medias res, as it were, and went on to complete his story (in the 1970s and early 1980s) with the last two episodes. The first three segments, however, which include the story of Luke's parents and the wars between antagonistic forces in the Galaxy, had remained untold, and the three "prequels," as they are called for lack of a better term, became the subjects of the second trilogy, not filmed until sixteen years later. Thus, the entire story may be considered two trilogies told in reverse order, a "hexalogy" (a hexad), as the whole might be called.

Only time will tell whether such a colossal scheme of storytelling in film is possible, for future generations resorting to home viewing (or conceivably new theatric releases) could see the entire story beginning with *Star Wars: Episode I, The Phantom Menace*, which chronicles the early adventures of Anakin Skywalker, the father of Luke, as he and his beloved Queen Amidala toil to save their planet from external threats. Generations from now may not be able to see the huge differences in technique, mainly in special effects, that evolved from the plain animations of the 1970s into the digital effects of the late 1990s and early 2000s. Had the story been told in natural chronological sequences and without the significant gap between trilogies, the story might have been more organically connected and followed by audiences that were relatively in the same age groups. Youth today may not have the same enthusiasm for a story that is told at the relatively leisurely pace of movie-telling twenty five years ago or feel empathetic for Luke as they do for his progenitors now. It is not surprising that the last three episodes (the prequels) have not done as well as their earlier counterparts, although DVD sets sell them as a package.

Of all the sequels and prequels, *Episode V, The Empire Strikes Back* has achieved more unity of action and better special effects, while the principal actors (Mark Hamill, Harrison Ford, and Carrie Fisher, in particular) have matured into their roles, play them with more ease, and connect better with one another and the whole. This movie also connects better with the sequel/prequel, *Star Wars: Episode III, Revenge of the Sith* (2005). For the new viewer, it would actually be better if he or she started with *Episode I, The Phantom Menace*, progress to its sequels, and then go back to the original *Episode IV, A New Hope* and take it from there. The whole could better fit into its parts. With today's DVD and Bluray editions, this is actually quite possible, even for the older, nostalgic viewers whose memories may have faded. CS

STAR WARS: EPISODE VI, RETURN OF THE JEDI (1983)

Director: Irvin Kershner
Writers: Leigh Brackett, Lawrence Kasdan, George Lucas
Producers: Howard G. Kazanjian, Rick McCallum, George Lucas (Lucasfilm)
Cinematographer: Alan Hume
Editors: Sean Barton, T. M. Christopher, Marcia Lucas, Duwayne Dunham, George Lucas (uncredited)
Production Design: Norman Reynolds
Art Direction: Fred Hole, James L. Schoppe

Set Decoration: Michael Ford, Harry Lange
Costumes: Aggie Guerard Rodgers, Nilo Rodis-Jamero
Music: John Williams
Sound Mixers: Ben Burtt, Gary Summers, Randy Thom, Tony Dawe
Visual Effects: Richard Edluand, Dennis Muren, Ken Ralston, Phil Tipett
Cast: Luke Skywalker: Mark Hamill. Princess Leia Organa: Carrie Fisher. Han Solo: Harrison Ford. Lando Calrissian: Billy Dee Williams. C-3PO: Anthony Daniels. Darth Vader: David Prowse. Chewbacca: Peter Mayhew. Anakin Skywalker: Sebastian Shaw. The Emperor: Ian McDiarmid. R2-D2/Paploo: Kenny Baker. Yoda (voice): Frank Oz. Ben Obi-Wan Kenobi: Alec Guinness. Boba Fett: Jeremy Bulloch. Teebo: Jack Purvis. Adm. Piett: Kenneth Colley. Bib Fortuna: Michael Carter. Jabba the Hut (voice): Larry Ward (uncreidted)
AA: Special Achievement Award–Visual Effects (Richard Edlund, Dennis Muren, Ken Ralston, Phil Tipett)
AAN: Best Art Direction–Set Decoration (Norman Reynolds, Fred Hole, James L. Schoppe, Michael Ford), Best Music–Original Score (John Williams), Best Sound (Ben Burtt, Gary Summers, Randy Thom, Tony Dawe), Best Effects–Sound Effects Editing (Ben Burtt)
DVD: Wide-screen edition, 20th Century Fox Home Video, 2006. Star Wars Trilogy (*Episode IV, A New Hope*; *Episode V, The Empire Strikes Back*; *Episode VI, Return of the Jedi*), 20th Century Fox Home Video, 2011.
Blu-ray: Star Wars Trilogy (*Episode IV, A New Hope*; *Episode V, The Empire Strikes Back*; *Episode VI, Return of the Jedi*), 20th Century Fox Home Video, 2011.
Duration: 124 minutes

If placed in chronological order, *Return of the Jedi* is the last episode of the hexalogy, and perhaps the most dramatic, at least in story continuity, for it brings the battle of good and evil in the fictional Galaxy, where it takes place, to its logical conclusion. If seen in sequence with its later prequels, this effect is amplified, for the hexalogy, in its totality, gives the narrative additional depth and dimension, as well as dramatic power.

The Galactic Empire has, by now, dominated the Galaxy and, under orders by Palpatine, the new and ruthless emperor, is undertaking the task of building a new and more efficient Death Star, one that will destroy the Alliance of Rebels once and for all. The evil part of the Force will also have won a decisive victory, tilting the world of the Galactic cosmos toward a regime of absolute power.

The Rebels organize under the leadership of Luke Skywalker (Mark Hamill), aided by Leia (Carrie Fisher), and both save Han Solo (Harrison Ford), who is being held captive by Lord Jabba the Hut (Larry Ward). After several battles, they return to Dagobah, where they hear the voice of Yoda saying that Darth Vader was once Anakin Skywalker, Luke's father, while the dead Obi-Wan Kenobi (Alec Guinness), in a holograph, also reveals that Princess Leia is Luke's twin sister. They also learn that, under the leadership of Darth Vader and Palpatine, a new and more dangerous Death Star is being constructed. Thus, the Rebel Alliance is threatened with annihilation. When the Death Star is about to be completed, the main battles begin.

Luke gathers his forces of resistance, aided by a tribe of Ewoks, on the moon Endor, but before a battle, he is desirous of meeting with Darth Vader (David Prowse) to convince him to change sides and use the Force for good. Instead, Darth Vader, still under the influence of Palpatine, battles Luke in a lightsaber duel, and when Luke cuts off his right hand,

Palpatine urges him to kill his father, who by now is also conscious that Leia is his daughter, and take his place. When Luke refuses Palpatine's entreaty, Darth Vader changes heart and kills Palpatine, throwing him down into a precipice, but, in the process, he is also mortally wounded. Before dying, he asks Luke to remove his mask—a symbol of his transformation into someone evil—so he can look at his son without it. He declares that there is still good in the Galaxy and instructs Luke to convey his message to his daughter. After fierce battles at Endor, the Rebels destroy the Death Star, and Luke, with the body of his father, soon joins them. Anakin's body is cremated with appropriate honors on a funeral pyre, brother and sister are recognized as such (rather than as allies), and peace returns to the Galactic cosmos.

If the hexalogy of Star Wars is seen as an entire work that took a quarter of a century to complete, one can marvel at the tremendous imagination of George Lucas as the creator of a magnificent cosmos where good and evil do battle, and where good prevails, but not without loss and pain. Not quite a Manichean universe, the hexalogy is a reminder that imagination, aided by advanced technology, is a prelude to even greater works in the future, cinematic or otherwise. In earlier ages, George Lucas, warts and all, might have been an Aeschylus or a Dante, whose works broadened the horizons of humankind both on Earth and in the heavens.

Bibliography

Arnold, Alan. *Once Upon a Galaxy: A Journal of the Making of* The Empire Strikes Back. New York: Ballantine, 1980.

Campbell, Joseph. *The Power of Myth.* New York: Anchor Books, 1991.

Henderson, Mary. *Star Wars: The Magic of Myth.* New York: Bantam, 1997.

Larsen, Stephen. *Joseph Campbell: A Fire in the Mind.* New York: Inner Traditions, 2002.

***SUPERMAN* (1978)**

DIRECTOR: Richard Donner

WRITERS: Jerry Siegel, Joe Shuster, Mario Puzo, David Newman, Leslie Newman, Robert Benton, Tom Mankiewicz, Norman Enfield

PRODUCER: Pierre Spengler (Warner Bros., DC Comics)

CINEMATOGRAPHER: Geoffrey Unsworth

EDITOR: Stuart Baird, Michael Ellis

PRODUCTION DESIGN: John Barry

ART DIRECTION: Ernest Archer, Philip Bennet, Stuart Craig, Leslie Dilley, Norman Dorme, Tony Reading, Norman Reynolds

SET DECORATION: Peter Howitt

COSTUMES: Yvonne Blake

MUSIC: John Williams

SOUND MIXERS: Gordon K. McCallum, Graham V. Hartstone, Nicolas Le Messurier, Roy Charman

VISUAL EFFECTS: Les Bowie, Colin Chilvers, Denys N. Coop, Roy Field, Derek Meddings, Zoran Perisic

CAST: Jor-El: Marlon Brando. Lex Luthor: Gene Hackman. Superman/Clark Kent: Christopher Reeve. Otis: Ned Beatty. Perry White: Jackie Cooper. Pa Kent: Glenn Ford. 1st Elder: Trevor Howard. Lois Lane: Margot Kidder. Eve Teschmacher: Valerie Perrine. Ma Kent: Phyllis Thaxter. Lara: Susannah York. Young Clark Kent: Jeff East. Jimmy Olsen: Marc McClure

AA: Special Achievement Award–Visual Effects (Les Bowie, Colin Chilvers, Denys N. Coop, Roy Field, Derek Meddings, Zoran Perisic)

AAN: Best Film Editing (Stuart Baird), Best Music–Original Score (John Williams), Best Sound (Gordon K. McCallum, Graham V. Hartstone, Nicolas Le Messurier. Roy Charman)

DVD: Warner Bros., 2009

BLU-RAY: Warner Bros., 2006

DURATION: 137 minutes

Superman begins with the image of the June 1938 edition of *Action Comics*, in which the character Superman debuted, the very first of the comic-book superheroes. On the distant planet of Krypton, Jor-El (Marlon Brando) sends his infant son to safety on Earth before his home world explodes. On Earth, the aging Kents (Pa is played by Glenn Ford, and Ma by Phyllis Thaxter) raise the boy as their own. Although the young Clark Kent (a less than engaging Jeff East) has great powers, his parents teach him restraint and responsibility.[1] As an adult, Clark (Christopher Reeve) travels to the city of Metropolis, where his day job as a reporter for the *Daily Planet* is a cover for his superhuman crime fighting activities. Meanwhile, Lex Luthor (Gene Hackman) is scheming to blow California into the sea to make his inland purchases the new, lucrative seaside strip. He lures Superman only to disable his abilities with Kryptonite, but Lex's companion Eve (Valerie Perrine) sets him free when she realizes that her own mother will be killed in Lex's scheme. Superman stops the bombs, but his colleague, Lois Lane (Margot Kidder), is killed. Ignoring his birth father's warnings, Superman reverses time and resurrects the woman he loves.

Jerry Siegel (Superman's cocreator, along with artist Joe Shuster) conceived of Superman as a "character like Samson, Hercules, and all the strong men I have ever heard of rolled into one,"[2] updated to give the mythic, heroic mold a science-fictional alien origin. The first Superman feature film was actually *Superman and the Mole-Men* (Lee Sholem, 1951), starring George Reeves from the television series (1952–1958). The 1978 delightfully cheesy version of *Superman* is better known for its critical and commercial success. DB

Notes

1. The origins and early life of Superman are conveyed in only three panels in the original comic, with the rest being expanded on later. See Jerry Siegel and Joe Shuster, *Superman: The Action Comics Archives*, vol. 1 (New York: DC Comics, 1997), 11.

2. Quoted in Richard Reynolds, *Super Heroes: A Modern Mythology* (London: B. T. Batsford, 1992), 9.

Bibliography

Reynolds, Richard. *Super Heroes: A Modern Mythology*. London: B. T. Batsford, 1992.

Siegel, Jerry, and Joe Shuster. *Superman: The Action Comics Archives*, vol. 1. New York: DC Comics, 1997.

SUPERMAN II (1980)

Directors: Richard Lester, Richard Donner (uncredited)
Writers: Jerry Siegel, Joe Shuster, Tom Mankiewicz, Mario Puzo, David Newman, Leslie Newman
Producer: Pierre Spengler (Warner Bros.)
Cinematographers: Geoffrey Unsworth, Bob Paynter
Editor: John Victor-Smith
Production Design: John Barry, Peter Murton
Art Direction: Terry Ackland-Snow, Ernest Archer, Charles Bishop, Norman Reynolds
Set Decoration: Peter Howitt, Peter Young
Costumes: Yvonne Blake, Susan Yelland
Music: Ken Thorne, John Williams
Cast: Lex Luthor: Gene Hackman. Superman/Clark Kent: Christopher Reeve. Otis: Ned Beatty. Perry White: Jackie Cooper. Ursa: Sarah Douglas. Lois Lane: Margot Kidder. Non: Jack O'Halloran. Eve Teschmacher: Valerie Perrine. Lara: Susannah York. Sheriff: Clifton James. The President: E. G. Marshall. Jimmy Olsen: Marc McClure. Gen. Zod: Terence Stamp
AA: None
AAN: None

DVD: Warner Bros., 2009
BLU-RAY: Warner Bros., 2006. *Superman II: The Richard Donner Cut.*
DURATION: 122 minutes

Director Richard Donner was shooting both *Superman* (1978) and *Superman II* but was fired and replaced by Richard Lester for the second feature (although Donner's version is now available on DVD and Blu-ray). At the beginning of *Superman*, Jor-El (Marlon Brando) sentences three criminals to exile from Krypton, and they are not seen again in the film, being, rather, a setup for this sequel. Superman (Christopher Reeve) saves Lois Lane (Margot Kidder) in Paris, where she is investigating a terrorist threat. He removes an activated nuclear bomb and safely takes it into space, unaware that the explosion causes the release of the criminals General Zod (Terence Stamp), Ursa (Sarah Douglas), and Non (Jack O'Halloran).

Back on assignment as Clark Kent, Lois finally realizes his true identity, and at the Fortress of Solitude, Superman relinquishes his powers to be with her and consummate their love (Richard Schickel of *Time* jests, "In the next film they will doubtless negotiate a prenuptial agreement and buy a co-op together."[1]) In the meantime, upon discovering their powers on Earth, Zod wreaks havoc and claims leadership of the planet. Lex Luthor (Gene Hackman) escapes from prison and, upon learning that Zod was imprisoned by Superman's father, offers to help Zod exact his revenge in return for Australia. Superman regains his powers but is outnumbered, only prevailing after he tricks his adversaries into having their own powers removed. Realizing that the truth is too great a burden on Lois, Superman removes her memory of his true identity.

General Zod (originally Dru-Zod) is a character introduced into the Superman story in *Adventure Comics* #283 in 1961, during what is known as the Silver Age of Comic Books, but it is Terence Stamp's bored, haughty version of the psychopath Zod in *Superman II* that has prevailed in popular culture, along with his (now trademark) line, "Kneel before Zod!" Stamp's Zod influenced later comic-book versions of the character, when he was reintroduced with Richard Donner as cowriter for *Action Comics* #845 in 2007. Somewhat ironically, Stamp became the voice of Zod's old adversary, Jor-El, in the television series *Smallville* (2001–2011). Zod is the main villain of the latest feature film, *Man of Steel* (Zack Snyder, 2013). DB

Note

1. Richard Schickel, "Flying High," *Time*, 8 June 1981, 84.

Bibliography

Schickel, Richard. "Flying High." *Time*, 8 June 1981, 84.

SUPERMAN III (1983)

DIRECTOR: Richard Lester
WRITERS: Jerry Siegel, Joe Shuster, David Newman, Leslie Newman
PRODUCER: Pierre Spengler (Warner Bros.)
CINEMATOGRAPHER: Robert Paynter
EDITOR: John Victor Smith
PRODUCTION DESIGN: Peter Murton
ART DIRECTION: Terry Ackland-Snow, Brian Ackland-Snow, Bert Davey
SET DECORATION: Peter Young
COSTUMES: Evangeline Harrison
MUSIC: Ken Thorne, John Williams
CAST: Superman/Clark Kent: Christopher Reeve. Gus Gorman: Richard Pryor. Perry White: Jackie Cooper. Jimmy Olsen: Marc McClure. Lana Lang: Annette O'Toole. Vera: Annie Ross. Lorelei: Pamela Stephenson. Ross Webster: Robert Vaughn. Lois Lane: Margot Kidder. Brad: Gavan O'Herlihy
AA: None
AAN: None
DVD: Warner Bros., 2006

BLU-RAY: Warner Bros., 2011. *The Superman Motion Picture Anthology.*
DURATION: 119 minutes

Unemployed Gus Gorman (Richard Pryor) undertakes training as a computer programmer and discovers he has a natural talent for it, using his skills to embezzle money at his new job. Gorman is found out, but his employer, Ross Webster (Robert Vaughn), sees the potential of such skills. Gorman is sent to Smallville with the assignment of hacking into a computerized weather station to ruin Colombian coffee crops and give Webster control of the coffee industry. Clark Kent (Christopher Reeve) is also visiting Smallville for his high school reunion, where he reunites with Lana Lang (Annette O'Toole), who (unlike Lois Lane) seems to genuinely prefer the homespun Clark to Superman. When Superman stops the tornado that Gorman has created, Webster decides that he needs to neutralize the superhero before he can prevail. Gorman locates Krypton debris in space, but the computer cannot identify 1 percent of the rock, so the manufactured Kryptonite is not pure and fails to kill Superman. But it does have an effect, turning Superman into a destructive, antiheroic force (writing for the *New Yorker*, Pauline Kael argues that this "dangerous" Superman is somehow more "attractive" as well,[1] prefiguring the darker vision of superheroes that would emerge in later decades). Webster takes over oil supplies, and Gorman designs a supercomputer. Meanwhile, Superman splits into two personas, and the evil Superman does battle with the good Clark Kent. Clark finally prevails, and the good Superman can finally go back to work. He seeks out Webster's hideout in the Grand Canyon, where the supercomputer has been built. Just as a Kryptonite beam seems set on killing him, Gorman has a change of heart, attacking the computer and freeing Superman. When the computer becomes self-aware and turns on its creators, Superman destroys it. Lois Lane (Margot Kidder) returns from holiday to find Lana Lang as a new arrival at the *Daily Planet. Variety* summed up the prevailing feeling about *Superman III* when it proclaimed that the film puts "emphasis on broad comedy" and, as a result, "has virtually none of the mythic or cosmic sensibility that marked its predecessors."[2] DB

Notes

1. Quoted in Gary Gumpert, "The Wrinkle Theory: The Deconsecration of the Hero," in *American Heroes in a Media Age*, edited by Susan J. Drucker and Robert S. Cathcart (Cresskill, NJ: Hampton Press, 1994), 60.
2. "Review: *Superman III*," *Variety*, 1983, http://variety.com/1982/film/reviews/superman-iii-1200425419/ (29 June 2013).

Bibliography

Gumpert, Gary. "The Wrinkle Theory: The Deconsecration of the Hero." In *American Heroes in a Media Age*, edited by Susan J. Drucker and Robert S. Cathcart, 45–61. Cresskill, NJ: Hampton Press, 1994.

"Review: *Superman III*." *Variety*, 1983, http://variety.com/1982/film/reviews/superman-iii-1200425419/ (29 June 2013).

SUPERMAN IV: THE QUEST FOR PEACE (1987)

DIRECTOR: Sidney J. Furie
WRITERS: Jerry Siegel, Joe Shuster, Christopher Reeve, Lawrence Konner, Mark Rosenthal
PRODUCERS: Menahem Golan, Yoram Globus (Warner Bros.)
CINEMATOGRAPHER: Ernest Day
EDITOR: John Shirley
PRODUCTION DESIGN: John Graysmark
COSTUMES: John Bloomfield
MUSIC: John Williams, Alexander Courage
CAST: Superman/Clark Kent: Christopher Reeve. Lex Luthor: Gene Hackman. Perry White: Jackie Cooper. Jimmy Olsen: Marc McClure. Lenny: Jon Cryer. David Warfield: Sam Wanamaker.

Nuclear Man: Mark Pillow. Lacy Warfield: Mariel Hemingway. Lois Lane: Margot Kidder
AA: None
AAN: None
DVD: Warner Bros., 2006
Blu-ray: Warner Bros., 2011. *The Superman Motion Picture Anthology.*
Duration: 89 minutes

The Christopher Reeve *Superman* movies got sillier as they progressed, such that *Superman IV: The Quest for Peace*, despite its ostensibly serious theme of nuclear disarmament, is so ridiculous, so bad, that with the passing of years it has become terrific camp fun. A little boy, scared at the Cold War nuclear standoff, asks Superman to help. Superman takes all the nuclear bombs and hurls them into the sun to be destroyed. He does not realize that one of the missiles harbors a genetics experiment by Lex Luthor (Gene Hackman), who uses Superman's own DNA and the power of the sun to create another superbeing called Nuclear Man. Meanwhile, the *Daily Planet* has been taken over by a tabloid tycoon, who puts his daughter Lacy (Mariel Hemingway) at the helm. The worldly Lacy has an immediate attraction to the homespun Clark Kent, resulting in an amusing "double date" with Clark, Lacy, Superman, and Lois. When Nuclear Man confronts Superman, Superman is badly injured, but he is saved from death by Krypton's last power source. Nuclear Man sees a picture of Lacy in the *Daily Planet* and (we are left to infer) becomes immediately obsessed with her. Nuclear Man succeeds in abducting Lacy into space (where she is apparently able to breathe) before she is rescued by Superman. Realizing the source of his opponent's power, Superman pushes the moon to create an eclipse, and Nuclear Man becomes powerless without the sun's rays. Superman then disposes of him in a nuclear reactor at a power plant. Lex and Lenny (Jon Cryer) are sent to jail, and the world is left to hope for a future of peace and lament the loss of a mullet-haired supervillain so finely adorned in Lycra. Reviews were mostly damning,[1] box-office returns were poor, and the first superhero of them all went quietly into temporary retirement from the big screen. DB

Note

1. For an amusing example, see Desson Howe, "*Superman IV: The Quest for Peace*," *Washington Post*, 31 July 1987, www.washingtonpost.com/wp-srv/style/longterm/movies/videos/supermanivthequestforpeacepghowe_a0c8a7.htm (2 July 2013).

Bibliography

Howe, Desson. "*Superman IV: The Quest for Peace*." *Washington Post*, 31 July 1987, www.washingtonpost.com/wp-srv/style/longterm/movies/videos/supermanivthequestforpeacepghowe_a0c8a7.htm (2 July 2013).

TOY STORY **(1995)**

Director: John Lasseter
Writers: John Lasseter, Pete Docter, Joe Ranft, Joss Whedon, Andrew Stanton, Joel Cohen, Alec Sokolow
Producers: Bonny Arnold, Ralph Guggenheim (Pixar Animation Studios, Walt Disney Pictures)
Editors: Robert Gordon, Lee Unkrich
Music: Randy Newman
Cast (voice): Woody: Tom Hanks. Buzz Lightyear: Tim Allen. Mr. Potato Head: Don Rickles. Slinky Dog: Jim Varney. Rex: Wallace Shawn. Hamm: John Ratzenberger. Bo Peep: Annie Potts. Andy Davis: John Morris. Sid: Erk von Detten. Andy's Mom: Laurie Metcalf. Sargent: R. Lee Ermey. Hannah: Sarah Freeman. Shark/Rocky Gibraltar: Jack Angel
AA: Special Achievement Award (John Lasseter)
AAN: Best Music–Original Song (Randy Newman for "You've Got a Friend in Me"), Best Music–Original Musical

or Comedy Score (Randy Newman), Best Writing–Screenplay Written Directly for the Screen (John Lasseter, Pete Docter, Joe Ranft, Joss Whedon, Andrew Stanton, Joel Cohen, Alec Sokolow)
DVD: Disney-Pixar, 2000
BLU-RAY: Disney-Pixar, 2011
DURATION: 81 minutes

John Lasseter, creative director at Pixar, has reinvented the epic form for a digital audience with the creation of the *Toy Story* series. Matching award-winning innovative technique with classic narrative form, he has managed to return storytelling and its methods back to their rightful place at the center of children's film.

The *Toy Story* animated film series (*Toy Story*, 1995; *Toy Story 2*, 1999; and *Toy Story 3*, 2010) narrate the coming-of-age of a young boy through the action of his cadre of cherished childhood toys, whose adventures comprise the episodes. The series follows the frame narrative of the chronological life of the fictional American boy Andy Davis from his seventh birthday party and family move (*Toy Story*) to his sojourn away to college (*Toy Story 3*). *Toy Story 2* takes place while Andy is about ten years old, and he is going away to cowboy camp.

Although each film achieves narrative and technical merit in its own right, when taken together, the series explores the epic themes of loss and search for self-identity, culminating in *anagnoresis* (self-knowledge) within the action of the episodes, leading to transformation through the gaining of self-determination and love. The cultural interest in the series explores the implicit understanding of the role toys play as tokens of our collective imagination from a generational perspective.

There are numerous popular references, tokens, and images imbedded within the visual and narrative frames to deliver thick cultural intertextual discussion without impeding the literal animation of the story, which reinforces the epic themes for adults, sometimes more so than for children. In short, the Toy Story series is the epic of a young America, reminding in subtle foreshadowing through the use of objects of play that although the child is father to the man, the hand that rocks the cradle rules the world.

Toy Story is a story of firsts. It was the first full-length animated feature film produced at Pixar Animation Studios and the first full-length animated feature film to be created in its entirety by artists using computer technology and tools. It was the first animated film to be nominated for an Academy Award for writing, and in its first year of eligibility (2005), *Toy Story* was added to the National Film Registry as being "culturally, historically, or aesthetically significant." The film has been widely acclaimed by critics and was top grossing at the box office its opening weekend. It also received numerous awards and nominations. They included a special achievement Academy Award; Academy Award nominations for Best Music–Original Song for "You've Got a Friend in Me," Best Music–Original Musical or Comedy Score, and Best Writing–Screenplay Written Directly for the Screen; eight Annie Awards; and two Golden Globe nominations. The cast includes several accomplished and familiar actors, namely Don Rickles, John Ratzenberger, Annie Potts, Laurie Metcalf, Tom Hanks, and Tim Allen (Hanks and Allen play Woody and Buzz Lightyear, respectively), both fittingly cast in their first animated film roles.

Dubbed a "buddy film" by director John Lasseter, the original *Toy Story* narrates the adventures of Woody and Buzz Lightyear, two of seven-year-old Andy Davis's (John Morris) favorite toys.

Although they begin as rivals, Woody (a 1950s-styled rough-and-tumble soft cloth cowboy figure with a pull-string voice feature) and Buzz (a Space Age–inspired action figure astronaut complete with a locking wrist communicator, karate-chop action, space wings, a voice simulator, and pulsating laser light) learn and teach the values of friendship and self-determination through the action of the episodes and the reinforcement of the Disney-inspired theme song "You've Got a Friend in Me."

While set in a contemporary era, the film surprises adult viewers at the outset by the unique cast of supporting characters who come to life on the screen, namely the collection of other toys in Andy's room. While children find awe and charm in the premise of animated toys (which speak and come alive only when out of the presence of most humans—the sinister child Sid being the only exception), adults experience a nostalgic return to childhood through the clever introduction of period toys from a previous generation. These " old friends" joining Woody and Buzz include Slinky Dog (Jim Varney), who is one of Woody's best friends; Rex (Wallace Shawn), a plastic dinosaur who is actually reactive, insecure, and nervous; Hamm (John Ratzenberger), a piggy bank who is a know-it-all and busy body; Mr. Potato Head (Don Rickles), who is the first to call Woody out and wrongfully blame him for things; and Sarge (R. Lee Ermey), the little green army man who is, well, mostly honorable, except for when he suggests fragging (a military term for a planned assassination of one's leader, popular during the Vietnam era) Woody when he thinks Woody has been reckless in dealing with Buzz. In the key episodes and adventures surrounding the plot, their relatively stable characteristics contrast those of the two stars and allow for the dual denouement of the plot to become evident: Woody's need to overcome his fear and anxiety of losing Andy and Buzz's search for self-realization.

However, linguistic reinforcement notwithstanding, and despite the recurrent language of filial piety, adults who move past this initial nostalgic joy of remembering some childhood friends in the opening scenes can't help but recognize the obvious contradictory action of the characters and ironic tone of the comedic plot, and they will quickly seek resolution in a didactic subtext. At face value, one is hard pressed to find any immediate thematic sense of true friendship in the film, but for the type that comes with the alternative of sheer abandonment.

For example, we learn from the first dialogue of the film after the opening song that Andy's birthday party will soon be taking place and that the family is moving away shortly thereafter. Just as we begin to marvel at Woody and the other toys coming to life, we become engaged in a flurry of angst among the toys because there is an unexpected party, which means new toys will be coming. Woody is afraid he'll be replaced by a new toy (Buzz Lightyear) and, sadly, he is; however, that's not the worst part.

The saga of the Buzz Lightyear toy is the cathartic element of this movie, for Buzz thinks he's lost in space and is trying to get home, only to finally discover that he doesn't know who he really is, so he truly doesn't care about much, much less who Andy even is until late in the series. Speaking of Andy, he takes forever to realize his toys are even missing. When Buzz is accidentally knocked out of the window, the other toys in Andy's room don't believe Woody when he says that it was an accident, and they actually plot against him for most of the film. In the end, it is not Woody's "friends," but the mutant toys next door (whom Woody at first misjudges as cannibals), that actually help save him and Buzz. In fact, for all his love for Andy, the only human that Woody ever communicates with is Andy's next-door neighbor, the evil Sid (Erk von Detten), albeit by scaring him into treating his toys better.

Yet, despite all this, Woody proclaims the "we gotta stick together 'cause we're all Andy's toys" mantra as if it were one of his pull-string lines. As for his pal Buzz, who is known for his prepackaged adage, "To infinity and beyond!" he completes his heroic escapade in the movie with a dashing free fall to safety with Woody in tow to the now-familiar, "It's not flying; it's falling with style," quoting Woody's earlier pragmatic observation with an ironic twist in farcical style. Were it not for the genius of Lasseter's storytelling talent—the use of tokens, recognition scenes, spectacle, and, most importantly, peripeteia (reversal of the two lead characters as the plot progresses) so masterfully crafted within the animation—this epic tale of a hero's adventure could have been concealed and not revealed to a new generation of seekers. It is truly only within the scope of the three films together that one can begin to see the larger story of the coming-of-age of the child who was born amid those toys, in that place, during those days, and, likewise, in that generation. MC

TOY STORY 2 (1999)

Director: John Lasseter
Writers: John Lasseter, Pete Docter, Ash Brannon, Andrew Stanton, Rita Hsiao, Doug Chamberlin, Chris Webb
Producers: Helene Plotkin, Karen Robert Jackson (Pixar Animation Studios, Walt Disney Pictures)
Cinematographer: Sharon Calahan
Editors: Edie Bleiman, David Ian Salter, Lee Unkrichn
Music: Randy Newman
Cast (voice): Woody: Tom Hanks. Buzz Lightyear: Tim Allen. Mr. Potato Head: Don Rickles. Slinky Dog: Jim Varney. Rex: Wallace Shawn. Hamm: John Ratzenberger. Bo Peep: Annie Potts. Andy Davis: John Morris. Andy's Mom: Laurie Metcalf. Sargent: R. Lee Ermey. Barbie: Jodi Benson. Jessie: Joan Cusack (Mary Kay Bergman, yodeling voice). Wheezy: Joe Raft (Robert Goulet, singing voice). Stinky Pete: Kelsey Grammer. Mrs. Potato Head: Estelle Harris. Al: Wayne Knight. Squeeze Toy Aliens: Jeff Pidgeon. Evil Emperor Zurg: Andrew Stanton
AA: None
AAN: Best Music–Original Song (Randy Newman for "When She Loved Me")
GG: Best Motion Picture–Comedy/Musical
GGN: Best Original Song–Motion Picture (Randy Newman for "When She Loved Me")
Grammy Award: Best Song Written for a Motion Picture, Television, or other Visual Media (Randy Newman for "When She Loved Me")
Grammy Award Nomination: Best Score Soundtrack Album for a Motion Picture, Television, or other Visual Media (Randy Newman)
DVD: Disney-Pixar, 2000. 3D digital rerelease, Disney-Pixar, 2009.
Blu-ray: Disney-Pixar, 2010
Duration: 92 minutes

Toy Story 2, the 1999 sequel to *Toy Story*, continues the frame narrative of the life of young Andy Davis (John Morris), now approximately ten years old, and his faithful collection of animated toys. In this second installment of the Toy Story series, the themes explored are loss, self-identity, purpose, and love, not only within an individual's perspective, but through an intergenerational eye as well, namely between parent and child. This is seen ironically in the *Empire Strikes Back* references, allegorically in the story line of Woody, and tragically in Jessie's story.

This plot centers on the adventures of the toys while Andy is away at cowboy camp without Woody (Tom Hanks)—much to Woody's dismay—because he was accidentally torn. Rex (Wallace Shawn) is upset because he is unable to successfully complete a Buzz Lightyear video game mission and defeat the Evil Emperor Zurg. Woody gets shelved and finds Wheezy (Joe Raft), a long-lost toy who had been shelved and was then taken by Ms. Davis (Laurie Metcalf) to the dreaded garage sale to be sold. Woody attempts a search and rescue of Wheezy (successfully) but gets kidnapped by Al, the owner of Al's Toy Barn, in the process.

While the other toys, led by Buzz, plan their own search and rescue for Woody, Woody discovers a new life at Al's apartment: he is a valuable collectible and the star figure of a series of figures from the once-popular TV show *Woody's Roundup.* Woody meets his other family: Jessie (Joan Cusack), the cowgirl; Bullseye, his loyal horse; and Stinky Pete (Kelsey Grammer), the prospector, who has never even been removed from his box. Woody learns who he really is, but he also learns of their plans to be memorialized in a Japanese museum as a complete set now that he's with them. When Woody realizes this, he attempts to leave but learns of Jessie's story about her abandonment by her owner, Emily, and reconsiders, especially after Stinky Pete's admonition that the same fate awaits him someday.

Meanwhile, the toys are, for the most part, successful at locating Al's Toy Barn and figuring out how to get to Woody, with one minor problem: Buzz is captured in the Toy Barn by a newer model of Buzz (the other toys don't realize it), and the real Buzz has to escape and meet up with the others (which he does, but in the process he activates his archenemy toy, Zurg, who follows him). The real Buzz finally meets up with the other toys and is recognized by revealing Andy's name written on the sole of his shoe. Woody, who at first refuses to leave, later changes his mind and offers for the other toys of *Woody's Roundup* to join him in Andy's room. They plan to leave when Stinky Pete seals their exit. He explains that it's unfair that he has spent his entire life on a shelf and was never sold, and that his dream now is to live in a museum and be admired by children forever. Al comes in and prepares the toys for their trip. The other toys follow them down the elevator, but Zurg (Andrew Stanton) meets them, and the new Buzz battles him, reenacting the "I Am Your Father" scene from *Star Wars: Episode V, The Empire Strikes Back.* Rex defeats Zurg. (In a later scene, outside Al's apartment, the new Buzz and Zurg are seen playing ball together.) Al leaves for the airport with the toys; the toys from Andy's room find a Pizza Planet delivery truck, and with the help of some of the Squeeze Toy Aliens (Jeff Pidgeon), another wild adventure and chase scene occurs. Bullseye and Woody are finally saved, Stinky Pete is put in the backpack of a little girl so he can be played with, Woody rescues Jessie from inside a plane, and Buzz and Bullseye rescue Jessie and Woody from the plane as it is taking off.

Once safe in Andy's room, the new team of toys greets Andy when he returns from cowboy camp, sans Stinky Pete. Woody is no longer afraid of Andy outgrowing him because even if he does, they will always have each other, "for infinity and beyond," thus completing his heroic escapade. Wheezy, all fixed up, sings Woody's theme song, "You've Got a Friend in Me." The toys are seen coupled: Mr. and Mrs. Potato Head, Jessie and Buzz, Woody and Bo Peep. MC

TOY STORY 3 (2010)

DIRECTOR: Lee Unkrich
WRITERS: John Lasseter, Andrew Stanton, Lee Unkrich, Michael Arndt
PRODUCERS: Darla K. Anderson (Pixar Animation Studios, Walt Disney Pictures)
CINEMATOGRAPHERS: Jeremy Lasky, Kim White
EDITOR: Ken Schretzmann
MUSIC: Randy Newman

SOUND EDITORS: Tom Myers, Michael Silvers
CAST (voice): Woody: Tom Hanks. Buzz Lightyear: Tim Allen. Mr. Potato Head: Don Rickles. Slinky Dog: Blake Clark. Rex: Wallace Shawn. Hamm: John Ratzenberger. Ken: Michael Keaton. Lotso: Ned Beatty. Andy Davis: John Morris. Andy's Mom: Laurie Metcalf. Sargent: R. Lee Ermey. Barbie: Jodi Benson. Jessie: Joan Cusack. Bonnie: Emily Hahn. Mrs. Potato Head: Estelle Harris. Squeeze Toy Aliens: Jeff Pidgeon. Chuckles: Bud Luckey
AA: Best Animated Feature Film (Lee Unkrich), Best Music Written for Motion Pictures–Original Song (Randy Newman for "We Belong Together")
AAN: Best Picture (Darla K. Anderson), Best Writing–Adapted Screenplay (John Lasseter, Andrew Stanton, Lee Unkrich, Michael Arndt), Best Sound Editing (Tom Myers, Michael Silvers)
DVD: Disney-Pixar, 2000. 3D digital rerelease, Disney-Pixar, 2009
BLU-RAY: Disney-Pixar, 2010
DURATION: 103 minutes

Toy Story 3 is a film known for bringing grown men to tears. Produced more than a decade after the second part, this highly anticipated third installment begins with Andy Davis (John Morris) preparing to move away again. The tone is nostalgic; there are clips of home movie reruns and old photos of little Andy throughout the years running through the opening credits in montage. We see, for example, clips from his birthday party from the original *Toy Story* narrative. There are no toys visible in the contemporary shots. They are in a box. Time has passed. Now Andy is seventeen, and he is leaving for college.

The familiar family of toys has been relegated to a large toy box in Andy's stark room, and the opening scenes find the old team concocting a scheme to get noticed by stealing Andy's cell phone and calling it so that he has to open the toy box to see them again and they can hopefully get some play time with him once more before he goes away. The plan fails, although for a moment Rex (Wallace Shawn) gets some handling, for which he is temporarily elated. Then, back in the box. Woody learns he's going with Andy to college, but the others' fates are left open: the attic, the garbage, or the donation box. Sarge (R. Lee Ermey) and the green army men call it quits first, saying, "We've done our duty; Andy's grown up." When his younger sister tries to appropriate the toys, Andy shoos her away, calling the toys junk. The toys hear Andy's comment, and later, although Andy packs up the bag of toys (except Woody) and begins to place them in the attic, he is distracted, and the bag is left in the hallway, where Ms. Davis (Laurie Metcalf) mistakes it for trash and puts it on the curb. Woody realizes what has happened and attempts a search and rescue, but with little help from a now-too-old Buster, the family dog. Woody can't save his friends this time; however, they manage to escape by themselves, and Woody finds them en route to Ms. Davis's car and jumping into the donations box. Despite Woody's best efforts at trying to reason with the crew that Andy was not trying to discard them, they don't believe him, and they insist that they want to go to the daycare as donations because they know they will get playtime there and will be wanted again. Woody gets stuck in the box with them when Ms. Davis gets into the car before they can escape, and they land at Sunnyside Daycare.

The daycare appears to be a paradise; the rooms are named according to the ages of the children: caterpillar for the less experienced children and butterfly for the better behaved ones. Lots-o'-Huggin' Bear (Lotso, voiced by Ned Beatty), a cuddly, soft-spoken teddy bear with a southern accent who carries a big stick/cane, runs the center from the toy perspective. He and his associate, Big Baby, introduce the gang to the caterpillar room, and the toys soon realize that they are not in paradise. Woody immediately escapes with Bonnie (Emily Hahn), the daughter of the receptionist. At Bonnie's house, while in her bedroom, Woody learns about the conditions at the daycare and the backstory of Lotso from another one of Bonnie's toys, Chuckles the Clown (Bud Luckey). Like Jessie, from *Toy Story 2*, Chuckles, Baby Doll, and Lotso once belonged to a little girl named Daisy. Lotso was the favorite of the three. One day, while on a trip, the toys were accidentally left behind by Daisy's mom. They managed to find their way home only to discover that Lotso had been replaced (although the others had not). Lotso refused to allow Chuckles to return to Daisy, and he lied to Big Baby, saying that the little girl had replaced all of them. Then the three of them made their way to Sunnyside Daycare, where Lotso's heart turned cold, and he started running the daycare as a tyrant, never allowing anyone to escape.

As usual, Woody plans the search and rescue of his mates left at the daycare. In the meantime, Lotso turns Buzz (Tim Allen) against the others by reprogramming him. During the rescue, Buzz gets partially fixed; he's now Spanish Buzz Lightyear. The only known escape route is the garbage Dumpster, but once they all arrive, Lotso and the gang are there to meet them. Woody reveals the truth about Lotso to Big Baby, who throws Lotso into the Dumpster; Lotso catches onto Woody, who then gets caught in the Dumpster. Everyone else falls in trying to save Woody, and they all end up at the landfill. Buzz regains his old self after getting hit with a TV in the dump while trying to save Jessie (Joan Cusack). The toys manage to land on a conveyor belt moving toward a fiery red incinerator. Lotso gets help from the others to push the stop button, but he escapes without pushing the button to stop the conveyor belt. His final words to Woody are, "Where's your kid now, Sheriff?" He then walks away as the group free-falls toward the wall of fire.

Once they land in the garbage and other debris also about to be incinerated, they hold hands and close their eyes, waiting to be sucked into the flames. Suddenly the giant crane claw (a literal deus ex machina), operated by the three Squeeze Toy Aliens, scoops them up, and they land safely in the landfill. Lotso is seen being picked up by a sanitation collector (possibly Sid from the first *Toy Story*), who recognizes the toy from childhood and displays it on the front of his sanitation truck.

The toys make their way home in time. They wash up, and Woody jumps in the college box for Andy to take with him, while the others go into the donations box. Woody leaves a note for Andy on the donations box. Thinking it's from his mom, Andy takes the toys to Bonnie's house and introduces his toys to her. He donates them to her because he "heard" that she takes good care of her toys. Woody is at the bottom of the box, to Andy's surprise, and when Bonnie recognizes him by his famous pull-toy phrase, and calls him *her* cowboy, Andy reluctantly hands Woody over to Bonnie. Then they begin to play together for a time until Andy finally says his goodbyes and leaves his toys with Bonnie. The conditions at the daycare improve, as evidenced by a letter sent home for the gang with Bonnie from Ken. The film ends with the camera panning over a collage of pictures drawn by Bonnie of toys that formerly lived in Andy's room and her toys together on her wall; Rex has a new dinosaur playmate, and the new family of toys are acting together in theatrical renditions of Shakespeare at Bonnie's house. The concluding song is a Spanish rendition of "You've Got a Friend in Me," starring Jessie and Buzz Lightyear.

The series closes with a poignant phrase that Andy delivers through the mouth of Woody as he prepares to leave Bonnie's house; in effect, it's Andy's testament to Woody, and perhaps the didactic message of the series itself for the adults watching with their children: "Now Woody, he's been my pal for as long as I can remember. He's brave, like a cowboy should be . . . and kind, and smart. But the thing that makes Woody special is he'll never give up on you . . . ever. He'll be there for you, no matter what." It's the kind of moment that'll bring a grown man to tears. MC

WRATH OF THE TITANS (2012)

DIRECTOR: Jonathan Liebesman
WRITERS: Dan Mazeau, David Leslie Johnson, Greg Berlanti. Based on characters created by Beverley Cross.
PRODUCERS: Basil Iwanyk, Polly Johnsen (Warner Bros., Legendary Pictures, Thunder Road Film)
CINEMATOGRAPHER: Ben Davis
EDITOR: Martin Walsh
PRODUCTION DESIGN: Charles Wood
ART DIRECTION: Raymond Chan, Mark Swain, Mike Stallion, Stuart Kearns, Tom Brown, Paul Kirby, Jordan Crockett
SET DECORATION: Lee Sandales
COSTUMES: Jany Temime
MUSIC: Javier Navarrete
CAST: Perseus: Sam Worthington. Zeus: Liam Neeson. Hades: Ralph Fiennes. Ares: Edgar Ramirez. Agenor: Toby Kebbell. Andromeda: Rosamund Pike. Hephaestus: Bill Nighy. Poseidon: Danny Huston. Helius: John Bell. Korrina: Lily James. Mantius: Alejandro Naranjo. Clea: Sinéad Cusack. Cyclops: Martin Bayfield
AA: None
AAN: None
DVD: Warner Bros., 2012
BLU-RAY: Warner Bros., 2012
DURATION: DVD, 96 minutes; Blu-ray, 99 minutes

A 3D sword-and-sandal sequel to *Clash of the Titans* (Louis Leterrier, 2010), itself a remake of the 1981 Desmond Davis film, *Wrath of the Titans* sees the mythical Greek hero Perseus (Sam Worthington) return to do battle with beasts and gods. Mourning the loss of his wife Io, Perseus is raising their son Helius (John Bell) alone and attempting to live a quiet life as a fisherman, but his plans are once again thwarted when his father, the great god Zeus (Liam Neeson), comes to him for help. With humans turning away from worship, the gods have grown weak and are struggling to keep the underworld in check. Zeus's father Kronos enlists the help of gods Hades (Ralph Fiennes) and Ares (Edgar Ramirez), the god of war, to help him escape his underworld imprisonment.

Perseus at first resists the call to heroism, but with his village attacked, the life of his son in danger, and Zeus taken captive in the underworld, he undertakes a quest to reform the ultimate weapon to defeat Kronos. He is joined by Poseidon's (Danny Huston) ne'er-do-well son Agenor (Toby Kebbell) and the Greek warrior queen Andromeda (Rosamund Pike, replacing Alexa Davalos from the earlier film), helped along the way by the god Hephaestus (Bill Nighy). They do battle with a group of Cyclopes, before defeating a minotaur who is protecting the labyrinthine entry to the underworld. Although the time of the gods comes to an end, as Kronos is defeated, Perseus looks forward to a new life with Andromeda, training his son to be the next hero.

The 3D underwhelmed reviewers, and the guitars and electronic elements to Javier Navarrete's otherwise orchestral score are sometimes jarring. Yet, overall, *Wrath of the Titans* makes for a more enjoyable romp than *Clash of the Titans*, courtesy of a lighter script, with hammy lines served up by the charismatic Bill

Nighy and Toby Kebbell. The film is just as free with the Greek mythological tradition as its predecessor, but it alludes to the heroic grandeur of myth without ever taking itself too seriously or overstaying its welcome. DB

APPENDIX B: FOREIGN-LANGUAGE EPICS

ANDREI RUBLEV: "THE PASSION ACCORDING TO ANDREI" (1969)

DIRECTOR: Andrei Tarkovsky
WRITERS: Andrei Mihkalkov Konchalovsky, Andrei Tarkovsky
PRODUCER: Tamara Ogorodnikova (Mosfilm)
CINEMATOGRAPHER: Vadim Yusov
EDITORS: Lyudmila Feiginova, Olga Shevkunenko, Tatyana Yegorycheva
PRODUCTION DESIGN: Yevgeni Chernyayev
SET DECORATION: E. Korablev
COSTUMES: Lidiya Novi, Maya Abar-Baranovska
MUSIC: Vyacheslav Ovchinnikov
SOUND: Inna Zelentsova
MAKEUP ARTISTS: Vera Rudina, Maksut Alyautdinov, S. Barsukova
CAST: Andrei Rublev: Anatoly Solonitsyn. Kirill: Ivan Lapikov. Daniil Chyoryy: Nikolai Grinko. Theophanes the Greek: Nikolai Sergeyev. Durochka (the Girl): Irma Raush Tarkovskaya. Boriska (the Bell Boy): Nikolai Burlyaev. The Grand Prince: Yuri Nazarov. The Jester: Rolan Bykov. Patrikei: Yuri Nikulin. Foma: Mikhail Kononov. Head Bell-Founder: Stepan Krylov. Tatar Kahn: Bolot Beyshenaliev
AA: None
AAN: None
DVD: Criterion, 2002
BLU-RAY: Currently unavailable
DURATION: 205 minutes

In Russia, Andrei Tarkovsky has been called the "poet of the cinema," and *Andrei Rublev*, also known as *The Passion According to Andrei*, is recognized as his masterpiece, an epic made explicitly for the sake of art and not for any commercial purpose. "Cinema," Tarkovsky claims, "is an unhappy art because it depends on money and it is marketed like cigarettes."[1] Films for a large audience cannot be produced, "for it is now difficult to surprise the spectator," and "good films are not seen by the masses." But Tarkovsky feels, and hopes, that "cinema will see a brighter day."[2]

It is hard to argue with such definite and straightforward views, especially since the director, now nearly three decades dead, has delivered a work that not only stands up to time, but validates nearly all his points. *Andrei Rublev* is a stunning work, combining breathtaking photography and deeply emblematic and emotionally charged images, provoking ideas about the relevance of art to life, while unearthing a corner of history when atrocities were committed of such magnitude as to make one doubt that the evil hidden in the human heart can be uprooted. Above all, *Andrei Rublev* is a deeply religious movie that manages, without a shade of irreverence, to equate the passion of an artist with the compassion of the West's greatest religious leader. Here the artist does not merely "imitate life," as a painter aloof and safe in his studio does, but mingles with his society's sufferers, undergoing their suffering himself, doubting dogmas he has cherished, witnessing unspeakable horrors, questioning faith and purpose, and even dreaming of what kind of resurrection humanity can achieve after the inferno on Earth it has created. These are not weak-kneed questions, and Tarkovsky interweaves them in this film with conviction and force.

To this it must be added that *Andrei Rublev* is not just a product of its director and his collaborators expressing particular views, but also a product of its period, the 1960s, when the Soviet Union was at its peak in terms of power, its leaders holding quite definite views as to what art could and should be made, leaving no doubt that it preferred art that conformed to or was created for the benefit of official political dogma. Boris Pasternak's being unable to visit Sweden to receive the Nobel Prize for *Doctor Zhivago* in 1958 is an example that partly validates this point.[3] Within this context of such comparisons, one can mention the Soviet-sponsored making of the seven-hour *War and Peace* in 1966, based on Leo Tolstoy's celebrated novel, which was officially promoted and distributed throughout the world and shown on U.S. screens. It won worldwide recognition and was hailed as a masterpiece, one that could be produced under the auspices of the socialist system; however, *Andrei Rublev* was not allowed to be entered in the Cannes Film Festival in 1971, under pressure by the Soviet Union, but it gained recognition by the International Film Critics and received the Critics Award of the French Syndicate of Cinema Critics and other international awards.

Andrei Rublev is substantial by epic standards (205 minutes), although it was reduced to 184 minutes by the Soviet authorities because of its violent content (!) and other material that must have appeared offensive. The missing passages have been restored on the 2002 Criterion Collection DVD version, and the film can be seen in its entirety, as it was meant by its maker, while the viewer can enjoy a wide-screen digital transfer, observations on cinema art by Tarkovsky, and a running and a video commentary by various scholars.[4] These observations not only shed light on the techniques used by Tarkovsky, but on the nature of film as art, the aims of a filmmaker, the distinctions between commercial and artistic aim, film and painting as artistic media, and the life of the artist related to his art, while a significant period of Russian history is seen in retrospect, within the contexts of the Soviet regime. It is no coincidence that two great historical epochs—the invasion of the Mongols in the fifteenth century and the Napoleonic Wars in the nineteenth—are seen from such different, and disparate, points of view, for one (the latter) is shown as a heroic endeavor, a triumph of Russia over the massive French invasion, whereas *Andrei Rublev*'s creator sees the Mongolian massacres of Russian populations as failures of the human spirit, man's inhumanity to man, and he is ardently advocating a rejection of tyranny in any form.

Although it is perhaps not a good idea to make comparisons by citing censored materials by any authority, it is a useful criterion for observing divergences of approach. *War and Peace*[5] was celebrated as the film adaptation of one of the greatest works in Russian literature. It is definitely a great work in film, with huge casts, elaborate sets, and great battles scenes that simulate the original battles in Russia during the Napoleonic Wars. It is the longest film epic in history, excluding TV miniseries. But Tolstoy, embraced by the Soviets (who hardly ever extended a literary hand to Fyodor Dostoyevsky, their other great writer of the time), principally critiqued the upper class, the crusty, failing, decadent aristocracy of nineteenth-century Russia, which contained in itself the genesis of a revolution. Marxism and Leninism embraced Tolstoy, whom they promoted in literary studies and film.

By contrast, Tarkovsky was an inheritor of Dostoyevskian trends, and *Andrei Rublev* seems to depict the doubter of faith, without the Dostoyevskian neurotic split persona[6] or Ingmar Bergman's sardonic self-flagellation.[7] But unlike Dostoyevsky's characters, Tarkovsky's do not doubt their faith, walk the path of their Golgotha, and give their lives to defend it. Tarkovsky's subject is mother Russia, her unconquerable soul, despite the atrocities that nearly annihilated her during the transition years after the Middle Ages, when Tatars invaded in an attempt to crush Christianity, then taking root in Russia and trying to uproot its spirit and the compassion and humanity of its new religion. It is no exaggeration to say that *Andrei Rublev* is a religious movie, despite the overt theme, which is the role and destiny of the artist and art in society. The premise seems to be accepted as that of the artist living his art, rather than the artist simply depicting life from a distance. Andrei Rublev was Russia's greatest painter, but he left the monastery, where he could paint safely—as many painters in the West did—to experience life. In the process, he discovered life's ungodliness, its barbarity, contradictions, and unbelievable cruelty. The epic reveals humanity's, and Russia's, greatest asset: that the end of the spirit, the collapse of the belief in God—and thence of Christianity—would mean the end of the world. The action is apocalyptic, for no one could witness cruelty and inhumanity of those dimensions and not think of the end of the world. Film can redeem, however, for it is capable of being unflinching in showing such truths.

Andrei Rublev was filmed in black and white; it is episodic in nature, and portions of it are told from a subjective/oneiric point of view, as the protagonist, wandering through the vastness of Russia, in the early fifteenth century (from approximately 1402 to 1425), witnesses scenes of unbelievable cruelty, miserable living conditions, acts of faith, pagan rituals, a massacre of a Russian village by Tartars, and atrocities where the weak and innocent are crushed by the strong and ruthless. Anyone but Rublev (played by Anatoly Solonitsyn) would have retreated to the monastery and painted his pictures in peace. His mission combines the idealism of a Don Quixote (but not comedic), the passionate faith of Dante (both experience hell), and the curiosity of artist dedicated to his subject matter. We never see him painting; the action is the panoramic view of his experiences. To that end, Tarkovsky uses the long shot, panning the landscape as if flying from a helicopter, surveying the action with an objectivity that in itself becomes a means of witnessing the cruelty of action. Cruelty is indeed the thematic lever that propels the story. A man beats a dog to death; a cow is seen burning (and mooing desperately); and a horse falls from a wooden staircase (a scene deleted in the shorter version), breaking its back and agonizingly trying to right itself. During the Tartar raid, a man, supposedly knowing where gold is, is tied, his eyes taped, and burning lead is poured into his mouth. Famine forces people to eat rotten horse meat or snow. The camera relentlessly records these horrors, leaving the viewer stunned, unrelieved by any acts of mercy on the part of the raiders.

The wanderings of Rublev are given in seven episodes, the first an attempt to hoist a balloon, in a semiscientific experiment, followed by the exodus of Andrei and his two companions, Kirill (Ivan Lapikov) and Daniil (Nikolai Grinko), from the monastery and the start of their wanderings; the last episode shows the casting of a bell under the orders of the prince, undertaken by a boy, Boriska (Nikolai Burlyaev), the son of a famous bell-maker, now dead. It is an enormously complicated process, with no guarantee of success (the penalty for failure is death), but brought to completion; it will perhaps symbolize resurrection. Two episodes show an oneiric (dreamlike) state, where Rublev is engaged in discourses with Theophanes the Greek (Nikolai Sergeyev), Rublev's teacher, who appears to be debating the role of the artist in society. The middle episode details the cruelties of the Tartar Invasion, and it is the longest. Tarkovsky's technique allows for lengthy takes, said to be the opposite of Eisenstein's, whose montages and frequent crosscutting include only shortened versions—or glimpses—of photographed objects, and thus only a momentary emotional response. The long takes and avoidance of crosscutting give a fuller picture of reality, enhancing the subjectivity of the picture, as a viewer, like Rublev, would be likely to experience when he views a picture of horror. For instance, as the Tatars ram the door of a church, where the village crowd has assembled, the camera shows only their efforts, the relentless pounding of the door, and we only hear the wailing of the people expecting to die inside. Later, when the invasion is accomplished, the camera has plenty of opportunity to witness the massacre in detail, but close-ups of the suffering victims are by and large avoided.

Tarkovsky's technique stresses the whole rather than the part. Thus, the viewer witnesses this period from a distance, never fully participating in the action, as would happen in a modern action movie where dismemberments are seen in close-up. But Tarkovsky does not forget that his protagonist is present, looking on in judgment, never taking his eyes off the horrors he sees. His faith is unshakable, despite all this, and when he hears victims cursing their captors and wishing them eternal hell, he feels the justice of the divine power. In the pagan ritual, Jesus is indeed seen as being nailed to the cross. His sufferings are for our sins. Russians—and all suffering victims—will survive, while their tormentors will burn in hell. Rublev, for all his suffering, is painting the story of Russia, a country tormented by its enemies and nearly exterminated by cruel winters, passionate and ruthless enemies, and inner conflict. Yet, he sees its spirit triumphing, because its faith in Christ is deep and rooted.

Thus, the painter paints, and his canvas is life itself. The canvas is the mingling of the bestial and the spiritual, both parts of life as it is, and that is the purpose of an artist, not to sit secluded in his cell and imagine what he will paint, for then he would know life only remotely. The artist needs to see it firsthand and live it as intensely as possible, even if his life is endangered in the process. A painter is not as Plato's painter, who is inferior to a carpenter, who has made the table, while the painter can only render a lesser truth, having only observed it; here a painter is one who lives what he knows. In a more complicated sense, cinema is not a Platonic entity, as the filmmaker and the cinematographer, his recorder, only copies life directly. A war is staged, and so is a massacre, or whatever else. There is no way that a real murder must happen to film one. Tarkovsky pushes this limitation to an extreme; he films in the most harrowing conditions, in a snowy steppe, in a cold forest, in a scene that resembles real torture and suffering as much as possible. There is, of course, no other way. But Rublev's method reflects an artistic dilemma nevertheless. Can the artist remain detached, academic (in a sense)? Or is he one who plunges into the life he describes and tells what he knows and what he has suffered firsthand. The artist must remain a recorder, even a sculptor, working with stone. Tarkovsky throws out an idea, however, a challenge to all artists: stay close to experience as much as you can, be honest, and ruthless if you must. That is not a bad message for an art that seems increasingly repetitive, and spurious. CS

Notes

1. Andrei Tarkovsky, "A Poet of the Cinema," *Andrei Rublev*, directed by Andrei Tarkovsky (Criterion, 2002), DVD.
2. Tarkovsky, "A Poet of the Cinema."
3. He was told that if he went there to accept the award, he could not come back to Russia. He did not go and died two years later (1960).
4. Vlada Petric, "Introduction" and "Commentary," *Andrei Rublev*, directed by Andrei Tarkovsky (Criterion, 2002), DVD. Tarkovsky, "A Poet of the Cinema."
5. Direction and screen adaptation by Sergei Bondarchuk.
6. As in Raskolnikov, in *Crime and Punishment.*
7. See Ingmar Bergman's *The Seventh Seal* (1955).

Bibliography

Johnson, Vida T., and Petrie Graham. *The Films of Andrei Tarkovsky: A Visual Fugue*. Bloomington: Indiana University Press, 1994.

Le Fanu, Mark. *The Cinema of Andrei Tarkovsky*. London: British Film Institute, 1987.

Turoskaya, Maya. *Tarkovsky: Cinema as Poetry*. London: Faber and Faber, 1989.

DAS BOOT (THE BOAT) (1981)

DIRECTOR: Wolfgang Petersen

WRITER: Wolfgang Petersen. Based on the novel by Lothar-Günther Buchheim.

PRODUCER: Gunter Rohrbach (Bavaria Film, PSO International)

CINEMATOGRAPHER: Jost Vacano

EDITOR: Hannes Nikel

MUSIC: Klaus Doldinger

SOUND EDITOR: Klaus Doldinger

SOUND MIXERS: Milan Bor, Trevor Pyke

CAST: Capt. Heinrich Lehmann-Willenbrock: Jürgen Prochnow. War Correspondent Werner: Herbert Grönemeyer. Chief Engineer Fritz Grade: Klaus Winnemann. 1st Watch Officer: Hubertus Bengsch. 2nd Watch Officer: Martin Semmelrogge. The Navigator and 3rd Watch Officer: Bernd Tauber. Chief Mechanic: Erwin Leder. Senior Cadet Ullman: Martin May. Petty Officer Hinrich: Heinz Hoenig. Chief Bosun: Uwe Ochsenknecht. Ario, the Mechanic: Claude-Oliver Rudolph. Petty Officer Frenssen: Ralf Richter. Schwalle, the Torpedo Man: Oliver Stritzel. Captain of the *Weser*: Günter Lamprecht

AA: None

AAN: Best Director (Wolfgang Petersen), Best Writing–Screenplay Based on Material from Another Medium (Wolfgang Petersen), Best Cinematography (Jost Vacano), Best Film Editing (Hannes Nikel), Best Sound (Milan Bor, Trevor Pyke, Mike LeMare), Best Effects–Sound Effects Editing (Mike Le Mare)

DVD: Sony Pictures Home Entertainment, 2004

BLU-RAY: Sony Pictures Home Entertainment, 2011. Director's cut.

DURATION: 150 minutes (208 for director's cut)

Das Boot is considered one of the greatest war movies of all time, made nearly forty-five years after World War II ended. It has few similarities with war movies that preceded (or followed) it. Its uniqueness lies in its classic structure. The film has the three unities: time, place, and action. What is more, it contains a unique point of view. *Das Boot* has a beginning, middle, and end, and each scene follows logically from the one that preceded it. In addition, it has unrelenting suspense that pins viewers to their seats from start to finish, despite the lengthy nature of its several releases throughout the years.[1]

The time frame is only a few weeks, from the time the *U-Boat 96* left its base in the harbor of La Rochelle, France, in the year 1941, until its arrival in Vigo, Spain, around Christmas, until its attempt to pass through the Straits of Gibraltar, its perilous plunge to the bottom of the ocean under British fire, and its return to La Rochelle, where it was bombed and sunk by British bombers. The place is the submarine itself, with its cramped quarters, its claustrophobic environment, the constant dangers from depth charges dropped by the enemy, and the necessity to battle both weather and enemy. The exceptions are three scenes outside the submarine: the beginning at a La Rochelle nightclub, where drunken sailors are carousing; a brief stop on board a luxury liner, the SS *Weser*, in Vigo, Spain, where they are offered a short reprieve from their hardships; and the last scene, where they are sunk as they are being welcomed as heroes. They stop at Vigo, and the boarding of the *Weser* is the crucial middle, where there is also the important complication that turns the fortunes of the *U-Boat 96* around. There, the captain, Heinrich Lehmann-Willenbrock (Jürgen Prochnow), who expected to be ordered to return home after his victorious sinking of several enemy ships, including a large tanker, instead receives orders to enter the Straits of Gibraltar and head for Italy. Furthermore, the captain, who had requested the have Correspondent Werner (Herbert Grönemeyer) and the chief engineer, Fritz Grade (Klaus Winnemann), return home, has his request overturned. These orders dishearten the crew, for they now know that they are headed toward certain doom, trying to pass through the narrow, heavily guarded, seven-mile-long Straits.

The most important element in this war adventure is point of view. Here, point of view can be considered in two senses. First, we have the point of view of the "narrator," Correspondent Werner, who came aboard the *U-Boat 96* to document a naval war mission, take photos, and presumably write about the experience. He carries a camera with him, and as soon as they are at sea, he starts taking photographs of the sub's crew members, but the captain reminds him that it would be best for him to wait until the crew grows beards and looks battle-tested. Incidentally, the film was shot sequentially[2] just for that reason, so the crew members would show the wear and tear of intense war scenes. Werner, of course, as he witnesses war in a submarine, changes from an eager, carefree reporter into a full participant and cosufferer. His initial detachment is completely lost and replaced by the utter seriousness of anyone who expects death at any moment; however, his point of view is never lost, and as he is ordered to stay aboard, he sees all until the very end, as he stays alive to see the sinking of the U-boat, and the death of its captain.

Point of view is also carried on by the entire crew. This is out of necessity, for the filmmaker never lets the viewer off the hook. As the sub sails into the high seas, it is exposed to bad weather, and the captain orders the crew to submerge the vessel to 150 meters—or more—below the surface to test its endurance under water pressure. Then come the several encounters with British convoys, which subject the U-boat to depth charge attacks that shake the sub, and the men undergo severe psychological traumas, but, miraculously, there is no substantial damage. Throughout the commotion, the captain remains calm, laconic, vigilant, and in full command at all times, expressing no emotion. He is no quitter. He has tested his boat, and he believes in its sturdy build.

In trying to escape air attacks as they attempt to pass Gibraltar and following the order for the boat to be submerged as deep as possible, the crew loses control. The vessel fails to respond and sinks below 150 meters. It continues to go deeper into the ocean until it reaches 220 meters and an unsustainable level of water pressure. The bolts come loose, water pours in, and the boat is about to be crushed to pieces. The sub is running out of oxygen, and the men are breathing through masks. But mostly through the heroics of the chief engineer, the holes are repaired and the water ballast is ejected. The needle showing depth slowly begins to rise.

The men cheer as the sub begins to ascend toward the surface. The captain is proud of his boat, which is what matters most to him in all this adventure, for he is not the one to offer congratulations to men, although he is fully conscious of both their terror and heroism. He lacks neither compassion nor humanism. The crew is presented as fully human, not as Nazis who cheer for victory. Not one picture of Hitler is shown on the vessel—or elsewhere for that matter—and no "Hail Hitler!" is heard. No mention of the Führer is made outside of the scene when the crew is on board the *Weser* and Gunter Lambrecht, who plays the captain, mouths it, but not its entirety.[3] The film seems scrupulously neutral, attempting to show human beings under extreme stress, especially from the brutality of war. An example is the sinking of a British supertanker, already in flames, and presumably abandoned. The captain orders one more torpedo to hit it, but, as the tanker is now cut in half and sinking fast, its crew members are jumping into the water, in flames, and swimming toward the German sub. The captain, who has been directed to take no prisoners, gives orders to retreat. The crew is horrified at the thought of leaving men drowning but is unable to do anything about it.

Point of view is finally that of the viewer himself, who, in watching this movie, is forced to witness the tragedy of war, regardless of who is fighting it or what side one is on. The movie oversees horrors objectively, judging neither the individual members of the crew, some of whom falter, nor the captain. The latter is proud of his work, and that of his men, but, above all, he is proud of his ship. The ship—*Das Boot*—is the real hero of this story. It is personified, it has endured beyond what one would imagine it could, and it has taken its crew members back. The captain is identified with it as a Greek mythologist would identify with Atropos,[4] one of the Three Fates. He is proud of a machine that was built to last—and it lasted under 280 meters of water pressure. But it could not outlast the bombs that eventually hilled it, and him with it. CS

Notes

1. The original theatrical release in 1981 spans 150 minutes, while the 1997 director's cut lasts 208 and the BBC miniseries goes for 300.
2. Wolfgang Petersen, "Commentary," *Das Boot*, directed by Wolfgang Petersen (Sony Pictures Home Entertainment, 2004), DVD.
3. In the subtitles, this comes out as "Fü . . ."
4. One that "could not be turned back." The others were Clotho, the Spinner, and Lachesis, the Disposal of Lots.

Bibliography

Buchheim, Lothar-Günther. *Das Boot*. London: Cassell & Co, 2007.

———. *U-Boat War*. New York: Random House, 1978.

CONTEMPT (LES MEPRIS) (1963)

DIRECTOR: Jean-Luc Godard
WRITER: Jean-Luc Godard. Based on the novel *Disprezzo*, by Alberto Moravia.
PRODUCERS: Carlo Ponti, Georges de Beauregard, Joseph E. Levine (Les Films Concordia, Rome Paris Films, Compagnia Cinematografica Champion)
CINEMATOGRAPHER: Raoul Coutard
EDITOR: Agnes Guillemot
PRODUCTION DESIGN: Philippe Dussart, Carlo Lastricati
ART DIRECTION: Christine Ditrio
TECHNICAL DIRECTOR: Lee Kline
MUSIC: Georges Delerue
CAST: Camille Javal: Brigitte Bardot. Paul Javal: Michel Piccoli. Francesca Vanini: Giorgia Moll. Jeremy Prokosch: Jack Palance. Fritz Lang: himself
AA: None
AAN: None
DVD: Criterion, 2002. Special edition (Studio Canal), two-disc restored version with high-definition digital transfer, supervised by cinematographer Raoul Coutard, with audio commentary by Robert Stam.[1]
BLU-RAY: Lion's Gate, 2010
DURATION: 104 minutes

The Criterion Collection's 2002 release of Jean-Luc Godard's *Contempt* on DVD offers viewers a chance to look at this seminal work by the legendary French New Wave director from a number of angles, the technical aspects of this edition not being the least important. Aside from a high-definition new digital transfer, the two-disc edition contains a conversation between Godard and Fritz Lang, a short film on Lang, a documentary on Godard, an interview with cinematographer Raoul Coutard, and a running commentary by Robert Stam. Although often referred to as a "mainstream" work, and on the whole not as an atypical Godard work, *Contempt* offers challenges to the viewer worth looking into on at least three levels: it is a story of the disintegrating marriage of a sex goddess; it is a film about the making of a film—Homer's *The Odyssey*; and it is a confrontation between two generations of directors, the older (Lang) and the younger (Godard). It is also an epic, if only by indirection.

A stage writer named Paul (Michel Piccoli) undertakes to write a movie script for an American producer named Jeremy Prokosch (Jack Palance), mainly to be able to afford the luxury apartment where he and his young, beautiful wife Camille (Brigitte Bardot) live. Their relationship is on the rocks, lacking ardor—as seen in the opening scene, in which Bardot, her backside bared as she lies on their bed next to him, is exchanging trivial remarks about their waning love habits. Later, both are seen at the studio, where Prokosch is making unabashed advances toward her, ignoring her husband and inviting her to ride in his red Alfa Romeo with him. The couple is again seen in their apartment, squabbling and venting their frustrations, Paul obviously being jealous, while Camille struts about aimlessly in a scene reminiscent of Antonioni marital alienation—a cinematic factoid to which Godard alludes in his commentary. She of course cheats on Paul with Prokosch. Prokosch, who is employing the services of an older-generation director (Lang), is presented as a crude but shrewd American in the business, who is out to prove that no American producer can be resisted when he eyes the wife of a foreigner. Be that as it may, he invites Paul and Camille to his villa in Capri and, after the film is finished, elopes with her—or steals her away in his red (phallic) car. The two are shown near the end of the film, the Alfa Romeo seen wedged between two sections of a truck—both killed instantly in a collision.

As for the story within a story—or film inside a film—there is innovativeness here, and this is not a repetition of Federico Fellini's *8½*, although the two films were done within the span of a year. This is not exactly a movie about making a movie (as Fellini's is), but the making of the movie is rather a secondary part—having bearing on the theme. Paul and Camille visit the studio (at Cinecittà), where there is a brief meeting with the movie's director—Fritz Lang playing himself in a confrontation with the mogul Prokosch, who is financing the film. The director has not followed the script exactly, and has rather innovated, including such things as statue heads of gods (Minerva) and a naked mermaid swimming. Prokosch protests that this will not do for American audiences. Lang declares that the script is the written word, which becomes different when given in pictured images. The debate erupts in violence, when Prokosch, discus-thrower-like, hurls film canisters across the room. The crew, actors, and director are all later transported to Capri, where the last part of the picture is to be filmed.

There is little shown as action in *The Odyssey*. Aside from brief shots of the heroes/Odysseus and Penelope, nothing is shown of the story. Godard intends the story of the Odyssey to be subservient (a subtheme) to the story of the two lovers (husband/wife) and her infidelity, but the actual story of the Odyssey thematically dominates *Contempt*. *The Odyssey* is the story of the relation between a man and his wife. In his fictional re-creation of *The Odyssey*, Fritz Lang maintains that Ulysses left Ithaca to go to Troy because he was bored with Penelope, and that the delays of his return were mere excuses to avoid being with her (after the war). Presumably, he preferred the nymphs he encountered along the way.

Likewise, while at the studio, Paul seems to have a flirtation with the interpreter, Francesca (Georgia Moll), a fact noticed by Camille. In fact, her "contempt" for him may have begun at that moment. When back at the flat, a simple design with gaudily bright colors, she is difficult, capricious, teasing, and unloving at the same time, while he, utterly frustrated, tries to cajole her, win her over again, and flatter her. Then, bursting into mild violence, he slaps her. Both become vindictive and irritable, drawing apart by the moment. Later, at Capri, Camille does not even try to hide her acceptance of Prokosch's not-so-subtle advances. This Odyssey ends up in infidelity, breakup, and disaster. Whether the two stories merely overlap or dovetail perfectly is an open question of interpretation; Godard comments that, "Whereas the Odyssey of Ulysses was a physical phenomenon, I filmed a spiritual odyssey: The eye of the camera watching these characters in search of Homer replaces that of the gods watching over Ulysses and his companion."[2]

Raoul Coutard's camera maintains an objective near indifference to what is going on in a scene. With few static shots (one lingering on Bardot's naked backside), few if any close-ups (unlike those of Bergman or Antonioni), Coutard photographs the entire action in the apartment at a distance, thus framing the moving figures within the apartment's rectangular shapes, establishing no sympathy either between the couple, or between the couple and the viewer. We see them simply (Godard's word) unemotionally, their concerns not our concerns, their passions trivialized, and child's game to the gods (camera). Again, Godard explains, "A simple film without mystery, an Aristotelian film, stripped of appearances, *Les Mepris* proves in 149 shots that in the cinema, as in life, there is no secret, nothing to elucidate, merely the need to live—and to make films."[3]

This is, of course, not a simple film, although the action of its main story is straightforward enough. The artfulness of its subtheme (*The Odyssey*) begs the overall concept of this type of filmmaking: Why is it necessary to insert another story in the story? And why bring in a famous director (Lang) to play the director of this movie, but not change his name into a fictional one? What is Lang doing there—not to speak of Palance and Bardot? We will leave the question of the last two (especially Bardot) for later and concentrate on Lang.

Godard had an interview with Lang entitled "The Dinosaur and the Baby," which is featured in the "Special Features" section of disc two of the Criterion DVD; deferentially, Godard asks the legendary director of *M* (and many other masterpieces) whether filmmaking should have elements of "entertainment" in it, trying to please a wider audience, or whether film should be considered an art in itself, regardless of its success at the box office. This is more or less a question tossed about for a while between the two men, for the interview lasts nearly an hour, showing numerous segments from *M* to illustrate Lang's points.

Here, of course, Lang is the "dinosaur," while Godard, nearly forty years younger, is the "baby." Lang insists on design and preconception of a scene down to its last details; Godard is for spontaneity and improvisation. The conversation is not particularly focused, but both offer insights into the art of filmmaking, and both agree that film is an art, albeit a popular one. Lang offers the opinion that the public—and time—is the ultimate judge of a film that is called a classic, and there is no way of telling whether a film will be a classic at the time it is being made, or that its maker himself knows whether he has made a movie that will last. He maintains that the art of film is mainly visual and refers back to the early silent era, when dialogue did not inhibit visual expression to the extent that it did later with sound. He also observes that only in France is a director called an "author" (auteur), which to him means that a director is one who does not merely tell an actor where to stand during a shot, or how to move from one place to the other, but who, like the novelist, imagines an entire scene—and an entire story—in visual terms, "finishing" the work before he starts shooting in his mind. Lang, who started out in the silent era in Germany and moved to Hollywood, where he worked for more than two decades, approaches filmmaking as a compromise, a necessity to please a common denominator, a necessity that does not invalidate the possibility of serious social/psychological (or other) themes crossing into the path of the action, or expressed in photography. The dinosaur can still deliver, while the baby can still revel, and learn. This is a genial confrontation between two giants of the cinema, more so than dialogue, for when egos clash, the result can be either a disintegrating discourse or a creative one in its disagreements.

Now for a note on Palance and Bardot, two opposing cinematic symbols, seemingly incongruous by nature, size, and screen appeal. Palance was chosen to play the American barbarian (in Godard's eyes at least), crude, overbearing, uncultured, and incapable of even understanding what he is doing, but he targets Bardot, a European sex symbol, in a way (but a much different way) equivalent to Marilyn Monroe, her contemporary in the United States. The difference is that Bardot bares it all before a gaping European and world audience, whereas Monroe looked sexy fully dressed. The larger point is tied up in the film's premises: Bardot hates her husband—here the Odysseus theme comes back in reverse—and finds him tedious, ordinary, too jealous and constricting, too unable to understand a sex goddess's expansive desires to conquer and subdue all maledom. Palance can tame her (temporarily), take her from her husband, insulting the husband and not caring, and take her away in his sports car—although in typical Godard fashion, all sexual desire is a pointless exercise that leads to tragedy, separation, or death. Beauty and Beast do not transcend their differences (as in Cocteau), but they are crushed to death as they flee; however, the Bardot glamour is so universal this hardly matters. Cinematically, she is the queen of the drones. The clips of filming at Capri, shown in one of the special features on the DVD, show Bardot being practically hunted down by the paparazzi, who had besieged the island and took various shots of her, as they could, wearing a bikini or moving around filming scenes. Bardot's image as an actress filters into the film, presenting to the audience an idea in imagery—a woman for whom marriage is a chain and for whom interest lies in adventure. In *The Odyssey*, Penelope is the opposite—faithful and satisfied only with a husband; the contemporary sex symbol (of the 1960s) points to a direct flight from such a concept.

This is *The Odyssey* in reverse. The heroes of Homer live in the natural world, part of which is a marital adventure that ends with reunion. The heroes of Moravia/Godard are wrecked in it. Godard says so himself:

> *Les Mepris* seems to me, beyond its psychological study of a woman who despises her husband, the story of castaways of the Western world, survivors of the shipwreck of modernity who, like the heroes of Verne and Stevenson, one day reach a mysterious deserted island, whose mystery is the inexorable lack of mystery, of truth that is to say. Whereas the Odyssey of Ulysses was a physical phenomenon, I filed a spiritual odyssey: the eye of the camera watching these characters in search of Homer replaces that of the gods watching over Ulysses and his companions.[4]

CS

Notes

1. Disc two contains "The Dinosaur and the Baby," a conversation between Fritz Lang and Jean-Luc Godard, and two documentaries by Jacques Rozier, featuring Godard on the set of *Contempt—Bardot and Godard* and also *Paparazzi*—among numerous other features. *Contempt*, directed by Jean-Luc Godard (Criterion, 2002), DVD.
2. Jean-Luc Godard, *Godard on Godard*, translated and edited by Tom Milne (New York and London: Da Capo, 1972), 201–2.
3. Godard, *Godard on Godard*, 200.
4. Godard, *Godard on Godard*, 201.

Bibliography

Godard, Jean-Luc. *Godard on Godard*. Translated and edited by Tom Milne. New York and London: Da Capo, 1972.

DOWNFALL (*DER UNTERGANG*) (2004)

DIRECTOR: Oliver Hirschbiegel
WRITER: Bernd Eichinger. Based on the book *Inside Hitler's Bunker: The Last Days of the Third Reich*, by Joachim Fest, and Melissa Müller and Traudl Junge's *Until the Final Hour: Hitler's Last Secretary*.
PRODUCER: Bernd Eichinger (Constantin Film Produktion, Norddeutscher Rundfunk, Westdeutscher Rundfunk)
CINEMATOGRAPHER: Rainer Klausmann
EDITOR: Hans Funk
MUSIC: Stephan Zacharias
CAST: Adolf Hitler: Bruno Ganz. Traudl Junge: Alexandra Maria Lara. Magda Goebbels: Corinna Harfouch. Joseph Goebbels: Urlich Matthes. Eva Braun: Juliane Köhler. Albert Speer: Heino Ferch. Heinrich Himmler: Ulrich Noethen. Gen. Alfred Jodl: Christian Redl
AA: None
AAN: Best Foreign-Language Film
DVD: Sony Pictures Home Entertainment, 2005
BLU-RAY: Momentum Pictures, 2005
DURATION: 155 minutes (178 for extended cut)

Hitler and his Nazi regime have provided cinema (and TV) with ample opportunities for moviemaking on the subject during the last sixty years, but not a single one of these movies has managed to raise itself above the ordinary and the unmemorable. One reason is the plethora of documentaries that have preserved the Führer's raw image on film, presenting him as he was, and movies found it hard to match the original footage. Another reason may be the existence of the one masterpiece in the genre, Leni Riefenstahl's controversial *Triumph of the Will*, made in 1934, at the height of Hitler's power. The film paints a definitive, if flattering, picture of Hitler, putting to rest any subsequent attempts to portray the dictator fictionally. Some efforts have been made to represent Hitler as a farcical or comic figure, including Charlie Chaplin's famous burlesque *The Great Dictator* (1940), a self-exhibitionist film that busies itself more with Chaplin's pranks than Hitler's, as well as Ennio De Concini's *Hitler: The Last Ten Days* (1973), with Alec Guinness in one of his poorest performances.

Oliver Hirschbiegel's *Downfall* belongs to a different order of filmmaking, taking its subject matter with utter seriousness and describing Hitler's final days with historical exactitude, while adding a touch of regret for the sufferings that this hated figure caused Germany and the rest of the world. Here, history is not merely duplicated, but rather given in terse dramatic form through the use of plot, characterization, and the development of ironic and complex themes. It is a "march of doom" type of story, unrelenting in its descriptions of painful events and unsparing of one's particular orientations and panoply of biases. It is not an easy story to judge, but the viewer is certain to be caught in a gripping tale where watching becomes a bumpy, emotional roller coaster.

Hirschbiegel states that he sought to give the "human" side of Hitler (played by Bruno Ganz), presenting him not as the world had known him at the height of his power, but in his harrowing last moments, trapped in the depths of his bunker, sunk in despair, and practically powerless.[1] The movie makes almost no references to Hitler's crimes during the war, aside from incidental bits and pieces of information inserted into the action and dialogue during the short span of time the movie covers. By presenting Hitler at the weakest point of his career, the film deftly avoids the tiresome task of repetition of materials audiences have grown accustomed to seeing for more than half a century. In *Downfall*, Hitler is given not as the supreme commander of the Third Reich, scoring quick triumphs and overwhelming Europe, but as a hunched, shaking, and bitter weakling, with occasional sparks flying when, in the grip of acute paranoia, he still imagines himself undefeatable, giving orders that cannot be carried out. To those still around him, he is a fallen idol—reduced in stature and vainly groping for a solution, finding no exit from the hole he has literally dug for himself. By focusing on a single incident, his last few days, the movie depicts a little cosmos of chaos and despair, but it does so with detachment, unmaliciously, as a means of catharsis from the guilt and dishonor that has haunted the German nation for sixty years. The somewhat abstract title becomes a verbal node, signifying the fall of an entire group, the justifiable end of those who helped a dismally inept figure wreak havoc in the world.

While we believe in the director's intentions to give Hitler's portrait objectively, it is hard for a viewer to determine exactly what he has in mind. We see a haunted man who is sympathetic to his dog (calling it "more intelligent" than most humans) and gentle with those who stood by him in his last hours, but we are also exposed to his verbal abuse, mad outbreaks of temper, and ever-present and unquashed delusion that he is still in charge. He raves like a maniac against those who have betrayed him but also displays moments of dignity when he dismisses any idea of attempting to escape or negotiate a surrender. There are even a few touching moments, for instance, when he marries Eva Braun (Juliane Köhler) when all is lost, tells those working closely with him that they may to go if they wish, and gives orders to have his body burned beyond recognition after he kills himself.

However one interprets Hitler's last actions, the film does not spare him otherwise. It shows him as a madman whose tragic illusions never left him, even in the very end. He raves about being betrayed by his senior officers and demands their execution. He believes in the German people and in final victory, hanging on to this delusion despite concrete evidence that his last armies were being wiped out by the advancing Russians, and that the last soldiers around the capital were either children or old men. It's questionable whether Hitler ever understood the causes of his failure, and it is this intense paranoia that the movie is good at demonstrating. For Hitler and those close to him, there is no exit, and he prepares, in desperation, to commit suicide with the loyal (but dissolute) Eva Braun, Joseph Goebbels (Urlich Matthes), and Magda Goebbels (Corinna Harfouch). Goebbels' wife Magda, tragically deluded as she is in believing in Hitler's and her husband's ideals, prepares to kill her own six children before she and her husband commit suicide, while Traudl Junge (Alexandra Maria Lara), his young secretary, remains there until Hitler is dead.

The movie tells the story of these people from the inside, from the point of view of Junge, who was hired personally by Hitler two and a half years before the downfall of the dictator, which she witnesses firsthand, thus offering a unique perspective of those fateful events. But the movie strives for objectivity, minutely following factual and historical evidence, and it includes the points of view of the numerous participants, thus giving a broader picture of that event. In style, the movie is close to a documentary, minutely detailing the last days of the German Reich, but this is also a drama of a group of individuals trapped inside a bunker and awaiting destruction, which historical evidence, if not the movie itself, tells us was self-inflicted. Although Junge witnesses the events and structures the narrative, Hitler is the center of attention, for the story is essentially about him. Hirschbiegel's stated intent to present Hitler's "human" side seems like an obligation of a historian, and Bruno Ganz, whose uncanny resemblance to Hitler gives him additional credibility, delivers the chronicles of the dictator's final hours with an authenticity that is hard to challenge. Everything the film tells is true, for all the evidence needed exists, and its makers did not want false facts to distract the audience with foreign matter usually inserted into film narratives to facilitate dramatic structure.

Two points can be made here: First, the film achieves a dramatic structure that can be called tragic. Second, the final result is a "decentering" of the historically given Hitler and the Nazis around him, if not revisionist version of them—at the least a "readjustment" of history.

The story is relentlessly tragic, although the term should be applied in a collective or general sense, for the film does not try to present Hitler as a tragic figure. Such a characterization may be reserved for such eminent fictional types as Oedipus, Hamlet, or King Lear, figures who were basically well intentioned but fell short of achieving their goals because of a fatal flaw. Hitler is the opposite: he had no redeeming qualities to speak of (despite his love of dogs and his mistress, and his fondness for his secretary); he had only the realization of his failure—which he always, at least verbally, attributed to others. The story is tragic because of what happened to those innocent victims (a word to be used advisedly here) of his entourage, especially those who were subjected to the horrors of imminent destruction either because of misguided loyalty (one example being Junge herself) or because they were innocent bystanders. The former included most of Hitler's senior officers still around him at the end, who preferred to kill themselves rather than surrender, as did Heinrich Himmler, an SS official. The latter group included soldiers in the streets of Berlin, including young boys and old men, who fought or were caught in the crossfire, or servants and functionaries who had remained in the bunker out of necessity or loyalty.

The most tragic figures, however, were Joseph Goebbels, Hitler's minister of propaganda, and his wife Magda, especially the latter. While Goebbels seems more preoccupied with dictating his will to Junge, after Hitler has done so, declaring that the "light" of Nazism will not be extinguished after his death, he seems sternly worn out, but still firm in his belief that his children must die. But he leaves the task of poisoning their six children to his wife. Remaining unwavering, erroneously but magnificently, staying loyal to Hitler and his ideals, she carries out her gruesome decision personally, not wanting her children to grow up in a world where the ideals of the German Reich do not exist. Corinna Harfouch is memorable as Magda Goebbels, a modern Medea who oversees the preparation of the liquid drug that would put the children to sleep prior to her placing poison capsules in their mouths. In the film, her oldest daughter senses the meaning of this and resists the drink, but she is forced into the act. This is the most dramatic scene of the entire movie—and the one that makes it fully tragic in the collective sense. To sum up the tragic tone of *Downfall*, one can add the relentless bombardment of Berlin, the indiscriminate slaughter of people in the streets, the terror of the bunker, and the final price of loyalty when many of Hitler's senior officers commit suicide. The picture of the disintegration of a regime, however malevolent, inspires mixed feelings, for a segment of humanity, although justifiably, suffers untold agonies and extreme mental anguish, worthy of some of the scenes described by Dante in *The Inferno*. Told without comment, the story of this collective tragedy is left to speak for itself.

As for Hitler's portrait, it is given in a deliberate attempt to show him dichotomized, often human and gentle to the point of sentimentality, at other times a raving lunatic shouting curses against the "traitors" who abandoned him and futilely ordering them to obey. The once almighty Führer is now humbled and impotent, subjected to the relentless bombardment of the approaching Red Army, giving orders and planning counterattacks that have no meaning. His subordinates still respect him and make a show of obedience, but they realize long before he does that all is lost. The loyal ones persist in remaining close to him to the end. Those who see his delusion, Albert Speer (Heino Ferch), for instance, decide to leave while there is still time. Hitler himself advises his young secretary to go, but she refuses and only leaves after he is dead. Alternately "human" and obsessive, Hitler keeps repeating his worn-out motto of the "superiority" of the Arian race. It is the law of nature that he follows: let the weak perish and the strong prevail. All animals in the animal kingdom follow this law—an idea that appears in the first paragraphs of *Mein Kampf*. Hitler blames his generals who abandoned him, Heinrich Himmler (Ulrich Noethen) in particular, whose "execution" he orders. Hitler is fully aware of the futility of ordering his remaining armies to attack and defeat the Russians—who relentlessly approach, although they make no actual appearance until the end.

The film does not dwell on Hitler's atrocities, although it does make reference to them. Hitler, rather, spends his remaining time bragging that he conquered Europe, even though his militarily trained officers failed him, and he himself had not attended any military academies. He thus vacillates between being "human" with his servants and lower echelons, while brutally attacking his generals for their continued failures. He cannot accept defeat, but he knows it is coming and that suicide is the only choice that remains for him. He marries Eva Braun just moments before they both commit suicide, a well-planned chain of events, for he wants one of his loyal bodyguards to find gasoline and burn his body so that it will not be "exhibited in Soviet museums" as a trophy. By the time the end comes, he is physically a wreck, his left hand shaking, his body bent, and his eyes rolling in anger and mad despair.

The film strives for objectivity, and in that sense it will offend those who think that any effort to be revisionist with the greatest monster of all time should not be allowed. But this is a German production, and perhaps the producers made it out of feelings of guilt, for Hitler did not act alone; he had the support of his people, otherwise he would not have risen to absolute power as he did. And he was proud of that as a man, as he said to his remaining subordinates, who did not go to the military academies, but who conquered all of Europe. CS

Note

1. Oliver Hirschbiegel, "Commentary," *Downfall*, directed by Oliver Hirschbiegel (Sony Pictures Home Entertainment, 2005), DVD.

Bibliography

Bischof, Willi, ed. *Filmri:ss: Studien über den Film "Der Untergang.* Münster, Germany: Unrast Verlag, 2005.

Fest, Joachim. *Inside Hitler's Bunker: The Last Days of the Third Reich.* New York: Farrar, Straus and Giroux, 2005.

Fischer, Thomas. *Soldiers of the Leibstandarte: SS-Brigadefuhrer Wilhelm Mohnke and 62 Soldiers of Hitler's Elite Division.* Winnipeg, Manitoba, Canada: J. J. Fedorowicz, 2008.

Junge, Traudl, and Melissa Müller. *Until the Final Hour: Hitler's Last Secretary.* Translated by Anthea Bell. New York: Arcade, 2004.

Vande Winkel, Roel. "Hitler's Downfall, a film from Germany." In *Perspectives on European Film and History*, edited by Roel Vande Winkel and Leen Engeleen, 182–219. Gent, Belgium: Academia Press, 2007.

FANNY AND ALEXANDER (FANNY OCH ALEXANDER) (1982)

Director: Ingmar Bergman
Writer: Ingmar Bergman
Producer: Jörn Donner (Cinematograph AB, Svenska Filminstitutet, Gaumont)
Cinematographer: Sven Nykvist
Editor: Sylvia Ingemarsson
Art Direction: Anna Asp
Set Decoration: Susanne Lingheim
Costumes: Marick Vos-Lundh
Music: Daniel Bell
Cast: Alexander Ekdahl: Bertil Guve. Fanny Ekdahl: Pernilla Allwin. Helena Ekdahl: Gunn Wållgren. Oscar Ekdahl: Allan Edwall. Gustav Adolf Ekdahl: Jarl Kulle. Carl Ekdahl: Böerje Ahlstedt. Emilie Ekdahl: Ewa Fröling. Lydia Ekdahl: Christina Schollin. Alma Ekdahl: Mona Malm. Bishop Edvard Vergerus: Jan Malmsjö. Isak Jacobi: Erland Josephson. Justina: Harriet Anderson. Maj: Pernilla August. Petra Ekdahl: Maria Granlund. Blenda Vergerus: Marianne Aminoff. Henrietta Vergerus: Kerstin Tidelius. Aron Retzinsky: Mats Bergman. Ismael Retzinsky: Stina Ekblad
AA: Best Art Direction–Set Decoration (Anna Asp, Susanne Lingheim), Best Cinematography (Sven Nykvist), Best Costume Design (Marick Vos-Lundh), Best Foreign-Language Film
AAN: Best Director (Ingmar Bergman), Best Writing–Screenplay Written Directly for the Screen (Ingmar Bergman)
DVD: Criterion, 2004. Theatrical version.
Blu-ray: Criterion, 2011
Duration: 188 minutes

Fanny and Alexander, Ingmar Bergman's last theatrical film, can be considered both a comedy and a tragedy, a mixed genre, somewhat unusual in the grand opus of Bergman, who was known for his gloomy tales, but also for his occasional comedies. At three-plus hours,[1] it is a lengthy work of epic proportions, but in some ways it is a work of relatively narrow scope, containing the story of a single family, although it is rich in themes, imagery, and complex human characterization. As his last and longest cinematic work, Bergman combines themes explored in many of his previous movies—marital relations, Oedipal interactions, questions of faith (always inevitable in Bergman), and, especially here, the circuit of theater (and consequently of film) as an art form and a way of life. The movie, episodic at first, develops a clear line of plot, with a sudden complication, a fully tragic development, and a denouement providing a catharsis of pity and fear combined with a happy ending. Despite its rather narrow compass, it is a cinematic work of large dimension, summing up Bergman's previous works, but also introducing new notes—of optimism, love, and reconciliation. It is lushly photographed in color by Sven Nykvist, with attention to detail, costuming, and period setting.

The story begins on 24 December 1907, Christmas Eve, which in Sweden is a celebration of Christmas itself, when relatives arrive for a dinner at the Ekdahl household, an affluent, upper-middle-class environment. Family members arrive at about 4:30 p.m., after a stage production of the Christmas nativity, played at the Ekdahl-owned theater, and they proceed with a lavish Christmas dinner that goes through most of the night. This is the household of the Ekdahl matriarch, Helena Ekdahl (Gunn Wållgren), whose family consists of her three sons, Oscar (Allan Edwall), Carl (Böerje Ahlstedt), and Gustav Adolf (Jarl Kulle), who come in with their wives, children, and some other friends, including Helena's old (and current) lover, Isak Jacobi (Erland Josephson), who has come to share in the celebration of Christmas, even though he is Jewish. The children open presents and the entire company joins in a dance, including the numerous female servants.

The plot evolves slowly, the dinner party itself lasting nearly one-fourth of the movie (45 minutes), but it already foreshadows some crucial events, all having to do with relations between the various members of the family. Oscar, the eldest son, runs the family theater, has put on the Christmas production, and evidently runs a successful business, although loans from his affluent mother are occasionally needed. His vivacious and beautiful wife Emilie (Ewa Fröling) is much younger than he is, and she seems happy with her role as a mother and is on good terms with the other members of the family. But Oscar is apparently not in sound health, for he nearly faints and has to sit down during the dance. He recovers to read a passage from the gospel at a postdinner prayer gathering. The next son, Carl, a professor, is married to a German girl named Lydia (Christina Schollin), and their relationship seems rugged; he is unhappy and often drunk, but he can entertain the children with vulgar jokes. The youngest son, Gustav Adolf, lusty, boisterous, and playful, carries on an affair with a young servant girl, Maj (Emilie's nursemaid, played by Pernilla August), and before the night is out he has an assignation with her in one of the bedrooms, giving her a note promising to help her open a café later in life, securing her financial independence. She sulks at the idea and refuses his offer. The party ends with the guests gradually departing around 3:00 a.m. and the children going to bed. Alexander (Bertil Guve) has a kinetoscope, through which he is able to show pictures on a projector to his siblings. Alexander is the protagonist of the story, but, at least in the first part, the point of view is omniscient, for the viewer sees and knows more than he does.[2]

Until this juncture, the story has crawled along, leisurely paced with the description of the endless Christmas party, introduction of various characters and their private liaisons, and details of the ceremonial dinner. In a somewhat abrupt transition, we find ourselves at a rehearsal of *Hamlet* at Oscar's theater, where Oscar, playing the ghost of Hamlet's father, suddenly collapses. He soon dies, pronouncing various aphorisms about life, promising to always be with his family, for death cannot separate him from them. Crushed, Alexander refuses to enter his dying father's room and has to be dragged there to hear his father's last words. A state funeral is followed by a grand dinner in the Ekdahl parlor, with a small circle of guests and family members.

Among the guests is Bishop Edvard Vergerus (Jan Malmsjö), who officiated at the funeral and is now sitting next to the bereaved widow and constantly talking to her. Astonished, Alexander notices that his mother, who screamed in agony during the night of her husband's death, is now receiving the overly intimate attentions of the bishop, while a faint smile comes to her face. Vergerus seems impressive: dignified but boyishly handsome, authoritative, dressed in austere black, a large cross ostentatiously decorating his chest. His are words of sympathy, no doubt, but his face betrays the vulturelike grimace of a man ready to pounce on his exquisite prey.

Another complication occurs in the next scene, although one is to understand that several months have passed after Oscar's funeral. Emilie summons her son to see Vergerus, who reprimands Alexander for having lied at school, gives him a severe lecture about truth and falsity, and asks him to beg his mother's forgiveness. Vergerus speaks cajolingly, in grave tones, but slaps Alexander on the back of the head in a mock caress, as if to underscore his growing authority over him. As he exits the room, Vergerus leans over intimately and whispers some words to Emilie, who rewards him with a broad smile. A moment later, she announces to her dumbfounded children that she has accepted the bishop's offer of marriage "with gratitude and joy." Alexander turns and sees the ghost of Oscar nodding gravely from the next room, as if disapproving of what is going on. Vergerus, now engaged to Emilie, asks her not to bring any of her possessions with her, nor allow her children to do so. Emilie gives in, although she protests that she cannot decide for her children. A brief wedding ceremony follows at the Ekdahl house, during which Alexander again sees his father's ghost watching the proceedings. He runs away from the ceremony and falls on his bed in a furious outburst. As Emilie and her new husband, with the children following behind, walk away in the street, Helena, who senses that this will be an unhappy union, predicts that Emilie will soon return.

As they move into their new residence, the transition is a shock to the children, and even to Emilie. The bishop's house, built in the fifteenth century, is an austere place with bare walls and devoid of furniture, a sharp contrast to the comfortable household the children are accustomed to. They are introduced to a forbidding-looking group of women: two unsmiling women in black who seem to be duplicates of one another; Edvard's mother Blenda (Marianne Aminoff) and his sister Henrietta (Kerstin Tidelius); and several stern-looking, older female servants, while a sick aunt is kept immobile in bed upstairs. The first dinner at home is a gloomy gathering during which Henrietta dictates the house rules, indicating how the children are to behave, adding that everyone must be up at 6:00 a.m. for prayer at the bishop's office. Shocked at this intrusion of her authority, Emilie begs to differ, stating that she will be the one to give her children orders. Later, as the children are seen in their beds, the bishop comes in and asks Alexander what he is reading. He snatches the book away in an expression of his displeasure. Vergerus also grabs his teddy bear, something that Alexander brought from his old home, against the bishop's wishes. When he leaves, Emilie, in tears, and sensing that a war has begun between her son and his stepfather, tells Alexander that she is not

Queen Gertrude, nor should he try to be a Hamlet. Moments later, Alexander shows Fanny, who seems to share her brother's thoughts, that the windows are barred, and that they are practically in a prison.

The plotline is now doubled (and later tripled), as crosscutting shows Helena, asleep, being visited by her dead son Oscar, who always appears impeccably dressed in white (in contrast to the bishop's black). He speaks, soothing his mother in her loneliness, but he confirms her fears about the children. Helena has two more visitors. One is Major Gustav Adolf's girlfriend, now pregnant, who breaks down in sobs, worried not about herself, but about the children. Emilie comes next, changed: she, too, is pregnant and declares her hatred for the bishop, whom she cannot leave, for he would sue her for desertion and take her children from her.

While Emilie is absent for this visit, a scene back at the bishop's house shows Justina (Harriet Anderson), the kitchen maid, bringing the children their dinner. As they eat, she tells them the story of the drowning of the bishop's former wife and children in the river next to the house. The bodies of the children were so tightly intertwined that they had to cut their arms off to place them in their different coffins. Alexander tells the story from this point onward and goes on to say that the bishop had locked his former wife and her children in a room without food for five days, and they drowned in the stream. A treacherous Justina tells the bishop about Alexander's story. Vergerus summons two of the children; stages a "trial," with his mother and sister and Justina present; and asks Alexander to admit his lie. At first he refuses, but seeing punishment coming, he states that he prefers caning to castor oil or being shut in a cubbyhole to be nibbled on by rats. Alexander is lashed on his bare backside ten times, but he still refuses to seek forgiveness. After being lashed once more, he relents, begs forgiveness, and kisses the bishop's hands, but he shouts defiantly as he admits his guilt. Emilie returns from her visit; grabs the key from Henrietta; and goes to the attic, where Alexander is lying prostrate. She embraces her son.

Then the story takes an unexpected turn. Isak Jacobi reappears on the scene as he is driving a carriage to the bishop's residence. He pretends that he wants to buy a chest that the bishop owns for a large sum of money and cleverly manages to hide the children in it and take them away to his place. At Jacobi's residence, the children are accommodated for the night and introduced to Isak's assistant, Aron (Mats Bergman), who runs a puppet show with its weird assemblage of puppets that scare Alexander when he wanders into the labyrinthine chambers during the night.

There is parallel action developing here. The story cuts back to Emilie, showing her away from the bishop's bed, drinking (or about to drink) a cup of hot broth, as she suffers from insomnia. The bishop joins her and asks her to give him some of the broth, for he, too, cannot sleep. She has put sleeping pills in it, and when the bishop is summoned upstairs by his sick aunt, she adds three more. She later tells Vergerus, while he is in a deep sleep, that she is leaving him; he begs her to stay and threatens to poison her life, persecute her children, and destroy their lives if she does not.

The action cuts back to Alexander, who has a final encounter with his father's ghost. Oscar speaks to him this time, begging forgiveness for the troubles he has caused his family. Alexander replies that he should go away and hide in heaven, since he can do no good for anyone anyway. He asks him to explain why God does not kill the bishop. Oscar caresses his son's head and tells him to be tolerant of people. A few moments later, Aron invites Alexander to meet his sick brother, Ismael (Stina Ekblad), who is considered dangerous and kept locked up. Ismael is an androgynous creature[3] who possesses telepathic qualities. He tells Alexander what is happening at this precise moment at the bishop's house. Aunt Else overturns the lamp next to her. It catches fire, and she runs through the house screaming.

There is yet another cut, back to Emilie, now at Helena's house, dressed in black and lying in bed. She is summoned by Helena, who tells her that the police want to talk to her. An inspector tells her that her husband has died under terrible circumstances: his aunt, engulfed in flames, had run to the bishop's bedchamber and embraced him, and he caught fire. His mother found him charred and dying in agony. The inspector knows that Emilie had given him a "soporific" the previous night, which may have made matters worse, but he cannot ascribe any blame to her; it was an extremely unfortunate accident.

The next scene reveals two infants lying side by side in baskets, while the Ekdahls, reunited, celebrate. Gustav Adolf is in charge, making a long speech, Maj sitting on one side and Emilie on the other. He is happy—they all are—to have Emilie back. We later see Emilie with her baby, visited by two women, Petra (Maria Granlund) and Maj; they have decided to move to Stockholm, where a job awaits them. Maj will leave Gustav, and Helena tells Emilie that Oscar wanted her to run the theater for him. She will stage a new play by August Strindberg, in which Helena will also act. Alexander sees one more ghost, the bishop's, who grabs him by the neck and tells him that he will never escape him. Alexander crawls onto his grandmother's lap, and she reads him a passage from the Strindberg play: "Everything can happen. Everything is possible and probable. Time and space do not exist. On a flimsy framework of reality, the imagination spins, weaving new patterns."

This quotation is both directly and indirectly related to the developing themes in the story. As film historian Peter Cowie claims in his lengthy commentary, this movie directly reflects Bergman's recollection of his youth in his austere household, run by his Lutheran father, whose image is represented in the diabolically oppressive Bishop Vergerus.[4] It is also a reflection of the rare happy moments, which are shown in the Ekdahl household. Thus, it is both a comedy and a tragedy. According to this interpretation, Bergman's gloomy films are attempts by the director to exorcise the devils of his childhood and his torments by his cruel father, who had actually locked his son in a cubbyhole with the mice, something Vergerus threatens to do to Alexander. The comedy exists in the family gatherings, the joyous Christmas dinners, or the pleasures of the attractive summer home. Art thus acquires a therapeutic quality, the healing of wounds—cruelties, deprivation of freedom, harsh religious practices—all of those embodied in the bishop, whose phantasm will always shadow Alexander. It is also a filial tribute to a parent (and parents) whom, as a grown man, Bergman recognizes simply as human beings rather than specters of cruelty and dominance.

Burdened as he is by his two fathers' ghosts, the good and the evil one, Alexander, unusually gifted with a supersensory imagination, weaves his tales of woe and occasionally of happiness—which is confined to moments. "Time and space do not exist" could mean that the present is in the past and vice versa, and death, as Oscar says, does not end life in those with an extraordinary imagination. Alexander cannot get rid of his fathers—or the split persona of a good/evil father—but he can re-create them and kill the evil one at will, as the telepathic scene with Ismael suggests. Ismael predicts—one can even say causes—the death of Vergerus precisely at the moment it happens. "Everything is possible and probable" could mean that ghosts can actually govern our lives, and a dead person can come back from the dead, if a telepathic or extrasensory imagination summons it. "The imagination spins, weaving new patterns" dependent "on a flimsy framework of reality," for any incident in life can be expanded and re-created at will and ad infinitum; thence, the gifted filmmaker can spin his tales out of a rather small body of materials—for how many tales can be told derived from the precious few years of a single childhood?

For Bergman, art is a bifurcation of two mediums: theater of the stage and film. He once said that theater was his wife and cinema his mistress. Pressed for an explanation a few years later, he responded, "Now I am a bigamist."[5] A third element is added in the film: the theater is a family. Just as the Ekdahls—Oscar in particular—own and run a theater, so is the theater a world of its own, delimiting a social existence that can be found nowhere else. It is a closed circle, operating with laws entirely its own, a microcosm, for it reflects the outside world in one way or another. When Oscar dies, that microcosm vanishes with the intrusion of the bishop, who becomes the means of destroying that order, thereby destroying the work of the imagination. Alexander can no longer read his books or look through his kinetoscope into imaginary worlds, and the tales he spins are mortal sin, punishable by caning (or other cruel means). When the evil Vergerus is removed from the scene (whether one regards Emilie's act a crime or not), that order is restored and imagination is again free to create. Now freed from the shackles of a restrictive agent, Emilie becomes the natural head of the theater company, to continue her good husband's creative work. In the end, Bergman brings us face-to-face with the work of the artist, as part of the redemption of human beings who are able to exorcise the evil spirit. Alexander asks Oscar's ghost to ask God to kill the evil bishop. If everything can be imagined as possible, that becomes a possibility, too. CS

Notes

1. The theatrical version runs 188 minutes. The TV version is much longer, at five hours, reduced to 240 minutes for the theatrical edition, and again for the final cut. The Criterion Collection editions offer both versions, both with commentaries by Peter Cowie.
2. This point is debatable.
3. In fact, this character is played by a woman.
4. Peter Cowie, "Commentary," *Fanny and Alexander*, directed by Ingmar Bergman (Criterion, 2004), DVD.
5. Cowie, "Commentary."

Bibliography

Baxter, Brian. "Obituary: Ingmar Bergman." *Guardian*, 30 July 2007, www.guardian.co.uk/film/2007/jul/30/ingmarbergman.obituaries (23 October 2013).

Brooks, Xan. "*Fanny and Alexander*: No. 8 Best Arthouse Film of All Time." *Guardian*, 19 October 2010, www.theguardian.com/film/2010/oct/20/fanny-alexander-bergman-arthouse (23 October 2013).

Canby, Vincent. "Movie Review: *Fanny and Alexander*." *New York Times*, 17 June 1983, www.nytimes.com/movie/review?res=9F51A0C01138F935A35750C8BF67 (23 October 2013).

Lamont, Tom. "The Film That Changed My Life: Matthew Macfadyen." *Guardian/Observer*, 20 August 2011, www.theguardian.com/film/2011/aug/21/matthew-macfadyen-fanny-and-alexander (23 October 2013).

Moody, Rick. "*Fanny and Alexander*: Bergman's Bildungsroman." *Current*, 8 November 2011, www.criterion.com/current/posts/347-fanny-and-alexander-bergman-s-bildungsroman (23 October 2013).

FITZCARRALDO (1982)

DIRECTOR: Werner Herzog
WRITER: Werner Herzog
PRODUCER: Werner Herzog, Lucki Stipetic (Werner Herzog Filmproduktion, Project Filmproduktion, Filmverlag der Autoren)
CINEMATOGRAPHER: Thomas Macuh
EDITOR: Beate Mainka-Jellinghous
MUSIC: Popal Vuh

CAST: Brian Sweeney Fitzgerald (Fitzcarraldo): Klaus Kinski. Molly: Claudia Cardinale. Cholo: Miguel Ángel Fuentes. Don Acquilino: José Lewgoy. Captain Orinoco: Paul Hittscher. Cook: Huerequeque Enrique Bohorquez. Opera Manager: Peter Berling. Chief of Campa Indians: David Pérez Espinosa. Rubber Baron: Ruy Polanah. Old Missionary: Salvador Godínez
AA: None
AAN: None
BAFTA AWARD NOMINATION: Best Foreign-Language Film
GGN: Best Foreign Film (Werner Herzog)
CANNES FILM FESTIVAL AWARD: Best Director (Werner Herzog)
CANNES FILM FESTIVAL AWARD NOMINATION: Palme D'Or (Werner Herzog)
DVD: Kinowelt Home Entertainment, 2003. In German, with English subtitles.
BLU-RAY: Currently unavailable
DURATION: 157 minutes

Sometimes the travails of making an epic are similar, or even exceed, the feats that the epic itself describes. Whether there is some masochism involved in an effort that requires the collaboration of two people who intensely dislike one another is a question that might be best left unanswered, but it is a fact that the brilliantly fruitful association between Werner Herzog and Klaus Kinski was a tortured one, beginning with *Aguirre, the Wrath of God* (1972), followed by the making of three more movies together.[1] *Fitzcarraldo* is, perhaps, Herzog's definitive epic, the word *definitive* being used here in a double sense, for it was an epic of moviemaking, as well as one of epic action. Here, fiction and reality merge, for Herzog admits that he would have played the role of the movie's protagonist himself had Kinski refused or been disabled before the film was finished.

After making *Aguirre, the Wrath of God* in the Amazon jungles with Kinski, one of the most volatile actors in movie history, one wonders why Herzog would bother making another film with him in the same jungles, especially since the locations and the risks of shooting were practically the same. But Kinski was not Herzog's first choice, and only extreme circumstances forced him to resort to using him once again. In his DVD commentary, Herzog states that he always had Kinski in mind, but he was hesitant knowing the actor's temper, which would add to the difficulties of shooting in a jungle environment, for a project that was extremely hazardous to begin with.[2]

The shooting had started with Jason Robards in the key role, with Mick Jagger as his sidekick, and the film was nearly finished when Robards became ill and withdrew. Practically the entire film had to be reshot, while the scenes with Jagger were cut out altogether, for Herzog thought Kinski could combine the two characters. Although he admits that Kinski turned out to be right for the part, most of his fears also proved true. Herzog had to exercise all his professional skills to control an actor known for his wild tantrums and moments of "freaking out" during shooting. In the process, he also had to alter Kinski's personal image—from an actor who had played villains and madmen throughout his career (he had made as many as 200 films up to this time) to an idiosyncratic but sympathetic hero facing impossible odds to achieve his ends.[3] As it turned out, the cooperation, while admittedly taxing, worked out well, producing a story of daring and heroism, and victory on a difficult, if "mad," mission, against all odds. Perhaps making this film under the circumstances it was made—weather delays, dangerous environment, actors' problems, and finances—was as heroic as the story it depicts.

The similarities between *Fitzcarraldo* with *Aguirre* cannot be ignored, for, in both cases, the action involves one man whose scheme is rooted in a grand idea. Aguirre aspires to reach the mythical land of Eldorado, defining it in his deranged, but possibly noble, imagination as a new world dominated by a "pure" race that he would start by marrying his own daughter. He is obviously mad, with unmistakable affinities to the Nazi ideals, but his obsession carries him to the limits, where he and his companions find death and extinction. Whether the trip up the Amazon branching off to the Peruvian jungles and mountains to found an empire would inspire such a story is another question, but the conquistadors had conceived it, and adventurers, ranging from the most insane to the most idealistic, pursued it throughout the centuries. In the beginning of the twentieth century, however, it was not Eldorado, with its abstract boundaries, but the concrete pursuit of wealth in the Amazon jungles—obtaining rubber from the rubber trees hidden in unapproachable areas of the jungle—that motivated daring businessmen to navigate to the river region and exploit its riches. In the city of Manaus, where native residents had lived in huts of mud, the rubber barons had flourished, building palaces, gambling houses, brothels, and an opera house[4] for the culturally minded, so that the jungle and river city would be transformed into an oasis of civilization. Fitzcarraldo was one of those people, but his ambition went beyond obtaining wealth for its own sake; he wanted to bring the great opera singers of Europe to the jungle, and to that he devoted all his energies.

The character of Fitzcarraldo, as he was called by the natives, is based on a real person, Brian Sweeney Fitzgerald, who conceived the idea of building a grand opera house at Iquitos, 800 miles up the river, near the Peruvian border, to accommodate the greatest tenor of the early twentieth century, Enrico Caruso (1873–1921), whose voice had been recorded on phonographs, and who had become a cultural phenomenon equal only to the great rock and pop stars of today.

Fitzcarraldo had proposed to the barons a scheme to get far greater quantities of rubber by sailing into a dangerous area near Ucayali Falls and taking an alternate route to avoid the perilous rapids. Don Acquilino (José Lewgoy), one of the richest barons and a considerable gambler, saw Fitzcarraldo's scheme as unrealizable and refused to support it. Fitzcarraldo, a pure opera lover, conceived the dream of bringing Caruso from Europe to sing in the jungles of the Amazon, but he wanted to build an opera house that would be commensurate with the supreme talent of the great opera star. His dream seemed outrageous to the barons, who refused to have anything to do with it, although the interest of some was piqued.

Here again, there is a story of a strong-willed individual, a character partially based on a real person, a near madman who seems determined to sail up the Amazon, into the Peruvian jungles, to a location rich in rubber that would make him wealthy enough to realize his dream. Fitzcarraldo seems obsessed with this one idea, but he is unable to convince the barons to finance his plan, for to them he seems an impractical madman, whose preoccupation with bringing culture into the wilderness is too far-fetched and not worth serious consideration. But the viewer may also perceive him as a cultural philanthropist, a hero of sorts. In contrast to Aguirre (and the comparisons seem unavoidable), who is a murderous tyrant, and whose scheme to find Eldorado ends in tragedy, Fitzcarraldo seems a benign madman, whose love of the art of singing, and particularly that of the phenomenally celebrated Caruso, redeems him; however, Kinski plays this character with such neurotic intensity that, as one follows the film's action, one senses that another tragedy is bound to happen at any moment before the story ends.

The trip begins at Manaus, a newly built town thriving in the middle course of the great Amazon River, where rubber barons had built palaces, and an opera house, for the entertainment of the rich people, and where celebrities from Europe occasionally visit and sing. Fitzcarraldo is late for one of these performances, escorted by his girlfriend, Molly, played by a middle-aged but still beautiful Claudia Cardinale, a luxury brothel keeper. After failing to persuade the wealthy rubber barons to finance his rubber scheme, Fitzcarraldo persuades his girlfriend to purchase and finance the repair of a decrepit boat, which he names the *Molly-Aida* and sails up the river with a small crew, most of whom abandon him in the middle of his trip; however, a tribe of natives is willing to help him, for reasons that seem mysterious, perhaps having being impressed by the largeness of the ship or the voice of Caruso, whom Fitzcarraldo constantly plays on his phonograph, possibly because they think such singing will exorcise the evil spirits.

But the expedition comes to an untimely halt when a peninsula blocks the progress of the ship. Fitzcarraldo comes up with the ingenious idea of hauling the big vessel up the hill and down the other side, pulling the huge structure with pulleys and revolving levers. It seems like Herculean task, but the idea is successful, against all odds. Nonetheless, when the ship is floating on the water again, it encounters a series of whirling currents that nearly wreck it. The travelers manage to reach their destination and then make it back to Iquitos again. Fitzcarraldo does not succeed in his rubber forest venture, but he demonstrates that feats that may appear impossible to accomplish become achievable when one is willing. One of the rubber barons is so impressed that he buys back the boat, and the exuberant Fitzcarraldo uses the proceeds to purchase the services of an opera ensemble touring the region at that time. As they play from Bellini's *I Puritani* (other operas are played throughout), Fitzcarraldo puffs on a cigar, enjoying his triumph. The same Kinski who had played the demented Aguirre in the previous film is now a content, happy, and vindicated man, although he has the look of a satisfied madman with ambition of getting rich. But perhaps a mad aesthete is saner than a zealous rubber baron, whose aims are not so lofty. Maybe this was Herzog's tribute to art and artistic pursuit, more so than the conquest of lands and the ensuing destruction of the environment for the sake of riches. CS

Notes

1. The others were, *Nosferatu the Vampyre* (1979), *Woyzeck* (1980), and *Cobra Verde* (1987).
2. See "Extras," *Fitzcarraldo*, directed by Werner Herzog (Kinowelt Home Entertainment, 2003), DVD.
3. See Werner Herzog, "Running Commentary," *Fitzcarraldo*, directed by Werner Herzog (Kinowelt Home Entertainment, 2003), DVD.
4. Herzog was himself an opera director and had directed such operas as *Lohengrin*, *The Flying Dutchman*, *Norma*, *Tannhäuser*, *The Magic Flute*, *Fidelio*, and many others. "Werner Herzog: Opera." *Werner Herzog.com*, 2013, www.wernerherzog.com/opera0.html (23 October 2013).

Bibliography

Cronin, Paul. *Herzog on Herzog*. London: Faber and Faber, 2002.

Herzog, Werner. *Conquest of the Useless: Reflections on the Making of* Fitzcarraldo. New York: HarperCollins, 2004.

GRAND ILLUSION (LA GRANDE ILLUSION) (1937)

Director: Jean Renoir
Writers: Charles Spaak, Jean Renoir
Producers: Albert Pinkovitch (uncredited), Frank Rollmer (uncredited) (Réalisation d'art cinématographique)
Cinematographer: Christian Matras
Editor: Marguerite Hullé
Production Design: Eugène Lourié
Set Decoration: Eugène Lourié
Costumes: René Decrais
Technical Advisor: Carl Koch

Music: Joseph Kosma
Cast: Lt. Maréchal: Jean Gabin. Lt. Rosenthal: Marcel Dalio. Capt. de Boeldieu: Pierre Fresnay. Capt. von Rauffenstein: Erich von Stroheim. Elsa: Dita Parlo. Cartier: Julien Carette. Sgt. Arthur: Werner Florian. Lt. Demolder: Sylvain Itkine
AA: None
AAN: Best Picture (the first foreign-language film ever nominated for an Oscar)
Venice Film Festival Award: Best Overall Artistic Contribution (Jean Renoir)[1]
Venice Film Festival Award Nomination: Mussolini Cup (Jean Renoir)
DVD: Criterion, 1999. With audio commentary and an introductory essay by film historian Peter Cowie.
Blu-ray: Studio Canal Collection, 2012
Duration: 114 minutes

Grand Illusion made its debut in the United States in 1938, and immediately won praise from President Franklin D. Roosevelt, while it was banned by Mussolini in Italy and the minister of propaganda in Germany, Joseph Goebbels, on the eve of World War II, for reasons that might be self-explanatory.[2] The movie has since won numerous honors, among which is its selection by *Sight and Sound* as one of the ten greatest movies of 1962. In its 1999 Criterion DVD issue, one can watch the film in its nearly pristine condition, with commentary by scholar Peter Cowie[3] and a short feature where Renoir himself, following World War II, explains the loss and total disintegration of his film, as well as its miraculous recovery (it had been stolen from Paris during World War II by the Germans) and subsequent restoration and rerelease. Renoir briefly and succinctly explains the film's contents and main theme, that the "grand illusion" is man's false notion that war is going to solve human problems; we must abolish war (he implies) before our "beautiful world" is in ruins. He also states that the film is about human relationships, which are capable of abolishing artificial boundaries of race and nationhood (or ideology) and binding people together. *Grand Illusion* is not an epic of size and spectacle, but one of grand dimension.

The story stresses both points: A group of French POWs held by German forces in a medieval castle make attempt after attempt to escape, and finally two of them, Maréchal (Jean Gabin) and Rosenthal (Marcel Dalio), make it into the German countryside, where they are befriended by Elsa (Dita Parlo), a German woman whose husband had been killed in the Battle of Verdun. Maréchal falls in love with the woman and promises to come back after the war. Erich von Stroheim plays Captain von Rauffenstein, a physically disabled German officer, humane and civilized, who befriends one of the French officers, Captain de Boeldieu (Pierre Fresnay), with whom he attended military school in England, and whom he sees as an aristocrat and a peer, rather than as an enemy. He has to shoot that officer, however, when the latter fakes an escape, using himself as a ploy to allow the others to go. The two men who have escaped and are given shelter by Elsa finally make it to the border. They cross into Switzerland and are saved.

Grand Illusion has been seen as a POW film, and there are several other POW films of note,[4] but, in essence, it is an antiwar film, and even much more than that. For one, it is about the passage of an era, early twentieth-century Europe, and a comparison of the two world wars, although World War II had not started yet and was only being anticipated. In World War I, what was dominant was the ethos of the aristocratic Europe of the nineteenth century, which had produced officers who adhered to codes of honor, the humane treatment of prisoners of war, for instance, a practice that was abandoned during World War II, what with Nazi atrocities, and the Japanese violations of the Geneva Conventions rules that excluded, among other things, officers from manual labor. Here, the aristocratic von Rauffenstein, played brilliantly by Stroheim, laments the passing of the code as he befriends Captain du Boeldieu, an officer with whom he shares values, and perhaps, as the movie shows, friendly, even affectionate, sentiments. Von Rauffenstein blames, appropriately, given his frame of mind, the French and the French Revolution, which was the historical convulsion that became the main social force that abolished aristocracy. In the film, Renoir seems to express a yearning for the passing of a social order that was capable of superior behavior even in the face of the forced enmities that war brings about.

On the other hand, Renoir not only mixes social classes, but he seems to favor the idea and superimposes it on the action that a common humanity can be developed by enforced captivity. Here, German guards are not the Nazi brutes one encounters in similar situations during World War II, and the film was made in 1937, when Renoir had witnessed the Nazi ascendancy and suspected that the storm would follow in just a few years. In that sense, the film seems to apply to both wars, World War I and World War II, and compares the two. In the film, the captors are quite aware of their duties, although they are perhaps presented to be not as mentally alert as their captives, who outsmart them on several occasions. The captives never forget that their primary duty is to escape—an extremely difficult task in the medieval castle where they are being held—and use ruses to achieve their ends. The most heroic act, however, proves to be that of Captain de Boeldieu, who pretends to escape, plays his flute as he is climbing the castle bulwarks, and ignores—or rather defies—the pleadings and orders of von Rauffenstein to surrender or be shot. His delaying tactics thus give the others the chance to outdistance themselves and finally make it to the farm where Elsa lives. The fact that she does not betray them is also significant, for she could have done so immediately, as a German detachment stops and knocks on her window to ask for directions. She has lost a husband and her brothers, practically her entire family. She and Maréchal fall in love and celebrate Christmas together, and Rosenthal, who comes from a wealthy Jewish family, participates.

Again, Renoir thinks of the abolition of the borders and borderlines that break up humanity's essential unity. Renoir was a philosopher/filmmaker, one who takes pains to show how people can live together, given a chance, and that the bad guys are not bad, or not worse than any of us. The grand illusion, the title of the film, is an elusive concept, for it emphasizes the bitter irony of having understood the inhumanity of war but not having been able to achieve its abolition. The illusion is the illusion of peace, tolerance, bonhomie, while the absurdity of war—which separates people artificially—is implied (and rejected) in just about every scene in this film.

The film uses innovative techniques, highly praised and admired by André Bazin, who thought that Renoir's use of depth of field and deep-focus photography and camera movement give the narrative of the story a natural look that quick cuts and excessive montage, a technique highly promoted at the time by Russian filmmaker and aesthetician Sergei Eisenstein, could not have achieved. Bazin stressed the simplicity of means and the group empathy that develops as these characters get to know one another and develop bonds in captivity, connections they may not have developed in a different situation. Philosophy and technique dovetail to produce a cinematic work of undiminished relevance, more worthy of viewing with the passing of decades. When *Grand Illusion*, in its restored version, was rereleased in theaters in May 2012, Chris Vognar wrote, "It's the most understated antiwar film ever made, effortlessly humanistic but far too subtle to indulge in preaching."[5] CS

Notes

1. Notoriously fascist, according to historian Barry Norman. Barry Norman, *The 100 Best Films of the Century* (New York: Carol Publishing Group, 1993), 134.
2. Peter Cowie, "Introductory Essay," *Grand Illusion*, directed by Jean Renoir (Criterion, 1999), DVD.
3. Peter Cowie, "Commentary," and Jean Renoir, "Introductory Note," *Grand Illusion*, directed by Jean Renoir (Criterion, 1999), DVD. Renoir had been an aviator in World War I.
4. *Stalag 17* (1953), *The Great Escape* (1963), and *The Bridge on the River Kwai* (1957) easily come to mind.
5. Chris Vognar, "*Grand Illusion*," *Rotten Tomatoes*, 7 June 2012, www.rottentomatoes.com/m/la_grande_illusion/ (23 October 2013).

Bibliography

Ebert, Roger. *The Great Movies*. New York: Broadway Books, 2002.
Mayo, Mike. *War Movies*. Farmington Hills, MI: Visible Ink Press, 1999.
Norman, Barry. *The 100 Best Films of the Century*. New York: Carol Publishing Group, 1993.

THE HIDDEN FORTRESS (KAKUSHI-TORIDE NO SAN-AKUNIN) (1958)

Director: Akira Kurosawa
Writers: Shinobu Hashimoto, Ryûzô Kikushima, Akira Kurosawa, Hideo Oguni
Producers: Sanezumi Fujimoto, Akira Kurosawa (Toho Company)
Cinematographer: Masaru Sato
Editor: Akira Kurosawa
Music: Masaru Satô
Cast: Gen. Rokurota Makabe: Toshirô Mifune. Princess Yuki: Misa Uehara. Tahei: Minoru Chiaki. Matashichi: Kamatari Fujiwara. Gen. Hyoe Tadokoro: Susumu Fujita
AA: None
AAN: None
DVD: Criterion, 1987, 2001
Blu-ray: Currently unavailable
Duration: 129 minutes

George Lucas claims that seeing *The Hidden Fortress* inspired him (in part) to write the script for the Star Wars series,[1] and that statement must not remain unnoticed. For one thing, both movies involve groups of people cast out of their previous authority positions and hiding in remote locations until they can regroup, plan a counterattack, and reclaim their previous authority. To do so they must traverse vast distances (expressed in relative terms); elude or confront numerous natural obstacles or hostile hordes; and, in the process, show bravery, courage, cunning, the ability to conceal their true identities, and the readiness of wit needed to face the adversity that often comes their way. Theirs are difficult, arduous, and exhausting tasks that, more often than not, go beyond the pale of human endurance. And the feats are performed, and the people on the right side (those winning our sympathies) are victorious and achieve their ends. It is a story in which new archetypal formulas have been repeated since the beginning of time, from Gilgamesh to Odysseus, King Arthur, Robin Hood, Hamlet, Hercules (in movies), and Harry Potter. Audiences delight to see heroes win in the end, especially if their ends coincide with those of the tribe.

Although Lucas achieved enormous popular success with his first trilogy (of the 1970s and early 1980s) and won numerous Oscars, if one plays the two movies today, one is struck by one big difference: while *Star Wars: Episode IV, A New Hope* has lost some of its glitter, and even looks arcane, *The Hidden Fortress* is still fresh, as if minted from the mind of its creator just yesterday, although *The Hidden Fortress* preceded *Star Wars* by nearly twenty years. This is the impression I got by watching the two movies simultaneously (that is, within the span of twenty-four hours), and I attribute it to at least three causes. The first is the stunning use of landscape to create a sense of realism that is beyond the reach of computerized animation and digital effects, then (1977) still in their infancy. The second is the presence of Toshirô Mifune, at the time at the height of his power. The third is the mastery of film techniques of the new CinemaScope format, used by Kurosawa for the first time, in black and white. There are, of course, similarities. Both are "frame" stories, that is, stories told from the point of view of secondary characters, whose adventures we follow up to a certain point, when the main heroes take over. Let us examine these points, more or less in that order.

Star Wars, clearly a fantasy, is a story that takes place in the Galaxy, and involves fantastic shapes of planets, asteroids, intergalactic vehicles, robots, weapon-like beams, and other such paraphernalia, most of which would be suited for a James Bond adventure transferred to the heavens. Only a limited amount of realism could be achievable in such a context and narrative format, where only the main heroes are human, and where animals are exotic forms and could not be shown except in animated form. Vehicles of transportation are fantastic objects that, at this point in history, can exist only in the human imagination. Although Lucas says that he wanted everything to look "used" (a "used universe"), a fantasy has its own visual codes, admittedly welcome, in this and other cases, by a fascinated public. Exactly the opposite is the case in Kurosawa's movie, where codification relies almost entirely on the familiar, although not less exotic in a certain sense, objects, like ravines, mountains, flowing rivulets, ponds, waterfalls, and gravelly, arid deserts. Kurosawa, quite capable of using the fantastic (as in *Dreams*,[2] 1990, for instance), prefers shooting on location, making a limited use of sets—and when he does use sets, he paints painstakingly accurate images.

The Hidden Fortress takes place in actual locations, on rocky slopes, ravines, and hills, with real flowing water and small springs, and in a countryside that actually looks impoverished and war-ravaged. When a group of people try to scramble up a hill, for instance, carrying heavy loads of gold on their backs and end up tumbling backward, or when a princess sleeps under a rock to protect herself from the rain while the others are being drenched, that realism lends credibility to the whole and evokes a more intense emotional response from the viewer. Although this may be a relative concept, that is how I felt, and it is a feeling others share. Commentator David Ehrenstein calls *The Hidden Fortress* "one of the greatest action adventures ever made,"[3] and Arnold White states that this movie holds its position comparable to John Ford's *Stagecoach* (1939).[4]

In *The Hidden Fortress*, the actors are generally used as a contrast—and enhancement—of the central character and the depiction of the heroic stature undertaken by Mifune. His previous performances in Kurosawa films included a bandit in *Rashomon* (1950) and a fake samurai in *Seven Samurai* (1954), where his attempt to deceive the other samurai as to his identity (he is a farmer) is redeemed by his heroic death at the end of the film. With his successes in *Yojimbo* (1961) and *Sanjuro* (1962) yet to follow, here Mifune plays a defeated general, Rokurota Makabe, a legendary fighter whose side has been overthrown in an internal conflict within the Akizuki clan, and Makabe is forced into hiding, protecting the young princess Yuki and her treasure of 200 golden pieces. His intent is to transport the princess to the friendly territory of the Hayakawas, where, under the protection of Lord Hayakawa, she will be safe and recover her throne.

Makabe is the leader of a small group hiding in a fortress, in a small building at the depth of a valley surrounded by gravelly hills, where an old soldier and his wife have undertaken to take care of the princess, then only sixteen and high-spirited. The group includes the princess herself and two guards. Makabe uses a ruse, selling his own sister, who is of the same age as the princess, to his enemies, and he soon learns that she has been beheaded. This will buy him time until the opportunity presents itself for him and the princess to make their escape across the border.

Mifune plays the general as an utterly loyal subject, a stern professional soldier dedicated to his duty to protect the princess and restore her to her legitimate throne. Although a defeated man at this point, he is an incomparable fighter in the samurai style and a wily veteran of the war, agile in body and mind, moving with ease and self-confidence, and determined to fulfill his mission at any cost to himself. The princess, played by a young Misa Uehara, is, by her own admission, a "handful," a willful, proud, stubborn young woman, dressed like a boy but moving like a princess, and exerting complete authority, even over the proud general, who is both the commander of the group and her loyal subject. But she cannot hide her noble looks, her bodily movements—abrupt and authoritative—and especially her speech, which would immediately reveal her identity. Makabe is stumped trying to find a way to transport her across the border when a solution is suddenly offered, as if by a deus ex machina.

The story is "framed" by two vagabonds, Tahei (Minoru Chiaki) and Matashichi (Kamatari Fujiwara), riffraff peasants who had gone to the war in search of riches, but, after the defeat of the Akizuki clan, became grave diggers. They constantly bicker, calling one another names, while roaming the countryside in search of better luck. They are seized by the Yamanas, now occupying the Akizuki, and are forced to dig with a large crowd of captives for the 200 gold pieces gone with the disappearance of the princess. During an uprising, they escape and run into the country, and just by chance, as they boil their meal, they discover that one stick of firewood will not burn. Matashichi finds a blade of gold in it. The men start searching for more and soon find another stick containing gold bearing the insignia of a crescent moon, the insignia of the Akizuki clan. As they are fighting over the ownership of the pieces, Makabe appears and shows them another piece of gold similar to what they have found.

Tahei and Matashichi reveal to Makabe that they intend to cross over from Akizuki to Hayakawa, but because the border is guarded by Yamana soldiers, they draw a map on the ground, suggesting that they could cross first to Yamana, for in that direction the border is unguarded, and then slip into the Hayakawas from that side, a far easier task, although not without risks. Makabe instantly conceives a plan to use the same route to get the princess and her gold treasure there. He will cross into Yamana, using the two men to carry the gold (promising them a share if they do), while the princess, pretending to be a mute to disguise her speech, will accompany them, also carrying a smaller portion of the gold. Makabe also plans on using the three horses he has captured to help carry the main part of the load.

The gold is hidden inside similar wood sticks sunk in a pool, where the two men are led to drink, and where they first meet the princess. They acquiesce to Makabe's scheme, and the group soon starts their trek to Yamana, where they have to pass through a city unrecognized and use various deceptions to escape notice. Makabe exhibits not only the bravery of a general, good in fighting, but also his wily, foxy nature, for he always finds a way to elude the various risks the journey entails. He knows that the best way to hide is to blend with the crowd ("to hide a stone you must place it among stones"), but when guile fails, he has to take chase and kills three soldiers. In the process, he encounters another general, Hyoe Tadokoro (Susumu Fujita), against whom he has fought before. This Yamana solider recognizes him immediately and challenges him to a duel. Makabe wins but does not kill his defeated opponent, who resents not being finished by Makabe, for a defeated man who still lives is considered dishonorable.

Makabe and his small group then pass through a town, where they blend with the crowd to hide their identity, and where they pick up a new companion, a young girl from the defeated Akizukis whose services (like those of other women) have to be sold to the highest bidder. Yuki is saved from such a fate when Matashichi says she is a mute, but the group suffers many hardships, enduring days of rain without cover and having to join a "fire festival" procession while being watched by guards who suspect that the gold might be hidden in the bundles of wood carried by the group for the fire ceremony. To avoid being caught, Makabe orders the firewood they are carrying to be thrown into the fire, and they later have to dig it up in the ashes and carry it themselves.

By this point the travelers are being hunted down by troops who have discovered the ruse, and when Matashichi and Tahei turn traitors to save themselves, they are informed that the fugitive princess, the general, and the girl they saved and who has loyally followed them are all under arrest. The gold is taken. The three are tied to posts and told that princess will be beheaded the next day, when help unexpectedly arrives. General Tadokoro, the man Makabe defeated, who is in charge of the execution, appears, a terrible scar on his face, and explains that he has been shamed and dishonored by his lord because the enemy who had beaten him had spared his life. Yuki angrily calls both him and his lord fools, for a man spared in defeat by a friend is indeed honored. Then she sings the fire song, a deeply symbolic chant that equates fire with immortality. Tadakoro has a change of heart, and the next day, as the arrestees are being led to their executions, he lets the horses carrying the gold go and then fights his own troops, frees the princess and Makabe from their bonds, and urges them to cross the border. Makabe shouts for him to follow them. Tadakoro does so and joins them on a hill overlooking Hayakawa.

In the next scene, we see Yuki in full regalia, sitting between her two generals, while Matashichi and Tahei, bowing before them, are told the truth about who she really is. Makabe generously thanks the two for their services and rewards them with one piece of gold, while he explains that the gold they had carried must be preserved to restore the princess to her Akizuki throne. The men, who had previously bickered and fought among themselves regarding how to divide their loot, walk down the stairs of the palace while speaking in friendly tones, offering the gold piece to one another.

As we began with two vagabonds, so we end. It is from their point of view that the story is told, for they are the ones who express their thoughts, Makabe speaking only as much as is needed to carry the action forward, while the princess is true to her disguise and is almost mute throughout. The framing of the action in this way is obviously a principal way of coding the story. Through action, Kurosawa argues against war, division, and greed, and his approach, found in many of his films, is codified by the two lowly characters who embody the worst in the human being. If Matashichi and Tahei are the signifiers, the signified are the heroic statures of Makabe, the princess, and eventually Tadokoro, who are the ones capable of putting an end to bickering, bringing about the restoration of justice, and reaching for peace and humanity. The variance between these codes is the changes effected in human character—the weaker the people, the greater the changes.

Tahei and Matashichi are constantly at one another's throats when good luck appears to be with them (when they find, or think they have found, the gold), but they unite in adversity, when their lives are threatened. They are anything but noble characters, but common danger makes them friends of necessity, and they will probably stay at that level—or learn generosity, as is the case at the end. The common crowd, soldiers, and so forth, around them are indeed neutral forces, like the forces of nature, and except for the fire dance, where they unite, they have no moral status in action or in society; that is left to individuals, who have to make the hard choices.

Yuki does not accept Makabe's sacrifice of his sister for her sake; is thought cruel and unemotional by her guardians, but she cries when alone, thinking of the sacrifice of the young girl who gave her life for her. Makabe does not need correction, for his instincts, bearing, and behavior, as well as his status as general and fighter, make him the leader of the tribe. But Tadokoro, weak in defeat and full of resentment, shows he is capable of change. Moved by Yuki's song and fearless facing of her death—she will die with the dignity befitting of a princess—he reverses his decision. His defeat at the hands of Makabe is no longer dishonorable, and, after being told that a defeated man can still have his dignity and honor, he chooses to help the rightful owner of the throne and a true leader. He then follows them. In fact, as was the habit of Kurosawa, he allowed a secondary character, who has flaws and who has entered the action late in the game, so to speak, to become the true hero. Reformation is as good as heroism.

Techniques to be mentioned are the unerring instinct of Kurosawa as filmmaker to make full and meaningful use of the entire screen. He was the master of the long shot, staging such events as the duel between Makabe and Tadokoro with full view of the fighters in the middle of ring, while the crowd around them watches and reacts. The same thing occurs in the fire dance scene, as the participants in the dance are part of the celebratory events meant to bind the tribe together, while reminding that all life is the same, that death is omnipresent, and that immortality awaits everyone. The camera embraces the entire crowd, and motion is both multiple and unified. Kurosawa's shooting methods were meant to exploit the screen as it was afforded him, in all its depth, avoiding too many close-ups and using that device only when absolutely necessary, as, for instance, when the princess, seen from an angle, suddenly turns and stares at the two rascals who have designs on her. Only her head is shown, and her glance is like a bolt of lightning. Mifune moves with his usual strut, enhanced here to fit a general, and while such abruptness may seem unnatural to western audiences, the shots of him do not lose their fluidity, for his body is always organic to the context—his domination over his environment—and he maintains that attitude even when he is seen captured. Use of space on the screen is of primary importance and plays a major role in what has been called "decodification" of imagery, or interpretation. The screen is restricted space, not all life in general, not what one actually sees: it is a directional device. To tell a story effectively, a director must know how to use it effectively, not wasting the opportunity that the art of cinema—with its kinship to photography—allows him to do. CS

Notes

1. George Lucas, "Commentary," *The Hidden Fortress*, directed by Akira Kurosawa (Criterion, 2001), DVD.
2. Coming late in his career, this is an unappreciated movie, told in eight episodes, some of which, like the demons in hell, for instance, are quite fantastic.
3. David Ehrenstein, "Commentary," *The Hidden Fortress*, directed by Akira Kurosawa (Criterion, 1987), DVD.
4. Arnold White, "Commentary," *The Hidden Fortress*, directed by Akira Kurosawa (Criterion, 2001), DVD.

Bibliography

Stempel, Tom, and Philip Dunne. *Framework: A History of Screenwriting in the American Film.* Syracuse, NY: Syracuse University Press, 1997.

INDOCHINE (1992)

DIRECTOR: Régis Wargnier
WRITERS: Erik Orsenna, Louis Gardel, Catherine Chen, Régis Wargnier
PRODUCERS: Eric Heumann, Jean Labadie (Paradis Films, La Générale d'Images, Bac Films)
CINEMATOGRAPHER: François Catonné
EDITORS: Agnès Schwab, Geneviève Winding
MUSIC: Patrick Doyle
CAST: Eliane Devries: Catherine Deneuve. Camille: Lihn Dan Pham. Jean-Baptiste: Vincent Perez. Guy: Jean Yanne. Yvette: Dominique Blanc. Emile: Henri Marteau. Castellani: Carlo Brandt. The Admiral: Gérard Lartigau. Raymond: Hubert Saint-Macary. Hebrard: Andrzej Seweryn.
AA: Best Foreign-Language Film
AAN: Best Leading Actress (Catherine Deneuve)
DVD: Arrow Films, 2011
BLU-RAY: Currently unavailable
DURATION: 159 minutes

In *Indochine*, Catherine Deneuve plays a rubber plantation owner in Indochina, when that country was under French rule in pre–World War II days and known by that name (previously the kingdom of Siam). The action occurs early in the century, in the late 1920s or early 1930s, judging from the cars and costumes. It moves through several generations to the mid-1950s, just before the French lost Indochina in the Battle of Dien Bien Phu, a war that looms in the background as the movie ends. In any case, the French are fighting a lost cause, since it is evident that corruption, abuse, cruelty toward the natives have begun to bear (negative) fruit. Revolution is in the air, and one easily connects this episode to those of Vietnam stories, although this is not really a war episode as such. It is rather a story—an epic—of love found and lost between one of the occupiers and a native girl, Jean-Baptiste (Vincent Perez) and Camille (Lihn Dan Pham).

Here, Deneuve, as Eliane, plays a central role, a role she shares to a large extent with her adopted daughter Camille. As the story progresses, the lovers become the leads. While Camille is Eliane's adopted child and has been brought up in Western fashion, she is caught up in one of the many skirmishes between the French police and the rebels, and she is apparently mortally wounded. When Jean-Baptiste, a young French officer, rescues her and attempts to wipe the blood from her bare chest (he bares it), he discovers that she has only been wounded, and he instantly falls in love with her—and she with him. But the romance seems an affront to Eliane, who had already formed a liaison with the same younger man herself.

After several emotional confrontations with Eliane, Camille escapes to join Jean Baptiste, who has been sent to an outpost and ends up becoming friends with an Indochinese family who had escaped from bondage. Camille is imprisoned and awaits judgment, but Jean-Baptiste spots her in the prisoners' group and rushes toward her. When he exchanges blows with another French officer, Camille grabs the latter's gun and shoots him in the head. She and Jean-Baptiste escape. They go on to live together with a group of fugitives and have a baby, but he is eventually taken prisoner while christening the baby in a pool. Camille soon sells the plantation and returns to Europe. Her defeat embodies and symbolizes the defeat of the French in Indochina, in a crucial era in history, an event that, together with the independence of Algeria, put an end to the claim of France as a Western empire. In a matter of days, the country was divided into North Vietnam and South Vietnam.

But the film still offers its rewards to today's viewer. Although Deneuve's role is somewhat limited,[1] as she is the focus of the story, she remains an integral part of it. The story is ultimately about her. In her fifties (in this film), the actress continues to be fascinating. Once called the "most beautiful woman in the world" (a title that was repeated on certain TV shows in the United States), in *Indochine* she shows herself as more than just a beautiful face. She has a graceful, commanding presence of the screen, a quality lacking in many of her contemporaries and the younger generation of actresses. Deneuve deserves to be called a "goddess," equal in "divine" graces to her predecessors of the silver screens—Greta Garbo, Ingrid Bergman, Katharine Hepburn, Audrey Hepburn, Joan Fontaine, Bette Davis, and others, women whose acting abilities were matched by a special charisma, a beauty that possessed a "high seriousness"—to use the well-known term of Aristotle and Matthew Arnold.

Both of these critics were speaking of poetry—that which possesses "mark" or "accent"—as Arnold put it. There is a depth and resonance, not only in sound (of music or poetry), but also in the human face—but it has a special quality in the female face; in the male this quality is found in sculpture, for instance in Michelangelo's *David*, and the *Hermes of Praxiteles*. Both have female faces. Both are nude statues, and the grace of the whole culminates in the "purity" of the face—but then the body expresses that ideal, too. Screen goddesses possess that quality, which actually consists of a complex of qualities: beauty (that need not always be perfection, that ideal of high seriousness noted by the aforementioned critics and others, that special look of intelligence—as in the face of Joan Fontaine, or Greer Garson, for instance). The whole—face, body—is complemented with a special movement—a stately step, a gesture, a look, the pronunciation of a word or phrase.

Deneuve achieves nearly all these qualities in *Indochine*—more than any movie of hers before or since. In some ways, she parallels the images of speech and movements established in *Out of Africa* by Meryl Streep, as the indomitable Baroness Karen Blixen. Both women were heroines out of their native lands; both dealt with intractable authority figures; both were compelled by circumstances (or conscience) to fight for the rights of natives and the liberation of their own sex. Both were awakening factors to the evils caused by Western civilization in its blind and overbearing conquests of other cultures. Although the stories in which they are present differ in many ways (*Indochine* is basically a romance), the central figures—both women—are heroes by acting out their inner convictions in the face of brutal realities. The female heroism, in this sense, is not expressed by acts of aggression—a characteristic of so many macho types, from Stallone to Schwarzenegger—but by words of compassion, arguments for human rights, and female comportment, of which beauty is only a special ingredient. Thus, beauty is not unrelated to character.

The critic Roland Barthes once said that the face of Garbo is a "Platonic idea."[2] That is also the face of Catherine Deneuve, but the idea is not an abstraction; it is something that is related to, and actually derived from, the inner self: knowledge, wisdom, feeling, emotion, and a conviction that good is better than bad and right preferable to wrong. These inner qualities of character are reflected in the face, the body language, and the speech of the female person. Thus, facial beauty only complements what is already inside the person—inviting the eye not to miss the beauty within. CS

Notes

1. Even so, this was the only time she was nominated for an Academy Award.
2. Gerald Mast and Marshall Cohen, eds., *Film Theory and Criticism: Introductory Readings*, 2nd ed. (New York: Oxford University Press, 1979), 720–21.

Bibliography

Mast, Gerald, and Marshall Cohen, eds. *Film Theory and Criticism: Introductory Readings*, 2nd ed. New York: Oxford University Press, 1979.

THE LADY AND THE DUKE (L'ANGLAISE ET LE DUC) (2001)

DIRECTOR: Eric Rohmer
WRITER: Eric Rohmer. Adapted from Grace Elliott's memoir *Ma vie sous la révolution*.
PRODUCERS: François Ivernel, Léonard Glowinski, Pierre Cottrell, Pierre Rissient (Pathé Image Production, Compagnie Eric Rohmer, KC Medien)
CINEMATOGRAPHER: Diane Baratier
EDITOR: Mary Stephen
PRODUCTION DESIGN: Antoine Fontaine
ART DIRECTION: Hubert De Forcade
SET DECORATION: Lucien Eymard
COSTUMES: Pierre-Jean Larroque, Gilles Bodu-Lemoine, Maritza Reitzman
SPECIAL EFFECTS: Dominique Corbin
CAST: Grace Elliott: Lucy Russell. Philippe, Duke of Orleans: Jean-Claude Dreyfus. Duke of Biron: Alain Libolt. Pulcherie the Cook: Charlotte Véry. Nanon: Caroline Morin. Madame Meyler: Héléna Dubiel. Robespierre: François-Marie Banier. Franchette: Rosette
AA: None
AAN: None
CÉSAR AWARD NOMINATIONS: Best Costume Design (Pierre-Jean Larroque), Best Production Design (Antoine Fontaine)
EUROPEAN FILM AWARD NOMINATION: Best Director (Eric Rohmer)
DVD: Sony Pictures Home Entertainment, 2002
BLU-RAY: Currently unavailable
DURATION: 129 minutes

Eric Rohmer, an editor in chief of *Cahiers du Cinéma*[1] (1957–1963), and a member of the French New Wave early in his career, was known for his small, intellectually challenging, dialogue-laden movies that could not be further removed from the epic form as was known in Hollywood or elsewhere, then and now. His most celebrated collection of movies, *The Six Moral Tales*,[2] was made during the 1960s and early 1970s, but Rohmer continued to make films for several more decades. *The Lady and the Duke*, made toward the end of a distinguished career, is thus one of his most unusual films, a period drama/costume piece, of which he made very few (*The Marquise of O*, 1976, is one), and it is as close as Rohmer came to the epic form. It is set in the period of the French Revolution and is based on the autobiography of Grace Elliott, a Scottish aristocrat who had resided in France during the Revolution. She had been a rather notorious personage, having married early to Sir John Elliott, then having become the mistress of the Prince of Wales, later King George IV. Elliott had spent her early years receiving an education in France, having been brought there by Prince Philippe, second cousin to Louis XVI, and the Duke of Orleans. The story is told in the form of a diary, a "Diary of the Revolution," as she calls it, a technique familiar to Rohmer, who often announces an event on the screen in the form of a title note and then proceeds to elaborate in a scene that follows.

Despite its epic format, the movie bears several typical Rohmer characteristics. It is a battle of wits—even a dialectic—between a man and a woman, who are also involved in a romance. In this case, while the romance has practically ended, Grace (played by Lucy Russell) still receives the Duke (Jean-Claude Dreyfus) in her apartment in Paris on a social basis, and at first their conversations seem to be typical social banalities; however, as the Revolution looms, the executions begin, and the king is about to be put on trial. The tension increases as she begs him, as a member of the Assembly, to vote against the king's conviction. He promises that he will, but he does the opposite. He loves her to the end, protects and hides her for as long as he can, and passionately begs her to leave the country, but when she decides to do so, he no longer can obtain passage for her, for he is himself under suspicion, being the first cousin of the king. Both are to be executed, but she is spared at the last moment because of the fall of Robespierre (François-Marie Banier) and the end of the "Reign of Terror."

The point of the story is not romance, as is often the case with Rohmer tales, for romance is only a starting point to explore the more complicated aspects of the relations between men and women. Here, for instance, Grace, a well-lettered, intelligent woman familiar with the doctrines of the French philosophes, severely castigates the Duke for siding with the Jacobins in the face of the bloodshed and murder in the name of the Revolution. The sight of an impaled head of a female friend of hers in the streets of Paris shocks her profoundly and forces her to totally relinquish the abstract principle of liberty and freedom for mankind preached by the likes of Rousseau and the other Enlightenment philosophers that has degenerated into the monstrous dogmas and action of the Jacobins.

The Duke, grounded in the reality of politics, has no defense to offer and has long given up principle in favor of mere survival—his and hers. At the beginning of the story, knowing what is to come, he entreats Grace to leave for England, while it is still possible, but she refuses out of loyalty for the queen and other friends of hers. She has chosen life in France, believing in French freedom and the emancipation of women, impossible in England, where she has become notorious because of her infidelities. The Duke, however, also has enemies, who, despite his votes in the Assembly in favor of Louis's execution, still regard him as a royalist. He loves Grace to the end, however, but his ambivalence and inability to stand up for what he believes in reduces his stature in her eyes. She, on the other hand, is unshakable in her belief that one must fight for humane causes no matter what the circumstances. She appears superior to him, for she risks her life to save a former friend of the Duke's, a hunted aristocrat, by hiding him under her mattress while a search is going on. She is a woman of superior wit, unremitting loyalty, and capacity for compassion in the middle of a chaotic, unraveling society. The Duke, loyal to her, seems weak and opportunistic, although still unable to save himself in the end.

Like almost all Rohmer movies, this also is a "moral tale," in which the parameters of allowable human transgressions are tested. Is it right to kill thousands of your opponents that happen to be on the other side, merely because they are positioned there, not because they have committed any crimes? The aim of the French Revolution was to free the French people from an oppressive aristocratic and royal regime—a worthwhile idea—but the murder of thousands of innocents, whose only crime was being an aristocrat, was an absurd, if not morally reprehensive, idea. Rohmer brings this contradiction—the aims of the noble philosophers and the hideous results of their ideas—to the forum in the fullest possible sense.

Some other typical Rohmer traits include the near-total absence of a music score (except music associated with the reading of credits) and the typical sets and action sequences that usually characterize period pieces. Here the sets are evidently (and ostensibly) digitally constructed backdrops, and so are the few mob scenes that our heroine finds herself in on one or two occasions. The movie, longish for Rohmer, at 129 minutes, is a series of scenes staged inside, where practically nothing other than dialogue occurs. The film could very well be told as a stage play, with cardboard scenery backdrops. Individuals, either alone or in groups, are photographed in medium-long shots, as one would photograph a play on the stage. Still, the movie is entirely cinematic, thanks to Rohmer's expert use of the camera, which fluently captures facial and body movements in a way that reveals the characters' deepest emotions.

As in all Rohmer works, there is far too much talk and little action—all right in the romantic stories we are used to seeing from him—but in this epic/history-based story, one would expect something more than symbolic representation of the horrors of the French Revolution during its most intense period. Here Rohmer seems to reverse and even attack the Hollywood (and some of the French) traditions that revel in blood and graphic beheadings by the guillotine.[3] The horror of the guillotine, however, as the most barbaric of human inventions is not only mentioned in Rohmer's story, it is actually highlighted in key parts of the dialogue, and for the reclusive Grace Elliot, it is the most repulsive event in the mob actions of the Revolution. Yet, not one beheading is shown, although several are mentioned. People are shown arrested, thrown in jail, tried by a tribunal, and led to execution, but the executions themselves are not shown to the audience.

In fact, *The Lady and the Duke* is an anomaly in the canon of violent epics, which are routinely imagined and produced with spectacle in mind—the word *spectacle* in modern terms meaning violent action, battle scenes, canons exploding, buildings and other structures being blown up, and human parts flying in space. Special effects have conditioned modern audiences to expect these things as a means of producing terror, and because of the demands of realistic cinema, the roots of which are shared by both Hollywood and French cinema. A director like Martin Scorsese—witness *Gangs of New York*—would have made a showcase of the guillotine's triangular sharp blade if he had made such a movie. He has a point, for realism of such intensity has won a place after the "liberation" of Hollywood from the various censorship codes that dominated cinema for decades in the late 1960s. Now you can show everything. Rohmer, however, challenges this idea with this movie. The horror one feels at the beheadings is felt even deeper in the despair, compassion, and disappointment of the noble Grace Elliot; in other words, the visual image—as Aristotle claimed centuries ago—is not as powerful as the story itself. One's heart can melt with pity even if one only hears the story of Oedipus.

The fact that Lady Grace has experienced the horror and the barbarity of killing translates into horror that an audience can feel; like a magnet that attracts, the audience is drawn into her feelings, in part due to Lucy Russell's fine acting and screen presence. Rohmer transforms the epic from what Hollywood has conditioned us to believe is screen mayhem of monumental proportions to an equally horrifying story told in purely cinematic terms, with meager budgetary demands, but with superior results. For here we are placed in a position to share the emotion of those who experienced the evil, rather than being faced with the shock of blood practically spilled in our laps. This technique was employed by Euripides in *Medea*, where a messenger tells the audience of her murder of her two children. This is a technique almost totally abandoned today by the bloodthirsty action epics. Rohmer has challenged this notion with a movie far superior to its rivals in depth, contemporaneity, and emotional impact. CS

Notes

1. The famous journal, founded by André Bazin, provided the theoretical basis for a number of French film critics and directors in the 1950s, among them François Truffaut, Jean-Luc Godard, and Claude Chabrol, all of whom were contributors and later noted directors associated with what came to be known as the French New Wave.
2. Based on a number of novellas, *Six Moral Tales* (*Six contes moraux*) became the basis for Rohmer's first collection of six movies from 1962 to 1973. For details, see *Six Moral Tales*, directed by Eric Rohmer (Criterion, 2006), DVD. Contained in the package is *Six Moral Tales*, by Eric Rohmer, translated from the French by Sabine d'Estrée (New York: Penguin, 2006).
3. Philip Kaufman's *Quills* (2000), which abundantly exhibits beheadings, is a case in point.

Bibliography

Rohmer, Eric. *Six Moral Tales*. Translated by Sabine d' Estrée. New York: Penguin, 2006.

METROPOLIS (1927)

DIRECTOR: Fritz Lang
WRITERS: Thea von Harbou, Fritz Lang (uncredited). Based on the novel by Thea von Harbou.
PRODUCER: Erich Pommer (Universum Film)
CINEMATOGRAPHERS: Karl Freund, Günther Rittau, Walter Ruttmann
PRODUCTION DESIGN: Otto Hunte, Erich Kettelhut, Karl Vollbrecht
COSTUMES: Aenne Willkomm
MUSIC: Gottfried Huppertz
CAST: Joh Fredersen: Alfred Abel. Freder Fredersen: Gustav Fröhlich. C. A. Rotwang: Rudolf Klein-Rogge. The Thin Man: Fritz Rasp. Josaphat: Theodor Loos. Georgy, Worker 11811: Erwin Biswanger. Grot: Heinrich George. Maria: Brigitte Helm
AA: None
AAN: None
DVD: Madman, 2010; Kino International, 2010. Reconstructed and restored edition.
BLU-RAY: Kino Video, 2010
DURATION: 150 minutes

Fritz Lang's monumental, dystopian epic vision of the future, with its "36,000 extras" and "200,000 costumes,"[1] was the most expensive silent film made in Germany as of 1927. A spectacular example of German Expressionist styling (with its surreal images and dramatic chiaroscuro lighting), *Metropolis* has become a profoundly influential film, particularly in the science-fiction genre, its cityscape towers reappearing in Ridley Scott's *Blade Runner* of 1982. But *Metropolis* was a complete financial disaster and was savagely edited for release, only being partially reconstructed when a more complete 16mm version was discovered in 2008.

Metropolis begins by proclaiming, "The mediator between the head and the hands must be the heart!" a message that is repeated at the close of the film. In the depths of a futuristic cityscape, a mass of undifferentiated workers descend into the underground city of workers. Heads bowed, they move as one mass, as mechanical as the machines they will soon man for ten straight hours. Contrasted with this subterranean world of toil, the aristocratic class enjoys frivolous hours in the Eternal Gardens above. Freder (Gustav Fröhlich), son of the city's leader, Joh Fredersen (Alfred Abel), is enjoying his privileges when he is interrupted by a woman named Maria, who has brought children up from the depths, declaring both to her charges and directly to Freder, "These are your brothers." Freder is entranced, but when he later searches for her, he instead finds the electrical power plant, where he is so shocked at the conditions that he envisions the plant as a gigantic consuming mouth of the god Moloch. Freder later swaps places with worker 11811, Georgy (Erwin Biswanger).

Meanwhile, in an old gothic house around which the new city has been built, Fredersen visits his old rival, the inventor Rotwang (Rudolf Klein-Rogge), who has created a humanoid robot. In one of the reinserted 16mm sequences, we learn that the pair once competed for the same woman, Hel, who became Freder's mother. Fredersen now wants Rotwang to decipher some plans that keep being found on his workers, and Rotwang identifies them as the layout of the catacombs even farther below the city. Here they discover that Maria is preaching to the workers and telling them to wait for a mediator to help them. Among them is Freder, having finished his shift, and Maria recognizes him as the promised mediator. Fredersen asks Rotwang to make his "machine-man" look like Maria, planning to destroy the workers' faith in her. Rotwang kidnaps Maria and transforms the robot into her likeness, an alchemic process of science and magic suggested by the inverted pentagram in the lab. The vengeful Rotwang orders the robot to destroy Fredersen, his city, and his son.

If Maria is the virginal, maternal Madonna, the robotic Maria is her opposite, the whore of Babylon (in an exquisite dual performance by Brigitte Helm), whipping up discord among the men. When Freder sees her in the arms of his father, we experience his subjective madness. Robotic Maria incites the workers to abandon and destroy the machines, despite the resistance of the foreman Grot (Heinrich George), an informant for Fredersen. The workers' city begins the flood, and the human Maria, having escaped Rotwang's clutches, saves the workers' children with Freder's help. While the workers burn one Maria on a pyre (soon revealed to be the robot), the other is dragged by Rotwang onto the roof of the gothic cathedral, where he is overcome by Freder. On the steps of the cathedral, Grot and Fredersen are brought together by the mediator Freder, at Maria's urging.

In 1927, science-fiction writer H. G. Wells reviewed the film for the *New York Times*, famously declaring, "I have recently seen the silliest of films."[2] Wells saw the future more optimistically, proclaiming, "The hopeless drudge state of human labor lies behind us."[3] Yet, in 2013, the Western world exports much of its drudgery and factory accidents overseas into the Third World rather than into the depths below, as we get in *Metropolis*, but they are nonetheless similarly (and conveniently) located elsewhere and out of sight.

The film attempts a perfunctory happy ending by unifying the classes, but as Tom Gunning notes, the participants are the leader himself, his son, and his spy Grot, perhaps suggesting the continuation of vested aristocratic interests.[4] Lang himself soon changed his mind about the film's framing message, declaring in a 1965 interview, "It is absurd to say that the heart is the intermediary between the hands and the brain, that is to say, the employer and the employee. The problem is social and not moral."[5] Despite distancing himself from the film and its ending, *Metropolis* remains the film for which Lang is perhaps most popularly known, its halo-surrounded robot an enduring icon of the cinema. DB

Notes

1. Artem Demenok, "Journey to Metropolis," *Metropolis: Reconstructed and Restored*, directed by Fritz Lang (Madman, 2010), DVD.
2. H. G. Wells, "Mr. Wells Reviews a Current Film," *Fritz Lang's* Metropolis*: Cinematic Visions of Technology*

and Fear, edited by Michael Minden and Holger Bachmann (New York: Camden House, 2000), 94.

3. Wells, "Mr. Wells Reviews a Current Film," 94, 96, 97, 99.

4. Tom Gunning, *The Films of Fritz Lang: Allegories of Vision and Modernity* (London: British Film Institute, 2000), 78–79.

5. Quoted in Gretchen Berg, "The Viennese Night: A Fritz Lang Confession, Parts One and Two," *Fritz Lang Interviews*, edited by Barry Keith Grant (Jackson: University Press of Mississippi, 2003), 69.

Bibliography

Berg, Gretchen. "The Viennese Night: A Fritz Lang Confession, Parts One and Two." In *Fritz Lang Interviews*, edited by Barry Keith Grant, 50–76. Jackson: University Press of Mississippi, 2003.

Gunning, Tom. *The Films of Fritz Lang: Allegories of Vision and Modernity*. London: British Film Institute, 2000.

Wells, H. G. "Mr. Wells Reviews a Current Film." In *Fritz Lang's* Metropolis*: Cinematic Visions of Technology and Fear*, edited by Michael Minden and Holger Bachmann, 94–100. New York: Camden House, 2000.

L'ODISSEA (HOMER'S ODYSSEY) (1911)

DIRECTORS: Francesco Bertolini, Adolfo Padovan, Giuseppe de Liguoro (Milano Films)
WRITER: Homer. Based on Homer's epic poem *The Odyssey*.
CINEMATOGRAPHER: Emilio Roncarolo, E. Beretta, Romolo Galli
COSTUMES: La Scala Theatre, Milan
CAST: Ulisse: Giuseppe de Liguoro. Also featuring Ubaldo Maria Del Colle, Eugenia Tettoni Fior.
AA: None
AAN: None
DVD: Currently unavailable
BLU-RAY: Currently unavailable
DURATION: 44 minutes

L'Odissea, a three-reel, $200,000 film released in the United States in 1912, as *Homer's Odyssey*, was one of many ancient-world epics being produced in Italy during this period. It claimed to feature a 1,000-strong cast. Although the advertising advice in the trade journal the *Moving Picture World* suggested that exhibitors draw customers to the film by emphasizing its spectacular elements, the movie was also proclaimed as marking a "new epoch in the history of the motion picture as a factor in education."[1] An essay-writing competition for students was one of many strategies employed to convince the public of the respectability of *Homer's Odyssey*, and more generally the film medium itself.[2]

The film begins as Odysseus is departing for Troy, bidding farewell to his distressed wife Penelope, infant son Telemachus, and father Laertes. While he is away, Penelope is imposed upon by would-be suitors who take up residence in her home. Although she promises to wed one of them once she finishes her tapestry, the suitors catch her unpicking it at night.

After we witness the final stages of the siege of Troy, Odysseus begins his journey homeward. His first stop along the way on the island of the Cyclops Polyphemus, an effective sequence in which the giant is depicted by virtue of a split-screen technique. Polyphemus encloses the entourage in his cave, until Odysseus and his men blind him and escape his detection by hiding under his sheep. When the ship nears the enticing sirens, here presented as delectable mermaids,[3] the men block their ears, but Odysseus is bound to the mast to hear their song.

Their next challenge is to get through the channel between the monstrous Scylla and the whirlpool Charybis. Some of Odysseus's men are eaten by the six beastly heads of Scylla, but the rest sail onward. On the island of Thrinakia, Odysseus's men ignore instructions not to eat the cattle and sheep, and Zeus punishes them with a storm when they set sail. Only Odysseus survives, to be washed ashore on the island of Calypso, where he remains as her lover for seven years. Upon his departure, he is shipwrecked in a storm, yet again brought forth by Poseidon, this time washing up on Scheria, land of the Phaeacians. He is found by the young maiden Nausicaa, who takes him to court, and Odysseus tells his story to her father, King Alkinoos.

When Odysseus is taken home, the goddess Athena appears to him and transforms him into an elderly beggar so that he may arrive undetected, but she allows the disguise to be lifted temporarily so that Odysseus can be reunited with his grown son, Telemachus. As the suitors each attempt to draw Odysseus' bow in competition for Penelope, it is the old beggar who is able to achieve the feat, and revealing his identity, Odysseus and his son slay the suitors. Odysseus and Penelope are finally reunited, much to the joy of their son.

At the time of its release, *Homer's Odyssey* was part of a larger agenda to improve the cultural status of film (and through this, also its wider commercial potential), "to bring the great treasures of art and literature within the reach of the general public" and, in the process, achieve the "highest mission and destiny of the cinematograph."[4] While this suggests that the best qualities of film were thought to come from those borrowed from older, more esteemed media, it is, in fact, the special effects in *Homer's Odyssey* that bring the epic poem to life—in other words, qualities specific to film itself. The sequence with the goddess Athena are particularly effective, as she fades in and out of the mortal realm to help her cherished hero. DB

Notes

1. Epes Winthrop Sargent, "Advertising for Exhibitors," *Moving Picture World*, 24 February 1912, 763; W. Stephen Bush, "*Homer's Odyssey*. Three Reels (Milano Films)," *Moving Picture World*, 16 March 1912, 941.
2. Sargent, "Advertising for Exhibitors," 666.
3. The sirens of Homer's *The Odyssey* (c. 750–700 B.C.E.) are not located at sea at all, but rather on a "flowery meadow" (12.159), a setting that had sexual connotations in Greek poetry. Lillian Eileen Doherty, "Sirens, Muses, and Female Narrators in the Odyssey," in *The Distaff Side: Representing the Female in Homer's Odyssey*, edited by Beth Cohen (New York: Oxford University Press, 1995), 84; Seth L. Schein, "Female Representations and Interpreting the Odyssey," in *The Distaff Side: Representing the Female in Homer's Odyssey*, edited by Beth Cohen (New York: Oxford University Press, 1995), 21. It is this sexual element that has tended to dominate cinematic representations of the sirens from the outset, rather than their main weapons in the poem, knowledge and flattery.
4. Bush, "*Homer's Odyssey*," 941.

Bibliography

Bush, W. Stephen. "*Homer's Odyssey*. Three Reels (Milano Films)." *Moving Picture World*, 16 March 1912, 941–42.

Doherty, Lillian Eileen. "Sirens, Muses, and Female Narrators in the Odyssey." In *The Distaff Side: Representing the Female in Homer's Odyssey*, edited by Beth Cohen. New York: Oxford University Press, 1995.

Sargent, Epes Winthrop. "Advertising for Exhibitors." *Moving Picture World*, 24 February 1912, 666, 763.

Schein, Seth L. "Female Representations and Interpreting the Odyssey." In *The Distaff Side: Representing the Female in Homer's Odyssey*, edited by Beth Cohen. New York: Oxford University Press, 1995.

ROME, OPEN CITY (ROMA, CITTÀ APPERTA) (1945)

DIRECTOR: Roberto Rossellini
WRITERS: Sergio Amidei, Federico Fellini, Alberto Consiglio, Roberto Rossellini
PRODUCERS: Giuseppe Amato, Ferruccio de Martino, Rod E. Geiger, Roberto Rossellini
CINEMATOGRAPHER: Ubaldo Arata
EDITORS: Eraldo Da Roma, Jolanda Benvenuti (uncredited)
PRODUCTION DESIGN: Rosario Megna
MUSIC: Renzo Rossellini
CAST: Don Pietro Pellegrini: Aldo Fabrizi. Pina: Anna Magnani. Giorgio Manfredi (aka Luigi Ferraris): Marcello Pagliero. Piccolo Marcello: Vito Annichiarico. Maj. Bergmann: Harry Feist. Ingrid: Giovanna Galletti. Francesco: Francesco Grandjacquet. Marina Mari: Maria Michi. Lauretta: Carla Rovere. Capt.

Hartmann: Joop van Hulzen. Austrian Deserter: Ákos Tolnay. Police Commissioner: Carlo Sindici. Agostino the Sexton: Nando Bruno
AA: None
AAN: Best Writing–Screenplay (Sergio Amidei, Federico Fellini)
Cannes Film Festival Award: Grand Prize of the Festival (Roberto Rossellini)
National Board of Review Awards: Best Actress (Anna Magnani), Best Foreign Film
New York Film Critics Circle Award: Best Foreign-Language Film
DVD: Criterion, 2009
Blu-ray: Flamingo Video, 2011
Duration: 103 minutes

Robert Rossellini's movie *Rome, Open City*, partly based on history, can be—and often is—called a docudrama, because it takes place during a historical period, 1943, after Benito Mussolini was overthrown, and General Pietro Badoglio, who sided with the Allied Forces, became head of a liberated Italy. During that year, however, Rome was still occupied by the Germans, and declared an "open city," that is, a non-war zone city that could not be bombed, or attacked directly, in an effort to preserve its valuable antiquities and the treasures in the Vatican, which remained neutral.[1] But while Rome was occupied, partisans from disparate political groups, communists, leftists during the fascist regime of Mussolini, and even fugitives from the Nazis in Europe, and some Catholics, joined in the resistance movement against the Germans. The story is mostly about the persecutions of members of these groups, particularly one, Giorgio Manfredi, an alias for Luigi Ferraris, a prominent leftist leader. Manfredi had eluded the Germans and was present in Rome trying to organize the resistance in the city. The story is intermixed with some groups of locals, who either sheltered or betrayed this leader and his friends, while trying to survive widespread hunger and deplorable conditions during that still war-ravaged city.

Filmed and hastily put together in studios, as well as in the streets of Rome, with both professional and amateur actors, the movie became the prime example of what was later called the "cinema of neorealism," which had its roots in the Mussolini era but developed during the postwar years, with Rossellini being its leader. The movie had a lukewarm reception at first, but it has since become the most celebrated example of that movement, which aimed at presenting real life, as opposed to the glitter and fantasies of Hollywood.

The story begins with a riot, as the Germans are searching for Manfredi (Marcello Pagliero), who escapes and soon joins a neighborhood woman, Pina, who is raiding a bakery and grabbing bread with a mob of other hungry women so that they can feed their starving families. Pina, a stubborn, powerful woman, played magnificently by Anna Magnani, is engaged to Francesco (Francesco Grandjacquet) and several months pregnant by him. Francesco is also involved in the resistance movement, and she is to marry him the next day. Manfredi asks her to get in touch with a priest, Don Pietro (Aldo Fabrizi), who, although a Catholic, has allied himself with the resistance, most of whom are Marxists, including Francesco. Pina dispatches her young son Marcello (Vito Annichiarico) to find the priest, who is refereeing a boys' soccer game.

At this point, the connection of the plot between the resistance leader Manfredi and Pina's family is established, and the two strands are soon to be added to by the third, as the plot shifts to the Gestapo headquarters, and Major Bergmann (Harry Feist), a monstrous homosexual[2] Nazi whose purpose is to capture Manfredi and force him by any means, including torture, to reveal who his collaborators are. In a highly dramatic scene, when the Italian troops working for the Germans enter the apartment where Pina and her family live to arrest collaborators, Francesco is seized and driven away after being loaded in a truck. Annoyed when a German makes advances at her, Pina becomes hysterical when she sees her husband-to-be being taken by the Germans on the day of their wedding. She runs after him and is shot in the middle of the street. This scene is possibly the most memorable in the film, and Magnani's intensity made her an international star.

The plot is further complicated when Marina (Maria Michi), Manfredi's girlfriend, who collaborates with the Gestapo in exchange for drugs and other gifts, and who is hiding Manfredi and Francesco in her apartment, betrays him to the Gestapo. Marina is carrying on a relationship with Ingrid (Giovanna Galletti), Bergmann's henchwoman, and a lesbian, who supplies her with drugs and various other luxury gifts. Lauretta (Carla Rovere), Pina's sister, who sells her favors to the occupiers for an easy living, shares Marina's apartment, where the two fugitives are hiding to evade the Gestapo. An Austrian deserter (played by Ákos Tolnay) from the German Army joins them, begging to be taken in as the third member of the fugitive group. Soon thereafter, Marina reveals their hideout, and Manfredi is arrested and tortured to death in a series of scenes of wrenching cruelty. The torture, which includes a blowtorch that scorches his side and the extraction of his nails, is not shown directly; only Manfredi's torn body is presented to the viewer. A telling image shows him with his arms outstretched, as if in a crucifixion, suggesting a religious theme, which is ironic given the fact that he was a communist and an atheist. Many commentators have noticed the juxtaposition between Don Pietro's religious faith and the communist groups that comprise a large part of the resistance.[3] This also suggests the unity of the resistance Italians, who have distanced themselves from Mussolini's fascist regime and the Axis alliance. Don Pietro is involved in an important mission, transferring a large amount of money, hidden in three books in large denominations, to the rebels.

But three of the four men are arrested while fleeing Marina's apartment, including Don Pietro, Manfredi, and the Austrian refugee, while Francesco, having lingered behind to say good-bye to Pina's son Marcello, manages to escape. He will be Marcello's adopted father, and it is implied that he will give the orphan a home and a new life after the war. Bergmann interrogates Manfredi, offering him a "reasonable alternative" to revealing the names of the National Resistance Committee, Badoglio's generals, in particular, but Manfredi stays calm while confronting the major. In a gesture of faked gallantry, the latter offers him a cigarette before he is escorted into the next room, where he is tortured. Don Pietro is then brought in and asked the same question, but he also declines to answer. Sadistically, Bergmann leaves the door open, and a deep-focus shot shows Manfredi about to be burned with a lighted blowtorch, but Don Pietro's glasses were broken as he was being shoved into Bergmann's room by the guards, and he can hardly see.

Meanwhile, news comes in that the Austrian refugee has hanged himself. The infuriated Bergmann goes into the next room, where officers gather to drink and relax, and from where the screams of tortured men can be heard. Marina and Ingrid are lying together on a couch in a lascivious embrace, while Captain Hartmann (Joop van Hulzen), quite drunk, spouts out words of regret, predicting the inevitable fall of the Nazis and their ideology as the "superior race," words that infuriate Bergmann, who leaves the room with a violent shrug of his shoulders. His assertion of a superior race has been proven wrong: Manfredi has defeated it by withstanding his merciless torture.

The story ends with the execution of Don Pietro in a field by an Italian execution squad, which fails to kill him, so an enraged Hartmann has to come close and finish the job with a shot to the head. A group of boys active in the resistance is watching the execution of the martyr from behind a wired fence, witnessing the martyrdom of their hero and religious leader, whose death will herald Italy's new birth. The boys are the new generation who will live to see Italy be freed from two decades of fascism and suppression by the Nazis, thus making the last scene of the film symbolic of a brighter future.

Rossellini's *Rome, Open City* has thus borne witness to the sadism and cruelty of the oppressor, whose false theory that "superior" races will dominate the "inferior" ones collapses as the film exposes, in plain and dark colors, all the barbarism and inhumanity—and insanity—that goes with it. The heroism of the resistance groups, and the eventual unity of families that have been torn apart by the war, is heralding a new era. The events the movie depicts are fully tragic; what is more tragic than an innocent woman being gunned down before witnesses in the middle of the street, or a martyr's swollen face and mangled body whose spirit stays alive as his body is destroyed? The fact that the resistance brings together religious leaders, communist partisans, and family members seems to be the goal of a movie that appears to lack focus on only one goal: how to liberate Italy. This goal can be achieved only by unity among a divided nation, but also it demonstrates that war paralyzes ethics, discredits good people, and leads the most vulnerable members of a tortured society to resort to any means to survive. This is a complex movie, an epic of the common man and woman, one might say, who strive for decency and a new national identity amid the chaos of political, moral, and financial paralysis. CS

Notes

1. During the war between Greece and Italy, in 1940–1941, both capitals, Athens and Rome, were declared "open cities," meaning that they could not be bombed to preserve their valuable classical treasures. During the German occupation of 1944, Rome remained an "open city" (*città apperta*), although resistance groups remained active, and the Gestapo continued to hunt them down.

2. Here the term *homosexual*, applied to Bergmann, is given in derogatory terms, as is the word *lesbian*, used to refer to his henchwoman Ingrid.

3. One such comment that appears continuously throughout the movie is made by scholar and historian Peter Bondanella, who makes it clear that this "alliance" is not forced, but it is credited to the desire of the suppressed Italians, aside from the police, who are bonding to get rid of the Nazis. Peter Bondanella, "Audio Commentary" *Rome, Open City*, directed by Roberto Rossellini (Criterion, 2009), DVD.

Bibliography

Crowther, Bosley. "The Screen; How Italy Resisted." *New York Times*, 26 February 1946, www.nytimes.com/movie/review?res=940CE7DE1239E23ABC4E51DFB466838D659EDE (23 October 2013).

Gottlieb, Sidney, ed. *Roberto Rossellini's* Rome, Open City. New York: Cambridge University Press, 2004.

Wakeman, John. *World Film Directors*, vol. 2. New York: H. W. Wilson Company, 1987.

A ROYAL AFFAIR (EN KONGELIG AFFÆRE) (2012)

DIRECTOR: Nikolaj Arcel
WRITERS: Rasmus Heisterberg, Nikolaj Arcel. Based on Per Olov Enquist's historical novel *The Royal Physician's Visit.*
PRODUCERS: Meta Louise Folgater, Sissy Graum Jorgensen, Louise Vesth (Zentropa Entertainments, DR TV, Trollhättan Film AB)
CINEMATOGRAPHER: Rasmus Videbaek
EDITOR: Kasper Leik, Mikkel E. G. Nielsen
MUSIC: Cyrille Aufort, Gabriel Jared

CAST: Johann Friedrich Struensee: Mads Mikkelsen. Queen Caroline Mathilde: Alicia Vikander. King Christian VII: Mikkel Folsegaard. Enevold Brandt: Cyron Bjorn Melville. Prince Frederik VI: William John Nielsen. Ove Høegh-Guldberg: David Dencik. Schack Carl Rantzau: Thomas W. Gabrielsson. Louise Von Plessen: Laura Bro. J. H. E. Bernstoff: Bent Mejding. Juliane Marie (Queen Dowager): Trine Dyrholm
AA: None
AAN: Best Foreign-Language Film
GG: None
GGN: Best Foreign-Language Film
DVD: Magnolia Home Entertainment, 2013
BLU-RAY: Magnolia Home Entertainment, 2013
DURATION: 137 minutes

Filmed the same year as *Anna Karenina*,[1] *A Royal Affair*, by the Danish director Nikolaj Arcel, bears some similarity to the former in that both examine fundamental changes in the social fabric (although a century apart), while an adulterous love affair tears apart family relationships. Both are filmed in epic scale, but *A Royal Affair* preoccupies itself less with spectacle and choreography and more with a straightforward telling of a royal intrigue that ends in tragedy. Point of view varies, but the narrative line begins with a retrospective of the queen's marriage and ends with its conclusion—the letters she had written to her children and their effect on them as the narrative reverts to its beginning. *Anna Karenina* carries a double plot, Anna and Vrosnky's story paralleled by Levin and Kitty's, with opposing endings, while Queen Caroline's (Alicia Vikander) begins with a conflict,[2] a complication at the palace court, and several reversals, which add a tragic note to the epic sweep of turbulent changes in a European nation during the Age of Enlightenment. The screenplay is based mostly on Per Olov Enquist's historical novel *The Royal Physician's Visit*,[3] which describes in great detail the "Struensee Era" (1770–1772), the period during which a German doctor, Johann Friedrich Struensee (Mads Mikkelsen), ruled Denmark with absolute power. The action of the movie, however, takes place in a broader chronological context, the latter part of the eighteenth century, between 1769 and 1778, a time when Rousseau and Voltaire were still alive and changing the intellectual and social fabric of European life. The divine right of kings was mostly intact, as were the excesses of the aristocracy and the tight ideological supremacy that kept "dangerous" ideas from invading tightly controlled royal courts. Royalties exchanged brides and grooms, mainly to keep alliances going, and marriages between individuals totally unknown to one another constantly occurred, often with disastrous effects.

A Royal Affair opens with such a marriage between Caroline Mathilde of England, sister of King George III, and Danish king Christian VII of Denmark, as Caroline travels to Copenhagen to meet her husband, already being the queen there. At first, Caroline is seen writing letters to her children, and the action soon shifts to nine years earlier, when the young queen, only fifteen at the time, arrives in Copenhagen. It does not take her long to realize that her husband is unbalanced. His State Council dictates all his actions, and she has to bear the humiliations she is subjected to. But she shows grace under pressure and is resigned to her fate, knowing she can change nothing. The royal environment consists of Queen Dowager (Trine Dyrholm) and a suffocating circle of courtiers who seem to take their king's lunacy for granted, afraid to imperil his royal status—and thence their own existence. Among them is the diminutive Ove Høegh-Guldberg, a religious fanatic who pulls the string of whatever happens, and the haughty and jealous Queen Dowager, Juliane Marie, whose younger son would succeed Christian (Mikkel Folsegaard), should he die childless.

After an erratic nuptial night, during which Christian subjects his wife to sexual perversions, he announces a tour of Europe, which might last two or three years. On his way home, his advisors recommend that he employ a personal physician and a delegation of two courtiers in a low status at the court. Count Rantzau (Thomas W. Gabrielsson) and Enevold Brandt (Cyron Bjorn Melville) arrive at Altona, a Danish colony in Germany, and Doctor Johann Friedrich Struensee is summoned to audition for this position. Struensee soon ingratiates himself with the king, who seems to suffer from some sort of bipolar disease, suppression of sexual desires, and erratic behavior, but Struensee perceives almost right away that the sullen young king possesses a brilliant gift. He can remember entire passages from *Hamlet* (ironically a Danish prince) and quotes verbatim from Shakespeare's most famous play. Struensee responds, quoting more lines from several plays, and the two soon become close friends.

As Christian cannot seem to control his court, Struensee advises him "to act" as a real king, and Christian suddenly asserts his power and dismisses his entire State Council, thus invoking their enmity. Among them are the head of the council, J. H. E. Bernstoff (Bent Mejding); Ove Høegh-Guldberg; and Queen Dowager. Struensee also inevitably rises in power, thus becoming Denmark's "second king," while Christian gives orders to clean up the city of its filthy streets. He employs the poor, abolishes censorship, and brings a breath of new ideas to Danish society. When small pox breaks out, Struensee recommends general inoculation, which saves many lives. He is so successful in elevating the status of the lower classes that the king receives a letter of congratulations from Voltaire himself.

But Struensee's fortunes soon change, as he and the queen embark on a passionate love affair, resulting in the queen's pregnancy. As she and the king have not been together for quite some time, Struensee proposes that the king visit the queen's quarters one night. When the king protests that he is incapable of normal sex, Struensee recommends that he still can "act." But things soon come to a head, as Queen Dowager, the king's stepmother, begins to suspect an affair between the two, and when the secret is out, the king is forced by those who surround him to sign Struensee's arrest and the queen's removal from the palace. Struensee is imprisoned and tortured, and then taken out and led to believe that he has been pardoned; however, he soon knows by the gathering crowds that he is being taken to a public place to be beheaded.

The queen is forced into exile, and many years later she writes to her son Frederick, now fifteen, and her young daughter, Louise, Struensee's child, the truth of what happened, and that Denmark has regressed socially and people have lost their rights since Struensee's death. In an epilogue, the screen shows that sixteen-year-old Frederick, the king, aided by his father, led a coup against his courtiers and reclaimed his powers, leading Denmark back to modernity.

Mads Mikkelsen, who plays Struensee, remarks in an interview that this movie is based on historical facts, but the details of his character's death and his actual liaison with the queen are vague, and details had to be filled in.[4] In the same interview, Nikolaj Arcel explains that the movie could have been done in English, but they preferred Danish for authenticity, although at that time in Denmark people spoke French and German, and some English.[5] The movie, of epic proportions, offers lavish spectacle and choreographed court scenes, although never in excess, for the story takes precedence over stylization, so one sees the deplorable conditions of people living in the capital as the queen enters Copenhagen, the streets filled with filth, rats running around, and horrendous poverty. During the small pox epidemic, sick and dying people are shown in realistic shots, a sharp contrast to the luxurious life of the palace and the ruling class. During Struensee's execution, which comes after he witnesses his friend's, Brandt's, killing, crowds are gathering to witness the beheading, as it was a common spectacle in those days, but the movie does not dwell on these atrocities, building the climax of the unfolding drama in clear lines, without most of the excesses of the modern blockbuster epic. There are some sexual scenes between Struensee and the queen, but the camera treads delicately between overt exposure and sanctimonious puritanism. What is treated more plainly is that this was something that routinely prevailed in European societies, but that the Age of Enlightenment was about to bring the old order of the king-aristocracy-church to a crashing halt—at least for a while. Young King Frederick reigned for fifty-five years, and he brought the Danish nation into the modern world. CS

Notes

1. Alicia Vikander, who plays Kitty in *Anna Karenina*, is Queen Caroline here, with a reversal of roles, for she is now the adulteress.
2. Vikander, a Swedish ballet dancer turned actress, also plays a woman of the Enlightenment, studying Rousseau and influencing her husband in adopting new ideas.
3. Per Olov Enquist, *The Royal Physician's Visit*, 2nd ed., translated by Nina Nunnally (Woodstock, NY: Overlook Press, 2012).
4. Mads Mikkelsen, "Special Features," *A Royal Affair*, directed by Nikolaj Arcel (Magnolia Home Entertainment, 2013), Blu-ray.
5. Nikolaj Arcel, "Special Features," *A Royal Affair*, directed by Nikolaj Arcel (Magnolia Home Entertainment, 2013), Blu-ray.

Bibliography

Enquist, Per Olov. *The Royal Physician's Visit*, 2nd ed. Woodstock, NY: Overlook Press, 2012.

SEVEN SAMURAI (SHICHININ NO SAMURAI) (1954)

DIRECTOR: Akira Kurosawa
WRITERS: Akira Kurosawa, Shinobu Hashimoto, Hideo Oguni
PRODUCER: Sôjirô Motoki (Toho Company)
CINEMATOGRAPHER: Asakazu Nakai
PRODUCTION DESIGN: Takashi Matsuyama
ART DIRECTION: Sô Matsuyama
COSTUMES: Kôhei Ezaki, Junjirô Yamada
MUSIC: Fumio Hayasaka
MAKEUP ARTIST: Midori Nakajo, Junjirô Yamada
CAST: Kambei Shimada: Takashi Shimura. Kikuchiyo: Toshirô Mifune. Shino: Keiko Tsushima. Wife: Yukiko Shimazaki. Farmer Manzo: Kamatari Fujiwara. Shichiroji: Daisuke Katô. Katsushiro: Isao Kimura. Heihachi: Minoru Chiaki. Kyuzo: Seiji Miyaguchi. Farmer Mosuke: Yoshio Kosugi. Farmer Yohei: Bokuzen Hidari. Gorobei Katayama: Yoshio Inaba
AA: None
AAN: Best Art Direction–Set Decoration–Black-and-White (Takashi Matsuyama), Best Costume Design (Kôhei Ezaki)
DVD: Criterion, 1998. Includes an essay and running commentary by David Ehrenstein.
BLU-RAY: Criterion, 2010
DURATION: 207 minutes

Akira Kurosawa's eleventh film, *Seven Samurai* (*Shichinin no samurai*) has been the most influential and was certainly one of the most popular Japanese epics to hit Western screens in the 1950s. The film not only gained audience acceptance, being shown in both art houses and on mainstream screens, but it was copied a few years later by Hollywood with the highly popular western *The Magnificent Seven*

(John Sturges, 1960), which itself has left its mark on subsequent movies in the genre. More important than anything in our context, *Seven Samurai* illustrates the perfect epic form, as it displays the main epic characteristics known to narrators in the West since antiquity: length (200 minutes), battle scenes, tribal conflicts, and heroic action. It is an epic where guile (or strategy) joins bravery—as in both *The Odyssey* and *The Iliad* of Homer.

Kurosawa learned epic film techniques, in part, from his Japanese mentor, Kajir Yamamoto, a director of both comedies and epics in Japan during the 1940s, and partly from his American model and master of Western epics, John Ford, whose film methods he adopted and imitated.[1] As a director of note who rose to fame in the West with his *Rashomon* in 1950, a film that won both a foreign film Oscar and the Grand Prix at the Venice Film Festival, Kurosawa embraced Western ideas and took "his cinematic inspiration from the full store of world film, literature, and music."[2] His mastery of the epic form is shown not only in *Seven Samurai*, but also in such later monumental works in the genre as *The Hidden Fortress* (1958), *Kagemusha* (1980), and *Ran* (1985), the last being an adaptation of Shakespeare's *King Lear*.

Seven Samurai shows the conflicts of a war-torn Japanese society in the sixteenth century, when warlords ruled the country, leaving anarchy behind when their rules ended. Then marauders raided villages, took the farmers' crops, raped the women, and left devastation and chaos behind. The villagers had a last resort: they could hire unemployed, and often starving, samurai to protect them. Thus, the legend of the samurai that emerged from these particular circumstances was not that of a swordsman at the service of a warlord, but of the defender of the weak. The "ronin," as he calls himself, is a roaming independent man of arms, who, in need of a meal, makes it his business to protect the tribe, leading it to victory and then once more dissociating himself from it. He has no master and no social connections, and the tribe has adopted him only momentarily. With the end of his task, he is again alone to roam the countryside, wiser perhaps and independent, but shiftless and homeless. His only satisfaction is to accomplish the task. He knows that the defeat of the villains is only a momentary triumph and that evil is cyclic and bound to return—and fought and defeated again to ensure survival. By the skillful blending of philosophical and technical elements, Kurosawa achieves a perfect aesthetic whole, offering unity of action, characterization of both the individual and the group, and a concept of a hero who achieves mythical/archetypal dimensions as the defender of the tribe.

Despite its great length (more than three hours), *Seven Samurai* is distinguished for its economy and relative leanness of action, which is achieved through quick editing, expert montage of battle scenes, and details confined to the absolutely essential points in describing character. There are few establishing shots here, so frequent in the gratuitous spectacle offered by the grandiose Hollywood epics of the time. Unity of action is achieved by focusing on only one episode, the saving of a village from bandits, in what must have been a prolonged civic strife that devastated Japan in the sixteenth century. As usual in the great narrative epics of the past, for example, *The Iliad*, war is given in capsulated form, and the viewer is informed indirectly, through dialogue and action, of the social unrest caused by the shifting of power from the aristocracy to the peasants, and the resulting dispossession of the professional warrior—the samurai. *Seven Samurai* achieves its unity of plot through the singleness of purpose that a group of peasants exhibit when they decide to enlist the help of these unemployed ragtag warriors to help them save their village from bandits.

This initial action precipitates a sequence of episodes organically connected and conforming to this general idea. After a brief shot of the bandits, who stop short of raiding the village but whose presence is known, the desperate peasants call a meeting. They consult an old wizard, who tells them that they must hire unemployed samurai to protect them from the outlaws. They go to the nearest town (or central village), where samurai are known to flock, presumably in search of employment. Here, the samurai are individually introduced and a distinct characterization of the principals is achieved. Kambei Shimata (Takashi Shimura) is the first samurai to come to the viewer's attention when he rescues a young baby that was abducted by a thief and is being held hostage in a hut. Kambei has his head shaven and is wearing a priest's robe, and in a lightning-quick move, he kills the thief, who is seen staggering out of the hut and drops dead in front of an amazed crowd.

Watching him is Katsushiro (Isao Kimura), a young man who aspires to become a fighter of equal valor, asking the latter to take him on as a disciple. Kambei declines modestly but soon agrees to take him under his wing, suspecting that Kikuchiyo (Toshirô Mifune), a vagabond competing for attention, might lead him to unworthy habits. Kambei has considered the farmers' request to hire samurai to protect them, but he thinks that the plan is unrealistic if only two or three samurai were to fight a band of forty bandits; however, he soon, revises this decision when Corobei, one of the numerous unemployed (and hungry) samurai roaming the villages, joins the group. He says he wants to join not for the job, which pays no wages and will bring no fame, but because, as he tells Kambei, "your character fascinates me."

Three other samurai soon join the group: Heihachi (Minoru Chiaki), who cuts wood for a living; Shichiroji (Daisuke Katô), an old friend and fellow fighter (the "right hand") of Kambei; and Kyuzo (Seiji Miyaguchi), a swordsman with dazzling skills. The six men head for the village, followed at a distance by Kikuchiyo, a laughable character carrying a fake document to prove his claim to be a samurai. After many jokes at his expense, they good-heartedly accept him as one of their own, and Kikuchiyo becomes the seventh member, although he is never officially titled as a samurai. Kambei, who possesses a strategic mind, plans the defense, making a camp of the village and devising a map with signs for the fortifications, which will include a flooded field as a ditch. Each samurai is assigned a post and is responsible for his position.

Villagers are recruited and trained in the handling of weapons—bamboo spears. They have not shed their fear of the samurais, and Manzo (Kamatari Fujiwara), always suspicious of their motivations, cuts his daughter Shino's (Keiko Tsushima) hair and makes her dress as a boy. His measure does not prove effective, however, for Shino and Katsushiro meet accidentally in a field of blossoms—a staple in Kurosawa films—and fall in love. This marks the young warrior's rite of passage, for now he will fight as a "complete man," as his colleagues will tease him later.

The number of the samurai is reduced by one when Heihachi is killed during a raid while trying to protect Richichi, whose wife had been abducted by the bandits. Kyuzo, meanwhile, has killed two bandits who came to scout, and Kikuchiyo kills one and captures a gun. The assault soon begins in earnest, and the village is in a state of commotion. Kambei methodically eliminates the bandits one by one, letting them pass through an opening in the fortifications to be killed by his troops, as the villagers gradually become expert warriors. But in the final and decisive battle, which is fought (and masterfully shot) during a downpour, the chief bandit forces his way into the women's quarters, and from there he shoots and kills both Kyuzo and Kikuchiyo. Before he dies, in an act of extreme heroism, Kikuchiyo, although fatally wounded, spears the chief bandit to death. Corobei has also died in the battle. The four samurai are buried in the burial mound outside the village, their swords wedged into each individual grave. "Again we have survived," Kambei says to Shichiroji, as they are about to depart from the village. Kambei, Shichiroji, and Katsushiro linger briefly before the mounds to look at the villagers now working on the rice pads, singing their tribal song of victory and harvest. Katsushiro looks wistfully at Shino, who passes by him to join her group. "Again we have been defeated," Kambei mutters. "These villagers are the winners."

Kurosawa's concept of the ronin in this film is the vital part of his vision. Here the ronin is presented in the person of Kambei, who proudly declares that he is one when the young, aspiring warrior Katsushiro begs him to take him as a disciple. When Kambei humbly declines, he is thus implying that he does not consider himself worthy enough to have followers, but also declaring his independent nature. Kambei, however, is not aloof, and he soon allows Katsushiro to follow him, seeking to protect him from the unmannerly Kikuchiyo. Kambei is proud, but also hungry. The request of the villagers, which promises "neither reward nor fame," attracts him, for in it he sees a challenge that will allow him to put to use his wily warrior's nature, but he also seems to be moved by the villagers' desperate plea. Although a skilled warrior, he is also a planner who can calculate the odds, and the impossible situation of the villagers—a handful of untrained farmers against a band of forty trainer warriors—seems to him a great challenge, no doubt as great as or greater than those he has faced before.

Kambei's previous life, never revealed in any detail, seems to have been a series of hardships and defeats. He is a hard-bitten realist, used to losing, but not disheartened, not a pessimist. His inner strength is untouched by the everyday rampant evil he has seen and faced. He is stoic and self-assured, approaching each adverse development with determination and firmness. During a moment of panic in the village, after someone has sounded an alarm signal, he remains firmly in command, beginning by asking rational questions. His sharp mind matches his inner courage; he is tough, courageous, compassionate, and unpretentious. Even-tempered and calm in a storm, he is endowed with a strategic mind, characteristically scratching his shaven head in a dilemma, keeping to himself rather than voicing his troubles. He is good-natured, devoid of the usual arrogance and hubris of warriors, never making condescending remarks, assuming leadership but also treating his fellow fighters with respect, as equals.

The other samurai exhibit similar traits: they are brave and even-tempered, accepting their leader's superiority and working flawlessly as a group, each offering to serve when called upon by necessity or his leader's command. As warriors and village guests, they are admirably disciplined, respecting the farmers' privacy and social customs. Their dangerous mission leaves them undaunted, and they are willing to die for an unworthy crowd, honoring their commitment even after the tragic revelation of the villagers' treachery. The samurai are not a faceless crowd blindly following their leader, but rather identifiable characters, each having his own distinctive personality and idiosyncrasies.

Heihachi is expansive and good-humored, always looking on the bright side (even if there isn't one). He is the first to die, while trying to save Richichi, who had rushed to save his wife from the bandits. Shichiroji, Kambei's old friend and again his right-hand man during this new venture, is busy training the farmers to be battle-ready. Corobei helps Kambei in his strategic planning, while Kyuzo practices constantly, even in the rain, to perfect his swordsmanship. And Katsushiro, the "kid," as they affectionately call him, is fully dedicated to the group's mission, although he pays as much attention to love as he does to learning the art of war. He is the admirer of the samurai in general and the hero-worshipper of both Kambei and Kyuzo, to whom he expresses his admiration after he sees him come back from a successful foray, during which he killed two bandits.

A departure from the disciplined samurai bunch is the unruly Kikuchiyo, who joins the group despite their initial rejection of him but who is eventually accepted as the "seventh" in the company. When help is needed and he follows them to the village loyally (and somewhat inexplicably), they are hardly in a position to argue, and they let him join the group even though they decidedly regard him as inferior. Kikuchiyo, played, of course, by the famous Japanese star Toshirô Mifune (born in Mongolia) is considered the "lead" in the movie, and in the final count he proves a worthy warrior. As a character, he is as individualistic as the others are group-oriented. He is the rebel in the group, and the only one who displays flaws. He is rude and, on occasion, drunk; fakes a samurai identity with a stolen document; and is laughed at and scorned for his lack of skill and refinement. He is awkward and blundering, and is caught sleeping while on guard duty. Yet, Kikuchiyo is the only member of the group who changes and develops as a character, and who eventually reveals his inner self. He is moody, emotionally violent and anxiety-ridden, and unpredictable.

In an emotional scene, after he has disclosed the villagers' true character by the discovery of hidden armor in the huts, he bitterly tells the group that these are the weapons of slain samurai. Kambei then guesses that Kikuchiyo is the son of a farmer. As such, he has knowledge of the farmers' mean-spiritedness and murderous nature, knowledge that the samurai lack, but he also knows that samurai, at different times, have reduced the farmers to this state by raiding their villages and robbing them. And after a fire destroys the water mill and a woman holding a baby is stabbed to death and dies, Kikuchiyo takes the child in his arms and breaks down and cries, saying, "I was like this child once!" He had been an abandoned orphan, the son of a farmer from a destroyed village, and although ignorant and untrained, he strove to become as brave and good as his superiors. He began to rise in the samurais' esteem when he sounded the danger alarm, an ingenious trick that induced the village crowd to accept the arrival of the samurai.

His buffoonery is matched by feats of bravery, like catching one of the bandits and stealing a gun, and even his reckless taunting of the enemy helps to raise the spirits of the embattled group. His heroic and redeeming death is the most telling event in the story, a release for the audience and a catharsis of emotions, for no great victory could have been accomplished without the tragic sacrifice of life. Unlike Kambei, who is even-tempered and calm, Kikuchiyo displays a different brand of heroism—that of emotions—a victory over casual weaknesses, as well as sacrifice for humanity. He is a pivotal character in the film, for he possesses an understanding of the farmer that the samurai do not have, while drawing the farmers into trusting those whom they had once considered enemies. Thus, he attains a status of one who balances the two antithetical groups. When he dies, he is buried on the mount of worthy heroes, a fit tribute to his sacrifice and a signal honor to his equality as a samurai.

The farmers as a whole are downtrodden, disloyal (to anything but their own cause), treacherous, inhospitable, fatalistic, distrusting of authority, and amoral. Kikuchiyo calls them "foxy beasts," while adding that it is the samurai who are responsible for their plight. It was the samurai who plundered their land, stole their crops, and violated their women. Having learned their hard lessons, the farmers are distrustful, striving for survival and nothing else. Outside their immediate tribal concerns, they have no interest in anything else. And yet, Kurosawa does not present them as hateful or despicable. They are the end result of the chaotic times they live in and the indifference of the outside world. Authority has betrayed them, and religion does not succor. "God has abandoned us," the group complains at the beginning of the action, as soon as the bandits have left. The magistrate, if appealed to, will arrive only after the destruction is done. Only the old man sees the solution ("Hire hungry samurai," he admonishes), and the frightened villagers find in him the only reliable counsel.

Although the struggle of the villagers against marauders encompasses a large time frame, for it is repeated yearly, this particular battle covers only a certain segment of this time period, the victory of the united forces of villagers/samurai against the attackers. Some of the villagers hold the samurai suspect and try to hide provisions and their womenfolk, but when the danger becomes imminent, they unite to defeat the outlaws. Some of the samurai are killed and buried with honors, while the rest depart with some philosophical observations.

In the modern sense, *Seven Samurai* offers viewers what they crave most, a suspenseful story, albeit with only minimal spectacle, not the "big show" that one finds in the Hollywood epics. Kurosawa's style is noted for its economy, which applies to the famous final battle scene, which goes on for nearly twenty minutes. For its effectiveness, the film relies on its own means of expression—the language of film—which includes montage, panning, crosscutting, deep-focus photography, and brilliant camera work. *Seven Samurai* is a film that redefines the epic; it is action-filled to appeal to a broader public, but also thoughtful enough to be a draw for discriminating audiences who seek levels of meaning beyond the easy allure of immediate gratification. Above all, it is a redefinition of the modern action hero, whose violence-prone nature often deprives him of the means to seek self-knowledge and self-exploration. Here the hero of thought combines with the hero of action, whose service to tribal interests has expanded considerably to include those of humanity. CS

Notes

1. Audie Bock and Rob Edelman, "Kurosawa, Akira," in *The St. James Film Directors Encyclopedia*, edited by Andrew Sarris (New York and London: Visible Ink Press, 1998), 255.
2. Bock and Edelman, "Kurosawa, Akira," 255.

Bibliography

Bock, Audie, and Rob Edelman. "Kurosawa, Akira." In *The St. James Film Directors Encyclopedia*, edited by Andrew Sarris, 255. New York and London: Visible Ink Press, 1998.

SOLARIS (SOLYARIS) (1972)

DIRECTOR: Andrei Tarkovsky
WRITERS: Fridrikh Gorenshtein, Andrei Tarkovsky. Based on the novel by Stanislaw Lem.
PRODUCER: Viacheslav Tarasov (Janus Films, Mosfilms)
CINEMATOGRAPHER: Vadim Yusov
EDITORS: Lyudmila Feiginova, Nina Marcus
PRODUCTION DESIGN: Mikhail Romadin
COSTUMES: Nelli Fomina
MUSIC: Eduard Artemyev
CAST: Hari: Natalya Bondarchuk. Kris Kelvin: Donatas Banionis. Dr. Snaut: Jüri Järvet. Henri Berton: Vladislav Dvorzhetskiy. Kelvin's Father: Nikolay Grinko. Dr. Sartorius: Anatoliy Solonitsyn. Kelvin's Mother: Olga Barnet.

André, Berton's son: Vitalik Kerdimun. Dr. Gibarian: Sos Sargsyan. Gibarian's She-Guest: Olga Kizilova. Kelvin's niece: Tatyana Malykh. Shannahan: Aleksandr Misharin. Professor Trajet: Bagrat Oganesyan. Anna, Kelvin's Aunt: Tamara Ogorodnikova. Chairman of Investigation Commission: Yulian Semyonov. Young Kris Kelvin: V. Statsinskiy. Professor Messenger: Georgiy Teykh
AA: None
AAN: None
Cannes Film Festival Award: FIPRESCI Prize (Andrei Tarkovsky), Grand Prize of the Jury (Andrei Tarkovsky)
Cannes Film Festival Award Nomination: Palme d'Or (Andrei Tarkovsky)
DVD: Criterion, 2011
Blu-ray: Criterion, 2011
Duration: 167 minutes

Besieged by problems with Soviet censorship and curtailed by an early death, director Andrei Tarkovsky made only seven feature films, of which *Solaris* is one of the best known (although in later years he changed his mind about the film and declared it his least favorite).[1] Tarkovsky disliked what he saw as the technological coldness of Stanley Kubrick's *2001: A Space Odyssey* (1968) and designed *Solaris* in opposition to this work.[2] Instead, he uses the science-fiction scenario of *Solaris* to contemplate our yearning to correct the irretrievable past.

At the beginning of the film, psychologist Kris Kelvin (Donatas Banionis) is visiting the lakeside home of his father and aunt (played by Nikolay Grinko and Tamara Ogorodnikova, respectively) before departing for the planet of Solaris. Scientists at the space station orbiting the planet have been sending strange messages, and Kelvin is to assess their status and the viability of the mission itself. His father's friend, Henri Berton (Vladislav Dvorzhetskiy), interrupts the awkward family farewell to show them the report from his own controversial mission to Solaris many years prior. Kelvin is skeptical of his seemingly wild claims of apparitions in the oceans of the planet. In any case, Kelvin is weighed down by his tense relationship with his father and his somber contemplation of the natural world he must leave behind (shown in Tarkovksy's signature long takes, although they are relatively restrained in their use here).

When Kelvin arrives at the space station, he finds it in disarray. His former colleague, Dr. Gibarian (Sos Sargsyan), has committed suicide before his arrival, leaving only two remaining inhabitants, Dr. Snaut (Jüri Järvet) and Dr. Sartorius (Anatoliy Solonitsyn). But Kelvin is intrigued by the glimpse of a young boy in Snaut's quarters, and a girl wandering around the station. He cannot make sense of Snaut's cryptic warnings until he is visited by a replica of his wife, Hari (Natalya Bondarchuk), who committed suicide ten years earlier. The distressed Kelvin quickly dispatches her in a rocket, only to find that another version of her returns to him. Snaut explains that the "guests" seem to be drawn from their minds and started appearing after they bombarded the planet with X-rays.

Hari exhibits a desperate need to be with Kelvin, even breaking through a metal door to reach him, but her bloodied wounds miraculously heal themselves almost immediately. As Hari begins to remember more from her former human life, it is Kelvin who cannot bear for them to be apart. This development is treated with disdain by Dr. Sartorius, who would gladly subject Hari to an autopsy. As she is not human, he sees no ethical problem with this.

While Sartorius works on a method to destroy the guests, an encephologram of Kelvin's mind is sent to the ocean in an attempt to make contact with the planet's apparent consciousness. When Sartorius tells Hari what she is, she becomes increasingly distressed and tries to commit suicide, an attempt that fails because, like all the other guests, she simply resurrects. Although Kelvin tries to tell this copy of Hari that she has become the real Hari, the real woman he loves, she nonetheless uses Sartorius's annihilator while Kelvin is in the midst of a fever.

After the encephologram, the guests stop returning, and instead islands start appearing on Solaris, suggesting that communication has been achieved on some level. The grieving Kelvin returns to Earth, embracing his estranged father. The steaming rainfall inside his father's house, along with Eduard Artemyev's electronic sound track, makes us suspicious of this apparent homecoming, and as the camera pulls out, we see that he is on an island in the Solaris ocean.

Polish author Stanislaw Lem, on whose 1970 novel of the same title the film was based, was not pleased with Tarkovsky's cinematic rendition of his work. For Lem, it is the challenge of encountering an unknowable alien consciousness that is central to the story.[3] But for Tarkovsky, the significance of this encounter lay in its ability to bring to the fore *human* difficulties of connection, with one another, and with the home planet, whose artifacts haunt the space station as much as the guests themselves. Tarkovsky writes that in the face of a thwarted "quest for knowledge" and personal disappointment, a "way out" is provided with an "illusory" reconnection with Earth, which itself has "already become unreal."[4] It may be *2001: A Space Odyssey* that, through its name at least, seems to hark back to the ancient epic of Homer (c. 750 B.C.E.), but it is *Solaris* that connects more forcefully with its painful longing for home and family. DB

Notes

1. Vida T. Johnson and Graham Petrie, *The Films of Andrei Tarkovsky: A Visual Fugue* (Bloomington: Indiana University Press, 1994), 99–100.
2. Johnson and Petrie, *The Films of Andrei Tarkovsky*, 100.
3. "Stanislaw Lem Documentary Excerpt," *Solaris*, directed by Andrei Tarkovsky (Criterion, 2011), DVD; Stanislaw Lem, *Solaris*, translated by Joanna Kilmartin and Steve Cox (London: Faber and Faber, 1970, 2003). See also Nariman Skakov, *The Cinema of Tarkovsky: Labyrinths of Space and Time* (New York: I. B. Tauris, 2012), 80.
4. Andrei Tarkovsky, *Sculpting in Time: Reflections on the Cinema*, translated by Kitty Hunter-Blair (London: Bodley Head, 1986), 198–99.

Bibliography

Johnson, Vida T., and Graham Petrie. *The Films of Andrei Tarkovsky: A Visual Fugue*. Bloomington: Indiana University Press, 1994.

Lem, Stanislaw. *Solaris*. Translated by Joanna Kilmartin and Steve Cox. London: Faber and Faber, 1970, 2003.

Skakov, Nariman. *The Cinema of Tarkovsky: Labyrinths of Space and Time*. New York: I. B. Tauris, 2012.

Tarkovsky, Andrei. *Sculpting in Time: Reflections on the Cinema*. Translated by Kitty Hunter-Blair. London: Bodley Head, 1986.

ULYSSES (ULISSE) (1954)

DIRECTOR: Mario Camerini
WRITERS: Franco Brusati, Mario Camerini, Ennio De Concini, Hugh Gray, Ben Hecht, Ivo Perilli, Irwin Shaw. Based on Homer's epic poem *The Odyssey*.
PRODUCERS: Dino De Laurentiis, Carlo Ponti (Lux Film, Point-De Laurentiis, Paramount Pictures)
CINEMATOGRAPHER: Harold Rosson
EDITOR: Leo Cattozzo
PRODUCTION DESIGN: Flavio Mogherini
SET DECORATION: Andrea A. Tomassi
COSTUMES: Giulio Coltellacci, Madame Gres
MUSIC: Alessandro Cicognini
CAST: Ulysses: Kirk Douglas. Circe/Penelope: Silvana Mangano. Antinoos: Anthony Quinn. Nausicaa: Rossana Podestà. Alicinous: Jacques Dumesnil. Euriloco: Daniel Ivernel. Euriclea: Sylvie. Telemachus: Franco Interlenghi. Cassandra: Elena Zareschi. Anticlea: Evi Maltagliati. Arete: Ludmilla Dudarova. Eucalicanto: Tania Weber. Achilles:

Piero Lulli. Mentor: Ferruccio Stagni. Diomede: Alessandro Fersen. Calops: Oscar Andriani. Polyphemus: Umberto Silvestri. Laerte: Gualtiero Tumiati. Melanto: Teresa Pellati. Eurimaco: Mario Feliciani. Leodes: Michele Riccardini
AA: None
AAN: None
DVD: Lionsgate, 2009
Blu-ray: Currently unavailable
Duration: 104 minutes

Based on Homer's *The Odyssey* and starring Hollywood exports Kirk Douglas and Anthony Quinn, *Ulysses* was shot during the boom period for the Italian film industry. As *Time* magazine reports, "In 1948, the Italian moviemakers produced only fifty-four feature films," but, in 1953, "they made 145, almost half as many as the major Hollywood studios released, and a third of them were in color."[1] The rapid expansion of the Italian film industry had its drawbacks, however, with many crew members still learning on the job. This proved a liability in the making of *Ulysses*, when it took three days to get replacement pants for Anthony Quinn after his costume was torn. "Meanwhile, the company sat around and did nothing, with the result that the $3.95 pants cost $22,000."[2] Later, in the editing room, significant gaps in continuity were found, but the company had already been disbanded. The necessary additional scenes again caused the costs to spiral.[3] The international market for Italian sword-and-sandal films would take off in 1959, when Joseph E. Levine spent $1 million promoting *Hercules* (Pietro Francisci, 1958) and created a worldwide box-office hit.[4] As Berne Schneyer reported in *Film Bulletin* in 1959, *Ulysses* might have been a contender if Paramount had similarly invested in its promotion (particularly as it had a major Hollywood star)[5]—or, perhaps, if it had been released after *Hercules*. But in 1954, and despite Douglas's charms, *Ulysses* was not a hit.

The film begins as Penelope, Queen of Ithaca (Silvana Mangano) is lamenting the fate of her husband Ulysses (Douglas), who has failed to return from the Trojan War. Taking advantage of her predicament, an array of hopeful suitors (and would-be kings) have made themselves at home. Penelope agrees to remarry once she finishes a tapestry she is working on, but, unbeknownst to the suitors, she unravels it each night to buy herself time.

Meanwhile, we learn of Ulysses' fate. Taken into the city of Troy in the wooden horse, the Greeks are finally victorious, but the oracle Cassandra (Elena Zareschi) curses him for desecrating the temple of Neptune, god of the sea. On his homeward journey, he washes up on a shore, having lost his memory, but he is rescued by the smitten princess Nausicaa (Rossana Podestà) and welcomed into the Phaiakian court. As his memory returns, we see his adventures in flashback.

On their way back from Troy, Ulysses and his men stop at an island to stock up on provisions, reassured by Greek custom to expect hospitality, but the island is home to the Cyclops Polyphemus (Umberto Silvestri), who instead begins to eat his guests. The ever-cunning Ulysses offers the giant copious amounts of wine, and when the giant lies down in a drunken stupor, Ulysses takes the opportunity to blind him. The men are able to escape in the ensuing chaos.

They are soon drawn by the otherworldly singing of the sirens, who lure sailors to their doom on the rocky shore. Ulysses quickly orders the men to put wax in their ears, but he has himself tied to the ship's mast so that he may hear the sirens' song. The voices of his wife and son come to him, telling him that he has reached home. The men ignore Ulysses' pleas to untie him, and the ship passes by unharmed.

When they arrive at the island of the sorceress Circe, she seduces Ulysses with her likeness to his wife (both parts are played by Mangano) and turns his men into pigs. Although she agrees to restore their human form, the men cannot persuade Ulysses to return home, and they depart without him, only to die at sea in a storm. Circe (taking on some of the characteristics of *The Odyssey*'s Calypso, who is not depicted in the film) offers Ulysses immortality if he remains with her, bringing forth the shades of his deceased friends to convince him. The shade of Ulysses' mother appears to tell him that he is needed at home, and the hero departs.

At home, Penelope's suitors, among them the ingratiating Antinoos (Quinn), discover her trick with the tapestry and demand that she decide on a husband through a contest. Returning in disguise, Ulysses suggests that she set the challenge of stringing Ulysses' own bow, a feat that proves beyond all of them, except Ulysses himself. Alongside his son Telemachus (Franco Interlenghi), Ulysses slays the suitors and is reunited with his wife.

While *Variety* praises Kirk Douglas's "virile performance" (albeit he was not in the same good shape he would be in for Stanley Kubrick's 1960 *Spartacus*), it notes that Mangano was "unfortunately limited by both parts to expressing monotonous unhappiness until the finale,"[6] and this, along with the poor English dubbing, detract from the piece, despite some good effects (for its time), in the Cyclops sequence, in particular. DB

Notes

1. "Hollywood on the Tiber," *Time*, 16 August 1954, 56–63, 0040781X, http://connection.ebscohost.com/c/articles/54158448/hollywood-tiber (14 June 2013).
2. "Hollywood on the Tiber," 56.
3. "Hollywood on the Tiber," 56.
4. Anthony T. McKenna, "Joseph E. Levine: Showmanship, Reputation, and Industrial Practice, 1945–1977" (Ph.D. diss., University of Nottingham, 2008), 99, http://etheses.nottingham.ac.uk/549/1/complete_thesis.pdf (14 January 2012); Jon Solomon, *The Ancient World in the Cinema* (New Haven, CT: Yale University Press, 2001), 117.
5. Quoted in McKenna, "Joseph E. Levine," 99.
6. "Review: *Ulysses*," *Variety*, 1954, http://variety.com/1953/film/reviews/ulysses-2-1117795987/ (14 June 2013).

Bibliography

"Hollywood on the Tiber." *Time*, Vol. 64, Issue 7, (16 August 1954): 56-63, 0040781X, http://web.ebscohost.com.ezp.lib.unimelb.edu.au (14 June 2013).
Lattimore, Richard, trans. *The Odyssey of Homer*. New York: HarperCollins 1965, 1991.
McKenna, Anthony T. "Joseph E. Levine: Showmanship, Reputation, and Industrial Practice, 1945–1977." Ph.D. diss., University of Nottingham, 2008, http://etheses.nottingham.ac.uk/549/1/complete_thesis.pdf (14 January 2012).
"Review: *Ulysses*." *Variety*, 1954, http://variety.com/1953/film/reviews/ulysses-2-1117795987/ (14 June 2013).
Solomon, Jon. *The Ancient World in the Cinema*. New Haven, CT: Yale University Press, 2001.

WAR AND PEACE (VOYNA I MIR) (1966)

DIRECTOR: Sergei Bondarchuk
WRITERS: Sergei Bondarchuk, Vasili Solovyov. Based on the novel *Voyna i mir*, by Leo Tolstoy.
PRODUCERS: Viktor Tsirgiladze, Nikolai Ivanov, G. Meerovich, V. Krivonoschenko (Mosfilm)
CINEMATOGRAPHER: Anatoliy Petritskiy, Aleksandr Shelenkov, Yu-Lan Chen
EDITOR: Tatyana Likhachyova
PRODUCTION DESIGN: Mikhail Bogdanov, Aleksandr Dikhtyar, Said Menyalshchikov, Gennadi Myasnikov
SET DECORATION: Georgi Koshelev, V. Uvarov
COSTUMES: Vladimir Burmeister, Nadezhda Buzina, Mikhail Chikovani, V. Vavra
MUSIC: Vyacheslav Ovchinnikov

CAST: Pierre Bezukhov: Sergei Bondarchuk. Andrei Bolkonsky: Vyacheslav Tikhonov. Natasha Rostova: Ludmila Savelyeva. Nikolai Rostov: Oleg Tabakov. Petya Rostov: Sergei Yermilov. Ilya Rostov: Viktor Stanitsyn. Natalya Rostova: Kira Golovko. Sonya Rostova: Irina Gubanova. Hélène Kuragin: Irina Skobtseva. Anatol Kuragin: Vasili Lanovoy. Fedor Dolokhov: Oleg Yefremov. Vasili Kuragin: Boris Smirnov. Kyril Bezukhov: Nikolai Tolkachev. Nikolai Bolkonsky: Anatoli Ktorov. Platon Karataev: Mikhail Khrabrov. Napoleon: Vladislav Strzhelchik. Mikhail Kutuzov: Boris Zakhava

AA: Best Foreign-Language Film

AAN: Best Art Direction–Set Decoration (Mikhail Bogdanov, Gennadi Myasnikov, Georgi Koshelev, V. Uvarov)

DVD: Image Entertainment, 1999. Five-disc set.

BLU-RAY: Currently unavailable

DURATION: 373 minutes (405 for 1999 restored version)

Sergei Bondarchuk's monumental adaptation of Leo Tolstoy's massive novel *War and Peace* is considered one of the greatest adaptations of a literary work ever filmed, and it has kept its status as a celebrated work in cinema history in the nearly half century since its initial release in 1966, especially after its complete restoration by Russian scholars[1] and distribution on DVD in its original length, in acceptable shape. The film required four years of preparation and production of the original epic, and it was released in four parts, which lasted a total of nearly seven hours (in its cut version in the United States just more than six hours). It was shown in sections of two or four parts, depending on location. In some large U.S. cities, Chicago, Illinois, for example, it was shown in one day, part one in the morning and part two in the afternoon or evening.

Bondarchuk's masterpiece was produced by Mosfilm, a Moscow-based studio, under the sponsorship of the Soviet Union, which financed it and supplied large units of the Soviet Army to accommodate the filming of battle scenes, for which the director used up to 20,000 troops, a veritable army in itself, while trained circus horses and other facilities were used for cavalry scenes, along with thousands of other extras and technicians. *War and Peace* was made for the staggering sum of 8,500,000 Soviet rubles, but that does not take into account the massive help Mosfilm received from the Soviet state. The state was supportive of the project and poured resources into it, considering Tolstoy a national hero and the greatest writer that ever lived, an opinion that some of its makers and critics still hold.[2]

The film loyally follows Tolstoy's story, which recounts the relationship between two families of the Russian aristocracy, the Rostovs and the Bolkonskys, and the romance between Natasha Rostova (Ludmila Savelyeva) and Prince Andrei Bolkonsky (Vyacheslav Tikhonov), while the main character of the story, Pierre Bezukhov (Sergei Bondarchuk), gains ascendance as an aristocrat when his dying father, Count Kyril Bezukhov (Nikolai Tolkachev), bequeaths his fortune and title to his illegitimate son. Pierre is a large, bespectacled, ungainly man who marries the enticing but dissolute enchantress Hélène Kuragin (Irina Skobtseva). After his marriage fails, he wanders aimlessly through Moscow society, falling in love with Natasha then visiting the battlefield at Borodino, to see what war is like. He is the mouthpiece of Tolstoy (as Konstantin Levin is in *Anna Karenina*), often uttering apothems on life and death, the abhorrence of violence and war, and the existence of God (which he often doubts[3]), becoming the "second" eye of the viewer, being the one who witnesses the horrors of war firsthand as the vast canvas of the war scenes unfold before his eyes.

The plot comes in four parts, divided by many years, beginning in 1805, when the Napoleonic Wars were raging in Europe, and finally ended with the invasion of Napoleon's army, his battle at Borodino, his occupation of Moscow, and his final defeat and retreat in 1812. In the first part, the principals are revealed. Young Natasha Rostova, barely thirteen, follows, with some envy, the doings of the high society of Moscow, eager to participate in it but still too young to do so. Her father, Ilya Rostov (Viktor Stanitsyn), is a well-respected but impoverished aristocrat, and the prospects of a good marriage for his young daughter are meager. An orphan cousin, Sonya (Irina Gubanova), lives with them, and she and Nikolai (Oleg Tabakov), Natasha's older brother, seem to be in love. Natasha's young brother, Petya (Sergei Yermilov), still a boy but quite impetuous, aspires to be a soldier and go to war, envious of his older brother, who will have all the glory.

Pierre Bezukhov and Prince Andrei live in St. Petersburg, both reluctant participants of social life, which both men abhor, thinking of it as superficial and aimless. They are close friends but quite different in aspirations and attitude. While Pierre admires Napoleon, considering him a force that will sweep Europe and wipe out its corrupt monarchies, Andrei is a staunch, unbending patriot who joins the army during the military campaign, in which Russia joins Austria and England to oppose Napoleon. Andrei bravely throws himself into the Battle of Austerlitz, and he is almost fatally wounded, ironically rescued by Napoleon himself, and freed when the conflict is over. Upon his return to Moscow, he finds his wife dying in childbirth, after which he renews his friendly relations with the Rostov family. He is secretly attracted to Natasha, still young and impressionable, not suspecting that Pierre is also in love with her.

Several years elapse, and Natasha is now (in 1809) a young woman attending her first grand dance, a scene magnificently filmed in the Mosfilm studios, where she falls in love with Andrei after she dances with him; however, Andrei's father, Prince Nikolai Bolkonsky (Anatoli Ktorov), a man of the Enlightenment who toys with inventions, objects to Andrei's marrying an impoverished girl and asks him to wait a year before he commits himself. Andrei goes back to the army, and meanwhile, Natasha, still youthful and impulsive, falls in love with Hélène Kuragin's reckless brother, Anatol Kuragin (Vasili Lanovoy), who, although married to a Polish woman, proposes an elopement. Natasha is about to run away with him when Pierre, informed of these developments by Sonya, interferes and saves her from certain destruction. Embittered, Natasha stays close to her family, and Andrei appears to be forever alienated—although it seems that he is still in love with her—but so is Pierre, whose depraved wife is cheating on him. Pierre's life seems to stall, complicated as it is by a bad marriage.

The year is now 1812, and Napoleon's vast army, estimated at 200,000 men and considered invincible, has invaded Russia. Andrei is asked by Field Marshall Kutuzov (Boris Zakhava) to join his staff, but he declines and decides to lead a regiment in the field. Pierre joins the army, but as an observer, not a fighter, even though his life is still endangered. He witnesses the horrors of the Battle of Borodino, during which both Napoleon's army and the Russian troops suffer heavy losses. The battle is staged as one of the most spectacular war scenes ever filmed, with thousands of troops positioned at a site not far from the actual Borodino,[4] but when Kutuzov inspects the unacceptably heavy losses of the Russian Army, he orders a retreat and indeed relinquishes Moscow to Napoleon, who invades only to find it empty and burning. Large crowds are seen leaving the city, among them the Rostov family. Natasha sees Pierre, who has returned to Moscow, and asks him to go with them, but he obstinately refuses. He stays in the burning city, and when he tries to defend a woman being attacked by Russian troops, he is seized and thrown into prison, where he meets a weird little person with a dog called Platon Karataev (Mikhail Khrabrov), a wretch who seems both resigned and prophetic, as a Tiresias predicting doom. The scenes of the burning Moscow are staged as in real life, the entire stage built for the film burning and vanishing into flames. This was a moment in the film where artifice and real life merge, for the vast scale of the operation is staggering in its staging of a momentous event in history.

Pierre has stayed behind and is soon being dragged along as a prisoner of Napoleon's forces, which begin to retreat, suffering, but enduring, the hardships of the Russian winter, although Pierre's companion Platon dies. The population of Moscow, now outside the city in the distance, sees their city burning, and Kutuzov is seen in a somber mood, a man who prays to God to save Russia, unlike his counterpart in King Vidor's earlier Hollywood version of *War and Peace* (1956), in which the foxy Oskar Homolka foresees Napoleon's retreat and is passively (and somewhat merrily) waiting for his destruction. Andrei has been mortally wounded and is being carried along with the sick. Natasha, now fully knowing how much she loves him, attends to him and asks to be forgiven, and their last reunion, the most touching scene in Tolstoy's novel, is well given here, simple but heartrending.[5] Another disaster befalling the Rostovs is the death of Natasha's young brother, Petya, who mixes with the soldiers and rushes into battle, only to be killed in the Battle of Krasnoi, where the Russians attack the remnants of Napoleon's retreating army. Natasha is finally free to marry Pierre, who has survived war, retreat, and torture, to become the leader of a new generation.

Tolstoy's novel lives in this superproduction, well but not gloriously restored by its present adherents, and preserved as a monument of filmmaking by Russians, who today continue to safeguard and cherish their national treasures, some of which are Tolstoy's works, their greatest achievements in literature. Here, film, state-sponsored but made by honest workers and expert filmmakers, survived an era of irresolute and state failure, only to be revived by those lovers of film that still believe in it. CS

Notes

1. Anatoly Petrinsky and Vasili Lanovoy, who plays Anatol Kuragin, recall the filming of *War and Peace*, both giving good details of the production and filming.
2. Karen Shakhnazarov, film director and general director of Moslem Studios, describes the restoration process of the film, part of which had started before the collapse of the USSR in the early 1990s.
3. Henry Fonda, playing Pierre Bezukhov in King Vidor's *War and Peace* (1956), abstains from ever crossing himself as a sign of his faith, while others around him do. In Bondarchuk's epic, this ritual never occurs, although Russian Orthodox ceremonies abound.
4. Petrinsky explains that modern-day Borodino was filled with monuments and other historical places, and staging a large battle there would be obstructive to the city.
5. By contrast, the same scene in King Vidor's version, between Audrey Hepburn's Natasha (who is generally excellent) and Mel Ferrer's Andrei (who does not manage to appear sufficiently responsive playing his late scenes), is weakly given.

Bibliography

Aitken, Ian. *European Film Theory and Cinema: A Critical Introduction.* Edinburgh, Scotland: Edinburg University Press, 2001.

Anninsky, Lev. *Shestidesiatniki i my: Kinematograf, stavshii i ne stavshii Istoriei.* Moscow: Soyuz Kinematografov, SSSR, 1991.

Balio, Tino. *The Foreign Film Renaissance on American Screens, 1946–1973.* Madison: University of Wisconsin Press, 2010.

Beumers, Birgit. *A History of Russian Cinema.* Oxford, U.K., and New York: Berg, 2009.

Liehm, Miera, and Antonin J. Liehm. *The Most Important Art: Soviet and Eastern European Film after 1945.* Los Angeles: University of California Press, 1977.

Pevear, Richard, and Larissa Volokhonsky. "Introduction." In *War and Peace*, translated by Richard Pevear and Larissa Volokhonsky. New York: Vintage, 2008.

APPENDIX C: EPICS MADE FOR TELEVISION

Of necessity, this is a short list. Hundreds of miniseries have been made for television, but few qualify as feature-film epics, since most are descriptions of historical events, many of them covering entire seasons, with multiple directors and dozens of characters, impossible to cite here. A more important reason is that the epic film is not suited for television, for it demands wide theater screens, large casts, high production values, and prominent stars (for the most part) as the major and even minor characters; however, television has contributed its share to the epic film endeavor. Some of its worthiest samples are briefly given here.

BAND OF BROTHERS

Release Date: 2001
Production Company: DreamWorks SKG
Distributor: HBO
Cast: TSgt. Donald Malarkey: Scott Grimes. Maj. Richard D. Winters: Damian Lewis. Capt. Lewis Nixon: Ron Livingston. Cpl. Eugene Rowe: Shane Taylor. Sgt. Floyd "Tab" Talbert: Matthew Leitch
Duration: 705 minutes

THE COUNT OF MONTE CRISTO

Release Date: 1975
Production Company: Incorporated Television Co., Norman Rosemont Productions
Distributor: NBC
Cast: Edmond Dantes: Richard Chamberlain. Abbe Faria: Trevor Howard. De Villefort: Louis Jourdan. Danglars: Donald Pleasence. Fernand Mondego: Tony Curtis. Mercedes: Kate Nelligan. Jacopo: Angelo Infanti. Morell: Harold Bromley
Duration: 119 minutes

THE COUNT OF MONTE CRISTO

Release Date: 1999
Production Company: Film and Arts Bravo Network
Cast: Abbé Busoni: Gérard Depardieu. Mercedes: Ornella Mutti. Fernand De Morcef: Jean Rochefort. Villefort: Pierre Arditi. Danglars: Michel Aumont. Bertuccio: Sergio Rubini
Duration: 400 minutes

I, CLAUDIUS

Release Date: 1976
Production Company: BBC
Cast: Claudius: Derek Jacobi. Livia: Siân Phillips. Herod Agrippa: James Faulkner. Augustus: Brian Blessed. Tiberius: George Baker
Duration: 669 minutes

THE JEWEL IN THE CROWN

Release Date: 1984
Production Company: Granada Television
Cast: Ronald Merrick: Tim Pigott-Smith. Sarah Layton: Geraldine James. Susan Layton: Wendy Morgan. Barbie Batchelor: Peggy Ashcroft
Duration: 778 minutes

THE MAHABHARATA

Release Date: 1990 (United States)

Production Company: Channel 4 Television Corporation, Brooklyn Academy of Music, Centre National e la Cinematographie

Distributor: MK2Productions (1990, theatrical), Image Entertainment (2002, DVD, United States)

Cast: Hidimbi: Erika Alexander. Kitchaka: Maurice Bénichou

Duration: 318 minutes (six episodes); 171 minutes (theatrical)

LES MISÉRABLES

Release Date: 2000

Production Company: GMT Productions

Cast: Jean Valjean: Gérard Depardieu. Thénardier: Christian Clavier. Javert: John Malkovich. Cosette: Virginie Ledoyen

Duration: 360 minutes

ROOTS

Release Date: 1977

Production Company: David L. Wolper Productions, Warner Bros.

Cast: Mathilda: Olivia Cole. "Chicken" George Moore: Ben Vereen. Kunta Kinte: LeVar Burton. Toby: John Amos

Duration: 600 minutes

SHOGUN

Release Date: 1980

Production Company: Asahi National Broadcasting Company, Jardine Matheson Co. Ltd., NBC.

Cast: Anjin-San: Richard Chamberlain. Lord Yoshi Toranaga: Toshirô Mifune. Lady Toda Buntaro: Yôko Shimada

Duration: 600 minutes

For further readings, consult www.imdb.com/search/title?genres=history&sort=moviemeter,asc&title_type=mini_series.

APPENDIX D: WHO'S WHO AMONG DIRECTORS AND THEIR WORK

This list is intended to help the reader check the contents of this book by director and the movies he or she has directed. The works of each director are given chronologically, beginning with the earliest.

Robert Aldrich
The Flight of the Phoenix (1965)

Robert Altman
Nashville (1975)

Alejandro Amenábar
Agora (2009)

Jean-Jacques Annaud
The Name of the Rose (1986)
Seven Years in Tibet (1997)

Nikolaj Arcel
A Royal Affair (*En kongelig affære*) (2012)

Richard Attenborough
Gandhi (1982)

Roy Ward Baker
A Night to Remember (1958)

Michael Bay
Armageddon (1998)
Pearl Harbor (2001)

Ingmar Bergman
Fanny and Alexander (*Fanny och Alexander*) (1982)

Francesco Bertolini
L'Odissea (*Homer's Odyssey*) (1911)

Bernardo Bertolucci
The Last Emperor (1987)

Sergei Bondarchuk
War and Peace (*Voyna i mir*) (1966)

John Boorman
Excalibur (1981)

Tinto Brass
Caligula (1979)

Richard Brooks
The Brothers Karamazov (1958)
Elmer Gantry (1960)
Lord Jim (1965)

Tim Burton
Batman (1989)
Batman Returns (1992)

Mario Camerini
Ulysses (*Ulisse*) (1954)

James Cameron
Titanic (1997)
Avatar (2009)

Frank Capra
Lost Horizon (1937)
Mr. Smith Goes to Washington (1939)

Michael Caton-Jones
Rob Roy (1995)

Don Chaffey
Jason and the Argonauts (1963)

Richard A. Cola
Battlestar Gallactica (1978)

Chris Columbus
Harry Potter and the Sorcerer's Stone (2001)
Harry Potter and the Chamber of Secrets (2002)

Merian C. Cooper
King Kong (1933)

Francis Ford Coppola
The Godfather (1972)
The Godfather Part II (1974)
Apocalypse Now (1979)
The Godfather Part III (1990)
Apocalypse Now Redux (2001)

Sofia Coppola
Marie Antoinette (2006)

Kevin Costner
Dances with Wolves (1990)

Alfonso Cuarón
Harry Potter and the Prisoner of Azkaban (2004)

Michael Curtiz
The Adventures of Robin Hood (1938)
The Egyptian (1954)

Delmer Daves
Demetrius and the Gladiators (1954)

Desmond Davis
Clash of the Titans (1981)

Basil Dearden
Khartoum (1966)

Giuseppe de Liguoro
L'Odissea (*Homer's Odyssey*) (1911)

Cecil B. DeMille
The Ten Commandments (1923)
The King of Kings (1927)
The Sign of the Cross (1932)
Cleopatra (1934)
The Crusades (1935)
Samson and Delilah (1949)
The Greatest Show on Earth (1952)
The Ten Commandments (1956)

Tarsem Singh Dhandwar
Immortals (2011)

Andrew Dominik
The Assassination of Jesse James by the Coward Robert Ford (2007)

Roger Donaldson
The Bounty (1984)

Richard Donner
Superman (1978)

Clint Eastwood
Letters from Iwo Jima (2006)

Atom Egoyan
Ararat (2002)

Roland Emmerich
Independence Day (1996)
The Patriot (2000)

John Favreau
Iron Man (2008)
Iron Man II (2010)

David Fincher
The Curious Case of Benjamin Button (2008)

Richard Fleischer
The Vikings (1958)
Barabbas (1961)

Victor Fleming
Gone with the Wind (1939)

John Ford
The Grapes of Wrath (1940)
Fort Apache (1948)
The Searchers (1956)
How the West Was Won (1962)
Cheyenne Autumn (1964)

Milos Forman
Amadeus (1984)

Pietro Francisci
Hercules (*La Fatiche di Ercole*) (1958)

Antoine Fuqua
King Arthur (2004)

Sidney J. Furie
Superman IV: The Quest for Peace (1987)

Terry George
Hotel Rwanda (2004)

Mel Gibson
Braveheart (1995)
Apocalypto (2006)

Lewis Gilbert
The Spy Who Loved Me (1977)

Peter Glanville
Becket (1964)

Jean-Luc Godard
Contempt (*Le Mepris*) (1963)

D. W. Griffith
The Birth of a Nation (1915)
Intolerance (1916)

John Guillermin
The Blue Max (1966)
The Towering Inferno (1974)

Henry Hathaway
How the West Was Won (1962)

Howard Hawks
Land of the Pharaohs (1955)

Werner Herzog
Fitzcarraldo (1982)

Charlton Heston
Antony and Cleopatra (1972)

George Roy Hill
Hawaii (1966)

Oliver Hirschbiegel
Downfall (*Der Untergang*) (2004)

Ron Howard
Apollo 13 (1995)

Howard Hughes
Hell's Angels (1930)

John Huston
The Bible: In the Beginning (1966)

Rex Ingram
The Four Horsemen of the Apocalypse (1921)

James Ivory
The Remains of the Day (1993)

Peter Jackson
The Lord of the Rings: The Fellowship of the Ring (2001)
The Lord of the Rings: The Two Towers (2002)
The Lord of the Rings: The Return of the King (2003)
King Kong (2005)

Charles Jarrott
Lost Horizon (1973)

Roland Joffè
The Mission (1986)

Elia Kazan
Viva Zapata! (1952)
America, America (1963)

Irvin Kershner
Star Wars: Episode IV, The Empire Strikes Back (1980)

Henry King
David and Bathsheba (1951)

Henry Koster
The Robe (1953)

Stanley Kramer
Judgment at Nuremberg (1961)

Stanley Kubrick
Paths of Glory (1957)
2001: A Space Odyssey (1958)
Spartacus (1960)
Barry Lyndon (1975)

Akira Kurosawa
Seven Samurai (*Shichinin no samurai*) (1954)
The Hidden Fortress (*Kakushi-toride no san-akunin*) (1958)

Fritz Lang
Metropolis (1927)

John Lasseter
Toy Story (1995)
Toy Story 2 (1999)

David Lean
The Bridge on the River Kwai (1957)
Lawrence of Arabia (1962)
Doctor Zhivago (1965)
Ryan's Daughter (1970)
A Passage to India (1984)

Ang Lee
Hulk (2003)

Rowland V. Lee
The Count of Monte Cristo (1934)

Spike Lee
Malcolm X (1992)

Sergio Leone
The Good, the Bad and the Ugly (1966)
Once Upon a Time in the West (*C'era una volta in West*) (1968)
Once Upon a Time in America (1984)

Mervyn LeRoy
Anthony Adverse (1936)
Quo Vadis (1951)

Richard Lester
Superman II (1980)
Superman III (1983)

Louis Leterrier
Clash of the Titans (2010)

Henry Levin
Journey to the Center of the Earth (1959)

Jonathan Liebesman
Wrath of the Titans (2012)

Frank Lloyd
Mutiny on the Bounty (1935)

George Lucas (director/producer)
Star Wars: Episode IV, A New Hope (1977)
Star Wars: Episode V, The Empire Strikes Back (1980)
Star Wars: Episode VI, Return of the Jedi (1983)
Star Wars: Episode I, The Phantom Menace (1999)
Star Wars: Episode II, Attack of the Clones (2002)
Star Wars: Episode III, Revenge of the Sith (2005)

Kevin Macdonald
The Last King of Scotland (2006)

John Madden
Captain Corelli's Mandolin (2001)

Terrence Malick
The Thin Red Line (1998)
The New World (2005)

Joseph L. Mankiewicz
Cleopatra (1963)

Anthony Mann
El Cid (1961)
The Fall of the Roman Empire (1964)

Richard Marquand
Star Wars: Episode VI, Return of the Jedi (1983)

George Marshall
How the West Was Won (1962)

Rudolph Maté
The 300 Spartans (1962)

Ronald F. Maxwell
Gettysburg (1993)

John McTiernan
The Hunt for Red October (1990)

Lewis Milestone
All Quiet on the Western Front (1930)
Mutiny on the Bounty (1962)

Anthony Minghella
Cold Mountain (2003)

Ronald Neame
The Poseidon Adventure (1972)

Mike Newell
Harry Potter and the Goblet of Fire (2005)

Fred Niblo
Ben-Hur (1925)

Christopher Nolan
Batman Begins (2005)
The Dark Knight (2008)
The Dark Knight Rises (2012)

Trevor Nunn
Lady Jane (1986)

Adolfo Padovan
L'Odissea (*Homer's Odyssey*) (1911)

Wolfgang Petersen
Das Boot (*The Boat*) (1981)
Troy (2004)

Roman Polanski
The Pianist (2002)

Sydney Pollack
Out of Africa (1985)

Michael Powell
The Life and Death of Colonel Blimp (1943)

Otto Preminger
The Cardinal (1963)

Sam Raimi
Spider-Man (2002)
Spider-Man 2 (2004)
Spider-Man 3 (2007)

Nicholas Ray
The King of Kings (1961)

Jean Renoir
Grand Illusion (*La grande illusion*) (1937)

Kevin Reynolds
Robin Hood: Prince of Thieves (1991)
The Count of Monte Cristo (2002)

Eric Rohmer
The Lady and the Duke (*L'anglaise et le duc*) (2001)

Roberto Rossellini
Rome, Open City (*Roma, città apperta*) (1945)

Robert Rossen
Alexander the Great (1956)

John Schlesinger
The Day of the Locust (1975)

Ernest B. Schoedsack
King Kong (1933)

Joel Schumacher
Batman Forever (1995)
Batman & Robin (1997)

Martin Scorsese
Goodfellas (1990)
The Aviator (2004)

Ridley Scott
The Duellists (1977)
Alien (1979)
Blade Runner (1982)
Gladiator (2000)
Kingdom of Heaven (2005)
Robin Hood (2010)
Prometheus (2012)

George Sidney
Scaramouche (1952)

Brian Singer
Superman Returns (2006)

Zack Snyder
300 (2007)

Steven Spielberg
Close Encounters of the Third Kind (1977)
Raiders of the Lost Ark (1981)
Indiana Jones and the Temple of Doom (1984)
Indiana Jones and the Last Crusade (1989)
Schindler's List (1993)
Indiana Jones and the Kingdom of the Crystal Skull (2008)
Lincoln (2012)

George Stevens
Giant (1956)
The Greatest Story Ever Told (1965)

Oliver Stone
Alexander: Director's Cut (2004)

John Sturges
The Great Escape (1963)

Andrei Tarkovsky
Andrei Rublev: The Passion According to Andrei (1969)
Solaris (*Solyaris*) (1972)

J. Lee Thompson
The Guns of Navarone (1961)

Richard Thorpe
How the West Was Won (1962)

Lee Unkrich
Toy Story 3 (2010)

W. S. Van Dyke II
Marie Antoinette (1938)

Charles Vidor
A Farewell to Arms (1957)

King Vidor
War and Peace (1956)

Erich von Stroheim
Greed (1924)

Régis Wargnier
Indochine (1992)

Marc Webb
The Amazing Spider-Man (2012)

Peter Weir
Gallipoli (1981)
Master and Commander: The Far Side of the World (2003)

Orson Welles
Citizen Kane (1941)

Robert Wise
The Andromeda Strain (1971)

Joe Wright
Atonement (2007)
Anna Karenina (2012)

William Wyler
Ben-Hur: A Tale of the Christ (1959)

David Yates
Harry Potter and the Order of the Phoenix (2007)
Harry Potter and the Half-Blood Prince (2009)
Harry Potter and the Deathly Hallows: Part 1 (2010)
Harry Potter and the Deathly Hallows: Part 2 (2011)

Robert Zemeckis
Beowulf (2007)

Jerry Zucker
First Knight (1995)

Edward Zwick
The Last Samurai (2003)

SELECTED BIBLIOGRAPHY

Alexander, Caroline. *The Bounty: The True Story of the Mutiny on the Bounty*. New York: Viking, 2003.

Andrew, J. Dudley. *The Major Film Theories: An Introduction*. New York: Oxford University Press, 1975.

Beaver, Frank E. *Dictionary of Film Terms*. New York: McGraw-Hill, 1983.

Brownlow, Kevin. *David Lean: A Biography*. New York: A Wyatt Book for St. Martin's Press, 1996.

Campbell, Joseph, with Bill Moyers. *The Power of Myth*. New York: Anchor Books, 1991.

Carnes, Mark C., ed. *Past Imperfect: History According the Movies*. New York: Henry Holt and Company, 1995.

Conrad, Joseph. *Lord Jim: An Authoritative Text*. Edited by Thomas C. Moser. New York: Norton, 1968.

———. *Nostromo: A Tale of the Seaboard*. Edited with an introduction and notes by Martin-Seymour Smith. London: Penguin, 1990.

Cook, David. *A History of Narrative Film*. New York: W. W. Norton and Co., 1991.

Crowther, Bosley. *The Great Films: Fifty Golden Years of Motion Pictures*. New York: Putnam, 1967.

Donnelly, Judy. *Titanic, Lost . . . and Found*. New York: Random House, 2012.

Earley, Steven C. *An Introduction to American Movies*. New York: New American Library, 1978.

Ebert, Roger. *The Great Movies*. New York: Broadway Books, 2002.

Eco, Umberto. *Postscript to the Name of the Rose*. Translated by William Weaver. San Diego, CA: Harcourt Brace Jovanovich, 1984.

Elley, Derek. *The Epic Film: Myth and History*. Boston: Routledge and Kegan Paul, 1990.

Fisher, Andrew. *William Wallace*. Edinburgh, Scotland: John Donald Publishers, 1986.

Geraghty, Christine. *Now a Major Motion Picture: Film Adaptations of Literature and Drama*. Lanham, MD: Rowman & Littlefield, 2008.

Gish, Lillian, with Ann Pinchot. *The Movies, Mr. Griffith, and Me*. Englewood Cliffs, NJ: Prentice Hall, 1969.

Godard, Jean-Luc. *Godard on Godard*. Translated and edited by Tom Milne. New York and London: Da Capo Press, 1972.

Gottlieb, Sydney, ed. *Roberto Rossellini's* Rome Open City. New York: Cambridge University Press, 2004.

Grant, Barry Keith, ed. *Film Genre Reader II*. Austin: University of Texas Press, 1995.

Hamilton, Edith. *Mythology: Timeless Tales of Gods and Heroes*. New York: Penguin, 1942.

Kazan, Elia. *The Anatolian*. New York: Alfred A. Knopf, 1982.

Keneally, Thomas. *Schindler's List*. New York: Scribner's Paperback Fiction, 1982.

Leon, Christopher, ed. *International Dictionary of Film and Filmmakers*. New York: Putnam, 1984.

Lovell, Glenn. *Escape Artist: The Life and Films of John Sturges*. Madison: University of Wisconsin Press, 2008.

Mast, Gerald, and Marshall Cohen, eds. *Film Theory and Criticism: Introductory Readings*, 2nd ed. New York: Oxford University Press, 1979.

Mayo, Mike. *VideoHound's War Movies: Classic Conflict on Film.* Detroit, MI: Visible Ink Press, 1999.

Mitchell, Lee Clark. *Westerns: Making the Man in Fiction and Film.* Chicago: Chicago University Press, 1996.

Monaco, James. *How to Read Film: The Art, Technology, and Theory of Film and Media.* New York: Oxford University Press, 1981.

Morris, Robert L., and Lawrence Raskin. Lawrence of Arabia*: The 30th Anniversary Pictorial History.* New York: Doubleday, 1992.

Murray, Gilbert. *The Rise of the Greek Epic.* Oxford, UK: Clarendon Press, 1907.

Norman, Barry. *The 100 Best Films of the Century.* New York: Carol Publishing Group, 1993.

Orrison, Katherine. *Written in Stone: Making Cecil B. DeMille's* The Ten Commandments. New York: Vestal Press, 1999.

Phillips, Gene D. *Beyond the Epic: The Life and Films of David Lean.* Lexington: University Press of Kentucky, 2006.

Pointer, Michael. *Charles Dickens on the Screen: The Film, Television, and Video Adaptations.* Lanham, MD: Scarecrow Press, 1996.

Powell, Michael. *A Life in Movies: An Autobiography.* London: Heinemann, 1996.

Rayner, Jonathan. *The Films of Peter Weir*, 2nd ed. London and New York: Continuum, 2003.

Sackett, Susan. *Box Office Hits: Hollywood's Most Successful Movies.* New York: Billboard Books, 1990.

Santas, Constantine. *The Epic in Film: From Myth to Blockbuster.* Lanham, MD: Rowman & Littlefield, 2008.

Sarris, Andrew. *"You Ain't Heard Nothing Yet": The American Talking Film History and Memory, 1927–1949.* New York: Oxford University Press, 1998.

Scorsese, Martin. *The Making of 2001: A Space Odyssey.* Series editor Stephanie Schwam. New York: Modern Library, 2000.

Siegel, Scott, and Barbara Siegel. *The Encyclopedia of Hollywood.* New York: Facts on File, 1990.

Stokes, Melvyn. *D. W. Griffith's* The Birth of a Nation*: A History of "the Most Controversial Motion Picture of All Time."* New York: Oxford University Press, 2007.

Taylor, Philip M. *Steven Spielberg: The Man, His Movies, and Their Meaning*, new ed. New York: Continuum, 1992.

Thomson, David. *A Biographical Dictionary of Film*, 3rd ed. New York: Alfred A. Knopf, 1996.

Turner, Adrian. *The Making of David Lean's* Lawrence of Arabia. London: Dragon's World, 1994.

Winkler, Martin M. Troy: *From Homer's Iliad to Hollywood Epic.* New York: Blackwell, 2006.

INDEX

ABOUT THE AUTHORS

Djoymi Baker teaches screen studies in the School of Culture and Communication at the University of Melbourne, where her dissertation won the Chancellor's Prize for Excellence. Her articles (on topics including stardom, science fiction television, the sword-and-sandal epic, and fandom) have appeared in such journals as *Popular Culture Review*, *Senses of Cinema*, and *Refractory*, and in such anthologies as *Millennial Mythmaking: Essays on the Power of Science Fiction and Fantasy Literature, Films, and Games* (2010) and *Star Trek as Myth: Essays on Symbol and Archetype at the Final Frontier* (2010). Baker previously worked for many years in television news and current affairs.

Maria Colavito, Ph.D., is professor of philosophy/humanities at Florida State College (FSC) at Jacksonville. Her employment background includes thirty years of clinical and administrative experience in positions in the private sector, higher education, and social services, most recently as director of St. Johns County Health and Human Services Department in Florida. A certified philosophical counselor, Colavito also serves as director of the Biocultural Research Institute, where she researches, writes, and consults on intertextual and extratextual biocultural didacticism in philosophy and healthcare. She is author of three books, including *Pythagorean Intertext in Ovid's Metamorphoses* (1989) and *The New Theogony: Mythology for the Real World* (1992). Her research on the Biocultural Paradigm has been cited by sources in the fields of child welfare, medical ethics, and culture studies. Colavito teaches the didactic epic as one of her humanities courses at FSC.

Constantine Santas received his B.A. at Knox College, his M.A. at the University of Illinois at Urbana, and his Ph.D. in American literature at Northwestern University. He taught at Milwaukee Downer College (1962–1964) and the University of Illinois at Chicago (1964–1971), and served as chairman of the English Department at Flagler College, in St. Augustine, Florida, from 1971 to 2002, when he retired as professor emeritus. At Flagler College, Santas initiated a program of film studies in 1987, which continues today. His publications include *Aristotelis Valaoritis* (1976), *Responding to Film* (2002), *The Epic in Film* (Rowman & Littlefield, 2007), and *The Epics of David Lean* (Scarecrow Press, 2011). Santas has published literary and film articles and authored translations of three ancient Greek plays, performed at the Flagler College Auditorium. He was a recipient of a Danforth Foundation Teacher Grant (1967–1969). Santas was also included in *Choice* as an Outstanding National Teacher in 1983, in *American*

Hellenic Who's Who in 1990, and in *Who's Who among American Teachers* in 2002. He is currently working on a translation of Homer's *The Odyssey.*

James M. Wilson teaches film, American literature, and creative writing at Flagler College in St. Augustine, Florida. He teaches and writes about film and has published short stories in the *Southwestern Review*, *Prairie Winds*, and other literary magazines and journals. He has written and presented on films by the Coen brothers, cinematographer Roger Deakins, and screenwriter Joss Whedon, among others. A creative writer, Wilson has given presentations about writing at the Association of Writers and Writing Programs, the Florida Institute of Technology, and the University of North Florida, and he has held workshops at the Deep South Writer's Conference and the UNF Writers Conference. He is president of the Florida Literary Arts Coalition and coorganizer of the "Other Words" Conference. Wilson is currently working on a novel.